SHIPBUILDING in NORTH CAROLINA

1688–1918

WILLIAM N. STILL, JR.
RICHARD A. STEPHENSON

© 2021 the North Carolina Office of Archives and History
All rights reserved.

ISBN 978-0-8652-6494-6

NORTH CAROLINA DEPARTMENT OF NATURAL AND CULTURAL RESOURCES
D. Reid Wilson
Secretary

Office of Archives and History
Sarah Koonts
Acting Deputy Secretary

Division of Historical Resources
Ramona Bartos
Director

Historical Research Office
Joseph A. Beatty
Research Supervisor

Historical Research Office
Sheilah Barrett Carroll
Designer

North Carolina Historical Commission
David Ruffin (2023)
Chair

Mary Lynn Bryan (2023)	Malinda Maynor Lowery (2025)
David C. Dennard (2021)	Susan Phillips (2025)
Samuel Bobbitt Dixon (2025)	Noah Reynolds (2023)
Valerie A. Johnson (2021)	Barbara Blythe Snowden (2023)

Darin J. Waters (2025)

Emeriti: Millie M. Barbee, Narvel J. Crawford, Alan D. Watson, Max R. Williams

Front Cover Photo: The sailing yacht *Roma* under construction at a shipyard at the foot of the old bridge in Beaufort, N.C. in 1897. The original photograph is owned by Nat Smith of Gloucester, N.C.. One of the ship carpenters was George W. Gaskill, Smith's grandfather. *Source:* State Archives of North Carolina. Photo also on p. 232.

Beaufort Harbor, Carteret County, N.C. in September, 1893 as depicted on Sanborn map. *Source:* Joyner Library, East Carolina University.

Back Cover Photo: The brig *Pyomingo*. The extraordinary ship was built in Hyde County in 1799 but wrecked off a Nassau reef circa 1806. This watercolor, by Antoine Roux, is the only known rendering of a North Carolina built vessel during the Federal period. *Source:* Peabody Essex Museum, Salem, M.A.. Photo also on p. 57.

Distributed by the University of North Carolina, Chapel Hill

Contents

Foreword	VII
Preface	IX
List of Abbreviations	XI

1	Introduction: North Carolina's Maritime Heritage	XIII
	We Are a Maritime People	1
	Discovery and Settlement	1
	North Carolina as a Maritime State	5
	Sources	5
	Building Boats and Ships	8
	Types of North Carolina Vessels	13
	Notes	14
2	The Colonial and Revolutionary Period, 1585–1783	18
	Early Eastern North Carolina	19
	Colonial Maritime Trade	20
	Settlement along the Colonial Carolina Coast	21
	The Nature of British Regulations in Colonial Carolina	23
	Colonial Shipbuilders and Shipwrights	24
	The Business of Colonial Shipbuilding	27
	Colonial Shipyards and the Natural Resources for Shipbuilding	29
	Colonial Ships and Boats	34
	A Description of Vessels Built during the Colonial Era	35
	The Earliest Vessels	39
	The End of the Colonial Era	41
	Notes	42
3	The Federal Period, 1784–1815	50
	Commerce in the Federal Period	51
	North Carolina's Relative Location, Natural Attributes, and Improvements	52
	Custom Houses and Ports of Entry in Coastal North Carolina	52
	Trade during the Federal Period	53
	Ports and Shipbuilding in the Federal Period	53
	Shipwrights and Shipbuilders	56
	Ship Craftsmen	59
	The Shipbuilding Business	59
	The Materials for Shipbuilding	62
	Shipyards	63
	Ship Types	64
	Ship Dimensions	65
	Shipbuilding Trends and the Wars	67
	The End of the Federal Period	71
	Notes	71

4 The Advent of the Steamboat, 1816–1860 — 79
- Languishing Commercial Development — 80
- Navigational Improvements — 81
- Developments along the Coast — 82
- Steamboats in Eastern North Carolina — 84
- Steam Engines for Water Navigation — 90
- The Railroads — 90
- Dredges — 91
- Launchings — 92
- The Business of Steamboating — 92
- Shipbuilding: Iron and Such — 94
- Notes — 95

5 The Antebellum Period, 1816–1860: Expansion, Prosperity, and Crises — 102
- The Workforce: Artisan, Laborer, Businessman — 104
- Shipbuilding and Shipyards in North Carolina — 108
- Ship Repair — 109
- Marine Railways — 109
- Shipbuilding in Beaufort and Carteret County — 110
- Shipbuilding in New Bern and the Neuse River Estuary — 111
- Shipbuilding in Swansboro and Onslow County — 113
- Shipbuilding in Washington and Beaufort County — 114
- Shipbuilding in Hyde County and the Outer Banks — 116
- Shipbuilding in the Albemarle Sound Region — 116
- Shipbuilding in the Cape Fear River Area — 122
- Collateral Shipbuilding Activities — 124
- Special Vessels for Special Needs — 125
- The Centerboard — 128
- Ship Dimension Analysis — 129
- The End of the Antebellum Period — 130
- Notes — 131

6 The Civil War, 1861–1865 — 142
- Preparations for War in North Carolina — 143
- The Battles in Coastal North Carolina — 143
- The Union Occupation and Blockage of Coastal North Carolina — 144
- Shipbuilders and Shipbuilding during the War — 144
- The Building of Documented Vessels — 145
- Coastal Defenses: Too Little, Too Late — 146
- Military and Naval Contracts for Shipbuilding — 149
- The Confederate Navy and Its Problems Ashore — 150
- Shipbuilding Facilities during the War — 151
- The Scarcity of Resources for War — 153
- Shipbuilding Activities during the War — 155
- The End is Near — 164
- Union Shipbuilding Activities in North Carolina during the War — 165
- Notes — 166

7 The Expansion Period, 1866–1892 — 175

- A Time for Recovery — 176
- Shipbuilding — 182
- Quantitative Analysis of Shipbuilding — 182
- Wilmington and the Cape Fear Region — 185
- Shipbuilding Activities in Onslow County — 188
- Boats and Fishing in Carteret County — 188
- Shipbuilding on the Tar/Pamlico — 189
- Shipbuilding in Hyde County and the Pamlico Sound — 190
- Shipbuilding on the Albemarle — 192
- The Outer Banks and Roanoke Island — 193
- The Business of Shipbuilding — 194
- The Apprenticeship System and Shipyard Employment — 196
- Shipbuilding: Facilities, Materials and Vessels — 198
- The Importance of Fishing — 202
- Lifeboats and Surfboats — 203
- The Pilot Boats — 204
- Races and Regattas in North Carolina Waters — 206
- The Boat Business — 206
- Water Navigation Improvements — 207
- A Problem of Capital — 208
- Pleasure Boats — 212
- The Industrial Age — 213
- Notes — 213

8 The Industrial Era, 1893–1914 — 227

- Shipbuilding Sites — 229
- The Business of Building Ships and Boats — 231
- Shipbuilders and Shipbuilding — 233
- Vessel Descriptions — 241
- Steamboat Building — 242
- Building Pleasure Craft — 244
- Building Commercial Fishing Boats — 244
- Building Ships for the Government — 245
- Auxiliary Craft — 246
- The "Infernal" Combustion Engine — 246
- Sails — 247
- Showboats or Floating Theaters — 247
- Notes — 247

9 Prologue to the Future — 255

- Shipbuilding During the Great War, 1914–1918 — 256
- The *Hauppauge* and *Commack* (photos) — 257
- Shipbuilding Data through Six Eras — 259
- Conclusion: The Importance of Shipbuilding — 261
- Anticipating the Future — 261
- Notes — 262

APPENDICES 263
Appendix A Stephenson-Still Ship List: Alphabetical 265
Appendix B Stephenson-Still Ship List: Chronological 372
Appendix C Notes Related to Naming Shipbuilding Locations 455
Appendix D Listing of Colonial Shipbuilders and Shipwrights 459

INDEX
In lieu of an index, readers are able to perform a full-text search on this volume through assistance of the State Library of North Carolina. Please visit https://www.ncdcr.gov/shipbuilding-nc for a link to the search page.

Foreword

Shipbuilding in North Carolina, 1688–1918 is not a scientific investigation or a statistical analysis. Neither is it simply a chronology of regional events. The approach is similar to that of critical thinkers like Fernand Braudel, Christer Westerdahl, and others, incorporating a concept of historical time, geographical space, and economic structure. In this case, the authors explore the connection between the ocean, inlets, and waterways that define Eastern North Carolina and the people who lived along and around those shores in order to create a maritime cultural landscape of North Carolina shipbuilding.

The authors have produced a seminal study that likely will boost ongoing research in North Carolina and encourage similar research in other coastal regions throughout the United States. Their project has spanned four decades and countless hours in libraries and regional and national archives. Often, material was discovered while working on other research projects: court records here; newspaper articles, diaries, and letters there. Everything was copied and filed. Over the years, an ever-growing corpus of primary sources indicated North Carolina contributed far more to regional, national, and international maritime industry than was commonly accepted.

Formerly, North Carolina was overlooked as a "maritime state," and its maritime industries considered insignificant. Those of eastern North Carolina have received little attention. Nevertheless, for centuries, maritime and related industries were the backbone of "Down East" economy and culture. The Piedmont region depended on the east to import necessities and export products regionally, nationally, and internationally. This is the broad context in which the authors tell the story of ship and boatbuilding in North Carolina and the frequent adaptations of vessel design and construction necessitated by the ever changing coastal, inlet, sound, and estuarine conditions of state waterways.

In 2009, David Perry, then with the University of North Carolina Press, contacted me with the idea of starting a North Carolina Maritime Series of monographs by historians, archaeologists, and other specialists on various aspects of the state's maritime heritage. Time passed, David retired, and nothing further developed. Subsequently, in late July 2013, Bill Still and Dick Stephenson visited the North Carolina Maritime Museum in Beaufort, bringing a box that had previously held a ream of typing paper and asking whether I would be willing to "look over" the first half of a manuscript they were hoping to publish. Four years, several meetings, and dozens of emails later, the North Carolina Office of Archives and History, which has a distribution agreement with UNC Press, added the book to their publication list.

Individually and as integral components of a continuing narrative, the following chapters will appeal to both professional and avocational readers. Intellectually stimulating and genuinely entertaining, the scope and depth of this work is remarkable. Whether amateur, student, or established scholar, those interested in history, archaeology, geography, genealogy, sociology, Black studies, urban development, ecology, resource management, commerce, North Carolina, or Southern studies will discover numerous subjects worthy of further exploration.

It has been a privilege and a pleasure to work with Bill Still and Dick Stephenson. The dedication, enthusiasm, and depth of knowledge of these distinguished scholars is exceptional. Throughout the project, their objectivity and patience facilitated each step toward publication. Special thanks are also due to Deputy Secretary Kevin Cherry and Research Supervisor Michael Hill of the Office of Archives and History and UNC Press Editorial Director Mark Simpson-Vos for their support.

Over the years, each of Dick's emails ended with the same salutation, and I can think of no better wish for all who embark on the journey incorporated in these pages– *Enjoy!*

Joseph K. Schwarzer, II
Director, North Carolina Maritime Museum System

Preface

This study has been evolving for many years, starting in the 1970s. There were frequent trips to Washington, D.C. to gather information for a variety of planned research projects undertaken by the authors over those years. Ship and boat building was one of these projects. Early on, an archivist at the National Archives, the late Ken Hall, introduced us to an important group of documents, Records of the Bureau of Marine Inspection and Navigation, which became the basis for this work. Those records include such data as a ship's name, place and date of construction, and dimensions. The authors created a form to record the data, a laborious process since the original documents were handwritten and at times difficult to decipher. Today, those documents are available on microfilm.

Since 1867, the Government Printing Office annually has published the data taken from these records in *Merchant Vessels of the United States*. To supplement these documents, we began researching other records in the National Archives such as those of the U.S. Army Corp of Engineers and the other military services that constructed vessels in North Carolina. We also examined local and state records, contemporary newspapers, manuscripts in various repositories, as well as published works. As academicians at East Carolina University, we had to integrate the research with our teaching and other responsibilities. Upon our retirements, we were able to devote more of our time to completing the work.

We have shared and divided responsibilities in the preparation of this research and writing. We looked upon the project as a prototype to encourage an examination of maritime industries in the other southern states. Like so many research projects, it grew over time from what we originally envisioned. From an article for a journal, then to a manuscript on shipbuilding in North Carolina up to the present, we have ended with a volume on ship and boat building from very early in the colonial period to the virtual end of the construction of large wooden commercial sailing and steam-powered vessels at the outbreak of the First World War.

Professor Still wrote most of the narrative, based on customhouse records, government documents, newspapers, and private papers. Professor Stephenson assumed responsibility for handling the numerical data, analyzing maps and charts, and incorporating spatial and quantitative information into the narrative. The volume, however, is more than just a study of vessels documented as constructed in eastern North Carolina. It is, we hope, a comprehensive study of the North Carolina ship and boat building industry that includes documented, non-documented, and government vessels; the industries associated with ship and boat building; and the builders and artisans who constructed the vessels across the coastal plain. There are probably as many if not more non-documented vessels than those that were documented in the customhouses. A great many watercraft of limited tonnage, including those employed in inland waters, were constructed through the years. Many federal government vessels such as warships, revenue cutters, and lightboats were built in the state, as were warships constructed by the Confederate government.

We have endeavored to learn as much as we could about the economic volatility of the maritime scene in North Carolina and to convey that volatility by describing the often precarious situations of the builders, as well as the shipwrights, who comprised the labor force. The impressive work done by genealogists was a major factor in this aspect of the study. Finally, the integration of quantitative data with the narrative was a major undertaking, as were the spatial aspects of the maritime activities in a sometimes stormy, hostile environment.

Very simply, a work of this magnitude could not be accomplished by the authors alone. Through the years, many students, colleagues, library staff members, friends, and others throughout eastern North Carolina and other locations have all been involved. Unfortunately, we cannot mention them all, as some names have been lost and forgotten. It comes to mind that the late Ken Hall may have started us on our way to learning so much about shipbuilding in eastern North Carolina. His knowledge about the holdings at the National Archives, his helpfulness, and his devotion to his job, inspired us to no end. In the early years of gathering data and other information, many students at East Carolina University contributed their time and talents to bring things meaningfully together.

Because this book has been in the works for a long time, many of those who helped, like Ken Hall, have died or retired. Bill Reaves, Tucker Littleton, Charles Pearson, Tom Parramore, and George Stephenson, among others who are no longer with us, provided invaluable help. It is doubtful whether this volume could have been written, certainly not in its present form, without their assistance. Among those who have retired during the process are Susan Charboneau Holland, staff member of the North Carolina Collection at East Carolina University; Sam Newell, local historian and retired Pitt County school teacher; and Roger Kammerer, local historian in

Greenville, North Carolina. No words can express our appreciation for their inestimable help.

Others who provided us with assistance include Ralph Scott, Chris Fonvielle, Mike Alford, Jack Dudley, Nathan Richards, Richard Lawrence, Victor Jones, Barbara Snowden, Larry Babits, Bob Holcombe, Paul Fontenoy, Peggy Jo Cobb Braswell, Frank Stephenson Jr., Ed Combs, Karen Underwood, Harry Thompson, Henry Mintz, Steven Goodwin, Bryan Blake, Gordon Watts, Robin Arnold, Fred Harrison, Maury York, Wayne Willis, Bob and Barbara Cain; Pam Morris; and Karen Willis Amspacher. Also assisting were Rebecca Livingston, John Vandereedt, and other staff members of the North Carolina Office of Archives and History, Dale Sauter and other staff of the East Carolina University Manuscript Collection, those at the Southern Historical Collection at UNC-Chapel Hill, and the National Archives.

Besides those already mentioned, many special people generously provided additional help. Regarding the geographical and quantitative details, special thanks go to Valli and Ivan Caballero, Dr. Stephenson's daughter and son-in-law, for their "working" the database into graphs showing trends and changes in the ship data. A special thank you goes to Jennifer Mann, and then to Professor Scott Wade, in the Department of Geography, Planning and Environment at East Carolina University for bringing the ship data into spatial form. The analysis of the data, as simple as it may be, could not have been accomplished without their help and support.

Last, but certainly not least, we are grateful for the support, encouragement, and assistance of Joseph K. Schwarzer, Director of the North Carolina Maritime Museums. With a research effort of this magnitude and the resultant written words, there is a tendency toward redundancy, if not downright confusion. We are pleased that Joe offered his valuable time to assist us by reading the entire manuscript and suggesting badly needed changes. Further, Joe became an advocate for our research project.

This work is dedicated to our wives. Mildred, Bill's wife, and Ann, Dick's wife, have supported the authors in many, many ways through the years. It is most appropriate that we pay homage for so much support of our research and writing efforts. Unfortunately, toward the end of our writing this manuscript, Mildred fell ill and passed away.

WILLIAM N. STILL, JR.,
and RICHARD A. STEPHENSON,
Professors Emeriti

Thomas Harriot College of Arts and Sciences,
East Carolina University

ABBREVIATIONS

DNCB	Dictionary of North Carolina Biography
DC	District of Columbia
ECU	East Carolina University
GPO	Government Printing Office
LOC	Library of Congress
NA	National Archives
NMCWNH	National Museum of Civil War Naval History
NCDAH	North Carolina Division of Archives and History
NCHR	North Carolina Historical Review
NCOAH	North Carolina Office of Archives and History
RG	Record Group
SANC	State Archives of North Carolina
SecNav	Secretary of the Navy
SHC	Southern Historical Collection
UNC-CH	University of North Carolina at Chapel Hill

Chapter 1

Introduction: North Carolina's Maritime Heritage

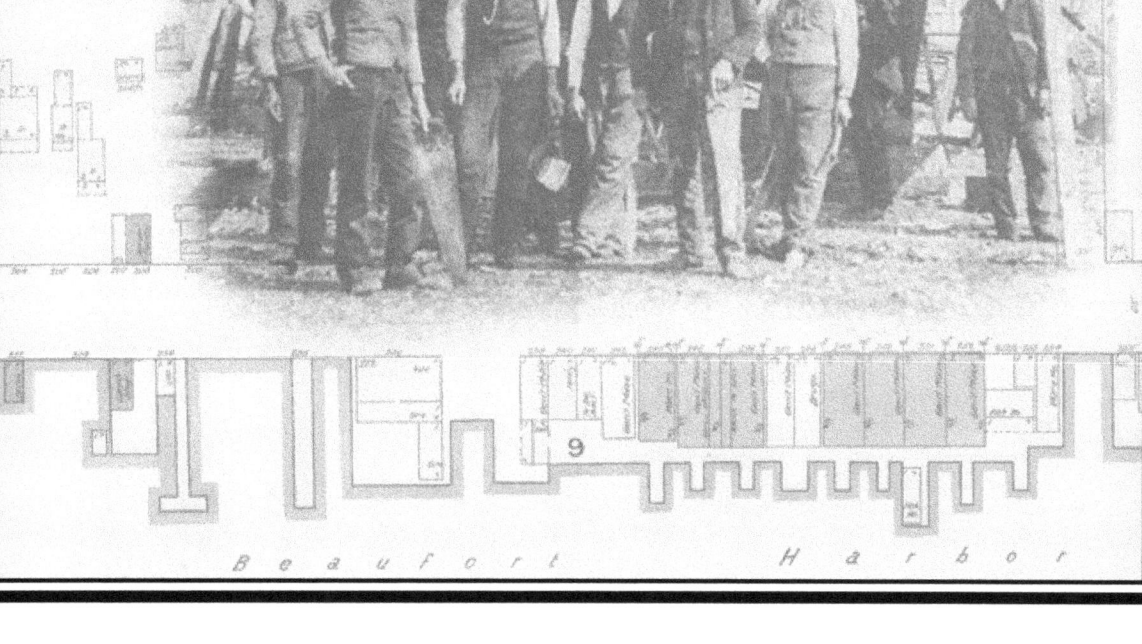

FIGURE 1–1 The 1676 map attributed to John Speed shows eastern North America including the Outer Banks and vicinity with a mix of English and Paleo-Indian place names. This map may have been published as early as 1611, and subsequently updated until 1676, even though John Speed died in 1629. His description of the colony illustrated the enormous natural resources available for shipbuilding and settlement. Notice the Speed map as compared to the Wimble and Moseley maps of 1733 and 1738 in Chapter 2, as the Outer Banks significantly changed their orientation. Historical records reveal a series of storms in the 1690s which probably prompted the alteration of the coastline. The map, like others of its time is oriented with east to the bottom and north to the right, as the exact measurement of time, was not determined until 1738 with the invention of the chronometer. *Source:* Newberry Library, Chicago.

We Are a Maritime People

Much of America's maritime heritage has been thoroughly recorded in published works and the media. Dramatic events such as "tall ships" sailing and the discovery and exploration of the USS *Nevada*, *Titanic*, USS *Monitor*, *Queen Anne's Revenge*, and the submersible CSS *H. L. Hunley* have attracted the attention of millions. The importance of New York, Boston, and San Francisco as ports is indisputable and maritime museums attract millions of visitors every year. Nevertheless, the maritime heritage of the southern states is not well known. Emory Thomas states, "To the extent that an American maritime tradition survives in art, scholarship, and popular imagination, it survives exclusively north of [the] Mason and Dixon line".[1] With a sizable portion of North Carolina's population living in the interior and overwhelming emphasis placed on agriculture and forestry, little attention has been paid to the state's maritime traditions. This is especially true of shipbuilding. Yet, from earliest times, North Carolina has sustained strong maritime industries of major consequence, including ship and boat building. The intent here is to prove this as fact.

- Construction of vessels has always been an important industry in the United States.
- A major reason for this is the extensive system of navigable rivers, lakes, and coastal waters.

Although most Americans are primarily land-oriented, the nation has always depended on its coasts and waterways. We are bordered on the east and west by two great oceans, the Atlantic and Pacific, on the south by the Gulf of Mexico, and, on the north by the Great Lakes and St. Lawrence River. Since our colonial beginnings, water transportation has been vital to America's development and economy. The discovery, exploration, and early settlement of this continent is a maritime story, especially so in North Carolina.

Discovery and Settlement

The early settlement of North America was largely determined by water (Figure 1). Upon exploration, the French settled along the St. Lawrence, the Dutch along the Hudson, and the English along many bays and rivers, such as the Delaware, Chesapeake, Roanoke, Cape Fear, Ashley, and Savannah. These colonies facilitated communications with their respective mother countries, as the early economic growth of the new United States focused largely on the Atlantic Ocean and the streams that flowed into it. In his *Maritime History of the United States*, K. Jack Bauer says, "The factors that controlled the direction and rate of flow of settlement in the great central heartland of the country were intimately related to the western rivers, lakes, and canals that traversed the Mississippi Basin."[2] Numerous communities owe their growth and greatness to these waters. It is doubtful the United States would have attained its eminent global position without waterborne commerce, and it was through this necessary mechanism that the United States became a naval power.

North Carolina possesses approximately three thousand miles of tidal shoreline, some of the most extensive barrier islands and estuaries in the world, and some of the most dangerous waters on earth. Bountiful inland forests afforded valuable resources for the ship and boat building industry. The state's streams, estuaries, sounds, and near-shore waters contain an abundance of marine life, providing sustenance and subsistence from the earliest times to the present.

Extending along the North Carolina coast for more than 175 miles, from the Virginia border to below Cape Lookout, is a chain of low, narrow, sandy barrier islands known as the Outer Banks, a geomorphologic phenomenon that has had far reaching effects on the economic development of the state. The Outer Banks are separated from the mainland by broad, shallow sounds of up to thirty miles in breadth and are cut by numerous inlets created by tidal surge and winds associated with hurricanes and northeasters. Kept open by the tides and flooding from the sounds and streams, the inlets constantly change location, size, shape, and orientation.[3] Few of them have been consistently navigable throughout the years, constituting a curse for mariners seeking a safe haven.

At Cape Hatteras, the Florida Current or Gulf Stream from the south meets the Labrador Current from the north, creating extensive, ever shifting shoals. In some four hundred years, more than two thousand vessels have run afoul of the Hatteras storms, shoals, and unstable inlets, earning the area the title, "Graveyard of the Atlantic" (Figure 2). Long recognized by mariners, these dangers were cited in the 1860 edition of the *American Coast Pilot*:

> We decline giving directions for sailing into many ports in North Carolina, as all of the harbors are barred, and always subject to alteration by every gale, particularly in the equinoctial storms; but the bars create only a part of the danger in sailing to those ports; it is the vast bed of shoals that lie within the bars, with their innumerable small channels, which give to tide so many different directions that even the pilots who live on the spot find it difficult to carry a vessel in without some accident.[4]

From the outset, North Carolina's maritime commerce was profoundly affected by this geographical phenomenon. The small hamlets and farms that sprang up along the many streams flowing into the sounds found themselves nearly isolated. Direct trade with small river ports was compromised. The Cape Fear River, located in the southeastern part of the state, is the only one in

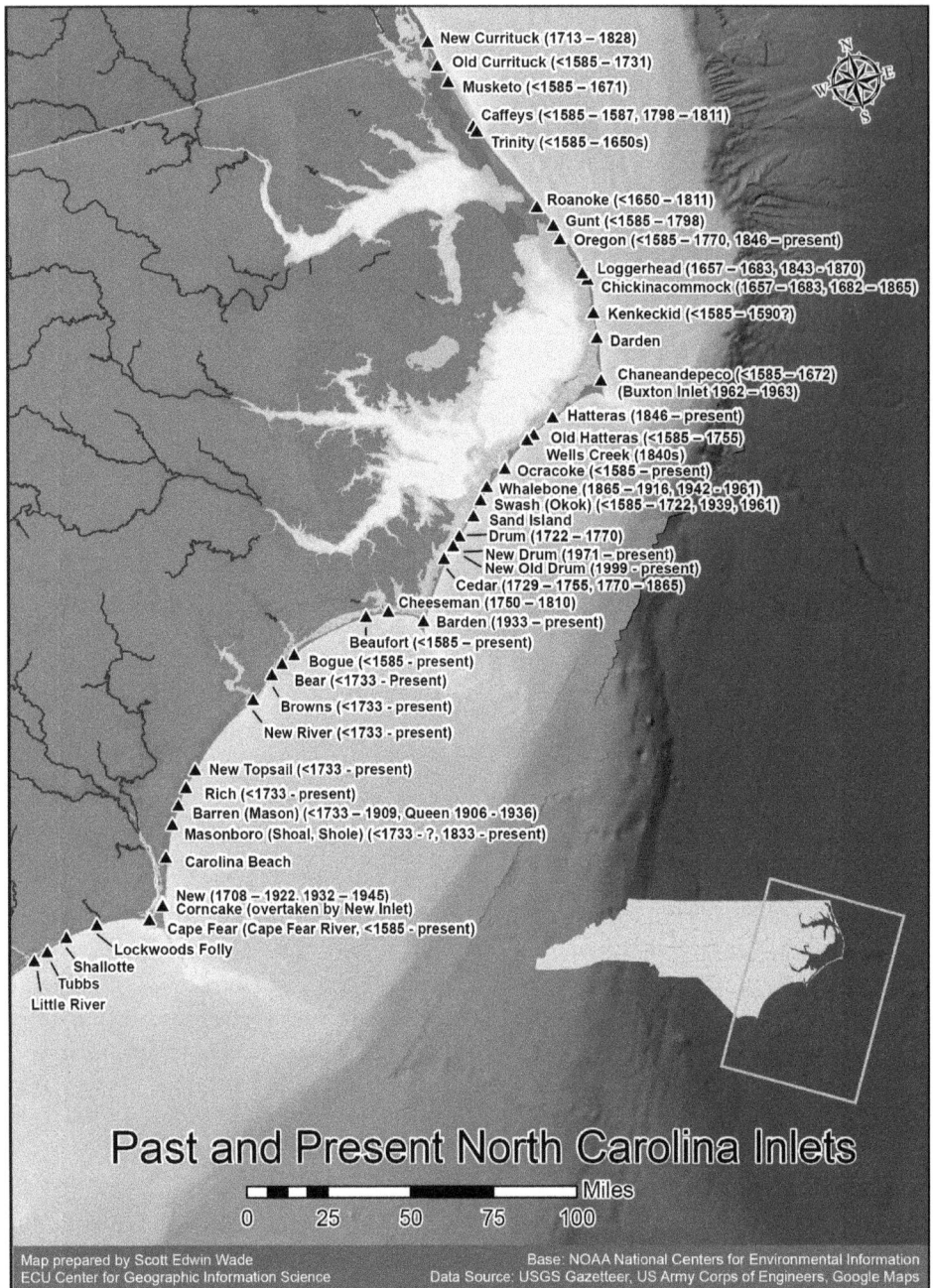

FIGURE 1-2 The present orientation and shape of the barrier islands shows inlets from a much earlier time to the present, so the location of the inlets in the 16th and 17th centuries are relative. Some of the inlet locations are not accurate insofar as time or space, due to the lack of historical records. Here, there are 41 inlets, with 24 north of Cape Hatteras. The Outer Banks is defined as the barrier islands north of Bogue Inlet, which has 27 inlets. Some inlets are related to rivers of which there are eight; and some inlets are related to the major North Carolina ports of which there are about seven. Inlets should be considered one of the more important factors in the success or failure of shipbuilding and the development of ports. *Source:* Joyner Library, East Carolina University.

North Carolina that flows directly into the ocean. Even this potential entrepôt is marked by shoals that extend eighteen miles into the Atlantic. From 1790 to the present, periodic efforts by the state and the U.S. Army Corps of Engineers to improve navigation achieved only limited success. However, the completion of the Dismal Swamp and the Albemarle and Chesapeake Canals in the nineteenth century created an intracoastal waterway and funneled water-borne commerce inside the barrier islands and away from the dangerous oceanic routes.

The state's unique coastal geography also handicapped the development of land transportation. Until the twentieth century, roads were poorly surfaced, improperly drained, and inadequately marked. Most ran in a northeast to southwest direction between Virginia and South Carolina. A good example of such a link was the "nine foot road" between Norfolk and Wilmington, parts of which still exist today. The few that ran east to west were of little benefit in the development of eastern North Carolina. The same was true of railroads. By 1860, there was only one north to south railroad in the region, and it was near the fall zone, where the coastal plain meets the piedmont. Economically, it was extremely difficult for North Carolina to overcome these conditions because:

> "North Carolina was sandwiched in between two states with navigable rivers and good harbors which drew off its products.... Hogs and tobacco were driven or hauled to Virginia markets, and cotton and rice were floated to South Carolina centers. Transportation costs delayed the development of commercial agriculture."[5]

Water transport was critical in carrying produce to markets outside North Carolina, and the state's leading export, naval stores, was carried exclusively by water. Water transportation required vessels.

North Carolina as a Maritime State

It would be impossible to exaggerate the importance of water transportation to the inhabitants of eastern North Carolina. Many wills and estate documents in northeastern counties up to 1850 included one or more vessels, and the deceased were usually carried to cemeteries by water, a practice still current. In 1880, a visitor to Carteret County observed, "The only mode of transportation in some portions of this county is by water. The judge, the lawyers, and the jurors attend Court by water; the sheriff takes his prisoner to jail by water, and often goes by water to collect his taxes or to serve his writs; the people frequently attend church by water; the young gallant often goes by water to get his marriage license; and to secure the minister to perform the marriage ceremony."[6] As late as 1884, every farmer but one in Carteret County lived within a half-mile of navigable water.[7] Some areas would not have adequate roads until the second decade of the twentieth century. Consequently, those on islands and in isolated hamlets depended heavily upon water transportation. Vessels that serviced the colony/state were from other parts of the country and world as well as from North Carolina. Over the centuries, a variety of vessels were made by local boatbuilders dispersed across the coastal plain (Figure 3).

Historians and geographers have long debated the importance of shipbuilding in North Carolina.[8] Noted southern historian Clement Eaton characterized southerners as "agricultural and unskilled in the ways of ships."[9] At the outset, most of the oceanic shipping in colonial North Carolina was managed by outside interests. Later, shipwrights migrated to the colony and small vessels were built. Observations made by various travelers during the colonial and early Federal periods suggest that North Carolina had a substantial shipbuilding industry. Well over a century later, this culminated during World War II when, at one time, the North Carolina Shipbuilding Company in Wilmington employed more than twenty-one thousand people and was the largest employer in the state.[10] However, shipbuilding in North Carolina was not on a scale with the industry in New England. Nevertheless, between 1688 and 1914, more than three thousand documented vessels were built in the colony and the state (Figure 4).

The volatility of the shipbuilding industry seems to be intricately related to economic, geographical, and political factors. Year-by-year annual fluctuations in tonnage of North Carolina-built ships are characterized by the same volatility; this fluctuation is usually a reflection of the number of vessels built, although, sometimes it simply indicates more tons per ship (Figure 5). The explanation for the volatility of shipbuilding with respect to space and time carries major consequences for this study. Some locations became more important than others. Over the years, many shipbuilding sites appeared, disappeared, and even reappeared, sometimes in the same place. Only a few survive today.

Sources

This study of North Carolina-built vessels is based on an accumulation of data from various sources. Data for the colonial period come from shipping lists of vessels entering and leaving British ports in the colonies and the West Indies. Copies of these records are in the State Archives of North Carolina in Raleigh. Five volumes of Port Roanoke (Edenton) records are in the Manuscript Department, University of North Carolina at Chapel Hill. Virtually no useful port records exist for the Federal period, but in 1789, Congress established customs districts and required officials to register vessels engaged in foreign trade and to enroll those engaged in coastal commerce. Vessels under five tons were usually not documented. Vessel documents for each customhouse, which included information on where and when ships were built, are found in the records of the Bureau of Maritime Inspection and Navigation, Record Group 41 at the National Archives in Washington, D.C. (hereinafter cited as RG41). These records are not always accurate or complete. For example, it was not uncommon for a customhouse official to record a vessel as being built in the port where recorded, although, in fact, it was constructed elsewhere in the district. Nevertheless, they provide important, primary evidence regarding the extent of North Carolina ship and boat building. This includes, but is not limited to: (1) name of vessel, (2) shipbuilding location, (3) year built, (4)

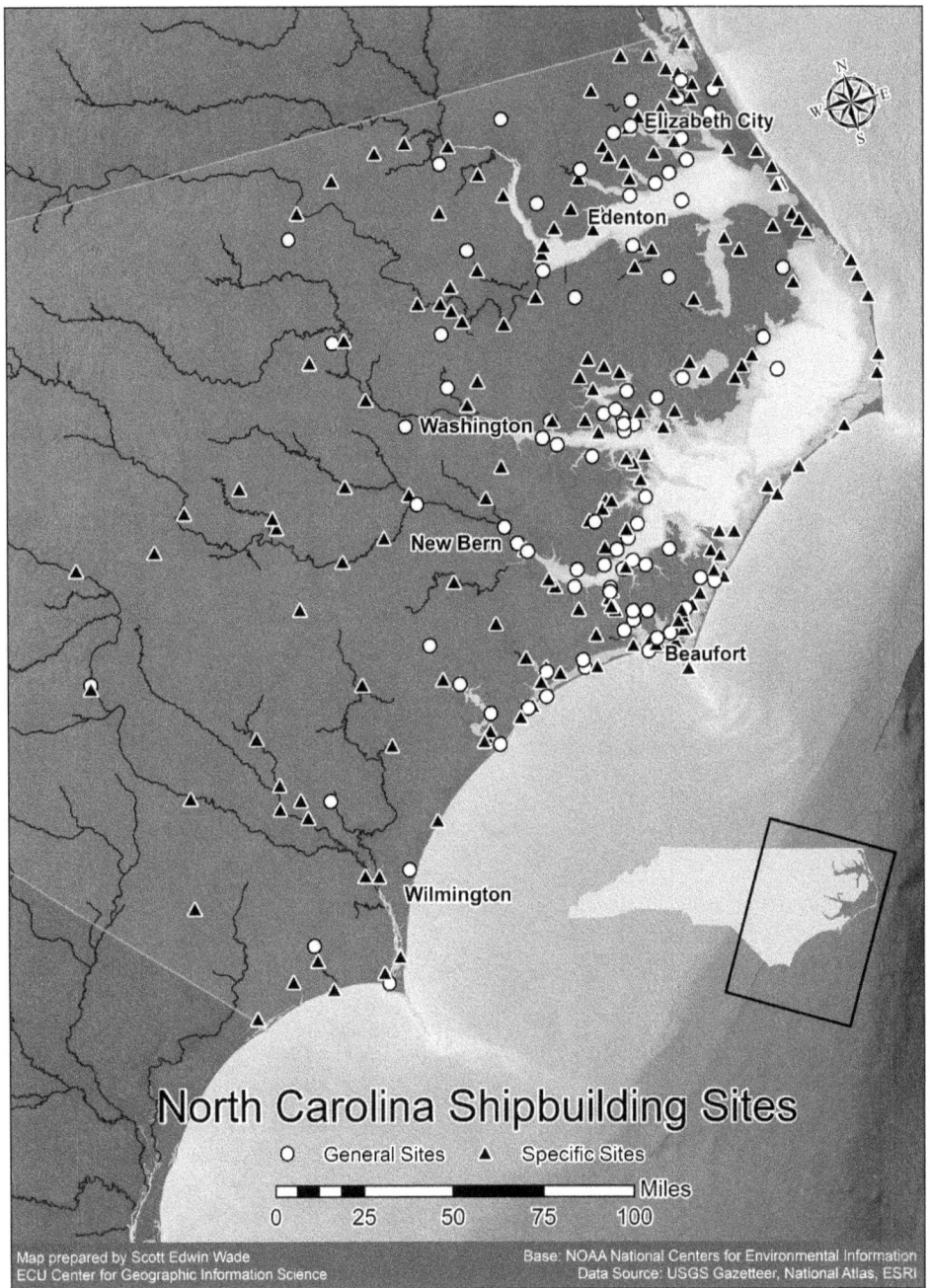

FIGURE 1-3 There were a total of 288 shipbuilding sites in North Carolina between 1688 and 1914. Some are site specific such as plantations or villages, while others are not, such as streams or sounds, for which the geographic center was chosen as a location. *Source:* author's database.

tonnage, (5) length, width, and depth of vessel, and (6) type of vessel.[11]

Appendix A contains the "Stephenson-Still List," which records, alphabetically, vessels built in North Carolina from the first in 1688 to the last in 1914. Appendix B contains a list that records, chronologically, vessels built in North Carolina. The use of 1914 as the cutoff date for inclusion in this quantitative study of documented North Carolina ships and boats is arbitrary, but marks the beginning of World War I. The nature of shipbuilding and the type and use of vessels in the state changed significantly after that date.[12] Nonetheless, there are over three thousand vessels for the period under consideration, and this is by no means a complete accounting of vessels built in the colony and state during this time. Hundreds, if not thousands, of undocumented vessels, including those under five tons, were constructed, but listed only in newspapers, state records, and private papers. These

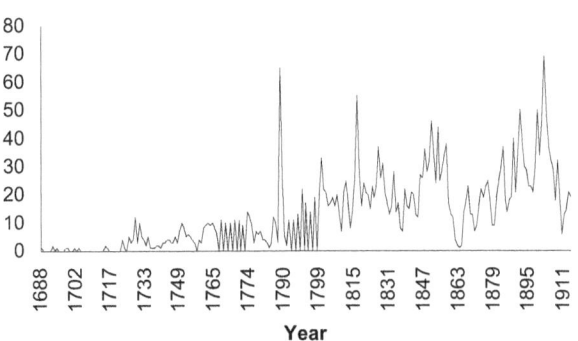

FIGURE 1-4 The trend in the number of ships built in North Carolina appears rather volatile, particularly around 1770 and the 1790's. Generally, low points can be related to wars and business downturns, while high points can be related to economic booms. With respect to the number of ships built, tonnage is an equally important consideration. *Source:* author's database.

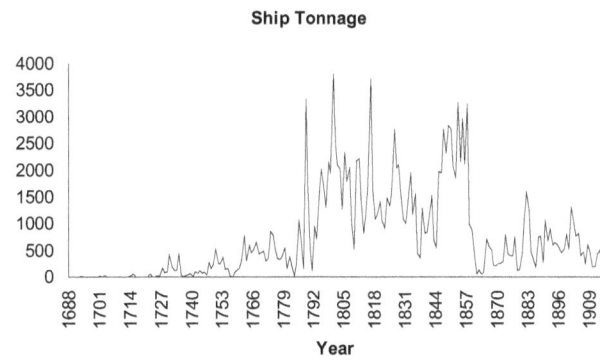

FIGURE 1-5 The trend in the tonnage of ships built is volatile, not necessarily correlated to the number of ships built. Ship tonnage, to a certain extent, could be related to the adaptation of size, as it is related to the local navigational conditions. But also oriented toward business cycles. *Source:* author's database.

were usually river and coastal craft of every type from flats and barges to small sailboats and steamers, engaged in intrastate waterborne activities. Small boats such as canoes, periaugers, bateaux, small fishing vessels, and skiffs used for domestic purposes were built by the thousands without documentation, sometimes by shipwrights or in shipbuilding facilities. Until roads existed and were passable, virtually every house had some kind of boat. In addition, ferries, surfboats, revenue cutters, lightboats, warships, and other vessels were built in the state for government service.

Little attention has been focused on small boat construction in North Carolina; indeed, maritime historian Ben Ford has written, "small craft were not recognized as an important part of our maritime heritage." Yet, a careful examination of the state's boatbuilding history indicates that, with regard to construction, ship and small boat building cannot be separated. Shipwrights built small craft as well as large vessels. Of course, the absence of documentation may be one reason for this lack of interest, and even federal documents rarely include data on vessels under five tons. Also, some North Carolina counties, such as Camden and Currituck, had scattered populations, no newspapers, and, although rarely having sites for the building of large vessels, were centers for small boat construction.[13]

The State Archives of North Carolina houses an extensive collection of county records for all periods including court papers, deeds, wills, inventories, and some correspondence. These resources provide important insight into colony/state shipbuilding activities.[14] Although by no means consistent from county to county or even within a single county, deeds and abstracts recorded vessels bought and sold, many while still under construction, and constitute a valuable primary source. Contracts provided insight into building procedures, the agreement between potential owner(s) and builder, and details about the vessel to be built. Wills and court records were equally valuable. Court records included not only local and state courts, but federal district court records as well.[15]

Determining where vessels were built within the colony/state is a taxonomic problem (see Appendix C for place name notations). Early documents are often difficult to read and interpret--some are faded, and others partially burned, torn, or fragmented. Customhouse officials frequently noted the construction site as the district rather than the exact location. A vessel documented as built in New Bern might have been constructed anywhere in the district. North Carolina was originally divided into three counties: Albemarle, Bath, and Clarendon. Over time, county names changed as boundaries were modified and new precincts and counties were created. By the twentieth century, twenty-eight counties bordered or contained eastern North Carolina seashores, sounds, and rivers. A vessel built in what today is Tyrrell County could have been constructed in Washington, Dare, or Tyrrell; one built in then Halifax could have been in present-day Martin, Edgecombe, or Halifax County. Was a vessel constructed in Washington or Washington County? Multiple place names create problems. There are fourteen Mill Creeks, ten Broad Creeks, seven Goose Creeks, at least four South Creeks, and two North Rivers. When first documented, vessel owners or captains often gave a local name where their vessel was built, a location that cannot now be identified—for example, Mouse Harbor, Bell's Buoy, Blue Rock, Polly's Point, Float Bridge, Pott's

Point, Tombstone, Richard's Creek, and Horne River. Moreover, documents themselves may contain significant inaccuracies; the customhouse official might record that a vessel was constructed in his district or the port where originally registered or enrolled, rather than the actual site where it was built, which might have been up a stream or along a sound.[16]

In the colonial period, port officials would frequently list a vessel as being plantation-built rather than identify a specific place of origin. In many cases, vessels would be identified with a river or broad geographical area; terms such as "Cape Fear built" or "Carolina built" were used. It is often difficult to determine whether a vessel was built in Beaufort, North Carolina, or Beaufort, South Carolina, or Camden, New Jersey, or Camden County, North Carolina. There were vessels with the same name and similar dimensions built at different places and times.

Other variables include additional discrepancies within customhouse records, vessel name changes, and changes in type, such as from a sloop to a schooner, due to rebuilding or rerigging.[17]

Newspapers are an extremely important source of information. Eastern North Carolina papers considered boat and ship building newsworthy and frequently had articles about vessels under construction, launchings, the importance of the industry, and even about the builders and owners. Colonial papers and those published during the early years of statehood often mentioned vessels for sale but rarely where they were built.

In North Carolina, as elsewhere, most shipbuilders did not leave written records. This was true of large and small shipyards and the larger domestic sites as well. Even when records were kept, they were often destroyed by fire, a constant danger in the industry. Furthermore, many shipwrights were intelligent, but illiterate. With few exceptions, artificers, mechanics, and shipwrights seldom left written records of their experiences. It appears they had neither the time nor the incentive to write, as this would only hinder their progress. Also, writing about one's own work has rarely been a part of the culture.[18] Moreover, there were quite often no plans or blueprints, models or half models; instead, shipwrights depended upon the eye to design and build a vessel. Designs and patterns were commonly used in the Civil War, and blueprints became standard construction features during the two world wars, but builders in the state, particularly those engaged in "backyard" or cottage industry construction, employed "eye design." This is just as true in North Carolina today as it was in the past. "Most old time, eyeball-only shipwrights could freehand a hull with near perfect lines," responded Julian Guthrie, a well-known shipbuilder from Harkers Island, to a question about using the "rack of an eye" to build a vessel. "I just go off a ways and look at her," he added, "and if she don't look right, I change her."[19]

There are no known photographs of North Carolina-built vessels prior to the Civil War. What is known about these early vessels comes from a painting in the Peabody Essex Museum depicting a Hyde County-built brig, an illustration of the *Tuley* on a vase in the North Carolina Museum of History, two drawings of vessels built by Charles Grice in Elizabeth City, and lithographs of Albemarle Sound fishing flats.[20] In recent years, archaeologists have studied the remains of vessels in North Carolina waters, including those from a number of ships built in the state, and have been able to project their general appearance. Archaeological investigations have also determined that the overwhelming majority of sailing vessels built in the state after 1820 included centerboards due to the state's shallow waters. In fact, there may have been more centerboard-constructed vessels in North Carolina than in any other state. There is little evidence and no known photographs or illustrations of pre-Civil War steamboats. Regarding river ferries, "the most important source for data on ferry architecture and construction is the archaeological record."[21]

Similarly, no illustrations of North Carolina boat or ship building facilities prior to the Civil War have been discovered, but there are photographs of late nineteenth and early twentieth century boat and ship yards. Beginning in 1885, Sanborn's maps of the state's small ports occasionally include the location of buildings and railways at a shipyard.

Building Boats and Ships

Until World War I, there were few large shipbuilding firms in the state, the largest being Beery's and Cassidey's at Wilmington. Eastern North Carolina had few plantations and fewer urban centers. The coastal plain was populated largely by small freeholders, the majority of whom sought only to wrest a modest living from the soils or waters. Communities were scattered and small.; Wilmington and New Bern were the only centers that could be characterized as towns until the middle of the nineteenth century. A large number of vessels were built on farms, plantations, and by individuals for their own use.[22] Shipwrights constructed vessels for both domestic use and sales. Nonetheless, few of these construction sites can be characterized as established yards.

The initial development of a ship and boat building industry in North America was influenced by New England fishing, highly protective navigation laws, and an abundance of ship timber in the British colonies, but these were not major factors in establishing the industry in North Carolina. The majority of vessels built in North Carolina responded to specific needs, rather than as planned factors in the state's economic growth. This was the case from the earliest settlement to the twentieth century. Historically, surplus capital was scarce throughout the South. Vessels were built under contract or speculation within the colony and state and elsewhere in North America and abroad. In the colonial period, British merchants occasionally purchased North Carolina-built vessels. In the nineteenth century, pilot boats, sailing merchantmen, and even steamers were exported to other states. Between 1786 and 1866, a total of 326 sailing vessels built in the state were registered or enrolled in the port of New York.[23] What few records are available suggest that the established yards gradually came to be concentrated in the state's small urban ports.

The exact number of shipyards is difficult to determine. As mentioned earlier, official documents and newspapers frequently use the term shipyard. Deeds and court cases often included shipyards in real estate surveys. Maps show the location of shipyards. Eastern North Carolina names and folklore often allude to the presence of shipyards in various localities.

There are the communities of Shipyard in Camden County and Launch in Currituck. Elizabeth City has Shipyard Road and, six miles to the north on the Pasquotank River, Shipyard Ferry Route. Bertie and Carteret Counties had Shipyard Landings; Currituck County residents also claim that Tull Bay at the mouth of the Northeast River was the site of a shipyard; residents of Bettie in Carteret County claim that a shipyard was located on "Deep Hole Run."

Beaufort County documents mention a shipyard on South Creek, but there are two South Creeks in the county. Local lore says that Perquimans County's Sutton Creek was the location of a shipyard. A local newspaper mentioned a shipyard on the Perquimans River six miles above Hertford that built vessels for the West India trade. Morehead City's City Hall is rumored to be the site of a shipyard. Local tradition says that the Barret farm on the Meherrin River, seven miles below Murfreesboro, was the site of a nineteenth century shipbuilding facility. At Edward's Ferry, near Palmyra, "a man named Gurkin operated a boat-building yard on the north shore a short distance above Williamston after the Civil War." Most of the coastal counties claim one or more shipyards.[24] The term "boat house" was used to identify not only where a boat was stored, but also where small craft were constructed. George Washington Creef, the famous Dare County boatbuilder, called his facility a boat house.[25]

Often, there is little evidence to back up these claims. Frequently, deeds and other records mention shipyards only in order to identify property and boundaries. Newspaper articles mention shipyards but usually do not describe them.[26] It is important to understand that although boats and boat building were present throughout these counties until the advent of roads, there is little published evidence. Water transportation may not have been mentioned because it was so common: "It has been said, and not without some truth, that nearly every man in Carteret County is either a half sailor or a full-fledged ship carpenter." Quite literally, there seems to have been "[a] boat with every cottage."[27]

In many cases, what constituted a shipyard was simply where one or more vessels were built, not an established shipbuilding facility with sheds, timber storage, sail loft, forges, docks, and, by the mid-nineteenth century, a marine railway and a sizeable workforce. As stated above, no large shipbuilding facilities were located in North Carolina until World War I. There were medium-sized yards in the ports, numerous small yards and backyards where one vessel at a time was built, and individuals who built vessels for their own use.[28] Although initially the state's shipbuilding facilities were relatively small in comparison to shipyards in the northeast, when steamboats began to appear, new facilities were all "created for the construction of a single river-going commercial steamer."[29] Usually, ship and boat yards in North Carolina were not permanent or even seasonal enterprises but established at a particular location for a specific purpose or because of the availability of land and/or timber. This was especially true of small yards in rural areas. Evidence, such as deed books, suggests boat builders often did not own the property where the yard was located but rather leased it. This may have been done to avoid paying taxes. Conversely, at least in Carteret County where there was much intermarriage and "everyone knew everyone else," a builder was allowed to construct one or more vessels on property simply through verbal agreement.[30]

A shipyard was often located on the site of an earlier shipbuilding establishment.

These locations were used and reused because they were the most suitable for a particular area, and/or the sites were owned by a family that engaged in boat and ship building for two or more generations. The John A. Meadows Shipyard in the 1880s and the J. A. Meadows Steam Marine Railway and Ship Yards in 1907 were at the same location in New Bern, and there is evidence that a shipyard was on this site as early as the colonial period.

North Carolina builders often found it more economical to locate their construction sites near available timber. It was not unusual to find shipyards located far up rivers and even smaller streams. In fact, wooden vessels were actually built above the fall line and floated down to navigable waters during freshets.

Subsidiary naval industries were also scarce or nonexistent in North Carolina. There were few ropewalks and even fewer sail makers. Iron ore was available in substantial amounts in the Piedmont, but efforts to mine and smelt it never really materialized. A one hundred-ton vessel usually required one ton of iron fittings, and although nearly all large plantations, farms, and communities had forges, there were no ironworks capable of fabricating that weight of metal parts for ships until the middle of the nineteenth century.[31] Many blacksmiths were capable of making nails, spikes, and other small ship parts, "if one had a supply of wrought-iron rods," but often, even nails had to be imported.[32] Rigging, sails, anchors, and chains all had to be obtained from outside the colony or state. Until the latter decades of the nineteenth century, steamboat machinery was contracted with northeastern ironworks. There was, though, no shortage of sawmills. North Carolina had an abundant supply of timber, and timbering became an important industry in the state. The production of naval stores, particularly of tar and pitch, was the most profitable commerce in eighteenth and nineteenth century North Carolina.[33]

Shipyards were most vulnerable to fire, since combustible materials were always present. This was particularly true in yards that built wooden vessels using lumber, rosin, turpentine, and paint. Dozens of accounts in local newspapers describe destructive fires in shipyards. In 1833 James Cassidey, a Wilmington shipbuilder, lost blacksmith and carpenter shops and a warehouse where rigging for new vessels was stored. In 1856 the Cassidey building site was hit by two more fires; one in March and the other in April. The latter did little damage, but the March blaze destroyed several buildings and a wharf. Then in May 1861 Cassidey, who for some unknown reason had more than his share of ill fortune from fires, lost his marine railway to fire. Benjamin W. Beery, another Wilmington shipbuilder, lost his marine railway and ship carpenter tools in a fire that started in a nearby sawmill. A new vessel on the ways was far enough along to be shoved into the river and saved. Beery nearly lost his shipyard in another fire that burned right up to his marine railway before being extinguished. A disastrous fire occurred in 1864, when several blocks of the Wilmington waterfront, including a shipyard being operated for the Confederate government, were engulfed in flames.[34] In 1858, Elizabeth City lost an entire block to fire, including C. M. Laverty's shipbuilding facilities.[35] Nor were New Bern builders spared the devastation of fire. In 1847, Thomas Sparrow lost his marine railway, a small vessel on the stocks, and all his buildings and tools to fire. Early in the twentieth century, Thomas Howard's shipyard and the Meadows marine railway and buildings were damaged by blazes.[36]

Although not as common, violent storms and hurricanes were just as devastating.

A 1769 storm drove every vessel and craft into the woods at New Bern: "So great is the scarcity of small boats . . . that the people cannot travel." In 1795 a large vessel recently launched was "driven so far on the marsh that it is doubtful that she can be got off."[37] A hurricane in 1806 sunk two revenue cutters at Ocracoke Inlet. In September 1815, in what was clearly a hurricane, vessels on the stocks in Beaufort, Washington, and Swansboro were "driven into the woods," and two vessels on the stocks at the Pigot and Otway Burns shipyard were destroyed.[38] Cassidey's shipyard was struck by a gale in August 1851, and a steamer on his railway "took [an unexpected] launch."[39] In 1913, due to another September hurricane, the woods in Carteret County were "full of boats."[40] There were similar accounts describing the results of storms in 1879, 1889, and 1933.[41] Often ship and boat builders profited from storms; destroyed vessels needed to be replaced or repaired. Repairing was considered more lucrative than new construction, and there were builders who preferred to concentrate on this alone. North Carolina shipbuilders usually operated on a slim financial margin and had little or no insurance to cover losses from storms, fires, or other disasters.

Colonial North Carolina had few ship and boat builders and artisans; skilled craftsmen and unskilled laborers, of European and African descent, were included in the work force.

In Maryland and other states, convict labor was used in shipbuilding.[42] According to census returns, the number of ship and boat builders in North Carolina increased to more than a hundred by the middle of the nineteenth century. Nevertheless, "difficulties in maintaining a skilled labor supply . . . retarded the rise of shipbuilding in the southern states."[43] This was certainly true in North Carolina. A distinction should be made between a shipwright and a shipbuilder, although a craftsman could be both. Shipwrights were artisans, whereas shipbuilders were often the shipyard owners. Shipwrights or master ship carpenters frequently became shipbuilders through apprenticeships, family connections to the trade, or by entering the profession from other livelihoods such as fishing boatman or house carpenter.[44] Yards were owned and operated by businessmen, merchants, and planters, as well as ship carpenters. Shipbuilders were prosperous and prominent businessmen in New England, but generally not so in North Carolina. Even the permanent establishments were frequently in debt with mortgages and silent partners. Quite often several individuals agreed to share the cost in the building and ownership of a vessel.[45] Bankruptcy was common.

Small facilities were often family-owned and operated enterprises, with shipyards often passing from one generation to the next, or, in some cases, to the spouses of children. Regardless of the yard's size or the type of vessel under construction, skilled workers were required. Building a ship is not like building a house. A large, well-equipped shipbuilding facility in eighteenth and early nineteenth century New England would employ dozens of specialized trades, including sawyers, joiners, spikers, daubers, caulkers, blacksmiths, riggers, glaziers, painters, guilders, ropemakers, blockmakers, and sailmakers, all working under the supervision of a master builder, superintendent, or foreman.[46] North Carolina's shipbuilding industry included a number of these trades, but rarely all. Nonetheless, there were workers specifically identified as sailmakers, caulkers, and other skilled craftsmen employed in the state's shipbuilding industry. The few sailmakers in North Carolina were concentrated in small ports. Some evidence suggests that the trades were not attractive, creating a scarcity of skilled artisans until the late nineteenth century. According to

1860 census records, there were only 570 ship carpenters and mechanics and 4,570 laborers in machinery works throughout the eleven states that would soon make up the Confederacy.[47]

Obviously, the percentage of North Carolina workers employed in shipbuilding was small. It is difficult to determine the exact number of such workers since an unknown number made their living in some other capacity: carpentry, farming, fishing, or another maritime activity. Ship carpenters were often employed in constructing houses, including those of their employers. One Salter Path shipwright built coffins in his spare time. They were, as one boatbuilder described them, "jacks of all trades." In many, if not most of the North Carolina yards, various shipbuilding skills were filled by a single craftsman: "In general a skilled shipwright was expected to be able to do any task to which he might be assigned."[48] This was particularly true in the colonial period because of the paucity of craftsmen. This circumstance blurred divisions of labor. Frequently, carpenters were not identified as house or ship carpenters but simply as carpenters. They also undertook the task of joinery. In 1810, Thomas Trotter, a most versatile craftsman and mechanic, wrote planter Ebenezer Pettigrew from Washington, "I am as the old saying is up to my B. side in business. I cannot have sawing done to go about my house . . . and have engadged [sic] to finish the iron work of a new Ship, and also expect to do the Cabbin [sic] work, etc. . . . These things are also new to me." He went onto say that he had "cut 3600 lb. of Nails."[49] Skilled shipwrights and other experts in shipbuilding were often transients. In more recent years, the use of automobile engines in fishing craft required builders/watermen to become mechanics in order to install and modify the engines. In rural areas like coastal North Carolina, most tradesmen, including those engaged in ship and boat building, farmed for subsistence. Jobs that required their skills were scarce.

Census returns can be notoriously inadequate and do not list all the shipbuilding trades. Ropemakers, mastmakers, riggers, and glaziers are rarely recorded, and boatwrights only occasionally. One Pasquotank deed listed a "canoewright." County death certificates often listed as ship carpenters individuals who do not appear in that category in census returns. In the nineteenth century, the term "mechanic" was generically used to designate all those occupied in iron and other metalworking trades, including those engaged in shipbuilding. The returns do not list any boilermakers, an important skill for steam-powered vessels. Apprentice papers sometimes provide relevant information on shipbuilding trades. For example, between 1784 and 1835, fifteen sailmakers, six blockmakers, two riggers, three caulkers, and thirteen ropemakers apprenticed in Craven County.[50]

It is often difficult to determine when the term "builder" denotes a "shipbuilder" or "shipwright," as opposed to a "contractor" or "capitalist" with the means of production but without the skill or knowledge to design and build a vessel himself. The craftsman who oversaw the actual building was usually a master ship carpenter. Newspapers, though, often credited the vessel's owner with its construction. Customhouse documents usually included a master carpenter's certificate and initial enrollment and registration papers bearing the builder's name. Unfortunately, most pre-1860 North Carolina carpenter certificates were destroyed during the Civil War, but some builders' names did survive on official vessel enrollment and registration documents. Of these, the most complete for North Carolina are the Elizabeth City vessel documents that record thirty-two carpenters or builder's names between 1815 and 1830.

The names of ship and boat builders and shipwrights may also be gleaned from newspapers, memoirs, genealogical accounts, and information provided by local residents and descendants. Curiously, census returns and other records do not list many of these names as involved in vessel construction.[51]

Apprentices were important, skilled artisans in the colony and state until after the Civil War. Apprenticeship was a type of indenture, essentially a contractual relationship between a master craftsman and a young man in order that the latter learn the master's craft. It was an exchange of technical training and maintenance for work. The term of service was usually seven years, although it could be less, and the apprentice had to be under the age of twenty-one. The system had two basic objectives: to provide skilled labor and to relieve the community of the burden of supporting poor orphans and other dependent children. In 1701, North Carolina established "orphan courts" to bind poor orphans to such apprenticeships. Although the law would be amended, it would remain in effect well into the nineteenth century. A large percentage of apprentices, including those in the various shipbuilding trades, were orphans.[52]

Apprentices in the shipbuilding trade were found in all the state's shipbuilding counties. They were highly valued and sought by builders. Some shipwrights, such as the Sparrows of New Bern, were able to persuade the court to apprentice a number of youths over a period of several years.[53] Apprenticeship in the shipbuilding industry declined in the years before the Civil War and disappeared shortly thereafter.[54]

In the American colonies, slaves were involved in the maritime trades, including shipbuilding, as early as the later decades of the seventeenth century. As in the rest of the South, the "peculiar institution" was an economic factor in North Carolina. Throughout the colonial period, there was a shortage of labor in North Carolina, skilled and unskilled. Slaves were imported to fill the need. No statistics are available on the number of slaves involved in North Carolina's ship and boat building, but the evidence suggests that by the nineteenth century, they were used in large numbers. Many builders owned slaves, who, presumably, were employed in the yards. A large number of North Carolinians of African descent, slave and free, were involved in all the maritime industries, including boat and ship building.[55] It is not clear whether these workers were skilled shipwrights or boat builders, or were semiskilled artisans in trades such as caulking, sailmaking, and ropewalking. A study of black craftsmen indicates the largest group were carpenters, of whom fourteen were listed as ship carpenters.[56] As with all craftsmen, slaves were often trained in several skills, such as house and ship carpentry. Many were probably trained in all shipbuilding skills. A skilled slave shipwright was worth nearly twice as much as a prime field hand, and they were often hired out.[57] A study of South Carolina's maritime history concludes that slaves probably did most of the ship repair and construction on the large plantations in the state.[58] This may well have been true for North Carolina as well, particularly in the building of flats and small craft such as canoes. Blacks also dominated the blacksmith and caulking trades, important subsidiaries to ship and boat building.[59] In Craven County between 1783 and 1835, there were few white apprentices compared to blacks. White backlash against black competition in various trades occurred throughout the coastal South, but there is little evidence of this in North Carolina shipbuilding.[60] After the Civil War, blacks were employed in large numbers in the state's shipbuilding industry. Most were part of the labor force, but there were black shipbuilders and a few black businessmen who had built one or more vessels.

In the United States, the later decades of the nineteenth century witnessed a rapid increase in iron and steel shipbuilding. Those trained in ship carpentry and related skills were of little use in building iron and steel vessels. Skilled metal workers, boilermakers, and foundrymen were required to build such ships, and North Carolina had very few such workers. It is not surprising that only one iron vessel, a steamer constructed in Wilmington in the late nineteenth century, was built in the state. With the exception of armored warships built during the Civil War, iron and steel ships were not constructed in North Carolina until World War I. From 1917 to 1919, the large steel ships built in the state were constructed by metal workers from outside the state. Despite metal ship production during the World Wars, wood continued to be the principal material used for ship construction in North Carolina until recent years.

Historians and geographers have long emphasized the enormous resource represented by North America's immense virgin forests. By the time the American colonies were settled, the timber supply in the British Isles was rapidly disappearing, and shipbuilders there were importing much of it from the Baltic region and elsewhere.[61] The government quickly realized the potential of the colonies in providing badly needed timber. Of the more than five hundred tree species found in North America, only a few were desirable for ship construction, and most of these could be found in North Carolina. White and live oak, red and white cedar, locust, ash, beech, chestnut, and southern pine were all native. Shipwrights looked for different types of trees for different parts of the ship. Large, straight trees were used for keels, keelsons, and masts. Crooked trees with many angled limbs were used for knees and breasthooks.[62] Inevitably, intense exploitation of popular building timbers depleted the resource; in some areas, they almost disappeared.[63]

Some timbers were preferred over others. New Englanders often used white oak, but according to British naval officials, it tended to rot. Longleaf yellow (pitch) pine was popular with southern builders because of its durability, strength, and long, straight grain, but northern shipbuilding interests were critical of it for hull construction.[64] Red and white cedar (juniper) and live oak were the most preferred timbers for wooden ships. The cedars, never as plentiful as pine, were used in hull construction and planking. Live oak was considered the best for futtocks, knees, transoms, breasthooks, and other curved timbers.[65] Tar Heel boat and ship builders used the Atlantic white cedar, which grew in huge stands in eastern North Carolina, extensively. These, along with other ship and boat building timbers, were depleted by the late nineteenth century.[66]

Vessels were constructed at various locations, usually depending upon their size and use. Small craft could be built anywhere and transported to the launching site. Larger vessels had to be constructed near navigable water. The authors have identified 288 sites in the colony and state of North Carolina where documented vessels, five tons or over, were built.[67] The yard itself was often a field by a stream, creek, or sound; or a lot next to a dock; or even on the grounds of a sawmill. Space to work and store timber, solid ground, and adequate water depth for launching at the end of the ways or slip were essential. The builders called the ground on which the ship was to be laid down the "building slip." In North Carolina, along rivers that were shallow, builders usually held launchings during freshets, a rising of the stream caused by heavy rains or the melting of snow in the mountains. Occasionally, they used inclined skidways, but more often, rollers formed from felled trees. Launchings have been described as popular events, attracting crowds of spectators to watch a vessel as it glided into the water. This was certainly true of the yards located in Wilmington and other large ports, but the many small, temporary facilities established to take advantage of nearby timber often launched vessels with little fanfare.[68] Launchings in North Carolina were generally fore and aft, but occasionally sideways launching was carried out. During World War I, this technique was used with the launching of concrete vessels in New Bern and Wilmington. Railways, first wood and later iron, were used in the larger yards, but it was not until the early twentieth century that a railway dry dock was erected at a state shipyard.[69]

Types of North Carolina Vessels

Vessels have been classified in various ways: as documented or undocumented; by materials—wood, composite, iron, steel, concrete, or, recently, fiberglass; by motive power—sail, oars, poles, motor, steam, gasoline, or diesel; by use—transport, naval, fishing, or utility; by rig—sloop, schooner, brig, ketch, or ship; by number of guns or function—ship of the line, frigate, and, in the modern era, battleships, cruisers, destroyers, or aircraft carriers. At a workshop held by the North Carolina Maritime Museum in Beaufort, participants grouped boats (rather than ships) as small craft, work boats, class boats, or modern boats.[70] The term "domestic boats" was used in court cases from 1870 to 1890 for undocumented vessels. A "market boat," according to the New Bern customs director, was one "of less burthen than five tons."[71]

Vessels can also be classified by design. Until the mid-nineteenth century, for vessels, and much later than that for most small craft, North Carolina ship and boat builders generally did not use plans, drawings, blueprints, models, and half models. The vast majority of vessels were custom-built by "rule of eye." One Dare County boat builder remarked that "imagination is the first law of nature . . . in constructing a vessel."[72] Boatbuilding in eastern North Carolina was, and is, a traditional folk craft, and "backyard" boatbuilding is a cultural phenomenon. Usually living adjacent to the water, all watermen knew something about boatbuilding or possessed the necessary skills to construct a vessel. In the Core Sound area of Carteret County, the tradition of "build your own" persisted into the twentieth century.[73] With an inherited or an acquired skill, each generation learned by observing and helping in the construction of ships and boats. "Joe Ease" Taylor of Sea Level built a sizeable vessel near his home located a quarter mile from water. When asked how he planned to move the boat to water, he replied, "I had enough sence [sic] to build her, so I reckon I can lanch [sic]."[74] "Down East" residents emphasize the importance of family in the craft, and certain families have a long history of unusual skill in boatbuilding:

> Pat O'Brien was the best boatbuilder in Tidewater, And every O'Brien that I ever saw around this section was a boatbuilder. James O'Brien, brother to Pat, is a good boatbuilder, and he's about seventy. His grandfather and his father and his father before him, all the O'Briens just had the knack to build a boat. Pat could take a piece of wood to build a stem lining and he'd take it and lay it out with a pencil and his finger against it as a guide, and lay it out, and take a hatchet and chop it out, and dress it off. When he put the side planks on, damn if they wouldn't fit. He just knew what he was doing.[75]

Custom-built vessels, even those constructed by the same man, were rarely alike. Each builder had his own method and insisted that his way was the best. Builders frequently disagreed, not only on building methods, but on the type of wood used, the setting of masts and sails, and, if a steamer, whether it should be side or stern wheel. Neal Easley, who photographed boats and interviewed residents in Atlantic, was impressed to discover that the names and peculiarities of various craft, even those built decades ago, were known not just to the builders, but to nearly every local. It has been suggested that builders had "little overt aesthetic interest" in their boats.[76] There is probably some truth in this, as most watermen were primarily interested in sailing and working qualities rather than appearance. Nevertheless, builders took great pride in the appearance and performance of their vessels.

The terms "vernacular," "indigenous," and "traditional" have been used to describe vessels built in the state.[77] There is some disagreement over what constituted a "vernacular" or "traditional" vessel, but the terms generally indicate a boat or ship type peculiar to a particular geographical location. Still, even local types were often affected by outside influences. The bateau and periauger were probably introduced into Canada and the American colonies by the French. Both appeared in North Carolina waters in the eighteenth century and, in improved models, continued to ply state waters throughout the nineteenth century. African slaves also brought with them knowledge of small craft used on that continent. The New Haven (Connecticut) sharpie was introduced into North Carolina waters in the 1870s. In a modified form, it became the most important freight boat in the Core and Pamlico Sounds, in time acquiring the distinction of being a Core Sound sharpie.[78] Hundreds, probably thousands, of small shallow-draft boats were constructed out of local materials in eastern North Carolina. Next to the dugout canoe, the deadrise skiff was the most popular shallow-draft vessel among watermen. Although skiffs were common along the Atlantic seaboard, the North Carolina deadrise skiff equipped with a spritsail is unique to the area. The earliest version of the skiff appeared in North Carolina waters in the last quarter of the eighteenth century and increased in popularity over the next hundred years. Until the 1880s, skiffs were either poled or rowed with oars. At some point after the Civil War, the deadrise skiff acquired its characteristic spritsail. By that time, the boats had become the workhorse (the "model T and taxi," as one Down East waterman described it) in the region between Albemarle Sound and the Cape Fear River and would continue in that capacity well into the twentieth century when the sail would be replaced by a gas engine and propeller.[79]

Ferries were essential to the residents of eastern North Carolina. Boats used for ferriage included canoes, periaugers, flats, and scows. In the twentieth century, power vessels began to be used on longer trips.

The dugout canoe is the earliest known workboat in North Carolina. It has the distinction of being the most commonly used craft in the state until the twentieth century. Called "cunners" by local inhabitants and fashioned from logs, they were extensively employed by Native Americans. Early settlers in the colony quickly adopted them for their use, and, in time, would increase their size and add sails.[80]

Identifying a particular type of vessel or a specific vessel itself can be more difficult.

The authors have compiled a list of one hundred different vessel designations used by North Carolina customs officials from 1688 to 1914: for example, screw (freight), screw steamer (tow), screw steamer (passenger).[81] Of course, the records do not include undocumented vessels such as flats (pole, sail, and steam), ferries (sail, horse drawn, pole, etc.), or small craft (skiffs, canoes, etc.). Other variables include whether a vessel had a figurehead, a centerboard, or more than one mast. Small craft might be round-bottom or flat, decked or partially decked, clinker or carvel built.

In general, geographical factors determined the type of vessels used in a particular area. Flats were commonly employed on the rivers in North Carolina. In fact, deed books and other records suggest that in the eighteenth and nineteenth centuries, many farms and plantations built and owned their own flats. Riverboats could be adapted to tow flats. Lighters, scows, and barges were similar to flats and used on streams. Some carried sails, and, in time, would be motorized. North Carolina steamboats, like their western river counterparts, were flat-bottom, capable of "steaming on a heavy dew."[82] The majority of these were stern wheelers designed to navigate the state's narrow meandering rivers. Vessels that plied the shallow sounds could not be deep-bottomed. Sailing vessels of the colonial and early national period were broad in beam, relatively flat-bottomed, and had little keel. The shad boat, indigenous to North Carolina waters, was designed for negotiating rough waters near inlets on windy days and incorporated a deep V-shaped, sweeping, curving keel attached to a wide hull.[83] Vessels constructed in the northeastern section of the state were usually long and narrow with a relatively deep draft compared to those built at Harkers Island and in the vicinity of Beaufort where the waters were much more shallow. Shrimp trawlers built in Brunswick County in the southeastern part of the state were quite different from the "Core Sounders" launched in the Pamlico and Core Sounds areas. Fishing for rockfish on the Roanoke River required flat-bottomed boats, "easy to walk in."[84] The steam flats used in the Albemarle Sound fisheries after the Civil War were indigenous to that area.

Each period in American history produced distinctive vessel designs determined by geographical factors, use, building materials, and technology. Distinctive types often overlapped historical periods with modifications and improvements to structure and power plants. The single-masted sloop first appeared several hundred years ago and the basic type is still in use today. Despite chronology's relevance, though, Lincoln Paine aptly declares, "[r]egardless of the period in question, the importance of a ship lies in the historical milieu in which she lived and worked. . . . The disappointing thing about so many ship books is that they tend to separate specifications or the most basic movements of a ship from the reality of the world in which she sailed."[85] Ships constructed in North Carolina generally employed European building techniques. However, Michael Alford has suggested that North Carolina boats were built by methods "distinct from others in the U.S. regardless of time period," although he does agree that, during the early colonial period, there was French influence on Carolina boatbuilding.[86] To understand the complexities of ship and boat building in North Carolina, it is necessary to place the vessels built there within "the reality of the world in which" they sailed. And it must be remembered that the geographic spread (this is an ancient term) of an innovation took much longer than it does today.

Fishermen and other coastal residents often claim that, for small craft, the greatest change was from sail to the internal combustion engine. This assessment could be applied to larger craft as well. The transition began late in the nineteenth century and gained momentum early in the twentieth century. By World War I, with few exceptions, sailboats and sailing ships were no longer constructed for commercial purposes in North Carolina.

Notes

Please refer to the List of Abbreviations; for additional publication information on works cited in the Notes for this and subsequent chapters, refer to the Bibliography.

1. Emory Thomas, "The South and the Sea: Some Thoughts on the Southern Maritime Tradition," *Georgia Historical Quarterly* 67 (Summer 1983): 160.
2. K. Jack Bauer, *A Maritime History of the United States*, xi.
3. David Stick, *The Outer Banks*, 1.
4. E. M. Blunt, *The American Coast Pilot*, 229.
5. Paul Gates, *The Farmers' Age: Agriculture, 1815-1860*, 6-7.
6. Rodney Barfield, *Seasoned By Salt*, 169.
7. *Goldsboro Messenger*, citing *Carteret Telephone*, January 28, 1884.
8. "What do you think was the state's biggest industry? It was the building of ships," wrote Samuel A. Ashe in a story from an unidentified newspaper, dated February 7, 1927, copy in the New Hanover County Public Library, Wilmington, N.C.
9. Clement Eaton, *A History of the Southern Confederacy*, 173. John G. B. Hutchins in *The American Maritime Industries and Public Policy, 1789-1914*, 190-191, wrote that despite an abundance of excellent ship timber, the southern states failed to develop a shipbuilding industry. Joseph Goldenberg agreed and stated, "North Carolina…launched relatively little tonnage" (*Shipbuilding in Colonial America*, 120). For similar observations, see Bern

Anderson, *By Sea and By River*, 16. Even one of the co-authors of this work accepted this argument in explaining the southern states' difficulties in building warships during the American Civil War (William N. Still Jr., *Confederate Shipbuilding*, vii). North Carolina historians accepted this premise. Charles C. Crittenden in his study, *The Commerce of North Carolina, 1763-1789*, 13, wrote that shipbuilding was of little significance, although it "did play some part in the life of her people"; Enoch Lawrence Lee determined that it did "not appear to have flourished to any great extent" in the colonial period (Enoch Lawrence Lee, *The Lower Cape Fear in the Colonial Period*, 156). More recently, Rodney Barfield agreed: "North Carolina did not develop a large shipbuilding industry, as other Atlantic coastal states did" (*Seasoned by Salt*, 167-168). Duncan Peter Randall wrote in his dissertation on Wilmington that shipbuilding was of no importance before the Civil War ("Geographic Factors in the Growth and Economy of Wilmington, North Carolina," PhD diss., UNC-CH, 1965, 38).

10 Travelers occasionally noted the presence of shipbuilding activities. John Brickell, who published an account of his meanderings in the colonies before the American Revolution said, "Almost every planter may have a convenient Dock upon his Plantation and a sufficient quantity of good Timber to build Ships and Boats withal" (*Natural History of North Carolina*, 260-261). In 1783, a German traveler, touring the newly established United States, wrote, "Washington [North Carolina] on the Tar River [is] a new settled little place of perhaps thirty houses.... [T]he chief occupation is the building of small ships and vessels which are put together entirely of pine timber." Twenty-three years later, William Tatham, one of the commissioners appointed to survey the coast of North Carolina from Cape Hatteras to Cape Fear, wrote, "[T]he town of Beaufort is situated at the junction of Bogue and Core Sounds.... [T]he inhabitants of this place build many ships of inferior [size].... there being five on the stocks while I was in Beaufort" (William Tatham, "The Separate Report of William Tatham, One of the Commissioners Appointed to Survey the Coast of North Carolina from Cape Hatteras to Cape Fear inclusive," manuscript in the Library of the U.S. Coast and Geodetic Survey, Washington, D.C., n.d.) See also Johann D. Schoepff, *Travels in the Confederation, 1783-84*, I: 124-125. A recent report listed fifty-five "vessel construction sites" along the lower Cape Fear (Wilmington and vicinity) alone. The report covers the entire historical period (Claude V. Jackson, III, *The Cape Fear-Northeast Cape Fear River Comprehensive Study: A Maritime History and Survey of the Cape Fear and Northeast Cape Fear River, Wilmington, Harbor, North Carolina*, Vol. 1, *Maritime History*, 209). For information about the Wilmington shipyard, see Ralph Scott, *The Wilmington Shipyard*. The authors have identified 288 shipbuilding sites for documented vessels (see Appendix C).

11 Not all of this information is available for each historical period. Most of North Carolina's customhouse records, including vessel documents, were destroyed during the Civil War. For an example of a study of shipbuilding using virtually the same records, see Peter J. Wrike, "Mathews County Shipbuilding Patterns, 1780-1860" (master's thesis, Old Dominion University, 1990).

12. The onset of World War I resulted in a temporary, significant increase in ship construction in the state.

13. Bonnie J. Wilkinson, "Building Wooden Boats: A Lost Chapter in Maritime History," *Association for Preservation Technology* 20 (1988), 61. Ben Ford wrote that small vessels (he does not define small) "do not constitute shipbuilding." "Wooden Shipbuilding in Maryland Prior to the Mid-19th Century," *American Neptune* 62, no. 1 (2002), 69–70. Even craft such as barges engaged in coastal trade, were usually not documented. Burbank to Chief Engineer, Wilmington District, March 8, 1877, file 19834, Entry 103, RG 77, NA. See also Ann Merriman, "North Carolina Schooners, 1818–1901, and the S. R. Fowle Company of Washington, North Carolina" (master's thesis, ECU, 1996), 134 note 9.

14. New Hanover County Estate Records, 1741-1759, July 1760, SANC. For example, the inventory of the estate of John Walker, a shipwright, includes tools such as irons for caulking, a box of other shipbuilding tools, a cradle used for launching ships, and shipbuilding lumber.

15. Federal court records and Record Group 21 for the North Carolina districts are found at the Regional Archives in Atlanta, Ga. Many of these vessels were not documented.

16. See Appendix C for a discourse on coastal North Carolina place names.

17. William Henry von Eberstein Papers, Manuscript Collection, Joyner Library, East Carolina University. A North Carolina mariner recalled a not uncommon occurrence: "I took her to the ways of Captain Wm. Farrow and after unrigging her and taking the masts out we hauled [her] up on his ways. She was then cut in two and a piece 18 feet long put in the center of her." He also re-rigged the vessel.

18. Robert B. Gordon, "The Interpretation of Artifacts in the History of Technology," *History from Things: Essays on Material Culture*, ed. Steven Lubar and W. David Kingery, 75.

19. Dara McLeod, "Backyard Boatbuilding," *Outer Banks Magazine*, 1995-1996, 28-31, 76-77; Norfolk *Virginian-Pilot*, February 26, 1996; Susan West and Barbara J. Garrity Blake, *Fish House Opera*, 84.

20. Edmund Ruffin, "The Great Fisheries of the Albemarle," *The State*, XXV (February 1958), 13-14.

21. Gordon P. Watts Jr., and Wesley K. Hall, *An Investigation of Blossom's Ferry on the Northeast Cape Fear River*, ECU Report No. 1, 38. See also G. J. Scofield, "The Boathouse," *Waterline*, 14 (1980), 1-2.

22. Ben Ford called these small yards "shade tree" yards. "Wooden Shipbuilding in Maryland," 62.

23. Forrest R. Holdcamper, *List of American Flag Vessels ... at the Port of New York, 1789-1867*.

24. *Beaufort News*, February 26, 1931; *Perquimans Record*, November 4, 1891; *Perquimans County History Yearbook*, 11; *State vs. Twiford*, Supreme Court of North Carolina, October 4, 1904, in 136 N.C. 603; 48 S.E., 1904 N.C. Lexis 311; Bland Simpson, *Into the Sound Country*, 95; *New Bern Daily Journal*, May 20, 1908; William S. Powell, *North Carolina Gazetteer*, 451; Raleigh *News and Observer*, August 18, 1957; Bill Sharpe, *A New Geography of North Carolina*, 871, 876.

25. See Connie Mason to Vaden Cudworth, February 2, 1995, and enclosures, copies in the North Carolina Maritime Museum, Beaufort, N.C.

26. A note in the *New Bern Journal*, November 26, 1896, states only, "at the shipyard." See also Steve Goodwin to authors, May 3, 2006.

27. Jonathan Havens, *The Pamlico Section of North Carolina*, 44. For an example of the presence of boats and vessels in nearly every household, see Gordon C. Jones, comp., *Abstracts of Wills and Other Records, Currituck and Dare Counties, North Carolina, 1663-1850*, passim.

28. Henry Hall's *Ship-Building Industry of the United States* (1882), 130, mentions shipyards in Elizabeth City, Washington, New

Bern, and even Bell's Ferry (modern Grifton), but Wilmington, which had at least two sizeable shipbuilding establishments and marine railways, is not mentioned.

29. Maurice K. Melton, "Shipyards," *Encyclopedia of the Confederacy*, IV, 1424-1425.

30. Wayne Willis interview, August 6, 2006.

31. Ford, "Wooden Shipbuilding in Maryland," 72; Lester J. Cappon, "Iron-Making, A Forgotten Industry of North Carolina," *North Carolina Historical Review* 9 (October 1932): 331-348.

32. Quoted in Diana Barbara Powell, "Artisans in the Colonial South: Chowan County, North Carolina, 1714-1776 as a Case Study" (master's thesis, UNC-CH, 1982), 49.

33. Percival Perry, "The Naval Stores Industry in the Ante-Bellum South, 1789-1861" (PhD diss., Duke University, 1947).

34. James Sprunt, *Chronicles of the Cape Fear River*, 534-535; *People's Press and Wilmington Advertiser*, July 31, 1833; *Wilmington Daily Journal*, May 19, 1854; *Wilmington Weekly Journal*, March 28, April 18, 1856; May 27, 30, 1861; Wilmington *Tri-Weekly Commercial*, May 20, 1854; New Hanover County Deed Book (June 1858), 400, SANC.

35. Elizabeth City *Old North State*, September 18, 1858.

36. *Fayetteville Observer*, May 4, 1847. The *Weekly Raleigh Register* on November 23, 1859, mentioned a fire at the shipyard of T. L. Skinner in Edenton.

37. William Gaston to Brother, August 11, 1795, William Gaston Papers, ECU; *Quarterly Review of the Eastern North Carolina Genealogical Society* 9 (Winter 1982), 112-113.

38. *Raleigh Minerva*, September 15, 22, 1815.

39. *Wilmington Commercial Weekly*, August 29, 1851.

40. *Carteret County News-Times*, September 3, 1948.

41. For other storms see Edenton *Gazette*, January 12, 1811, September 10, 1821; Edenton *Fisherman and Farmer*, April 19, 1889; *Wilmington Journal*, June 7, 1860; and Samuel W. Newell, "A Maritime History of Ocracoke Inlet, 1584-1783" (master's thesis, ECU, 1987), 57-58. One writer surmised that an unusual increase in the number of vessels built in 1898 and 1899 was a result of the destruction generated by severe storms (Barfield, *Seasoned by Salt*, 106-113). For a history of the state's hurricanes, see Jay Barnes, *North Carolina's Hurricane History*.

42. See Ford, "Wooden Shipbuilding in Maryland," 74. It was more difficult to obtain information on shipbuilders than ships. Builders left no journals, and papers only rarely; newspapers were vague, frequently not indicating whether an individual was the one who had a vessel built or the builder. Census returns also are not clear, and because of the destruction of records, master carpenter certificates are generally missing, though some can be found in NA RG 41. Genealogical research and writings were the most valuable source for obtaining information about shipbuilders and shipwrights.

43. Hutchins, *American Maritime Industries*, 95.

44. For an example of how one Maryland shipbuilder entered the profession through the apprenticeship system, see Pete Lesher, "Apprenticeships and the Shipbuilding Trade: Robert Lambdin of St. Michaels," *Weather Gauge* 36 (Fall 2000), 19-26.

45. See, for example, agreement dated May 9, 1829, New Hanover County Deed Book T, 260, SANC.

46. A Newport, R.I. shipbuilder in 1740 listed twenty-three separate crafts that he employed in his shipyard. See Carl Bridenbaugh, *Colonial Craftsman*, 94.

47. Still, *Confederate Shipbuilding*, 61.

48. Frederick G. Fassett, *Shipbuilding Industry in the United States of America*, 29; "Riverfront Restoration," Wilmington *Star-News*, November 24, 2004.

49. Quoted in Catherine W. Bishir, et al., *Architects and Builders in North Carolina: A History of the Practice of Building*, 103.

50. Victor Jones, "Apprentice Bonds of Craven County, N.C.," copy in the Craven–Pamlico-Carteret Regional Library, New Bern, N.C. Blockmakers made blocks, wheel-like devices for working lines and ropes. Ropemakers worked at a ropewalk, where cordage needed to rig a ship was made.

51. Correspondence with Tucker Littleton of Swansboro provided the authors with a long list of individual boatbuilders in Onslow and Craven Counties who, at one time or other, were involved in boat and ship building, including Alton Phillips, Louis Matthews, Luther Harrison, Walter Marine, Wiley Marine, Ollie Marine, Nanza Covil, Reinhold Foster, Ed Foster, Monte Lee Hill, Isaiah Willis, Van Buren Willis, John Woodhull, John Rodgers, John Riggs, Ed Hill, Alex Moore, Calvin Kirkman, Vance Mathews, Will Pridgen, M. T. Maness, Leon Styron, George W. Littleton, Dewey Salter, Lee Smith, and a Mr. Lockhart. See also William N. Still, Jr., "Shipbuilding and Boatbuilders in Swansboro, 1800-1950," *Tributaries* (October 1995), 7-14. Jack Dudley published a pictorial history of maritime activities in Swansboro including shipbuilding, *Swansboro: A Pictorial Tribute*. Barbara Snowden provided the authors with a long list of boatbuilders in Currituck County, as did Rebecca Swindell for Hyde County. A series of heritage volumes for coastal counties includes family histories and genealogical information that mention boat and ship builders. These include families with a long history of vessel construction, such as the Pigotts (Pigots), Willises, Gaskills, and Lewises of Carteret County (*Carteret County Heritage*, two vols.). Sources, at times, are quite vague: "The Clarks from Connecticut; members of a colony that settled in Currituck, N.C. & they are reported to have had a shipyard." (J. E. Warren, "Tomkins Family," *William and Mary Quarterly* 10, no. 1 (January 1930), 34.

52. In Chowan County, of fifty-six apprentices listed in county records between 1717 and 1776, thirty-eight were orphans. An examination of apprentice bonds for Craven County, from the 1740s to the middle of the nineteenth century, suggests that the number of orphans apprenticed in that county was nearly two-thirds of all apprentices. In all the counties, mulattos were frequently apprenticed. For Craven County, see "Apprentice Bonds of Craven County, N.C." abstracted by Victor T. Jones Jr. For Chowan County, see Diana Powell, "Artisans in the Colonial South: Chowan County, North Carolina, 1714-1776 as a Case Study" (master's thesis, 1983, UNC-CH), 61; for Perquimans County, see Dru Gatewood Haley and Raymond A. Winslow Jr., *The Historic Architecture of Perquimans County, North Carolina*, 26. See also Richard B. Morris, *Government and Labor in Early America*, 363-364; and Joseph G. Rayback, *A History of American Labor*, 18-19. A recent study of the indenture system in North Carolina is Karen L. Zipf's *Labor of Innocents: Forced Apprenticeship in North Carolina, 1717-1919*.

53. Apprentices were so valued that at least one was persuaded to run away from his master for a promise of paid employment. Bishir, *Architects and Builders*, 36. See also James H. Craig, *The Arts and Crafts in North Carolina 1699-1840*, 250-266.

54. The system, however, would continue in North Carolina until the end of the nineteenth century. Zipf, *Labor Of Innocents*, focuses on the state-sanctioned apprenticeship programs and their effect on children and their families, including those involved in shipbuilding.

55. David S. Cecelski, *The Waterman's Song: Slavery and Freedom in Maritime North Carolina*.
56. Gale Farlow, "Black Craftsmen in North Carolina," *North Carolina Genealogical Society Journal* 6, no. 1 (February 1985), 8.
57. Farlow, "Black Craftsmen," 4; Brendan Foley, "Slaves in the American Maritime Economy, 638-1865: Economic and Cultural Roles."
58. H. Tibbetts, "Rise and Fall and Rise, South Carolina's Maritime History," *Coastal Heritage* 17, no. 2 (Fall 2002), 8.
59. Census returns between 1783 and 1835 list only three white caulkers in Craven County and very few in the other ship and boat building counties.
60. Some backlash may have taken place. Hull Anderson, a successful black shipbuilder in Washington, migrated to Africa in the 1830s because of discrimination. Competition with whites in the local shipbuilding industry may have contributed to his decision to relocate.
61. See Robert G. Albion, *Forests and Sea Power: The Timber Problem of the Royal Navy, 1652–1662*; Brooke Hindle, *America's Wooden Age: Aspect of Early Technology*, 8, 32-33; Hindle and Steven Lubar, *Engines of Change: The American Industrial Revolution, 1790-1860*, 34-36.
62. Amy M. Mitchell, "A Comparison of Wood Use in Eighteenth Century Vessels" (master's thesis, ECU, 1994), 11. For the live oak industry see Virginia Wood, *Live Oaking: Southern Timber for Tall Ships*.
63. Brian Lavery, *Nelson and the Nile: The Naval War Against Bonaparte 1798*, 47. According to K. Jack Bauer, wooden ships required four to five hundred board feet per ton and five hundred board feet per tree, *Maritime History of the United States*, 33-34. See also Roger E. Simmons, *Wood Using Industry in North Carolina*, 52. For a good concise description of the basic shipbuilding timbers, see Richard Steffy, *Wooden Ship Building and the Interpretation of Shipwrecks*, 256-259. The construction of a typical Indiaman might have consumed almost six hundred fully grown hardwood trees spread over as much as twenty acres of old growth forest. Although ships the size of an Indiaman or even a large warship were never built in North Carolina, consider the resources consumed in constructing a major warship of the eighteenth century. For a seventy-four gun ship of the line, three thousand trees spread over ninety acres of forest, were required.
64. William C. Fleetwood Jr., *Tidecraft: The Boats of South Carolina, Georgia, and Northern Florida, 1560-1950*, 142; Goldenberg, *Shipbuilding*, 110-11; Wood, *Live Oaking*, 12; James M. Cox, "The Pamlico-Tar River and Its Role in the Development of Eastern North Carolina" (master's thesis, ECU, 1989), 30; "The Building of the Ship," *Harper's New Monthly Magazine* 24 (1862), 616.
65. Wood, *Live Oaking*, 25.
66. Jim Senter, "Live Dunes and Ghost Forests: Stability and Change in the History of North Carolina's Maritime Forests," *North Carolina Historical Review* 80 (July 2003): 365, passim.
67. There were, of course, a great many additional sites where undocumented vessels and those under five tons were constructed.
68. Charles Thompson, ed., *Cyclopedia of Useful Arts*, II, 603, 613; F. Roy Johnson, *Riverboating in Lower Carolina*, 120; Dana Story, *Frame-Up: The Story of the People and Shipyards of Essex, Massachusetts*, 68-69; Hutchins, *American Maritime Industries*, 118-119.
69. For railway dry docks, see *A Short History of Railway Dry Docks since Their Inception in 1854* (1967).
70. "Selected Notes from the First North Carolina Maritime Workshop, April 9, 1986," copy in authors' possession. The *New Bern Weekly Journal* occasionally used the term "wood boat," not referring to building material but their use in carrying wood. See also Michael Alford and Mark Wilde-Ramsing. *North Carolina Small Craft Historical Context: An Underwater Archaeology Unit Management Plan* (North Carolina Maritime Museum, 1990).
71. Director to Mayor, December 12, 1865, Records of the Treasury Department, E90, "From Collector of Customs," G Series, 1865, RG56, NA.
72. Elizabeth City *Independent*, June 30, 1922.
73. Pat D. Davis, et al., *The Heritage of Carteret County North Carolina*, 1, 58.
74. Quoted in Sonny Williamson and Steve Goodwin, *Maritime Reflections of Carteret County*, 51.
75. Quoted in John Forrest, *Lord I'm Coming Home: Everyday Aesthetics in Tidewater North Carolina*, 108.
76. Forrest, *Lord I'm Coming Home*, 107.
77. Barfield, *Seasoned by Salt*, 159.
78. Michael B. Alford's *Traditional Work Boats of North Carolina* is the best introduction to North Carolina work boats, particularly small craft. For building a replica of a periauger, see Ryan Reynolds, "The Odyssey of the Periauger," *Coastwatch* (Winter 2005): 27-29.
79. The best account of the deadrise skiff is Paul E. Fontenoy, "North Carolina Deadrise Skiffs," *Tributaries* 13 (October 2005): 29-33. See also Wesley N. Jones, "The Spritsail Skiff," *The State* 28, no. 5 (August 1960): 13; Phil Bowie, "A Flair for Raging Inlets," *Wooden Boat* 17 (1991): 23-25; Wayne Willis interview, August 6, 2006.
80. William S. Powell, "Tar Heels Good Ship Builders," Raleigh *News and Observer*, August 23, 1953. Deed books, wills, and estate papers listed canoes as property. They also indicate how universally popular these vessels were. See, for example, Jones, "Abstracts of Wills," passim; Margaret Johnson, "They're Still Used," *The State*, 49 (August 1971) 10; *Beaufort News*, July 21, 1932; Senter, "Live Dunes and Ghost Forests," 365.
81. The *James of Virginia*, built in 1688, is the first documented vessel known to have been constructed in North Carolina, although the colonists undoubtedly built small boats before that date.
82. See *Life on the Mississippi* for this quotation and others by Mark Twain.
83. David E. Griffith, *The Estuary's Gift: An Atlantic Coast Cultural Biography*, 16; Ted Dossett, "Boats That Fit," *Wildlife in North Carolina* 61, no. 1 (January 1997): 8-13.
84. Peggy Jo Cobb interview with James Wilson, January 5, 1982.
85. Lincoln Paine, "Aspects of a Global Maritime History," *Nautical Research Journal* 43 (1998): 131. See also J. Richard Steffy, *Wooden Ship Building and the Interpretation of Shipwrecks*, 11.
86. Michael Alford, "Tracing Colonial Carolina Boats to Their European Roots," unpublished paper presented at the Seventh International Symposium on Boat and Ship Archaeology, July 22, 1994, in Tatihou, France.

Chapter 2

The Colonial and Revolutionary Period, 1585–1783

The maritime history of North Carolina begins with the discovery and exploration of its coastline. Recorded on sixteenth-century maps and described in period manuscripts, the coast was very different from what we know today (Figure 1). Nature is dynamic, not static. Only remnants exist of Cape Kendrick from 1585, as it is now Wimble Shoals. The present location of Cape Hatteras came about toward the end of the seventeenth century.[1]

In 1525, a Spanish expedition led by Lucas Vazquez de Ayllón settled long enough in the Cape Fear region to build a small vessel, replacing one wrecked as the fleet entered the river.[2]

Sir Walter Raleigh's famous "Lost Colony" on Roanoke Island may have built a vessel toward the end of the century, but no evidence exists of this. However, the "Cittie of Ralegh" on Roanoke Island was the first planned town in America, which despite its defensive character focused on economic activities such as farming, fishing, trade, and, perhaps, shipbuilding. Shipbuilding, along with other maritime industries, would develop and expand with increased colonization.[3]

EARLY EASTERN NORTH CAROLINA

After Sir Walter Raleigh's failed attempts on Roanoke Island, the colonization of North Carolina proceeded by way of Virginia. Maps of the area record place names in aboriginal languages, such as Wococon for Ocracoke and Hararask for Hatteras, which suggests discovery and exploration as opposed to settlement. In the years after the founding of Jamestown in 1607, hunters, trappers, and traders roamed the area south of the James River, but few actually settled. Maps in the early seventeenth century continued to record aboriginal place names, but English names began to appear, indicating some degree of permanent settlement (see Appendix C for some explanation about place names).

According to John Speed's description of the Albemarle colonies, first published in 1611 but with revisions until its last edition in 1676, plantations had been established:

> by setling therein two considerable Plantations; the one at *Albemarl-Point*, which lying to the North, borders upon *Virginia*, and whither very many Families have transplanted themselves from *New-England*, and other of our *American* Plantations: the other at *Charles-Town* or *Ashly* River, almost in the center of the Countrey: which being the better Plantation of the two, may in all likelihood invite a far greater, as well from *New England* and other parts that way, as from *Barbadoes* and *Bermudas* many have already removed their effects hither.[5]

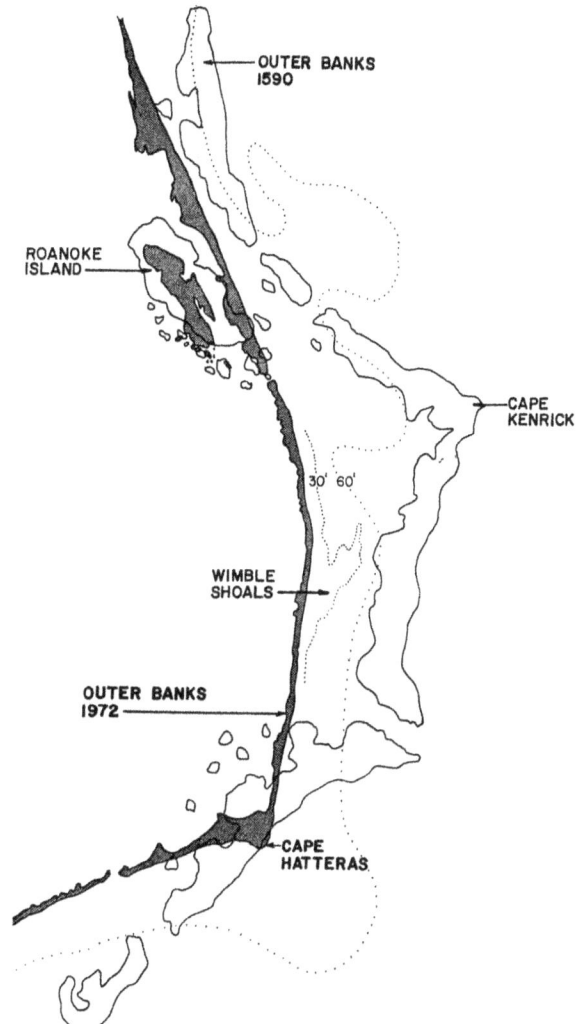

FIGURE 2-1 Four hundred years of change on the Outer Banks. The location of the Outer Banks in 1590, taken from De Bry's publication of the accounts of Thomas Harriot (likely using his triangular surveying method) can be compared to the location taken from the 1972 navigation chart. Both use a Mercator projection which has been in use for navigation since 1569. Very noticeable is the landward movement of the barrier islands and their decreasing width. The comparative cartography also shows a decrease in the areal extent of Roanoke Island, this too, in part, due to a rising sea level. Map by Richard Stephenson.

From the Albemarle to the Cape Fear region, sparse settlement spread south, hugging the sounds and rivers. By the mid-seventeenth century, numerous colonists had pushed into the Albemarle region settling as close to navigable waterways as possible. Nevertheless, the Comberford map of 1657 indicates much of coastal Carolina had yet to be explored.

In 1663, the first land grants in the vicinity of Albemarle Sound and adjacent rivers were recorded.[4] The major inlet, Port Ferdinando, was on Hatteras Island. The name was soon changed to Trinite or Trinety Harbor, the only English place names recorded on early charts. Published in 1672, John Ogilby's *First Lords Proprietors' Map of Carolina* documented a large number of English place names for the first time, although many aboriginal names were still used (see Figure 1 in Chapter 1, and Appendix B). Attesting to the dynamics of the coast, Trinity Inlet no longer existed; Roanoke and Musketo Inlets were now viable passages.

In 1705, the town of Bath was founded on the Pamlico River, becoming the first incorporated community in the colony. Within a few years, Port Roanoke (also known as Roanoke and finally Edenton) and Beaufort were established, followed by New Bern in 1710. Farms and larger settlements extended from the Virginia border to the sounds and rivers of North Carolina and many of these featured shipbuilding sites.

As overland travel was difficult if not impossible, colonists depended on the waterways. Usually, the most perishable crops were planted near the settlements, less perishable crops and pastures near forests. Most ports were surrounded by somewhat fertile, sandy soil interspersed with swamps and marshes. The barrier islands were colonized well before the beginning of the eighteenth century. There were runaways, a few whalers and stockmen, and at least one plantation.[6] Regardless, Native Americans continued their summer migrations to the barrier islands, returning to their permanent villages on the mainland in the fall. The southeastern section of the colony was the last to be settled, but it would rapidly become the most populated. There were a few people living along the Cape Fear estuary prior to 1720; however, Brunswick Town, the first organized settlement along the west bank of the river was not founded until 1726. In 1739, Wilmington was established on the east bank just below the confluence of the Northeast Cape Fear and Cape Fear Rivers.[7]

Despite this growth, overall settlement in eastern North Carolina was rather sporadic. Available population figures for the region suggest that, by the end of the first quarter of the eighteenth century, there were probably less than forty thousand inhabitants, apart from Native Americans. Some colonists migrated directly from Europe, such as the Germans brought to New Bern by Baron Christopher von Graffenried. Nonetheless, the majority arrived from New England and other English possessions.

From the outset, the barrier islands were a handicap to European immigration.

The Albemarle Sound and Cape Fear River regions grew more rapidly than the Pamlico Sound, Tar River, and Neuse River areas located inland, west of the central barrier islands. The vast coastal plain was dominated by large sounds and expanses of swamps or lowlands considered unsuitable for farming. Subsequently, some of the wetlands would be drained by digging ditches and canals and farming then flourished. The pace of colonization was also seriously affected by the Indian wars that did not end until 1725. After the threat of incessant war decreased, the colony's population grew more rapidly.

COLONIAL MARITIME TRADE

Maritime trade was important to the settlers. It may have been crucial to their survival, and their economic prosperity depended upon it. Historians have rightfully emphasized the tremendous handicaps faced in overcoming problems created by Carolina coastal features. Although the barrier islands were cut by many inlets, most of them were treacherous and not navigable. Currituck Inlet was close to the Virginia line and was used essentially by small sloops trading with the Chesapeake Bay settlements. Roanoke Inlet, which appeared in the mid-eighteenth century, was also shallow with only six and a half feet of water at low tide. It was considered treacherous, but was the closest to the Albemarle Sound, and later, to the important entrepôt of Port Roanoke, later called Edenton. Ocracoke Inlet had the advantage of thirteen feet of water at low tide as well as being the closest to Bath and New Bern; it was "the best Inlet and Harbor in this Country."[8] Further south was Topsail Inlet (present-day Beaufort Inlet), which had a low water depth of twelve feet, allowing Beaufort to thrive as a significant port. All the inlets were surrounded by shoals and sand bars. Ocracoke had the "swash," a nearly three-mile-long sandbar lying inside the inlet with a water depth of approximately nine feet. Larger vessels, up to 250 tons, were able to pass these obstructions by utilizing lighters to ferry their cargoes to and from the ports.[9] Lightering was time consuming, increased insurance rates, escalated the danger to ships at anchor waiting to load or unload cargoes, and may have discouraged shipping interests from outside the colony.[10] No vessel was safe along the North Carolina coast. As early as 1665, proprietors were warned that vessels arriving through Roanoke Inlet, "which for ought we can perceive must always be of very small butthen for although Capt Whitties vessel this winter at her coming in found fifteen feete water, yet her going out she had but eleaven feete and though she drew not eight foote water, struck twice or thrice notwithstanding they had Beatoned the Chanell and went out in the best of it, at full sea."[11] Conditions in the inlets changed constantly, and ships trying to navigate them did so at great peril.

In 1673, a Rhode Island ship captain was sued by an Albemarle merchant for damage to his tobacco. The captain responding to the suit stated that in attempting to pass through an inlet he ran aground. He worked free, but ran aground twice more while trying to get out on the other side of the inlet. His efforts to find a free passage led him

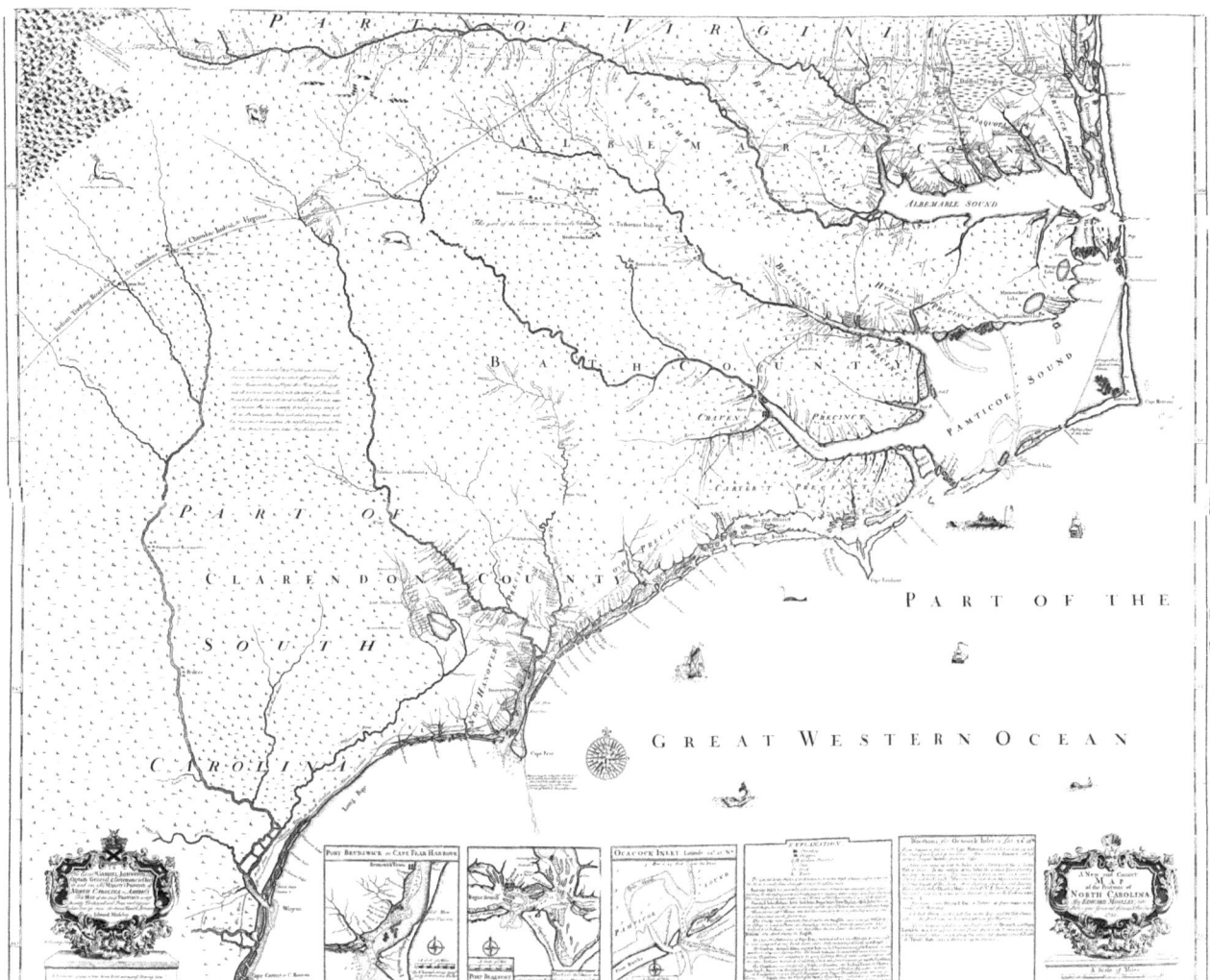

FIGURE 2-2 The Moseley Map of 1733 shows the numerous precincts and ports of entry during the colonial period. While no shipyards are noted, a sawmill is located near Kendrick Creek which is near the confluence of the Roanoke River and Albemarle Sound. It is likely ships were built nearby. Also noticeable are fewer Native American place names as compared to earlier maps. See too, the orientation of the Outer Banks as compared to the John Speed map of 1676 in Chapter 1. The original map is in Joyner Library Special Collections at East Carolina University.

to run into shoals and aground again. Hours later, having been pounded by heavy seas, "with great labor & paines & with the help of the flood wee got her off In which time wee received three or foure extraordinary knockes."[12] These groundings were common and quite often vessels were not so fortunate. Although inlets created short-term havoc for transporting goods, storms tended to disrupt shipping for a longer period with greater loss. Summer hurricanes, winter northeasters, and the uncertainty of currents and tides along the coasts, caused shippers to bypass the capes, inlets, and ports between False Cape, Virginia, and Cape Fear, a distance of approximately 300 miles.

With each storm, it was likely that the shape of the barrier islands and the nature of the inlets changed significantly. Old inlets closed as new ones opened. Each winter, northeasters, with wave heights greater than five feet and lasting several days to a week or more, generated disastrous conditions for shipping. As a result of winter storms during the last decade of the seventeenth century, particularly one in 1697, the shape of the barrier islands was completely changed; Cape Kendrick disappeared and Cape Hatteras was created.[13] In 1773, fourteen vessels were lost during a single "gale."[14] Nevertheless, maritime trade continued to be a mainstay of the colony.

Settlement along the Colonial Carolina Coast

As settlements were established along the waterways, landings were constructed to load and offload vessels. Well up rivers, where larger vessels could not venture due to their drafts, small watercraft were used to transport goods and commodities to and from such landings. Early in the seventeenth century, much of this trade was carried out at individual plantations and a few small communities. As a result, the legislature divided the colony into trading districts and designated five settlements (Bath, Roanoke, Beaufort, New Bern, and Brunswick) as official ports of entry due to their trade, provisioning, ship repair, and shipbuilding activities (Figure 2).

Bath on the Pamlico River served the Hyde Precinct and was the first port with a customs official. Officially, Bath became a port of entry in 1715. It was the closest town to Ocracoke Inlet, one of the most used channels through the barrier islands. In 1709, an unidentified writer noted that Bath "consists of about 12 houses. . . . In all probability, it will be the centre of trade, as having the advantage of a better inlet for shipping."[15]

Early in the eighteenth century, two ports were established in the Albemarle area: Port Currituck and Port Roanoke. Port Currituck, near Currituck Inlet, which was located near present-day Currituck Court House, was not a designated port of entry and remained the smallest of the duty collection districts throughout the colonial period.[16] As early as 1653, a small sloop entered Albemarle Sound by way of Currituck Inlet in search of cargo.[17]

The port of entry for the Albemarle Precinct was Port Roanoke (later known as Edenton). The town was founded in 1712 on Albemarle Sound at the junction of two small tributaries, Queen Anne and Pembroke Creeks, just a few miles from the Chowan River and across the sound from the confluence with the Roanoke River. The Roanoke is the largest drainage basin on the eastern seaboard. The bay at Edenton was a natural site for docking ships and for small wharves to serve the plantations along the various rivers and streams. The town was also the closest port to both Currituck Inlet and the more important Roanoke Inlet. However, it was more than 140 miles from Ocracoke Inlet, the entry point for larger vessels. On the eve of the Revolutionary War, the port had approximately 160 residences, but a large number of warehouses and other buildings involved in shipping lined the waterfront. Maritime industries, including shipbuilding, were vital to the port's economy. Forty-four Port Roanoke shipowners owned vessels that were built there.[18] It became the most active shipping center in the colony. In the first half of the 1770s alone, 827 vessels cleared port carrying a multitude of cargos.[19]

Beaufort was founded in 1713 and incorporated in 1723. The town's origin was due to its proximity to Topsail Inlet roughly two miles southward.[20] Although mariners considered Beaufort a "safe port," its growth was slow. In 1737, John Brickell described the seaport as "small and thinly inhabited," and, as late as 1765, the town had only twelve houses.[21] Its slow growth was a result of the location. The port's trading area was severely handicapped by its inaccessibility by land. It was on a peninsula less than fifteen miles in length and bordered by two shallow rivers. The nearby sounds, Core and Bogue, were also shallow. Although there were roads linking the port to the interior, swamps and creeks west of the town made them problematic for the transportation of bulk cargoes. In addition, the port could not depend much on its small hinterland, as it was not particularly suitable for agriculture except for growing fresh produce used in the provisioning of ships. Despite the proximity of Beaufort to the ocean and its official status as a port of entry, New Bern at the confluence of the Neuse and Trent Rivers, forty miles to the north, quickly surpassed it in size and importance.

New Bern struggled back from the destruction caused by the Tuscarora War (1711-1715). The town was strategically positioned to tap the trade in a much larger hinterland. Despite its distance from the ocean, it became a transshipment point. By mid-century, it had outstripped Beaufort and Bath as a major port. However, growth remained slow.

The passage of a series of acts designed to improve navigation between New Bern and Ocracoke Inlet in 1739 signaled "the rise of New Bern as a port town."[22] Certainly, the designation of New Bern as the capital of the colony in 1746 provided a stimulus to the port's economic and maritime activities. That New Bern remained in Beaufort's jurisdiction makes it difficult to determine the number of vessels that actually traded there. What information exists makes it clear that New Bern's trade increased steadily until the Revolutionary War.[23] During this period, New Bern's maritime trade equaled that of the Cape Fear region and its port of Wilmington, and challenged Port Roanoke as the leader until the mid-1770s.[24]

Founded in 1726, Brunswick Town was Cape Fear's port of entry. The town remained small. In 1731, it consisted of ten or twelve houses, "hardly worth the name of a Village."[25]

It was quickly eclipsed as the strategic location by Wilmington, the deep estuary of which was instrumental in its growth and economic activity. In addition, the rise in the region's population before the Revolutionary War surpassed the other sections of coastal North Carolina, aided Wilmington's development as a port, and further spurred its economic growth.

It is a mistake to assume North Carolina's maritime commerce, especially its inland trade, was monopolized by the ports. Although vessels engaged in oceanic trade had to declare their cargo at the ports of entry, and later at customhouses, a considerable percentage of trade was with the plantations, landings, and small hamlets scattered along the sounds and streams. In 1734, a traveler on the Cape Fear River noted "two ships, two sloops and a brigantine, loaded with lumber for the West Indies" at a plantation landing.[26] In 1775, two hundred hogsheads of tobacco were transported downstream from Halifax. Tobacco, wheat, lumber, and other products were carried on piraguas or dugouts, flatboats, and small sailing vessels from warehouses in Halifax to Port Roanoke. Murfrees Ferry (Murfreesboro) on the Meherrin River was the site of a landing where produce from upstream, including nearby Virginia, and downstream, by way of the Chowan River, was transshipped by sailing vessels.[27] This trade pattern would continue well into the nineteenth century.

The Nature of British Regulations in Colonial Carolina

The Navigation Laws, regulations which governed colonial economic activities, were drafted in order to provide England with raw materials. Most North Carolina settlers engaged in agriculture and forestry. The majority of the crops were for local consumption. However, as more land was cleared and crops planted, colonists began to export their surplus. Corn led the list in agricultural exports, followed by peas and rice. In the Pamlico and Neuse River basins where there was little arable land, livestock was raised. Salted pork and beef were exported in barrels. Salted fish was shipped out of Beaufort. As early as 1709, seafood, primarily red drum, was exported to other colonies. Beaufort, Currituck, and Hatteras residents also engaged in whaling, to export oil, but the amount was small.[28] All North Carolina ports exported hides and furs obtained from traders and Indians. New Bern and Wilmington exported tanned leather, skins, tallow, and lard.[29] Port Roanoke monopolized the transport of tobacco and hemp. In 1769, the Albemarle port exported twenty-six tons of hemp. Four years later, the port shipped between 3,000 and 5,000 hogsheads of tobacco.[30] However, timber products, rather than tobacco, were the most important export.

The American colonies had the resources to provide raw materials for various industries, particularly ship construction. From earliest exploration and settlement, it was clear that harvesting the wilderness could generate income and even wealth. British and colonial officials recognized that North Carolina had an abundant supply of timber. When Bath was designated a seaport, the assembly informed the Lords Proprietors that it was "the most proper place within the . . . province for the ships to take in Masts, Pitch, Tar, Turpentine and other Naval Stores for the use of His Majesties Fleet." In 1720, 8,000 barrels of tar and pitch were shipped through Port Bath.[31] Naval stores such as tar, pitch, and turpentine, derived from longleaf or pitch pine, became North Carolina's chief contribution to colonial commerce. North Carolina became Britain's largest supplier of naval stores. Bath would be joined by other ports of entry, Port Roanoke, Beaufort, and New Bern, in the shipping of naval stores. Exports from Beaufort in 1764 consisted of 30,043 barrels of tar, 3,303 barrels of turpentine, 3,721 barrels of pitch, 1,279 barrels of spirits of turpentine, and 619 barrels of rosin. However, by 1770, Brunswick Town and Wilmington led the way in this commercial venture, providing approximately half of all such stores shipped to England.[32]

In 1761, Governor Arthur Dobbs reported that the abundant forests were "excellent for Ship timber."[33] Sawmills appeared on colonial maps well before shipyards. The forest industry developed rapidly as sawmills were erected throughout the coastal plain. Pine, oak, walnut, cypress, and cedar were all used for commercial purposes. Shingles, barrel staves, masts, spars, and sawn lumber, materials used in ship construction and goods for maritime commerce, were produced and shipped. Of these, only shingles, staves, and sawn lumber were of major importance. All the ports exported lumber and timber products, but they differed in the degree of what was shipped. Port Roanoke led the export of staves and Brunswick dominated the sawn lumber trade. Port Roanoke exported more than a million staves in one year. In addition to staves and boards, New Bern shipped shingles and scantlings, mostly to the West Indies.[34]

North Carolina's oceanic commerce followed four routes: coastal, West Indies,

trans-Atlantic, and the slave trade or traditional triangular trade route.[35] Although few records are available for the period prior to the 1760s, it seems clear that New Englanders and Virginians dominated the colony's shipping from the beginning. They owned most of the vessels engaged in the trade. Vessels with North Carolina cargoes traded throughout the Chesapeake Bay region and the rivers flowing into the bay. Norfolk was the most important port engaged in trade between the two colonies. Trade between Norfolk and North Carolina "was the principal reason for the growth of that seaport."[36] The New England trade with North Carolina generally followed a similar pattern, shipping the goods from North Carolina elsewhere. The colony's direct trade with Europe was not substantial, but it is worthy of note. In 1769, seventeen schooners and one sloop cleared Port Roanoke for British and Irish ports. From 1768 to 1773, a total of 117 schooners and twenty-six sloops with cargoes from Port Roanoke engaged in transoceanic trade. Imports to the Roanoke District generally followed a coastwise route. Significantly, imports accounted for approximately one-third of Port Roanoke's maritime trade. In 1768, sixty percent of Brunswick and Wilmington's trade was with the British Isles. The colony's maritime trade patterns depended on the complex geographical features of the coastline. Each of North Carolina's five colonial ports of entry supported distinct trade routes. Brunswick and later Wilmington, with relatively deep water, concentrated on the overseas trade. The four remaining ports depended heavily upon coastwise trade, as direct commerce with Britain was negligible.[37]

Nevertheless, the colony's overall trade was far from negligible. A 1768 tabulation of shipping recorded that 472 vessels entered the colony's ports compared to 491 for South Carolina and 625 for Virginia during the same year.[38] Shipping from North Carolina tended to be more expensive. Planters frequently complained about insurance, freight costs, and the dependence upon out-of-state vessels, particularly large oceangoing ships. Throughout much of the colonial period, North Carolina interests owned few vessels engaged in trans-Atlantic trade. Charles Pollock complained that "as our navigation is bad, so we have very few Vessels except those that are very small, which makes freight excessive dear and very often not to be had at any rate."[39] Pollock later wrote that he was considering building his own vessel "if it will not cost to[o] dear."[40] The cost was "dear," in fact so "dear" to many merchants and planters that consortiums or partnerships were often arranged to build and own vessels.

Historians have argued that the majority of vessels engaged in North Carolina's oceanic trade were owned, registered, and built outside the colony, primarily in New England. This may be correct. Nonetheless, complete statistics are not available for the entire colonial period. Only the decade leading up to the Revolutionary War is well documented and even the interpretation of evidence for this period is not without controversy.[41] Historian Alan Watson has concluded that Montego Bay in Jamaica constructed most of the vessels that visited Port Brunswick during this period, and notes that forty-one percent of the vessels that entered the Cape Fear in 1776 were from Jamaica. The remaining registered vessels were from other North American colonies and Great Britain.[42] However, Watson and others have paid little attention to British records in the North Carolina State Archives, records copied from the Public Records Office and other repositories in Great Britain, as well as the vast number of county records from the colonial period. These indicate that ship and boat building was far more extensive in the colony. There is also considerable evidence that far more North Carolina merchants engaged in shipping than has previously been thought.[43] There is considerable evidence that far more vessels were built for the oceanic trade in North Carolina than previously recognized.

Colonial Shipbuilders and Shipwrights

Shipbuilding is one of the oldest colonial industries in America. Small watercraft were built for local transportation. A Dutch builder on Manhattan Island in 1614 constructed the first decked vessel built in the North American colonies. In that same year, Captain John Smith, of Jamestown fame, built several fishing vessels in what today is the state of Maine.

The Virginia Company sent several skilled boatwrights to their colony and the first vessel was launched in 1611. In order to encourage this industry, Virginia and Massachusetts Bay colonies gave grants of free land to shipbuilders willing to locate in their colonies.[44] Shipbuilding grew rapidly, especially in New England. "In all the American Plantations, his Majesty has none so apt for the building of Shipping as NewEngland."[45] The industry continued to expand throughout the seventeenth century, particularly in the 1680s, with the outbreak of war in Europe.

Whether shipbuilding or ship repairing started first in the colonies is not known, but ship repairing was no less an integral and lucrative aspect of the shipbuilding trade. Every vessel, large and small, at one time or another, requires repairs and overhaul. Wooden vessels need constant attention. Ship carpenters and other associated tradesmen, such as sailmakers and blockmakers, were primarily involved in ship repairs rather than new construction. Existing records suggest the industry was extensive, probably more so than new construction.[46]

It has been claimed that "there is no record of any shipbuilding" in seventeenth century North Carolina.[47] Admittedly, records are incomplete. Nevertheless, available sources indicate vessels were built in the colony prior to the eighteenth century. As elsewhere in the colonies, small craft such as canoes and sailing vessels were constructed for local transportation. Deed books list a "boatbuilder," a "boatright," [sic] and a "canoe builder," among the first vessel craftsmen in North Carolina. Four shipwrights and one boat builder settled in the colony during the later years of the seventeenth century. When the first ship was built in the colony is not known. English naval officer records list five vessels built in the colony in the seventeenth century, the earliest, the *James of Virginia*, completed in 1688. Small sloops and shallops of less than six tons were documented in the West Indies. Colonial leaders from Baron Christoph von Graffenried to Governor William Tryon all recognized the need for vessels.[48]

Small craft and nondescript vessels were built by individuals for their own use. The builders often had little or no experience. However, larger vessels required a variety of skilled artisans: ship carpenters, sawyers, blacksmiths, sailmakers, blockmakers, and caulkers. Records identify only one individual as a caulker, although slaves were used as caulkers as well. Three blockmakers have been identified as working in the colony, along with two rope makers in Port Roanoke; there were three sailmakers, one in Wilmington, another in New Bern, a third in an unidentified location, and several joiners. Joiners were employed in house building as well as ship construction.[49] Nearly every shipbuilding site had a forge, as did most plantations, so blacksmiths were fairly common. The same was true of sawyers. Fortunately, ship carpentry was a valued trade and often identified in the records.[50] Court records, deed books, and other documents often indicate that individuals either changed occupations or had multiple business interests. Shipwrights were often mariners, farmers, fishermen, and/or house carpenters. One became an innkeeper; others entered government service as sheriffs, mayors, council members, legislators, and even a governor. Traditional European guilds separated trades, but professional lines were often blurred in colonial North Carolina.

Shipwrights began migrating to the colony in the seventeenth century. According to several accounts, shipwrights from Bermuda settled along the Pasquotank River in the 1660s.⁵¹ There is also evidence that shipbuilders from Virginia migrated to the Albemarle region. This is confirmed by the 1714 disposition of Thomas Barwick, who stated that, forty-eight years earlier, Thomas Keele, a Virginian, built a vessel for William Crawford on the Pasquotank River.⁵²

In 1678, Timothy Biggs, a North Carolina planter in the Albemarle region, petitioned the proprietors to "issue land grants in order to . . . induce shipbuilding so the people might ship their tobacco to Virginia and England without having to sell to Virginia boats directly."⁵³ All but two of the shipwrights listed for the seventeenth century were residing in the Albemarle Sound region. In fact, eighteen of the twenty-seven builders living in the colony before 1721 were in the northeastern section of the colony, specifically, the Albemarle Sound area. In the last decade of the seventeenth century, two shipwrights, William Barkely and John Watts, were located in Perquimans County. In 1698, the first listed apprentice for learning the trade of shipbuilding was in Perquimans County under Watts's direction, and William and Johann Veendam established themselves on the Roanoke River.⁵⁴ Shipwrights and builders migrated to the colony not only from Virginia and Bermuda, but from other colonies and from the British Isles.⁵⁵ A number of them came from New England, several from Philadelphia, and at least one from Maryland.⁵⁶ The immigration of ship carpenters from the British Isles to the American colonies reached such proportions by 1764 that the master shipwrights of Thames River represented to the King that since 1710, the number in Great Britain had diminished by one-half.⁵⁷ The drain continued up to the Revolutionary War. In 1767, the *Virginia Gazette* reported that a "great number of shipwrights were engaged [in Great Britain] to embark . . . to North America, where artificers in that branch are greatly wanted."⁵⁸ The large majority of these settled in New England, but some made their way to North Carolina.

There were a surprisingly large number of shipwrights and shipbuilders living in North Carolina in the eighteenth century, particularly from 1770 to 1783. Altogether, some 168 who listed themselves as shipwrights or ship carpenters were found in deeds and other documents (Appendix C).⁵⁹ Some family names occur frequently but with different surnames, for example, the Sparrow family in Craven County, and the Bell and Smith families in Hyde County. Some are clearly different generations; others are relatives. Probably a large number moved to North Carolina from other colonies. Virginia was a principal source of many, but others came from Maryland, South Carolina, and New England. At least two were sent from the British Isles specifically to build vessels. In 1724, Matthew Rowan arrived in North Carolina under contract with two Irish merchants to build vessels. A Welsh shipwright by the name of Ogden took passage to the colony and built a brig near New Bern. With the outbreak of the Revolution he scuttled the vessel, and after the war ended raised her.⁶⁰

Between 1700 and 1725, thirty-four settlers in North Carolina claimed to be shipwrights or builders of vessels. Twenty-four listed the Albemarle Sound area as their home or place of business, nine claimed residence in the Pamlico region, and one in Craven County. A number of shipwrights were listed for different counties at different times. They either owned land in more than one county or moved from one to another. At least two of them moved out of the colony but continued to hold property in North Carolina. From 1726 to 1760, an additional fifty-eight shipwrights/boatbuilders are listed in thirteen locations excluding two, for whom no location was found.

Port Roanoke and the Albemarle Sound area list thirty-six, Hyde County seven, Bertie County five, Craven County four, eight were in Wilmington and New Hanover County, and two in Brunswick County. The decline of Bath as a port is demonstrated by the fact that only one shipbuilder is listed for that port. From 1760 to 1776, sixty-four shipwrights/boatbuilders are listed. This suggests that, in the years preceding the American Revolution, shipbuilding was a thriving enterprise. Shipwrights were locating farther into the interior during this period: two in Pitt and Halifax counties, one in Northampton County, and others up the Cape Fear River.⁶¹ New Hanover and Chowan counties continued to lead in the number of ship carpenters, but Hyde County, with nine, began to emerge as an important shipbuilding center.⁶² There were at least five shipbuilders in Chowan County during this period, and thirteen during the Revolutionary War years. There were nine shipwrights/shipbuilders in Carteret and Craven counties.

Wilmington, in New Hanover County on the Cape Fear River, is the only port with depth enough to handle trans-Atlantic vessels directly. It was accessible to trade from the hinterland and had a number of shipwrights. Few vessels that engaged in the oceanic trade were built on the Cape Fear River. A large percentage of vessels engaged in this trade were owned by non-residents.⁶³ There is some debate over who was the first shipwright in Wilmington. Most authorities consider Michael Dyer to be the first as he is granted property along the river in 1734. Nevertheless, in 1733, Richard Dyer (kin?), a shipwright, was working in the vicinity. In 1737, Michael Dyer purchased a river front lot called the "Ship Yard" somewhere between Castle and Church Streets. Apparently, his shipbuilding activities lasted about two years. In 1739, he sold the "Ship Yard" lot as well as his other personal property. In 1740, he tried to establish a grist mill but failed. In debt, he fled before the sheriff could arrest him.⁶⁴ From the mid-

1730s to the mid-1770s, thirteen shipwrights plied their trade in the Wilmington area. Joshua Grainger, probably the most prominent shipbuilder in the region, located his shipbuilding business at the foot of Church Street. A number of them were located along the river between Orange and Dock Streets. Some of the shipwrights sold out to others.[65] Deeds record a shipyard at Cogdells Landing on the Black River which flows into the Cape Fear River west of Wilmington.[66]

There is no evidence that Brunswick County, or the Cape Fear estuary below Wilmington, developed a notable shipbuilding industry prior to the nineteenth century.[67] Shipwrights were often mariners, farmers, fishermen, or simply house carpenters. In 1702, Thomas Blount of Kendricks Creek near Plymouth, was both a ship carpenter and a blacksmith, while another was considered a caulker.[68]

Despite the number of shipbuilders and carpenters residing in North Carolina during the colonial period, there is evidence that skilled labor was scarce. The rural nature of North Carolina, with a sparse and scattered population, simply did not attract skilled craftsmen in adequate numbers. Such professionals were certainly wanted and needed in the Carolinas. The South Carolina governor wrote the Board of Trade in 1719 that "[w]e are come to no great matter of [ship] building here for want of persons who undertake it."[69] In 1753, a planter noted a brig under construction at Nixonton on the Little River in Pasquotank County: "Very little done since I was here last. Carpenter coming however."[70] Hugh Williamson, who was having a vessel built at Winton in 1778, wrote that "a single carpenter is hard to be get."[71] In 1783, a merchant from Beaufort County informed an acquaintance that a vessel being built would not be completed on time "mainly by the want of a sufficient number of carpenters."[72] The ship *Elizabeth*, in need of repairs, put into Beaufort, but "for want of skillful and experienced shipwrights ... could not be done or performed there."[73]

One way of alleviating this shortage was through the apprenticeship system which was a well-established institution in Great Britain long before the English first arrived in North America.[74] In fact, it was the predominant entry point into many trades and professions, including those involved in ship and boat building. Bound as youngsters to work until their twenty-first birthday, apprentices learned the art and mystery "in ye building of Vessells."[75] They received room and board, minimal clothing, and instruction in reading and writing; in turn, they provided shipwrights with cheap labor. At their "graduation," they received a letter of recommendation and a chest of shipbuilding tools.[76] Often they were hired by the shipwright who trained them. It was quite common in North Carolina, as elsewhere, to apprentice orphans to shipbuilders. Of thirty apprentices listed in the county records, thirteen were orphans. The earliest recorded apprentice to a shipwright was Thomas Cockrey, a freeman, who bound himself to John Watts in 1698.[77] Abell Miller and Nathaniel Matthias, both of Chowan County, Thomas and Samuel Smith of Hyde County, and Roderick Sparrow of Craven County trained more than one apprentice, occasionally more than one at the same time. At times, neither master nor apprentice honored the terms of the agreement. The Craven Court of Pleas and Quarter Sessions freed two boys from their bondage to a ship carpenter claiming that they had not been taught to write. In 1713, George Fox of Prince County, Virginia, was apprenticed to Chowan County shipwright John Avery. Fox fled his apprenticeship to work for a planter. At Avery's request, the court ordered Fox to resume his apprenticeship. In Wilmington, apprentice William Martin claimed that his master, shipwright Michael Dyer, refused to teach him the trade of ship carpentry. An apprentice in Chowan County testified before the court that his master, William Harper, "starved [him] and put him to work in a corn field instead of training him in shipbuilding."[78] Several of the apprentices were blacks and mulattos, some enslaved and some free.

It is reasonable to assume that black laborers and craftsmen, usually slaves, were involved in the building of vessels in colonial North Carolina. They were in New England and Virginia, from which many of the North Carolina shipwrights originated.[79] A great number of vessels, large and small, were constructed on plantations where the labor force usually consisted of slaves. It is conceivable that slaves on plantations were responsible for constructing the small boats and dugouts. Businessmen involved in shipping and shipbuilding often possessed slaves.[80] Traditionally, blacks were used as caulkers. In 1752, six carpenters and nine caulkers labored on HMS *Scorpion* in the Cape Fear River. The nine caulkers were probably slaves; one itemized note mentions that on November 4th, four black slaves worked on the vessel.[81] However, the most revealing documentary evidence for the involvement of slaves in shipbuilding is in regard to the MacKnight shipyard in Currituck County. MacKnight had approximately forty-five slaves, including ship carpenters, blacksmiths, and caulkers, employed in his shipyard. A Norfolk merchant and acquaintance of MacKnight, Colonel Jacob Ellegood, stated: "he [Ellegood] knew their Blackes very well, they were almost all Tradesmen & House servants & the most valuable collection of Blackes in that Country - They were able to build a ship within themselves [i.e., by themselves] with no other assistance than a Master Builder."[82]

Social mobility was characteristic of colonial society in general and was evident in the shipbuilding trade. The Veendam family, in the Albemarle region, included some of the earliest entrepreneurs to engage in shipbuilding activities. By 1680, they had established a sawmill, a naval stores trade, and a shipbuilding business. They also leased vessels to merchants and mariners to carry naval stores, deer skins, hides of fur bearing animals, cypress shingles, and oak staves to the West Indies and England.[83] In 1717, William Downing, a shipwright and merchant in Chowan County, sold his property, "houses, shops, shipyards" on Wiccacon Creek to his brother-in-law William Sharp.[84] Evidently, Downing went out of the shipbuilding business. He called himself "Captain" and a mariner. In 1722, Sharp sold his brother-in-law a plantation of about 2,000 acres with cattle and horses.[85] Downing's will in 1736 left his property to his son who in turn sold it to Sharp.[86] Captain James Wimble learned the shipbuilding trade in England where "with the aid of friends" he built an ocean-going vessel. After immigrating to North Carolina, he built, or had built, at least one vessel, the brigantine *Rebecca*, on the Cape Fear River. Whether or not he actually engaged in the shipbuilding industry is unclear. He referred to himself not as a shipwright, but as a mariner. At other times, he called himself an innkeeper and distiller. He is best known as a real estate promoter, one of those responsible for the settlement of Wilmington, and as an accomplished cartographer.[87]

New England immigrants to Carteret County laid the foundation for what would become an important ship and boat building industry. Ebenezer Harker, a native of Boston, moved to Carteret County early in the eighteenth century. Calling himself a mariner, he purchased the island that bears his name in 1730. Subsequently, referring to himself as a shipwright, he established a shipyard on the island.[88]

The most extensive shipbuilding in Carteret County took place on the Newport River. There, a colony of transplanted Quakers from Rhode Island established a number of business enterprises, including at least one shipyard. Henry Stanton, a minister and shipwright, moved to the county in 1721 and purchased property which eventually totaled more than 2,000 acres, most of which was placed under cultivation. Stanton founded a number of businesses, including turpentine stills, a brickyard, and a shipyard. He was joined in the settlement by other Rhode Island Quakers including William F. Borden. Borden and his family arrived in Beaufort in 1732 and joined the Quaker colony on the Newport River, named after their community in Rhode Island. There, he entered the shipbuilding business. Whether he established a new yard or joined with Stanton is not clear.[89]

Apparently, Borden was involved in shipbuilding in Rhode Island. He also manufactured duck cloth used for sails, but there is no evidence that he made duck cloth in North Carolina. He contracted to construct vessels for business acquaintances in New England. William Borden died in 1748, leaving his property, including the shipyard, to his son. William Jr. continued the shipbuilding business but became far more interested in running his plantation, other businesses, and, in later life, entering politics. At some time before the American Revolution, the shipyard came under Benjamin Stanton's ownership.[90]

A distinction can be made between a shipwright and a shipbuilder. Shipwrights were artisans; shipbuilders were often shipyard owners. Occasionally, they were businessmen, merchants, mariners, and planters. However, such distinctions are often blurred in the colonial period. Few businessmen and planters were directly involved in shipbuilding. Generally, they contracted for one or more vessels with builders or shipwrights. Joseph Hewes, signer of the Declaration of Independence and a well-known businessman and merchant, owned a shipyard in Port Roanoke. It was said to be at the point where Pembroke Creek meets the bay at Edenton.[91] Thomas Clark and John Rutherford of Wilmington were merchants, millers, and shipbuilders. Rutherford was also a planter and sawmill owner, as well as Receiver General of the Kings Quitrent in the province. In the early 1760s, Cornelius Moore, a Perquimans merchant and shipwright, purchased property in Nixonton on the Little River from Joshua Guyer, where he established a shipyard. For unknown reasons, it failed, and he had to sell it and other property to pay off his creditors.[92]

The Business of Colonial Shipbuilding

Shipbuilding required land and capital. Four shipwrights joined together and moved from Virginia to Tyrrell County in 1761. They jointly purchased land for a ship construction site.[93] William Haly, a Bertie County shipwright, contracted with John Campbell, an Edenton merchant, to "frame, Build, Compleat and Launch [a vessel] when compleated and finished . . . as well as my Right . . . procured of Mr. Thomas Ryan a certain Tract and Parcel of Ground for a Ship Yard laying on Salmon Creek . . . and Previledge . . . to cut Down Timber necessary for Building . . . the said Vessell." Campbell also agreed to provide credit for tools and "Tackel."[94] However, like so many colonial merchants, Campbell found himself in court unable to pay his debts.[95] Campbell's 1777 will suggests that he had considerable property when he died.[96]

Campbell, like most merchants and businessmen, either had the capital or could borrow it. Livelihood depended on trade and trade depended on vessels. Merchants often entered the shipbuilding business as a profitmaking enterprise and as a means of providing necessary water transportation. In 1733, Francis Pugh, a Bertie County merchant and owner of several vessels, added a codicil to his will:

> I have begun to build a briganine [sic] which is now on the stocks in Bertie Precinct. My executors are to finish the brigantine from the money from my estate, with anchors, masts, cables, sails, and all other appurtenances. After this vessel is finished my executors and trustees shall purchase a loading of tobacco, black

walnut or other merchandise fit for the british market and send this vessel to great Britain.

He added that the ship and profits from the cruise were to go to his family.[97] In that same year, Richard Sanderson Sr. of Perquimans County bequeathed his vessels to his son and son-in-law, including a "small vessel" he was also building.[98] William Gray of Bertie County was a man of many interests. He was a large landowner, merchant, businessman, politician, and shipbuilder. He apparently owned a shipyard on "a high bluff" on the Cashie River. Richard Blackledge, a successful New Bern merchant and land owner, left a large inventory of vessels when he died in 1776, including a brig under construction at Beaufort and a schooner being built at Otter Creek.[99]

Records indicate that colonial shipwrights in North Carolina usually owned the shipyard or the site where they constructed and repaired vessels. William and John Smith, ship carpenters in Pasquotank County, contracted to rebuild a ship for Peter Brock. It is clear from the records that the Smiths were both shipwrights and owners of the site where the work was to be performed.[100] In 1716, Richard Alban of Albemarle County established one of the first shipyards in Edenton when he purchased a half-acre at the fork of Queen Anne's Creek, a section of the waterfront that was historically utilized for shipbuilding.[101]

Some shipwrights entered politics and became government officials. Matthew Rowan rose to become a colonial governor. Charles Cogdell, who lived in the Beaufort area, rose from an apprentice ship carpenter in 1713, to a juryman in 1723, and in 1726, Justice of the Peace. In 1733, he was elected to the General Assembly.[102] William Borden of Carteret County was elected to the General Assembly, but, as he was a Quaker, declined the office. In 1764, Josiah Nash represented Pasquotank County at the Provincial Assembly and held various local offices. He owned considerable property in Camden and Perquimans Counties as well as in Pasquotank County.[103] Joshua Grainger was not only one of the founders of Wilmington but served as Justice of the Quorum. He also became a prosperous real estate developer and owned approximately one-quarter of all Wilmington property.[104]

North Carolina colonial county records include numerous deeds of transfer for land involving shipwrights. Most of them likely purchased the land for farming, but it was also important for political and economic reasons. In the British Isles, the freeholder or yeoman who cultivated his own land was entitled to vote and, in the New World, he was also entitled to hold public office. Land was much less expensive in the North American colonies and it was not unusual for an individual to own several hundred acres. An undetermined number of ship carpenters were farmers. In addition to farming, shipwrights often leased or purchased land for timber, built one or more vessels, and then sold the land or gave it up. The land purchased or leased by shipwrights was usually adjacent to a stream or swamp. Swampland was usually a good source of white cedar, also known as juniper.[105]

In a number of instances, a shipbuilding contract required the client to provide everything necessary to complete the vessel except the timber. It seems reasonable that, in some cases, the builder would provide the necessary ship timber, either by purchase from a sawmill or by providing it from his own land. In 1753, William Haly, a shipwright in Bertie County, obtained a parcel of land from a local planter "for a ship yard laying on Salmon Creek . . . and privileges to cut down timber necessary for building compleating and launching of the said frame and vessel."[106]

In 1774, a contract agreement was negotiated between the merchant firm of Scott, Irwin and Cowpers with John Smith, shipbuilder of Hyde County:

> [T]he said John Smith should and would build finish launch and complete to a cleet a Vessell of the following dimensions in a strong neat and workmanlike manner according to the best mode of Building now in Practice - that is to say Sixty feet keel eight feet four inches Lower Hold and three feet nine Inches between Decks. Twenty feet four Beam fourteen feet floor . . . Seven Inches deadrise. Thirteen feet rake forward seventeen feet six Inches Transom and on those Dimensions to be moulded to draw as little Water as possible to her burthen by giving her a long floor and round Rib and that the said Smith should find and furnish Masts Yards Bowsprit and Booms likewise Tops, Capes and every other material belonging to the Carpenters business that the said Vessell might want to complete her and to bring in no after Bill. And that the said Smith would Launch the said Vessell and complete her in as aforesaid on or before the twentieth of November next . . . That the said Vessells floor timbers were to be red oak of sufficient size her lower futtocks fifteen on each sides. The bilge to be the best natural grown white oak the remainder to be of Pitch Pine two and half inches thick for bottom sides and Deck (except as follows) in the turn of the bilge on each sidegood white oak three and half Inches thick three Streaks on each side and where the turns forward. . . and aft to be of white oak. the beams to be pine except in the Hatchway and all the Windless bitts and middle futtocks and upper Timbers to be pine except in the breast of the chains. The Quarter Deck to take in the Pumps and to rise fourteen Inches above the Main Deck the quickwork eleven inches high. The whole of the Plank beams and Timbers to be free from Sap or decay and to be of strong and sufficient sizes according to the best mode of Building . . . Vessells that are to take the ground. In consideration where of the said Scott, Irwin and Cowpers for themselves . . . to find and furnish to the said Smith with Iron Oakhum and Pitch Tar and Turpentine as might be necessary to

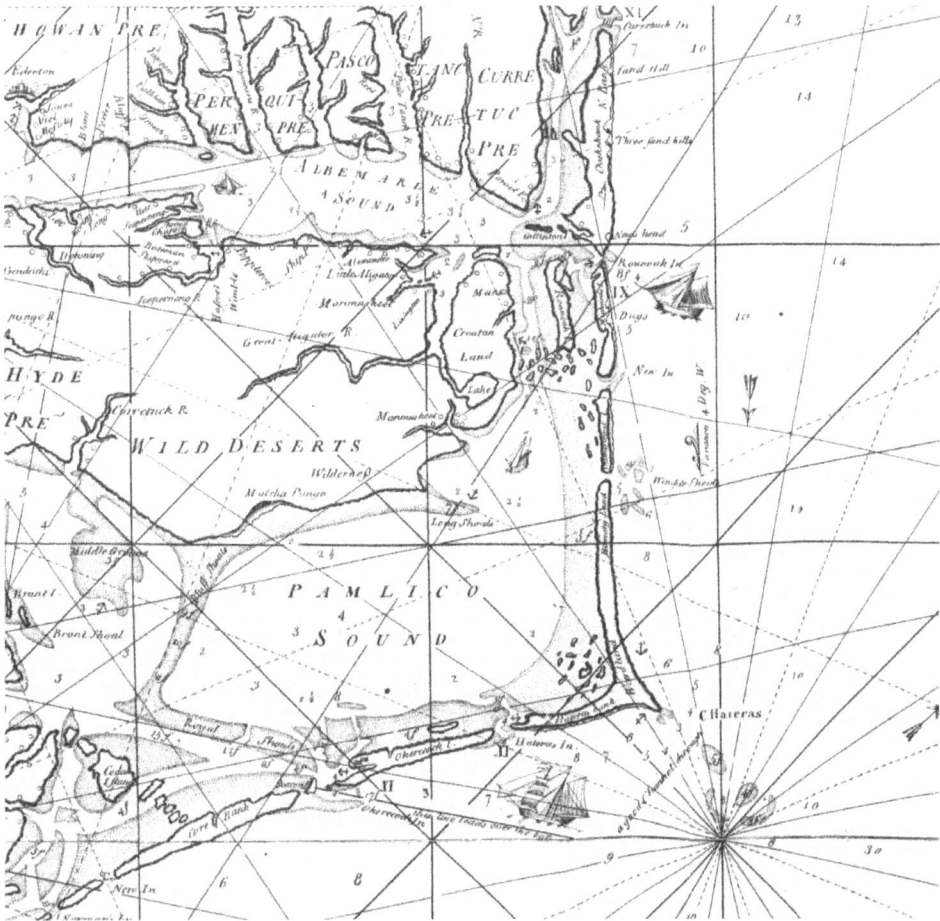

FIGURE 2-3 This portion of the Wimble Map of 1738 shows the Bateman Shipyard on the Scuppernong River. However, compared to other maps, the Scuppernong River appears to be located too far to the west. Also, compare the orientation of the Outer Banks with the Wimble map in Figure 2, the Ogilvy map in Figure 5, and the Speed map in Chapter 1. *Source:* Joyner Library, East Carolina University.

complete and furnish the said Vessell and also to pay the said John Smith the Sum of Three Pounds seven shillings and sixpence per ton for every ton the said Vessell might tonnage allowing the depth of hold to be ten feet six Inches and also to allow the said Smith for any extraordinary expenses he might be at . . . the Payment to be as follows one half in dry goods at one hundred and forty six and two thirds per first advance on the sterling cost and at the other half in Proclamation money one third of the money to be paid at the laying of the Keel one third at the planking and the balance at the delivery of the Vessell.[107]

This is an extremely interesting document. It is far more detailed than others examined in the records. It indicates that either the builder or contractors or both had a specific design concept for the vessel, and knew the material that needed to be included in the agreement. Further, that either they, or perhaps a lawyer who drew up the document, had experience in preparing such a construction document. Moreover, it disproves the idea that North Carolina-built vessels in the colonial period were roughly planned. On the contrary, it reflects a relatively high degree of professionalism in shipbuilding.

COLONIAL SHIPYARDS AND THE NATURAL RESOURCES FOR SHIPBUILDING

Shipyards are frequently mentioned in official documents. However, given the number of ship carpenters in North Carolina during the colonial period and the number and type of vessels built, it is difficult to determine whether these were established yards or individual vessel construction sites. Joseph Goldenberg describes a typical colonial shipyard as "simply a vacant lot upon which . . . [a boatbuilder] . . . could assemble a ship." Often, there were few or no buildings, and all work was carried on in the open.[108] Under this definition, any site where one or more vessels were constructed could be called a shipyard. A North Carolina colonial shipyard might have a tool shed, forge, sawpit, and possibly a wharf. Hyde County civil and criminal papers mention Jonathan Jasper's Shipyard. Bertie County confiscated property papers list William Lowther's property on Cashoke Creek at a place called the "Ship yard." Perquimans County deeds of 1767 describe property "where the shipyard is."[109] At least two colonial maps show the location of shipyards. The Wimble map of 1738 (Figure 3) clearly shows the presence of a shipyard on the north bank of the Scuppernong River. The yard is listed as belonging to a planter, Jonathan Bateman.[110] In 1767, William Churton, a surveyor, produced a plat of Sir Nathaniel Duckenfield's land. He detailed, among other possessions, a shipyard on Salmon Creek located between the Roanoke and Chowan Rivers (Figure 4).[111] Despite the date, it would be incorrect to describe the Duckenfield shipyard as "probably the earliest definitely located shipyard in the State."[112]

Vessels were constructed in North Carolina prior to the eighteenth century, but there is no evidence an established shipyard existed in the early colony. However, in the eighteenth century, a number were operating at one time or another. Thomas MacKnight owned a well-laid-out shipbuilding facility in Currituck County. He described his facility as "commodious" and claimed that it was the best shipyard "in the province." The Stanton/Borden shipyard on Newport River in Carteret County qualifies as an early, established yard because of its founding and longevity.[113]

Unquestionably, the majority of shipbuilding sites in colonial North Carolina were small, and the majority of them were probably temporary sites. An undetermined number of such sites were located at plantations, wherever suitable timber was available, and, of course, in the ports. Plantation yards were usually a cleared site on the riverbank and of brief duration. This may be why customs officials often recorded "Cape Fear Built," "Carolina built," or "plantation built" as a designated origin. Ship carpenters were hired to supervise the building with gangs of the planter's slaves providing the labor.

At times, the location of shipyards is mentioned in the records by referencing property next to a shipyard or "shipyard landing." A New Hanover County deed book cites " 4 acres at a "place called Sloop Point including the Shipyard." A 1762 land patent records "Shipyard Point" on Adams Creek. A 1730 land deed concerns property "in Scuppernong called Viniard Island, joining Mathew Caswell and the River on the E. side of the shipyard."[114] A Hyde County deed describes acreage on the "W side Smith Creek, beg small gut near ship yard." A 1750 Pasquotank deed dated states that the lot in Nixonton was "on the main Street adjacent to the Shipyard." Another Pasquotank deed places a shipyard on "Windmill Point."[115]

Occasionally, shipyard sites are found on maps and plans, such as the 1738 Wimble map and 1767 Churton plan (see figures 3 and 4). Some shipyard sites were so well situated, particularly in ports such as Port Roanoke (Edenton), that they would continue in that capacity, under different ownership, for a great many years. In 1837, the Wimble yard in Wilmington, between Church and Castle Streets, was sold to Michael Dyer and would continue to be a shipyard site for years. In turn, Dyer may have sold the yard to ship carpenter John Doughty.[116] Josiah Grainger, another Wilmington shipwright, established a yard at the foot of Church Street, a yard that was later sold to John Walker, and, in fact, would continue to be a shipyard site into the twentieth century.[117] In 1702, Thomas Lee and Thomas Blount settled on Kendrick's Creek, near what is now Roper in Washington County. There, Blount, a blacksmith, established a sawmill, and, with Lee, a shipyard. When Lee died in 1716, he left instructions for William Downing, presumably another ship carpenter, to complete a ship, or pink, then on the stocks.[118] The shipyard was probably at the mouth or confluence of the creek with Albemarle Sound. Contemporary with the yard on Kendrick's Creek, Thomas Harding established a yard in the port of Bath. Although Harding purchased land in other counties, he continued to call himself a ship carpenter until he died in 1726.[119] The yard was probably on Main Street along Bath Creek. In 1712, Matthew Midgett, a native of Maryland, established a shipyard on the Scuppernong River in Tyrrell County. He gave it up nine years later, moved to Bodie Island, and turned to raising cattle. In 1722, there may have been a shipyard at the small settlement of New South Wales on the Trent River.[120] In the 1730s, John Smith established a shipyard on the Pungo River in Hyde County, perhaps at Woodstock, which may have been the first in that area. He evidently continued to build vessels until his death. His brothers and sons, William, Samuel, and Thomas, were all shipwrights and owned property on the Pungo River. Whether the family operated one shipyard or several shipbuilding facilities is not clear. The brigantine *Happy Luke*, built in 1734 for Edward Salter, was among the first large vessels launched on the river.[121]

As stated above, Richard Alban and Ebenezer Harker established shipyards at Port Roanoke in 1716 and Harkers Island in 1740, respectively.[122] In 1774, John Pearson wrote that he had recently launched a new vessel, "esteemed one of the finest ever Built in this part of the World. She cost 3,000 [pounds]. She is called the *Penelope* 200 tons." The vessel was built at Duckenfield's shipyard on Salmon Creek in Bertie County (Figure 4). When Duckenfield died, the estate passed on to his widow, Margaret, who married John Pearson. Despite the appeals of Margaret Pearson in 1778, the Duckenfield property was seized by the state as belonging to a Loyalist.[123]

Thomas MacKnight, another prominent North Carolina Loyalist, also lost his shipyard. MacKnight moved to North Carolina in 1757. He may have been an experienced businessman, for in that year, he entered into a

FIGURE 2-4 Churton's 1767 plan of the Duckenfield tract shows a shipyard on Salmon Creek. The site marked is the approximate location of the Salmon Creek shipyard. This may or may not be the same shipyard as indicated on the Moseley and Wimble maps. *Source:* State Archives of North Carolina.

partnership with a Virginia merchant to cut and transport shingles. MacKnight may well have been from Virginia as he owned property in the Norfolk area. In Currituck County, he bought large tracts of land, built a plantation known as "Belville," and established a shingle mill along the North River's headwaters, known as Indiantown Creek. The large swamps in northeastern North Carolina, particularly the Great Dismal Swamp, were abundant in white cedar or juniper, an important timber for shingles as well as planking for vessels because of its resistance to rot. The shingle business was successful and, along with his plantation, made him one of the wealthiest individuals in northeastern North Carolina.[124]

MacKnight's decision to enter the shipbuilding business was a logical business decision. He needed vessels to transport shingles and other cargoes such as naval stores, to market. MacKnight hired a master carpenter and bought a large number of slaves trained as skilled artisans for his shipyard. In his efforts to gain compensation for his property seized by the state during the Revolutionary War, he wrote a description of his yard: "on the north side of the [North] river, at a very great expense [I had erected] the most commodious, and I will venture to say the best ship yard in the province, where I had every conveniency for careening as well as for building vessels. From this yard I have launched a ship (one hundred feet long) into fourteen feet water, upon sliding boards not more than thirty feet in length; the whole run did not exceed twenty-five feet; and from the top of the keel blocks to the surface of the water was a fall of little more than two feet."[125] MacKnight also erected wharves, warehouses and probably other buildings associated with the shipbuilding and shipping business.[126]

Four vessels, the *Belville*, the brigs *Betsy* and *Johnston*, and an unnamed sloop were owned and operated by MacKnight's businesses. Twelve additional vessels built in Currituck County in the early 1770s may well have been constructed at the MacKnight yard.[127] There was evidently another vessel either on the stocks or in the preliminary stages of construction when the yard was seized by "rebels."[128]

In the early 1770s, MacKnight became caught up in the friction between Great Britain and her North American colonies. He unsuccessfully tried to straddle the controversy. Considered a "Tory" by many in northeastern North Carolina, he fled his plantation in October 1775 to seek sanctuary with other Loyalists in Norfolk. Years later he sought restitution for his lost property, including his shipyard.[129]

MacKnight's success in the shingle business was a result of North Carolina's abundant timber, particularly juniper. Juniper, live oak, and especially pine were found throughout eastern North Carolina in the colonial period. Although travelers and royal officials lauded these timbers as excellent for shipbuilding, in general, their recommendations were ignored. Governors Arthur Dobbs and William Tryon urged that North Carolina oak be used by the British navy. Dobbs considered the wood "excellent for ship Timber being all crooked and very lasting." Although American oak was considered inferior to English oak, naval officials were not unaware of its potential value. "We have hitherto failed in our attempt of obtaining any importations of live or other oak timber from America, though we have used every means in our power to effect it," the Navy Board reported to the Admiralty in 1771. The Admiralty did order an investigation of oak timber "particularly . . . called live oak, whether useful for Royal Navy from islands along the North Carolina, South Carolina and Georgia coasts."[130] The report to the Admiralty stated that the timber from the southern colonies, including live oak, had good qualities, citing a ship built in South Carolina twenty-three years before with little or no decay, but the report's author, Charles Inglis, did not recommend that it be exploited since it was too expensive."[131]

Undoubtedly, shipyards were located in close proximity to a sufficient supply of natural resources such as timber and naval stores. Southern longleaf yellow pine was one of the most plentiful species found in eastern North Carolina. In 1765, Governor Tryon wrote the commissioner of the dockyard at Portsmouth, England that "ships built in America are now very commonly planked with the yellow pine, and which is reckoned to last as long as English oak plank." He wrote two years later to the Board that "It is the received opinion in this part of the world that the yellow and pitch pine is admirable for ships decks or any work under water."[132] Despite this endorsement, British shipbuilders and their counterparts in the northern American colonies were critical of the wood because they believed it was "apt to splinter." Nonetheless, yellow pine, live oak, juniper, and cypress, were the most common shipbuilding timbers used in North Carolina.[133]

Most vessels were built with milled timber. In the colonial period, such basic shipbuilding material may have been cut on the site of the shipyard, or purchased from timber merchants, sawmill owners, or local farmers/planters. Some sawmills were operated by shipbuilders.[134] The earliest shipbuilding establishments may have produced their own planks and other pieces.[135] Sawpits were quite common and required gangs of two or three men working together. The "tiller man" stood above the log and guided the ripsaw or cross-cut, or thwart saw while the "pit man" stood in the pit drawing the saw down. Pit work was dirty and laborious. The pit man was usually covered with sawdust, and the members of the crew usually rotated in the pit. Trestles were also used to square timbers and form knees and other pieces. Shipwright inventories list a variety of tools from augers and axes to various saws and chisels.[136]

Sawmills were established quite early in the colonies.[137] They were built in all parts of eastern North Carolina, but by the mid-eighteenth century, were most prominent in the Cape Fear Valley. Captain Thomas Blount, a blacksmith and shipwright by trade, came to Perquimans County and erected a sawmill in 1702, probably the first in the colony. By 1733, there were several such establishments in Craven County along the Neuse and Trent Rivers and their tributaries.[138] A sawmill is located near the Scuppernong River on the Moseley map of 1733. During the first half of the eighteenth century, nearly forty mills were erected in this region. In 1767, Governor Tryon reported that there were fifty in operation in the Cape Fear River drainage basin "and more constructing." The mills depended upon waterpower, utilizing dams, water wheels, and even tidal movements.[139] Although mill owners did raft their timber and float it to various destinations, North Carolina shipyards were frequently located at or near sawmills. This was true in the colonial period and increasingly so in the nineteenth century. Primarily, such mills produced pine.

Pine was also the source of other important shipbuilding materials. In the eighteenth century, naval stores had a very broad meaning and included not only tar, pitch, and turpentine, but also masts, spars, hemp and other articles. Almost every plantation in the coastal area had a "tar pit" where pinewood was fired up. However, other naval stores became even more important during this period. Although few spars and masts were exported beyond the colony, North Carolina became the leader in the naval stores industry.

Hemp for cordage was in much demand, not only for local shipbuilders, but for the British navy as well. Despite a bounty and other encouragements, very little hemp was grown in North Carolina.[140] The same was true of ropewalks, sites where hemp fiber was spun first into yard, then into twine, cordage, and rope, used for rigging. There was only one ropewalk in North Carolina, established in 1783 in Edenton, although operations were located in South Carolina, Virginia, New York, and elsewhere in the colonies.[141]

As mentioned earlier, blacksmiths could be found throughout the colony. Although there are a few instances of blacksmiths or "shipsmiths" in the records, there is little

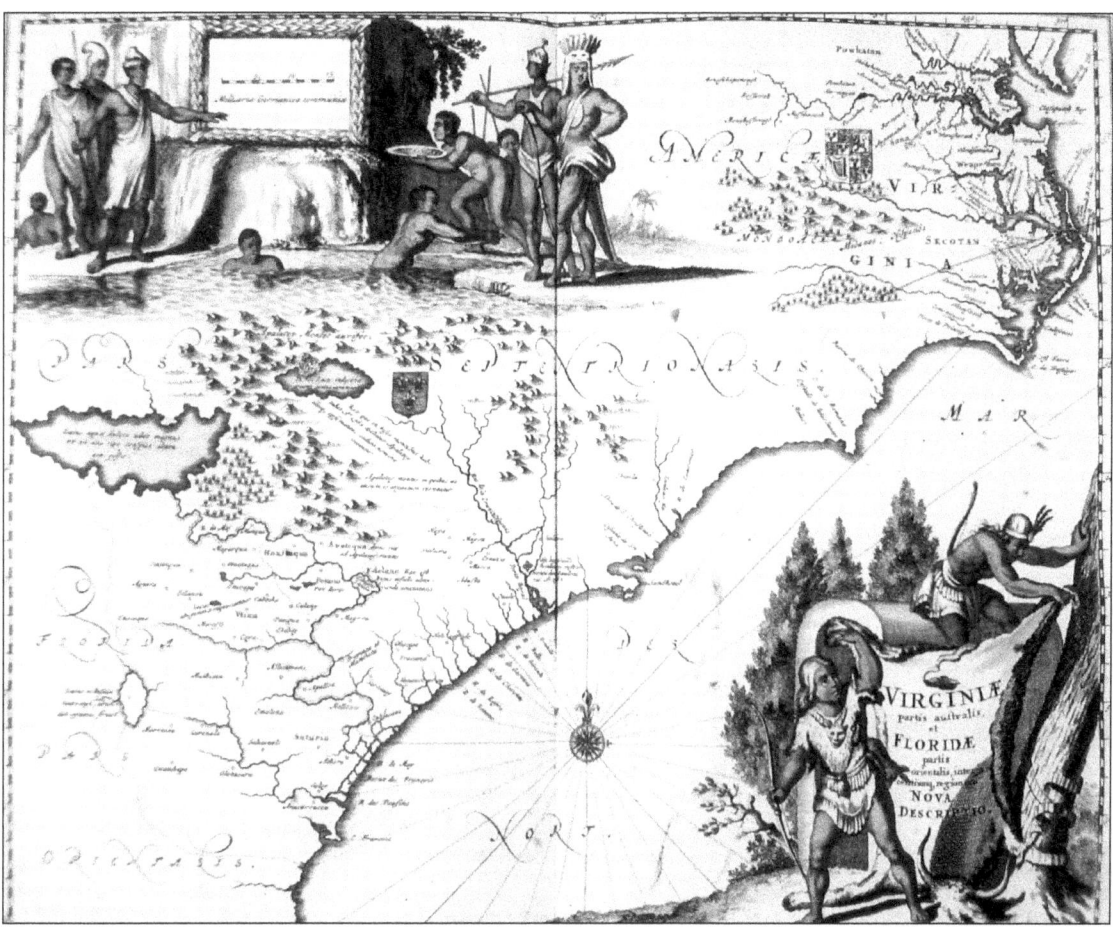

FIGURE 2-5 The John Ogilvy map of 1672 is somewhat similar to the 1676 John Speed map. Neither cartographer ever set foot on the North American continent. The Ogilvy map shows the Outer Banks extending outward to Cape Kendrick. Today, only Wimble Shoals remains of Cape Kendrick. *Source:* Newberry Library, Chicago.

information on them and their role in shipbuilding. In the colonial period, North Carolina produced virtually no iron ore in the coastal area, and due to British restrictions, erected no large forges or furnaces for forging large metal objects, not even bar iron.[142] There was a "plentiful supply of iron in the colonies," but this was certainly not true of coastal North Carolina.[143] All iron used in ship construction, anchors, chain, and various castings was imported, primarily from the British Isles.[144] However, wood was substituted for iron wherever possible, especially in joining planks and other pieces to heavy members. Oak pins or treenails were usually employed for this. As stated previously, a one-hundred-ton wooden ship in the eighteenth century needed approximately one ton of ironwork.[145] Local blacksmiths were probably able to forge hand wrought nails and spikes, but there is no specific record of this.

Canvas for sails, rope for rigging and cables, even cabin furniture, had to be imported. A Wilmington newspaper advertised for sale anchors "from 100 to 420 weight, grapnells for petriaugers, [sic] small cables & cordage of all sizes . . .[and] mariners compasses."[146]

Available records do not mention the importation of materials necessary for building vessels prior to the eighteenth century. Nonetheless, at least five oceanic trading vessels were built in the colony prior to 1700. In 1691, William Barkely, a shipbuilder, sold the hull of the shallop *Tryall* in Perquimans Precinct.[147]

Although North Carolina shipbuilding increased in the eighteenth century, it remained "a minor industry" until 1783. "As our navigation is bad," a merchant wrote, "so we have very few vessels except those that are very small." In 1767, Governor Tryon wrote the Board of Trade that, "[t]he ship building is not considerable, the largest built vessel not exceeding two hundred tons burden."[148] In his study of shipbuilding in the American colonies, Goldenberg states "North Carolina . . . launched relatively little tonnage according to the records." Other studies on shipbuilding in colonial North Carolina substantially agree with this conclusion stating that, in 1769, the tonnage for North Carolina was only one-fourth that for New Hampshire and one-thirteenth that for Massachusetts, and of all the colonies, from New Hampshire to Georgia inclusive, only two built fewer ships than North Carolina.[149] However, this conclusion is erroneous since virtually all scholarship has relied on only one source: Lord John Sheffield, *Observation on the Commerce of the American States*, published in London in 1794, which provides colonial shipbuilding figures only for 1769 through 1774. Using this primary source and a few port records, Goldenberg concludes that, of the 229 vessels built between 1710 and 1739 that engaged in North Carolina maritime trade, only thirty-eight were launched in the colony.[150] The present study has identified sixty-six vessels built in the colony during that period. For the period from 1688 to 1776, this study shows that 329 documented vessels were built in North Carolina (Appendices A and B). As determined by Robert Cain, "An examination of various shipping lists . . . yielded a total of fifty-nine different vessels built in North Carolina between 1730 and 1767."[151] North Carolina's total is respectable. Between 1688 and 1783, an average of almost four documented vessels a year were built in North Carolina, an impressive number considering the colony's sparse population.

COLONIAL SHIPS AND BOATS

There were only five documented vessels built in the colony in the seventeenth century (see Appendices A and B). In the eighteenth century, only two documented vessels were built prior to 1710. The schooner *Ann of North Carolina* was built in the Pasquotank area in 1701 and the sloop *Otter*, owned by Frederick and Thomas Jones, was built in 1703 somewhere in the Pamlico area. In 1706, Thomas Harding, a shipbuilder, signed a contract to build a sloop "forty six feet by the keel, eighteen feet by the beam and eight feet in the hold." Thomas Cary, who had contracted with Harding for the vessel, was obligated to provide the timber, iron, and everything needed to equip the sloop. He was also to provide food and lodging while the vessel was being built.[152] This un-named vessel is not documented. It is possible that, in 1715, the first vessel was built in Port Roanoke (Edenton). One of the carpenters working on a new courthouse took time to build a sloop on the waterfront.[153] However, the first official record of a vessel being built in Edenton is in 1722, when a twenty-ton cargo and passenger sloop, *Carolina Venture*, was built for John Lovich.

In 1727, an ocean-going vessel was built on the Cape Fear River. Three years later the brig *Rebecca* was launched on the same river. Owned by Captain James Wimble, a prominent planter and mariner, the vessel, at 128 tons (documented at seventy tons in the ship list) and armed with ten guns, was the second largest ship built in the colony up to that time. The largest was the 140-ton ship, *North Carolina*, built at Bath in 1727.[154] Often, colonial vessels were sold to British interests. They were either built under contract in a colony or, at times, sold after disposing of a cargo in Britain or the West Indies. At that time, North America had the best supply of timber in the world; consequently, it was less expensive to obtain vessels from the colonies. It is estimated that vessels could be built at a cost per ton of from one-fifth to one-half less than in Great Britain. The industry developed rapidly—so rapidly in fact that quite early in the development of the colonies, ships were sold abroad. The sale of American-built vessels in England was so great that, by the outbreak of the Revolution, it amounted to more than a third of total British tonnage. Although British shipbuilders complained about losing skilled personnel as well as business to the colonies, the government made no effort to stop it.[155]

North Carolinians did engage in this enterprise, but the extent of their participation is unknown. The sale of vessels to buyers outside of Britain and her colonies was not recorded in North Carolina custom records, but there are a few references to this activity.[156] The percentage of vessels sold abroad was limited. Construction costs were higher in North Carolina than in New England, skilled labor was scarce, and, with the exception of timber, the materials needed to build and outfit a vessel had to be imported. A recent study suggests that it cost less to build a fore-and-aft rigged vessel in Philadelphia than in colonial North Carolina. However, there is evidence indicating the cost could be the same.[157] English interests purchased most of the North Carolina-built vessels that were sold abroad, but at least two were sold in Ireland and two in Scotland. In 1730-31, at the small port of Bath, the 100-ton brig *John & David* and the sixty-ton sloop *Carolina* were both built for and purchased by John Rieusett of Dublin. In the 1750s, Archibald Corbett of Wilmington agreed to build a vessel for the firm of James Baird Jr., and Alexander Walker of Glasgow, England. In 1765, the sixty-five-ton brig *Edinburgh* was built for a group of merchants that included three from Charleston and one from Bristol. Matthew Rowan, who would rise to become a colonial governor, supposedly came to the colony in the 1720s "to build a ship or two for some persons in Dublin."[158] With the exception of at least one sloop and a few schooners, the majority of North Carolina-built vessels engaged in the trans-Atlantic trade were brigs.

If vessel registration is any indication, a good number of North Carolina vessels were sold to merchants in other colonies. It was not uncommon for North Carolina vessels to be advertised for sale in the *Virginia Gazette*. In 1780, the paper carried an advertisement of an auction to be held in Edenton to dispose of the property of Joseph Hewes, including vessels belonging to the firm of Hewes and Smith. A new brig of 100 tons, three schooners, a sloop of sixty tons, a "schooner decked boat," a large sailing flat, and four bay flats were offered for sale.[159] The ship register for South Carolina lists seven North Carolina-built vessels—three brigs, three schooners, and a sloop—owned by Charleston merchants. In 1779, a North Carolina-built sloop was advertised for sale in the *Charleston Gazette*. The ad described the sloop as capable of carrying one hundred barrels of flour.[160] It is not known if vessels were built in the colony for speculation; however, ads and correspondence record builders wishing to sell their vessels while still on the stocks.

Joseph Goldenberg states that shipbuilding in the South stagnated until 1730 because of the emphasis on agriculture.[161] However, shipbuilding in North Carolina steadily increased until the Revolution. According to ship registers, no fewer than 317 were built in North Carolina between 1720 and 1776. A French traveler noted in his journal that in Bath "there are several vessels built here, and on other parts of this (Pamlico) as well as the Neuse River, but all small."[162]

Shipbuilding records from 1688 to 1783 show considerable activity in coastal North Carolina, during the early colonial period, primarily in the Albemarle Sound region. In the later part of the colonial era, there was a subtle shift to the Pamlico, Beaufort, and Brunswick areas.

It is unfortunate there is not more precise data about shipbuilding sites, ships, and ports, particularly regarding plantation-built vessels, during this period.

A Description of Vessels Built during the Colonial Era

There were 365 vessels registered or documented as being built in North Carolina at thirty-six different locations between 1688 and 1783 (Appendix B). The number of ships built annually during this period reflects the variation in shipbuilding activity for the era (Figure 6).

There was an average of 3.8 vessels built per year and probably many more were repaired or "recycled," with some parts being salvaged for further use. Shipbuilding in the colony was slow to begin and the building of vessels was sporadic with numerous highs and lows. There is little doubt that economic conditions contributed to the volatility, but the number of colonial wars could also be a factor. During the first two wars in the colonies, shipbuilding was minimal. Between Queen Anne's War and King George's War, a period of thirty-one years, a sporadic increase in shipbuilding activity took place. Also, between King George's War and the French and Indian War, there was a significant increase in shipbuilding. Similarly, between the French and Indian War and the Revolution, shipbuilding increased to the highest levels. During the wars, shipbuilding activity slowed. However, between 1743 and 1751 (a period roughly coinciding with King George's War), thirty-two armed ships were built.

Between 1762 and 1780, twenty-one armed vessels were built. Many of these ships were primarily blockade runners and privateers. Many more were plantation-built and therefore not in the database. The total tonnage per year indicates that relatively small ships were being built. Nonetheless, vessel tonnage increased during this period ranging from three tons to 170 tons (Figure 7). The 170-ton vessel was the *Fair American*, a privateer built in

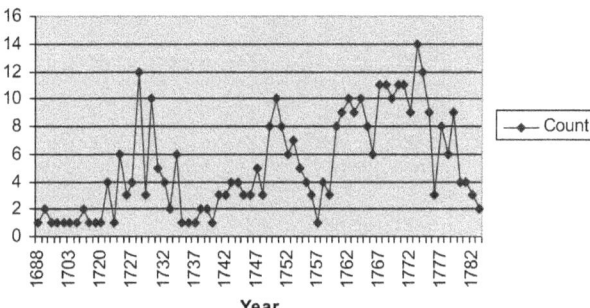

FIGURE 2-6 The total number of ships built for the colonial period is less than a hundred. The trend appears to be upward, but volatile. It must be realized that documentation of vessels and recording of information at that time was less than thorough. *Source:* Author's database.

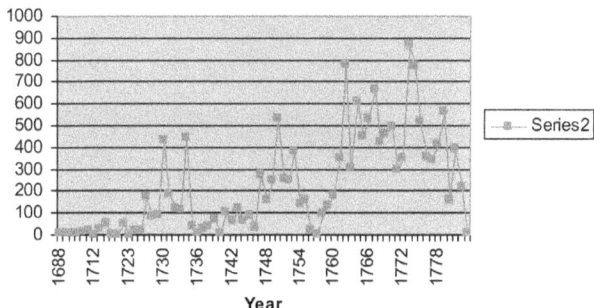

FIGURE 2-7 Documented vessels totaled slightly less than 16,000 total tons for the colonial era. Notice that the vessel count (Figure 6) and tonnage per year is similar in trend and volatility. *Source:* Author's database.

Hertford in 1778. The smallest vessels were the periaugers, a few schooners, and sloops.[163]

John Speed's 1611 description (with several revisions until 1676) of early activities in North Carolina does not specifically mention shipbuilding. Only five small ships of less than six tons were recorded as being built in the seventeenth century in North Carolina. That documented or registered ships were not recorded until 1688 is a mystery. It is entirely possible that the colonial government had not yet recognized the importance of shipbuilding. Most port activities were related to loading and unloading ships, making ship repairs, and provisioning ships and sailors. It is well known that fruits and vegetables were grown and harvested around the larger ports, and forests were a source for timber and naval stores.

Port Roanoke (Edenton) was the major North Carolina port during the colonial era. Situated up the

FIGURE 2-8 Shipbuilding sites during the colonial era were scattered, but there seems to be clustering around the Albemarle Sound area, and increasing in sparseness toward the south. *Source:* Author's database.

Albemarle Sound near the confluence of the Roanoke and Chowan Rivers on a protected bay, it was an ideal port. It was also a shipbuilding center. Out of the 365 vessels built, 296 were designated as North Carolina built or port unknown, with forty-one listed as being built in Edenton, which included Port Roanoke and the Roanoke River. The Albemarle region had more than 59% of these vessels, demonstrating its maritime activity. The list shows that only twenty-eight vessels were built at other known shipyards in the colony (Figure 8).

During the colonial era, there were fourteen inlets along the Carolina coast, most of them on the barrier islands north of Cape Hatteras. The navigability of New Currituck Inlet, Old Currituck Inlet, Trinity Inlet, and Roanoke Inlet varied, but they were available throughout the period. Most ports were positioned in relation to these inlets.

The building of ships in the Pamlico region was secondary to that in Albemarle and was centered on Port Roanoke. Port Bath and Bath County accounted for twenty-one vessels. An additional six vessels are attributable to the region bringing the total number of vessels built on the Pamlico to twenty-seven.[165] The remaining thirty-two vessels were primarily built along the coast to the south, at Beaufort, Brunswick, and Wilmington. Apparently, the Neuse, including New Bern, and points south, was not as important as the Albemarle or Pamlico regions for shipbuilding. However, most of the documented vessels are recorded simply as being built in North Carolina, in the four precincts, or in the counties.

For trans-Atlantic trade, many sloops, schooners, shallops, snows, brigantines, and ships were constructed in North Carolina during the colonial period. Descriptions of specific North Carolina-built vessels during the era are virtually non-existent and it is impossible to generalize about hull forms, rigs, and even size.[166] Sloops, schooners, and brigs ranged from four tons up to fifty. They were custom-built and designs were influenced by a variety of factors, including the intended purpose of the vessel, whims of builders and buyers, and, in North Carolina, the presence of unusual geographical features. During the early years of the colony's settlement, most of the vessels were sloops. The first vessel registered as being built in the colony was a sloop of four tons. Between 1688 and 1725, at least fourteen sloops were built. Between 1725 and 1751, of a hundred vessels built in the colony, at least twenty-seven were small sloops. The registry of Port Beaufort, which included New Bern, recorded 127 vessels between 1763 and 1764; seventy-two (57 percent) were sloops and forty-three (34 percent) were schooners.[167] As in England, sloops were the most popular vessel type built for coastal trade. In North Carolina, shoal waters and a dangerous coastline were the major reasons for this. During the five-year period, 1768 to 1773, some 632 sloops entered Edenton.[168]

For the purposes of this study, the coast of North Carolina has been partitioned into five areas, the Albemarle, the Pamlico, the Neuse, the Cape Fear, and the Outer Banks. A total of 134 vessels can be attributed to these specific areas. Of the remaining vessels, 229 were listed only as being North Carolina-built and two were without a precise geographical origin (Figure 7).

In the Albemarle area, the known shipbuilding sites were Currituck, Port Roanoke (Edenton or Roanoke), Hertford, Pasquotank, and Quistna (Appendix A). More general areas of construction were in the counties of Albemarle, Bertie, Camden, Chowan, Currituck, Pasquotank (including the prior precincts), and Tyrrell, and along the Roanoke, Little, and Perquimans Rivers. By far, the port with the most shipbuilding activity was Port Roanoke with forty vessels. Seven vessels were constructed in Pasquotank and six in Currituck. Only one or two vessels were built in the other locations during the colonial period.

With a boat built in Pasquotank in 1693, the Albemarle area, generating seventy-five vessels, appears to be the earliest shipbuilding region followed by a site

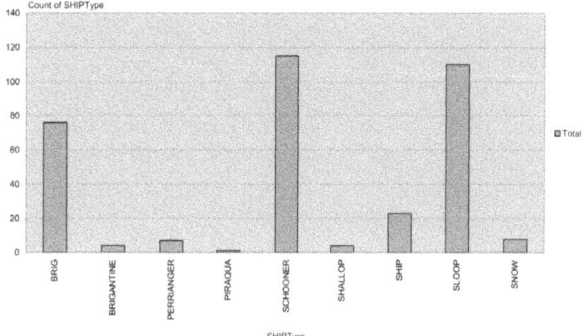

FIGURE 2-9 Vessel types built during the colonial era. The most popular riggings being employed were the schooners, sloops and brigs. *Source:* Author's database.

on the Little River in 1720. In the Pamlico area, there were twenty-seven vessels built during the colonial era. Beginning in 1725, the leading shipbuilding site was Port Bath with eighteen vessels. Bath County, Hyde County or Hyde Precinct, and Pitt County had a collective total of seven vessels. Washington and, in 1727, the Machapongo (known later as the Pungo) River had one site each. The area of the Neuse produced six vessels. New Bern had two. In 1703, one was built at Pamlico. Smith Creek and Otter Creek had one each, and, in 1750, a vessel was built on Adams Creek. In third place, the Cape Fear region had seventeen vessels built during this period. In this area, Wilmington was the leading shipbuilding site with eight vessels, followed closely by Brunswick or Port Brunswick, and Cape Fear with four each. The Cape Fear River had one vessel built somewhere along its course in 1727 and another in 1730. Four were built in Beaufort, the earliest in 1725. The Outer Banks produced but a single vessel at Cape Hatteras in 1777.

In summary, according to the database, major shipbuilding began in the Albemarle area in 1693 and soon spread to the Pamlico area. The Cape Fear region began shipbuilding in 1727. Shipbuilding in the Neuse area started in 1703, but was not as significant as were the Albemarle, Pamlico, or Cape Fear production sites. Schooners, sloops, and brigs were the most popular types of vessels being built (Figure 9). Other vessel types included the brigantine, ship, snow, periauger, shallop, and piragua.[169] Brigantines or brigs were probably the first to be built, followed by the sloop, shallop and schooner. Early in the eighteenth century, shipwrights introduced the periauger, ship, and snow. Toward the end of the colonial period, schooners and sloops were the dominant type.

It is thought that ship dimensions changed significantly during the colonial era, particularly in depth and width, but data are unavailable. Shipwrights had to alter dimensions in order for vessels to navigate successfully in shallow waters and have maneuverability through inlets and shoals, without decreasing cargo capacity.[170]

In general, periauger and shallops were between three and six tons (the smallest range in tonnage), schooners between three and fifty tons, and sloops between three and eighty-two tons. The few brigantines that were built during this period were between four and seventy tons. Brigs ranged between thirty-five and 150 tons. The smallest snow was sixty tons; the largest was 112 tons. Ships ranged between eighty and 150 tons (Appendix A). Although the range in tonnage is considerable, the different types of rigging were less variable.

A sloop may be defined as a single-masted vessel having a bowsprit, with a fore and aft sail, one gaff mainsail, two or three headsails, and possibly a square topsail. The sloop may be a transitional vessel adapted from, and combining elements of, a ketch, pinnace, and shallop. Over time, it may have developed into the schooner or, at least, the distinctive American schooner.[171]

Eight shallops were registered in colonial North Carolina ports, the first in 1688 and the last in 1736.[172] All were small; four were registered at four tons but were probably used in oceanic as well as inland trade. There was really no clear line of demarcation between shallops, sloops, and schooners.[173] The two-masted fore and aft rig was basically the same for shallop, schooner, periauger, and ketch. Chapelle described the shallop as a "nondescript small boat" both open and half-decked. There is no description of a North Carolina-built shallop.[174] By 1736, the term "shallop" disappeared from North Carolina port records.

With few exceptions, brigantines, or brigs, were the largest vessels built in the colony. They were used primarily in the West Indian and British trades. Joseph Goldenberg estimates that twenty-three vessels registered and built in North Carolina in the colonial period were brigs. Between 1720 and 1776 at least sixty-six brigantines were launched in North Carolina.[175] According to colonial records, the first North Carolina-built brig, the *Endeavour*, was launched in 1720. Subsequently, North Carolina-built brigantines were constructed on a regular basis; six in the 1730s, seven in the 1740s, and six in the 1750s. Twenty-eight brigs were launched in the 1760s, and eight between 1770 and 1776. *Lloyd's Register of Ships* for 1776 included twenty-one brigs built in North Carolina.[176] Theoretically, brigs and brigantines are different types; in reality, the names were interchangeable in the colonial period and are treated so herein. In general, they were two-masted, with square sails on both masts, and a fore and aft gaff on the mainmast. To complicate matters even further in identifying types, it was quite common for owners to change their rig from schooner to brig, or from brig to schooner. As with the sloops, no descriptions of brigs constructed in colonial North Carolina have been located.

Snows were another type of vessel built in North Carolina. Some have classified them as a type of brigantine depending on the rigging. Essentially, snows were oversized brigantines with square sails on both masts and a small fore and aft sail set on a shorter mast directly behind the mainmast. According to the records, six snows were built in the colony.[177]

Schooners first appeared in American waters early in the eighteenth century. By the end of the century, the schooner would replace the sloop as the most popular vessel type built in the colonies.[178] As with the sloop, there is disagreement regarding the origin of the schooner, as to whether it was Dutch or American. A schooner was not only a type of vessel, it was also a type of rigging that was carried on other vessel types such as pilot boats and periaugers. A schooner was a vessel with two or more masts and fore and aft sails on each mast. In the colonial period, there were only two-masted schooners. Some schooners also carried a small square sail on the mainmast. Between 1770 and 1783, thirty-one schooners were built in North Carolina, with twice the number of sloops built during the same period.

Ships were the largest vessels built in the colonies. At least nineteen ships were constructed in North Carolina in the colonial period. At least two more in the appendices were probably ships, the *North Carolina* of 201 tons and the *Penelope* of 200 tons. A 104-ton ship was built in Bath in 1727. North Carolina-built ships were generally smaller in size than those built in the British Isles or other colonies. Only two ships registered as having been built in the colony were 200 tons, the remainder ranging from 100 up to 200 tons.

Occasionally, it is not possible to identify the type of vessel. The Wilmington/New Hanover Safety Committee minutes mention an invoice for a new vessel on the stocks on the Cape Fear. Newspaper advertisements would often state only vessel or craft for sale: "The subscriber has for sale at the town of Beaufort, Carteret County, a new vessel on the stocsts [stocks], well calculated for a fast sailer, and will be completely finished the 15th of May next. Her dimensions are 55 feet keel strait rabbet, 11 feet rake forward, 18 and a half feet beak, and 7 feet and a half hold."[179] A letter from a British subject instructed his agent in Wilmington to sell his property including a "boat with burthen of 140 barrels."[180] At times, even court records would be vague mentioning only a vessel. The inventory of Richard Sanderson of Perquimans County dated July 22, 1722 included "a small vessel on the stocks."[181] Some correspondence suggests the addressee knew the type of vessel. Henry Tuley, a ship carpenter, wrote John Gray Blount, a merchant, "I am sory to inform you that the Vessel is not complet but will carey on as fast as posebel when soplied with Oachum & Iron whitch we air at present with out."[182]

Pilot boats were also not identified as to type. Usually, they were small sloops or schooners. These vessels were "sharp," that is designed for speed and seaworthiness. They were also frequently built for speculation. In 1778, the *Virginia Gazette* advertised two or three for sale in Beaufort, and, in 1780, the paper carried an advertisement for four to be sold in Edenton.[183]

Vessel type may not be mentioned, particularly with reference to "ships on the stocks" because the purchaser was responsible for the rig and the rig defined the type. In 1774, a suit was filed against the estate of John Smith, a Hyde County shipbuilder. Smith had agreed to build a vessel for a firm of New Bern merchants. He died before the vessel was completed. Although the dimensions as well as the type of wood to be used in the proposed vessel were described, the type was not mentioned.[184] Robert Palmer, Surveyor-General of North Carolina, wished to pay off his debts to Neil Jamison, a merchant of Norfolk, by offering him a new vessel being built at Bath. In July 1764, Palmer wrote to Jamison:

> If you would take a vessel I have now upon the stocks and will be launched in February or beginning of March at furthest. She is sixty foot keel, twenty four beam or near it, twenty two and a half from outside to inside, about ten feet in the lower hold and four feet 6 inches from the lower deck to the upper....
>
> You may have her viewed and I require no more than I pay. I give three pounds five shillings our money per ton.... expense you might be eased of.... finish her from Virginia. All the Iron work for her upper works, deck nails, dead eyes, etc. might be sent from you.... I beg to have answer as to the vessel soon for I have some offers from Philadelphia for her hull completed.... I shall certainly sell her on the stocks if I can.[185]

When he received no reply from Jamison, he wrote in September again giving dimensions; the vessel, he wrote, "is said to be the best that was ever built here." Nothing has been found to indicate whether Jamison agreed to buy the vessel or what happened to it. Another vessel, the *Penelope*, built on Salmon Creek and described as "one of the finest ever Built in this part of the World," was two hundred tons, possibly a brig or schooner, but more probably a ship. When finished, she carried a cargo to the West Indies and, subsequently, to Bristol, England, where she was sold.[186]

Navigating North Carolina's inland waters required a variety of small craft. It was a common practice to off load cargo at Portsmouth, for example, and load smaller vessels to complete the shipments across the shallow sounds to ports such as New Bern on the Neuse River. Although the construction of small vessels may be considered separate from building larger oceanic vessels, in North Carolina, small craft and larger vessels were frequently built at the same construction site and by the same builders. Often, many of the vessels used on the rivers and streams were the same type, such as sloops and schooners, but smaller. Oceanic vessels traded with plantations and inland communities as well. However, it is extremely difficult to quantify the craft used exclusively in inland transportation. As a general rule, such vessels, although extremely numerous, were not required to register with the port authorities.

The Earliest Vessels

By the time North America was discovered and explored by Europeans, the art of boat building had already existed in North Carolina for centuries. The first among the many boats and ships built in North Carolina were dugouts or logboats.[187] Natives in North Carolina created and used dugouts for transportation between their permanent settlements on the mainland and the barrier islands they inhabited during the summer. They worked the sound waters and streams for subsistence and processed some of their catch for storage. Dugouts were an integral part of their existence.[188]

Cypress, cedar, and pine were used to build the dugouts. These species grew abundantly throughout most of the Tidewater area. The dugout was fashioned by carefully burning the tree, then scraping out the burned portion with shells. The process usually took weeks before the canoe was finished. Natives crafted these vessels to meet specific needs. This involved many years of experimentation in order to produce the best watercraft. They ranged in length from about nine feet to more than sixty feet, with variations in hull shapes. Some were small and built to move swiftly through the water; others were large to carry cargo and were not as swift. It was these vessels that the early explorers of America first observed, and when they did, they no doubt marveled at the workmanship.[189]

Earliest explorers, Spanish and Portuguese adventurers from the south, as well as Dutch, English, and others from the north, brought with them European boat-building tradition combined with concepts of boat construction gleaned from the Caribs, Arawaks, and other natives living along the waters of the Caribbean and Florida. In addition, slaves applied their knowledge of African boat-building traditions to this artistry. How these different aspects of boat building fused together is not known, but a synthesis is reflected in the variety of dugout types, sizes, modifications, and alterations throughout the period.[190] According to county and state records, the dugout canoe, also known as 'cunner' or 'kunner', was by far the most popular craft used in the colony. Commonly propelled by paddles or oars, some dugouts also had sails, although the natives never used them.[191] Dugouts did not normally require the skills of a shipwright, but, at times, professional craftsmen were employed for this work.[192]

The eight dugouts recorded in the database, designated as periaugers or piraguas, were built between 1722 and 1745 (Appendix B). Five were built at Bath near the Pamlico

River, Port Roanoke and Pasquotank near the Albemarle Sound; another was built in Albemarle Country, adjacent to the Albemarle Sound; and another on the Pungo River off the Pamlico. It is not possible to ascertain their specific use, but, since they were documented, it may be assumed they were used in coastal trade. Evidently, the colonists built large canoes that were somewhat similar to periaugers with planking and two masts, capable of carrying a dozen or more people or cargos.

Periaugers, piraguas, or pettiaugers, derivatives of the pirogue, were one- or two-masted sailing vessels with fore and aft rigs, and between the "kunners" and sloops in size. The periauger was nearly as popular as the canoe. As with canoes, colonial records frequently mentioned periaugers. They were modified log canoes, probably derived from native dugouts. Although periauguers could be found up and down the Atlantic coast, the majority of them were located in the Carolinas and Georgia. It is possible that North Carolina periaugers were patterned after those built in South Carolina, although some were found in Virginia. Periaugers were flat bottomed and excellent for North Carolina's shoal waters. Although most of them were small (three to six tons), two built on the Cape Fear River were twelve and sixteen tons respectively.[193] It is estimated that a five-ton periauger with an eight-foot beam, like most of those built in North Carolina, would be approximately thirty-five or more feet in length, with a draft less than four feet. This would require a very large log, suggesting that, while small dugouts may only require one log, the larger dugouts needed two or more. In addition, strakes may have been attached to increase depth. These larger vessels were usually split down the middle with a sort of keel log placed between the two halves. They also carried oars and paddles "according to . . . size and bigness."[194] John Brickell noted that some of them were so large that they could carry forty to fifty barrels of pitch or tar. Others could carry up to a hundred barrels. They often carried horses and cattle from one plantation to another one. John Brickell wrote, "They frequently trade in them to Virginia and other places on this continent."[195] Eight periaugers were registered in North Carolina between 1722 and 1828 (Appendix B). No dimensions were available for these vessels, but they may have been used for fishing and transporting goods from inland locations to the ports, or perhaps from the ports to ships, or even from inland places directly to the ships. At times, they may have engaged in coastal trade.[196]

Flats were another craft frequently found in colonial North Carolina. Wills and inventories often record flats, bay boats, canoes, periaugers, and small sailers. Sometimes called rafts, pole boats, or scows, they were found on virtually every river and stream in North Carolina. They were propelled by poles, oars, and, at times, by sail. Surprisingly, some, specifically on the Cape Fear River, relied completely on the tides. Janet Schaw wrote, "They must lay to between tide and tide, it having no power to

FIGURE 2-10 Vessel types built during the colonial era. The most popular riggings being employed were the schooners, sloops and brigs. *Source:* Author's database.

move but by the force of the stream."[197] They were simply a box-like craft with a flat bottom and square ends. They were used to carry cargoes of tar, pitch, corn, tobacco, and even wood products like shingles.[198] It was the best means of transportation on the Cape Fear River and was "adopted by all the people up the country."[199] Some of the rafts were broken up and sold along with the cargo upon reaching the destination; others were taken by upstream to be used again.[200]

Flats were also used as ferries. Although small boats were used to ferry people across the many rivers and streams in eastern North Carolina, only flats, scows, and periaugers could be used to haul wagons, horses, cattle, and large loads. In 1725, John Brian built a ferry flat which he said could "carry over four horses in good weather or two horses in bad weather." They were moved by poles, horses, ropes, and even sails. There are numerous accounts of colonial ferries. Government-licensed ferries operated in the colony as early as 1699.[201]

There were also numerous unidentified row boats and small sailing craft, some large enough to carry cargo. Tobacco was transported by open boat through Currituck Inlet, some thirty-five miles to Cape Henry, and then to Norfolk or other Hampton Roads ports.[202] Row boats were also used in whaling and in the waters off of Beaufort.[203] In Onslow County, a shipwright agreed to build a thirteen-foot boat for Dr. Isaac Guion. The order might be related to Dr. Guion's responsibility to transport some prisoners of war to the island of Providence. Inventories and wills often contained such items as bay boats and "Sailing boat Sail Oars & Anchor." Small sailing skiffs were quite common in colonial North Carolina.[204]

The extent of colonial North Carolina-built and -owned vessels is unclear. With regard to oceanic vessels, data for such an assessment is not available.[205] Craft for domestic use were generally North Carolina-built and -owned. After 1783, North Carolinians would own an increasing percentage of oceanic vessels constructed in the state.

THE END OF THE COLONIAL ERA

With the onset of the Revolutionary War, the North Carolina government, concerned about protecting its shipping from the British navy, purchased and outfitted three armed vessels. They were brigs converted from merchant ships and commissioned as the *General Washington, King Tammany,* and *Pennsylvania Farmer.* The brigs were purchased in Edenton, New Bern, and Brunswick. They may have been built in the colony, but no information has been found to substantiate this.[206] In cooperation with Virginia, the state later added two rowing galleys, built at South Quay, Virginia. They were deployed to protect Ocracoke Inlet.

Fortunately, the British generally ignored North Carolina in its blockading operations. There were simply not enough naval vessels to adequately blockade the entire North American coast and little priority was given to North Carolina with its small ports.[207] Throughout most of the war, Loyalist owned and manned privateers cruised up and down the Outer Banks seizing merchant vessels. In the spring of 1777, a loyalist privateer crossed the bar at Ocracoke and took several prizes, but this occurred before the two rowing galleys had been completed. Occasionally, the Cape Fear River would be invaded by one or more British navy ships and privateers, and in 1780 Wilmington was occupied by British troops. Cape Fear area shipping was stifled throughout the conflict nevertheless. During the early years, an occasional prize was brought into the estuary. Shipbuilding for oceanic trade was also brought to a standstill in the Cape Fear area. Although records are incomplete, only one vessel, the brigantine *Hunter,* was built in Wilmington during the war.[208] In April 1782, a British raiding force captured Beaufort. William Borden's house and shipyard were burned along with a brig on the stocks.[209]

North Carolina's contribution to naval defense during the war was negligible, but privateering was popular among the colony's seafaring population. Privateers were privately owned vessels sailing under a commission or letter of marque, authorizing them to attack enemy merchant ships. Virtually every maritime nation took part in this legalized *guerre de course,* but it had a particular appeal in the American colonies.[210] Before 1783, approximately two thousand privateers sailed under commissions from Congress, diplomats abroad, and state governments; eighty-four North Carolina vessels saw service as privateers.[211] The number of these built in North Carolina is uncertain. The *Anne,* a twenty-ton vessel, was built on Smith Creek by Craven County merchant John Wright Stanly. The *Rising State,* a ninety-ton brigantine was built in 1781 in Edenton.[212] A brig named the *Fair American,* not to be confused with the more famous South Carolina brig by that name, was built in Hertford County on the Chowan River. Launched in 1779, the 180-ton vessel carrying a battery of twelve guns received her letter of marque in 1780. Her career as a privateer was short. After sailing out of Edenton, she captured one prize before being captured by a British frigate.[213] Others identified as probably North Carolina-built include the brigs *Governor Burke, Eclipse, General Washington,* along with the *Betsy, Heart of Oak, General Caswell, General Nash, Willing Maid,* and *Sturdy Beggar.*[214] Abiel Chaney, a Beaufort shipbuilder, supposedly constructed some privateers.[215] Undoubtedly, others were built.[216]

North Carolina's shipping was interrupted, but not totally halted, by the British and their Loyalist allies. Despite the blockade, considerable maritime trade was carried on with West Indies ports. In December 1781, General Jethro Sumner was informed of several vessels on the Chowan River loading cargos destined for the West Indies and of another vessel, recently completed at Winton, nearly ready to sail.[217] Merchant ships continued to be constructed during the war. In fact, the conflict may well have stimulated shipbuilding. There were at least thirty-eight vessels built for oceanic trade between 1776 and 1783. Most of them were built in the Port Beaufort and Port Roanoke districts, as Brunswick and Wilmington were either blockaded or occupied by the British for much of the conflict. The *North Carolina Gazette* carried advertisements of sales for three new vessels in 1778.[218] Four pilot boats were offered for sale in 1778. Three of them were built in Beaufort and the fourth on the Pungo River in Beaufort County.[219] In time, however, even the ports that depended upon the inlets for their oceanic trade were affected by the war. A German visitor to Edenton found the harbor in 1783 "a graveyard of many large and small craft...which at the outbreak of the war had run in here and were not half gone to pieces."[220]

An unknown number of North Carolina-built vessels were captured by the British.

In 1776, the schooner *Hiram* of Edenton was taken in the West Indies. In 1779, the brig *Lucy* from Camden County was seized.[221]

In 1777, Hugh Williamson, a prominent North Carolina physician, merchant, statesman, and a future signer of the U.S. Constitution, entered into a mercantile business at Port Roanoke. He believed that there was a great opportunity in building vessels for "a trade that might be carried on here by help of considerable capital . . . I have but 2 small vessels for the inland trade and am building 2 or 3 boats of about 70 tons." In addition to capital, he needed skilled labor and admitted, "a single carpenter is hard to be got."[222] His vessels were laid down at Winton in Hertford County. Josiah Collins, another Edenton businessman, also recognized the potential in shipping. He belonged to the firm Collins, Stuart and Muir. In 1782, they contracted with Richard Dawson, who owned a shipyard at Windsor in Bertie County, for two brigs, and evidently two other vessels with different builders.[223] The outcome of these two ventures is unknown.

During the conflict, Loyalists, including shipwrights, left the colony. Obediah Simpson went to Canada. A shipwright by the name of Ogden built a brig in New Bern, and, to keep it from being taken by the "rebels," he scuttled it in a creek. He returned after the war ended and raised the vessel to enter trade.[224]

At the beginning of the Revolutionary War, William Scarborough was a Justice of the Peace in Camden County and a Loyalist. According to his testimony he was "mobb[ed]... abuse[d] Insult[ed]" by the local populace. He built a brigantine of 100 tons on the Pasquotank River in order to flee the colony. Although the local militia closely watched the construction site, the building of the *Lucy*, as she was named, was not interfered with, mainly, as one testified, because "the people in general appeared to be glad when a Tory was about to leave North Carolina." In 1779 the brigantine was launched and with Scarborough and family on board sailed for Cadiz, Spain.[225] With the Peace of Paris in 1783, North Carolina's shipbuilding industry continued to thrive, although it would be affected by the new nation's economy and international problems.

Notes

1. Richard A. Stephenson, "Comparative Cartography and Coastal Processes: Four Hundred Years of Change on the Outer Banks of North Carolina," *Terrae Incognitae*, 22:1 (1990): 29-40.
2. This may be the first ship constructed in what became North Carolina, but no permanent settlement was established, and the expedition eventually returned to Spanish possessions in the Caribbean. See Roy Davenport and Cornelius D. Thomas. "America's First Ship," *The State* 20 (August 1952): 1-2, 15.
3. David Beers Quinn. *The Roanoke Voyages, 1584-1590*, 2 vols; Richard A. Stephenson, "The First Planned Town in America: The Cittie of Ralegh," *Tributaries*, 15 (October 2008), 7-12.
4. Hugh Talmage Lefler and Albert Ray Newsome, *North Carolina: The History of a Southern State*, 32-33. The 1672 Ogilvy map provides information on the land grants of 1663.
5. For a description of Carolina see John Speed, *The Theatre of the Empire of Great Britain* (original available in the Library of Congress). However, this treatise was first published in 1611, with numerous printed editions through the years, even after Speed's death in 1629.
6. Stick, *Outer Banks*, 23-24.
7. For the maritime history of Wilmington and the lower Cape Fear see Alan D. Watson, *Wilmington: Port of North Carolina*.
8. Wilson Angley, "A History of Ocracoke Inlet and Adjacent Areas," Research Branch, North Carolina Division of Archives and History, 3.
9. Crittenden, *Commerce of North Carolina*, 5.
10. See James Cox, "The Pamlico-Tar River and its Role in the Development of Eastern North Carolina" (master's thesis, ECU, 1989), 28.
11. Thomas Woodward to Sir John Colleton, June 2, 1665, William L. Saunders (ed)., *Colonial Records of North Carolina*, I:99.
12. Lindley S. Butler, *North Carolina Genesis: Seventeenth-Century Albemarle County*, 40-41.
13. See Stephenson, "Comparative Cartography and Coastal Processes."
14. *Virginia Gazette*, November 23, 1773.
15. Saunders (ed,), *Colonial Records*, II: 396. A small hamlet was laid out in 1738 called "Woodstock" on the Pungo River close to Bath, and briefly rivaled that port in maritime trade. It never developed as envisioned mainly because of the growing importance of other towns in the colony.
16. F. Roy Johnson, *Sail and Steam: Navigation of Eastern Carolina*, 9.
17. Ray E. Lamb, III, "The Maritime History of Edenton, North Carolina, 1768-1773," copy in possession of the authors.
18. Wilson F. Angley, "Port Roanoke, North Carolina in the Eighteenth Century: A Compilation of Records," Research Branch, North Carolina Division of Archives and History, 884-887.
19. These included ten million staves, sixteen million shingles, 320,000 bushels of corn, 100,000 barrels of tar, 24,000 barrels of fish, and 6,000 hogsheads of tobacco. Bruce S. Cheeseman, "A Brief History of the Edenton Waterfront," Research Branch, North Carolina Division of Archives and History, 1980); Katherine I. Goodall, "The Burroughs Wreck: A Key to Eighteenth Century Ship Construction Techniques and the Life and Death of the Port of Edenton" (master's thesis, ECU, 2003).
20. Beaufort was originally known as "Fishtown," presumably because its primary export was fish.
21. Charles L. Paul, "Factors in the Economy of Colonial Beaufort," *NCHR* 44 (Spring 1967): 113; Report of Peter Knight, December. 19, 1780, Case 70, Revolutionary War Prize Cases: Records of the Court of Appeal in Cases of Capture, 1776-1787, Reel 8, Duke University Library, Durham, North Carolina.
22. Alonzo T. Dill, "Eighteenth Century New Bern: A History of the Town and Craven County, 1700-1800," *NCHR* 23 (January 1946): 64.
23. In 1739-1740, thirty vessels entered the district annually. By 1764, a total of 127 ships discharged cargoes there, probably most of them in New Bern. Alan Watson, *A History of New Bern and Craven County*, 58; Dill, "Eighteenth Century New Bern," 66.
24. Watson, *History of New Bern and Craven County*, 38.
25. Watson, *Wilmington: Port of North Carolina*, 6.
26. Wilson Angley, "An Historical Overview of the Black River in Southeastern North Carolina," Research Branch, North Carolina Division of Archives and History, 1983, 2. The Black River is a tributary of the Cape Fear River.
27. Thomas C. Parramore, *Murfreesboro, North Carolina and the Founding of the American Republic 1608-1781*, 21; William S. Price Jr., "Nathaniel Macon, Planter," *NCHR* 78 (April 2001), 193.
28. Paul, "Factors in the Economy of Colonial Beaufort," 116-121; Watson, *History of New Bern and Craven County*, 56.
29. Robert Cain, ed., *Colonial Records of North Carolina* (Second Series), VI: xvii.
30. Crittenden, *Commerce of North Carolina*, 74; Lamb, "Maritime History of Edenton," 26.
31. Cox, "The Pamlico-Tar River," 12; Saunders, ed., *Colonial Records*, II: 236-237. Exports from Beaufort in 1764 consisted of 30,043 barrels of tar, 3,303 barrels of turpentine, 3,721 barrels of pitch, 1,279 barrels of spirits of turpentine, and 619 barrels of rosin.
32. Watson, *History of New Bern and Craven County*, 56; Watson, *Wilmington: Port of North Carolina*, 12.

33. Saunders, ed., *Colonial Records*, VI: 606-607.
34. William N. Still, Jr., "Croatan Forest Study," manuscript copy in possession of author; Lamb, "The Maritime History of Edenton," 27; Harry Roy Merrens, *Colonial North Carolina in the Eighteenth Century*, 94-95. See also Lee, *The Lower Cape Fear in Colonial Days*, 149-150. About seventy to seventy-five percent of these exports went out of the Cape Fear region. In 1769 alone, 547,540 shingles and 91,054 feet of scantling were exported from New Bern.
35. At least two North Carolina-built vessels were involved in the slave trade. See Elizabeth Donner, ed., *Documents Illustrative History of Slave Trade*, 16:611, 622.
36. In 1733, Virginia's governor estimated that imports from North Carolina totaled some 50,000 pounds; from there the goods were transshipped to Europe or the West Indies. Thomas J. Wertenbaker, *Norfolk: Historic Southern Port*, 35; Arthur P. Middleton, *Tobacco Coast: A Maritime History of Chesapeake Bay in the Colonial Era*, 201.
37. Edwin L. Combs III, "Trading in Lubberland: Maritime Commerce in Colonial North America, *NCHR* 80 (January 2003), 1, passim. See also Watson, *Wilmington: Port of North Carolina*, 11; Lamb, "The Maritime History of Edenton," 22-23; Joseph Goldenberg, "Names and Numbers: Statistical Notes on Some Port Records of Colonial North Carolina," *American Neptune*, 155-157; Robert J. Cain, ed., *Records of the Executive Council, 1755-1775*, xxvii.
38. Goldenberg, "Names and Numbers," 155-157.
39. Pollock to Nathaniel Duckenfield, December 20, 1741, Thomas Pollock Letterbook, SANC. See also Combs, "Trading in Lubberland," 24; Bradford J. Wood, *This Remote Part of the World; Regional Formation in Lower Cape Fear, North Carolina, 1725-1775*, 24-25; and A. Roger Ekirch, "'Poor Carolina'": Society and Politics in North Carolina, 1729-1771," Ph.D. diss., Johns Hopkins University, 1979).
40. Pollock to Duckenfield, July 4, 1743. Thomas Pollock Letterbook, SANC.
41. Joseph Goldenberg, *Colonial Shipbuilding*, shipping tables in appendix, and 291. See also Goldenberg, "Names and Numbers." Goldenberg, the most recent authority, was able to utilize only records for the years preceding the American Revolution as well as selected shipping records.
42. Watson, *Wilmington: Port of North Carolina*, 16.
43. Cain, ed., *Colonial Records of North Carolina* (Second Series) VI: xxiv; Watson, *Wilmington: Port of North Carolina*, 22-23; Lamb, "Maritime History of Edenton," 15.
44. For North Carolina, see New Hanover Deed Book C, 112, SANC. The District Court Records, Edenton, 1760, Vol 2, SANC, has several cases concerning ship repair.
45. Goldenberg, *Colonial Shipbuilding*, 9, 12; John Anthony Eistenhold, "Lumber and Trade in the Seaboard Cities of the Old South, 1607-1860, Ph.D. diss., University of Mississippi, 1979, 1.
46. Goldenberg, *Colonial Shipbuilding*, 23.
47. Goldenberg, *Colonial Shipbuilding*, 25.
48. See the English/British Naval Office Records, copies in SANC.
49. Writ of *cepi corpus* against Francis Howard, caulker, October 1750, Chowan County Civil Action papers, SANC.
50. Edward Moseley, "Southern Built: Wilmington's Maritime Construction Industry, 1717-1860," copy of unpublished manuscript in possession of authors, 9-10; William Atmore Papers, SHC, UNC-CH.
51. Francis Xavier Martin, *History of North Carolina*, I:142; George Bancroft, *History of the United States*, II:151, citing Martin. Martin's account is the one that provides the basis for this statement.
52. Keele obtained a patent for 800 acres on the southwest side of the Pasquotank River. The vessel was probably built there, possibly from timber on this land.
53. William S. Price Jr., ed., *North Carolina Higher Court Minutes, 1709-1733*, 247, 492-498; Samuel Ashe, *History of North Carolina*, I:91; *Pasquotank Historical Society Yearbook*, I:41.
54. Information about these shipbuilders and others in the colonial period has been obtained from a variety of sources including the published colonial records, unpublished wills, estate papers, inventories, deed books, land entries, and court papers from North Carolina and Virginia. An incomplete list can be found in James H. Craig, *The Arts and Crafts in North Carolina, 1699-1840*, 250-253. Considerable use has been made of abstracts of various county records.
55. This migration was mentioned by John Speed in 1676 (see note 5 above).
56. W.B. McKoy, "Incidents of the Early and Permanent Settlement of the Cape Fear," *Quarterly Review of the Eastern North Carolina Genealogical Society*, II:130; (Raleigh) *News and Observer*, June 29, 1980.
57. Middleton, *Tobacco Coast*, 234.
58. September 3, 1767.
59. This number included two who called themselves boatbuilders, and one canoe builder. The number is undoubtedly conservative as those listed were property owners; obviously there were shipwrights who did not own property. Although the deeds indicated that they owned plantations, they rarely called themselves planters. In addition to colonial and county records, see Diana Barbara Powell, "Artisans in the Colonial South. Chowan County, North Carolina, 1714-1776" (master's thesis, UNC-CH, 1983); Jean B. Kell, ed., *Coastal Carteret County during the American Revolution, 1765-1785*, 98; Dru Haley and David Winslow Jr., *The Historic Architecture of Perquimans County North Carolina*, 253, 255; Thomas R. Butchko, *Edenton: An Architectural Portrait*, 4; *High Tides: Hyde County Historical Society Journal*, Vol. 8 (Spring 1987): 22; Weynette Parks Haun, comp., *Chowan County North Carolina Miscellaneous Papers 1685-1744*; Mrs. Watson Winslow, *History of Perquimans County*, 239, 251.
60. Ship *Fanny* file, 1785, Colonial Office Record 101/8, copy in SANC. For Rowan, see William S. Powell, *Dictionary of North Carolina Biography*, V:258. Rowan later became a prominent official in the colony and served briefly as acting governor.
61. Luke Mounts and George Every owned property on Tranter's Creek, close to the Beaufort County line. A.B. Pruitt, comp., *Abstracts of Land Entries: Pitt Co., NC 1778-1797*, 67; Pitt County Deed Book F, 319.
62. "[L]ess than five percent of all vessels were constructed there, leading us to believe that shipbuilding was not one of the extensive activities of these men of commerce and business." Ira Wilson Barber Jr., "The Ocean-borne Commerce of Port Roanoke, 1771-1776" (master's thesis, UNC-CH, 1931), 8.
63. Wood, *This Remote Part of the World*, 229-230.
64. Alexander M. Walker, comp., *New Hanover County Court Minutes 1738-1769*, 16, 22; New Hanover County Deed Book A-B, 57-60, 247-248, 250-253, 304-305, 342-343, SANC; Donald Lennon and Ida Kellum, eds., *The Wilmington Town Book, 1743-1778*, xvii.
65. For a discussion of shipbuilding localities as well as other town lot uses, see Elizabeth McKoy, *Early Wilmington Block by Block from 1733 On*. See also A. B. Pruitt, comp., *Abstracts of Deeds, New*

Hanover County, N.C., Books C, D, and E, pp. 35, 36, 51, 52, 64, 79, 136, 197,; Janet Schaw, *Journal of a Lady of Quality*, Evangeline Walker Andrews and Charles M. Andrews, eds., 148; Alfred Moore Waddell, *A History of New Hanover County and the Lower Cape Fear Region*, I:205.

66. Elizabeth McKoy, comp., *Early New Hanover County Records*, 66, 70. No information has been found associating a shipwright with the site or describing what shipbuilding activities occurred there.

67. Wilson Angley, "A Brief Biography of Thomas Mulford, Sometime Mariner of Brunswick Town," Research Branch, North Carolina Division of Archives and History, 1987, 8-10.

68. For Howard Chowan County Civil Actions, 1730-1756, SANC; for Blount see Francis Jones, et al, *Washington County: A Tapestry*, 71.

69. From Wilmington a businessman listed occupations that were needed in the Cape Fear region including ship carpenters. Quote about South Carolina in William J. Rivers, *A Chapter in the Early History of South Carolina*, 99-100.

70. September 1, 1753, John Saunders Notebook, SANC.

71. Hugh Williamson Letter to John Mease, February 25, 1778, SANC.

72. Blount to Sir William, December 29, 1783, John Gray Blount Papers, SANC.

73. H.C.R. 16/62, British Records, SANC.

74. Sir Wescott Abel, *The Shipwright's Trade*, 31.

75. Saunders, ed., *Colonial Records*, VI:429.

76. Robert Cain, ed., *Records of the Executive Council 1664-1734*, VII of *The Colonial Records of North Carolina*, 62; Goldenberg, *Colonial Shipbuilding*, 111.

77. Craig, *The Arts and Crafts in North Carolina*, 250-253. Six additional apprentices were found in addition to those in Craig's work. For a somewhat unusual arrangement see Cockrey's agreement with Watts, in Weynette Parks Haun, ed., *Perquimans County Deed Abstracts, 1681-1729*, 29.

78. Chowan County Miscellaneous Records, vol.7, July 26, 1762, SANC; Walker, comp., *New Hanover County Court Minutes 1716-1769*, 11, 16; Wood, *This Remote Part of The World*, 94; Saunders, ed., *Colonial Records of North Carolina*, II: 31; Cain, ed., *Records of the Executive Council 1664-1734*, 62.

79. Lorenzo J. Greene, *The Black in Colonial New England*, 100-101; Raymond B. Pinchbeck, *The Virginia Black Artisan and Tradesman*, 29.

80. A. Alexander Bontemps, "A Social History of Black Culture in Colonial North Carolina," Ph.D. diss., University of Illinois-Urbana, 1989, 152-157.

81. ADM 36/3902, British Records, SANC; also see Wilson Angley to Richard Lawrence, August 28, 1992, copy in Underwater Archaeology Branch, North Carolina Division of Archives and History, Kure Beach, NC.

82. Loyalist Claims Papers 1782, P.R.O. Audit Office 13, Bundle 121, copy in British Records, SANC.

83. Howard A. Hanlon, *The Bull-Hunchers: A Saga of the Three and a Half Centuries of Harvesting the Forest Crops of the Tidewater Low Country*, 72.

84. At that time, the property on Wiccacon Creek was in Bertie County; today, it is in Hertford County. Chowan County Deed Book B, No. 1, 524-537, SANC.

85. Chowan Deed Book B, 1067, 1073; C, No. 1, 281, ibid.

86. *Hertford County: The First Two Hundred Years 1584-1789*, 17.

87. For Wimble see William P. Cummings, *Captain James Wimble, His Maps, and the Colonial Cartography of the North Carolina Coast*.

88. Wilson Angley, "An Historical Overview of Harkers Island," copy in the Core Sound Waterfowl Museum, Harkers Island, North Carolina; Robert G. Lewis, *Ebenezer Harker: Island Namesake*, 1-3; Pat Davis et al., eds., *The Heritage of Carteret County North Carolina*, I:40.

89. The two families were close. Henry Stanton and William Borden Srs. were brothers-in-law. Henry Stanton Jr. married one of William Borden's daughters, Rebecca Willis Sanders. *Carteret County Wills 1700-1880*, 2, SANC; Davis, et al., eds., *The Heritage of Carteret County, North Carolina*, I: 188; (Morehead City-Beaufort) *News-Times*, October 3, 1974; M. Marsh Wilson, *Beaufort, North Carolina*, 78-79; William R. Boyd, ed., "William Borden's Address to the Inhabitants of North Carolina," *NCHR* 2 (April 1925), 188-225.

90. Davis, et al., eds., *Heritage of Carteret County North Carolina*, I: 429-430, 187-188; *Beaufort News*, February 29, 1929; Borden will, 1749, Carteret County Deed Book D, 12; "North Carolina Bordens," 12.

91. W. P. Pruden statement, Sept. 19, 1936 in the Joseph Hewes Papers, SANC. In 1936, a severe gale caused the bay to recede approximately eight to twelve feet uncovering the remains of a shipyard, including an old wooden railway. A local resident claimed that it was the Hewes Shipyard, although other shipbuilding facilities would have been located in the same general location. There is some question that it might be the remains of the Robert Treat Paine Shipyard, a mid-nineteenth century facility. See George Stevenson to author, November 13, 2001, copy in authors' possession. East Carolina University's Maritime Studies Program held an underwater archaeological field school in Edenton during the summer of 2001, including an examination of the remains located in 1936. Possibly this investigation will determine the age of the shipyard and whether or not it was that of Hewes.

92. Cornelius Moore Deed of Trust, July 13, 1767, Perquimans Co. Deed Book H, No. 5, 11, SANC; Deed of indebtedness, March 21, 1771, Norfolk County, Va., Deed Book 25, 62; *News and Observer*, November 19, 1935; Murray to Bennet, July 3, 1751, in James Murray Papers, Massachusetts Historical Society, Boston, Mass.; Eisterhold, "Southern Lumber," 75. See also Winslow, *History of Perquimans County*, 211, for shipbuilding activities in Nixonton, Perquimans County, of the merchant and ship carpenter Cornelius Moore. See also Perquimans County Deed Book No. H., no.5; Deed Book D, No. 17; and Deed Book G, No. 92, SANC, for background to Moore shipyard.

93. Tyrrell County Deeds, 4, 121, 161, 146, 492, SANC.

94. May 1753, Bertie County Deed Book G, 516, SANC.

95. Chowan County Miscellaneous Papers, 1685-1744, Book I, 460, SANC.

96. Bertie County Wills, SANC.

97. J. Bryan Grimes, *North Carolina Wills and Inventories*, 362-363.

98. Alan D. Watson, *Perquimans County: A Brief History*, 13,15; Sec. of State Papers, Wills, Vol. 27, 62, SANC.

99. For Gray see Harry Thompson, *The Windsor Story, 1768-1968*, http://www.rootsweb.com/~ncbertie/windsor.htm; for Blackledge see the inventory of his Real and Personal Estate taken October 1777, Carteret County Civil Action papers, SANC. See also Marguerite Butler McCall, ed., *Business as Usual: Edenton Merchant Ledgers, 1759-1819*, 30-31.

100. The court case Brock v. Smith resulted when the Smiths evidently backed out of the contract and Brock demanded restitution. Cain, ed., *North Carolina Higher Court Minutes, 1709-1723*, 435-436.

101. Chowan Country Deed Book B-l, 230, SANC; Wm. Haly to John Campbell, May 1753, in Bertie County Deed Book, Vol. 5, Book G, 516, ibid.
102. Charles L. Paul, "Colonial Beaufort: The History of a North Carolina Town" (master's thesis, ECU, 1965), 99; Wilson, *Beaufort, North Carolina*, 79.
103. Jesse Forbes Pugh, *Three Hundred Years Along the Pasquotank: A Biographical History of Camden County*, 60; Pasquotank County Deed Book C, 415-416, SANC. See also ibid., Book C, 159; E, 364.
104. Susan Block, *The Wrights of Wilmington*, 18; McKoy, *Early Wilmington Block by Block from 1733 On*, 110; Lennon and Kellam, eds., *The Wilmington Town Book 1743-1778*, xvi.
105. Rarely does a document mention land use: residence, business (including shipbuilding if in a port), agriculture, or timber if in a rural area. James Story to Thomas Gaines, October,15, 1765, Tyrrell County Deed Book 4.1, 492, SANC; John Spear to John Cherry, March 6, 1753, Tyrrell County Deed Book 3, 21, ibid.; John Cherry to Joseph Biggs, January 29, 1755, Tyrrell County Deed Book 4.1, 127, ibid.; Thomas Grimes Indenture, August 19, 1766, Norfolk County, Va., Order Book 23, 34a; Thomas Grimes Will, May 12, 1769, Norfolk County Va., Will Book l, 191; James Cleeves to John Cleeves, September 18, 1761, Norfolk County, Va., Deed Book 20, 26a; John Scott to Joseph Hackett, April 21, 1725, Pasquotank County Deed Book A, 238, SANC; Joseph Hackett to John Jones, April 21,1726, Pasquotank County Deed Book B, 203,; John Powell to Arthur Johnson September 18, 1741, Arthur Johnston to Joseph Balch, October 20, 1742, Craven County Deed Book, l, 331k, 171; John Spear to John Cherry, March 6, 1753, and John Cherry to Joseph Biggs, January 29, 1735, Tyrrell County Deed Book, 4.1, 21, 127,; John and Ann Smith to William Sharp (shipwright), March 28, 1715 and William Sharp to William Downing, August 10, 1722, Chowan County Deed Book, B-l, 1650, and Deed Book C-1, 281; William Green to Robert Trawick, September 12, 1769 and Robert Trawick to William Green, July 3, 1774, in Hargett Gwynn, *Records of Onslow County*, 196, 221.
106. May, 1753, Bertie County Deed Book, vol. 5, Book G., 516, SANC. See also Robert Cain, ed., *North Carolina Higher Court Minutes, 1709-1723*, V:497.
107. North Carolina District Superior Court, Estate Records, SANC. John Smith died before the vessel was built and the plaintiffs were asking for restitution.
108. Goldenberg, *Colonial Shipbuilding*, 112. See also C. Stevens Laise, "Interpreting the Colonial Shipyard," *Society of Naval Architects and Marine Engineers,"* reprint of paper presented November 11, 1976, 5.
109. Thomas Parramore claimed that two gullies adjacent to the Meherrin River in Hertford County were sites of shipbuilding. He based this claim on documents. Winslow, *History of Perquimans County*, 211; A. B. Pruitt, comp,, *Abstracts of Sales of Confiscated Loyalists Land and Property in North Carolina*, 7. For Jasper see *High Tide: The Journal of the Hyde County Historical Society*, XI (Spring 1990), 13.
110. Copy of the map in William P. Cummings, *The Southeast in Early Maps*. Hoffmann, *Province of North Carolina 1663-1729: Abstracts of Land Patents*, 237; Bateman's will in Tyrrell County Wills, I:20, SANC.
111. Duckenfield was a wealthy planter and member of a noble family in England. Cummings, *The Southeast in Early Maps*.
112. Ibid. See note 359, 238. In 1987, an underwater archaeological survey of Salmon Creek located the shipyard and determined it was also active in the nineteenth century. Michael Hill and Mark Wilde-Ramsing, "Historical Documentation and Underwater Archaeological Reconnaissance of Salmon Creek in the Vicinity of Batts- Duckenfield – Capehart Site, Bertie County," March, 1987, Research Branch, North Carolina Division of Archives and History, Raleigh, N.C.
113. Jeffrey D. Morris, "An Intensive Survey of a Proposed Location for Thomas MacKnight's Shipyard Currituck County, North Carolina," June 1994, Underwater Archaeology Branch, North Carolina Division of Archives and History, Kure Beach, N.C.
114. Wilson Angley, "A Brief History of the Scuppernong River," Research Branch, North Carolina Division of Archives and History, Raleigh, N.C., 1986, 2-3; McCoy, *Early New Hanover County Records*, 26; Hofmann, *Colony of North Carolina 1735-1764*, 443. Neither Viniard nor John Adams Creek are listed in William S. Powell's *North Carolina Gazetteer*.
115. J. H. Stevens, *Albemarle People and Places*, 356-7; Gwen Boyer Bjorkman, *Pasquotank County North Carolina, Record of Deeds 1700-1751*, 419; Allen Wilkinson Hart Norris, *Hyde County, North Carolina Record of Deeds B, 1762-1783*, 90.
116. Jackson, *The Cape Fear–Northeast Cape Fear River Comprehensive Study*, I: 210; William P. Cummings, "The Turbulent Life of Captain James Wimble," *NCHR* XLVI (January 1969): 6; James Wimble to Michael Dyer, June 18, 1837, New Hanover County Record Book AB, 60; Lennon and Kellam, eds., *The Wilmington Town Book, 1743-1778*, xxxvi.
117. McKoy, "Incidents of the Early and Permanent Settlement of the Cape Fear," 130; Jackson, *Cape Fear–Northeast Cape Fear River Comprehensive Study*, I: 211.
118. *North Carolina Historical and Genealogical Register*, Vol 2, No. 2: 313; Thomas Blount, "Buncombe Hall," *North Carolina Booklet* (December 1902), 14-16.
119. Articles of Agreement, January 8, 1709, Beaufort County Deed Book l, 162,; and Harding to John Snead, May 17, 1744, Onslow County Deed Book B, folio 11,SANC; Harding vs Ellsey, Mar. 1723, Cain, ed., *North Carolina Higher Court Minutes, 1709-1723*, 394; C. Wingate Reed, *Beaufort County: Two Centuries of Its History*, 46; Gwynn, *Abstracts of the Records on Onslow County, North Carolina, 1734-1850*, 33.
120. A. T. Dill, *Governor Tryon and His Palace*, 31.
121. Grimes, *North Carolina Wills and Inventories*, 388; Allen Wilkinson Hart Norris, comp., *Hyde County, Record of Deeds, A, 1736-1762*, 24, 35, 45, 48, 54-55,; Margaret M. Hofmann, *Colony of North Carolina, 1735-1764*, 82; A. B. Pruitt, comp., *Colonial Land Entries*, III:117; Russell note, May 28, 1774, New Bern District Court Estate Records, SANC; Albert W. Cowper to authors, Feb. 1, 1982, copy in possession of authors. Deeds suggest that a considerable number of shipwrights were concentrated on the Pungo River and vicinity during this period.
122. Whether or not Alban actually built vessels on it is not known. Nathaniel Chevin to Richard Alban, Mar 29, 1716, Chowan County Deed Book B-1, 230, SANC; George Stevenson to Still, Nov. 16, 2001, copy in possession of authors. Onslow County Deed Book A, 38, and Beaufort County Deed Book E, 299, SANC.
123. To Willson and Carr, October 1774 in Chowan County Ferriage Docket, 1781-1783, SANC; William Cummings, "The Earliest Permanent Settlement in North Carolina, Nathaniel Batts and the Comberford Map," *American Historical Review*, 92-99; Hill and Wilde-Ramsing "Historical Documentation and Underwater Archaeological Reconnaissance of Salmon Creek in the Vicinity of the Batts-Duckenfield-Capehart Site, Bertie

County"; W. Churton Map, August 22, 1767, in English Records, SANC; Loyalists Claims, Duckenfield, Sir Nathaniel, SANC. There is no information as to the number of vessels built at this yard.

124. Merrens, *Colonial North Carolina in the Eighteenth Century*, 105; Barbara Snowden, "Thomas MacKnight, Local Tory," in JoAnn Bates, ed., *The Heritage of Currituck County*, 101-102. MacKnight's deposition describing his property and explaining what attracted him to the area, in the English Records, Audit Office Loyalist Claims, Box 8, Thomas MacKnight, SANC.

125. MacKnight deposition, English Records, SANC.

126. Since 1992, the MacKnight shipyard and his other properties have been the subject of a number of archaeological investigations. They have found the remains of his wharves, shipyard, and a vessel(s) near Indiantown in Currituck County. Mark Wilde Ramsing, "Underwater Archaeological Examination of North River, Currituck and Camden Counties, August 28, 1992; Sheridan R. Jones, "Historical and Archaeological Investigation of the MacKnight Shipyard Wreck," May 1996, copies of these reports in the Underwater Archaeology Branch, North Carolina Office of Archives and History, Kure Beach, NC.

127. Jones, "Historical and Archaeological Investigation of the MacKnight Shipyard Wreck," 18, 21-22.

128. Loyalist Claims Papers, 1782, PRO Audit Office 13, Bundle 121, copy in English Records, SANC.

129. Snowden, "Thomas MacKnight, Local Tory," 101-102. See also Pugh, *Three Hundred Years Along the Pasquotank*, 103-104.

130. Navy Board to Admiralty, October 17, 1771, a copy in British Records, 74.1088, 1-3, SANC; Inglis to Board of Admiralty, July 11, 1772, ADM1/484, copy in British Records, SANC. Virginia Wood in *Live Oaking*, mentions this document but leaves out North Carolina from the survey, 13. Roger Fiske to Navy Board, September 3, 1771, 1-3, British Records, SANC; Tryon to Cdr. Hughes, April 24, 165, ibid.; Commissioner of Dock Yard, Portsmouth to Tryon, August 27, 1765, in Saunders, ed., *Colonial Records*, vol. 7:112-113; Bricknell, *The Natural History of North Carolina*, 59-64; Middleton, *Tobacco Coast*, 224-225.

131. Inglis Report to Board of Admiralty, July 11, 1772, ADM1/484, copy in British Records, SANC.

132. Tryon to Board of Trade, February 22, 1767; Saunders, ed.; *Colonial Records*, VII: 440-441; Tryon to Hughes, April 24, 1765, British Records, SANC.

133. Amy Mitchell, "A Comparison of Wood Use in Eighteenth Century Vessels" (master's thesis, ECU, 1994), 169.

134. Laise, "Interpreting the Colonial Shipyard," p.5.

135. Joseph Goldenberg, "Saw, Axe, and Auger: Three Centuries of American Shipbuilding," in *Material Culture in the Wooden Age*, Brooke Hindle, ed., 107, hereinafter cited as "Saw, Axe, and Auger."

136. Abell, *Shipwright's Trade*, 90; Inventory of effects of John Mitchell, July 15, 1774, in New Hanover County Records,; Inventory of Estate of Hatten Williams, Dec 7, 1773, Chowan County Estate Records,; and Inventory of goods of John Walker, Nov 15, 1769, Washington Co. Estate Records, SANC.

137. Albion, *Forests and Sea Power*, 233.

138. Dill, "Eighteenth Century New Bern," 73, 74, 171; *North Carolina Booklet* (December 1902), 14-16.

139. Paul, "Colonial Beaufort: The History of a North Carolina Town," 98-99. Merrens, *Colonial North Carolina in the Eighteenth Century*, 96-99; Tryon to Board of Trade, January 30, 1767, William S. Powell, ed., *The Correspondence of William Tryon and Other Selected Papers*, I:410; Eisterhold, "Lumber and Trade in the Seaboard South," Ph.D. diss., 8, 74; Donald E. Becker, "North Carolina, 1754-1783, An Economic, Political, and Military History of North Carolina During the Great War for the Empire," Ph.D. diss., 49, Tucker Littleton, "A Civilian History of the Camp Lejune Area From Earliest Settlement to 1941," 68.

140. C. Robert Haywood, "North Carolina Advocates of Mercantilism," *NCHR* 33 (April 1956), 153; Moseley, "Southern Built," 12.

141. George Stevenson, "Ropewalks," unpublished manuscript, copy in possession of authors.

142. Cappon, "Iron-Making--A Forgotten Industry of North Carolina," *NCHR* 9 (October 1932), 331-332.

143. Goldenberg, "Saw, Axe, and Auger," 109.

144. Pollock to Borland, April 13, 1711, Pollock Letterbook; similar letter and date to Welstead; and Wm Russell to (unclear), May 28, 1774, New Bern District Estates, Superior Court, D.S.C.R., SANC.

145. James A. Mulholland, *A History of Metals in Colonial America*, 84.

146. *Wilmington and Cape Fear Mercury*, December 29, 1773; entry for December 30, 1774, in Leora McEachern and Isabel Williams, eds., *Wilmington-New Hanover Safety Committee Minutes*, 7; James Smith to William Miller, April 2, 1776, "Notes from the Archives of Scotland Concerning America," in J. Franklin Jameson, ed., *Annual Report of the American Historical Association for the Year 1930*, I, 56.

147. Secretary of State Records, Council Minutes, Wills, and Inventories 1677-1701, SANC. According to an archivist at the North Carolina State Archives, there was no Barkely living in Perquimans at the time. Possibly, Barkely came from another colony to build the vessel and left afterwards.

148. Saunders, ed., *Colonial Records*, VII; 429; Cain ed., *North Carolina Higher Court Minutes, 1724-1730*, xxiv; Pollock to Sir _____, December 20, 1741, Thomas Pollock Papers, SANC.

149. Hugh T. Lefler and William S. Powell, *Colonial North Carolina: A History*, 164-165; Lee, *The Lower Cape Fear in Colonial Days*, 156; Simeon Crowther, "The Shipbuilding Industry and the Economic Development of the Delaware Valley, 1681-1776," Ph.D. diss., 98-99; Hawk, *Industrial History of the South*, 113; Charles C. Crittenden, "Ships and Shipping in North Carolina," *NCHR* 8 (April 1931), 7; Goldenberg, "Names and Numbers: Statistical Notes on Some Port Records of Colonial North Carolina," 155-156.

150. Joseph Goldenberg, *Shipbuilding in Colonial America*, 52. Lefler and Newsome, *The History of Southern State: North Carolina*, 100, cites the same statistic.

151. The ship list is taken from port records. North Carolina-built vessels mentioned elsewhere such as newspapers, court records, and the like are not included. The number of ships built in North Carolina does not compare with the number built in New England during the colonial period. Between 1703 and 1708 Massachusetts alone built 374 vessels. Cain, ed., *Records of the Executive Council 1735-1754*, xxxii; Goldenberg, *Shipbuilding in Colonial America*, 141.

152. Beaufort Co. Deed Book l, SANC. See also Norris, comp., *Beaufort County, North Carolina Deed Book I, 1696-1729*, 53-54.

153. Elizabeth Van Moore, "Report on the Cupola House for the Edenton and Chowan Historical Commission," n.p. See also Chowan County Deed Book B., SANC.

154. Cumming, "Turbulent Life of Captain James Wimble," 6.

155. Robert A. Kilmarx, *American Maritime Legacy*, 17; Goldenberg, "Saw, Axe and Auger," 117; John G.B. Hutchins, "History and Development of the Shipbuilding Industry in the United States," in F.G. Fassett Jr., ed., *The Shipbuilding Business in the United States*

of America, I:22-23; Howard Chapelle, *History of American Sailing Ships*, 10.

156. James Shepherd and Gary Walton, *Shipping, Maritime Trade and the Economic Development of Colonial North America*, 96.

157. The 1774 contract that John Smith of Hyde County made with a mercantile firm set the cost at six pounds and three shillings per ton, the same as in Philadelphia. Robert Palmer of Bath asked three pounds, and five shillings for a vessel on the stocks. See District Court Estate Records, New Bern, May 1774; Robert Palmer Letters, P.C. 1198.1; and Josiah Collins Papers for 1782, SANC. For Philadelphia see Joshua H. Howard, "'The Most Abandoned Sett of Wretches': North Carolina Privateering Efforts During the American Revolution, 1778-1783" (master's thesis, ECU, 2004), 39.

158. Saunders, ed., *Colonial Records*, III:123; New Hanover County Deed Book D, 403; New Hanover County Deed Book F, 303; CO5/1035, British Records; and Court Records, New Hanover Country, XXI, 24, SANC; Goldenberg, *Shipbuilding in Colonial America*, 92.

159. February 12, 1780.

160. January 26, 1779.

161. Goldenberg, "Saw, Ax and Auger," 117.

162. Thirty-one ships were built in the 1720s, forty in the 1730s, thirty-five in the 1740s, fifty-one in the 1750s, seventy-seven in the 1760s, and fifty-two between 1770 and 1776. The outbreak of the War of the Austrian Succession (French and Indian War) may account for the marked increase in launchings in the period after 1754. March 24, 1765 entry, "Journal of a French Traveler in the Colonies, 1765," *American Historical Review* 26 (July 1921), 736.

163. It is assumed that larger vessels were built at large shipbuilding sites at or near the larger settlements, while the smaller vessels were built at the more isolated sites such as plantations and small hamlets as shown on the map in Figure 8.

164. Bertie County, Camden County, Albemarle County, Chowan County, Currituck and Currituck County, Hertford, Little River, Pasquotank County or Precinct, Perquimans County and Perquimans River, Quitsna, Tyrrell County, and the Roanoke River were all a part of the Albemarle region.

165. The Pamlico region included Hyde County or Precinct, the Pungo River, Pitt County and Washington.

166. Unfortunately, we do not have a detailed description of a North Carolina-built vessel for the colonial period. Undoubtedly, there were vessel variations depending upon the shipbuilder. Defining vessel types were, at least, somewhat arbitrary. Ship carpenters migrated to the colony from Virginia, Bermuda, and New England. They undoubtedly introduced the type of hull and rig with which they were familiar.

167. Watson, *A History of New Bern and Craven County*, 57; Goldenberg, *Shipbuilding in Colonial America*, 217. The statistics for 1688 to 1725 come from port records. See Appendix A.

168. Lamb, "Maritime History of Colonial Edenton," 43; Book of Register, Collectors Office, Port of Roanoke, 1725-1751, microfilm, ECU; *North Carolina Historical and Genealogical Register*, (July 1900), 436; Roger Kammerer, "Early Shipbuilding in Pitt County," *Greenville Times*, March 1, 1989.

169. Appendix A shows that seventeen vessels were recorded without any type being given.

170. From Appendix A, only three vessels had dimensions other than tonnage. These vessels were the *Rebecca* in 1730, the *Mary* in 1780, and the *Kener* in 1782. The *Rebecca* was a brig of seventy tons built at Cape Fear. It was fifty-four feet long with a width of twenty-one feet, and a depth of ten feet. The *Kener*, also a brig, was much larger at 107 tons, but a length of seventy-six feet, and a width of twenty feet and a depth of eight feet. The comparison of these two vessels is interesting with the trend being toward longer and heavier brigs, but shallower, indicating the need for capability to navigate the shoals. The *Mary* was a sloop of eighty-two tons, like the *Kener* built someplace in North Carolina, with a draft of seven feet, a width of twenty feet, and a length of sixty-two feet. It is thought that shipwrights very early on saw the need for adapting to the shallow waters of the North Carolina coast, as compared to the deeper waters of more northerly ports.

171. Chapelle, *History of American Sailing ships*, 11; Fleetwood, *Tidecraft*, 26-28; Goldenberg, *Shipbuilding in Colonial America*, 39; Middleton, *Tobacco Coast*, 215-225. Regardless, the best that can be said of the North Carolina-built sloop is that it was a single-masted vessel, often much smaller than those built in other colonies.

172. Pollock to Jordan, October 3, 1712, Thomas Pollock Letterbook, SANC. See also bill of sale of the shallop *Tryall* in 1691. Secretary of State Records, Council Minutes, Wills, and Inventories, 1677-1701, SANC. Another shallop, apparently not registered, was built at Bath to carry supplies to militia fighting the Indians in 1712. It seems likely that an undetermined number of shallops engaged solely in inland navigation were not registered.

173. William Baker, *Sloops and Shallops*, xi.

174. Chapelle, *History of American Sailing Ships*, 15.

175. Goldenberg, "Names and Numbers: Statistical Notes on Some Port Records of Colonial North Carolina," table IV. Goldenberg estimates that twenty-three vessels registered and built in North Carolina in the colonial period were brigs.

176. The twenty-eight North Carolina brigs were evidently insured by Lloyd's (of London) Goldenberg, *Colonial Shipbuilding*, 241. In 1730, James Wimble had the brigantine *Rebecca* built on the Cape Fear River. In 1734, North Carolina built brig *Two Brothers*, 150 tons, carried a load of immigrants from Germany to Savannah, Georgia. In 1734, John Smith's shipyard in Bath launched the brigantine *Happy Luke*. Two years later a Bertie County merchant in his will instructed his executors to complete a brig on the stocks, fill it with a cargo of "tobacco, Black Walnut or other merchandize fit for the British market" and send it there. In 1769, a brig was built at the "Forks of the Tar River," at the location of a small community that would be named Washington. George F. Jones, ed., *Henry Newman's Salzburger Letterbooks*, 497-498; Grimes, *North Carolina Wills and Inventories*, 364-365, 388; Cumming, "Turbulent Life of Captain James Wimble," 1-18.

177. Goldenberg, *Shipbuilding in Colonial America*, 80. Only one snow was built in North Carolina after 1752.

178. Goldenberg, *Shipbuilding in Colonial America*, 79.

179. *North Carolina Gazette*, August 15, June 13 and 20, 1787; *North Carolina Magazine for 1764*, 159; McEachern and Williams, *Wilmington-New Hanover Safety Committee Minutes*, 7.

180. Parker to Parker, October 31, 1771, copy in file on ships/shipbuilding in the eighteenth century, Lower Cape Fear Historical Society Archives, Wilmington, N.C.

181. Grimes, *North Carolina Wills and Inventories*, 543.

182. July 4, 1783 entry, Alice Keith and William H. Masterson, eds., *The John Gray Blount Papers*, I:67.

183. Advertisement for three boats to be sold in Beaufort, October 16, 1778, and advertisement for sale of four boats in Edenton, March 11, 1780, *Virginia Gazette*. A number of North Carolina-built pilot boats were sold to interests in Charleston, S.C.

184. New Bern District Court Records, Craven County Courthouse, New Bern, N.C.

185. Robert Palmer Papers, SANC.

186. John Pearson to Messrs. Willson and Carr, October 1774, Chowan County Ferriage Docket, 1781-1783, SANC; Capehart Family Papers, Reel 3, folder 102, SHC, UNC-CH.

187. David Sutton Phelps, *Ancient Pots and Dugout Canoes*, 1-11. As the name suggests, logs were dug out using tools of shell, bone, or stone. The area to be hollowed out was burned and the charred wood was scraped out. In 1985, a number of canoes were discovered in Lake Phelps, located in Washington and Tyrell Counties. In all, thirty canoes ranging in age from the early woodland period, 900 B.C.E. to the fifteenth century C.E., were found. Other dugouts, discovered in Florida and the Caribbean, are 5,000 years old. They varied in size from a few feet to thirty-seven feet. According to archaeologist David Phelps, they were made by first splitting a cypress log, then alternately burning and scraping the interior until the desired shape and size were obtained.

188. Louis Arthur Norton, "The Native American Canoe-wright and Mariner", *Northern Mariner/le marin du nord*, XXIII, No. 4 (October 2013): 399-411, indicates that the spatial diffusion of the canoe building artistry shows a barrier between the north and the south, perhaps due to the difference in the species of vegetation, the nature of the streams and coasts, and perhaps, cultural differences. Also, Lynn Harris, *Patroons and Periaguas*, passim.

189. Arthur Barlowe, a member of the Sir Walter Raleigh expedition in 1584, was impressed with the natives' methods of constructing a dugout. Barlowe claimed that it was made out of pitch pine, unlike the Lake Phelps canoes.

190. In the Caribbean, a dugout was known as a canoa, and the Spanish called the dugout, a piraqua. Sometimes, the dugouts were called periagua, pereauguer, pereaugur, periagoe and pettyagua. A 1587engraving by DeBry shows such a vessel in North Carolina coastal waters. It is likely that Europeans learned how Native Americans built their dugouts and the natives may have learned something from the Europeans, such as the use of iron tools.

191. Inventory of possessions of William Reed, and Will of Thomas Clark, Secretary of State Papers, Series XIX, Box 43: Deeds, Wills, and Inventories, III:178, 68, SANC.

192. Mattie Erma Edwards Parker, ed., *North Carolina Higher-Court Records 1670-1696*, 363; Hyde County Civil Action Papers, 1750-1753, SANC; Fleetwood, *Tidecraft*, 40

193. Sale of two boats, June 2, 1746, and sale of a periauger, January 25, 1750, New Hanover County Deed Book C, 112, 349, SANC.

194. Johnson, *Riverboating in Lower Carolina*, 11; Alford, *Traditional Workboats of North Carolina*, 31.

195. Brickell, *Natural History of North Carolina*, 260-261.

196. Travelers frequently observed this type of vessel. There were a fairly large number plying North Carolina's rivers. However, there is little information on them. In 2004, a replica of a periauger was built at the North Carolina Maritime Museum in Beaufort. For the building and a general discussion of these early vessels see Michael B. Alford and Lawrence E. Babits, "Reproducing a Periauger," *Sea History*, 15-17, 31; Alford, *Traditional Work Boats of North Carolina*, 29-31. See also *Carteret County News Times*, July 21, 1932; F. W. Clonts, "Travel and Transportation in Colonial North Carolina," *NCHR* 3 (January 1926), 10-35; Fleetwood, *Tidecraft*, 32-40. South Carolina periaguers were considerably larger than those built in North Carolina. A twenty-ton South Carolina periagua was described as having an eight-foot beam and being more than forty-five feet in length, with 1,200 cubic feet of cargo space.

197. [Janet Schaw], *Journal of a Lady of Quality*, Evangeline Walker Andrews and Charles McLean Andrews, eds., 185.

198. J. Kelly Turner and John L. Bridgers Jr., *History of Edgecombe County, North Carolina*; 321; Johnson, *Sail and Steam*, 15.

199. Watson, *Wilmington: Port of North Carolina*, 15.

200. *North Carolina: A Guide to the Old State*, 65. One scow was listed in the port records. However, it is recorded as being a hundred tons. This does not seem reasonable. It is possible that the record meant a hundred barrels.

201. Michael B. Alford, "The Ferry from Trent: Researching Colonial River Ferries," *Tributaries* (October 1991), 10. This article discusses an archaeological investigation of a colonial ferry, a flat found on the Trent River. Alan Watson, "The Ferry in Colonial North Carolina," *Quarterly Review of the Eastern North Carolina Genealogical Society*, 5.

202. Saunders, ed., *Colonial Records*, I:219.

203. Charles L. Paul, "Factors in the Economy of Colonial Beaufort," *NCHR* 44 (Spring 1967), 118.

204. Gwynn, comp., *Records of Onslow County, North Carolina, 1734-1850*, 278; Walter Clark, ed., *State Records of North Carolina*, XXII: 960.

205. Combs, "Trading in Lubberland: Maritime Commerce in Colonial North Carolina, 24.

206. William N. Still Jr. *North Carolina's Revolutionary War Navy*, 6; Howard, "Most Abandoned Sett of Wretches,'" 54; William S. Powell, "Tar Heels Good Ship Builders," *News and Observer*, August 23, 1953; R. D. W. Connor, *History of North Carolina*, I:448; Earl Dean, "Carolina-Built Ships," *The State*, 11, 17-18.

207. Still, *North Carolina's Revolutionary War Navy*, 3-4.

208. Watson, *Wilmington: Port of North Carolina*, 28-29; Moseley," Southern Built," 13-14.

209. Jean Bruyere Kell, *When the British Came to Beaufort*, 6, 19; Jeffrey Crow, "What Price Loyalism? The Case of John Cruden," *NCHR* 68 (July 1981), 226-227.

210. In the late seventeenth and early eighteenth centuries, the colony, especially the Outer Banks, was a focus of piratical activity most notably with the notorious Blackbeard. When the time came for privateering, it was a logical step and was widespread. There is no evidence that North Carolina-built vessels were outfitted as privateers prior to the American Revolution, but it certainly is possible.

211. Howard, "'The Most Abandoned Sett of Wretches,'" 70.

212. Lawrence E. Babits and Joshua Howard, *"Fortitude and Forbearance": The North Carolina Continental Line in the Revolutionary War, 1775-1783*, 213; British Records, H.C.A. 32/328, SANC; Thomas Parramore, "The Great Escape from Forten Gaol: An Incident of the Revolution," *NCHR*, 349-351; British Records, H.C.A. 32/328, SANC.

213. Barry Fyre, "Privateering in North Carolina Waters During the American Revolution" (master's thesis, ECU, 1980), passim.

214. Connor, *History of North Carolina*, I:448-449.

215 Jean B. Kell, *Carteret County During the American Revolution*, 98; Powell, "Tar Heel Good Ship Builders," *News and Observer*, August 23, 1953.

216. According to the authors of *"Fortitude and Forbearance,"* privateers were constructed in Perquimans County. e-mail to author, November 30, 2006.

217. Murfree to Sumner, December 5, 1781, Clark, ed., *State Records of North Carolina*, XIX:886.

218. George W. Troxler, "The Homefront in Revolutionary North Carolina," Ph.D. diss, 78; Dill, "Eighteenth Century New Bern," 74.

219. October 16, 1778, *Virginia Gazette*; Bill of Sale, H.C.A. 32/282, British Records, SANC. Pilot boats were utilized to guide vessels across shoals and channels. In other colonies, or states as the case may be, they were usually small schooners, but we have no statistical information on these four.

220. Troxler, "The Homefront in Revolutionary North Carolina," 78.

221. Various volumes of William Bell Clark et al., eds., *Naval Documents of the American Revolution*, mention vessels out of North Carolina ports that were taken by the British, but there is no mention of where the vessels were built.

222. Williamson to Mease, February 11, 1778, unpublished letter of Hugh Williamson in *Historical Papers of Trinity College Historical Society*, Series XIII:112-113; John L. Humber, "Williamson, Hugh," in Powell, ed., *Dictionary of North Carolina Biography*, VI: 218.

223. Thomas Parramore, *Cradle of the Colony. The History of Chowan County and Edenton, North Carolina*, 38; "Memo of sundre goods put in a joint stock fund by subscribers under firm of Collins, Stuart and Muir," October 7, 1782, Josiah Collins Papers, SANC. See also note of payment to Richard Dawson, May 1782, and purchase note, August 1782, SANC; Troxler, "The Homefront in Revolutionary North Carolina," 119. The two brigs were named the *Alliance* and the *Nonsuch*.

224. CO101/8 British Records, SANC.

225. Papers in the British Records, SANC.

Chapter 3

The Federal Period, 1784–1815

The Treaty of Paris gave the American people their independence. The Revolutionary War had seriously disrupted the economy, particularly foreign trade. A great many merchant vessels had been seized or destroyed. The colonies could no longer depend on business interests in Great Britain to provide capital. American merchants had to compete without the benefit of tariff protection. They no longer had the protection of the British navy. American vessels no longer had unrestricted access to traditional markets in the British Isles and the West Indies. As the regulation of trade was left to individual states, the fledgling national government could do little to control the situation. Nonetheless, maritime commerce resumed as soon as peace was declared and many shipowners overcame these limitations by establishing new trade patterns in various parts of the world. Unfortunately, this was not the case in North Carolina. In 1783, the British government issued an Order in Council declaring only British ships were allowed to engage in trade between the United States and the West Indies. This had an especially serious impact on North Carolina as the bulk of its foreign trade was with the West Indies.

The state's agriculture, industries, and trade had deteriorated during the war. Edenton (Port Roanoke), which had been a small but prosperous port, experienced a significant decline in maritime trade. The harbor became cluttered with abandoned vessels: "At the time there were lying in the harbor but three ships . . . but many large and small craft were there which . . . were now half gone to pieces." In 1789, it was noted that the business of the port "is Verry [sic] Inconsiderable."[1] The same was true of the other state ports. North Carolina was in debt, virtually without finances, and had little means of quickly stabilizing its economy. Its limited English markets were lost and the West Indian trade would take years to return to its prewar level. Agricultural products, especially naval stores and lumber, remained the most viable trading commodities but required transportation and markets; and vessels did enter North Carolina ports.

In 1783 alone, sixty-four vessels, mostly British, entered the Cape Fear. Once again, Norfolk became the entrepôt for northeastern North Carolina, as naval stores, tobacco, and other agricultural produce were transported overland or by small coastal vessels and disseminated from that port.[2]

In 1789, the adoption of the Constitution led to the enactment of legislation that substantially improved the nation's maritime trade and industries. At the recommendation of Secretary of the Treasury Alexander Hamilton, Congress passed a tariff on imports and an additional act that discriminated in favor of imports carried by American ships. Although the acts did not exclude foreign vessels from engaging in American trade, duties were so high that few ventured into coastwise commerce. The "Navigation Acts" were designed to stimulate, protect, and regulate shipping, shipbuilding, and manufacturing in the new nation.[3] Concurrently, revolution in France and the consequent collapse of the old order escalated into almost constant international warfare until 1815. These events had an enormous impact on American commerce, shipping, and shipbuilding. The United States became the principal neutral carrier, which precipitated a substantial expansion of American maritime industry despite serious dislocation and losses from belligerent violations of American neutrality, piratical activities, an undeclared "quasi" war with France, and a declared war with Great Britain in 1812.

Commerce in the Federal Period

North Carolina's maritime commerce recovered from the effects of the long conflict with Great Britain. Initially, this trade essentially mirrored that of the late colonial period.[4] However, closure of West Indies ports to American trade and restrictions on trade with the British Isles necessitated significant adjustment. North Carolina vessels did trade in the West Indies but with non-British colonies. In 1788, nearly half of those North Carolina vessels engaged in overseas trade carried cargos to and from Danish, Dutch, and French islands.[5]

With the outbreak of the French revolutionary wars in 1793 and French seizure of Holland, British warships began to interdict American trade with French and Dutch possessions. Jay's Treaty, ratified in 1795, reopened British West Indies ports to American trade, but only to vessels of less than seventy tons. The French felt betrayed by the treaty and began to seize American vessels.[6] North Carolina merchants and ship captains lost a sizeable number of vessels during these years. John Gray Blount, a Washington merchant, lost several, including the brig *Russell*, the *Tuley*, and the *Grampus*. New Bern and Wilmington shipowners also lost vessels. The sloop *Rainbow* based in New Bern had the unwanted distinction of being taken by French privateers and, two days later, being seized from the French by a British warship.[7]

Violations of American neutrality by the French and British persuaded President Thomas Jefferson to employ economic coercion, which he believed had been successful against the British during the crisis leading up to the American Revolution. Through his efforts, which culminated in the embargo of 1807, American ports were closed to foreign trade. This had a dramatic impact on American maritime trade, and when the tactic failed, the President agreed to alternative coercive acts that were not as detrimental to American shipping.[8]

Throughout this period, North Carolina's trade reflected the national trend. It increased significantly until the embargo of 1807.[9] The Embargo Act devastated the state's foreign trade. It recovered in 1809 but was still relatively weak in 1811, with a total of only 29,033 tons. Overall, the embargo spurred growth in coastal trade. From 1787 to 1809, approximately two-fifths of North Carolina's maritime commerce was coastwise trade, primarily with ports outside the state. In addition, considerable overland trade existed with Virginia and South Carolina ports. During the late eighteenth century, as much as a half of the state's exports were sent through neighboring states, and this pattern may have continued throughout the first decade of the nineteenth century.[10]

American trade and shipping suffered severely during the War of 1812. Some 1,407 merchant vessels, a large percentage of them engaged in West Indies trade, were seized by British warships and privateers. North Carolina's maritime trade was adversely affected.

The state's total tonnage dropped more than a third from its prewar average and coastal shipping was significantly restricted. Although the British naval blockade of the American coastline concentrated on northeastern ports, there were several raids along the Outer Banks, and a British naval force under Admiral George Cockburn briefly occupied Ocracoke and seized a number of vessels in 1813. In that same year, the Cape Fear was also blockaded. Nevertheless, in 1814, North Carolina's tonnage was 27,959, of which approximately a third was coastwise trade.[11] Earlier in the Federal period, 1790 to be exact, the Revenue Cutter Service, which later became the U.S. Coast Guard, was founded for the protection of the ever-increasing American commerce. That meant building cutters in North Carolina as well as other useful watercraft for government service.

North Carolina's Relative Location, Natural Attributes, and Improvements

As viable transportation arteries, North Carolina's rivers varied considerably. Most were navigable for many miles inland, some as far as the fall zone (see Figure 1). However, flats and other small craft were needed to traverse the vast swamps, forests, and shallow, narrow, meandering streams, and to carry goods from the state's hinterland to the ports. Indeed, the difficulty and expense of maritime trade persuaded many Piedmont merchants to transport their goods overland. Periodically, private companies and state and local governments attempted to improve navigation, particularly on inland waterways. Although some improvements were made on nearly every major waterway in the state, the Cape Fear and Roanoke Rivers were the major focus of activity. Several canals were planned. Toll companies were authorized by counties to clear obstructions and maintain watercourses. Nevertheless, despite the emphasis placed on internal improvements by governmental officials, very little was accomplished until after the War of 1812.[12]

In 1795, two North Carolina merchants constructed extensive shipping facilities on Shell Island inside Ocracoke Inlet. The complex included wharves, a warehouse, gristmill, windmill, small store, and a fishery. Primarily, it was a lighterage center where cargoes were exchanged between large oceangoing vessels and smaller craft capable of navigating the sounds and rivers aligning Ocracoke with inland areas. The establishment lasted until the War of 1812 when its principal channel began to shoal significantly.[13]

Custom Houses and Ports of Entry in Coastal North Carolina

During the Revolutionary War, the state maintained the same custom districts that had been authorized by the British government in the colonial period: the ports of Brunswick, Beaufort, Bath, Roanoke, and Currituck. Following the war, a number of changes took place.

In 1786, the area incorporating Bogue, Bear, and New River Inlets was separated from Beaufort and organized into a new official port of entry under the name Swansborough.[14] In 1790, Washington, at the head of the Pamlico estuary, replaced Bath as an official port. In the 1770s and 1780s, Washington developed as a trading center where products from the Tar River basin were loaded on oceangoing vessels.[15] Sometime prior to 1800, the number of custom districts, or ports of entry, increased from five to eight. In the Albemarle region, Currituck was replaced by Camden near the mouth of the Pasquotank River. In 1806, a customhouse was established in Plymouth on the Roanoke River, a short distance upstream from the confluence of the Chowan River and the Albemarle Sound. Wilmington replaced Brunswick as the port of entry on the Cape Fear River.

With the establishment of Swansborough as a port of entry and the creation of the Customs Office in New Bern, Beaufort rapidly declined as a port. Between 1804 and 1815, its trade averaged less than twelve hundred tons. By 1810, it was principally a marine village with a few hundred citizens primarily engaged in fishing.[16] Between 1783 and 1815, Wilmington, New Bern, Edenton, and Washington were the most important ports. From 1783 through the early 1790s, Wilmington led all ports, clearing approximately thirty-eight percent of export tonnage.[17] By 1794, Edenton had surpassed Wilmington followed by New Bern, Washington, and Camden. Until the War of 1812, Edenton continued to be the leading port in the state.[18]

Travelers were not impressed by Edenton. J.F.D. Smyth thought the harbor "indifferent," and Johann D. Schoepff, a German physician touring the United States, described it as "ordinary."[19] Nevertheless, the port's maritime traffic was brisk. On September 9, 1788, twenty-five small sloops and schooners cleared Edenton for various ports from Virginia to Philadelphia. Between 1790 and 1800, twenty brigs, primarily used in the West Indies trade, were registered at Edenton.[20] Coastal trade was widespread from Savannah and Charleston in the south to New York, Philadelphia, and Baltimore. Virginia ports, particularly Norfolk, dominated trade with Edenton.[21] By 1793, the port of New Bern on the Neuse River had become the largest community in the state. At the turn of the century, it was second to Edenton in maritime trade.[22] During the first decade of the nineteenth century, New Bern tonnage would average five to six thousand tons per year, the bulk being with the West Indies. On the eve of the War of 1812, New Bern experienced a boom in maritime trade. An average of eight to ten vessels per week entered the port, and the February 29, 1812 issue of the *Carolina Federal Republican* reported eighteen vessels had cleared the port during the previous week.[23]

Although only shallow draft vessels could navigate the Roanoke River, Plymouth was a relatively important small port when it was designated as a port of entry in 1806. In that year, twenty-six vessels, of twenty tons or more, from Plymouth, Williamson, and Windsor, cleared the Roanoke River for various foreign ports, primarily in the West Indies.[24]

Murfreesboro on the Meherrin River engaged in foreign and coastal trade prior to the Revolutionary War. Murfree's Ferry at King's Landing was the site of a moderate amount of shipping before the Revolution. Although this trade continued in the postwar years, the port's West Indian trade was decimated by the European wars. From 1790 to 1791, twenty-one vessels brought cargos from the West Indies. Ten vessels cleared the port for the West Indies in 1792, three in 1793, two in 1794, and, by 1799, there were none at all. The trade would continue to be negligible until 1815.[25]

Other small ports emerged during this period. Fayetteville on the Cape Fear River became an increasingly important transshipping point from the state's interior to Wilmington and the coast. Washington replaced Bath because ocean-going vessels could reach the head of Pamlico Sound, but not ascend the narrow, shoaling, and winding Tar River.[26] Elizabeth City, on the Pasquotank River, replaced Nixonton on Little River as well as the forgotten town of Jonesborough as the most important port. Originally named Redding, it initially emerged as a shipping center because the Pasquotank's depth at the town's site could accommodate relatively large vessels.[27]

Trade during the Federal Period

As in pre-Revolutionary War years, North Carolina's chief commodities were still naval stores, lumber, produce, and tobacco. However, naval stores lost their British market, and their preeminence as an export declined, with 128,000 barrels shipped in 1763 and 95,000 barrels in 1788.[28] Shipping in the Albemarle Sound area briefly surpassed that in the Cape Fear region, but, by 1800, activity had shifted to the middle coastal plain counties and those that surrounded the Roanoke, Tar/Pamlico, and Neuse Rivers became dominant. All North Carolina ports shipped farm produce, especially corn, wheat, flour, rice, peas, and bacon, and lumber was exported on a much larger scale. The most striking change in North Carolina's export trade was in tobacco. The amount jumped from 360,000 pounds in 1768 to 6,000,000 pounds in 1790.[29] Although the West Indies continued to be an export market, particularly in lumber and produce, the northeastern United States became the most important market for naval stores.

From 1783 to 1815, despite fluctuations in maritime trade resulting from economic and political weaknesses and European conflicts, the nation's shipbuilding industry, including that of North Carolina, prospered. This was particularly true after the adoption of the Constitution and various trade regulations in 1789. In that year, shipwrights from Baltimore, Maryland, and Charleston, South Carolina, petitioned Congress for legislation to protect American commerce as well as shipbuilding. These protective measures, combined with the conflicts in Europe which stimulated trade, generated a boom in the nation's shipbuilding industry. In 1795, ninety-two percent of American imports and eighty-six percent of American exports were carried on American-built vessels.[30]

Ports and Shipbuilding in the Federal Period

In 1783, Johann Schoepff observed, "Washington [is] on the Tar river, a new-settled little place of perhaps 30 houses.... The trade of Washington is as yet trifling; the chief occupation is the building of small ships and vessels; which are put together entirely of pine timber quickly, rotting under water, but lasting well above ground."[31] In 1806, William Tatham, member of a commission appointed to survey the North Carolina coast from Cape Hatteras to Cape Fear, reported that "the town of Beaufort is situated at the junction of Bogue and Core sounds.... [T]he inhabitants of this place build many ships of inferior [size]... there being five on the stocks while I was in Beaufort.... Is it not desirable to order a few <u>Core Sound Boats</u>." He also mentioned the town of Swansboro on the White Oak River near Bogue Inlet as being "chiefly employed in shipbuilding for the West India and coasting trade."[32] In 1809, Thomas Henderson was impressed by shipbuilding in Beaufort: "The principal trade carried on here is shipbuilding in which they have acquired a very considerable reputation both on account of the solidity of the materials and the judgment and skill of their workmen as well in modeling as in completing their vessels.... Some of the swiftest sailers and best built vessels in the United States have been launched here, particularly the Ship *Minerva*, a well-known Packet between Charleston and New York. There are at present five vessels on the Stocks two of which are to be launched."[33]

FIGURE 3-1 There were approximately a hundred Federal period shipbuilding sites recorded. There continued to be a concentration of sites in the Albemarle area, particularly in the east near Currituck Sound, which probably is due to the construction of the Dismal Swamp Canal. Also, there was an increase in sites in a southerly direction. It is highly likely that sites where undocumented vessels were built are scattered throughout the coastal area as well. *Source:* Author's database.

During the Federal period, ninety-nine shipbuilding sites were located in eastern North Carolina (Figure 1). The average distance between these sites was approximately thirty miles, compared to an average distance of seventy-five miles during the colonial era. The pattern of shipbuilding site locations reflects the topography of shoreline and river courses. More specifically, the navigability of inlets, sounds, and rivers determined the relative locations where ship repairs, provisioning, and new ship construction took place. If, in addition, ports were adjacent to a productive hinterland, they were successful in every respect. Unfortunately, many ports were poorly capitalized, which may also help to explain the broad dispersal of shipbuilding sites along the more isolated areas of the North Carolina coastline. Many colonial shipbuilding sites remained active throughout the Federal era.

The Albemarle Sound region had nineteen shipbuilding sites including those established in the colonial period, including Camden, Edenton, Elizabeth

City, Nixonton, Plank Bridge, Powells Point, and Plymouth. In the Pamlico Sound area there were seven sites, including the colonial ports of Bath and Washington. The area in and around Beaufort continued to be an active shipbuilding center as well. In addition to established colonial sites such as New Bern, Sneads Ferry, and Swansboro, there was an increase in shipbuilding sites from New River along the coast to the Neuse River estuary. In the Cape Fear area, only Smithville, Elizabethtown, and Wilmington supported shipbuilding. During the late eighteenth and early nineteenth centuries, shipbuilding migrated farther inland, expanding up the major rivers such as the Roanoke, Tar, Neuse, and Cape Fear toward the fall zone.

Customhouse records from 1784 to 1815 document 558 vessels constructed in North Carolina. The number excludes most vessels under twenty tons and most of those engaged in intrastate trade, linking farms, plantations, and small hamlets inland with various ports. Nevertheless, the Federal period is characterized by an average of eighteen ships built per year compared to only 3.8 per year for the colonial era. Perhaps to some extent, improved record keeping provided a reason for such a substantial increase.

Names of builders and owners changed, types of rigging changed, and even the exact location and identity of construction sites are problematic. Records list Bell's Buoy, Tombstone, and Polly's Point as places where vessels were built, but these locations are not found on available maps or in the *North Carolina Gazetteer*.[35] In fact, of all recorded North Carolina-built vessels, 121, or approximately one fifth, are listed without a specific construction site (Appendix A).

In the first few years after the Treaty of Paris, fewer than nine ships were constructed annually in North Carolina. However, sixty-five vessels were built in the state in 1788, a number that would not be surpassed for nearly half a century. Port records from 1787 indicate that nearly seven hundred vessels used Ocracoke Inlet, and an undetermined number entered the Cape Fear River. Although a large percentage of these ships, especially those trading with Brunswick and Wilmington, were constructed out of state, this extraordinary boom in shipbuilding within the state was undoubtedly related to expanding maritime commerce.[36] Of seventy-eight vessels clearing Port Roanoke (Edenton) during the three months ending September 9, 1788, forty-four vessels were built in-state.[37] Twenty-six vessels were launched in 1789, but, for a number of years thereafter, few were constructed as belligerent nations began to prey on American shipping. However, as the United States became the most important neutral trader, with North Carolina's foreign trade concentrated in the West Indies, ship construction gradually increased. In 1800, twenty-nine ships were built. Even the embargo in 1807 stimulated shipbuilding as coastal trade increased dramatically. The number of ships built would continue to fluctuate until the declaration of war in 1812. Nevertheless, there was a shortage of vessels for the coastal trade.[38]

Very little construction for the oceanic trade went on in Wilmington. Only one commercial vessel engaged in foreign trade, the *Chance,* was built there during the Federal period. River craft as well as numerous small boats and flats were built along the Cape Fear. Wilmington's shipbuilding was centered on what was called "Fayetteville boats." These vessels were sized in terms of what could be carried: hogsheads, barrels, and shingles.[39] Only four were built in Brunswick County, three in Smithville, and one at Lockwood's Folly.[40] Three counties led the state in the construction of ocean-going ships: forty-two were built in Currituck, forty-three in Craven County (including New Bern), and fifty in Carteret County (including Beaufort). Others were constructed at more than thirty sites scattered throughout the coastal region and into the Piedmont. Swansboro with seventeen construction sites, Beaufort with sixteen, and Washington with eleven led the ports in the industry (see Appendix A). A 1795 newspaper article reported that "thirty sail of vessels . . . are now building in the district of Edenton," which encompassed a large region, including Murfreesboro and Windsor where a number of vessels were built. In 1798, "ship building was carried on extensively" in New Bern.[41]

As in the colonial period, vessel construction sites could be found along almost any shore or stream bank in coastal North Carolina. In fact, because of the need for timber, builders were pushing farther and farther inland. This movement to the interior was happening all along the Atlantic seaboard.[42] Fayetteville, the head of navigation on the Cape Fear River, and Murfreesboro, on the Meherrin River, became boatbuilding centers. Small vessels were even constructed above Fayetteville.[43]

The drainage basin of the Tar River, including the Pamlico estuary, was also a center for vessel construction. As mentioned by Schoepff, shipbuilding was Washington's major industry, and business interests outside the state often contracted with local shipwrights. John Gray Blount, a prominent Washington businessman, not only owned a fleet of vessels, but acted as an agent for vessels constructed in the region. In 1784, he agreed to sell a vessel still on the stocks at James Maxwell's farm outside Washington. In 1799, a vessel was built under Blount's direction for a ship captain in Edenton. David Adams, a Washington shipwright wrote Blount that he had a "small schooner on the stocks . . . burthen about 41 tones[sic] . . . to send to the West Indies to sell."[44] Shipbuilding was just as prosperous during the first decade of the nineteenth century. In 1810, Thomas Trotter, a jack-of-all-trades and mechanic in Washington, wrote, "I am as the old saying up to my B. sided in business. I cannot have sawing done to go about my house &c. and have engaged to finish the Iron work of a new Ship, and also expects to do the Cabb in work &c., these things are all new to me...it is as the saying is a Cash job. my Blacke men will clear me one dollar pr. Day.... I have cut 3600 lb. Of Nails."[45]

At least three vessels were built in Pitt County on the Tar River. Two were built at Yankee Hall and a third in Greenville. The Greenville vessel was constructed for a New York firm. Two vessels, including a 153-ton brig, were built at Yankee Hall near Pactolus by an Irishman named Samuel Ralston. Ralston operated a large mercantile and shipping business there.[46] Vessels "carrying from 200 to 400 Barrels of a particular construction," were built on the Tar River close to the fall line.[47] Beaufort County deeds suggest that Hyde County builders were just as prolific as those farther up the Tar and Pamlico rivers. The Pungo River, which flowed into the Pamlico River in Hyde County, had long been a center of shipbuilding. Shipwrights, working along its banks, continued to build ocean-going vessels.[48]

Shipwrights and Shipbuilders

There was no shortage of shipwrights and shipbuilders during this period, although the number of master carpenters/foremen was limited.[49] At least 117 men who listed themselves as shipbuilders or ship carpenters lived in the state.[50] Their places of residence or work generally coincided with the areas where vessels were constructed. During the shipbuilding season, generally from the spring through the fall, workers who had some experience in putting up a vessel were also scarce. Trying to complete a vessel in Hyde County, John Gaylord frequently complained of his inability to obtain enough workers. He even traveled all the way to Currituck County searching for "hands."[51]

The largest centers of ship construction during the period were Hyde, Craven, and Currituck Counties. Only four ship carpenters and three apprentices were listed in Wilmington.[52] However, there were some inconsistencies. Currituck County, where forty-two vessels were built, listed only seven ship carpenters and seven apprentices. Smithville, where at least three vessels were built, listed no ship carpenters. The coastal village of Swansboro was home to at least six shipwrights. There is no record of vessels being constructed in Duplin County, but one ship carpenter resided there. Considerable shipbuilding took place in the Albemarle region, but few ship carpenters have been identified as residing in the area. Clearly, shipwrights must have been somewhat itinerant, moving to different localities where work was available.

Some families were heavily involved in the shipbuilding business. This was particularly true in Hyde County. Bounded by the Pamlico Sound, with numerous streams, and endowed with an abundance of shipbuilding timber, Hyde was the scene for construction of an impressive number of vessels. More ship carpenters and apprentices were listed in Hyde and Craven Counties than elsewhere in the state. Thirty-two vessels were built in Hyde County between 1783 and 1815, and twenty-two ship carpenters as well as twenty-nine apprentices listed that county as their place of work. In 1799, the *Pyomingo* (Figure 2) was launched from an unknown shipyard in Hyde County. The vessel, 183 tons with a length of 81 feet, was brig-rigged, and traded in the Mediterranean and the West Indies.

Most of the construction took place along Broad Creek and the Pungo River, although John Gaylord probably did his shipbuilding on Rose Bay. Some building also occurred on Wyesocking Bay. Benjamin Russell had a shipyard on Broad Creek, now known as Scranton Creek. He owned considerable property and was the largest slaveowner in the county.[53] In the latter years of the eighteenth century, Henry Tuley was a successful shipbuilder. The Tulle family, also spelled Tuley or Tooley, first appears in the Hyde County records in 1709, but there is no evidence of any member of the family engaging in shipbuilding until Henry entered the trade, probably sometime before the Revolution. He owned sizeable tracts in Hyde County, much of it along Slade's Creek and the Pungo River.[54] It is possible that Adam Tooley, who built the schooner *Ellinor* in 1777 on Otter Creek in Pitt County, was a member of the family. William Tuley is listed as a shipwright in 1788-89 when he took two apprentices. In 1804-05, William Tuley, or his son, and Zach Fortescue Tuley were apprenticed to John Winfield. Thereafter, the Tuleys disappear from the shipbuilding record. James Leath also built vessels on the Pungo River, or on Pungo Creek, which flows into it.[55]

The Bell family was the most prominent Hyde County shipbuilding family in the nineteenth century. From the end of the Revolutionary War until the outbreak of the War of 1812, there were at least ten Bells involved in shipbuilding. The Bells apparently trained family members without formal indentures of apprenticeship. However, they did apprentice four young boys from the county. The family would continue to be involved in shipbuilding after the War of 1812.[56]

There were fifty documented vessels constructed in Carteret County during the early national period. A number of families on The Straits, a body of water between North River and Core Sound, and along the Newport River dominated the trade. The Stanton/Borden shipbuilding enterprise remained in business until the end of the century.[57]

The Pigot (possibly Pigott) family was the best-known shipbuilding family in Carteret County during the first half of the nineteenth century. In 1808, William Tatham mentioned the family: "several ingenious brothers, excellent ship-wrights."[58] They had at least one shipbuilding site on The Straits. Elijah had a large shipyard at Gloucester, where, in 1790-91, more than twenty hands either worked for him or furnished materials. Micajah worked for Elijah. He also built vessels in Beaufort along

FIGURE 3-2 The brig *Pyomingo* (watercolor by Antoine Roux). The extraordinary ship was built in Hyde County in 1799 but wrecked off a Nassau reef circa 1806. This watercolor is the only known rendering of a North Carolina built vessel during the Federal period. *Source:* Peabody Essex Museum, Salem, Mass.

with his brother Jeconias.[59] Ambrose Jones built vessels on Sleepy Creek between Gloucester and Marshallberg. He was still building vessels in the 1820s.[60] John Fulford also had a shipbuilding works on The Straits. He may not have been a shipwright but owned considerable property and a porpoise fishery; he was sheriff and served in both houses of the state legislature.[61]

New Bern and vicinity emerged as an important shipbuilding center after the Revolution. It was the most populous community in the state and served as state capital from 1746 until 1792. Its maritime trade grew rapidly during this period, and its economic ties encompassed a wide area reaching as far as Raleigh and the Neuse River headwaters. Flats and other small craft plied the Neuse and Trent Rivers, bringing lumber, naval stores, and other products to the port where cargo was loaded on ocean-going vessels, many of which were constructed locally. New Bern succeeded Beaufort as a port of entry and rivaled the Carteret County port in building vessels. At least thirty-six documented vessels were built in New Bern and Craven County. The county listed thirty-three shipbuilders and forty-six apprentices, more than any other county in the state. The shipbuilding trade was strong in New Bern but also along the various waterways in the county.[62] Bay River, now located in Pamlico County, was a location for shipbuilding activities. Henry Tillman was the most prominent builder in that area. An inventory of his personal estate in 1814 included a recently finished vessel, four canoes, and ship carpenter tools.[63]

The Sparrow family of Craven County was equally prominent in shipbuilding in the late eighteenth and early nineteenth centuries. In 1783, Samuel Sparrow was a New Bern ship carpenter. His father, Peter, also a shipwright, owned land in Norfolk County, Virginia.[64] Francis Sparrow, another New Bern shipwright, was involved in shipbuilding during the Revolutionary War. Francis died in 1786, but Samuel, Thomas, Roderick, and William were involved in the shipbuilding business in the latter years of the century. One or more of them learned the shipbuilding business from Francis Sparrow on Smith Creek. Thomas was evidently the most prosperous. A number of apprentices worked under him. In 1810, he built a three-story brick townhouse in the port. In the years leading up to the War of 1812, ten more Sparrows were listed as ship carpenters. They engaged a number of apprentices, including members of their family. Like the Bells in Hyde County, the Sparrows would continue in the shipbuilding business in the decades after the War of 1812.[65]

The Albemarle Sound region in the northeastern section of coastal North Carolina also continued to be a center of ship and boat building. Construction sites were scattered throughout the region. The names of less than a dozen shipwrights are recorded but there were certainly others. A Hyde County builder hired a number of ship carpenters from Currituck to work on a vessel. Thomas B. Tillett at Nags Head "built ships" but was probably a businessman rather than a shipwright. Thomas Jarvis called himself a blacksmith and a ship carpenter. Joseph Farrow, who may have learned the trade from his father, Hezekiah, moved to Hyde County.[66] Lemuel Gregory, Jonathan Downes, and Charles Grice were the only shipbuilders/shipwrights listed in Camden County deeds. Downes had a shipyard on "shipyard road," also called Shipyard Ferry Road, which ended on the Pasquotank River. Grice may have had a yard there, or he may have purchased the property at an auction when Downes got in financial trouble and the property was seized by the sheriff in 1811.[67]

Charles Grice owned extensive property in Pasquotank County. He was one of the founders of Elizabeth City and was in the real estate business, owning and renting a number of houses in the town.[68] Apparently, he was not as successful in his shipbuilding endeavors.

He owned two yards, one on the Camden County side of the river at Shipyard Ferry Road and the other in Elizabeth City. Grice's son, James, was in charge of the Camden facility. His Uncle Francis, a ship constructor at the Gosport Navy Yard in Norfolk for much of his career, may have had some involvement with these enterprises, possibly as a silent partner.[69]

Although eleven documented vessels were built in Pasquotank County, only three shipwrights, in addition to Grice, are recorded there. At least sixteen vessels were constructed in Edenton, but the name of only one probable shipwright is recorded and it is illegible.[70] William Rombough was a carpenter in Edenton. He also did cabin work, manufactured blocks and tackle, and did vessel repairs.[71] Ships and boats were built in Bertie County, but the names of only two ship carpenters have been discovered.[72] Customhouse records indicate vessels were built in Perquimans, Washington, Tyrrell, Hertford, Martin, and Northampton Counties, but the names of shipwrights, except one for Tyrrell, are unknown.

An undetermined number of Blacks, free and slave, were involved in shipbuilding. A large number of slaves, skilled and unskilled, labored in the shipbuilding industry during the Federal period. Shipbuilding and related occupations were trades in which Blacks were allowed to excel. Later in the nineteenth century, plantation owners employed their slaves in a variety of tasks, including building flats and other vessels.

An Edenton shipbuilder paid off a debt with four slaves, one of them a ship carpenter.

Henry Tuley, who built vessels on the Pungo River, had at least one slave, a blacksmith, involved in his shipbuilding activities. In Hyde County, Tillman Farrow's heirs sold slaves to two local shipbuilders. Hyde County records identify nine free blacks apprenticed to learn the shipbuilding trade. Records for other counties are not as complete, but they do indicate free blacks were apprenticed to shipbuilders. Wilmington shipbuilder John Telfair employed at least three slaves working in his Cape Fear yard; two of them were caulkers and the third was listed as a laborer. A Wilmington newspaper advertisement refers to an escaped slave who was a ship carpenter. The *Norfolk Herald* carried notice of an escaped slave who was a shipwright. Virginia newspapers also noted two slaves, shipbuilders, and caulkers, who ran away from John Drew, a Bertie County businessman. William Bell, a Hyde County shipbuilder, employed several of his father-in-law's slaves to help complete the ship *St. Thomas*. Elijah Pigot's account of expenses in building a schooner listed "Blacks" working on the vessel, but the document does not state whether they were enslaved or free. Blacks, free and enslaved, probably dominated the caulking trade.[73]

Shipbuilding was a popular and prosperous profession during the Federal period.

General Benjamin Smith, in his efforts to hire shipwrights, wrote, "Ship Carpenters of all other People got (for their rank) rich fastest. . . ."[74] At this time, the industry was essentially a handicraft, easily entered by capable and enterprising individuals. Shipbuilding professions included caulkers, joiners, sparmakers, sailmakers, riggers, blockmakers, ropemakers, gravers, blacksmiths, as well as shipwrights. In North Carolina, these professions were often combined and/or practiced by non-professionals under the supervision of a master carpenter or foreman.

As in other rural states, labor, although less skilled, was cheaper and ship/boat building was an occupation of farmers and fishermen in the off season. Until the Revolutionary War, there was a steady stream of English-trained shipwrights into the American colonies, but after independence, this migration sharply declined. As in the past, shipbuilders occasionally moved to the state. Ebenezer Paine left Massachusetts for opportunities in Edenton. The number of individuals who entered the shipbuilding trade from other occupations is unknown. In 1810, Thomas Trotter of Beaufort County entered the shipbuilding business: "I . . . have engaged to finish the Iron Work of a new ship, and also expect to do the Cabbin work, etc . . . . these things are all new to me, but

I must be doing something, it is as the saying is a Cash job.... I have more business than I can do."⁷⁵ Nevertheless, not all prospered in the shipbuilding business or were even successful.

Ship Craftsmen

Often, shipbuilders hired various craftsmen for piece work on a particular vessel.

Elijah Pigot's account of expenses for building a schooner mentions more than twenty different individuals employed for specific tasks.⁷⁶ Blacksmiths were frequently involved and not just for shipbuilding. Martin Ettinger of Wilmington was a blacksmith, but he was also a gunsmith and a "Nail manufacturer."⁷⁷ Blacksmiths are listed in wills, estate records, and land deeds, but this is rarely true of other shipbuilding trades such as blockmakers, riggers, sailmakers, and caulkers. However, these trades are often listed in apprentice records.⁷⁸ William Rombough, a blockmaker in Edenton, kept detailed account books which attest that he, like many other craftsmen in the eighteenth and early nineteenth century, performed a variety of tasks from making or repairing blocks and other shipboard items to manufacturing household furniture.⁷⁹

North Carolina gained most of its skilled shipwrights through the apprenticeship system. Between 1783 and 1815, a total of 124 boys, from age three to twenty-one, were bound to shipwrights to be trained as ship carpenters. In Craven County alone, from 1787 to 1789, apprenticeship indentures indicate that no fewer than seventeen boys were bound to twelve different masters to learn the art of a "ship carpenter or sail maker."⁸⁰ Although a number of ship carpenters accepted one or two apprentices, none matched Hyde County shipbuilder John Winfield, who agreed to take six between 1797 and 1805.

The Shipbuilding Business

As in the colonial period, businessmen and planters were rarely directly involved in shipbuilding. They engaged in the industry as an economic enterprise, built vessels for their own use, or both. They preferred local builders and employed a master ship carpenter to supervise the work. However, there were exceptions. Willis H. Gallop was a wealthy Currituck businessman and landowner, Maurice Moore of Martin County was a judge, and Andrew Wilson owned a plantation on the White Oak River. All engaged in shipbuilding among their many activities.

On the New River, the Dudley family owned and operated a shipyard. Christopher Dudley, merchant and planter, owned more than ten thousand acres in 1827. Edward Bishop Dudley inherited his father's business interest, and he eventually became governor as well as congressman. Whether or not Edward Dudley took an active interest in the shipbuilding facility is not known. In 1815, a 600-ton vessel built at their yard was advertised for sale. More than likely it was built for privateering, but the War of 1812 ended before it was launched. John Drew evidently engaged in boat and ship building, as he advertised for two runaway slaves who were ship carpenters and caulkers. He was a prosperous merchant with vessels and mercantile establishments in Halifax, Scotland Neck, and Louisburg. Drew was widely known for his thoroughbred racehorses. He lived on Salmon Creek in Bertie County, but the site of shipbuilding activities is unknown.⁸¹

In 1792, William Guy and his brother Henry moved from Martin County to Johnston County and leased and purchased land just above Smithfield on the Neuse River. As suitable timber was available locally, he entered the shipbuilding business. In 1798, Guy hired shipwrights to construct a ninety-five-ton vessel on his property. On April 6, 1799, the *Norfolk Herald* noted, "This was the first vessel ever built so high up [on the] Neuse, being one hundred miles by land from Newburn (sic) It will be a spectacle as interesting as it will be novel, to see a vessel of such magnitude. Floating ... on waters which have heretofore been navigated only by small Boats and canoes." The vessel was never completed but was burned by some "villain."⁸²

Guy wasted no time in laying the keel of a second vessel. In January 1801, the *Raleigh Minerva* announced the launch of a 120-ton vessel at Guy's shipyard. The vessel was towed to New Bern to be fitted out. "We are happy to find this persevering industry ... as it promises from the peculiar circumstances of the situation in which the vessels were built; very far in the interior of the country ... [that] it will encourage others to undertake ship building in a part of the country where the best of materials can be easily had, and where all the incidental expenses must be much less than in places where this business is usually carried on." Guy Williams died in Johnston County in 1815 leaving his property to his son. There is no evidence that he built additional vessels after the first two. Nothing has been found to indicate the name of the vessel completed or what happened to it.⁸³

In 1802, General Benjamin Smith, the influential and irascible politician, planter, and businessman, decided to establish a shipbuilding enterprise. He wrote to John Gray Blount requesting advice on establishing a shipyard in Smithville (Southport), hiring workers, their pay, etc.:

> God knows I have enough Irons in the fire & Ship Building is a new business altogether to me but I think by engaging in it I may assist others, benefit our little town at the mouth of the [Cape Fear] River & employ my Resources of timber plank Jobbing carpenters & Blacksmiths to advantage. I have the offer of a Man from the Kings yard at Sheerness who writes to me he can bring out as many others as I want... [but] I prefer an American to head the business believing one from your part of the country will probably possess more

ingenuity in drafting or moulding—Capt. Eastwood says the vessel He proposes to build viz a Ship or Brig of 100 Tons may be done in 4 months by two White workmen capable of carrying up the side of a vessel who must be procured for One hundred Dollars pr Month.

He also listed the need for two "Black hands ... [and] 4 handyfellows." In a "PS" he added, "What do you think ... I may fairly expect will be the cost of Timber Plank Iron work & Nails ... & then what would the Vessel *easily* sell for in *Cash*? Do not you think from Peace being made Vessels will probably fall in Price? And that Carpenters Wages should will fall? Will it not be best to begin on a small scale first?"[84]

At Blount's recommendation, Benjamin Smith considered hiring James Smith and the Tuleys, probably Hyde County shipbuilders Henry Tuley and son. James Smith would provide an Black ship carpenter. According to Benjamin Smith, he and Eastwood were to be joint owners. Smith would finance building the hull and the captain would superintend fitting the vessel out: "Riggins, Ironwork, Sails rigging, anchors & Cables suitable." In September 1802, Blount learned Smith had apparently decided against the enterprise; Eastwood was unavailable or unwilling to go personally and search for a replacement, and the proposed ship or brig would not be built. However, Smith was still interested in building one or two small schooners and had sent an inquiry to Philadelphia in hopes of obtaining a qualified builder. This, too, was unsuccessful. His next effort, as recorded in the Blount papers, was somewhat bizarre. He wrote Blount in November that he had received a letter from a man in England who claimed to be a brother. Smith explained he had had only one brother and neither he nor his brother had ever left America. What attracted the General's attention was that his supposed brother described himself as an experienced shipwright, "but cannot draft," who could bring with him all the workmen needed to establish a shipyard and build ships. General Smith wrote his "Brother that *will* be" to come on and bring with him several skilled ship carpenters. He (Smith) would hire six or eight Blacks as laborers. Smith even advanced money to enable the supposed brother's family to travel to Wilmington. Although a schooner was built in Smithville in 1807 and a brig in 1810, there is no evidence that they were built or financed by the General. In fact, there is no record that the General pursued shipbuilding as one of his many enterprises after 1802. The General died in poverty in 1826.[85]

Benjamin Smith was not the only North Carolina businessman to approach John Gray Blount for help in building a ship. In 1803, Blount received a letter from David Clark, a Plymouth merchant, stating that "General William of Martin [County] and myself are about building a vessel of 70 to 80 tons. We are in want of a master carpenter. I am told there are some about Washington and Pungo. Please let me know whether we can get one from either of those places and what is the customary wages."[86] Christopher Deshon, an Edenton merchant and ship captain, engaged Blount to outfit a vessel:

> I must beg you will go on as fast as possible with the Spars of the Ship: the Riggin of the Ship will be round next week, and hope you have Engaged the rigers (sic)to be ready.... .[I] wish you ... to Imploy as many hands to work on the Ship as can work to advantage in getting the Ship finished. If you can not borrow Iron to keep the Smiths at work I wish you to purchase as much as will keep them at work till I can get some round from Baltimore.[87]

When merchants had vessels built "to order," they understandably preferred construction sites near enough to allow them some degree of personal oversight. In addition, local builders understood the types of vessels needed for their particular geographical area. A few engaged in shipbuilding as an adjunct to their main business. Although farmers and planters occasionally contracted for vessels, most of those who negotiated with shipbuilders were merchants.[88]

In Edenton, the firm of Collins, Stewart and Muir had several ships built for the West Indies trade.[89] In the 1780s, Richard Blackledge, a Washington merchant, was engaged in shipping to the British Isles and the West Indies with two partners in Great Britain. During this period, Blackledge built a number of vessels for the partners. In 1784, a schooner was completed on his order, but, as he admitted, it had too "grate [sic] a draft of water for our use in this country." The following year, he negotiated an agreement with Adam Tuley, a shipbuilder on Pungo Creek, to build a vessel for the firm and in 1786 reported, "I have also in Pungo a fine new Brigg I have just ready to launch," adding "Burden 150 tons." In 1790, Blackledge and his partners purchased an unfinished vessel under construction in Carteret County and had it towed to Washington to be completed.[90] Philip Reilly and Richard Fahey were Washington businessmen who owned a store and other property, including a vessel on the stocks. In 1786, they sold all of their property to a Baltimore merchant and moved out of the county.[91]

John Gray Blount was Blackledge's friend and rival. Blount and his two brothers owned a mercantile firm in Washington, N.C. The Blount firm was probably the most prominent in the eastern part of the state, certainly one of the most important in the years preceding the War of 1812. During nearly twenty years of trading, they owned, or were partners in ownership of, nineteen vessels. An undetermined number of these were built in the state. Blount contracted with a number of local builders for his vessels. John Young built the lighters that were used at Shell Island. He also built the brigantine *Young* for the Blounts. Benjamin Russell constructed the *Russell*, a 173-

ton brig in 1789. Henry Tuley, who built vessels on Slades Creek and the Pungo River, constructed most of their vessels. He launched the brig *Tuley* in 1783 and continued building for the Blounts until 1798.[92]

The Blounts contracted with John Gaylord during the first decade of the nineteenth century. Gaylord, who changed his occupation from a plantation overseer to shipbuilder, built vessels on Broad Creek in Beaufort County. He constructed at least two vessels for the Blounts, who employed John Winfield, a master ship carpenter, to supervise construction of the first. A Mr. Lacy was hired as foreman for the second. Lacy and Gaylord did not get along. Lacy complained to John Gray Blount that Gaylord refused to hire additional workers needed to complete the vessel. When launched, the brig drifted on a mud bank and became hard aground on a falling tide. Before the vessel could be pulled free, it stranded, gradually filling with water "up to the gunnel," causing the vessel to careen over on one side. Pumps were not available locally and had to be ordered. Gaylord tried to use a kedge anchor and even tried to sail her off but without success. Three months after running ground, she broke free. The incident ruffled feelings between Gaylord, John Gray Blount, and Lacy. Blount and Gaylord became involved in a controversy over who would pay for the extra expense. When Blount threatened to abort the contract, Gaylord insisted that he keep the vessel or be compensated as originally agreed with land and ownership of a sawmill. In December 1805, Blount assumed ownership of the vessel, but this was the last vessel that Gaylord built for the Blounts.[93]

Blount's agreement with his builders called for him to provide all the material but the lumber. Periodically, he received requests for nails, spikes, and oakum for caulking. He provided the rigging and sail canvas for Tuley. On several occasions, Blount was urged to send iron and coal for Tuley's blacksmith, a slave, to forge into various parts.[94] For Gaylord's vessels and the one for Christopher Deshon, the rigging was to be done in Washington by workers hired by Blount. He also had to provide blacksmith work for the Gaylord vessels.

John Gray Blount's arrangement with his builders was not unusual. In a proposal to construct an eighty-ton vessel, one builder included clauses requiring the contractor to provide the timber, iron, joiner work, and qualified workers. Also, he was to find "for every carpenter sufficient diet, lodging."[95] In 1794, Jonathan and Daniel G. Marsh contracted with John Winfield to build a 156-ton brig on Pungo Creek in Hyde County. The contract detailed the ship's dimensions as well as the type of wood to be used for planking, upper works, etc. The Marshes were to provide the timber, the iron to be delivered to the blacksmith, the pitch, and oakum for calking. Nothing was said in this contract about workers so, presumably, Winfield was to employ them.[96]

Gideon Willis of Greenville contracted to build a vessel for a New York merchant. Willis agreed to have the work completed with all possible dispatch, "to have her caulked, entirely on the outside, her main and quarter decks laid, her windless compleat; cat head, etc. [finished] but it is understood that her decks are not to be caulked." Willis agreed to these terms and also said he would launch the vessel as soon as the water was high enough. Inexplicably, the contract was not fulfilled. Willis finished the vessel, now named the *Carolina*, and he used her in the coastal trade. Willis was sued and had to pay compensation to the New York merchant.[97] Contractual disputes were not uncommon and usually arose over altering a vessel under construction or adding something not called for in the original contract, thereby increasing costs. A New Bern businessman sued Edward Carraway, a shipwright, for failing to "give the vessel a bottom of Pitch" before launching. The shipwright claimed that he did so, but the merchant wanted additional "pitch" and the foremast moved further aft because of certain changes in the rigging. The judgment was in favor of the shipwright. The brig, named the *Eagle*, was sold to Baltimore interests.[98]

John Gray Blount and many other owners of newly built vessels often preferred to contract for a bare hull and then outfit it themselves. Sails, rigging, blocks, chain, anchors, and other parts were normally obtained from independent contractors. When the planking stage was reached, such vessels were usually advertised for sale in local papers. The *North Carolina Gazette* issue of August 15, 1787 included this ad: "For sale and now ready to be launched, at Bogue, A NEW VESSEL, built of live oak and cedar. . . . She will be sold CHEAP, for cash, and the remainder in goods." The April 14, 1796 edition of the *Wilmington Chronicle* advertised the "frame of a Boat about thirty-four feet keel. . . . with timbers . . . sufficient to complete her. . . the greater part of bolts and nails are ready."[99] The *Edenton Gazette* carried an ad on January 12, 1810: "For sale, a vessel now on the stocks, the carpenter work compleat and can be launched at any time within 2 or 3 days, her masts and spars ready to go up." An ad in the *North Carolina Gazette* of New Bern of May 21, 1796 mentioned a vessel of 163 tons for sale, intended for a brig, with all joiners work completed. In 1803, the brig *Nancy Bell* was sold in New Bern at sixteen dollars per ton, one-half in cash and the balance in six months. The ad mentions that she was double-decked.[100]

Maurice Moore, who had a shipyard on Gardners Creek in Martin County, advertised a vessel of "400 barrels burthen—with masts, main boom and bow." Wilmington papers often included advertisements for vessels, usually flats and vessels engaged in the Fayetteville trade.[101] One ad listed four "Petty-Augors," with sails, tackle, and rigging for sail.[102] The hull of a new vessel, 253 "custom house measure," was advertised for sale in a New Bern newspaper: "The frame is of picked white oak of the best quality; plan of best pitch pine, the butts of every plank on the bottom, ringed and keyed; she has double biding, is abundantly ironed throughout, decks of best quartered pitch pine plank."[103]

Advertisements were also carried in Norfolk papers.[104] The ads occasionally mentioned the type and amount of cargo that could be carried. Vessels were sold at auctions and as a result of wills.[105] Because of the various problems generated by the Napoleonic Wars, some vessels remained unsold for an extended period. Ambrose Jones of Greenville ran an ad for over a year and a half, 1810-1811, before his ship was finally sold.[106]

The lucrative British market for vessels was lost with independence, but occasionally, North Carolina builders sold vessels to other buyers outside the state. Richard Blackledge sold vessels and cargos in New York and the West Indies. David Adams, a Washington shipwright, wrote John Gray Blount that he had "a small schooner on the stocks ... burthen about 41 tons ... to send ... to the West Indies to sell." The brig *Pyomingo*, built in Hyde County in 1799, was sold to a New York firm. It traded extensively throughout the Mediterranean for several years. Other vessels were sold to Baltimore merchants. The schooner *Hummingbird*, built in Bertie County in 1811, belonged to a New Bedford, Massachusetts firm.[107]

The payment for work done varied. Blount compensated his builders with land, goods such as rum, corn, and the like, or, as with Gaylord, a sawmill. The Marshes agreed to pay Winfield in goods and money, two-thirds "in time of building," and the remainder when delivered. A builder on Bogue Sound offered a vessel for cash "or part cash and the remainder in goods." "She will be sold cheap," he added in his advertisement.[108] Blackledge and his partners agreed to pay eight pounds per ton or its equivalent in imported goods. Another merchant agreed to sixty-three pounds, ten shillings in sugar for part ownership of a vessel still on stocks.[109] The vessel advertised in the *Edenton Gazette* on January 12, 1810 was for sale at "$22 per ton." The ad also included dimensions and type of wood used in her construction.[110] A New York merchant contracted to pay twenty dollars per ton for a 140-ton vessel to be built in Greenville.[111]

Perhaps the most unusual agreement was in Tyrrell County where the purchaser gave the builder all the property he owned, including slaves, household furniture, books, kitchen utensils, animals, and the like for building a "small vessel of fifteen tons."[112] Other contracts called for a one-third payment after the keel was laid, a third upon launching, and a third when delivered. Apparently, a merchant believed he was overcharged and sued. A shipwright testifying for the merchant declared that he did not believe "that a frame for a vessel of one hundred thirty tons ... would cost from twenty or thirty pounds."[113] Hard currency was always scarce and negotiations usually included compensation in kind.

Building a vessel of any size was expensive. If a business firm were not the contractor, costs were often shared by several individuals. Ownership of vessels was frequently divided into halves, thirds, fourths, fifths, sixths, or eighths, and these shares were usually sold. Ownership of the schooner *Hazard* was divided into thirds. A schooner, the *Elizabeth*, built on Roanoke Island in 1795, was owned by the builder and one other.[114] Owners often willed their shares to other members of their family or to relatives.[115] Occasionally, shared ownerships were contested. The schooner *Panther* was involved in a rather bizarre affair. At a meeting of the owners to "settle the building of the said schooner," the Perquimans sheriff served a writ on one of them who, in turn, threatened him and the others present with a pistol. Subsequently, he commandeered the unfinished vessel, even though, according to the deposition of co-owner Andrew Donaldson, it had not been caulked, and took her to the West Indies. What happened after that is not stated in the records.[116]

The Materials for Shipbuilding

In 1808, a naval officer wrote the Secretary of the Navy that southeastern North Carolina "abounds with live oak of the best quality and well afforded which renders this a very convenient place for building vessels of any description under frigate."[117] Although he was probably not aware of it, his observation applied to the entire coastal region. Pine was particularly abundant and periodically was offered to the Department. In 1813, John Gray Blount had twenty-five to thirty hands cutting timber, "pitch and yellow pine for planking ... and rails" for the Navy.[118] Large quantities of white cedar, or juniper, were still available in the northeastern coastal area, particularly around the Albemarle Sound and Dismal Swamp. However, by 1810, supplies of juniper and live oak were declining in Carteret County and in the low areas of the middle coastal counties.[119] Pine, live oak, and white cedar continued to be the most popular shipbuilding timber used by North Carolina builders. Frequently, for certain pieces such as the stem and sternpost, white oak was used and, occasionally, ash and mulberry. Yellow or longleaf pine, also called "pitch pine," remained the timber most used for planking, ceiling, keelsons, rails, and, occasionally, for decking and spars. It was available in abundance throughout eastern North Carolina. Shipbuilding timber was so valuable that, at times, land transactions separated the timber from the land itself.[120]

Until the American Revolution, cordage for hawsers, cables, and other rope used for rigging had to be imported from New England or the British Isles. In 1783, Josiah Collins Sr. and Samuel Johnston, a silent partner and one-third owner, established a rope walk in Edenton.

The site would eventually include the walk, probably six hundred or more feet in length, situated under an open shed, along with yarn houses, a warehouse, and a wheel house. It did a very good business. In 1795, Collins wrote John Gray Blount that he was unable to immediately send the required cordage: "Such has been the demand for Cordage at this place for a month or two past that I have not been able to keep even a coil of Rope on hand." The ropewalk and other Collins property were sold at public auction in 1806.[121]

Francois X. Martin operated a ropeyard in New Bern. He is listed as taking an apprentice in 1806.[122] Nonetheless, the state's shipbuilders and merchants continued to obtain cordage as well as other materials from outside the state.[123] Although some shipbuilders and merchants employed blacksmiths to forge fastenings, chain, anchors, and other iron parts were often imported.[124] Iron was used in countless places, in the fastenings of the frames and other pieces, as well as the rigging. Each vessel usually carried two or more anchors. Large iron objects such as anchors were imported, but nails and small iron objects were frequently manufactured by local blacksmiths. Wrought iron bars were imported from outside the state.[125] Copper was expensive and there is no evidence the hulls of commercial vessels built in North Carolina were sheathed. Canvas for sails was also imported. Flax was universally used for sails prior to the nineteenth century, but cotton sails were beginning to appear before the War of 1812.[126] In all probability, some of the North Carolina-built vessels carried cotton sails.

The technical methods employed by most North Carolina shipbuilders were unscientific and generally the product of trial and error. With only two exceptions, no evidence has been found that builders used models, half-models, or drawings in their work. Ebenezer Bell, a Hyde county shipbuilder, was able to draft vessels and create moulds.[127] Elijah Pigot of Carteret County listed the preparation of a draft of the schooner in his account of expenses for building the vessel.[128] In general, the majority of North Carolina builders used the "eye" method of construction. More than likely, many of the vessels were poorly designed as a result. In 1794, one of John Gray Blount's ship captains wrote, "Damn Carolina for Ship Building, for the *Tuley* kept us well Employ'd at the pumps & Tar. The *Russell* Tom says Behaved worse than Ever."[129]

Spending some time in New Bern, Charles Biddle of Philadelphia observed, "Many of the vessels that were sent to sea were not sufficiently secured to sail with safety in a River."[130] John Gaylord's inadequate caulking of Blount's brig and another vessel, locally constructed for Blount, the stern of which "was not well secured," attest to poor workmanship.[131] In later years, American Lloyd usually gave North Carolina-built vessels a low insurance rating, occasionally because of workmanship but primarily because of the pine used in construction.

Shipyards

As in the colonial period, shipyards in the Federal era are difficult to identify. North Carolina shipbuilders rarely mention shipyards in correspondence or other documents. The yards were not elaborate facilities. Often, they were located in a field adjacent to a shore or riverbank or on a vacant lot next to a dock in an established port. The shipyard frequently consisted of no more than a graded launching site and a set of bed logs and ways. There was space to work and store timber and other shipbuilding materials. Occasionally, there was a saw pit and blacksmith shop. A characterization of a shipyard at the beginning of the nineteenth century can best be described as simple and mobile. Usually, there was a small pier where launched vessels could be fitted out. The small rural yards were easily dismantled. In North Carolina, builders often moved their ship construction sites to a timber resource. At times, they purchased or leased the land.[132] Usually, they depended upon sawmill owners to provide the timber they required.

Intermittently, shipyards are recorded in deed books, petitions, and on maps. Jonathan Jasper's shipyard is mentioned in a 1787 land entry for Hyde County.[133] There was a shipyard owned by Maurice Moore on Gardner's Creek in Martin County. Others may have been located on the Roanoke River in Williamston, Jamesville, and Hamilton.[134] Shipyards were also across the Roanoke in Bertie County. A shipyard belonging to John Drew in 1804 was located on Salmon Creek. Two were located where the Cashie Farm is located today. George Lockhart, a planter, had a shipbuilding facility on his plantation.[135]

Although shipbuilding was an important industry in Edenton, the only mention of a shipyard is in a note from Thomas Benbury to Richard Mitchell: "I was yesterday at the shipyard." He mentions an appointment to go into the woods to select timber for spars and masts.[136] Further south, in 1810, Thomas DeVane, a plantation owner on the Black River, deeded tracts of 520 acres to each of his two daughters, and each of the two deeds mentions that the land was "close by the Ship Yard on Cogdell's Landing." A New Hanover County deed book records a tract of land on the Cape Fear River between New Topsail and Stumpy Inlets that included a landing called "the Ship Yard."[137] In 1788, William Gray operated a shipyard at Windsor in Bertie County. Christopher Dudley owned a shipbuilding facility on New River near Jacksonville. Howard's Shipyard was also on New River.[138]

The Potter map records a shipyard, possibly one associated with Benjamin Smith, on the Cape Creek near Smithville (Figure 3).[139] Under Benjamin Stanton, the

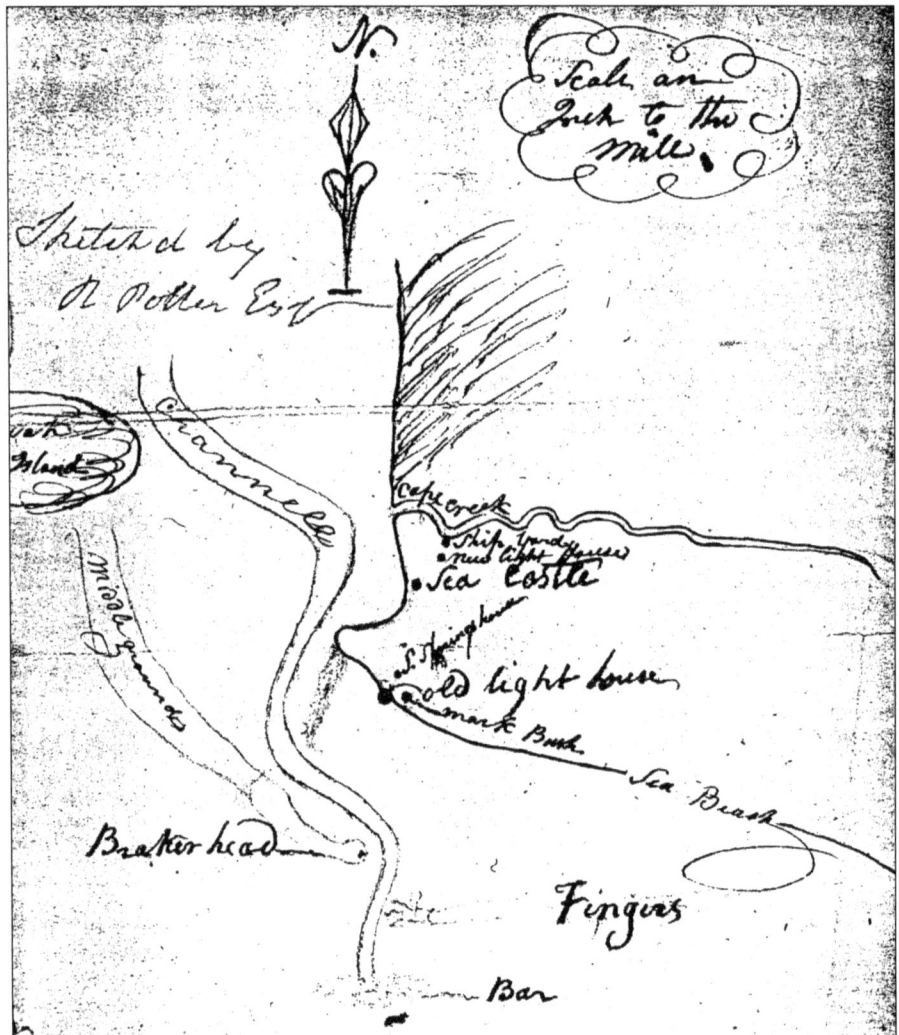

FIGURE 3-3 Map sketched by Potter circa 1814. The map records the sites of the old and new lighthouses as well as that of the Potter shipyard on Smith Island. The shipyard was on Cape Creek which flows into the Cape Fear River. Southern Historical Collection, UNC-CH.

colonial Stanton/Borden shipyard was still in business on the Newport River.[140] Local lore and place names provide clues identifying sites of shipyards such as "The Old Shipyard Field" near Princeton on the Meherrin River in Hertford County. Nathaniel Downes owned a small yard north of Camden. Charles Grice owned two shipyards, one in Camden County and the other in Elizabeth City. According to a land warrant, Nixonton in Perquimans County was the site of a shipyard. A Perquimans County deed book records the "Newby shipyard," thirty acres in size, as located at Belvidere about six miles above Hertford.[141] It is often difficult to determine how long a particular yard or site continued to function. The operational life of some yards or sites, particularly those located in ports, spanned various periods.

While minor repairs were usually done by the crew or by the owner's employees, major repair was usually turned over to shipwrights. The latter was a fairly prosperous business. In fact, far more repair work was carried out than new construction. However, records of such work, are quite scarce. The account book of William Luten, an Edenton ship carpenter, includes details of his work on repairing vessels. In addition, court papers often included lawsuits concerning repairs.[142]

Ship Types

In contrast to the colonial era, there is considerably less information on Federal era small craft. Canoes, periaugers, and flats continued to be the most popular vessel types. Commissioner William Tatham mentioned seven large canoes, possibly periaugers, used for fishing on the Outer Banks. Occasionally, canoes and periaugers were advertised for sale. Newspapers also announced the construction of new ferries. Albemarle fisheries used large flats to carry fishing seines.[143] Designed to draw very little water, flats and scows were found in great numbers on all rivers and streams. These vessels could carry as many as two hundred barrels or hogsheads of tobacco. "Flat-bottomed keel boats" was the description applied to the vessels on the Tar River before flats came into common use.[144] An undetermined number of lighters were built by Blount and Wallace for use on Shell Island. Wallace wrote to Blount about lighters: "two hundred & fifty Barrels are the right size for this navigation. The *Sisters* which Wade owns half of is of that Size & one that Reuben Wallace is gone upon today to Launch which will be down in a few weeks.... I can have as many of them built as will do for this Navigation on good terms."[145] Canoes are frequently mentioned in estate papers and wills. Indentures and deeds, particularly those for New Hanover County, often included negotiations for lighters and flats. These small craft were essential for the river trade.[146] Barges were also found on North Carolina waters. The *New Bern Sentinel* carried an advertisement for a sail-powered flat large enough to carry five hundred bushels of grain and a barge "eight oars calculated to carry 40 men conveniently."[147]

SHIP DIMENSIONS

Merchant vessels generally remained under a hundred feet in length, regardless of type. Despite the state's shallow waters, some large, deep drafted vessels were constructed. In his letterbook, Washington merchant Richard Blackledge recorded building two vessels that were too large for use in his trade. A traveler passing through Washington noted in his journal that "They are now building here a ship of six hundred hogsheads, rather too large, I fancy for the navigation of this river." In 1814, a New Bern newspaper published an advertisement that a "ship now on the stocks [at Swansboro] of about 600 tons, nearly completed ... will be sold."[148]

Full-rigged ships, such as brigantines, schooners, sloops, and a variety of small craft were built. Throughout the eighteenth century, schooners gradually replaced the sloop as the most common vessel in North American maritime trade. During the nineteenth century, the two-masted schooner emerged as the most popular vessel built for coastal and foreign trade. From 1783 to 1815, there were 346 schooners constructed in the state.[149] Between 1801 and 1815, 114 brigantines, the most popular vessel used in the West Indian trade, were built. Thirty-one ships were launched from the state's shipyards. A bark, sailing barge, and a scow were documented in the state's customhouses. Builders and customhouse records often stressed if a particular vessel was "sharp" built or built for speed.[150]

The number and tonnage of ships built indicate significant growth in shipyard activities during the Federal period (Figure 4). Most of the vessels were schooners

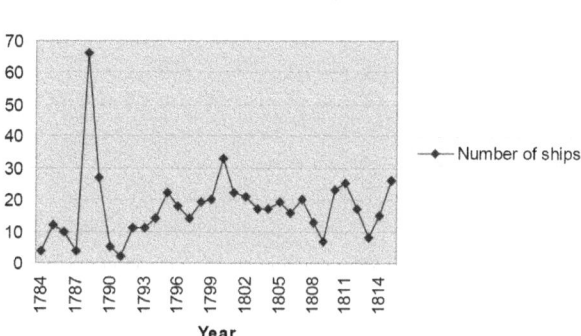

FIGURE 3-4 Number of ships built during the Federal Period shows a freedom newly found with a spike after the adoption of the U.S. Constitution, then a moderately increasing trend in shipbuilding. *Source:* Author's database.

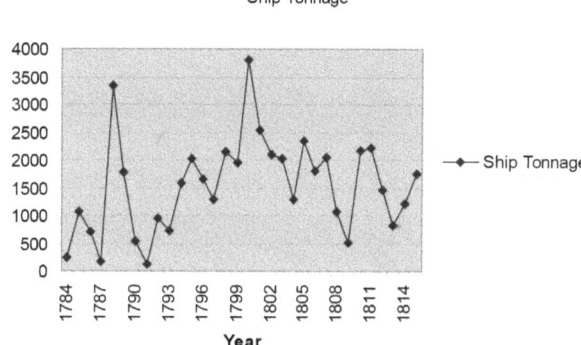

FIGURE 3-5 Amount of ship tonnage during the Federal period shows an increasing trend, with a spike after the adoption of the U.S. Constitution, and then another at the turn of the century. *Source:* Author's database.

and sloops. There are two dramatic increases in tonnage (Figure 5). One increase may be related to the ratification of the U.S. Constitution; the other may be a result of the Quasi-War with France.

Ship dimensions include width, depth, length, width/depth ratio and volume, and certain relationships between these dimensions. Ship width and depth remained relatively constant during the Federal period (Figures 6 and 7). Ship length decreased slightly during the period but stabilized from 1805 to 1814 (Figure 8).

The width/depth ratio is an interesting dimension (Figure 9). It illustrates the relationship between width and depth. A higher ratio or value shows that the vessel has greater width compared to depth. A lower ratio or value indicates the vessel has greater depth compared to width. A vessel with a value near one has a large hull depth; a vessel with a value of five has a small depth. During the Federal period, the width/depth ratio averaged

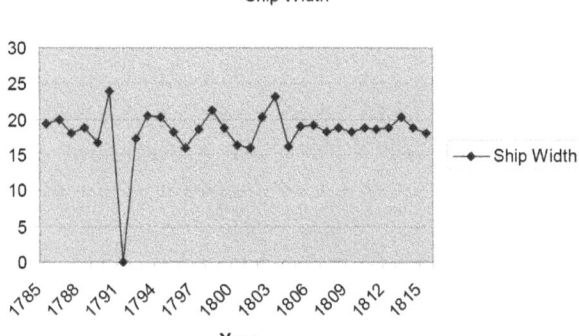

FIGURE 3-6 Ship width during the Federal period is steady; the glitch about 1792 should be disregarded. This steadiness shows that a somewhat normal width had been adopted for the local maritime conditions. *Source:* Author's database.

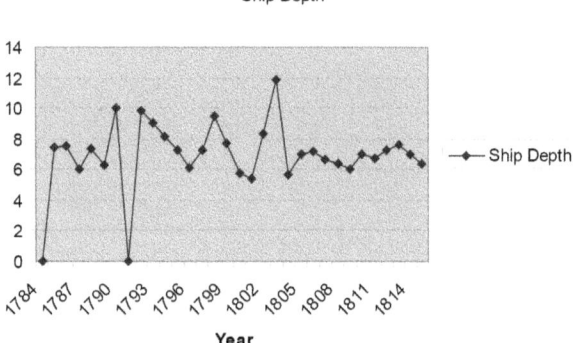

FIGURE 3-7 Ship depth during the Federal period shows some variation early on, but steadies between six and eight feet in the early 1800s. This seems to indicate a shallow depth to conform to the local waters. *Source:* Author's database.

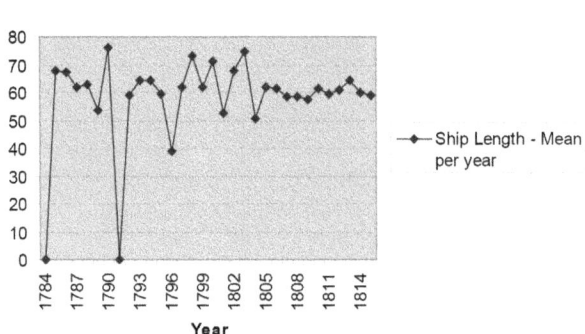

FIGURE 3-8 Ship length during the Federal period is somewhat erratic early on, but settled near sixty feet in the 1800s. The adaptation of building ships to match local water conditions seems clear. *Source:* Author's database.

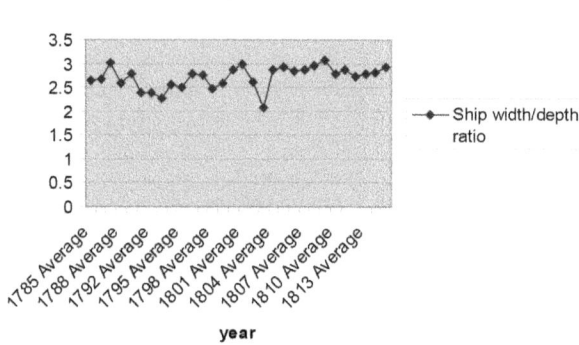

FIGURE 3-9 Ship width/depth ratio during the Federal period appears rather steady. The adaptation of shallow hulled ships for coastal North Carolina waters is evident. *Source:* Author's database.

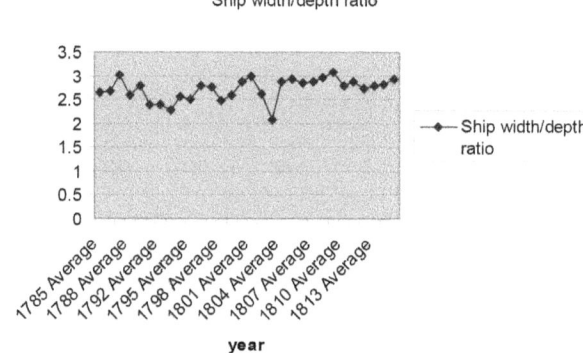

FIGURE 3-10 The scattergram indicates an expected strong relationship between ship tonnage and ship length. *Source:* Author's database.

2.5 to 3, suggesting a shallow depth as compared to width was favored. Generally, this means that a vessel's draft was shallow as compared to its beam.

Vessel volume is the product of the vessel's width times depth times length. The general trend reflects a moderate increase in volume compared to a slight increase in ship tonnage. This may indicate an increase in the number of smaller ships being built. In general, shipbuilding during this period shows considerable volatility; all graphs show considerable variation from year to year. This fluctuation may be the result of either supply and demand or variation in available capital, workforce, and materials, or poor number crunching.

It is interesting to note a positive relationship between ship tonnage and ship length in Figure 10 and ship tonnage and ship width in Figure 11, but a slight

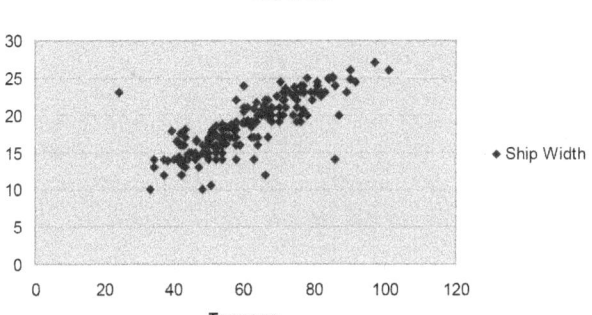
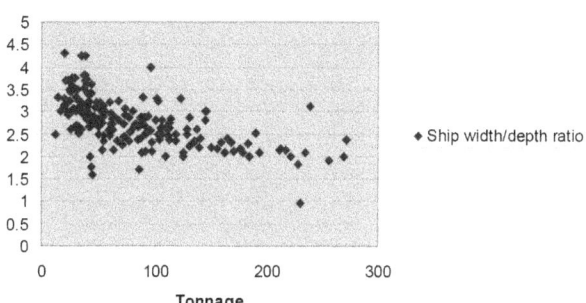

FIGURE 3-11 The scattergram indicates an expected strong relationship between ship tonnage and ship width. *Source:* Author's database.

FIGURE 3-12 The scattergram indicates a fairly strong inverse relationship between tonnage and the width/depth ratio. This means that tonnage decreased as the ship's hull became wider and shallower. *Source:* Author's database.

negative relationship between ship tonnage and the ship width/depth ratio in Figure 12. This may be due to tonnage decreasing with deeper draft vessels. In sounds and inlets, the draft of vessels was limited by the depth of the water, and the width was limited by the need for maneuverability. These positive relationships were expected and support shipbuilding trends.

Vessel types were similar to those of the colonial era. Schooners and sloops were the preferred vessels for plying the waters of North Carolina. Adaptation of vessel types and size to shallow sounds, inlets, and overall coastal environment suggests vessels of a certain type and size were needed for a successful and profitable operation. Moreover, hurricanes in the late summer and fall and nor'easters in the winter had a direct, significant impact on trade and commerce. Clearly, it may be concluded that shipbuilding and all it entails was rather volatile during the Federal period.

Shipbuilding Trends and the Wars

During the intercolonial wars of the seventeenth and eighteenth centuries and into the early decades of the nineteenth century, the British, Spanish, and French governments encouraged the arming of private naval vessels to prey on enemy commerce. Americans followed suit with considerable success. International law required that privateers have a commission or "letter-of-marque" from the government under which they sailed; otherwise, they would be regarded as pirates. American-built privateers were of various types—ships, brigs, and schooners. The large schooner was the most popular type and speed the most important characteristic.[151]

Occasionally, vessels built in North Carolina were outfitted as privateers. There may have been some during the French and Indian War, and there were at least three during the American Revolution.[152] During the period of the Quasi-War with France, 1798-1800, and the War of 1812, a number of vessels built in the state were either built for privateering or converted from merchantmen to privateers.[153] Advertisements appeared in newspapers offering "sharp" (fast) vessels. In 1799, Ralph Pigot, a shipbuilder of Beaufort, wrote a local merchant that he was selling his new schooner *Harmine*, "68 tons built for a privateer. She is very sharp and sails remarkably fast."[154] Records of naval operations during the Quasi-War cite two vessels named *George*. One was a 120-ton schooner built in 1786 with fifteen guns; the other, a 135-ton brig built in 1800 with sixteen guns. They may have been the same vessel; a brig re-rigged as a schooner was a fairly common practice.[155] From 1798 to 1800, American privateers had little success in taking prizes. British warships had swept up much of the French shipping in the West Indies and along the American coast.

American privateers had far more success in the War of 1812. Five hundred privateers were commissioned in the nation and took some thirteen hundred prizes. Four North Carolina-built privateers have been identified, but there were undoubtedly more built for this purpose. In Swansboro, two schooners, the *Paul Jones* and the *Salmagundi*, were built during the war with characteristics that suggest both were privateers. Another unnamed vessel of approximately six hundred tons, much too large for normal coastal or West Indian trade, may have been built as a privateer.[156] Other vessels which were probably constructed as privateers include the *General Jackson*, a nearly two hundred-ton brigantine built on Clubfoot Creek; the ship *Industry* built in Washington; the *Joseph*, a hermaphrodite brig and the brig *Perseverance* at 212 tons, both built at Smith's Creek; and the *Gleaner*, a nineteen hundred-ton "sharp" schooner built on Adams Creek. Evidence suggests a number of privateers were laid down in Washington. In October 1812, the naval secretary was notified by a North Carolina congressman that Lewis

Leroy, a Washington merchant, "was the only person I know of in this part of the country who has had the spirit . . . to engage in fitting out a privateer. . . . He has now a very fine vessel built for this purpose of 240 tons ready for sea." However, he needed cannon, and whether or not they were provided is not known. The privateer *Hawk* out of Washington sortied against British shipping but with little success.[157] At least two privateers were fitted out in New Bern and one in Wilmington. The *Lovely Lass* of Wilmington captured only one prize before being taken by a British naval vessel.[158] The *Snap Dragon* was by far the most successful privateer sailing out of North Carolina. Under the command of Otway Burns, she hunted British merchant ships from Newfoundland to South American, capturing an impressive number of merchant vessels.[159]

North Carolina shipbuilders also constructed vessels for the Navy and the Treasury Department. Alexander Hamilton, first Secretary of the Treasury, created the Revenue Cutter Service to enforce revenue laws. The Service was to make sure custom duties were collected and smuggling eliminated. In 1790, Hamilton proposed that ten cutters from forty to fifty feet "keel" be built. "To avoid dissatisfaction it may appear best to build them in different parts of the Union . . . One in North Carolina for the sounds & coasts of that state." For political reasons, he felt it expedient to construct the cutters in the states where they were to be used.[160]

In 1792, the cutter *Diligence* was built in Washington. Nothing is known of the vessel's dimensions other than that she was a forty-ton schooner armed with four swivel guns.[161] Most of the cutters were similar in size, measuring forty to forty-eight feet in length, with a fifteen to seventeen-foot beam.[162] As the other cutters were schooner rigged, it is reasonable to suggest that the *Diligence* was as well. The choice of shipbuilder was left to the local collector of customs. Secretary Hamilton appointed the commanding officers for each of the cutters and assigned them the responsibility of building the vessel. William Cooke was commissioned to build the *Diligence*, but there is some confusion as to the actual builder. The collectors for New Bern and Washington both corresponded with the Treasury Department about the vessel. In May 1791, Nathan Keais, the collector at Washington, informed Hamilton that he was in the process of contracting "with some person of ability" to build the vessel. It is reasonable to surmise that a local shipbuilder constructed the *Diligence*, and Cooke superintended the project as this was a common procedure at the time. There is also some confusion regarding where the cutter was built. The New Bern collector wrote the Secretary that some of the materials needed to complete the cutter could not be obtained locally.[163] In February 1791, the *Diligence* was taken down the Pamlico River, through Pamlico Sound, around to the Neuse River, and up to New Bern.

There, she was fitted out for active service. Later that year, she was reassigned to the customhouse in Wilmington. She remained there until 1798 when she was replaced by *Diligence II*, a much larger vessel.

The initial cutters were considered too small for their intended duties. *Diligence II*, a 175-ton cutter, was built in Wilmington in 1802. A third *Diligence* may well have been built in the state, also in Wilmington and probably by Amos Perry.[164] In 1807, the cutter *Mercury* was constructed at Ocracoke to replace the *Governor Williams*, a galley built in Wilmington in 1799, and transferred to the Revenue Cutter Service the following year. In 1809, *Mercury* was transferred from the Outer Banks to New Bern.[165] In 1800, a second galley, also named for the state's governor, the *Governor Davie*, was transferred to the Revenue Service. The Service chartered other vessels that were probably built in North Carolina. In 1807, the schooner *Vigilant*, constructed in Swansboro, was commissioned as a cutter. She remained in the Service until sold in 1816.[166]

The Quasi-War with France and the possibility of its escalation into a much larger conflict led Congress to authorize funding for coastal defense vessels as early as 1794, but two years later, the money was reallocated to the construction of new frigates. In May 1798, Congress authorized the Navy Department to purchase or construct up to ten small vessels of the galley type to be manned by a local naval militia.[167] Two of these galleys, the *Governor Williams* and the *Governor Davie*, would be built in Wilmington.

The Navy Department appointed Ameziah Jocelin to supervise construction of the North Carolina galleys. Keels were laid down sometime in the late spring or early summer of 1798. The vessels were approximately fifty-two feet long, coppered, and propelled by sails and oars. In September, the naval secretary informed Jocelin that two twenty-four pounders, as well as fifty muskets, powder, and ordnance stores were to be sent for their armament. The galleys were launched in the fall but were still being fitted out in 1799. In January 1799, the muskets and ordnance stores were lost in a fire and had to be replaced.[168] In December of that year, the Navy Secretary named the two galleys, the *Governor Davie* and the *Governor Williams*, after two North Carolina governors. The galleys apparently were placed in ordinary until needed. In 1801, with the end of the crisis, the *Governor Williams* was turned over to the Revenue Cutter Service. She sank with the *Diligence II* in a storm off Portsmouth Island in 1806. The *Governor Davie* was sold in 1802.[169]

During the first decade of the nineteenth century, President Thomas Jefferson recommended the construction of a number of small gunboats for harbor defense. Three were built in North Carolina. The gunboats were deemed an economical means of protecting the nation's vast coastline. They were far less expensive to build than the large frigates and sailing sloops of war, could be easily maintained by placing them in ordinary or hauling them out, and would not require a permanent crew but could be manned by local naval militia.[170] Eventually, 107 of the 188 vessels authorized were built in various parts of the country. Jefferson and his Secretary of the Navy, Robert Smith, wisely decided to distribute contracts to most of the Atlantic seaboard states as well as the Great Lakes. Congress authorized the construction of twenty-five in 1805 and fifty the following year. Jefferson proposed 200 be built and Smith recommended 257, including nine to be stationed in North Carolina waters.[171]

In June 1807, the *Chesapeake* incident, deemed a "recent outrage committed by a British Squadron off Norfolk," led to the decision to construct gunboats in North Carolina. Jefferson recognized the vulnerability of the American coast, and in July, at his recommendation, Congress authorized an additional 188 gunboats. Of these, three gunboats, designated numbers 166, 167, and 168, were to be built in Smithville, North Carolina.[172]

Smithville was selected as the building site due to the influence and contrivance of Benjamin Smith. Smith was a Brunswick County planter, businessman, prominent politician, and a former Revolutionary War officer. Although wealthy by reason of inheritance and marriage, he spent much of his considerable energy promoting various enterprises to increase his fortune. He owned thousands of acres of land along North Carolina's southeastern coast, including what is now Bald Head Island.

In early July 1807, in a public meeting held in Wilmington to consider what should be done, a committee was appointed and a resolution drawn up appealing for defense, both military and naval. Benjamin Smith volunteered to write a letter to the Secretary of the Navy, enclosing a copy of the resolution along with a request that a brig or schooner of sixteen guns and three gunboats be stationed in the Cape Fear.[173] Early in August, the Secretary replied explaining the Navy had no ships to spare and available funds for gunboat construction were already allocated. He went on to say there was a bill before Congress for new gunboat construction, he was confident that it would pass, and the Department would agree to use these funds to build three gunboats in Wilmington. He recommended that Smith, acting as naval agent, solicit contracts "providing that the contractors will be willing to wait for payment until money shall be therefore appropriated" for the materials needed in constructing the gunboats. The Secretary included a general description of the type of vessel to be built. At Smith's suggestion, Thomas N. Gautier was appointed a sailing master to supervise the project.[174] Smith agreed to serve as Naval Agent but questioned the propriety of this since he had suitable timber which he wanted to sell to the Department for the gunboats. "I certainly prefer using live oak and cedar and it will be quite as agreeable to purchase the necessary timber of you as of any other gentleman," the Navy Secretary replied. Informed of the Secretary's decision, the committee began to advertise for contracts in Wilmington newspapers.[175]

In December 1807, Congress overwhelmingly approved the construction of additional gunboats, including the three in North Carolina. This news and the fact the new naval construction bill was for far more than just gunboats persuaded several North Carolina businessmen to seek contracts for the rebuilding and the new construction of ships. In January 1808, a Washington merchant wrote Congressman Thomas Blount that he had a rebuilt eighty-ton schooner that he wanted to sell the navy for stationing at Ocracoke Inlet. Later that month, a New Bern shipbuilder, Magar Jones, informed William Blackledge that he could "carry on the building of at least five [gunboats] at a time." He added, "I have a great quantity of timber of every kind ... and have also workmen at my command, and ship yards."[176] Representative Blount also informed the Secretary that his brother, John Gray Blount, "has on the stocks [at Washington] ... and nearly finished a vessel ... which he supposes would make ... an excellent Gun Boat." Nothing came from these inquiries. Even a resolution from Beaufort citizens appealing for one or more gunboats had no effect.[177] Although the Secretary did order a gunboat stationed at the Washington Navy Yard on the Anacostia River to North Carolina waters, the only new construction approved was for the three gunboats at Smithville. The contract was finally signed in March 1808.

Amos Perry, presumably a local shipbuilder, received the contract. General Smith wrote the Secretary that, although he had inquired in Raleigh while attending a legislative session, no prospective builders had been located. However, Gautier located and hired "a man to build the cutters."[178] Although Perry had some experience in constructing vessels, he evidently had never built a gun boat. Inspecting the completed vessels, including those in Smithville in 1813, Captain Hugh Campbell, observed, "nothing more has been required contracting for them than to agree on the price and have them built, leaving the construction entirely to the fancy of the builder, who perhaps had never in his life seen a gun vessel, without taking into consideration the service required of them, the metal they are to carry, or water in which they are to act."[179]

The Smithville-built boats certainly illustrate Campbell's observation. They were modified a number of times before being commissioned. In fact, at least one of the three Smithville-built boats differed from the other two. The original specifications approved by the Secretary were those drawn up by Captain James Barron. The design called for a boat sixty feet on deck, fifty-six feet on the keel; 16' 6" beam, and 6'6" in the hold. It was to be sloop rigged and carry one bow gun.[180] Amos Perry later modified the vessels to be schooner rigged and carry two guns. Gunboat 167 was later rerigged as a ketch.[181]

In July 1808, Captain Campbell arrived in Smithville and, after inspecting one of the gunboats, found it was almost ready to launch except for being coppered on the bottom. However, he recommended changes for the other two. "The present draft is certainly handsome and form most beautiful vessels, but as the service required of gun boats is so different from that of pilot boats which the present vessel too much resembles, I would recommend following alterations in their frame. The stem should not have more than one foot rake, the stern post perpendicular or nearly so. Two feet more beam which should be carried as far forward and aft as possible." He stated these changes would make the vessels more seaworthy.[182] The Secretary approved the recommended changes, but they were not carried out. In July 1809, a year after Campbell made his recommendation, he informed the Secretary that a second boat was ready to be launched. "She is a fine vessel and more like a Gun Boat than anything I have seen in this country, and would have been more so had the Builder carried into effect my directions in the alteration of the plan from the General Draft."[183] Unfortunately, there are no detailed descriptions of the three Smithville-built gunboats.

The Secretary agreed to the changes, in part, because there was to be no additional cost. However, in the same letter approving these changes, he turned down the request for coppering the bottoms, stating that Congress had not approved funds for this. Nonetheless, at least one of the boats was coppered and the department charged for the expense. In fact, the history of the building of the three gunboats is a litany of financial chicanery and fraud, most of it engineered by General Smith.

The original contract called for the three boats to be built for $4,000 each. According to the Secretary, this was about the same cost as for the ones being constructed in Virginia. The builder was to provide everything but the armament, the boatswain, carpenter, and cooper stores. These would be provided by the Navy and, in fact, were sent from the Washington Navy Yard.[184] In January 1808, General Smith wrote the Secretary that the specified contract price was too low. When the Secretary replied that the quoted price was to be met or the project cancelled, the General evidently persuaded Amos Perry to accept the amount. However, in March, the Secretary learned the department was being billed $700 more per vessel than the contracted price. He wrote General Smith: "I should be disposed to make a reasonable allowance for the superior quality of your timber which you state to be live oak and cedar, but I cannot consistently with my official duty make such an allowance as 700 each hull." Once again, the Secretary threatened to abort the contract. Evidently, General Smith agreed to the builder's price of $4,700 per vessel and was determined to get that amount from the department. In July, he submitted a bill which included copper, nails, etc. The Secretary, concerned over what was going on in Smithville, ordered Captain Campbell to investigate. Campbell found nothing out of order and was impressed with the General and Smithville as a building site. In October, the first boat was ready to be launched and the other two were on the stocks. However, Campbell was not present. After his trip in July, he returned to South Carolina to recuperate from a leg injury.

In January, Campbell received an abrupt order to return to Wilmington as soon as possible. General Smith had written the department that the gunboats could not be finished without $10,000 in additional funds.[185] Campbell returned in February 1809 and was shocked at what he discovered:

> General Smith has not conformed to his contract with the Builder in making the stated payments. . . . In consequence of which the builder withdrew his workmen and left the boats in the unfinished state they are in ... I inquired of General Smith . . . why the boats were kept so long on the stocks. His answer was that from . . . your instructions he thought himself authorized in delaying the business, but the fact is he refused making the first payment previous to my leaving Smithville that induced the builder to stop the work.

When Gautier questioned the General, he reported to Campbell that the General said that "it was none of my business." In March, Gautier wrote the Secretary that "[n]ot a stroke of Work has been put on them for the last Four months." Gautier also complained to the Navy Department that he was unable to get stores and supplies from General Smith, nor could he get the General to pay his bills.[186]

Paul Hamilton, the new Secretary of the Navy, immediately instructed General Smith to "turn the Public moneys" to Gautier, in effect firing him as naval agent.[187] In September, Gautier sought proposals to build gun carriages. He requested that he be provided with the necessary funds as the carpenters would not work if General Smith was in charge of the funding.[188] When General Smith negotiated with the Department for the three gunboats, the Secretary informed him that he could advance the builder a third of the contract price. Apparently, the General did not do this. Even after he became governor, the General continued pressing the Department for funds. In November 1811, he said that from six to seven thousand dollars were needed immediately to complete the boats. "No money has been sent me for years." In December, he insisted that he had handed over to Gautier "every shilling, other than what he was due in reimbursement.[189] Naval officials from the Secretary on down were disillusioned with General Smith. The Secretary no longer corresponded directly with him but through Captain Campbell or Gautier. Campbell wrote to Charles Goldsborough, Chief Clerk in the Navy Department, that Benjamin Smith was "one of the cleverest fellows in North Carolina but a very improper person for a publick agent." He told the Secretary the same thing. Even fellow North Carolinians, especially residents of Wilmington, were unhappy with him. In June 1809, a town meeting was held to discuss the continued absence of adequate port defense. "[We are] aware that large sums of money have from time to time been forwarded here for the public service; we are rather induced to ascribe our present exposed situation to some incapacity neglect, mismanagement ... on the part of the contractors or public agents and superintendents." A navy clerk accused merchants in Wilmington, and presumably Smithville, of making extraordinary profits from the timber sold for boatbuilding.[190]

Gunboat No. 166 was launched on the first day of April 1809; Gunboat No. 167 followed on September 19, 1809; and Gunboat No. 168 was launched in October of that year. Rigging and sails for the three vessels were not provided until the fall of 1811. They were ready when war was declared in 1812. No. 166, renamed the *Alligator*, was transferred to Charleston and sold after the war. No. 168 was transferred to the St. Mary's Station in Maryland. She remained in service until 1823. No. 167 apparently remained in Wilmington during the war.[191]

The War of 1812 engendered limited new naval construction in the state. Thomas Gautier remained in command of the North Carolina station. In May 1812, he reported to the

Department that, in addition to the three gunboats, he needed at least two more gunboats and a heavy brig to defend Wilmington. He did not even mention the other state ports, did not get his requested brig, and lost one of his gunboats. However, Gunboats No. 147 and No. 148 were ordered to Ocracoke. In 1813, these were withdrawn, causing Congressman William Blackledge to write bitterly to the Secretary of the Navy that "[t]he removal of your gunboats from Ocracoke and Beaufort has completely destroyed all hopes of success which a Republican candidate could have had in this district."[192]

Some minor construction took place at the beginning of the war. In June, the Navy Department contracted with William E. Jury of Smithville to construct three guard boats to be used in conjunction with the gunboats. The guard boats were to be thirty-five feet in length, eight feet in beam, and to be both sail and oar propelled. The contract did not mention any armament. They were apparently completed and turned over to the navy by the end of August. In January 1814, Jury received a second contract to build small boats for the navy "for the use of the gunboats on this [Smithville] Station."[193] In 1813, Congress appropriated $250,000 for the construction of fifty-five barges/galleys. Of these, the Secretary authorized five for North Carolina.[194] Secretary Jones did not favor barges or galleys. He gave in to congressional pressure but later rescinded authorization for many of them, including all but one for North Carolina. He informed Gautier that he preferred small sailing vessels to barges for the North Carolina coast.[195] Although Congress specified that they were to be at least forty-five feet in length and large enough to carry heavy guns, there is no information

on the Wilmington barge. The guard boats, gunboats, and the barge all remained on active duty in North Carolina waters until the end of the war when they were sold.

The End of the Federal Period

Shipbuilding in the early Federal period was similar to that during the colonial period. The same types of vessels were built. Shipbuilding facilities were generally small and unpretentious. The yards were distributed in at least sixteen counties in the eastern part of the state, not only in the small ports but far up the rivers, up to and even above the fall line. Adequate lumber continued to be available, but deforestation affected the supply. Although some iron parts and rope could be manufactured in the state, most materials needed to outfit a vessel were imported. The state's shipbuilding community was generally adequate. Despite handicaps imposed by wars and trade restrictions, the industry on the whole thrived. It would continue to thrive throughout most of the nineteenth century.

Notes

1. Johann D. Schoepff, *Travels in the Confederation, 1783-84*, 112; Katherine Goodall, "The Burroughs Wreck: A Key to Eighteenth Century Ship Construction and the Life and Death of the Port of Edenton," (M.A. thesis, East Carolina University, 2003), 22.
2. Thomas J. Wertenbaker, *Norfolk: Historic Southern Port*, 76; Alan Watson, *Wilmington: Port of North Carolina*, 31.
3. John J. B. Hutchins, *The American Maritime Industries and Public Policies, 1789-1914*, 38, 170-171.
4. Charles C. Crittenden, *The Commerce of North Carolina, 1763-1789*, 155.
5. Crittenden, *Commerce of North Carolina*, 158-159. Shipping between North Carolina and British ports did resume on a reduced level but only in British vessels. In 1769, nearly a third of North Carolina vessels engaged in foreign trade went to the British Isles; in 1788, approximately a tenth did so.
6. Hutchins, *American Maritime Industries*, 224-225; Alexander DeConde, *The Quasi-War: The Politics and Diplomacy of the Undeclared War with France, 1797-1801*, 9. In 1795 alone, French privateers and warships captured 316 American ships. From 1796 to 1798, French ships seized and carried into Spanish ports some 136 American vessels.
7. W. Stuart Morgan, "The Commerce of a Southern Port, New Bern North Carolina, 1783-1812" (M.A. thesis, East Carolina University, 1985), 62-68; Ursula Loy and Pauline M. Worthy, *Washington and the Pamlico*, 234. Records of the United States Court of Claims in the National Archives include the records of the French Spoliation Cases. These are claims filed by individuals that arose from the depredations committed by French warships and privateers. Many North Carolina vessels are included in the claims.
8. On the eve of the Embargo Act, registered tonnage in the United States was 840,000 gross tons. It dropped to nothing during the period the Act was in effect, but quickly recovered afterwards. In 1811, registered tonnage engaged in foreign trade was 768,852, and coastal tonnage was 420,678.
9. Total tonnage of vessels clearing the state's ports in 1788

amounted to more than 47,000 tons, an increase of over one hundred percent since 1769. Crittenden, *The Commerce of North Carolina*, 158.

10. Alan Watson, "North Carolina and Internal Improvements, 1783-1861: The Case of Inland Navigation," *NCHR* 84 (January 1987), 37.

11. *American State Papers, Series IV: Commerce and Navigation*, 1:1018-1019; Hutchins, *American Maritime Industries*, 228.

12. As early as 1784, and again in 1801, Governors Alexander Martin and Benjamin Williams made internal improvements a priority in messages to the legislature. The most complete study of internal improvements in the state is Alan D. Watson's *Internal improvements in Antebellum North Carolina* 57, passim. See also: Watson, "North Carolina and Internal Improvements," 45; Watson, *Wilmington: Port of North Carolina*, 35-37. One canal, the "Somerset Canal," linking Lake Phelps with the Scuppernong River was completed and in operation by 1791.

13. Wilson Angley, "A History of Ocracoke Inlet and Adjacent Areas," Research Branch, North Carolina Division of Archives and History, 25-26; see also Phil McGuinn, "Shell Castle, a North Carolina Entrepot: A Historical and Archaeological Investigation," (M.A. thesis, East Carolina University, 2000).

14. William N. Still Jr., "Shipbuilding and Boatbuilders in Swansboro, 1800-1950," *Tributaries*, No. 5 (October 1995), 7. Swansborough would later be shortened to Swansboro.

15. James Cox, "The Pamlico-Tar River and Its Role in the Development of Eastern North Carolina," (M.A. thesis, East Carolina University, 1989), 24.

16. A. R. Newsome, ed., "A Miscellany from the Thomas Henderson Letter Book, 1810-1811," *NCHR*, 398-399; Wilson Angley, "Historical Overview of the Beaufort Inlet," Research Branch, North Carolina Division of Archives and History, 25. Although Beaufort's coastwise trade was negligible, in 1814 Samuel Leffers, writing from Beaufort, noted that "[t]he inland navigation between our Inlet and Virginia has been very profitable to those who own some vessels. [Also] great quantities of goods are brought in here in neutral vessels or transported through the sound to Virginia." Tonnage statistics are taken from *American State Papers, Series IV*, 1:455-456, 625-626, 824-826, 1018-1019. Tonnage figures do not include vessels under twenty tons.

17. Watson, *Wilmington: Port of North Carolina*, 32.

18. Morgan, "Commerce of a Southern Port," 69. In 1794, Edenton was first, with 5,671 tons, followed by Wilmington with 5,407 tons. In 1805, Wilmington led the state in duties collected; however, in 1806, Edenton's total tonnage exceeded 10,000 tons and was more than twice as large as any of the other state ports. Charles William Janson, *The Stranger in America, 1793-1806*, 485.

19. Wilson Barber, "The Ocean Borne Commerce of Port Roanoke, 1771-1776" (M.A. thesis, University of North Carolina, 1931), 8.

20. F. Roy Johnson, *Sail and Steam Navigation of Eastern North Carolina*, 10. Average tonnage per brig was 121 tons. Approximately half of the total tonnage was foreign, nearly all with the West Indies.

21. In general, the trade was balanced, as New England did not dominate the trade with Edenton.

22. *American State Papers, Series IV*, 1, 496. In 1800, 6,729 tons cleared the customhouse. Of this, only 822 tons were engaged in coastal trade.

23. Alan Watson, *A History of New Bern and Craven County*; Morgan, "Commerce of a Southern Port," 33, 41, 43.

24. "Report –The Committee of Commerce and Manufacturing, 1806," copy in the Roanoke River Maritime Museum, Plymouth, N.C.

25. Thomas C. Parramore, *The Ancient Village of Murfreesboro, 1787-1825*, 44; Thomas C. Parramore, *Murfreesboro, North Carolina, and the Great Intracoastal Waterway, 1786-1814*, 24-25; John F. Foote, *Memoirs of The Life of Samuel E. Foote*, 22-23.

26. William N. Still Jr., "The Shipbuilding Industry in Washington, North Carolina," in *Of Tar Heel Towns, Shipbuilders, Reconstructionists and Alliancemen*," Joseph Steelman, ed., 27-28; Bradley A. Rodgers and Nathan Richards, *The Castle Island Ships' Graveyard: The History and Archaeology of Eleven Wrecked and Abandoned Watercraft*, 13-15. For Fayetteville, see Watson, *Wilmington: Port of North Carolina*, 32-33; *Fayetteville and Raleigh Minerva*, January 20, 1801.

27. James Pugh, *Three Hundred Years Along the Pasquotank: A Biographical History of Camden County*, 105; J. H. Stevens, *Albemarle, People and Places*, 355-356.

28. Percival Perry, "The Naval Stores Industry in the Ante-Bellum South, 1789-1861" (Ph.D. diss., University of North Carolina, 1947), 230-231.

29. Crittenden, *Commerce of North Carolina*, 159-161; Watson, *Wilmington: Port of North Carolina*, 32; John Anthony Eisterhold, "Lumber Trade in the Seaboard Cities of the Old South, 1607-1860" (Ph.D. diss., University of Mississippi, 1979), 21-22; Cox, "Pamlico-Tar River and its Role in the Development of Eastern North Carolina," 9.

30. Robert A. Kilmarx, *America's Maritime Legacy: A History of the U.S. Merchant Marine and Shipbuilding Industry Since Colonial Times*, 28.

31. Schoepff, *Travels in the Confederation, 1783-1784*, I:124-125.

32. William Tatham, "The Separate Report of William Tatham, One of the Commissioners Appointed to Survey the Coast of North Carolina from Cape Hatteras to Cape Fear Inclusive" (1806), Records of the Coast and Geodetic Survey, R.G. 23.2: General Records, NARA. This is possibly the first time that boats built along this waterway are distinctly identified. *Beaufort News*, February 14, 1929. For Swansboro, see (New Bern) *Carolina Federal Republican*, October 11, 1813; *Wilmington Gazette*, May 27, 1806, August 31, 1815.

33. Newsome, ed., "Miscellany from the Thomas Henderson Letterbooks," 399.

34. Carraway vs. Brinton in New Bern District Court Records, Civil Action papers 1800-1801, SANC.

35. William S. Powell and Michael Hill, *North Carolina Gazetteer*, 2nd Edition.

36. Crittenden, *The Commerce of North Carolina*, 158.

37. Ibid., 14.

38. As mentioned earlier, an Elizabeth City merchant in 1801 complained that a shortage of small vessels handicapped his trade. Arthur Jones, an Edenton businessman echoed this sentiment. Both letters are in the Clifford Correspondence, Pembroke Papers, Historical Society of Philadelphia. See also Grice to E. Fisher and Co., September 20, 1801 in the same collection. For a similar observation see Leffers to brother, May 15, 1815, in Frank C. Salisbury Collection, ECU.

39. *Wilmington Gazette*, March 30, 1797, August 31, 1797, September 14, 1797, and April 16, 1805. See also New Hanover Deed Book O, 264, and Deed Book P, 85, SANC; Edward Moseley, "Southern Built: Wilmington's Maritime Construction Industry, 1717-1860," unpublished manuscript in authors' possession.

40. *Wilmington Chronicle and North Carolina Weekly Advertiser,* April 14, 1796.
41. (Halifax) *North Carolina Journal,* April 27, 1795; *Edenton Gazette,* January 6, 1810. For other vessels in the Edenton District see the *Norfolk Herald,* June 16, 1801; Parramore, *Murfreesboro, North Carolina, and The Great Intracoastal Waterway,* 19, 55; Charles Francis Hannigan, *An Architectural Monograph: New Bern, "The Athens of North Carolina."*
42. Goldenberg, "Saw, Axe and Auger," 121.
43. *Fayetteville and Raleigh Minerva,* June 10, 1800; (Raleigh) *North Carolina Star,* October 4, 1811. In 1795, a brig and a pilot boat were built at Hill's Ferry on the Roanoke River near Halifax, close to the fall zone and near the end of navigation on the river. (New Bern) *North Carolina Gazette,* May 23, 1795; Parramore, *Murfreesboro, North Carolina and The Great Intracoastal Waterway,* 19, 54.
44. Quoted in Still, "Shipbuilding Industry in Washington, North Carolina," 30; Maxwell to Gladden, June 1786, Beaufort County Deed Real Estate Conveyances, Vol. 6, 3-4, SANC.
45. Quoted in Catherin W. Bishir, et al., *Architects and Builders in North Carolina: A History of the Practice of Building,* 103.
46. Roger Kammerer, "Early Shipbuilding in Pitt County," *Greenville Times,* March 1, 1989.
47. A. R. Newsome, "Twelve North Carolina Counties in 1810-1811," *NCHR* 6 (April 1929), 74.
48. Hyde County Deed Book K, 95-97 (1796), 307-308 (1797), SANC; Beaufort County Real Estate Conveyances, vol. 6, 1784, SANC; Russell to John Gray Blount, Aug 6, 1789, in Alice B. Keith and William H. Masterson, eds., *The John Gray Blount Papers,* I:496.
49. Two Martin County businessmen interested in having a vessel constructed had some difficulty in hiring a master carpenter. Clark to Blount, February 15, March 15, 1803, Box 39, John Gray Blount Papers, SANC.
50. The number is taken primarily from land deeds and apprenticeship indentures, and vessel documents in Records of the Bureau of Marine Inspection and Navigation, NARA. The archival list is undoubtedly incomplete. Craven County marriage bonds identify a number of individuals as ship carpenters who are not found in either the apprenticeship records or land deeds.
51. Yet, his foreman said Gaylord refused to hire additional workers: "I begged him to get [more] hands." Lacy to Blount, May 8, 1805, John Gray Blount Papers, SANC; Gaylord to Blount, February 2, 8, August 15, September 2, 1805, in Keith and Masterson, eds., *John Gray Blount Papers,* IV: 54; Hyde County Deed K, 307-308, 438-439, SANC. Gaylord's will does not mention shipbuilding. His ship construction was probably on Rose Bay.
52. Very few vessels were built in Wilmington and along the Cape Fear River during this period. In 1803, James Mitchell of Fayetteville constructed three vessels for a Wilmington firm. John Hogg Account Books, SHC, UNC-CH.
53. Hyde County Deed Book K, 303-304, and Book L, 478-480, SANC; Russell to Blount, 1787, Hyde County Wills, 3, 492-493, SANC; Russell to Blount, August 8, 1789, Keith and Masterson (eds.), *John Gray Blount Papers,* I:496; *Hyde County Historical and Genealogical Society,* XV (Spring 1994), 11-12. Deed books and other documents suggest that he was a prolific builder. For Wyesocking Bay see Bannister Midyett, *Hyde County History: A Hyde County Bicentennial Project,* 88.

54. Hyde County Deed Book K, 8, 34, 65, SANC; (Belhaven) *Beaufort-Hyde News,* September 11, 1975; Hyde County Will Book 3, 447-448, SANC; Grimes, *Wills and Inventories.*
55. *High Tides,* XI (Fall, 1990), 31.
56. Some were fathers and sons, some cousins, but most resided in Hyde County. However, there were also Bells in Carteret County involved in shipbuilding. One, Eden Bell, listed his residence as Carteret County. Not all the Bells in Hyde County were in shipbuilding, and, like many families, not all members were harmonious. There were suits concerning ownership of vessels, estates, and land ownership among immediate members of the family as well as members by marriage. For documents concerning the Bell family as shipwrights see the Hyde County Estate Records, 1745-1904, SANC; Hyde County Court Minutes, 1798-1804, VI, SANC. An article on the Bells in Fisher, *One Dozen Pre-Revolutionary War Families,* 490-493, does not mention any Bells in shipbuilding. However, a court case in 1790-91 mentioned three Bells involved in building a schooner. Stephen E. Bradley Jr., comp., *New Bern District North Carolina Loose Estate Papers, 1775-1810,* 29.
57. *Beaufort News,* February 29, 1929; Pat Davis et al., eds., *The Heritage of Carteret County North Carolina,* I:188, 429; Carteret County Deed Book N, 107-108, 110-111, 141-142, SANC; Carteret County Deed Book O, 168-169, SANC; Rebecca Willis Sanders, *Carteret County Wills, 1700-1880,* 2-3; Fletcher Pratt, *Stanton: Lincoln's Secretary of War,* 3-4. After Benjamin Stanton died, his widow sold their property and moved to Ohio. William Borden Jr. had inherited his father's share in the yard in 1749, and the partnership was dissolved when she sold the property. Borden was still building vessels at the turn of the century. Edwin Stanton, Lincoln's Secretary of War was the son of David Stanton, one of Benjamin's children who migrated from Carteret County to Ohio.
58. Quoted in David Stick. The Outer Banks of North Carolina, 1584-1958, 83. See also William Tatham."The Separate Report of William, One of the Commissioners appointed to survey the coast of North Carolina from Cape Hatteras to Cape Fear inclusive under the Act of Congress of the 10th of April last." MSS in the library of the U.S. Coast and Geodetic Survey, United States Department of Commerce, Washington, D.C.
59. The Pigots include Ralph, Jechonias, Micajah, Jick, Culpepper, and Elijah. See the New Bern District Court Records, SANC; Mrs. Fred Hill, ed., HISTORIC CARTERET COUNTY, NORTH CAROLINA, 1663-1975, 133; Giles W. Willis, Jr. HISTORY OF LANDS AT GLOUCESTER; THE FIRST 150 YEARS, 43; Stephen E. Bradley, Jr., Comp., NEW BERN DISTRICT NORTH CAROLINA LOOSE ESTATE PAPERS, 1775-1810, 29; Tom Howland. "Pigot History, Part I, THE RESEARCHER, XVII (Spring, 2001) 13-16; French Spoliation Claims, NARA, Baltimore, MD.
60. Willis, *History of Lands at Gloucester,* 7
61. Willis, *History of Lands at Gloucester,* 7, 36-37; Barry Munson, comp., *Citizens of Craven County, North Carolina, and Vicinity,* 27.
62. Craven County Deed Book 32, SANC.
63. The vessel was apparently one advertised for sale in a New Bern newspaper. Henry Tillman Estate Papers, SANC; (New Bern) *Carolina Federal Republican,* May 30, 1815. For his property see Craven County Deed Book, 32.599, SANC; A. B. Pruitt, comp., *Abstract of Land Entries: Craven County, N.C., 1778-1796,* 63, 83, 90, 93, 118.
64. Norfolk County Deed Book 28, 1783-85, 73. Smith Sparrow was a shipbuilder in Norfolk in 1761; Wertenbaker, *Norfolk,* 42.

65. W. Keats Sparrow, "Dr. William Tucker Sparrow: Builder of the Octagon House in Hyde County, North Carolina: A Biographical Sketch of the Builder and His Family," *Hyde County Historical and Genealogical Society North Carolina*, XV (Spring, 1994), 3-6; Linda Vestal Herzog, "The Early Architectural History of New Bern 1750-1850," (Ph.D. diss., UCLA, 1977), 347-351; Victor Jones, comp., "Apprentice Bonds for Craven County, N.C.," New Bern-Craven County, Public Library, New Bern, North Carolina.

66. Elizabeth Baum Hanbury, *Currituck Legacy*, 76-77; Currituck County Deed Books 3-10, SANC.

67. Gregory moved to Currituck County. He also owned land in Tyrrell County. Currituck County Deed Book 3, 530-537, SANC. It is not clear whether Downes and Grice had yards on "shipyard road" at the same time.

68. Charles Grice was from a prominent shipbuilding family in Philadelphia and was undoubtedly trained as a shipwright. He came to North Carolina by way of Norfolk and settled along the Pasquotank River in the 1780's. Some researchers believe he was from Delaware but his descendants identify Philadelphia as his birthplace. For Delaware as the site of his birth see (Elizabeth City) *Daily Advance,* November 6, 1948; *The State,* 22 (April 29, 1950), 13. There is also some confusion as to his initial location in North Carolina. At least one source claims that he settled in Edenton before moving to what became Elizabeth City. Wayne H. Payne, "The Commercial Development of Elizabeth City" (M.A. thesis, Old Dominion University, 1971), 16-17. See also "The Story of the 'Little Charles,'" copy in the authors' possession. The name of the author is not known but it was clearly a member of the Grice family, possibly his daughter, Mrs. Gilbert Elliott. (Elizabeth City) *North Carolinian,* September 16, 1869; E. O. Baum, *Albemarle's Historical Genealogy Researcher,* January 29, 1962; Wilma Cartwright Spence and Edna Morrisette Shannonhouse, *North Carolina Bible Records Dating from the Early Eighteenth Century to the Present Day*, 133-134; William A. Griffin, "Ante-Bellum Elizabeth City: The History of a Canal Town," (M.A. thesis, East Carolina University, 1969), 45-46; J. H. Stevens, *Albemarle, People and Places,* 212-214; Camden Deed Book G, 41, Deed Book N, 151, and Deed Book P, 325-336, SANC. Francis Grice II, a nephew of Charles, was one of the best-known ship constructors in the U.S. Navy. For Francis Grice's career see Howard I. Chapelle, *The History of American Sailing Ships,* 112, passim; Howard I. Chapelle, *The History of the American Sailing Navy: The Ships and Their Development,* 256, passim. Francis Grice owned a house in Elizabeth City as well as in Norfolk. Griffin, *Ante-Bellum Elizabeth City,* 46.

69. In an 1806 newspaper advertisement, Charles Grice listed property for sale including "one piece of ground back of lots occupied by a shipyard" as well as two vessels on the stocks. Jesse F. Pugh and Frank T. Williams, *The Hotel in the Great Dismal Swamp, and Contemporary Events Thereabouts*, 83-84; (Elizabeth City) *North Carolinian,* September 9, 16, 1869.

70. A brig, enrolled in 1800, was the first recorded vessel built in Elizabeth City. The document refers to the Edenton shipwright as a mariner, but he agrees to finish the hull of a "boat that he is now building." Chowan County Shipping Records, June 24, 1784, SANC.

71. William Rombough Account Book, 1799-1814, SANC.

72. Michael Evans, *Bertie County Records of Estates*, May 23, 1796. Steven Butler, "The Butler Family," Biographicalindex.com, mentions Jacob Kennehorn, ship carpenter.

73. Bill against the William Bell estate, May Term, 1799, Hyde County Estate Records, 1745-1904, SANC; *Norfolk Herald,* September 25, 1800; *Gazette,* July 17, 1810; Tuley to Blount, Keith and Masterson, eds., *John Gray Blount Papers,* III:80. Mortgage Deed, October 19, 1805, Chowan County Deed Book D, 388, SANC; Moseley, "Southern Built," 16; Farrow Estate Records, SANC; R. S. Spencer Jr., "Hyde County Apprentice Papers," Part l, 14; Gale Farrow, "Black Craftsmen in North Carolina," *North Carolina Genealogical Society Journal,* XI (May 1985), 91-103; New Bern District Court Estate Records, SANC; Beaufort County Real Estate Conveyances, Vol. 11, 109, 373, SANC. Caulking was a particularly dirty kind of work throughout the nineteenth century.

74. General Benjamin Smith to Blount, Nov 4, 1802, in Keith and Masterson, eds., *John Gray Blount Papers,* III:551.

75. Thomas Trotter to Pettigrew, Aug 10, Sept. 13, 1810, in Sarah Lemmon, ed., *The Pettigrew Papers,* I:428-432.

76. New Bern District Court Estate Records, SANC; Still, "The Shipbuilding Industry in Washington, North Carolina," 30.

77. Moseley, "Southern Built," 15.

78. Six blockmakers, ten sailmakers, ten blacksmiths, and two riggers are listed in the apprentice bond records for Craven County. Two blockmaker apprentices are listed for Hyde County. William Smeeton, a blockmaker in Wilmington, advertised for an apprentice to learn the "pump and block-making business." *Wilmington Gazette,* March 29, 1798; Victor T. Jones Jr., comp., "Apprentice Bonds of Craven County, N.C.", *Quarterly Review of The Eastern North Carolina Genealogical Society,* VI (Winter, 1979), 201-202.

79. Peter Jennings Wrike compiled and edited the account books (unpublished) examined by the authors.

80. For apprenticeship listings, see James H. Craig, *The Arts and Crafts in North Carolina, 1699-1840*; Jones, comp., "Apprentice Bonds of Craven County, N.C.," 201-202; Dru Haley and David Winslow Jr., *The Historic Architecture of Perquimans County, North Carolina,* 253; apprenticeship indentures housed in county records in the SANC. Undoubtedly, there were more apprentices. Thirty-six, or nearly a third of the 124 recorded, were orphans; eight were free Blacks or mulattos. Records for Craven County are fairly complete, but no systematic examination of the other counties has been made. Johnson, *Sail and Steam,* 45.

81. Jo Ann Bates, ed., *The Heritage of Currituck County,* 236; Francis M. Manning and W. B. Booker, *Martin County History,* 1:195; *Edenton Intelligencer,* April 9, 1788; *Wilmington Gazette,* August 31, 1815; Daniel M. McFarland, "Edward Bishop Dudley," in Powell, ed., *DNCB,* 2:113-114; P. W. Fisher, *One Dozen Pre-Revolutionary War Families of Eastern North Carolina and Some of Their Descendants,* 277; Christopher Dudley Will, Sept 17, 1828, Onslow County Wills, Book 1, SANC; Onslow County Court Minutes, April Term, 1800, SANC; Alan Watson, *Onslow County; A Brief History,* 47, 57; "Rayner," Sally's Family Place website, https://sallysfamilyplace.com/rayner-2/.

82. Johnston County Deed Book S1, 262, 291, 296, Deed Book V1, 139, 141, 414, Deed Book W1, 208, and Deed Book X1, 77, SANC; *Norfolk Herald,* April 6, 1799. The quest to identify the villain resulted in accusations and a court case. William Guy brought suit against Daniel Dees, a neighbor, accusing him of destroying the vessel. In the trial and retrial that followed, Dees claimed he was innocent and hinted that Guy himself burned the vessel. His witnesses were later convicted of perjury and Dees was forced to pay 600 pounds in restitution to Guy Williams. Evidently, a

squabble over property was the cause. New Bern District Court Records, SANC.
83. (Raleigh) *North Carolina Minerva*, January 20, 1801; (Raleigh) *Star*, April 14, 1815; Guy Williams Will, May 9, 1812, Johnston County Records, SANC; "Sale Estate of William Guy, Aug 12, 1815," Johnston County Record of Estates, Vol. VIII, SANC; *Helm and others v. Guy*, Supreme Court of North Carolina, 6 N.C. 341 (1818), SANC.
84. Smith to Blount, July 10, 1802, Keith and Masterson, eds., *John Gray Blount Papers*, III:520-521. Captain Eastwood has not been identified but may have been a local businessman. The town of Smithville was founded by Benjamin Smith and named after him. Today the name of the town is Southport.
85. Smith to Blount, October 8 and November 4, 1802, Keith and Masterson, eds., *John Gray Blount Papers*, III:538-539, 551-553; Dorothy F. Grant, "Benjamin Smith," Powell, ed., *DNCB*, V:370-371.
86. Clark to Blount, February 15, 1803, Box 39, John Gray Blount Papers, SANC.
87. Deshon to Blount, May 14 and 20, 1799, Keith and Masterson, eds., *John Gray Blount Papers*; III:292-293.
88. Parramore, *Murfreesboro, North Carolina and the Great Intracoastal Waterway*, 30; "Report –The Committee of Commerce and Manufacturing, 1806,"copy in Roanoke River Maritime Museum, Plymouth, N.C.; suit for building the *Hazard* in the Edenton District Superior Court Papers, 1798-1799, SANC; will of Abraham Ferguson, June 23, 1795, Bertie County Wills, SANC. William Rea, a Boston merchant and shipper who relocated to Murfreesboro, had the schooner *Belinda* built for him in 1794. On the *Belinda*, see the Boston Customhouse Records, Peabody Museum Library, Salem, Mass.
89. Josiah Collins Papers, SANC; communication from George Troxler to authors, March 2, 1983.
90. New Bern District Court Records of Ships and Merchants, SANC; Blackledge to Dennis, June 10, 1786, Blackledge to Cooke, December 1, 1784, and Blackledge to Tuley, July 1, 1785, Richard Blackledge Letterbook, Tryon Palace, New Bern, N.C.; Morgan, "Commerce of a Southern Town," 31-32.
91. Indenture of Fahey and Reilly to George Grundy, October 15, 1784, in the Elizabeth Moore Papers, East Carolina University Manuscript Collection. In 1783 Fahey and Reilly purchased the brig *Friendship*. The vessel is not mentioned in the 1784 property agreement with George Grundy. Beaufort County Deed Book, Vol. 9, SANC. Joel Wilkinson, another Beaufort County Businessman sold all his property in 1811 including five vessels. Beaufort County Deed Book 9, 147-148, SANC.
92. Tuley to Blount, July 4, 1783, July 23 and December 6, 1793, September 8, 1795, and March 3, June 16, and August 9, 1796, in Keith and Masterson, eds., *John Gray Blount Papers*, I:xv, 67, II:290, 337, 590; and III:66-67, 89.
93. Gaylord to Blount, Feb 2, April 14, Aug 2, Sept 2, Oct 21, Nov 2, Dec 30, 1805, in Keith and Masterson, eds., *John Gray Blount Papers*, IV:34, 58, 69-74, 76; Gaylord to Blount, February 8, March 8, August 15, September 28, November 19, 1805, and Adam Lacy to Blount, May 8, 1805, John Gray Blount Papers, NCDAH.
94. Tuley to Blount, July 4, 1783, July 23 and December 6, 1793, September 8, 1795, and March 3 and August 9, 1796, Keith and Masterson, eds., *John Gray Blount Papers*, I:67, II:290, 337, and III:30, 89.
95. Captain Shaw, n.d. (late eighteenth or early nineteenth century), Shaw Papers, SANC.
96. Jonathan and Daniel G. Marsh were natives of Rhode Island who migrated to Bath and opened a commission business. The pitch pine for planking was to be water soaked for eight weeks; white oak was to be "clear of sap." The pitch was a mixture of tar and resin, often used on the bottom of wooden vessels to seal the cracks. Contract dated Dec 4, 1794, in Brown Library, Washington, NC. For another example, see the 1782 agreement between Joseph Mann and John Clarke to build a vessel in Nixonton. Chowan County Shipping Records, 1736-1818, SANC.
97. Craven County Superior Court and District Court Records, Vol. I, 1800-1820, SANC.
98. Elizabeth Moore Papers, Affidavit, September 1800, ECU Manuscript Collection; New Bern District Court Records, Civil Action Papers, 1800-1801, SANC.
99. (New Bern) *North Carolina Gazette*, August 15, 1787; *Wilmington Chronicle and North Carolina Weekly Advertiser*, April 14, 1796.
100. (New Bern) *North Carolina Circular and New Bern Weekly Advertiser*, September 23, 1803.
101. *Wilmington Gazette*, March 30, 1797, April 16, 1805.
102. *Wilmington Gazette*, May 29, 1800. Obviously, the advertisement was for periaugers.
103. (New Bern) *Carolina Federal Republican*, March 20, 1815. For other ads, see (New Bern) *North Carolina Gazette*, May 30, 1795; (Halifax) *North Carolina Journal*, January 18 and March 26, 1806; *Wilmington Gazette*, May 27, October 7, and December 2, 1806; *Newbern Herald*, September 17, 1807.
104. Advertisement for a brig built in Washington, *Norfolk Gazette and Public Ledger*, November 12, 1810; advertisement for a vessel on the stocks at Windsor, *Norfolk Herald*, June 16, 1801, and December 14, 1814.
105. *New Bern Federal Republican*, November 12, 1814; *New Bern Sentinel*, May 28, 1814; Bill Reaves, *Southport (Smithville): A Chronology*, I, 13; Charles C. Crittenden, "North Carolina Newspapers Before 1790," in *James Sprunt Historical Studies* 20 (Number 1), 48.
106. See ads in the (New Bern) *Carolina Federal Republican*, 1811.
107. John S. Carter, *American Traders in European Ports*, 16; Still, "The Shipbuilding Industry in Washington, North Carolina," 30.
108. *Martin's North Carolina Gazette*, August 1, 1787.
109. Pasquotank County Court Records, SANC.
110. *Martin's North Carolina Gazette*, January 12, 1810.
111. Craven County Superior Court and District Court Records, Vol. 1, 1800-1820, SANC.
112. Agreement and Inventory, September 24, 1804, Tyrrell County Record of Estates, 1802-1837, 62-65, SANC.
113. William Ferrand affidavit, July 1801 Term, New Bern District Superior Court of Law, Craven County Estates, SANC.
114. Agreement, June 23, 1795, Bertie County Land Papers, 1736-1819, SANC; suit brought by Telemachus Washington, October 1799, Edenton District Superior Court Records, 1798-1799, 46-47, SANC.
115. William Bell Will, February Term, 1800, Book 1, 2, 3, 312-313, Hyde County Wills, SANC; Nathan Fuller will, 1801 Term, Beaufort County Deed Book, Book D, 176, SANC.
116. Deposition of Andrew Donaldson, March 31, 1784, Perquimans Court Miscellaneous Records, 1710-1933, SANC; Deposition of Henry Ramsey, October term, 1799, Edenton District Superior Court Records, Civil and Criminal Action Papers, 1799, SANC.
117. July 17, 1808, Letters Received by the Secretary of the Navy: Captains' Letters, Microfilm M125 (hereinafter cited as M125), Roll 12, NARA.

118. Blackledge to Secretary of the Navy, March 24, 1813, Letters Received by the Secretary of the Navy: Miscellaneous Letters, Microfilm M124 (hereinafter cited as M124), Roll 54, NARA; Blackledge to Secretary of the Navy, March 15, 1809, Roll 28, NARA.

119. Newsome, "A Miscellany from the Thomas Henderson Letterbook," Jacob Henry to Thomas Henderson, December 16, 1810, 399.

120. Craven County Deed Book, Vol. 32, February 1, 1794, SANC.

121. George Stephenson, "Ropewalks," unpublished manuscript in authors' possession. See also entry for June 14, 1783, which suggests that the ropewalk was under construction prior to 1783. Probably Collins bought it out and completed it. An article in the *North Carolina Journal* mentions that "eighteen hands are constantly employed in the rope-walk." The ropewalk was taken over by Josiah Collins Jr., who bought out Johnston. It remained in operation at least until 1839. Hugh B. Johnston Jr., ed., "The Journal of Ebenezer Hazard, in North Carolina, 1777 and 1778", *NCHR*, 35 (July 1959), 362; Edenton *Gazette*, October 29, 1806, May 19, 1795; Keith and Masterson. eds. *John Gray Blount Papers*, II:549; Deshon to Blount, III:318; Miller to Blount, September 24, 1805, Blount Papers, SANC; *North Carolina Journal*, April 27, 1795.

122. Jones, comp., "Apprentice Bonds of Craven County, N.C." Craven-Pamlico-Carteret Regional Library, New Bern. It was bought out by John Snead in 1812.

123. Schoonmaker to Blount, Oct 26, 1802 SANC; Gladden to Blount, June 19, 1786, Beaufort County Deed Book C, SANC; Stevenson, "Ropewalks."

124. Martin Ettinger, "Black Smith, White Smith, Gunsmith and Nail Manufacturer" advertisement, *Wilmington Gazette*, August 8, 1799; Gaylord to Blount, November 4, 1802, and Deshon to Blount, May 14, 1799, in Keith and Masterson, eds., *John Gray Blount Papers*, III:551, 292; Spaight to Blount, August 20, 1792, Tuley to Blount, July 4, 1783, December 6, 1793, September 8, 1795, II:206, 67, 337, 590; August 6, 1796, III:89; Gaylord to Blount, March 8, 1805, Blount Papers, SANC; contract dated Dec 4, 1794, George H. and Laura Brown Library, Washington, N.C.; Hyde County Estate Papers, SANC.

125. Lester J. Cappon, "Iron Making—A Forgotten Industry of North Carolina," *NCHR* (October 1932), 339.

126. Hutchins, *American Maritime Industries*, 121-123; Orr to Blount, June 15, 1799, in Keith and Masterson, eds., *John Gray Blount Papers*, III:299.

127. Testimony of Nimrod Meakins, 1815, William Bell Records, Hyde County Estates Records, 1745-1904, SANC.

128. New Bern District Court Estate Records, SANC.

129. John Smith to Blount, November 8, 1794, Keith and Masterson, eds, *John Gray Blount Papers*, II:456-457.

130. Jas S. Biddle, ed., *Autobiography of Charles Biddle*, 195; *Ashel Sikes v. Robert T. Paine, et al.*, December Term, 1849, N.C. Supreme Court, 208-210.

131. Still, "Shipbuilding Industry in Washington, North Carolina," 30.

132. Henry Tuley, a shipbuilder along the Carteret and Hyde county line, mentioned the difficulty he had in securing workers "to work in the woods at this season of the year." Tuley to Blount, July 23, 1793, in Keith and Masterson, eds., *John Gray Blount Papers*, II:290.

133. A. B. Pruitt, comp., *Abstract of Land Entries: Hyde Co. North Carolina, 1778-1795*, 35; Hyde County Deed Book W, 176-178, SANC.

134. Elizabeth Roberson, "A History of Ships and Shipping on the Roanoke River," *History of Williamston, 1779-1979*; *Edenton Intelligencer*, April 9, 1788. A map in the Pollock-Devereux papers shows the location of a shipyard on the Roanoke River. John Devereux Papers, SANC.

135. David B. Gammon, (comp.), *Abstracts of Wills, Bertie County, North Carolina, 1774-1797*, 51; Harry Thompson, "*A History of Windsor – 1768-1968*"; Stephen E. Bradley Jr., (comp.), *Deeds of Bertie County, North Carolina, 1785-1794*, 54; *Raleigh Register and North Carolina Gazette*, June 4, 1804.

136. February 27, 1785, Chowan Miscellaneous Records, Vol. XVII, SANC.

137. New Hanover County Deed Book S, 47, SANC; Wilson Angley, "A Historical Overview of the Black River in Southeastern North Carolina," Research Branch, North Carolina Division of Archives and History, 16.

138. July 11, 1791, Onslow Co. Miscellaneous Papers, C.R. 072.928.5, SANC; Tucker Littleton to author, September 11, 1976; Thompson, "*History of Windsor*," 83; William A. Griffin, *Ante-Bellum Elizabeth City: The History of a Canal Town*, 39.

139. Copy in the Reaves Collection, New Hanover County Public Library, Wilmington, N.C.

140. Sanders, *Carteret County Wills*, 59; Pruitt, comp., *Abstract of Land Entries: Carteret County, North Carolina, 1778-1803*, 25, 46; Benjamin Stanton Will Book D, 360, 1799, SANC.

141. For Grice's yard see Stevens, *Albemarle People and Places*, 212-213, 437-438; Elizabeth City *Independent*, November 1, 1935; Edenton *Gazette*, October 8, 1811. For Nixonton, see Stevens, *Albemarle People and Places*, 355-356. The Newby shipyard may have belonged to Thomas Newby, a prominent merchant in the area. May Term, 1815, Perquimans County Deed Book T, SANC; A. B. Pruitt, comp., *Abstracts of Land Warrants: Chowan County (1778-1932), Gates County (1778-1888), Hertford County (1778-1904), and Perquimans County (1778-1940)*, 73; Raymond A. Winslow Jr. to author, February 23, 1979; Haley and Winslow, *Historic Architecture of Perquimans County*, 73.

142. Case file dated January 16, 1801, New Bern District Court Record, SANC; *Hunter vs. McAuslan*, Supreme Court of North Carolina, Wilmington, 3N.C. 560, 1805, 366. For Luten, see his account book, SANC.

143. *Edenton Gazette*, October 29, 1806, November 4, 1818; Stick, *Outer Banks*, 81; Ryan to Pettigrew, 1805, Lemmon (ed.), *Pettigrew Papers*, I:366-367.

144. Lida T. Rodman, ed., "Journal of a Tour in North Carolina," Lida T. Rodman, ed., in *James Sprunt Historical Publications*, XVII:28; Newsome, "Twelve North Carolina Counties in 1810-11," 185; Jeremiah Battle, "The County of Edgecombe in 1810," in *Our Living and Our Dead*, I (1874-1875), 153; John Hogg Account Book, vol. 10, SHC, UNC-CH, for extensive mention of the use of flat boats.

145. Wallace to Blount, November 20, 1800, in Keith and Masterson, eds., *John Gray Blount Papers*, III:448-449, and Wallace to Blount, February 12, 1792, II:182.

146. New Hanover Deed Book O, 264, and Deed Book P, 85, SANC. There are no descriptions for these lighters, but they did carry sails. A note in the *Fayetteville Gazette*, June 4, 1793, announced the invention of a "cheap method of Carrying BOATS AGAINST the CURRENT"; there is no description other than that it was machinery.

147. *New Bern Sentinel*, October 16, 1813.

148. *New Bern Sentinel,* October 25, 1814; entry for June 14, 1786, Louis B. Wright and Marion Tinling, eds., *Quebec to Carolina in 1785-1786: Travel Diary of R. B. T. Hunter,* 275; Blackledge to Dennis, June 10, 1786, and Blackledge to Cooke, Dec 1, 1784, Richard Blackledge Letterbook, Tryon Palace, New Bern, N.C..
149. During the same period only forty-six sloops were built and between 1801 and 1815, only eight were registered or enrolled according to Appendix A.
150. Howard Chapelle, *The Search for Speed Under Sail, 1700-1855,* 145-146; Richard Pigott to Peter Fabre, July 17, 1799, Craven County Records, C.R. 028.928.4 SANC.
151. Chapelle, *History of American Sailing Ships,* 131.
152. For privateers, see William N. Still, Jr., *North Carolina's Revolutionary War Navy,* 18-22.
153. It is difficult to determine, or even estimate, the number of North Carolina-built privateers. Some vessels constructed in the state but purchased by outside interests engaged in privateering. Watson, *Wilmington: Port of North Carolina,* 40.
154. Pigot to Fabre, July 17, 1799, Craven County Records, C. R. 028.928.4, SANC; *Edenton Gazette,* October 8, 1811.
155. U.S. Office of Naval Records and Library, *Naval Documents Related to the Quasi-War Between the United States and France,* II:168, VI:400.
156. Still, "Shipbuilding and Boatbuilders in Swansboro," 8.
157. Still, "The Shipbuilding Industry in Washington, North Carolina," 32; William Blackledge to Secretary of the Navy, October 11, 1812, M124, Roll 51, NARA; (Washington) *American Recorder,* May 5, 1815; Sarah Lemmon, *Frustrated Patriots: North Carolina and the War of 1812,* 157.
158. Watson, *Wilmington: Port of North Carolina,* 44.
159. There is some confusion over the origin of the privateer *Snap Dragon.* The biographical sketch of Otway Burns in the *Dictionary of North Carolina Biography* suggests that the vessel was originally the schooner *Zephyr* built in 1808 in West River, Maryland. However, a Philadelphia customhouse document mentions a schooner *Snap Dragon* built at Smith's Creek, North Carolina, in 1806.
160. Hamilton to Washington, Sept 10, 1790, in Harold C. Syrett, ed., *Alexander Hamilton Papers,* VII:31-32.
161. Irving H. King, *George Washington's Coast Guard: Origins of the U.S. Revenue Service, 1789-1901,* 33-37; *Record of Movements: Vessels of the United States Coast Guard, 1790 – December 31, 1933.*
162. *Record of Movements,* 59.
163. Keais to Hamilton, May 6, 1791, John Dawes to Hamilton, Nov 12, 1791, in Syrette, ed., *Hamilton Papers,* VIII:328, IX:497; Chapelle, *History of American Sailing Ships,* 179-181. Chapelle mistakenly wrote that the North Carolina cutter was built in New Bern. Collectors Office, Port of New Bern to Hamilton, June 12, 1791, M178, roll 15, NARA.
164. See Smith to Secretary of the Navy, December 10, 1807, M124, Roll 18, NARA.
165. Gallatin to Taylor, April 6, Nov 24, 1807, M178, NARA; "Record of Movements, United States Coast Guard,"I, U.S. Coast Guard History Office, Washington, D.C.; Chapelle, *History of American Sailing Ships,* 189; Horatio Davis Smith, *Early History of the United States Revenue Marine Service,* 22.
166. For the *Vigilant,* see Register of Vessels, Wilmington, 1816, NARA; Don Canney to the authors, July 30, 2002. Both the *Governor Williams* and the *Diligence II* were sunk during a hurricane in 1806 at Ocracoke.

167. Marshall Smelser, *The Congress Founds the Navy,* 75-76, 78, 142-147; Chapelle, *History of the American Sailing Navy,* 151. Although the rowing galley, one of the earliest types of warships, had lost its supremacy to sailing vessels, it was still utilized in various parts of the world. Galleys had been used with some success in the Revolutionary War.
168. Navy Department to Jocelin, September 12, 1798, January 4, March 23, 1799; Navy Department to William Crafts, September 14, 1798, March 20, 1799, U.S. Office of Naval Records and Library, *Naval Documents Related to the Quasi-War Between the United States and France,* I:396-397, II:211, 506-507,; 391, 493; Secretary of the Navy to Gilt, September 13, 1798, M149, Roll l, NARA.
169. Navy Department to Jocedlin, December 11, 1799, June 6, 1801; Smith to Jocelin, December 16, 1801; Navy Department to Jocelin, July 17, 1801, in U.S. Office of Naval Records and Library, *Naval Documents Related to the Quasi-War Between the United States and France,* III:536-537, VII:246, 282,and IV:, 169-270; *Dictionary of American Fighting Ships* (hereafter cited as DANFS) III, 125, 127. To place a vessel in ordinary was essential to de-commission the vessel, equivalent to "mothballing" a vessel after World War II.
170. For in-depth studies of Jefferson and his gunboats, see Spencer C. Tucker, *The Jeffersonian Gunboat Navy;* and Gene A. Smith, *"For the Purposes of Defense: The Politics of the Jeffersonian Gunboat Program.* Dean A. Mayhew, "Jeffersonian Gunboats in the War of 1812," *American Neptune,* 101-117, is a good summary but marred by some unfortunate errors.
171. Tucker, *Jeffersonian Gunboat Navy,* 28-29.
172. Gene A. Smith, "'A Force of Being': North Carolina and Jefferson's Gunboat Navy." *Tributaries,* no. 4 (October 1994), 32. The *Chesapeake,* an American frigate, was forced to strike to a British warship in the waters off Norfolk after the frigate's commanding officer refused to heave to while a boarding party examined the ship's crew for deserters. The incident resulted in an uproar, and a demand for war on the part of the American people.
173. Copy of resolution dated July 8, 1807, Governor Nathaniel Alexander Papers, SANC; Smith to Secretary of the Navy, Miscellaneous Letters Received by the Secretary of the Navy, M124, Roll 16, NARA.
174. Smith to Gautier, August 31, 1807, Officer Letters, M149, Roll 7, NARA; Robert Smith to Benjamin Smith, August 6, 1807, Entry 173, Gunboat Letters, RG45, NARA. Gautier, who would supervise their construction, was a native of Bristol, England, who had served in both the Royal and U.S. Navies. He had retired to Wilmington in 1801 where he evidently had some business interests. The naval background of Gautier apparently qualified him for the position as superintendent in the eyes of both Smith and the Secretary of the Navy. As a sailing master and later acting lieutenant, he would serve on the Carolina station until retiring in 1814. He would reside in Wilmington until his death in 1848. Sarah M. Lemmon, "Gautier, Thomas Nicholas Boudet," in Powell, ed., *Dictionary of North Carolina Biography,* II:289; William S. Dudley, ed., *The Naval War of 1812: A Documentary History,* I:98; Alan Watson to author, April 10, 2002.
175. R. Smith to B. Smith, September 25, 1807, entry 173, Gunboat Letters, RG45, NARA; B. Smith to R. Smith, September 18, 1807, M124, roll 17, NA; *Wilmington Gazette,* September 29, 1807.
176. Magar Jones to William Blackledge, January 22, 1808, and John Alderman to Rep. Thomas Blount, Jan 6, 1808, Roll 19, M41, Roll 19, NARA.
177. William Blackledge to Thomas Jefferson, February 2, 1808, in Keith and Masterson, eds., *John Gray Blount Papers,* IV:101-

102; T. Blount to Robert Smith, January 23, 1808, M124, Roll 19, NARA; T. Blount to Secretary of the Navy, April 23, 1814, M124, Roll 62, NARA. It is possible the *Blount*, owned by the Blounts and transferred to the navy in 1814, was the ship on the stocks.

178. B. Smith to Secretary of the Navy, December 10, 1807, M124, Roll 18, NARA. The only other information we have on Perry is that he died in Smithville in 1812. Reaves, *Southport (Smithville): A Chronology*, 17.

179. Tucker, *Jeffersonian Gunboat Navy*, 36. Captain Hugh Campbell would later command the naval stations in the two Carolinas. He was from South Carolina, had an injury to his leg, and probably requested the Carolina command because of that. For his career see Christopher McKee, *A Gentlemanly and Honorable Profession: The Creation of the U.S. Naval Officer Corps, 1794-1815*, 183-185. Captain Hugh Campbell, nicknamed "Cork", had been a most successful commander of the USS *Constitution*, the most famous ship in American history, but as the ship's historian noted, little is known about him. Tyrone G. Martin, *A Most Fortunate Ship: A Narrative History of Old Ironsides*, 124.

180. Chapelle, *History of the American Sailing Navy*, 223-224, 226; R. Smith to B. Smith, August 8, 1807, Entry 173, RG45, NARA.

181. Gautier to Secretary of the Navy, October 27, 1814, M173, Roll 13, NARA.

182. Campbell to R. Smith, July 17, August 11, 1808, M125, Roll 12, NARA.

183. Campbell to Secretary of the Navy, July 11, 1809, M625, Roll 200, NARA; R. Smith to Campbell, August 2, 1808, and Goldsborough to Campbell, August 26, 1808, Entry 173, RG45, NARA.

184. R. Smith to B. Smith, January 13, 1808, Entry 173, RG45, NARA; R. Smith to Gautier, February 8, 1808, M149, Roll 8, NARA; Tingley to Secretary of the Navy, July 26, 1808, M125, Roll 12, NARA.

185. Smith to Secretary of the Navy, January 29, 1809, M124, Roll 26, NARA.

186. See various letters dated 1809-1811 in the Thomas Nicholas Boudet Gautier Letterbook, Southern Historical Collection, UNC-CH; Gautier to Campbell, March 7, 1809, Roll 14, M125, NA; Campbell to SECNAV, February 26, `809, Roll 14, M125, NA. See also Campbell to SECNAV, Jan 2, 1809, *ibid*.; B. Smith to SECNAV, July 19, 1808, Roll 22, M124, NA; R. Smith to B. Smith, March 9, Jan 20, 1808, Entry 173, RG45, NA; Tucker, *The Jeffersonian Gunboat Navy*, 63: Gautier wrote the Department: "Independent of any public document I wish to beg you to place funds in the hands of someone else than the gentleman who is in possession of them in order to enable me to liquidate several considerable demands against the boats under my charge. You have no idea Sir for nothing short of experience could evince to you the trouble, vexation that I have to procure money from General Smith." See various letters dated 1809-1811 in the Thomas Nicholas Boudet Gautier Letterbook, SHC, UNC-CH; Gautier to Campbell, March 7, 1809, M125, Roll 26, NARA; Campbell to Secretary of the Navy, February 26, 1809, January 2, 1809, M125, Roll 14, NARA. B. Smith to Secretary of the Navy, July 19, 1808, M124, Roll 22, NARA; R. Smith to B. Smith, March 9, January 20, 1808, Entry 173, RG45, NARA; Tucker, *Jeffersonian Gunboat Navy*, 63.

187. Hamilton to Smith, June 28, 1810, M 209, Roll 4, NARA; Gautier to Turner, June 14, 1810, M142, roll 36, NARA.

188. Gautier to Secretary of the Navy, September 22, 1811, Gautier Letterbook, SHC, UNC-CH.

189. B. Smith to Secretary of the Navy, December 25, November 11, and December 5, 1811, M124, Roll 45, NARA. There is no evidence that he pursued shipbuilding as one of his many enterprises after 1802. The General died in poverty in 1826.

190. Sarah M. Lemmon, *Frustrated Patriots*, 74; Callender to Secretary of the Navy, January 9, 1809, M625, Roll 197, NARA.

191. Tucker, *Jeffersonian Gunboat Navy*, 200. See also Gautier to Department, October 5, 1811, Gautier Letterbook, SHC, UNC-CH. President Jefferson and Secretary Smith had originally wanted the gunboats to be placed in ordinary but agreed to their remaining in the water even after being fitted out.

192. Blackledge to Secretary of the Navy, March 24, 1813, M124, Roll 54, NARA. See also Blount to the President, January 6, 1812, Roll 46, NARA; Pigott to Secretary of the Navy, November 4, 1812, Roll 51, NARA; Tucker, *Jeffersonian Gunboat Navy*, 102.

193. Contract dated January 24, 1814, Entry 235, RG45, NARA. See also Contract, June 24, 1812, NARA; Josuah Potts to Secretary of the Navy, May 16, June 30, 1812, M124, Roll 22, NARA.

194. According to Tucker, seven barges/galleys were to be built in Wilmington. Tucker, *Jeffersonian Gunboat Navy*, 105-107.

195. Secretary of the Navy to Gautier, March 31, 1814, M149, Roll 11, NARA; Samuel Smith to Secretary of the Navy, June 10, 1813, Secretary of the Navy to Smith, June 17, 1813, Dudley, ed., *Naval War of 1812: A Documentary History*.

Chapter 4

The Advent of the Steamboat, 1816–1860

The United States, during the first half of the nineteenth century, witnessed a revolution in maritime transportation.[1] Emphasis was on internal improvements, especially the construction and linking of canals, rivers, and sounds along the eastern seaboard. The development of steam propulsion accelerated the growth of waterborne commerce. As technology improved, the American merchant marine gained status worldwide. The extensive coastline, sounds, rivers, canals, and Great Lakes supported a remarkable maritime network that included road and rail. But, water transport was not possible in much of the nation. Significantly, the era witnessed the emergence of the railroads and of the telegraph. The two innovations challenged the primacy of the maritime economy and themselves became competitive means for the circulation of people and goods.

The shipbuilding industry in America quickly recovered from the War of 1812 and enjoyed accelerated prosperity during most of the period.[2] Within a few years, there were hundreds of small shipyards scattered along the coast from New England to Louisiana. These yards were supported by one of the most extensive timber supplies in the world. Little capital was required to build wooden vessels. The industry's growth was facilitated by discriminatory port duties, and after 1817 by a federal statute whereby foreign vessels were restricted from trading between American ports. American coastwise trade operated without competition. Between 1815 and 1818, the American coastal fleet grew from 475,666 gross tons to 842,906 tons.[3] Though not similarly protected, foreign trade continued to prosper, partly because of bilateral agreements eliminating barriers to trade with other nations such as Great Britain. The wooden shipbuilding industry, however, fluctuated with the economic cycles. By mid-century, it was seriously affected by the decline in the nation's supply of shipbuilding timber and the increased use of iron for frames and hulls, particularly in northern shipyards. Investments in the shipbuilding industry declined sharply.[4]

After the War of 1812, North Carolina's maritime industries prospered. The use of the long seine was a major factor in North Carolina commercial fishing becoming the second most productive in the South. The Dismal Swamp Canal was completed. Steam propulsion was adopted. The centerboard, a significant innovation in North Carolina-built sailing vessels, was introduced. Marine railways were established in several ports, providing a means of shipping seafood to other parts of the state and region, bringing in needed resources, and generating an economic boost for shipbuilders.[5] All of these factors stimulated North Carolina's maritime industries, including ship and boat building. Nevertheless, navigating the coastal waters was still dangerous. Cautious skippers gave the "Graveyard of the Atlantic" a wide berth.[6]

Languishing Commercial Development

North Carolina was overwhelmingly rural during the period. Most of the ports were small and somewhat isolated. The coastal environment made competition with neighboring states difficult. For years after the war, North Carolina's economy, based largely on agriculture, was stagnant at best and in periods of recession or depression, very poor. "No state was less developed or had more serious problems relating to agriculture, transportation, commerce, manufacturing, finance, education, and emigration than North Carolina."[7] Manufacturing was nearly non-existent. An 1830 legislative report concluded that North Carolina was "a state without foreign commerce, of want of seaports or a staple; without internal communications by rivers, roads, or canals; without a cash market for any agricultural product; in short, without any object to which native industry and active enterprise could be directed." A contemporary New Bern newspaper editorial noted business was dismal: "Insolvency is the order of the day, and the tide of ruin is sweeping onward with fearful rapidity. Merchants who, a few years ago, were wealthy, who have, all their lives, been industrious and economical, are overwhelmed."[8] Vessels, warehouses, and other property were sold for a fraction of their value. Referred to as the "Rip Van Winkle State," North Carolina's prospects were so poor that there was a steady migration to the West and other parts of the country. Nevertheless, although North Carolina's ports may "have outwardly resembled backwater outposts on minor trade routes," trade was important and certainly not provincial.[9]

In 1816, one and one-third million dollars of produce was shipped from North Carolina ports. Of this, 40,000 tons was in maritime trade, an amount that increased gradually until it peaked at 55,000 tons in 1855.[10] However, tonnage figures are not the only criteria in evaluating the state's commercial activity. Much of the state's trade was still funneled through Virginia and South Carolina by road and, later, by rail. At the expense of the state's ports, Norfolk continued to be an important entrepôt for North Carolina's products. "There are a great quantity of Produce, Lumber, and Naval Stores coming down the Roanoke [River] right by Plymouth and making Norfolk the depot, of a great portion of the production of North Carolina! Why is it, that North Carolinians had rather enrich and build up Cities in other States, than have even respectable towns within their own borders," Governor Edward B. Dudley declared. "Our sister states are . . . drawing from us the life-blood of our existence; and unless we act, and act efficiently, we become the humble tributary, a mere Province of our neighbors."[11]

North Carolina focused efforts on improving "the navigability of the river system."[12] Most of the rivers were shallow and all had obstructions that seriously hampered waterborne transportation. Problems, including those

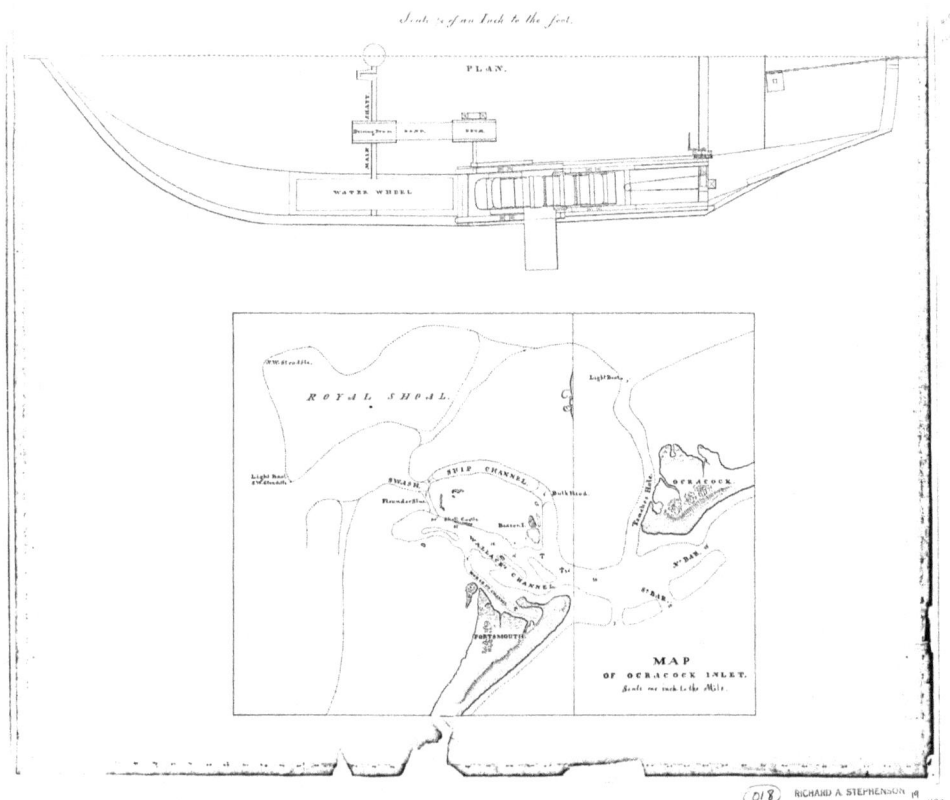

Figure 4-1 The early 1800s plan of a dredge to be used at Ocracoke Inlet and a map of the channel. Ocracoke Inlet was the most important inlet for ports from Port Roanoke (Edenton) to the north, and southward to New Bern. The dredge is thought to have been built in 1829 at the Howard and Sparrow shipyard in New Bern. Courtesy Cartographic Branch, National Archives.

relating to waterways, were addressed in various legislative sessions. Between 1784 and 1861, eighty-six laws were passed relating to improving the waterways. Private navigation companies were engaged to clear obstructions from state waters but little public funding was appropriated. The companies depended primarily on voluntary financial contributions.[13] "Navigation is not much attended to in N.C. They make a great noise about it but do nothing. The house of assembly granted $20,000 in 1822 to clear out the river below Wilmington. A countryman and a free Black took up the contract ... and began to clear away obstructions in their own way by clearing in one place and filling up the other.

So it is now said to be worse than ever."[14] Under the leadership of state senator Archibald DeBow Murphey, a comprehensive program of internal improvements was approved by the legislature, but it included no funding to improve navigation. An uninterested public and the priority placed on railroads were perennial challenges.[15] Improvements were made, particularly on the Cape Fear and Roanoke Rivers. The Cape Fear River was opened to traffic throughout the year between Wilmington and Fayetteville and, later, as far upstream as Averasboro for flats and small vessels.[16] However, on the whole, this did little to improve the state's maritime commerce.

Navigational Improvements

In addition to improving the state's rivers, efforts were made to maintain coastal inlets, which were shallow, shoaling, and moving as a result of sporadic storms and variations in tidal energy. Aside from Wilmington, state ports were often cut off as inlets migrated and shoaled, restricting navigation to inland waters. By the early nineteenth century, Roanoke Inlet was effectively closed to all but very small vessels. Efforts to reopen it were to no avail. The closing of Currituck Inlet in 1818 rendered Ocracoke Inlet the only remaining navigable passageway through the Outer Banks north of Beaufort. Murphey's plan included inlet improvements on the Outer Banks, especially Wallace's Channel at Ocracoke Inlet.[17]

As early as 1817, the federal government surveyed the sounds and inlets and made recommendations to improve navigation. Two surveys were completed before Congress passed a general survey act in 1824. The North Carolina surveys were the first undertaken by the U.S. Army Corps of Engineers. The corps initially dredged Ocracoke Inlet and the Swash, but the results were disappointing.[18] The plan of a bucket dredge for Ocracoke Inlet (Figure 1) illustrates the type of mechanism employed to keep inlets open during this period.

In 1846, an earthquake centered in Charleston, South Carolina, combined with a hurricane that swept the North Carolina coast, created Oregon and Hatteras Inlets which were navigable for vessels having less than an eight-foot draft. Navigation through these and other inlets remained hazardous, a circumstance which adversely affected the state's commercial development.

The years following the War of 1812 were known as the "Canal Era." North Carolina interest in canal construction stemmed, in large part, from the hazards of sailing near the state's shore waters and sounds.[19] Thoughtful North Carolinians understood the need for these artificial waterways as a means of solving their transportation problems. Originally proposed in the 1760s, construction of two canals, the Clubfoot and Harlow Creek Canal and the Dismal Swamp Canal, was not completed until after the War of 1812. The Clubfoot and Harlow Creek Canal, between the Neuse River estuary and Beaufort Inlet, was intended to direct oceanic commerce from New Bern and the Neuse River area to Beaufort, rather than Ocracoke Inlet. The canal, from the head of Clubfoot Creek to the head of Harlow Creek, was completed in 1828, but its width and shallow depth limited its use to small vessels only.[20]

The Dismal Swamp Canal, between the Elizabeth River in Norfolk and Albemarle Sound, was far more complex and successful. The concept of digging a canal through the nearly impenetrable swamp that covered parts of southeastern Virginia and northeastern North Carolina was far more appealing to Virginians than most North Carolinians. It would benefit commercial and agricultural interests in both states, but many resident Tar Heels were convinced that although it "may be of incalculable benefit to Virginia, it was 'to North Carolina, a blood-sucker at her very vitals.'"[21] In 1793, construction started on the fifty-mile stretch which would link Norfolk and the Pasquotank River. Although the first recorded passage of a vessel other than a small flat occurred in 1814, it was not until the 1820s that the canal attracted considerable traffic.[22] Throughout the period from 1821 to 1860, Norfolk newspapers continually ran notices of flats, schooners, sloops, and steamboats carrying cargo to Norfolk on the canal. However, most of the steamboats were too large to navigate the canal and, usually, towed rafts and lighters up to the first lock.[23]

The Roanoke Canal was started in 1823, largely completed by 1834, and, in terms of engineering, was the most challenging of all North Carolina canals.[24] Designed to bypass the fall zone on the Roanoke River, a series of locks was utilized to raise and lower vessels of up to fifty tons by approximately forty-four feet, providing uninterrupted navigation between upriver locations and the sounds. The objective was to provide an alternative outlet for North Carolina goods that previously had been transported overland to Virginia ports. It worked, but the completion of the Raleigh and Gaston Railroad in 1841 led to its decline.

The Albemarle and Chesapeake Canal was the most successful canal in North Carolina and the easiest to build.[25] Designed to link the Chesapeake Bay via the Elizabeth River and Currituck Sound, it provided a safe inland passage for vessels from North Carolina ports northward. Although the canal was chartered in the eighteenth century, digging did not begin until the mid-1850s. It was opened in 1859 but the Civil War delayed its full use. Nonetheless, the canal was a major factor in diminishing the importance of the Ocracoke and Hatteras Inlets, which continued to suffer due to shoaling and inadequate maintenance.[26] By the Civil War, Hatteras Inlet traffic had far surpassed that of Ocracoke Inlet, and in 1895, the last commercial vessel passed through Hatteras Inlet.[27]

Developments along the Coast

Internal improvements—canals, navigable rivers, steamboats, and railroads—were major factors in the growth and prosperity of most North Carolina ports but contributed to the decline of others. Wilmington thrived as a steamboat and rail center, becoming the state's largest city by 1860.[28] In 1816, eighty percent of the state's oceanic trade went through Wilmington and it was the first state port to benefit from railroads. The Wilmington and Weldon and the Raleigh and Gaston railroads linked the port to the interior and to other states. Later, other railroads provided additional lines to the piedmont carrying naval stores and other products to Wilmington for export. The railroads supported "Tar Packets," most of which were brigs, schooners, and, later, steamers.[29] By the 1850s, "there were frequently as many as ninety vessels in the port of Wilmington loading or unloading, or waiting for berths at anchor in the stream."[30]

Beaufort was often touted as having the best harbor in the state but lacked adequate transportation to the interior. The Clubfoot Canal was intended to resolve this problem, but neither the canal nor Beaufort's potential were realized. In 1839, "[a] half dozen schooners—more or less were lying at anchor...from the shore—wharves there were none, or next to none.... The coasting vessels that came into the port were generally owned by residents of the town. The fact is, Beaufort in those days, was as nearly out of the world as a town could be."[31] In 1835, tonnage was so negligible that Beaufort was not even listed among North Carolina ports trading with northern cities.[32] In 1857, twenty-one schooners and ten steamers cleared the port. In 1859, the completion of the Atlantic and North Carolina Railroad to Shepherd's Point (Morehead City), which lay across the Newport River, provided little help to Beaufort until years later when a spur line was built to link the two ports. New Bern opposed the railroad fearing Beaufort, always a rival in maritime shipping, would benefit.[33]

Located at the confluence of the Neuse and Trent Rivers, New Bern was well situated for maritime trade. The Trent River was navigable all year round up to a few miles above Pollocksville. Steamboats could ascend the Neuse River most of the year as far as Goldsboro, and to Smithfield when the river was fresh; above Smithfield, trade was carried on as far as Raleigh by flats. Contentnea Creek, which flowed into the Neuse River near Kinston, was navigable by flats and other small craft as far as Stantonsburg in Wilson County.[34] From 1812 to 1830, New Bern's maritime trade was second only to Wilmington. Shipping to the West Indies was particularly lucrative. In 1815, New Bern was the largest town in the state and its economy was built around maritime trade. By 1818, the port had two steam sawmills, a ropeyard, a number of distilleries, and shipbuilding facilities.[35] However, inland rivers were shallow, restricting steamboat traffic, and Ocracoke Inlet was not the only feasible outlet to the ocean, factors which contributed to New Bern's decline as a port. After 1830, its share of commerce dropped. In 1859, only twelve of 233 ships clearing North Carolina ports for the West Indies and other foreign destinations departed from New Bern.[36] Nonetheless, in 1860, the Neuse River port had nineteen distilleries, two large sawmills, and a shipyard with a marine railway.[37]

Washington on the Pamlico River was a small but thriving port during the transportation revolution but would be bypassed by railroads until the late nineteenth century.[38] It was the shipping center for settlements and communities east and west. For much of the year, the Tar River upstream from Washington was navigable as far as Tarboro in Edgecombe County. Efforts to make it navigable throughout the year proved disappointing despite private, state, and federal efforts. The Tar River shoaled more than any other river in the state. Although an occasional vessel reached Norfolk by way of the canals, Washington, like New Bern, had to rely on Ocracoke Inlet for access to the ocean.[39] In 1846, the *Raleigh Register* reported that Washington had seven turpentine distilleries, several steam sawmills running twenty-four saws, one vessel now being built and preparations "are underway for building several more," and that approximately thirty thousand tons of shipping were exported annually.[40] Throughout this period, average tonnage was from five to six thousand tons. In 1860, the value of exports was estimated to be more than a million dollars.

With more than fourteen thousand square miles in its drainage basin, the largest on the east coast, the Roanoke River was considered the most important watercourse in the state. Plymouth, just above the confluence of the Roanoke with the Chowan River, should have benefited from this location. However, the small port never reached its full potential. Until the 1850s, Plymouth's maritime trade was inconsequential; most of it was from New England.

The completion of the canal around the fall zone on the Roanoke River channeled products downstream. Much of this cargo was carried on steamboats and vessels under tow and passed by Plymouth on the way to the Dismal Swamp Canal. Sailing vessels, especially small schooners, continued to utilize the port. In 1860, Plymouth, with the only federal customhouse in the northeastern section of the state, was the second busiest port in North Carolina.[41]

The Port of Edenton suffered the greatest setback during this period. In 1816, it was observed that the port was "well situated for commerce, but it does not appear to be flourishing."[42] Nevertheless, total tonnage that year was slightly more than six thousand tons, more than most other state ports. Shipping gradually increased after the War of 1812 but never reached its pre-war level. The opening of the Dismal Swamp Canal in the 1820s initially stimulated the port's commerce.[43] However, this prosperity ended in the 1830s. In 1828, Currituck Inlet shoaled up; no railroad reached the town; and Edenton lost its supremacy in the Albemarle Sound area to Elizabeth City and later Plymouth.[44] In 1860, total tonnage through Edenton was only two thousand tons.

Elizabeth City was a small port on the Pasquotank River fourteen miles above the confluence of the Pasquotank River and the Albemarle Sound. Its maritime activity was of little consequence until the Dismal Swamp Canal was completed. The canal connected Elizabeth City with Norfolk, making it the most important commercial center for northeastern North Carolina.[45] In 1827, Elizabeth City's growing importance as a port led to the transfer of the customhouse from Camden. Thereafter, Elizabeth City enrolled more vessels than any other North Carolina port except Wilmington. However, not all shipping traffic in the Albemarle Sound went through the canal.[46] Regardless, Elizabeth City's prominence as a port steadily increased.[47] Even the completion of the Albemarle and Chesapeake Bay Canal in 1859 had little adverse effect on its maritime trade.

A number of river communities acted as transshipping points for maritime trade. The "fall zone" towns at the head of navigation, particularly Fayetteville on the Cape Fear River, and Weldon and Halifax on the Roanoke River, were important centers where flats, lighters, and other small craft brought cargos to be loaded onto steamboats and larger vessels.[48] Most of the river towns that acted in this capacity were below the fall zone: Tarboro and Greenville, on the Tar River; Goldsboro and Kinston, on the Neuse River; Williamston and Hamilton, on the Roanoke River; and Murfreesboro, on the Meherrin River, were all important transshipment points. When the Wilmington and Weldon Railroad was in operation, steamboats carried barrels of fish to the railheads, especially to Weldon, where they were transported to markets in Richmond.

Although limited amounts of fish had been exported prior to 1815, it was in the antebellum period that it became commercially profitable. By 1860, North Carolina ranked second in the south in commercial fishing. This was due to the introduction of the long-haul seine in Albemarle Sound in 1816, which enabled fishermen to harvest fish, particularly shad and herring, in large quantities, and the introduction of steam transportation, trains and vessels, which permitted the highly perishable products to reach markets relatively quickly.

Of all the southern states, North Carolina had the most diversified economy. Agriculture predominated but was primarily for subsistence, local trade, and supplying ships. Agricultural products such as corn, peas, rice, tobacco, and cotton were exported, but from 1835 to 1860, naval stores, lumber, and lumber products "were the dominant part of North Carolina's economy and her 'peculiar stable,' in the coastal areas."[49] In 1840, North Carolina accounted for ninety-six percent of the nation's production of naval stores. After 1840, turpentine gradually replaced tar and pitch in commercial importance. Initially, central, coastal, and northern counties on the headwaters of the Tar and Roanoke Rivers led the industry, but by the 1850s, the counties bordering on the Cape Fear River basin took the lead in naval stores production.[50]

In northeastern North Carolina, large amounts of lumber, staves, and shingles were shipped from other coastal counties either through the Dismal Swamp Canal or Ocracoke Inlet. In concert with railroads and steam packets, sailing vessels, particularly schooners, provided the chief means of transporting lumber to markets in the northeast and the West Indies.[51] In the 1850s, agricultural products, mostly cotton, gradually replaced naval stores, particularly in the central coastal area, largely as a result of the depletion of the immense pine forests.[52]

Imports remained essentially the same. Most manufactured goods had to be shipped into the state.[53] The majority of imports were brought in by vessels owned out of state, which included most of the manufactured items related to the shipbuilding industry.

Steamboats in Eastern North Carolina

The years from 1816 to 1860 constitute the "golden age of the river steamboat" in North Carolina. By 1830, the vessels dominated river transportation and did so until challenged by the railroads.[54] North Carolina's internal transportation system was significantly affected by this new mode of transportation. The rivers and sounds throughout the state provided the incentive to develop steam navigation. Only five years after Robert Fulton's *Clermont* made its successful run on the Hudson River, efforts were made to introduce steam navigation in North Carolina. The state legislature granted John Stevens of New Jersey the right to establish steamboat lines in the state. John D. DeLacy, representing Fulton and his partner, Robert Livingston, challenged Steven's grant by organizing several steamboat companies. None of these early efforts were successful.[55] Steam navigation in state waters started in 1818 with the arrival of the steamboat *Norfolk* purchased by the chartered Newbern Steam Boat Company to run between New Bern and Elizabeth City.[56] Although this enterprise failed, others quickly followed. Between 1817 and 1861, the legislature chartered twenty-seven steam navigation companies.[57] Steam navigation had a significant impact on eastern North Carolina's economy. In 1849, the steamboat *Amaidas*, towing four flats laden with merchandise, made its inaugural trip on the Tar River from Washington to Tarboro. Prior to that time, goods were carried by small boat to Greenville and, from there, to Tarboro by wagon.[58]

Nearly all of the early steamboats operating on North Carolina waters were constructed outside the state.[59] The lack of facilities to build the engines and other machinery was a major factor in the failure of these initial efforts. Fulton's agent, DeLacy, wrote to John Gray Blount: "Mr. Fulton has agreed with me that it is best to build all the boats for the Southward in North Carolina ... but the want of Competent Iron works is a great obstacle."[60] John Stevens, Fulton's rival, in justifying his failure to construct a steamboat in North Carolina, wrote, "a vessel might have been built in any part of that state, but it would have been almost impracticable to construct the engine any other place than New York or Philadelphia."[61] The state's shipbuilders and carpenters had no experience in the construction of steamboats. As late as 1835, the builders of the first steamboat in Washington contracted with Samuel Peabody to build the vessel, and with Mr. Baxley of Baltimore to install the machinery.

Two exceptions were the *Henrietta* built in 1818 by James Seawell on the Cape Fear River, and the *Prometheus* built by the famed mariner and privateer Otway Burns in Swansboro. The *Prometheus* was launched in May 1818 and left early in June for Wilmington. The vessel was towed to Wilmington where her machinery was installed. She evidently was purchased by a group of businessmen to run between Wilmington and Smithville. She was not a financial success and was accidentally burned at a wharf and abandoned about 1825.[62]

The *Henrietta* was built by James Seawell at his plantation a few miles west of Fayetteville. Seawell was a prominent merchant, businessman, politician, and promoter of improved transportation for the region.63 He recognized the potential of steam navigation on the Cape Fear and played a key role in making the river and its tributaries the primary area for its early development in the state. The General Assembly granted Seawell a seven-year monopoly on steam navigation on the Cape Fear River between Wilmington and Fayetteville. The *Henrietta* was laid down in 1817 and completed in July 1818. She was 110 feet long on deck, twenty feet in beam and looked more like a steam flat, with no superstructure above deck except her machinery. Unlike the *Prometheus*, Seawell's vessel was a sidewheeler and her hull was similar to a Hudson River steamboat drawing seven and a half feet. She may have had cabins and part of her machinery below the main deck. At first, that machinery, manufactured out of state, presented considerable difficulties. She was "geared to work with cogwheels like a mill." At times, her crew had to use a line to pull her around a sharp bend in the river.[64] The steamboat's engineers modified the machinery, installing a connecting rod and crank more typical of steamboats of the period. The *Henrietta* had an unusually long life. In 1858, she was put up for sale in Wilmington but simply rotted and rusted away.[65] In 1823, Seawell launched another steamboat, the *North Carolina*, which was constructed for a stock company. The *North Carolina* was designed to tow flats loaded with cargo from Fayetteville to Wilmington. In 1826, another steamboat, *Ann Francis*, was launched in Fayetteville, and two more boats were being built to run between Wilmington and Fayetteville during low water.[66] That same year, the *Raleigh Register* reported that the "Cape Fear is once more in boatable order" and mentioned the launching of the steamboat *Henry Clay*. By 1860, thirteen steamers were running between Wilmington and Fayetteville on a regular basis.[67]

During the years *Prometheus* and *Henrietta* were operated on the Cape Fear River, steamboats were introduced in New Bern and the Albemarle Sound area. These vessels were built out of state and generally were unsuccessful. More than a decade passed after the launch of these first two steamboats before one was constructed outside the Cape Fear region.

Steamboats were expensive to build, maintain, and operate, particularly the machinery, which had to be manufactured and shipped in from out of state. Hulls could be built by local ship carpenters, but their structure was quite different from that of a sailing vessel. In some ways, steamboats, with their flat hulls, fewer bends, and reduced superstructure, were simpler to construct. Builders could adapt their lifetime of experience, techniques, and imagination to steamboat hulls, but the manufacture of the necessary machinery required quite different skills. Even installation often required mechanics from out of state. Early steamboats in the Albemarle Sound area drew too much water to operate year around. It would be years before advances in engineering made practicable the construction of small, shallow-draft steamboats capable of operating efficiently in North Carolina's ever shoaling waters. Moreover, most early steamboats were financial failures. State builders found it more convenient and profitable to construct schooners, brigs, and an occasional sloop.[68]

Fayetteville, the seat of Cumberland County and a commercial center of some importance, became a center of steamboat construction. Goods flowed into the river town from the Piedmont counties and from there were transshipped to Wilmington. Before steamboats, cargos were shipped by flats, rafts, and an occasional sailing vessel. Between 1816 and 1860, sixteen vessels, nearly all steamers, not counting flats and other small craft, were launched there.[69] Initially, Fayetteville was bypassed by railroads and depended on plank roads and the river for the transportation of goods and people. The completion of the Wilmington and Weldon Railroad provided an additional incentive for Fayetteville merchants to expand steamboat transportation. The Panic of 1857 precipitated the sale of navigation companies and steamboats on the Cape Fear River and elsewhere in the state.[70] The Panic and subsequent recession adversely affected the state's economy. Nevertheless, transport of people and goods by steam and sail continued unabated in North Carolina.[71]

It is difficult to determine the exact number of steamboats built in North Carolina during this period. Unless engaged in coastal or foreign trade, they were not usually documented at the customs office. However, of the sixteen vessels constructed in Fayetteville, twelve were enrolled with customs officials. Of fourteen built in Wilmington during the same period, only seven were enrolled. Five were constructed in New Bern and Craven County and four were documented. At least six were built in Washington but only one, the *Edmund McNair*, was enrolled.[72] Elizabeth City, Plymouth, Smithville, and a location on the New River in Onslow County each produced one steamboat; all were documented. Many of the documented vessels, especially from locations other than the Cape Fear River region, were purchased by interests outside of the customhouse district where they were originally recorded and had to re-enroll at new locations. The *Walter Raleigh* was built for a Norfolk concern but was burned in Georgetown, South Carolina, in 1835. The *Edmund McNair* also ended up in South Carolina.[73] In 1829, the *North Carolina* was sold to a firm that put her in service on the Altamaha River in Georgia. The *David St. John*, built at New River in 1836, was sold to a Savannah firm and abandoned there in 1844. The *Duncan McRae*, built in Wilmington, exploded at Johnson Landing in Georgia in 1841.[74] Steamboats were under construction in Wilmington, New Bern, and Plymouth at the start of the Civil War.

Although the majority of North Carolina-built steamboats were freight and passenger vessels, others were used as excursion craft, engaged in salvage business, and even served as a floating shingle mill.[75] Configuration, architecture, and machinery developed throughout the period. Design varied according to location and function. Those constructed in Washington were different from those built in Wilmington. The Corps of Engineers built steamers for river improvement projects. Small steamboats were constructed to tow flatboats with cargos of fish from Albemarle Sound to Norfolk. Cape Fear steamers were built to transport sailors to and from sea as well as tow flats upstream.[76] They differed considerably from northeastern boats and western river boats.

American steamboats are usually divided into two distinct types quite different from each other in design, construction, and machinery. The northeastern steamers, particularly those developed on the Hudson River and Long Island Sound, were distinguished by low pressure engines, fine lines, appearance, and speed. They were primarily passenger boats and carried little freight except baggage and express goods.[77] Western river steamboats, those found on the Mississippi, Missouri, and Ohio Rivers, shipped cargo such as cotton. The majority of North Carolina-built steamboats placed a premium on freight capacity but were designed to carry passengers as well. Nearly all North Carolina steamboats were designed to tow flats, barges, sailing vessels, and other small craft. Some of the tow boats were nearly as long as the towing steamer.[78] North Carolina newspapers usually described all types of steam vessels simply as steamboats; terms such as towboat, mail boat, ferry boat, relay ferry, flat boat, excursion boat, light boat, work boat, and dredge boat were added subsequently for clarification.

Unfortunately, there are no known contemporary drawings or paintings of antebellum North Carolina-built steamboats, with the exception of generic depictions of steamboats for sale in newspapers. In the northeast and the west, different structural methods were used to compensate for the long, light hulls of steamboats. In the east, longitudinal trusses known as "hogframes" were used, while in the west, builders attached "hog chains" or iron rods that connected bow to stern. North Carolina-built steamboats were light and, at times, long, but there is no evidence that either method was used by state shipbuilders.[79] The remains of a steam-powered vessel in the Pamlico River has large, wooden, longitudinal stiffeners.[80] In contrast to "hog frames" and "hog chains," stiffeners are located inside the hull and were used as an early method of preventing hogging and sagging on steamboats. No description of a North Carolina-built steamboat examined has mentioned or described external trusses. There is only one known reference to the prevention of hogging in a North Carolina-built steamboat. On August 2, 1861, while developing plans for a new vessel, Angelo Garibaldi wrote his employer, James Cathcart Johnston, recognizing the need for a "strong keelson etc. so as to make sufficient strength to keep her from hogging," but stated, "the strength to keep her from hogging will be iron braces which will run from one end of the boat to the other."[81]

Vessel descriptions often appeared in newspapers, especially on the occasion of a launching, and they usually provided some information regarding size and design. The *Henrietta* was described as plain and practical, even "ugly," nothing like the ornate steamboats that plied the eastern and western rivers: "She had no upper deck at first ... her cabin was set down in her hold" and she drew six to seven feet of water.[82] With her draft, a length of 152 feet, and a twenty-foot beam, she obviously resembled the narrow steamboats built in the northeast. If the cabin were in her hold, like eastern boats, her boilers, furnaces, and engine were also in the hold. The drawing of the *Prometheus* (Figure 2), though not contemporary, suggests one possible configuration for the *Henrietta*. However, none of the early steamboats, from 1807 through the late 1820s, had that much superstructure.[83] Even the early western river boats had deep hulls with keels and little superstructure.[84] It is also doubtful early steamboats were completely flat bottomed. Hulls were probably slightly rounded and, like their eastern counterparts, were long, narrow, and had a deep hold of six or more feet.

The North Carolina-built steamboat developed into a very different vessel from these early boats. Considerable attention was focused on the problem of draft. Documented North Carolina steamboats in the antebellum period had an average draft of 4.85 feet. Newspaper articles often cited new boats of "very light draught." Articles from the 1820s describe a newly built steamboat that drew so little water it could be used year round.[85] Launched in 1850, the *Union* was "of very light draught and ... intended for use on the Cape Fear above Wilmington."[86] On September 22, 1860, the Tarboro *Southerner* referred to a steam flat boat being built in Pitt County.[87] Sloan considered the "'steam flat' to be a distinct type of ... barge like construction to ply the upper rivers." Steam flats were usually without superstructure and were designed to carry only cargo.[88]

The draft of the boats built in the 1820s and 1830s was usually measured in feet; those built in the late 1840s and 1850s had drafts usually measured in inches, indicating a move toward shallower drafts. Sometimes the draft is not given and only the depth of hold is mentioned. At times, the stated draft of a vessel, typically printed before the machinery was installed and before the vessel was loaded with cargo and passengers, could be misleading. Some of the very light draft steamboats included: the *Charles Henry*, in 1854, with eighteen inches; the *Southerner*, in 1852, at twelve inches; the *Sun*, in 1853, with thirteen inches; the *John Dawson* with sixteen inches; the *Chatham*, in 1850, at twelve inches; and the *New Wayne*, in 1848, with fifteen inches. Designers and builders wrestled with the engineering problem of length and width of the hull versus draft. The *Raleigh Register* reported that the newly constructed steamer *Utility* "is built upon a new principle of Captain Patrick's own design and is very light draft of water."[89]

Builders often experimented in their design and construction techniques. Two steamboats built in Fayetteville in 1851 had no frames, and strakes were joined with iron fasteners that were driven edgewise through the planks; "[t]his made them much lighter."[90] The ultimate solution was formulated by western steamboat designers:

Figure 4–2 The *Prometheus*, one of the first steamboats to ply coastal North Carolina waters. The precise design and look of the steamboat is unknown but this rendition is believed to be a very close approximation. The sketch is by Roger Kammerer, with his permission.

a flat bottom hull with virtually no hold and everything carried above the deck, including machinery, cargo, and passengers. The superstructure and, eventually, additional decks were added. In 1835, the *Edmund McNair*, with one deck, was launched in Washington. The *Wayne II*, built in New Bern, "differs in several particulars from the other boats on the [Neuse] river, one very important one is, that her cabin and all her machinery are on deck."[91] A steamboat still on the stocks near Clarendon Bridge in Cumberland County was to have "a cabin 80 feet long on deck." The *Chatham*, built in New Bern for the Cape Fear River trade, was designed as a passenger vessel; 250 persons could be seated on the promenade deck, and her cabin was neatly fitted with a stained-glass skylight. The *Chatham* had berths for twenty-four passengers and accommodations for thirty. The helmsmen, and presumably the pilot, were housed on the promenade deck as well.[92] The *Union*, a small boat of only fifty tons burthen built in Wilmington, was described as having a "large superstructure." In 1859, a large steamboat, probably the *Kate McLaurin*, was "built after the modern style of passenger boats . . . with the cabin or salon on the upper deck where they are kept cool and airy, and ample room for the storage of freight on the main deck. . . . Her boilers are situated well forward and at a considerable distance from the salon, adding much thereby to the safety, comfort and convenience of the passengers." She had two cabins and a "saloon, also used as a dining room or promenade deck. Length of ladies' cabin 16 feet; gentlemens' cabin 19 feet . . . with a passage of 3 feet between saloon and cabin."[93] Boat architecture varied according to function and, particularly, operating area. The Cape Fear River from Wilmington to Smithville was a relatively wide and deep estuary. Above Wilmington, it became increasingly a more shallow, narrow, and winding stream; above Fayetteville, it was even more so. Other North Carolina rivers were similar. None of them were close to being as wide as the Mississippi, Missouri, Ohio, or most of the eastern rivers, and the width of canals and locks imposed further restrictions. Consequently, North Carolina hulls had a narrow beam.

Conventional rounded hulls developed into box-like structures with flat bottoms. Two light draft steamers launched in Fayetteville in 1851 were "about 115 feet long and fifteen feet wide, and flat bottomed."[94] Some of the early side wheelers had rounded sterns (tucks). A few carried one or two masts, but there is no evidence that sails were used.

Most of the passenger/freight steamers built and operating on North Carolina inland waters were between 100 and 130 feet in overall length. The *Fayetteville*, constructed in the port of that name, was the largest at 264 tons; the *Enterprise*, of forty-four tons, was probably the smallest. During the antebellum period, width averaged between fifteen and twenty-five feet, depth in hold from three to nine feet, and draft from a foot to two feet when light. The *Samuel Beery* drew approximately six feet and was built to carry freight and passengers from Wilmington to Smithville on the relatively deep water of the lower Cape Fear River. However, draft was rarely mentioned in accounts of the early steamboats.

North Carolina steamboats had to operate on narrow, shallow, meandering rivers. Sternwheelers were practical for narrow rivers but sidewheelers were more maneuverable. There were considerably more sidewheelers built in North Carolina than sternwheelers. The *Wayne II*, completed in New Bern in 1848, had rudders on both the stern and the bow.[95] The sternwheeler *Chatham* had three rudders extending forward as well as aft of the sternpost, a characteristic of the western river sternwheelers. By the 1850s, Cape Fear-area builders were incorporating three rudders on most of the new steamers. The *Tarboro Press* described sternwheelers as "Marine Wheel-Barrows . . . going wrong end foremost."[96] Approximately a third of North Carolina steamboats were sternwheelers; sidewheelers made up the majority. However, sidewheelers had the disadvantage of being rather wide amidships with huge wheels often protruding above the hurricane deck.[97] Despite obvious similarities between later North Carolina steamers and those used on the western rivers, only one North Carolina-built boat was advertised as being of the "western style." The *Governor Graham*, built for use on the Neuse and Tar Rivers in 1847, had sides of wood two and a half inches thick with the interior ribs of the hull placed only a foot apart. The *Graham* was 125 feet long and 37 feet wide. She was probably a sternwheeler.[98] With a thirty-seven-foot beam, the *Graham* would have had a most difficult time on the narrow, crooked Tar and Neuse Rivers.

Two screw-powered steamers were constructed in North Carolina before the Civil War. The *Fox*, a small thirteen-ton vessel, was built in 1861 in Elizabeth City for the Dismal Swamp Canal route. As with all vessels that used the canal, she had a narrow beam of 9.8 feet. The *Fox* survived the Civil War and, until 1876, carried passengers and freight from Elizabeth City to Norfolk.[99] The *Chowan*, later renamed the *Southern Star*, was built in Murfreesboro and launched in 1857.

Difficulties in the design of a North Carolina-built steamboat can best be illustrated by a series of letters written between Angelo Garibaldi and James Cathcart Johnston.[100] In 1849, Angelo Garibaldi, or Garibaldo as he called himself, became a sort of shipping agent for planter Johnston. He was instrumental in negotiating the contract and supervising the building of Johnston's first steamboat, *Caledonia*, named after his plantation, but not completed for some time. The *Caladonia* was towed to Wilmington, Delaware. When the vessel was finished by Pusey and Jones it was a screw-propelled steamer and launched in 1854.[101] Garibaldi was not only the planter's agent in this transaction but held a fourth interest in the vessel. The *Caledonia* was never satisfactory to Johnston because her draft was too deep to ascend the river to his plantation.102 She was sold in 1861.

Subsequently, Johnston commissioned Garibaldi to supervise the construction, including the planning and design phase, of a steamboat in Plymouth. In 1861, Garibaldi wrote Johnston regarding the retainment of Jesse Herrington as the shipwright:

> Mr. Herrington says that he will build you a boat and do all the joiner's work complete (say cabin, steering house, cooking house, upper deck, etc.), but would not furnish any of the iron for braces that she would require to strengthen her. He says that he will build the boat out of the very best of wood that he can get—say a good white oak frame and a portion of her bottom of good white oak and the balance of good pine . . . at forty dollars ($40) per ton carpenter's measure, complete. . . . I herewith enclose you a rough drawing of the plan of the boat—deck, hold, and side view as to give you some idea of how she will look when built.
>
> Judging from your letter that you would want her to carry a considerable load of corn and cotton, I have concluded that it would be best, if agreeable with you, to building 110' keel, 24' beam, and 4' hold. Her length and width will be an advantage in her draft of water, as your object is to have her draw as little as possible, and Mr. Herrington thinks that she will not draw over 20" when light. According to the above dimensions she would be about 110 or 112 tons, and if you think that the above will be a longer boat than you would wish, she can be made smaller on the same plan as you may prefer. [In that] kind of boat I see they generally have the engine aft and the boiler in the forward part of the boat. That plan, I think will make them draw less water. . . .[It] would probably consume more fuel, [while] the objection to having the boiler aft [is that it will] make her draw a little more water. But this can be arranged at any time. . . . If this is satisfactory with you I will close it with him as soon as I get your answer, and have a proper contract drawn up and send [it] to you for your signature . . .
>
> As soon as I hear from you I will go directly to Washington and take Mr. Herrington along with me, and probably go as far as Wilmington as they have some of that class of vessels there . . . When I get all straight with Mr. Herrington I will go on to Petersburg and Richmond to see about the engines. I think that 2 engines will be preferable to one.

Garibaldi also mentioned that the steamboat would be a sternwheeler. Resulting correspondence addressed additional issues regarding the steamboat's design:

> [Y]ou think her bow rather too full, which of course can be made sharper, but the sharper the bow, the more water she would draw, and unless she is partly full she will draw too much water. . . . As to her full bow will not injure her running, the running of the boat depends entirely on the formation of her stem. I also notice that you think she will be too long, but judge from your letter of the 13th that you wish her to carry a good load, and that the dimensions sent you would be about what you wanted—but you can have her 100' long and about 19' beam. You will see that she will be very shallow in the hold. I do not think that 110' would be too long for the Roanoke. As to having her bottom plank of cypress, I do not think that would answer as well as oak and pine, for the reason that cypress is so very soft that she would be too easily snagged in case she should strike a log or anything on the Roanoke. Besides, it's so soft that being constantly underwater, [cypress] would absorb so much water that it would be heavier than oak and pine, but . . . the deck, and the upper deck, and all the joiner's work, of course, would be of cypress.

Garibaldi and Herrington did make a trip to Washington and Wilmington to examine steamboats that they considered similar to the one they planned to build.

> We saw several boats at Wilmington of the class that you wish, but saw only one that suited my notions, and she was about 100' long, 15' beam, and some 4 1/2' hold, and drawed [sic}a very light draft, they said about 16" when light, but would not carry over 200 or 300 barrels very deep loaded. I have requested Mr. Herrington to make the model that we could get by making this alteration, say 100' keel, 23' beam, and 4 1/2' hold. The extra width will, I think, make her draw less water besides the advantage in her carrying. But when deep loaded will draw from 4 to 4 1/2 feet. Her loading would have to be governed by the water over the bar. I should think when light that she would be able to navigate the river at nearly all the seasons of the year.

> ... I think a boat of these dimensions well calculated to turn the bends well on the river as I find the boats on the Cape Fear River are considerably longer and the same proportion than the one I propose to build for you will be—say some five of six feet wider, which will be an advantage to her turning. She will have 3 rudders, the same they have."[103]

On August 12, Garibaldi sent a contract to Johnston. In the enclosed letter, he mentioned he was going to Petersburg, Richmond, "and probably Charleston" to negotiate for engines.

> I have not made up my mind fully what size to have them. I think they had better be of sufficient power to force her through the water—say from 13" to 14" cylinder and about 4' stroke, and a locomotive boiler of sufficient size for the 2 cylinders.... I understand all kinds of mechanics in Richmond are busily engaged. I may have some difficulty in getting the engine in Petersburg or Richmond. I understand that they build them in Charleston and probably Georgia, but I am afraid in the latter place that the expense of getting them there would be too expensive." In a letter sent a week later, he discouraged Johnston's enquiry about obtaining a secondhand engine and decided a single engine was sufficient. He may have determined either that two engines would be too costly or, perhaps, due to the war, that he would be fortunate to get even one.[104]

Surprisingly, Garibaldi's letters concerning the steamboat do not mention the secession crisis or the resulting war. He obviously had little or no idea of the difficulties they would face in constructing the vessel given current military and naval operations and logistical needs. In September, he traveled to Virginia searching for suitable engines. He first went to Norfolk and from there to Petersburg and then to Richmond. On September 14 he wrote Johnston:

> I stopped on my way at Petersburg, and I could not do anything there in the way of getting machinery, all the machine shops being busily employed in work for government, making cannon shells and all sorts of other machinery, and about the same thing in Richmond. I can get an engine there by waiting some three months for the completion of it at a very high price—say an engine with 2 cylinders, 3' stroke, and 4" diameter, between $7,500 and $8,000, delivered at Richmond, and that is provided they can get the iron for the boiler (which seems to be very doubtful). I, therefore, in consequence of the difficulties on our coast and the very high prices, and being anxious to get home, I thought I would prefer waiting in contracting for an engine until I heard from you.... Messrs Talbert & Co., of Richmond, have promised to make me out an estimate of an engine, and that they would let me know the very best that they could do in a few days, and whether or not they could get the boiler iron to make the boiler. They say that the tubes to make locomotive boilers with are not to be had.
>
> Therefore, if they can make a boiler it will have to be a flue boiler.... If there were any chance of getting one from England [one] might get [an engine] there for half the money that one can be made at Richmond at this time.

He also mentioned that no secondhand engines were available. In early October, Garibaldi learned that Dibble and Brothers of New Bern had a secondhand engine for sale and wrote them about it. It is not known if the Dibbles replied as the matter is not mentioned again in correspondence. Considering the problems in getting machinery, Garibaldi was undoubtedly somewhat relieved when Johnston wrote him that he was not in a "hurry about building the boat" and that he had given up buying the engines at that time because of the high prices.[105]

Herrington, however, was already building the vessel. Garibaldi informed Johnston on September 4 that the shipbuilder planned to lay the keel, stern, and stem posts the following day, "making the first payment ($500.00) due." Shortly after work commenced, his carpenters were requisitioned to go to Edenton and work on the two steamers, formerly belonging to the state, but taken over by the Confederate Navy for conversion to gunboats; "Mr. Herrington had to let all his hands go." They were back at work in Plymouth nine days later. On the 27th, Johnston was informed that the vessel should be completely framed in about two weeks. Three weeks later Garibaldi wrote that "Mr. Herrington is going on with her very well. He has her all in frame and 2 strakes of bends run, and by seeing her now you can about judge how she will look." After that, however, work slowed down and eventually halted altogether. His final letter concerning the steamboat was dated January 20, 1862. "Owing to the rainy and bad weather Mr. Herrington has not done much to the boat since the 24th of December. He has had a few hands on her only commencing today week."[106] Whether work continued on the vessel after that date is unknown. With the approach of Union forces, Garibaldi fled Plymouth to Caledonia, Johnston's plantation, and remained there for the duration of the war. Presumably, Herrington and his workers fled as well. The vessel, still on the stocks, was probably destroyed by Union naval forces occupying the town in May, but this is not clear.[107] In a court suit after the war, Garibaldi stated that the vessel was destroyed "by some agency, to the plaintiff unknown, but not by his default." Johnston died in 1865 and, according to Garibaldi in a later court case, owed him $4,046.81 for his work on the steamboat. Garibaldi's case eventually reached the State Supreme Court but was not decided in his favor.[108] What he did after the war until his death is unknown.

Steam Engines for Water Navigation

The *Henrietta* began blowing its steam whistle on the Cape Fear River in 1818, quite a while since Hero had experimented with steam in Greece around 130 BC. The transfer of heat energy to mechanical energy was found to be dangerous and difficult, which was learned early on with many explosions. In order to make steam, all that is needed is a fire box and a boiler with water, but to harvest that energy to do work is another problem. That problem was partially solved by Thomas Savery and Thomas Newcomen in England in the late 1600s. But, these "steam engines" required manual labor to turn valves for the steam to produce mechanical energy. At the same time in France, Denis Papin developed a cylinder and piston pump.

The early steam engine, with its fire box, boiler, and cylinder with a piston, is basic for the transfer of energy from heat to mechanical energy. It was not until the late 1700s that stationary steam engines were placed in boats or on rails to add motion. For about a hundred years, dangerous and difficult experiments ensued involving many inventors. But it was not until 1763 that James Watt improved the steam engine with pressure valves which operated from cranks attached to the piston arm in the cylinder. This stationary steam engine proved to be very successful, and one of its first uses was to pump water out of coal mines in England. Nevertheless, it was not long before Marquis de Jouffroy operated a paddlewheel steamboat on the Saone River in France, and William Symington was steamboating on the River Clyde in Scotland. Meanwhile in America, John Finch had fashioned a steamboat and started a steamboat line on the Delaware and Schuykill Rivers. All these successes ensued before Robert Fulton fashioned a paddlewheel steamboat using a Watt and Bolton engine from England in 1807.

With the beckoning expansive, shallow waters of North Carolina, the steamboat came south. Information about steamboat power plants is extremely scarce and incomplete. Newspaper articles rarely mention steam machinery, although it is well known that no locales in the state had manufactured machinery of any kind. The one known contract for a steamboat refers only to required horsepower.[109] The steamboat built by Jesse Herrington and Angelo Garibaldi in Plymouth was designed to have two engines, 13" to 14" cylinders and about 4' stroke, and a locomotive boiler of sufficient size for the two cylinders.[110] Boilers were occasionally mentioned in some sources, but usually there are no detailed descriptions or number.

The streams and sounds of North Carolina are usually turbid with high amounts of suspended sediments, commonly known as "mud." There was a tendency for boilers to explode due to the accumulation of "mud" in the valves; also, the pressure gauge to warn of excessive pressure was not invented until 1850.[111] Scaling was also a clogging problem, as the iron used had a tendency to exfoliate.

Experimentation was the order of the day, as low- and high-pressure boilers were being used. The early low-pressure engines, which were preferred, were usually the condensing type, designed to recover exhaust steam. The steamer *Caldwell*, built in Beaufort in 1858, had a low-pressure engine of thirty-five horsepower.[112] As time went on, however, the high pressure non-condensing type became more popular, particularly on the western rivers. The high-pressure engine usually weighed less and operated better in muddy waters. These steam engines would have been better for the North Carolina waters, but there is no evidence that any were used.

The experimentation continued with all sorts of adaptations in the engine room, including the use of two engines instead of one. With two engines, sidewheel steamers could make very short, quick turns, which was important for river navigation. There were various schemes such as the walking beam, the side lever, the crosshead, and the half beam.[113] Vertical engines were poorly adapted for sternwheelers and propeller-driven vessels and had to be connected by a series of levers. The *Rowan* and the *Cotton Plant*, built in the 1820s, had walking beam engines. The *Chowan (Southern Star)* was the exception (Figure 3),[114] where her two inclined engines and cylinders was placed athwart ship and screw propeller.[115] Neither Elizabeth City nor any other shipbuilding community possessed the facilities to fabricate steamboat power plants.

What we do know is that steamboat builders had to go elsewhere to find their power plants. For example, Pusey and Jones of Wilmington, Delaware, was contracted to provide engines, boilers, propellers, and other metal parts. The firm also provided the machinery for the *James Petteway*, built in Wilmington, and the *Chowan*, constructed at Murfreesboro. It is interesting that the *Fayetteville*, launched in 1842, had six boilers. Even so, most steamboats in North Carolina were underpowered, ranging between twenty and 130 horsepower.[116] And, again, machinery for steamboats in North Carolina was so scarce, that some entrepreneurs were known to have adapted locomotive engines for use in steamboats.

The Railroads

Compared to the Grand Trunk region in the northeastern United States, southern railroads, particularly those in the coastal area, were few. The need was not as great along the south Atlantic coast as compared to the mid-Atlantic or northeast. Consequently, compared to roads, fewer railroads were built in coastal North Carolina.[117]

The lack of railroads in the state led to the introduction of ferries to carry cargo, passengers, and even a train or two, across rivers from port to port. In 1853, James Cassidey's shipyard in Wilmington contracted with the Wilmington and Manchester Railroad to build a

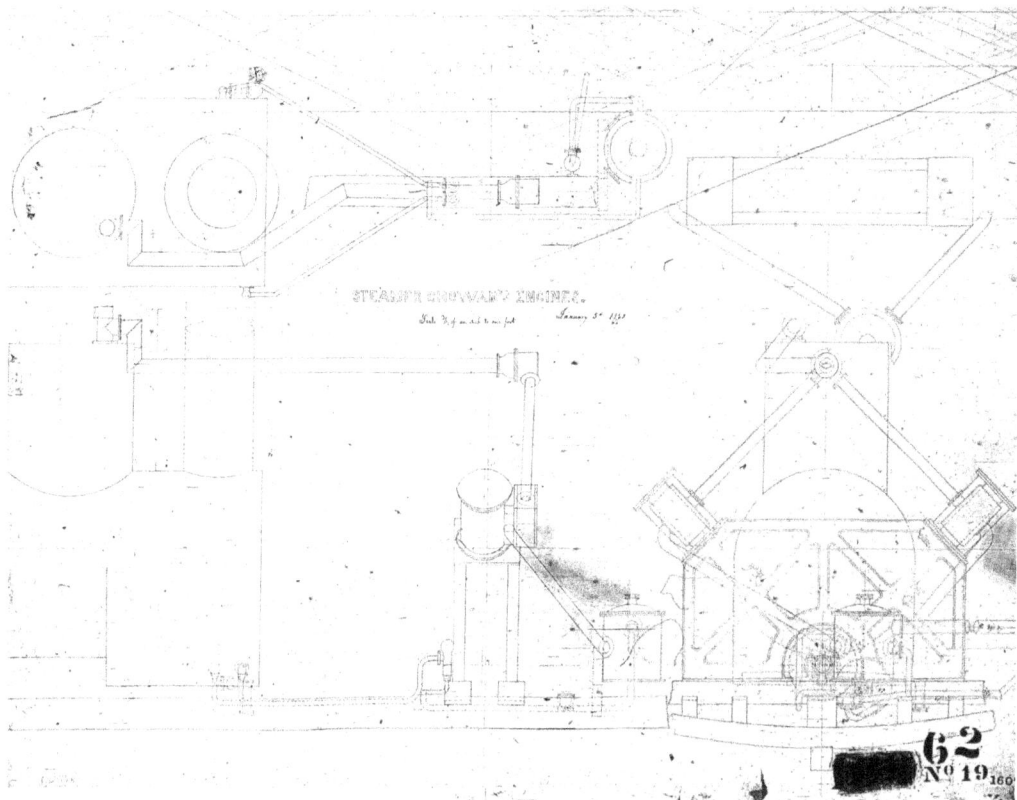

Figure 4-3 The engine of the *Chowan*, originally named the *Southern Star*, built in 1856. Later, it became the U.S.S. *Crusader*. This is the only known drawing of a marine steam engine in a North Carolina-built vessel during the antebellum period. *Source:* Pusey & Jones Drawings on Microfilm at the Hagley Museum, Wilmington, Delaware; with permission.

ferry to carry passengers across the Cape Fear River to the company's terminal. The vessel was a double ender with a rudder on both bow and stern. "One acts as a cutwater, while the other steers the Boat." Newspaper articles reported she was built "after the model of the Ferry Boats at the North."[118] The ferry *Clarendon*, completed in Wilmington in 1860, incorporated railroad tracks, centered on the main deck, to enable the train to be conveyed across the river.[119]

Generally, with respect to railroads, the south was a decade behind the north, although their introduction came about the same time. In 1828, the Baltimore and Ohio Railroad linked the port of Baltimore with the port of Wheeling on the Ohio River. Subsequently, the South Carolina Railroad connected Charleston and Memphis on the Mississippi River. In each case, the first stretch of track was not completed inland until 1830.[120]

In eastern North Carolina, and other parts of the eastern seaboard, railroading was controlled by the RF&P (Richmond, Fredricksburg, and Potomac) between Washington and Richmond, as all north- and south-oriented train traffic had to use that line. South of Richmond, the Atlantic Coast Line eventually dominated southern rail movement. By 1843, the only railroads in eastern North Carolina were the Portsmouth and Roanoke Railroad between Portsmouth and Weldon, the Wilmington and Weldon Railroad, and a line between Raleigh and Hicksford on the Meherrin River in Virginia. Except for Wilmington, the ports of eastern North Carolina were without rail service.

Dredges

Steam-powered dredge boats were widely used in North Carolina by the Army Corps of Engineers, the state, and private firms. There is little information on the origin of dredge boats. Before the Army Corps of Engineers was given the responsibility of maintaining navigable waters, the state and private companies attempted to clear streams and harbors using a variety of methods. The advent of the steam engine led to the development of the steam-driven dredge boat. The state's attempt to build a dredge in the early 1820s was a failure.[121] The first successful North Carolina-built dredge boat was constructed by Cassidey in 1826 with machinery from New York.[122] In 1828, the Corps of Engineers advertised for bids to build a dredge for Beaufort harbor. The proposed vessel was to be sixty feet long at the keel and twenty feet at the beam, with "such rakes as will best adapt her to float lightly on the water, and ride and roll easily in a sea."[123] Three years later, Congress appropriated funds to construct dredge boats for the mouth of the Cape Fear River and Ocracoke Inlet.[124] Private companies also had dredge boats built. In 1852, Cassidey built a bucket dredge named the *Elephant* to clear the Cape Fear River of sand and mud bars all the way to Fayetteville. The following year, the Neuse River Navigation Company Board of Directors voted to build a dredge boat and flats. They agreed to build the vessels in New Bern as it would save money.[125]

Launchings

More than a simple event, the launching of a vessel was often a festive occasion in North Carolina. Except for masts, spars, rigging, and furnishings, wooden sailing vessels typically were complete at launching. Steamboats were usually launched without superstructure until machinery was installed. Ships were generally launched fore and aft, but in 1846, at his shipyard in Elizabeth City, Timothy Hunter constructed a marine railway that employed sideway launching. There is no evidence that similar launching ways were installed elsewhere in the state.[126] Steamboat launchings were especially popular, particularly if they were the first in a region. The *Henrietta* was launched in 1818 in Fayetteville with hundreds lining the banks to witness the event, and an open house was held onboard the new vessel with refreshments provided.[127] The launching of the *Chowan* (*Southern Star*) in Murfreesboro in April 1857 was considered such a big event that the student bodies of local Chowan and Wesleyan colleges were dismissed to attend the launching.[128]

The initial appearance of a steamboat in a river town was also an exciting event, much like court week and holidays, and quite often attracted farmers, peddlers, politicians, and families from miles around. Spectators usually brought everything they needed for the gala occasion, including a picnic. When the *E. D. McNair*, the first steamboat to ply the Tar River, reached Tarboro on her maiden run, the local paper noted that as the vessel "anchored in our harbor amidst the roaring of cannon and other testimonials of joy with which our citizens who thronged in crowds to the river, greeting this novel and welcome visitor. On Thursday evening the public spirited and enterprising proprietors gave a general invitation to the citizens to take a short excursion in the steamer. A large number of ladies and gentlemen were hospitably received on board, and the steamer went down the river. . . . [M]usic, dancing, and refreshments gave a zest . . . to the occasion."[129] The steamboat *Fayetteville* was launched in 1842. "As she touched the water, her name was pronounced with the customary honors . . . and a streamer thrown to the wind, told the crowd on shore" her name."[130]

Occasionally, launchings did not go as planned. In an 1895 newspaper column, James G. Burr mentioned a ship launched in Wilmington that abruptly went aground. The British consul was on board, fell overboard, and much to the amusement of the assembled crowd, was hauled out of the water without his wig. A poem about his misfortune was published in the local papers.[131] The *Ellen Belle* was to be launched from the Paine shipyard in Edenton on July 4, 1853. The local militia, a drummer, and fifer attended but the vessel was not launched until October. As she slipped down the ways, she stuck fast. When workers finally freed the vessel, they forgot to cast off from the wharf, which went into the water with her.[132] Constructed at Murfreesboro, the *Chowan* (*Southern Star*), at 545 tons, was evidently too large for her launching ways. On April 17, 1857, she broke through to lie partially on the river bank until "shoved" into the river.[133] It was described as a miserable day, cold with even a few snowflakes the day before. "Notwithstanding this, men, women and children came flooding into the borough on every road, in almost every kind of conveyance." An estimated four thousand people witnessed the launching.[134] The steamboat *Wayne* took a group of passengers on an "excursion" from New Bern down to Bay River to witness the launch of a vessel at the Nichols shipyard.[135] In New Bern, a ship was launched with a bottle of "pure cold water," not with the usual christening bottle of champagne. "Three cheers were given for the Sons of Temperance. Success to the Cold Water Vessel."[136]

The Business of Steamboating

Steamboats usually required more initial capital investment than one individual could assume. The majority of steamboats in North Carolina waters were owned in partnerships or by joint stock companies. Early ventures by outside interests, often a steamboat captain and presumably the owner, generally failed.[137] Setting a precedent in 1822, James Seawell of Fayetteville and his associates created the Cape Fear Steam Boat Company to operate the *Henrietta*, the first steamboat built on the Cape Fear River, and other vessels to transport their products between Fayetteville and Wilmington. The end of Seawell's monopoly in 1825 opened the door for others eager to enter the business. Between 1825 and 1860, eleven steamboat companies were chartered by the General Assembly to ply their trade on the Cape Fear River.[138] Steamers were built and purchased from a variety of places in and out of state but the majority were built in Fayetteville and Wilmington. Similar consortiums financed the building of steamboats on the Neuse, Tar, and Pamlico Rivers, and the Albemarle Sound. William Tannahill and Benjamin A. Lavender, chandlers and commission merchants in Washington, received a fifteen-year monopoly from the legislature to operate steamboats on the Tar and Pamlico Rivers. In 1835, they launched the *Edmund D. McNair*, the first steam vessel to navigate those rivers. In 1860, a joint stock company was formed in Greenville to build a steam flat.¹³⁹ Launched in Beaufort in 1856, the sternwheeler *Wilson* had owners from Plymouth and New Bern.¹⁴⁰ Builders often purchased one of more shares in their own steamboats.¹⁴¹

The Cape Fear and Deep River Navigation Company was chartered in 1849 to improve the Cape Fear River above Fayetteville and the Deep River as far north as Sampson County. The company contracted with Nathan King and Elias Bryan in 1853 to build a steamboat, the *John Haughton*, and up to six tow boats, each one hundred feet in length, to carry construction materials, workmen, and supplies for the construction of locks and the implementation of other river improvements in Chatham County. The contract price included shares in the company.¹⁴² In 1855, King refused to accept a contract to build a second steamboat for the company. The company used its own employees to construct several towboats, but not a steamer. In 1859, the company did contract for a second steamboat, which was completed in 1860.¹⁴³ The Cape Fear Steamboat Company built two iron steamers in Wilmington, Delaware, for service on the Cape Fear.¹⁴⁴

In 1855, the joint stock North Carolina and New York Steamboat Company was formed in Hertford County and received a charter from the state. The company built one steamship, the *Chowan* (*Southern Star*), and voted to add additional vessels as needed. Unfortunately, the company failed and the steamer was sold at public auction.¹⁴⁵ In 1858, a group of Hyde and Craven County businessmen formed the Hyde County Steamboat Joint Stock Company. They purchased the small open deck steam-powered flat *Post Boy* to carry cargo between Hyde County landings and New Bern.¹⁴⁶

Dibble and Brothers, a prominent mercantile company with offices in New Bern and Kinston, owned a line of steamers on the Neuse River.¹⁴⁷ Initially shipping cotton and naval stores to New York and importing a variety of goods, the firm purchased a brick building which became a retail store and a warehouse on the Trent River. Later, a warehouse was leased in Goldsboro.¹⁴⁸ Calvin Dibble eventually moved to New York City and opened an office for their firm sometime in the 1850s.

In 1843, Dibble and Brothers purchased the *Wayne*, built in their home state of Connecticut, to run on the Neuse between New Bern and Waynesboro, near present-day Goldsboro. Later, the company added additional steamboats on the Neuse River, including several built within the state. The company also placed the New Bern-built *Chatham* on the Cape Fear and Deep River run; the *Wayne II* and the *Johnston* on the Neuse River; and the *Governor Graham* on the Tar and Pamlico Rivers. In 1851, the General Assembly approved a charter that incorporated the Dibble Steamboat Company.¹⁴⁹

Only five steamers were built in Murfreesboro and Hertford County, but these included the *Chowan* (*Southern Star*), one of the largest vessels constructed in the state during the nineteenth century. In 1855, a group of businessmen and planters, principally from the Albemarle Sound area, met in Murfreesboro to consider what could be done to revitalize oceanic trade and regain "the ancient commercial spirit once so noticeable among the sons of Hertford."¹⁵⁰ The participants formed an association, concluding that "the introduction of steam propelling suited to navigation similar to ours" could help alleviate their problem. They agreed to create a joint stock company, seek a charter of incorporation from the state, and build a steamship which "can be successfully and profitably maintained between this place and New York, embracing . . . when sufficient freight to justify—the intermediate landings and towns below this place including Edenton and Plymouth, N.C."¹⁵¹ The association met a second time in February 1856 and adopted the name The North Carolina and New York Steamboat Company. With more than $25,000 pledged, including a sizeable amount from the New York firm of Glines and Graham, they directed Jesse Jackson to superintend the construction of a steamer and authorized him to begin initial preparations: selecting the shipyard site, hiring labor, and obtaining the required lumber and other materials.¹⁵²

Jackson evidently had no experience in shipbuilding. Two days after the association's Valentine's Day meeting, Jackson was empowered to journey to Wilmington, Delaware, to contract for the vessel's plans and machinery. He was also to obtain housing for the workmen. In the following weeks, John A. Kirkman, a New York shipwright, agreed to build the vessel and drafted the vessel's plans.¹⁵³

The Panic of 1857 precipitated the collapse of Glines and Graham. The unpublished history of Pusey and Jones mentions that the vessel was still on the stocks at Murfreesboro when the company failed. Stockholders refused to invest more money. Kirkman, the ship's builder, brought suit, presumably because he did not receive what was owed to him as the builder and a stockholder. The court agreed with him, attached the vessel, and the incomplete hull was put up for auction.¹⁵⁴ In October of that year, John Southall and Thomas W. Badger purchased the hull.¹⁵⁵ The steamer changed owners and her name changed from *Chowan* to *Southern Star*.

The *Southern Star* was initially rigged as a three-masted schooner but was completed as a sailing bark with three masts and sails. She was launched in 1857 and was sailed or towed to Wilmington, Delaware, where her machinery was installed and additional ironwork, anchor, sails, and rigging added.¹⁵⁶ Badger, impatient with the Wilmington firm, took her to Norfolk where the shipyard of Thomas Nash finished the upper works and finally got her ready for sea. In September, she steamed to Petersburg, which was listed as her homeport. The *Southern Star* was the only steamship, as opposed to steamboat, built in North Carolina prior to the Civil War. She was one of only two screw steamers built in the state before 1861. The enrollment paper, as well as records from Pusey and Jones, lists her at 545 tons. She was 160 feet in length and twenty-four feet in beam. Her machinery consisted of two direct-acting inclined engines of eighty horsepower geared to a single propeller.[157]

The *Southern Star* made trips between Wilmington, North Carolina, and northern ports.[158] The original company had planned for the steamer to carry passengers as well as freight. However, her enrollment papers clearly state that she was not cleared to carry passengers. The Petersburg *Daily Express* also mentioned that her "cabin accommodations are not as yet complete."[159] In 1858, Badger leased her to the navy. In December of that year, she made an expedition to South America. A letter printed in the *Norfolk and Portsmouth Herald* stated that the ship "is buoyant, pitches very easy, rolls very deep and quick, and yet without straining herself much . . .[and]. . .withstood heavy gales en route." In 1859, she was purchased by the navy and commissioned as the *Crusader*. After a trial run, the navy's chief engineer reported, "I consider the trial highly satisfactory, and the vessel a good specimen of the auxiliary screw steamer."[160] She spent nearly two years on antislavery patrol before joining a unit of the North Atlantic Blockading Squadron during the Civil War. At times, she was stationed off the North Carolina coast. After the war, the steamer was decommissioned and sold at auction to J.P. Morgan. Later, she was taken around Cape Horn to the Pacific and there, as the *Kalorama*, engaged in shipping. She sank in 1876 south of San Buenaventura, California.[161]

Shipbuilding: Iron and Such

Practically every community in every county had certain amenities, such as post office, gristmill, store, and blacksmith shop. Local blacksmiths forged nails, spikes, and a few other metal parts and fastenings for various shipbuilding facilities.[162] There were a few machine shops in the state prior to the Civil War, one each in New Bern and Elizabeth City, but none were manufacturing large metal parts such as steamboat machinery. The state's principal manufacturers of steam engines were Silas Burns's Iron Works in Raleigh and the Snow Camp Machine Shop and Foundry in Alamance County, and they produced agricultural and sawmill parts rather than marine engines.[163] There were eight furnaces in the state in 1840, but together they produced less than a thousand tons of cast iron.[164] The 1860 census lists twenty-five iron manufacturing sites in North Carolina. Facilities were quite small, employing only 129 workers, and manufactured bar iron. There were at least three machine shops in Wilmington before the Civil War, including one of the most developed ironworks in the state established in 1840 by Samuel Polly and Levi Hart. Polly retired in 1857 and was replaced by John C. Bailey, an immigrant machinist and experienced pattern maker from Norway. The company was then known as Hart and Bailey or the Wilmington Iron and Copper Works. The firm gradually branched out into ship construction and repair and was apparently beginning to do heavy forge work on the eve of the Civil War.[165]

Hart and Bailey were also involved with a second iron works founded in the Port City. The Clarendon Iron Works was incorporated in 1854. The company opened for business the following year, advertising in local and other newspapers that they could make steam engines, boilers, castings of all kinds, and repairs.[166] However, the firm never got off the ground. It was sued for indebtedness in 1856, then reorganized under Hart, who sold it to two of the defenders in the suit. In 1857, they in turn sold it to a Mr. M. London. He could not or did not make the business a success. In 1861, a New York firm sued the company for unpaid bills. "The said corporation has been utterly insolvent," the suit said. The war interrupted their efforts to gain restitution, and they tried again in 1867.[167] There is no evidence that Clarendon did any major work in steamboat construction. Steamboat machinery was imported from outside the state, or vessels were taken to iron works for installation. The steamer *Southern Star*, built in Murfreesboro, and the *James Petteway*, constructed in Wilmington by James Cameron, were towed to Wilmington, Delaware, where Pusey and Jones fabricated and installed their engines, boilers, and other parts.

As in the past, most of the iron parts such as anchors, chain, steamboat machinery, and shafts, came from out of state.[168] North Carolina was severely handicapped by its lack of iron works. In 1838, there were only twenty-two steam engines in the state; eleven of them were in steamboats. Thirteen were built in Baltimore, six in New York, one in Philadelphia, and two are of unknown origin.[169] Two Baltimore firms, the Reeder Works and Watchman and Bratt, made most of the North Carolina-built steamboat machinery. The firms were two of the most reputable iron works on the east coast. Charles Reeder and his son and later grandsons built more than eighty engines for steamboats. Watchman and Bratt, whose works were adjacent to those of Reeder's, provided more than thirty steamers with engines and other machinery in the pre-Civil War years.[170] In the 1850s, Pusey and Jones of Wilmington, Delaware, and probably Tredegar Ironworks of Richmond, Virginia, provided machinery and other iron parts for North Carolina vessels. Pusey and Jones opened for business in 1849 and began building machinery for North Carolina shortly thereafter. Firms often sent machinists or mechanics along with the machinery to supervise installation.[171] This added considerable expense to the building of steam vessels in the state. The situation may have changed in the 1850s. A Wilmington newspaper article announcing the launching of a new steamboat said that "all the work was done in the State (except the machinery) and ere another six months we shall have no occasion to send elsewhere for [machinery]."[172] Although the Wilmington Iron Works was established in 1840, it did not have the ability to make steam machinery until 1859. As late as the 1850s, steam machinery was still being ordered from Baltimore.[173] The outbreak of the Civil War in 1861 halted most commercial ship construction in the state, including steamboats. Emphasis shifted to naval vessels, and available shipbuilding and auxiliary facilities concentrated on the war effort.

Notes

1. George Rodgers Taylor, *The Transportation Revolution, 1815-1860*. In North Carolina, rail progress was slow as compared to the states to the north. In eastern North Carolina, the location of swamps determined where rails could be laid and bridges were rather expensive.
2. Although considerable ship and boat building took place in North Carolina between the War of 1812 and the Civil War, Ben Ford, in his article "Wooden Shipbuilding in Maryland Prior to the Mid-Nineteenth Century," *American Neptune*, 62 (Winter 2002), 69-70, does not consider the construction of small craft part of the shipbuilding industry. However, since North Carolina shipwrights built all kinds of watercraft, small craft construction is included in the present study. Examination of the documents in RG41 indicates 1,013 vessels were constructed in the state during this period. Of course, records can be misleading or incomplete; vessel names change; ships and boats are rebuilt (a sloop to a schooner or a schooner to a brig); and undocumented vessels such as flats, lights, scows, bateaux, yachts, small sailing vessels, and steamboats used exclusively in intrastate activities are not included. For example, vessel documents record thirty-five steamers constructed in North Carolina before the Civil War, but thirty steamboats were built in Fayetteville alone, and only thirteen of these are included in the vessel document papers. Even the *Prometheus*, the first steamboat built in the state, is not listed in the documents. Steamboats were built from Smithville and Wilmington to Elizabeth City. An examination of newspapers and other records indicate that at least twice that many were constructed in the state during the antebellum period. According to the Raleigh *Weekly North Carolina Standard*, of March 2, 1853, North Carolina had approximately forty-five percent of the South's steamboat tonnage. On June 27, 1855, the *Daily Wilmington Herald*, reported sixteen steam vessels were in operation on the Cape Fear River alone, an observation corroborated by Hugh Thompson in "Early Steam Navigation on Albemarle Sound," unpublished manuscript, copy in the author's possession.
3. John J. B. Hutchins, *The American Maritime Industries and Public Policy, 1789-1914*, 229.
4. In 1859 the gross tonnage of all vessels built in the United States fell to one-third of the 1856 total.
5. Railroads included the Wilmington and Weldon, running north-south, and the North Carolina Railroad, running east-west.
6. A survey of Diamond Shoals in 1823 showed the original Cape Hatteras Light 1,297 yards inland from the surf. By 1974 the foundation of that same light was in the surf. On the average, that's about twenty-five feet of change or erosion per year. This signifies the dynamic environment in and around the Carolina capes and inlets.
7. Hugh Talmage Lefler and Albert Ray Newsome, *North Carolina: The History of a Southern State*, 314.
8. "Report of Legislative Committee on Internal Improvements," *Journal of the Senate and the House of Commons of the General Assembly of the State of North Carolina*, 220-221; *New Bern Spectator and Literary Journal*, May 15, 1830.
9. David S. Cecelski, *The Waterman's Song: Slavery and Freedom in Maritime North Carolina*, 141.
10. Robert Albion, *The Rise of the Port of New York, 1815-1860*, 403.
11. *Plymouth Weekly*, October 21, 1849; Alan D. Watson, "Battling 'Old Rip': Internal Improvements and the Role of State Government in Antebellum North Carolina," *NCHR*, 181.
12. Alan D. Watson, *Internal Improvements in Antebellum North Carolina*, 56.
13. Watson, *Internal Improvements in Antebellum North Carolina*, 57, 59.
14. Thomas O. Larkin, "My Itinerary: U.S. America," *California Historical Society Quarterly*, vol. 16, no. 1, part 1, 13; Watson, "Battling 'Old Rip,'" 190; Charles Clinton Weaver, *The History of Internal Improvements in North Carolina Previous to 1860*; John R. Ross, "The Cape Fear River and Internal Improvements in North Carolina," (M.A. thesis, Duke University, 1965).
15. Alan D. Watson, *A History of New Bern and Craven County*, 270-272.
16. Robert B. Outland III, "Suicidal Harvest: The Self-Destruction of North Carolina's Naval Stores Industry," *NCHR*, 316; Watson, *Internal Improvements in Antebellum North Carolina*, 18, 65, 69-71, 74.
17. Forest G. Hill, *Roads, Rails, and Waterways: The Army Engineers and Early Transportation*, 24-25, 154-155.
18. Robert B. Hartzer, *To Great and Useful Purpose: A History of the Wilmington District U.S. Army Corps of Engineers*, 20-21; Wilson Angley, "A History of Ocracoke Inlet and Adjacent Areas," Historical Research Office, North Carolina Division of Archives and History, 39; David Stick, *The Outer Banks of North Carolina, 1584-1958*, 86-88.
19. In the colonial and Federal periods, various canal schemes were proposed, but only about one hundred miles were constructed. The best studies of North Carolina canals are Watson, *Internal Improvements in Antebellum North Carolina*, 81-96; and Clifford Reginald Hinshaw Jr., "North Carolina Canals before 1860," *NCHR*, 156.
20. Watson, *History of New Bern and Craven County*, 272-274.
21. The canal was somewhat of a pet project of George Washington. *Edenton Gazette*, February 27, 1830. The best study of the canal is Alexander Crosby Brown, *The Dismal Swamp Canal*.
22. A Norfolk newspaper, the *American Beacon*, recorded in the March 19, 1833 issue that in the month of February, 194 schooners and sloops averaging about forty-five tons passed through the canal from Virginia and ninety-eight from North Carolina.
23. Brown, *Dismal Swamp Canal*, 202
24. Peggy Jo Cobb Braswell, *The Roanoke Canal: A History of the Old Navigation and Water Power Canal of Halifax County, North Carolina*.
25. Alexander Crosby Brown, *Juniper Waterway: A History of the Albemarle and Chesapeake Canal*.
26. In 1836-37, more than 1,400 vessels passed through Ocracoke Inlet. In 1892, 4,061 steamers, 1,807 schooners, 1,150 barges, 329

sloops, 198 rafts, and 62 lighters went through the Albemarle and Chesapeake Canal.

27. Stick, *Outer Banks*, 94, 182.

28. Catherine W. Bishir and others, *Architects and Builders in North Carolina: A History of the Practice of Building*, 133.

29. Albion, *Rise of the Port of New York*, 397; Watson, *Wilmington: Port of North Carolina*, 66-67. In 1835, twenty-nine brigs and ninety schooners arrived in New York; nine brigs and twenty-two schooners in Boston, and six brigs, and thirty-one schooners in Philadelphia. In 1854, 111 vessels arrived in Boston from Wilmington, while even more docked in New York.

30. Edward Chase Kirkland, *Men, Cities and Transportation: A Study in New England History, 1820-1900*, II:157.

31. *Beaufort News*, November 29, 1923. Despite such statements, other articles such as that in the September 22, 1858, issue of the *Greensboro Patriot* described the port in glowing terms: "We found the waters covered over with vessels of various sizes and descriptions, freighted with produce of every section of the state."

32. Cargo clearing Beaufort in 1832-1833 amounted to only 316 tons and, in 1849, was still well under a thousand tons. Watson, *Wilmington: Port of North Carolina*, 67; Albion, *Rise of The Port of New York*, 395; *Elizabeth City Star*, November 14, 1824.

33. (New Bern) *Daily Progress*, March 10, 1860; Watson, *History of New Bern and Craven County*, 262.

34. *History of Wilson County and Its Families*, 14; Kate Ohno, *Wilson County's Architectural Heritage*, 107-108; Patrick M. Valentine, *The Rise of a Southern Town: Wilson, North Carolina, 1849-1930*, 8; (New Bern) *Daily Journal*, July 16, 1882; Gallaway to Stanton, August 22, 1895, Entry 113, Box 32, RG77, NARA.

35. Watson, *History of New Bern and Craven County*, 261-263; (Elizabeth City) *Old North State*, May 31, 1851; Stephen F. Miller, "Recollections of New Bern North Carolina Fifty Years Ago," copy in the New Bern-Craven County Public Library, New Bern; *Raleigh Register and North-Carolina Gazette*, September 30, 1828; *Elizabeth City Star*, November 14, 1827; Peter Sandbeck, *The Historic Architecture of New Bern and Craven County, North Carolina*, 37; Lynda Vestal Herzog, "The Early Architecture of New Bern, North Carolina, 1750-1850" (Ph.D. diss., University of California at Los Angeles, 1977), 34.

36. Watson, *History of New Bern and Craven County*, 262.

37. Sandbeck, *Historic Architecture of New Bern and Craven County*, 100.

38. There are three excellent M.A. theses on the maritime history of Washington: Christopher P. McCabe, "The Development and Decline of Tar-Pamlico River Maritime Commerce and Its Impact upon Regional Settlement Patterns" (East Carolina University, 2007); Ann M. Merriman, "North Carolina Schooners, 1815-1901, and the S.R. Fowle and Son Company of Washington, North Carolina" (East Carolina University, 1996); and James Cox, "The Pamlico-Tar River and Its Role in the Development of Eastern North Carolina" (East Carolina University, 1989); Henry Clark Bridgers Jr., "Steamboats on the Tar," manuscript copies in the Henry Clark Bridgers Papers, ECU Manuscript Collection, Greenville, N.C., and the Outer Banks History Center, Manteo, N.C.

39. (Norfolk) *American Beacon*, March 19, 1833.

40. *Raleigh Register and North Carolina Gazette*, January 26, 1846.

41. See Wayne K. Durrill, *War of Another Kind: A Southern Community in the Great Rebellion*; Merriman, "North Carolina Schooners, 1815-1901, and the S.R. Fowle and Son Company", 44, 52; Braswell, *Roanoke Canal*, 39-42; Plymouth records in RG41, NARA; Francis Jones and S. B. Phelps, eds., *Washington County, North Carolina: A Tapestry*, 67.

42. (Norfolk) *American Beacon*, June 21, 1816.

43. In February 1833, 194 sloops and schooners passed through the canal; forty-eight of these were from Edenton. In 1835, the port's trade with New York was six brigs and thirty schooners. One Edenton merchant owned six vessels regularly trading between New York, Edenton, and the West Indies. Haughton to Mangum, Jan 13, 1836, in Henry T. Shanks, ed., *The Papers of Willie T. Mangum* (hereinafter cited as *Mangum Papers*), II:376-377; Albion, *Rise of the Port of New York*, 297.

44. This was a result of the proximity of Elizabeth City to the Dismal Swamp Canal, what the *Edenton Gazette* called the "Dismal Ditch." In 1856, the Edenton *American Banner* editorialized: "and what was Edenton of old? A place of commerce and trade. . . .Then Edenton harbor was filled with vessels. . . . Now [our wharves] . . . lie rotting in the sun." Bruce S. Cheeseman, "A Brief History of Edenton Waterfront," copy in author's possession, 18, 19; Thomas R. Butchko, *Edenton: An Architectural Portrait: The Historic Architecture of Edenton, North Carolina*, 21.

45. In 1820, Elizabeth City had a population of 677; by 1830, it approached a thousand. Edenton's population declined over the same period. Wayne H. Payne, "The Commercial Development of Ante-Bellum Elizabeth City" (M.A. thesis, Old Dominion University, 1971), 24, 50.

46. In 1825, twenty-three vessels carried cargo to New York City and eight to Boston through the inlets. Albion, *Rise of New York Port*, 367; Merriman, "North Carolina Schooners, 1815-1901, and the S.R. Fowle and Son Company," 44; William A. Griffin, *Ante-Bellum Elizabeth City: The History of a Canal Town*, 74.

47. An 1856 report on the port's commerce recorded that 119 vessels were home ported there. Griffin, *Ante-Bellum Elizabeth City*, p. 79.

48. For Fayetteville see John A. Oates, *The Story of Fayetteville and the Upper Cape Fear*.

49. Percival Perry, "The Naval-Stores Industry in the Old South, 1790-1860," *Journal of Southern History*, 34 (November 1968), 525.

50. Percival Perry, "The Naval Stores Industry in the Ante-Bellum South, 1789-1861," (Ph.D. diss., University of North Carolina, 1947) 294; Cox, "Pamlico-Tar River and Its Role in the Development of Eastern North Carolina," 50; Watson, *Wilmington: Port of North Carolina*, 67–69.

51. In the 1840s, J. D. Steele observed: "Elizabeth City furnishes a good deal of pine timber for the Navy Yard at Norfolk which is taken through the Dismal Swamp Canal." J. D. Steele Journal, Huntington Library, San Marino, Calif.; Perry, "Naval Stores Industry in the Ante-Bellum South," 125-126, 129; Wilson Angley, "A Brief History of the Scuppernong River," Research Branch, North Carolina Division of Archives and History, 12.

52. Perry, "Naval Stores Industry in the Ante-Bellum South," 284, 286-287, 291–292.

53. As Thomas S. Larkin recorded in his journal, "Every article wanted [is] brought from the North." These included ice first imported from New England in the mid-1850s. See Larkin, "My Itinerary: U.S. America," 9; Kirkland, *Men, Cities And Transportation*, II:153.

54. Taylor, *Transportation Revolution*, 58; Robert Gardiner, ed., *The Advent of Steam: The Merchant Steamship before 1900*, 44-82.

55. Alan D. Watson, "Sailing Under Steam: The Advent of Steam Navigation in North Carolina to the Civil War," *NCHR*, 30–32; Thomas H. Sloan, "Inland Steam Navigation in North Carolina 1818-1900" (M.A. thesis, East Carolina University, 1971), 11-13;

Sarah Woodall Turlington, "Steam Navigation in North Carolina Prior to 1860" (M.A. thesis, University of North Carolina, 1933), 2-5. For Stevens's efforts to establish steam navigation in the state, see Archibald D. Turnbull, *John Stevens: An American Record*, 333-345. See also several letters in Alice B. Keith and William H. Masterson, eds., *The John Gray Blount Papers*, IV:223-232; Sloan, "Inland Steam Navigation in North Carolina"; Watson, "Sailing Under Steam."

56. In 1818, steamboat construction south of Chesapeake Bay was relatively new. In 1815, the first one was built in Norfolk and, a year later, one was launched in Savannah. William C. Fleetwood Jr., *Tidecraft: The Boats of South Carolina, Georgia and Northern Florida*, 93; John C. Emmerson Jr., comp., *The Steamboat Comes to Norfolk Harbor, and the Log of the First Ten Years*, 43-53; Watson, "Sailing Under Steam, The Advent of Steam Navigation in North Carolina to the Civil War," 33.

57. Watson, *Internal Improvements in Antebellum North Carolina*, 128; Sloan, "Inland Steam Navigation in North Carolina," 13-14.

58. J. Kelly Turner and John L. Bridgers Jr., *History of Edgecombe County*, 23-24.

59. Emmerson, comp., *Steamboat Comes to Norfolk Harbor*, 28, passim; see also John C. Emmerson Jr., *Steam Navigation in Virginia and Northeastern North Carolina Waters, 1826-1836*; (New Bern) *Daily Journal*, May 28, 1882.

60. Keith and Masterson, eds., *John Gray Blount Papers*, IV:231.

61. Turnbull, *John Stevens*, 344.

62. Unfortunately, there is no information as to where Otway Burns and Joseph Seawell got their ideas to build a steamboat. No known description of *Prometheus* has been found. Apparently, she was a sternwheeler and her engines were too weak to make headway against a strong tidal current. Many writers believe Burns built the *Prometheus* at his shipyard in Beaufort but the evidence clearly indicates that the steamboat was built in Swansboro. Watson, *Wilmington: Port of North Carolina*, 52; Sloan, "Inland Steam Navigation in North Carolina," 18-19; F. Roy Johnson, *Sail and Steam Navigation of Eastern North Carolina*, 16; F. Roy Johnson, *Riverboating in Lower Carolina*, 31; Tucker R. Littleton, "North Carolina's First Steamboat," *The State*, 45 (November 1977), 8-10; *Jacksonville Daily Times*, March 27, 1976.

63. More than likely Seawell also hired outside experts to build the boat and install the machinery. *Raleigh Recorder*, May 15, 1818; (Raleigh) *Star and North-Carolina State Gazette*, May 2, 1818.

64. Johnson, *Riverboating in Lower Carolina*, 36; *Raleigh Minerva*, April 17, May 15, 1818; (New Bern) *Carolina Sentinel*, May 9, 1818; Oates, *Story of Fayetteville*, 91, 122, 192-193.

65. Our understanding of the appearance of the *Henrietta* is based on the picture of Norfolk's first steamboat shown in Emmerson, *Steamboat Comes to Norfolk Harbor*; (Wilmington) *Daily Herald*, October 13, 1856; (Wilmington) *Daily Journal*, November 25, 1874; *Wilmington Chronicle*, April 2, 1846.

66. *Raleigh Register and North-Carolina Gazette*, October 13, 1826.

67. Wilson Angley, "An Historical Overview of the Black River in Southeastern North Carolina," Research Branch, North Carolina Division of Archives and History, 20; *Raleigh Register and North-Carolina Gazette*, October 17, 1826.

68. Fleetwood, *Tidecraft*, 93.

69. Most of these vessels were built between 1840 and 1860. According to the census of 1820, there were four boat carpenters employed in Cumberland County.

70. New Hanover County Civil Action Papers, SANC. Some vessels were taken over by interests in other southern states. One of these, the *Scottish Chief*, may have ended up in the Florida Keys. An archaeological survey at Bird Key in the Dry Tortugas off the Florida Keys, uncovered a wreck that the investigator claims was the *Scottish Chief*. However, there are discrepancies between his description of the vessel surveyed and that of the *Scottish Chief* derived from other sources. Specifically, his report of a composite hull and description of the machinery is at variance with official records and other accounts. Richard A. Gould, "The Bird Key Wreck, Dry Tortugas National Park, Florida," *Florida Keys Sea Heritage Journal*, 7 (Summer, 1997), 1-14; (Wilmington) *Daily Herald*, May 28, 1855; Bailey to Welles, October 24, 1863, *Official Records of the Union and Confederate Navies in the War of the Rebellion*, (hereinafter cited as ORN) Series I, vol.17, 570-571; Gordon Watts, correspondence to authors, June 14, 2004, copy in possession of authors.

71. Taylor, *Transportation Revolution*, 350-351.

72. (Tarboro) *Southerner*, September 22, 1860; *Tarborough Press*, December 26, 1835, March 9, 1839; (New Bern) *Daily Journal*, September 17, 1893.

73. Emmerson, *Steam Navigation in Virginia and Northeastern North Carolina Waters*, 178, 197, 200; *North Carolina Journal*, May 13, 1831.

74. William M. Lytle, comp., *Merchant Steam Vessels of the United States, 1807-1968*, 46; *DeBow's Commercial Review*, X, 579.

75. (Wilmington) *Daily Herald*, June 12, 1860; (New Bern) *Journal*, January 23, 1856.

76. (Raleigh) *News and Observer*, May 6, 1984; Barbara M. Howard Thorne, ed., *The Heritage of Craven County, North Carolina, Vol. I, 1984*, 22; *Fayetteville Observer*, May 19, 1853.

77. Louis C. Hunter, *Steamboats on the Western Rivers: An Economic and Technological History*, 62.

78. Unlike on the Hudson River and elsewhere in the northeast, for safety reasons passengers were not carried on towed craft; towing in North Carolina was done exclusively to increase cargo tonnage. Wade H. Hadley Jr., *The Story of the Cape Fear and Deep River Navigation Company, 1849-1874*, 30.

79. For the two methods see Hunter, *Steamboats on the Western Rivers*, 96-98; Adam Isaac Kane, "The Western River Steamboat: Structure and Machinery, 1811-1860" (M.A. thesis, Texas A.&M. University, 2001), 111-128.

80. Bradley A. Rodgers et al., "Underwater Archaeological Investigation and Data Recovery of Ten Vessel Sites Near Castle Island in Washington, North Carolina" (draft report, April 2002, Program in Maritime Studies, East Carolina University).

81. Hayes Collection, SHC, UNC-CH.

82. Her enrollment paper said six feet. Vessel documents rarely differentiate between steamboat and steam flat. Johnson, *Riverboating in Lower Carolina*, 35-36.

83. She had a pronounced superstructure; the pilot house and passenger cabin were forward, engine and boiler room aft. Cargo was apparently stowed between the two structures. The vessel was plain and practical, not difficult to build. However, this is a speculative reconstruction and
may prove overly imaginative. It resembles more so a steamboat built a decade or so after the *Henrietta*. See the illustrations in John H. Morrison, *History of American Steam Navigation*.

84. Hunter, *Steamboats on the Western Rivers*, 65-66.

85. For comments on the *Enterprise's* draft, see *Raleigh Register and North-Carolina Gazette*, September 30, 1828, and (New Bern) *Carolina Sentinel*, January 20, 1820.

86. *Wilmington Chronicle*, April 24, 1850. An earlier *Union* was constructed in 1834. Newspapers accounts referred to her as a "flat boat." No additional information was given. It is not known if this boat was called "flat" because of her hull configuration or lack of superstructure. *People's Press and Wilmington Advertiser*, April 9, 1834; *Fayetteville Observer*, April 15, 1834.

87. (Tarboro) *Southerner*, September 22, 1860. No additional information, including the vessel's name, has been discovered.

88. Sloan, "Inland Steam Navigation in North Carolina," 42.

89. *Raleigh Register and North-Carolina Gazette*, December 17, 1841.

90. *Wilmington Journal* (daily), November 17, 1851; *Fayetteville Observer*, April 27, 1852; Perry, "Naval Stores Industry in the Ante-Bellum South," 88.

91. *Newbernian*, August 1, 1848.

92. *New Bern Republican*, Oct 2, 1850.

93. *Wilmington Journal* (weekly), August 19, 1959; (Wilmington) *Daily Herald*, August 15, 1859.

94. Fayetteville (North) *Carolinian*, November 17, 1851.

95. *Newbernian*, August 1, 1848.

96. *Tarborough Press*, October 25, 1850; (New Bern) *Republican*, October 2, 1850; Hunter, *Steamboats on the Western Rivers*, 66.

97. Gallaway to Stanton, August 22, 1859, Entry 113, Box 32, RG77, NARA; (Wilmington) *Daily Herald*, September 7, 1859. Whether the tall stacks, that is, the boat's chimneys, protruded skyward from the superstructure or were separate and forward of the superstructure is unknown. At least one description of a boat mentioned that the boilers were forward of the cabins suggesting that the stack were also forward. Hinges were often attached to the chimneys (stacks) so they could be lowered in order to pass under bridges. Sloan, "Inland Steam Navigation in North Carolina," 43.

98. (New Bern) *Republican*, November 27, 1847.

99. Brown, *Dismal Swamp Canal*, 113, 205. No information has been located as to the *Fox's* machinery, and nothing has been found to indicate where she was or what she was doing during the war.

100. The letters provide a rare look at the problems in building such a vessel in North Carolina. The 1850 census lists Angelo Garibaldi as a thirty-two-year old mariner. He was born in Italy and came to the United States sometime in the 1830s. He arrived in Plymouth in the 1840s, and engaged in a shipping business. He contracted with James Cathcart Johnston, a prominent planter, to ship produce from Caledonia, Johnston's large estate on the Roanoke River in Halifax County, to markets in New York and elsewhere in the northeast. This business association continued until the Civil War and the Union occupation of the region.

101. Garibaldi wrote that Betts and Pusey was the firm that contracted to build the vessel but Pusey and Jones was the actual name of the company. Edward Betts was one of the founders of the firm. Garibaldi to Johnston, July 12, 22, August 30, 1854, Hayes Collection, SHC, UNC-CH; David B. Tyler, *The American Clyde: A History of Iron and Steel Shipbuilding on the Delaware from 1840 to World War I*, 13-14.

102. Garibaldi to Johnston, June 12, July 12, 22, August 20, 1854, Hayes Collection, SHC, UNC-CH.

103. The rough drawing of the proposed vessel and the contract mentioned by Garibaldi have not been discovered. However, he mentioned the necessary carpenters and other workers. "I think he would allow you $10 per month for your steamboat hands and find them, or $13.50 per month and you find them.... He will take your 2 carpenters ... and allow the same as he will have to pay for others.... Mr. Herrington will want some money, as he goes on with the work, to pay off his hands." Garibaldi to Johnston: July 17, 22, August 2, 1861, Hayes Collection, SHC, UNC-CH.

104. August 12, September 13, 14, 1861, Hayes Collection, SHC, UNC-CH.

105. September 13, 14, October 4, 1861, Hayes Collection, SHC, UNC-CH.

106. September 18, 1861, November 20, 1861; Jan 20, 1862; Hayes Collection, SHC, UNC-CH.

107. The expedition's commanding officer was instructed to destroy any vessel on the stocks. Interestingly, the Union naval officer later reported that no private property had been harmed. In fact, he specifically mentioned finding a vessel on the stocks, "but being assured that it was the property of a private individual, did not destroy it." Quackenbush to Rowan, May 3, 1862, and Rowan to Quackenbush, April 30, 1862, *ORN*, Series I, vol. 7, 305-306, 287-88.

108. Garibaldi's claim was only one aspect of one of the "most sensational legal proceedings in state history." *Angelo Garibaldi v. C.W. Hollowell and Edward Wood*, Case No. 10,392, Supreme Court Original Cases, SANC; Max R. Williams, "The Johnston Will Case: A Clash of Titans," *NCHR* 67 (July 1990), 358; Powell, ed., *DNCB*, 3:302-303.

109. Contract dated April 1, 1853, Henry Adolphus London Papers, SHC, UNC-CH.

110. Garibaldi to Johnston, August 12, 1861, Hayes Collection, SHC, UNC-CH.

111. Hunter, *Steamboats on the Western Rivers*, 121-142.

112. *Wilmington Journal* (daily), November 9, 1860. Other descriptions include two "disconnected engines" on the *Charles Henry*; the *Evergreen* had "double engines"; the *Scottish Chief* and the *Carolinian* had two engines each.

113. Sloan, "Inland Steam Navigation in North Carolina," 42.

114. Unpublished history of Pusey and Jones, Hagley Museum and Library, Wilmington, Del. The Hagley Museum holds drawings of both vessel's machinery, but most of those for the *James Petteway* are faded to the point where they are unreadable. The company records also include information on the machinery fabricated for North Carolina vessels that were built by Pusey and Jones, and other firms.

115. *Crusader* file, Ships History Division, Naval History and Heritage Command, Washington, D.C.; unpublished history of Pusey and Jones, Hagley Museum and Library, Wilmington, Del. For the *Southern Star's* engines see the drawings and unpublished history of Pusey and Jones in the Hagley Museum.

116. (New Bern) *Daily Journal*, July 16, 1842, referring to the *Fayetteville*.

117. A railroad requires a roadbed to lay the ties upon which to spike the rails. The sandy and
marshy soils of the coastal plain are not the best for a solid bed, so special care is needed. The same is true for stagecoach routes. The famed nine-foot (wide) road, parts of which are still found today between Washington and New Bern, was first a plank road and was then made into a brick road in colonial times. Railroads needed to be high and dry, and bridged over wetlands and water; vastly more expensive and time consuming to construct and maintain than other forms of land transportation.

118. *Wilmington Herald*, March 9, 1853; *Wilmington Journal* (daily), March 19, 1853;
Wilmington Journal (weekly), March 11, 1853. She burned at the docks in 1857.

119. *Wilmington Journal* (daily), December 17, 1860.
120. Earlier, George Stephenson constructed a track from Perth Amboy to Trenton for the purpose of connecting the two ports. North from New York came the Mohawk and Hudson in 1831, which eventually became the New York Central System stretching to Buffalo, followed by the demise of the Erie Canal, and then the road continued on to Detroit and Chicago. A good treatise on railroading is found in Albro Martin's *Railroads Triumphant*, an excellent account of the growth of American steam railroads.
121. Sloan, "Inland Steam Navigation in North Carolina," 25.
122. *Raleigh Register and North-Carolina Gazette*, June 30, 1826.
123. *Newbern Spectator and Literary Journal*, November 29, 1828. The name of the successful contractor has not been found.
124. Captain Blaney of Smithville wanted to bid on the Cape Fear boat and was told that information on construction could be obtained from Baltimore where a number had been built. The Howard and Sparrow shipbuilding firm of New Bern received a contract to build the Ocracoke dredge. The ninety-one-ton boat was completed in 1829, but it proved a failure, its fifteen-horsepower engine unable to cope with the amount of sand that had to be moved. The Corps contracted with a Baltimore firm for a larger and more powerful dredge boat. In 1835 the Howard and Sparrow boat was auctioned off in New Bern. Chief, Corps of Engineers to Blaney, May 10, 30, 1829, Letters Sent by Office of Chief of Engine Relating to Internal Improvements, 1824-30, M65, Reel 3, NARA; *New Bern Spectator and Literary Journal*, January 2, 1835; Chief, Corps of Engineers to Dutton, November 6, December 28, 1829, February 15, April 13, 1830, and Chief, Corps of Engineers to Sparrow and Howard, December 28, 1829, M65, Reel 3, NARA; Dutton to Chief, Corps of Engineers, August 2, 1831, Office of Chief Engineers, Letters Received, 1826-37, "D-709," records of the Corps of Engineers, RG77, NARA; Dutton to Chief, November 4, 1832, E18, General Correspondence File D870, RGG77, NARA; *Edenton Gazette*, January 20, 1831; (New Bern) *Carolina Sentinel*, June 1, 1832.
125. (Raleigh) *News and Observer*, March 9, 1941; (Wilmington) *Weekly Commercial*, September 24, October 12, 1852; (Elizabeth City) *Democratic Pioneer*, November 20, 1855; Thorne, ed., *Heritage of Craven County*, I:22.
126. *Raleigh Register and North Carolina Gazette*, April 28, 1846.
127. (Raleigh) *Star and North-Carolina Gazette*, May 15, 1818.
128. Frank Stephenson, *Hertford County, North Carolina*, 107.
129. *Tarboro Press*, May 13, 1836. For similar events, see the *Raleigh Register*'s account of the launching of the *Cotton Plant*, April 28, 1826.
130. *Raleigh Register and North-Carolina Gazette*, February 15, 1842.
131. *Southport Leader*, December 26, 1895.
132. Anne M. Tunstall, "Memoir of Edenton," Reel 2, Cupola House Papers, Shepherd-Pruden Memorial Library, Edenton, N.C.
133. In her diary Mrs. Jethro Darden wrote, "just as the bottle was raised to be broken to sprinkle and name the boat, the underworks gave way." F. Roy Johnson, *Sail and Steam*, 44.
134. (Petersburg) *Daily Express*, April 15, 1857. Copies of this and other articles in the Petersburg paper were provided by Thomas Parramore. See his article, "The Ironic Fate of the *Southern Star*," 42 NCHR (Summer 1965): 335-344.
135. (New Bern) *Republican*, June 13, 1849.
136. (New Bern) *Republican*, April 10, 1850. See also the *Newbernian*, April 9, 1850. For another New Bern launching, see the *Raleigh Register and North-Carolina Gazette*, October 24, 1828.
137. There were exceptions. The *Enterprise*, built in 1818 to run between Fayetteville and Wilmington, was owned jointly by the builder John K. McIlhenny and General (later governor) Edward B. Dudley. (Fayetteville) *Carolina Observer*, October 2, 1818. Dudley later bought out McIlhenny and used the steamboat to carry mail and passengers between Wilmington and Smithville. New Hanover Deed Book T, p. 386, SANC. Thomas Snipes Lutterloh, a Fayetteville merchant, owned a line of steamers on the Cape Fear for more than twenty years. They included the *Magnolia* and the *Fanny Lutterloh*. (Wilmington) *Weekly Commercial*, July 9, 1852; (Wilmington) *Weekly Herald*, August 15, 1859; (Wilmington) *Daily Herald*, September 7, 1859; *Wilmington Journal*, July 7, 1852; *Wilmington Journal* (weekly), June 8, 1855, August 19, 1859; J. S. Tomlinson, *Tar Heel Sketch-Book: A Brief Biographical Sketch of the Life and Public Acts of the Members of the General Assembly of North Carolina (Session of 1879)*.

For another example concerning the Cape Fear, see *Peoples Press and Wilmington Advertiser*, February 27, 1833. In 1854, the *Charles Henry* was launched. "She is owned by gentlemen on Black River," a newspaper article stated. *Wilmington Journal* (weekly), September 4, 1854; Watson, "Sailing Under Steam," 46; Cox, "Pamlico-Tar River and its Role in the Development of Eastern North Carolina," 45; (Goldsboro) *North Carolina Telegraph*, May 9, 1850; *Wilmington Journal* (weekly), July 12, 1850; *Newbernian*, July 2, 1850; *New Bern Republican*, May 22, October 2, 1850; Emmerson, *Steamboat Comes to Norfolk Harbors*; Emmerson, *Steam Navigation in Virginia and Northeastern North Carolina Waters*; Watson, "Sailing Under Steam," 334-340.
138. Typical of these companies was an announcement that "a company has been formed & considerable portion of material collected, for the building of a 60 horsepower steamboat, intended for towing vessels down the [Cape Fear] River, and to seas, during the prevalence of Southern winds & also for performing trips to Fayetteville during the winter season." *Raleigh Register and North-Carolina Gazette*, April 28, 1831. For a discussion of these companies see Watson, "Sailing Under Steam," 29-68; Hugh Thompson, "Early Steam Navigation on the Albemarle Sound," unpublished manuscript, copy in the author's possesion.
139. Bridgers, "Steamboats on the Tar," 21-22; (Tarboro) *Southerner*, July 14, September 22, 1860. There is no information as to when the vessel was finished, nor do official records of the Civil War mention such a vessel being destroyed in Pitt County.
140. Craven County Deed Book 60, SANC. There were two steamers named *Wilson* built in 1856. In addition to the one in Beaufort, Wiswall and Havens built one in Washington, N.C. Neither was documented. Ursula Loy and Pamela M. Worthy, *Washington and the Pamlico*, 230; (Tarboro) *Southerner*, September 13, 1856.
141. Sixteen vessels, all steamers, were launched in Cumberland County during this era. According to the censuses of 1820 and 1850, there were four boat carpenters employed in Cumberland County. Five are listed in the 1860 census. However, there were clearly more carpenters working in the county in the 1850s. Vessel document papers record L. L. Lutterloh as the builder of the *Magnolia* in 1855, John Banks as the builder of the *Scottish Chief* in the same year, and R. M. Orrell as builder of the *Kate McLaurin* in 1859. None of these are listed in either the 1850 or the 1860 custom records.
142. A copy of the contract dated April 1, 1853, is in the Henry Adolphus London Papers, SHC, UNC-CH; Elsie Faye Russ, "The Cape Fear and Deep River Navigation Company" (M.A.

thesis, Wake Forest University, 1970), 48. The *John Haughton* and several of the towboats, completed and placed in operation, later were used on regular runs between Chatham County and Wilmington transporting cargos of coal and other products. Watson, *Wilmington: Port of North Carolina*, 60-61. Receipt for money paid King and Bryan, November 23, 1853, Henry Augustus London Papers, SHC, UNC-CH; Hadley, *Story of the Cape Fear and Deep River Navigation Company*, 30.

143. This may have been the *Enterprise II*. London to Board of directors, July 5, 1855, Engineers report, June 1856, London Papers, SHC, UNC-CH.

144. J. Worth to B.G. Worth, July 20, 1859 and April 15, 30 1860, B.G. Worth to J. Worth, December 2, 1862, Jonathan Worth Papers, SANC.

145. Parramore, "Ironic Fate of the *Southern Star*," 335-344.

146. (New Bern) *Daily Journal*, July 16, 1882.

147. Sometime around 1840, Harlow and Calvin B. Dibble moved from Connecticut to New Bern. The two were followed by three more brothers, James, John, and Franklin (Frank). They evidently arrived with funds to go into business. In 1841, Calvin joined with John and Stillman W. Mildrum to manufacture iron and tin ware, cutlery, and other metal items. The partnership was dissolved by mutual consent in 1843. James arrived in 1842 and established his carriage manufactory works in Kinston. James and Frank settled in Kinston. By 1845, John had joined his brother in North Carolina and the partnership of Dibble and Brothers was formed. *New Bern Times*, December 14, 1865; Craven County Deed Book 60:289; SANC; *Newbernian*, September 2, 1843. For other genealogical information on the family, see correspondence from Stephenson to Still, December 9, 2002; Craven County Deed Book 57:212.

148. 1840 and 1850 censuses for Craven County; deed from Calvin B. Dibble to John and Stillman W. Mildrum, July 8, 1843, SANC; correspondence from Victor Jones to author, November 20, 2002; 1860 Census Manufacturing Schedule, Lenoir County.

149. Watson, *History of New Bern and Craven County*, 277-278; Johnson, *Riverboating in Lower Carolina*, 46; Goldsboro *News-Argus*, November 16, 1975; (New Bern) *Daily Journal*, July 16, 1882; William S. Powell, *Annals of Progress: The Story of Lenoir County and Kinston*, 64; (New Bern) *Daily Progress*, January 2, 3, 1860. The paper carried frequent advertisements announcing items for sale by the Dibbles. (Tarboro) *Southerner*, May 23, 1856; *Fayetteville Observer*, June 27, 1853. John Dibble also sold insurance for the New York Mutual Fire Insurance Company. For the *Wayne's* history, see (New Bern) *Daily Journal*, June 18, 25, July 2, 16, 1882.

150. Oceanic trade had been steadily declining due to shoaling of the inlets, particularly Ocracoke Inlet. Benjamin B. Winborne, *The Colonial and State Political History of Hertford County, N.C.*, 192.

151. Minutes, October 10, 1855, Wynns Family Papers, Murfreesboro Historical Association Collection, ECU.

152. Minutes, February 14, 1856, Wynns Family Papers, Murfreesboro Historical Association Collection, ECU. Apparently, Jesse Andrew Jackson, a native of New Jersey, came south for opportunity. For several years, he owned a store in Pine Tree, possibly located in Wilson County, before moving to Murfreesboro. He gained a contract to make bricks for two female colleges in the town and, later, established a sawmill. At some time in the mid-1850s, he became fascinated with the idea of building a sea-going vessel capable of being a packet between Murfreesboro and New York City. He persuaded a number of local people to contribute money and even convinced a New York commission house that the project was feasible. Parramore, "Ironic Fate of the *Southern Star*," 336. Parramore's article is a detailed account of this vessel and its early history. See also *Murfreesboro Enquirer*, January 24, 1878.

153. Whether Jackson met him in Wilmington, or possibly New York, is not known. It is even possible that the New York firm of Glines and Graham, which held stock in the company, recommended him. (Petersburg) *Daily Express*, May 2, 1857, copy provided by Thomas Parramore. See also Parramore, "The Ironic Fate of the *Southern Star*," 337-339; and Association Minutes, February 16, December 9, 1856, Wynns Family Papers, Murfreesboro Historical Association Collection, ECU.

154. Jesse Jackson never recovered from the disaster and eventually left North Carolina.

155. Badger, whose real name was Thomas Churn, was a native of Virginia who became a "forty-niner," journeying to California during the gold rush. There, he became a sea captain and operated a successful shipping business. He was passenger captain on the ill-fated *Central America* when she went down off the South Carolina coast in 1857. Supposedly, he lost $20,000 in gold but evidently retained enough funds to purchase the *Chowan*. Stockholder John Southall informed Badger that "I wrote you on the first inclosing a transfer from our court setting forth the sale of the steamer *Chowan* . . . with the necessary papers to show that you purchased the same at publick auction under John Kirkman's attachment." June 3, 1859, copy in Subject File AY, RG45, NARA; Austin D. Kilham and Fannie M. Clark, eds., *Badger and Tankard Families of the Eastern Shore of Virginia*, 21; (Murfreesboro) *Daily Express*, October 27, 1857, copy in a file on the *Southern Star*, Mariners' Museum, Newport News, Va.; Norman E. Klare, *The Final Voyage of the Central America, 1857: The Saga of a Gold Rush Steamship, the Tragedy of her Loss in a Hurricane, and the Treasure Which is Now Recovered*, 46; (Petersburg) *Daily Express*, October 27, 1857.

156. Unpublished history of Pusey and Jones, Hagley Museum and Library, Wilmington, Del.

157. *Lloyd's Register of Ships*, 541; Chief of the Bureau of Statistics, *List of Merchant Vessels of the United States*, 1875 edition; *Southern Star* enrollment paper dated August 12, 1858, Petersburg, Virginia, RG41, NARA; correspondence from Franklin Smallman to Still, May 16, 1984; Parramore, "Ironic Fate of the *Southern Star*," 340. Evidently, the steamer was a well designed and built craft. One Murfreesboro resident wrote: "a prettier craft I never saw on water." Long to Secretary of the Navy, September 29, 1859, Letters Received by the Secretary of the Navy from Commandants of Yards, Philadelphia, RG45, NARA; (Petersburg) *Daily Express*, May 2, 1857; (Norfolk) *Southern Argus*, August 20, 1858; copy in the Charter, Bylaws and Proceedings of the North Carolina and New York Steam Boat Company file, Mariners' Museum, Newport News, Va.

158. The *Southern Star* did not return to Murfreesboro. Possibly, her thirteen-and-a-half-foot draft was considered too deep. However, it is more probable that Badger realized the steamer would be more profitable employed in trade between larger ports.

159. September 7, 1858; *Southern Star* Enrollment, August 12, 1858, Petersburg Virginia, RG41, NARA; (Norfolk) *Southern Argus*, August 20, 1858, copy in file on the *Southern Star*, Mariners' Museum, Newport News, Va.

160. Guion Grifis Johnson, *Ante-Bellum North Carolina: A Social History*, 98-99.

161. Correspondence from Smallman to Still, May 16, 1984; Parramore, "Ironic Fate of the *Southern Star*," 340-344; *Crusader*

file, Ships Histories Division, Naval History and Heritage Command, Washington, D.C.

162. Bishir and others, *Architects and Builders in North Carolina*, 210; Griffin, *Ante-Bellum Elizabeth City*, 79.

163. Robert B. Gordon, *American Iron, 1607-1900*, 260.

164. Edwin L. Combs III, "Confederate Shipbuilding on the Cape Fear River," *NCHR* 62 (October 1996), 416; (Winston-Salem) *Journal and Sentinel*, February 7, 1937; (Wilmington) *Morning Star*, April 23, 1907; Wilmington Iron Works Charter, 1859, Wilmington Iron Works Records, ECU. Tony P. Wrenn in *Wilmington, North Carolina: An Architectural and Historical Portrait*, 232, states that Hart founded the business in 1838 as a tin shop.

165. *Wilmington Journal* (daily), March 16, 1855; (Tarboro) *Southerner*, May 26, 1855; (Raleigh) *North Carolina Star*, February 20, 1856.

166. "The Clarendon Iron Works are now prepared to receive orders for Beam, Vertical, Horizontal, or Oscillating Steam Engines, high or low pressure and adapted to all purposes. . . [including] . . . equipping of Steamers," *Kemble and Warner vs. the Clarendon Iron Works Company, A.H. Van Bokkelen, and Others*, March 1867, Case #9099, Original Case Files, Supreme Court Records, SANC; Wrenn, *Wilmington*, 20.

167. (Wilmington) *Morning Star*, August 14, 1888; (Elizabeth City) *Democratic Pioneer*, February 21, 1854, April 8, 1856; (Washington) *North State Whig*, September 11, 1850; C. Alexander Turner III, "An Historical and Archaeological Investigation of the *Scuppernong*: A Mid-Nineteenth-Century North Carolina-Built Centerboard Schooner" (M.A. thesis, ECU, 1999), 39-41.

168. A one hundred-ton vessel required at least a hundred tons of iron. Iron pintels and gudgeons attached the rudder to the vessel. Iron fastenings were used to attach the rigging to the hull. Iron ore was available in North Carolina but, with the exception of spikes and a few small miscellaneous pieces, all manufactured iron came from out of state, much of it from Norfolk and Richmond, Virginia; Baltimore, Maryland, and New York City. Copper for ship bottoms was also imported. Carroll Pursell Jr., *Early Stationary Steam Engines in America, A Study on the Migration of a Technology*, 146.

169. Norman G. Rukert, "Federal Hill: A Baltimore National Historic District," 42-49; unpublished information provided by the Maryland Historical Society, Baltimore, Md.

170. Bridgers, "Steamboats on the Tar," 22; Tyler, *American Clyde*, 13-14; unpublished history of Pusey and Jones, Hagley Museum and Library, Wilmington, Del.; Charles B. Dew, *Ironmaker to the Confederacy: Joseph R. Anderson and the Tredegar Iron Works*, 2-3, 19.

171. *Wilmington Journal* (daily), September 5, 1854.

172. (Raleigh) *News and Observer*, March 9, 1941. For Baltimore, see also the *People's Press and Wilmington Advertiser*, March 6, 1833.

173. (Elizabeth City) *Democratic Pioneer*, November 20, 1855.

Chapter 5

The Antebellum Period, 1816–1860: Expansion, Prosperity, and Crises

In North Carolina, as in the South as a whole, the term "antebellum" has special meaning. In many ways, it marks the end, rather than a beginning, of an era. It is defined as the period before the Civil War; yet, for many, it alludes to the "Old South." As the revolution in transportation began and accelerated, the aristocratic agrarian system continued to dominate the economy and the institution of slavery was a critical factor.

From 1815 until secession in 1861, much of North Carolina's maritime commerce depended on vessels from other states.[1] This, coupled with various contemporary publications, has led to the conclusion that relatively few ships were built in North Carolina during the period. In *The American Maritime Industries and Public Policy*, John G. B. Hutchins endorsed this assumption, stating, "One of the notable facts was the failure of the shipbuilding industry to develop in the South." Citing a lack of skilled labor, he asserted only one brig and two schooners were built in the South from 1829 to 1830.[2] For North Carolina, this is simply not the case. The Records of the Bureau of Marine Inspection and Navigation in the National Archives note nineteen schooners, two brigs, and three sloops built in the state from 1829 to 1830.

In *The Rise of the Port of New York 1815-1860*, Robert Albion includes an appendix on shipbuilding by state from 1833 to 1866, which is based on published commerce and navigation records. Similarly, he concludes that vessels totaling only 34,600 tons were constructed in North Carolina during this period and that there was an "almost complete absence of shipbuilding in the far south," including North Carolina. However, a detailed examination of vessel documents indicates 643 vessels totaling 43,438 tons were built in the state. Furthermore, relying on tonnage figures alone (Figure 1), also presents a false picture because most of the vessels built in North Carolina were small.

Certainly, North Carolina's shipbuilding industry did not compare with that north of Cape Henry and the Chesapeake Bay area, but due to discrepancies in available sources, it is impossible to formulate an accurate comparison.[3] Nevertheless, although susceptible to fluctuating economic conditions, the state's shipbuilding during this period was far more extensive and important than has been recognized.

The late eighteenth century innovation of the steam engine engendered managerial chaos. North Carolina was ill-prepared for the industrial and transportation revolutions. Volatile conditions prevailed during the antebellum period as the state moved slowly from an agrarian-based economy toward one marked by increasing mechanization. The ship data from 1688 to 1914, found and collected from various archival sources, tends to bear this out.

From 1816 to 1860, the level of North Carolina shipbuilding activity was directly affected by the intent

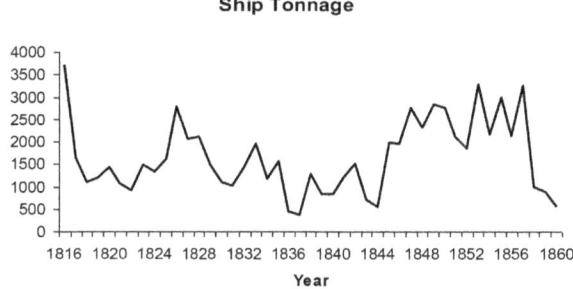

Figure 5-1 Ship Tonnage during the antebellum era shows volatility between the War of 1812 and the Civil War, likely related to economic ups and downs. *Source:* Author's database.

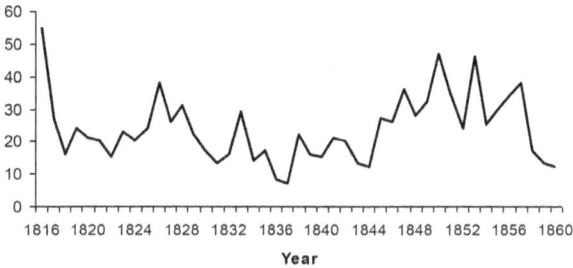

Figure 5-2 Number of Ships Built in North Carolina during the antebellum era tends to mirror the volatility of ship tonnage, and economic panics. *Source:* Author's database.

of the builders; instabilities of local, regional, state, and national economies; a rapidly changing technology; and unique coastal geography (Figure 2). As already noted, shipbuilding sites appeared and disappeared across the coastal plain of North Carolina. Workers at shipyards commonly had to revert to other types of employment during downturns in the economy. Still, some communities had relatively stable shipbuilding sites, as repair work and the like were always needed. Many shipbuilding sites continued business patterns established during the federal period.

The decline in the number of ships built after the War of 1812 is not unusual. The need to repair existing ships surpassed the need to build new ships. In addition, money was scarce and the financial services industry was corrupt. There was an entrepreneurial preoccupation with reconstruction and periodic financial panics. Nevertheless, there was a total of 1,049 ships built in North Carolina during this period, ranging from a high of fifty-five in 1816 to a low of eight in 1837. Fourteen peaks and just as many dips over forty-four years suggest an approximate three-year cycle underscoring the volatility of the ship and boat building industry in coastal North Carolina.

The Workforce: Artisan, Laborer, Businessman

Although at least fifteen vessels were built in North Carolina in 1840, an unpublished summary in that year's census on manufacturing and agriculture includes no mention of shipbuilding in North Carolina. The introduction to the census states that "[t]he attempt to gather the industrial and commercial census was looked upon with great disfavor in some sections of the country," including the South.[4] The 1850 agricultural and industrial census for North Carolina listed nine shipyards in the state but none for Carteret County. Yet, fifty-five of the 195 ship carpenters living in the state in 1850 resided in Carteret County. Customshouse records list eighteen ships built in Carteret County in 1850, but according to Emory Q. Hawk's *Economic History of the South*, only eight vessels were built in the entire state in 1850.[5] In addition, the 1850 census on manufacturing and agriculture does not include Bertie, Brunswick, Cumberland, New Hanover, or Pasquotank Counties, although vessels were constructed in all these districts. Similarly, vessels were built in Beaufort, Carteret, Bertie, and Craven Counties in 1860, but the census from that year does not mention shipbuilding. Many of these vessels may have been constructed on temporary sites located on plantations, near saw mills, or near sources of timber.

Population censuses are plagued by similar inconsistency. Ship carpenters in North Carolina are not listed prior to 1850, and evidence indicates that data may not be accurate for 1850 and 1860. The censuses list only one ship carpenter in Chowan County, but there were two shipyards in Edenton throughout the 1850s. Craven County lists nine ship carpenters and four caulkers in 1850 (the only time caulkers are listed in North Carolina), and twelve ship carpenters in 1860; Currituck County lists seven in 1850 and none in 1860; Cumberland County had eight in 1850 and five in 1860; Onslow County lists none in 1850 and two in 1860; Brunswick County had five in 1850 and four in 1860; Hyde County listed one in 1850 and none in 1860; Pasquotank County listed eleven in 1850 and nine in 1860; Martin County lists none for either census; and New Hanover County lists eleven in 1850 and twenty-one in 1860. The 1850 census does not include William Brumble, although his obituary mentions that he was "good at blacksmithing, coopering, and boatmaking." Sailmakers are recorded and all the ports had one or more, but only one rigger and no blockmakers are listed.[6] The building of steamboats required different occupations, such as mechanics and engineers. Although engineers are not listed in the 1850 and 1860 censuses, mechanics are listed, but their involvement in steamboat construction is not clear. A careful examination of this data and a comparison with vessel statistics indicate the validity of census returns is questionable. Few or no ship carpenters are listed in counties where vessels were regularly constructed during the 1850s.

During this period, ship carpenters were frequently itinerant. Moreover, population returns rarely include more than one occupation for an individual, and it was common, in coastal North Carolina, for individuals to be farmers or fishermen in one season and boat and ship carpenters in another. Fishermen, ship carpenters, and anyone with a maritime occupation were often referred to as "boatmen" or "mariners." The 1850 population census for Camden County lists sixteen boatmen and that for Onslow County, in 1860, lists fourteen mariners.

Individuals also changed occupation. Edan Morse was a shipbuilder and merchant in Onslow County, but when he moved to New Hanover County, he listed himself as a seaman.

On Ocracoke Island, Simon H. Garrish, who inventoried only shipbuilding tools in his estate papers, was registered as a pilot in the 1850 census.[7] The 1850 and 1860 censuses listed a large number of mechanics in various counties, including Hyde. Christopher C. Flowers was a ship carpenter in 1840 when he took on an apprentice, but in the 1850 census, he is listed as a mechanic.[8] A vessel could also be built by one master ship carpenter using free, skilled, and unskilled labor as well as slaves. Ebenezer Pettigrew, who owned a plantation in Tyrrell County, hired seven ship carpenters from Beaufort, including a master carpenter, and employed neighboring farmers along with his slaves in order to build a schooner at a site on his property.[9]

Master carpenter or foreman became a popular profession among North Carolina shipbuilders. In the 1850s, William Shaw Jr. was the master carpenter at William Farrow's shipyard in Washington. George Smith was the master carpenter for the Paine shipyard in Edenton, and a Mr. Vandazen held the same position for James Sewell at his yard near Fayetteville.[10] In New Bern, Daniel Diamond was the builder for the Nichols Shipyard, and Ephrian B. Hackburn for O.S. Dewey's facility.[11] In 1856, John A. Kirkman, a New York shipwright, was employed in Murfreesboro to build the steamer *Chowan*.

Available records for this period, including census records, clearly document that a substantial number of ship carpenters came from out of state and even from outside the country.

The New Hanover County population census for 1850 lists ship workers, such as ship carpenters, sailmakers, and riggers, from Maine, New York, Connecticut, Pennsylvania, Massachusetts, Virginia, plus two from Sweden, and one from Scotland. The 1860 census for the county lists one from England, two from Ireland, and two from Sweden, in addition to a large number from out of state. In the Elizabeth City shipbuilding trade, there were a substantial number of out-of-state ship workers but few at other shipbuilding sites in the area. Prominent shipbuilders such as Ezra Cornell and his sons from New York; Timothy Hunter and John Boushell from Virginia; Ebenezer Paine and James Cassidey from Massachusetts; and Captain

Vandasen of Philadelphia established shipbuilding facilities because abundant timber was available.[12] The 1850 Pasquotank County census lists fourteen ship carpenters, of which three were born out of state. Brunswick County lists five ship carpenters in 1850, two of whom are from out of state; and four out of eleven ship carpenters in New Hanover County were from out of state. However, of the fifty-five shipbuilders and ship carpenters listed in the Carteret County population census for 1850, none were listed as being from out of state.

The typical work force in North Carolina consisted of free whites and Blacks and slaves. As in the past, the apprentice system provided the state with experienced shipwrights. Between 1815 and 1840, at least forty-five boys, of both races, from age three to eighteen were apprenticed as ship carpenters to learn the trade. Of these, twenty-two were orphans. Many of the others were sons or relatives of a ship carpenter. Three of the apprentices were free Blacks, one of whom was an orphan.[13] The apprenticeship system declined in the 1850s because it was considered too expensive; nevertheless, it continued into the twentieth century.[14]

Many shipbuilders turned more and more to inexperienced labor. Only two bonds for ship carpenter apprentices were issued for Hyde County after 1840, and none after 1853. In New Bern, most apprenticeships were issued between 1815 and 1830; nearly all went to the Sparrows, but in 1848, two were at the Howard and Robinson Shipyard. From 1815 to 1860, there were ten ship carpenters, five sailmakers, five caulkers, and four ropemakers apprenticed in Craven County. Nonetheless, apprentices were never a major source of labor in North Carolina.[15] Indeed, slaves were the preferred labor force throughout the antebellum era.

In the shipbuilding industry, artisans and laborers, slave and free, worked together in a variety of roles and relationships. Blacks were involved throughout the antebellum period. Enslaved artisans, like free craftsmen, often entered their trades through apprenticeships.[16] Blacks unquestionably made up a substantial segment of the labor force in shipbuilding and, in fact, were involved in most maritime trades in the South during this period. Between 1800 and 1860, Blacks made up approximately 45 percent of the total population of nineteen tidewater counties in North Carolina and were preeminent in the state's maritime industries, including caulking and rebuilding vessels.[17] In the Albemarle Sound area "the African-American, both free and enslaved, played a prominent role in the nineteenth-century economy," their "artistic" occupations including ship rigger and ship carpenter.[18] Evidence suggests white tradesmen were concerned about competition from Blacks. Organizations such as "mechanics' associations" were formed in Wilmington and other coastal communities to control or limit Black involvement in maritime industries.[19]

There were few industries in the agrarian, antebellum south and few slaves worked in them.[20] Generally, slaveholding records do not list occupations, skills, or duties, but slaves were widely employed in shipbuilding as laborers and as skilled artisans. Deeds often mention the sale of male slaves to an individual who, at one time or another, claimed to be a shipwright. John Burgess, an Elizabeth City shipbuilder, owned seventeen male slaves, but, other than their ages, no information is provided. Thomas Howard, a prominent New Bern shipbuilder, furnished living quarters in his house located on his shipyard property for six slaves who apparently worked there. Ulysses Ritch, a Washington shipbuilder, owned a "lot of Blackes," many of whom were presumably engaged in shipbuilding. According to the 1830 census, the Cornells, shipbuilders in Washington County, had twenty-four slaves in their households. Of these, eleven were engaged in manufacturing, much of it likely related to ship construction. Their father in Martin County had six slaves working for him.[21] Malachi Roberson, in Craven County, received ten dollars a month by leasing his slaves for ship construction.[22] The Tarboro N. Carolina Free Press advertised two "flat caulkers" for sale, presumably slaves who specialized in working on flats.[23] An article in the New Bern Daily Progress mentions "a beautiful boat, of large size" built by a slave in Wilmington and stated that "[t]he Black has never served at any trade; nor had access to tools prior to the commencement of the boat."[24] Otway Burns owned eleven slaves who were employed in shipbuilding and his other businesses.[25]

The majority of men employed in Jonathan Havens's Washington shipyard were slaves. According to the 1850 slave schedule, John Boushall, in Edenton, owned eleven male slaves, ages eighteen to fifty, but there is no indication they were employed in his shipyard. However, two of Ebenezer Paine's four slaves worked in his Edenton shipyard. An 1816 issue of the New Bern Carolina Federal Republican mentions a shipbuilder on Clubfoot Creek who had a large number of slaves working as ship carpenters, caulkers, and blacksmiths.[26] Skilled slaves were considered valuable. In Elizabeth City, Timothy Hunter owned twenty-two male slaves and employed a number of them in his shipbuilding activities, including seven ship carpenters, a blacksmith, a caulker, and a sawyer. He considered them so important that they were insured for $5,800.[27] James Cathcart Johnston, a planter in Pasquotank County, remarked that by using his own slave labor, it would not "cost me much" to build a canal boat. Contracting for a steamboat in 1861, he persuaded the shipbuilder to employ two of his slaves to cut timber and work on the vessel.[28] At times, enslaved Black shipyard workers fled and rewards were offered for their return. Occasionally, runaway slave notices described an escaped slave as a ship carpenter or caulker.[29]

Frequently, Black artisans, slave and free, were competent in more than one trade. This is particularly the case with regard to shipbuilding and house construction. Felling, hewing, and hauling ship timber was a part of the shipbuilding trade and slaves were often employed in these activities. Blacks also dominated the caulking trade and were sailmakers and shipjoiners.[30] Skilled slaves with shipbuilding expertise were often hired out. The May 19, 1837 edition of the *Newbern Spectator* advertised a number of slaves available for hire for a year. They included ship carpenters, caulkers, and a blacksmith. Josiah Collins of Somerset Plantation possessed a caulker and a shipwright, valued at $500 each, both of whom he hired out.[31] In 1856-1857, a case entitled *James W. Bell v. Caleb L. Walker et al.* was brought before the state Supreme Court. Caleb Walker and Jesse Herrington, shipbuilders of Plymouth, agreed to employ three of Bell's slaves for four years and teach them the ship carpenter and caulker's trades. Bell sued at the end of the stipulated period, claiming that the defendants (Walker and Herrington) had not done as they agreed, but instead used the slaves primarily to cut and haul timber. Bell claimed, and the court agreed, that because the training had not taken place, the slaves were worth considerably less in value.[32]

Free Blacks engaged in many of the shipbuilding trades. In 1830, Hull Anderson, a former slave and ship carpenter, bought a waterfront lot in Washington and established a shipyard. Anderson owned extensive real estate in Washington. His workforce included four black slaves. There is little information on the number of vessels he built or repaired. However, he retained ownership of the shipyard until 1841, when he sold his property in Beaufort County and, with his family, moved to Liberia. He built two ships to carry his family and others to Africa under the auspices of the American Colonization Society.[33] Sutton Davis, who became a shipbuilder and fisherman in Carteret County, was trained as a ship carpenter by a small planter and shipbuilder, Nathan Davis.

Clearly, Blacks had a significant role in North Carolina ship and boat construction. Those who were free not only worked for wages but saved enough to purchase land, become entrepreneurs themselves, and even owned or utilized slaves at their shipyards.

Obviously, this was a rare occurrence in the antebellum South. Census returns list riggers, sailmakers, blacksmiths, caulkers, and, of course, ship carpenters. Master carpenter is listed on vessel document papers but not in census returns, nor are shipyard manager, foreman, or superintendent listed. Master carpenters, such as Timothy Hunter of Pasquotank County and Thomas Howard of Craven County, owned their own shipyards. Other shipbuilding trades mentioned in North Carolina papers and documents include blockmakers, joiners, sawyers, carvers, gilders, painters, and glaziers.[34]

Shipbuilders and shipyard owners' names appear in newspapers and official documents but are not found in population or manufacturing census returns as being involved in the shipbuilding business. The shipbuilder was a businessman; the shipwright was an artisan.

The occupation of "businessman" is not listed in the returns. A more appropriate description would be either merchant or contractor.[35] Many ship carpenters aspired to be shipbuilders and a considerable number reached that goal.

North Carolina shipbuilders were generally small businessmen who had considerable difficulty making a living. They were often in debt and had to borrow money, sell property, or accept partners who were willing to invest in the business. The vessels they built were small compared to those constructed in the Northeast. With rare exceptions, even the more successful builders constructed few vessels throughout their careers. The more prominent shipbuilders in the Northeast rarely constructed small craft such as barges, lighters, or flats. North Carolina builders welcomed opportunities to build such vessels. They also actively pursued vessel repair; built bridges, houses, and buildings; and inspected damaged and salvaged sunken vessels.[36] Nevertheless, shipyard ownership often changed, and a large number of shipbuilders gave up vessel construction as a living.

A large number of shipbuilders engaged in a variety of business activities. Shipbuilders were listed in census returns or other legal documents as merchants. Many owned one or more vessels or a share in one or more vessels.[37] At times, businessmen engaged in building vessels simply by employing a master carpenter and the necessary labor, often slaves.[38] Virtually all owned farms or plantations and many owned sawmills. Charles M. Laverty operated a lumber yard in addition to his shipbuilding facility. A few took out shares in navigation companies.

In 1836, two Washington businessmen, William Tannehill and Benjamin A. Lavender, obtained a monopoly of steam navigation on the Tar and Pamlico Rivers for fifteen years from the General Assembly. They owned a sawmill, four turpentine distilleries, and were also ship chandlers and commission merchants. In the 1850s, John Myers and Son, another Washington firm, also became involved in shipbuilding.[39] In 1856, Hertford County planters and merchants hired a New York shipwright to build a steamer. Deed books for various counties suggest that shipbuilders owned extensive property and it is likely that mariners built and operated their own vessels as well.[40]

Businessmen, merchants, and planters purchased or contracted for vessels in and out of state. Samuel R. Fowle and his brothers owned a shipping business in Washington. During the nineteenth century, the company would either purchase or build twenty vessels, of which half were built in-state.[41] The practice of planters building their own vessels continued in the antebellum period but not to the degree as in the colonial and early national periods.

Samuel S. Simmons, a wealthy planter and businessman in Tyrrell County, owned and operated a fleet of sixteen vessels. How many were built in North Carolina is unknown; a majority of them, including thirteen canal boats, probably were. Just before the Civil War, the J. C. Blanchard and Company of Nixon Bridge in Hertford County contracted for vessels, including a two-masted schooner.[42] William Hollister, a native of Connecticut who migrated to New Bern about 1800, went into the import-export business there. Over the years, he gradually accumulated a fleet of sailing vessels. Three of the vessels were built in North Carolina: the brig *Jason*, constructed by Gideon and Thomas Sparrow at their shipyard on Jack Smith Creek in Craven County, and the schooners *Cygnet* and *Julia*, built by Freeman Ellis, a Beaufort shipbuilder.[43] The Dibble Brothers of New Bern and Kinston (formerly of Connecticut) built and operated a fleet of steamboats and lighters.[44] Nevertheless, many considered building their own vessels to be unprofitable. When Ebenezer Pettigrew, a planter of Tyrrell County, wrote a friend that he was building a vessel at his plantation, the friend replied, "have nothing to do with vessels or vessel building the latter cannot end profitable to you, the holding and running them is [sic] would bed still more so.... Again with the very best management by merchants who devote their time and attention to them they are expensive and unprofitable.... A farmer who spread his bread on the land may after many days gather it to gather it again but when he scatters it on the water I fear he will not again find it at all." Pettigrew replied that had he received the above in time, he would have given "its due weight," but "the keel is laid, the stern, sternpost & are up, the spars got & so far we are going well."[45]

Pettigrew made the decision to build this vessel in partnership with John Dunbar shortly after Christmas 1828. He felt he had little choice. He had to have transportation to get his crops to market; "[p]rocuring a vessel was more important to the planter than the crop price."[46] At times, vessels were not available, and when they were, the commission merchants and ship captains drove hard bargains realizing the hold they had on planters and farmers. Pettigrew's friend and fellow planter, James Cathcart Johnston, agreed that adequate shipping was crucial:

"...I know well the motive that prompts you to build [a vessel].... I have felt the inconvenience myself but never that of owning a vessel a river or canal boat was the sumit [sic] of my ambitions." Johnston was also convinced that even merchants, much less farmers, had a difficult time making profits from vessels that they owned.[47] However, the Pettigrew/Dunbar schooner did make a profit. In 1837, the vessel was crippled in a storm and abandoned after forty-six voyages.[48] Pettigrew considered building a second vessel but, ultimately, opted to purchase a used one. Johnston would later purchase a steamer and had a steamboat under construction at the onset of the Civil War. Not all planters made a profit. Samuel Simmons, a Tyrrell planter and businessman with sixteen vessels, accumulated so much debt that he lost all his vessels and plantation in 1856.[49]

A substantial number of North Carolina-built vessels were in operation outside the state. Pilot boats constructed in Wilmington and Smithville were utilized in Charleston harbor. Six sailing vessels engaged in coastal trade were owned by Savannah interests. Others operated out of New York and New England ports. The steamboat *North Carolina*, built on the Cape Fear in 1829, was the first steam-powered vessel to navigate the Ocmulgee River up to Macon, Georgia.[50]

Shipbuilders, who built vessels to order, usually negotiated a contract or indenture, specifying in detail the type of vessel, dimensions, type of wood and other materials to be used, date of delivery, and schedule of payment. Some contracts were more detailed than others. Contracts for flats and, at times, for larger vessels were brief. An agreement negotiated in 1815 between Jonathan Havens and Josiah Hawk of Washington simply stated dimensions, type of wood to be used, that the builder was to provide the necessary ironwork, that the construction be done in a workmanlike manner, and the schedule of payment.[51] However, contracts for larger vessels were usually more complex. Thomas Sparrow and James Howard of New Bern agreed to build a vessel for Thomas and Alonzo T. Jerkins. The contract read:

> 60 feet keel strait rabbit—22 feet Beam, 8 1/2 feet hole and out of the following materials, Timber and Stanchions of prime live oak and red cedar, the bends of prime white Oak, Bottom, Deck and Side planks of prime pitch pine, the fore and main hatches to be of prime white or Live oak or red cedar, the pawl bitts and knees of prime white or live oak, knees of prime live oak or red cedar, the keel, the keelson, bottom planks ... to be spiked and bolted with copper, all the bolts in the bends and Bottom to be bolted with copper except as much of the stem and stern postand upper breast hooks to be bolted with iron bolts, the deck plank, waterways and knees to be well fastened with iron spikes and bolts, the two lower breast hooks and transom log to be bolted with copper bolts, the ... windlass, knees and bitts to be bolted with iron bolts, all the heads of the spikes in the sides and deck and waterways, to be plugged with wood, all the trunnels to be of the locust wood.... W. Thomas Sparrow and James Howard have agreed to furnish the said vessel, free of Charge with the following articles, rig, main mast, foremast, main boom, foreboom, jibb Boom, Tiller, Bow Sprit, and Cat heads, main and foregaft – the main boom, foreboom And two gafts to be jawed. [the builders] ... bind ourselves to deliver the aforesaid Vessel during the month of June and July 1833.... We ... also agree to fit the Rudder in The patent style and to hang it with composition braces, pindles, and gudgeons

– We . . . {agree to pay twenty five} Dollars per Ton for the aforesaid vessel. One half at the time of delivery and the other half in a note payable six months after the delivery of the vessel with interest from the date.[52]

Payment was often in kind, bartering being a characteristic feature of the state's economy. Occasionally, those contracting for the vessel provided lodging and food, which resulted in reduced compensation.

Verbal agreements were common, particularly when they involved individuals in the same community. However, occasionally, they were not sufficient. In 1826, William Gregg, a ship carpenter, and William Woodhouse, a ship captain, both of Currituck County, agreed to joint ownership of a sloop. Gregg built the vessel and Woodhouse agreed to provide the ironwork. One unusual condition that would later create problems between the two was that the agreement was to be in secret "so that his [Gregg's] creditors would not sell vessel for little or nothing." Before the vessel was completed, one of the creditors applied for restitution. Woodhouse was at sea at the time, and in order to pay the debt, sold a share in the vessel. When Woodhouse returned, Gregg requested that he pay for part of the labor in building the vessel. Woodhouse refused. The disagreement went to trial, but there is no record of judgment.[53] The sloop was completed and named the *Entered Apprentice*.

Shipbuilding and Shipyards in North Carolina

There is no doubt that considerable ship and boat building took place in North Carolina during the antebellum period.[54] Examination of vessel documents in at the National Archives has revealed 1,013 vessels were constructed in the state between the War of 1812 and the Civil War. However, as already stated, records can be misleading. Names changed, vessels were rebuilt, and undocumented vessels were not listed, including steamboats used exclusively in intrastate activities. Vessel documents list thirty-five steamers constructed in North Carolina before the Civil War, but thirty steamboats were built in Fayetteville alone and only thirteen of those are included in the vessel document papers. Not even the *Prometheus*, the first steamboat built in the state, is listed. Steamboats were built from Smithville and Wilmington to Elizabeth City. An examination of newspapers and other records indicate at least twice that many were constructed in the state during this period. In 1853, North Carolina was supposed to have approximately forty-five percent of the South's steamboat tonnage.[55] In 1855, sixteen were in operation on the Cape Fear River alone.[56]

The shipbuilding industry was highly decentralized in North Carolina during the antebellum period. The state was overwhelmingly rural.[57] As late as 1860, none of the ports had a large population, although Wilmington's population had nearly doubled to 9,552 and New Bern had approximately 5,000 residents. Shipbuilding facilities were located in nineteen counties of the coastal plain. Customhouse officials recorded ninety-five sites where vessels were built in the state, including counties, various ports of entry, rivers, creeks, bays, sounds, and eleven islands. Four of the five top shipbuilding centers were ports of entry: Beaufort, New Bern, Elizabeth City, and Washington. The fifth center, which was actually the second most active on the list, was Currituck County, which had numerous sites. Information regarding the location and other specific aspects of shipyards is rather vague. An Onslow County land survey mentions a shipyard located on the east shore of the mouth of Queen Creek. The survey and other documents bear the date 1839. A notice of property for sale in Chowan County states that it was "commonly called the shipyard plantation." The ad notes that the shipyard, probably at Cashoke Landing, was on the north side of Cashoke Creek, a tributary of the Cashie River, which in turn flows into the Chowan River, all within Bertie County. In Thomas Bowen's will, a shipyard was described as being located between Jarvis Creek and Bailey Creek.[58] As Jarvis Creek is in Hyde County and Bailey Creek is in Beaufort County, it is not improbable that the shipyard was located along the shore of the Pamlico River between the two streams.

Throughout the era, over a thousand vessels were registered as being built at 123 different sites. Eighteen counties had shipyards and the state had three, but the locations of the latter are not known. Twenty-two sites were located on known rivers and streams, and forty-one sites were situated along a shore, bay, bank, island, strait, or some other land-water interface.

The remaining thirty-nine were located in known villages or towns. The county that produced the most vessels was Carteret with 183. Beaufort produced seventy-seven vessels, and Swansboro sixteen. This was the most active shipbuilding area in the state. The Albemarle Sound region hosted another concentration of shipbuilding activity. Elizabeth City alone produced eighty-six vessels; thirty-six were built at Plymouth; and thirty-four at Edenton. On the Neuse River, New Bern produced fifty-eight vessels, and Washington, on the Pamlico, produced fifty-six. Seventy percent of all the vessels built during the antebellum period were constructed at only thirteen sites, seven of which are known: Wilmington, Edenton, Plymouth, Washington, New Bern, Beaufort, and Elizabeth City.

As in the eighteenth century, the actual number of established shipyards in North Carolina is unclear. Changes in ownership, abandonment, new construction, and inaccurate records make it difficult to determine. The 1850 census on manufacturers lists seventy-one establishments in the state, but shipyards are not specifically mentioned. Nevertheless, it does record that John Boushell's shipyard in Edenton was the second largest industry in the county, with twenty-seven men. The 1860 census lists sixty-eight establishments for Craven County alone, but again, shipyards are not specifically mentioned, including the Sparrow and Thomas S. Howard shipbuilding facilities. For Howard, only the sawed lumber produced by his steam sawmill is reported. Discrepancies were common for other counties as well. At the beginning of the antebellum period, a shipbuilding site might be located on a plantation or, perhaps, on a temporary site and be abandoned after launching. Many sites consisted of one or more lots in a port town or on a piece of land on the bank of a stream or on the shore of an estuary, sound, or island. Most were small, accommodating a small sloop or schooner hull that could be built by as few as three men, with much of the specialized work being subcontracted. A few framed sheds housing tools, a blacksmith shop, a carpenter shop, a timber storage area, and a shipway, usually consisting of wide pine boards placed on bed logs, were all that was needed. Sometimes, sawpits and wharves were added if sites possessed high ground and deep water. After 1819, steam mills became increasingly common.[59]

Later, ports required larger, more complex ship construction and repair facilities. Several of the yards were sizeable, employing twenty or more ship carpenters, caulkers, riggers, sailmakers, blacksmiths, and even sparmakers and pump and block makers. In the 1850s, Elizabeth City had two large shipyards, one employing seventeen hands, the other twenty-five. Washington had three yards with marine railways. Beaufort had at least one large shipyard. In Wilmington, there were two large facilities and Fayetteville had at least one. The Sparrow Marine Railway, later taken over by William Robinson, was a leading employer in New Bern.

Steam boxes, for bending wood to required shapes, were introduced in the 1840s and at least one shipyard, on Bay River in Craven County, had one in 1849.[60] The Beery Shipyard, on Eagles Island across the Cape Fear from Wilmington, had a rigging loft, and John Boushall had a sail loft in his Elizabeth City warehouse. One of the Elizabeth City yards may have had a molding loft. The estate of John Cox, a Chowan shipbuilder, included "molding plans."[61]

A "designer" is occasionally noted in the construction of steamboats. The *Cape-Fear Recorder* reported that a Captain Patrick was the designer of the *John Walker*, launched in 1831.[62] This suggests that some North Carolina shipbuilders were using plans rather than laying out a vessel by eye as had been the tradition. The building of steamboats required skilled laborers, such as mechanics, who knew how to work with metal. Although lathes, drills, circular and band saws, and other mechanized tools were in use by the 1840s, there is no evidence that North Carolina shipyards had machine shops. Marine railways began to replace the traditional method of careening to overhaul a vessel. Their value in ship construction as well as repair was quickly realized.

Ship Repair

Ship repair and maintenance was an important source of income, probably more so for builders in the ports. The introduction of marine railways in the 1830s was a valuable addition to shipyards. Hauling a vessel completely out of the water, rather than careening it, provided workers easy access to the ship's bottom and side planking. It was more useful for repairs than for new construction. Repair costs were itemized: from hauling the vessel up on the railway to relaunching. Spikes, caulking, lumber, and other materials were listed. Workers were paid by the hour and by the shipowner rather than the supervising shipwright. Costs, of course, varied depending on the type of vessel and extent of repairs. Vessels with coppered bottoms were more expensive to repair if plates had to be removed. Of course, there were disputes over payment, inferior materials, and quality of work.[63]

Marine Railways

The first marine railway built in the United States was at Salem, Massachusetts in 1824.[64] In 1828, Thomas Sparrow constructed a railway powered by horses at his yard near Union Point in New Bern. The railway was built on the plan of a Long Island, New York, railway. In a court suit, Joseph Robinson, who was one of several partners in a shipbuilding firm, testified that their "railways are attached to the ground by battering logs into the ground and bolting . . . the ways to them." In 1844, the Howard Shipyard in New Bern installed new steam-powered railways "of the most improved plan."[65] Within two years, Washington boasted a new marine railway. The *Washington Times* reported that a schooner with her entire cargo was hauled up on the railway and repaired: "Under the old plan of heaving down, she would have to unload, and loaded again; besides incurring much more expense and double the detention."[66] Another steam railway was installed in Washington in 1847, and in the mid-1850s, this railway was enlarged to haul vessels weighing up to 400 tons. Washington obtained a third railway when the Pamlico Railway Company opened in 1855. The railway was specifically designed to build or repair steamboats.[67]

In 1837, Wilmington received its first marine railway. The *Wilmington Advertiser* announced: "We understand our enterprising fellow citizen J. Cassidey, is erecting a marine railway, to be worked by horse power."[68] A second one was built in 1851 by Samuel Beery and Son. In that same year, Bath, in Beaufort County, was the site of a small railway of sixty tons capacity.[69] Edenton and Elizabeth City obtained marine railways in the 1850s. The Elizabeth City railway was at the James Grice shipyard. As stated in the *Elizabeth-City Star and North-Carolina Eastern Intelligencer*: "A horse and a few men were able to raise vessels of 100 to 200 tons in two of three hours. . . . The great expedition, safety, and absence of strain on the vessel's

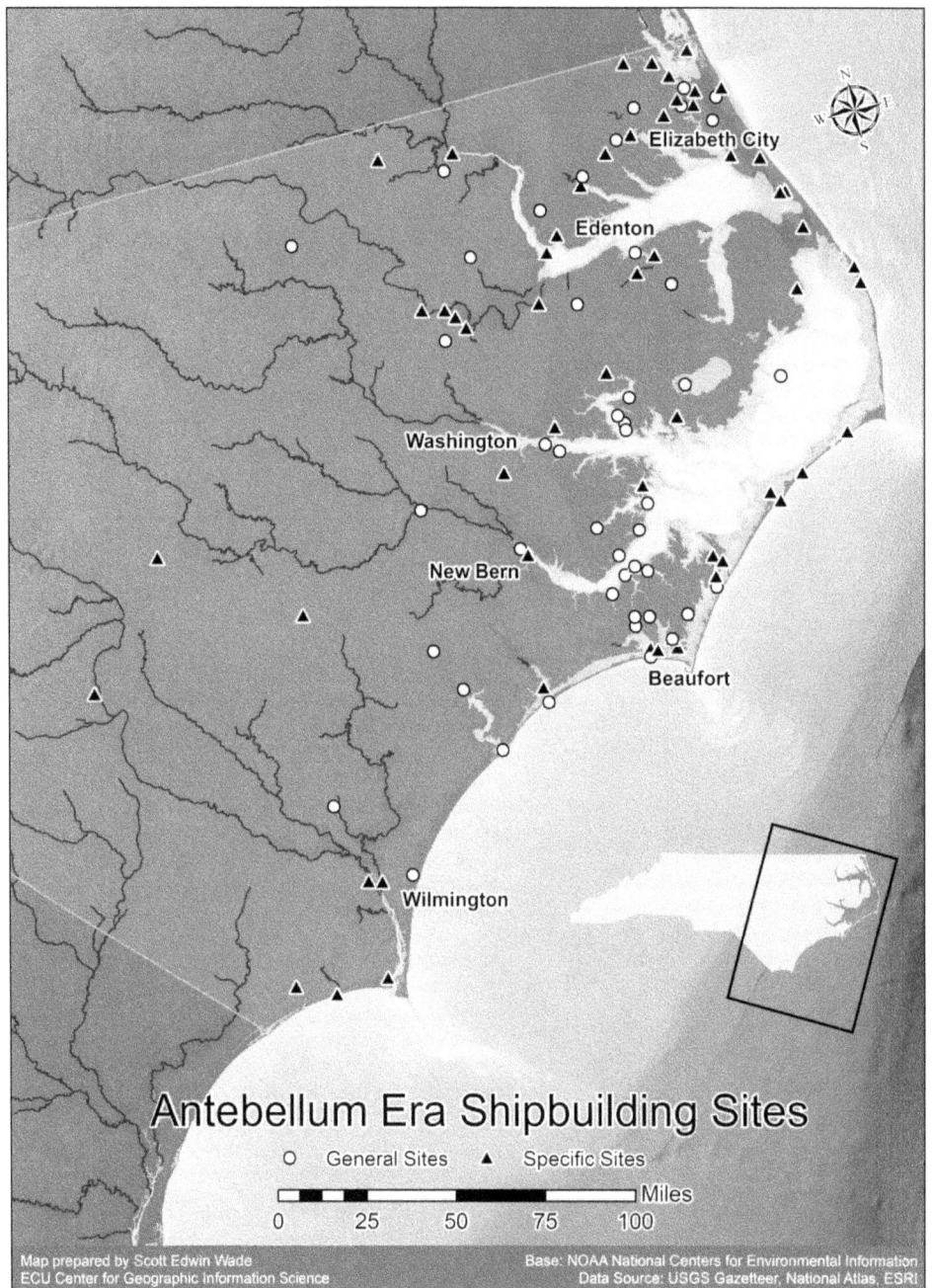

FIGURE 5-3 Antebellum Era Shipbuilding Sites in North Carolina lacks the concentration around the Albemarle as compared to the colonial era, with more ship construction shifting a little to the Beaufort area. *Source:* Author's database.

frame ... unite in giving a preference over the heretofore pursued of heaving vessels out."[70] Other railways used windlasses to haul vessels. With the exception of Bath, all North Carolina marine railways were located in small urban ports. No railway was installed in Carteret County, a center of shipbuilding during the period.[71]

Shipbuilding in Beaufort and Carteret County

Among shipbuilding sites throughout the state's coastal plain (Figure 3), fifteen vessels were constructed in Martin County on the Roanoke River, and two at Halifax. One of the largest vessels was built at Murfreesboro, on the Meherrin River. In the southern portion of the state's coastal zone, a number of vessels were built on branches of, and streams running into, the Cape Fear River. In 1829, Captain Vandazen of Philadelphia built a schooner of 100 tons at Fayetteville in the Sandhills region. According to the *Raleigh Register and North-Carolina Gazette*, this was "the first rigged vessel ever built upon the Cape Fear River above the head of the tidewater."[72]

Carteret County maintained the lead in shipbuilding during the antebellum period. With a total of 276 documented vessels, Beaufort led the state in ship construction.⁷³ However, specific vessels and shipbuilding establishments are rarely mentioned. The 1850 census lists fifty-five ship carpenters and three sailmakers in the county.⁷⁴ The 1820 census on manufacturing lists only two yards for the state, both in Carteret County. The census uses the term "regular yard" to distinguish between an established yard and a temporary site where vessels were built. The 1820s were peak years for Carteret County shipbuilders. In 1828, eighteen vessels were launched by builders, including Ambrose Jones, Benjamin Williams, Joseph Fulford, Freeman Ellis, and the Pigott family. Ellis was probably the most prominent builder in the county during the 1820s. He constructed a number of vessels for merchants in New Bern and elsewhere.⁷⁵

Although Otway Burns, the famous privateer, built his first vessel, the steamboat *Prometheus*, in Swansboro, he sold his shipyard there, purchased property on Core Creek and North River in 1820, and established a shipyard in Beaufort, where he also had a residence.⁷⁶ The *Warrior* in 1823, the *Henry* in 1831, and possibly the 272-ton brig *Rambler* were built there. He also constructed a small, two-masted sailing vessel that he named the *Snap Dragon*, after his War of 1812 privateer. He probably built other vessels there as he owned the schooner *Venus*, the flat *Elizabeth*, and a small fishing craft.⁷⁷

The Pigott (Pigot) family was also well known for shipbuilding. They built an undetermined number of vessels during the period including the *Pigott* in 1816, the *John Myers* in 1828, the *Elizah Pigott* in 1835, the *Dolphin* in 1845, and the *David Ireland* in 1854. Two of the three shipbuilders, not ship carpenters, listed in the 1850 census were Pigotts.⁷⁸ The Pigotts owned considerable property on the north side of the straits, presumably where most of the shipbuilding occurred.

Members of the Brooke family, who emigrated from Ireland in the 1840s and also settled on the Straits, were shipbuilders.⁷⁹ The Willis family was another prolific boat and shipbuilding family. According to the 1850 census, Benjamin, Washington, John, Edgar, Horatio, and Gabriel Willis were all ship carpenters. Members of the Bell family, well-known Hyde County shipbuilders, also constructed vessels in Carteret County.⁸⁰ In addition to the Pigotts, R. Howland, H. Willis, M. Longest, and M. B. Robertson, were building vessels in Beaufort in the 1840's. A notice in the *Raleigh Star and North Carolina-Gazette* mentions five schooners built there in 1845, and documents indicate two additional vessels were built in the county. Four vessels were under construction in 1854.⁸¹ Although there must have been other shipyards in the county, the location, names, and owners are unknown. There were no newspapers in the county, and legal documents do not cite shipbuilding facilities. Most of the shipbuilding facilities in the county were scattered along the many waterways and not concentrated in Beaufort. There was no marine railway in Beaufort or the county before the Civil War. The 1850 agricultural and industrial census does not record any shipyards in the county despite the large number of ships built and the equally impressive number of ship carpenters residing there. Moreover, no ship carpenters are listed in the 1860 census, but seventy-four mechanics are recorded.⁸²

Shipbuilding in New Bern and the Neuse River Estuary

According to vessel document records in the National Archives, eighty-eight vessels were built in New Bern and the immediate environs between the War of 1812 and the Civil War.⁸³ Little construction, much less trade, took place for more than a decade after the War of 1812. Wilmington rapidly surpassed New Bern as the leading port in the state. Nonetheless, there were shipbuilders and sail makers in the county.⁸⁴ Between 1815 and 1828, only six small schooners and one brig were built on Adams Creek, Smith Creek, or elsewhere in the county. In 1824, a 149-ton brig, built by Henry Carraway for his own use, was offered for sale.⁸⁵ In 1815, John Burney constructed the schooner *John Burney* on Broad Creek. That same year, another small schooner, the *Valentine*, was launched by Christopher D. Delmac on Richard Creek. Only one shipyard is recorded for New Bern in 1836. By 1841, five of twenty-six documented vessels constructed in the state were built in New Bern, and by 1850, eight of thirty-three were built there.⁸⁶

Sparrow family members were the most prominent shipbuilders in New Bern during the first four decades of the nineteenth century. The Sparrow and Howard property is shown on an 1849 map of the New Bern waterfront (Figure 4). From the 1780s until the 1840s, a considerable number of Sparrows entered the shipbuilding trade: Francis, Gideon, Joseph B., Robert R., Roderick, Samuel, William S., William T., Smith, and Thomas Sparrow II.⁸⁷ The Sparrows settled on Smith Creek in Pamlico County, the main site of their shipbuilding activities. In 1815-1816, they launched two schooners, the *Gideon Sparrow* and the *Sally Sparrow*. Although Gideon and other members of the family continued to build vessels on Smith Creek, at least two Sparrows, Smith and Thomas, moved to New Bern. In 1828, Smith announced in the local newspaper that he had established a shipyard near Union Point at the confluence of the Neuse and Trent Rivers.⁸⁸

The most prolific builder was Thomas Sparrow II who was born in 1783 at Smith Creek. Members of the Sparrow family included shipwrights who moved to Craven and Hyde Counties. Thomas Sparrow II was evidently the last of the family to build vessels on the creek before moving to New Bern in the 1820s. As early as 1826, he relocated to New Bern where he engaged in shipbuilding and repair work until his death in 1853.⁸⁹ There is no record of the total number of vessels he built, although local newspapers often carried notices of their launching. He not only constructed vessels for the North Carolina trade but out of state interests as well.⁹⁰ At some time prior to 1830, he entered into a partnership with

James Howard, son of Josiah Howard, owner of a large plantation in Jones County.[91] They built at least three vessels: the *Panther*, the *Lion*, and the *John L. Durand*. In 1829, Sparrow launched the large schooner *Tiger*. In 1836, with the death of James Howard, the partnership dissolved. Thomas Sparrow bought out Howard's share of the business from the heirs.[92]

The shipyard at Union Point consisted of various shipbuilding facilities, including a railway. A second facility was built several years later. Sparrow also built a three-story brick house on the premises where he and his family lived. The Sparrow yard was the only one in New Bern until after 1836, when John Darling established a shipyard on the Trent River to build steamboats, and John Osgood and John Noe, both from Beaufort, formed a shipbuilding business, purchasing lot 11 in New Bern as the site for a shipyard, which remained active well into the twentieth century. Darling built the *Wayne*, the first steamboat constructed on the Neuse River. In 1839, Osgood sold his interest in the business to Malachi B. Roberson, also from Beaufort. Noe remained in the shipbuilding business until he died in 1841.[93]

Ownership of the shipbuilding site continued to change. On December 8, 1841, Malachi, "surviving partner of the firm of Noe and Roberson," sold part ownership in the shipbuilding facility to his brothers Joseph and William, and the firm became known as Roberson Brother (some accounts use Robinson, not Roberson). Evidently, there were other investors in the business. In 1843, Malachi, who also built vessels in Beaufort, sold his interest to Thomas S. Howard, and the yard became known as Howard and Roberson's Shipyard.[94] Howard's brothers, James Jr. and Samuel, were also shipwrights.[95] They moved to New Bern, entered the "shipbuilding trade," and later joined their brother in the Craven County shipbuilding business.[96] In 1843, Howard and the two Roberson brothers advertised in a local newspaper for shipbuilding and repair business.[97] That same year, a fire damaged the shipyard and marine railway. Two years later, Joseph Roberson sold his interest to James Pittman, and the firm's name was changed to Roberson, Pittman and Company. Thomas Howard's name was not included in the firm's title at this time, possibly because he owned a relatively small interest in the business. In 1848, he purchased a larger interest from three other investors: Thomas Wallace, Oliver Dewey, and James Howard, his brother.[98]

Thomas Howard owned cotton gins, gristmills, sawmills, warehouses, wharves, the waterfronts of lots numbers 9, 10, 11, and 12, which included the shipyard and adjacent property, as well as other property in the town. From the mid-1850s until the 1940s, the property remained in the Howard, Ellis, Wade, and Meadows families with its shipyards, marine railways, sawmills, gristmills, wharves, and warehouses.[99] In 1848, William Roberson bought out the interest of his brother, Malachi, and retained interest in the yard until 1859. Nonetheless, the yard was known as: "Messers Howard, Pittman and Company."[100] According to testimony by the company's clerk, Howard actually managed the yard. Roberson was the master carpenter, and Pittman and his brother worked as carpenters. However, Pittman was listed as master on three vessels built between 1848 and 1850. In 1857, there were at least two shipyards in the port: Howard and Roberson, and the Sparrow facility leased by Joseph Roberson. In 1848, Howard and Roberson launched at least four vessels, including a sailing yacht, and the 240-ton schooner *Napoleon*. The Howards built two large schooners, the *Cassandra* in 1848 and the *Laura E. Johnson* in 1852, the latter designed to run as a packet between New Bern and New York, and at the time, the largest vessel home ported in New Bern. The *Cassandra* was engaged in trade to South America when she was lost in 1852.[101]

Despite these impressive accomplishments, the yards remained in debt. In 1849, Alexander Miller tried to take over Roberson, Pittman and Co. because of debts owed by Pittman. Although he did not succeed, he did obtain Pittman's interest in the shipyard.[102] In 1852, Pittman's former interests were purchased from Miller by Howard.[103] However, as early as 1848, the business was in a precarious financial situation. Howard claimed that in the 1850s, he had to use personal funds to pay off debts. In an 1857 foreclosure suit, Howard and Roberson admitted that the firm "proved to be unfortunate in business and became and is utterly insolvent." No doubt the panic of that year and the recession that followed significantly contributed to the firm's insolvency. In 1859, an auditor appointed by the court determined that Howard owed the firm and its creditors $2,125 and Roberson $1,167. The firm was sold at public auction and purchased by Elijah W. Ellis, a turpentine distiller. Later that same year, a deed was worked out whereby Ellis and Howard each owned half of lot number eleven.[104] Ellis, who was not a shipbuilder, formed a partnership with Howard that lasted for several years. In 1856, Howard married Ellis's daughter, Nancy. Prior to the Civil War, Howard again came into sole possession of the waterfront properties including the shipyard.[105]

The Sparrow shipyard was also put up for sale in 1859. Joseph Roberson had leased the yard for many years. In 1854, the New Bern *Journal* reported that the "ship-yard, formerly owned and conducted by . . . the late Thomas Sparrow; but at present [is] under the auspices of our newly adopted fellow citizen, Mr. Stephen Fulford." Fulford, a merchant, may have assumed Robeson's lease as Sparrow still owned the property.[106] At that time, the property included the brick house, shipyard with railway, fall house, blacksmith shop, and other buildings. Lack of evidence to the contrary suggests the shipyard was inactive from 1859 to the outbreak of the Civil War.

The shipbuilding industry in New Bern declined during the 1850s.[107] Financial difficulties explain some, but not all, of the problems the Sparrow shipyard experienced under various owners from 1841 to 1859. Testimony in court cases cites contracts and verbal agreements among the different parties. Pittman was an illiterate ship carpenter who secretly mortgaged his part of the firm in order to buy out Joseph Roberson's interest. Pittman and Howard built private residences on the shipyard property and charged it to the company.

When Ellis obtained the property, it included a wharf, blacksmith shop, saw pit, marine railway, and a long working shed in addition to the two residences. In 1847, the firm leased a shop to Benjamin Swindell to make blocks and pumps.[108]

There were other shipyards and builders in New Bern and Craven County that competed with the Sparrow and Howard facilities. The Ritch brothers, Isaac and Ulysses, were building vessels there as early as 1842. Thomas B. Wallace built lightships in 1828 and 1831, as well as a schooner in 1834. In 1829, Jonathan G. Calley built a small vessel for use on the Dismal Swamp Canal.[109] The 120-ton schooner *Wade* was launched in 1832 from the shipyard of Mr. Ellis.[110] Thomas McLin was also a New Bern shipbuilder. The brig *Julia* was to have been completed and launched in 1835, but on the day of her launching, "owing to some imperfection in the structure of the 'ways' the more the workmen 'tried' the 'more she wouldn't go'." She never left the shipyard because of a misunderstanding between the builder and owners, "which put the vessel into the legal dry dock." Before the legal fight was over, "she had gone to decay" and, eventually, sank at her moorings. The wreck was discovered and removed in 1881.[111] John Darling owned a shipyard on the Trent and is supposed to have constructed the first steamer on that river. O. S. Dewey established a shipyard on Smith's Creek and built a number of large vessels, including the 175-foot schooner *Henrietta*.[112] Due to discrepancies in customhouse records, it is difficult to determine the exact number of vessels he built. Some were built on Smith's Creek, and some in Craven County. In 1840, the bark *William Henry Harrison* was constructed at the shipyard of Mr. Floyd on South Front Street in New Bern.[113]

The schooner *Henry Clay* was constructed at "Cobert's Shipyard."[114] The Dibble Brothers were not shipbuilders but employed shipwrights to construct the steamer *Chatham*. There was also a large shipyard owned by an unknown planter in the southern part of the county.[115] In the year ending June 1850, four schooners, one ship, and three steamboats were built in New Bern.[116]

Bay River, about twenty miles downstream from New Bern, was in Craven County until 1872, when Pamlico County was organized. As early as 1815, a shipyard was located on Bay River. The yard was owned and operated by Colonel Henry Tillman.[117] Fourteen ships, including the bark *Maintonomah* of 427 tons, were built on Bay River between 1815 and 1860. The bark, named after an Indian chief of the Narragansett tribe, was built for a New Bedford, Massachusetts firm by William H. Nichols who had established a shipyard on his plantation in 1847. During its existence, in addition to the *Maintonomah*, the Nichols shipyard constructed five large vessels of 200 tons or more, including at least two others for Massachusetts firms. He employed thirty men, evidence of a relatively large shipbuilding facility. Because of debts, the Nichols property on Bay River, including the shipyard, was sold at public auction in September 1849. In addition to the shipbuilding facility and plantation, a pleasure boat with sails and the frame of another 200-ton vessel on the stocks was sold. Although there is no evidence that he had a railway, he did have "a patent steamer for steaming plank" and about everything else needed to build large vessels. In February 1850, a Dun and Company report bluntly stated that Nichols was "[o]ut of business; insolvent and gone."[118] The village of Jackson (later Stonewall) had a boatworks in the 1850s. Josephus Daniels Sr., the father of Josephus Daniels Jr., editor of the Raleigh *News and Observer* and later Woodrow Wilson's Secretary of the Navy, was a shipwright for a number of years, resided in the vicinity of Bayboro, and engaged in boatbuilding. In the 1850s, he moved to Beaufort County.[119]

An ad in the May 25, 1832 issue of the *New Bern Spectator* appealed for four or five ship carpenters to report to Durham Creek Mill on the Pamlico River.[120] On October 11, 1833, the *New Bern Spectator and Literary Journal* reported that "[d]uring a ramble around our wharves and ship-yards the other day, we were forcibly impressed with the advantages [in shipbuilding] we possess." The April 4, 1834 edition of the (New Bern) *North Carolina Sentinel* stated that four new vessels had been constructed in the port in the course of a year. On October 6, 1858, the (New Bern) *Daily Progress* noted that "[s]hipyards are crowded with work at present."[121] Nevertheless, this activity was primarily for the repair of vessels because, in fact, there was very little construction during the year.

Shipbuilding in Swansboro and Onslow County

Onslow County was not as important a shipbuilding center as some other coastal counties, but nonetheless produced a considerable number of vessels. Swansboro, the major town in the county, is at the confluence of the White Oak River and Bogue Sound at Bogue Inlet. The White Oak River basin is relatively small. Its resources and navigational advantages were limited. Nevertheless, from 1815 to 1861, at least thirty-five oceangoing sailing vessels and two steamboats were built in Onslow County. Eight were constructed on New River, one each on White Oak River and at Bogue Inlet, and eleven others are listed for the county.[122] During this period, builders in the county included Caden Cooper, who owned a tract of land in the Stump Sound area, Eden Bell, John M. Pigott, Samuel Wiley, C. H. Barnum, George W. Willis, and Captain Eden Morse. Morse was a prominent mariner, merchant, and shipbuilder whose business enterprises were located in Swansboro in the 1820s and 1830s. In 1833, he sold his shipyard in Swansboro and established a store and shipyard on the northeast branch of New River. The New River, with a smaller drainage area than the White Oak River, did not support any large communities. Nevertheless, Morse constructed a number of vessels, two of which were the schooner *Caleb Nichols*, launched in 1833, and the brig *Caroline*, launched the following year.[123] Edward Bishop Dudley inherited a shipyard on New River and listed his occupation as shipbuilder. He was a prominent politician who served as governor and in the U.S. House of Representatives.[124] Census records for 1860 listed only two shipwrights, Samuel Wiley and Ross Moss, as residents of Onslow County.

Shipbuilding in Washington and Beaufort County

Beaufort County was third in shipbuilding with seventy-seven documented vessels. Hyde County was a close fourth with seventy-five. Although Washington was the center of ship construction, vessels were built elsewhere in the county, on the Tar and Pamlico Rivers and Pamlico Sound, on Goose Creek, North Creek, Durham Creek, and Bath Creek. In 1819, Thomas Bowen owned a shipyard on Bailey's Creek.[125] Bath, the old port of entry, still had a shipyard in 1853, but it was used primarily for repairs, not for new construction.[126]

Until the mid-1850s, between one and four documented vessels were built in Washington annually. Between 1815 and 1820, only nine small vessels were constructed in the entire county. Abner P. Neale and Jonathan Havens were the only two shipbuilders able to sustain steady business. In May 1815, Neale advertised a new, 160-ton vessel for sale, and Havens contracted to build a seventy-foot vessel for a local merchant.[127] Neale's shipbuilding facility was located on Castle Island opposite the point where the Tar widens into the Pamlico River. In 1847, he sold the island to Benjamin Hanks.[128] Havens employed eight workers, principally slaves. He was a "born ship builder, and had this talent been cultivated would have been one of the foremost of the times." He built at least three vessels before his death in 1828.[129] The name Havens disappears from the list of shipbuilders until the mid-1850s, when the firm of Havens, Wiswall, and Havens built the steamer *Wilson*.[130] The 1820 census of manufactures mentions two "regular" shipyards in Washington employing fourteen men. The census taker reported shipbuilding was "formerly good but now little demand and declining," and probably used the term "regular" to mean "established." Another shipbuilding facility, on Bailey's Creek in the vicinity of Pamlico Point, was owned by Thomas Bowen, but the name disappears from the list of shipbuilders in 1830.[131]

In 1830, Captain Hezekiah Farrow built the first marine railway in Washington. Initially, the railway was used only for repairing vessels. Farrow's shipyard, railway, and wharf lay on the water in front of his house. He also owned a blacksmith shop and other property in the town. He died in 1833. Subsequently, the shipyard and marine railway were rented out, possibly to Burton Shipp who, in 1837, purchased an "undivided seventh part in Farrow's property" including the shipyard and railway.[132] With the exception of the portion sold to Shipp, the heirs of Hezekiah Farrow held the family property as owners in common for twenty years. It is probable that Shipp worked at the shipbuilding facilities for most of this period, either leasing what he did not own or paying a percentage of the profits. Like many other builders in the state, he continuously had financial difficulties.[133] Joseph Farrow, who was one of the family's trustees for the property, also leased the facilities during this period. Joseph Farrow, like his father William, was a ship carpenter. In 1847, the Washington *North State Whig* reported that "[t]hree vessels have been recently launched here [including] the schooner Benjamin F. Hanks by our young townsman Joseph Farrow.... Besides [this one] ... Mr. Farrow has two vessels under way at the Railway yard."[134]

In 1856, Joseph Farrow purchased the shipyard and marine railway from David Farrow, who had himself bought the waterfront lots with the railway and other buildings from the other Farrow heirs.[135] Except for the years when Union troops occupied Washington, Joseph Farrow would own the shipyard and railway until his death early in the twentieth century. In 1860, Dun and Company reported that Joseph Farrow "is worth no property but is solvent. His yard has a fine share of work. Is now building a small vessel and is preparing to build another. I hear that like his father he does his business loosely and is not a thrifty man." The 1861 report was far more complimentary: he "paid strict attendance to business."[136]

The 1840 census listed six shipbuilders in Washington: Joseph Farrow, Abner Neale, Burton Shipp, Hull Anderson, Benjamin Styron, and William Tannehill. Hull Anderson was a free Black who owned and operated a shipyard in Washington from 1830 to 1841 when he disposed of his holdings and migrated to Liberia. Born enslaved and later freed, he became prosperous, owning in addition to the shipyard, a dozen lots in the town and at least four slaves who worked with him in the yard.[137]

In 1835, Tannehill and Benjamin A. Lavender built the *Edmund D. McNair*, the first steamboat constructed in Washington. Lavender, a local businessman, was not a shipwright. Tannehill was a shipbuilder, and along with Lavender, was a commission merchant as well as the latter's partner in a sawmill, turpentine distilleries, and a shipyard.[138] Two years later, they leased the shipyard to John Myers, a native of Pennsylvania, who arrived in

Washington in 1825. He opened a mercantile business and, with his sons, leased and then purchased the Tannehill and Lavender shipyard, which was renamed the Washington Marine Railway. The firm employed carpenters, caulkers, sparmakers, blacksmiths, and other artisans. In 1837, Myers and Sons were virtually bankrupt and had to sell their property, including the shipyard and an unfinished marine railway, to pay their debts.[139] Within a few years, the Myers family would regain control of the shipyard and marine railway and retain it until the twentieth century.

In 1854, Myers purchased waterfront property, including the shipbuilding facilities. In 1858-1859, the firm constructed a new railway of four hundred tons called the Pamlico Railway Company. Myers and Son was primarily a shipping and commission business, but, as with many firms, it initially engaged in shipbuilding to provide vessels for its own use. Gradually, it became a profitable enterprise. Although the Myers organization built sailing vessels, it specialized in steamboat construction. One of the Myers-built schooners, the 144-ton *Herndon* (later, the *Jane Campbell*), was a blockade runner in the Civil War until it was captured by a Union naval vessel in December 1861.[140]

An 1845 article in the *Tarboro Press* reported that "Washington is a delightful place . . . wharves and shipping give it the appearance of a commercial city. About midway of the River is an island [called the Castle] owned by Abner Neale covered with workshops . . . for shipbuilding." An 1847 article in the Washington *North State Whig* stated: "We are gratified to see that the business of shipbuilding is exciting more and more daily attention of our citizens. Three vessels have been recently launched here.... two are . . . schooners, both built by one G. Floyd. ... Besides these, Mr. Farrow has two vessels under way at the Railway yard, and two are being built down the river, one by Paul Cornell, and the other by E. Ellis."[141]

The *Whig* described Paul Cornell as a "Master builder," having constructed forty-six vessels by 1850. Many of these boats were built in Martin and Washington Counties on the Roanoke River.[142] For a number of years after Cornell and his family settled in Washington, he was employed by Shipp's shipyard as a master ship carpenter, superintending construction. When Shipp went out of business in the early 1850s, Cornell either found work with another shipbuilder or opened his own establishment. He died in 1858 at age sixty-three. Paul Cornell was survived by his wife, Keturah, and three sons, Paul Jr., John, and Ezra. In the 1860 census, Paul Jr. was listed as a ship carpenter; the other two brothers were not listed as having occupations.[143] The schooner *Pacific*, launched in 1850 at the Shipp shipyard, is the only named vessel known to have been built by Cornell.[144]

The Cornells were residents of Washington when shipbuilding became a thriving business. According to the 1850 population census, there were twenty-three ship carpenters in Beaufort County. The 1850 census also lists four sailmakers, three blockmakers, one ship joiner and one caulker (black). Seven of the shipwrights, as well as several of the other artisans, were from other states. There were three marine railways in the town by 1855. In 1856, the Tarboro *Southerner* reported that Myers and Sons had finished a new marine railway; Farrow had replaced his first railway with a larger one; and Ulysses Ritch had recently renovated his railway.[145] Farrow also took on a partner, William Shaw Jr. They built at least two large schooners before the partnership fell on hard times and dissolved in 1858.[146]

The railway owned by Burton A. Shipp was bought out by Isaac W. and Ulysses H. Ritch, natives of Long Island, New York.[147] They entered the state's shipbuilding business in New Bern in 1841 and moved their business to Washington where they were able to purchase the Shipp railway and shipyard.[148] There is little in the records to indicate how successful the Ritches were. An 1853 article in the *North State Whig* boasts of a schooner with a length of ninety-three feet and a width of twenty-seven feet being built by the Ritches. In the same year, they obtained a contract to repair the deck of the Ocracoke lightboat from the local customs collector. Isaac Ritch died in 1853. Dun and Company reports for 1858 to1860 described Ulysses as "a man of good habits and good standing, industrious, consciousness and honest."[149] However, the business may not have prospered. Ulysses is not listed as a shipbuilder in the 1860 census. He had become a merchant, purchasing the "Beamer store" in 1858.[150]

Shipbuilding reached its peak in Washington in 1855, when twelve vessels were built there: nine schooners, two steamboats, and one flat designed to carry 550 barrels. An editorial in the *North State Whig* of Washington pretentiously claimed that their shipbuilding facilities were surpassed "by no place on the globe." The Panic of 1857 seriously affected Washington's shipbuilding industry. Only six vessels were completed between 1857 and 1860.[151] The 1850 census lists twenty-three shipwrights; the 1860 census lists only five in all of Beaufort County. Among these, neither Ulysses Ritch nor the Cornells are included. In fact, of all the shipbuilders mentioned above, only Joseph Farrow is listed. Interestingly, the recession had little effect on the major builders in Washington. In January 1859, the Tarboro *Southerner* reported that Myers and Sons, Farrow, and Ritch had all either erected new railways or improved the ones they already had. Recognizing the importance of the shipbuilding industry to their community, Washington newspapers gave it considerable coverage in the decades prior to the Civil War and, at times, promoted rivalry with other shipbuilding centers.[152]

Shipbuilding in Hyde County and the Outer Banks

In the antebellum period, shipwrights often migrated back and forth between Beaufort and Hyde Counties depending on where they could find employment. Hyde County's boundaries included the Pamlico and Neuse Rivers, as well as the Outer Banks. Although coastal North Carolina has numerous suitable sites for shipbuilding, Hyde County had more than any other location due to its long, crenulated shoreline. County shipwrights continued to be prolific builders. Between 1815 and 1860, at least seventy-five vessels were launched, including those built on Ocracoke Island and that portion of the Outer Banks encompassed by Hyde County. Builders on Ocracoke Island constructed sixteen vessels in the years immediately after the War of 1812, despite very little, if any, locally available shipbuilding timber. Ten were built between 1824 and 1847.[153] At least ten ship carpenters were residents of the county between 1815 and 1830, and the 1850 census lists two ship carpenters on Roanoke Island. The Midyettes built small vessels at Chicamacomico and Hatteras Village.[154] The Farrow family produced numerous boat and ship carpenters not only on the Outer Banks but on the mainland in Hyde, Beaufort, and Craven Counties. William Farrow lived on the Outer Banks before moving to Beaufort County. At Kinnakeet, on Hatteras Island, Tilman and Abraham Farrow were engaged in constructing vessels. In 1825, Tilman moved to Oyster Creek on the southwest shore of Roanoke Island and purchased "a piece of marsh by the name of the Ship Yard" from William Farrow. Later, he moved to Ocracoke and continued his boat building there.[155] Abraham was also a prominent shipbuilder in the county. Both he and his son, Abraham C. Farrow, are listed as shipbuilders in the 1850 census. This is probably an error as Abraham died in 1847. His shipbuilding tools and even his saw pit were sold upon his death.[156] The Farrow family, including Pharoah Farrow of Kinnakeet, were well-to-do. Pharoah Farrow was not only a shipbuilder but owned a number of vessels as well as a plantation and slaves.[157]

Other well-known Outer Banks families that periodically listed shipbuilding as one of their economic activities included Meekins, O'Neal, Fulcher, Gaskin, Garrish, and Flowers. Interestingly, they were also listed as mariners, or even mechanics.[158] Builders on Ocracoke Island included William and Wahab Howard, James Brooks, and Josephus Willis, as well as Tilman Farrow.[159] Although fishing rather than shipbuilding was the major occupation on Portsmouth Island, at least two vessels, the seventy-four-ton schooner *Elizabeth* and the twenty-one-ton *Elizabeth* were built there.[160] Wooden vessels did not have long lifespans but the schooner *Paragon* was an exception. Built on Ocracoke in 1838, she lasted more than fifty years. In 1885 she was still afloat, the oldest vessel registered in North Carolina.[161]

A large percentage of vessels built in Hyde County were probably constructed on the mainland. Documents and newspapers mention several shipyards: one on the Pungo River, a second at Swan Quarter operated by William Farrow and, later, Tilman Farrow, and a third near Germantown, the early county seat. In 1835, a visitor to Germantown mentioned the "Dunerly Ship yard."[162]

Shipbuilding in the Albemarle Sound Region

As in the past, considerable shipbuilding took place in the Albemarle Sound region, on the Roanoke River, and upstream on the Chowan River, to the Virginia border. The region constitutes one of the largest drainage basins on the eastern seaboard and, consequently, is one blessed with natural resources. The area supported a large number of small shipbuilding sites along the shores of the sound and coastal streams. There were large commercial facilities located in Plymouth, Edenton, and Elizabeth City. In contrast to previous years, there was little building in Perquimans County during the antebellum period.[163]

An article in the (Williamston) *Enterprise* mentions a shipyard owned between 1820 and 1850 by "the Slades" above Williamston on the Roanoke River but supporting information is not available. Another article from the Robersonville *Weekly Herald* states that a shipyard was located on the north side of the Roanoke River near Williamston in 1860.[164] Six documented vessels were constructed in Hertford County, including the large steamer *Southern Star*.[165]

The Currituck Sound area, located in the extreme northeastern section of the state, was a leader in the state's ship and boat building industry before the War of 1812. This trend continued during the antebellum period. Next to Beaufort, Currituck County led the state in ship construction with 106 documented vessels. Most of these were constructed during the first thirty years after the War of 1812; only eleven were launched between 1845 and 1860. Forty-nine different shipwrights are listed as building vessels in Currituck County from 1815 to 1830.[166] The 1850 census lists only six and the 1860 census only three. Some of the more prolific builders were Albert, William and Nathan Walker; James Prior; Caleb Ethridge; William Gregg; and Richard Knight. Knight and Ethridge constructed six vessels each prior to 1830. The Walkers, Prior, Lemuel Gregory, and others also built vessels in other counties in the Albemarle Sound area. This was a fairly common practice. If work was not available in one county, shipwrights simply went to another. In the 1850s, Dempsey, Isaac Tillett, Christopher Flowers, and Joseph B. Daniel were constructing vessels in the county. At his plantation on Martins Point, near Jean Guite Creek on the northern Outer Banks, William Hodges Gallop used slave labor to build several vessels that he employed in the West Indian trade. His son, in partnership with the Reverend Samuel Dutcher from New York, continued in

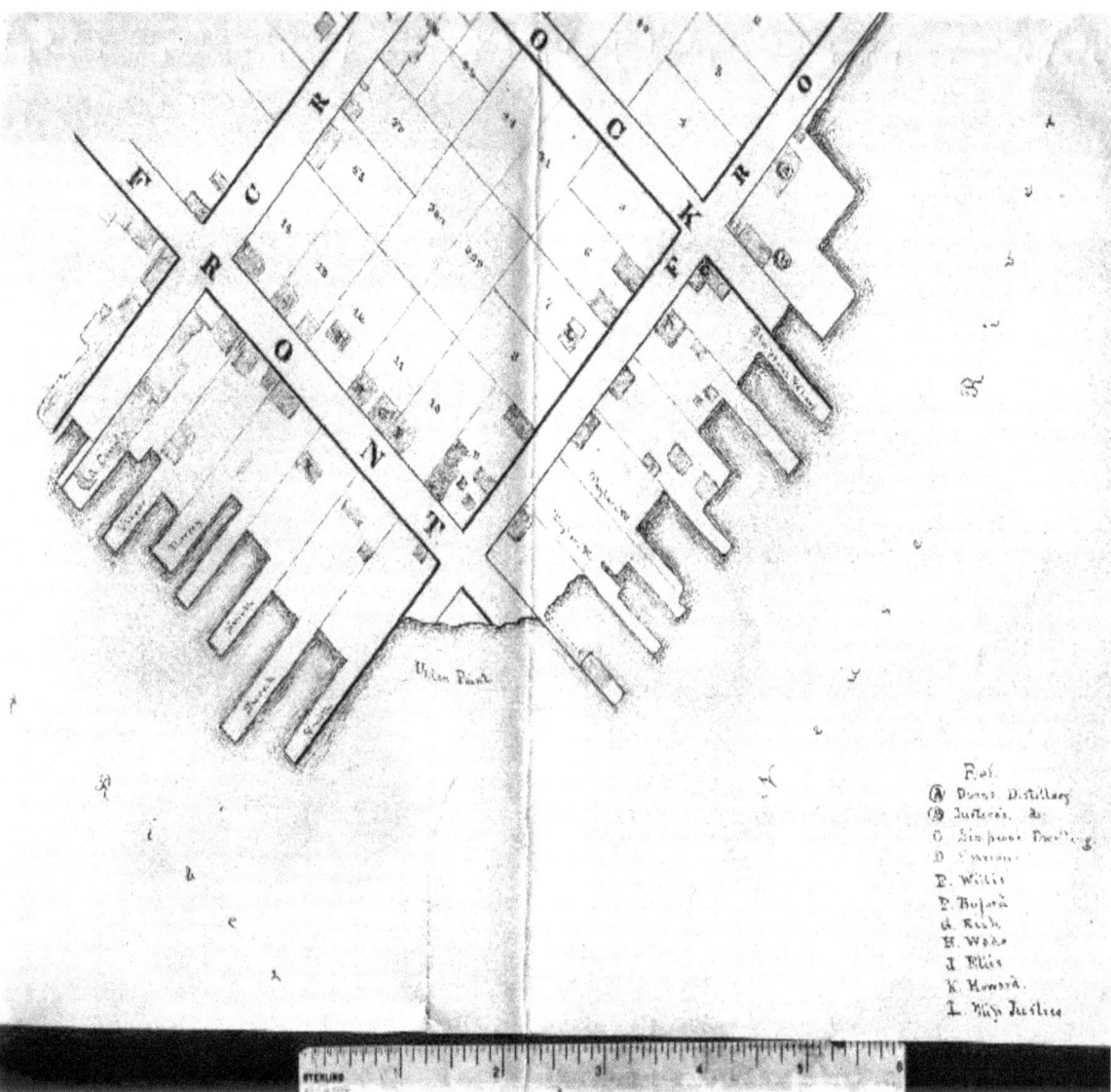

FIGURE 5-4 The New Bern waterfront in 1849 shows a few shipyards, as well as other port activities. Courtesy State Archives of North Carolina.

the ship and boat building trade. Much of the construction occurred on Knotts Island, a peninsula which protrudes south into Currituck Sound.[167] There are no records of large shipyards in the county. Most of the vessels were built on plantations or in small communities. A number of vessels were launched at Currituck Court House, the county's seat of government.[168] At least three schooners and probably other vessels were constructed at the Gallop plantation.[169]

Northeastern North Carolina reflected the industry's volatility. Waterborne traffic shifted due to politics, navigational improvements, and natural forces. The Edenton customhouse was relocated to Camden as a result of the closing of the Currituck and Roanoke Inlets to navigation and the opening of the Dismal Swamp Canal. The canal altered the area's sailing patterns, shipbuilding centers, and even vessel design. Local builders continued to construct vessels for the West Indian trade but began building vessels specifically designed for the Dismal Swamp Canal. Canal vessels, primarily schooners, were limited to a seventeen-foot beam and a six-foot draft based on the canal's width and depth. The bows were bluff rather than sharp in order to increase cargo capacity. Canal vessels were also limited in tonnage and length. As many of these vessels were not limited to Chesapeake ports but provided service to New York and other northern cities as well, they had centerboards, which improved their sailing abilities.[170] Elizabeth City, at the Pasquotank River entrance to the canal, became a transshipping entrepôt for cargoes between West Indian and other southern and North American ports. The small community also became a shipbuilding center.

From 1815 to 1830, there were at least seven ship carpenters working in Pasquotank County: Josiah H. Barker, Herman T. Hinds, John Shannon, John Bushee, Simon Walker, Alpheus Forbes, and Charles Grice. The latter constructed at least one vessel before the War of 1812 but only a few after 1815. Between 1815 and 1817, only two small vessels were built in Elizabeth City; it is not known if Grice was the builder. In 1829, the eighty-ton schooner *Madison Barge* was launched, probably the best known of Grice's vessels. Grice also built a vessel that was too large and drew too much water to pass over the bar at the inlet.[171] The fate of this vessel is unknown. Prior to 1829, he closed his shipyard, but his son, James, reopened it later that year.[172] He also expanded it by adding a marine railway. Charles Grice died in 1833.

In 1831, John Boushell purchased waterfront property from Thomas Butler, and immediately laid down a vessel. In that year, shipbuilding presented a "scene of bustle and activity such as we have never witnessed before…. The keels for two brigs of about 300 tons have been laid at the yards of Mr. Jno. Boushall and Mr. J.W. Grice and from the number of workmen employed these vessels will probably be ready to launch in three weeks. Mr. Grice has also at his yard, in 'full tide of success,' a Marine Railway."[173]

Elizabeth City developed as a shipbuilding center largely due to the completion and ever-increasing importance of the Dismal Swamp Canal. The trend began in the 1820s, accelerated after 1830, and, through 1860, Elizabeth City produced two to six documented vessels per year in addition to an unspecified number of barges and other undocumented watercraft. By the mid-1830s, there were at least two full-time yards and probably several part-time shipbuilding and repair facilities in the port and along the nearby shoreline. From 1830 to 1850, the many changes in shipyard ownership in Elizabeth City reflect the speculative nature of the industry.

By 1849, there were three established yards in Elizabeth City. Timothy Hunter had bought one owned by John Boushell; Charles. M. Laverty was operating the old Grice yard and railway; and John S. Burgess and Samuel D. Lamb had a third yard with a marine railway. An 1848 advertisement announced the opening of their shipyard and railway at Pleasant Point in Elizabeth City. Burgess and Lamb constructed at least four vessels by 1856. There were also builders who constructed vessels outside established facilities.[174] From August through early November 1849, three vessels were launched in the city: the *John A. Gambril* by Laverty, the *Huntress* by Timothy Hunter, and the *Samuel B. Lamb* by Burgess and Lamb. All three were schooners, two for the West India trade and the third built for the canal.[175] The 1850 census on industry for the county listed three shipyards, including the Burgess and Lamb and the Hunter facility, but the Laverty facility is not listed. A small yard, with only $500 in capital, is listed under Richard Numann; this is probably a spelling error, as his name was probably Richard Overman. An 1854 article mentions four shipyards in the city.[176]

The absence of Laverty's shipyard is surprising. A native of Ireland, he worked for several shipbuilders in Elizabeth City and vicinity before going out on his own. In the 1850s, he built at least three schooners, including a three-masted vessel. He also repaired a number of vessels, including at least one light boat. In 1850, Dun and Company reported that he owned a shipyard and vessels, had twenty to thirty employees—mostly Blacks, was dependable, and "never failed." However, the 1858 report stated that he had failed and was "perfectly insolvent."[177] In 1858, Laverty had to sell his real and personal property because of indebtedness. This included his interest in several vessels, his marine railway and shipyard, a new schooner on the stocks, and even eight slaves who were presumably workers in his shipyard.[178] The 1860 census lists him as a merchant. Laverty also owned a store and lumber yard, both destroyed by fire in 1852. Before the Civil War, Laverty retired to New York City; he was still living in 1869.

John Boushell was involved in ship construction in Elizabeth City and elsewhere in the Albemarle Sound area for over thirty years. As early as 1827, the *Elizabeth-City Star and North-Carolina Eastern Intelligencer* reported he was constructing the schooner *Mary Ann*. In 1828, he launched the schooner *A. Haddocks* and completed his first brig, the *George Loring*. The following year, he launched the *John Bartlett* and the *Henry Clay*, and in 1831, he built the 300-ton brig *Flora*. In that same year, he laid the keel of another large brig and purchased two lots along the Pasquotank River that became his shipyard. There is some evidence that he borrowed money from Matthew Cluff, a local businessman, to purchase the lots. Four years later he sold his shipbuilding facility to Timothy Hunter and moved to Edenton where he started another shipbuilding business. His relocation may have been a result of financial losses.[179] Sometime prior to 1853, he returned to Elizabeth City and reentered the shipbuilding business there. In 1853, he launched the schooner *Independence* and, the following year, the schooner *Ann G. Sikes*. He was still listed as a ship carpenter in Elizabeth City in the 1860 census. In 1855, Boushell built a schooner in Plymouth. It is possible that he did this with a brother or son as Benjamin F. Boushell is listed as a shipbuilder in Washington County in the 1860 census.

In the 1840s and 1850s, Timothy Hunter was the most productive shipbuilder in Elizabeth City. Between 1839 and the Civil War, he constructed at least twenty-eight vessels and several flats.[180] He also had an extensive repair business and, along with Boushell, contracted to inspect and report on the condition of damaged vessels.[181] Hunter was a native of Nansemond, Virginia, who moved to North Carolina and lived in New Bern before moving to Elizabeth City. Since he started building in Elizabeth City prior to 1839, it is conceivable that he constructed even more vessels. Nevertheless, Hunter, like so many other shipbuilders, had financial problems. In 1835, as a result of debts, he deeded land, "the railway blocks and falls, screws, augers, saws, timber, ring bolts . . . and all such other tools as he the said Timothy Hunter has" to Horatio Williams. Williams was not a shipbuilder and simply held the deeds in trust until Hunter paid off the debts. Interestingly, in the same year, Hunter and Lemuel C. Moore signed a management agreement regarding the prices and management of each builder's yard. In 1836, a fire destroyed his blacksmith and carpenter shops. Despite this, he prospered for, in 1838, he paid off his debt to Williams and purchased the yard owned by Boushell. Moreover, Hunter and Gilbert Elliott, a local lawyer, were partners in real estate transactions, acquiring various lots in Elizabeth City.[182]

Prior to the mid-1830s, Dr. William Martin, the first physician in Elizabeth City, entered the shipbuilding business as an owner, not a builder., but nothing is known of this enterprise. In 1834, William Martin bequeathed his shipyard property to his son Charles and Lemuel Moore.[183] Charles Martin, like his father, was not a shipbuilder, although he apparently learned the shipbuilding trade. Moore was a shipbuilder and ran the facility. However, Moore is not identified as a shipbuilder in the 1850 census, and the shipyard is not listed under either name in the industrial census for that year. What happened to the Martin shipyard during those years is unknown. Three shipyards are listed: Burgess and Lamb, Timothy Hunter, and R. Murmann.

Between 1850 and 1852, John Black purchased the Martin shipyard. According to vessel documents in 1853, he launched the schooners *Georgianna* and *L.D. Starke*. In 1857, he purchased a lot adjacent to his shipyard. However, within four months, he was insolvent and had to sell all his property at auction. William F. Martin bought the Black residence and shipyard that his family had once owned.[184] After the Civil War, Black became an insurance agent in the city. Although he was a lawyer, not a shipwright, Martin clearly took an active role in the yard and tried to make it a success. In 1859, he is listed as the master carpenter for the schooner *Planter*.

In January 1833, Elisha Nash and John Burgess became partners in a shipbuilding business.[185] What happened to Nash is not known. He probably died prior to 1850, but his heirs retained his property, including his share in the shipyard, until it was sold in 1858. Burgess remained in the shipbuilding business for more than thirty years. Sometime before 1850, Burgess and Samuel D. Lamb became partners. When Lamb died, Burgess, along with the Nash heirs, took ownership of the yard. The Nash, later Burgess, shipyard was adjacent to that owned by William F. Martin. In the post-Civil War years, Burgess filed a claim with the Southern Claims Commission for losses incurred due to the Federal occupation of Elizabeth City. The claim was filed in the name of Burgess and Martin, suggesting that they had become partners. There is a real estate conveyance dated April 1858, in which a James Hinton sold at public auction a piece of property originally owned by Elisha S. Nash that was "joining the Ship yard of W.F. Martin and Jno L. Burgess known as the Nash Ship Yard."[186] In 1857 or 1858, Martin and Burgess must have become partners. Whether their two shipyards were joined is not clear; at least that portion of the Burgess yard owned by Nash was not jointly owned. Burgess is not listed as a shipbuilder in the census of 1860, nor was he a party to the contract signed by William F. Martin with the Confederate government in 1861.

Martin, Griffin and Black, E. S. Nash, and J. S. Burgess were in the shipbuilding business in 1850.[187] The 1850 population census for Pasquotank County also lists fourteen ship carpenters. The 1860 census lists no commercial shipyards for the city, although small yards existed, and only nine ship carpenters are recorded for the county. Timothy Hunter and John Boushell are listed as ship carpenters, but C. M. Laverty is listed as a merchant and Burgess as a farmer. William Martin is not listed at all. He was a prominent lawyer in the city, and his shipyard was probably operated by one of the listed ship carpenters.[188] Between 1850 and 1860, five shipbuilders are listed in ship documents as master carpenters for vessels built in Pasquotank County: Willoughby Donald, Crandy Harris, John Sawyer, Joseph Lawrence, and Zephaniah Burgess. Two of these, Lawrence and Burgess, constructed two vessels each between 1855 and 1857.

The Elizabeth City shipyards produced thirty-five documented vessels from 1849 to 1859. A November 3, 1849, report in the (Elizabeth City) *Old North State* noted that in "less than three months, three fine vessels, two of them of large size and intended for the West India trade and the other for the Canal, has been launched from the ship yards of E. City."[189] In 1850, Hunter launched the *A. C. Williams* and a sixty-foot ship named the *Newman*. Five years later, Laverty launched the 336-ton *Charles M. Laverty*, "the largest ship ever built in Elizabeth City" up to that time. In 1856, 119 vessels were then "in commerce" from Elizabeth City shipyards. These included: one brig, ninety-three schooners, five sloops, four sloop boats, and sixteen lighters.[190] In 1858, eight vessels were launched by Elizabeth City builders. As with other North Carolina ports, the Panic of 1857 and resulting recession severely impeded the industry in Elizabeth City. Most of the builders went out of business. Only two additional vessels were constructed there before the state seceded.[191]

Edenton had been one of the leaders in the state shipbuilding industry prior to the War of 1812 but experienced a decline during the antebellum period. Only three small schooners were built there between 1815 and 1820. Each was constructed by a different ship carpenter: Phillip Millary, Jamy Prior, and Thomas Brownrigg. According to vessel document papers, these three schooners are among the twenty-nine small sloops and schooners constructed in Chowan County between 1815 and 1860.[192] In 1841, George Smith ran a shipyard in the city, and until 1849, his was the only established shipbuilding facility in Edenton. Later, Smith managed a yard owned by Robert Treat Paine.[193] In 1846, John Master, listed as a master ship carpenter, constructed a schooner in the port but his name does not appear in the 1850 population census. In 1850, shipbuilding may have been the second largest industry in Chowan County with as many as ten schooners produced there annually, most of them for the fishing industry. This may be accurate as small, local, fishing vessels were rarely recorded in custom house records. However, in 1852, only three small schooners, totaling 215 tons, were launched in Edenton.[194]

These three may well have been constructed by John Boushell, who moved there from Elizabeth City in 1849. He built three vessels in 1849-1850 and two more in 1851. According to the 1850 population census for the county, he was the only ship carpenter in Edenton. The 1850 industrial census reported that Boushell's shipyard employed twenty-seven men. In 1849, Boushell and Robert Trent Paine were partners. Paine was not a shipbuilder but a businessman. Boushell probably entered the shipbuilding business before forming a partnership with Paine. Sometime prior to 1853, he returned to Elizabeth City and reentered the shipbuilding business there. Paine remained in the shipbuilding business in Edenton with George Smith as his foreman and, in 1855, launched the schooner *Harriet Ryan*. Robert Paine's father, Ebenezer, a native of Massachusetts, had established a shipyard in Edenton early in the nineteenth century. In 1850, the Paine shipyard was offered for lease but no agreement was reached.[195]

In the mid-1850s, there were two shipyards in the town, one owned by Paine and the second by John Cox. Neither man was a shipbuilder. Cox was a local businessman who promoted a railroad for the town. Paine was a lawyer who owned shipping and shipbuilding businesses. He was also a prominent politician serving in both the state legislature and U.S. Congress. Cox died in 1856 and his shipyard, with railway, ways, and warehouse, along with a vessel on the stocks, a flat, and a bateau, were purchased by Tristram L. Skinner.[196] In 1860, the Paine yard was also sold to Skinner, and Paine moved to Texas. According to the 1860 census on manufacturing, the Paine shipyard was worth $20,000, with ten men employed, and the Skinner yard was worth $11,400, with fifteen men employed. The 1860 population census for the county lists only two ship carpenters. The operation of both shipyards came to a halt shortly after the start of the Civil War. Skinner was commissioned in the Confederate Army and was killed in 1862. His will makes no provision for the shipyards, but they were included in his property.[197]

The Roanoke River supported considerable traffic and was navigable for vessels drawing six feet of water for approximately a hundred miles upstream. Vessels were built all along the Roanoke River in Halifax, Martin, and Bertie Counties during the eighteenth century and before the War of 1812. Shipbuilding continued in those counties and in Washington and Tyrrell Counties in the antebellum period. Although there is no documentary evidence, vessels were certainly constructed in the latter two counties prior to 1815. Tyrrell County was the leader in the area, producing thirty-nine documented vessels. The Roanoke River was navigable for vessels drawing six feet of water or less for approximately a hundred miles upstream. In Halifax, near the head of navigation, two small schooners were constructed. In 1816, William Johnson launched a small schooner, and John Phelps built a schooner at Bull Pond fishery on the Chowan River. In the same year, two schooners, the *Sam Potter* and the *Sarah Potter*, were launched in Bertie County.[198] In 1820, a shipyard was established in the county, and small craft and undocumented vessels were built there for a number of years.[199] Only two small documented vessels are listed as being constructed there during the antebellum period. The 1850 census lists two shipwrights for Bertie County. No shipwrights are listed for either Martin or Perquimans Counties in the 1850 and 1860 censuses. Nonetheless, vessels were built there. Eleven were constructed in Martin County, including the 107-ton schooner *Joseph I. Williams* built in 1847 by Gilbert Floyd, and the *Melvina* built by T. Phelps in 1849.

An undetermined number of vessels were also constructed across the Roanoke River along a higher bluff in Martin County. In 1855, "Gilbert L. Moore ... launched above Williamston Landing a new vessel of about 150 tons burthen called *Martha Moore*." Gilbert Moore was identified in a court suit as both a shipbuilder and a sailor. He contracted to construct a coastal sailing vessel for New York interests. They were to provide sails, cordage, blocks, etc. to complete the vessel, later named the *Corrine;* Moore was sued for not paying his bills. Altogether, fifteen documented vessels were built on the Roanoke River above Washington County between 1815 and 1860. A large percentage of these were probably built by Ezra Cornell.[200]

In 1807, Ezra and his brother were ship carpenters building a vessel in Westchester County, New York. The vessel, which the two brothers owned, was lost on her first voyage. Shortly after the War of 1812, Ezra and his family moved to North Carolina in order to start a shipbuilding business. Initially, they resided in Martin County, probably on Welch's Creek, the dividing line between Martin and Washington Counties.[201] In 1817, Ezra Cornell wrote his brother:

> Paul and John are to work with me. We have boarded with the men that we are building for. My wife and Mary [daughter] have been down country all winter. ...I finished the vessel That I was at to good satisfaction. The owner sold her. I am now building another for the

Same man and have got her will forward. I have got the timber and planks nearly ready for my self of a good size [vessel] and shall be able to complete her hull with the means I have got here.... I live to get her finished. I will show you a vessel worth with all her upper works will be mulbary.... I can have frate for her as soon as she is done. If I have a chance to sell her I will sell and come and build again. I Can build vessels here To a grate advantage. Timber costs are nothing handy to the river. I get a teem (team) at one Dollar per day. I get plank sawd at one dollar per hundred by the plank and get hands at fifty cents per day ... we get bord at five dollars per month. I wish that thee would take every step possible to collect that money from Brower (says has to have it for rigging and sails).[202]

This ship may have been the *Alpha and Omega*, first documented in 1818. Cornell purchased property on the Roanoke River, probably in the vicinity of Jamesville. In 1830, he sold the property to pay debts and moved farther up the Roanoke to Poplar Point. In 1831, he launched the schooner *Margaret*. While this vessel was still on the stocks, his ship carpenters sued for back wages, and the court decreed that, once completed, the vessel should be sold, along with other property owned by Ezra, to compensate the workers. Ezra Cornell died in 1833.[203]

Approximately forty vessels were launched in Plymouth and Washington County during the antebellum period. The schooner *John Armstead*, built by Joel Thorp, was the first documented vessel constructed in Plymouth after the War of 1812. In 1821, a shipyard, owned by Horace Edy, built the 100-ton schooner *General Iredell*. An 1837 deed records a sailing vessel on the stocks at Mackey's Ferry.[204] Most shipbuilding activity occurred in the 1820s and 1830s after the Cornells relocated to Washington County. Exactly when the Cornells moved to Plymouth is unknown but the sons, Paul, John, and Elijah, all trained as shipwrights, were there by 1823. They also continued to help their father build vessels in Martin County until 1831. In that year, the brig *Hiram*, built under the direction of Paul Cornell, was launched. In 1830, the *Edenton Gazette and Farmer's Palladium* published a letter that was somewhat critical of the three steamboats navigating the Roanoke River. They drew too much water and were too slow. "I do not much admire the steam boats the Transportation Company have in our water ... the Messrs Cornell are now drawing the draft of a boat for them, which, it is confidently believed, will not draw over two feet; and from their well known judgment and skill, I am satisfied if they are employed by the company to build a boat, they will not, either in the quality of the materials, the excellency of their work, or the taste with which it is executed, be behind any other part of the country."[205] This may refer to the seventy-ton sidewheel steamboat *Plymouth* that was launched in 1835. In 1833, one of Elijah Cornell's sons, John, wrote a relative in New York: "Paul, Elijah and my self are engaged in business together. We are doing well. We employ from five and twenty to thirty five workmen constant the year round. We build from two to three new vessels a year. We also have [a] Railway for hauling up vessels and have as much as can do at that. We have lately purchased half of one of the greatest mills in this county about four miles from our town with navigation wright (sic) to her.... Father at this time is building a small vessel."[206] The Cornells probably built the schooners *Elijah* and *Indian Queen*, both completed that year.[207]

In 1829, Plymouth businessman Thomas Turner wrote that he had twelve men overhauling a vessel "on the rail ways."[208] Turner was not a shipbuilder. The vessel was on the Cornell railway. In 1830, the Cornells had to cede one-half of the shipyard as well as some other property to Plymouth merchants Joseph and William Norcom because of debts.[209] Two years later, "Paul Cornell and Brothers" bought back Norcom's holdings. They would continue their shipbuilding business in Washington County until sometime in the late 1840s.

In 1844, on Welch's Creek in the vicinity of the Chowan and Gates County line, Edgar Hanks, John Cornell's son-in-law, bought a share in the steam sawmill, ship yard and dry docks, and presumably the railway. This may have been due to Paul moving to Washington, North Carolina in 1838, leaving John and Elijah to run the railway and shipyard, or to the fact the shipbuilding business was not what it once had been. Hanks later rejoined the Cornells in Plymouth; what happened to his facilities on Welch Creek is unknown. Elijah Cornell visited his Plymouth cousins in 1843 and, in a letter to his wife, observed that shipbuilding was no longer the prosperous business that it had been for the past ten years: "There used to be considerable shipbuilding down here by our cousins and also a large one of repairing but this business has become very limited."[210] According to customhouse records, only two new vessels were built in the 1840s, the schooners *Charity* and *Edmund F. Hanks*. However, the marine railway remained active largely because of repair work.[211]

The firm was successful in obtaining several contracts to repair lightboats. Edgar Hanks, an engineer in 1850, certainly contributed to gaining the contracts. Before Hanks joined the firm, John Cornell surveyed the Roanoke River lightboat and submitted a lengthy list of needed repairs. He also urged that the work be awarded locally, not by contract for the entire project but on a day-to-day basis. He observed: "the pine timber is of a far superior quality to that used in the first instance in building the vessel and as commonly used at the place where she was built, which is called swamp or short leaf pine (if I am not mistaken) which soon decays.... Also I am informed, and am of the same opinion myself, that the carpenters in this place are superior workmen to any that are in this section of the country...." Of course, he requested that he be awarded the contract. However, under government regulations, the collector had no choice but put the project out for bid.[212]

The Cornells were awarded the contract. Five years later, John Cornell and Hanks surveyed the Roanoke River lightboat a second time and reported that it needed "extensive repairs." They recommended the vessel be hauled up on the railway, the bottom copper removed, and the planking thoroughly examined. Hanks stated that he could use iron rollers "made for the purpose" and reroll the copper "as new." The local collector of customs recommended that the Cornells and Hanks do the work: "In this place, there is but one shipyard and to have the work done under private contract . . . would be the cheapest plan...."[213] The custom collector highly praised the Cornell's workmanship as it was well respected in Plymouth. Nevertheless, they moved to Washington, and eventually gave up shipbuilding. Elijah died in 1845 and John in 1851.[214]

Hanks bought out the Cornells, and later sold their sawmill to Joseph A. Spruill. In 1852, the collector of customs in Plymouth informed the Lighthouse Board that he could no longer get lightboats repaired in Plymouth as "there are no boatbuilders here" willing to do it.[215] However, the 1850 census lists John Cornell, Madison Frazier, Charles Barber, William Everett, and Jesse Herrington as ship carpenters residing in Plymouth. In the same year, Caleb Walker and Jesse Herrington purchased the marine railway and shipyard previously owned by Hanks and the Cornells.[216] The 1850 industrial census lists the Walker and Herrington firm with $5,000 capital employing twenty-two workers, all slaves. Walker, as master carpenter, built at least one vessel, the sloop *Martha Ann*, while he was in Plymouth. Walker and Herrington also surveyed two lightboats.[217] The partnership survived only two years before Walker sold out to Herrington and to his new partner Angelo Garibaldi.[218] Garibaldi joined with Herrington in the purchase of a marine railway in Plymouth as an investment. He was not a shipbuilder but was involved in maritime shipping. Between 1851 and 1852, Herrington launched at least two small schooners, the *Charles Addams* and the *Spruill Moore*, but Garibaldi's name is not included on the vessel documents. Between 1852 and 1860, five vessels were built in Plymouth. Of these, Herrington constructed the 230-ton schooner *John W. Maitland*, and the *M.C. Etheridge* at his shipyard. In October 1857, Herrington's yard was doing well and had the frame of a schooner on the stocks, but it is unclear if Garibaldi was still a partner.[219] In 1859, the schooner *M.C. Etheridge* was launched, the last documented vessel built in Plymouth before the Civil War. The schooner was seized by the Confederate government, armed, and commissioned as the *Black Warrior*. She was destroyed during the military action at Elizabeth City in the spring of 1862.[220]

Following the War of 1812, there were seven shipwrights, including Michael Walker and his sons Caleb and John, residing in Columbia and Tyrrell County on the south shore of Albemarle Sound. The Walkers owned a shipyard on the Scuppernong River where they built a number of small schooners ranging from twenty to twenty-three tons. After Michael's death, his sons continued to operate the shipyard. Caleb spent several years in Plymouth constructing vessels before returning to Tyrrell County in 1851. The 1850 Tyrrell County population census lists five ship carpenters in the county, but neither of the Walkers is included. Also not reported are three other shipwrights: Cary and Davis, and a Mr. Hackburn who launched schooners in Columbia between 1850 and 1851. Since they are listed in the vessel document papers as master carpenters, it is possible that they were in the county temporarily to supervise the building of one or more vessels.

A schooner was also built in Perquimans County by Eliza Felton in 1847, and two others were built by unknown builders.[221] Surprisingly, no shipbuilders are listed for Camden County. Yet, at least nine enrolled vessels were constructed there between 1815 and 1860. Lemuel Gregory built several vessels after the War of 1812, and Job Garrett launched what was characterized as a boat. Charles Grice owned a shipyard across the Pasquotank River from Elizabeth City that was operated by his son. Hertford County listed one shipwright in the 1850 census, but four vessels were built in Winton, the county seat, the first in 1821.

Shipbuilding in the Cape Fear River Area

In the southern coastal area of North Carolina, the Cape Fear River was navigable from the bar near Cape Fear all the way to Fayetteville and, at times, upstream as far as Harnett County. Smithville, known as Southport since 1889, in Brunswick County, near the mouth of the estuary, was a thriving port. However, according to 1820 Brunswick County census records, no ship carpenters resided there. Census records for 1830 to 1840 list only Francis Morse and Uriah Morse as shipwrights. No vessels of any size were built in the county until 1823 when a 104-ton schooner was launched. In 1825, the sixty-seven-ton sloop *James F. McRae* was built and launched in Smithville. Between 1815 and 1860, nineteen documented vessels were built in the county, nearly all in Smithville. The schooner *James Buchanan* was built by Cornelius Gallaway at Lockwood Folly in 1856. In the 1850 population census, two ship carpenters and three "boat makers" are listed. The 1860 census recorded four ship carpenters and one sail maker. In the 1850s, the most prominent ship carpenter in the county was Robert B. Potter, who built at least two schooners for the oceanic trade—the 110-ton *S. R. Potter* and the seventy-ton *Robert B. Potter*. Both vessels were constructed for his shipping line. Like many others, Potter had various occupations—shipwright, farmer, shipping merchant, ship captain, and, at one time, inspector of customs for the district of Wilmington.[222] The 1850 agricultural and manufacturing census records one boat yard employing two "boat makers" building an average of twenty boats a year, probably small, undocumented vessels. In fact, many of the pilot boats that worked out of Smithville were built in Wilmington.[223] Brunswick County, with its wealth of navigable waters, undoubtedly had a much larger boat and ship building industry than has been documented.

Fayetteville, once known as Campbellton, became a steamboat building center. In addition, flats and lighters, designed to be towed by steamboats, were constructed there. In North Carolina, towing small flats or lighters was first introduced on the Cape Fear River. In 1829, the *North Carolina Journal* reported that a 100-ton schooner, a full rigged vessel, was constructed in Fayetteville.[224] The 1850 census lists four ship and boat carpenters in the city. There is no evidence that organized boat yards existed. Newspaper accounts of steamboat construction mention two brothers, William and Harrison Driver, as the builders. The 1850 population census lists them as laborers, but in 1860 they are listed as ship carpenters.

Shipbuilding was not a strong industry in Wilmington during this period. Although the port led North Carolina in maritime commerce, the majority of vessels were from out of state. From 1815 to 1860, twenty-seven documented vessels were built there, most of them in the 1850s.[225] The *Charlotte Farquhar* was launched in 1818. Three steamboats were being built in the port in 1826. Three years later, a full-rigged ship, two brigs, and a steamboat were under construction in the city.[226] Nevertheless, the industry was slow to develop. In 1856, it was suggested that the absence of large-scale shipbuilding in the port was due to a lack of shipbuilders and that they be imported from the north. A local shipbuilder stated there was no need to import shipwrights:

> There is one shipyard in the place that has been in successful operation for more than thirty years and I find that the proprietor of that yard has been offered but two contracts in that length of time. . . . There is also another yard that has been in operation for at least twelve years, the proprietor of which has, during that time, built about ten vessels, ranging from forty to two hundred and fifty tons, and but three of that number by contract; and these three were for gentlemen in Charleston. From the citizens of Wilmington he has yet to receive the first contract.

In 1856, the absence of vessel construction in Wilmington was blamed on the lack of shipbuilders. It was suggested to import them from the north[227]

There were at least seven ship and boat yards established in Wilmington at one time or another during the antebellum period. There were also small facilities in the county, but their location and owners are rarely identified.[228] One establishment described as a boatyard owned by W. J. Price was located at Wrightsville Beach in the 1850s.[229] Members of the extended Farrow family, particularly Jesse, were known as expert boat builders in the Masonboro Sound area. In Wilmington, Thomas Hunter owned a shipyard and dock on the north side of Castle Street which, in 1819, was sold to Doyle O'Hanlon. In 1831, the Doyle O'Hanlon Shipyard specialized in constructing steamboats.[230] Joshua Toomer was still building small sailing vessels as late as 1829. His son, Jack, was also a ship carpenter and supervised the building of a large vessel for John K. McIlhenny. In the early 1820s, John K. McIlhenny entered the city shipbuilding industry. A local businessman, he owned a rice mill and a sawmill before establishing a shipbuilding facility at his sawmill near Queen Street. He had a canal dug to provide a waterway for launching and erected his shipbuilding facility at the canal's head. He built a number of vessels including the *Elizah and Susan*, a 316-ton full-rigged ship. The vessel eventually entered the Pacific Ocean whaling industry. McIlhenny constructed the 181-ton brigantine *Eliza* in 1824, and the following year he launched the *Sarah*, a 136-ton brig.[231] In the mid-1830s, McIlhenny left the shipbuilding industry. However, he provided timber for the construction of the 120-gun ship of the line *Pennsylvania*.[232] Shipbuilding establishments owned by James Cameron and Richard Price built steamboats for the Cape Fear River trade. In addition, Cameron built the schooners *Robert Edens*, launched in 1833, and the *James Crow*, launched in 1837.[233] In 1845, he abandoned shipbuilding in Wilmington and moved to Brunswick County where he took up farming. In 1852, he sold that property to pay his debts and moved back to Wilmington. The 1850 census lists him as a farmer, but in 1860, he is listed as a shipbuilder. He repaired several vessels in the 1850s and built at least one steamer, the *James Petteway*. He moved his family to Onslow County in 1862 and died there two years later.[234] Vessel enrollment papers for 1854 list A. H. Van Bokkelin as being associated with the Cameron Iron Works and as the master carpenter for the construction of the sidewheel steamer *Black River*. However, he is not listed as a shipbuilder in either the 1850 or 1860 census returns.

For decades, flats were important to the river's maritime trade. A great many were built but all are undocumented. Several boat builders specialized in building flats. A boatyard owned by Simon and James Lewis built flats. In 1841, Isaac Reynolds, the owner of a sawmill on Eagles Island, advertised that he was willing to build flats and "flat boats." S. P. Ivey, who owned the Eagles Saw Mill, also advertised to build flats.[235]

Two yards established in the 1830s lasted beyond the Civil War. James Cassidey, (sometimes spelled Cassidy) established a yard and marine railway near downtown Wilmington. A few years before his death, James Cassidey wrote a brief memoir. He stated that his father emigrated from Ireland to Massachusetts. His father was a shipbuilder, having learned the trade in Ireland. James was born in Massachusetts and eventually bound to a boatbuilder in Bath, Maine. Subsequently, he worked at a shipyard in New Brunswick, Canada, and as a deck hand on a sailing vessel before settling in Brunswick County, North Carolina. He built two vessels near Shallotte for a local businessman who sold them to Charleston interests. In 1818, James moved to Wilmington. He later wrote that "[t]he first contract I undertook was to haul up and lengthen a steamer (stern-wheel) called the *Prometheus*."[236] As a ship carpenter, he was building vessels in New Hanover County in the 1820s. By 1830, Cassidey had established a shipyard on Church Street where he built two steamboats. In 1837, he added a horse-powered marine railway to his shipyard. Cassidey, like other shipbuilders, often engaged in other business activities to bring in additional revenue, including contracting to build a bridge.[237] In 1852, he signed an agreement with a shipping firm to permit them to use a warehouse and wharf at his shipyard; in return, he was hired to repair and maintain the firm's vessels.[238] In 1855, James Cassidey announced his retirement and that his son would take over the shipyard.[239] However, the 1860 census listed sixty-eight-year-old James and his two sons as shipbuilders, the youngest as an apprentice. In that same year, Dunn and Company reported that James Cassidey was "good as Gold … a man of … excellent character," and that he was considered to be an excellent shipbuilder. James Cassidey continued in the shipbuilding business until he died in 1867. His son Jesse, having been trained in a New England shipyard like his father, took control of the facility.[240]

In 1839, Samuel Beery owned a sawmill west of Wilmington. He built and repaired flats and luggage boats. A newspaper reported that year that "his method is to take the flat completely out of the water on ways, and is thus able to render them perfectly tight." At that time, he lived in Smithville.[241] He later moved his boatyard to Harrison's sawmill next to the Cassidey facility and, in 1844, constructed a marine railway. He built ocean-going vessels, including the steamer *Col. John McRae*, for Captain Thomas Marshall, late master of the famous steamer *Vanderbilt*.[242] In 1848, Beery and his two sons, Benjamin and William, purchased land on Eagles Island and moved their shipbuilding establishment and railway there. They also established a steam sawmill adjacent to the yard. The Beerys later advertised that they were capable of building any size vessel from a pilot boat to a ship. Despite financial difficulties, the shipyard remained in business during the post-Civil War years. They built an impressive number of vessels before the war including a whaler for a Bedford, Massachusetts firm, the 250-ton brig *John Dawson*, the schooner *Ella*, and a number of pilot boats.[243] The 1850 census lists only two yards for Wilmington, the Cassidey and Beery facilities. According to the census, Beery and Sons employed thirty men and Cassidey fifteen. In 1852, the Beery partnership was dissolved with one son, Benjamin, obtaining sole ownership of the shipyard. Benjamin also purchased the site at Harrison's Saw Mill near Wilmington which included a railway, shipyard, blacksmith shop, and rigging loft. Samuel Beery bought out his son's gristmill and plantation, where he died less than a year later.[244]

Benjamin Washington Beery was born in 1822 in Brunswick County. When he was nineteen, his father sent him to Baltimore to learn the shipbuilding trade. Benjamin was also trained in machinery, at least that which related to steamboats. The Eagles Island establishment was known as the Cape Fear Marine Railway. A fire at a nearby sawmill destroyed the marine railway and Beery went into debt to rebuild it. He sold his house on the island and other personal property, including six slaves, to pay off the debt.[245] In 1859, Michael Robbins purchased the Cape Fear Marine Railway, "formerly the property of B. W. Beery," but William Beery regained ownership in 1861. It would remain in his hands during the Civil War and after.

Although the 1860 census mentions only the yards of Cassidey and Beery, there was a third. The yard of Morse and Ellis specialized in building pleasure craft, including racing yachts. Eden Morse owned and operated a shipbuilding facility on New River in Onslow County before relocating to Wilmington. On April 1, 1834, he launched a large brig. On that same day, a vessel built at the Doyle O'Hanlon yard was launched in Wilmington. Unlike Morse, O'Hanlon moved his shipbuilding activities up the Cape Fear from Wilmington to Fayetteville.[246]

Collateral Shipbuilding Activities

There were three ropewalks in the state in 1819: one at Plymouth, a second in New Bern, and a third in Edenton. New Bern and Edenton had ropewalks dating back to the eighteenth century. The Edenton establishment had been in continuous operation since 1783 and did not close until 1839. Ropewalks manufactured hawsers, cables, and cordage for ship rigging.[247] Canvas and duck for sails had to be imported, mostly from New York or Baltimore.[248] In turn, sailmakers in North Carolina's ports finished them for specific vessels. In 1850, Wilmington had six sailmakers, Washington three, Beaufort two, and Elizabeth City at least one.[249]

The first steam sawmill was erected in the state in 1819. By the 1840s, such facilities were established throughout the coastal region. Many shipbuilders purchased steam sawmills for ship construction and other traditional commercial purposes. Samuel Beery and John McIhenny in Wilmington; Tannahill and Lavender, Myers, and Abner Neale in Washington; Thomas Howard in New Bern; John Cornell and Edgar Hanks in Plymouth; and several Elizabeth City builders all owned steam sawmills.[250] Shipbuilders who did not own sawmills tried to establish their shipbuilding facility as close to a source of timber as possible. On the Cape Fear, logs were rafted down to sawmills near Wilmington.

Local supplies of shipbuilding timber in the state were still adequate. Live oak, white oak, and cedar, as well as red and white juniper, were still relatively inexpensive and, in fact, periodically offered for sale to the Navy. In 1849, the Navy sent an officer to examine shipbuilding timber resources in Chatham County and headwaters of the Cape Fear River basin.[251] However, after the War of 1812, live oak became much less popular because of its great weight. North Carolina was rich in pitch pine, and this timber came to be used more and more by North Carolina shipbuilders.[252] By the 1840s, the scarcity of suitable timber in New England caused builders in those states to purchase an increasing amount from North Carolina. Steamboat builders used all of the timbers mentioned above, but to a degree, what they used depended on where the steamer was built. Cape Fear River builders used red cedar, pine, and live and white oak. At least one steamboat, the *Fayetteville*, launched in 1842, was built primarily of red cedar.[253] New Bern builders used these timbers as well as cypress and mulberry. The frame of *Wayne II* was mulberry and cedar, her bottom planks of white oak. A newspaper in 1848 reported "her sides above the light water mark are planed with cypress."[254] The *Chatham* was built of juniper and cedar. Locust was used occasionally. On the Outer Banks, "chinquapin oak" was popular.[255] The increasing scarcity of shipbuilding timber nationwide did not significantly affect shipbuilding in North Carolina until after the Civil War. An article in the *Wilmington Daily Journal* in 1854 reported that everything needed to build a new steamer came from within the state but the machinery. Nonetheless, timber resources were depleting. Between 1850 and 1860, approximately eighteen million board feet were processed.[256]

Special Vessels for Special Needs

As in the past, a large variety of vessels and small craft were constructed in the state. No military vessels were built, but the federal government contracted with state shipbuilders for revenue cutters, dredge boats, and lightboats. Other special need vessels included pilot boats, racing craft, commercial fishing vessels, flats, and bateaux.

Small vessels equipped with some sort of warning device and a distinctive navigational light were common in Great Britain and North America prior to the nineteenth century. The first lightboats did not appear in American waters until the 1820s. The first such vessels to receive Congressional approval were for southern waters and New York. In 1819, funds were appropriated for two light boats to be placed in the lower Chesapeake Bay. In 1820, a Washington, D.C. shipbuilder contracted to construct and deliver a lightboat to Ocracoke Inlet. In 1823, funding was authorized for a light vessel off Cape Hatteras. It was in operation on Diamond Shoals in 1825 and was the first light vessel in state waters. The Diamond Shoals light vessel was driven ashore in a gale in 1837 and replaced with a buoy. In 1826, the two lightboats constructed in New York were placed on station at Wades Point Shoal, at the entrance to the Pasquotank River, and at Ocracoke Inlet.[257]

Due to North Carolina's treacherous waters, at least twelve light vessels were stationed along the coast during the antebellum period.[258] Eight of these were constructed by North Carolina shipbuilders between 1827 and 1844: three by Thomas B. Wallace, one in Portsmouth and two at his shipyard in New Bern; two by Beaufort shipwrights Elijah Whitehurst and Elijah Pigott; one by Ralph Howland and M. B. Robinson, also of Beaufort, for Long Shoal on Pamlico Sound; and, in the northeastern section of the state, one each by Horace Williams and the firm of Paine and Boushall, both of Elizabeth City.[259]

Generally, the collector of customs in each district determined what type of navigational aids were needed (lighthouses, lightboats, or buoys), where they were to be located, and controlled the acquisition process from bidding through acceptance.[260] They prepared advertisements for local and regional newspapers and signed off on contracts. From 1820 through 1844, the wording and content of contracts were remarkably similar, suggesting the Treasury Department prepared and distributed a standard form as a model. Advertisements mirrored contract language, down even to specifying the type of wood to be used for different parts of the vessel (hull, deck, masts, etc.). There were two exceptions to this. One builder was allowed to use stone rather than pig iron as ballast, and the Carteret County light vessels incorporated considerable yellow pine. Builders were also expected to provide the lighting equipment. Despite such standardization, designs were flawed; neither the Treasury Department, the collectors, nor the builders possessed sufficient understanding of light vessel requirements.[261]

North Carolina-built lightboats were small, ranging from seventy-two to 160 tons. Dimensions also varied. They were entirely of wood and fastened with iron and copper bolts. Rigged to carry sails, in reality they rarely were able to sail on their own. All North Carolina light vessels, constructed in and out of state, had two masts three feet apart, primarily used to carry lights. They were usually towed into a predetermined position, anchored, and remained on station until they needed repairs, were lost, or the station was abandoned.

Because of the materials used in their construction, environmental conditions, and even neglect by crews, light vessels required frequent repairs. The Roanoke River lightboat was built in 1835, rebuilt in 1839, had the bottom of the hull replaced in 1844, and needed extensive repairs in 1849. In 1854-1855, the Neuse River, Roanoke River, and Wade's Point lightboats all had to be removed from their stations for repairs.[262] Typically, a collector, responding to a report from the lightboat keeper, would authorize an inspection by a shipbuilding firm or shipwright. If repairs were recommended, as they nearly always were, detailed advertisements for bids were published, the wording of which was almost identical to that used in construction documents. In the case of North Carolina light vessels, the inspector(s) almost always received the contract. Light vessel repair contracts paid well and were eagerly sought. In 1828, Thomas Sparrow and James Howard of New Bern were paid $3,680 for repairing the Long Shoal lightboat. In 1838, Charles Laverty of Elizabeth City received $5,400 for extensive work on the Wade's Point vessel, and in 1839, John Cornell of Plymouth got $4,704 for rebuilding the Roanoke River lightboat.[263] The Cornell shipbuilding business thrived on the repair of lightboats throughout North Carolina. The Plymouth collector justified awarding so many contracts to the Cornells by claiming: "[i]n this place . . . there is but one shipyard." Moreover, they were superior carpenters and used much better timber than the "swamp or short leaf pine" timber used elsewhere.[264]

On one occasion, the collector requested that the authority forgo the published bid process and award the contract directly to John Cornell. He also recommended that Cornell be paid on a day-by-day basis rather than a contracted amount, as he feared there would be more work required than reported by the examiner. As might be expected, the Treasury Department refused to disallow the bidding process. Nevertheless, only two bids were received and that submitted by John Cornell was accepted.[265] In 1850-1851, Jesse Herrington, who bought out the Cornells, received a number of contracts to repair lightboats.[266] However, in 1852, the collector informed the Treasury Department that there were no boat builders in Plymouth willing to undertake such repair work.[267] After 1851, although bids for repairs and caulking were received from Beaufort and Washington, most lightboat repairs were done in New Bern.[268]

The North Carolina-built lightboats were stationed in inlets, sounds, and rivers because, along with lighthouses and buoys, they provided navigational aids for ships at sea entering the shoaling waters along the treacherous coast. Light vessels in the sounds generally lasted approximately thirty years. In some cases, shoaling closed an inlet and a light vessel was no longer needed. In a number of instances, lightboats were replaced by larger vessels.[269] In time, lighthouses and buoys would replace nearly all of the sound area lightboats. The last North Carolina-constructed lightboat was decommissioned in 1867. The 1871 Lighthouse Board annual report was critical of the standard wooden light vessels then in use: they were too small "for exposed positions," and they were poorly designed for this work. The report further stated that "[t]he first cost, large annual expense for maintenance and repairs, and the rapid decay of light-vessels, render this mode of lighting very objectionable. . . . The rapid decay of timber, especially on our southern coast, would seem to suggest the propriety of employing more durable materials." As a result, the board recommended that, in the future, iron be used in the construction of light vessels.[270] The board's recommendation was adopted, and after that date, iron, and later steel, was the principal construction material. Iron and steel ship construction did not become an industry in North Carolina until World War I; no other light vessels were built in the state.

Revenue vessels were also under the direction of customhouse officials. In 1816, revenue cutters were stationed at New Bern and Ocracoke. In 1820, a cutter built in Wilmington operated out of Smithville. These vessels were under the control of the customs official at New Bern. In 1820, the New Bern collector of customs recommended discontinuing the Ocracoke cutter as being "too large" for the services required and replacing it with one or two small "decked" boats. They were contracted and built in Carteret County. From time to time, additional boats were constructed to replace older vessels or add to the number of those operating on the North Carolina coast due to increased trade.[271] In 1846, the New Bern collector indicated that he wanted to commission a customs boat similar to the ones "used upon the waters of this District. . . . They are made of large cypress logs trimmed out and strongly put together with knees and copper fastened. . . . With proper care will last 25 years I am told . . . [and] are preferable to the clinker built boats being so much stronger."[272]

Builders in the Wilmington and the Cape Fear area seem to have specialized in the construction of pilot boats for local use and export as well. Charleston pilots had a number of pilot boats built in the Cape Fear area. Two were built by Beery, the *John C. Calhoun* in 1852 and the *William Y. Leitch* in 1854. In 1853, the sixty-three-ton *Charleston* was constructed for that port's pilots.[273] Ocracoke Inlet pilot boats were generally constructed in Carteret County.[274] Pilot boats have been defined according to vessel type and use. Their sole purpose was to transport port pilots, who guided vessels into and out of the harbors. Pilotage is an old profession and appeared in North America during the colonial period. Americans developed a distinct type of pilot boat. By the nineteenth century, they were usually schooner-rigged, sharp-bowed vessels, and unusually fast. The average size of these vessels increased from approximately forty feet in 1800 to sixty feet by 1860.

Rowing and sailing regattas appeared in North Carolina ports in the 1840s and may have migrated north from the Charleston Races. Regattas were held off Wrightsville Beach in the early 1840s, leading to the organization of the Carolina Yacht Club in 1853. In 1852, two North Carolina-constructed boats, the *North State*, a ten-oared clinker-built forty-five-foot boat, and the forty-four-foot *Wrecker's Daughter*, raced against some twenty-three other boats. In one race, the *North State* came in second.[275] In 1856, a North Carolina-built sailing skiff, the *Razor*, beat a New York boat. "North Carolina boatbuilders can now hold up their heads, after having beaten a vessel from the commercial emporium of the Western hemisphere," crowed a North Carolina newspaper.[276] In the late 1850s, Wilmington and New Bern caught the racing spirit. The editor of the New Bern *Daily Progress* described a sailing yacht under construction at the Howard and Robinson yard and challenged a local rival editor to put his money behind a sailing racer. "We have heard that a club of gentlemen have contemplated giving [the]. . . fastest craft on Masonboro Sound next season a trial of speed for a silver pitcher or something of the sort."[277] The club was undoubtedly the Carolina Yacht Club. In 1859, Cassidey launched two small sailing vessels approximately seventeen feet in length. A Wilmington paper reported, "Both vessels are beautiful specimens of work, and will be valuable additions to the large fleet owned by the Carolina Yacht Club."[278] In addition to racing craft, other small vessels and boats continued to be constructed in the state, including scows, many with sails; canoes, periaugers, log boats, fishing craft, and flats.[279]

In the nineteenth century, commercial fishing became an important maritime industry particularly in the sounds, along the coast, rivers, and in the ocean.[280] No boat specifically designed for commercial fishing was developed until the 1840s when the haul seine industry for shad and herring became a large-scale enterprise in in Albemarle Sound. "Shad galleys," large flat-bottomed skiffs, were introduced in a local fishery. Seine flats were used in river fisheries early in the century and the Albemarle Sound flat probably derived from this design. The Albemarle "galleys" had eight to ten oars, were approximately forty feet in length, and had a platform on the stern from which to haul the net. Although the number of these small vessels that were built is unknown, by 1852 there were at least some seventy fisheries, both large and small scale, operating in the sounds and tributaries.[281] Most of these fisheries probably had at least two of these vessels to haul the seines. The boats were probably built by the fishermen themselves and were "a very simple form of construction that local builders would undertake."[282]

In the nineteenth century, flatboats were the most common vessels found on eastern North Carolina rivers and streams. Local newspapers frequently carried ads and notices concerning flats for sale, under construction, or about their arrival and departure.[283] In 1820, the Tar River was only navigable by "large flat bottomed boats," and for the upper Tar River beyond Tarboro, this continued to be the case as late as 1860.[284] The preponderance of vessels that plied the Dismal Swamp Canal were flats, ten to forty feet long, four to six feet wide, and drawing from eighteen to twenty-five inches, loaded.[285] Flats were the principal craft in transporting cargos of naval stores from up the rivers to the ports. In the 1840s, two steamboats on the Neuse River towed large flats capable of carrying up to 600 barrels each. Flats monopolized river traffic on the Northeast Cape Fear, the Black, and the Deep Rivers, all flowing into the Cape Fear River and downstream to Wilmington. By the late 1850s, because of improvements on the upper Cape Fear River, including locks, flats up to 105 feet in length carried freight as far as Summerville in Harnett County.[286]

Flats were also called lighters and barges, although, at times, lighters were distinguished from flats. The *Daily Wilmington Herald* advertised two lighters for sale: *J. R. Blossom* and *Republican* of seven and nine hundred barrels capacity respectively and "[a]lso, two flats."[287] In 1829, at William Borden's shipyard on Bogue Sound, a forty-six-foot centerboard lighter was offered for sale. Some lighters carried sails.[288] Flats were propelled by sails, oars, poles, and even the tide and current.[289] Until the advent of steam navigation on state rivers, flats were the principal means of transporting goods. Even after steamboats began to ply North Carolina's inland waters, flats continued to carry the bulk of waterborne cargoes. Steamboats towing flats or lighters loaded with cargoes were common on all the state rivers. They were particularly important in areas where steamboats could not navigate and during periods of low water. They ranged in size from approximately twenty to more than 100 feet in length. The size of flats increased over the century, and by midcentury, sixty to a hundred-foot-long flats were common. Size also depended upon use. Drafts varied depending upon vessel size and where the flats were employed. Large flats, operating on the Cape Fear above Fayetteville, often drew two feet fully loaded. Those built for the Dismal Swamp Canal were usually narrower and had greater draft. Tonnage also varied considerably. The fifty-five-ton *Cofu*, used on the Dismal Swamp Canal, had a capacity of 3,000 bushels of grain. Often, lighters that plied the Albemarle and Chesapeake Canal were considerably larger.[290] Frequently, large lighters were decked; smaller ones usually had a wide walkway from stem to stern along the gunwale for the crew or were entirely open.[291] Various procedures were employed to ensure they were water tight. Traditionally, they were caulked but smaller vessels were sunk so they would "swell."[292]

Some flats were named. The flat *Andrew Jackson* was sold in Wilmington in 1833. In 1851, the new and beautiful flat boat *General McRae* was launched at the Cassidey shipyard.[293] Other Cape Fear flats included *Uncle Sam*, *David Lewis*, *Stevenson*, *The General Taylor*, *Dried Apple*, *James Ellis*, *J. L. Cassidey*, *David Reed*, *Jackson*, *General Cass*, *Macmillan's Boat*, and *Robinson's Boat*.[294]

Flats were used for a variety of purposes. Steamboats routinely towed large barges, usually two but as many as six at a time.[295] For safety reasons, the practice of carrying passengers in towed barges was not allowed in North Carolina. By the 1850s, lighters towed by steamers on the Neuse River carried an average of 600 barrels each.[296] Reporting on the building of steamboats, newspaper articles occasionally mention the construction of their towing flats as well.[297] Flats were used in the construction of dams, locks, and even the forts at the entrance to the Cape Fear River. In 1837, the Corps of Engineers advertised for the building of two sixty-foot flats for work on Fort Caswell.[298] The Cape Fear and Deep River Navigation Company contracted for the construction of three flats, two 100 feet in length, and a third 104 feet in length.[299] Steamers towed large flats called "tanks" full of salt on the lower Cape Fear River, and ferries were usually flats.[300]

Flats were relatively inexpensive to build. Timothy Hunter contracted to construct one sixty feet in length, ten feet in beam, and three feet four inches in depth for $460. The flat was probably intended for use on the Dismal Swamp Canal.[301] In Fayetteville, a flat measuring eighty-five feet by seventeen feet cost $550. Navigation companies involved in clearing obstructions from rivers and streams used flats. In 1846, a New Bern shipbuilder completed a boat of 250 barrels for $250.[302] These vessels could be built easily and quickly. Even house carpenters constructed them.[303] In 1842, John H. Brooks of Greenville informed businessmen and farmers of Edgecombe County that he had built a flat and planned to operate it himself.[304] Three "corn flats" that could carry 300 barrels of corn were built for a number of farmers and businessmen in Hyde County.[305] Flats were also popular with established shipyards. In Wilmington, Simon and James Lewis, S. P. Ivey, Samuel Beery, and James Cassidey all advertised for flat contracts. In Hyde County, flats were built by Ebenezer Bell and Timothy Hunter in Elizabeth City, and by B.F. Hanks in Washington. All were well-known shipbuilders.[306] A large number were also built in Fayetteville.[307] This vessel type was built throughout eastern North Carolina. A Craven County merchant contracted for a "wood boat" that was probably a flat type vessel used to haul lumber.[308]

The bateaux, though similar to flats, were distinct vessels. They were usually small, open, light craft up to six feet in beam and pointed at bow and stern. They were flat bottomed and keelless like the barge, usually propelled by oars, steered by long oar-like sweeps at the stern, and, occasionally, carried sails. They were not as popular as flats. They were found on the upper reaches of the Dan, Roanoke, Neuse, and Cape Fear Rivers, but they were much more famous on the James River in Virginia. The best known was the *Experiment*, built in Raleigh, and famous as the first vessel of any size with a cargo to run the river as far as New Bern.[309] In 1816, there were six bateaux operating on the upper reaches of the Roanoke River, four of which had been built in Virginia. By 1829, twenty bateaux were working the river and more were under construction.[310] The bateaux were also a popular vessel type for freighting on the Dan River in North Carolina and Virginia.

The overwhelming majority of documented sailing vessels built in the state were schooners. Of just over a thousand documented vessels built in the state during the antebellum period, 876 were schooners. After 1840, with the exception of steamboats, nearly all the vessels built were schooners.[311] This surpasses the national average, although schooners were the most common vessel type in all the seafaring states. The nineteenth-century schooner was the most manageable sailing vessel afloat.[312] It was admirably designed for moderate voyages along the Atlantic coast and to the West Indies, destinations of most North Carolina-built oceanic vessels. Descriptions of North Carolina-built schooners are very general. Dimensions are given and the number of masts: usually two, although three-masters were not uncommon.[313] Often, documents also included a description of the stern as square or round, the structure and number of decks, the presence or absence of a figurehead, and whether the vessel was sharp or bluff bowed. Other features such as rigging or the use of a centerboard are not included. Nevertheless, the centerboard was a significant improvement for sailing vessels navigating North Carolina's shoal waters.

The Centerboard

The centerboard was a revolutionary feature. It was a retractable, pivoting board that was lowered into the water through a watertight case built inside the vessel. The centerboard increased a vessel's sailing qualities, particularly going into the wind. More importantly for North Carolina, it could be raised, enabling a vessel to navigate shallow waters, and lowered when in deeper water. The centerboard affected ship design, resulting in flatter hulls. The device probably derived from the leeboard used extensively by the Dutch in the seventeenth and eighteenth centuries and the dropped keel introduced into North America in the later years of the eighteenth century.[314]

North Carolina builders first included centerboards in their vessels shortly after the War of 1812. According to one account, Otway Burns introduced the centerboard in the state.[315]

He incorporated it in his two-masted sailboat, *Snap Dragon*. Alternatively, Ezra Cornell, a Martin County shipbuilder, claimed to have introduced it. In an 1817 letter to his brother, he describes a vessel he was building: "… she is a vessel with a leaboard in the middle which, people here are not acquainted with, but I think it will introduce the fashion here, which will be a grate advantage to this Country, the navigation be shole. . . ."[316] By 1825, centerboards were being used in American-built sloops and schooners.[317] Regardless, it is obvious that the centerboard was adopted quickly by owners as well as builders. The centerboard was adopted quickly by owners as well as builders and was of such importance for navigating North Carolina's shoal waters that, within a few years, it was found on all sailing vessels plying coastal waters north of the Cape Fear River.[318]

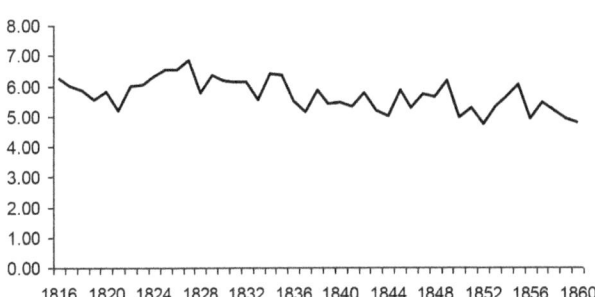

FIGURE 5-5 Ship Depth, measured in feet, during the antebellum period, shows that depth was decreasing. Likely, this is a response to the shoals and shallow wateras of the local waters. *Source:* Author's database.

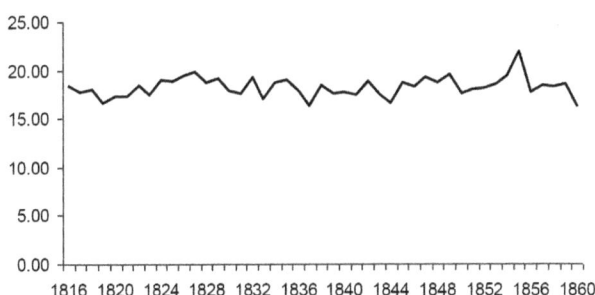

FIGURE 5-6 Ship Width, measured in feet, during the ante-bellum period, showing little change with time. *Source:* Author's database.

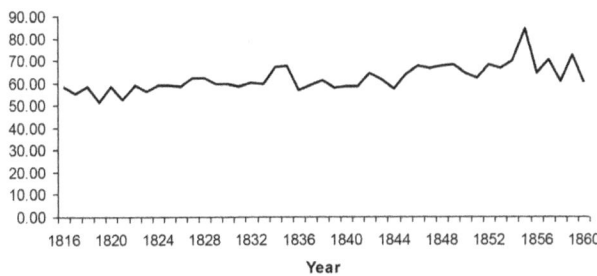

FIGURE 5-7 Ship Length, in feet, during the antebellum period, revealing a slight increase with time. This could be related to the decrease in depth in order to maintain a profitable tonnage. *Source:* Author's database.

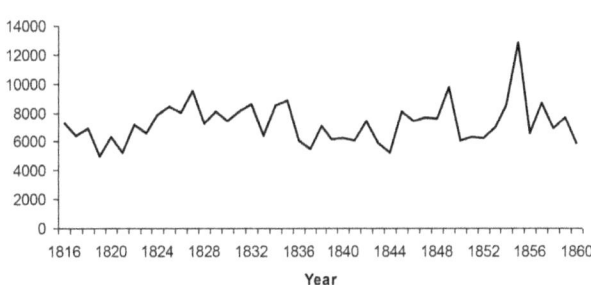

FIGURE 5-8 Ship Volume (length times width times depth) during the antebellum period shows a volatility similar to ship tonnage, with a very slight increase. *Sources:* Author's database.

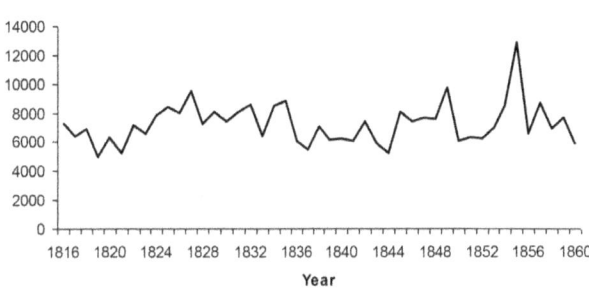

FIGURE 5-9 The Width/Depth Ratio during the antebellum period shows a slight increase. This indicates that ships are becoming wider as compared to depth. This is likely due to the shoals and sounds where a shallower drafted vessel is more appropriate. *Source:* Author's database.

Ship Dimension Analysis

Early settlers from New England and Europe brought construction concepts and techniques that were familiar to them. The design and technology of ships and boats changed as they adapted to the treacherous coastal waters of North Carolina. Generally, deep drafted vessels or those with a large hull depth were the norm, but these easily ran aground on shoals and in shallow sounds, rivers, and inlets. Consequently, over time, the draft of North Carolina vessels decreased. Although this is not noticeable in the federal period, data indicate it did occur in the antebellum era (Figure 5).

Shipbuilders were forced to respond to a new and different environment. Overall, hull depth decreased from more than six to about five feet during the period but fluctuated as experimentation continued. The decrease may have been due to the introduction of steamboats on shoaling sounds and rivers. Design criteria shifted from

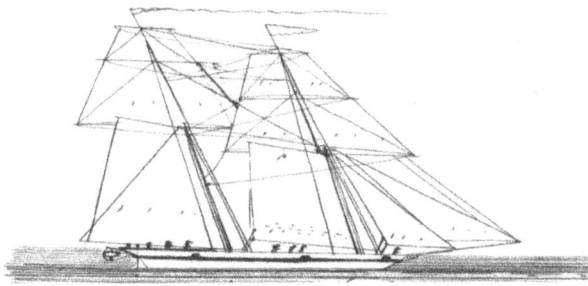

FIGURE 5-10 Ship built at the Grice shipyard in Elizabeth City during the antebellum period. Notice the degree of strake, and a hull built for speed. *Source:* State Archives of North Carolina.

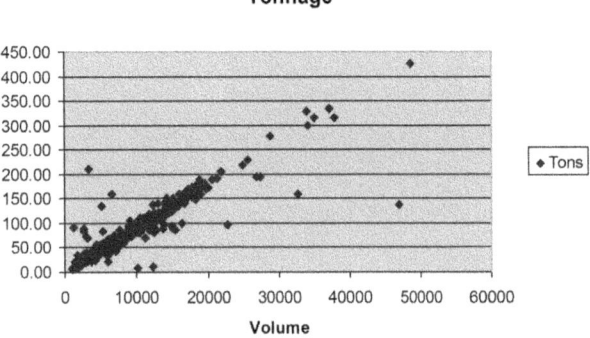

Figure 5-11 Scattergram revealing an expected strong positive relationship between vessel volume and tonnage. *Source:* Author's database.

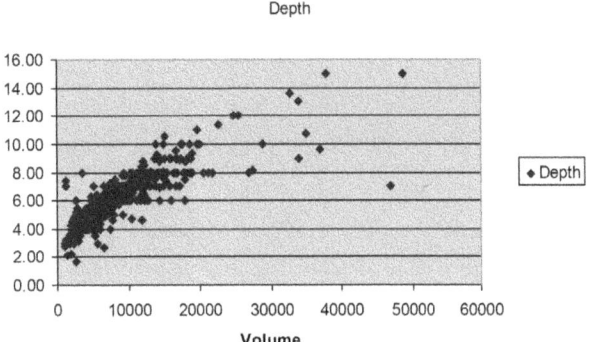

Figure 5-12 Scattergram showing an expected positive relationship of vessel volume with depth. With depth decreasing, vessel width or length increased. *Source:* Author's database.

deep-drafted vessels to those that seemed to float on only a few inches of water. Ships and boats had to carry sufficient cargo to make a voyage or cruise profitable. Generally, steamboats carried their cargo above the water line.

Reducing depth required an increase in length and width in order to maintain a similar volume. Unfortunately, North Carolina's narrow and meandering rivers restricted length and width (Figure 6). Vessel width varied during the antebellum era but averaged a little less than twenty feet. In comparison, vessel width was slightly greater during the federal period and slightly less the decade before the Civil War.

As vessel width remained essentially consistent and draft decreased, vessel length had to increase in order to maintain or expand cargo capacity and economic viability. Average length increased from less than sixty feet during the federal period to almost sixty-five feet during the antebellum period (Figure 7). Twists and turns in channels, rivers, and streams limited vessel length. A wide vessel on the sounds improved stability, but on rivers and streams, a wide vessel was difficult to maneuver and increased length made navigating meandering waterways dangerous, if not impossible. However, steamboats pushed or towed flats or barges, improving their capacity many times over. Consequently, although vessel length did not in increase substantially, vessel utility did. Despite limited length, beam, and draft, vessel volume (cargo capacity) was maximized to sustain economic feasibility (Figure 8).

Ship width/depth ratio increased, indicating that vessels were built with a broader beam and less draft (the greater the value of the ratio, the wider the beam as compared to the draft of a ship). A shift from the narrow, deep vessels of the federal period, to the wider, shallower vessels of the antebellum era suggest a real effort was made to maximize maneuverability within the confines imposed by environmental conditions (Figure 9).

Charles Grice's ship exemplifies antebellum vessels (Figure 10). These ships were sleek and fast, designed for maximum efficiency in local waters and on the high seas. Obviously, dimensions complement one another. Vessel length, width, and draft determine increase in volume (cargo capacity) and generate the expected good correlation between volume and tonnage (Figure 11) and volume and draft (Figure 12).

The End of the Antebellum Era

Few large sailing vessels were built in the state prior to 1860. In the 1850s, ship size was limited to 400 tons on the Pasquotank River due to shallow inlet depths.[319] It is not known who imposed the limit or if it applied to other parts of the state. A small number of brigs, barks, schooners, and full-rigged ships over 200 tons were constructed, but none reached the size of the merchant vessels constructed in the northeastern United States between 1840 and 1860. By the 1850s, merchant vessels of a thousand tons were typical.[320]

The financial crises of 1819, 1837, 1839, and 1857 affected every aspect of the national economy, including the shipbuilding industry. Because North Carolina was overwhelmingly agrarian, lacked a strong banking system, and was dependent on outside shipping for manufactured goods, the state's shipbuilding and other maritime activities were not seriously affected by the first three crises. The same was not true in 1857. As a result of the crash that year and subsequent recession, the gross tonnage of vessels built in the United States in 1859 dropped to approximately a third of the tonnage constructed in 1856.

The Panic of 1857 and resulting recession clearly hurt North Carolina's shipbuilders. Beery in Wilmington and Howard in New Bern, two of the largest yards, were sold. Many other shipbuilders went into debt. Although not entirely to blame for these events, the financial crisis was certainly a major factor. Between 1850 and 1860, the number of ship carpenters in the state declined significantly. Only four new vessels were launched in 1857; ten vessels were launched in 1859 and the same number in 1860. Altogether, thirty-nine documented vessels were built between 1857 and 1860, nearly all small schooners. Vessels were left on the stocks. The Dibbles had a steamboat under construction at New Bern, but it was still unfinished in 1865. The steamer under construction by Garibaldi in Plymouth was destroyed during the Civil War while still on the ways. The small screw steamboat *Fox* was launched in 1861.[321] Oceanic trade also suffered. Benjamin B. Lavender had to auction off his entire fleet of vessels, including the schooners *Sabine*, *Laura E. Johnson*, *Isaac W. Hughes*, *Midas Platt*, *Howard*, and *Benjamin Maitland*, three-fourths of the schooner *Elizabeth* and seven-eighths of the schooner *Napoleon*. In 1857, "upward of 60 vessels" were lying in Wilmington owing to difficulties of getting freight.[322]

In 1861, North Carolina seceded from the United States and joined the Confederate States of America. The war that followed seriously affected the state's shipbuilding industry. Shipwrights and other shipbuilding workers volunteered for the armed forces, were impressed, or were conscripted. Shipyards and shipbuilding sites were taken over by Union or Confederate forces. Other shipbuilding sites were destroyed. Union forces also destroyed vessels on the stocks whenever they were discovered. Vessels afloat were seized and few escaped.

Notes

1. According to these reports, state-owned vessels included a few "miserable coasters; and a few keel and steam boats of inconsiderable burthen and value." In Washington, it was lamented that in the past few years "seven vessels have been bought at the North by gentlemen living here.... [T]hese vessels probably cost their owners $40,000 every dollar of which has thus been taken out of the town.... And yet whilst our merchants are going to the North to buy vessels readymade, we have every facility for building them here." A week later, it was noted in Wilmington that those "remarks are equally applicable to this place as to Washington." *Newbern Spectator*, June 13, 1834; *Wilmington Chronicle*, February 25, 1849; (Washington) *North State Whig*, February 19, 1853.
2. John G. B. Hutchins, *The American Maritime Industries and Public Policy, 1789-1914: An Economic History*, 190, 193; Philip G. Davidson, "Industrialism in the Ante Bellum South," *South Atlantic Quarterly*, 27 (1938), 423.
3. Robert Albion, *The Rise of the Port of New York, 1815-1860*, 406, 420. Such conclusions derive from a dependency on two, incomplete sources: the reports on commerce and navigation published by the U.S. government annually since 1821 which include information on vessels built in each state, and the census reports, particularly the agricultural and manufacturing reports which, beginning in 1840, record shipyards. In the *Report on Commerce and Navigation for 1850*, thirty-three vessels were listed as having been built in North Carolina. This is less than half the total built in that year according to customhouse records. Similar discrepancies have been discovered for other years. Why this discrepancy exists is unknown. It is possible that the destruction of customhouse records in a number of North Carolina ports during the Civil War may provide at least some explanation. In addition, an examination of vessel documents found in NARA Record Group 41 (Records of the Bureau of Marine Inspection and Navigation) provide a very different picture. For example, traditional sources indicate only one vessel was built in Wilmington in 1848-1849; yet, the Secretary of the Treasury informed Congress that five vessels were built there during the fiscal year ending June 30, 1849. House of Representatives, 31st Congress, 1st Session, *Ex. Document No. 15*. See also Thomas P. Kettell, *Southern Wealth and Northern Profits*, 65. Furthermore, for the 1860 list, Albion does mention shipbuilding companies in Georgia but not North Carolina, which had more companies than Georgia.
4. 1840 Census on Manufacturing, 38.
5. Emory Q. Hawk, *Economic History of the South*, 281.
6. *Wilmington Journal* (weekly), April 23, 1852.
7. Ellen Fulcher Cloud, *Old Salt*, 40-41.
8. Flowers died in the fall of 1850 and included in his estate papers was a boat frame on the stocks. Hyde County Estate Records, 1735-1933, SANC.
9. Sarah Lemmon, ed., *The Pettigrew Papers*, I: 112, 117; Ebenezer Pettigrew, Lady of the Lake Account, August 21, 1829, Pettigrew Papers, SANC. See also *Quarterly Review of the Eastern North Carolina Genealogical Society*, V (Winter 1978): 10-181.
10. (Raleigh) *Star and North-Carolina State Gazette*, May 15, 1818; *Fayetteville Observer*, February 22, 1853.
11. (New Bern) *Republican*, July 16, 1847, and September 13, 1848.
12. *Raleigh Register and North-Carolina Gazette*, June 19, 1829.
13. James H. Craig, *The Arts and Crafts in North Carolina, 1699-1840*, 262-266.
14. Hutchins, *American Maritime Industries and Public Policy*, 393. For a recent study of the system see Karen L. Zipf, *Labor of Innocents: Forced Apprenticeship in North Carolina, 1715-1919*.
15. Zipf, *Labor of Innocents; Forced Apprenticeship in North Carolina, 1715-1919*, 35-36.
16. Gale Farrow, "Black Craftsmen in North Carolina, Part II," *North Carolina Genealogical Society Journal*, 91-103. See also David Cecelski, *The Waterman's Song* (2001).

17. David S. Cecelski, "The Shores of Freedom: The Maritime Underground Railroad in North Carolina, 1800-1861," *NCHR*, 193-194; Freddie L. Parker, *Stealing a Little Freedom: Advertisements for Slave Runaways in North Carolina, 1791-1840*, 21-22; Catherine W. Bishir, "Black Builders in Antebellum North Carolina," *NCHR*, 423-458. Although Bishir's study does not mention the shipbuilding industry, it is an excellent account of Blacks involved in building. Her analyses and conclusions are applicable to shipbuilding as well.

18. C. Alexander Turner III, "An Historical and Archaeological Investigation of the *Scuppernong*: A Mid-Nineteenth-Century North Carolina-Built Centerboard Schooner" (M.A. thesis, ECU, 1999), 14. See also Horace James, *Annual Report of the Superintendent of Black Affairs in North Carolina, 1864*, 10, 27; Vincent Colyer, *Report of the Services Rendered by the Freed People to the United States Army, in North Carolina*, 9.

19. Guion Griffis Johnson, *Ante-Bellum North Carolina: A Social History*, 174. See also Catherine W. Bishir and others, *Architects and Builders in North Carolina: A History of the Practice of Building*, 111.

20. In "Cooperation and Contention: Slave-Poor White Relations in the Ante Bellum Period," (Ph.D. diss., University of Delaware, 2003), 51, Jeffrey P. Forrest claims that only about five percent of slaves worked in industry but it is unclear if he considered ship/boat building an industry. See also Robert S. Starobin, *Industrial Slavery in the Old South*, 28-30.

21. Their father, in Martin County, had six slaves working for him. Martin County Deed Book I-J, 135-137, SANC.

22. Joseph I. Roberson Collection, SANC.

23. Tarboro *N. Carolina Free Press*, April 17, 1829. See also *James W. Bell v. Caleb L. Walker, et al.*, Supreme Court of North Carolina, Raleigh 50 N.C. 43, 1857 N.C. Lexis 15, 5 Jones Law 43; David Cecelski, *The Waterman's Song: Slavery and Freedom in Maritime North Carolina*, 141; James Howard Estate, 1840, Craven County Estate Papers, SANC.

24. (New Bern) *Daily Progress*, October 19, 1858.

25. Lindley S. Butler, *Pirates, Privateers, and Rebel Raiders of the Carolina Coast*, 90.

26. (New Bern) *Carolina Federal Republican*, October 16, 1816.

27. Slavery Insurance Registry by name of Slave, 9, California Department of Insurance.

28. Lemmon, ed., *Pettigrew Papers*, I:115. See also Turner, "Historical and Archaeological Investigation of the *Scuppernong*." For other examples of slaves as shipbuilders, see George P. Rawick, ed., *The American Slave: A Composite Autobiography*, Vol. 14, Part 1, 450; Cecelski, *Waterman's Song*, passim.

29. See *Norfolk and Portsmouth Herald*, June 18, 1817; *Fayetteville Observer*, August 18 and 22, 1859, and June 30, 1862.

30. The 1850 census lists only three Black caulkers in the state, but this figure is clearly incorrect; the 1860 census lists only two. The 1850 census for Pasquotank County lists only four Black ship carpenters; the 1860 census lists two Black ship carpenters and one caulker. John Hope Franklin mentions two Black shipbuilders, five ship carpenters, and two caulkers in Craven County between 1800 and 1860. Gale Farrow in her articles on Black craftsmen lists seven caulkers in the state. She also lists a number of Black ship carpenters. Cecelski, *Waterman's Song*, 173; 1830 bill in the John Grey Blount Papers, SANC; 1850 and 1860 United States census for Beaufort County; (Washington) *American Recorder*, December 21, 1821; John Hope Franklin, "The Free Black in the Economic Life of North Carolina," *NCHR*, July 1942, p. 243; Farrow, "Black Craftsmen in North Carolina," *North Carolina Genealogical Society Journal*, 2-13, 91-103.

31. Itemized account of workers for repairing brig *Cygnet*, May 14, 1832, Mrs. V. J. McKnight Papers, SANC; *Newbern Spectator*, May 19, 1837; correspondence, George Stevenson to "Alice," September 18, 1997, copy in author's possession. See also (New Bern) *Carolina Federal Republican*, October 26, 1916; (New Bern) *Carolina Federal Republican*, December 6, 1817, February 1, 1817; Bishir, "Black Builders in Antebellum North Carolina," 442, 444.

32. Case 7801, North Carolina Supreme Court Original Cases, SANC; *James W. Bell v. Caleb L. Walker, et al.*, 50 NC 43, 44, 48 NC 320, June term 1856, 321-323; 50 NC 43, December term 1857, 43-47; Supreme Court Original Case, file 3124 and 7358, SANC.

33. See the Hull Anderson Files, George H. and Laura Brown Library, Washington, N.C. A list of emigrants to Liberia that included Anderson and his family records his profession as a caulker; William N. Still Jr., "The Shipbuilding Industry in Washington, North Carolina," in Joseph F. Steelman, ed., *Of Tar Heel Towns, Shipbuilders, Reconstructionists, and Alliancemen: Papers in North Carolina History*, 33; Cecelski, *Waterman's Song*, 54.

34. (New Bern) *Daily Progress*, December 30, 1858; *Newbern Spectator*, February 2, 1838.

35. Jonathan Havens informed the editors of the Raleigh *News and Observer* in 1893 that the first steamboat to sail the Pamlico was built by a shipbuilder named Peabody, working as a contractor. (Raleigh) *News and Observer and State Chronicle*, September 15, 1893.

36. North Carolina customhouse records have a large number of documents concerning the repair of vessels in North Carolina yards. North Carolina customhouse records in Box 30, Entry 17C, Record Group 26: Records of the United States Coast Guard, NARA.

37. Turner, "Historical and Archaeological Investigation of the Scuppernong," 55-57. Coastal county deed books and real estate conveyances are replete with legal documents concerning partial sale and ownership of vessels.

38. Account book of Culpepper Piggott for constructing a vessel in 1828. He kept a daily log of his master carpenter and others who worked on the vessel. He also listed other expenses. Mrs. V. J. McKnight Papers, SANC. See also Henry Clark Bridgers Jr., "Steamboats on the Tar," manuscript copies in the Henry Clark Bridgers Jr. Papers, ECU Manuscript Collection, Greenville, N.C., 32.

39. Myers was a native of Pennsylvania who opened a mercantile business in Washington in 1825. Still, "Shipbuilding Industry in Washington, North Carolina," 36; Alan D. Watson, "Sailing Under Steam: The Advent of Steam Navigation in North Carolina to the Civil War," *NCHR*, 48-49; James Cox, "The Pamlico-Tar River and Its Role in the Development of Eastern North Carolina" (M.A. thesis, ECU, 1989), 7; William A. Griffin, "Ante-Bellum Elizabeth City" (M.A. thesis, ECU, 1996), 105.

40. *Wilmington Chronicle*, December 22, 1844. It is not known if Captain Kirkpatrick, who built and sailed his own steamboat, the *Utility*, was a mariner or a shipbuilder.

41. Ann M. Merriman, "North Carolina Schooners, 1815-1901, and the S.R. Fowle and Son Company of Washington, North Carolina," (M.A. thesis, ECU, 1999), 149-158; Cox, "Pamlico-Tar River and its Role in the Development of Eastern North Carolina," 18-19.

42. This company is not listed in the state gazetteers. J. C. Blanchard and Co., *Over a Century of Merchandising, 1832-1954*,

8; Turner, "An Historical and Archaeological Investigation of the *Scuppernong*," 51-52.

43. Rose Goode McCullough, *Ghosts on the River: The Sailing Ships of William Hollister of New Bern*, 1-50.

44. Thomas H. Sloan, "Inland Steam Navigation in North Carolina, 1818-1900" (M.A. thesis, ECU, 1971), 35.

45. Pettigrew to Johnston, March 30, 1829, Ebenezer Pettigrew Papers, SHC, UNC-CH; Lemmon, ed., *Pettigrew Papers*, I:115; Bennett H. Wall, "Ebenezer Pettigrew: An Economic Study of an Ante-Bellum Planter" (Ph.D. diss., UNC, 1946), 353-355.

46. Wall, "Ebenezer Pettigrew," 341.

47. Johnston to Pettigrew, February 17, 1829, Pettigrew Papers, SHC, UNC-CH.

48. Wall, "Ebenezer Pettigrew," 356-357, 362.

49. Turner, "Historical and Archaeological Investigation of the *Scuppernong*," 52-54.

50. Carlton A. Morrison, *Running the River: Poleboats, Steamboats and Timber Rafts on the Altamaha, Ocmulgee, Oconee and Ohoopee*, 58. Other steamboats were sent out of state.

51. Dated December 8, 1818, in George H. and Laura Brown Library, Washington, N.C.

52. Contract dated October 5, 1832, Joseph I. Roberson Papers, SANC. For another contract see Joseph R. Roberson, William Roberson and Thomas Howard with William Dunn, May 8, 1844, copy in the Roberson Papers. Their contract called for thirty dollars per ton which seems to be the accepted price until mid-century.

53. Deposition, May 2, 1828, Box 6, General Assembly Session Records, SANC.

54. Not all scholars consider the construction of small craft as shipbuilding. However, as shipwrights in North Carolina built all kinds and all sizes of watercraft, the current study adopts a more comprehensive approach. Ben Ford, "Wooden Shipbuilding in Maryland Prior to the Mid-Nineteenth Century," *American Neptune* 62 (Winter 2002):69-70.

55. (Raleigh) *Weekly North Carolina Standard*, March 2, 1853.

56. (Wilmington) *Daily Herald*, June 27, 1855; Hugh Thompson, "Early Steam Navigation on Albemarle Sound," unpublished manuscript, copy in the author's possession.

57. In 1850, the total population was 869,039 of which only 21,109, or 2.4 percent, were classified by the census as urban. Hugh Talmage Lefler and Albert Ray Newsome, *North Carolina: The History of a Southern State*, 391.

58. *Edenton Gazette and North Carolina General Advertiser*, April 13, 1819; transcript of land dispute in possession of Mrs. Daisy Smith, Swansboro, N.C., Carteret County Wills, 1819, SANC.

59. "The Building of the Ship," *Harper's New Monthly Magazine*, 24 (April 1862), 609; *Newbernian*, September 14, 1847.

60. (New Bern) *Republican*, September 16, 1849.

61. John Cox Estate, 1858, Chowan County Estate Records, 1728-1951, SANC; Pasquotank County Deed Book CC, 7-8, SANC.

62. *Cape-Fear Recorder*, November 12, 1831.

63. Documents on repairs are extensive. *Ashe Sikes v. Robert T. Paine, et al.*, Supreme Court of North Carolina, Raleigh 32 N.C. 2809; 1849 N.C. Lexis 106; 10 Iredell. Law 280; *James Cameron vs. The Brig Marcellus*, ibid. 48 N.C. 83; 1855 Lexis 123; 3 Jones Law 83; *Whitehurst v. Lincoln*, Sept 11, 1851, Craven County Civil Action Papers, SANC; itemized account for repairing a vessel, Mrs. J. V. McKnight Papers, SANC; itemized account, Sparrow and Howard, June 10, 1837, James Howard Estate, Craven County Estate Papers, SANC; Bill of Sparrow and Howard, 1830, Joseph Nelson Estate, Craven County Estate Papers, SANC; To Sparrow and Howard, Oct 5, 1828, Francis M. Manning Papers, ECU; To Joseph Farrow for repairing schooner *Catherine Howard*, Mary Farrow Credle Papers, SHC, UNC-CH; McRae to Beery, June 9, 1843, New Hanover County Deed Book Z, 636, SANC; (Halifax) *Roanoke Advocate*, May 15, 1830; William Hollister Journal, June 30, 1824, March 9, 1825, William Hollister Account Books, SANC; June 23, September 20, 1845, January 1846, October 30, 1849, May 15, 1850, Ballance Family Papers, ECU.

64. Hutchins, *American Maritime Industries and Public Policy*, 108-109.

65. *Newbern Journal*, October 4, 1854; *John N. Hanff v. Thomas S. Howard and others*, Supreme Court Case Papers #7344, SANC; *Newbern Spectator and Literary Journal*, August 23, October 18, 1828; (New Bern) *North-Carolina Sentinel*, September 6, 1828

66. *Roanoke Advocate*, reprinted from *Washington Times*, May 13, 1830.

67. (Washington) *North Carolina Times*, January 25, 1860; *Tarboro Press*, March 4, 1837.

68. *Wilmington Advertiser*, April 14, 1837.

69. (Washington) *North State Whig*, June 4, 1851.

70. *Elizabeth-City Star and North-Carolina Eastern-Intelligencer*, June 3, 1831.

71. Small yards were scattered throughout the county with its maze of waterways. During the Civil War, Union forces occupied Beaufort and established a coal depot there. However, except for minor work, Union vessels were repaired elsewhere in the state, where marine railways were available. William Danford Blair, "'One Good Port:' The Union Navy and Beaufort Harbor, NC, 1862-1865", (M.A. thesis, ECU, 1999).

72. *Raleigh Register and North-Carolina Gazette*, June 29, 1829.

73. At least five additional vessels were built in Beaufort. Local documents such as deeds and court records frequently mention vessels. For example, an 1828 deed mentions the purchase of a vessel on the stocks in Beaufort built by Solomon Ward and Needham Canaday. Carteret County Deed Book U, 300, SANC.

74. This is somewhat surprising considering the area's limited maritime trade but may be a continuation of Beaufort's dominance established prior to the War of 1812. Although a report issued before the War of 1812 mentions a decrease in ship timber in the area, supplies must have been extensive enough to support the industry. Sonny Williamson in *Sailing with Grandpa* included a list of forty-one ship carpenters and boatbuilders from 1815 to 1860 but the list is far from complete; see 117-118.

75. McCullough, *Ghosts on the River*, 29-44; Carteret County Deed Books S, 300, 31 and T, 30, SANC.

76. Carteret County Deed Book S, 364, SANC.

77. The best study of Burns is in Butler, *Pirates, Privateers, and Rebel Raiders on the Carolina Coast*, 73-93, and 236-239. See also *Beaufort News*, August 11, 1821; Walter F. Burns, *Captain Otway Burns: Patriot, Privateer and Legislator*, 106. Otway Burns closed his shipyard down in 1842 because of the lack of business and moved to Portsmouth Island where he died in 1850.

78. Curiously, Williamson does not include any of the Pigotts in his list of ship carpenters and boatbuilders; see *Sailing with Grandpa*, 117-118. For the Pigotts, see the miscellaneous accounts of Piggott, Mrs. J.V. McKnight Papers, SANC; extensive correspondence and other documents in the Piggott estate papers, Carteret County Estate Papers, SANC. See also Carteret County Deed Books S, 303-304, and T, 109, SANC; bill of sale for the schooner *Pigot* of Newbern, in the Wynn Family Papers, Murfreesboro Historical

Association Collection, ECU.

79. *Beaufort News*, September 12, 1946; Pat Davis and others, eds., *Heritage of Carteret County*, I:298; James Brooke Estate Papers, Carteret County Estate Papers, SANC.

80. (New Bern) *Atlantic*, August 20, 1854; enrollment for the 315-ton *Laura Gertrude*, Port of Savannah, RG41, Records of the Bureau of Marine Inspection and Navigation, NARA.

81. (*New Bern*) *Atlantic*, August 30, 1854; *Raleigh Star and North Carolina Gazette*, November 19, 1845. Deed books mention ships built in the county. Craven County Deed Book 51, 277; 66, 27; 60, 356, SANC.

82. The lack of a marine railway in Beaufort is the major reason why the federal navy, which established a fairly extensive logistical base in Beaufort, repaired its vessels in New Bern. Fred M. Mallison, *The Civil War on the Outer Banks*, 17. The county shipbuilding industry, like others in the state, was probably hurt by the Panic of 1857 and the recession that followed. There is also the possibility that ship carpenters were listed as mechanics. Jean B. Kell in *North Carolina's Coastal Carteret County during the Civil War* suggests that the census taker may have visited when individuals were either farming or fishing.

83. This does not include Bay River, but it does include Smith Creek, just northeast of the port where at least ten schooners and brigs were built, and another twenty more in outlying Craven County on Adam and Garbacon Creeks and the South River. Peter B. Sandbeck, *The Historic Architecture of New Bern and Craven County, North Carolina*, 563.

84. Stephen Miller, "Recollections of New Bern," I (1875).

85. (New Bern) *Carolina Sentinel*, May 8, 15, 1824.

86. Virginia Kirwan, "The Impact of the Lumbering Industry on the Economy of New Bern and Craven County, 1710-1988," *Journal of the New Bern Historical Society*, III (May 1990):28-29. Craven County Deed Book 63, SANC, has information on more than a dozen vessels built in the state from 1842 to 1854. See also *Raleigh Register and North-Carolina Gazette*, November 29, 1836.

87. George Sparrow of Princess Anne County, Virginia, had three sons, Smith, Peter, and Henry, who "put to the ship carpenter's trade." Smith had two sons who moved to Craven County, North Carolina in the 1780s. W. Keats Sparrow, "Sparrow, Thomas II," in Powell, ed., *DNCB*, V:405-406. William S. Sparrow built vessels at Dawson's Creek which is in Pamlico County today.

88. (New Bern) *Carolina Sentinel*, April 5, 1828; McCullough, *Ghosts on the River*, 18.

89. Genealogies of the Sparrow Family by Margaret Jarvis, vertical files, State Library of North Carolina; Keats Sparrow to authors, June 8, 1976, copy in author's possession; W. Keats Sparrow, "Dr. William Tucker Sparrow: Builder of the Octagon House in Hyde County," *Hyde County Historical and Genealogical Society North Carolina*, XV (Spring 1994):3.

90. Sparrow, "Sparrow, Thomas, II," in Powell, ed., *DNCB*, V:406. See also the *Raleigh Register and North-Carolina Gazette*, October 24, 1828; *Newbern Spectator and Literary Journal*, October 18, 1828; April 16, 1833; June 26, 1835. Sparrow apparently built a lightboat for Galveston, Texas. Box 8, Entry 17 C, RG26, Records of the United States Coast Guard, NARA.

91. Sandbeck, *Historic Architecture of New Bern and Craven County*, 262.

92. James Howard Estate, 1840, Craven County Estate Papers, SANC; Sparrow, "Sparrow, Thomas, II," *DCNB*, V:406; *Fayetteville Observer*, June 30, 1835.

93. December 11, 1838, Craven County Deed Book 53, 453, SANC; *Newbernian*, July 29, 1848. A ship carpenter by the name of Thomas B. Wallace built the schooner *Kimberly* in 1833. November 2, 1839, Craven County Deed Book 54, SANC; John B. Green III, *Perfect Hurricanes and Awful Conflagrations: The Historical Significance and Archaeological Potential of the Craven County Convention Center Parking Lots Sites, New Bern North Carolina*, 30; *Newbernian*, August 1, 1848; John Whitford Memoir, copy in New Bern-Craven Public Library, New Bern, N.C.; Thomas Sparrow Property including map, Box 322, folder marked R. Duffy and Appleton Oaksmith, Elizabeth Moore Collection, ECU.

94. Thomas S. Howard was the son of James Howard and presumably got his ship carpenter training under his father's tutelage. Howard was born in 1821 in Portsmouth and came to New Bern with his father in 1827. Thomas later claimed that he was a seaman before becoming a ship carpenter. *Hanff v. Howard and others*, Supreme Court of North Carolina, Raleigh, 56 N.C. 440, 1857 N.C. Lexis 217, 3 Jones eq. 440; *Newbernian*, June 24, 1843.

95. *New Berne Weekly Journal*, December 4, 1890; Whitford Memoir, SANC; *Historical and Descriptive Review of the State of North Carolina*, II:84.

96. Howard later claimed that he built his first vessel in New Bern in 1843, but the Howard and Roberson firm was repairing vessels before then. Accounts of John Brissington, July-November, 1841, and receipt for repairs to schooner, April 3, 1842, Roberson Papers, SANC; *Historical and Descriptive Review of the State of North*, II:81; Sparrow, "Sparrow, Thomas, II," in Powell, ed., *DNCB*, V, II:406.

97. *Newbernian*, June 24, 1843.

98. According to the 1850 census, James Roberson, was no longer in the shipbuilding business. He was a roadmaster for the Atlantic and North Carolina Railroad. December 11, 1848, Craven County Deed Book 59, SANC.

99. File of Thomas S. Howard, RG 94: Records of the Adjutant General's Office, 1762-1994, NARA, Microfilm Publication M1003: Amnesty Papers: 1865-1867, Roll 62; *New Berne Weekly Journal* December 4, 1890; Joseph Tomlinson and wife to Howard, November 12, 1856, Craven County Deed Book 86, 319, SANC; William Roberson and Harriet Roberson to Thomas Howard, December 2, 1859, for waterfront lot 10; John A. Meadows and Louisa Meadows to Thomas Howard, December 2, 1859, for western half of waterfront lot 10; James Howard to Thomas Howard, December 2, 1859, for fifth part of lot 10; Samuel Howard to Thomas Howard, December 2, 1859, a fifth part of lot 10 including wharf; and John F. Hanff to Thomas Howard, one sixth of lot number 10, Craven County Deed Book 66, 295, 296, 299, 301, SANC.

100. (New Bern) *Republican*, April 12, 1848, February 21, 1849; Malachi Roberson and Elizabeth Roberson to William Roberson, December 11, 1848, Craven County Deed Book 59, SANC.

101. John D. Whitford, "The Home Story of a Walking Stick: Early History of the *Biblical Recorder* and Baptist Church in New Bern, N.C., Told in Every Day Talk," unpublished typescript, Whitford Papers, SANC; (New Bern) *Atlantic*, May 17, 1854; (New Bern) *Daily Progress*, September 21, 1858. See also the (Washington) *North State Whig*, May 23, 1853; Craven County Deed Book 66, 27, SANC; (New Bern) *Republican*, April 10, 1850; enrollment for the schooner *Alexander Doyle*, Savannah Enrollments, RG41: Records of the Bureau of Marine Inspection and Navigation, NARA.

102. February 19, 1849, Craven County Deed Book 59, 1849, SANC.

103. Miller claimed that, as a result of buying out Pittman's interest in the shipyard, he was a partner in the firm. Pittman's suit was

dismissed by the State Supreme Court. *Hanff v. Howard*. . . 56 N.C. 440, 1857 N.C. Lexis 217, 3 Jones Eq. 440. The original is Supreme Court Case 7344, SANC; it includes lengthy testimony. See also February 9, 1852, Craven County Deed Book 63, 1020, SANC.

104. December 3, 1859, Craven County Deed Book, 86, 293-294, SANC. See also Benjamin Ellis (Elijah's son) to Howard, November 3, 1859.

105. Ellis, who was a silent partner off and on in the shipyard for several years, died in 1880 at the age of seventy-seven. At different times, in addition to the shipyard, he owned interests in various sailing vessels, and other commercial interests in New Bern. His impressive home still stands in the city. *Newbernian*, June 5, 1880; (Raleigh) *Observer*, June 1, 1880. For his fleet of sailing vessels, see the shipping papers in the Mrs. V. J. McKnight Collection, SANC; (New Bern) *Daily Progress*, March 1, 1859; Case No. 7801, Supreme Court Records, SANC. See also *Hanff v. Howard and others*, Case No. 7344. The litigation was long and complex. *Newbernian*, June 24, 1843; Craven County Deed Book 56, 130, SANC; *Hanff v. Howard and others*, December Term, 1857, Supreme Court 56 N.C.418-421); (New Bern) *Union*, January 19, 1857.

106. The 1860 Census lists Sparrow as a ship carpenter, age sixty-seven. See *New Bern Journal*, October 4, 1854; Palmer to Smith, June 24, 1864, Area File 7, RG45: Naval Records Collection of the Office of Naval Records and Library, 1691-1945, NARA, Microfilm Publication M625: Area Files of the Naval Records Collection, 1775-1910; (New Bern) *Daily Progress*, February 15, 1859.

107. In 1859, no ships were built in New Bern, probably a result of the recession following the crash of 1857. In 1850, the census listed sixteen shipwrights, seven sailmakers, and three caulkers. The 1860 census listed only six carpenters, including the two Howards and William Roberson, one sailmaker, and no caulkers. Alan D. Watson, *A History of New Bern and Craven County*, 255-256. A Craven County death certificate for Valentine W. Paul stated he was a ship carpenter. He was born in 1835 and died in 1915.

108. *Newbernian*, September 14, 1847.

109. (New Bern) *North Carolina Sentinel*, June 13, 1829.

110. (New Bern) *Sentinel*, September 21, 1832. Possibly Richard Ellis or one of his family or relatives was the shipbuilder.

111. (New Bern) *Commercial News*, November 19, 1881. See also the *New Bern Spectator and Political Register*, May 15, 1835. For other McLin-built vessels, see the (New Bern) *North Carolina Sentinel*, April 14, 1834, and *Goldsboro Messenger*, December 1, 1881.

112. (New Bern) *Republican*, September 13, 1848; September 26, 1849.

113. *New Bern Spectator*, August 22, 1840.

114. *Newbernian and North Carolina Advocate*, December 3, 1851.

115. Watson, *History of New Bern and Craven County*, 236; Case no. 7801, Supreme Court Records, SANC; *Newbernian*, August 1, 1848.

116. (Elizabeth City) *Old North State*, May 31, 1851.

117. (New Bern) *Carolina Federal Republican*, July 15, 1815.

118. July 3, 1849 and April 24, 1849, Craven County Deed Book 59, 387-388, SANC; (New Bern) *Republican*, September 26, 1849; *Newbernian*, June 16, 1847; February 13, May 30, 1848; June 26, July 4, 1849; Craven County Deed Book 59, 348, SANC; Watson, *History of New Bern and Craven County*, 236.

119. Josephus Daniels, *Tar Heel Editor*, 9; Joseph L. Morrison, *Josephus Daniels: The Small-d Democrat*, 3-4; Joe A. Mobley, *Pamlico County: A Brief History*, 29.

120. *New Bern Spectator and Literary Journal*, May 25, 1832.

121. *New Bern Spectator and Literary Journal*, October 11, 1833; (New Bern) *North Carolina Sentinel*, April 4, 1834; (New Bern) *Daily Progress*, October 6, 1858.

122. William N. Still Jr., "Shipbuilding and Boatbuilders in Swansboro, 1800-1950," *Tributaries* 5 (October 1995); 8-9.

123. (Wilmington) *People's Press and Wilmington Advertiser*, April 10, 1833, April 9, 1834.

124. Michael Hill, ed., The Governors of *North Carolina*, 37-39.

125. Beaufort County Will Abstracts, December 27, 1819, 45, SANC; (Washington) *North State Whig*, February 24, 1847.

126. A newspaper ad stated that the shipyard would "take a contract to build." (Washington) *North State Whig*, January 18, 26, 1853. Hugh Toland, a ship carpenter from Rhode Island, leased the yard. He, like many others, moved to North Carolina looking for opportunities to better himself financially. Toland arrived in the county in the 1850s but had moved to Hyde County by 1860, where he continued to list his profession as a ship carpenter. He was no longer there in 1870, and, like others from northern states, may have left the area with the secession of North Carolina.

127. Still, "Shipbuilding Industry in Washington, North Carolina," 32.

128. Beaufort County Deed Book 24, 132, 138, SANC; *Raleigh Register and North Carolina Gazette*, February 11, 1845.

129. Havens was a native of Long Island, New York. He first settled in Hyde County, married a local lady in 1804, and went into shipbuilding with James H. Smith, either his wife's uncle or brother. He moved to Beaufort County sometime before the War of 1812, served in a militia unit during the war, and subsequently established his own shipyard in Washington. The notes on Jonathan Havens in possession of Peter Wirke, copy provided to the authors.

130. This was probably Benjamin Franklin Havens, the son of Jonathan. Ursula Loy and Pauline Worthy, *Washington and the Pamlico*, 230.

131. Beaufort County Deed Book 19, 219, SANC.

132. Beaufort County Deed Book 19, 219, SANC.

133. Shipp sold off property that he owned in the port. In 1849, he sold a one-third interest in a vessel on the stocks; a few months later, he had to sell another third to a creditor. In 1850, he had to make Benjamin Hanks his trustee and creditor, and gave over the last third of the unfinished vessel and the lumber and other materials intended for her completion, his long-term lease on the shipyard, shipbuilding tools and machinery, and even the remaining half-year's hire of two slaves. Beaufort County Deed Book 24, 15, Book 25, 450, 462, and Book 26, 13, 29, SANC; (Washington) *North State Whig*, February 6, June 1, 2, 1850, for ads placed by Shipp.

134. William Farrow must have been involved in shipbuilding in some capacity as owner, partner or lessor. In 1850, he was master carpenter for the schooner *Pacific*, launched that year. Dun and Company considered Farrow a failure. *Washington Gazette*, November 1, 1889.

135. Beaufort County Deed Book 34, 299, SANC.

136. One of Farrow's ship carpenters was Josephus Daniels Sr.

137. Still, "Shipbuilding Industry in Washington, North Carolina," 33; C. Wingate Reed, *Beaufort County: Two Centuries of its History*, 172.

138. Copy of interview in the Myers Papers, George H. and Laura E. Brown Library, Washington, N.C.; Beaufort County Deed Book 28, 626, and Deed Book 29, 624, and 431, SANC.

139. Beaufort County Deed Book 9, 73-76, SANC; Percival Perry,

"The Naval Stores Industry in the Ante-Bellum South, 1789-1861, (Ph.D. diss, UNC, 1947), 234; *Tarboro' Press,* March 4, 1837.

140. Admiralty Case 17:59, Dec 31, 1861, U.S. District Court for the Southern District of New York. Copies of the case, including the vessel's enrollment document, are in the George H. and Laura E. Brown Library, Washington, N.C. See also the T.H.B. Myers memoir in the Myers Papers, George H. and Laura E. Brown library, Washington, N.C.; *Wilmington Journal* (weekly), October 16, 1857; (Washington) *North Carolina Times,* October 8, 1856; Loy and Worthy, *Washington and the Pamlico,* 241.

141. Still, "Shipbuilding Industry in Washington, North Carolina," 34.

142. Paul Cornell left Plymouth and his two brothers sometime before 1838. The 1840 census for Beaufort County lists Paul, Keturah (his second wife), and Paul's three sons by his first marriage: Beaufort County Deed Book, 19, 418-419, SANC; (Washington) *North State Whig,* September 11, 1850.

143. When North Carolina seceded, Ezra E. and John W. Cornell enlisted in Company K, 10th Regiment N.C. State Troops (lst Regiment N.C. Artillery); Paul Cornell Jr. enlisted in (2nd) Company G. 36th Regiment N.C. Troops (2nd Regiment N.C. Artillery) in September 1861. Ezra and John were deployed to Fort Hatteras on the Outer Banks and surrendered with their unit when the fort fell. Incarcerated successively in various prisoner-of-war camps, they were paroled upon appeal from their family in New York under oath not to leave that state without permission from the U.S. Secretary of State nor engage in activities or correspondence hostile to the Union. In letters written to their New York relatives in April 1861, they expressed clear Unionist convictions. Writing to Secretary of State Seward, their uncle Ezra Cornell insisted that they "were forced against their will to take up arms against the Union." Learning of this from a Boston newspaper article, Thomas Sparrow, their commanding officer imprisoned with his men, angrily denied they were forced to take up arms. His journal states: "They took no oath of allegiance and they were not forced into the service. They were volunteers in the strictest sense of the term." However, with this single exception, Sparrow's journal entries were not critical of the Cornells. An April 17, 1861 letter from Ezra E. Cornell, in Washington, North Carolina, to his uncle, in New York, confirms his sentiments, indicating that he wanted to be "neutral but I cannot and remain here and I have not the means to get away with my mother and family." Ezra died in 1863; John took a bounty and joined a Michigan unit. Paul was discharged from the service in May 1862 and, after Washington was occupied by Union troops, became a commission merchant buying up corn and, later, cotton, and shipping it north. In February 1864, he wrote a cousin that he was in the baking business. When Washington was evacuated by Union troops, he fled first to Hyde County, then to Beaufort. In June, he was in New Bern, and wrote that he had had no work since Washington was evacuated. He mentioned that his mother and her companion Susan Fagan were still in Washington. Paul and John disappear from the historical record after the war. Their mother Keturah and Susan Fagan remained in Washington. When Keturah died she willed her property to Susan Fagan. Her sons are not mentioned. Entry for November 6, 1861, Thomas Sparrow Journal, Thomas Sparrow Papers, SHC, UNC-CH; see also entries for October 18, 19, 1861; Cornell Papers, SHC, UNC-CH. See also John Cornell to E. Cornell, April 22, 1861, Cornell Family Papers, Cornell University Libraries; E. Cornell to Seward, October 11, 1861, Updegraff to Loomis, October 18, 1861, Seward to Loomis, October 21, 1861, Memo of Political Arrest, n.d., *O.R.* Series II, 2:100-101, 108-109, 114-115, 296.

144. New Bern Enrollments, RG41: Records of the Bureau of Marine Inspection and Navigation, NARA; *New Bern Republican,* September 18, 1850.

145. (Tarboro) *Southerner,* Feb 23, 1856.

146. (Washington) *North State Whig,* February 25, 1853.

147. A genealogy of the Ritch family records that the Ritches of Washington were from Middle Island on Long Island. The entry also mentions that a third brother, Simon, came to North Carolina with his two brothers to engage in shipbuilding. He moved to Hyde County but there is no evidence that he engaged in shipbuilding. In 1859, Simon sold land in Hyde County to cover debts. Balance Papers, ECU.

148. (Washington) *North State Whig,* March 12, 1851; bill for sale of wood from Samuel and John S. Brinson of Craven County to the Messer's Ritch, 1842, Henries Collection, SANC. Ulysses Ritch married Adeline Long in Washington, November 27, 1850. This may have been a factor in the move.

149. Ulysses Ritch to Collector, July 10, 1853, letterbook 16, Entry 17C, RG26: Records of the United States Coast Guard, NARA; (Washington) *North State Whig,* May 23, 1853.

150. Beaufort County Deed Book 30, 342, SANC.

151. Still, "Shipbuilding Industry in Washington, North Carolina," 36; Cox, "The Pamlico-Tar River and its role in the Development of Eastern North Carolina," 47.

152. (Washington) *North State Whig,* May 5, 1853; *Fayetteville Observer,* March 5, 1860.

153. Cloud, *Old Salt,* 41.

154. Hyde County Deed Book 4, 1, SANC; War of 1812 Widow's Pension File #24657, Dare County, SANC. See also "The Hayman Family," *Swamproots,* XI (Spring, 1984), 65.

155. After the Civil War, Tilman applied to the Southern Claims Commission for reimbursement of goods seized during the war. The claim was not approved. Agreement between William Farrow and Tilman Farrow, February 14, 1825 in the Credle Papers, SHC, UNC-CH; *High Tides: Hyde County Historical and Genealogical Society North Carolina,* XX (Fall, 1999), 8, and XIII (Spring 1992), 39, 41; *Carteret County News-Times,* July 9, 1948.

156. Abraham Farrow Estate property, September 20, 1847, Hyde County Estate Records, 1735-1933, SANC; Cloud, *Old Salt,* 42.

157. For Pharoah see also the *Dare County Times,* August 11, 1936; Hyde County Estate Papers, , SANC. For other Farrows, see Estate of Isaac Farrow, Hyde County Estate Papers, SANC.

158. Cloud, *Old Salt,* 42. For the Outer Bank families see Stick, *Outer Banks,* 73. Tilmon Farrow was listed as a seaman in the 1860 census.

159. (New Bern) *Daily Journal,* December 15, 1885; Collector of Customs, New Bern to Secretary of Treasury, October 15, 1845, Letters from Collectors on Revenue Boats, January 1 to December 31, 1845, RG26: Records of the United States Coast Guard, NARA.

160. Kenneth Burke, "The History of Portsmouth, North Carolina from Its Founding in 1753 to Its Evacuation in the Face of Federal Forces in 1861," 33; Carteret County Deed Book U, 463, SANC.

161. (New Bern) *Daily Journal,* December 15, 1885.

162. This is probably not the actual name of the yard but there is no information as to the real owner. *High Tides: Hyde County Historical Society Journal North Carolina,* I (Fall, 1980):7; Moore to Bell, January 10, 1835, Bell Family Papers, Rubenstein Rare Books and Manuscripts Library, Duke University; deed, February 14, 1825, Credle Papers, SHC, UNC-CH; *Dare County Times,* August 11, 1936.

163. It is possible that the extreme shallowness of the Perquimans River made it impracticable to build there. An 1891 issue of the *Perquimans Record* recorded that a shipyard operated several miles above Hertford and built vessels for the West Indies trade. An 1833 deed mentions a shipyard, but this may well have been one that previously existed on the property. Perquimans County Deed Book X, 256, SANC; Alan D. Watson, *Perquimans County: A Brief History*, 48.
164. Williamston *Enterprise*, November 14, 1902; (Robersonville) *Weekly Herald*, August 20, 1941.
165. For the Southern Star, see Thomas Parramore, "The Ironic Fate of the *Southern Star*," *NCHR*, 335-344.
166. List provided authors by Barbara Snowden, Currituck County, N.C.
167. (Elizabeth City) *Independent*, February 22, 1935; *Journal of Currituck County Historical Society*, I (1973):55.
168. *Edenton Gazette and North-Carolina General Advertiser*, May 26, 1818; Ellen F. Cloud, *Portsmouth: The Way It Was*, 15.
169. Jo Ann Bates, ed., *The Heritage of Currituck County*, 27.
170. Turner, "A Historical and Archaeological Investigation of the *Scuppernong*," 44-56.
171. (Elizabeth City)*North Carolinian*, July 8, 1869.
172. Quoted in Jesse F. Pugh and Frank T. Williams, *The Hotel in the Great Dismal Swamp and Contemporary Events Thereabout*, 49-50.
173. *Elizabeth City Star*, June 3, August 20, 1853.
174. For example, John Sawyer built the *Trader* in 1853 and Grady Harris launched the *William Franklin* the same year.
175. *Elizabeth City Star*, November 3, 1849; 1850 unpublished industrial census, copy in Joyner Library, ECU.
176. Griffin, "Ante-Bellum Elizabeth City," 106.
177. Contract, June 4, 1838, Box 30, entry 17c, RG26: Records of the United States Coast Guard, NARA; (Elizabeth City) *Democratic Pioneer*, May 29, September 25, 1855, and August 25, March 4, 1857.
178. December 3, 1858, Pasquotank County Deed Book MM, SANC. For the Burgess and Lamb yard, see the (Elizabeth City) *Democratic Pioneer*, November 5, 1850.
179. Turner, "Historical and Archaeological Investigation of the *Scuppernong*," 48-49; account of payment, Boushell to Hunter, May 7, 1835, Timothy Hunter Papers, ECU; Pasquotank County Deed Book BB, 398-399, Real Estate Conveyances for Cluff, Pasquotank County Records, and Pasquotank County Deed Book CC, 7-8, SANC; *Elizabeth City Star and North-Carolina Eastern Intelligencer*, July 21, November 21, 1827, June 3, 1831.
180. (Elizabeth City) *Democratic Pioneer*, November 19, October 8, 1850; (Elizabeth City)*Old North State*, July 14, October 20, 1849.
181. See Pasquotank County Records in the SANC for several examples of the inspection reports.
182. March 30, 1834, and April 9, 1849, Pasquotank County Deed Book LL; May 7, 1835, SANC; copy of deeds, Timothy Hunter Papers, ECU. See also Turner, "Historical and Archaeological Investigation of the *Scuppernong*," 35-36.
183. Pasquotank County Wills, 1709-1917, William Martin, 1834, SANC.
184. Deeds and real estate conveyances, August 8, September 17, May 24, 1857, Pasquotank County Deed Book MM, SANC.
185. Pasquotank County Deed Book LL, SANC.
186. April 8, 1858, Pasquotank County Deed Book MM, SANC.
187. Earl Dean's account of early Elizabeth City, copy in possession of author. See also Wayne H. Payne, "The Commercial Development of Elizabeth City" (M.A. thesis, Old Dominion University, 1971), 63.
188. Martin served as a colonel in the Confederate Army. Hunter had his only vessel confiscated by the Confederate government and, later, served in the army. What happened to the other shipbuilders is not known.
189. (Elizabeth City) *Old North State*, November 3, 1849, February 24, 1849; Griffin, *Ante-Bellum Elizabeth City*, 74, 78, 82; *Pasquotank Historical Society Yearbook*, I (1954-1955):25; Wood, *Brief Sketch of Pasquotank County*, 13.
190. (Elizabeth City) *Democratic Pioneer*, October 8, 1850, November 19, 1854, September 25, 1855, May 20, 1856
191. Vessels were evidently built elsewhere in the county but only one, in Nixonton, is known. *Pasquotank County History Yearbook*, III:8
192. *Newbernian*, September 12, 1848; *Wilmington Morning Star*, March 21, 1906.
193. Anne M. Tunstall, "Memoir of Edenton," Reel 2, Cupola House Papers, Shepherd-Pruden Memorial Library, Edenton, N.C.; *Edenton Sentinel and Albemarle Intelligencer*, November 6, 1841; N.C. Supreme Court Original Case Papers, File 6745, SANC.
194. *New York Herald*, June 13, 1852; Bruce S. Cheeseman, "A Brief History of Edenton Waterfront," 19, copy in the author's hands; Thomas R. Butchko, *Edenton: An Architectural Portrait*, 21.
195. (Edenton) *Albemarle Bulletin*, December 25, 1850; *North Carolina Reports*, 32 NC 280, 208-210; File 6745, N.C. Supreme Court Original Case Papers, 1800-1909, SANC; Turner, "Historical and Archaeological Investigation of the *Scuppernong*," 48-49; 1850 census for Chowan County; George Stevenson to Alice, September 18, 1997, copy in author's possession.
196. John Cox Estate, 1858, Chowan estate Records, 1728-1951, SANC; (Edenton) *American Banner*, May 15, 1856; *Biographical Dictionary of the American Congress, 1774-2005*, 1505-1506; Butchko, *Edenton: An Architectural Portrait*, 21.
197. Badham, William disposition, Superior Court, Spring term 1886, Chowan County Records, 1728-1951, SANC.
198. Francis M. Manning and W.H. Booke, *Martin County History*, I:74.
199. (Williamston) *Enterprise*, undated clipping, (August?) 1941.
200. A court document claimed that Ezra Cornell alone built twenty vessels in addition to one that was currently on the stocks. Martin County Deed Book I-J, 135-137, SANC. For the Moore suit see *William E. Curtis and William Mitchell v. the Schooner Corinne*, United States District Court, May 1858 Term, Record Group 21, Records of the District Courts of the United States, NARA-Atlanta.
201. Martin County Deed Book H71, 428, SANC; Martin County North Carolina Abstracts of Will Books 1 and 2, 1774-1868, 135, SANC.
202. November 10, 1817, Cornell Family Papers, Cornell University.
203. Martin County Deed Books I-J, 135-137, SANC. For the Cornells in Martin County see numerous deeds in Martin County Deed Books F, G, I, J, SANC.
204. Washington County Deed Book H, 9-10, SANC; *Edenton Gazette and North-Carolina General Advertiser*, January 21, 1822.
205. *Edenton Gazette and Farmer's Palladium*, August 5, 1830.
206. Feb 5, 1833, Ezra Cornell Papers, Cornell University.
207. For the *Indian Queen* see the Timothy Hunter Papers, ECU. See also Plymouth Enrollments, 1833, RG41: Records of the Bureau of Marine Inspection and Navigation, NARA.
208. Turner to Blount, November 4, 1829, Alice B. Keith and William H. Masterson, eds., *The John Gray Blount Papers*, IV:513-514.

209. Washington County Deed Book G93 and G94, 93-96, SANC.
210. February 26, 1843, Cornell Family Papers, Cornell University; Betsy Burgess Lucas Modlin and Shirleyan Beacham Phelps, *My Home Is Washington County, North Carolina: A Local History for Students*, 127.
211. In 1831 they advertised in the *Edenton Gazette* for repair work. It was signed P[aul] Cornell & Bros. and dated June 1, 1831. R. G. Dunn and Company gave Cornell and Hanks good marks, "both responsible men."
212. Cornell to Collectors Office, April 3, 1839, Box 30, Entry 17C, RG26: Records of the United States Coast Guard, NARA. The newspaper announcement for bids went out on April 27, 1839. The lengthy detail of required work followed closely John Cornell's report and survey. There was at least one other bid, that of C. Fagan and Guyer, May 14, 1839. Both the call for bids and the bids are found in Box 30, Entry 17C, RG26, NARA.
213. Murray to Fifth auditor, June 5, 1844, and survey and report by John Cornell and Caleb Walker, July 4, 1849, Box 30, Entry 17C, RG26: Records of the United States Coast Guard, NARA.
214. John Cornell, *Genealogy of the Cornell Family*, 79, records the year of John's death as 1849. This is obviously not correct as he and his family are listed in the 1850 census. The August 5, 1830 issue of the *Edenton Gazette and Farmer's Palladium* states that the Cornells were planning to build a steamboat, but there is no evidence that this occurred.
215. Murray to Secretary, Lighthouse Board, November 24, 1852, letterbook 16, Entry 17C, RG26: Records of the United States Coast Guard, NARA. The document suggests that the collector actually wanted permission to build a new lightboat.
216. North Carolina Supreme Court, 50 NC 43, 44, SANC. Herrington was a shipwright in Beaufort before moving to Washington County. Caleb Walker was the son of a noted Tyrrell County shipbuilder, Michael Walker. He constructed at least two schooners in Tyrrell County before moving to Plymouth with his family.
217. Surveys, July 25, 1851 and September 19, 1851, Box 30, Entry 17C, RG26: Records of the United States Coast Guard, NA.
218. Copy of deed, March 10, 1852, in Angelo Garibaldi Papers, SANC. What happened to Caleb Walker is unclear. He is not listed in the 1860 census of either Tyrrell or Washington Counties.
219. In 1861, when Garibaldi was negotiating with James Johnston to build a new steamboat, he recommended Herrington, but mentioned that the shipbuilder needed money upfront: "Mr. Herrington has been unfortunate in business," and added that any contract would have to be negotiated with Herrington's agents or trustees. What happened to Herrington is unclear. He was alive in 1863 when his youngest child was born. However, according to the census he was not alive in 1870, as his widow and children were living in Lee's Mills Township, Washington County. (Petersburg) *Daily Express*, October 1, 1857. A local resident of Plymouth justified the need for a bank in 1855 by listing statistics including $50,000 in "ship Building, coach making, etc." (Raleigh) *Semi-Weekly Register*, February 10, 1855, August 12, 1861. See also Hayes Collection, SHC, UNC-CH; *Washington County Genealogical Society*, XI (January 2000):2; United States Census, Washington County census, 1850.
220. United States Naval History Division, *Civil War Naval Chronology*, VI:265.
221. Perquimans Deed Book X:44, SANC.
222. Ragnhild M. Bairnsfather, *The Potter Family of North Carolina, Indiana and Kentucky*, 29-30; *Wilmington Journal*, June 27, 1851.
223. Bill Reaves, *Southport (Smithville): A Chronology*, I:36.
224. Roy Parker Jr., *Cumberland County: A Brief History*, 57.
225. Alan D. Watson, *Wilmington: Port of North Carolina*, 67-69.
226 *People's Press and Wilmington Advertiser*, January 16, 1833; *Raleigh Register and North-Carolina Gazette*, October 13, 1826.
227. (Wilmington) *Daily Herald*, October 11, 1856, and, March 17, 1854; (Wilmington) *Daily Journal*, March 27, 1854; *Wilmington Dispatch*, October 8, 1917.
228. (Wilmington) *Daily Journal*, April 5, 1852. A ship carpenter, John Hendrick, a native of Switzerland who worked in a shipyard, was murdered. The victim was employed by A. D. Bordeaux whose establishment was about twelve miles from Wilmington. It does not state that Bordeaux was a shipbuilder and he is not listed as such in the 1850 census.
229. (Wilmington) *Tri-Weekly Commercial*, September 4, 1855.
230. There is little information about this yard. O'Hanlon built only a few steamboats and, by 1836, abandoned the industry for maritime trade. In the 1840s, he again entered the boat building trade, this time in Fayetteville. New Hanover County Deed Book U, p.359, SANC; Claude V. Jackson III, "The Cape Fear-Northeast Cape Fear Rivers Comprehensive Study: A Maritime History and Survey of the Cape Fear and Northeast Cape Fear Rivers, Wilmington Harbor, North Carolina," I: Maritime History, 216.
231. Vessel document papers, Wilmington Enrollments, 1826, 1829, RG41: Records of the Bureau of Marine Inspection and Navigation, NARA; (Fayetteville) *Carolina Observer*, October 27, 1825; *Raleigh Register and North-Carolina State Gazette*, October 25, 1825; *People's Press and Wilmington Advertiser*, January 16, April 10, June 5, 1833. James Sprunt in his *Tales and Traditions of the Lower Cape Fear, 1661-1896*, 34 wrote that the *Eliza and Susan* was the first sailing vessel built in Wilmington. This obviously was incorrect.
232. *Wilmington Morning Star*, August 20, 1947; *Fayetteville Observer Semi-Weekly*, April 16, 1863.
233. (Wilmington) *People's Press and Wilmington Advertiser*, April 10, May 1, 1833; *Fayetteville Observer*, April 16, 1833; *Wilmington Chronicle*, October 20, 1841.
234. George W. Willcox, *Camerons of Wilmington*, 117-131; North Carolina Supreme Court Records. Original Case Papers, File 4985(48 NC 85), SANC; *James Cameron vs. the Brig* Marcellus, Supreme Court of North Carolina, Raleigh 48 N.C. 84, 1855 N.C. Lexis 123, 3 Jones Law 83.
235. *Wilmington Chronicle*, January 29, 1845; *Wilmington Weekly Chronicle*, January 13, 1841; New Hanover County Registry Record, V, 13, New Hanover County Courthouse, Wilmington.
236. Copy in the Historic Plaque File, New Hanover County Public Library, Wilmington. See also Mrs. Brooke G. White interview, American Life Histories: Manuscripts from the Federal Writers' Project, 1936-1940: http://memoruy.loc.gov/bin/quer
237. *Wilmington Advertiser*, April 27, 1838; April 14, 1837; Wilmington Town Minutes, 1847-1855, SANC, 197.
238. New Hanover County Deed Boo KK, 14, SANC.
239. (Wilmington) *Tri-Weekly Commercial*, March 22, 1855.
240. In 1860 Jesse Cassidey also owned some sort of "store" called the "Rendezvous" in Wilmington but ran into financial difficulties, probably as a result of the economic instability following the Panic of 1857. He purchased goods from a New York firm on credit but was unable to pay them off before the Civil War. *Henning, et.al, vs. Cassidey*, 1867, Superior Court of New Hanover County, New Hanover County Papers, SANC; (Wilmington) *Daily Journal*, December 21, 31, 1860.

241. In 1841, Beery put his house in Smithville up for sale but still owned it in 1847. That year, the house was destroyed by fire and Beery announced a reward in the local paper for information leading to the conviction of the individual who set the fire. (Wilmington) *Commercial*, March 5, 1847; *Wilmington Chronicle*, November 10, 1841, March 9, 1842; *Wilmington Advertiser*, December 6, 1839; John Anthony Eisterhold, "Lumber and Trade in the Seaboard Cities of the Old South, 1607-1860." (Ph.D. diss., University of Mississippi, 1979), 112.

242. *Wilmington Advertiser*, April 14, 1837; (Wilmington) *Commercial*, November 24, 1846.

243. Although the Beerys called their shipbuilding establishment the "Commercial Mill and Ship Yard," it was popularly known as the "Beerys Shipyard," or "Beery & Sons Shipyard." *Wilmington Dispatch*, October 8, 1917; (Wilmington) *Weekly Commercial*, June 28, 1850; *Wilmington Chronicle*, Oct. 20, 1847, December 4, 1849, July 31, 1850; *Wilmington Journal* (weekly), December 7, 1849; August 2, 1850; New Hanover County Deed Book HH, 171, SANC; *Fayetteville Observer Semi-Weekly*, August 28 1851; New Hanover County Deed Book KK, Deed Book BB, 501; Deed Book HH, 131, 201, SANC.

244. (Wilmington) *Daily Journal*, February 18, 1852; *Wilmington Dispatch*, July 10, 1916, July 8, 1917. See also *DeBow's Review*, XIV (June 1853); G. N. Dunn, "Wilmington Shipyard Sites, 1860-1970," unpublished manuscript in possession of the authors; Edward H. Moseley III, "Southern Built: Wilmington's Maritime Construction Industry, 1727-1860," copy in Underwater Archaeology Unit's files, Kure Beach, N.C.; Samuel Beery's will dated January 31, 1852, copy in Beery Family file, Lower Cape Fear Historical Society, Wilmington.

245. (Wilmington) *Daily Journal*, May 15, 1861, and May 3, 1859; account of Mrs. Sarah C. Willson, and William A. Willson to his niece, n.d., in possession of Ida Kellum, Wilmington; notes on the Beery yard on file at the Underwater Archaeology Unit, Kure Beach, N.C.; New Hanover County Deed Book PP, 400, SANC.

246. (Wilmington) *Daily Herald*, April 3, 1860; (Wilmington) *Daily Journal*, May 5, 1860; *Fayetteville Observer*, April 15, 1834, September 10, 1836, and January 3, 1844.

247. George Stephenson, "Ropewalks," unpublished manuscript, copy in possession of authors. For the Plymouth facility see the census on manufactures for 1820, Washington County. For Edenton see Butchko, *Edenton: An Architectural Portrait*, 21. For New Bern see the *Carolina Centinel*, January 2, 1819; and Whitford, "Home Story of a Walking Stick," John D. Whitford Papers, SANC.

248. *Carolina Sentinel*, May 8, 15, 1824.

249. For a good study of the importance and economic viability of sailmaking, see Deirdre O'Regan, "Sailmaking in Nineteenth Century Southern New England" (M.A. thesis, ECU, 2001).

250. *Wilmington Messenger*, May 2, 1897; (Goldsboro) *Republican and Patriot*, August 28, 1851; *Tarboro' Press*, March 4, 1837; Cox, "Pamlico-Tar River and Its Role in the Development of Eastern North Carolina," 49; Percy, "Naval Stores Industry in the Ante-Bellum South," 234; Bill Reaves, comp., *Brief History of Wilmington*; Watson, *Wilmington: Port of North Carolina*, 47.

251. Whitford, "Home Story of a Walking Stick," John D. Whitford Papers, SANC. For an excellent study on the decline in timber for wooden vessels see Virginia Steele Wood, *Live Oaking: Southern Timber for Tall Ships*.

252. Reaves, *Southport (Smithville): A Chronology*, I:26; *Newbernian*, February 13, 1849; Chauncy to Board of Navy Commissioners, April 24, 1827, Entry 220, Letters, Board of Navy Commissioners Received from Commandants, RG41: Records of the Bureau of Marine Inspection and Navigation, NARA; Donald McAdoo and Carol McAdoo, *Reflections of the Outer Banks*, 58; *People's Press and Wilmington Advertiser*, October 16, 1833; (Wilmington) *Daily Herald*, March 12, 1855.

253. (Wilmington) *Weekly Commercial*, February 16, 1849. See also *People's Press and Wilmington Advertiser*, March 6, 1833; Moseley, "Southern Built: Wilmington's Maritime Construction Industry, 1717-1860," 22 - 23; *Fayetteville Observer*, October 22, 1833.

254. The article mentions the timber came from "high up the Neuse." *Newbernian*, August 1, 1848.

255. Treasurer and Commerce Papers: Ports, Box 24, SANC; *Aikwa v. Boushall and Paine*, Supreme Court Original Cases, 1800-1909, Case No. 6745, SANC.

256. *Wilmington Journal*, September 8, 1854.

257. Advertisements were placed in New York and Norfolk newspapers but not in North Carolina papers. Newspaper ads and contracts are in Box 005-006, Entry 153, RG217: Reports of the Accounting Officers of the Department of the Treasury, NARA. Contract between S. Pleasonton and William Doughty, dated August 31, 1820, Box 005, Entry 153, RG217, NARA; *Laws of the United States Relating to the Establishment, Support, and Management of the Light Houses, Light Vessels. . .of the United States from August 7, 1789 to March 3, 1855*, 60-61; Willard Flint, *A History of U.S. Lightships*, 1-2. See also information on early U.S. lightships prepared by the Coast Guard Historian's Office, Washington, D.C.; Robert F. Cairo, "Notes on Early Lightship Development," *Coast Guard Engineer's Digest* (July-August-September 1975), 3-12.

258. Stick, *North Carolina Lighthouses*, 30; David Stick, *The Outer Banks of North Carolina*, 84 (lists nine). In addition, at least one lightship, the *S. Pleasonton* constructed by Thomas Sparrow in New Bern, was built for the Galveston, Texas area. *Newbern Spectator and Literary Journal*, November 28, 1828; (New Bern) *Republican*, September 22, 1847, August 29, 1849; (Goldsboro) *Eastern Carolina Republican*, May 6, 1851; *Newbernian*, August 28, 1849. Proposal ads included details of the lightboats. See (New Bern) *Republican*, April 25, 1849; *Newbernian and North Carolina Advocate*, October 15, 1850.

259. Flint, Lightships of the United States Government.

260. Flint, Lightships of the United States Government.

261. Flint, Lightships of the United States Government. Contracts and bids for the North Carolina light vessels can be found in boxes 005-006, entry153, RG217: Reports of the Accounting Officers of the Department of the Treasury, NARA; Box 30, entry 17C, RG26: Records of the United States Coast Guard, NARA.

262. "Report of the Secretary of the Treasury of the State of the Finances," 34th Cong., lst Sess., House of Representatives, Ex. Doc. No 10, 355; Report of examination of Roanoke River light boat by John Cornell and Caleb Walker, July 4, 1849, Box 30, entry 17C, RG26: Records of the United States Coast Guard, NARA.

263. Custom Collector, Plymouth to Fifth Auditor, April 3, 1839, Box 30, entry 17C, RG26: Records of the United States Coast Guard, NARA; contract for repairing Long Shoal Light Boat, September 1, 1828, and Charles Laverty Contract, June 4, 1838, Box 005, entry 153, RG217: Reports of the Accounting Officers of the Department of the Treasury, NARA.

264. Letter to Fifth auditor, June 8, 1844, Box 30, entry 17C, RG26: Records of the United States Coast Guard, NARA.

265. Fagan and Guyer to Collector, May 14, 1839; John and Elijah Cornell to Collector, April 26, 1839; copy of the published bid, Box

30, entry 17C, RG26: Records of the United States Coast Guard, NARA. See the Plymouth bid for an example of ads calling for repairing light boats.

266. Box 30, entry 17C, RG26: Records of the United States Coast Guard, NARA.

267. Box 30, entry 17C, RG26: Records of the United States Coast Guard, NARA.

268. Contracts and correspondence, Box 30, entry 17C, RG26: Records of the United States Coast Guard, NARA.

269. "Building Light-Houses, Light-Boats, Beacons, etc.," Doc. No. 158, House of Rep., 128th Congress, 3rd Sess., 3.

270. *Compilation of Public Documents and Extracts from Reports and Papers Relating to Light-Houses, Light Vessels, and Illuminating Apparatus And to Beacons, Buoys and Fog Signals*, 626-631.

271. Crawford to Hawks, October 5, 1819, Nov. 21, 1820, March 5, 1821, roll 15; Crawford to Singleton, May 31, 1820; Taylor to McLane, June 27, 1832, RG56: General Records of the Department of the Treasury, microfilm series M178: Correspondence of the Secretary of the Treasury with Collectors of Customs, 1789-1833, NARA; *Wilmington Advertiser*, July 28, 1837; Collector, New Bern to Sec. of the Treasury, Oct. 15, 1845, Letters from Collectors. . . on Revenue Boats, Jan. 1 to Dec. 31, 1845, RG26: Records of the United States Coast Guard, NARA.

272. Rawls to Secretary of Treasury, July 9, 1846, RG26: Records of the United States Coast Guard, NARA. More than likely, the collector's recommendation was approved.

273. (Wilmington) *Daily Journal*, May 3, 1852; April 16, 1853; April 14, 1854.

274. Carteret County Deed Books, 1813-22, SANC; *Tarboro' Press*, September 28, 1839; (Wilmington) *Commercial Weekly*, May 4, 1852; *Wilmington Herald*, April 11, 1854; Fleetwood, *Tidecraft*, 126-128. Others were built for local pilots. *Wilmington Daily Journal*, January 20, April 11, 1854; *Wilmington Weekly Journal*, May 3, 1852; April 14, 1854; *Wilmington Commercial Weekly*, May 4, 1852; Reaves, *Southport (Smithville): A Chronology*, 50. See the *Tarboro' Press*, September 28, 1839, for the pilot boat *Washington*.

275. Fleetwood, *"Tidecraft,"* 118-119. There is no information where they were built, but *North State* was steered by a Cape Fear pilot. Lewis Philip Hall, *Land of the Golden River*, 46-49.

276. (Salisbury) *Western Carolinian*, June 27, 1856.

277. (New Bern) *Daily Progress*, September 21, 1858.

278. *Wilmington Daily Herald*, May 12, 1859.

279. Craven County Deed Book 63, 333, SANC; Roy F. Johnson, *Tales of Old Carolina*, 130-131; *New Bern Sentinel*, March 15, 1829.

280. Roy F. Johnson, *Tales of Old Carolina*, 130-131; *New Bern Sentinel*, March 15, 1829.

281 Charles L. Heath, Jr., "A Cultural History of River Herring and Shad Fisheries in Eastern North Carolina: The Prehistoric Period Through the Twentieth Century," (M.A. thesis, ECU, 1997), 93; "The Fisheries of Albemarle and Pamlico Sounds, North Carolina," *Harper's Weekly*, September 22, 1861; *Plymouth News*, October 12, 1840.

282. Although most of the works on the history of fishing in North Carolina mention the flats, the descriptions are extremely brief. There are no detailed descriptions nor are there references as to where and by whom they were built. In fact, very little has been written about flatboats in North Carolina. Letter from Michael Alford to authors, April 8, 2002; Mark Taylor, "Seiners and Tongers: North Carolina Fisheries in the Old and New South," *NCHR* 69 (January 1992); William J. Leary, Jr., "The Fisheries of Eastern Carolina," *North Carolina Booklet* XIV (April 1915), 183. For a study of flatboats beyond the Appalachians, see James Mark and Gary M. Walton, "The Persistence of Old Technologies: The Case of Flatboats," *Journal of Economic History*, 33 (June 1973), 292, 441-451.

283. *New Bern Sentinel*, April 5, 1828; *North Carolina Board of Internal Improvements, Annual Report, 1828*, 17-18.

284. J.D. Steele Journal, 1820, Huntington Library; Johnson, *Ante-Bellum North Carolina: A Social History*, 98.

285. Brown, *The Dismal Swamp Canal*, 460.

286. Sandbeck, *Historic Architecture of New Bern and Craven County, North Carolina*, 96; *Wilmington Weekly Journal*, February 20, 1857. See also Jennifer F. Martin, *Along the Banks of the Old Northeast: The History and Archaeology of Duplin County*, 16; Watson, *Wilmington Port of North Carolina*, 56. Flats were employed by the Army Corps of Engineers in river improvement projects. (Johnson to Bolles, August 11, 1855, Charles P. Bolles Papers, SANC.)

287. *Daily Wilmington Herald*, November 1, 1856; *Wilmington Weekly Journal*, October 17, 1845.

288. *New Bern Sentinel*, December 19, 1829; January 1, 1830; January 11, 1837.

289. Angley, "An Historic Overview of the Black River in Southeastern North Carolina," 17; Johnson, *Riverboating in Lower Carolina*, 16-17.

290. Sloan, "Inland Navigation in North Carolina 1818-1900" (M.A. thesis, ECU, 1971), 36; (Elizabeth City) *Old North State*, November 17, 1849.

291. Thomas H. Carrow, "Memoirs of Beaufort," *Carteret County Times-News*, July 13, 1948; *Wilmington Advertiser*, July 7, 1837.

292. Samuel Beery advertised that he took "the flat completely out of water on ways, and is thus able to render them perfectly tight." *Wilmington Weekly Chronicle*, March 23, 1842; Wall, "Ebenezer Pettigrew: An Economic Study of an Ante-Bellum Planter," 170.

293. *Wilmington Daily Journal*, December 2, 1851; Mortgage Deed, May 28, 1833, New Hanover Deed Book V, 13, SANC.

294. Johnson, *Riverboating in Lower Carolina*, 17. Two "tote" boats, the *Peter Ross*, and the *Fayetteville*, ninety-eight and eighty-eight feet in length respectively, probably were completed in Fayetteville in 1837. *Wilmington Advertiser*, June 30, 1837.

295. *Wilmington Daily Journal*, March 19, 1854, February 20, 1857; Sloan, "Inland Navigation in North Carolina, 1818-1900," 36, 92, 98.

296. Sloan, Inland Navigation in North Carolina, 1818-1900," 100.

297. *Wilmington Weekly Commercial*, April 26, 1850.

298. *Wilmington Advertiser*, July 7, 1837; Reaves, *Southport (Smithville): A Chronology*, I:26.

299. Contract, April 1, 1853, and Report of London, May 1, 1855, in the London Papers,
SHC, UNC-CH.

300. Williams and McEachern, *Salt-That Necessary Article*, 90.

301. Contract, May 29, 1837, Hunter Papers, ECU; New Hanover County Deed Book V, 13, SANC.

302. *Meadows v. Smith*, June Term, 1851, N.C. Supreme Court, Vol. 44, 27-29l; *Meadows v. Smith*, June Term, 1853, 44, 306-308; *Wilmington Weekly Journal*, February 20, 1857. The original case files are 5989 and 5990, SANC; *Raleigh Star*, July 18, 1817, July 17, 1818.

303. Cleophus Wiley and John Scott Account, July 26, 1819, Pettigrew Papers, SANC.

304. *Tarboro Press*, May 8, 1847.

305. Deed Book 4, October 16, 1853, SANC.
306. *North Carolina Times,* October 8, 1856; Taylor to Hunter, January 22, 1838; Hunter Papers, ECU; Singleton to Bell, Feb. 15, 1833, Bell Family Papers, Rubenstein Rare Books and Manuscripts Library, Duke University; *Wilmington Weekly Chronicle,* March 23, 1842; January 29, 1845; *Wilmington Daily Journal,* August 24, 1854; *Edenton Gazette,* January 28, 1822.
307. *Wilmington Weekly Commercial,* April 26, 1850; *Wilmington Weekly Journal,* August 19, 1859; *North Carolina Journal,* November 21, 1820; *Fayetteville American,* November 21, 1816; Sloan, "Inland Navigation in North Carolina 1818-1900," 3; Watson, *Wilmington: Port of North Carolina,* 56.
308. Craven County Deed Book, March 10, 1850, SANC.
309. *Raleigh Star,* June 23, 1819; *New Bern Sentinel,* June 5, 1818; *American Recorder,* June 25, 1819.
310. Bruce G. Terrell, *James River Bateau, 1745-1840,* 70; Peggy Jo Cobb Braswell, *The Roanoke Canal,* 30, 42.
311. A few brigs and sloops, three barks, and two full-rigged ships were also built. For an excellent account of the origin and evolution of the schooner as well as an archaeological examination of the remains of a small nineteenth century schooner in North Carolina, see Gordon P. Watts, Jr., *Underwater Archaeological Excavation and Data Recovery of the Hilton Wreck, Northeast Cape Fear River, Wilmington, North Carolina.* Two master's theses discuss the North Carolina schooner: Turner, "An Historical and Archaeological Investigation of the *Scuppernong,* and Merriman, "North Carolina Schooners 1815-1901, and the S. R. Fowle Company of Washington, North Carolina."
312. Macgregor, *Schooners in Four Centuries,* 10. See also Chapelle, *The History of American Sailing Ships.*
313. See, for example, the launching of a 300-ton three-masted schooner built by Thomas S. Howard and Company in the *New Bern Union,* November 24, 1866.
314. The centerboard may well have been developed in 1811 by two New Jersey builders. For the background to the centerboard see Edwin Doran Jr., "The Origin of Leeboards," *Mariner's Mirror,* 53 (February 1967), 39-53; and Henry B. Barkhausen, *Focusing on the Centerboard.* See also Gordon P. Watts, Jr., *Underwater Archaeological Excavation and Data Recovery of the Hilton Wreck, Northeast Cape Fear River, North Carolina,* 5.
315. Kemp Battle, "Otway Burns, Privateer and legislator," *North Carolina University Magazine,* 22.
316. Letter to his brother, November 13, 1817, Ezra Cornell Papers, Cornell University. Both accounts could be correct, as their shipyards were in different parts of the state. There is no way of knowing if it was independent invention or how quickly the innovation spread.
317. Chapelle, *American Small Sailing Craft,* 40.
318. Between 1984 and 1997, the staff and students in the Maritime History and Archaeology Program at East Carolina University examined a number of schooner and sharpie remains, nearly all of which had centerboards. The vessels were located at Washington on the Pamlico River, and at New Bern on the Trent River, as well as at Edenton and Beaufort.
319. (Elizabeth City) *North Carolinian,* July 8, 1869.
320. Taylor, *The Transportation Revolution,* 1815-1860, 109.
321. Still, "The Shipbuilding Industry in Washington, North Carolina," 37; *New Bern Times,* February 7, 1865; Brown, *Dismal Swamp Canal,* 113.
322. *Raleigh Register,* October 28, 1857; June 11, 1859; Craven County Deed Book 85, 199-201, SANC.

Chapter 6

The Civil War, 1861–1865

In December 1860, escalating tensions between southern and northern states polarized the nation, and state after state seceded from the Union. In February 1861, seven states formed the Confederate States of America; North Carolina was not one of them. Two months later, Confederates fired on Union forces at Fort Sumter in Charleston harbor. This precipitated President Lincoln's call for 75,000 volunteers to suppress the rebellion which, in turn, caused North Carolina to take military precautions.

On May 20, 1861, a convention called by North Carolina's governor unanimously approved secession from the United States of America. On the Capitol grounds and in the streets leading to it, thousands cheered the news. A military band started playing, and a hundred guns were fired in salute. Although the state had been badly divided over the issue, the convention's decision led to North Carolina joining the Confederate States of America and increased preparations for war.

The state legislature authorized the formation of ten regiments, as well as volunteer units. Even before secession, North Carolina "volunteers" seized Forts Caswell and Johnson on the Cape Fear River, and Fort Macon, which protected Beaufort Inlet and harbor. After May 20, 1861, work began on fortifying the vulnerable coast.

PREPARATIONS FOR WAR IN NORTH CAROLINA

As a consequence of the North Carolina legislature approving the creation of a state navy in 1861, four merchantmen were converted, armed with cannon, and turned over to the Confederate government in June 1861.[1] This "mosquito fleet" was the first Confederate naval force to see action in state waters. These vessels, as well as a number of converted merchant ships purchased by the Confederate government, were considered a stopgap measure. The newly-formed nation would have to build warships, not only to protect its harbors and rivers but to challenge the Union blockade.

Shortly after the bombardment of Fort Sumter, President Lincoln not only called out troops to suppress the insurrection but ordered an economic blockade of the southern coastline. The blockade became a principal duty of the Union Navy during the war and had an immediate and significant effect on North Carolina's maritime interests, including shipbuilding.

The war disrupted, but did not destroy, the state's maritime industry and commerce. The effectiveness of the blockade was erratic. In August 1861, a combined army and navy Union force captured Forts Hatteras and Clark at Hatteras Inlet. This single action virtually eliminated most Confederate shipping into the Pamlico and Albemarle Sounds. The Dismal Swamp and Albemarle and Chesapeake Canals remained opened, however, until a Union naval force entered the Pasquotank River and defeated a small Confederate naval flotilla, including vessels formerly belonging to the North Carolina navy, and seized Elizabeth City in February 1862.

THE BATTLES IN COASTAL NORTH CAROLINA

In May 1862, Union troops reconnoitered the Dismal Swamp Canal and discovered thirteen stranded schooners "ready for use."[2] The wider and deeper Chesapeake and Albemarle Canal was used extensively by the Confederates until it was captured. Between September 1 and December 15, 1861, more than two hundred army transports and "steam gunboats" passed through the canal.[3] However, by the time any new naval vessels in North Carolina were ready to be outfitted, the canals, much of the North Carolina coast, and most of eastern North Carolina outside of the Cape Fear region were firmly under Union control.

With the capture of Elizabeth City and the destruction of the only Confederate naval force in eastern North Carolina, combined Union military and naval units fanned out in the sounds and streams seizing various small ports. Only a few days after the battle at Elizabeth City, a small Union force raided Edenton, captured two schooners, and destroyed eight cannon and a vessel on the stocks. Plymouth was struck in early May. No vessels were discovered in the port, but one on the stocks was left alone being, according to the Union naval commander, the property of a "private individual."[4] Plymouth was not occupied until December, but with the control of the sounds, North Carolina's maritime trade was all but eliminated (see Figure 1).

In March 1862, Union transports, loaded with eleven thousand troops and escorted by fourteen gunboats, steamed up the Neuse River toward New Bern (Figure 2). Despite extensive fortifications, Federal troops under an umbrella of naval gunfire occupied the strategic port of New Bern, located at the confluence of the Neuse and Trent Rivers. On March 21, a Union naval force seized Washington on the Pamlico River. The port of Beaufort was guarded by Fort Macon, a well-built structure of brick and mortar completed in 1833 under the direction of Lt. Robert E. Lee. Beaufort was actually captured before Fort Macon, but on April 25, after an extensive bombardment by naval gunboats and shore-based artillery, the Confederate bastion surrendered.[5]

From the spring of 1862 until the end of the war, Union military forces controlled a large expanse of coastal North Carolina. From their bases in occupied ports, Union forces launched raiding expeditions up the various rivers, destroying private and Confederate States property, and disrupting inland water transportation: " ... the means of transportation across the [Chowan] river is completely broken up, as ... all the boats of every description ..." have

FIGURE 6-1 The invasion of Plymouth in October of 1864, with Federal gunboats attacking the CSS *Albemarle*, and the landing party moving forward. *Source: Harper's Weekly.*

been destroyed.⁶ The same was true of other waterways, with the exception of the Cape Fear River. Testifying before a House committee in 1862, Charles Foster, a Union sympathizer seeking Congressional support to form a "loyal government," described the plight of eastern North Carolinians: "Their commerce has been interrupted. Many of them own lighters and small schooners, by the use of which, in carrying cargoes and pursuing the coasting [and riverine] trade, they earned their livelihood. Now their ordinary avocations are at an end, and they have no means of support...."⁷

The Union Occupation and Blockade of Coastal North Carolina

Maritime trade was curtailed in May 1861 when state officials decreed that food and grain could no longer be exported outside the state. Marine insurance was cancelled. Moreover, surviving steamboats were commandeered by Confederate and state officials for military service. Maritime trade did not completely cease; however, except for the navigable upper reaches of rivers and streams under Confederate control, it was regulated by the Union army and navy.

The Cape Fear region was the single exception. Throughout 1861 and 1862, notices in Wilmington newspapers carried announcements of scheduled trips between Wilmington and Fayetteville. Cotton, naval stores, and other agricultural products continued to be transported to Wilmington, but eventually, trade did decline. Although the Union blockade off the Cape Fear River was ineffective until late in the war, state regulations against the exportation of these products resulted in a reduction of steamboat traffic on the river. In 1861, the number of steamboats in operation was half of what it had been in 1860. This number was further reduced when the Confederate government seized steamboats for "military necessities."⁸

A number of North Carolina-registered vessels, including some built in the state, engaged in blockade running. The schooner *Wingan*, built in Wilmington in 1856 and originally classified as a pilot boat, was sold to Canadians and renamed the *Albion*. In August 1861, she was captured by a Union naval vessel off the Charleston bar and condemned by a prize court.⁹ Another Wilmington schooner, the *William H. Northrup*, was captured off that port in December.¹⁰ The use of sailing vessels as blockade runners rapidly declined as they were simply too vulnerable to Union forces. Nonetheless, as late as 1863, the schooner *Polly Pigott* was advertised as being "suitable for running the blockade."¹¹ Although a large number of blockade running steamers utilized North Carolina ports, particularly Wilmington, none were constructed in the state during the war.

Shipbuilders and Shipbuilding during the War

In 1861, the state's commercial shipbuilding industry was still suffering from the effects of the 1857 financial panic that plunged the country into a depression. Only ten documented vessels, all schooners, were constructed in 1860, and only four, including the screw steamer *Fox*,

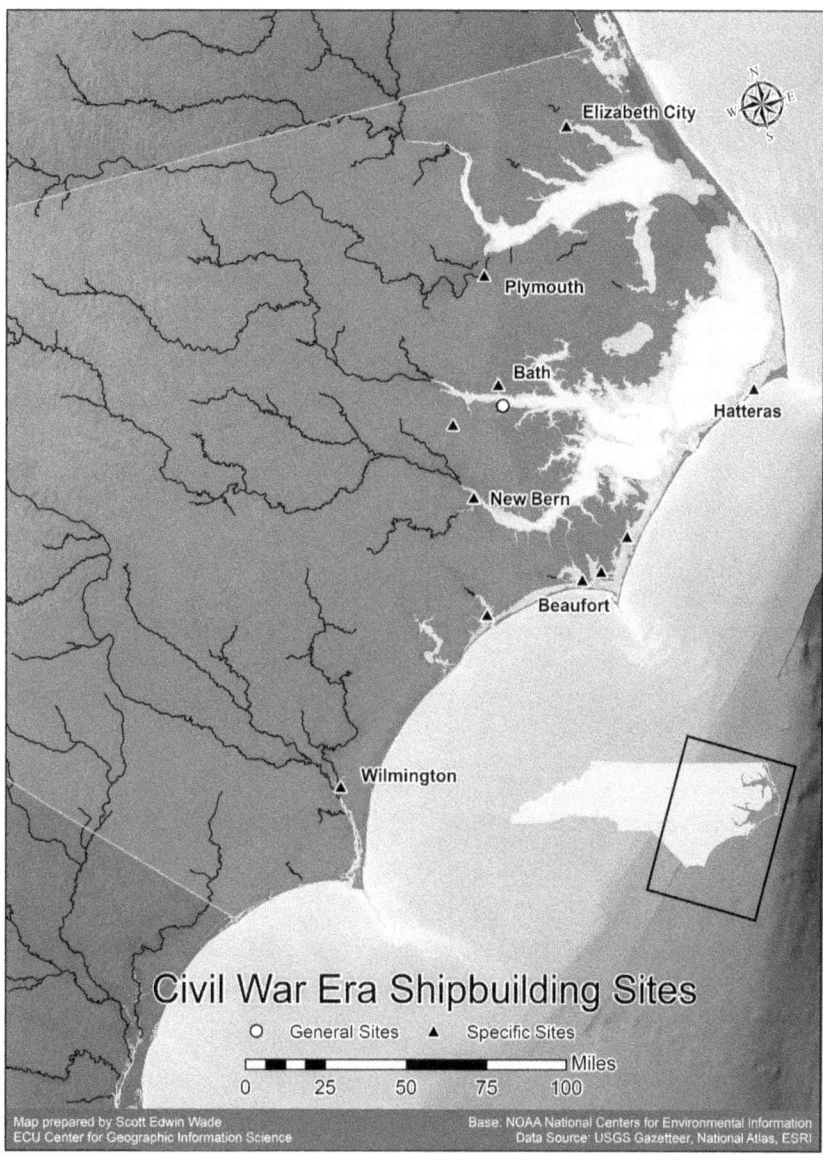

FIGURE 6–2 During the Civil War, the number of shipbuilding facilities and the number of documented vessels decreased significantly. It is likely that ships of war and undocumented vessels increased. The cluster of shipbuilding sites around the Beaufort area spreads toward the Neuse and Pamlico rivers. *Source:* Author's database.

were completed at Elizabeth City in 1861. The sidewheeler *James T. Petteway* was launched in April 1861. A large vessel, over 120 feet in length with machinery provided by Pusey and Jones of Wilmington, Delaware, it was the last steamboat built for private interests in the state until after the war.[12] A steamboat built for Dibble and Brothers of Kinston was seized on the stocks and partially burned when New Bern was occupied in 1862. The 445-ton sidewheeler was completed by the Union Army's Quartermaster Department and named the *Long Island*. A second Dibble vessel, also unfinished, was sold in February 1865 for $110.[13] In Plymouth, Angelo Garibaldi was contracted to build a steamboat for James C. Johnston of Edenton. According to Garibaldi's deposition in a suit to recover losses suffered in the shipbuilding project, the vessel was destroyed while still on the stocks sometime after 1863.[14]

THE BUILDING OF DOCUMENTED VESSELS

Ship and boat building for either Confederate or Union interests consumed a sizable share of economic resources during the war. A barge, of 119 tons, was built on Durham Creek near the Pamlico River. Twenty-three documented vessels were built for private interests, fourteen of those in 1865. As in other eras, schooners were the dominant type: nineteen were constructed along with three steamers and one barge. They were built at twelve sites (Figure 2). Active naval and military ports with established shipbuilding facilities during the conflict included Elizabeth City, Plymouth, New Bern, Washington, and Wilmington. Documented schooners were also built at Bath, Hatteras, Piney Point, the Straits, Beaufort, near Beaufort Inlet, and at Swansboro near Bogue Inlet.

Documented vessels built during the war showed a slight increase in dimensions. Vessel draft varied from one to five feet with a beam of approximately twelve feet. Draft/beam ratio also varied, decreasing over time, indicating greater draft in relation to beam. Ship volume increased slightly. The preference for a shallow draft of less than five feet continued, and schooners remained the dominant vessel type.

Several schooners constructed for private interests were seized and completed by Union forces. In April 1862, John Myers and Company towed a schooner to Tranters Creek, a tributary of the Tar River, upstream from Washington. She was captured by Union naval forces and renamed the *Renshaw*. The force commander reported that the vessel was without masts but was "well put together."[15] Josiah Farrow, also a Washington shipbuilder, had a schooner on the stocks that was seized and completed by the Union naval force. After the war, he tried, without success, to obtain compensation for the vessel.[16] At least one North Carolina shipbuilding firm built blockade runners. A Washington newspaper reported that Myers and Son had recently sold the schooner *Herndon* to a Virginia firm: "She was purchased . . . by or for English subjects and for a direct trade with England." The paper also mentioned that the Myers firm was planning to build a brig for the European trade. In 1864, the owners of the Columbia Rolling Mill agreed to provide coal for vessels operating out of Wilmington and contracted for the construction of a number of flats.[17] Union forces in the state's waters discovered other vessels under construction, and a majority of them were destroyed.

The Union occupation of eastern North Carolina, including its canals and sounds, along with the ever-tightening blockade off the state's coast, created a scarcity of building materials and labor. Priority was given to military and naval necessities, which contributed to the decrease in commercial/private ship and boat construction. By the beginning of 1862, there was little private construction; however, repair work continued in the shipyards. The state naval vessels turned over to the Confederate government were sent to various yards to be overhauled and strengthened as gunboats. Most of the vessels were taken to Norfolk, but some of the repairs were done by the Howard shipyard in New Bern, the T. L. Skinner facility in Edenton, and by at least one shipbuilder in Beaufort. Jesse Herrington of Plymouth was ordered to send his shipbuilding crew to Edenton for a week's work on one of the gunboats.[18] In October, the Howard facility repaired the gunboats *Ellis, Curlew, Beaufort,* and *Fanny*, the latter requiring extensive repairs. In November, the *Sea Bird, Forrest,* and *Winslow* were sent to Washington for overhaul on the Myers marine railway.[19] Vouchers indicate that local businesses were paid for work and supplies not provided by the shipyards. For example, W. E. DeMille of Washington provided a Franklin stove, pipes, furniture, hardware, and "housekeeping articles." William Church provided paint and painting.[20]

Coastal Defenses: Too Little, Too Late

Confederate and state governments recognized the need to strengthen coastal defenses and naval facilities. Initially, commercial vessels, including several constructed in the state, were purchased and outfitted. The schooner *Etheridge*, built in Plymouth in 1859, was sold to the Confederacy by the Etheridge family of Colerain in Bertie County. Renamed the *Black Warrior*, armed with two thirty-two-pounder smoothbores, and assigned to the small flotilla commanded by Commodore William F. Lynch, she was destroyed when Elizabeth City fell in 1862. The *Wilson*, a small steamboat built at Beaufort in 1856, was used by the Confederate government to transport men and supplies on the Roanoke River. She was captured in 1862 and similarly employed by the Union Army's Quartermaster Corps. In Wilmington, the lightship *Arctic* was converted into a receiving ship and floating battery. In December 1861, Thomas M. Crossan, a colonel in the state's coastal defense, wrote to Gilbert Elliott, agent for William Martin in Elizabeth City, requesting a construction estimate for a "Gunboat of Porter's Model, also of Graves...."[21] There is no evidence that Elliott and Martin agreed to build the gunboat. At that time, their resources were committed to completing a gunboat for the Confederate navy and they were considering a contract for another three gunboats.

In June 1861, Stephen Mallory, Confederate secretary of the navy, sent a memo to his chief of the Bureau of Orders and Details: "I want the services of a reliable and experimental officer for a few days to examine the ships of the North Carolina Navy. . . ." That officer was Commander Arthur Sinclair who examined the vessels and recommended that all of them be incorporated into the Confederate navy. It may have been the desperate need for anything afloat that could carry one or more guns and could be employed to guard the state's rivers and sounds that persuaded Sinclair to make the recommendation. The vessels were obviously not suited for naval combat. Captain William F. Lynch, appointed senior naval officer in North Carolina in September 1861, wrote the naval secretary that the state gunboats were "not very serviceable." Mallory sent a copy of the Lynch report to Governor Henry Clark and added,

"I am informed that good vessels can be built at Washington ... rough, strong, light draft boats planed with good hard pine and with substantial frames and decks ought to be built readily...."[22]

The Confederate army was also concerned about naval defenses in the state. Brigadier General Richard C. Gatlin, commanding the Department of North Carolina, wrote the War Department, in September 1861, that the naval force " here consist[s] of two inferior steamers without screws, and one of them two dull a sailer to be of any service...."[23] Brigadier General Daniel H. Hill expressed his concern for lack of naval vessels to Secretary of War Benjamin. Gatlin and Hill urged the construction of gunboats. Benjamin approved and informed the state's governor that efforts were underway to contract for gunboats in North Carolina.[24] Hill apparently obtained an agreement with Thomas Howard of New Bern to build two gunboats. Evidently, the order did not indicate that the vessels were to be constructed for the army. The first vessel was well underway by November. The November 2, 1861, edition of the *New Bern Daily Progress* noted that at Howard's shipyard there was "an immense amount of timber ... located between the keel and upper deck in the construction of a ship...."[25] Sinclair, assigned to oversee gunboat construction in North Carolina, visited all the state construction sites in the fall. Later that month, Howard wrote to the governor to inquire if they were being constructed for the state and, if so, when would they receive payment.[26] Early in the new year, a New Bern merchant wrote to his representative in the Confederate Congress, "Messrs. Howard & Ellis, of this place, commended some time ago the construction of a gunboat, by order of Brigadier General Hill, which is now ready for machinery and can be completed in thirty or forty days. They now visit Richmond to see the Secretary of the Navy in relation to her...." Representative Abraham Venable sent the letter to Mallory as an introduction.[27] The naval secretary does mention the New Bern vessel in a report, but it is not known if machinery was provided. In May, after Union forces occupied New Bern, Mallory instructed that Howard and Company be paid $1,320.[28]

In February 1862, the *Daily Progress* reported that "Mr. Howard, constructor at this place, has a vessel half done which finished and four more like it, he is willing to bet his life he could run the last Yankee vessel out of our sound in three days.... He could have built five since the Merrimac has been under way had the government authorized him...."[29] An editorial in the *New Bern Progress* lambasted the Confederate government for its inability to provide adequate naval defense for the state. "We have been urging these matters upon our authorities for months.... Two or three hundred thousand dollars expended in the proper time in armed vessels for our Sounds and rivers would have insured us against the inroads of marauders.... If the Confederate States cannot build and equip the boats, the State can, and certainly will not be denied the liberty of so doing by the former ...."[30] The state was not interested, but the Confederate government was attempting to build naval vessels to defend state waters.

All Confederate shipbuilding activities in North Carolina were essentially related.[31] Contractors, builders, and subcontracting firms (iron works, labor, and materials) for naval vessels were linked. Skilled labor had to be moved from one ship construction site to another, which, at times, seriously delayed the completion of a vessel.

Initially, North Carolina had the facilities, materials, and labor to build warships. There were a number of shipbuilding facilities scattered along the coast and along the inland waters. Abundant timber was available. Iron parts such as nails and spikes could be made locally, and machinery could be obtained from iron works outside the state. There were a few ironworks in the state with the capacity to manufacture parts for machinery, and no thought was given to armor plate. Adequate labor was available. The 1860 population census listed an impressive number of ship carpenters in the state, and slaves provided an essential part of the work force. These conditions created an optimistic picture that, in fact, proved to be illusory. This was especially true in regard to materials, particularly iron, and labor.[32]

In 1861 and the first quarter of 1862, shipbuilders had little trouble obtaining skilled carpenters and unskilled laborers. Gilbert Elliott in Elizabeth City, who had a contract to build wooden gunboats, was able to hire carpenters and caulkers from Edenton, Plymouth, and elsewhere. A number of shipwrights went to Norfolk to work on vessels under construction in the yards.[33]

Nonetheless, the Confederate navy's warship construction program required a large number of skilled carpenters and mechanics, far more than were available. A considerable number of skilled mechanics and other workmen were from the North or from foreign countries and left with the outbreak of hostilities.[34] More significant was the large number of artisans who, with patriotic enthusiasm, left their trade to join the army. In August 1861, Secretary Mallory began a long and frustrating effort to persuade the War Department to release as many ship carpenters and mechanics from the army "as may be willing to receive discharge ... to work for the navy...." The War Department half-heartedly cooperated, but in reality, few were released.[35] The scarcity of experienced shipwrights and other artisans forced naval officials to move workers from different construction sites and naval stations as they were needed. In time, the yards would work seven days a week, night and day. The War Department was also pressed for help. Blacks, free and slave, were employed in large numbers in the shipyards. Enslaved, skilled workmen were offered to contractors. Gilbert Elliott in Elizabeth City was offered several from

Edenton and Plymouth. All builders mention using slaves to work on vessels under construction. In an 1863 letter, Chief Constructor John Porter mentioned that drilling plates for the Wilmington ironclads was done primarily by "Black laborers."[36]

Mallory's decision to build armored vessels in North Carolina exacerbated the labor problem. Ironclads were laid down in Wilmington on the Neuse River, in Tarboro on the Tar, and at Edward's Ferry on the Roanoke. In September 1862, one of the builders in Wilmington, Cassidey and Son, advertised for fifty carpenters and laborers. Skilled workers were shifted from naval facilities in Richmond, Charlotte, Charleston, and Savannah to work on the vessels. Some carpenters and other craftsmen were moved from various stations within North Carolina as they were needed. Experienced seamen were even transferred from commissioned vessels to work at shipyards. Engineers and mechanics were in short supply and were sent from Richmond and elsewhere to install machinery. In September 1862, the Chief Engineer at the Wilmington naval station was ordered to Richmond to obtain mechanics. Commodore Lynch, in command of the station, ordered the engineer to travel to Selma, Richmond, Raleigh, Charleston, Savannah, Columbus, and Mobile for boilermakers.[37]

The Confederate navy yard (formerly Beery's shipyard) in Wilmington on Eagles Island had the least trouble obtaining laborers. Approximately 200 men from local military units were detailed to work at the yard and were enrolled in companies. The yard also employed a number of Blacks as mechanics (iron workers) and caulkers.[38]

Cassidey and Son shipyard had far more difficulty in obtaining and retaining skilled and unskilled labor. The yard employed whites and Blacks. According to a deserter, the Cassidey yard, at one time, employed from ninety-five to a hundred workers, but by September 1862, there were only thirty. He blamed the decrease on the fear of yellow fever and dissatisfaction over pay. The wage scale continued to rise, but the depreciating value of Confederate money resulted in increasing unhappiness throughout the Southern states. In June 1863, the station paymaster telegraphed the Department of the Navy that he had no funds to pay the laborers at the Cassidey yard. He stated that money was borrowed from a local bank to meet the payroll and keep the men working. Subsequently, the workers went on strike.[39] The strike was settled, but desertion at both yards became a serious problem. Commodore Lynch provided some workers, but in November 1864, the desperate need for men to fill depleted ranks led Generals Lee and Bragg to order all those detailed to shipbuilding facilities, including those in Wilmington, to return to active military service.[40]

Operating capital was just as much a problem at other shipbuilding sites. The paymaster reported that workers at the Halifax facility had not been paid in six weeks and were "destitute." The Cassidey and Beery shipyards in Wilmington competed for qualified workmen by frequently raising their pay scale.[41]

Construction of ironclads on the Roanoke and Neuse Rivers (the one at Tarboro was destroyed on the stocks) depended heavily upon the Confederate army, as well as volunteer state units, to provide a workforce. General Robert Hoke detailed a large number of men from his division to finish the armor-clad at Kinston. In 1863, seventeen conscripts were detailed to work on the *Albemarle* under construction at Edwards Ferry and, later, at Halifax. In 1864, Gilbert Elliott, one of the contractors, appealed to General Hoke for workmen. Hoke, planning to attack Plymouth, needed the ironclad completed. He detailed fifteen additional mechanics to work on the vessel. One of the unit commanders wrote the General: "I furnish good ship carpenters—the navy keep[s] the workers waiting for material…."[42] Master Ship Carpenter John Snell was one of the "conscripts" detailed to work on the *Albemarle*. In addition, twenty-two skilled workers were sent from Richmond. Elliott also recruited several farmers and approximately fifty Blacks from nearby farms and plantations. He even employed two supposed deserters. He later stated he had a workforce averaging two hundred men, "but few of whom, however, were skilled mechanics…."[43]

Thomas Howard superintended the construction of the armor-clad built at Whitehall on the Neuse River. In November 1863, he had eight carpenters, three caulkers, and an unknown number of laborers at work on the vessel. General Hoke, anxious to see the vessel *Neuse* completed, detailed ninety-five carpenters and mechanics and fifty laborers to assist in its construction. Howard agreed to pay the men from Hoke's brigade five dollars a day. Nine mechanics from the Charlotte navy yard were sent to help install the ironclads ordnance and machinery.[44]

The Charlotte facility was principally involved in manufacturing steam machinery, anchors, and various ordnance stores. When the equipment and machinery were moved from Norfolk to Charlotte, fifty-one skilled workers and their families moved with it. Nonetheless, like other naval facilities, the Charlotte navy yard was handicapped by a shortage of skilled artisans.[45]

Difficulties constructing warships in North Carolina mirrored those of the Confederacy as a whole. The Southern states had inadequate facilities, especially to build ironclads. There were two navy yards in the South, Norfolk and Pensacola; both were lost to Union forces in 1862.

The Confederacy had to depend on commercial yards for naval construction. Related facilities for the manufacture of iron, marine machinery, and ordnance were extremely limited. There were experienced shipbuilders throughout the South, but few had experience in military naval construction. The same was true of ship carpenters and other shipbuilding trades. Moreover, the transportation problem was profound. River transportation was available but inadequate. Railroads were vital, not just for naval construction but for the war effort as a whole, but these, too, were insufficient. Conflicting track gauges and lack of regional connections proved insurmountable.[46] Although Wilmington had much of what was needed to construct and outfit warships, no single facility or region possessed everything necessary. Shipyards were in various locations, ordnance stores and laboratories in others; foundries, machine shops, iron works, and ropewalks were in still others. A developed transportation system was needed to get raw materials such as iron to manufacturing facilities and finished products to building sites. This was certainly the case in North Carolina.

Military and Naval Contracts for Shipbuilding

The role of Naval Secretary Stephen Mallory in overall naval construction in North Carolina was significant. He made most of the decisions and negotiated nearly all of the contracts for vessels built in the state. His surviving correspondence indicates he was directly involved in the details of naval construction throughout the Confederacy.[47] With secession, several North Carolina shipbuilders travelled to Richmond to obtain contracts. Martin and Elliott of Elizabeth City; Howard and Ellis of New Bern; and John Myers and Company and Ritch and Farrow, both of Washington, were successful.[48] Although the Beery Brothers and James Cassidey are considered the builders of the naval vessels in Wilmington, they were not contractors. They were hired by the navy as "superintendents" and "master carpenters." Exactly why they did not receive contracts is not known. Commander William Muse, senior naval officer in Wilmington, received instructions relating to gunboats from the Secretary of the Navy in March 1862.[49] It is quite possible they were given an option of contracting for gunboats or leasing their shipbuilding facility to the Confederate government. This was the case with Martin and Elliott.[50] It was considered expedient to follow the same policy for other builders when their contracts ran out, as, for example, with Howard and Ellis building the ironclad *Neuse*, and Martin and Elliott contracting for vessels on the Tar and Roanoke Rivers.

Gilbert Elliott was seventeen and had little or no experience in shipbuilding. Elliott was a law clerk when the war broke out, but he "had been employed in a shipyard as a book keeper." It may be that he was both, as he was listed in the 1860 census as a lawyer's clerk. In both cases, William Martin, a prominent Elizabeth City lawyer, was his employer, for he owned a shipyard as well.[51] The relationship between Elliott and Martin continued during the war. When Martin was appointed to command the 17th North Carolina Regiment, Elliott was appointed lieutenant and adjutant. In August 1861, the regiment surrendered to Union forces on Hatteras. After being paroled, Elliott returned to Elizabeth City and Martin's employment. As his agent, Elliot sought a contract with the Confederate navy to build a gunboat.

Elliott was cosigner with Martin on all but the last contract that he received. Elliott's name was probably on the contract because he negotiated it with the navy department and would oversee the ship's construction, obtaining workmen and materials. Martin owned the shipyard in Elizabeth City and, under the initial contract, raised the necessary capital to purchase construction material. However, Martin remained in military service away from the construction site. This business relationship is made clear in their correspondence.[52] Martin tried to remain in control as much as possible.

Their first gunboat project was lost when Elizabeth City was taken and the shipyard and vessels on the stocks destroyed by Union forces. Subsequently, Elliott contracted to construct an ironclad at Deep Creek, Virginia, but, again, the occupation of the area by Federal troops ended the project. Elliott and Martin resumed their association when the former returned to the position of adjutant in Martin's regiment. While stationed near Drewry's Bluff, the secretary of the navy obtained a two year leave of absence for Elliott to construct a naval vessel. On September 17, 1862, Martin and Elliott signed a contract to build an ironclad gunboat at Tarboro on the Tar River. In early October, they received another contract for an ironclad to be constructed on the Roanoke River. As business associates, they signed a final contract on December 1 for an ironclad floating battery also to be built on the Roanoke River. In January 1863, in a long letter, Elliott suggested that Martin is still keeping a close eye on the gunboat construction. For whatever reason, the business association ended in 1864. Elliott contracted for one more ironclad, but the co-contractor was Peter Smith, not Martin.[53]

Elliott is usually given credit for building the ironclad *Albemarle*. In reality, he handled the logistical requirements, employing labor, establishing the building site at Edwards Ferry, and acquiring the tools and materials needed to build the vessel.[54] The navy provided the plans, maintained a supervising officer at the site, and after the contract date had expired, took control of construction with Elliott as an employee. Actual construction was under the direction of a master ship carpenter, James F. Snell. Peter Smith may have been in charge of construction while the vessel was on the stocks at Edward's Ferry, but certainly not at Halifax. Smith was an engineer, mechanic, and inventor, but there is no evidence that he had any experience in shipbuilding.[55] Elliott's relationship with naval officials was mixed. He got along with Commander James W. Cooke, the first naval officer assigned to the *Albemarle* construction site.[56] His relationship with Lieutenant John J. Gutherie, who briefly replaced Cooke, is unknown. His relationship with Flag Officer Lynch and, to some degree, with Secretary Mallory was far more troubling.

Lynch had little respect for Elliott, possibly because of the latter's youth and inexperience, but more probably because of the contractor's perceived avarice. On more than one occasion, Elliott demanded more money than his contracts originally called for, a demand that was somewhat reasonable considering his difficulties in acquiring materials, workmen, and the declining value of Confederate currency. However, Lynch's order to prematurely launch the *Albemarle* from her construction site at Edwards Ferry and remove the uncompleted vessel to Halifax resulted in an open breech between them. Elliott was outraged. He determined he was no longer responsible for the ironclad's construction and dismissed the workers.

In November and December 1863, virtually no work was done on the vessel, as Elliott, Lynch, Governor Vance, and Secretary Mallory wrote letters of accusation and recrimination. Eventually, for political reasons, Confederate naval activities were taken out of Mallory's control. Despite the naval secretary's criticism, Elliott received a new contract with a $15,000 increase and resumed work on the *Albemarle*. He remained with the ironclad as a volunteer when she made her famous sortie down the river to attack Union warships at Plymouth.[57]

In addition to Secretary Mallory and Flag Officer Lynch, Confederate naval construction in North Carolina involved a host of naval officials. Chief Constructor John Porter not only designed the vessels but made frequent trips to building sites in the state. At Halifax and later at Wilmington, he spent considerable time participating in decisions concerning the construction of ironclads.[58] William P. Williamson, the Confederate navy's engineer in chief, played a major role in designing the power plants for the vessels. The Confederate navy department employed numerous inspectors and superintendents such as J. J. Roberson, Hugh Lindsey, Edward Williams, and John A. Thomas to inspect and supervise various aspects of construction.

The Confederate Navy and Its Problems Ashore

Following traditional policy, the Confederate navy department assigned officers to supervise vessel construction. Usually, they were sent to a warship they were to command once it was commissioned. Those in North Carolina included lieutenants William T. Muse, William Sharp, Benjamin Loyall, and Commander James W. Cooke. Muse was a North Carolinian who was supervising officer for naval construction in Wilmington and commanded several vessels there. Virginians Sharp, and later Loyall, were ordered to the *Neuse*. Cooke gained fame by commanding the ironclad *Albemarle*.

Cooke, also a native Carolinian, entered the U.S. Navy in 1828.[59] In the Confederate navy, he gained early recognition as an able and aggressive officer. Wounded and captured in the Battle of Elizabeth City, he was later exchanged and recovered from his injuries. Returning to duty, he initially procured iron for armor plate used on armor-clads under construction in North Carolina. Subsequently, he supervised projects on the Neuse, Tar, and Roanoke Rivers. In 1863, with the destruction of the ironclad being built on the Tar River, and the slow progress of the one on the Neuse River, Cooke was ordered to concentrate his efforts on completing the Roanoke River vessel, CSS *Albemarle*.[60] He not only played a major role in completing the *Albemarle*, but took her into successful action against the Union forces at Plymouth.[61] Cooke got along with and was respected by all involved in naval construction except Flag Officer Lynch; but then, few got along with the flag officer.

For more than forty years in the United States Navy and throughout his few years in Confederate service, Commander William F. Lynch was a dedicated naval officer.[62] In prewar years, he gained recognition leading an expedition to survey the Black Sea, publishing an account, *Narrative of the United States Expedition to the River Jordan and the Dead Sea*, followed by a second book, *Naval Life, or Observations Afloat and on Shore*. He was one of the senior officers to resign his commission and serve his state, Virginia, when it seceded. Although he was known as gallant and courageous, his combat record was mixed. He did well at Aquia Creek in May and June 1861, but less so at Roanoke Island and Elizabeth City. At the Battle of Elizabeth City, Cooke, who commanded one of the Confederate gunboats there, accused Lynch of abandoning his flagship for a shore battery unable to fire its guns.[63]

The flag officer's career as a naval administrator in the Confederate navy is also questionable. In October 1862, he was assigned to command North Carolina's naval defenses, which consisted of converted wooden vessels on the Cape Fear River. The rest of his potential fleet was under construction. For the remainder of his tenure, he devoted his efforts to completing gunboats in the state. No one questioned his determination, but his methods were often criticized. At times, Lynch was his own worst enemy. His sensitivity over what he considered to be naval matters under his command, his inflexibility, and, at times, tactlessness often antagonized his associates.[64] Lynch's relationship with army officers was notoriously deleterious and ultimately led to censure by Confederate President Davis. In 1861, he squabbled with Brigadier General Henry A. Wise over the purchase of local steamers to be converted into gunboats, as well as numerous command decisions. However, it would be his disagreements with Brigadier General W. H. C. Whiting, in command of the Cape Fear defenses, which led to his trouble in Richmond. He challenged the general over control of railroads, the use of industrial facilities in Wilmington, building torpedo boats, and control of blockade running. What probably started as a lapse in communication eventually degenerated into open hostility between the two officers.

Although Whiting was censured by the secretary of war for interfering in naval affairs, the general was not apologetic nor moved to better relations. He clearly had little respect for the sister service; in fact, he considered naval forces on the Cape Fear to be under his command: "So far the gunboats have caused more trouble, interfered more with government business and transportation, been bound up more and accomplished less than any other part of the service. Here [in Wilmington] I do not permit them to interfere any longer."[65] It is difficult to assess the extent to which Lynch's disagreement with Whiting affected naval construction, but it certainly did not help. Nevertheless, Secretary Mallory stood by the flag officer.

What Lynch's own officers thought of him is not clear. Lieutenant John J. Guthrie, who commanded the Artic in the Cape Fear squadron, was impressed with him. James Randall, the flag officer's personal secretary, thought highly of him. However, as previously noted, Cooke did not care for him.[66]

Shipbuilding Facilities during the War

With few exceptions, shipbuilding facilities in the state were quite small. Initially the Confederate government attempted to utilize existing shipyards. Beery and Cassidey in Wilmington, Howard and Ellis in New Bern, Farrow and Ritch in Washington, and the Martin establishment in Elizabeth City were either considered for, or received, naval construction contracts. Union occupation of coastal North Carolina eliminated all these facilities except the ones at Wilmington. Builders then turned to *ad hoc* shipbuilding sites. Gilbert Elliott, agent for the Martin Company, selected Tarboro on the Tar River, and later, Edward's Ferry on the Roanoke River as building sites. Howard & Ellis established a yard at White Hall on the Neuse River. These sites were selected because of the availability of adequate timber and proximity to railheads. They were also considered far enough up the rivers to be safe from Union attack.[67]

These new yards were literally carved out of the wilderness. The land along the river was cleared, a few crude houses and buildings erected as living quarters for workers, storerooms, and offices. Each of the yards had at least one sawmill. There were no marine railways; instead the keels were laid on timber rollers. The *Neuse* building site was on a slope close to a swamp (Figure 3); the *Albemarle's* site was in a cornfield on a bluff sloping towards the river.[68] The uncompleted vessel was launched at an angle and towed twenty-two miles upstream to a newly established naval station at Halifax. The Halifax site was inadequate for construction but had a hospital, storehouses, and most importantly, was close to the Wilmington and Weldon Railroad. There is no information on the launching of the *Neuse*. However, she was towed to Kinston where adequate facilities for completing the ironclad were available. The Kinston naval station included three to five houses for offices and storerooms. At least one was built specifically for the navy; the others were rented. The navy also rented facilities and equipment from two carriage firms in the town, Dibble Brothers and M. W. Campbell & Co., and the officers of the *Neuse* rented a private house in Kinston. A temporary tram road was built to connect the shops with the ship. The Dibble Company provided not only space in their facilities but a variety of iron and steel hardware as well. M. W. Campbell & Co. did extensive iron work for the navy from October 1863 until the *Neuse* was launched. One voucher lists making iron blocks for tiller chains, plates and rings for steam pipes, spikes, and an assortment of cutting, drilling, and forging.[69]

Wilmington, by far, had the most extensive facilities for building gunboats; not only well-established shipyards, but ironworks and other concerns associated with shipbuilding. Although there were several yards along the Cape Fear River in the vicinity of Wilmington, two were used exclusively for Confederate naval construction: James Cassidey & Son on the Wilmington waterfront, and that operated by B.W. and W. L. Beery located directly across the river on Eagles Island.[70] The Cassidey yard included a marine railway, but there is no description of other facilities. The Beery Shipyard was on low land, barely above river level, and next to rice fields. The yard included a large steam sawmill, a marine railway, a blacksmith shop, rigging loft, and additional shipbuilding facilities. After the war, W. L. Beery insisted that the Confederate navy seized his shipyard. The yard's timekeeper and paymaster agreed that the Confederate government requisitioned it. Although it was known as the "Navy Yard," or "Confederate Navy Yard," it was still owned by the Beerys.[71]

Wilmington was the only location in the state with extensive iron and machinery works. Hart & Bailey, known as Wilmington Iron and Copper Works in 1861, did an extraordinary amount of work during the war, not only for the Confederate government but for the state, counties, and even private interests. The firm manufactured cartridge gauges, wheel hubs, shot furnaces, columbiad carriages, shot canisters, and small arms ammunition for the state's quartermaster department. A large assortment of items was sent to Fort Macon including cooking stoves, pumps, iron pipes, pie plates, wash basins, copper ladles, etc. The company provided Wilmington's Committee of Safety and several county militia units with canteens, drinking cups, tin plates, spoons, kettles, iron coffee pots, and other utensils. The Confederate army contracted for iron castings, repair to sawmill machinery, anchors for river obstructions, machinery on torpedo boats, and equipment used for hoisting sand at Fort Fisher. Throughout the war, Hart & Bailey continued to repair machinery for steamers such as the *Flora McDonald, Cornalia, Eugenie, Dawson, Cape Fear,* and *Virginia*.[72] However, the bulk of the work was done for the Confederate navy.

FIGURE 6-3 Construction of the CSS *Neuse*. Courtesy CSS *Neuse* Interpretive Center.

From repairing and overhauling the machinery of the *Uncle Ben* and lightship *Arctic* to manufacturing boilers for torpedo craft under construction, Hart & Bailey continued working for the Confederate navy until Wilmington's evacuation in spring of 1865. It was "indispensable to the naval effort at Wilmington."[73] Virtually every metal item needed to equip a man of war, with the exception of ordnance, was fabricated at the plant, including huge shafts linking machinery with propulsion systems, spikes, nails, bolts, steel washers, steam gauges, steam pipes, wrought iron stern and stem posts, wrought iron port shutters, stanchions, davits, pumps, boiler flues and grate bars, nozzles, elbows and hose connection links, sheet iron smoke and exhaust pipes, brass valves and boxes, copper fittings, water closet pipes, hawse pipes, eye bolts, rudder and anchor chains, boat hooks, flag staff, hatch plates, shovels, door locks, hinges, marine clocks, dust pans, wheel and clamps, crank pins, bridge and muzzle sights for ordinance, sponges for 32-pounders, rammers, sheet iron, strips for rudder frames, and a variety of tools. The company provided coppersmiths, pattern makers, and machinists. Hart & Bailey not only drilled armor plates for the Wilmington armor-clads, but for the *Neuse* as well. Company machinists assembled and installed the machinery for the Wilmington ironclads. The engines for the tender *Yadkin* may well have been built by the ironworks.[74]

The Clarendon Iron Works were organized before the Civil War but experienced financial difficulties until 1861. Thomas E. Roberts, a machinist from New Hampshire, migrated to Wilmington just before secession. He leased the Clarendon property, with its equipment and tools, from Mauger London. In 1867, Roberts purchased the Clarendon works outright and renamed it the Wilmington Manufacturing Company.[75]

Other than Hart and Bailey, the Clarendon Iron Works did most of the foundry and machinery work for the Confederate navy. Despite the prewar advertisements, it probably did not have the ability to manufacture steam engines. However, the firm did fabricate boilers. Like Hart & Bailey, it also did mechanical work for the ironclads under construction in Wilmington and on the Neuse River, including drilling and fitting the armor plate.[76]

As Wilmington was a busy port, it is not surprising that there were many vendors that carried items for the navy such as marine paint and red lead, chains, oakum, hemp and manila rope, blocks and tackle, marline spikes, anchors, compasses, adzes, and other tools. One provided a steering wheel; another, a hawser; a third, clocks; and a fourth, furniture. Joseph H. Neff, a ship chandler, had a large supply of what the navy needed, including log books. Although it is possible his inventory was replenished by blockade runners, it is still surprising that he did considerable business with the Confederate navy into 1864.[77] James Fleet was paid for the use of his blocks and tackle to hoist machinery into the steamer *Caswell*, and later, for seventy-five days employment, for "putting up and moving machinery of ironclad gunboats." P. E. Smith worked on the *Cora's* hull and machinery. William Sutton repaired the *Equator's* sternpost and rudder.[78]

THE SCARCITY OF RESOURCES FOR WAR

Nothing illustrates the Confederacy's difficulty in providing the material for fighting a war more than the scarcity of iron. In 1860, the southern states produced only fourteen percent of the total amount of iron ore mined in the United States. North Carolina produced so little iron that "hardly enough iron was smelted to shoe the horses...."[79] Confederate officials were all too aware that obtaining iron required for armaments and transportation would tax their efforts to the utmost. Indeed, the problem was never resolved and undoubtedly contributed to the ultimate defeat of the Confederacy.

The exact amount of iron ore produced by North Carolina during the war is unknown. The Confederate navy's Bureau of Ordnance and Hydrography made contracts with mine and blast furnace owners and operators in various states, including North Carolina, to provide iron ore for the navy's shops and contractors.[80] Much of what came from North Carolina came from Chatham County, particularly along the Deep River part of the Cape Fear River basin. After the war, George Washington, president of the Sapona Iron Company, testified that his company manufactured pig iron under contract with the Confederate government.[81] Some of the Deep River pig iron was transported by rail and boat to the ironworks in Wilmington.[82] However, most of it went to Charlotte and facilities out of state.[83]

From the outset of the war, shipyards and iron works, including those in North Carolina, found it extremely difficult to obtain the iron they needed. The Charlotte Navy Yard was the most important iron and engineering works in the state. Shortly before the fall of Norfolk in May 1862, machinery and tools at the navy yard there were shipped by rail to Richmond and Charlotte. The Confederate navy took over the former United States Mint and purchased the Mecklenburg Iron Works from a former naval officer. Charlotte was selected because of its interior location and excellent railroad connections. A number of large frame structures were erected to house various shops, including a gun-carriage construction facility, a large forge, a laboratory, and a torpedo shop. A cupola furnace, coke ovens, pattern shop, coppersmith shop, and an ordnance facility were soon added. The yard operated several steam hammers, including one which was reputed to be the largest in the south.[84] The navy yard was extremely important to the fitting out of warships, not only in North Carolina but throughout the Confederacy. The works did not manufacture complete engines but did produce many of the parts and nearly all of the shafts, propellers, and anchors. Although the goal to cast ordnance at the yard was never realized, wrought iron projectiles, ordnance stores, such as fuses and caps, and elevating screws for naval guns were manufactured there.[85]

Facilities like the Charlotte Navy Yard were available, or would be established, during the war, but they could only produce the needed bolts, ordnance, machine parts, and other stores if they had the raw iron. The Charlotte works had another significant shortage, that being leather, used in making fuse washers for projectiles. "We make what we use out of scraps of leather (upper is the best) by drawing it through a 'shaver' or 'splitting knife' used by harness makers...."[86]

Iron machinery, particularly engines, and armor plate, were most difficult to obtain. Although Hart & Bailey in Wilmington had the capacity to manufacture standard steam engines, as for the *Yadkin*, the firm certainly did not have the expertise to fabricate the large, powerful engines needed for ironclads. The *North Carolina's* engines came from the tugboat *Uncle Ben*, and the *Raleigh's* from Richmond.[87] In July 1862, a naval engineer stationed in Wilmington was ordered to Richmond to confer with the chief engineer about engines and boilers for the two ironclads under construction there. In August, Tredegar Ironworks shipped one nine-foot propeller and two boilers to Wilmington by rail. In July 1863, it sent a third boiler.[88] Machinery for the *Wilmington*, under construction at the Beery yard, was ready to be shipped from the Naval Iron Works in Columbus, Georgia when units of Sherman's army cut the railroad that linked the town to Atlanta and Wilmington. In June 1865, an inventory of captured materials in Columbus listed two high pressure engines and boilers intended for shipment to Wilmington.[89]

Naval construction crews in other parts of the state faced even greater difficulty in obtaining needed items. This was especially true after Union forces occupied much of coastal North Carolina. However, significant problems existed before the occupation. Gilbert Elliott, building wooden gunboats in Elizabeth City, had to go out of state to get what he required. He wrote Tredegar Iron Works requesting iron spikes, nails, and other items and was told to obtain them from Norfolk. Norfolk firms, when contacted, could not supply them. He had similar difficulties trying to obtain anchors, chains, linseed oil, metal parts, and machinery. Elliott wanted to use the engines and boilers from a steamboat, but the navy deemed them unsatisfactory. Subsequently, he approached Talbott and Brothers, who owned the Shockoe Foundry and

Machine Shops in Richmond, Virginia. The establishment manufactured steam machinery including engines and boilers. Their inventory of large engines had been sold to the navy, but they had two engines in New Orleans that could be modified. In addition, the Confederate navy's chief engineer informed Elliott that he would also try to get suitable engines for the gunboats being built in Elizabeth City. He added, "My greatest difficulty is in procuring boilers. . . ." The machinery was not received before Elizabeth City fell to Union forces.[90] Shoekoe was also to provide six engines for three gunboats under construction in Washington, North Carolina. As with the Elizabeth City vessels, the engines were not received before Washington was captured.[91]

The origin of the *Neuse* and *Albemarle's* machinery is unknown, although the propeller shafts were probably forged at the Charlotte Navy Yard.[92] Information on the *Albemarle's* engine and boilers is contradictory. One source claims the engine of a large sawmill was modified for the ironclad; a second states it came from the Tredegar Works in Richmond.[93] Nothing is known concerning the source of the *Neuse's* engine, nor is there information regarding the origin of the large, nine-foot propellers for the armorclads. They may have been manufactured in Charlotte.

The Confederacy's greatest challenge in building ironclads was obtaining the iron armor. Secretary Mallory estimated that it took a thousand tons of iron plate to armor the *Virginia* alone.[94] Although it did not take that amount to armor the smaller North Carolina ironclads, thousands of tons of iron plate were required for all of them. Three establishments in the Confederacy had the ability to roll iron plate: Tredegar Iron Works in Richmond, Scofield and Markham in Atlanta, and the Shelby Iron Works in Alabama. Rolling mills were converted to turn out two-inch plate.[95] Nevertheless, contracts for delivery of plate were not and could not be met because of the lack of raw iron. Foundries often waited months for this vital resource before the needed armor could be rolled.

The Tredegar and Atlanta facilities provided armor plate for North Carolina ironclads. Much of it came from rolled railroad T-rails. The naval secretary determined that ten to twelve miles of track, or two to three miles for each ironclad, would provide enough iron to armor the vessels under construction on the Roanoke, Neuse, Tar, and Cape Fear Rivers.[96]

Early in the fall of 1862, with two ironclads under construction in Wilmington, and three under contract on the Roanoke, Tar, and Neuse Rivers, Secretary Mallory approached Secretary of War George W. Randolph with the idea of removing rails belonging to the Portsmouth and Weldon or the Norfolk and Petersburg Railroads. When Randolph said it could not be done, Mallory instructed Commander James Cooke, the navy's senior officer in the area north of the Cape Fear River, to negotiate for the purchase of some rails in Kinston, as well as several miles of track between Kinston and New Bern. "If they refused to sell at any price you will notify them that you will take the iron for the public service, have it appraised and paid for. . . ."[97]

Subsequently, the secretary learned of iron belonging to the Atlantic and North Carolina Railroad Company, the principal stockholder of which was the State of North Carolina. Mallory requested help from Governor Vance and Vance agreed, specifying the iron be used to armor the vessel under construction on the Neuse River and other vessels being built in North Carolina.[98]

In January 1863, Cooke, with considerable exasperation, reported to the navy department that he was unable to obtain railroad iron. He recommended that "if no iron can be obtained to clad these boats . . . the entire work ought to be abandoned. . . ." A copy of this report was forwarded to the North Carolina governor with the notation that "the vessels would not have been undertaken had the Department not had good reason to believe the Rail Road iron could be obtained in North Carolina. . . ." Some iron for the Wilmington ironclads was acquired and rolled. In October, Flag Officer William Lynch was ordered back to North Carolina from Mississippi as commanding officer of the state's naval defenses. Upon arriving in Wilmington, he was immediately confronted with the problem of iron procurement. In the middle of December, officers were ordered to follow the railroad towards Atlanta in order to locate a shipment of plate sent from the rolling mill there and destined for Wilmington. The iron arrived, but there was not enough to armor the Wilmington vessels, much less the others being constructed in the state.[99] Armor plate trickled in, much of it from two rail lines that reached Wilmington and some from railroad iron acquired in South Carolina and Georgia. By March 1863, the ironclad *North Carolina* was completed and commissioned.[100]

Lynch was under pressure from Mallory to find iron for all armored warships under construction in the state. The navy had identified deposits of unused rails owned by several railroads, and Lynch turned to the governor for assistance. At first, Vance vacillated. The railroads protested that the rails were needed to replace worn out track. In March, Lynch met with the directors of the Wilmington, Charlotte & Rutherford Railroad and threatened to seize the rails with military force unless it was turned over to the navy. When the governor was made aware of this, he instructed the president of the railroad to turn the rails over to the navy. By the summer of 1863, four hundred tons of iron had been obtained, and by the end of the year, the amount had been doubled, but it would be months before the metal could be rolled into plate and transported back to North Carolina. The railroad owners and shareholders in the state pressed the governor to find replacements for the rails taken for armoring the gunboats. At times, they also absolutely refused to let the navy take up rails. Lynch appealed to General D. H. Hill to help persuade them to comply with the government's demands. There is no evidence that the general did so.¹⁰¹

Once the navy obtained the rails, they had to be shipped to rolling mills in Atlanta or Richmond and the finished armor plates transported back to the building sites. This proved to be as much of a problem as acquiring the rails. An inadequate rail system was a major factor in ultimate Confederate defeat. Despite increasing government control over the railroads, the logistical requirements, including those of the navy, could not be met. The Army virtually monopolized rail transportation. Understandably, the movement of troops, materiel, and food had priority. Naval commanders, responsible for completing the ironclads, had little control over rail movements. In exasperation, Flag Officer Lynch reported to Mallory that there were many cars loaded with armor plate in Wilmington, but he was unable to get them to Kinston and Halifax. He wrote, "The rights of the navy are not respected, its wants utterly disregarded and it is in the power of an acting assistant quartermaster to cause our transportation to be set aside at will...."¹⁰²

In February 1864, two carloads of armor plate intended for the *Neuse* disappeared on their way from Atlanta to Wilmington. Flag Officer Lynch had several naval officers ride the rails to discover what happened to the shipment. He wrote General W. H. C. Whiting, in command of the Cape Fear military defenses, who told him that he "had no authority over the trains...." Mallory appealed to the president of the Albemarle and North Carolina Railroad. On February 4, a local army commander wrote:

> "We have no two-inch iron here. The difficulty being to get transportation for it on the Wilmington Road. I have dispatched Elliott to Wilmington with an urgent appeal to the master of transportation to let the iron come on at once...." Approximately 25,000 pounds did arrive at Halifax towards the end of February, but considerably more was needed. In March 1864, the naval officer supervising the *Neuse* wrote, "The Neuse floats not—the first course of iron is complete-the second fairly begun ... the stop is at Wilmington, where there are several car loads of iron waiting transportation...."
¹⁰³ Not all could be blamed on the army or the railroads. Delays occurred at the rolling mill because of the lack of coal.¹⁰⁴ In time, the ironclads were completed, the *Neuse* only partially. In order to armor the *Wilmington*, a third ironclad under construction in the Cape Fear port, some of the plate was removed from the sunken armor-clads *Raleigh* and *North Carolina*.¹⁰⁵ With the approach of Union forces in 1865, the *Wilmington* was destroyed.

Even timber was in short supply, particularly seasoned lumber. North Carolina had an abundance of pine, oak, cypress, and other timbers used for shipbuilding, but by 1861, it was often some distance from the building sites. In fact, a major consideration in the location of ad hoc sites was the availability of timber. Shortly after receiving a contract to build a gunboat in Elizabeth City, Gilbert Elliott, of Martin and Elliott Shipbuilding, sought lumber from timber companies in Columbia, Plymouth, Winton, South Mills, and Camden. Dealers in Columbia and Plymouth initially agreed to provide cypress and pine but later declined. No reason was given. He had more luck in the other locations. A Camden sawmill owner wrote Elliott, "I commenced sawing your dry oak and have sawed three or four pieces and broke my saw which I would not have happened for all the timber here ... You had better send over your Boat and a lot of small rope and you can carry all the logs a float to your yard...."¹⁰⁶

Although Wilmington's two established shipyards had seasoned timber early in the war, it was quickly exhausted. Local citizens were unhappy with a decision to cut down some old live oak trees in the port. By 1864, builders were sending agents up river to Bladen County and even into South Carolina, searching for suitable timber.¹⁰⁷

Material for caulking was essential. Initially, oakum, the best substance for filling gaps between wooden planks, was used, but when it was no longer available, cotton was substituted.108 At first, rope was also readily available but quickly became scarce. In 1863, the navy opened a ropewalk in Petersburg, Virginia. It produced cotton rope, tarred cotton (a substitute for marlin or tarred hemp), and other cordage to meet the needs of the navy and the vessels under construction in North Carolina.¹⁰⁹

Shipbuilding Activities during the War

In June 1861, William Martin, an Elizabeth City lawyer and shipyard owner, sent one of his employees, Gilbert Elliott, to Richmond to look into the possibility of building a gunboat. In September, Martin wrote Elliott, "Send me at once the dimensions of the vessel you have on the stocks and when she could be launched.... The Confederate States want some Gunboats built. Could you build one or more. How soon and at what price per ton...."¹¹⁰ The Martin shipyard did not get a contract until October. Martin prompted Elliott to get something in writing "to show you were authorized to go on heavy hands and buying lumber to build the gunboats before any contract was made...the contract must be signed by me...."¹¹¹ A few days later, the contract was signed by Captain Lynch, calling for the construction of a 130-foot gunboat hull. Machinery for the vessel was provided by the Confederate government and came from the steamer *Empire*.¹¹² By this time, North Carolina builders had received contracts for five gunboats. There is some discrepancy over the total number of gunboats under contract, including the ones Howard agreed to build. These six gunboats, all for the Confederate navy, were laid down in established shipyards: three in Washington, one in Elizabeth City, and two in New Bern.¹¹³

The navy department also had gunboats built in Washington. Mallory wrote Lynch in September that he had been informed that "good vessels can be built at Washington. . . ." Subsequently, Arthur Sinclair was ordered there to contract for a steam powered gunboat "with propeller or side wheel of light draft suitable to navigate those waters. . . it is very important that she would be commenced at once...."[114] On October 5, a naval officer contracted with Myers and Company to build two gunboats, one to be completed in March and the other in May, 1862. A week later, he signed an agreement with Ritch and Farrow to build a gunboat to be finished by May 15. All three were to be vessels of 150 feet in length.[115]

Throughout the first year of the conflict, the naval defenses of Wilmington were mostly ignored by state and Confederate officials. Land defenses, strengthening Forts Fisher and Caswell, were stressed and thought to be adequate. The only naval defenses for the Cape Fear area were instigated by a group of local citizens who called themselves the "Committee of Safety of the Town of Wilmington."[116] Under instructions from Governor John Ellis, they seized the steam tug *Uncle Ben* and later removed the lightship, *Frying Pan Shoals*, from the river's mouth. Hauled up on the ways at the James Cassidey shipyard, the lightship was transformed into a naval vessel with her original name *Arctic*. Although Wilmington was home to two of the state's best known shipbuilding facilities, Cassidey and that of B. W. and W. L. Beery (Figure 4), no gunboat construction contracts were awarded or sought by the builders until the spring of 1862.[117]

The four gunboats built in Washington and Elizabeth City were designed by Confederate Naval Constructor John Porter. He developed three classes of wooden gunboats for shallow water operations. All three classes had common characteristics: ten feet depth of hold, propulsion provided by steam and sail, and either screw- or wheel-powered. All classes had the same configuration, the major difference being length and breath. Lengths were, respectively, 110 feet, 130 feet, and 150 feet. Porter was known for lengthening or shortening the same design by adding or subtracting at the midship section.[118] He instructed Elliott to cut twenty feet from the middle section of the gunboat he was building at Elizabeth City and thus reduce the length to 130 feet.[119] When Elliott complained about the change, Chief Engineer Williamson wrote him that Porter, not Lynch, had the final authority on hull design.[120] Elliott also attempted to gain other modifications, but the naval secretary firmly instructed him to abide by Porter's plans and specifications.

The Martin firm was also given the opportunity to build smaller gunboats. On November 26, Chief Engineer William P. Williamson wrote Elliott, "We are about to build a large number of gun boats to carry 2 guns each, and shall probably get you to build several. . . .They will be about 100 to 120 ft. long and 18 to 20 ft. beam. . . ." He later wrote Elliott that Porter had finished the drawings

FIGURE 6-4 Captain Benjamin Beery, a Wilmington shipbuilder, built ships at Eagle Island. *Source:* New Hanover County Public Library.

and that the vessels were to be 106 feet long, 21 feet in the beam, and have an eight-foot draft. Mallory approved contracting for fifty of these gunboats. In December, the Elizabeth City company agreed to build three of the smaller gunboats.[121] Elliott requested an advance on the contract but was told that no payment could be made until he met the deadlines. There is no evidence that any of these vessels were laid down.[122]

The Confederate government contracted for a large number of the Porter-designed wooden gunboats in the fall of 1861, but few were completed, and none in North Carolina. The successful Union occupation of most of coastal North Carolina in the spring of 1862 resulted in their destruction. The Battle of Elizabeth City in early February 1862 not only brought about the destruction of the small Confederate naval force but the burning of the gunboat and another vessel under construction at the Martin Shipyard.[123] The second vessel was the one that Elliott was unable to persuade the Confederate or

FIGURE 6-5 A sizable naval battle took place on the Roanoke River resulting in the capture of Plymouth. The CSS *Albemarle*, built in North Carolina, was sunk. *Source: Harper's Weekly.*

state governments to accept. A Union report stated that the vessels were destroyed "by the people of the place themselves...."[124] In March, New Bern was captured and Howard fled the city. His partner Ellis remained. What happened to the gunboat on the stocks there is not clear. It is possible she was completed by Union forces (Figure 5). A Federal soldier wrote in his journal, "In occupying the city we find they have a very active ship yard for repairs and building. A fine steamer on the stocks of 3 to 400 tons in quite an advance state...."[125] On March 21, 1862, Union forces occupied Washington. One of the gunboats on the stocks at Farrow's shipyard was destroyed. One of the Washington gunboats, probably being built by Myers, was launched and towed up the Tar River and into Chicod Creek.[126] Union forces would have burned the vessel on the stocks at Farrow's shipyard, "but they said they feared firing the town...."[127]

On May 7, 1861, Secretary Mallory stated in an oft-quoted report: "I regard the possession of an iron armored ship; as a matter of the first necessity... inequality of numbers may be compensated by invulnerability; and thus not only does economy but naval success dictate the wisdom and expediency of fighting with iron against wood...." Subsequently, the navy contracted for the construction of a number of ironclads. It was decided the captured and partially destroyed screw frigate *Merrimack*, at the Gosport Navy Yard, should be converted into an armored vessel and renamed *Virginia*. The Battle of Hampton Roads would change the nature of naval warfare forever. On March 8, 1862, the recently completed Confederate ironclad *Virginia* and her wooden escorts destroyed USS *Cumberland* and USS *Congress* and grounded USS *Minnesota*. On March 9, 1862, USS *Monitor* fought CSS *Virginia* for more than three hours with no clear victor. Success of the *Virginia* vindicated Mallory's faith in ironclads and virtually ended efforts to construct wooden boats in North Carolina. The secretary immediately contracted for more ironclads, including several to defend North Carolina's ports.[128]

A week after the battle between the *Monitor* and the *Virginia*, John M. Brooke, Chief of the Bureau of Ordnance and Hydrography, noted: "The Secretary desired me ... to give the proportions, etc. of a light draft vessel that could enter Pamlico Sound, pass through the [Albemarle & Chesapeake] canal. Secretary asked me if such vessels were iron plated...."[129] Four to eight flat-bottomed, light draft ironclads, presumably to be sent into North Carolina waters, were laid down in the tidewater region of Virginia. None of them were completed before the Confederates evacuated the area later that spring.[130]

Gilbert Elliott was the first North Carolinian contracted to build an armored vessel. Approaching Union forces caused him to flee from Elizabeth City. In April, he was able to negotiate a new contract with the navy department for the building of an ironclad gunboat. The construction site was in Virginia in the vicinity of Norfolk. He was still in the process of preliminary plans, assembling a work force, and obtaining the necessary materials, when Norfolk fell early in May.[131] Subsequently, Elliott was appointed a lieutenant in a North Carolina volunteer regiment stationed near Drewry's Bluff near Richmond, Virginia. He remained there until, once again, he became involved in gunboat construction.

The navy department turned to Wilmington for the initial effort to construct armored vessels within North Carolina. The Confederate government was also aware that Wilmington was without adequate naval protection. In the spring of 1862, the *Artic*, a receiving ship and floating battery, was the only naval vessel in the Cape Fear area. The Confederate government had focused its attention on defending the northeastern part of the state, an effort that generally proved futile as Federal forces defeated and gradually occupied most of the region.

On March 21, 1862, two weeks after the engagement in Hampton Roads, Mallory replaced Arthur Sinclair with Commander William Muse as naval officer in charge of gunboat construction in North Carolina.[132] Muse contracted with Cassidey and Sons to build one, later commissioned the *Raleigh*. B. W. and W. L. Beery agreed to construct a second one, originally the "Ladies gunboat," later commissioned the *North Carolina*.[133]

On March 24, a notice was published in the Wilmington *Daily Journal* that a Wayne County planter was willing to donate ten bales of cotton, half of his crop, to the construction of an ironclad steamer and that other local farmers and planters were willing to give "in proportions to their means...." A New Hanover planter followed suit and called for a meeting of "citizens on the subject...." He added that he had no money, but would donate his cotton, an offer noted in the March 29, 1862 edition of the *Raleigh Register*. The Wilmington news media then took up the mantle. In an editorial on March 27, the *Daily Journal* agreed that an organization was needed, one that would include representatives of each county in the Cape Fear region.[134] A lady from Duplin County endorsed a state drive. There is no evidence that an organization was created that encompassed the entire region, but a special committee of Wilmingtonians was selected to accept money for the "Gunboat Fund."[135]

On April 5, the *Raleigh Register* carried an announcement of the formation of a statewide "Ladies Gunboat Fund." In a letter to the editor, a local woman pointed out that in Virginia, South Carolina, and Alabama, ladies were already soliciting funds for gunboat construction. She appealed for funds to be collected through the *Register* for a gunboat to be named "The Old North State" and requested that "[a]ll the papers in the state ... give this as extensive a circulation as possible...." The *Register* agreed to help with holding the collected funds.[136] The *Wilmington Daily Journal* followed suit. "The ladies, ever foremost in good works, may be said to have initiated the movement in North Carolina...." An editorial appealed to citizens throughout the state to contribute to a gunboat fund under the jurisdiction of the local committee of safety emphasizing "[t]he fact that now the Cape Fear is the only unobstructed outlet in [North Carolina waters]... gives... a character not merely local, but co-extensive with the State...."[137] The *Journal* started carrying lists of subscribers to "The Gun Boat Fund." On the April 16, a town meeting was held at the City Hall and a committee appointed to receive the donations "that were pouring into the local paper...."[138] However, state wide coordination, which was envisioned by those behind the movement, never occurred. In August, the *Register* ran a notice that it was found to be "impracticable" to use the funds collected from the Raleigh, Chapel Hill, and Windsor area for gunboat construction, and instead, the monies would be diverted to helping the sick and wounded. According to the Wilmington paper, the money collected there was returned to the donors.[139]

Two Richmond-class armored vessels were laid down in Wilmington in June, one under contract with the firm of Cassidey and Sons and the second, which had been requisitioned by the Confederate government, at Beery's shipyard.[140] As with most of the Confederate naval vessels, this class was designed by John Porter. Six of this class, including the two in Wilmington, were constructed and commissioned into service. They were 150 feet in length, 34 feet in beam, and 11 feet in draft. The battery was enclosed in a box-like structure, a casemate or shield, with inclined armored sides. A pilot house and smoke stack were located on top of the casemate.[141] Work on both vessels was carried on seven days a week, twenty-four hours a day. Cassidey frequently ordered candles for night work. Nevertheless, the Wilmington ironclads were not completed until 1864. Along with the usual factors of inadequate labor, materials, and the like, discord between the military and naval commanders contributed to the delay. In September 1862, an Black ship carpenter, who fled to a Union vessel, reported that the two gunboats would have been ready for launching in a few weeks. He said that many of the workmen left either because of inadequate pay or yellow fever. In October, another reported that the epidemic had resulted in large numbers of the town's inhabitants becoming infected and that work on the gunboats had stopped. The epidemic ran its course by December, but work did not resume on the gunboats until January. The Cassidey shipyard was damaged by fire in the spring of 1861, and then the Beery facility in 1864. In both cases, naval construction and repair work was delayed.[142]

By April 1863, Lynch was in command of Confederate naval forces in the state. He wrote a state senator that the *North Carolina*, formerly called the "Ladies Gunboat," was nearly completed, and the *Raleigh* was waiting for her iron armor. After commissioning in the spring of 1864, the vessels proved disappointing. The *North Carolina's* draft was too great to permit her to cross the bar, and she was used as a floating battery until teredo worms cut short her usefulness. The *Raleigh* was able to cross the bar and engage Union blockaders, but in trying to re-cross the bar at the river's mouth, she ran aground and was abandoned.[143] The failure of the *North Carolina* and *Raleigh* left Wilmington with only a few, weak, wooden vessels as its naval defense. On May 23, 1864, Porter was ordered to Wilmington to supervise the construction of a new ironclad of his design. The new armor-clad named the *Wilmington* was to be 234 feet in length, 34 feet in beam, with a 9-foot 6-inch draft. Described by Mallory as a "fast light draft, double casemated steam ram," she was to have two octagonal shaped casemates with a pivot gun mounted in each. Most Confederate naval officers felt the oblong, heavily armored casemate characterizing the South's ironclads was a major factor in their deep draft, slowness, overall clumsiness, and general unseaworthiness. At any rate, the vessel was never completed.[144]

On June 3, a naval officer wrote his brother that a new ironclad was being built at the Beery yard. "She will have two shields, something like the yankee turrets... They say that they will finish her in 3 months, but I think if they finish her in 9 months they will surprise me very much...."[145] Iron plates, anchors, and other equipment were taken off the two ironclad "hulks" near the river's mouth for the new armor-clad. The Naval Iron Works in Columbus, Georgia fabricated the vessel's power plant. It was ready to be shipped to the building site in November 1864, but in February 1865, the navy secretary informed General Braxton Bragg that the machinery was still in Columbus. More than likely, it was never shipped. Mallory cabled Bragg, in command of Wilmington's defenses, that he needed assurance that the city would be held in time to complete the ironclad. "This place will be held so long as means enable us. . ." Bragg responded.[146] Still incomplete when the city fell on February 21, 1865, the *Wilmington* was destroyed.

A number of other Cape Fear built vessels were destroyed as Union troops approached the city's outskirts. The wooden tender *Yadkin*, built in 1863, became the Cape Fear Squadron's flagship.[147] A number of small craft were built by individual shipwrights as well. A flatboat was delivered in February 13, 1862, a sailboat and equipment in August 1862, and a cutter in February 1864. A clinker-built boat named the *Caswell* was also constructed for the navy, and a number of launches, some twenty feet long, were built, placed on a railroad flat car, transported to the Neuse River, and used in the expedition that destroyed the *Underwriter*.[148]

Wilmington was also a site for torpedo boat construction. The Confederate army and navy each contracted for at least two. The navy boats were destroyed by fire at the Beery yard: one in 1864 and the second shortly before the port fell to Union forces.[149] No description of the boats or record of their design has been located, but they were probably of the "David" type.

The army's decision to build torpedo boats was the brainchild of General W. H. C. Whiting, in command of Confederate military forces in the Wilmington area. In the spring of 1863, he sent one of his engineers to Charleston to confer with General P. G .T. Beauregard and Major Francis Lee about building torpedo boats. Although Beauregard was a strong supporter of torpedo boats, he was not a strong supporter of the Confederate navy. With the backing of Beauregard and the state, Lee, a Charleston architect in civilian life, had already designed a torpedo boat. In the fall, Whiting sent a second officer to Charleston to investigate the potential for building torpedo boats. On November 30, he wrote to the Secretary of War Seddon. He had heard the department had plans for a torpedo boat designed by Robert W. Dunn, a member of the Singer Submarine Corps. The Singer group had been directly involved in the construction of the submarine *R. L. Hunley*.[150] Whiting asked for Dunn's assistance in building the boats. The department replied that there were no plans, but that Dunn would be notified of Whiting's request. Dunn later recorded "we" (presumably the Singer group) were ordered by the Secretary of War to construct one boat at Selma, Alabama and one at Wilmington North Carolina of the following dimensions. 160 feet long 28 feet beam and 11 foot hold with flat decks—carrying all their machinery below—to be iron sheathed with no capacity for guns and only showing 2 feet above water when ready for work. They are to be armed with torpedoes, worked from below decks, and through tubes forward, aft and on both sides...."[151]

Whether he used his officer's plans or those provided by Dunn, Whiting ordered two to be built, one at Cassidey's yard, and a second at Beery's facilities. Machinery and other parts were manufactured by the Tredegar Iron Works in Richmond and Hart and Bailey in Wilmington. Tredegar provided at least one 42-inch propeller. Hart and Bailey provided hardware and machinery parts. There is no information as to who was to provide the power plants. Lumber was ordered from the vicinity of Smithville.[152] The total number of torpedo boats actually laid down in Wilmington is unknown. None became operational or were even completed.

Concurrently, additional vessels, including ironclads, were being built elsewhere in the state. In October 1862, Mallory ordered Commander James W. Cooke to investigate possible locations for building armor-clads. "The Department desires to construct vessels for the waters of N. Carolina wherever this can be done in security from the enemy. . . ."[153] Cooke and Commander

William T. Muse, fellow North Carolinian and naval officer assigned to Wilmington, emphasized the need to construct ironclads on the Roanoke River.[154] Three ironclads, of a design that was later designated the Albemarle class, were laid down in the fall of 1862. They were flat bottomed, light draft armor-clads, characterized by a diamond shaped hull designed to carry two gun batteries. Although there were minor variations within the same class, the vessels were approximately 140 feet in length, 34 feet in beam, with a 9-foot 6-inch draft.[155] As Union forces controlled the coastal regions, the ironclads were built at temporary shipyards established in the interior, as close as possible to the Wilmington and Weldon Railroad. Building materials, including heavy machinery and the iron plates, were easily transported to the construction sites.

Once more in business, the firm of Martin and Elliott obtained a contract from the navy department on September 17, 1862 to build an ironclad at Tarboro, on the Tar River. Elliott, who had taken a commission in a North Carolina regiment after the fall of Norfolk, received a leave of absence from his regiment "for two years on full pay" to construct the gunboat.[156] There is nothing to suggest that Elliott had any connections at Tarboro, as he later did at Edward's Ferry on the Roanoke River. It is possible that his co-contractor, and nominally his boss, determined the site.

There is little information on the construction of the Tarboro ironclad. Timber was cut in November. According to the diary of Joseph Bond, it was cut directly across the river from the town. By December, the keel had been laid and some of the frames put in place. In December, the shipbuilders received their initial payment provided by contract. In January 1863, the supervising officer recommended additional payments, but the money was not received until February. Construction was held up by yellow fever, snow, and the diversion of labor and materials to the other building sites. A Union sympathizer from Tarboro reported to Acting Rear Admiral S. P. Lee, in command of the North Atlantic Blockading Squadron, that:

> the work on the gunboat at Tarborough was begun in September last [1862], continued one month, then stopped in order to work on the iron-clads at Wilmington and afterward on the Roanoke; and was renewed only two weeks before General [E. E.] Potter destroyed it at which time, about 20 feet of its amidships section had been put up in six parts or the frame of bottom, four parts making sides and angles and tops. More of the frame, in sections, was ready to be put up.

The possibility of a Union attack up the Tar River, or by way of the Neuse River, concerned the navy, and the builder as well. As early as February, Commander James Cooke, the navy's supervising officer for the Tarboro ironclad, entertained an extremely problematic proposal to remove the uncompleted vessel as well as building materials to the Halifax Navy Yard on the Roanoke River. This was not done. In July 1863, the vessel, still on the stocks, was burned in a raid by Union forces.[157]

On October 10, 1862, Martin and Elliott proposed to build "an ironclad and ram" at Tilley's Farm on the Roanoke River seven miles below Halifax. Elliott suggested that an ironclad on the Roanoke River would contribute to the defense of Tarboro as well as the Roanoke River valley. In December, the Martin and Elliott firm agreed to construct a four-gun ironclad floating battery at Tilley's Farm. As with the Tarboro ironclad, Elliott continued to act as agent for Martin and must have spent considerable time shuttling back and forth between Tarboro and Halifax. Cooke actually authorized the agreement as he had been given the authority to contract for vessels without referring the matter to Richmond.[158] Although the contracts record "Tillery Farm" as the building site, only the floating battery was actually built at the location. The ironclad was laid down at Edwards Ferry, more than a dozen miles downstream. It is possible that Elliott originally selected Tilley farm as the site, but quickly moved operations to the land of E. W. Smith and his sons at Edwards Ferry. Elliott did contract with Tilley for timber and farm produce.

Priority was placed on the construction of the floating battery at the expense of the other ironclads. Convinced of an impending Union attack up the Roanoke, Confederate authorities contracted for the floating battery to be finished and turned over on February 1, and the ironclad hull on March 1, 1863. Neither deadline was met. In fact, the gunboat's keel was laid in April, a month after the contract date had passed.[159] The stationary floating battery was launched in March and towed below Edward's Ferry to await armor plate. Next, Elliott focused on completing the gunboat hull. With a growing threat of Roanoke River valley invasion, Commodore Lynch decided priority should be given to Elliott's vessel. Nonetheless, it was early October before the hull was launched.

There was some disagreement over the launching since the river was about six feet below normal, and the large, heavy vessel would have to drop from the ways into the river. The launching of a vessel was usually a festive event generally attracting a crowd. There was certainly a large audience present for this launching complete with a local southern belle chosen to bless the event with a bottle of wine. However, the newly christened Confederate vessel *Albemarle* would not slide down the ways. During the night, after the disappointed crowd had dispersed and gone home, the hull slid into the river. The drop caused some damage. Constructor Porter examined the vessel and reported that the launch was attempted "before she was in a proper state of forwardness and also when the water was too low... the consequence of which has been to hog the vessel 5 1/2 inches...."[160]

The incident resulted in censure from Secretary Mallory and constructor Porter and dissension among those involved in the vessel's construction, eventually further involving the secretary and even Governor Vance. On October 21, the situation was acerbated when, under Lynch's orders, Commander Cooke seized the recently launched ironclad hull and equally unfinished floating battery and moved them upstream from Edwards Ferry to Halifax.[161]

There followed a stalemate that lasted until January 1863. Lynch claimed the move was for the vessel's safety and said that the local military commander endorsed it, a statement later denied by the military commander.[162] Defense was certainly a factor. In defending Lynch's actions to the governor, Secretary Mallory emphasized that the fear of an enemy attack was the major reason for the removal. "He may have been mistaken as to the danger to be apprehended from the enemy...but he acted upon such information as was before him...."[163] Federal raids up the streams had increased, and in fact, late in July, one ranged within twelve miles of Edwards Ferry. Also, the commodore felt that the installation of machinery and the armor plate, all of which was to arrive by rail primarily from Atlanta and Richmond, would be expedited by being closer to the railroad.

Nonetheless, Elliott was convinced that this move took the vessels out of his hands. He tried to get the naval secretary to modify his contract relating to providing and securing the iron plating for the floating battery, probably because of the difficulties in getting the armor. He was angry because the first carload of iron plate was sent to the ironclad *Neuse* rather than to his vessel, although the *Albemarle* was further along. The secretary refused to modify the contract.[164]

Problems in communications could explain some of the confusion concerning Elliot's actions as well as the armor plate. Matters deteriorated when Elliott refused to continue work on the vessel and released a number of his work force, sending several back to their military units, and returning slaves, primarily caulkers, to their owners. Construction had virtually stopped while the vessels were moved to Halifax, and the iron armor could not be attached to the hull and casemate until the machinery was installed. In December, a Halifax County official wrote Mallory complaining that no work had been done on the ironclad for two months, since she had been brought to Halifax from Edwards Ferry.[165]

Lynch, who rarely if ever visited the site, concluded that Elliott was reneging on his contract and demanded that Cooke take control of the work. Elliott complained to the governor about Lynch; Vance in return complained to Secretary Mallory. The chief naval constructor was sent hurrying down to try to smooth over the difficulty. The result was that Lynch was directed to turn over complete control of naval construction on the Roanoke to Cooke. Mallory ordered constructor Porter to make an arrangement with Elliott "employing him and his force by the day.... It is clearly [in Elliott's] ... interest to protract the work, a circumstance which you will not fail to note...." Although, the naval secretary acceded to Governor Vance's demand and removed Lynch from control over the Roanoke ironclad, he was not altogether pleased with Elliot's performance.[166] Nevertheless, the new arrangement seemed to work. Elliott and Cooke got along well together. Finally, the naval secretary ordered William A. Graves, the assistant naval constructor, to supervise completing the ironclad.[167]

Despite the controversy and disagreements, construction picked up early in the new year. Tredegar Iron Works in Richmond supplied a bending machine. The navy department also obtained a small engine for drilling holes in the armor plates.[168] The iron was actually being drilled in the weeks prior to moving the *Albemarle* from Edwards Ferry to Halifax.[169] In November, machinists began installing the machinery, including the shafts to connect the propellers with the engines.[170] In January 1864, Elliott submitted a bill for, among other items, "hauling and loading engine."

By February, the machinery and propeller were installed, and workers concentrated on completing the armor. Nevertheless, President Davis and Secretary Mallory were unhappy with the progress of the North Carolina ironclads, especially those under construction on the Neuse and Roanoke Rivers. General Lee informed the president that an effort should be made as soon as possible to regain control of eastern North Carolina. Troops were available that would not be available when the spring campaign in Virginia began. He expressed concern about completing the ironclads, which would be key elements in an attack. Lieutenant Robert D. Minor was ordered to proceed to North Carolina, inspect the ironclads on the Roanoke and Neuse rivers, and make any recommendations that would hasten their completion. In mid-February, he visited the two construction sites. He reported the *Albemarle* nearly finished, with mechanics at work bolting the last layer of iron on her casemate. Minor wrote to Mallory that the ironclad should be ready early in March if the last of the armor plate and the two guns for her battery arrived on schedule.[171]

In March, the boilers arrived and were installed, but the last of the iron plate did not arrive until the end of the month. The original plan called for a coordinated movement against New Bern and Plymouth. However, the *Neuse* was not ready. Consequently, the plan was modified and Plymouth became the only objective. General Robert F. Hoke's division was selected to make the attack. Hoke was assured by Cooke, who was to command the ironclad in the operation, that the *Albemarle* would be ready. Less than twenty-four hours before Hoke's troops were to begin their assault, the ironclad got underway to join in the attack. She was not completed; mechanics were still working on her as she steamed slowly downstream.

FIGURE 6-6 A New Bern shipyard during the Civil War. Sketch made by Pvt. Herbert Valentine. *Source:* Herbert Valentine Collection, Southern Historical Collection, UNC-Chapel Hill.

Nonetheless, the *Albemarle* played a significant role in recapturing the town, sinking one gunboat and forcing the remainder of the Union naval force to withdraw to the sounds. Early in May, she engaged Union naval vessels in Albemarle Sound, and was severely damaged. Months later, she was sunk in a daring small boat attack by Lieutenant William B. Cushing (Figure 6).

Cooke, under instructions from the naval secretary, laid down another ironclad but she was never completed. As before, Gilbert Elliott was one of the contractors. He was joined by Peter and W. H. Smith, two of his subcontractors in building the *Albemarle*. They made considerable progress before having to destroy the vessel on the stocks. On February 20, 1865, a local planter and his wife visited the shipyard. "I had no idea how rapidly the work had gone on nor of what a fine large boat it is. ... [the builders] ... have carried it near completion...."[172]

With the approach of Union forces in early April, Cooke ordered that the uncompleted ironclad be set afire. The floating battery awaiting armor plate, the *Halifax*, probably built as a tender and still on the stocks, the screw steamer *Fisher*, and other vessels were also destroyed.[173]

An undetermined number of small craft were also built either at Edwards Ferry or elsewhere on the river during the war. Approximately thirty-five vessels were built to transport forage on the river and at least one flat was built at Edwards Ferry.[174] The ironclad *Neuse* was the only Confederate warship afloat in North Carolina waters after the destruction at Halifax.

On October 5, 1862, Secretary Mallory wrote commander Cooke and constructor Porter, informing them that the New Bern shipbuilding firm of Howard and Ellis had proposed to build an ironclad "on the Neuse River between Kinston and Goldsboro...." The naval secretary was confident that they could build the vessel as they were "practical men," but he was concerned about whether the water was deep enough for the proposed gunboat, as the vessel was to be the same design as the one approved for the Tar River.[175] Cooke reported that it was and the contract was signed twelve days later. The vessel was virtually identical to those built by Elliott and Martin. The hull was to be turned over to an agent of the navy department by March 1, 1863, "complete in all respects ready to receive the engine and machinery, and to put in place and fasten iron plating on said vessel. . . .the iron plates and the bolts for fastening the same are to be furnished by the part of the second part [navy department] ...."[176]

Whitehall, a small hamlet a few miles up the Neuse River from Kinston, was selected as the building site. A workforce had to be assembled and building materials acquired or contracted for, all of which was done by the end of November 1863. However, two months later, there was a serious setback when the vessel on the stocks was seriously damaged. In the middle of December, a Union raiding force reached the south side of the Neuse opposite the ironclad building site.

The gunboat on the stocks was hit repeatedly by artillery fire. Cooke was ordered to discontinue construction on the Neuse River and concentrate on completing the Roanoke River ironclad.[177] Eventually, work resumed. During the summer and early fall of 1863, carpenters worked on the interior of the hull-cabins, crew's quarters, mess rooms, shell rooms, magazines, berths, and furniture. At the same time, mechanics drilled the armor plate as it arrived. However, plate could not be bolted to the wood backing until launched. Governor Vance would claim that some iron plate was bolted to the hull before machinery was installed and it had to be removed in order to lower the engines, boilers, and the like into the hull.[178] Exactly when the vessel was launched is unknown but it was probably sometime in the fall of 1863. According to the contract, Howard and Ellis were to have turned the hull over to the navy on or before March 1, 1863, ready to receive machinery and armor. This clearly was not the case. Vouchers submitted by Howard indicate he continued as superintendent and chief carpenter well into 1864.[179] After launching, the gunboat was moved downstream to Kinston where machine shops and other facilities were available to complete the vessel. The ironclad's machinery started to arrive from Richmond and Charlotte early in January 1864, and machinists were sent from both naval ironworks to install it. The boiler was in place by the middle of February. The main deck was then laid and the guns mounted on March 7.[180]

Progress was slow, too slow for Richmond officials. Anxious to recover eastern North Carolina, General Lee considered the ironclads being built on the Roanoke and Neuse rivers a key element in the offensive operation. Commander John Taylor Wood, naval aide to President Davis, examined the *Neuse* after the Confederate raid that destroyed the *Underwriter* and reported to the President that progress on the *Neuse* ironclad was too slow. On February 10, Secretary Mallory ordered Lieutenant Robert Minor to proceed to Kinston immediately "and endeavor by every means in your power to hasten the completion of the gunboat...." Minor arrived in Kinston four days later and, after two days of inspecting the work, reported to Mallory:

Lieutenant Commander Sharp has a force of one hundred and seventy two men employed upon her.... As you are aware the Steamer has two layers of iron on the forward end of her shield, but none on either broadside, or on the after part.

The carpenters are now bolting the longitudinal pieces on the hull, and if the iron can be delivered more rapidly, or in small quantities [sic] with some degree of regularity, the work would progress in a much more satisfactory manner. The boiler was today lowered into the vessel and when in place, the main deck will be laid in. . . . If thematerial is delivered here as rapidly as I hope it will be ... I believe the steamer will be ready for service by the 18th of next month....[181]

When Cooke was ordered to concentrate on the ironclad *Albemarle*, Sharp was ordered to superintend the *Neuse*. Shortly after Minor's inspection, Sharp was replaced by Lieutenant Benjamin P. Loyall. Loyall was to finish constructing and fitting out the vessel, then assume command. On March 9, Loyall wrote, "The Neuse floats not—the first course of iron is complete—the second fairly begun—the Guns are in and mounted and I think will work well. . . . We have been working slowly for the past few days from want of iron, and I don't know how it can be helped. . . ." A Virginia soldier stationed near Kinston wrote that work on the gunboat was going on night and day as well as Sundays. In mid-March, an officer recently assigned to the ironclad wrote, "Her iron fixin's are not done, her engines are not ready, her quarters and storerooms are not ready. . . ." Even General Robert Hoke, commanding military forces in the area, took a personal hand in trying to get the ironclad completed. He requested the use of a machine for drilling holes in metal from the president of the Atlantic and North Carolina Railroad. According to Loyall, the general made two trips to Richmond and "brought back with him in his trunk certain augers and other tools necessary to carry on the work...."[182]

In mid-April, Loyall reported that the gunboat was nearly operational despite incomplete armor. Much to his disappointment, Loyall was then replaced by Commander Joseph Price.[183] However, Price had little opportunity to take his vessel into action. Her deep draft, more than eight feet, kept her in the vicinity of Kinston. His only engagement was in March 1865, when he was ordered to cover the retreat of army units. After firing a few shells at Union cavalry, the vessel was fired and abandoned.[184]

Kinston, or possibly Whitehall, was the site of some minor naval construction. Lieutenant Minor ordered the building of a lighter, or possibly a flat, to carry fuel and stores. He also authorized the construction of camels, designed to float the ironclad into deeper water. There is no evidence the camels were completed. If completed, they clearly did not raise the *Neuse* sufficiently to move her down the river.[185]

With few exceptions, facilities for the construction of naval vessels in North Carolina, particularly ironclads, were inadequate. This was true throughout the Confederacy. Shipyards of adequate size were scarce, as were facilities for the forging of iron anchors, propellers, shafts, and other required metal parts for ships, the manufacture of iron plate for armor, marine machinery, and ordnance.[186] North Carolina had few such establishments. In 1860, fewer than 200 workers were employed in iron works.[187]

Although all were destroyed before completion, the wooden gunboats undoubtedly would have been serviceable and would have compared favorably with others built within the Confederacy. They were built by experienced shipwrights and seasoned timbers were used in their construction. However, the same was not true of the ironclads. According to Chief Constructor Porter, the *Albemarle* was poorly built. Similarly, Lieutenant Benjamin Loyall evaluated the *Neuse* in 1864, stating: "Mark what I say—when a boat, built of green pine and covered with 4 inches of iron gets under fire of heavy ordnance she proves anything but bomb proof. This vessel is not fastened and strengthened more than a 200 ton schooner. Her upper deck is 2 inch pine with light beams and is expected to hold a pilot house. I should not be surprised, if said pilot house was knocked off. There is very little to hold it on...."[188] The two Wilmington ironclads were constructed of green timber, were slow and underpowered, with machinery frequently "out of repair" and drafts too deep. After the grounding and destruction of the *Raleigh*, a court of inquiry concluded that the vessel was poorly built, the "worst constructed of all the Confederate gunboats...."[189] Confederate ironclads were similar in design features and construction methods to the typical steamer of the period, major exceptions to this being armor and armament.

The Cassideys, Beerys, and Howard were experienced builders, certainly as experienced as most shipbuilders in the Southern states and more than some. Gilbert Elliott, for example, had no experience in building steam vessels. Nearly all Confederate armor-clads were slow, experienced frequent problems with their machinery, and were built of unseasoned wood. After the *Raleigh* was wrecked, a naval officer wrote his mother that "It was a great mistake in building them so heavy, which has rendered them utterly useless...."[190] The August 18, 1862 edition of the *Wilmington Daily Journal* editorialized: "If the vessels are completed of the draft which we know they will draw, and fitted with the machinery which we know is intended for them, they will be, like all our naval ventures, dead failures...."[191] Confederate naval officials, who designed the vessels and gave their stamp of approval, were partially responsible. The chief naval constructor prepared the plans, assisted by John Brooke and the chief engineer, William Williamson.[192] However, the poor performance of the vessels was a result of many factors, including poor design, inadequate machinery, and general inexperience in designing and building armored vessels.

The End is Near

Wilmington fell in February 1865. The vessels of the small squadron there, including several on the stocks at the two shipyards and others in the river, were torched. Later, Federal officials were able to raise the uncompleted steamer *General Whiting* and one of the torpedo boats. John Porter was supervising the construction of an ironclad at the Eagles Island shipyard when he was informed that Union troops were approaching Wilmington. He loaded what stores he could on flats and, with his workers, crossed the river and attempted, without success, to obtain rail transportation. Eventually, Porter, with some of the men and his tools, reached the naval facility at Halifax only to be told that it was being evacuated. Union forces also captured a number of flat boats that were sold at auction in 1866.[193]

The *Albemarle*, sunk by a torpedo boat in October 1864, was raised five months later, repaired, and the iron armor removed. She was then towed through the Albemarle and Chesapeake Canal to Norfolk. Three years after being raised, she was sold at auction for $2,500.[194] Up the river from Plymouth, the unfinished floating battery was sunk above Jamestown. Other vessels belonging to the Confederate navy were seized by Union forces at Halifax, including the *Halifax*, which was launched and towed to Norfolk.[195]

The remains of the *Neuse* were also auctioned by U.S. government officials with the sale taking place in New Bern. The *New Bern Daily Times* editorialized: "Don't forget to go to Polk's auction on Monday at the Bank Building. Mr. P. has been guilty of exposing to public auction almost every description of animal . . . except an elephant, b[u]t on Monday next he will sell one far superior to an elephant—it is a Ram—and a rebel ram at that...." A few days later, the paper reported the results: "The Rebel Ram fell yesterday . . . under the telling stroke of Polk's auction hammer and was taken by Mr. John Satterlee, of the well-known firm of Satterlee, Lyon & Co., of New York . . . Mr. S. now has a full grown Rebel Ram all to himself with guns, chains, rope, and tackle all complete, moved by two powerful engines with plenty of coal on hand for an extended cruise. What he intends to do with the brute has not transpired. . . ."[196] There is no record of what, if anything, the purchaser salvaged.[197]

The *ad hoc* naval facilities at Whitehall, Kinston, and Halifax were abandoned. Remaining equipment and materials were seized by Union forces. Gilbert Elliott later complained that the sawmill and lumber seized at Edwards Ferry, where the *Albemarle* was laid down, was private and "therefore not liable to seizure...." His claim was ignored.[198] Shipyards in Elizabeth City, Plymouth, and Washington were destroyed when the ports were captured by Union forces. In Elizabeth City, a Union regiment occupied and bivouacked on shipyard property for much of the war.[199] In July 1865, the Howard shipyard in New Bern was restored to its owner by the U.S. Army Quartermaster Department, which had utilized the yard during the war.[200] The Cassidey shipbuilding facility in Wilmington was not seriously damaged and was back in operation shortly after the war. However, the Beery yard on Eagles Island was burned by Beery, and much of it had to be rebuilt. The naval ordnance works in Charlotte occupied a former machine shop owned by John Wilkes. He wrote to his father that he hoped to get his property back and convert it into a shop to fabricate and repair agricultural equipment. He did so, and it became the Mecklenburg Iron Works.[201]

Union Shipbuilding Activities in North Carolina During the War

Union forces undertook a limited amount of shipbuilding in North Carolina, primarily repairing vessels, but also completing or converting a few that were seized. In the fall of 1862, Flag Officer Samuel P. Lee informed the senior officer in the North Carolina sounds that "all repairs possible should be made" in North Carolina.[202] The number of Federal naval vessels in the sounds was too small to allow one or more to be absent for repairs. Although major repairs and refits were frequently conducted in Norfolk, the bulk of such work was done in New Bern. Union forces destroyed or damaged shipbuilding facilities, including marine railways, in a number of North Carolina ports. Only those in Washington were repaired and utilized. Despite the fact that Beaufort became an important coaling and logistical base for the blockading squadron, Federal forces did not make use of the shipbuilding facilities in the port or those around Core Sound. The Union Navy attempted to use a small machine shop in Beaufort to replace some boiler tubes on a blockader, but the flag officer was informed that there were no competent machinists "for such work."[203]

Whenever possible, local artisans were hired. From New Bern, Commander J. Rowan wrote Flag Officer Louis Goldsborough that he was sending ship carpenters detailed from the fleet back to Fortress Monroe stating, "I think it best to employ mechanics from the town...."[204] The Union naval force in the Neuse employed white and Black workers in its shipbuilding activities. However, there were few available. The majority of white males, including those employed in shipbuilding, were either in the Confederate armed forces or working at shipyards in the interior.[204] There were skilled Black shipwrights and caulkers in the area occupied by Union forces and they were undoubtedly employed.[205]

Commander Henry K. Davenport, who commanded Union naval forces in the sounds, wanted to use Washington as a repair station. The port had marine railways as well as a small foundry and blacksmith shop. Two seized vessels were completed in the months after Federal forces occupied the town in March 1862.[206] In February 1863, after a formal survey, it was recommended that experienced machinists and other needed craftsmen as well as tools and materials be sent in order to utilize the facilities. After consulting the chief engineer, Flag Officer Lee initially decided against using Washington as a repair depot largely because the army was reluctant to garrison the port permanently.[207]

A combined Union force of warships and troops captured New Bern in March 1862.

Despite Confederate efforts to recapture it, the port remained in Federal hands and became headquarters for naval and military forces in coastal North Carolina. Because of the port's importance and Union interests in capturing Goldsboro and cutting the Wilmington and Weldon Railroad, a sizeable military presence was concentrated in the town and the surrounding area.

The Union army and navy stationed several gunboats and other vessels in the Neuse River. Union forces also seized two shipyards. The Federal force immediately made use of the marine railway and machine shops. One, formerly the Sparrow establishment, became the "Navy Yard." The other, owned by Thomas Howard and Elijah Ellis before the Civil War, was operated by the army's Quartermaster Corps as the "Government Shipyard."[208] There may have been a third small shipyard as well. When the town was occupied, Dibble and Brothers had a steamboat on the stocks, and for some unexplained reason, it remained on the stocks throughout the war. The army also took over a locomotive shop belonging to the Atlantic and North Carolina Railroad. The Union army and navy utilized its facilities. The navy sent most of its river gunboats there for repairs.[209] In July 1863, Commander Davenport requested help from Major Herman Biggs, the army's chief quartermaster in New Bern: "[T]here is a large amount of work, necessary to repair the several naval vessels in the Sounds, which can only be done by machinery, such as is at present at your disposal in the locomotive shop...." The army complied whenever possible.[210]

At the Sparrow shipyard, the navy had a ship carpenter in charge and hired local workmen on an *ad hoc* basis. In June 1864, the naval facilities in New Bern had to be returned to their owners under the president's property proclamation. However, Union forces could and did rent them for the remainder of the war.[211]

The army not only repaired its vessels but converted several barges and steamers into gunboats. The army's quartermaster department developed an extensive shipbuilding program throughout the occupied South during the war, including at New Bern.[212] With the exception of Black caulkers hired locally, the army brought in ship carpenters, blockmakers, and machinists to man the shipyard and machine works. In March 1863, there were twenty-four ship carpenters, one superintendent of shipbuilding, one boiler maker, one engineer, and seven caulkers working at the army's facility at New Bern. In September 1863, the Black caulkers complained of being sick and tired of North Carolina. The quartermaster complained that the Black workers at the shipyard were troublesome and that they were "free and could work or not work as they pleased...." Evidently, most of the local, skilled shipyard workers fled with Thomas Howard and were employed at Whitehall, building the Confederate ironclad *Neuse*. One local ship carpenter was kidnapped and threatened with tar and feathers "for taking the Union side...."[213]

A number of captured steamers such as the *Wilson* were taken to the New Bern shipyard and converted into army transports. The 445-ton steamer *Long Island*, which had been burned to the waterline at Washington, was towed to New Bern and completely rebuilt.[214]

The most ambitious project carried out by the army quartermaster's shipyard in New Bern was the conversion of canal barges *Bombshell*, *Shrapnel*, and *Grenade* into gunboats. The vessels were large "Laker" boats purchased by the quartermaster department in New York in 1861. They were used in the Burnside expedition to Roanoke Island and later towed to New Bern.

The *Bombshell* was the first one completed. The engineer who superintended the work described the process: "Altered . . . by cutting off both bow and stern, changing their form and lengthening to 114 feet. . . ." A turret was built on the deck and plated with planks twelve inches thick and the interior packed with coal. An eight-inch iron boiler was then bolted to the outer plank. The boiler and machinery were protected by three feet of coal in the bunkers and also plated with 3/8 inch boiler iron. "The pilot house is purposely built low and the lookout, while in action is reduced [so that] the pilot can see every point around him...." The sides of the vessel, above the waterline, were also plated. The report does not state where the machinery came from, but the quartermaster in charge at New Bern mentioned that he had located sawmill engines at Beaufort and Washington for the other canal boats.[215] One small steamboat, the *J.C. Slaght*, was constructed from the keel up at the New Bern shipyard.

In May 1865, the *New Bern Daily Times* announced that the government shipyard was closing up: "2 or 3 of the shops have already suspended operations. These changes affect business very materially...." [216] The navy yard had already suspended operations, giving up its lease on the former Sparrow shipyard. Two months later, Thomas Howard announced that he was back in business. At about the same time, John Myers and Co. did the same. By the end of 1865, the old established yards in the state were either back under their former owners or had been taken over by new owners. North Carolina's badly depleted maritime fleet needed to be rebuilt, but it would be several years before this took place.

Notes

1. The Confederate States Navy paid North Carolina for five steamers. Voucher, July 26, 1861, Reel 9, M1091, NA. The Confederate Congress authorized a navy in February 1861. Initially, it was a navy without ships. It did gain control of the *Fulton*, an old sidewheeler, as well as various state navies, including that of North Carolina.
2. Report of Charles Dodge, May 31, 1861, *The War of the Rebellion: A Compilation of the Official Records of the Union and Confederate Armies*, Ser. I, vol. LI, pt. I, 96, hereafter cited as *ORA*. For an account of the Dismal Swamp Canal in the Civil War, see Brown, *Dismal Swamp Canal*, 97-106.
3. The president of the canal informed the Confederate government and the local Confederate military commander that "the large fleet of gun-boats now being constructed at the various shipyards in North Carolina would need to pass through the canal in order to be fitted out at the Norfolk shipyard...." Brown, *Juniper Waterway*, 68-69.
4. The vessel at Edenton was spared as well, but the officer in command of the raiding expedition there made no distinction between private and public. Quakenbush to Goldsborough, May 3, 1862, *Official Records of the Union and Confederate Navies in the War of the Rebellion.*, ser. I, vol. 7, p. 305, hereinafter cited as *ORN*; Murray to Rowan, February 12, 1862, *ORN*, vol. 7, p. 638. For a contemporary view by a Union correspondent see the *New York Times*, September 23, 1861.
5. Robert M. Browning, Jr., *From Cape Charles to Cape Fear*, 31-38.
6. John W. Hinds, *Invasion and Conquest of North Carolina*, 169.
7. An undetermined number of fishing vessels were seized which seriously affected the livelihood of coastal residents. Report, Committee of Elections, June 16, 1862, Report No. 118, 37th Congress, Second Session, House of Representatives, 16; Delany, "Charles Henry Foster and the Unionists of Eastern North Carolina," *NCHR*, 354.
8. The *A. P. Hurt*, *John R. Grist*, and *Enterprise II*, among others, were taken over by either state or Confederate authorities. Watson, *Wilmington: Port of North Carolina*, 82-83; Johnson, *Riverboating in Lower Carolina*, 53-54; J. Worth to Brother, November 12, 1864, Worth Papers, SANC; Sloan, "Inland Navigation in North Carolina, 1818-1900," 50-51; *Wilmington Daily Journal*, February 5, July 9, November 30, 1861.
9. Pendergrast to Stringham, August 19, 1861, *ORN*, I, 6, 89; *Wilmington Daily Herald*, October 13, November 14, 1856.
10. Browne to Goldsborough, December 25. 1861, *ORN*, I, 6, 487-488. The *William H. Northrup* was built in 1859.
11. *Wilmington Daily Journal*, June 25, 1863.
12. *Wilmington Daily Journal*, April 25, 1861. For the Elizabeth City vessel see *Wilmington Daily Journal*, February 19, 1868.
13. *North Carolina Times*, February 7, 1865; *New York Herald*, March 19, 1862; Banks to Boyd and Boyd to Wing, May 18, 1865, Joseph F. Boyd Papers, Rubenstein Special Collections Library, Duke University; Rowan to Goldsborough, March 16, 1862, *ORN*, I, 7, 109; Charles Dana Gibson and E. Kay Gibson, comps., *Dictionary of Transports and Combatant Vessels Steam and Sail Employed by the Union Army, 1861-1868*, 203.
14. Deposition, January 1873, Angelo Garibaldi Papers, SANC; correspondence, Stevenson to Hoffman and Mitchell, November 13, 1980. This may well have been the vessel on the stocks that a Union expedition discovered early in 1862, but did not destroy "as private property."

15. Renshaw to Lee, June 12, 1863, Box 31, S.P. Lee Papers, Library of Congress, Washington, D.C.; Renshaw to Davenport, May 24, 1863, *ORN*, I, 8, 35; *ORN*, II, 191.
16. Farrow vs. United States Government, February 1901, William B. Rodman Papers, ECU. There is no record that he was compensated. A suit filed in July 1861 in the New Bern District Court mentioned two vessels under construction, one in Craven County and a second one in Onslow. A schooner was launched in Elizabeth City in 1864.
17. *Fayetteville Observer*, August 12, 1861. For the flats see Jackson to Mallett, November 2, 1864, Charles Mallett Papers, SHC, UNC-CH; *Wilmington Daily Journal*, February 13, 1868; J. Murphy Estate Record, Craven County Estate Papers, SANC.
18. Garibaldi to Johnston, January 1862, Hayes Papers, SHC, UNC-CH.
19. For the repairs to gunboats see the various warrants issued to the Navy Agent's Office, Governor's Office Records, Warrant book, 1857-1864, SANC; Vouchers, October 1861, Reel 8, 9, M1091, NA.
20. See various vouchers for Howard and Ellis, May-September 1861, reels 470 and 471, M346. NA. For Norfolk see vouchers for August through October 1861, Reel 8, M1091, NA. Shipbuilders were also doing other military work during this period.
21. December 10, 1861, William F. Martin Papers, SHC, UNC-CH; Powell, ed., *DNCB*, I, 463-464. Crossan was a former U.S. and state naval officer. Presumably, the gunboat was for the state. No reply from Gilbert Elliott has been located.
22. Mallory to Clark, September 14, 1861, Governor Henry Clark Letterbook, SANC; Mallory to Office of Orders and Detail, June 1861, Reel 34, M499, NA; Voucher, August 24, 1861, Arthur Sinclair file, ZB Files, Navy Department. Library, Washington D.C.
23. He was referring to the Pamlico Sound area, where two steamers of the five were turned over to the Confederacy for repair in New Bern, and deployed in the sound. The others were stationed further north in the state. Gatlin to Cooper, September 4, 1861, *ORA*, I, LI, 269-270; October 1, 1862, IV, 573-574. See also John G. Barrett, *Civil War in North Carolina*, 62.
24. Daniel Harvey Hill, ed, *North Carolina in the War Between the States, Bethel to Sharpsburg*, I:185-186.
25. *New Bern Daily Progress*, November. 2, 1861. See also travel voucher for Sinclair, November 6, 1861, ZB file, Navy Department Library, Washington, D.C.
26. Howard to Governor Clark, November 25, 1861, Clark Letterbook, SANC.
27. Dewey to Venable, January 6, 1862, *ORA*, I, VI, 433-434.
28. May 9, 1862, Reel 8, M1091, NA. Whether the payment was for repairs or new construction is not recorded.
29. *Daily Progress*, February 4, 1862.
30. *New Bern Progress*, February 24, 1862.
31. Correspondence from Edwin Combs to authors, June 2, 2002.
32. Joseph P. Reidy, Paul D. Escott, and others, "Skilled Labor," *Encyclopedia of the Confederacy*, II, 902-903. Edwin L. Combs, III, "Field or Workshop: A Study of Southern Industrial Labor in the Civil War," (Ph.D. diss.. University of Alabama, 2003), is the best study of maritime labor in the Confederacy. See also Maurice Melton, "Major Military Industries of the Confederate Government" (Ph.D. diss., Emory University, 1978).
33. *New Bern Progress*, May 18, 1862; Mallory to Lee, March 30, 1862, *ORN*, I, 7, 753; Perkins to Elliot, January 6, 30, 1862, and Skinner to Elliott, December 23, 1861, William F. Martin Papers, SHC, UNC-CH; Combs, "Field or Workshop: A Study of Southern Industrial Labor in the Civil War." Skilled workmen also journeyed to Edenton, Roanoke Island, and Washington to repair government vessels. See vouchers, 1861, Reel 8, M1091, NA.
34. Still, *Confederate Shipbuilding*, 89, note 2. Shipwrights from North Carolina were employed in Norfolk and elsewhere during the early months of the war. *New Bern Progress*, May 18, 1862.
35. In October 1861 a shipwright in a North Carolina state unit wrote a number of letters to Elliott appealing to him for help in getting a discharge in order to work on the vessels being built at Elizabeth City. There is no evidence that he was successful. Gilbert to Elliott, October 23, 28, 1861, Martin Papers, SHC, UNC-CH. For Mallory's efforts to secure workmen from the army see Still, *Confederate Shipbuilding*, 61-74.
36. Porter to Lynch, November 14, 1863, private collection, copy in authors' possession. See also Perkins to Elliott, January 6, 1862, and Skinner to Elliott, December 23, 1861, Martin Papers, SHC, UNC-CH. See vouchers, Reel 8, M1091, NA; Porter to Brother, March 29, 1863, *ORN*, I, 592; Combs, "Field or Workshop," 179. For a general discussion of the employment of Blacks in shipbuilding during the Civil War see Combs, "Field or Workshop," 145-185.
37. Lynch to Greene, August 30, 1863, Area 7 File, RG45, NA; Lee to Hunter, October 10, 1864, W.W. Hunter Collection, Rubenstein Special Collections Library, Duke University; Mallory to Graves, March 30, 1863, Reel 5, M1091, NA; Muse to Manning, September 17, 1862, Miscellaneous files, Wilmington folder, Subject File, RG45, NA; *Wilmington Daily Journal*, Sept. 17, 1862; travel vouchers, January-February 1864, Reel 3, September 1863, Reel 7, M1091, NA. The shipyards employed local boys as messengers and clerks in hopes of exempting them from military service. *Wilmington Weekly Journal*, September 4, 1862.
38. The men were on detached service from the army and received only their military pay, according to rank. Beery's Shipyard, Marker File, NCOAH; letter by Sarah Jane Beery Willson, in Genealogical Records of Ida Kellam, copy in author's possession; William A. Willson Memoir, copy in the Beery file, Lower Cape Fear Historical Society Archives, Wilmington; *ORN*, I, 9, 119.
39. Lynch to Mallory, March 18, June 8, 1863, September 27, 1864, June 8, 1863; Mallory to Secretary of the Treasury, June 19, 1863, September 27, 1864, Reel 34, M499, NA. For a discussion of the wage scale see Combs, "Field or Workshop," 74-75, 121-122.
40. Whiting to Pinckney, November 24, 1864, W.H.C. Whiting Letterbook, RG109, NA. Vouchers for work done, roll 6, M1091; *ORN*, I, 8, 90; Paymaster, Wilmington to Mallory, June 8, 1863, Reel 34, M499, NA; *Wilmington Daily Journal*, September 23, October 1, 1863.
41. The salary for a first class ship carpenter was $4.50 by 1864. Combs, "Field or Workshop," 77; Porter to Mallory, June 10, 1864; Mallory to Secretary of the Treasury, June 19, 1863, September 27, 1864, Reel 34, M499, NA.
42. Still, *Iron Afloat*, 157; Gilbert report to Adjutant General, North Carolina, Miscellaneous Records, folder 1, Box 78, SANC; Combs, "Field or Workshop," 194.
43. John W.H. Porter, *A Record of Events in Norfolk County, Virginia*, 223. The deserters were apparently spies and later slipped out of the yard and informed the Union naval commander of the ship's progress. John W. Hinds, *Hunt for the Albemarle*, 14. See also voucher, February 1864, reel 6, M1091, NA; (Robersonville) *Weekly Herald*, August 24, 1940; *ORN*, I, 8, 599.
44. Loyall to DeLeon, March 5, 1864, Area 7 file, RG45, NA; Howard and Ellis file, November 1863; voucher of pay to Hoke's units, March 1864, roll 3, M1091, NA. The ninety-five skilled

workers and fifty laborers mentioned in Hoke's report is probably a discrepancy or error in the document. William D. Blair compiled a study of records on the CSS *Neuse* and, based on vouchers in M1091, concluded that the exact number from Hoke's Brigade was 105 (unpublished manuscript in authors' possession). For the published Hoke report, see *ORA*, I, XXXIII, 97. Reels 3 and 7, M1091, NA, also include vouchers for machinists and engineers traveling to and from Richmond, Charlotte, and Wilmington transporting machinery. An appendix to the Blair manuscript lists 289 individuals who worked on the *Neuse* at one time or another. A number of these are listed in the 1860 census as ship carpenters. A *New Bern Weekly Journal* article dated January 13, 1864, lists a number of local individuals who worked on the vessel including a significant number from New Bern; report, February 15, 1864, Reel 10, M 1091, NA.

45. A July 3, 1865 article in the *New Bern Daily Times* reported that the facility employed approximately 250 men. Ralph W. Donnelly, "The Charlotte, North Carolina, Navy Yard, C.S.N.," *Civil War History*, 77; Violet G. Alexander, "The Confederate States Navy Yard at Charlotte, N.C., 1862-1865," *North Carolina Booklet*, 24-25; Barrett, *Civil War in North Carolina*, 361.

46. The deterioration and near collapse of rail transportation was undoubtedly a major factor in the Confederate defeat. The Confederacy underwent an industrial revolution as it sought to overcome such deficiencies. This included manufacturing facilities needed for military naval construction. Richard E. Beringer and others, *Why the South Lost the Civil War*, 59, 215-218.

47. See Joseph T. Durkin, *Confederate Navy Chief: Stephen R. Mallory*.

48. All were experienced shipbuilders except Elliott. Vouchers in Reels 6 and 9, M1091, NA. Petitions for pardon submitted after the war state that Beery, Cassidey, and Howard built gunboats for the Confederate government only reluctantly. Beery wrote that his shipyard was seized by the Confederate Navy: "…that I was not professionally engaged in the supervision of the construction of vessels repaired or built upon the said yard and that the extent of my service consisted in paying off the hands employed and receiving the money for that purpose…." He also stated that during the war he was engaged in farming. However, records in the National Archives indicate he was intimately involved in gunboat construction, including being listed as a supervisor. Cassidey, in his petition, stated "…your petitioner…has not been in any way engaged in the late war…." At least Thomas Howard admitted that he worked as a ship carpenter for the Confederate Navy, although he insisted that "…his services were required and demanded by the so called Confederate States in building Gun boats, and were reluctantly given; he having no other alternative than to render such service or be put into the Confederate Army as he was liable for conscription…." Elijah Ellis, his co-contractor in building the *Neuse*, did not apply for pardon. Ellis, a prominent Craven County businessman and investor, was not a shipbuilder. He remained in New Bern after the Union occupation until he was "sent through the lines for disloyalty having refused to take the oath of allegiance…." Joseph Farrow, of Washington, also did not apply for pardon, probably because he did not have property worth $20,000, but he did make claims for property seized by Union forces. U. H. Ritch, his associate, died shortly after the war. William Martin, of Martin and Elliott, had no direct role in Confederate naval construction but was involved indirectly through Elliott, his employee. Martin, a lawyer, also owned a shipyard in Elizabeth City. He served in a military capacity throughout the conflict and resumed his law practice after the war. For his petition for pardon, see M1003, NA. A copy can be found in the Military Collection, Civil War Collection, Petitions for Pardon, New Hanover County, SANC. Report of July 19, 1985, Box 124, Consolidated Correspondence File, 1794-1915, RG92, NA.

49 Combs, "Confederate Shipbuilding on the Cape Fear River," (M.A. thesis, ECU, 1996), 411; vouchers for payment in M1091, NA.

50. Martin to Elliott, October 10, 1861, Martin Papers, SHC, UNC-CH.

51. Gilbert Elliott, n.d., in Clipping File, North Carolina Collection, UNC-CH. Robert G. Elliott, *Ironclad of the Roanoke*, 11-12. For a somewhat more objective account of Elliott, see Hinds, *The Hunt for the Albemarle*. See also Powell, ed., *DNCB*, II:148-149. Elliott opened a law firm in New York City in later years and died there in 1895. *New Bern Weekly Journal*, May 16, 1895.

52. The first evidence of this is a set of instructions from Martin for Elliott to "go to Portsmouth and do everything you can to make a contract for a gunboat… If you cannot get work in the yard, close it and hire out the hands…." Elliott evidently went from Portsmouth to Richmond and had an interview with the naval secretary. "…I am inclined to prefer the building of the hulls alone…. If it is necessary however to do every thing as you say Mr. Mallory [insists] … and furnish the boat ready for use, we must be protected against any failure on the part of the contractor for engines and other equipment… Buy all the lumber you can to be paid for when the boats are delivered and paid for by the government. Let me know how much money you will need to begin and I will try to raise it …." Martin was clearly uneasy about building a gunboat. "…I feel some hesitation to undertake a regular contract not knowing anything about the business and suggest that you be very careful in your calculations and allow for contingencies. I am inclined to think it would be safe to rent the yard and here the hands to the Government." Nonetheless, he hired agents in Camden and other counties to purchase timber. Martin wrote to him on October 12, "You should have put the whole loss of lumber gathered for the boat on the government in case the enemy destroys it…." In November, Martin sent money to him to pay for lumber and other materials ordered. He added, "…When you get that first payment [from the Confederate government] pay the taxes." October 3, 10, 1861, Martin Papers, SHC, UNC-CH: Combs, "On Duty at Wilmington: The Confederate Navy on the Cape Fear River."

53. Although the authors do not always agree with Elliott's interpretation, *Ironclad of the Roanoke* is the best account of the Martin/Elliott association.

54. One of the Smiths, whose ancestors owned the property where the ironclad's hull was built and who were at times employed in building the vessel, later wrote that Elliott was in charge of finances. Burton H. Smith, "Carolina's Contribution to the Confederate Navy," *Confederate Veteran* 38 (1930), 376.

55. (Raleigh) *News & Observer*, February 27, 1868; Powell, ed., *DNCB*, V:386. Smith, "Carolina's Contribution to the Confederate Navy." The Peter Smith Collection, SHC, UNC-CH, includes a biographical sketch by Lena H. Smith.

56. Elliott to Martin, January. 11, 1863, Martin Papers, SHC, UNC-CH. Elliott complimented Cooke in an article he wrote after the war but, on one occasion during the conflict, referred to him as a "humbug." Elliott, *Ironclad of the Roanoke*; Catherine Ann Devereux Edmondston, *Diary of a Secesh Lady: The Journal of Catherine Ann Devereux, 1860-1866*, eds., Beth G. Crabtree and

James W. Patton. See entries for July 30, 1863, and October 15, 1863.
57. Vance to Mallory, November 28, 1863, Lynch to Vance, December 4, 1863, Mallory to Vance, December 11, 1863, in Joe Mobley, ed., *The Papers of Zebulon Baird Vance*, II, 1863, 330, 336-337, 339-341; Elliott to Vance, January, 27, 1864, Vance Papers, SANC; Gilbert, *Ironclad of the Albemarle*, 114-128.
58. See John Porter's papers in the ZB File, Navy Department Library, Washington, D.C. See also Porter's Papers and Journal, ECU. The Confederate Navy Department employed various inspectors and superintendents such as J.J. Roberson, Hugh Lindsey, Edward Williams, John A. Thomas, and Thomas Carr to inspect and supervise certain aspects of the construction. Carr superintended the assembling of machinery on both the *Albemarle* and *Neuse*. Voucher, March 22, 1863, Confederate Navy Files, Subject Files, machinery, RG45, NA.
59. Because of the anachronistic promotion system in the prewar navy, Cooke was still a lieutenant in 1861. In fact, he was frequently derided by his fellow officers as the "patriarch of the lieutenants." Nonetheless, he was admired by both Union and Confederate naval officers. Daniel Ammens, *The Old Navy and the New*, 291; Maffitt to Davis, August 17, 1874, John Newland Maffitt Papers, Rubenstein Special Collections Library, Duke University; Still, *Iron Afloat*, 163.
60. Butler, *Pirates, Privateers, and Rebel Raiders*, 135. Elliott would write that Cooke was ordered to observe the building of the ironclad. However, Cooke had orders to "superintend" construction. He spent so much time personally searching for iron to armor the vessel that he gained the sobriquet "Ironmonger Captain." Forrest to Cooke, December 1, 1862, ZB file, Navy Department Library, Washington, D.C.; Walter Clark. ed., *Histories of the Several Regiments and Battalions from North Carolina in the Great War, 1861-1865*, V:318.
61. Edmondston, who had an ability to accurately portray those individuals with whom she came into contact, characterized Cooke as "a plain sensible unaffected man" and later as "a gentlemanly, well informed and eminently practical man." Edmondston, "*Journal of a Secesh Lady,*" eds., Crabtree and Patton, 420, 424.
62 None who knew Lynch, including his detractors, denied this. Edwin Combs, "'On Duty at Wilmington,'" 22-55. See also Still, *Iron Afloat*, 150-156, and Maxine Turner's brief sketch in Paul Escott and others, eds., *Encyclopedia of the Confederacy*, 3, 962.
63. Mary Elizabeth Cooke's journal of her husband's life, copy in the National Museum of Civil War Naval History, Columbus, Georgia, (hereafter NMCWNH, Columbus, GA). See also Hinds, *Invasion and Conquest of North Carolina*, 102-109.
64. Gilbert Elliott, one of the contractors for naval construction on the Tar River, and, later, the Roanoke River, became so embittered toward the flag officer that he wrote Governor Vance, "Lynch is universally looked upon in this State as incompetent, inefficient and almost imbecile." The governor agreed with Elliott. "I am satisfied of his total and utter incapacity for the duties of his position…," he wrote to the naval secretary. Still, *Iron Afloat*, 151-152.
65. Combs, "Confederate Shipbuilding on the Cape Fear River," *NCHR*, 424; Still, *Iron Afloat*, 154-155.
66. Cooke stated: "I have been unfortunate in this struggle to have had incompetent commanders," clearly a comment aimed at Lynch. Mary Elizabeth Cooke's journal of husband's life, copy in NMCWNH, Columbus, GA; Combs, "'On Duty at Wilmington,'" 36; Still, *Iron Afloat*, 155; Hinds, *Hunt for the Albemarle*, 26.

67. Escott and others, ed., *Encyclopedia of the Confederacy*, 4, 1424-1425; voucher, February 5, 1864, Confederate Navy, Subject File, Transportation and Supplies, RG45, NA.
68. A descendant of the Smiths wrote that he had always heard the vessel was built "in a gut." C. T. Smith to Braswell, February 2, 1979, copy in author's possession; see also (Scotland Neck) *Commonwealth*, August 3, 1928, for comments by Lena Smith.
69. Vouchers in rolls 3, 30, 31, 41- M1091, NA. As early as September 1862, timber was cut for the vessel across the river from Tarboro. Entry, September 15, 1862, F.I. Bond Journal, F.I. Bond Papers, ECU. The Tarboro vessel never left the stocks. Bacot to "Sis," March 19, 1864, Richard H. Bacot Papers, SANC. In later years, James Webb claimed that he owned a foundry there that connected the iron plates to the vessel. However, the list of subcontractors in the Confederate Treasury Department Papers does not include him. Nor do they mention who installed the plates. Possibly Campbell leased the Webb facility. Gerald A. Patterson, *Justice or Atrocity*, 38; *Kinston Free Press*, April 24, 1940; James B. Webb, "Kinston in the Sixties," *Carolina and the Southern Cross*, I (November 1913), 199-201.
70. Combs, "Confederate Shipbuilding on the Cape Fear," *NCHR*, 409-434.
71. (Wilmington) *Morning Star*, May 23, 1917; Louis T. Moore, "Ships for the Confederacy Were Built in Wilmington," *The State*, XII (January 1945), 20-21. In April 1864, the Eagles Island shipyard was damaged by fire. Sprunt, *Chronicles of the Cape Fear River*, 535.
72. An examination of dozens of Hart and Bailey's vouchers and bills found in various record groups in the National Archives demonstrates the breadth of its proficiency. Considerable information about the company work can be found in Roll 5, M909 and Roll 416, M346, NA. Letter from General Whiting to Lynch, May 24, 1863, District of Cape Fear and North Carolina Letter Book (Sent), RG109, NA.
73. Combs, "Confederate Shipbuilding on the Cape Fear River," *NCHR*, 416.
74. Combs, "Confederate Shipbuilding on the Cape Fear River," *NCHR*, 416. For the vouchers see Rolls 5, 6, 7, and 9, M1091, NA.
75. Roberts partly financed the purchase with the proceeds from his wartime work. "An Act to Incorporate 'The Wilmington Manufacturing Company,'" *Private Laws, Session of 1866-67*, c. 42, 296; 1850 Census, Middlesex, Massachusetts; Thomas E. Roberts Petition for Pardon, New Hanover County, Military Collection, Civil War Collection, SANC; New Hanover County Deed Books SS, 1860, p. 266, and UU, 1867, p .678, SANC; Correspondence, George Stevenson to author, November 15, 2002. A Union map of Wilmington dated 1864 shows the "Roberts Factory" where Clarendon was located. Correspondence, Chris Fonvielle to author, November 23, 2002. Locally it continued to be known as the Clarendon Iron Works. Correspondence, William A. Burgess to "Dear Parents," June 13, 1863, in the John Haywood Papers, SHC, UNC-CH.
76. An examination of the vouchers for payments to the Iron Works suggests that Roberts produced many of the same type of items as Hart and Bailey. Combs, "Confederate Shipbuilding on the Cape Fear River, *NCHR*, 417; vouchers in Rolls 6, 8, 9, and10, M1091, NA. In something of a puzzle, Roberts was on board the blockade runner *Merrimac* when she was captured in July 1863. After a short imprisonment he was released. *Wilmington Journal*, October 23, 1863.
77. Vouchers in Rolls 6, 7, and 9, M1091, NA.
78. Vouchers in Rolls 6, 7, and 9, M1091, NA.

79. Still, *Confederate Shipbuilding*, 47-48; Barrett, *Civil War in North Carolina*, 17.
80. Charles B. Dew, *Ironmaker to the Confederacy: Joseph R. Anderson and the Tredegar Iron Works*, 140.
81. Washington to Andrew Johnson, August 5, 1865, in Military Collection, Civil War Collection, Petitions for Pardon, 1865-1868, SANC. Webb, "Kinston in the Sixties," *Carolina and the Southern Cross*, 169.
82. Combs, "Confederate Shipbuilding on the Cape Fear River," *NCHR*, 420-421.
83. Minor to Mallory, February 15, 1864, Reel 10, M1091, NA; Mallory to Gibbs, September 19, 1862, Reel 5, M1091, NA; *New Bern Daily Times*, July 3, 1865.
84. Minor to Mallory, May 7, 20, 1862, Reel 34, M499, NA; Donnelly, "The Charlotte North Carolina Navy Yard, C.S.N.," *Civil War History*, 72-75; V.G. Alexander, "The Confederate State Navy, Yard, at Charlotte, N.C., 1862-1865," *North Carolina Booklet*, 28-37; Still, *Confederate Shipbuilding*, 38, 42; *Charlotte Observer*, April 3, 1910; *New Bern Daily Times*, July 3, 1865. On May 31, 1862, the *Raleigh Register* reported that the Navy had purchased the foundry of Alexander and McDongold in Charlotte. Exactly how many steam hammers and where they came from is unclear.
85. In August 1864, the responsibility for making rifle shells was shifted to the Selma, Alabama, naval works. An undetermined amount of nitric acid, used in the manufacture of explosives, was found in the mint. Brooke to Jones, August 25, 1864, Reel 9, M1091, NA; Ramsay to Jones, September 1, 1864, reel 10, M1091, NA; Minor to Brooke, February 15, 1864, M1091, NA. *New Bern Daily Times*, July 3, 1865. Ramsay to Mallory, July 29, 1862, Reel 34, M499, NA.
86. Page to Brooke, December 8, 1863, Reel 9, M1091, NA.
87. Combs, "Confederate Shipbuilding on the Cape Fear River," *NCHR*, 416.
88. Tredegar Foundry Sales Book, August 18, 1862, July 31, 1863, 254, 351, Virginia State Library, Richmond; Muse to Manning, July 7, 1862, Reel 6, M1091, NA. Muse to Manning, September 11, 1862, Reel 6, M1091, NA. After the *Raleigh* was no longer serviceable her boilers were transferred to the CSS *Chattahoochee*. Maxine Turner, *Navy Gray*, 196.
89. Warner to Alexander, Captured and Abandoned Property, Case File No. 825, RG56, NA; Warner to Mullins, November 19, 1864; Warner to Lynch, June 23, 1864, J. H. Warner Letter Book, NMCWNH, Columbus, GA.
90. Correspondence concerning the machinery and related items is in the Martin Papers, SHC, UNC-CH.
91. Williamson to Elliott, November 9, 1861, and Reed to Elliott, November 2, 1861, Martin Papers, SHC, UNC-CH; Voucher, March 1, 1862, Roll 6, M1091, NA. Shoekoe was taken over by the Confederate Navy in 1862. John M. Coski, *Capital Navy*, 72.
92. Donnelly, "The Charlotte, North Carolina Navy Yard, CSN," *Civil War History*, 78. The article does not mention the *Neuse*, but it is logical that, if the Charlotte facility provided the shafts for the *Albemarle*, it also did so for the *Neuse*.
93. Elliott, *Ironclad of the Roanoke*, 141-142.
94. Williamson to Davis, February 27, 1862, ORN, II, 2, 151.
95. Still, *Confederate Shipbuilding*, 34-36; Maurice Melton, "Facilities," in *Confederate Navy: Its Ships, Men and Organization, 1861-65*, William N. Still Jr, ed., 72.
96. Combs, "Confederate Shipbuilding on the Cape Fear River," *NCHR*, 422.
97. October 31, 1862, James Cooke Papers, NMCWNH, Columbus, GA; Mallory to Randolph, September 1, 1862, RG109, NA; October 28, 1862, ORN, I, 8, 843.
98. Vance to Mallory, November 21, 1862, Reel 13, Zebulon B. Vance Papers, SANC; Still, *Iron Afloat*, 152; William N. Still, Jr., "The Career of the Confederate Ironclad '*Neuse*,'" *NCHR*, 4. Elliott was most unhappy when this iron was designated for the *Neuse*. In his reply to Mallory, Vance underlined "Neuse River." See November 21, 1862, Reel 13, Vance Papers, SANC; Lynch to Jack, December 16, 1862, Roll 6, M1091, NA.
99. Lynch to Jack, Dec 16, 1862, Roll 6, M1091, NA
100. Combs, "Confederate Shipbuilding on the Cape Fear River," *NCHR*, 422-423.
101. Mallory to Vance, December 11, 1863, Mobley, ed., *Papers of Zebulon Baird Vance*, II, 1863, 340-341; Combs, "Confederate Shipbuilding on the Cape Fear River," *NCHR*, 423. Lynch to Vance, January 24 and Vance to Lynch, January 28, 1863; Vance to Cooke, February 2, 1863; Lynch to Hill, March 9, 1863, Vance Letter Book, Vance Papers, SANC ; Vance to Whitford, Jan. 28, March 5, 1863, John D. Whitford Papers, SANC; Mallory to Hill, March 13, 1863, ORA, I, 18, 919; Still *Iron Afloat*, 153. Lynch appealed to Hill for help, but there is no evidence that he did so. Charles Price, "Railroads and Reconstruction in North Carolina," (Ph.D. diss., UNC, 1959), 50-52.
102. Hinds, *Hunt for the Albemarle*, 122.
103. Mallory to Whitford, February 8, 1864, Whitford Papers, SANC; Whiting to Lynch, February 6, 1864, RG109, NA; Peck to Butler, February 23, 1864, ORA, I, XXX, 589; Elliott, *Ironclad of the Roanoke*, 148; Still, "The Career of the Confederate Ironclad '*Neuse*,'" *NCHR*, 8; Still, *Iron Afloat*, 153.
104. Jackson to Jones, March 22, 1864, and Jackson to Jones, February 23, 1864, Reel 10, M1091, NA.
105. Charlie to "Sister," September 16, 1864, and to "Brother," June 3, 1864, Charles Peek Papers, private possession. Combs, "Confederate Shipbuilding on the Cape Fear River," *NCHR*, 423-424.
106. Dozier to Elliott, November 28, 1861, Martin Papers, SHC, UNC-CH. See also other correspondence concerning timber in Martin Papers.
107. *Wilmington Morning Star*, April 23, 1917; Report of Secretary of the Navy, April 30, 1864, ORN, I, 15, 733; Combs, "Confederate Shipbuilding on the Cape Fear River," *NCHR*, 417-420. After the seizure of much of coastal North Carolina, Union shipbuilders arranged to ship timber, especially pine, to their yards in the North. Heaton to "B.," January 23, 1864, Records of Civil War Special Agencies of the Treasury Department, Box 3, RG366, NA.
108. Elliott, *Ironclad of the Roanoke*, 96.
109. Still, *Confederate Shipbuilding*, 38; Voucher to Smith and Griffith, December 7, 1861, Reel 7, M1091, NA.
110. June 13, September 14, October 3, 29, November 9, 19, December 14, 1861, Martin Papers, SHC, UNC-CH. Martin tried to peddle the unfinished vessel on the stocks to the Confederate or state government, but without success. He persisted even after he was told that the engines were too small.
111. October 17, 1861, Martin Papers, SHC, UNC-CH.
112. October 22, 1861, Martin Papers, SHC, UNC-CH.
113. *Raleigh Register*, September 6, 1862, copied from the *Richmond Enquirer*.
114. Buchanan to Sinclair, September 25, 1861, Subject file AC, Reel 3, M1091, NA; Mallory to Lynch, September 14, 1861, copy in Governor Henry Clark Letterbook, SANC.

115. *Report of Evidence Taken Before a Joint Special Committee of both Houses of the Confederate Congress to Investigate the Affairs of the Navy Department*, 439-440, 443, hereafter cited as *Committee to Investigate the Affairs of the Navy Department*. The hull remains there today having been investigated by archaeologists.

116. Combs, "On Duty at Wilmington: The Confederate Navy on the Cape Fear River," 27.

117. Combs, "On Duty at Wilmington: The Confederate Navy on the Cape Fear River," 3. For efforts by the Confederates to build vessels in Wilmington, see Combs, "Confederate Shipbuilding on the Cape Fear River," *NCHR*, 409-434.

118. Still, *Confederate Shipbuilding*, 73; Robert Holcombe, "Types of Ships," in *Confederate Navy: Its Ships, Men, and Organization, 1861-65*, Still, ed., 45. A copy of the specifications for the Elizabeth City vessel can be found in the Martin Papers, SHC, UNC-CH. Although the *Chattahoochee* specifications were the same as the Elizabeth City vessel, because designs were often slightly modified by local contractors, it cannot be said that they were identical.

119. Porter to Williamson, November 26, 1861, Martin Papers, SHC, UNC-CH.

120. Williamson to Elliott, December 4, 1861, Martin Papers, SHC, UNC-CH.

121. Mallory to Elliott, December 28, 1861, January 4, 6, 1862, copies in the Martin Papers, SHC, UNC-CH. *Wilmington Journal*, April 3, 1862. Williamson to Elliott, November 26, December 4, 1861, Martin Papers, SHC, UNC-CH. Contract, signed January 13, 1862, in Confederate Contracts, RG56, NA; copy in *Committee to Investigate the Affairs of the Navy Department*, 444-445.

122. Mallory to Elliott, January 4, 6, 1862, Martin Papers, SHC, UNC-CH.

123. Rowan to Goldsborough, February 11, 1862, *ORN*, I, 6, 606-608.

124. Goldsborough to Fox, February 9, 1862, *Confidential Correspondence of Gustavus Vasa Fox*, eds. Robert M. Thompson & Richard Wainwright, I:240.

125. Levi Hayden Journal, 1838-77, 122, Library of Congress, Washington, D.C.

126. Gradually settling to the bottom, the unfinished hull remained there, until maritime archaeologists from East Carolina University examined the remains in 1985 and determined that it was indeed one of the Confederate gunboats. See "Chicod Creek Site, November 8-9, 1973," manuscript copy, Underwater Archaeological Unit, Kure Beach, N.C.; Glenn A. Forest, "Is the Chicod Creek Vessel a Macon-Class Porter Gunboat?," *Underwater Archaeology*, Denise C. Lakey, ed., 149-151; Rowan to Goldsborough, March 27, 1862, *ORN*, I, 7, 151; unpublished manuscript by Robert Holcombe, copy in possession of authors. Register of Civil, Military and Naval Contracts, entry 57, RG365, NA.

127. *Wilmington Weekly Journal*, April 3, 1862. This is confirmed in a letter to General Branch. Walker to Branch, April 11, 1862, L. O'B. Branch Papers, University of Virginia Library, Charlottesville, Va. Still, "The Shipbuilding Industry in Washington, North Carolina," 37-38. What happened to Farrow is unclear. He was paid for an anchor chain seized by the Confederate Navy, probably for the *Albemarle*. Voucher, August 1, 1863, Reel 7, M1091, NA. There is also evidence that he was working on the ironclad building at Tarboro in 1863. Voucher to Farrow and Thomas, August 3, 1863, roll 6, M1091, NA. Ritch remained in Washington and became a Union Treasury agent.

128. For the Confederate ironclad policy, see Still, *Iron Afloat*.

129. George M. Brooke, Jr., ed., *Ironclads and Big Guns of the Confederacy: The Journal and Letters of John M. Brooke*, 82.

130. The secretary also turned to builders in North Carolina for ironclads. Holcombe, "Types of Ships," in *Confederate Navy: Its Ships, Men, and Organization, 1861-65*," Still, ed., 55.

131. Elliott, *Ironclad on the Roanoke*, 55-56; Virgil C. Jones, *Civil War at Sea*, III, 68.

132. Mallory to Sinclair, March 21, 1862, Sinclair file, BZ files, Navy Department Library, Washington, D.C.

133. Combs, "Confederate Shipbuilding on the Cape Fear River," *NCHR*, 410-411. The *North Carolina's* construction may have been influenced by the Committee of Safety, a self-proclaimed defense group headed by the mayor. Undoubtedly, the disasters in the northeastern section of the state prompted action. The *Wilmington Daily Journal* blamed the Confederate government for the lack of an adequate naval defense in the Cape Fear area and called for a local citizens committee to be formed to collect funds to build one or more gunboats.

134. *Wilmington Daily Journal*, March 31, 1862; *Raleigh Register*, March 29, 1862. Combs, "On Duty at Wilmington: The Confederate Navy on the Cape Fear River," 12-13; Richard E. Wood, "Port Town at War: Wilmington, North Carolina, 1861-1865" (Ph.D. diss., Florida State University, 1978), 98-99.

135. Combs, "On Duty at Wilmington: The Confederate Navy on the Cape Fear River," 13.

136. Combs, "On Duty at Wilmington: The Confederate Navy on the Cape Fear River," 411. Patriotic ladies' societies with names such as Ladies Gunboat Fund, Ladies Gunboat Association, Ladies Defense Association, and Ladies Association for the Defense of North Carolina sprang up throughout the Confederacy after the Battle of Hampton Roads. Their goal was to raise funds to build ironclads. A number of them (at times including men) were organized in North Carolina, including Wilmington. As early as December 1861, a lady from Wilmington suggested that each woman in North Carolina contribute one dollar towards building a navy. *Wilmington Daily Journal*, December 11, 1861. The *Greensboro Patriot* carried the appeal, April 17, 1862. The Williamston paper and the *Raleigh Register* carried it on May 10.

137. *Wilmington Daily Journal*, April 10, 1862.

138. On May 24, the *Raleigh Register* listed thirty-two ladies who had forwarded their contributions to the local paper. A list of names was printed in the June 11 issue.

139. As early as April, the *Daily Journal* was discouraging further contributions as it might interfere with efforts by the Confederate navy to construct ironclads in Wilmington. *Wilmington Daily Journal*, August 13, November 12, 1862; January 7, 1863.

140. William A. Willison's account of the Beery shipyard, the Beery File, Lower Cape Fear Historical Society Archives, Wilmington, N.C. Article by Mrs. J. A. Fore, daughter of W. L. Beery, *Wilmington Star*, July 10, 1916.

141. For an in-depth analysis of the *Richmond* class, see Robert Holcombe, "The Evolution of Ironclad Design" (M.A. thesis, ECU, 1993); Still, *Iron Afloat*, 93-110.

142. Braine to Scott, September 22, 1862, *ORN*, I, 8, 90; Parker to Lee, January 23, 1863, *ORN*, I, 470; William F. Clayton, *A Narrative of the Confederate States Navy*, 67; Foster to Halleck, October 3, 1862, *ORA*, I, XVIII, 414-415; Whiting to Beauregard, January 8, 1863, *ORA*, I, XVIII, 827-830; Whiting to Cooper, January 15, 1863, *ORA*, I, XVIII, 849; *Wilmington Daily Journal*, May 27, 1861; Sprunt, *Chronicles of the Cape Fear River*, 534-535.

143. Lynch to Vance, November 15, 1863, Vance Papers, SANC;

Maffitt to Davis, June 7, 1880; Dunbar Rowland, ed., *Jefferson Davis, Constitutionalist: His Letters, Papers and Speeches*, VIII, 474; Charlie to "Sis," May 7, 9, 1864, Charles Smith Peek Papers, in private possession; National Archives Microfilm M1091, roll 6, contains extensive documentation in the form of vouchers, etc. concerning work on the two ironclads. They include payments to subcontractors for materials such as lumber, iron, oakum and paint. The *Raleigh* has been the object of underwater archaeological investigations. See Martin D. Peebles, "CSS *Raleigh*: The History and Archaeology of a Civil War Ironclad in the Cape Fear River" (M.A. thesis, ECU, 1996).

144. *Wilmington Daily Journal*, September 3, 1863.

145. Peek to "Brother," June 4, 1864, Peek Papers, in private possession; Mallory to Porter, May 23, 1864, Area 7 file, RG45, NA. Randall to "My Darling Katie," May 21, 1864, James R. Randall Papers, SHC, UNC-CH. In September 1863, an advertisement was included in local newspapers for proposals to construct a gunboat. Presumably, this was the vessel that was still incomplete when the city fell in 1865. *Wilmington Daily Journal*, August 8, 1863.

146. Mallory to Bragg, February 6, 7, 1865, ORN, I, 12, 179. Warner to Mullins, November 19, 1864, J. H. Warner Letterbook, NMCWNH, Columbus, Ga,; Holcombe, "Type of Ships," in *Confederate Navy: Its Ships, Men and Organization*, ed. Still, 55.

147. The only private construction of note in the port during the war was that of a number of flats or barges used in the salt works in the sound below Wilmington. See Ella Lonn, *Salt as a Factor in The Confederacy*, 102-103, 261.

148. Information concerning these boats can be found on Reel 8, M1091, NA. The Beery's bookkeeper mentioned the boats in a reminiscence published in *Wilmington Morning Star*, April 23, 1917. For the destruction of the Underwriter, see Barrett, *Civil War In North Carolina*, 208-211.

149. Charlie to "Bro.," December 30, 1863, Peek Papers, private possession; Richard E. Wood, "Port Town at War, Wilmington, North Carolina 1860-1865," 114; Combs, "Confederate Shipbuilding on the Cape Fear," *NCHR*, 412.

150. Mark K. Ragan, *Union and Confederate Submarine Warfare in the Civil War*, 151-152, 214; Whiting to Hawks, November 1, 1863, to Beauregard, November 25, 1863, to Gilmer, November 25, 1863, to Seddon, December 1, 1863, Letters Sent, General W.H.C. Whiting's Command, July 1863-August 1864, II, 336, RG 109, NA: Combs, "On Duty at Wilmington: The Confederate Navy on the Cape Fear River," 85; Combs, "Confederate Shipbuilding on the Cape Fear, *NCHR*, 412; Still, *Iron Afloat*, 115-116.

151. Ragan, *Union and Confederate Submarine Warfare in the Civil War*, 152, 214.

152. Ragan, *Union and Confederate Submarine Warfare in the Civil War*, 152; Combs, "On Duty at Wilmington: The Confederate Navy on the Cape Fear River," 85; various vouchers for Hart and Bailey in Reel 11, RG1091, NA; Whiting to James, December 1, 1863, Letters Sent, General WHC Whiting's Command, July 1863-August 1864, II, 336, RG 109, NA.

153. Cooke was wounded in the Battle of Elizabeth City, and was recuperating in North Carolina, October 5, 1862, Cooke Papers, NMCWNH, Columbus, Ga.

154. Muse, in command at Wilmington in the summer of 1862, wrote the governor recommending the construction of an ironclad gunboat on the Roanoke River. Mary Elizabeth Watts Cooke's journal of husband's life, Cooke Papers, NMCWNH, Columbus, Ga.; Muse to Governor Henry T. Clark, July 26, 1862, Clark Papers, SANC; and to Governor Zebulon Vance, May 8, 1863, Reel 17, Vance Papers, SANC.

155. Holcombe, "Types of Ships," in *Confederate Navy: Its Ships, Men and Organization*, ed., Still, 55; Holcombe, "The Evolution of Ironclad Design," 96-103. Various authorities provide different specifications. Overall length has been given as 156 feet and 158 feet. See Butler, *Pirates, Privateers and Rebel Raiders*," 242, note 29.

156. Porter, *A Record of Events in Norfolk County, Virginia*, 223. Information is based on an article by Elliott in the April 16, 1887, issue of the *St. Louis Republican*. Elliott, *Ironclad of the Roanoke*, 61, cites a special order giving Elliott a thirty-day leave of absence. Copy of the contract in *Committee to Investigate the Affairs of the Navy Department*, 461. The unique arrangement is curious. Elliott may have approached the Navy Department with a proposal. Since he was stationed at Drewry's Bluff at the time it was not difficult to do so. However, of the river systems leading into the interior and approaching the strategically important Wilmington and Weldon Railroad, certainly the Tar River was considered the least important. Confederate and state authorities considered the Neuse and Roanoke Rivers more vulnerable to Union attack.

157. Although the naval station was not in Halifax, it was designated as the Halifax Navy Yard. One officer described the site as a "God forsaken place," where the principal work was making wash tubs and repairing old buggies and wagons. Elliott to Martin, January 11, 1863, Martin Papers, SHC, UNC-CH; Cooke to Mallory, January 21, 1863, and Elliott to Cooke, February 6, 1863, Cooke Papers, NMCWNH, Columbus, Ga.; voucher, December 26, 1862, Reel 6, M1091, NA; Elliott to Colonel, October 20, 1863, Martin Papers, SHC, UNC-CH; Elliott, *Ironclad of the Roanoke*, 70, 83; Cohen to Lee, August 18, 1863, ORN, 9, 164-165; F. L. Bond Diary, entry date unclear, F.L. Bond Papers, ECU. For Potter's raid up the Tar River see Barrett, *Civil War in North Carolina*, 164-166.

158. Mallory to Cooke, October 10, December 7, 1862, Martin and Elliott, October 10, 1862, contract dated December 1, 1862, Martin Papers, SHC, UNC-CH; Joseph Bond Diary, ECU.

159. It is not known what tools and equipment were salvaged from Elliott's earlier, abortive gunboat building ventures. In his published reminiscence, he mentions having to scrounge up a blacksmith forge and portable sawmills. Much of the timber was apparently obtained in the vicinity of the building site, although Elliott wrote that some of it had to be hauled from a "long distance." Combs, "Field or Workshop: A Study of Southern Industrial Labor in the Civil War," 115; Burton H. Smith, "Carolina's Contribution to the Confederate Navy," *Confederate Veteran*, 38 (1930), 376. Carpenters were hired to not only work on the boats but to build houses for the workers as well. See invoices and vouchers, dated early 1863, Reel 2, M1091, NA. Elliott's reminiscence, "The Ram 'Albemarle': Her Construction and Service" was published in *Century Magazine* (July 1888) and reprinted in Walter Clark (ed.), *Histories of the Several Regiments and Battalions From North Carolina in the Great War, 1861-1865*, V, 315-323. Elliott, *Ironclad of the Roanoke*, is the most detailed account of the vessel. See also John W. Hinds, *The Hunt for the* Albemarle: *Anatomy of a Gunboat War* and *Invasion and Conquest of North Carolina*.

160. Mallory to Cooke, October 31, 1863, Cooke Papers, NMCWNH, Columbus, Ga. The letter quotes Porter. For the launching "disappointment," see entry for October 9, 1863, Edmondston, *"Journal of a Secesh Lady*," eds., Crabtree and Patton, 463-464. Mallory to Porter, October 14, 1863, ZB file.

161. Mallory was writing to Elliott and Lynch, whereas Lynch directed his correspondence to Cooke, and Cooke was not on the

building site all the time. According to Edmondston, Cooke was also unhappy with the decision to move the two vessels to Halifax. Entry for October 15, 1863, *"Journal of a Secesh Lady,"* eds., Crabtree and Patton, 477-478; Lynch to Cooke, October 12, 1863, Cooke Papers, NMCWNH, Columbus, Ga.

162. Martin to Mallory, November 7, 1863, Vance Papers, SANC.

163. December 11, 1863, *Papers of Zebulon Baird Vance*, II, ed. Joseph A. Mobley, 339-341.

164. Mallory to Elliott, October 12, 1863, Cooke Papers, NMCWNH, Columbus, Ga.

165. December 2, 1864, copy in the Zebulon B. Vance Papers, SANC.

166. Mallory to Cooke, January. 15, 1864, *ORN*, I, 9, 800. This evidently superseded the original contract awarded to Elliott to build the vessel. Elliott's and Hind's book on the *Albemarle* describes at length the disagreements. The originals concerning it are in the Cooke Papers, NMCWNH, Columbus, Ga.

167. Mallory to Cooke, January. 15, 1864, *ORN*, I, 9, 799-800.

168. After the war, Elliott recalled that it initially took approximately twenty minutes to drill a hole but Peter Smith, one of the subcontractors and something of a tinkerer and inventor, developed a twist drill that cut the time to around four minutes. There is no evidence that Smith's drill was introduced elsewhere in the state or Confederacy where armor plate had to be drilled. *Century Magazine* (July 1888).

169. Elliott Vouchers, September-November, 1863 Reel 2, 6, M 1091, NA; Porter to Lynch, November 14, 1863, Cooke Papers, NMCWNH, Columbus, Ga.

170. Elliott voucher, November 1863, Reel 2, M1091, NA.

171. Minor to Mallory, February 28, 1864, Robert Minor Papers, Virginia Historical Society, Richmond. Excerpts from his report can be found in *Civil War Naval Chronology*, IV, 24.

172. Edmondston, *"Journal of a Secesh Lady,"* 669-670; contract dated August 29, 1864, in Reel 7, M1091, NA. Cooke to Mallory and his reply, May 8, 26, 1864, *ORN*, I, 10, 627, 659.

173. Macomb to Radford, June 24, 1865, *ORN*, I, 12, 163-164.

174. A note in the J. Boyd Papers, Rubenstein Special Collections Library, Duke University; Hinds, *Hunt for the Albemarle*, 46.

175. Both letters are in the Cooke Papers, copies in the NMCWNH, Columbus, Ga. Ellis remained in New Bern while the ironclad was initially under construction. As mentioned previously, he was not a shipbuilder but a businessman who invested in Howard's shipbuilding business. He rented property to Union officials, possibly including the Howard shipyard. However, in 1863, he was ordered out of the port and was taken through the lines. Where his family went after that is unclear. He returned to New Bern in April 1865 and demanded compensation from the Federal government. Order, April 5, 1865, and claim for compensation, February 18, 1865, Army Quartermaster Records, Consolidated Correspondence file, 1774-1915, Box 724, New Bern folder, RG92, NA.

176. William N. Still, Jr. "The Career of the Confederate Ironclad *Neuse*," *NCHR*, 1. The contract can be found in *Report of Evidence Taken Before a Joint Special Committee of Both Houses of the Confederate Congress to Investigate the Affairs of the Navy Department*, 463-464. See also Leslie S. Bright and others, *C.S.S. Neuse: A Question of Iron and Time*.

177. Lynch to Cooke, January 3, 1863, Cooke Papers, NMCWNH, Columbus, Ga. Bright, *CSS* Neuse: *A Question of Iron and Time*, 78.

178. Vance to Mallory, November 28, 1863, Vance Letter Book, SANC.

179. Vouchers for January 1863-February 1864; voucher by Daniel Hilton for work, September-November 1863; voucher to J. H. Dibble for rent of machinery and shop, as well as assorted items, October 1863, Reel 3, M1091, NA. Both Hilton and Dibble were Kinston manufacturers. Clifford C. Tyndall, "Lenoir County During the Civil War" (M.A. thesis, ECU, 1988), 3-4. Hilton and his brother owned a large woodworking plant, and Dibble a carriage factory. "Kinston In the Sixties," *Carolina and the Southern Cross*," I (November 1913), 199.

180. Dan Blair, research report, December 1995, CSS *Neuse* State Historic Site, Kinston, N.C.

181. February 16, 26, 1864, Robert Minor Family Papers, Virginia Historical Society, Richmond, Va.

182. B.F. Loyall in Biographical Clipping File, North Carolina Collection, UNC-CH; letter from Hoke to Whitford, February 9, 1864, John D. Whitford Papers, SANC; Richard H. Bacot to "Sis," March 19, 1864, Bacot Papers, SANC; George Leitz to Aurelia Hooper, March 8, 1864, Aurelia Hooper Papers, Rubenstein Special Collections Library, Duke University; Loyall to Robert Minor, Minor Family Papers, Virginia Historical Society, Richmond, Va.: Bright, *CSS* Neuse: *A Question of Iron and Time*, 12-13.

183. Bright, *CSS* Neuse: *A Question of Iron and Time*, 16.

184. The remains of the *Neuse* were discovered, salvaged, and are now at the CSS *Neuse* State Historic Site, Kinston, N.C. For a detailed description of the recovery and artifacts, see Bright, *CSS* Neuse: *A Question of Iron and Time*.

185. Minor to Mallory, February 14, 1864, Minor Family Papers, Virginia Historical Society, Richmond, Va; vouchers dated March-April, 1864, Roll 3, M1091, NA; Bright, *CSS* Neuse: *A Question of Iron and Time*, 12.

186. For a study of shipbuilding facilities in the Confederacy, see Still, *Confederate Shipbuilding*, 23-46.

187. Barrett, *Civil War in North Carolina*, 17.

188. Loyall to Minor, April 16, 1864, Minor Family Papers, Virginia Historical Society, Richmond, Va.

189. William H. Parker, "The Confederate States Navy," in *Confederate Military History*, ed. Clement A. Evans, 85; statement of former seaman on the *North Carolina*, June 27, 1864, *ORN*, I, 9, 770; Combs, "Confederate Shipbuilding on the Cape Fear River," *NCHR*, 431.

190. W. Calder to "Mother," June 7, 1864, W. Calder Papers, SHC, UNC-CH.

191. *Wilmington Daily Journal*, August 18, 1862.

192. Naval Constructor Porter prepared the plans, but he had help from John Brooke and the Chief Engineer, William Williamson. For example, on March 17, 1862, Brooke wrote in his journal: "The Secretary desires me to make the computation of weights, etc. for small gunboats [and] iron clads...." Brooke, *Ironclads and Big Guns of the Confederacy*, 82.

193. John Porter Journal, ECU; "Sale of Captured and Abandoned Property," March 26, 1866, Entry 622, Heaton Papers, RG366, NA; Phelps to Porter, April 15, 1865, *ORN*, I, 12, 118; Chris E. Fonvielle, Jr., *Wilmington Campaign*, 422; *Fayetteville Observer*, February 27, 1865; *Wilmington Star*, July 10, 1916; Block, *Wilmington Through the Lens of Louis T. Moore*, 123.

194. Elliott, *Ironclad of the Roanoke*, 268-276; Hinds, *Anatomy of a Gunboat War*, 201.

195. For a contemporary account of efforts to raise the *Albemarle*, see the correspondence of Union soldier S.A. Shumway February-June 1865, copies in the Port O'Plymouth Roanoke River Museum, Plymouth, N.C. See also *ORN*, I, 12, 163-164, 148, 166.

196. In March 1865, the ironclad had been set on fire by her crew

near Kinston. However, because of the shallow water, she was not totally destroyed. *New Bern Daily Times,* October 3, 7, 10, 1865. See also Bright, *C.S.S. Neuse: A Question of Iron and Time,* 17.

197. Local lore has it that, at low water, various parts were removed including the machinery. The vessel remains and numerous artifacts were recovered and placed in a museum in the 1960's. For an account of the recovery see Bright, *C.S.S. Neuse: A Question of Iron and Time,* 19-28.

198. Macomb to Porter, June 19, 1865, *ORN,* 12, 159.

199. Case file of John Tatum, Case Files for Approved Claims of the Southern Commission, Records of the Accounting Officers of the Department of the Treasury, RG217, NA.

200. Howard and Ellis testimony, July 31, 1865, in Joseph Boyd Papers, Rubenstein Special Collections Library, Duke University.

201. "To father," May 20, 1865, Wilkes Family Papers, Duke University; Alexander, "The Confederate States Navy Yard at Charlotte, N.C., 1862-1865," *North Carolina Booklet,* 23 (1926), 33.

202. Correspondence to Davenport, October 4, 1862, *ORN,* I, 8, 115. Two days before, Lee sent a request to the naval secretary for an "…intelligent navy carpenter to repair naval vessels…" and mentioned that there was only one carpenter available to supervise such work. Correspondence to Welles, October 2, 1862, M89, NA.

203. Scott to Lee, December 4, 1863, M89, NA. Amelia Dees-Killette, "The Union Occupation of Coastal North Carolina," (M.A. thesis, North Carolina State University, 1991), 18. For Beaufort see William D. Blair, "'One Good Port,' The Union Navy and Beaufort Harbor, North Carolina, 1862-1865" (M.A. thesis, ECU, 1999); and Browning, *From Cape Charles to Cape Fear.* For an example of Union destruction of shipbuilding facilities, see Rowan to Goldsborough, February 11, 1862, *ORN,* I, 6, 608.

204. Husband to wife, September 6, 1864, Clarisa Phelps Hanks Papers, ECU; testimony of Henry Covert, n.d., Craven County Claim No. 104316, Records of the Southern Claims Commission SANC.

205. Slaght to Hoffman, January 23, 1863, E3238, Letters Received, Dept. of NC/VA, 1861- 63, RG393, NA; Vincent Colyer, *Report of the Services Produced by the Freed People to the United States Army in North Carolina*; James, *Annual Report of the Superintendent of Black Affairs in North Carolina, 1864,* 10, 27; Cecelski, *Waterman's Song,* 161.

206. Still, "The Shipbulding Industry in Washington, North Carolina," 38.

207. Davenport to Lee, May 22, 1863, March 3, 1864, and May 18, 1863; Isherwood to Lee, May 14, 1863; all in RG45, NA. See also Lay to Renshaw, February 2, 1863; Renshaw to Murray, February 3, 1863; Murray to Lee, March 1, 1863, 587; Murray to Lee, March 13, 1863; Lee to Davenport, March 20, 1863; Renshaw to Davenport, April, 22, 1863; Lee to Lay, March 12, 1863; Lay to Davenport, March 24, 1863; Lee to Davenport, May 12, 1863; Lay to Davenport, May 16, 1863; Lee to Davenport, May 18, 1863; all in *ORN,* I, 8. Samuel P. Lee Papers, Library of Congress, Washington, D.C.; Browning, *From Cape Charles to Cape Fear,* 163.

208. A letter dated May 9, 1862, from a Union soldier mentioned that when the Confederates evacuated the port, "…machine ships with engines for Gun Boats were fired…." so they could not he used "against the South." Paul Fay Letter, Collection No. 21867, New York State Library, Albany, N.Y.

209. Howell to Welles, June 27; Macomb to Welles, May 22, July 8, 1865; ORN, I, 12, 163-164, 148, 166.

210. For Navy repairs see Rowan to MacDiarmid, April 21, 1862, *ORN,* I, 7, 254; Davenport to Shubrick, October 4, 1862, *ORN,* I, 7, 8, 117-118; Davenport to Lee, September 22, October 15, 1862, *ORN,* I, 7, 83, 134; Flusser to Murray, January 17, 1863, *ORN,* I, 7, 448; Ottinger to Murray, March 20, 1863, *ORN,* I, 7, 609; Davenport to Lee, May 31, 1863, *ORN,* I, 7, 9, 54; Flusser to Davenport, May 8, 1863, *ORN,* I, 7, 11; Smith to Lee, May 7, 20, 1864, *ORN,* I, 7, 10, 32, 73; Davenport to Lee, April 28, 1864, Lee Papers, LC; Palmer to Smith, Entry 163, Area 7 file, RG45, NA; *Wilmington Journal* cited in *Fayetteville Observer,* March 27, 1862.

211. Stuart to Lee, October 26, 1863, and Stuart to Farrell, October 16, 1863, Lee Papers, LC; Davenport to Biggs, July 29, 1863, RG45, NA.

212. Smith to Lee, June 27, 1864, *ORN,* I, 10, 214; Davenport to Smith, June 5, 1864, *ORN,* I, 122; Browning, *From Cape Charles to Cape Fear,* 163.

213. Russell F. Weigley, *Quartermaster General of the Union Army: A Biography of M.C. Meigs,* 248-249.

214. "Articles & Persons Hired, March-August, 1862," New Bern File, Water Transportation, 1834-1900, RG92, NA; Smith to Hoffman, July 23, 1863, Box 3, Letters Received, Dept of NC/VA, E3238, Records of U.S. Army Continental Commands, 1821-1920, RG393, NA; testimony of Henry Covert, n.d., Craven County Claim No. 10,416, Southern Claims Commission Records, NA; Hanks to wife, September 8, 1864, Clarissa Phelps Hanks Papers, ECU.

215. Slaght to Meigs, June 23, 1863, Box 9, Water Transportation 1834-1900, RG92, NA. See also Hoffman to Davenport, July 21, 1863, *ORN,* I, 9, 101; Gibson and Gibson, comps., *Dictionary of Transports and Combatant Vessels Steam and Sail Employed by the Union Army, 1861-1868,* 39; Havenhurt to Meigs, June 10, 1865, Box 47, Water Transportation, 1834-1900, RG92, NA; Report of Biggs, December 1863, Box 21, Water Transportation, 1834-1900, RG92, NA.

216. *New Bern Daily Times,* May 10, 1865.

Chapter 7

The Expansion Period, 1865–1892

The political and economic collapse of the Confederate States of America in the spring of 1865 proved devastating. Banks and insurance companies were bankrupted, industry was nearly nonexistent, plantations burned out, fields were in weeds and most soils were exhausted. The main source of labor disappeared as Blacks gained their freedom and many became refugees. The maritime industries were totally disrupted, and the southern railroad system equally affected. Commercial fishing, oceanic and inland shipping, and shipbuilding were all severely distressed.

Simultaneously, there was a migration westward in the south as well as the north. Short line railroads were being consolidated throughout the nation, and industries were moving westward as well. In North Carolina the piedmont crescent dominated the manufacturing scene while on the coast shipyards became fewer but larger and more complex. This was a period of expansion, but also the beginning of industrial modernization.

A Time for Recovery

North Carolina's economy, like that of other southern states, was ravaged. Poverty was rampant from the mountains to the coast. Much of the fighting, destruction, and occupation had taken place on the coastal plain which was overwhelmingly agrarian, and now, essentially unattended.[1] To some degree, Union occupation and control sustained maritime activities in port communities such as New Bern, Plymouth, Elizabeth City, and Beaufort. However, federal authorities banned local maritime trade except for those few who remained loyal to the Union.[2] Domestic watercraft had been either destroyed or seized by military forces. By 1865, there were few vessels not in possession of Union forces. Few steamboats were in operation; those not destroyed were laid up because machinery had broken down and parts were not available.[3]

During the war, coastal prosperity had been heavily dependent on blockade running, with Wilmington being the most important blockade running port. The city remained in Confederate control until soon after the fall of Fort Fisher in January 1865. However, as a few steamboats were still privately owned, even the subsequent seizure of the port by federal troops did little to disrupt river trade in the Cape Fear region.[4] Federal occupation in eastern North Carolina did not end with the war; nevertheless, there was a steady increase of inland and oceanic trade. Wilmington and New Bern experienced significant economic growth.[5]

In 1866 the *Wilmington Dispatch* noted the river business was so good that there were not enough vessels to meet demand. A major reason for the resurgence was the revival of the naval stores trade. The cotton trade also became increasingly important and much of the cargo was transported on sailing ships.[6] New wharves and warehouses were constructed at the port. Maritime trade grew despite a lack of consistent economic stability.[7] Nevertheless, prosperity was fleeting. In 1885 the deputy collector of customs position in the port was eliminated because business had decreased.[8] The commercial recovery of the Cape Fear River basin was hampered primarily due to a scarcity of vessels.

From 1871 to 1873, low agricultural commodity prices and an insurance business slump slowed national postwar recovery. The resulting depression adversely affected North Carolina's economy including that based on maritime activities. A number of steamboat companies went out of business.[9]

Water transportation remained vital to the region's economy. Considerable emphasis was placed on internal improvements for navigation in state waters. Navigable rivers were badly obstructed by sunken vessels, pilings, and other objects. In 1865, a navigation company began the task of clearing thirty sunken vessels from the Cape Fear River. In the late sixties, river improvements were carried out by private firms.[10] Other than the Cape Fear River and its tributaries, few river improvements took place until the 1870s. In 1871, the U.S. Army Corps of Engineers began a program to clear obstructions in navigable waters in the former Confederate states. Systematic surveys were made of all the waterways that were considered potentially navigable. In addition to the Cape Fear River, attention was focused on the Neuse, Tar, and Pamlico Rivers, and the Roanoke River basin, the largest on the eastern seaboard. The Corps of Engineers also dredged navigable channels in state harbors and inlets. From 1872, Congressional representatives from the coastal region were constantly lobbied to provide support for this work.[11] Over ensuing decades, the Corps of Engineers expended considerable time and money on clearing obstructions, and on other projects to improve riverine navigation in North Carolina. Often an annual task, and one with limited success, this ongoing effort was a major factor in sustaining the state's maritime industries. Work on minor waterways such as the New River and Contentnea Creek, a tributary of the Neuse River and important to New Bern, was problematic, and depended on funding which was often inadequate (Figure 1). The Corps also had to address problems with bridges and even fishing nets placed in navigable waters. The extent of traffic depended, to a great degree, on the success of these improvements.[12]

The Dismal Swamp and the Albemarle and Chesapeake Canals were crucial to the revival of the state's maritime commerce. The Albemarle and Chesapeake (A&C), on the other hand, was important since it could accommodate vessels of up to 400 tons including side wheel steamers and those with screws. The Dismal Swamp Canal was narrow and shallow. Only small vessels could pass through, and they were usually towed. Periodically, the canal was dredged allowing small steamers to pass. Although traffic was nothing like that on

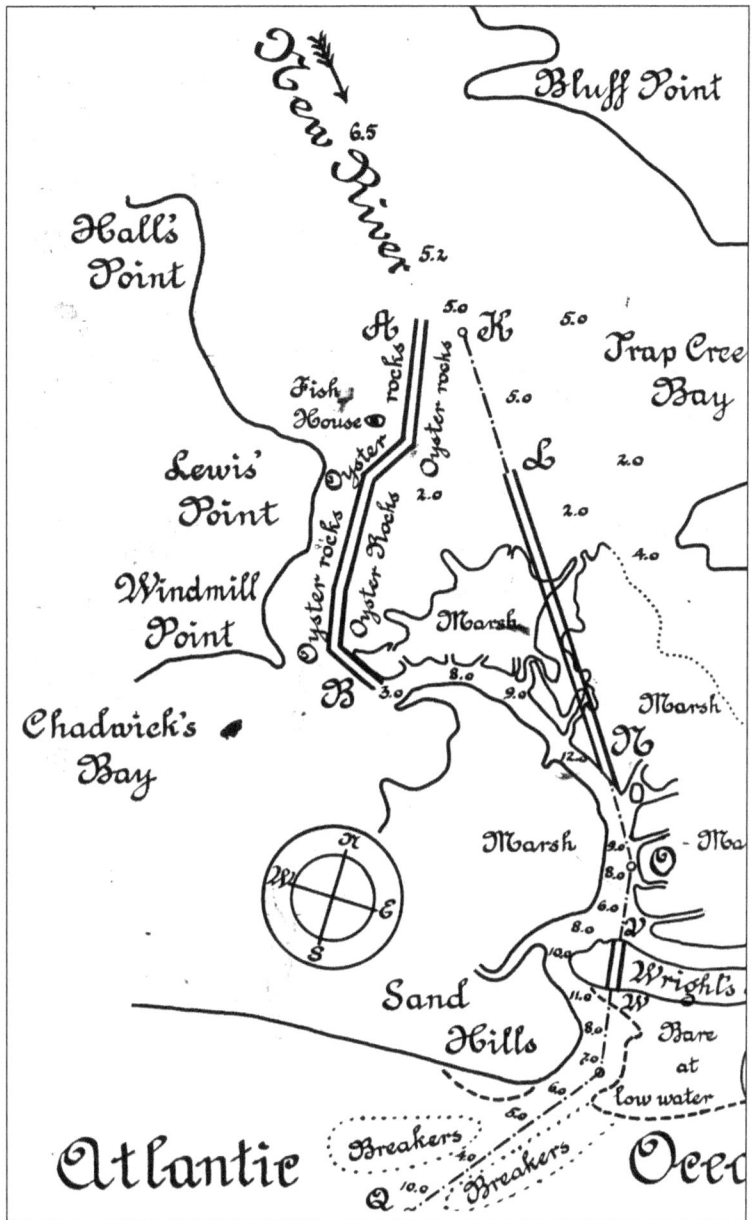

FIGURE 7-1 Map showing the improvements for the New River and New River Inlet is representative of the period. Dredging a navigational channel through the inlet bars was essential for small ports to survive. *Source:* Cartographic Branch, National Archives.

the A&C, 1,195 vessels, including rafts, travelled through the Dismal Swamp Canal in 1883.[13] Unlike the Dismal Swamp Canal, however, there were no tow paths as all the vessels utilizing the A&C Canal had to be self-propelled. During the war, few vessels other than those owned by the federal government navigated the canal. At war's end, the canal again opened to private business, but only about a dozen craft "of all classes" were available.[14] In 1866, there was a slow but steady increase in the number of vessels utilizing the waterway. In the following year, forty-one steamers as well as several hundred barges and other craft used the canal.

Most steamer traffic using the A&C Canal was from the Roanoke River and Albemarle Sound areas. In 1869, Norfolk businessmen contracted for three new iron vessels to lure traffic that, in the past, went from Washington, North Carolina and New Bern to New York City. Nearly all the steamers at that time were built and owned outside the state. A number of small shipping companies began to employ the canal to link up with local steamboats in North Carolina waters. Of these, the Old Dominion Steamship Company was the most important, continuing to serve the state well into the twentieth century. The company was organized in 1867, but did not engage in trade with North Carolina until 1872.[15] Sailing vessels, which had previously followed the coastal route through Ocracoke and Hatteras inlets, began to use the A&C Canal. Eventually, the railroad reduced the importance of canals and their associated ports.

In 1866, an article in the *Fayetteville News* reported that "the construction of Railroads has totally changed the conveying trade—the Cape Fear still rolls on, but she has lost the power to control; and the Iron horse is the master of the situation."[16] Before the advent of paved roads and highways, the railroad affected the state's maritime industries more than any other single factor. Before the war, there was only the Atlantic and North Carolina Railroad which linked up with the Wilmington and Weldon Railroad at Goldsboro. In decades after the war, railroad construction in eastern North Carolina was slow. The Norfolk and Southern reached Elizabeth City in 1880 and extended to Edenton the following year.[17] It did not reach Washington, NC until the first decade of the twentieth century. The construction of railroads connecting the coast to the piedmont was equally slow. Communities throughout the area appealed for rail links, stressing that their economic survival depended on such transportation.[18]

Throughout much of this period, river commerce, particularly that carried by steamboats, was important to the railroad's success in the eastern section of the state. This was the case on the Cape Fear and Neuse Rivers before 1865, and became all the more so as railroads expanded. Railroads depended on rivercraft to provide links with coastal regions and areas where rail lines were not available: "All the railroads projected or built...since the war have been located with reference to steamboat connections; and those counties not crossed by some line or railroad have all a steamboat service in operation, with the single exception of Onslow."[19] This marriage of convenience would continue into the twentieth century in the coastal areas and isolated communities that remained without rail service.

In the 1880s, the Norfolk and Southern went into the water transportation business. It purchased a small railroad and lumber company which owned and operated a number of vessels. The steamers of the Old Dominion Steamship Company and the Albemarle Steam Navigation Company were later added to its fleet. As late as 1890, the Norfolk and Southern had a contract with the Wilmington Steamboat Company of Delaware to operate freight steamboats on the Cape Fear River. The companies also contracted for the construction of transfer barges and other vessels.[20]

Competition was inevitable. Railroads had a number of advantages over water transportation that were apparent even to those communities with regular river trade. Railroads were better able to keep to a schedule than water transport. Usually, they were not affected by seasons, inclement weather, or low water. Trains could haul larger loads at less cost than steamboats and they were much faster, a definite advantage in the shipment of perishable produce and seafood. A roundtrip between Norfolk and New Bern by water usually took three days and two nights; by rail, it took approximately eight hours.[21]

Steamboat lines tried to be competitive and often cut rates. During low water, they would run small launches and even road vehicles to link up with steamboats. Fayetteville benefited from the Cape Fear River, but "railroads ... developed more wealth and resources and energies in 10 years than inland water transportation ever did in 100." Kinston repeatedly campaigned for a railroad rather than for navigational improvements on the Neuse River. Comparing the advantages of competing steamboat companies, a Murfreesboro editor candidly admitted it would recommend the one that provided the town with a rail connection: "...Steamboats don't bring trade like railroads...."[22]

As railroads reached a river community, water transportation declined or ceased. In 1883, the Corp of Engineers reported it was no longer economical to improve Edenton harbor as the arrival of the Norfolk and Southern Railroad "at this point changing entirely the conditions of travel of this place. The produce of the back country formerly brought to Edenton for shipment by water now generally now favoring...railroads."[23] Some communities, like Lisbon in Sampson County, virtually disappeared as river commerce gave way to rails. Although competition between railroads and water transport, particularly steamboats, was one sided, economic collapse of the latter did not occur until the twentieth century. By then, cotton and bulk agricultural goods were the only major commodities shipped by water.[24]

Ports were not always adversely affected by the presence of railroads. Some struggled more than others. Washington, Plymouth, Winton, and Elizabeth City were all partially destroyed during the war: "Certainly no town in North Carolina has undergone greater changes during the past three years than Elizabeth City...When the war ended...the little town was a wreck...square after square on the principal streets without houses or even a fence . . . In other places where houses were standing all was dilapidation and decay...bridges had been burnt...no business to any considerable extent was done for no one had money; vessels were seldom seen in the harbor."[25] As late as 1873, it was reported that, in Washington, "[m]oney was scarce before, and is more so now."[26] However, trade in Washington and up the Tar River saw considerable improvement in the late 1870s as a result of the work by engineers on the river. Through the Old Dominion as well as the Clyde Lines, trade also resumed with Norfolk and other eastern communities. Washington maintained a significant trade with the West Indies primarily by sail and local merchants owned six large sailing vessels that traded regularly with the Indies.[27]

Maritime trade in Beaufort, Morehead City, and environs was depressed not because of wartime destruction, but because federal occupation ended. A Union veteran returning to Beaufort observed: ". . . When we were stationed here. . . the harbor was usually well filled with vessels. . . to-day scarcely a sail is seen and little canoes and oyster boats glide about where the terrible 'kings of the sea' lay at anchor. . . ."[28] In 1866, a local resident wrote Governor Jonathan Worth that steamer traffic between Morehead City and New York had stopped. Ocean shipping virtually disappeared.[29] Beaufort and Morehead City blamed their lack of maritime trade on New Bern which monopolized the area's shipping. Even the resumption of rail traffic did little to alleviate the situation as most of the river business went to New Bern.

By 1870, the state's oceanic trade was nearly back to its prewar level. During that year, an average of two vessels a day were moving between some North Carolina port and New York City.[30] Ocean trade with Baltimore, Philadelphia, and New York continued to be important, but declined overall. New England ports, the West Indies, and Norfolk remained the state's most important out-of-state entrepôts.

Norfolk had strong economic ties with North Carolina. Norfolk newspapers mentioned periodic visits by the city's businessmen and journalists to various North Carolina ports. In early May 1870, the *Norfolk Journal* noted that twelve schooners arrived from North Carolina.[31]

However, the port's trade relationship with the state was not without critics. An Elizabeth City editor noted: "Norfolk has always injured the Eastern North Carolina merchants by sending out peddlers to undercut local businessmen...."[32]

Ocean shipping was important but domestic river trade was crucial to North Carolina's ports. Except for the Cape Fear River basin, this trade revived slowly. Each river system had inland ports on the major rivers and tributaries. For example, the Cape Fear River meandered far into the hinterland and was navigable as far north as Averasboro in Harnett County. In 1872 eighty rafts of timber as well as flats carrying naval stores were floated down the river to Wilmington.[33] The Northeast Cape Fear, the Black River, and others flowed into the Cape Fear River, and like the upper Cape Fear River, were navigable at least part of the year. Generally, only flats and other small craft used these rivers before the Civil War. However, in 1870, the first steamboat was put into operation on the Black River. By the mid-1870s, seven steamboats were in service. In addition, steamboat landings were established at Clear Run and Lisbon, and at Point Caswell in Pender County.[34]

Fayetteville continued to be the most important inland port in the Cape Fear River basin. Located 113 miles above Wilmington, the small city was considered the head of navigation on the Cape Fear River.[35] Fayetteville, like many other eastern North Carolina communities, was partially destroyed during the war. However, its river trade recovered quickly. By 1873, eight steamboats were running regularly on the river between Fayetteville and Wilmington and over the next decade and a half averaged more than a half-dozen at any one time.[36] This river trade continued into the twentieth century.

Without Wilmington, the Cape Fear River basin's maritime trade would have been greatly reduced. The port was rightly considered the "great commercial city of North Carolina" in the postwar years. Its ocean and river trade remained vigorous throughout the later decades of the nineteenth century. In 1871, 513 vessels engaged in Atlantic and foreign trade were registered at the port. In 1883, 673 vessels with an aggregate registered tonnage of 212,047 utilized the port.[37]

Smithville, renamed Southport in 1887, was the only deepwater port on the Cape Fear River. Editorials and letters to the editor in the *Southport Leader* expressed frustration at the number of vessels anchored off the port waiting tide or pilot before ascending the estuary to Wilmington and bemoaned the fact these vessels were not utilizing its port facilities. Despite a variety of schemes over the years to attract ocean commerce, "all efforts proved abortive [and] Southport remained a village in the shadow of the busy port of Wilmington...." Nonetheless, the small port's livelihood was tied to maritime industry.[38] The majority of trade with other Brunswick County communities also took their trade to Wilmington and steamboats made regular trips between Southport and Wilmington. In 1888, Lockwood Folly, on the river that bears that name, was served by one steamboat; two years later, the number had increased to three with one under construction. These vessels provided the only outlet for its products, usually fish.

In 1890, the schooner *William* was destroyed by fire. The local newspaper said, "No greater calamity could have befallen ... the ... county, as it was [the]... chief means of communication with the outside world."[39]

Communities along the New River in Onslow County also utilized Wilmington for their trade. Three small communities, Marines, Sneads Ferry, and Jacksonville, all on the New River estuary were connected by sail, and later by steam vessels to Wilmington and Morehead City. However, maritime activities were limited, consisting primarily of fishing, oystering, and some shipping of cotton, farm produce, lumber, and naval stores. In the mid-1880s, the Corps of Engineers made some improvements on the river but, by the end of the century, ceased to work on the New River because of negligible "ocean going commerce."[40]

Swansboro, on the White Oak River estuary, was by far the most important maritime community in Onslow County. Nonetheless, this small port of only a few hundred inhabitants struggled in the postwar years. Bogue Inlet, which gave Swansboro direct access to the ocean, often shifted and silted over until dredged by the Corps of Engineers. Oceanic shipping declined including the West India trade which had been lucrative in the pre-Civil War years. In 1894, a Swansboro lumber company owner wrote that the town was "dead because of the closure of the bar. . . ."[41] Nevertheless, Swansboro continued to be an important production center for naval stores until the end of the nineteenth century. In the colonial period, Swansboro was the only port between Smithville and Beaufort. Nearby forest resources, especially live oak and cedar, supported shipbuilding, but production of naval stores dominated the local economy. A shoaling inlet inhibited the growth of Swansboro. Bitter disappointment among local distillers, fishermen, and others, arose when the railroad between Wilmington and New Bern crossed the White Oak River at Maysville, almost fifteen miles upstream from the port.[42]

In the 1880s, steamboats began to navigate the White Oak River. It was claimed that the river was navigable a few miles into Jones County, but even small vessels rarely went as far as Maysville.[43] Much of Swansboro's maritime trade was with New Bern, primarily by sailing craft, but subsequently by steamers.

New Bern was the second most important port in North Carolina behind Wilmington. The Neuse River town had long been a prominent economic center, at one time leading the state in maritime shipping. During most of the war, New Bern's economy was sustained by Union occupation forces. Shipping was controlled by federal authorities. However, with the withdrawal of Union troops in the spring of 1865, maritime traffic began to decline. The local newspaper appealed to federal authorities to re-open the port to trade. This was done a few months later and, by 1866, oceanic trade was brisk, but river trade remained sluggish due to navigational obstructions in the Neuse River. In the mid-1870s only one small steamboat operated on the Neuse and Trent Rivers. However, river trade improved significantly in the late seventies as a result of improvements on the Neuse and Trent Rivers and their tributaries. Improvements on Contentnea Creek led to steamboat traffic increasing from one small boat in 1877 to several by 1883. At Snow Hill, located on Contentnea Creek, "natives were aroused and astounded by the terrific streaming of four steamers lying in our would be famous creek...."[44] Next to Wilmington, New Bern led the state in coastal trade into the twentieth century. The port was the leader in sailing ship tonnage throughout most of this period.[45]

By 1888, there were four steamers and four different steamboat lines with agents in New Bern. During the seventies and eighties, the Clyde Line ran weekly steamers from New Bern to Baltimore, Philadelphia, New York and occasionally, a New England port. The Old Dominion Line also ran steamers to northern ports, usually through the A&C Canal. In 1888, it was written that "with nine steamers per week to Philadelphia, Baltimore, Norfolk and Elizabeth City, and eight steamboats on the Neuse and Trent rivers, [the port]

. . . should be the Norfolk of North Carolina."[46] However, in the 1890s, this shipping disappeared. The head of the Clyde Line's traffic department in 1893 informed the Corps of Engineers that no ships were running between New York and New Bern. The company's vessels were ". . . doing mainly a local business as between Norfolk and Carolina Sound points."[47] Vessels from New Bern followed a route through the sounds and the A&C Canal to Norfolk.

New Bern's inland water trade was considerable, surpassing that of the Atlantic and North Carolina Railroad, which linked Morehead City with Goldsboro through Kinston and New Bern. Due to navigational problems, most of the traffic above Kinston was by pole boats.[48] Efforts were made to extend steamboat service to Goldsboro in 1889, and again ten years later, but with no success. Most of the time, the river beyond Kinston was simply too shallow to make steamer trade profitable. Settlements on the Trent River were equally handicapped, although in the 1890s one steamboat occasionally made runs between Trenton and New Bern. In the 1880s, vessels, including steamboats, ventured up Swift Creek to Vanceboro, and up Contentnea Creek to Hookerton, Snow Hill, and Grifton.[49] At best, steamboat traffic upstream from New Bern was sporadic.

New Bern also profited from trade with the lower Neuse River estuary, particularly with Hyde, Dare, Pamlico, and Carteret Counties. The port was an important market for fishermen and oystermen. Even though it was fifty-seven miles farther, the majority of Core Sound fishing and oystering vessels utilized New Bern because it was a better market than Beaufort.[50] Sailing vessels and, later, steamboats linked the Pamlico County communities with New Bern. Sailing vessels continued to dominate Hyde County traffic until the twentieth century.[51] The lower Neuse River trade significantly surpassed that above New Bern during the first decade of the twentieth century.

Carteret County had two seaports, Morehead City and Beaufort. Both could accommodate ocean-going vessels. Neither port realized its full potential, as they negated each other being only two miles apart. Beaufort was the oldest with a relatively deep harbor. Morehead City was established in the 1850s as a terminus for the Atlantic and North Carolina Railroad. Steamers docked at Morehead City; cargo was offloaded and carried inland by train. Occasionally, steamers also used Beaufort, but with no rail connection, only local produce was shipped. Between 1867 and 1880, only a hundred ships, most of which were sailing vessels engaging in coastal trade, entered Beaufort. In the 1880s, the number of vessels utilizing Beaufort began to decline. In 1885, the custom district was eliminated as "the business of the port has fallen off. . . materially."[52] Usually, residents along Core and Pamlico Sounds, and the North River carried their produce to Beaufort in small vessels with drafts under five feet.[53]

Washington, at the head of navigation where the Tar River widens to form the Pamlico River estuary, retained its customhouse after the war and disputed New Bern's claim as the second most important port in the state.[54] As before the war, oceanic trade was primarily with the West Indies and was carried on by small sailing vessels. Coastal trade also depended upon small sailing ships although in 1872, the Corp of Engineers reported that a weekly steamer linked the town with Norfolk. By the mid-1880s, the number of steamers utilizing the Pamlico River port increased to ten. In December 1894, a record seventeen steamers in one day were tied up at Washington docks.[55] Exports included cotton and other agricultural products, particularly lumber. Oysters and fish were also shipped from Washington. Imports included manufactured goods and fertilizer. In 1894 the port was "redolent with the odor of guano and oyster shells."[56]

The trade upstream of Washington was important as it supplied the largely agricultural counties of Pitt, Edgecombe, and Beaufort. For several years after the war, only two steamboats plied the Tar River, one venturing as far as Tarboro. By 1890, twelve steamboats worked the river trade, several going as far as Tarboro. Twenty miles upstream from Washington, Greenville developed a vigorous maritime trade, "The wharf at Greenville was assuming almost seaport-like appearance, comparatively speaking, last week.... There were four steamers, two large schooners, three oyster boats and three flats...."[57] Due to the shallow waters of the Tar River above Greenville, steamboat traffic to Tarboro was limited to periods of high water until A. W. Styron, a Washington businessman and shipbuilder, introduced extremely shallow draft boats on the upper Tar River. Occasionally flats reached Rocky Mount and the Atlantic Coast Line Railroad.[58] Most rivers in northeastern North Carolina supported navigation. As in the past, maritime activities in the area were extensive, and included shipping, boat building, and fishing.

Albemarle Sound continued to be the most important fishing grounds in North Carolina and one of the most important in the nation.[59] Many small communities along the sound and its tributaries heavily relied on these waterways. When water transportation was curtailed or discontinued, it resulted in hardship. In 1877, the only steamboat to Murfreesboro on the Meherrin River was withdrawn, and there was no "boat line to Norfolk or to the railroad...." Two years later, the steamer carrying the mail to various places along the Chowan River and its tributaries was seized by a federal marshal and business was almost paralyzed. Of course, this also affected all the communities and landings along the inland waterways, especially those without railroads.[60]

Plymouth was dependent upon the Roanoke River, and to a lesser extent on the Chowan River, for its economic survival. The Roanoke River was navigable upstream from Halifax. However, because of the Wilmington and Weldon Railroad, little maritime traffic went beyond Scotland Neck. Plymouth was among the most devastated North Carolina communities during the war, but recovery was rapid. By 1869, a steamer was making bi-weekly, later increased to tri-weekly, trips to a railhead at Franklin, Virginia. The schedule continued until the Norfolk and Southern Railroad reached Edenton. The Corps of Engineers reported nearly a hundred vessels clearing Plymouth in 1869. A Norfolk paper mentioned "huge sailing craft . . . moored continually to the [Plymouth] wharves." Traffic on the Roanoke was extensive. In 1877, eleven steamboats and steam tugs operated on the river.[61] In 1867, Congress passed an act reorganizing the custom districts in North Carolina. Those in Plymouth and the district of Camden were discontinued and the district of Albemarle was created at Elizabeth City. Despite a temporary decline in the 1890s caused by the Panic of 1893, subsequent river traffic continued into the twentieth century.

Historically, Edenton, on Albemarle Sound near the confluence with the Chowan River, was the most important port in northeastern North Carolina. After the Civil War, the port remained a regional shipping center for much of the Albemarle region. In 1881, the completion of the Norfolk and Southern Railroad spur to Edenton was a major factor in its economic prosperity. Steamers linked the Roanoke and Chowan River systems with the railroad. Perishable products, especially fish, were carried by fast freight trains to eastern cities. However, coastal steamers and small sailing vessels continued to serve the region. An 1891 newspaper noted that Edenton Bay was crowded with schooners "...waiting to load with watermelons for the northern cities."[62] The proximity of the Dismal Swamp and Chesapeake and Albemarle Canals to Elizabeth City led to the emergence of the Pasquotank River port as the preeminent shipping center.

Elizabeth City's economy depended on the canals. The port had extensive wharves on a mile-long waterfront.[63] Some commerce originated there, but most of it was transitory. The city was badly hurt by the war and economic recovery was slow. In 1871, prosperity still had not returned and the port's documented tonnage remained lower than that reported by other North Carolina customhouse districts throughout the period.

Cut off from the mainland and somewhat isolated, residents of the Outer Banks subsisted on account of husbandry, fishing, and other maritime subsistence activities. Federal occupation of Ocracoke, Hatteras, and Roanoke Islands brought change and, following the war, steamboat service reached Roanoke Island stimulating trade and tourism.

There are no statistics documenting the importance of maritime industries in the state between 1865 and 1893. As the state recovered from the war and the economic upheaval that followed, maritime-based commerce continued to mature. Albemarle fisheries reemerged. The menhaden fishery and oyster canneries were established. A sizeable northeast market for the region's seafood developed. Maritime trade, in and out of state, expanded. Water-related recreation and resorts became popular. Ship and boatbuilding increased.

Shipbuilding, Shipyards and Shipwrights

The state's maritime industries depended on the availability of vessels, from steamers to flats. An undetermined number of vessels were destroyed or seriously damaged during the war. As a result of wartime confiscation and seizure, the majority of watercraft was in northern hands, military and private. Few were returned to previous owners. New construction was needed. However, merchants and other potential customers lacked the finances to build or even repair vessels.

Unfortunately, many of the established shipyards and marine railways were destroyed or badly damaged. Benjamin Beery burned his yard on Eagle Island to prevent its use by federal forces. The Martin Marine Railway in Elizabeth City was dismantled and dumped in the river by retreating Confederates. The John Myers and Joseph Farrow yard and marine railway in Washington were also destroyed. Some shipbuilding facilities remained in working order throughout the war primarily because they were commandeered by Union forces. Two in New Bern, one in Washington, and possibly one in Plymouth were seized and used.

An undetermined number of builders and others associated with the ship and boat building trade failed to return to their prewar occupation. Some were casualties of the war. T. L. Skinner, who owned two shipyards in Edenton and was a major in the Confederate Army, was killed in 1862. Some simply disappeared, such as Jesse Herrington of Plymouth. Others lacked the necessary capital. Overall, the shipbuilding business was depressed for several years. After serving as a quartermaster in the Confederate Army, John Myers returned to Washington and, in the summer of 1865, advertised that his marine railways were ready for business. However, his company was out of business by 1870. Ulysses Ritch owned a shipyard in Washington before the war, partnered with Farrow during the early months of the war, and died in 1866. That same year, shipbuilder Timothy Hunter re-opened his yard in Elizabeth City but, two years later, declared bankruptcy. Hunter built two small vessels, one on speculation, and repaired several others. On more than one occasion, he had to go to court to obtain payment for the repairs.[64]

Those shipyard centers responsible for much of the construction in previous years produced very few vessels after the war. Between 1865 and 1870, Wilmington's two yards built three; Washington's two yards built two; Elizabeth City's one shipbuilding facility built four; and Thomas Howard's yard in New Bern launched nine. None of these facilities could remain economically viable constructing only one or two vessels a year.

Shipbuilders struggled. Most of the shipwrights, including those that had worked on building Confederate warships, were required to take an oath of allegiance to the federal government. However, the Beerys, Cassideys, and Thomas Howard, applied for presidential pardons. Former Confederates owning $20,000 or more were one of fourteen classes required to do so. All of them tried to de-emphasize or even lie about their Confederate service. Benjamin Berry professed he was "not professionally engaged in the supervision of the construction of [Confederate] vessels." He insisted he was occupied in farming during the war! His brother declared he never favored secession, and basically was a sort of paymaster at the shipyard. James Cassidey did not even mention his shipyard in requesting a pardon. Thomas Howard, in his petition, stated that although he did not believe he came under the $20,000 class, he was nevertheless, concerned his "conduct in the rebellion might be misunderstood." He claimed he was forced to work on Confederate warships or face conscription into the Confederate Army. Josiah Farrow claimed he was conscripted and detailed to work on warship construction in Wilmington.[65] However, as shipbuilders, they were exempt from conscription. All were evidently pardoned without question. A pardon was crucial to resuming business. Until it was received, a shipbuilder could not buy, sell, or recover his confiscated property. There is no evidence any other North Carolina shipbuilders applied for a pardon.

Quantitative Analysis of Shipbuilding

In the last decades of the nineteenth century, ships and boats built in North Carolina fell into two general categories, those documented in the customhouses and those not documented. An examination of official records, particularly customhouse returns, suggests the state's shipwrights constructed few documented vessels during this period. However, there is abundant evidence that a sizeable number of vessels built in the state were not documented. Vessels under five tons did not have to be documented and, generally, barges and flats were not documented. For several years after the war, new construction was essentially limited to a few steamboats, small sailing vessels, and flats (Figure 2). Between 1865 and 1900, nearly 3,000 documented vessels were built in the southern states.[66]

According to various customhouse and census records, only a small number were built in North Carolina. Between 1865 and 1899, a total of 623 documented vessels were built in North Carolina. Of these, seventy-six were schooners and sloops and ninety-four were steamers. Most of the steamers were built in Wilmington, Edenton, Washington, and New Bern. This represents about 18% of

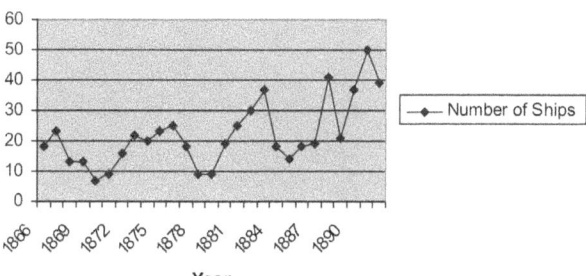

FIGURE 7-2 The number of vessels built during the Expansion Period trended upward. However, the climb was sporadic coinciding with economic panics. *Source:* Author's database.

all the vessels under fifty tons registered in the database. Three ships were over a hundred tons, the largest was the 300-ton schooner *Wave Crest*. Construction sites were scattered throughout the region, although a sizeable number of the smaller vessels were built along the sounds, probably for fishing purposes (Figure 3). Shipbuilding tended to concentrate around the Albemarle Sound specifically at Elizabeth City and Edenton (21 and 19 vessels respectively), and the Cape Lookout area specifically at Beaufort and Morehead City (55 and 18 vessels respectively). Nearby, Smyrna produced 55 vessels, Hunting Quarters 22 vessels, Core Straits 22 vessels, and Atlantic 7 vessels. On the Neuse River, 41 vessels were built at New Bern. On the Pamlico River, Washington produced 37 vessels. Along the Cape Fear River, 31 vessels were built at Wilmington; Smithville (Southport) produced 14 vessels. On the Outer Banks, 35 vessels were built at Hatteras, 11 vessels at Kinnakeet, and 7 vessels on Ocracoke. Overall, that is approximately one vessel for every 5.5 miles of tidal shoreline, or a shipbuilding site every 32 miles.

Between 1865 and 1869, thirty documented fishing vessels were constructed in Beaufort and along Core and Pamlico Sounds. Many of these vessels were constructed by builders for their own use. A few new steamers, all but two built outside the state, were added to the river fleet. In 1865, the *Bette* was built in New Bern and, two years later, the steamboat *Halcyon* was launched in Fayetteville.[67]

Despite a general depression in the 1870s, the industry slowly revived. In 1874, the Tarboro *Southerner* noted: "At one time, ship building was carried on as extensively in this State as in any other in the Union" and cited the need for vessels. A Wilmington editor echoed this view, saying, "Why is it that this business [shipbuilding] has been abandoned . . . there is the demand for good vessels and we cannot but believe this branch of mechanical art, if carried on extensively, would become one of the most important trades in the State."[68] By the mid-1880s, a modest boom in shipbuilding was taking place in the state. Business interests from the northeastern United States occasionally visited North Carolina investigating the possibility of investing in shipbuilding. In 1881, a large shipping company from Norfolk leased the Laverty marine railway in Elizabeth City to construct two steam barges. In 1882, a committee assessed New Bern for the same purpose. Another group examined a steamboat under construction in Washington and considered the possibility of building similar vessels there. Wilmington and Elizabeth City received similar attention. Thomas W. and William Fricks of Philadelphia established a shipyard in Murfreesboro to build steamboats and other vessels. However, there is no evidence the yard was ever set up. In fact, there is no evidence any these inquiries led to the establishment of shipyards.

Relatively cheap labor and an abundance of shipbuilding timber were motivating factors for these would-be ventures. It was claimed that a vessel's frame could be assembled in North Carolina for a third less than in the northeast.[69] A large number of vessels were built for northern interests at established North Carolina shipyards. S.W. Skinner's shipyard in Wilmington constructed two lighters for a company in Cuba.[70]

The census of 1880 listed eleven ship and boat building establishments in the state; five of them also repaired vessels. According to the census, only eight vessels of moderate size were built in the state, five of these in Washington. The report noted that Washington:

> could build large and good vessels. There are two yards in the town . . . but business is irregular . . . Since the war little has been done here. A schooner . . . and 3 barges were on the stocks in 1880, and a sloop of 29 tons and two steamboats were built.

Shipbuilding in New Bern, Beaufort, and Elizabeth City is mentioned, but little construction was taking place. The writer concluded, "business has been dull."[71]

Based only on documented vessels, these reports are inaccurate. Watercraft under twenty tons were rarely documented. Ships and boats were built throughout the coastal region, in ports, villages, on sound beaches, and at landings. Yards were often established to build one or more small vessels and then dismantled.[72] Fishing concerns and other maritime industries, such as towing and lightering enterprises, frequently constructed their own vessels. Lumber companies often found it more economical to establish their own shipbuilding facility.[73]

There was significant growth in the industry in the 1880s. The 1890 census listed the state as having sixteen shipyards, a third more than in 1880. In 1890, forty-six fishing boats, thirteen pleasure craft, nine barges, three steamboats, one sail boat, and three "ships" were built for a total of seventy-five vessels, and 177 vessels of all types were repaired.[74] In sum, data indicates shipbuilding resumed slowly after the war and was characterized by

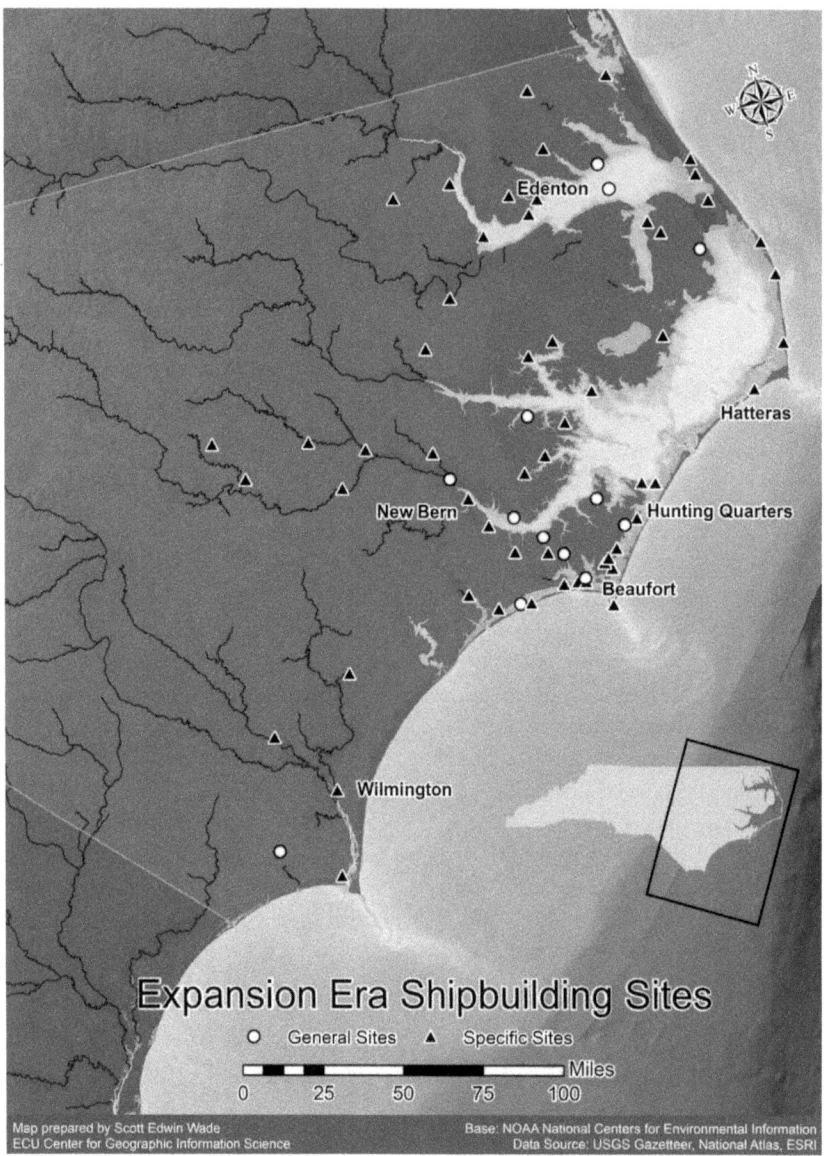

FIGURE 7-3 The spatial distribution of shipbuilding sites shows a wide spread across the coastal area. Some clustering can be noted in and around Beaufort and The Straits. *Source:* Author's database.

erratic growth; over a quarter century, 623 ships were built at 119 shipbuilding sites.

In general, the characteristics of the vessels changed very little. Shoaling, inlet migration, hurricanes, northeasters, flooding streams, droughts producing low streamflow, tides and currents influenced vessel design and construction. Vessel width decreased slightly but remained approximately the same (Figure 4). Desired capacity and maneuverability and canal dimensions also influenced hull design.

Vessel depth relates to its draft, the distance between the water line and the keel, and is largely dependent on the locale (Figure 5). North Carolina's shoaling waters at inlets, in sounds, and the shallow water of the streams and estuaries require a minimum vessel draft, and the depth did decrease during this period. This is not surprising particularly with the proliferation of the steamboat, some of which had a draft measured in inches rather than feet.

Although there was some fluctuation, the length of vessels remained approximately the same (Figure 6). The length of canal locks and the need to maneuver around tight bends in rivers were some of the controlling factors. In general, vessel length averaged fifty feet. However, vessel length, width (beam), and depth did not vary greatly, but there was considerable variation in vessel tonnage during this period (Figure 7). In 1866, and again in 1893, the average was 600 tons. However, from 1869

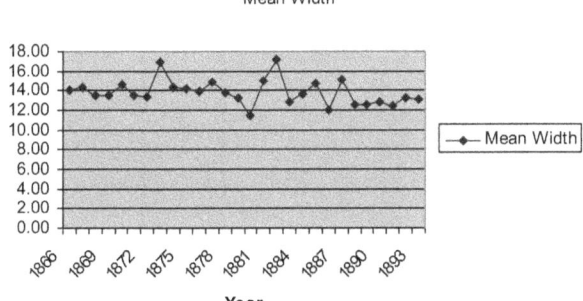

FIGURE 7-4 The mean width of vessels during the Expansion Period shows a very slight decrease. *Source:* Author's database.

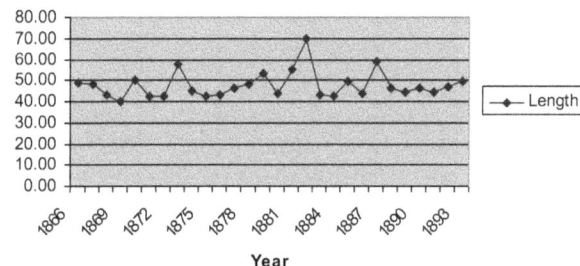

FIGURE 7-6 The mean length of vessels during the Expansion Period showed some variation, but little change with time. *Source:* Author's database.

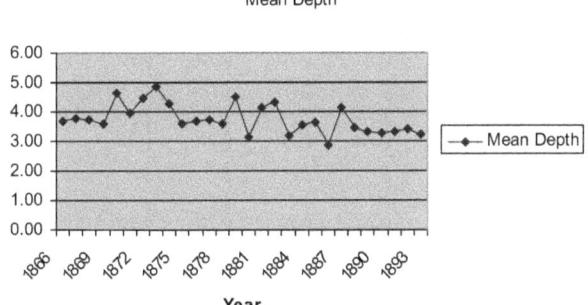

FIGURE 7-5 The mean depth of vessels during the Expansion Period shows a very slight decrease. *Source:* Author's database.

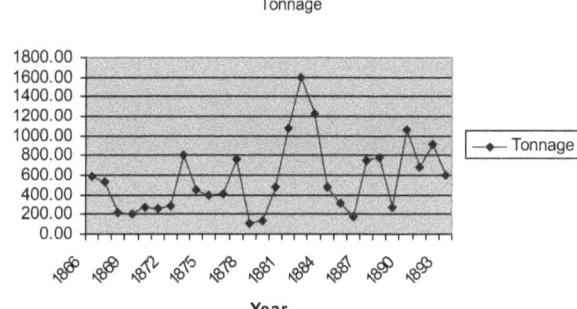

FIGURE 7-7 The tonnage of vessels during the Expansion Period shows considerable volatility, but also a slight increase. *Source:* Author's database.

through 1892, the variation between 200 and more than 1,600 tons is significant, and there is no correlation with ship dimensions or the number of ships built. In a weak economy, more tonnage was required at less cost and, in a strong economy, more ships were required which generated more tonnage. Consequently, there appears to be a correlation between tonnage and economic cycles. A further analytical category ratio is that between ship volume and length (Figure 8). Data substantiates the logical assumption that length, beam, and depth increase in proportion to increases in volume.

WILMINGTON AND THE CAPE FEAR REGION

Shipyard ownership and operation in Wilmington was kaleidoscopic in the post-Civil War years. This may have been due to the instability of the business. Census records and directories listed large established firms such as those of the Cassideys, Beerys, and S.W. Skinner, but smaller yards were not mentioned.[75] In the 1890s, many vessels were built, but few were documented by custom officials. Between 1865 and 1900, thirty-five documented vessels

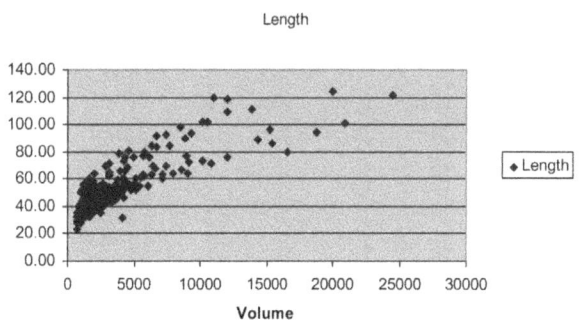

FIGURE 7-8 Scattergram showing a positive relationship between volume and length, with most vessels being less than sixty feet. *Source:* Author's database.

were constructed, but only eight were built prior to 1881.[76] Nevertheless, a large number of vessels of all types were built there. In 1884 there were two marine railways, two shipyards, and one dry dock in the port. In contrast to the prewar years, no ships were constructed for the oceanic trade. In 1888, despite the fact that all necessary resources, such as lumber and qualified labor were available, the repair of vessels occupied much of the ship and boat building activities in the city.[77]

With the destruction of the Eagle Island shipbuilding facility in 1865, the two Beery brothers worked elsewhere. Forty-six-year-old Benjamin, who had been a sea captain, shipbuilder, and farmer, recovered and rebuilt wrecked and sunken vessels. His brother, William, joined him. Benjamin also partnered with his old competitor, James Cassidey, at the latter's business on South Water Street. This association lasted approximately one year.[78] Subsequently, Cassidey leased the marine railway, but not the shipyard, to Beery for four years. Cassidy's son-in-law Robert Henning was co-lessee, but Henning was not a shipbuilder and was probably a financial partner instead. Later, Henning became a co-owner of the shipyard. William Beery, who was thirty-five in 1865, tried to rebuild the Eagle Island yard and is listed as the owner in the 1869 *Branson Directory*. Unfortunately, the yard burned again in that year.[79] The two brothers continued building and repairing vessels at different sites along the Cape Fear River. In 1871, they built a pilot boat in Smithville. They also constructed vessels on the east side of the river. In 1873, they leased the Cassidey property and converted a number of recovered wrecked vessels into lighters.[80] In 1873, Benjamin, William, and Benjamin's son Robert opened a new shipbuilding establishment in Wilmington at the foot of Castle Street. Robert operated the yard. The brothers continued their shipbuilding work in the port until the late 1880s and built a number of vessels. Benjamin also continued in the wrecking business until he died in 1892 at the age of seventy-two.[81] The Castle Street yard remained in business until 1889, with the last years under Robert's proprietorship. In that year, Northrop Sawmill purchased the property. At some time during the 1880s, William left shipbuilding for farming.

The Cassidey shipbuilding interests underwent a number of changes as well. James died in 1866. His four sons and son-in-law became co-owners. Two of his sons continued the family business at the shipyard, and when Beery's lease expired, took control of the marine railway. After breaking with Benjamin Beery, the Cassideys found another partner in Roderick G. Ross, a shipbuilder from Scotland. This affiliation lasted only a few months.[82] In 1868, Jesse Cassidey's one-fifth share in the shipyard was sold to John A. Parker, a local businessman. In 1870, Robert Henning sold his share to Francis Cassidey. Francis, a trained shipbuilder, tried to keep the struggling firm going. The Panic of 1873, and the depression that followed, hurt the Cassideys as it did the industry as a whole. They borrowed money from a local bank to stay in business. Unfortunately, in 1874 a fire destroyed most of the establishment. Although the shipyard and marine railway were rebuilt, the Cassideys could not meet their debts. Dunn & Co. reported they "were not desirable customers."[83]

Parker sued for his share in profits, and requested the firm be apportioned. The court ruled the property could not be divided equally and ordered it sold. In February 1875, the shipyard and marine railway were auctioned. The buyer was the banker who had loaned them money earlier. The Cassideys continued their shipbuilding activities under some sort of agreement with the new owner. In 1877, Ross was again in partnership with the Cassideys. From 1878 into 1879, the yard was extensively renovated, resulting in "...an almost new shipyard and marine railway." In 1880 another fire nearly destroyed the business. Francis Cassidey sold his share to Samuel W. Skinner and moved to Florida. Henry Cassidey continued working at the Skinner shipyard for several years.[84]

The Cassideys built few vessels. They specialized in repairs, claiming they had the best-equipped marine railway south of Baltimore. By the 1870s, their yard and marine railway were fairly expansive, occupying four large lots bounded on the west by the Cape Fear River and on the east by South Water Street. The Cassidey and Ross firm was responsible for one of the most unusual projects when they recovered the locomotive and tender from the Cape Fear River, and utilized their marine railway for repairs.[85] The Sanborn map of 1889, showing the Wilmington waterfront west of South Water Street, does not identify their facilities by name. The only shipyard so identified was Taylors Shipyard at the south end of South Water Street, which included a marine railway.[86]

Aside from the Beerys and the Cassideys, Samuel W. Skinner became the most prominent shipyard operator in the city. A former steamboat captain from Virginia, he entered the shipbuilding business in 1879-1880 as an associate of Thomas Evans. J. R. Blossom and Thomas Evans owned a distillery on the waterfront. In 1879, they secured a contract to construct a dry dock. Robert H. Beery was employed to supervise the project. The success of the venture persuaded Evans to build a marine railway. In 1880, along with Skinner, who identified himself as the "proprietor of a marine railway," Evans contracted with Henry C. Cassidey to build a steamer. Skinner left Evans the following year to become an associate with the Cassideys and Ross.[87]

Samuel Skinner and his son Louis were involved in a variety of successful business ventures. Their repair business was considerable. They were also accomplished "wreckers," purchasing, recovering, and rebuilding wrecked vessels up and down the coast as far as Florida. They operated vessels on the Cape Fear River, and on one occasion, received a government contract to transport a number of twelve-inch coastal guns to Fort Caswell. Like many other entrepreneurs, they were involved in maritime shipping, carpentry, marketing of steamboat machinery, and "general merchandising, including ... a paint company," as well as shipbuilding. They established a machine shop and iron foundry adjacent to their shipyard, and fabricated marine boilers, machinery, and other ironwork. In 1901, Samuel Skinner turned over management of their business enterprises to his son but continued to be involved in the firm's activities.[88]

In 1884, Skinner's marine railway was reconstructed. An 1888 account describes the rebuilt railway as being 175 feet long.[89] The 1893 Sanborn map does not show the Skinner shipyard, suggesting it was not in operation. Skinner certainly planned to continue in the business. He renewed his lease for ten years with the property owners in 1894 and agreed to rebuild the railway foundation and make other improvements.[90] The 1896 Sanborn map indicates the yard was in business. It may have been the Panic of 1893 and subsequent economic downturn that caused Skinner to close his facility temporarily.

Wilmington's inventory of shipbuilding facilities in the latter decades of the nineteenth century included several sawmills. At least one vessel was built at the A.Y. Wilson Saw & Planing Mill. The Colville and Company mill was the site of a more extensive construction operation. Between 1874 and 1879, a number of vessels were built at the latter site including a steamboat and a yacht.[91] George M. Summerall, a builder and contractor but not a shipbuilder, also had a small boat building operation adjacent to the J.W. Taylor Saw and Planing Mill property.[92] In 1879, Thomas Evans built a dry-dock used for repairing vessels. He later sold the drydock to a Haitian company. In 1889, Evans, a lawyer and businessman, erected a marine railway. He built at least one vessel there and repaired others.[93]

Periodically, local newspapers mentioned ship and boat building sites in Wilmington. These were identified as ship or boat yards but were simply locations where one or more vessels were constructed. Charles Wessell had such an establishment just north of the city limits. Charles and a brother, both natives of Germany, were in the towing and lighterage business. Occasionally, they also built vessels. In 1902, Charles sold his "river interest which included steamboats, flats, barges, pile driver and hoister and the marine railway to the Wilmington Towing and Construction Company," which was subsequently sold to the Stone Towing Company.[94]

Henry T. Lemmerman and Walter Coney were also in the lighterage business and also built several vessels. At times, newspapers identified individuals building boats in the city.

Samuel Morse built a yacht in 1869. Robert Otto constructed a sharpie for a Wrightsville Beach hotel. S. G. Northrop built a catamaran at his mill yard in 1879, and Henry H. Heide, son of the Danish vice-consul in the port, built at least one fishing boat. *Branson's Directory* of 1869 mentions Ellis and Welch as "builders of boats" but they are not mentioned elsewhere.

H.P. Bowdoin, a Wilmington builder and operator of a towing business, deserves mention. Whether or not he actually had a shipyard is not known. In the mid-1880s he designed and built several steamboats and flats for lightering on the Cape Fear and Black Rivers. Interestingly, they were unique for watercraft because they were not powered by wheels, but by propellers that could be raised or lowered depending on water depth.[95]

Wilmington's prosperity not only relied on vessels built in the city but on those that were constructed elsewhere in the Cape Fear River basin. Fayetteville was a site for steamboat construction. According to the 1850, 1860, and 1870 census, Duncan and Archibald Black, and William Driver were boatbuilders in Cumberland County. A large number of rivercraft were also built on the Black River. This waterway was shallow and prior to the war, inaccessible to all but pole boats and other small craft. Although construction on the Black River was concentrated in a few locations, principally the village of Point Caswell, there are no known shipyard sites. Most of the builders were involved in businesses other than shipbuilding.[96] D.J. Black, William Ellis, William and Luther Sherman, and R.P. Paddison were the most prominent boatbuilders on the Black River in Sampson and Pender Counties.

In 1865, Paddison, a Confederate veteran, introduced steamboats on the Black River. He has been credited with pioneering this maritime innovation on the shallow tributaries that flow into the Cape Fear River.[97] He either built or purchased the *Little Sam* in 1865, and the *John Dawson* built in 1880 at Point Caswell. In the mid-1880s, with the decline of the turpentine business, he rebuilt the *Governor Worth* and took her to the Indian River in Florida.[98]

Daniel J. Black, a steamboat captain, supervised the construction of several steamboats. Much of the actual work was probably accomplished by the Shermans. William Sherman was considered to be "an expert steamboat builder" with a "fine set of carpenters." By 1895, Black, Sherman, and several associates were credited with having built the *Lisbon I*, the *Lisbon II*, the *Frank Sessions*, and the *Hall*. Other members of the Sherman family, Luther, Stephen, David, and Ellis, were all in the steamboat building business at one time or another.[99] There were a number of other vessels built on the Black River by merchants, but their names are unknown. In nearby Pender County, Sloop Point on Topsail Sound was known for boat building. Douglas McMillan had a small shipyard there. He repaired vessels, and occasionally built fishing craft.

The 1880 manufacturing census lists two shipbuilding facilities in Brunswick County. The Enoch Daniels boatyard was located at Bald Head on Smith Island and was in business as early as 1869, when it was destroyed by fire and quickly rebuilt. Daniels primarily constructed pilot boats, a specialty of the lower Cape Fear region in prewar years. When Enoch Daniels died, his sons went into the house building business.[100] The 1870 census of Brunswick County does not list any shipbuilders. Samuel Morse owned a boatbuilding "shop" on the waterfront in Smithville (Southport) before the war and continued building boats until he died in 1877. W. R. Dosher also had a boatyard in Smithville (Southport) until he died in 1878 and William Weeks assumed operation of the establishment.[101]

Southport specialized in small craft, particularly pilot and racing boats. The 1880s witnessed a boom in sailing regattas in Southport. The 1890 *Branson Directory* lists five shipbuilders in Southport. In 1893, a local newspaper quipped: "the boat building fever continues and shows no signs of abatement. The only safe way not to catch the prevailing epidemic is to keep away from the boat houses." A few weeks later, the editor concluded the boat building boom would soon end as "there seems to be now about a boat for every family."[102] In the 1880s and 1890s, the most prominent shipbuilders were Emanuel Garcia, T.J. Piver, and A.M. Guthrie. Guthrie specialized in building racing bateaus.

There were no documented vessels built in Brunswick County until 1872. Between that date and 1900, at least twenty-five vessels were constructed. Approximately half of them were built in Southport. Lockwoods Folly and Shallotte had boatbuilders, although none are listed as such in census returns.[103]

Shipbuilding Activities in Onslow County

Onslow County was recognized for its boatbuilding, particularly fishing and coastal craft. Small sailing vessels were built on the New River from Sneads Ferry to Jacksonville. Skipjacks were introduced in the 1880s, and continued to be the largest sailing vessel constructed along the river until the early twentieth century. They were primarily coastal traders. Sharpies were also built along the river. The most important boat building sites were at Sneads Ferry and across the river at Marines. A newspaper reported that a dry dock was located at Jacksonville on the New River.[104]

Swansboro continued to be the most important shipbuilding site in Onslow County.

In contrast to the pre-Civil War years, few oceangoing vessels were built there. In 1866, three small schooners, the *May Queen, Susan,* and *Willie B.* were launched, but only five oceangoing vessels (all schooners) were constructed there over the remainder of the century. In 1877, a small shipyard was located in Swansboro. This was probably the Edward and Hall yard. No record of new construction has been found in the vessel document papers for Swansboro between 1880 and 1895. However, at least one steamboat was built there in 1895. A local correspondent observed that "ten years ago there were only 11 water craft here and now there are over 50. We mean owned and built by the citizens ... here." A month later, he noted, "very little improvements are going on except for a few fine boats being built by Mr. Van Willis and Captain E. M. Hill."[105] Hill was a Swansboro native who started building vessels shortly after the Civil War. Two of his sons would also become boat carpenters. Van Buren Willis was a ship carpenter in Carteret County before moving to Swansboro. Local legend has it that he was the first builder in the county to build boats with a lapstrake design. He continued building boats until his death in 1925.[106]

Reinhold Foster constructed at least one steamboat. He also built a number of sailing vessels at his yard on the Swansboro waterfront. Foster was a native of Germany who immigrated to the United Sates in the 1870s. He worked at shipyards in New York and New Jersey before moving to Swansboro in 1886. His first vessel, the sharpie *Edwin*, was probably launched the following year and he continued building boats until his death. As with many other North Carolina shipbuilders, he also farmed and fished. His son erected the first marine railway in Swansboro.[107]

Stella, originally named Barbers Bridge, was a small community a few miles up the White Oak River from Swansboro, and the site of a large lumber mill and shipyard where one steamer and a number of scows were built to transport lumber to Morehead City.[108] Killey E. Terry, from New Bedford, Massachusetts built the facilities in 1886. The following year he launched the steamer *Minnie B.* Ten years later, Terry's establishment went bankrupted and he returned to Massachusetts. In 1898, Terry was still trying to collect debts from the White Oak River Corporation.[109]

Boats and Fishing in Carteret County

Considerable ship and boat building went on in Carteret County in the post-Civil War years, with one observer noting, "nearly every man in Carteret County is either a half sailor or a full-fledged ship carpenter."[110] Before the war, "[d]uring the summer and fall seasons ...one might have seen as many as one-half dozen vessels varying from 60 to 300 tons burthen on the 'stocks' at the same time." However, since the war, the industry had "much declined." Many ship carpenters had abandoned the profession for other pursuits.[111] Moreover, vessels were being sent to New Bern for repairs, with this complaint noted, "We have no ways, nor dry dock in Beaufort harbor and because of this we are building up the industries in a sister town." Nonetheless, production rebounded quickly and strongly. A total of 294 documented vessels were built in Carteret County between 1865 and 1901, far surpassing all other counties. Nearly all were less than five tons, that is, small craft designed for commercial fishing. Fishing was the major source of income. In 1890, 704 boats and forty-two other vessels were engaged in fishing in the county, either transporting fish to markets or involved in the menhaden fishery. In 1889, over seventy boats from the county were engaged in hand line fishing. Oystering was equally important. New Bern newspapers often carried news of boats loaded with the shellfish arriving from down river. Introduced after the war, the menhaden industry soon became profitable. In the 1880s, Dye and Company and the Menhaden Oil and Fish Scrap Company introduced steamers to the fishery. In 1886, there were between fifteen and twenty schooners and one steamer engaged in menhaden fishing. By 1893, the number of steamers in the menhaden fleet surpassed those vessels under sail.[112]

The Carteret County population census for 1880 lists 5 boat builders, 37 ship carpenters, 5 sail makers, 1 caulker, and 376 fishermen. One of those listed, Thomas Thomas, continued to build vessels into the 1890s, and owned a fish packing business. The Pigotts, at their landing on the straits, remained the most prolific shipbuilding family in the county. David Brooks was a noted Harkers Island shipbuilder in the 1870s. The 1866-67 *Branson Directory* lists Joseph Swindell and David Brooks as "boss ship carpenters." The 1869 *Branson Directory* added C. Delamar. An 1872 newspaper identifies Edward and John W. Hill of Jarrotts Bay as "celebrated builders." The Willis brothers, especially Zephaniah, were noted boatbuilders in Williston. They built at least ten documented vessels and an undetermined number of undocumented vessels under five tons. Even Hog Island "boasted its own schooner-building facility."[113]

The 1870 census on manufacturing mentions no shipbuilding facilities in the county. However, there were a number of boat and ship yards not identified in census returns on manufacturing or in other directories. In 1872, Appleton Oaksmith became a resident of Carteret County.[114] His ownership of a shipyard, a building, and at least one vessel, confirms his standing. In 1876, he was building a "fast sailing yacht" to carry passengers to the centennial observance in Philadelphia. The vessel was never completed. In 1877 he sold her, still on the stocks, to a New York businessman. Two years later, the unfinished yacht was still on the stocks when it was totally destroyed by a hurricane. In 1878, Oaksmith incorporated the Beaufort Marine Railway Company as a joint stock company. In order to keep creditors off of his back, Oaksmith frequently listed property under the name of another family member. Although the shipyard clearly belonged to him, it was listed, owned, and operated by his sister-in-law, Ellen Mason. Ellen Mason's family was also involved in general merchandise and fish packing.[115] The Sanborn maps for the area show no shipyards in the port in 1885, but identifies the A.G. Hall Shipyard on the Newport River in 1893.[116]

Shipbuilding in New Bern and on the Neuse River

After the war, the bulk of New Bern shipbuilders' work was in repairing vessels. A barge was launched in New Bern in November 1865, but no light draft steamer was available to tow it up the Neuse River. It was urged that one be built, but capital was unavailable. The first ship of any size built in the port was a 210-ton, 105-foot schooner launched in 1873. The event was considered so novel that a large crowd was summoned by the ringing of a bell, and witnessed what was described as a "genuine old fashioned launch."[117] In the immediate postwar years, New Bern had two shipyards, one owned by A.R. Dennison and another operated by Thomas Howard. In 1866, Thomas Howard restored his shipyard and the sawmill he owned in partnership with Benjamin Ellis through permission of federal authorities. Howard advertised his business in the local paper on July 31, 1866, two days after he applied for the pardon. Howard purchased lumber and other material left behind when the Union army's quartermaster abandoned the yard.[118] However, there was no new construction for more than a year. The yard only repaired vessels. Dun and Company considered the Howard and Ellis facility a "very small business." In the same year, the U.S. District Court appointed Howard to appraise vessels caught in smuggling. This provided him with capital, but not enough to survive. According to census records, no vessels were built in 1869. The 1869 tax list valued the Howard and Ellis shipbuilding operation at $4,000 and it was sold that year at public auction to pay off debts.

Amos Wade, a local businessman married to Thomas Howard's sister, purchased the shipyard and other property belonging to Howard and Ellis. The shipyard was known as Wade and Howard until 1879 when Wade died. As with Ellis, Wade was simply a business partner and left shipbuilding to Howard. New Bern saw a strong surge in ship construction in 1872, with the paper noting that a "general impulse seems to have been given to vessel building of late."[119] The Wade and Howard yard built a small schooner, and one of the owners was the son and namesake of Howard's former partner, Benjamin Ellis. In lauding this vessel, a local editor wrote, "In the olden times (we mean prior to the war), New Berne was noted for the number, size, strength and beauty of ... the vessels built at her shipyards, but since that time little has been done in that branch of business. It is true that three, or perhaps more, schooners have been rebuilt or re-modeled from hulks, but until a few days past no effort has been made to build a vessel entirely new from truck to keel." Only the Wade and Howard firm is mentioned in the 1872 *Branson Directory*.[120]

Thomas Howard was joined by his son James, also a shipwright, and continued in the shipbuilding business for a number of years. In 1878 they bought out Wade, and, in 1879, Elijah W. Ellis, who had been a silent partner for many years.[121] They owned the Trent River ferry, as well as a steam saw and gristmill. Thomas Howard also owned considerable real estate in the city. He served at least one term as mayor.[122] His brother, James Howard, worked as a master carpenter at the shipyard. The Howard Shipyard and its successor is the only were the only ones that continued to appear in the papers and directories.

The 1880 census and Hall's report on the shipbuilding industry do not mention a shipyard in New Bern. Nevertheless, Hall stated that "vessels of the largest class can be built at one yard, which, however, produces only 3 or 4 fishing and sail boats yearly." The Howard yard is the only one mentioned in 1881 and 1882 city directories. The 1882 "Grey's New Map of New Bern" shows Howard's Shipyard and marine railway on the Trent River where it joins with the Neuse River. Next to it were the Elijah Ellis wharf and warehouses, and on the other side of Ellis's property, the gristmills and fertilizer warehouses of J. A. Meadows, Thomas Howard's son-in-law.[123] In 1885, the Howard shipyard included two marine railways, the most recent one erected after Thomas Howard visited dockyards in New England. In 1891, he rebuilt part of his yard, enlarged the marine railway, and added a fully equipped machine shop.

Other yards, or potential yards, are occasionally mentioned in newspapers and directories. In 1888, a local paper mentioned a death at the John G. Sutton Shipyard on South Front Street. According to *Branson's Directory* for 1896, this was the Sutton and Perkins Shipyard.[124] There is no record of vessels built or repaired at a facility owned by Sutton and Perkins. T.G. Dixon constructed at least three vessels, including one steamboat, at the foot of Pollock Street. F.T. Gaskill constructed a steamer for the Merchants and Farmers' Steamboat Company.[125] Tilman Farrow, who resided in Hyde County, built at least one vessel somewhere along the Neuse River. J.B. Hardison of Beards Creek in Craven County did as well. Few vessels were built in New Bern in the 1890s particularly after 1893. The Blades Lumber Company located in Craven County contracted out-of-state builders to construct schooners and barges.[126]

Vessels were built elsewhere on the Neuse River, its estuary, and tributaries. One shipyard was in the village of Oriental in Pamlico County, but it lacked a marine railway. It did little or no business. A second shipyard was at Bells Ferry, known today as Grifton on Contentnea Creek, a tributary of the Neuse River. Several steamboats were built for the Moccasin River Steamboat Company in this small village and floated downstream to New Bern for installation of machinery.[127] Steamboats were also constructed at Snow Hill. Businessmen in these small communities funded vessel construction and recruited skilled labor including master carpenters. The boats would be towed or floated down the creek to New Bern to be finished.[128]

Benjamin Webb superintended the building of two steamboats, the *Snow Hill* in 1882 and the *Carolina* in 1883-84. The 1880 census lists him as a manufacturer. The *Snow Hill* was built at the confluence of the Neuse River and Contentnea Creek, and the *Carolina* was constructed at Snow Hill. Webb and his wife mortgaged their property to fund the *Snow Hill*. The vessel was later sold to the Farmers and Merchants Steamboat Company of Snow Hill, who then contracted with Webb for the *Carolina*.[129]

Vanceboro, a small community on Swift Creek, which is another tributary of the Neuse River, was also a steamboat building site. James Madison Ipock, a steamboat captain, was the principal entrepreneur in the enterprise. At least five small steamboats and a number of flats were built there. Andrew Gatlin constructed a steamboat to replace the *Carolina*, the original Swift Creek built vessel.[130]

The *Wilmington Morning Star* mentions that the Hicks Boatyard was located in Waynesboro near Goldsboro. William Roberts Hicks had at least one vessel built there for a lumber company that he managed. Others were built at White Hall, Kinston, and Goldsboro on the Neuse River. Occasionally, flats and other small craft were built close to Raleigh. They rarely returned upstream, but were sold along with their cargos at the port.[131]

Shipbuilding in Hyde County, along Pamlico Sound and the Tar River

Hyde County, along Pamlico Sound, was consistently one of the preeminent shipbuilding areas before the Civil War. However, in the postwar years, in regard to documented vessels, its industry declined significantly. Only William and Tilman Farrow are known to have continued building during this period. The 1880 census lists only one ship carpenter.[132] What precipitated this decline is unknown. The census returns indicate that a significant majority of residents were farmers.

In the 1870 census, Washington listed only one shipyard, that of Joseph Farrow in business with two employees. Farrow was a master carpenter and shipbuilder. He constructed a number of vessels at his yard before the Civil War and had two gunboats under construction when federal forces occupied the town. He regained control of his facility after the war, although it would not regain its prewar value until the mid-1890s.[133] Other prewar yards in the port town had disappeared.

Before the war, John Myers established a shipyard, John Myers and Company, which included the Pamlico marine railway. The firm operated a number of steamboats and barges on the Pamlico and Tar Rivers, and later became the local agents for the Old Dominion Steamship Company.[134] John Myers and Company dissolved because of the death of the senior partner, but in 1875 it was reopened and the firm's name changed to John Myers' Sons. Although an 1873 report states that "[t]imes are dull here" in reference to Washington, one yard was rebuilding a schooner and constructing a small sloop while a large schooner was being built down river at Bath.[135] It is impossible to determine the number of vessels built in Washington during this period. The Pamlico Customhouse District included Washington and New Bern, as well as the surrounding territory. In the mid-1870s, approximately one hundred vessels under twenty tons were enrolled or licensed in the district. These were all small vessels undoubtedly built in the area.[136] For nearly ten years after the war, no vessel of any size was built in Washington. Hall's report in 1882 stated, "Washington, North Carolina could build large and good vessels. There are two yards in the town, but business is irregular."[137]

By the mid-1880s, business had improved. Three shipyards were in operation, those of Farrow, Myers, and Adepheus Whitehurst Styron. Nowitzky's 1885 Directory called Washington "North Carolina's Shipyard." A few years later a local newspaper headlined the city as the "Shipbuilding and Fish and Oyster Metropolis of North Carolina."[138] However, the 1885 Sanborn map shows only two yards in the city, those of Farrow and Myers. Styron, a local businessman, may have had a shipbuilding facility, for he did build a number of vessels. His shipyard was probably on the property of one of his warehouses. Probably, he did not own an established shipbuilding facility but employed shipwrights as needed, and at times, may have leased or contracted with Farrow and Myers for the use of their facilities. In 1885, a large steamboat was under construction at Styron's facility. Beaufort County records from 1886 include articles of incorporation for the Home Navigation Company. The company was formed to include the building of vessels, and one of the signatories was A. W. Styron.[139]

The national economic slowdown of the 1890s affected the shipbuilding business. In early 1890, the *Washington Gazette* reported the industry was not as large as it used to be. However, in August of that year, the paper noted "Ship building is assuming big proportions in our ship yards. There are about a dozen craft at each yard, and several applications could not be accepted this week." Repairs constituted much of the work. Nonetheless, a substantial number of vessels, barges, sail, and steam, were built in the small port. Some ship captains believed Washington could provide "better and cheaper work than anywhere else in the country." Local shipbuilders were encouraged to "bring more Yankee gold down this way."[140] Styron was certainly eager to do so.

Adepheus W. Styron formed a partnership with his brother-in-law, Lawrence Clark, and established a lime factory on Castle Island in the Tar River opposite the Washington waterfront. They purchased machinery and barges and had the steamer *Edgecombe* constructed in 1877. Styron later borrowed additional funds from the Clarks and others to purchase a new boiler and lengthen the steamer. He borrowed money from the Clarks yet again to rebuild the barge, *Red Ram*, as a steamer, which he renamed *Greenville*. He promised creditors he would ship their cotton at a discount. Subsequently, Lawrence Clark left the partnership, returned to cotton farming, and sued his former partner for the money borrowed to build *Edgecombe*.[141] The 1880 census listed Styron as a captain and he was clearly involved in the shipping business. In 1882, he organized the Tar River Line, incorporated as the Tar River Transportation Company in 1883, and leased waterfront property for warehouses and a shipyard. Despite financial difficulties and lawsuits, he continued building vessels into the twentieth century. He has been characterized as a "genius . . . who revolutionized the shipping on the Tar river and to Northern cities." It was said he started out "with a blind mule and ten galleons of honey and built the steamer *Edgecombe*." However, Styron was a businessman and not a shipwright. He was able to raise the capital necessary to finance the building of steamboats, but lacked the training or expertise to design and construct them.[142]

Joseph Farrow is the only Beaufort County antebellum shipwright who continued in the trade at his own waterfront lot facility with his own equipment and tools. In 1860, his small shipyard and marine railway had an assessed tax value of $2000. In 1866, its tax value has fallen to $500. This was probably a result of destruction at the facility during the Civil War, as well as the effect of three years of inactivity and lack of maintenance. By 1883, the tax value was back up to $1200. In 1884, he rebuilt and enlarged his yard to add a new railway. In 1887, Farrow then leased a part of the shipyard property for a small sawmill. Later, a machine shop and foundry were added. Although the shipyard was partially damaged by fire in 1890, it was rebuilt. By 1896, it was at its prewar value of $2000 and continued in business into the twentieth century. Joseph Farrow remained in the shipbuilding business until his death in 1906 at the age of eighty-four.[143]

The Farrow and Myers firms continued to be the principal builders in Washington. With the death of one son in 1878, John Myers' Sons was changed to John Myers' Son, and then to Pamlico Marine Railway, a name originally used by the firm's founder. The shipbuilding firm was the creation of a mercantile family, and not that of a shipwright. The family owned and operated a number of businesses in Beaufort County, but they were engaged primarily in shipping and shipbuilding.[144] After the war, under Thomas H.B. Myers' control, the shipyard constructed a large number of vessels for railroads, the Old Dominion Steamship Company, and out-of-state clients. In 1879, the shipyard launched the first *R. L. Myers* and in 1881 built five barges for New York interests. The facility was not as extensive as Farrow's, but the labor force was usually larger. In 1894, forty ship workers were employed in addition to office staff. The firm's connection with the Old Dominion line helped Myers secure contracts to build barges for railroads. The majority of the work said to have been done was for various railroads and steamboat lines.[145] T.H.B. Myers ran the business and continued building vessels until his death in 1906.

Myers employed a master ship carpenter to superintend the construction of vessels. Daniel S. Liddon worked for the Myers for many years as "boss carpenter." He started in 1858, and continued on and off until the mid-1890s, when he had a falling out with Myers over the division of profits from a contract. In a suit he brought against Myers, Liddon insisted he was a partner of Myers, although the contract does not substantiate this. Myers claimed Liddon was paid wages as an employee. Liddon either superintended for shipyard owners such as the Myers and Styron or leased facilities to build vessels under contract. He continued working in Beaufort County until 1903, when he moved to Carteret County. Liddon also worked as master carpenter on vessels throughout the east.[146]

In 1892, the Corps of Engineers established a depot on Castle Island for the construction and repair of vessels. During its three-year existence, several vessels were built there including the seventy-two-foot sidewheel steamer *General George Thom*, and the section dredge *Albemarle*. The facility lacked a marine railway and was moved to New Bern in 1893.[147]

Shipbuilding along Albemarle Sound

Although there were few established yards, ship and boat building took place at many sites in the Albemarle Sound region. *Branson's Directory* for 1890 lists William Core and Company in Hertford County as a boatbuilding firm, but there is no record of vessels being fabricated there. Watercraft may have been constructed on the Roanoke River, but again, there is no documentation. Plymouth is something of a mystery. Vessels were built in the river port before the war. In fact, a marine railway was located there, but there is no record of ships or boats being built in the small port between 1865 and 1900.[148] Four steamboats were constructed at Windsor in Bertie County, three by the Askew brothers and their partners. Correspondence suggests they were not built at a shipyard, but on the banks of the Cashie River. At least one vessel was built in Perquimans County.[149]

A few vessels were built on the Chowan River in Hertford County. The best known was the relatively large steamer *Ark*, built in Murfreesboro, on the Meherrin River, by W. C. Worrell, a prominent local businessman. Described as a jack-of-all trades, Worrell owned a steam sawmill, an ice house, and a coach manufacturing firm. He served as mayor of Murfreesboro and was something of an inventor. There is no evidence that a shipyard was located in the town. The *Ark* was built on the site of the sawmill.[150]

Before the war, Edenton was also a shipbuilding center. In 1862, Union forces discovered one vessel on the stocks there. Between 1865 and 1901, principally in the 1880s, nineteen documented vessels were constructed in the Albemarle port. Some construction went on in Chowan County in the immediate postwar years. The majority of vessels constructed in the county, including Edenton, were barges and small steam flats. The 1870 Chowan County census lists three ship carpenters. The Skinner, Hunter, and Paine shipyards were no longer in business after the war.[151] In 1888, the Roper Lumber Company purchased the old Skinner shipyard site owned by the Norfolk and Southern Railroad. It is possible this company built some of the barges. However, in 1889 the local paper sadly noted that the sound of a mallet or the ring of a calking iron was no longer heard. It reported, "The ways have been torn up . . . the sites of these yards . . . have become the home of the toad, the amphitheatre of the operatic bullfrog, or the safe asylum of the cold and sneaky lizard." In 1890, the paper deplored the absence of a shipyard.[152] Nonetheless, fishing vessels, continued to be constructed on the Albemarle Sound and its tributaries.

Most of the shipbuilding related to the region's most important industry—fishing. Fishermen such as Peter Warren, Edward Wood, and the Capeharts (Figure 9) employed shipwrights to build their vessels. Listed as a farmer in the 1870 census, Warren is credited with introducing steam flats to replace small, oar-propelled vessels in the sound. In 1876, he purchased a fifth of an acre of land known as the "Ship yard" tract on Yeopim River near Drummond's Point on Albemarle Sound and established a ship and boat building facility there. Warren was engaged in shipbuilding prior to 1876. He built two vessels and rebuilt at least one.[153]

Before the war, Elizabeth City was one of the most important shipbuilding centers in the state. The end of the conflict spurred a modest gain for the industry and in 1869 there was building at the ship yards. Timothy Hunter attempted to reopen his yard in 1866, but declared bankruptcy three years later. James Snell worked for Hunter before and after the war. Snell, trained as an apprentice carpenter in Washington County, moved to Elizabeth City before the war and was employed as a shipwright. During the war, he was a prominent master carpenter building Confederate warships. In 1871, a marine railway was added. In 1873, Hunter contracted with A.H. Whitcomb to sell the shipyard. Whitcomb agreed to purchase the facility, but in 1878 it was sold to R. Lukins, Jr., who in turn, sold it to Snell. Snell continued in the trade until he died in 1904 at the age of seventy-nine. He was considered one of the best, if not the best, ship carpenter in the state. In addition to constructing vessels he also built a number of bridges.[154]

A second yard, known alternately as the Elisha Nash Ship Yard or the John Black and Company Ship Yard was owned by the Martin family and resumed business under the management of Joseph Lawrence. Lawrence, originally a mariner from Pennsylvania, arrived in Elizabeth City before the war. Like Snell, he was employed by Hunter as a ship carpenter. In 1869, he purchased a half interest in the Martin shipyard. Shortly thereafter, he bought the rest of the property. Lawrence remained in business for thirteen years and built a number of vessels before his death in 1882. In 1884, the facility was sold to William J. Pailin and became known as the Pailin Brothers Shipyard. The Pailins were not shipbuilders. They operated several farms, a livery stable, a fishery on Albemarle Sound, and a gristmill. They established a cannery and a cotton gin

FIGURE 7-9 Capehart's Fishery in Edenton in 1880s. Here, long seines are being hoisted on sidewheel steamers. *Source:* State Archives of North Carolina.

on their shipyard property. They even introduced the first public transportation, an omnibus, in Elizabeth City. The Pailins recovered and rebuilt the old Laverty Marine Railway which had been destroyed and thrown in the river during the war. By 1896, the yard had been purchased by S. Willey, of Maryland, and was known as the William Pailin Shipyard.[155]

The shipbuilding business remained erratic. In 1885, Elizabeth City had only one active shipyard. New construction was negligible. In 1880, only one sloop and a small steamboat were built in the port. In fact, between 1865 and 1901, only twenty-two documented vessels were constructed in the city. In 1882, Hall reported that Elizabeth City yards "are good facilities . . . for building . . . but since the war business has been dull."[156] He also mentioned that most shipyard work was in repairs. No port in the state, other than Wilmington, did as much ship repair as the Elizabeth City facilities. The city was strategically located near the two major canals that connected with Norfolk and labor costs were cheaper.

Vessels were built in other coastal counties in the northeastern part of the state. For example, boats were built in Currituck County but none were documented. In the 1870s, four were constructed in Camden County, most at South Mills; and there was at least one in 1881, and another in the 1890s.[157] Four each were built in Bertie and Hertford Counties. Three steamboats were constructed in Bertie County at Windsor; the *Kalulu* in 1870, the *Bertie* two years later, and the *Tahoma* in 1884. Wilbur and Richard Askew contracted with a shipbuilder, Lafayette Thrower, to build the *Kalulu* . He also supervised the building of *Bertie*, which was jointly financed by the Askew brothers, the owners of *Kalulu*. Windsor merchant and jeweler Charles L. Harden joined the brothers in building the new steamboat. It is thought that Will Askew supervised the building of *Tahoma*. Whether or not any of his brothers were involved in the venture is unknown. In 1891, Richard Askew fatally shot Charles Harden who was captain of the *Bertie* at that time.[158]

SHIPBUILDING ACTIVITIES ON THE OUTER BANKS AND ROANOKE ISLAND

Small boatyards, "backyard building," or cottage building were characteristic along the Outer Banks from Portsmouth Island and Ocracoke to Kinnakeet and north to Currituck. Residents of the Outer Banks built boats out of necessity; "The reality of it was they were all just making a living, just like everybody else."[159] The majority were small, undocumented vessels primarily employed in fishing. The only established yards were on Roanoke Island. A resident of Roanoke Island wrote that "of [the island's] three thousand or more inhabitants there are practically none but fishermen or boat builders."[160] The same was true all along the Outer Banks. *Branson's Directory* for 1896 listed nineteen boat builders on the Outer Banks, and eight at Manteo on Roanoke Island. The list included three Creefs. A number of Creefs were in the boatbuilding business at

FIGURE 7-10 George Washington Creef at work on a shad boat at the Creef Boatworks at Wanchese on Roanoke Island around 1890. Small boats such as these are not documented, and literally thousands were built. *Source:* Author's file.

different times. The 1900 census of Dare County listed only Benjamin and George W. Creef, Jr.. Their father, George Washington Creef, Sr., was not mentioned. William Midgett was also listed as a shipwright.

George Washington Creef, Sr., was the most prominent shipbuilder on the Outer Banks (Figure 10). He was a legendary boat builder. Born in 1829 at East Lake, a small settlement not far from the Alligator River, he was the son of a boat builder. In fact, some credit his father with the original concept for the shad boat. His father specialized in building "kunners," the dugouts that were a popular means of water transportation on the Outer Banks for centuries. Around 1861, George Washington Creef moved to Roanoke Island and worked with a brother in repairing vessels and fishing. Their yard was located on Shallowbag Bay at the north end of the island. After the Civil War, he erected a small railway, the Manteo Machine Shop and Railway, which depended on a horse to pull vessels onto the railway. After a few years, he moved to Wanchese, and it is unclear what happened to the railway. His first boat shed in Wanchese was not on the water. Launchings required the use of wagons to carry the boat from the building site to the water. Later, Creef moved his boatyard to the waterfront. He constructed a variety of vessels, but is best remembered for designing and building shad boats, also called Albemarle Sound fishing boats. He usually constructed two boats at a time and the exact number of boats he built is unknown, but at least nine have been identified. The yard's name went through several changes from Creef, to Creef and Creef, to Creef Brothers.[161] George Washington Creef Sr. died in 1917, at the age of eighty-eight. His two sons continued in the boat building business into the 1920s.

THE BUSINESS OF SHIPBUILDING

Periodically, a newspaper would question why large vessels could be overhauled and even totally rebuilt in North Carolina, but the majority of vessels built in the state were small. For example, "With so many of the most important articles of manufacture used in the construction produced in the South we can see no reason why we can't build our ships."[162] Supporters of the state's shipbuilding potential failed to recognize the gradual dominance of iron and steel in the industry, a building material not readily available in the state.

North Carolina's ship and boat building industry predominantly produced wooden vessels. To a great extent, the American shipbuilding industry was dominated by wooden ship construction until the twentieth century. The technological advantages of metal ships were well known. Delay in transition from wood to metal was principally due to abundance of timber and a lack of trained labor in metal shipbuilding.[163] Iron, and later steel, vessels were built, but tonnage was small compared to wooden vessels. A few iron steamers plied North Carolina waters in the 1870s, but only one was constructed in the state, a thirty-foot steamer built at Cassidey's shipyard in Wilmington. As early as 1860, an iron sternwheeler built in Delaware began carrying cargo and passengers between Fayetteville and Wilmington. Others followed.[164]

Material requirements for wooden vessels were the same as they had been for decades, and included wood, metal spikes, nails, and other small fittings, sails, rope, and for steamers, machinery. Sailcloth, rope, and much of the machinery were imported. Small sail-making establishments were located in most of the larger ports. S.S. Fowler Net and Twine Mills was located in Elizabeth City. This relatively large establishment included one building that was listed on a Sanborn map as being for "ship carpentry." There may have been a ropewalk in Edenton. John Riggs of Swansboro operated a unique shop that manufactured oars.[165]

Timber, the basic shipbuilding material, remained abundant in North Carolina. By the 1880s, shipbuilding timber had largely disappeared from New England. Live oak was practically nonexistent. Shipyards in Maine were importing timber from as far as away as Oregon.[166] North Carolina's forests were still immense. After the war, lumber was the state's most important export. Almost every community had at least one sawmill. In 1888, there were twenty sawmills in New Bern and its vicinity. The availability of timber and cheap labor supported the shipbuilding industry well into the twentieth century. Yellow pine was the wood most favored by North Carolina shipbuilders. It is hard, strong, and resistant to teredos or shipworms because of its high resin content. However, yellow pine was subject to rot contributing to the short lifespan of many vessels. Increasingly, pitch pine was used particularly for frames. Saltwater treated timber was occasionally used but it was expensive. The resource was not inexhaustible. In the 1860s, there was a profusion of oak and white cedar, known locally as juniper, on the sound side of the Outer Banks, but by 1890, most of it was gone. In 1888, a steamboat under construction in Wilmington was delayed for several weeks until timber could be located.[167] Builders ranged inland searching for suitable timber. Some lumber was even imported. When storms drove coastal vessels carrying lumber ashore, shipbuilders up and down the coast salvaged the wrecks for lumber to use in ship construction.[168]

North Carolina shipbuilders and shipbuilding firms included established yards, fishery operators, steamboat lines, merchants, shipping concerns, and a large, undetermined number of individual builders including entrepreneurs and steamboat captains who constructed vessels for themselves. They were all small private enterprises, locally owned and operated with the exception of government shipyards under control of the Corps of Engineers. From 1865 until 1914, North Carolina's shipbuilding firms and subsidiary establishments, such as ironworks, eked out a marginal existence. Entry into ship and boat building required surprisingly little capital but the business was risky, particularly for individuals who attempted to build on borrowed capital. The majority had limited funds and often operated on borrowed money or mortgaged property including vessels. In 1876, a Washington shipbuilder borrowed $500 for lumber and labor, and $700 from a businessman for machinery in order to build a steamer. The unfinished boat was mortgaged to pay off the latter loan. Unfortunately, when put into service hauling cotton, the vessel did not make enough profit to pay off the former debt and mortgage. Builders who did not own a permanent shipyard either leased shipbuilding facilities or built on vacant property. A few builders survived. Occasionally, they were able to pass the property on to sons and other family members. However, most went out of business after a brief period.[169]

A number of vessels were built for out-of-state interests. Railroads, steamboat companies, fishing interests, and shippers were the principal buyers. In 1890, a ship owner from Baltimore negotiated with Washington shipbuilders for an undetermined number of vessels. John Myers and Company built a 200-foot sea transfer barge for New York harbor. A number of North Carolina-built steamboats were purchased to operate on Georgia and Florida rivers.[170] North Carolina builders also sold pilot boats, whale boats, and other sailing vessels to out-of-state buyers. Potential buyers, particularly from the north, were attracted to North Carolina shipbuilders because of lower labor cost and the availability of timber.

Throughout the nineteenth century, shipyard owners and shipbuilders who were not trained in the trade employed master carpenters to superintend construction. Individuals and firms building vessels usually hired a master ship carpenter and the necessary labor.[171] Superintendents, or boss ship carpenters, were often journeymen, traveling to various shipbuilding sites as needed. Among them were Daniel Liddon of Washington, Alford Ellis and A. Thomas of Wilmington, Archibald G. Black of Fayetteville, and a number from Carteret County listed in *Branson's Directory*. Experienced shipbuilders, such as the Beerys in Wilmington and the Howards of New Bern, occasionally supervised new construction in facilities other than their own. Rarely, a builder was brought in from out of state.[172]

It is difficult to generalize about shipwrights, the number of them in the state and different counties, where they came from, how they were trained, their pay, and whether they were full-time or part-time shipbuilding employees. Often, boat and ship building was only part-time employment. Fishing, farming, house carpentry, and working as boatmen, or on commercial vessels provided employment for many individuals. In 1880, Stephen Chadwick listed himself as a ship carpenter, but his neighbors always associated him with farming.[173]

Census records only document primary employment. Smyrna, in Carteret County, was a center for construction of small fishing boats. However, census returns list a great many carpenters, but no ship carpenters. The 1890 census listed 126 ship carpenters for the state. The 1900 census listed 178, but the figure includes part-time as well as full-time shipwrights. The 1900 census for Craven County lists nine ship carpenters, but county death certificates include four ship carpenters not on the list. The state published a few statistical volumes in the 1890s on labor, including shipbuilders. Nearly all of the coastal counties had one or more shipwrights. Predictably, counties with the most shipbuilding activity had the largest workforce.[174]

The Apprenticeship System and Shipyard Employment

The apprenticeship system continued after the Civil War, but there is no evidence regarding the shipbuilding trades. The 1870 census for New Hanover County listed one apprentice, the only one listed in a postwar census. The *New Bern Weekly Journal* noted, "…the old time way of apprenticing boys to learn a trade has about played out." In 1888, the clerk of the superior court in New Hanover County wrote, "You will scarcely find an apprentice bound anywhere." State labor officials wanted to revise laws concerning the apprentice system which they admitted had changed little in a hundred years.[175] Nothing came from this. In general, for ship and boatbuilding, it was on-the-job training.

As indicated by the number of ship carpenters and other related professions, Carteret County had by far the greatest number of boat and ship builders. The 1870 census lists five boat builders for the county, thirty-seven ship carpenters, five sailmakers and one caulker. Equally revealing, 376 residents identified themselves as fishermen. Traditionally, male residents were both fishermen and boatbuilders. In subsequent census records, few were listed as ship carpenters, but more commonly as carpenters. Individuals who were listed as carpenters in census returns were identified as ship carpenters on their death certificates.[176] The same relationship between shipbuilding activity and number of shipwrights and other associated professions was noted in New Hanover County. In 1868, the Cassideys employed forty-two workers, including caulkers, to repair one large vessel. Approximately half of the work crew were caulkers, or listed as both carpenters and caulkers. The 1880 New Hanover County census lists twenty-six shipwrights.[177]

Washington and Elizabeth City had relatively large shipbuilding facilities. Beaufort County's 1870 and 1880 census lists five shipwrights in each city which corresponds to the limited amount of construction during the period. However, as the shipbuilding business improved in the 1880s and 1890s, there was a corresponding increase in the work force.

In the state's labor report for 1894, Thomas Myers mentioned that he employed forty workers for shipbuilding projects. Other Washington shipbuilders certainly employed shipwrights and other craftsmen and laborers, but the complete number is unavailable. Fifteen shipwrights were employed in Elizabeth City in 1870. By the beginning of the twentieth century, the workforce had grown to approximately a hundred.[178]

Shipyard employment was dictated by the workload. The number of men employed in building or repairing a vessel depended on its type and size. Frequently, small craft could be constructed by one man. Larger vessels were often built by a ship carpenter and members of his family. At times, some of the larger yards employed more than twenty to work on a vessel. Three shipyard owners in Elizabeth City and others in the state agreed that shipyard work was seasonal. Thomas Myers stated he had no permanent employees, "In our report a year ago …we were employing a number of carpenters in our ship-yard. …Since the early spring there has not been a craft built here… this makes the demand for labor very uncertain." Ship carpenters complained about the irregular work, saying, "Our system in the shipbuilding line is pretty well regulated; the only trouble is, we do not have regular work." A Dare County resident testified that he was a mechanic and fisherman. He said, "I spend the balance of the year building fishing boats and skiffs and repairing small schooners."[179] Clearly there was a degree of mobility in the shipbuilding labor force.

In addition to ship carpenters, blacksmiths and mechanics, riggers, block makers, and caulkers were usually employed at ship building sites. Caulking was considered a separate skill, although it was not unusual for employees to perform multiple tasks. Sailmakers were usually self-employed. Beaufort, Washington, Wilmington, Elizabeth City, and New Bern each listed one or two sailmakers.[180] In 1870, Carteret County listed five. Mechanics, needed to assemble a steamers power plant, were usually independently employed as well.

The majority of ship carpenters and associated professionals in the state were from North Carolina. However, the 1880 New Hanover County census listed one carpenter from Scotland and a ship rigger from France. Wages varied. In Wilmington, first-class ship carpenters generally received $2.00 a day, second-class $1.50 to $1.75. A definition for a first and second-class ship carpenter has not been found, but $2.00 was standard pay for the majority of skilled carpenters. Nevertheless in 1887, a fishing company which constructed its own vessels, paid ship carpenters from $1.25 to $1.75 a day. In 1890, a boat carpenter in Dare County was paid $1.50 a day. In 1894, a Carteret County shipwright claimed he received from one to five dollars a day. The pay for skilled ship carpenters in Washington was $2.00 a day, and less for unskilled workers. Black laborers were paid a dollar a day. The work day was commonly ten hours. Caulkers generally received less than carpenters, but blacksmiths and riggers received more.[181]

In prewar years, slaves constituted a substantial percentage of the workforce for ship construction. Census returns for 1870 indicate Blacks were still employed in shipyards but the number was relatively small. A large number of freedmen had become refugees during the war and many were still displaced. This probably included former shipyard workers. Over 3,000 fled to Roanoke Island during the conflict where, among other crafts, boatbuilding was encouraged. Most of them left the island after the war.[182] Some Blacks may have settled in Elizabeth City and in small towns along Albemarle Sound. The 1870 Pasquotank County census lists nineteen shipwrights and caulkers, of which nine were black. Six were listed as ship carpenters and three as caulkers. Three years after the war, Timothy Hunter, in Elizabeth City, had a six-man work crew, four of whom were black. One was a blacksmith, but the others were not identified by trade.[183] The census lists several Blacks for Craven and New Hanover Counties, but none for Beaufort County. Carteret County is something of an enigma. There were so many Blacks engaged in maritime activities in Carteret County, that one contemporary referred to them as "aquatic animal[s]."[184] Yet, few ship carpenters are identified among them.

Sutton Davis, a Black shipbuilder who owned a menhaden factory on Davis Ridge (now known as Davis Island), built two schooners and some small purse boats. It is possible he was the owner or operator of a menhaden factory that reported building a number of vessels including one steamer in 1894.[185] Sutton Davis was born in 1825. Although black, he was adopted by James Davis, a white shipwright on Harkers Island. Sutton learned the trade from his adopted father. During the Civil War, James and Sutton worked at the shipyards in Wilmington. After the war, Sutton returned to Carteret County and, according to the census of 1870 and 1880, continued in the shipbuilding trade. His brother Thomas was also listed as a ship carpenter.[186]

New Bern shipbuilders employed four black shipwrights according to the 1880 census. At least six Blacks were listed as ship carpenters in Craven County. Qbert Perkins was not only a master carpenter but was hired as the superintendent for the construction of the steamer *Trent*. At one time, he was also co-owner of a shipyard.[187] By 1900, the number of blacks had increased to seven out of ten ship carpenters and caulkers listed. The 1900 census indicates that out of more than twenty shipwrights employed by Elizabeth City builders, only four were black. One out of every two shipwrights in Camden County was black. There is no record of black carpenters in Washington. Thomas Myers made it clear that he hired only whites in his shipbuilding establishment.[188]

A few Blacks owned and operated firms involved in ship construction. Sutton Davis certainly employed skilled workers to build vessels. Four freedmen, Benjamin McGee, Edward Brown, Samuel Nelson, and Benjamin Beasley, entered the shipbuilding business in New Bern by leasing land and establishing a marine railway and shipyard.[189] In 1873, McGee built a large flat and had a second one under construction.[190] The firm went through a number of changes in partners. In 1883, it was named McGee and Nelson, Shipwrights. Magee, a former slave, was trained as a house carpenter. None of the other original partners were trained shipwrights. No information has been found to indicate the number of vessels the firm built or repaired, although it was in operation for nearly a decade.[191]

Several Blacks constructed steamboats. Parker D. Robbins, whose father was a Chowan Indian, was a native of Bertie County and fought for the Union in a United States Colored Troops cavalry unit. After the war, he entered politics serving as a member of the state legislature and a local postmaster. He also gained some recognition as the inventor of farm machinery. Around 1879, he moved to Duplin County where he became the owner and operator of a sawmill. In 1887 and 1888 he built a steamboat, *St. Peter*, in the community of Hallsville. He had the timber sawed at his mill and worked on the steamboat at "odd times." He probably hired one or more shipwrights as he was not trained in carpentry.[192]

Needham E. Kennedy built a sidewheeler, *Rough and Ready*, at Waynesboro in 1883. The 1870 census listed him as a mechanic. He may have worked on a steamboat or at an iron-works, but there is no evidence that he had any experience in boat or house carpentry. Although a former slave, he had become a property owner in Wayne County in postwar years.[193]

In Elizabeth City, Abraham Wilder, a carpenter, laid down a keel and frame, but was unable to obtain adequate funds to finish it. According to one account, "it is alleged that the title was acquired by members of the White race who completed the boat and put in into operation." In 1883, Isaac N. Brown, "an enterprising colored man who has been engaged in steamboating on the Neuse River and Contentnea Creek," decided to build a steamboat that would be "owned entirely by Colored People." He was able to raise $700 from a number of blacks in a small community outside New Bern, but there is no evidence that the vessel ever became a reality.[194]

FIGURE 7-11 The Fearing-Hyman railway and shipyard was in operation from 1870 to 1885. The *Harbinger* is on the ways. Notice the sheds and the "junk pile." *Source:* Outer Banks History Center.

SHIPBUILDING: FACILITIES, MATERIALS AND VESSELS

There were few established yards but dozens of small boat building sites.[195] Occasionally, a "shipyard" is mentioned in newspapers and county records, but not identified. A newspaper article mentioned a shipyard in the "thriving little place" of Hubert in Onslow County. In a pension claim, the widow of Wallace D. Gray included an affidavit affirming that he worked in I.H. Scarborough's shipyard in Hyde County.[196]

Shipyards are frequently mentioned in connection with the construction or repair of a vessel. These are often sites where one or more vessels were built or repaired. Facilities remained somewhat primitive. There was little difference in the shipbuilding establishments of 1900 and those a hundred years earlier (Figure 11).[197] They usually included a frame building or two, a tool shed to protect material, a few pieces of machinery, and occasionally, even a marine railway. Power tools such as saws and drills were beginning to appear, although hand tools remained predominant.

Established shipbuilding facilities, some owned and others leased, are recorded on Sanborn maps of the 1880s and 1890s for Elizabeth City, Beaufort, Washington, New Bern, and Wilmington. Detailed descriptions identify marine railways, wharves, workshops, storage facilities, sail lofts, and usually a blacksmith forge (Figure 12). Marine railways were found in all the larger ports.

Before the war, nearly all the machinery on North Carolina-built steamboats was provided by out-of-state firms. Hart and Bailey, in Wilmington, had the ability to build power plants from boilers to shafts, and during the war, did so for Confederate vessels. After the war, the number of machine and ironworks in North Carolina ports increased. A few were able to forge and assemble steam machinery. Others had repair and limited manufacturing capability.[198] After 1865, two establishments operated machine shops and foundries in Wilmington: The Clarendon Works, which had been in operation before and during the war, attempted to re-open in 1867 under a new name, the Wilmington Manufacturing Company. It was in business for a number of years but did not again manufacture steamboat machinery.[199] Hart and Bailey, which had been in business in Wilmington before the war, also reopened. Through the years, it operated under various names. In the 1870s, Henry A. Burr, who married Hart's daughter, entered the firm and the company's name was changed to Hart, Bailey and Company. In 1879, the firm became Bailey and Burr, and later, Burr, Bailey and Company. In 1892, the firm officially became the Wilmington Iron Works although it was locally known by that name before then. As early as 1868, it fabricated steamboat machinery and continued doing so for decades.[200]

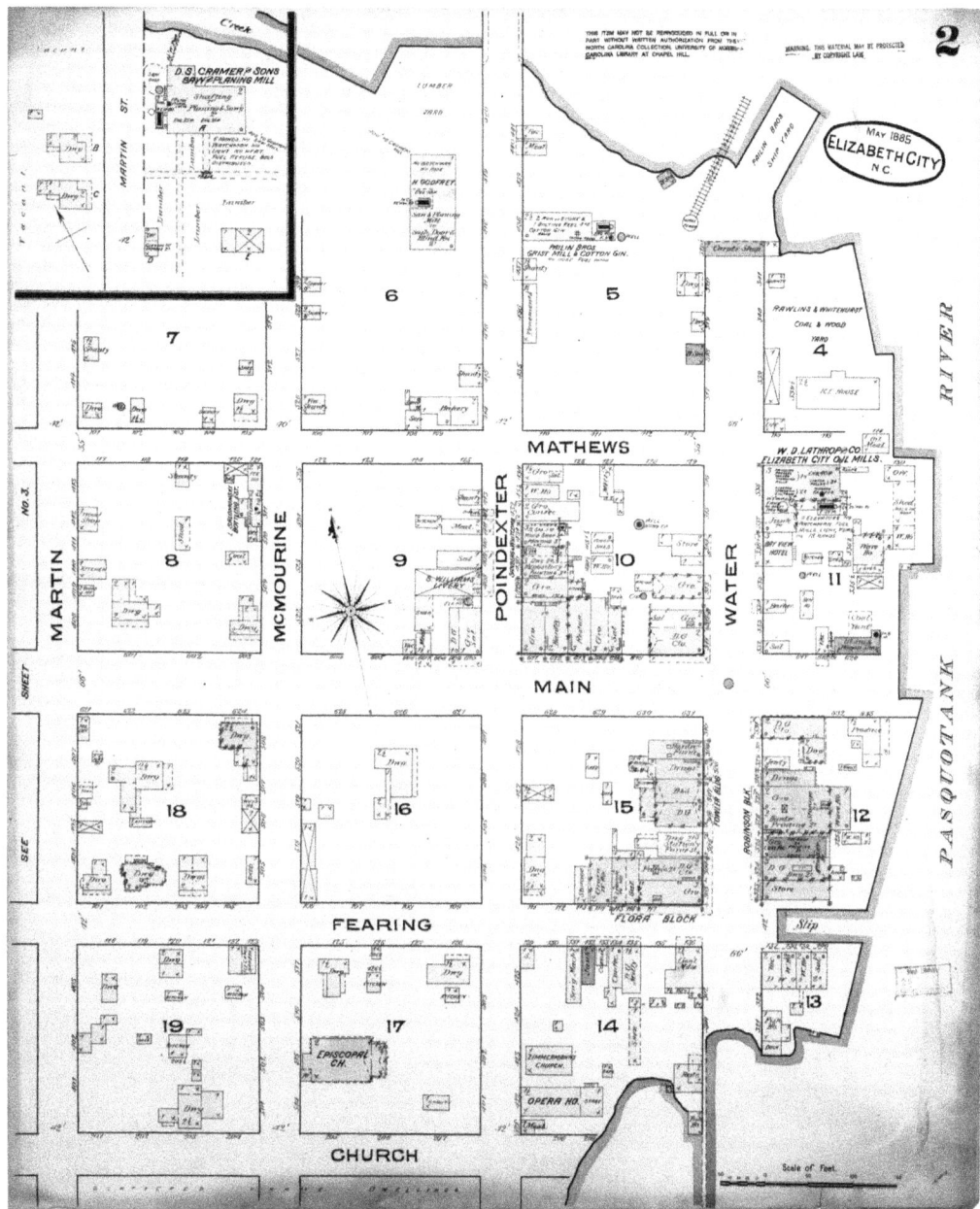

FIGURE 7-12 A portion of the Sanborn map of Elizabeth City in 1885 showing the Pailin Bros. holdings on the Pasquotank River. Notice the railway and power plant and the carpenter shop at the end of Water Street. Also, notice their grist mill and cotton gin to the left. *Source:* North Carolina Collection, Joyner Library, East Carolina University.

In 1878, Samuel W. Skinner, along with L.B. Lyons, purchased a small machine works previously owned by F.J. Lord. Skinner utilized the iron works for minor repairs and forgings for his shipbuilding activities. In 1891, he established machine shops and a foundry at his shipyard. An opening announcement stated that the works would be able to repair and rebuild steamer machinery.[201]

During the war, the Union Navy operated a machine shop at Union Point in New Bern. It was abandoned in the spring of 1865 and reopened under civilian ownership in August.

Advertisements stressed repairs on steamboat machinery. However, it was not listed in the 1870 city and state directories. In the 1870s, two machine shops opened in the city. E.H. Cuthbert initially rented space at Howard's shipyard but by 1882 had his own establishment. Howard continued leasing part of his shipyard property to machinists. The Manwell and Crabtree foundry and ironworks was the largest machine shop in the port. Later, Manwell sold his interest and the name was changed to John H. Crabtree and Company. Both establishments fabricated boilers, engines, and steamboat work of all kinds. There was also a boiler shop in New Bern. In 1890, the New Bern Iron Works was established with facilities to work on steamer machinery.[202]

The New Bern iron works competed with a much larger one in Goldsboro. W.F. Kornegay and Company manufactured farm and steamboat machinery as well as other ironwork. The company was also the dealer for boilers and engines marketed by northern firms. Kornegay, a machinist, opened a small shop in the mid-1870s to repair machinery, and within ten years had expanded to become the second largest ironworks in the eastern part of the state. In 1878, Kornegay journeyed to Jefferson, Indiana, to observe the production of steamboat machinery. He then expanded his business and successfully sought riverboat business. Kornegay's works provided machinery for several steamers before being dissolved in 1885. Kornegay opened a branch office in New Bern in 1883, but it was not successful.[203] Kornegay died in 1884. Charles Dewey took over management in 1885. Under Dewey, the firm began to specialize in building railway locomotives.[204] Herring and Rand also ran a machinist shop in Goldsboro that occasionally repaired steamboat machinery. In 1886, O. R. Rand, Jr., bought out his partner. The shop continued in business for several years.[205]

There were other machine shops and foundries in the eastern part of the state, but none made steamboat power plants. Washington had several ironworks. They repaired machinery, but there is no evidence of fabrication.[206] The Kinston Iron Works may well have repaired steam machinery. In the 1880s, Miller & Canady also owned a machine shop in Kinston that worked on steamboat machinery. T.A. Perry operated a machine shop in Plymouth that repaired farm and steam machinery. After the war, Elizabeth City had considerable vessel repair business, but, until the 1890s, only minor machinery repair work could be done in the port. E.S. Willey established the North Carolina Iron Works in connection with his shipbuilding establishment. The Elizabeth City Ironworks was also founded in the mid-1890s.[207]

Out-of-state firms continued to provide boatbuilders with engines, boilers, and other vessel machinery during the latter decades of the nineteenth century. Baltimore was a leading provider of machinery before the war years and continued to be so. E. H. Frazier and Company of Baltimore made and delivered several power plants for steamboats built in Windsor.[208] Out-of-state marine machinery establishments occasionally advertised in North Carolina newspapers. A Washington group, planning to build a steam flat, drew up a detailed outline of the machinery they wanted and contacted the Marine Iron Works in Chicago for a price.[209]

Ship repairs were more lucrative than new construction. Storms and hurricanes played havoc with coastal shipping, and with the fishing and shipbuilding industries. Ship and boat yards were destroyed or seriously damaged, as were vessels on the stocks and afloat, all of which provided ship and boat builders with work.[210]

From the end of the Civil War until the twentieth century, most of the shipyard work, by far, was in repairing and rebuilding vessels. By 1890, so many shipbuilding establishments were exclusively engaged in repair work that the census of that year, and that of 1900, had a separate category for them. Repairs were carried out at all shipyards and other building sites, even along wharves and on river banks. Shipbuilding facilities with marine railways generally repaired far more vessels than they built. Some small marine railways specialized in repairs. The Carroll marine railway in Wilmington specialized in repairs.[211] A number of the state's shipbuilding firms expanded their railways, allowing work on up to four vessels at a time. The war and the absence of capital for new construction resulted in a marked increase in this aspect of the industry. The war left dozens of vessels in need of repair, many in such disrepair that they had to be rebuilt. A surprisingly large number that had been sunk during the conflict were raised and rebuilt. Steamboats, which had outlived their use, were often converted to flats or barges. The state's yards also benefited from lower cost. As a Washington paper noted, "Many vessels are sent here from the North to be overhauled and repaired."[212]

The Wilmington builders were particularly successful in repairing and rebuilding vessels. Wilmington had the only marine railways in the Cape Fear region, including Southport. The port benefitted from the only dry dock in the state. It was constructed in 1879 by Blossom and Evans shipbuilders. When completed, the dry dock was comprised of six sections, each thirty-three feet long and seventy feet wide. It had a lifting capacity of 1,200 tons and was later sold to a firm in Haiti. Various Wilmington newspapers loyally carried reports about what was on the ways being repaired, at times even detailing what work was being done. The papers frequently mention the recovery of sunken craft as well as ship repairs. Evans later erected a marine railway at the dry dockyard.[213]

The Cassidey and Brothers Shipyard was reported to have had the largest marine railway south of Boston. In 1867, the yard repaired the 1,100-ton steamer *City Point*, and the following year the oceanic steamer *Lizzie Baker*. The Cassideys repaired a number of large sailing ships, including the German barque *Kosmos*, the Norwegian brig *Fred*, the Spanish barque *Cabieces*, and the French full-rigged ship *L'Amerique*.[214]

Samuel W. Skinner took over the Cassidey firm and was even more successful in vessel repair. In the twenty years he operated the shipyard, more than two hundred vessels of all types and sizes were repaired and rebuilt.[215] Work done at New Bern shipyards also demonstrated the importance of repairing vessels. In 1881, Thomas Howard's establishment reported that, in a two-month period, forty vessels were on the ways. His marine railway was large enough to handle the iron revenue cutter *Winona*.[216]

Washington yards were more involved in building than repairing vessels. Nonetheless, as in other port communities, overhauling was an ongoing business, particularly for vessels engaged in local trade. Over a two-week period in 1891, four steamboats as well as several vessels were on the ways. The *Washington Gazette* reported that "Myers' Shipyard presented quite a business like appearance last week. There were seven different schooners on the railway for repairs."[217]

Elizabeth City shipyards constructed a limited number of vessels between 1865 and 1893, but did a bustling repair business. The only marine railways in the northeastern section of the state were located there. In 1870, the port's shipyards were "busy repairing vessels." The Lawrence Shipyard and another owned by James Snell did well in ship repairs.[218] Newspaper articles, however, suggest that a great many vessels from the Albemarle region were taken to Norfolk for repairs.

Rebuilding a vessel was the most expensive work done on marine railways. In fact, it could cost as much or more than constructing a new vessel. Rebuilding could involve replacing all planking, enlarging by lengthening or widening the hull, or adding superstructure. Converting one type of vessel into another was a standard procedure such as steamers into flats, flats into steamers, schooners into brigs, and brigs into schooners. Virtually all of the established yards had occasion to rebuild one or more vessels.[219] Samuel Skinner actually went to Florida, recovered three wrecks, transported them to his facility in Wilmington, and converted them into barges.[220]

Disputes between vessel owners and shipbuilders over building and repairing a vessel were quite common and often had to be settled in court. Disputes involved nonpayment, accusations of poor workmanship, disagreements over scope of work, and schedule of completion.[221] After a long difficult voyage from Liverpool, the bark *Dunkeld* needed extensive repairs and was hauled up on the Cassidey and Brothers marine railway in Wilmington. The yard owners hired more than forty workers to carry out the repairs. Funds were quickly exhausted and an appeal to the ship's parent company for an advance to provide provisions and pay for the workers went unheeded. After several weeks, the Cassideys filed suit again to recover $4,000 owed them for the repairs. The vessel's owners could not or would not pay for the repairs so the court ordered the bark sold at public auction.[222]

At the turn of the century, wooden shipbuilding and repair was still a viable business in the coastal counties. Professional shipbuilders preferred new construction to ship repairs. It was more satisfying to see the birth of a vessel, a skiff, or large merchant steamer, than to replace rotten timbers or damaged spars.

North Carolina craftsmen continued to build small craft such as row boats, skiffs, canoes, and kunners in large numbers, but piraguas were rarely constructed. Even kunners began to disappear towards the end of the century.[223] The type and nomenclature of larger vessels built in the state changed after the Civil War. The construction of oceangoing ships declined in favor of craft that utilized inland waterways. Technological changes led to improved steamboat designs and the introduction of gasoline powered vessels. New types including the shad boat and sharpies were introduced.

After 1865, steamers increasingly dominated the oceanic trade with North Carolina ports. Between 1883 and 1893, a combination of steamboat and barge traffic utilizing the Dismal and Chesapeake and Albemarle Canals diminished North Carolina's coastal sailing trade by seventy-five percent.[224] Despite the growing importance of steamers and barges, sailing vessels, such as schooners remained competitive. They continued to carry much of the region's bulk cargos: such as lumber, naval stores, and fresh produce (watermelons, potatoes, etc.) to North American and West Indian markets. Relatively small coasters were cheaper to build and operate than steamers and they were often adapted to fishing and oystering. They also serviced areas where steam-powered vessels did not operate. In certain industries, such as fishing, they were overwhelmingly predominant. In the coastal trade, they were economical and operated on flexible schedules and rates. Fuel was not a problem, but sailing vessels were affected by weather and an increasing preference for shipment by railroad.

Customhouse officials documented vessel tonnage. However, builders and owners often preferred different measurements. Estimated tonnage of cargo that could be loaded and estimated number of barrels that could be carried were common standards. The *Minnie Ward*, built in Swansboro in 1873, was a "small two-masted schooner of only about 250 barrels capacity." A schooner, built in New Bern in 1868, was "of about 1000 barrels capacity." Barrels referred to the amount of turpentine that could be carried. Capacity was also measured in bushels of corn and other produce. Boats dredging for oysters were measured in terms of bushels or tubs of oysters.[225]

The North Carolina sailing vessel changed little during the nineteenth century, but center boards were a major improvement. Better sail cloth and other building materials were used, and there was a gradual increase in size, particularly in coastal freighters. North Carolina builders adapted center boards to large sailing vessels. In 1873, the Howards constructed an 88-foot, 210-ton schooner with a center board. Brigs gave way to skipjacks, sloops to schooners. North Carolina builders tended to cling to two-masted vessels, although those with three, four, and even five masts were being constructed in other sections of the country.[226] They also developed different vessel types such as the skipjack oyster sloop, schooner rigged scow, skipjack bateau, fishing smack, and schooner sharpie.

Sloops continued to be built in large numbers. They were usually small, seven tons or less, used for fishing and, to a limited degree, freight and passenger trade. A few were quite large. Garcia built a seventy-foot sloop in Wilmington for Brunswick County trade.[227]

Sixty-one are documented as being built between 1865 and 1900. Those under five tons were rarely documented. Various types of vessels from schooners and sloops to skiffs and sharpies used similar fore and aft rigs. However, specific sail patterns and rigging developed on particular vessel types.[228] Descriptions occasionally mention a vessel as having a flat or round bottom, or a center board. A small fishing boat built in Washington is described as having a "diamond bottom." Sloop-rigged skiffs were built in large numbers and often were the only transportation owned by a coastal family.[229] In contrast to pre-Civil War years, newspaper articles frequently mention boats as being constructed "expressedly for the fishing business."[230]

Sharpies or "Core Sounders", and shad boats, are probably the best known North Carolina-built sailing vessels. Both appeared in the 1870s. By the beginning of the twentieth century, the sharpie became the most popular sailing vessel in the Core Sound area, which included Carteret, Hyde, Craven, Onslow, Pamlico, and Beaufort Counties. They were also built in other parts of the state.[231] It was a most versatile craft, used in oystering, fishing, freighting, racing, carrying passengers, and recreation. Like most pre-twentieth century mass produced vessels, sharpies were designed and modified to meet local conditions and demands. They generally ranged from under twenty feet to sixty feet in length. Sharpies were popular with boat builders because of their simplicity in design and construction. Some builders specialized in building sharpies, but amateurs also built them.[232] How many were built in the state is undetermined. An article on North Carolina sharpies in *Field & Stream* stated that in 1879 there were at least 500 in the state, only five years after the first one was produced.[233] Large numbers of sharpies were under five tons, and federal document records are not consistent. Sharpies were occasionally listed, but at times they were listed as schooners or sloops.[234]

Sharpies were first built in Connecticut and migrated south. It is generally accepted that George N. Ives introduced the sharpie to North Carolina. The story has been told by Ives himself and others. Ives was a native of Connecticut, a successful businessman who migrated to Morehead City in 1874 to start a wholesale seafood business.[235] Realizing that the oyster industry in North Carolina waters had great potential, he had a typical Connecticut oyster sharpie built and transported to Morehead City. Racing fishing craft was quite common along the Atlantic coast and, as Ives recognized, often enhanced the popularity of a particular vessel.

He raced his Connecticut built sharpie, *Lucia*, successfully on Long Island Sound and, later, in the greater Core Sound area. This started what can only be described as a sharpie boatbuilding boom. It would be difficult to exaggerate the almost immediate popularity of the sharpie in North Carolina. A Core Sound resident recalled a family anecdote that "papa spent all of his money building 'sharpies' to lure husbands for his old maid sister."[236]

The sharpie commonly had a flat bottom, but the North Carolina shad boat had a round bottom. The shad boat was used primarily in the Albemarle Sound area, and is usually considered a craft indigenous to North Carolina waters. In 1987, the North Carolina General Assembly designated the shad boat as the official State Boat of North Carolina. George Washington Creef is usually credited with the design and construction of the first shad boat, which was built in the 1870s. Subsequent builders modified the original design. Like sharpies, they were all-purpose boats used in fishing, hauling freight, racing, and even by at least one North Carolina lifesaving station. Their building sites were concentrated on Roanoke Island and the surrounding area and large numbers were constructed. An observer counted 210 in Albemarle Sound during the 1901 shad season.[237] Sharpies and shad boats were widely employed in fishing and oystering. Throughout the nineteenth century, next to farming, fishing was the most important industry in eastern North Carolina.

The Importance of Fishing

Seventeen North Carolina counties front the ocean or sounds, and their primary industry was commercial fishing. Nine inland counties also counted commercial fisheries in their economic base. After the Civil War, the fishing industry experienced the transition from sail to craft powered by other means. Most commercial fishing after 1865 occurred in the sounds and rivers. The menhaden fishery was the only significant offshore industry. A group of northeastern fishermen, former Union veterans, recognized the potential of the fishery in North Carolina waters. Local fishermen and businessmen such as G.P. Day, H.C. Jones, and Sutton Davis entered the business. They had schooners and purse boats constructed. Day built a steamer "expressly for fishing at sea."[238] Between 1865 and 1900, at least twenty-four menhaden vessels were built in Carteret County. The *Southport Leader* mentioned an unusual fishing vessel, a sort of houseboat used as a headquarters. Small boats brought their daily catch to the anchored vessel, where the fish were iced down for shipment.[239]

The menhaden schooners were classified as vessels as they were over five tons. According to state records, there were actually few vessels engaged in fishing. In 1889, only forty-nine were listed, all in the Pamlico area. The number increased slightly in 1890.[240] The majority of fishing craft were classified as boats. In 1890, state records listed 3,616 boats. In 1897, the number increased to 3,827. However, these statistics are not complete. Data for seventeen coastal counties are included, but upriver counties such as Halifax, Martin, and Pitt are not, and many of these had commercial fisheries that employed small boats. County and state records such as court proceedings, deed books, and estate papers often mention fisheries. Reports also list twenty steam flats all employed in long haul seine fishing in the Albemarle Sound. According to W.R. Capehart, who owned one of the largest fisheries in the Albemarle region, the fisheries in the sound used about 125 boats and gave "employment to a large force of boat-builders." It is assumed that virtually all of the boats and most of the vessels were built in the state. One report said that boats "without number are being built . . . for the purpose of fishing."[241] Of course, a great many were small craft such as row and pole boats, and sailing skiffs. Canoes were still popular for fishing on the state's streams and lakes.

Into the twentieth century, sail was dominant in small family owned and operated fisheries. Literally thousands of small sail boats, shad boats and oyster schooners, including sharpies, gill netters, and other nondescript craft, were used in the fisheries. Some vessels designated as yachts were actually built for fishing.[242] In 1880, there were ninety-five vessels, including those that transported fish, and 2,714 boats engaged in commercial fishing. By 1896, the number of vessels remained approximately the same, but the number of boats had increased by more than a thousand. In 1890, Dare County listed the most boats, 1,184, and seven vessels, followed in order by: Carteret County, 704 boats plus 42 vessels; Onslow County, 307 boats; Currituck County, 271 boats, down from 306 the previous year; Chowan County, 123 boats and 8 steam flats; and Hyde County with 107 boats. The rest of the counties listed less than a hundred each. Surprisingly, Brunswick County listed only 16 boats in 1890.[243]

In the 1880s and 1890s, fishermen began to replace sail with internal combustion engines to power their craft. A few steamboats were built for the industry, primarily in the menhaden and Albemarle seine fisheries. A significant number of vessels transporting fish were propelled by steam and gasoline and the number increased annually.[244] Peter Warren is given credit for creating the steam flat in 1879, to replace the oared-propelled flats that carried the seines out into the sounds and rivers. However, in 1866, it was reported that a Norfolk firm was constructing six iron steamers designed for the fisheries in the sounds of North Carolina, "to be used in the work of hauling the seine."[245] It is possible that Warren started experimenting with steam powered vessels in the early 1870s. These steamers were quickly adopted by most of the haul seine fisheries.

As designed by Warren, they were shallow draft sidewheel steamboats with the machinery and wheels in the extreme stern, allowing the deck area forward open for the handling of the nets and the catch. An 1890 newspaper article provided a somewhat humorous description of the steam flat saying, "It's a cross between a vertical saw mill without the saw and a boiler afloat without the proper hold of a steamer." Some of them did not have rudders but backed up to a beach to take in the seine. Although not involved in coastal trade they were still given an annual inspection by the Steamboat Inspection Service.[246]

In 1895, William R. Capehart, owner and operator of one of the best-known Albemarle Sound fisheries, reported that the Albemarle Sound's fishing interests employed approximately 125 vessels of which twenty were steam-propelled flats.[247] In 1987, the Underwater Archaeology Unit of the North Carolina Department of Cultural Resources discovered and investigated several wrecks in and near the sites of former fisheries and found the remains of one steam flat *Little Winnie,* built in 1888 by Wilmington shipbuilder Benjamin Beery. It may well have been the first charter boat in the state. It was designed to take up to seventy people out as fishing parties.[248]

LIFEBOATS AND SURFBOATS

For many years, the federal government did not consider lifesaving worthy of its concern. More consideration was given to lost cargo than to the human victims of shipwrecks. It was not until 1848 that federal funds were committed to limited lifesaving efforts. For over two decades, volunteers staffed scattered facilities. A professional lifesaving service was finally created in 1871 as a unit of the U.S. Treasury's Revenue Marine Bureau.

The new United States Lifesaving Service (USLSS) suffered from an inadequate budget and widespread incompetence. Training and equipment were either poor or nonexistent, and many of its lifesavers were either inept landlubbers or corrupt political appointees. Sumner I. Kimball, head of the Revenue Marine Bureau, worked to correct these problems.

Two tragic shipwrecks along the North Carolina coast, the USS *Huron* at Nags Head in November 1877, and *Metropolis* at Currituck Beach in January 1878, sparked outrage. The press and public alike demanded Congress appropriate additional monies and implement reforms, including extension of the lifesaving patrol season and construction of additional lifesaving stations along North Carolina's coast and elsewhere. In June 1878, the USLSS was made an independent unit of the Treasury Department with Kimball as its first superintendent.

More than a hundred lifesaving stations were established on the Atlantic coast followed by others on the Great Lakes, Pacific coast, Gulf coast, and one at the Falls of the Ohio. The Atlantic coast stations commonly had lifeboats, surfboats, and utility boats. The most exposed were those on the Outer Banks of North Carolina, well-known as the "Graveyard of the Atlantic." (Figure 13.)

Lifeboats, surfboats, supply, and utility boats were made of wood. Well-constructed and heavily used, very few remain. Although a majority of them were provided by out-of-state builders, a few were constructed in North Carolina (Table 1). Lifeboats were 34 to 36 feet in length, and surfboats were 25 to 26 feet long. In 1887, William Payne of Rodanthe, built a 26-foot keel boat to supply the Pea Island station. In 1890, D.M. Pugh, also of Rodanthe, built a skiff to supply the Kinnakeet station. In 1898,

FIGURE 7-13 This is a 1882 or 1883 United States Life Saving Service station, and is typical of the era when twenty-nine were built on the Outer Banks. A number of the small boats at these stations were built locally. The exact location of this station is in question: That means, by the date, it can only be at New Inlet, Cape Hatteras, Ocracoke, or possibly Oak Island, although that would make it 1886. The Station Keeper (far right, double-breasted jacket) looks a lot like John Allen Midgett, Jr., although he did not serve at any of those. However, his father served at New Inlet. It seems that New Inlet might be the most likely location. A hurricane destroyed the station in 1916 (personal communication with James Charlet, OBHC). *Source:* Timothy Dring (U.S. Life Saving Service Heritage Society file)

Benjamin Creef in Manteo built a 25-foot sailing craft for the Oregon Inlet station.[249] Station crews along the Outer Banks were on constant watch, particularly during hurricanes and nor'easters. Many stations launched surfboats directly from the beach into the open, wave crested seas to save lives. It is believed that many more boats were built for the North Carolina lifesaving stations than those listed in Table 1.

THE PILOT BOATS

Pilot boats date back hundreds of years. They are designed for a particular task, that of transporting pilots to vessels entering inlets, rivers, and other navigable bodies of water. On the Outer Banks, pilots often built their own boats designed to pass through the strong tidal currents of inlets. Cape Fear pilot boats were usually built in Wilmington, Southport (Smithville), and on Bald Head Island. Between 1771 and 1884, at least fifteen pilot boats were built, more than half of these at Southport where pilotage was a principal occupation. The number of pilot boats built in North Carolina between 1865 and 1893 is not known. In 1875, a Wilmington newspaper reported that "Notwithstanding the dull times and scarcity of money, the pilots at the mouth of the Cape Fear are displaying commendable energy. . . . which is illustrated in the construction of two more pilot vessels."[250] Outer Banks-built pilot boats are not mentioned in the newspapers. At least two pilot boats were built for the lifesaving stations on the Outer Banks. Ira Stowe claimed to have designed a boat "especially for

TABLE 7-1 NORTH CAROLINA-BUILT BOATS FOR THE U.S. LIFE-SAVING SERVICE (reference: 1902 USLSS Boat Register)

Station	Type	Builder and Year Built	Comments
Pulling Surfboats			
Bodie Island	26 ft. Long Branch	Unk; 1878	Builder not recorded, but may have been local
Caffeys Inlet	26 ft. Jersey	Unk; 1878	Builder not recorded, but may have been local
Creeds Hill	26 ft. Long Branch	Unk; 1878	Builder not recorded, but may have been local
Durants	26 ft. Long Branch	Unk; 1878	Builder not recorded, but may have been local
Gull Shoal	26 ft. Long Branch	Unk; 1878	Builder not recorded, but may have been local
Kill Devil Hills	26 ft. Long Branch	Unk; 1878	Builder not recorded, but may have been local
Nags Head	26 ft. Jersey	Unk; 1875	Builder not recorded, but may have been local
Ocracoke	26 ft. Long Branch	Unk; 1878	Builder not recorded, but may have been local
Paul Gamiels Hill	26 ft. Long Branch	Unk; 1878	Builder not recorded, but may have been local
Whales Head	26 ft. Jersey	Unk; 1872	Builder not recorded, but may have been local
Station Supply Boats			
Chicamacomico	25 x 7.5 ft. sailing shad	Crief, East Lake, NC, 1892	
Durants	33 x 8 ft. dead-rise sailing pilot	JF Austin, Hatteras, NC 1885	
Little Kinnakeet	22 x 6.5 ft. dead-rise sailing skiff	DM Pugh, Rodanthe, NC 1890	
New Inlet	25 x 7.5 ft. sailing shad	Crief, East Lake, NC 1892	
Ocracoke	33.5 x 8 ft. sailing pilot	WK Gaskins, Hatteras, NC 1888	
Oregon Inlet	24 ft. 10 in. x 7.5 ft. sailing shad	Crief, Croatan, NC 1890	
Oregon Inlet	25.5 x 7 ft. sailing Squan surfboat	Crief, Manteo, NC 1898	
Pea Island	24.5 x 6.5 ft. sailing skiff	Wm. Payne, Rodanthe, NC 1887	
Cape Henry	Unknown length pilot skiff	Unk	Builder not recorded, but may have been local

Table 1: Surfboats in North Carolina (U.S. Life Saving Service Heritage Society).

rough water."[251] This was probably a pilot boat. In the 1890s, steam-powered pilot boats began to replace those powered by sail. In 1894, the Southport Pilot's Association decided to replace their sailing vessel with steam-powered tugs.[252] However, Outer Banks pilots continued to depend on sail well into the twentieth century.

Races and Regattas in North Carolina Waters

Sailing regattas or races were not common in North Carolina before the Civil War, but became increasingly popular in the later decades of the century. In the 1850s, the Carolina Yacht Club at Wrightsville Beach was the only organized racing association in the state. In the postwar years, the club picked up where it left off. As early as 1868, yacht races were held in Smithville (Southport), and, as early as 1872, in Masonboro Sound.[253] Although additional clubs were not established, organized races began to take place in Morehead City, New Bern, and Washington. Impromptu races often took place in other North Carolina waters. This was especially true on holidays such as the Fourth of July. The type of boats varied. In Washington, a Fourth of July event included yachts, which were all northern built, and canoes. Roanoke Islanders preferred shad boats. In New Bern and Morehead City, sailing skiffs and sharpies became most popular for regattas. In Southport, flat-bottomed skiffs, known locally as bateaus, were widely used. Sculling in the Cape Fear River off the downtown waterfront was also a popular racing sport.[254] Rowboats of all sizes were universally popular for racing. North Carolina-built vessels occasionally entered regattas in other states. There are no known statistics for racing craft built in North Carolina. Obviously, most of the smaller boats and skiffs, along with shad boats and sharpies, were constructed in the state.[255]

The Boat Business

Sailing bateaux carried a mainsail, jib, and occasionally a sprit sail. Sailing canoes, usually sloop-rigged, were still being built, especially in Currituck County where they were used by hunters. A Bertie County shipbuilder by the name of Thrower built a sailing canoe that was large enough to carry the builder and guests as far as Roanoke Island. Occasionally, unique sail craft were built in the state. Sailing skiffs were the most popular boats built in North Carolina after the Civil War. They were the Model T Ford, the taxis, for many in coastal regions. On the Roanoke River above the fall line, large bateaux-type keel boats were built to carry produce below the rapids by way of a canal. At Weldon, the cargo was transshipped to vessels, sail boats, and steamers.[256]

Often, nondescript watercraft such as scows, flats, lighters, and even barges carried sail. In 1872, the *Norfolk Journal* predicted that small sail boats engaged in the coastal trade would be eclipsed by barges using the canals.[257] Occasionally, scows were classified as sailing scows, scow schooners, sailing flats, lighters, and even barges.

Documented or not, it can be difficult to determine a particular vessel type. Often, they were interchangeable. One report indicated "A large lighter or scow is being built at Messers Cassidey's & Ross' shipyard..." while another stated "[a] lumber lighter is being built at the government yard, called a flat when launched. . . ." A suit in a federal district court mentioned "the barges or flats." Railroad car ferries were usually called barges but at least one built in Wilmington was called a scow.[258] Scows were flat-bottomed vessels with square ends, "the most primitive of the flat-bottomed hull forms," and were quite common throughout the country. In North Carolina, they were popular because of their shallow draft and low construction cost. The two-masted schooner scow *Swansboro* was built in Swansboro. *Centennial* was a sailing flat built in Beaufort.[259] It is equally difficult to determine the number built in the state. Customhouse records are inconsistent. Some scows are listed, but others are listed by rig, such as sloop or schooner. Newspapers rarely differentiated as to whether a scow was powered by sail or not.[260]

Scows, flats, lighters, and barges usually had to be towed. These North Carolina-built craft were used for a variety of tasks from carrying cargo to internal improvements. Wilmington papers mention lighters being constructed for wreck salvaging operations, moving phosphate rock and shingle blocks.[261] Flats that were poled or towed were probably the most common vessel of any size built in North Carolina. They had been constructed in large numbers before the Civil War and continued to be widespread until the twentieth century. They were especially useful on streams where steamboats could not run or where they could do so only when the water was high. A Hookerton correspondent noted that Contentnea Creek was too low for steamboats, "consequently our merchants have to rely upon the flats to bring up the goods."[262] Flats were also used to carry virtually any kind of cargo such as lumber, naval stores, cotton, produce, bricks, machinery, or even fish and oysters. Flats were built as ferries. One was built in Beaufort as an excursion boat to carry tourists. Two excursion barges were built in Wilmington. *Experiment*, was constructed by Lemmerman and Coney in 1874, and a 350-passenger barge was built by A. D. Wessell in 1900.[263]

Watercraft identified as barges or scows were also employed in the same manner as flats. They worked with steamboats and carried cargo. Some were quite large, over a hundred feet in length, and occasionally were decked over, enabling them to carry a deck load as well as cargo in the hold. A Wilmington paper described a newly built barge as having a house on it in order to carry hay and straw without "exposing them to the weather."[264]

After the Civil War, railroads began to expand in the eastern part of the state. At first, shipbuilders profited from this expansion receiving contracts to build steamers and barges. Steamboats and tugs were used to carry passengers and cargo to various railheads.[265] Transfer barges, also called scows, in addition to lighters, car floats, and even pontoons were required to carry trains across streams before the advent of bridges. Between 1889 and 1896, a number of barges for the Cape Fear and Yadkin Valley Railroad were constructed at S.W. Skinner's shipyard in Wilmington.[266] However, Washington benefited most from the construction of railroad barges. In 1881, John Myers and Company was contracted to build two barges for the Old Dominion Steamship Company with an option to build two more. The agent for the steamship company agreed to pay for the material and labor to build the barges which were completed and turned over to Old Dominion. Myers then purchased material for two additional barges, but the steamship company refused to pay for the material. Myers sued and a sheriff's sale provided Myers with reimbursement.[267]

In 1894, and again in 1895, Myers received contracts to build transfer barges to run between Edenton and Mackey's Ferry for the Norfolk and Southern Railroad. They were over a hundred feet in length and included two sets of tracks each to carry three coaches or cars. In 1895, his shipyard constructed a 155-foot transfer barge for the Danville and Atlantic Railroad.[268] In 1898, Chauncey and Farrow contracted to build three barges for the Norfolk and Southern. Only one was delivered to the railroad in Norfolk. At first, the railroad agent refused to receive the vessel claiming that Chauncey did not follow the contract building instructions and specifications. A protracted correspondence followed between the railroad and Chauncey, and later, his attorney William Rodman, until a compromise was reached. In one letter, Chauncey complained bitterly over individuals sent to inspect the barges, claiming one of them said North Carolina builders had no right to build a barge that should have been constructed in Norfolk.[269]

WATER NAVIGATION IMPROVEMENTS

Navigable rivers were vital to the state's economy. The war disrupted navigation. Immediately after the war, private enterprise did some work on the Cape Fear River and its tributaries. In the 1870s, the Corps of Engineers began work on the state's waterways. Vessels were needed. Some were built and brought in from out of state. Others, especially small craft such as flats, were constructed in the state. The Corps followed three procedures in building these new vessels. First, they were contracted out to shipbuilders. Next, they were built in their own yards in Washington, and, later, moved to New Bern and Wilmington. Finally, they were built by hired labor. Annually, the district chief requested funds to build vessels, outlining costs and recommending whether the Corps should construct the craft or outsource the contract. Generally, the Corps of Engineers in North Carolina preferred purchasing material on the open market and hiring local labor to build the requested vessels.[270] In time, nearly all types of vessels employed in river improvements by the Corps, including steamboats, snag boats, dredgers, hoisters, and supply vessels of various sizes, were constructed in the state.

The Wilmington District used hired labor under the supervision of Corps personnel to build flats and scows and other small craft.[271] A number of vessels including a steamer, a section dredge, and two steam launches were built at the Washington depot. In 1893, Major Stanton, in charge of the Wilmington District, requested permission to construct a side wheel steamboat and a hoister at the Washington yard. He said, "The depot recently rented at Washington, N.C., affords special advantages for the building of the hoister by hired labor at the same time that [a] light steamer is built there... Inasmuch as no expense will be entailed for superintendence, hire of shipyard and ways, and as the material can be cut and used to better advantage upon the two hulls than upon one."[272]

The Corps facility in New Bern primarily employed hired labor to construct vessels for the Neuse River and its tributaries. In 1881, a survey of the entry into Beaufort harbor determined that shoaling at Shackleford Point, across from Fort Macon, was a serious handicap to vessels using the harbor. The Corps decided building a stone wall at Shackleford Point would solve the problem. Three flats were built in Morehead City to carry the stones to the Point.[273] Following the policy of using hired labor under Corps personnel supervision, several quarter boats providing housing for workers, three derrick flats, one side dump scow, the snag boat *Trent*, a steam hoister, and the steamboat *General George Thom* were built at their facility in New Bern.[274]

The Wilmington District office and private firms engaged in dredging the Cape Fear River and its tributaries contracted with local shipbuilders to construct vessels. In 1879, the Corps employed local labor to build a derrick scow at a rented wharf. In 1880, J.W. Taylor received a contract to build two flats for the Corps. Two years later he received a second contract for lighters, a mud scow, a steam dredge boat, and water scow for the Corps. Taylor also built a large scow for the New York Dredging Company. G.M. Summerell leased a lot and wharf adjacent to J.W. Taylor's sawmill. He built five scows for the Corps.[275] In 1884, the 100-foot steamboat, *H. G. Wright*, was built in Fayetteville under private contract.[276]

In 1884, Samuel Skinner's shipyard received a contract to construct a self-propelled steam hoister and pile driver. *Hercules* was equipped with a 2,500-pound hammer and a steam pump launched in 1885. Skinner built a dredge boat and several large scows for the Corps as well as vessels for dredging companies. In 1890, he built a steam launch for the Corps in South Carolina. In 1887, Captain Bowdoin built a large mud scow and several flats for river improvement work.[277]

A Problem of Capital

Before the Civil War, the economic importance of steam power, railroads and steamboats was clearly recognized by the citizenry of eastern North Carolina. More than fifty steamboats were constructed in the state. The federal occupation of much of the east resulted in the virtual elimination of the state's steamboat fleet. A few did survive such as the *Fox* and several Cape Fear River steamers. Adequate transportation was needed to help restore normalcy, but rebuilding the fleet required capital and the state, like most of the former Confederacy, was bankrupt. Some private funds flowed in from northern interests, but national financial instability culminating with the Panic of 1873, tended to limit this. After the war, despite economic issues steamboat construction remained an important industry in eastern North Carolina. In the mid-1880s, there were between sixty and seventy steamboats owned and operated in the state, most of them built in North Carolina. Fourteen were on the Neuse River.[278]

Governor Jonathan Worth, along with his family, owned a shipping concern on the Cape Fear River, and negotiated an agreement with New York commission merchant Calvin Dibble, which provided needed capital to operate a steamboat line on the river.[279] In 1866, the Worths decided to build a new steamboat, but the vessel was constructed out-of-state. Nonetheless, the steamboat building industry resumed operation on the Cape Fear River in the immediate postwar years and, as in the 1850s, Fayetteville led the way.

In 1870, Fayetteville had seven steamboats operating on the river and all but one was Fayetteville-built. Four of these vessels were not documented at the Wilmington customhouse. Samuel Skinner, a local shipbuilder, was also constructing a steamboat for use on the Waccamaw River in South Carolina. Ship carpenters and steamboat owners such as Archie Black and R. C. Orrell resumed building vessels. Orrell laid down a new steamboat, *Orrell*, immediately after the end of hostilities and built a second one, *Halcyon*, in 1867. *Marion*, also launched in 1867, was an unusual river boat. It was sharp at both ends with twin wheels at the stern operating independently.

Between 1864 and 1870, four large steamers, *Juniper*, *North State*, *Robert E. Lee*, and *Cumberland*, were completed. These vessels were all stern wheelers over 115 feet in length with machinery taken from older boats or purchased out-of-state. Descriptions suggest they were more than "nondescript" steamboats. They had cabins and other accommodations for passengers. *Marion* provided separate male and female living spaces below deck for Blacks, the first North Carolina-built steamboat to do so. *Cumberland* was divided into eight watertight compartments. This steamboat fleet was the largest in the state, and the Cape Fear River vessels continued to be the largest into the twentieth century. After 1871, Fayetteville's shipbuilding industry collapsed, possibly because it was more economical to construct steamboats elsewhere on the river. The only known vessel built in Fayetteville after 1870 was the steamboat *Lily McFayden*, completed in 1882.[280] Undoubtedly, the Panic of 1873 affected the industry. At least one steamboat, *George Lobdell*, was built above Fayetteville for the upper Cape Fear River trade.[281] No new steamers for the Fayetteville to Wilmington trade were constructed until the 1880s.

For a number of years after the war, Wilmington made no effort to challenge Fayetteville in steamboat construction. Very little shipbuilding occurred in the port. The small steamer *Mary Eleanor*, built for the Black River trade, was launched in 1868 at Colville & Taylor's Lumber Company. In 1872, *Northeast* was built to operate on the river of that name. In 1877, *Colville* was built in Wilmington at the Colville (formerly Colville & Taylor) Lumber Company which was destroyed by fire in 1879.[282] In 1884, Captain H. P. Bowdoin built the steamer *Excelsior*, with a screw propeller that could be adjusted to any depth of water greater than thirteen inches. The Beerys, who had been the most prominent shipbuilders for the past quarter-century, did not construct a steamer until 1888. Charles H. Wessell, who managed a shipyard on property owned by a railroad, had a towboat constructed in 1890. In 1891, Thomas Evans also launched a steam-powered towboat at his facility.[283]

It was Samuel Skinner who became Wilmington's most prominent steamboat builder. In 1880, he constructed two steamers, a small fifty-foot stern wheeler to carry passengers on Wrightsville Sound, and a large vessel for the Bladen Steamboat Company. In 1882, he launched the first of several shallow water steamboats for navigating the Black River. His shipyard constructed at least one steam-propelled vessel a year from 1882 to 1892.[284]

In 1888, Parker D. Robbins built the steamboat *Saint Peter* at Hallsville in Duplin County for the Northeast Cape Fear River trade. Aside from the Northeast Cape Fear River, the Black River was the most important Cape Fear River tributary. Before the war, no steamboats had been able to navigate the river that links Pender, Sampson and Bladen Counties with Wilmington. However, after the war, the river was improved and navigation was possible for shallow draft steamboats. *Mary Eleanor* inaugurated steamer service on the Black River in 1869. She was the first of a number of shallow draft, flat-bottomed steamboats, most of which were constructed on the Black River for trade. R.P. Paddison, the father of steam navigation on the Black River, recognizing that new technology enabled these light steamers to operate on shallow water, purchased and captained *Mary Eleanor*. The following year he brought *Little Sam*, built in Fayetteville, to join *Mary Eleanor*. In 1871, Paddison entered the shipbuilding business at Point Caswell in Pender County. He designed and supervised the construction of a number of steamers, including

Caswell, *Lillington*, and *John Dawson*. D.L. Black followed Paddison, building *Lisbon II*, *Hall*, and *Frank Sessons*. At least sixteen steamboats were constructed for the Black River trade between 1871 and 1899, nearly all at Point Caswell. They were all stern wheelers, 65 to 110 feet in length. Although built on the Black River, they were usually towed to either Wilmington or Fayetteville for the installation of machinery and finishing. Others were built during the first two decades of the twentieth century. *Lisbon I*, *Isis*, *E.A. Hawes*, *Susie*, *Delta*, *Enterprise*, *Busy Bee*, *A.J. Johnson*, and *Clinton* were Black River built.[285] No steam-powered vessels were constructed in Southport. However, two were built at Lockwoods Folly to link that section of Brunswick County with Smithville and Wilmington.[286]

Steam navigation returned to the Neuse River slowly after the war. In 1865, the 140-ton steamer *Bette* was built in New Bern. There is no information on this vessel. It may have been the steamboat the Dibble Brothers laid down before the war. More than ten years passed before a second steamer was constructed on the Neuse River. The *Neuse* was built in Kinston in 1876, followed a year later by the steam flat *Contentnea*. The *Neuse* was limited to the navigable portion of the river between New Bern and White Hall. Above that point, the river and its various tributaries were plagued by obstructions. The *Contentnea* was designed to traverse the creek of the same name and was considered an experiment. Machinery was installed on an old flat at Kinston, and the resulting vessel towed to New Bern for completion. The light draft steam flat was successful. In 1879, *Contentnea* was converted into a steamboat by adding superstructure. In later years, she was referred to as the "pioneer steamer" for navigating the shallow tributaries.[287]

In 1882, the *New Bern Journal's* editor wrote, "Down to five years ago the only steamer that bore the port name of New Berne was the *Neuse* owned in Kinston, and ten years ago the arrival of a steamer of any kind in this port was a notable event." By 1884, there were ten steamboats navigating on the Neuse River and its tributaries. As usual, river improvements were the major factor.

In 1879, the Trent River Transportation Company was organized. The company owned the *Neuse* and *Contentnea*, and contracted with Thomas Howard to build a third steamer. Howard, who had been elected mayor of New Bern, was occupied with his official business and his shipyard had four vessels, including the steamboat under construction. Named *Kinston*, the 104-foot vessel was launched in the summer of 1882.[288] The following year, Howard launched the steamer *Blanche*. The Neuse River Transportation Company finished another steamer, the *Trent*, at a site in New Bern in 1882.[289] However, after that, no steam-powered vessels were constructed in New Bern other than a few tugboats and steamers operated by railroads. In general, they were not built for river trade, but to carry lumber and other products to markets outside the state. The exception was in 1887, when Thomas Howard built the steamer *Howard*, his last vessel.[290] Steamers were also being built in Kinston. In 1882, Ben Webb launched *Snow Hill*. The vessel was constructed at a site a quarter-mile from the river and a house mover was employed to use flatbed wagons pulled by oxen to carry the unfinished hull to the river. Three years later, Webb constructed the *Tom Parker* at the same site.[291]

Even before the war, Goldsboro wanted steam navigation to reach New Bern and upstream into Johnston County. The city was served by the Wilmington and Weldon Railroad, but local businessmen realized river transport was usually more economical than rail. Occasionally, particularly when the river was up, steamers from New Bern made the trip to Goldsboro. Beginning in 1880, newspapers reported individuals were either "contemplating" building a steamboat for the Goldsboro trade or were actually constructing one. In 1882, a sternwheeler, *Ransom*, was built at Barfield's Landing, five miles upstream of Goldsboro. In 1884, Needham Kennedy, an Black businessman, constructed *Rough and Ready* at Waynesboro downstream from Goldsboro. In 1889, a second steamer was built at Waynesboro. This was supposed to be the first vessel of a newly formed firm, the Neuse Navigation Company. When completed, *Sally Rand* was sold to another navigation company. Despite these efforts, the river was never deep enough to allow steamers to ascend it throughout the year. Stockholders in the navigation companies rarely received any returns on their investments. The 1890s witnessed limited steamboat travel between New Bern and Goldsboro. No additional vessels were built for this trade.[292]

A considerable number of steamboats were constructed on two shallow tributaries, Swift and Contentnea Creeks. Until the Corp of Engineers removed obstructions, particularly from Contentnea Creek, the small communities along those waterways had to depend on flats to carry their produce to New Bern. Five screw steamers were constructed in the small village of Vanceboro, located a few miles up Swift Creek from the Neuse River. *L H. Cutler* was built in 1882, *Vanceboro I* in 1888, *Vanceboro II* in 1891, *Carolina II* in 1893, and *Maggie H. Lane* in 1894. Ship carpenters were brought in from New Bern to construct the hulls which were subsequently taken to New Bern for machinery.[293]

Shipwrights were also hired in New Bern for projects at Bell's Ferry (Grifton) and Snow Hill. Like the Vanceboro-built boats, hulls were floated to New Bern for completion. As throughout eastern North Carolina, local merchants provided the inspiration for building steamboats at Bell's Ferry and Snow Hill. Two flat-bottomed steamboats were built at Bell's Ferry, *L.A. Cobb* in 1888, named after one of the two merchants who contracted for the vessel, and *May Bell* in 1891.[294] B.T. Webb, who constructed two steamboats at Kinston, agreed to build two at Snow Hill. *Snow Hill* was completed in

1883, and *Carolina I* in 1887. The arrival of steam navigation to these small communities was an economic boom. As one Snow Hill resident wrote in 1883, "Within the last eighteen months our steamship navigation of Contentnea Creek was begun. Snow Hill now has two steamship lines." In another letter, he mentioned four steamboats moored on the riverbank at the same time.[295]

The White Oak River in Onslow County is only twenty miles long, but it flows into Bogue Sound and the Atlantic Ocean through Bogue Inlet, providing an outlet to markets. Located at the juncture of the river and sound, Swansboro was small but important. Steam navigation first reached the port in 1884, when the small steamboat *Margie* made an excursion up the White Oak River. Local businessmen wanted to establish a steamboat route to New Bern. In 1885 construction of a little steamer was proposed. However, none were built until 1895, when Reinhold Foster constructed a steam tug for a lumber company. In 1887, at Stella, a small lumber community on the White Oak River, the steamer *Minnie B.* was built under the supervision of master ship carpenter Washington Willis.[296]

Washington had the facilities to build steamboats, but it was not until the 1870s that one was laid down. For nearly a decade after the war, only three steamboats made the Washington to Greenville run with occasional trips to Tarboro. All were from out-of-state all except the old *Cotton Plant* which had been built in Washington in 1860. Washington was economically destitute after the war. It was not until two out-of-state transportation lines, the Old Dominion and the Clyde, opened trade with the port that local shipbuilders were able to attract capital. Vessels were needed to link the Tar River trade with the two steamer lines. Between 1874 and 1896, at least fourteen steamboats were built in Beaufort County. Thirteen of them, *Pitt, Greenville, R.L. Myers, North East, Tarboro, Beaufort, R.L. Myers II, Alpha, Beta, Margie, Washington, Aurora,* and *Tar River* were constructed in Washington. Leachville, on Pungo Creek, was the building site for *Edgecombe*.[297] Why *Edgecombe* was built on the banks of the Pungo River in 1876 is unknown. Lawrence Clark, a prosperous farmer, and A.W. Styron, well-known Washington businessman, borrowed money to construct the vessel.[298]

All these vessels were riverboats designed to navigate the shallow Tar River, as far as Tarboro, and were built by Styron and R. L. Myers, prominent businessmen and shipbuilders before the war. Styron converted the large barge *Red Ram* into *Greenville*. Styron claimed that she was the "lightest draught propeller in America," drawing only twenty inches, despite the fact she was over 115 feet in length. In 1881, he made a similar claim for *Tarboro*. With her machinery, boilers, and ballast on board the latter drew only eight inches. The prestigious journal, *Scientific American*, substantiated this claim.[299] Styron went on to build a number of steamers. He built the *Margie* in 1883, *Alpha* in 1886, *Beta* in 1888, and *Aurora* in 1893. *Margie* was designed to operate on Bogue Sound and White Oak and New Rivers in Onslow County.[300] *Alpha* was the first of his "alphabet" vessels. Styron envisioned a fleet of these steamers, but only a second one, *Beta*, was constructed. In contrast to Styron's other steamers, *Alpha*, a large vessel more than 120 feet long, was built to navigate the waters between Washington and Baltimore. She made at least seven trips across Chesapeake Bay.[301] Styron may have constructed other steamers, but nothing is known about them. The *New Bern Weekly Journal* reported he was "… pushing work on a new steamer," and the Washington *Progress* noted he was building a light steamboat to run on Lake Mattamuskeet in Hyde County. In 1888, it was rumored he was building a 400-ton steamer. There is no other information on this large vessel.[302]

Myers's shipyard not as productive as Styron's, but the firm had exclusive rights in Washington to build vessels for the Old Dominion Steamship Company. Myers constructed *Pitt* in 1874, followed by *R.L. Myers* in 1879, *Washington* in 1881, *Myers II* in 1885, and *Tar River* in 1896. *Alma*, which may have been constructed by Myers, was launched in 1897.[303]

Few steam-powered vessels were built in the Albemarle Sound region. Most of the steamers that plied Albemarle Sound and its tributaries were Norfolk-built and owned. They were generally larger than North Carolina-built steamboats. Except in Elizabeth City, there was no established shipbuilding facility in the northeastern part of the state that built more than one steamboat. They were generally built at lumber companies and alongside wharves. As elsewhere in North Carolina, newspapers occasionally mention a steamboat being constructed, but additional information is scarce. One was supposedly built on the Yeopim River near Edenton. This may have been *Mary E. Roberts* launched in 1873.[304] A notice in the *Murfreesboro Index* refers to a "party of Virginians building a steam powered vessel at Eaton Ferry on the Roanoke River."[305] In 1870, *Helen Smith* was built in Edenton and later rebuilt in Norfolk. In 1881, the small canal steamer *Sue* was constructed in Edenton, and in 1893 another vessel built to navigate the Chesapeake and Albemarle Canal, *Sarah Drummond*, was launched there. A number of small steam flats employed in the Albemarle Sound fisheries were also constructed in Edenton.[306]

Two steamers were built in Hertford County, an unnamed one near Tunis on the Chowan River and *Ark* at Murfreesboro on the Meherrin River. E.C. Worrell, a local businessman, hired a Lieutenant Britton to supervise *Ark's* construction. A large paddlewheeler, she was 143 feet long and was completed in 1888.[307] The small steamboats *Cleopatra* and *Chowan* were not built on the Chowan River, but at Colerain in Bertie County. Several steam-powered fishing vessels were constructed in Colerain. As Colerain had a large fishery, *Chowan* was probably built for the fishing industry, but later rebuilt to carry freight.[308]

Three steamboats were constructed in Windsor on the Cashie River in Bertie County under the supervision of Wilbur Askew, who also captained them at different times. *Kalula*, launched in 1870, was the first of the three. Built by Askew and W.D. Mizelll, the sidewheeler was only forty-three feet long and provided a link with larger steamers at Plymouth. Along with one of his brothers and Charles T. Harden, Wilbur Askew decided a larger vessel was needed. *Bertie*, a 68-foot sidewheeler, was laid down in 1872. The vessel was designed and built by L. Thrower, a local ship carpenter. In 1884, the Askers built *Tahoma*, a 100-foot screw propelled vessel.[3]

Between 1865 and 1893, despite having several shipyards, Elizabeth City produced few steamers. The *Elizabeth City* was completed at the Lawrence shipyard in 1879, the 65-foot paddlewheeler *Bettie* in 1884, and the screw steamer *G.F. Derickson* in 1894. Steam-powered towboats and fishing vessels were also built in Pasquotank County.[310] Small steamboats were constructed across the Pasquotank River in Camden County. The *Enterprise*, *Hattie*, and *Dauntless* were all built at South Mills for the canal trade.[311] Two were built in Manteo, probably by one or both of the Creefs. The *Cumberland* was launched 1883, and the *Hattie Creek* in 1888. The *Cumberland* was documented as being 119 feet in length an unusually large vessel to have been constructed in Manteo.[312]

In the decades after the Civil War, the all-purpose steamboat was gradually superseded by tugs, freight boats, steam-propelled flats and barges, and later, gasoline-powered small craft. Steamboats continued to be constructed into the twentieth century but in decreasing numbers. This may have been a result of the increase in railroads throughout the south and the west. Over the same period, the use of steam flats as cargo vessels grew in popularity. Some prewar steamboats were little more than paddlewheel flats, but it was in the postwar years that the flat as a distinctive type emerged in large numbers. While a great many were built, the exact number is difficult to determine. Vessel documentation records usually use the term steamboat as opposed to steam flat. Moreover, an undetermined number were involved in the state's internal trade and were not documented. In 1886, at least ten steam flats were transporting naval stores and other commodities from the backcountry to Wilmington.[313] Flats were practical and economical to build. They were usually built without knees or superstructure. They might have a small pilot house, and at times, superstructure was added in order to carry passengers. Flats could navigate on extremely shallow water even with a cargo. On several of the state's rivers, particularly the Cape Fear River and its tributaries, they were able to navigate in waters previously plied only by small craft such as pole and row boats. Steam flats were also used in the fishing industry, particularly in Albemarle Sound.[314]

After the war, steam-powered tow or tug boats were also built in North Carolina in large numbers. Vessel documents do not identify a steam towboat until 1890. As with steam flats, many were listed as steamers. The first mention of building a towboat was in 1881 when a combination passenger and tow boat was constructed in Wilmington for the Cape Fear River trade. The majority of North Carolina-built tow boats were constructed for the lumber business.[315]

In 1869, a steam tug was repaired at the Cape Fear marine shipyard, but it is not known where it was built. Vessel documents list eleven towboats built in the state between 1890 and 1899. The 1895 annual report of the Steamboat Inspection Service lists nine that were constructed between 1890 and 1895. Others were built that were not documented.[316] Paddlewheels and propellers were utilized but the majority were screw steamers.

Steam barges and lighters, like flats, were economical to build and operate. A few were documented. In 1895, one was constructed to carry freight on Lake Mattamuskeet. At 340 tons and 165 feet in length, *Glide* was the largest barge built in the state. The vessel was constructed at Tunis in Hertford County for a local lumber company.[317] There was a considerable increase in the use of self-propelled barges on the Dismal Swamp and the Chesapeake and Albemarle Canals at the end of the nineteenth century. North Carolina shipbuilders constructed miscellaneous steam-powered vessels including Corp of Engineers dredges and even a fireboat. In 1878, Colville and Taylor built a self-propelled cotton compress for use on the Cape Fear River. In 1882, the floating compress was rebuilt as a water-borne sawmill. In 1889, a steam hoisting boat was constructed to lift heavy cargos on and off vessels.[318] Several floating saw and shingle mills were constructed for use on the state's rivers. One was constructed in Fayetteville. A local newspaper quipped that it "will be a big thing on wheels—no, no, on water, we mean." The Murfreesboro *Index* referred to one built there as a "lumber boat." Christened *Ark*, it serviced the timber industry on the Chowan and Meherrin Rivers for several years. A floating saw mill was launched in Hertford where the local paper wrote erroneously that it was a "novel" invention.[319]

Local newspapers often referred to a new steamboat as a "thing of beauty." Available descriptions suggest that their appearance had improved over those built before the Civil War, but they were hardly things of beauty, at least in comparison to steamers elsewhere in the country. Larger boats were constructed to carry more cargo and passengers. In addition to staterooms, many of the new boats had galleys, dining halls, and even lounges or sitting rooms. Nevertheless, a large percentage of the steamers, especially those constructed to operate on the narrow curvy channels, were short and stubby, giving the appearance of "large wheelbarrows going backward."[320] There was some improvement in hull design. Vessels with screw propellers usually had sharp sterns and bows. Bottoms remained relatively flat but some designs incorporated modifications to increase speed: "The beautiful, blunt headed [vessels] . . . are too slow and monotonous. We want something to plow the water, with sufficient speed to make twelve knots."[321] Wooden steam-powered vessels constructed in North Carolina generally had short lives. They were built with local timber, usually pine. Maintenance was regular, and at times, expensive. Steamboat accidents were frequent and often resulted in sinkings.[322] Frequently, a steamboat was rebuilt or its machinery was removed and it was converted to a flat or barge. Corps of Engineers records are particularly revealing on this aspect as many of their North Carolina-built vessels had to be rebuilt within a few years of original construction.[323] It is difficult to generalize about steam-powered vessels built in North Carolina between 1865 and 1893. Other than a major change in propulsion after the war, the only shared characteristic was their relatively flat bottom. Only two screw-propelled steamers were built in North Carolina before the Civil War. Nearly all were paddle wheelers with the wheel in the stern. After the war, a significant majority of those constructed in the state were screw- propelled. The *Contentnea*, built at Kinston in 1879, was the first to use propellers on the Neuse River and its tributaries.[324] Much of the machinery was then manufactured in North Carolina, principally by Kornegay and Company in Goldsboro, and the machine works in Wilmington. However, evidence suggests the majority was still imported from outside the state. All the propellers were cast out-of-state. Baltimore firms provided much of it. Some came from New York, Richmond, Virginia, and Waynesboro, Pennsylvania. A Chicago firm was contacted regarding engines for a Washington built vessel.[325] Occasionally, there are brief descriptions of machinery.

The steamboat *Snow Hill* had an "Eclipse engine" that had a unique power system in which the engine used a "lochner attachment for transmitting power." Another Contentnea Creek vessel employed machinery in which the engine and boiler were "…so constructed as to generate its own steam without the use of fire." One of the local steamers was powered by a high pressure vertical engine. Although engine design had improved, they were primarily the non-condensing type, as used in North Carolina-built boats before the war. The sound of steam exhaust from steamboats is described as being similar to that of railroad locomotives. The power plants made enough noise "…to awaken the dead in the National Cemetery [in] Newberne." Apparently, the Eclipse power plant did not work well as it was removed from *Snow Hill*, and sold the following year.[326] Horsepower varied considerably depending upon a variety of factors including vessel size. The Eclipse engine was 15 horsepower, but a number of engines generated more than 100 horsepower.[327]

Pleasure Boats

In the 1880s, North Carolina-built vessels began to use the internal combustion engine fueled by both naphtha and gasoline. The state's commercial fishermen were the first to convert their sailboats to motor boats as well as construct them from the keel up.[328] Both fuels were derivatives of petroleum, and both were developed in Europe in the 1880s. The naphtha engine was a transition between the steam power plant and the gasoline-powered engine. It was smaller, lighter, and more economical than the steam engine, but the fuel was dangerous. It was first manufactured and sold commercially in the United States in the 1880s by F. W. Olfeldt. As early as 1891, a pilot boat based in Southport was equipped with a naphtha engine. Naphtha powered craft were introduced in Carteret County in the 1890s. Boats using naphtha engines were certainly built elsewhere in the state, but as they were used primarily on small non-documented craft, information about them is scarce.[329]

As with naphtha engines, the installation of gasoline-powered engines did not require a licensed engineer. They were lighter, more economical than steam engines, took up less space, and consequently, became increasing popular. As with naphtha-powered vessels, there is little information on those either converted to, or built to be powered by, gasoline engines. Even before the twentieth century, there were clearly a sizeable number. Not surprisingly, this new technology created problems for builders: "The gas boats built in this place by Messers Sterling and Blake do not nearly meet expectations, the motors are not good." Between 1886 and 1890, nine menhaden vessels built in North Carolina were converted from sail to gasoline or naphtha.[330]

Pleasure craft also experienced a transition. The 1900 manufacturing census reported that the construction of pleasure boats had become an important aspect of boat building. Yachts and recreational craft were constructed before the Civil War, but few in North Carolina. Workboats were multipurpose and used for other activities including leisure. In 1898, a New Bern newspaper reported "not in the memory of the oldest inhabitants were there any boats constructed entirely for pleasure and put upon the Neuse for sailing and rowing." In the decades after the Civil War, the construction of "pleasure boats" became a lucrative business for North Carolina shipbuilders. In the 1870s, this was particularly true for sailing vessels. However, business was generally confined to established yards in the ports. Newspapers occasionally mention the construction of a sailing yacht or small boat built for racing or recreation. A few were built in New Bern and Carteret County. In 1871, two New Bern boat builders were planning to construct pleasure yachts of from six to nine tons.[331]

The catamaran type, which originated in Polynesia, was first constructed in the United States in the 1870s.

As with other types, it quickly spread to North Carolina where two were built in Wilmington, one in 1879 and a second one in 1882.³³² These were the only two catamarans built in the state prior to the twentieth century. By far, Wilmington was the center of pleasure boat construction in the 1870s. At least one a year was launched by the port's shipbuilders. As early as 1860, Solomon Morse and Alford Ellis formed a partnership to construct pleasure boats. The partnership was dissolved in 1869 and Ellis formed a new partnership. Both men continued building small yachts. The Beerys and Cassideys also built yachts. Occasionally, locally constructed yachts raced on the river opposite the town.³³³

There is no information on pleasure boats being built in Wilmington during the 1880s. In the 1890s, the brilliant boatbuilder, Emanuel Garcia, moved from Southport to Wilmington and promptly began building yachts, which he continued to do until his unexpected death.

At least three yachts were built in the state for purposes other than racing. The yacht *Eagle* was constructed to carry passengers from Carteret County to Philadelphia for the Centennial. *Governor Jarvis* was intended for the shad trade, and *George Slover* for the oyster fishery.³³⁴

Regattas and races contributed to the growing popularity of pleasure craft. Wrightsville Beach was a particularly popular location for periodic regattas.³³⁵ Small craft propelled by oars also participated in regattas. Wilmington had a rowing club and Southport had a small organization devoted to sculling. Row boats and canoes were the most common small craft in North Carolina waters and, at times, were involved in racing activities.³³⁶ Not all rowing craft were built for racing. The New Hanover County sheriff had a large forty-foot barge or gondola built for fishing and hunting. It was furnished with sleeping and cooking facilities, and except in propulsion, was not that different from modern pontoon boats.³³⁷

THE INDUSTRIAL AGE

After the Civil War, shipbuilding in North Carolina became more of a science than an art. More vessels were powered by engines, and those engines became increasingly efficient. Shipwrights discarded the traditional methods of designing and building by eye and adopted plans and models. Designers, sometimes from out-of-state, were frequently employed to draw up plans.³³⁸

Launching a vessel was still a popular event in North Carolina. If such an event was publicized, crowds often lined the banks or beaches to witness it. The tradition of christening with champagne was usually followed, although occasionally, a non-alcoholic beverage or water was substituted. When the steamer *Kinston* was launched at Howard's Shipyard in New Bern, a bottle of champagne was broken on both the stern and bow by co-owners. On at least one occasion, the editor of a local newspaper announced the name of a newly-built vessel before the launching, which elicited criticism from the builders. At times, launchings were delayed because of inclement weather or some fault with the ways or launching mechanism. Accidents happened. A large barge was launched in Washington and floated to the opposite side of the Pamlico River, destroying twenty feet of a wharf.³³⁹

The state's water transportation initially benefited from railroads. Vessels of all types carried produce to rail terminals. Railroads owned and operated steamer lines with established routes to all state ports. As late as 1893, the Norfolk and Southern Railroad owned seven steamboats operating in state waters. However, the rail-water transportation relationship, shifted from cooperation to competition, and precipitated the collapse of maritime commerce in the state. As railroad rates increased, newspaper editorials called for the use of barges and other vessels. Water transportation just barely survived into the twentieth century. The railroads, "administered the coupe de grace," to canal traffic.³⁴⁰

Gradually, the growing importance of the railways spurred major changes in the region's economy, and the role of water transportation diminished. This, coupled with the volatility of the United States economy, generated major downturns such as the panics in the 1870s and 1890s. These were of major consequence. However, there were consolidations, not only among railroads, but with major industrial and financial institutions as well. Economic volatility affected the ship and boat building industry in North Carolina and elsewhere. Although railroads developed rapidly, the ship and boat building industry was more conservative. The Panic of 1893, and its immediate aftermath, precipitated changes in North Carolina's boat and ship building industry. However, despite increasing competition from railroads, and the ever-shifting business climate, it would recover. It would be a recovery in a new form.

NOTES

1. As one middle class farmer wrote: "The people. . . have . . . scarcely bread to supply them to harvest." Paul D. Escott, *Many Excellent People*, 52.
2. The Dibbles brothers are a good example. According to records in the New Bern file, Quartermaster records, RG92, NA, they were able to utilize coastal shipping from New Bern after Union occupation.
3. *ORN* is replete with reports of capturing and destruction of vessels in North Carolina streams. For seizure of fishing vessels, see Norman C. Delaney, "Charles Henry Foster and the Unionist of Eastern North Carolina," *NCHR*, 354.
4. Fonvielle, *Wilmington Campaign*.
5. "Wilmington has changed much since we came here," a union medical officer wrote, "The stores are being opened and there is a large amount of shipping here." Fonvielle, *Wilmington Campaign*,

453; *New Bern Times*, December 21, 1873 reported "about thirty sailing vessels were in port yesterday." Watson, *History of New Bern and Craven County*, 443.

6. James Sprunt, *Chronicles of the Cape Fear River*, 501; Robert Miller, *The New York Coastwise Trade, 1865-1915*, 12; Roberta Alexander, *North Carolina Faces the Freedmen*, 120.

7. "It is not necessary to tell the citizens of Wilmington the difference between today and five years ago. The signs of prosperity are everywhere manifest. Our harbor is full of ships of all nations constantly coming and going." *Wilmington Daily Journal*, February 11, 1874.

8. Deputy Collector of Customs, E. Hubbs, stated further "there is no reason to suppose there will be an increase in the immediate future." E. Hubbs to Secretary of the Treasury, June 25, 1885, Box 275, Special Agent Reports, RG36, NA.

9. Sloan, "Inland Navigation in North Carolina, 1818-1900," 57.

10. *Wilmington Herald of the Union*, May 2, 1865; Fayetteville *Eagle*, October 6, 1870; Angley, "An Historical Overview of the Black River in Southeastern North Carolina."

11. Senator Matthew W. Ransom, who for many years served on the Commerce Committee, was extremely effective in obtaining funds for river and harbor projects in North Carolina. Nancy Revelle, "Matthew Whitaker Ransom's Political Career," M.A. thesis, 45-47, 59, 62-63. See also Cox, "The Pamlico-Tar and its Role in the Development of Eastern North Carolina," M.A. thesis, 86-99; Sloan, "Inland Navigation in North Carolina 1818-1900," 59-60; *Goldsboro Messenger*, January 12, 1885; *New Bern Democrat*, October 8, 1879; Watson, *Wilmington Port of North Carolina*, 118-119. The Ransom Papers, SHC, UNC-CH, have correspondence concerning the state internal improvements. See particularly boxes 5 and 6.

12. *Goldsboro Messenger*, January 12, 15, 1885; also, correspondence and reports in Box 95, Entry 1117, Wilmington District Office, RG77, NA. Local newspapers for the last decades of the nineteenth century carried information on these improvements including editorials, letters to editors and reports. See, *Goldsboro Messenger*, June 5, 1876; March 14, 1878; January 9, April 17, October 16, 1879. In 1884 H. C. Carter of Hyde County was granted a patent for an improved dredging machine: Patent Number 292732, January 29, 1884, Patent Office, Washington, D.C. There is no evidence that it was used but dredging was done in Hyde County and adjacent waters after 1884.

13. Gay to Chief Engineer, 1884, Records of the Chief, RG77, NA; and, Brown, *Dismal Swamp Canal*, 123, 130.

14. Brown, *Juniper Waterway*, 84.

15. Thomas M. Southgate, "Personal Recollections of Thirty Years' Service in the Old Dominion Steamship Company," Mariners Museum, Newport New, Va. See also Brown, *Juniper Waterway*, 92; Watson, *History of New Bern and Craven County*, 529-530; J. Henry Chataigne (comp.), *Raleigh City Directory Containing a General Directory of the Citizens of Raleigh, Together with a Complete Business Directory of the Cities of Raleigh, Charlotte, Durham, Fayetteville, Greensboro, Newbern and Wilmington*, 1883-84, 75, hereafter cited as *Directory*; (Elizabeth City) *Fisherman & Farmer*, June 22, 1888; *Norfolk Journal*, February 9, September 1, 1869. See also the *Norfolk Journal*, May 12, 1872, for statistics and other information on the canal in 1871, and *Murfreesboro Enquirer*, April 10, 1877.

16. *Fayetteville News*, September 25, 1866.

17. Richard Prince, *Norfolk Southern Railroad, Old Dominion Line and Connections*; Brown, *Juniper Waterway*, 126-135.

18. In 1889 the *Washington Progress* reported: "Our citizens are talking railroads continually." The *Raleigh Observer* editorialized for railroads as "cheap transportation," and the *Goldsboro Messenger* advocated "lateral lines of narrow gauge railroads" to open up isolated sections such as Greene County. In another editorial, the Goldsboro paper referred to Greene County as "walled in," unsuitable to water navigation because the Moccasin River (Contentnea Creek) was navigable only during the "wet season." (August 10, 1885; January 6, 1879). See also the (New Bern) *Daily Journal*, January 8, 1886.

19. *Goldsboro Messenger*, November 9, 1885.

20. Still, "The Shipbuilding Industry in Washington, North Carolina," 41-42; Johnson, *Sail and Steam Navigation of Eastern North Carolina*, 25-26; Brown, *Juniper Waterway*, 129-131; Thomas H. Sloan, steamboats notes in author's possession.

21. Brown, *Juniper Waterway*, 149; Tarboro *Southerner*, February 10, 1881; *Kinston Free Press*, September 19, 1888.

22. *Murfreesboro Enquirer*, November 1, 1877, August 22, 1878; *Fayetteville Eagle*, February 23, 1871.

23. Schubert to Wright, December 3, 1885, Entry 1116, RG77, NA.

24. *The State* XXI (May, 1954), 16; Brown, *Juniper Waterway*, 149-150.

25. *North Carolinian*, May 30, 1871; *Norfolk Journal*, August 4, 1870.

26. *New Bern Times*, June 4, 1873.

27. Article 1888 Norfolk newspaper reprinted by *The Connector*, 9 (Fall, 2005), 14; *Historical and Descriptive Review of the State of North Carolina, II, The Eastern Section*, 134.

28. Joseph C. Carter was a Union soldier who had been stationed in Beaufort from 1862 to 1864. He returned to Beaufort after the war and remarked upon differences observed. Joseph C. Carter, *A Union Vet Revisits the Former Confederate States*, 65.

29. Brown, *A State Movement for Railroad Development*, 122; A. E. Rhodes to Worth, July 26, 1866, Hamilton (ed.), *Correspondence of Jonathan Worth*, II, 694-695. The *State Agricultural Journal* called Beaufort "North Carolina's natural outlet to the sea... the most magnificent port on our sea-coast," but admitted that as a port it was a "failure"; (Wilmington) *Morning Star*, December 27, 1874.

30. Miller, *The New York Coastwise Trade, 1865-1915*, 13.

31. *Norfolk Journal*, May 14, 1870; *New Bern Daily Journal*, February 23, 1886; (Tarboro) *Southerner*, October 3, 1878.

32. (Elizabeth City) *Fisherman & Farmer*, January 24, 1889; *Norfolk Journal*, January 10, February 15, 27, 1866; December 25, 1867; June 9, 1868; May 14, 1870.

33. The small community of Averasboro would disappear late in the nineteenth century partly because maritime trade ceased. *Fayetteville Eagle*, June 16, 1873.

34. Angley, "A Historical Overview of the Black River in Southeastern North Carolina," 26-27; nomination form for Clear Run for the National Register of Historic Places, copy in the Underwater Archaeology Branch, Kure Beach, N.C.; Johnson, *Riverboating in Lower Carolina*, 71-77; *Fayetteville Semi-Weekly Eagle*, June 7, 1873.

35. *Wilmington Daily Journal*, September 4, 1868. Flats carried cargo as far as Averasboro, and steamboats could reach the small Harnett County town during high water. Four steamboats brought cargo to Averasboro in February 1872. *Fayetteville Eagle*, February 22, 1872.

36. *Fayetteville Eagle*, September 16, 27, 1873; Parker, *Cumberland County: A History*, 99; Watson, *Wilmington: Port of North Carolina*, 118.

37. *Fayetteville Eagle*, May 11, 1871; *Goldsboro Messenger*, March 8, 1880, March 27, 1884; Watson, *Wilmington: Port of North Carolina*,

104-135.

38. Susan S. Carson, *Joshua's Dream: A Town with Two Names*, 58; Watson, *Wilmington: Port of North Carolina*, 121.

39. Lockwood Folly supposedly got its name because a Mr. Lockwood built a vessel so far from the water that it could not be launched. W. W. Storm, *Wilmington—Where the Cape Fear Rolls to the Sea*, 74; *Southport Leader*, April 3, 1890, May 29, 1890.

40. Assistant Engineer to Captain E. Lucas, June 20, 1899, Entry 1113, Box 33, RG77, NA; Littleton, *Camp Lejeune*, 144-148; (Wilmington) *Weekly Star*, December 7, 1883, September 17, 1897, March 14, 1890, October 2, 1891; (Wilmington) *Morning Star*, May 23, 1884, August 3, 1898; (Wilmington *Messenger*), October 12, 1889, November 22, 1899, May 14, 1891; *Goldsboro Messenger*, May 20, 1886.

41. "Pettyman to Grady, June 11, 1894, copy in Ransom Papers," SHC, UNC-CH; *New Bern Weekly Journal*, January 8, 1883.

42. Archaeological surveys revealed evidence of many activities related to turpentine distilling. In order to ship the turpentine, tar, and pitch, barrels and kegs were manufactured. Numerous wharves beneath the estuary and on adjacent land have been identified and reflect past economic activities of the small port. Richard A. Stephenson and William N. Still, Jr., *The Submerged Cultural Resources of Swansboro*.

43. In the mid-1880s a Massachusetts businessman established a large lumber mill on the river at a place he named Stella. It became a boom town for a number of years but declined with the depletion of the local timber. Davis and others, *Heritage of Carteret County*, 153-154. Also, see Still, "Shipbuilding and Boatbuilding in Swansboro," 10.

44. *Goldsboro Messenger*, March 5, November 12, 1883. For Contentnea and the Neuse see Creek see *Goldsboro Messenger*, June 5, 1876, January 14, 1778, April 9, 1882, February 22, August 20, 1883; Roger Kammerer, "A History of Grifton," *Greenville Times*, June 7, 1789. Kammerer's article lists eight steamboats trading up the stream. Watson, *History of New Bern and Craven County*, 443; *North Carolina Times*, March 21, April 11, 14, 1865.

45. Merriman, "North Carolina Schooners, 1815-1900, and the S. R. Fowle Company of Washington, North Carolina," 54; Cox, "The Pamlico-Tar and Its Role in the Development of Eastern North Carolina," 124, 106.

46. (New Bern) *Daily Journal* reported the arrival of a schooner from New York with a cargo of turnips, cabbage and Irish potatoes. "This sounds like bringing coal to New Castle," the editor wrote, January 2, 1886.

47. Eyes to Stanton, February 1, 1893, Entry 1113, Box 32, RG77, NA; *Kinston Free Press*, November 15, 1888, *New Bern Weekly Journal*, March 3, 1887.

48. Regarding the idea of a steamboat from Kinston to Goldsboro the *Mount Olive Advertiser* editor quipped, "The way is now open for the formation of the Amphibious Sprinkling Co., to sprinkle the river bed at low water, so the boat won't kick up so much dust." (New Bern) *Weekly Journal*, October 31, 1899; *Goldsboro Weekly Argus*, January 19, June 29, September 21, 1899; (New Bern) *Weekly Journal*, September 19, October 24, 1899.

49. *Goldsboro Headlight*, July 24, 1889; *Kinston Free Press*, April 5, 1888; October 3, 1889; (New Bern) *Daily Journal*, January 15, 1884; (New Bern) *Weekly Journal*, July 19, 1899; (Wilmington) *Morning Star*, September 11, 1883; Watson, *History of New Bern and Craven County*, 530. For Contentnea Creek see (New Bern) *Daily Journal*, February 28, March 11, 1883. For a personal account of New Bern's maritime trade during the latter part of the nineteenth century see letter from W.G. Boyd to editor of the *Greensboro Daily News*, November 2, 1924. Grifton was originally known as Bell's Ferry.

50. Corps of Engineers, Stanton to Casey, January 26, 1896, Entry 1117, Box 76, RG77, NA. Since most were under five tons and not required to obtain a license, the exact number of vessels is impossible to determine. On Christmas Eve of 1885, the (New Bern) *Weekly Journal* reported that twenty-nine oyster boats were moored at one canning establishment.

51. (New Bern) *Weekly Journal*, April 16, 1896. For the Pamlico County trade see Angley, "A Brief Maritime History of the Oriental Area of Pamlico County"; (New Bern) *Weekly Journal*, July 25, 28, 1899.

52. E. Hubbs report, June 23, 1885, Box 275, Special Agents Reports, RG36, NA; *Goldsboro Messenger*, April 5, 1880, February 11, 1886; (Wilmington) *Morning Star*, July 16, August 14, 1879.

53. Corps of Engineers, Stanton to Casey, January. 26, 1896, Entry 1117, Box 96, RG77, NA.

54. Washington's claim was supported by George Nowitzky, Norfolk newspaper writer in the 1880s. In 1888 he asserted that Washington, next to Wilmington, was the busiest "water-front" in the state. George I. Nowitzky, *Norfolk: The Marine Metropolis of Virginia and the Sounds and River Cities of North Carolina*, 187.

55. *Washington Progress*, April 13, 1989; (New Bern) *Weekly Journal*, December 20, 1894; Merriman, "North Carolina Schooners, 1815-1900, and the S. R. Fowle Company of Washington, North Carolina;" (New Bern_ *Daily Times*, November 24, 1872; (New Bern) *Journal*, June 8, 1882; Still, "The Shipbuilding Industry in Washington, North Carolina"; *Historical and Descriptive Review of the State of North Carolina*, I, 1885, 149-150, 183-184; Cox, "The Pamlico-Tar and its Role in the Development of Eastern North Carolina," 139. Only a small percentage of barges and flats were documented.

56. *Washington Gazette*, November 1, 1889, February 15, 1894.

57. (Greenville) *Eastern Reflector*, January 30, 1889; Turner and Bridgers, *History of Edgecombe County*, 353; *Washington Progress*, June 21, 1887.

58. *King Weekly*, June 19, 1896, Turner and Bridgers, *History of Edgecombe County*, 353; (Tarboro) *Southerner*, August 26, 1880.

59. W. Scott Boyce, *Economic and Social History of Chowan County, North Carolina*, 91-102; North Carolina State Board of Agriculture, *North Carolina and its Resources*, 150-151; Brown, *Juniper Waterway*, 136-138; *Murfreesboro Enquirer*, April 3, 1878.

60. *Murfreesboro Enquirer*, May 15, 1879, February 8, 1877, May 8, 1879.

61. *Norfolk Journal*, August 1, 1873; Corps of Engineers Report, October 11, 1870, File 154, RG77, NA; *Albemarle Times*, August 24, 1874; (Robersonville) *Weekly Herald*, August 10, 1949; unpublished history of Williamston, copy in author's possession.

62. (Elizabeth City) *Fisherman & Farmer*, November 7, 1890, July 21, 1891, January 17, February 3, 1893, November 1, 1895; Corps of Engineers Report, November 16, 1883, File 987, RG77, NA.

63. (Elizabeth City) *North Carolinian*, September 2, 1869.

64. Timothy Hunter Bankruptcy File, Case File 259, Record Group 21, NA –Atlanta. Myers died in 1870 and his oldest son died in 1878. He listed six employees (four black people) for back pay. Among his property he listed the shipyard as worth $500. For one of his debtors see *Timothy Hunter vs. Kenneth Pendleton*, February 1866, Admiralty, Elizabeth City, RG21. He sold his shipbuilding establishment to Margaret Snell, the wife of another Elizabeth ship carpenter. Copy of Deed in Hunter Papers, ECU; Jakes(?) to Hunter, July 20, 1868, Hunter Papers, ECU; Turner, "An

Historical and Archaeological Investigation of the *Scuppernong*," 43; various bills and other documents in the Hunter Papers, ECU; (Elizabeth City) *North Carolinian*, December 9, 1869.

65. Affidavit of Josiah Farrow, February 1901, copy in the Rodman Papers, ECU; Howard to the President, July 29, 1865, Reel 62, M1003, NA; Cassidey to the President, July 11, 1865, Reel 37, M1003, NA; William L. Beery to the President, August 8, 1865, copy in Petitions for Pardon, New Hanover County, Civil War Collection, SANC; Benjamin Beery to Andrew Johnson, August 1, 1865, Reel 37, M1003, NA.

66. William N. Still, Jr., "Southern Maritime Heritage," in *Encyclopedia of Southern Culture*, 637-638.

67. *Fayetteville News*, October 23, 1866. The large steamboat *Governor Worth* was built in Delaware for the Cape Fear trade. Jonathan Worth to "Brother," January 9, 1866, Worth Papers, SANC; Johnson, *Riverboating in Lower Carolina*, 146. For the construction of the schooner *Johnny* in Beaufort see the William Clarke Papers, ECU.

68. (Tarboro) *Southerner*, November 29, 1874; *Wilmington Weekly Journal*, December 4, 1874.

69. Jonathan Havens, *New Bern and the Pamlico Sound Region*, 43; *Wilmington Star*, October 15, 1873; *New Bern Journal*, April 13, 1882, February 21, 1887; *Washington Progress*, January 14, 1896; (Elizabeth City) *Economist*, July 19, 1881.

70. (Wilmington) *Weekly Star*, February 20, 1891; *Wilmington Messenger*, September 19, 1890.

71 Henry Hall, *Report on the Ship Building Industry in the United States*, 130, 256-264.

72. Benjamin Webb built at least one steamboat in Kinston a quarter-mile from the river. A house mover hauled it to the river for launching. (New Bern) *Daily Journal*, June 16, 22, 1882.

73. (New Bern) *Journal*, May 11, 1893; White Oak River Corporation Account Book, May 1898, Carteret County Court Records, SANC.

74. Although the 1890 census records were destroyed, the report on manufacturing, based on the 1890 census, was published in 1895.

75. As an example, the 1900 census does not mention the well-known boatworks of Emanuel Garcia.

76. This may be why Hall's *Report of the Shipbuilding Industry in the United States*, based on the census of 1880, does not mention Wilmington among North Carolina's shipyard locations.

77. (Wilmington) *Messenger*, Special Edition, June 7, 1888; *Fayetteville Observer*, June 5, 1884.

78. A "Mr. Sink" partnered with Benjamin for a brief period in the wrecking business. (Wilmington) *Star*, October 11, 1868, November 28, 1872, February 12, 1873; *Branson and Farrar's North Carolina Business Directory, 1866-1867*, 103.

79. (Wilmington) *Morning Star*, December 14, 1869. The yard never re-opened. The 1870 census on manufacturing does not list a Beery establishment on Eagle Island. The 1872 directory lists the yard as still in operation, although a newspaper notice the year before indicates that it was no longer in use as a shipyard. One authority suggests that it continued to be used by "small boatbuilders until 1911 when the Wilmington Iron Works purchased the property." An employee of the yard wrote years later that only a smokestack remained after the yard was destroyed in 1865, and that it was still standing overrun by vines in 1917. Jackson, *The Cape Fear-Northeast Cape Fear Rivers Comprehensive Study*, 220; (Wilmington) *Morning Star*, May 23, 1917.

80. *Cassideys vs. Washington*, April 1873, Wilmington District Court Records, RG21, NA-Atlanta; Jackson, *Cape Fear-Northeast Cape Fear Rivers Comprehensive Study*, 225; (Wilmington) *Morning Star*, October 31, 1871; Tony P. Wrenn, *Wilmington North Carolina: An Architectural and Historical Portrait*, 266-267.

81. Benjamin Beery's obituary noted that "his skill in removing grounded vessels off the shoals or beach was unsurpassed." (Wilmington) *Messenger*, April 26, 1892.

82. In 1867, one of the brothers, Jesse Cassidey, received a patent for developing a ship building mold used for the shaping of wooden timbers "for the frame of a vessel laid out on the floor." Patent number 68487, September 8, 1867, Patents Office, Washington, D.C. The R.G. Dun report of 1868 described Jesse as not having the energy of his father. In 1860 Jesse's brother, James, allowed him to use his credit with New York merchants to purchase goods for a store that Jesse owned. In 1868, the merchants sued. Jesse borrowed money mortgaging his one-fifth share in the shipyard and marine railway as collateral. The debts were evidently paid off, but when he was unable to pay back the loan, his partnership in the shipyard was sold.

83. Francis Cassidey's daughter, who visited the shipyard frequently, wrote that her father was a sort of jack of all trades there. He drafted the plans, built half models, and worked as ship carpenter on the vessels. R.G. Dun and Company, report, June 1874.

84. *John Seymour, et. al., vs. Jesse Cassidey*, 1868, New Hanover County Estate Papers, SANC; 1880 census does not mention Ross as still in the county. New Hanover County Deed Books KKK, 287-289; UU, p. 225, SANC; New Hanover County (original) Wills, 732-1961, *SANC*; Censuses of 1870, 1880; Isaac. B. Grainger Estate, New Hanover County Estate Records, 1878, SANC; (Wilmington) *Morning Star*, January 14, 31, 1875; *Wilmington Daily Journal*, August 29, 1874; Jackson, *Cape Fear-Northeast Cape Fear Rivers Comprehensive Study*, 214-215; *Branson's Directory for 1877-78*, 215; Brooke G. White Interview, March 23, 1939, American Life Histories, Manuscripts from the Federal Writers Project, 1936-1940, American Memory.com; Helen Moore Sammons, *Marriage and Death Notices from Wilmington, North Carolina, 1866-1870*, 32. James Cassidey, Jr. was not in the shipbuilding business but was a merchant.

85. (Wilmington) *Morning Star*, September 28, 1878.

86. See list of maps in bibliography. Sanborn maps are available for 1889 and several other years. However, shipyards are not clearly designated. The Taylor Steam Saw Mill boatyard built a steam dredge, a yacht, and a number of scows. A Sanborn map of 1889 positions the Taylor sawmill and yard adjacent to the Skinner establishment.

87. Skinner was a shipbuilder and a skilled mechanic. Initially, he was a shipbuilder in Fayetteville after the Civil War. In the 1870s, he moved to Wilmington. *Wilmington Star*, April 8, August 16, 1879.

88 Skinner built the smokestack and machinery for the city's electric railway company in 1892. Until he died in 1907 in Jacksonville, Florida, the elder Skinner engaged in "some special marine work." and often took on jobs outside the state. For information on the Skinner's business activities, see Vol. 66, Series I, Bill Reaves Collection, New Hanover County Public Library; Jackson, *Cape Fear-Northeast Cape Fear Rivers Comprehensive Study*, 226-229.

89. An archaeological survey of the Skinner property found two marine railways, a small one and the one rebuilt in 1884. *Society for Historical Archaeological Newsletter*, 24 (October 1991), 32-33. Mark Wilde-Ramsing, "Underwater Archaeologists Dig Up Clues,"

Tar Heel Junior Historian, 31 (Spring 1992), 34-38. The article includes reconstructed drawings of one of the railways. Ramsey to Marshall, March 14, 1881, copy in Underwater Archaeology Branch, Kure Beach, N.C.; Jackson, *Cape Fear-Northeast Cape Fear Rivers Comprehensive Study*, 227; (Wilmington) *Weekly Star*, August 1, 1884. Skinner told a reporter in 1888 that he planned to erect a second railway. (Wilmington *Messenger*), Special Edition, June 7, 1888, July 1, 1887.

90. New Hanover County Deed Book 14, 429-431, NA. Skinner had signed a five-year lease in 1892, but he wanted a longer lease, warning the property owners that he might take his shipbuilding business elsewhere. New Hanover County Deed Book 11, 140-142, SANC; (Wilmington) *Weekly Star*, September 11, 1891. A newspaper article reported the yard resumed operation in 1895.

91. The steamboat was built by Henry Efamy, a carpenter from Buffalo, New York, who traveled to Wilmington in a small skiff. Jackson, *Cape Fear-Northeast Cape Fear Rivers Comprehensive Study*, 222; (Wilmington) *Morning Star*, November 9, 1877. For Wilson boatyard see (Wilmington) *Morning Star*, October 8, 1882, and Sanborn map, 1884-1886; (Wilmington) *Star*, April 12, 1876.

92. (Wilmington) *Star*, August 21, October 10, 1883, Jackson, *Cape Fear-Northeast Cape Fear Rivers Comprehensive Study*, 231.

93. Jackson, *Cape Fear-Northeast Cape Fear Rivers Comprehensive Study*, 230-231; (Wilmington) *Messenger*, May 8, 1889.

94. For Wessell see Vol. 77, Series, I, the Reaves Collection New Hanover County Public Library, Wilmington, N.C.; Jackson, *Cape Fear-Northeast Cape Fear Rivers Comprehensive Study*, 232.

95. (Wilmington) *Star*, September 17, 1886; Johnson, *Riverboating in Lower Carolina*, 120, 144-145.

96. Johnson, *Riverboating in Lower Carolina*, and Angley, "An Historical Overview of the Black River in Southeastern North Carolina" offer detailed descriptions of the maritime activities on the Black River. However, neither mentions a shipyard site. Angley does state that a "shipyard of at least some size and sophistication must also have been located at Clear Run in Sampson County by the late 1890s" (23) but no other information is given. At least one steamboat, the *A. J. Johnson*, was built there. Some of the vessels were floated to Wilmington where machinery was installed and they were fitted out. The same is true for Fayetteville.

97. Johnson, *Riverboating in Lower Carolina*, 71. Paddison's memoir, Richard P. Paddison Papers, ECU. Paddison is listed in the 1880 census for Pender County as a merchant.

98. Paddison Memoir, Paddison Papers, ECU.

99. *History of North Carolina*, IV, 284-285. Black family file, series I, vol. 8, Reaves Collection, New Hanover County Public Library; also see Angley, "An Historic Overview of the Black River in Southeastern North Carolina" and Johnson, *Riverboating in Lower Carolina*, 85, 87, 120. The Shermans are listed in the Pender County census returns for 1880 and 1900 as carpenters. Stephen is listed as a mechanic. Sherman family file, Series II, Reaves Collection.

100. *Wilmington Journal*, January 21, 1869; Jackson, *Cape Fear-Northeast Cape Fear Rivers Comprehensive Survey*, 223.

101. *Wilmington Sun*, October 23, 1878.

102. *Southport Leader*, June 15, 29, 1893; *Goldsboro Messenger*, May 8, 1884; April 5, 1894.

103. *Southport Leader*, May 29, 1890. See also Crockette W. Hewlett and Mona Smalley, *Between the Creeks, Revised, Masonboro Sound, 1735-1985*.

104. Victor K. Padgett, "Ship Building Along the New River," manuscript in author's possession; *King Weekly*, March 11, 1898; (Wilmington) *Morning Star*, August 21, 1876.

105. (New Bern) *Daily Journal*, April 12, 1893; (New Bern) *Weekly Journal*, May 9, 1895; *Wilmington Evening Dispatch*, February 27, 1896.

106. Still, "Shipbuilding and Boatbuilders in Swansboro, 1800-1950," *Tributaries*, 10; (New Bern) *Weekly Journal*, July 12, 1894, October 3, 1895.

107. (New Bern) *Weekly Journal*, September 6, 1894, July 22, 1897.

108. According to one erroneous account, this yard, had the "first elevated marine railway in the state." *Beaufort Weekly Record*, August 18, 1887; Still, "Shipbuilding and Boatbuilders in Swansboro, 1800-1950," *Tributaries*; (New Bern) *Daily Journal*, August 11, 1886, February 26, 1887. For acquisition of the land see Carteret County Real Estate Conveyances, NN, 308-310, SANC.

109. There is a large file on this in Carteret County Civil Action Papers, SANC.

110. Havens, *Pamlico Section of North Carolina*, 44.

111. A new shipbuilding firm owned by William Brooks and M.C. Phelps was mentioned. *Carteret County Telephone*, October 14, 1881.

112. (New Bern) *Weekly Journal*, February 4, 1886, August 24, 1882; memoirs of Thomas Carrow of Beaufort, *Carteret County News Times*, July 13, 1948. According to the owner of the Menhaden Oil and Fish Scrap Company, "Within five years we have built two steamers, a schooner and many small boats." *First Annual Report of the Bureau of Labor Statistics. . . for the year 1887*, 63-64; (New Bern) *Daily Journal*, August 19, 1882, January 23, 1890; *New Bern Times*, November 6, 1893.

113. Unpublished document in the Core Sound Waterfowl Museum, Harkers Island, N.C. *Pigott vs. Willis*, 1879, Carteret County Civil Action Papers, SANC; *Mailboat* (Fall 1991), 23.

114. Appleton Oaksmith has been called an adventurer. He was that, and much more. Various writers have described his many activities and schemes from filibustering, shipping, and running slaves before the Civil War to development and other economic ventures. Among several biographical sketches see Robert G. Lewis, "Appleton Oaksmith, Man of All Trades," *The Researcher*, 20-27; Ruth P. Barbour, "Appleton Oaksmith, A Doomed Dreamer," *The State* (April 1985), 20-22, 31-32; Nona (Blanchard) Lockhart, "Appleton Oaksmith," Davis and others (eds,), *Heritage of Carteret County North Carolina*, II, 177-178. However, none of these mention his shipbuilding activities.

115. There is no evidence that the company had any business and probably went defunct with Oaksmith's death in 1887. *Branson's Directory*, 1885, 186; *Ellen Mason vs. Charles Milner*, September 19, 1878, Superior Court, Carteret County, SANC; *New Bern Daily Times*, May 26, 1872; Williamson, *Sailing with Grandpa*, 32; *Beaufort Eagle*, May 17, 1876; Davis and others (eds.), *Heritage of Carteret County North Carolina*, II, 411; Beaufort County Incorporation Plan, May 20, 1878, Carteret County Incorporation Records, Carteret County N.C. Courthouse; Ellen Mason Deed, October 1, 1878; Carteret County Deed Book 2, 323-324, SANC; *Ellen Mason vs. Charles Milner*, Superior Court Fall Term 1878, copy in the Appleton Oaksmith Papers, SHC, UNC-CH; Oaksmith to Clerk of the Superior Court, November 11, 1880, Carteret County Civil Action Papers, SANC; Jim Willis, "Tales of a Confederate Yankee: Appleton Oaksmith and His Dream of Atlantic Beach," *The Researcher*, 17; (Tarboro) *Southerner*, May 12, 1876.

116. Carteret County Court Records, November 11, 1880, SANC; Beaufort Marine Railway Company, May 20, 1878, Carteret County Incorporation Records, I, 1-3, Carteret County Courthouse. Beaufort, N.C..

117. *New Bern Daily Times*, November 22, December 12, 1865; *New*

Bern Times, December 10, 11, 1873.

118. It is most doubtful that Howard could have received a presidential pardon from Washington in that length of time. He obviously reopened his shipbuilding facility before he was notified of his pardon but with approval of local federal authorities. Howard to Joseph Boyd, July 31, 1865, Joseph Boyd Papers, Rubenstein Special Collections Library, Duke University; *New Bern Daily Times,* July 6 and September 4, 1865.

119. John B. Green III, *Perfect Hurricanes and Awful Conflagrations: The Historical Significance and Archaeological Potential of the Craven County Convention Center Parking Lot Sites, New Bern, North Carolina,* 32-33, hereafter cited as Green, *The Historical Significance and Archaeological Potential of the Craven County Convention Center Parking Lot Sites; New Bern Daily Times,* May 21, 1872.

120. Although the local newspaper notes a schooner being built at the Dennison yard, Dennison must have left the shipbuilding business for in 1878 he is mentioned as a cotton broker and, later, as the sheriff. *Wilmington Weekly Star,* May 31, 1872; *New Bern Daily Times,* May 21, 1872, May 24, 1873, December 11, 1873; *New Bern Times,* December 9, 11, 1873; Sparrow to Wade, 1866, Craven County Deed Book 67, 460; Howard to Wade, November 8, 1869, Craven County Deed Book 70, 359-362, SANC; District of Pamlico Court Records, RG21, NA-Atlanta; *Branson's Directory,* 1869, 46. Wade also owned considerable property including the former shipyard of Thomas Sparrow. The will of William D. O'Leary in Craven County Wills, July 21, 1854; and Craven County Deed Book, vol. 69, 461, SANC.

121. Craven County Deed Book Book 80, 512, SANC. In 1878 Ellis loaned his son-in-law money, not for the first time. It is probable that J. A. Meadows at this time became a silent partner of Howard. See Craven County Deed Book 79, 180, 194, SANC. Amos Wade Estate Papers, Craven County Estate Papers, SANC.

122. *New Bern Times,* June 10, 1873; Whitford Papers, SANC; *New Bern Weekly Journal,* December 4, 1890; Green, *The Historical Significance and Archaeological Potential of the Craven County Convention Center Parking Lot Sites,* 32-33.

123. In his memoir, Whitford refers to Meadows as Howard's nephew. Whitford Papers, copy in the Craven-Pamlico-Carteret Regional Library, New Bern, N.C.

124. Dorcey Perkins is listed in the 1870 census as a ship carpenter. If he died in 1888, either the yard was at least partly owned by a member of the Perkins family or the name was retained. (New Bern) *Weekly Journal,* January 8, February 26, June 29, December 8, 1891; *Historical and Descriptive Review of the State of North Carolina,* I, 81; *New Bern Daily Journal,* August 15, 1888.

125. (New Bern) *Weekly Journal,* September 21, November 27, 1890; November 23, 1900; *New Bern Daily Times,* August 27, October 8, 1872.

126. The firm under Howard and later Meadows did more repairs than new construction and other shipbuilders did the same. (New Bern) *Weekly Journal,* April 5, 1894; January 10, 1895; December 15, 1899.

127. (New Bern) *Journal,* July 31, 1901; (New Bern) *Weekly Journal,* November 2, 1893. In 1888 a writer in the *Kinston Free Press* boasted that Bell's Ferry "now [has] a ship yard." Actually, there must have been one located there earlier, large enough in 1882 to be mentioned in Hall's report. *Kinston Free Press,* June 21, 1882, April 23, August 23, November 29, 1888; Hall, *Report on Shipbuilding Industry of the United States,* 130. Moccasin River was the original name of Contentnea Creek.

128. *Goldsboro Messenger,* June 12, 1884.

129. Webb was the son of a Kinston carriage manufacturer. He followed a variety of careers from farming to working at his father's carriage plant to becoming a steamboat captain and builder and finally to managing a planing mill in Birmingham, Alabama. *F.W. Kornegay & Co. vs Farmers and Merchants Steamboat Co.,* Supreme Court Original Case papers, File No. 16, 409, SANC; Lenoir Co., Deed Book 3, 640-641, SANC; crop lien to W.S. Bell, Jr., March 24, 1869, in Carteret Co., Deed Book II, 402, SANC; 1880 census for Lenoir County; notes provided by George Stevenson, September 9, December 18, 2003, copy in author's possession.

130. (New Bern) *Weekly Journal,* November 2, 1893. J.C. Price was the master ship carpenter for the construction of many of these vessels. No information has been found on him.

131. (New Bern) *Daily Journal,* June 1, 11, July 2, 1882; April 30, 1884; August 25, 1885, October 18, November 9, 1888, March 20, 1889; (Wilmington) *Morning Star,* July 2, 1882, April 14, 1889; (Goldsboro) *Headlight,* March 27, April 10, 1889; Stevenson to authors, December 19, 2003, copy in authors' hands; (Raleigh) *North Carolina Star,* November 6, 1878.

132. See various documents in Credle Papers, SHC, UNC; Tilman Estate Papers, Hyde County Estate Papers, SANC.

133. Still, "Shipbuilding Industry in Washington, North Carolina," 39; *New Bern Daily Times,* July 3, 1865; correspondence, Stevenson to authors, August 29, 2003.

134. *Branson Directory,* 1869, 17; Still, "Shipbuilding Industry in Washington, North Carolina," 39. For Myers see petition dated July 26, 1875, and commission to sell the property, John Myers Estate, Beaufort County Estate Papers, SANC. R.G. Dun and Company had several comments about Farrow before the war but none afterwards.

135. *New Bern Times,* June 4, 1873.

136. Cox, "Pamlico-Tar River and Its Role in the Development of Eastern North Carolina," 103-104.

137. Still, "Shipbuilding Industry in Washington, North Carolina," 39.

138. *Washington Gazette,* December 25, 1893.

139. (New Bern) *Daily Journal,* November 23, 1883; Still, "Shipbuilding Industry in Washington, North Carolina," 45; *Washington Gazette,* November 3, 1993, February 8, 1893.

140. *Washington Gazette,* May 29, August 11, 1890; *Washington Progress,* July 16, 1889.

141. Styron was born on Portsmouth Island in 1847. His father, a mariner, fled to Washington with his family during the Civil War. The 1870 census lists him as a merchant. In the 1870s, he married into the Caleb Clark family. Clark was a prominent landowner in the county. For an account of Styron see Christopher P. McCabe, "The Development and Decline of Tar-Pamlico Maritime Commerce and its Impact upon Regional Settlement Patterns," 153-154, 156-158; Cox, "Pamlico-Tar River and its Role in the Development of Eastern North Carolina," 108-109. "Clark vs. Styron and Steamer *Edgecombe,*" draft for suit in the Rodman Papers, ECU.

142. Styron engaged in a number of enterprises, even at one time selling stock for a hotel on Ocracoke Island. He was the type of local entrepreneur who constantly sought new business ventures, some of which were successful, but many of which failed. William Styron, the novelist, was Adepheus's grandson. A biographer of William Styron wrote that the elder was energetic and did not fear hard work, but tended to overreach himself and attempt too many things at once. Adepheus's sons recalled that he was a "persuasive talker." Not surprisingly, Styron was involved

in litigation on more than one occasion. In 1895 a Washington lawyer who had frequent dealings with Styron and his creditors, wrote that "Styron is a great brag, and expects to do many things which are purely visionary." He added, "Styron himself is utterly insolvent and there is no hope of getting anything out of him." James L. West III, *William Styron: A Life*, 8, 10; Still, "Shipbuilding Industry in Washington, North Carolina," 45; notes on *Lawrence Clark vs. Steamer* Edgecombe, n.d., in Rodman Papers, ECU; Beaufort County Deed Book 42, 273, 278-280; Book 44, 440; Book 54, 293, SANC; Supreme Court Original Case Papers File #16,2545, SANC. For the *Margie* controversy see the Beaufort County Deed Book 77, 480, SANC.

143. (New Bern *Journal*), January 18, 1887; Still, "Shipbuilding Industry in Washington, North Carolina," 42; *Washington Gazette*, Industrial Edition, November 1, 1889; Sanborn map of Washington, 1896; *Washington Progress*, November 22, 1906; (Raleigh) *News and Observer*, November 22, 1906.

144. (Tarboro) *Southerner*, September 12, 1878; Connor, *North Carolina Rebuilding an Ancient Commonwealth*, IV, 442-443; *Washington Progress*, March 8, 1906.

145. Still, "Shipbuilding Industry in Washington, North Carolina," 44; *Washington Gazette*, Industrial Edition, November 1, 1889; *Washington Progress*, January 14, 1896.

146. *Liddon vs. Myers*, 1894, copy in Rodman Papers, ECU; Supreme Court Original Case file #19,220, SANC; *Washington Evening Messenger*, December 7, 1898; *Beaufort News*, March 10, 1921; *Washington Gazette*, April 28, 1892, November 28, 1895; (Wilmington Weekly Star), March 11, 1887.

147. Still, "Shipbuilding Industry in Washington," 44-45; Improvements for the Tar River, Entry 96, file 6259, RG77, NA.

148. In reference to Plymouth, an 1874 letter to the editor of a Murfreesboro newspaper stated that "The Navy yard has ... been discontinued for some reason." No naval yard was established in Plymouth by either Union or Confederate forces during the war. The writer may have been referring to prewar years. *Albemarle Times*, August 24, 1874.

149. Considerable information about two of these vessels can be found in the Askew Family Papers, ECU. The papers do not mention a shipyard. *Perquimans Record*, October 28, 1891.

150 *Murfreesboro Enquirer*, April 5, 1877; *Murfreesboro Index*, May 4, 1888, May 2, September 12, 1890. See also *Virginian-Pilot*, September 22, 1899, for additional shipbuilding activity on the Chowan River.

151 (Elizabeth City) *Economist*, January 5, 1876; William Badham Estate, Chowan County Estate Records, SANC. In 1874 it was reported that a shipyard would be established in Edenton to build barges but there is no record this actually occurred. (Wilmington) *Morning Star*, March 28, 1874.

152. (Elizabeth City) *Fisherman and Farmer*, September 19, 1890, August 17, 1888, October 11, 1889; Chowan County Deed Book A, 1889, SANC; correspondence, George Stevenson to author, November 14, 2001, copy in author's possession.

153. "Expenses Building Boat," July, August 1865, Hayes Papers, SHC, UNC; (Elizabeth City) *Fisherman and Farmer*, May 17 and 19, 1889; Warren to Wood, August 24, 1870, Wood Family Series, Hayes Papers, SHC, UNC.

154. Hunter deed, December 25, 1869, Pasquotank County Deed Book PP, 49, SANC; (Elizabeth City) *Economist*, November 22, 1901; communications to authors from Jean Hiebert, March 29, 2005, and George Stevenson, November 7, 2005, copies in authors' possession. Snell may have leased the yard until he purchased it. *Elizabeth City Tar Heel*, January 28, 1902; (Elizabeth City) *Weekly Economist*, November 22, 1901, April 22, 1904; receipt from Snell for lumber, 1872 in Hunter Papers, ECU. Hunter retained ownership of his lumber after declaring bankruptcy. *Snell vs. Schooner Sarah*, February 1894 session, U.S. District Court, Eastern District, Admiralty, Box 1, Elizabeth City, RG21, NA-Atlanta.

155. Lawrence Deed, October 27, 1869, Pasquotank County Deed Book PP, 297, SANC; *North Carolinian*, October 14, 1869; 1850 and 1870 censuses; petition of Elizabeth Lawrence, November 16, 1883, Pasquotank County Estate Papers, SANC; *Economist*, October 12 and July 19, 1881, February 20, 1883; Wilmington *Weekly Star*, November 21, 1890; Thomas R. Butchko, *On the Shores of the Pasquotank: The Architectural Heritage of Elizabeth City and Pasquotank County, North Carolina*, 124. In 1876 divers recovered the railway. *Economist*, January 5, 1876; (Wilmington) *Weekly Star*, November 21, 1890; (Elizabeth City) *Fisherman and Farmer*, March 22, 1889; Stevens, *Albemarle People and Places*, 141-142, 144, 369-370, 534.

156. Hall, "Report on the Shipbuilding Industry of the United States," 130; *Branson's Directories*, 1885-1896; (Elizabeth City) *North Carolinian*, October 27, 1870; Sanborn maps, 1885-1900; (Wilmington) *Messenger*, December 6, 1895; (Elizabeth City) *Economist*, November 22, 1901.

157. (Elizabeth City) *Economist*, June 3, 1879; (Elizabeth City) *Carolinian*, May 2, 1879.

158. Various documents and notes in the Steamers Exhibit, Eastern North Carolina Digital History Exhibits, Joyner Library, ECU; (Elizabeth City) *Economist*, January 31, 1882; *Wilmington Morning Star*, February 12, 1884; *Murfreesboro Index*, September 25, 1891; *Roanoke Beacon*, September 18, 1891, March 25, 1892.

159. Dara McLeod, "Backyard Boatbuilding," *Outer Banks Magazine* (1995-1996), 28-31.

160. (Elizabeth City) *Fisherman and Farmer*, June 30, 1901.

161. (Elizabeth City) *Fisherman and Farmer*, July 7, 25, 1899; Stick, *Dare County*, 19; *Coastland Times*, February 17, March 15, 1977; *Branson's Directories*, 1890, 1896; Donald and Carol McAdoo, *Reflections of the Outer Banks*, 88-89. Communication, Connie Mason to Vaden Cudworth, February 2, 1995, and enclosures, copies in the North Carolina Maritime Museum, Beaufort, N.C.; *North Carolina Labor Statistics*, 1898, 119; Angel Ellis Khoury, *Manteo: A Roanoke Island Town*, 75-77; Milford R. Balance, *The Hands of Time*; 1900 Census, Dare County.

162. *Wilmington Weekly Star*, July 23, 1875; *New Bern Weekly Journal*, July 9, 1900.

163. For an examination of this issue see C. K. Harley, "On the Persistence of Old Technologies: The Case of North American Wooden Shipbuilding," *Journal of Economic History*, 372-397.

164. *Fayetteville Eagle*, November 4, 1869, September 20, 1873; (New Bern) *Daily Journal of Commerce*, April 25, 1867; (New Bern) *Daily Journal*, May 31, 1892. For the Cassidey iron steamer see (Wilmington) *Morning Star*, July 26, 1868.

165. Sanborn Map, 1885; (New Bern) *Weekly Journal*, January 4, 1894; Warren to Shepard, September 9, 1891, William B. Shepard Papers, ECU; interview with Leon Weatherington, copy in Onslow County Historical Society Papers, SANC.

166. Hall, *Report on the Shipbuilding Industry of the United States*, 244-246; Wood, *Live Oaking*, 64-65; Charles C. Carroll, "Wooden Ships and American Forests," *Encyclopedia Preview*, 215; Hutchins, *American Maritime Industries*, 99-100.

167. (Wilmington) *Star*, April 27, 1888; McAdoo, *Reflections of the Outer Banks*, 58; Stick, *Dare County*, 19.

168. *Southport Leader,* January 24, 1894; (Norfolk) *Pilot,* November 24, 1899; (New Bern) *Weekly Journal,* February 20, 1896; (New Bern) *Daily Journal,* June 10, 1882. For statistics of material used in North Carolina shipbuilding in 1890, see the 1900 Manufacturing Census.

169. *Lawrence Clark v. Styron and Steamer* Edgecombe, *et al.,* Rodman Papers, ECU; *Kornegay v. Everett and Kennedy,* Supreme Court of North Carolina, 99 N.C. 30; 5 S.E. 418; 1888 N.C. Lexis 238; *Washington Gazette,* August 14, 1889; May 28, 1896; *Murfreesboro Inquirer,* March 21, 1878.

170. *Washington Gazette,* October 2, 1890; see Edward A. Mueller, *St Johns River Steamboats,* 193, 202, 206, 214; (Wilmington) *Morning Star,* November 9, 1877; (Wilmington) *Weekly Star,* January 23, 1880; September 11, 1891; (Wilmington) *Messenger,* November 26, 1881; *Washington Gazette,* October 2, 1890; (Greenville) *Eastern Reflector,* May 25, 1887; *Southport Leader,* January 12, 1893; *Washington Progress,* January 14, 1896; (New Bern) *Journal,* July 15, 20, 1897; Certificate of Enrollment for steamer *Colville,* April 4, 1880, U.S. Customs Records, Collection 648, Georgia Historical Society, Savannah, Georgia; Still, "The Shipbuilding Industry in Washington, North Carolina," 41-42; Johnson, *Riverboating in Lower Carolina,* 142, 145, 146; (New Bern) *Weekly Journal,* November 1, 1894; (Wilmington) *Messenger,* October 29, 1897; *Southport Leader,* October 4, 1890.

171. (Hertford) *Eastern Courier,* April 2, May 28, 1896; *New Bern Commercial News,* November 16, 1881; *Goldsboro Messenger,* September 18, 1882; *Wilmington Daily Journal,* October 24, 1868; (Wilmington) *Star,* December 12, 1868, June 8, 1870; Bridgers, "Steamboats on the Tar," n.p.

172. (Wilmington) *Morning Star,* September 13, 1890, mentions H. A. Wendell from Philadelphia, hired to superintend construction of two large flats. *Kinston Free Press,* April 5, 1898 mentions a steamer being built under the auspices of a "Commodore Lawhorne."

173. Amy Muse, *Grandpa Was a Whaler,* 29.

174. *Twelfth Census on Manufacturers,* Vol. X, 216, 236; North Carolina Department of Labor (NCDL), *Eighth Annual Report of the Bureau of Labor Statistics,* 236-237; NCDL, *Ninth Annual Report of the Bureau of Labor Statistics,* 331-332.

175. Zipf, *Labor of Innocents,* 67; NCDL, *Second Annual Report of the Bureau of Labor Statistics,* 212 - 227; (New Bern) *Weekly Journal,* December 9, 1886.

176. Havens, *New Bern and the Pamlico Sound Region,* 41.

177. *Cassidey Brothers vs. Barque* Dunkild, Wilmington June District Court Records, RG21, NA-Atlanta. Statewide, an average of ten shipwrights worked on a particular vessel. NCDL, *North Carolina Labor Statistics for 1890,* 130; notes for Onslow County provided by Tucker Littleton, copy in possession of author.

178. NCDL, *North Carolina Labor Statistics, 1894,* 331; (Elizabeth City) *Economist,* November 22, 1901. The 1900 census listed twenty-four ship carpenters in the county.

179. NCDL, *Eighth Annual Report of the Bureau of Labor Statistics for the Year 1894,* 118, 331; (Elizabeth City) *Economist,* November 22, 1901; NCDL, *North Carolina Labor Statistics, 1888,* 67.

180. *Cassidey Brothers vs. Barque* Dunkild, 1868, Wilmington District Court Records, RG21, NA-Atlanta; *Carteret County News-Times,* July 2, 1948; T. M. Haddock, *Haddock's Wilmington, N.C., Directory,* 1871, 41; Tilman Farrow Estate, Hyde County Estate Papers, SANC.

181. These figures were obtained from a variety of North Carolina labor reports.

182. Gary S. Dunbar, *Historical Geography of the North Carolina Outer Banks,* 43.

183. Hunter Bankruptcy File, Elizabeth City District Court, Box 21, RG21, NA-Atlanta.

184. Horace James, *Annual Report of the Superintendent of Black Affairs in North Carolina,* 19; Cecelski, *Waterman's Song,* 273.

185. Cecelski, *Waterman's Song,* 206; Davis and others (eds.), *Heritage of Carteret County,* I, 57; NCDL, *North Carolina Labor Statistics,* 1894, 118-119.

186. Davis and others (eds.), *Heritage of Carteret County,* I, 212.

187. *New Bern Commercial News,* November 16, 1881.

188. NCDL, *North Carolina Labor Statistics,* 1894, 331-332.

189. These four are listed as shipyard shipwrights and caulkers on reel 18 of the Register of Signatures of Depositors of the Freedman's Savings and Trust Company Records, National Archives Microfilm Publication M816. They had business initially, but are not mentioned in the 1878 *Branson Directory.* However, they are listed in the 1883-84 *Chataigne Directory.*

190. *New Bern Daily Times,* September 14, 1873.

191. Correspondence from George Stephenson to author, September 11, 2003, copy in author's possession; Craven County Deed Book, 77, 315-318; 81, 2-3, SANC; *New Bern Daily Times,* August 15, September 14, November 14, 1873. What happened to the firm is unknown.

192. (Wilmington) *Weekly Star,* November 23, 1888; *Kinston Free Press,* July 19, 1888; (Wilmington) *Messenger,* September 11, 1888; notes in the Roy Johnson Collection, SANC. He later claimed that he was of "Portuguese or Arab descent." (Wilmington) *Messenger,* January 13, 1889.

193. What happened to the steamboat is unknown. Presumably he sold it, or lost it, because of bad debts, as the vessel is not mentioned when he died in 1894. In 1888 W. R. Kornegay provided a boiler and probably other machinery parts for the *Rough and Ready* when she was under construction. Kennedy had to sell property to pay off his debts to the machine works. *W.F. Kornegay vs. N.K. Everett and Charles Kennedy,* February 1888 term, North Carolina Supreme Court, Vol. 99, 53-57, SANC; (New Bern) *Daily Journal,* April 30, 1884; correspondence, George Stevenson to authors, August 4, 2003.

194. Roland C. McConnell, "The Black in North Carolina since Reconstruction," 117; (New Bern) *Daily Journal,* December 7, 15, 1883.

195. An article in *Tributaries* suggested that the "demands of commercial fisheries after the Civil War placed the traditional 'cottage industry' occupations such as boatbuilding and net making in competition with large organized factories." Rodney Barfield, "A View of History…Faces of the Outer Banks," *Tributaries,* 16.

196. Sanders P. Gray file, http://www.rootsweb.com; (New Bern) Daily Journal, September 8, 1896.

197. The September 24, 1981, issue of the *Coastland Times* features a photograph of the Otis Dough boatyard, showing the site of two small vessels where were under construction under a tree with a small shed in the background. Some photographs show buildings such as the Howard and later Meadows facility in New Bern; in others, just vessels under construction or repair as at the Fearing and Hayman and the Willey yards in Elizabeth City.

198. An article in the (New Bern) *Journal,* for July 30, 1896 declared that boat builders would "…be surprised to find how few concerns there are who actually build [steamboat] … machinery."

199. *Private Laws, Session of 1866-67,* 296; (Wilmington) *Semi-Weekly Messenger,* February 20, 1900.

200. *Wilmington Dispatch,* November 23, 1894; (Wilmington) *Morning Star,* August 23, 1789. W.W. Storm, "Historical Sketches, Wilmington Iron Works," copy in Wilmington Iron Works Collection, ECU; Tony P. Wrenn, *Wilmington, North Carolina: An Architectural and Historical Portrait,* 20; *Wilmington Daily Post,* April 12, 1868.

201. (Wilmington) *Weekly Star,* September 11, 1891, April 20, 1878. Skinner apparently continued his partnership with Lyons.

202. (New Bern) *Weekly Journal,* December 8, 1891; *Steamer* Sadie Rand *vs. the Newbern Iron Works,* District Court, Admiralty, Box 1, RG21, NA-Atlanta; (New Bern) *Daily Journal,* May 13, 1882; (New Bern) *Weekly Journal,* December 25, 1890, January 17, 1895, March 26, 1896; *New Bern Daily Times,* August 18, 1865.

203. *W.F. Kornegay vs. the Farmers and Merchants Steamboat Company,* Supreme Court Original Case Papers, No. 16, 409; *W.F. Kornegay vs. A.W. Styron and Thos. Duncan,* Supreme Court Original Case Papers, No.16, 254, copy in the Rodman papers, ECU; (New Bern) *Daily Journal,* May 24, 1882; *Goldsboro Messenger,* February 28, March 25, 1878, May 19, 1881, June 8, 1882, January 25, 28, 1884.

204. *Goldsboro Argus,* May 26, 1898; *Goldsboro Messenger,* February 22, 1883; January 5, 1885.

205 *Goldsboro Weekly Transcript & Messenger,* Industrial Issue, May 1887.

206. (Greenville) *Eastern Reflector,* July 25, 1883; repairs on *Shiloh* by Pamlico Iron Works, Machine Shop and Foundry, March 28, 1899 in Tar River Oil Company Records, ECU.

207. *Goldsboro Messenger,* copy of advertisement in the Steamboat Exhibit, Eastern North Carolina Digital History Exhibits, ECU. Major repairs and the fabrication of steamboat engines and boilers had to be carried out in Norfolk and elsewhere. (Elizabeth City) *Fisherman and Farmer,* February 28, 1894; notice in Box 5, Elizabeth City, RG41, NA- Atlanta; *E.S. Willey vs. steamer* D.K. Neal, U.S. District Court, Eastern District of North Carolina, Admiralty Records, Elizabeth City, RG21, NA-Atlanta.

208. *New Bern Commercial News,* December 11, 1881. For a New York firm see (Murfreesboro) *Index,* August 31, 1888. There is considerable correspondence, a contract, and drawings of machinery for the steamer *Bertie* in the Askew Papers, ECU. Frick and Company of Waynesboro, Pennsylvania, provided boilers. Correspondence, Stevenson to authors, August 29, 2003.

209. Rodman to Marine Iron Works, May 5, 26, 1900, Rodman Papers, ECU; (New Bern) *Journal,* March 12, 1896.

210. *Murfreesboro Enquirer,* April 19, 1877; *Goldsboro Messenger,* September 21, 1876, August 29, 1879; *Kinston Free Press,* August 30, 1899; *Beaufort News,* August 30, 1942. See also Barfield, *Seasoned By Salt.*

211. *Wilmington Morning Star,* February 9, 1873; October 31, 1882; September 21, 1889; *Southport Leader,* May 22, 1890; Farrow Account Book, Credle Papers, SHC, UNC-CH.

212. *Washington Progress,* October 15, 1889; (New Bern) *Daily Journal,* June 2, 1896; *Kinston Free Press,* October 17, 1891.

213. (Wilmington) *Star,* April 8, May 9, 17, 28, July 9, 10, August 13, September 13, 14, October 2, 1879; (Wilmington) *Weekly Star,* April 20, 1888; Jackson, *Cape Fear-Northeast Cape Fear Rivers Comprehensive Study,* 223; *New Bern Daily Times,* August 16, October 11, 1866.

214. *Wilmington Daily Journal,* June 18, September 15, 1868; (Wilmington) *Morning Star,* October 27, 1875; August 24, November 3, 1878.

215. *Wilmington Dispatch,* June 15, 1899.

216. (New Bern) *Weekly Journal,* November 19, 1891; *New Bern Commercial News,* October 9, 1881.

217. *Pamlico Enterprise,* July 27, 1883; *Washington Gazette,* July 1, 1891.

218. (Elizabeth City) *North Carolinian,* July 28, 1870; *Jennings vs. Schooner* Jenny & Alice, 1866, Admiralty, Elizabeth City District Court Records, Box 2, RG21, NA-Atlanta.

219. (New Bern) *Daily Journal,* April 13, 1893; June 2, 3, 1896; (New Bern) *Weekly Journal,* August 31, 1893, May 15, 1900; *New Bern Daily Times,* May 26, 1872, November 14, 1873; *New Bern Commercial News,* December 9, 1881; (Wilmington) *Morning Star,* October 2, 1880, June 3, 1885; *Wilmington Daily Journal,* May 11, 1873; (Wilmington) *Messenger,* April 19, 1888; *Beaufort Weekly Record,* March 24, 1887; *Washington Progress,* August 24, 1898; (Elizabeth City) *Fisherman and Farmer,* February 23, 1900; Ellen F. Cloud, *Abstracts From Miscellaneous Newspapers Published In Beaufort, N.C., 1876-1983,* 37; *Mason vs. Milner,* September 10, 1878, Carteret County Supreme Court Records, SANC.

220. *Wilmington Dispatch,* September 9, 1899.

221. *Moore vs. Benjamin Beery and His Son,* 1874, Wilmington Court Records, RG21, NA-Atlanta; *Woods vs. Jones and Ireland,* January 20, 1866, Craven County Civil Action Papers, SANC; *Donaldson vs. Skinner,* n.d., Perquimans County Misc. Records, Vessels, SANC; *Farrow vs. Short,* November 28, 1882, Beaufort County Civil Action Papers, SANC; *Farrow vs. Windley,* October 7, 1883, SANC; *Linguish vs. Johnson,* August 1876, Carteret County Civil Action Papers, SANC; *Hart and Bailey vs. Lutterloh,* October 1, 1868, New Hanover Civil Action Papers, SANC; *Wilmington Daily Journal,* May 11, 1873.

222. An extensive file on the case is in the Wilmington Federal District Court Records, Admiralty, RG21, NA-Atlanta. The records give a detailed account of the difficulties encountered by shipbuilders.

223. Clarence Robinson, *The Core Sounder,* 8; (New Bern) *Daily Journal,* December 24, 1874.

224. Cox, "The Pamlico-Tar and its Role in the Development of Eastern North Carolina," 142.

225. *New Bern Republican,* December 19, 20, 1868; (Wilmington) *Morning Star,* February 18, 1868, September 12, 1873; (Tarboro) *Southerner,* August 1, 1878; *Washington Progress,* February 5, 1889.

226. *New Bern Times,* June 10, 1873. Ralph Pigott, a Carteret County boatbuilder received a patent for an improved centerboard (No. 498082), May 23, 1893, Patent Office, Washington, DC; McGregor, *Schooners in Four Centuries,* 52; Hutchins, *American Maritime Industries,* 553-557; Fassett, *Shipbuilding Business in the United States,* I, 33; Chapelle, *History of American Sailing Ships.* A few three-masted schooners were built. Fowle Notes, Brown Library, Washington, N.C.; *Economist,* May 30, 1898.

227. *Wilmington Semi-Weekly Messenger,* March 29, 1898; *New Bern Daily Journal,* November 12, 1885; (Elizabeth City) *North Carolinian,* October 27, 1870. Occasionally in describing a new vessel, newspapers simply cited sailing boat or sailing craft. *New Bern Weekly Journal,* June 24, 1886.

228. For a good discussion of sail patterns on small craft see Alford, *Traditional Work Boats of North Carolina,* 5-9.

229. *Washington Gazette,* March 12, 1896; *Carteret County News-Times,* June 22, July 13, 1848; Kay Holt Roberts Stephens, *Judgment Land: The Story of Salter Path,* I, 30; (New Bern) *Weekly Journal,* November 14, 1895. For illustrations of various types see Barfield, *Seasoned By Salt,* and Jack Dudley, *Beaufort: An Album of Memories;*

Wilmington Morning Star, June 6, 1886; *Kinston Journal,* March 17, 1881.

230. *Washington Gazette,* May 28, 1896; (New Bern) *Daily Journal,* June 3, 1896; *New Bern Times,* November 6, 1873; (Wilmington) *Messenger,* April 14, 1889; (Wilmington) *Star,* March 31, 1882.

231. *Southport Leader,* August 24, 1890.

232. An "up-country preacher" built a sharpie "with his own hands." (New Bern) *Journal,* July 17, 1884. An article in the (Wilmington *Star),* July 1, 1879, called the vessel a skiff and a sharpie. One sharpie builder mentioned that he planned to construct a steamer on the sharpie model. (New Bern) *Daily Journal,* July 12, 1882. Coastal county newspapers are full of announcements of sharpies being constructed.

233. *Field and Stream,* 13 (November 13, 1879), 876.

234. For good studies of sharpies, see: Howard I. Chapelle, *The Migration of An American Boat Type;* Howard I. Chapelle, *American Small Sailing Craft,* 122 -124; Reuel B. Parker, *The Sharpie Book;* and "New Haven Oyster Sharpie," in the Frank C. Salisbury Collection, ECU. Michael Alford's writings are the best accounts of the North Carolina sharpie: Michael Alford, *Traditional Work Boats of North Carolina;* Michael Alford, "A Story of Shoal Water: Sharpies in the Carolinas," *Wooden Boat,* 62-71. See also John S. McCormack, "North Carolina Oyster Sharpie Schooner," *Nautical Research Journal,* 3-8; *Goldsboro Messenger,* April 10, 1884. Barfield's *Seasoned by Salt,* and Dudley's *Beaufort: An Album of Memories* have a number of photographs on North Carolina built sharpies.

235. *History of North Carolina,* VI, 248-249; (New Bern) *Weekly Journal,* September 6, 1894.

236. Jean Day, *Cedar Island: Past and Present,* II, 72; (New Bern) *Weekly Journal,* November 6, 1896; *Carteret County News-Times,* August 9, 1957; Michael Alford, 'How the Sharpie Came to North Carolina," *The Waterline,* 1; Charles Ives, "A Tale of Two Cities," *The State* (June 18, 1949), 9; (New Bern) *Weekly Journal,* August 16, 1882; *Cyclopedia of Eminent and Representative Men of the Carolinas of the Nineteenth Century,* II, 562-563. Ives wrote a letter describing the introduction of the sharpie in North Carolina in *Forest and Stream,* March 17, 1881, copy in the authors' possession. Sonny Williamson writes that the first North Carolina-built sharpie was constructed at Cedar Island in 1867 by Jackson Goodwin. Williamson, *Sailing With Grandpa,* 9.

237. For the shad boat see Alford, *Traditional Work Boats of North Carolina,* 18-21; Alford, "Shad Boats & Sharpies," 42-44; McLeod, "Backyard Boatbuilding," 76; Chapelle, *Small Sailing Craft,* 122; Duncan, *Historical Geography of North Carolina,* 56-57; Morris, *The Fore and Aft Rig,* 69; Fleetwood, *Tidecraft,* 164; Boats at Stations, 1892, RG26, NA; *Elizabeth City Daily Advance,* December 7, 1983. For a reminiscence concerning a shad boat see Fred Mallison, "Shad Boat," *Coastal Cruising,* (April-May 1993), 220-223.

238. (New Bern) *Daily Journal,* August 19, 1882.

239. Information on the menhaden vessels provided by Steve Goodwin. *Southport Leader,* March 21, 1895.

240. NCDL, *Ninth Annual Report of the Bureau of Labor Statistics of the State of North Carolina for the Year 1895,* 379.

241. *North Carolina and its Resources,* 145; NCDL, *Ninth Annual Report of the Bureau of Labor Statistics,* 238; *Perquimans Weekly,* July 7, 1887; Potter suit, *North Carolina Reports,* Vol. 74, 44.

242. NCDL, *Annual Report of the Bureau of Labor Statistics, 1894,* 252-256; (Elizabeth City) *Fisherman and Farmer,* June 3, 1893.

243. It must be remembered that vessels were those documented over five tons berthen; boats were under that number. NCDL, *Eighth Annual Report of the Bureau of Labor Statistics of the State or North Carolina,* 252-256; (Elizabeth City) *Fisherman and Farmer,* June 9, 1893.

244. (New Bern) *Daily Journal,* December 31, 1901.

245. *Wilmington Weekly Journal,* November 8, 1866. The source for the Warren introduction of steam flats in 1879 is William J. Leary, "The Fisheries of Eastern Carolina," *North Carolina Booklet,* XVI (April 1915), 188; Sloan, "Inland Navigation in North Carolina 1818-1900," 72. Warren's patent for "steam machinery for seine-hauling," # 89717, was approved May 4, 1869, Patent Office, Washington, D.C.; *Perquimans Weekly Record,* October 28, 1891, August 19, 1992; (Elizabeth City) *North Carolinian,* January 4, 1877.

246. Elizabeth City *Fisherman and Farmer,* March 6, 1890. One authority suggests that originally they were basically the same as the oared skiff/flats, with the steam machinery replacing the oars. "It would be the simplest of all mechanization conversions," Michael Alford to authors, April 8, 2002.

247. These flats were first introduced in the 1870s. NCDL, *Annual Report of The Bureau of Labor Statistics, 1896,* 382-384; *Pamlico Enterprise,* November 2, 1883; (New Bern) *Daily Journal,* September 5, 1882; (Elizabeth City) *North Carolinian,* December 21, 1887, January 4, 1888.

248. See Hill and Wilde-Ramsing, "Historical Documentation and Underwater Archaeological Reconnaissance of Salmon Creek in the Vicinity of the Batts-Duckenfield-Capehart Site, Bertie County"; (Wilmington) *Morning Star,* June 23, July 15, 1888.

249. Boats on Station, RG26, NA.

250. (Wilmington) *Weekly Star,* October 1, 1875; Reaves, *Southport (Smithville), A Chronology,* I, 59, 60, 64, 66, 67, 68, 87.

251. The 1880 census lists Stowe as a pilot. *Washington Progress,* December 12, 1893; Boats on Station Volume, 1885, 1888, RG26, NA.

252. Reaves file, Underwater Archaeological Unit, Fort Fisher, N.C.

253. Reaves, *Southport (Smithville): A Chronology,* I, 54; (Wilmington) *Morning Star,* August 26, 1872; Hall, *Land of the Golden River,* 46.

254. (Wilmington) *Morning Star,* August 4, 1875.

255. Fleetwood, *Tidecraft,* 152. The *Southport Leader* reported on June 1, 1893 that "...Orders for new sail boats continue." *Southport Leader,* March 6, 1890, August 20, October 15, 1891, April 24, 1890, March 31, June 2, 1892, April 17, April 24, June 1, July 6, 1893, January 1, April 26, May 17, June 24, 1894, April 4, 1895; (New Bern) *Weekly Journal,* September 19, 1895; Williamson, *Sailing with Grandpa,* 9-11; *Goldsboro Messenger,* July 17, 1882; (New Bern) *Weekly Journal,* January 5, 1896; Hall, *Land of the Golden River,* 50-52; *Goldsboro Daily News,* September 12, 1866; (New Bern) Weekly *Journal,* August 20, 1896; *Kinston Free Press,* July 24, 1890; (New Bern) *Nut Shell,* August 13, 1878; (Greenville) *Eastern Reflector,* June 25, 1890; *Wilmington Star,* July 26, 1876; June 9, 24, 1877; May 31, 1878.

256. Collector of Customs, Edenton, to Chief of Engineers, File 154, E71, RG77, NA; Alford, *Traditional Work Boats of North Carolina,* 4-5, 12; (New Bern) *Weekly Journal,* July 11, 1895; Outlaw, *Old Nag's Head,* 56; *Journal of the Currituck County Historical Society,* I (1973), 67.

257. Sloan, "Inland Navigation in North Carolina 1818-1900," 132.

258. (Wilmington) *Messenger,* July 31, 1895; (New Bern) *Daily Journal,* May 15, June 21, 1902; (New Bern) *Weekly Journal,* May 26, 1892; (Wilmington) *Weekly Star,* October 2, 1895; *Chauncey vs. A. W. Styron,* June 1891, District of Pamlico, Admiralty, RG21, NA-Atlanta; (Wilmington) *Star,* March 26, April 28, 1882; January 2,

1884; August 12, 1887.

259. *Beaufort Eagle*, October 7, 1876; (New Bern) *Weekly Journal*, November 14, 1895; Chapelle, *American Small Sailing Craft*, 45.

260. In her study of a North Carolina sail flat, Merriman listed eleven built between 1865 and 1900 that were documented and eight others that had scow characteristics. Ann M. Merriman, *The Cypress Landing Shipwreck of Chocowinity Bay: A North Carolina Sail Flat*, 38-47.

261. (Wilmington) *Star*, March 2, 1874, May 17, 1898.

262. *Kinston Free Press*, June 25, 1891; *Wilmington Daily Herald*, October 10, 1865; (Wilmington) *Morning Star*, June 2, 1872, December 24, 1889; *Tarboro Enquirer*, November 2, 1872; (New Bern) *Weekly Journal*, September 17, 1895; *New Bern Daily Times*, September 14, 1873.

263. *Murfreesboro Index*, February 10, March 25, August 17, 1888; (Wilmington) *Star*, January 14, 1869, September 28, 1878, October 9. 1882; October 19, 1897; *Wilmington Sun*, January 25, 1899; (New Bern) *Weekly Journal*, October 8, 1885; *Wilmington Daily Journal*, April 20, 1894; *Washington Progress*, November 8, 1882; Gordon P. Watts and Lesley K. Hall, *An Investigation of Blossom's Ferry on the Northeast Cape Fear River*, *Mace vs. Ramsey*, January 1876, Supreme Court of North Carolina, Raleigh 74 N.C. 11; 1876 N.C. Lexis 3; (Wilmington) *Messenger*, June 19, 1900; (Wilmington) *Star*, May 11, 1874; Reaves, *Southport (Smithville): A Chronology*, 89.

264. (Wilmington) *Morning Star*, May 5, 1883; (New Bern) *Weekly Journal*, September 26, October 3, 1895, (Tarboro) *Southerner*, October 18, 1877; *Washington Progress*, October 28, 1890; (Wilmington) *Messenger*, February 23, July 31, 1889.

265. *Washington Progress*, May 18, 1899; Still, "The Shipbuilding Industry in Washington," 39-45; (Wilmington) *Morning Star*, May 5, 1872.

266. (Wilmington) *Morning Star*, November 1, 1889, July 17, 23, August 2, 3, 1890, April 10, July 31, 1895; (Wilmington) *Messenger*, July 31, 1895; (Raleigh) *News and Observer*, September 13, 1890.

267. Beaufort Civil Action Papers, SANC; *Goldsboro Messenger*, March 6, 1882; (New Bern) *Daily Journal*, June 8, 1882.

268. *Washington Gazette*, January 18, April 12, October 25, 1894; *Washington Progress*, February 12, July 9, August 13, October 24, 1895; (Elizabeth City) *Fisherman and Farmer*, February 23, 28, 1894; (New Bern) *Weekly Journal*, March 15, 1894; October 30, 1895; *Roanoke Beacon*, September 21, 1894; Myers damage, February 5, 1895, Box 74, Entry 1116, RG77, NA-Atlanta.

269. The entire file on this incident is in the Rodman Papers, ECU. See particularly Chauncey to King, December 1, 12, 1899; Rodman to King, December 15, 20, 1895, January 22, February 20, 1900, King to Rodman, January 1, 22, February 16, 1900. *Washington Evening Messenger*, December 7, 1898; *Washington Progress*, September 28, 1898.

270. Phillips to Chief, April 29, 1879, Letters received, 1879, file 148, RG77, NA.

271. Bixby to Chief, August 25, 1884; Bixby to Chief, September 19, 1884; Stanton to Chief, August 30, 1894, all in RG77, NA; (Wilmington) *Star*, May 14, 1883.

272. Bixby to Chief, April 24, 1893, Box 36, RG77; Schuster to Stanton, April 6, 24, 1893, Box 73,; Stanton to Casey, April 8, 1893, Box 21, file 2140; July 13, 1893, Box 32; Bixby to Chief, January 17, 1885, RG77, NA; Return of Vessels, June 30, 1897, RG77, all in NA-Atlanta.

273. (New Bern) *Daily Journal*, May 18, 1882; *Goldsboro Messenger*, June 26, 1882; Mercer to Chief, March 30, 1882, RG77, NA-Atlanta.

274. Phillips to Chief, October 22, 1878; Chadbourn to Lucas, June 5, July 31, 1879; Phillips to Chief, August 16, 1879, September 2, August 2, 1884; Lucas to Chief, May 6, 1899; Craighill to Chief, August 20, 1897, Chadbourn to Stanton, May 6, 1895; Chadbourn to Lucas, June 25, September 8, 11, 1899, all in RG77, NA-Atlanta; (Wilmington) *Morning Star*, August 29, 1879; (New Bern) *Daily Journal*, July 9, September 6, 1899; (New Bern) *Weekly Journal*, June 15, August 31, 1893; September 8, 1899. A report dated January 26, 1894 from Schuster to Stanton, January 26, 1894, RG77, NA-Atlanta. gives a detailed description of the construction and characteristics of the *General George Thom*.

275. Craighill to Chief, July 10, 1883, Craighill to Chief, August 22, 1883, RG77, NA-Atlanta; (Wilmington) *Morning Star*, March 27, 29, 1874; December 9, 1879, April 25, 28, June 2, 13, 17, July 13, August 1, 27, 31, September 6, October 12, December 1, 1882, March 20, August 21, September 9, October 10, 1883; July 30, 1889; *Southport Leader*, July 12, 1894; Jackson, *The Cape Fear Northeast Cape Fear Rivers Comprehensive Study*, 231.

276. (Wilmington) *Star*, January 16, 1885; *Annual Report of the Corp of Engineers*, 1883, 167, and 1884, 1043.

277. No information has been found to identify Bowdoin. He may have received a contract to do the work. (Wilmington) *Messenger*, July 28, August 6, 17, 1887; (Wilmington) *Morning Star*, February 4, 1885; August 12, October 15, 1887, July 30, August 7, September 31, 1889, January 31, 1890, August 29, 1891; *Wilmington Daily Review*, January 10, 21, 1890.

278. *Goldsboro Messenger*, January 19, 1885; *Fayetteville Eagle*, July 2, 1874; (Raleigh) *Farmer and Mechanic*, June 5, July 17, October 16, 1879; (Raleigh) *News and Observer*, May 18, 1940.

279 Richard L. Zuber, *Jonathan Worth: A Biography of a Southern Unionist*, 195-196, 291-292; Worth to Dibble, July 26, November 27, 1865, Hamilton (ed.), *Correspondence of Jonathan Worth*, I, 384, 454-455.

280. (Wilmington) *Morning Star*, October 17, 1871, June 17, 1882. For steamboat construction, 1865 to 1870, see *Fayetteville News*, March 12, August 20, December 31, 1867; *Fayetteville Eagle*, December 2, 1869, January 20, March 31, June 16, December 22, 1870, March 9, 1871; *Wilmington Dispatch*, March 9, 1867; *Wilmington Semi-Weekly Post*, September 28, 1868; (Wilmington) *Morning Star*, November 12, December 21, 1867, September 4, December 12, 1868, October 1, 1869, June 8, 1870, March 21, 1871; *New Bern Daily Times*, June 6, 1869; *Goldsboro Messenger*, June 6, 1869; *Washington Index*, March 14, 1867; Carter lien on the *Halcyon*, n.d., Wilmington District Court Records, RG21, NA-Atlanta.

281. The (Wilmington) *Morning Star* mentioned a steamboat under construction in the city, but no additional information as to whether it was finished or named has been found. (Wilmington) *Morning Star*, copy in the Reaves files did not include date, Underwater Archaeological Unit, Fort Fisher, N.C.

282. (Wilmington) *Morning Star*, February 8, April 12, 19, 24, August 19, 1868; March 20, 22, 1872.

283. Cora Bass, *Sampson County Yearbook, 1956-1957*, 141; (Wilmington) *Star*, April 25, 1884; (Wilmington) *Messenger*, July 15, 1888, May 8, 17, 18, August 25, November 22, 1899, June 7, 1891.

284. (Wilmington) *Star*, April 20, June 3, 1880; March 23, April 29, 1883; January 10, 1884; April 30, May 18, June 24, July 29, 1886; November 4, 1887; January 1, 1888; November 26, 1889; (Wilmington) *Messenger*, August 29, 1891; *Wilmington Post*, June 19, October 2, 1881; *Southport Leader*, December 3, 1891; *Fayetteville Evening News*, August 2, 1887; *Goldsboro Messenger*, February. 23, May 11, 1882.

285. Wilson Angley, "Historical Overview of The Black River in

Southeastern North Carolina," 20-48; Johnson, *Riverboating in Lower Carolina*, 71-78, 141-152; Roy Johnson Collection, SANC. Oscar M. Bizzell (ed.), *Heritage of Sampson County, North Carolina*, 457; *Clinton Sampsonian*, February 26, 1970; Tom Butchko, *An Inventory of Historic Architecture of Sampson County, North Carolina*, 36-37. Wilmington newspapers for the 1869-1899 period, especially the *Star* and *Messenger*, have a great deal of information on the building of Black River steamboats. Much of this can be found in the Bill Reaves Collection at the New Hanover County Public Library, Wilmington, N.C., and the Underwater Branch of the state's Office of Archives and History, Fort Fisher, N.C.; *Fayetteville Eagle*, March 16, 1871.

286. Southport *Leader*, May 29, 1890.

287. Brown, *Juniper Waterway*, 88; *New Bern Commercial News*, December 9, 1881; *Pamlico Enterprise*, July 21, 1882; (New Bern) *Daily Journal*, December 31, 1886; (New Bern) *Weekly Journal*, January 6, 1887; *New Bern Democrat*, July 12, 1879; *Goldsboro Messenger*, June 8, September 18, 25, 1876.

288. (New Bern) *Journal*, January 8, 1882; *Goldsboro Messenger*, April 12, 1883. One article reported *Kinston* was 122 feet in length. For *Kinston*, see (Kinston) *Journal*, July 28, September 15, 1881; *New Bern Commercial News*, September 29, 1881; (New Bern) *Daily Journal*, May 24, 28, July 22, 1882, December 31, 1886; Wilmington *Morning Star*, July 23, 1882.

289. *New Bern Commercial News*, November 10, 16, 1881; (Kinston) *Journal*, March 16, 1882; *Goldsboro Messenger*, April 16, 1882.

290. *Goldsboro Messenger*, March 23, 1883; (New Bern) *Daily Journal*, July 27, 1897.

291. (New Bern) *Daily Journal*, June 1, July 2, 1882; November 21, 1883; August 25, 1885; *Goldsboro Messenger*, June 29, 1882; (Wilmington) *Morning Star*, July 2, 1882; *Pamlico Enterprise*, July 21, 1882.

292. (New Bern) *Daily Journal*, June 8, 1882, April 30, 1884, October 23, 29, 1891, December 29, 1892, September 18, 1899; *Goldsboro Messenger*, March 14, 1878, August 29, 1882; (Kinston) *Journal*, August 5, 1880; (Goldsboro) *Headlight*, April 12, 1889; (Wilmington) *Messenger*, April 12, 1889; (Wilmington) *Morning Star*, April 14, 1889; *Kinston Free Press*, August 20, October 22, 1891.

293. (New Bern) *Daily Journal*, June 13, 1882, June 2, 11, 13, Oct 18, 18, November 9, 1888, August 27, November 5, 1891, April 13, August 31, 1892, October 1, November 1, 1893; (New Bern) *Weekly Journal*, December 20, 26, 1894, October 3, 1895; (Wilmington) *Star*, June 15, 1882; (Wilmington) *Messenger*, August 28, 1891, November 3, 1893; *Pamlico Enterprise*, June 23, 1882; *Kinston Free Press*, August 20, 1891. The (New Bern) *Daily Journal*, September 7, 1882 reported that the *L. H. Cutler's* builder had a second steamboat under construction but there is no information as to what happened to it.

294. *Kinston Free Press*, April 5, 19, July 19, September 6, 15, December 29, 1888; (New Bern) *Daily Journal*, September 5, October 14, 1888, October 24, 1890; (New Bern) *Weekly Journal*, November 24, 1892. For a brief history of Grifton and when the town received that name see Roger Kammerer, "A History of Grifton," *Greenville Times*, June 7, 1989. One source claims that the *Contentnea* was built at Bell's Ferry rather than Kinston.

295. *Goldsboro Messenger*, March 5, 26, April 9, 11, June 11, 28, August 20, 27, October 4, 25, 30, November 1, 1883; (New Bern) *Daily Journal*, March 18, 1883; *Pamlico Enterprise*, July 27, 1883.

296. *Goldsboro Messenger*, March 15, 31, 1884; (New Bern) *Daily Journal*, December 21, 1887, June 7, July 2, 1895, April 22, October 26, 1897; July 11, 1897; (New Bern) *Weekly Journal*, April 18, June 20, 1895, June 2, 9, 1899; *Beaufort Weekly Record*, September 9, 1887; *Wilmington Evening Dispatch*, February 27, 1896; Still,

"Shipbuilding and Boatbuilders in Swansboro, 1800-1950," 10-11.

297. Bridgers, "Steamboats on the Tar," 133. Bridgers wrote extensively on steamboating on the Tar River, and his manuscript includes brief histories of each of the vessels that operated on that river. Roger Kammerer, "'Yonder She Comes Rounding the Point': A History or Steamboats on the Tar," *Greenville Times*, June 28, 1985. Newspaper coverage on the construction of these vessels was fairly extensive.

298. In addition to Bridgers manuscript, see notes of William Rodman, n.d., in the Rodman Papers, ECU. This rather lengthy manuscript concerns a suit instigated over payment for the vessel. See also Styron to Clark, December 1, 1876, Beaufort County Deed Book 42, 278-279, SANC; Styron and Clark to Frick and Co., November 30, 1876, SANC, 280; Styron to Fulford, December 1, 1876, SANC, 273; Styron mortgage, April 1881, Beaufort County Deed Book 77, 480, SANC.

299. Still, "The Shipbuilding Industry in Washington, North Carolina," 40; *Goldsboro Messenger*, October 20, 29, 1879, February 14, 1881; (Tarboro) *Southerner*, October 16, December 25, 1879, June 10, August 12, 19, 26, September 23, October 18, 20, 1880, January 13, February 10, March 31, 1881, (Kinston) *Journal*, January 20, 1881; Styron to Lawrence, September 23, 1879, Beaufort County Deed Book 47, 130, SANC; Bridgers, "Steamboats on the Tar," 139.

300. (Wilmington) *Star*, September 15, November 29, 1883, March 26, 1884; (New Bern) *Daily Journal*, September 13, 20, November 23, 1883; *Pamlico Enterprise*, November 30, 1883. See also long suit concerning the *Margie* in 1885, Beaufort County District Court Records, SANC.

301. *Norfolk Ledger*, June 4, 1887; *Norfolk Landmark*, March 19, 1887; (Greenville) *Eastern Reflector*, January 25, 1888; *Washington Progress*, November 1, 1887; (Wilmington) *Weekly Star*, March 4, 1887; (New Bern) *Weekly Journal*, March 3, 1887.

302. *Washington Progress*, October 8, 1895; *Connector*, Newsletter of the Tar River Connection Genealogical Society, IX (Fall 2005), 14; Prince, *Norfolk Southern Railroad*, 205; *Washington Gazette*, January 25, 1894; Turner and Bridgers, *History of Edgecombe County, North Carolina*, 23.

303. (Tarboro) *Southerner*, January 5, 8, 1880, December 1, 1881; *Goldsboro Messenger*, March 2, 1881; (Wilmington) *Star*, August 15, 1879; (New Bern) *Daily Journal*, August 27, October 2, 1879, January 8, 1880; *Reveille*, December 4, 1885; Prince, *Norfolk Southern Railroad*, 120, 225; *Washington Progress*, October 29, 1895; (New Bern) *Weekly Journal*, August 15, 1895; Still, "The Shipbuilding Industry in Washington, North Carolina," 39-40.

304. (Elizabeth City) *Independent*, January 21, 1927.

305. (Murfreesboro) *Index*, June 10, 1887.

306. For the *Helen Smith* see (Wilmington) *Daily Journal*, September 10, 1873; notes on the *Helen Smith* in "Charter, By Laws and Proceedings of the North Carolina and New York Steam Boat Company. . .," manuscript in Mariners Museum, Newport News, Virginia.

307. (Murfreesboro) *Index*, May 20, December 2, 1887, May 4, August 3, 10, November 9, 1888.

308. Bridgers, "Steamboats on the Tar," 166.

309. Most of the information on the first two vessels comes from the Steamer *Bertie* Collection, ECU. The collection includes a number of letters concerning the steamboat's construction. See also (Wilmington) *Morning Star*, February 12, 1884. According to vessel documents, the *Tahoma* was built at Elizabeth City. She was registered at the custom house there but built in Windsor.

310. (Elizabeth City) *Economist*, October 21, 1870.

311. The writer of a letter to the editor in (Elizabeth City) *Economist*, June 3, 1879, insisted that the *Enterprise* was built in the Newland Township not South Mills. Brown, *Juniper Waterway*, refers to them as "home-made products of a country shipyard" (121). See also (Wilmington) *Morning Star*, April 30, 1879; (Elizabeth City) *Economist*, April 15, 1879.

312. For a pencil drawing of the *Cumberland* see Eldredge Collection, Mariners Museum, Newport News, Virginia. The file includes additional information and a photograph of this vessel.

313. Johnson, *Riverboating in Lower Carolina*, 17; See also (Wilmington) *Star*, September 12, 1886. For descriptions of other steam flats, see (Kinston) *Journal*, June 19, July 24, 1879; *Kinston Free Press*, September 18, 1890; *New Bern Times*, September 14, 1873; (New Bern) *Daily Journal*, June 19, 1879, January 1, August 27, 1885, December 31, 1886; (Tarboro) *Southerner*, October 18, 1877.

314. Bizzell (ed.), *Heritage of Sampson County, North Carolina*, 136. For steam flats in process of construction, see *Perquimans Record*, February 10, 1892; (Windsor) *Ledger*, February 27, March 19, 1896; (Murfreesboro) *Index*, April 29, 1557; (Hertford) *Eastern Courier*, March 12, 1895; (Kinston) *Journal*, June 19, 1879; *Elizabeth City Falcon*, January 20, 1888.

315. *Wilmington Post*, March 13, 1881; (Wilmington) *Star*, November 23, 1900.

316. *Steamboat Inspection Service*, 1895, 163-164, RG41, NA; (Wilmington) *Morning Star*, May 29, 1869; *Washington Progress*, June 16, 1896, February 28, 1899; *Washington Gazette*, March 9, 1893; (Hertford) *Eastern Courier*, January 16, 1896; Reaves, *Southport (Smithville): A Chronology*, 98; (New Bern) *Daily Journal*, June 3, 1896; *Perquimans Record*, February 11, 1891; (Wilmington) *Messenger*, April 20, 1893; (Murfreesboro) *Index*, June 10, 1887, May 17, 1889; *Beaufort Weekly Record*, September 9, 1887. For tow boats listed in vessel documentation papers, see *Washington Gazette*, March 2, 2893; *Washington Progress*, February 28, April 30, 1899; (New Bern) *Daily Journal*, May 4, 1893, September 1, 1896, July 13, 1898; (New Bern) *Weekly Journal*, May 11, 1893; (Hertford) *Eastern Courier*, November 26, 1895, April 16, 30, May 14, July 16, October 15, 1896; Gerald A. Patterson, *Perquimans County, North Carolina*, 101; contract between Whatley and T.H.B. Myers, January 9, 1899, copy in Rodman Papers, ECU.

317. (Edenton) *Fisherman and Farmer*, August. 2, 1889, June 6, 1890.

318. (Wilmington) *Morning Star*, December 17, 1878; (Wilmington) *Messenger*, April 14, 1889; Jackson notes, Underwater Archaeology Branch, Fort Fisher, N.C.

319. *Perquimans Record*, January 20, February 3, 1892; Haley and Winslow, *Historic Architecture of Perquimans County*, 56. For *Ark*, see (Murfreesboro) *Index*, December 2, 1887, May 4, July 13, August 3, 5, 10, 19, November 9, December 14, 1888; *Fayetteville Messenger*, January 6, 1888; (Wilmington) *Morning Star*, July 13, 1882. In 1886 a number of "seamen" brought suit in federal district court in Elizabeth City challenging a floating sawmill as a vessel. The court ruled that it was a vessel since it "engaged in navigation or commerce on navigable waters." District Court of the United States Eastern District of North Carolina, March 1886 term, Admiralty, Box 3, Elizabeth City, RG21, NA-Atlanta; (New Bern) *Weekly Journal*, April 29, May 6, 1886. The newspaper's April issue mentioned that this suit was of particular interest to local business interests as there were a great many in this area; "…it is quite important to the owners to know whether or not they own a vessel…."

320. White, *Carolina Riverboats and Rivers*, 20. For a detailed description of the interior arrangement of a new steamboat, see *Fayetteville Eagle*, March 9, 1871.

321. *Goldsboro Messenger*, October 27, 1879; (New Bern) *Weekly Journal*, February 13, 1900.

322. As a Greene County letter writer wrote, "Give us a boat that won't sink." *Goldsboro Messenger*, January 24, 1884.

323. Schuster to Stanton, January 26, 1894, RG 77, NA-Atlanta; *Annual Report of the Corp of Engineers*, 1885, 109; *New Bern Daily Journal*, September 11, November 19, 1896.

324. (Kinston) *Journal*, November 27, 1879.

325. For the Washington vessel see correspondence between William Chauncey and Marine Iron Works of Chicago in the Rodman Papers, ECU. See particularly Chauncey to Willard, May 24, 25, 1900, and Rodman to Marine Iron Works, May 5, 1900. The correspondence gives a detailed description of the desired machinery. July 19, 1868 clipping on steamer *Halcyon* in Reaves files, Underwater Archaeology Unit, Fort Fisher; Styron indenture, November 30, 1876, Beaufort County Deed Book 42, 380; (Murfreesboro) *Index*, August 31, 1888; *Washington Progress*, February 29, 1899; *Kinston Free Press*, April 19, 1882; *Pamlico Enterprise*, July 21, 1882; *Fayetteville Eagle*, March 9, 1871.

326. Stanton, *Steam Navigation on the Carolina Sounds*, 17; Sloan, "Inland Navigation in North Carolina, 1818-1900," 63; *Goldsboro Messenger*, August 9, 1883; *Kinston Free Press*, April 19, 1882; (New Bern) *Daily Journal*, June 1, 1882; *Jones vs. Farmers and Merchants Steam Boat Company*, Carteret County Civil Action Papers, SANC. For description of the location of machinery on a typical paddle steamboat, see *Fayetteville Eagle*, August 24, 1871. By far the most detailed description, including drawings, of steamboat machinery placed in North Carolina-built vessels is the series of letters from Wilbur Askew to E. H. Frazier and Company and the company's replies concerning the *Bertie*. See Steamboat Collection, ECU. For another account of steamboat machinery, see the case file *Kornegay vs. Farmers and Merchants Steamboat Company*, Craven County Superior Court Original Civil Action Papers, SANC.

327. (Wilmington) *Morning Star*, October. 24, 1891; *Goldsboro Messenger*, October 27, 1879; *Pamlico Enterprise*, July 21, 1882.

328. (Edenton) *Fisherman and Farmer*, October 23, 1891.

329. *Beaufort News-Times*, June 22, 1948; *Southport Leader*, January 15, 1891; (Wilmington) *Messenger*, May 16, 1899.

330. Between 1886 and 1890, nine menhaden vessels built in North Carolina had been converted from sail to gasoline or naphtha. Information provided by Steve Goodwin. (New Bern) *Daily Journal*, June 3, 1896; *Washington Gazette*, August 6, 1896; *Kinston Free Press*, October 28, 1899; (Elizabeth City) *Fisherman and Farmer*, July 31, 1896; (Greenville) *Eastern Reflector*, October 17, 1899.

331. (New Bern) *Nut Shell*, August 9, 1898; 1900 manufacturing census, 16. Vessel documents do not list a yacht until 1897. Only two (both built in Carteret County) were listed between 1865 and 1900; *New Bern Times*, October 10, 1871, May 22, 1872.

332. (Wilmington) *Morning Star*, May 13, 14, June 6, 1879; September 18, 1881; March 25, 1882.

333. (Wilmington) *Daily Journal*, October 28, 1868; *Kelley's Wilmington Directory*, 1860; (Wilmington) *Morning Star*, August 13, 1873, July 29, 1876, May 20, June 6, 24, 1877, May 31, June 14, 28, July 10, 1878; *Wilmington Sun*, April 22, 1879.

334. *Wilmington Dispatch*, April 27, 1897, August 26, 1898; (Wilmington) *Messenger*, April 4, 1895; (New Bern) *Weekly Journal*, June 5, 1900; (Wilmington) *Morning Star*, April 28, 1876, March 1, 1879.

335. *Goldsboro Messenger* of April 10, 1884, lists the sharpie fleet at Morehead City.

336. (Wilmington) *Messenger*, July 20, 1888; Reaves, *Southport (Smithville): A Chronology*, 94.

337. (Wilmington) *Star*, January 7, April 22, 1883.

338. (Wilmington) *Morning Star*, July 26, 1868, July 1, 1879;,July 20, 1883; (Hertford) *Eastern Courier*, June 27, 1895, April 16, May 28, 1896; *Wilmington Daily Journal*, October 24, 1868, May 7, 1882; (Wilmington) *Star*, December 16, 1873; (Elizabeth City) *Economist*, June 6, 1877; (Tarboro) *Southerner*, August 20, 1880; (New Bern) *Weekly Journal*, September 8, 1892.

339. (New Bern) *Daily Journal*, July 23, 25, 27, 1882; Myers's agreement to pay for damage to wharf, February 5, 1895, RG77, NA-Atlanta.

340. *Pender Chronicle*, March 7, 1973. Ironically, a photograph of a Cape Fear-built steamboat shows the vessel being loaded with railroad crossties. The caption under the photo reads: "Self Destruction." *Clinton Reporter*, January 8, 1874; Robert Zoeller, "Steamboats on the Tar," *The State*, XI (February 5, 1944), 22; *Murfreesboro Enquirer*, December 5, 1898; *Clinton Reporter*, January 8, 1874; *Norfolk Journal*, August 14, 1868; *Norfolk Landmark*, March 4, 1887; (Edenton) *Fisherman and Farmer*, December 2, 1887.

Chapter 8

The Industrial Era, 1893–1914

Eastern North Carolina was characterized by change in the 1890s, with a transition from wooden to steel-hulled vessels, from sail and steam to gas engines, and an ever-increasing dependence on rail and roadway infrastructure. The coastal plain economy remained overwhelmingly agrarian. In the Piedmont, a crescent of industries arose from Raleigh to Durham, Greensboro, Winston-Salem, and Charlotte, but there was little economic growth east or west.

Railroads and roadways increasingly eroded the viability of the state's maritime trade. After the Panic of 1893 and during the subsequent economic downturn, railroads paralleled most of the rivers draining toward the coast and provided an alternate means of transportation. As a result of railroad competition, steamboat traffic between Wilmington and Fayetteville slowly declined in the 1890s. By 1900, only two companies were still running steamers on the Cape Fear River.[1] The same was true for the Neuse and Roanoke Rivers. In 1900, there were 3,381 miles of railroad track approximating the length of shoreline, providing a majority of communities, even those along rivers, with rail access. More than 5,000 miles of track crisscrossed the state by the beginning of World War I, but rail mileage along the shoreline remained constant.

In 1906, the Norfolk and Southern Railroad was formed by consolidating short lines connecting Norfolk with various communities, principally Elizabeth City, Edenton, Morehead City, and New Bern. In 1907, the Norfolk and Southern reached New Bern and "various water services of the company.... were greatly curtailed." With two railroad lines passing through the port, shipping by water almost ceased. The editor of the New Bern *Daily Journal* began a crusade to restore water transportation to the city and offered this estimation: "There is no local market as there was once, and the empty docks where no one looks for the steamer, are sad features of a departed river business." Editorial after editorial decried "vanishing shipping," blaming the railroads. Other newspapers took up the cause. The *Charlotte Observer* wrote, "There is scarcely a city on the Atlantic Seaboard that has better facilities for water transportation than New Bern... and strange to say, in this commercial age, the waters of the Neuse are floating no vessels of any consequence."[2] At a meeting of local residents in Morehead City, the president of the Chamber of Commerce remarked that they no longer had any vessels to ship their fish, "the railroads own everything.... The freight rates have increased so much that it is almost impossible to pay the rates charges."[3] The Corps of Engineers became increasingly reluctant to approve dredging and the removal of obstructions in rivers and harbors with rail connections. Edenton's efforts to have the harbor area and Pembroke Creek dredged proved futile. Despite Congressional efforts, the Corps also refused to continue improving the upper Neuse River.[4] In 1913, a report to President William Howard Taft concluded that railroads had "destroyed competition on many of the water highways of commerce."[5]

The development of automotive transportation expedited the collapse of the maritime shipping business. By 1910, there were approximately 2,400 motor vehicles traveling on 48,000 miles of largely unimproved roads in the state. Although nearly unusable for bulk trade in major exports such as forest and farm products, roads carried an increasing percentage of produce and passengers that, in the past, were conveyed by water transport.

Seafood was exported, but the absence of adequate refrigeration imposed severe limitations. The state's small ports ceased to engage in foreign trade. Wilmington, which became the state's largest port, did benefit from some foreign shipping. Trade with the West Indies, particularly in lumber and naval stores, disappeared early in the twentieth century. By 1910, local newspapers ceased reporting West Indies shipping. It was more economical to ship lumber to Norfolk, and then by freighter to the islands of the Caribbean.

West Indian trade completely disappeared in the first decade of the twentieth century. However, water transportation was still vital on some rivers and sounds, particularly in areas without rail connections. In 1905, the Roanoke River, despite having the largest drainage area on the eastern seaboard, handled only 9,055 commercial tons compared to that of the Tar River with 567,331 tons, and the Neuse and Trent Rivers with a combined total of 731,700 tons.[6] Reduced tonnage on the Roanoke River was largely due to railroads usurping water borne commerce. The Norfolk and Southern Railroad reached Washington in 1907, and freight rates were considerably lower by rail than by water. In addition, there was an increase in farm-to-market roads. Markets were relocated from local ports to railheads, such as those in the Piedmont Crescent, and to regional ports, such as Norfolk and Charleston. Despite rail competition, steamboats remained an important means of transportation linking various North Carolina communities with each other and with Norfolk.

The importance of the Chesapeake and Albemarle Canal increasingly surpassed that of traditional coastal routes. In 1892, tolls were collected for 4,061 steamers, 1,817 schooners, 1,150 barges, 61 lighters, 329 sloops, and 298 rafts.[7] Inlets that had been so vital to North Carolina's maritime trade were now utilized only by small sailing vessels. The Dismal Swamp and Chesapeake and Albemarle Canals handled the bulk of coastal traffic. The completion of the Intracoastal Waterway (ICW) system in 1912 and 1913 resulted in a significant increase in tonnage for the Chesapeake and Albemarle Canal, but the Dismal Swamp Canal could not compete with the toll-free system.

Community business groups (chambers of commerce, steamboat lines, and even railroads) appealed to Congress and the Corps of Engineers for improvements to rivers, streams, and harbors. Generally, Corps engineers determined the viability of each request for funding based on usage. Obstructions were removed and channels deepened in the Cape Fear, Neuse, and Trent Rivers annually. Occasionally, other navigable waters in the state received internal improvement funds. Morehead City was ignored until the creation of the ICW. With a terminus at Beaufort Inlet, funds to deepen the Morehead City harbor became available.[8] The Corps made no effort to work on inlets.

In 1895, Wilmington's export tonnage was off by nearly twenty percent from its peak in 1880 and continued to dwindle through the end of the century. Smaller ports, such as New Bern, Washington, Beaufort, and Elizabeth City continued to depend heavily upon water transportation. Nevertheless, their water borne trade gradually disappeared. The decline in New Bern's maritime industries and trade caused the local Chamber of Commerce to characterize the port's economic condition as "stagnant."[9] Steamers out of Norfolk maintained maritime routes to North Carolina ports, and small steamboats still linked those ports with settlements along navigable waterways. However, by 1906, much of this inland trade was accomplished with sailing and gasoline powered craft. The Old Dominion Steamship Company and other lines abandoned their North Carolina routes. In 1907, the President of the John Roper Company wrote the District Chief of the Corp of Engineers, "the traffic on the Albemarle Sound . . . is decreasing yearly and very shortly will be eliminated with the exception of very small sailing or fishing craft and motor boats."[10]

The shipbuilding productivity of the 1880s did not continue. Nationally, new vessel construction declined thirty percent during in the 1890s.[11] The state's shipbuilding industry was hurt by the depression and the economic instability that accompanied it. In 1895, the owner of a Washington shipyard observed, "Like all sections of the country we are having a very dull season . . . Since the early spring there has not been a craft built here."[12] The 1900 census recorded fourteen yards building ships and boats in North Carolina, a loss of four since 1890. Four of the remaining yards built only small craft, and five others were listed as repair yards. The census noted only nine small vessels launched in the state and Wilmington as the only location where a vessel was built in that year. Of course, there may have been far more vessels constructed in the state than documented in the census which itself is inconsistent. Although nine small boats, launches, pleasure boats, and row boats are recorded as being built in the state, another statistical source cited in the census states that an additional 156 gasoline power craft were constructed. On Shackleford Bank, residents built double-ended whale boats until the hurricane of 1899 virtually destroyed the fishery. Ferries were built and rebuilt.[13] Lifeboats were built, as regulations required that all steamers including riverboats were required to carry at least one. In 1883, a lifeboat built entirely of galvanized iron was constructed in Wilmington.[14] Even so, vessel construction remained erratic during much of the 1890s and into the new century.

Between 1900 and 1915, the state's ship and boat building industry began to recover and thrive. According to vessel document papers, nearly four hundred wooden vessels of all types were built in the state during this period. Three steel ships were rebuilt in North Carolina facilities, and in 1913, *C. W. Lyon* was totally rebuilt at the Wilmington Iron Works. In 1917, the hulls of two vessels were towed from Baltimore to Elizabeth City where they were completed.[15] Of course, a large number of non-documented vessels and small craft should be added to the total. Rowboats, skiffs, and other small craft were built in large numbers.[16] The type of vessels constructed changed. Steamboat construction declined as more and more gasoline-powered vessels were launched. According to vessel document papers, a large percentage of sailing vessels over five tons were converted to gasoline power. This was the national trend. Sailing vessels of five tons or over, built in the United States, declined from 526 in 1901 to 134 in 1908.[17] In contrast, the construction of sailing vessels in North Carolina was sustained because small sailing craft dominated the state's fishing industry. National and regional economic factors, including meager crops and poor fishing, frequently affected the industry and other manufacturing sectors.

Shipbuilding Sites

The locations of ship and boatbuilding sites changed over time (Figure 1). There was a marked decline in the number of vessels built at sites scattered along interior rivers and streams. Construction sites were concentrated in coastal counties and ports. Not all established shipbuilding sites continued to produce vessels. Fayetteville built only two steamers during this period. Washington produced twenty-four vessels, only a few of these after 1910. Twenty-three documented vessels were built at Wilmington where much of the work was in repairs. Twenty-nine were constructed in New Bern and thirty-four in Elizabeth City, the yards also concentrating on ship repairs. Carteret County, with many small yards, continued to be a boat building center and, in fact, overwhelmingly led the state in the number of documented vessels constructed. Morehead City produced eighty-two and Beaufort thirty-four. Other "Down East" communities built seventy-one, and a few were built elsewhere in the county, generating a total of a total of 187 documented vessels. In the northeastern part of the state, the Outer Banks (principally Roanoke Island) produced thirty documented vessels, an impressive number, as previously, the area had been noted for building only small fishing craft. Similarly, Southport, known for building small boats, produced eighteen documented vessels.

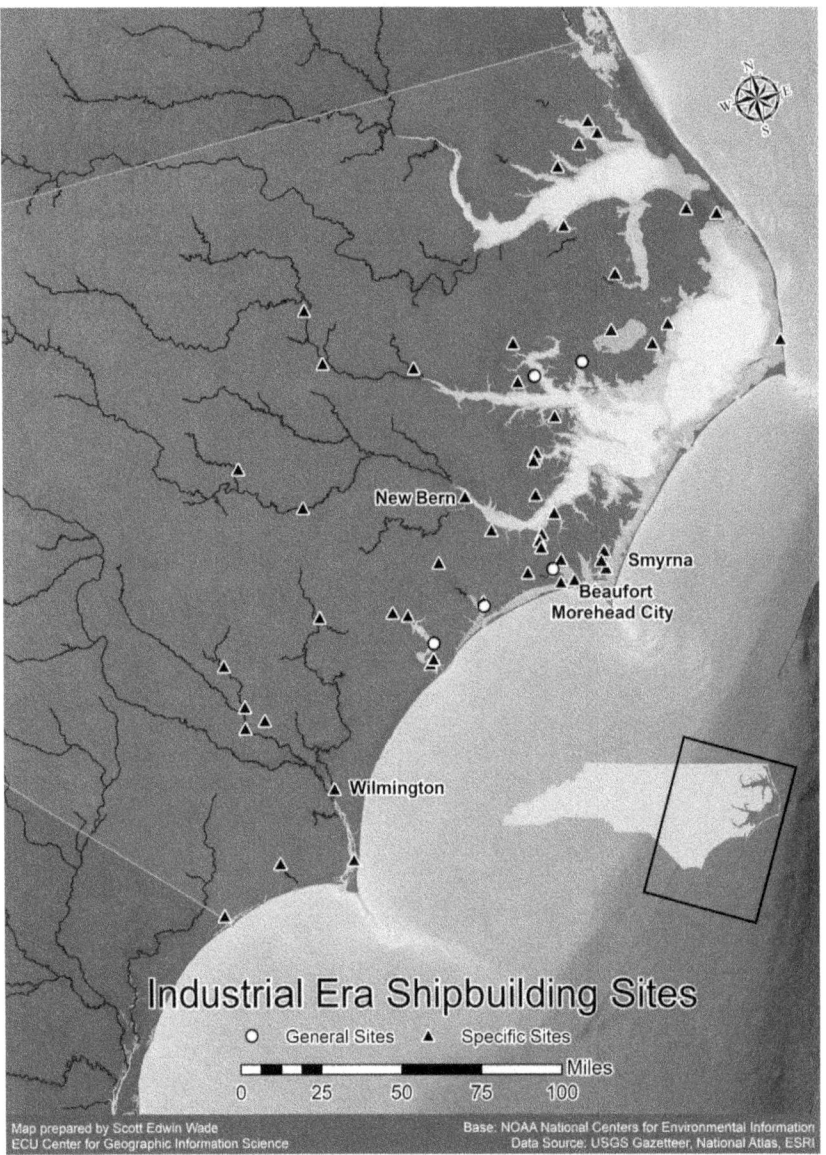

FIGURE 8-1 The shipbuilding sites during the Industrial Era were scattered with very little clustering. *Source:* Author's database.

There was an average of one shipbuilding site for every thirty-one miles of tidal shoreline, and thirty-one vessels built per year, one for every five and one-half miles of shoreline. The Beaufort area led the state in vessels built. The majority were gas- and steam-powered screw vessels. The Albemarle Sound area followed; the Cape Fear area, centered on Wilmington, was third. The Outer Banks area continued to build fishing schooners. The Pamlico area, centered in Washington on the Tar River, produced mostly steamers, as did New Bern on the Neuse River. There were 256 steamers constructed during this period, accounting for 42% of the total number of vessels built; 289 schooners and sloops were built, amounting to 47% of the total.

Nonetheless, some vessels were built at inland sites. The small community of Belhaven produced twenty-seven vessels and led Beaufort County in ship and boat construction. The Hertford *Eastern Courier* references the Jewell Marine Railway in Elizabeth City operated by Walter M. Jewell, who died on June 2, 1896. However, no information has been found on a marine railway by that name and there is no evidence that Jewell's shipbuilding activities were successful.[18] Steamboats continued to be constructed on the Black River in Pender County. In 1909, a steam dredge was built by the Roanoke River and Power Company and launched near Roanoke Rapids. This event was considered so unusual that a large crowd lined the river bank to witness the launching.[19]

Two steamers were constructed in Edgecombe County close to the head of navigation on the Tar River. *Shiloh* was built in 1895 by the Shiloh Oil Company. The company was bought out by the Tar River Oil Company shortly after *Shiloh* was launched. The screw steamer's construction was supervised by David Liddon, the well-known ship carpenter from Washington.[20] The paddle wheeler *Tarboro*, not to be confused with a steamboat by the same name built in Washington, was constructed in 1898 in Tarboro. The Tar River Oil Company had the vessel built to carry passengers and freight between the town and Washington. Although David Liddon was the master carpenter on this vessel, Robert Zoeller claimed to have superintended the work.[21]

The number and tonnage of vessels built declined from 1894 to 1914 (Figures 2 and 3). Construction peaked at the turn of the century. As in previous years, industry productivity continued to be erratic.

The Business of Building Ships and Boats

The 1905 manufacturing census recorded shipbuilding data including repairs and labor. Census returns incorporated a table illustrating the value of repairs by state. Of twenty-three states listed, North Carolina was near the bottom in estimated value of repair work in private yards for 1890, 1900, and 1905. The report also concluded that most of the repair work was done in facilities with marine railways.[22] This was certainly true for North Carolina. No evidence has been found to indicate that any significant amount of vessel repair, rebuilding, or overhauling was done at boat or shipyards without railways. Although repairs were done at these yards and even alongside wharves, river banks, and other coastal locations, such work is unrecorded. Newspapers frequently mentioned vessels undergoing repairs or overhauling, but rarely at ship or boat building facilities outside a port. Modifying a sailing vessel for a gasoline-powered engine often required the use of a shipyard's equipment and labor.[23]

The Meadows marine railway in New Bern was one of the busiest ship repair facilities in the state. J.A. Meadows concentrated exclusively on repair and rebuilding from the time he assumed ownership in 1892 until early in the twentieth century. He added a second railway to allow more repairs to be done at one time. One of the railways could hold four vessels at a time and the other could accommodate two. They were usually full during the summer and fall months. After the 1899 hurricane, there was a large number of vessels waiting in line to be hauled up and repaired. In September 1910, twenty-five vessels were placed on the ways. The local papers frequently mention repairs and rebuilding taking place at the facility.[24]

The Elizabeth City marine railways did a profitable repair and overhauling business because of their proximity to the two canals in the area, and the fact that many vessels

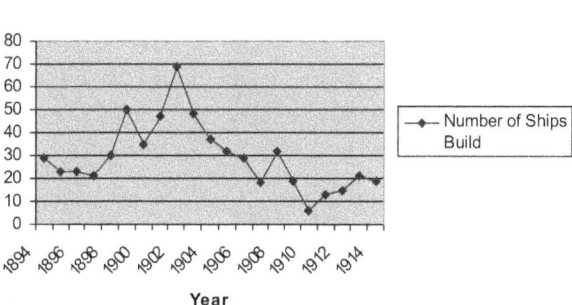

FIGURE 8-2 The number of vessels built declined from the turn of the century. This shows a recovery from the Panic of 1893, an economic boom, then a substantial decline. *Source:* Author's database.

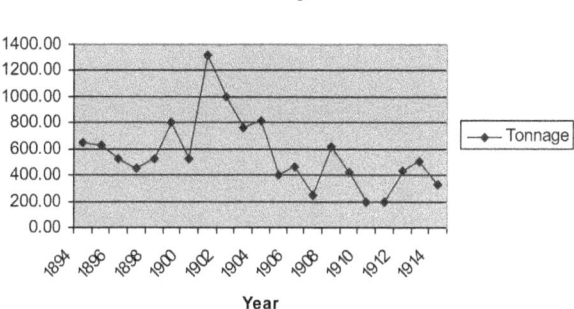

FIGURE 8-3 The tonnage of vessels built during the period 1894–1914 shows a similarity to the number of vessels built. *Source:* Author's database.

went aground or were involved in collisions in Albemarle Sound. Between 1893 and 1917, the Scott, Fearing, Pailin, Williams, Hayman, and Willey railways were all involved in the repair business, although not all at the same time. Willey's marine railway was the busiest. Willey had a railway that was large enough to take care of at least three vessels at a time.[25] Typical shipyards did not have railways (see Figure 4).

The state's shipbuilding force continued to be largely itinerant. In 1898, the Wilmington Iron Works, which had a contract to rebuild the monitor *Nantucket*, advertised in local, state, and even out-of-state newspapers for fifty ship carpenters. Ship workers often moved from location to location. At isolated sites, where an occasional vessel was built or repaired, workers were hired and brought in from remote places. The March 5, 1896, the Hertford *Eastern Courier* reported that two ship carpenters had arrived from Carteret County to help build a new steam tug.[26]

The 1905 U.S. manufacturing census recorded 200 North Carolina wage earners as the "greatest number employed at any one time during the year" in

FIGURE 8-4 The sailing yacht *Roma* under construction at a shipyard at the foot of the old bridge in Beaufort in 1897. The original photograph is owned by Nat Smith of Gloucester, N.C. One of the ship carpenters was George W. Gaskill, Smith's grandfather. *Source:* State Archives of North Carolina.

shipbuilding, and seventy-three as the average number so engaged. Ship carpenters are specifically identified in population census returns. In 1910, twenty-two are listed for Wilmington, fifteen for Washington, seven for other sections of Beaufort County, eighteen for Craven County, nineteen for Pasquotank County, and twenty for Carteret County. The number for Carteret County was consistent for several years. Sailmakers, block makers, caulkers, and marine railway mechanics are also listed. However, ship- or boatyard laborers are usually not recorded.[27] In 1915-1916, Whitehurst and Rice shipyard employed five, Willis marine railway had three, and the John Bell Company had twelve. In 1908, the superintendent of the Meadows marine railway in New Bern stated he had a workforce of twenty-seven, and had to "import several ship carpenters from an adjoining county because he could not find them in the city." The November 19, 1909 New Bern *Daily Journal* reported that twenty-five men were working at the Meadows marine railway and shipyard repairing a vessel. In 1912, the Hunt Barge Building Works was established in Elizabeth City and three "expert boat builders were brought in to supervise the barge construction."

The company planned to hire an additional fifty local carpenters and other workers.[28]

City directories often listed professionals. The New Bern directory for 1904-05 listed several ship carpenters and sail makers. Occasionally, photographs were taken of individuals working on a particular vessel. A 1900 photo showed twenty-three workers posing alongside a vessel under construction at the Fearing-Hayman Boat Works in Elizabeth City (Figure 5). A 1915 photo showed ten in front of a steamboat being repaired at an Elizabeth City shipyard.[29] A special industrial edition of the Elizabeth City *Economist* notes that Wiley's shipyard employed from ten to sixty hands depending on the number of vessels under construction or repair. Snell's shipbuilding facility employed from five to fifteen workers "according to the season," and the Hayman work force varied from less than ten to as many as thirty.[30] When work was scarce, Elizabeth City shipwrights were able to find work in Virginia yards.[31] There is little data on the boatbuilding force on the Outer Banks (Figure 6). North Carolina's report on labor statistics for 1915 stated that the Wanchese marine railway on Roanoke Island employed four

FIGURE 8-5 Workers at the E.S. Willey Marine Railway and Shipyard in Elizabeth City, ca. 1915. Courtesy Ernest Saunders, Elizabeth City, N.C..

workers. Calvin Burrus, in Buxton, and brothers Frank and Irving Stowe, in Hatteras Village, were shipbuilders. Considering the number of documented vessels built during the period, there must have been ship carpenters scattered up and down the Outer Banks.[32]

Period photographs show that black laborers continued to be employed in shipbuilding. The 1910 census listed five in Pasquotank County, six in Craven, eight in Washington, and one in Wilmington. The Wilmington census also listed a black man as a shipyard porter. In November 1898, in the wake of the Wilmington race riot, a Raleigh newspaper reported that white ship carpenters and other workers had been discharged at the government shipyard in Wilmington, and blacks were hired in their place. The engineer in charge denied this, pointing out that workers of both races had been discharged as an economy measure, "It just happened at a most unfortunate time."[33] Carteret County listed no blacks involved in the shipbuilding trade.

With the exception of Wilmington, the number of workers employed in the shipbuilding industry fluctuated from year to year. Overall, the number declined. In 1915, the Wilmington Marine Railway, a subsidiary of the Wilmington Iron Works hired sixteen workers, but the following year the number had grown to approximately a hundred.[34] The number increased with the outbreak of World War I.

SHIPBUILDERS AND SHIPBUILDING

As noted, it can be difficult to distinguish between a shipbuilder and an individual having a ship built. Census returns do identify shipbuilders as a separate category, but often builders identified themselves as ship carpenters. Businessmen or merchants, sawmill and lumber company owners and managers, and even representatives of shipping lines employed a shipbuilder or a master ship carpenter to build a vessel. This practice was commonplace throughout the nineteenth century. A. W. Styron of Washington is perhaps the best example, but there were dozens scattered throughout the coastal plain region. Moreover, shipbuilders and ship carpenters often engaged in other business activities such as building houses and bridges, farming, fishing, salvaging stranded ships and wrecks, and captaining a vessel. One was a well-known cabinetmaker and another a part time police officer.

Wilmington shipbuilders continued to dominate the industry, although vessels were constructed elsewhere along the Cape Fear River and its tributaries (Figure 7). The Skinners, Samuel W. and his son Louis, were the most successful. Samuel, who established and expanded the business in the latter years of the nineteenth century, died in 1907. Louis took over the Skinner businesses in 1905, including shipbuilding, and managed them until 1913 when the shipyard became the site of the Cape Fear Machine Works.[35]

FIGURE 8-6 The Creef Boatworks at Manteo in 1898. Source: Outer Banks History Center.

Charles Wessell, a native of Germany, announced his retirement from the shipbuilding business in 1902, then changed his mind and began work on a new vessel. He entered the towing business on the Cape Fear River before retiring a second time in 1917.[36] In 1915, the Wilmington Iron Works entered the shipbuilding business and master builders were employed to carry on the work. R. P. Paddison, Walter Taft, John B. Robinson, and the Shermans, especially Luther, were noted shipbuilders along the Black River. Luther Sherman was the most prolific, constructing at least eight steamers as well as other vessels. He built the majority of the vessels at Point Caswell, and under contract, supervised other projects on the river. Vessels were constructed at Clear Run, Beattys Bridge, and Strawhorn Landing. Launch Johnson was the only known boatbuilder along this section of the river. In Bladen County, the Johnson brothers built a gasoline-powered tug.[37]

Jeff Piver, who was also a sail maker, was the only known boat builder in Brunswick County during this period.[38] In Swansboro, Reinhold Foster continued boat building. His son Joseph erected the first marine railway in Swansboro. In 1895, Foster constructed a 130-foot steamer for a lumber company. Nearly all steam-powered vessels built in Swansboro were for the lumber business. Several vessels were constructed at Swansboro lumber and saw mills. In 1897, two steamboats, *Onslow* and *Nina*, were launched for the lumber trade. Both were built for the Swansboro Lumber Company which contracted for a third steamboat in 1899. That year, a barge was completed in the town, probably by the same firm. The lumber company also repaired vessels. A Baltimore lumber firm had a large steamboat built in Swansboro and, after launching, the hull was towed to Baltimore for her machinery and superstructure. J.F. Pettyman, owner of the Swansboro lumber company, also owned a mill across the river from New Bern where other vessels were built.[39]

The 1903 *North Carolina Yearbook* lists Van Buren Willis as a Swansboro builder. He relocated there from Carteret County along with his son Isaiah. They launched an impressive number of small craft. Van Buren died in 1925. Robert Lee Smith and Edward Hill were recognized small craft builders prior to World War I. Elsewhere in Onslow County, Walter Marine and Luther Harrison were the most prominent builders on the New River. In the small community of Marine, Harrison constructed several vessels including houseboats, sailboats, and gasoline-powered boats. In a 1906 letter, Louis C. Brown of Gilletts mentioned that he built vessels near Snead's Ferry.[40]

The people of Carteret County take great pride in their maritime culture. Ship and boat building is a traditional industry and way of life, practiced by a sizable number of county residents. This was particularly true in the small, "down east" communities of Marshallberg,

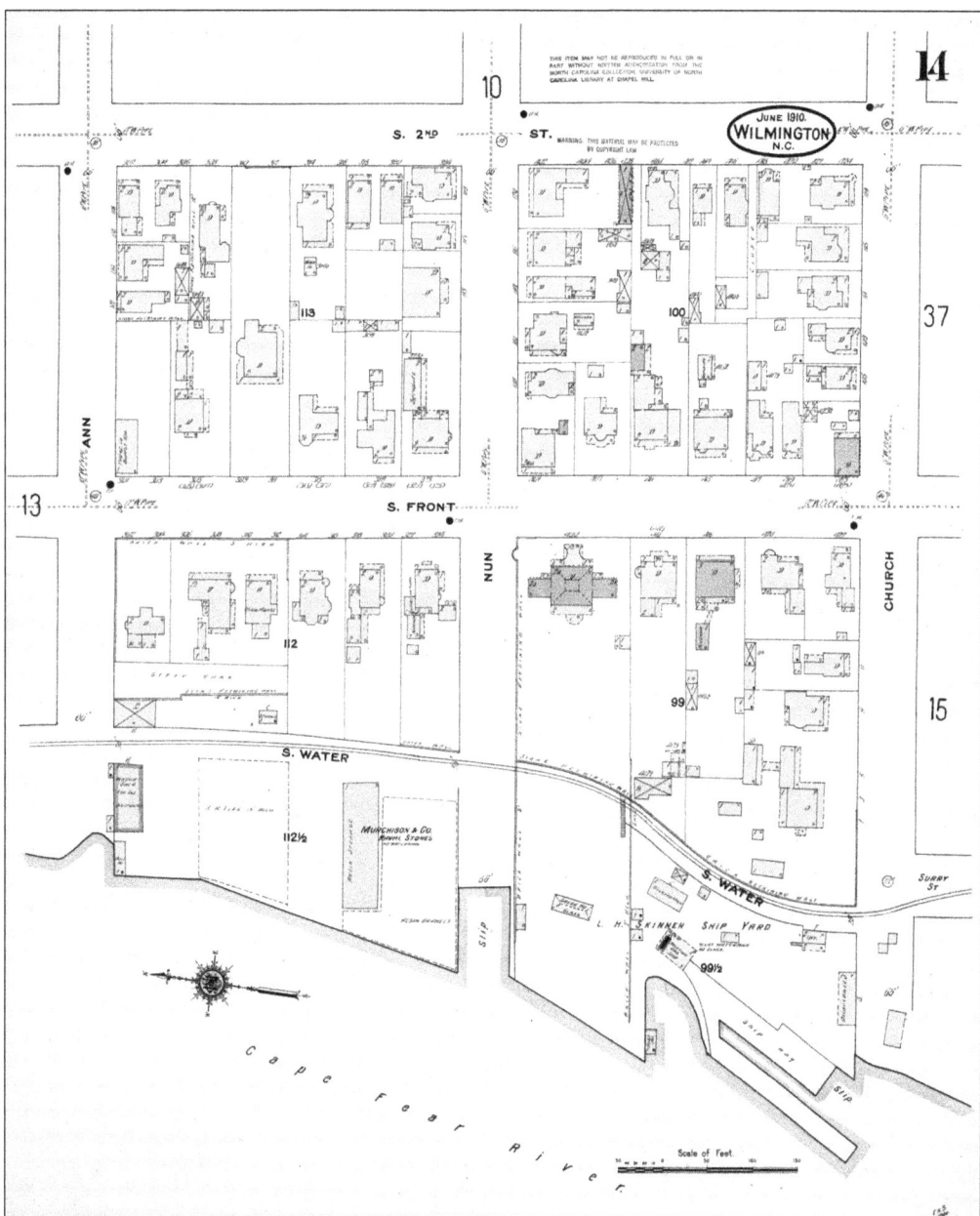

FIGURE 8-7 Skinner Shipyard in Wilmington in 1910 as depicted on Sanborn Map. *Source:* Joyner Library, East Carolina University.

Williston, Gloucester, Atlantic, Smyrna, and along the islands, straits, sounds, and streams. Vessels continued to be built in Beaufort, and a shipyard was opened in Morehead City in the 1890s. Boatbuilding in Carteret was most productive in the 1890s. Twenty boats were built in 1890, twenty-nine in 1891, and seventeen in 1892. A.G. Hall, from New England, was the only listed Carteret shipbuilder in the 1890s.[41]

Certain families were particularly prominent in the boat building business. An undetermined, but considerable number of Willises were boatbuilders. In Marshallberg, Mildon Willis started building in the early 1900s and, along with his sons, was still launching vessels after World War II. Zephania (Zeph) Willis and his brothers operated a boatyard near Williston. Zeph was a master boat builder. According to vessel document records, he constructed fourteen sailing vessels over five tons. He also built many undocumented small craft until his death in 1934. Other Willises noted as boatbuilders included: Abner, Benjamin, Samuel, and O. C. Willis. George Gaskill, born in 1835, was still building vessels early in the twentieth century. Micajah Adams was also a well-known master boat builder in the county. He was born in 1877 and started building small craft in 1896 when his family

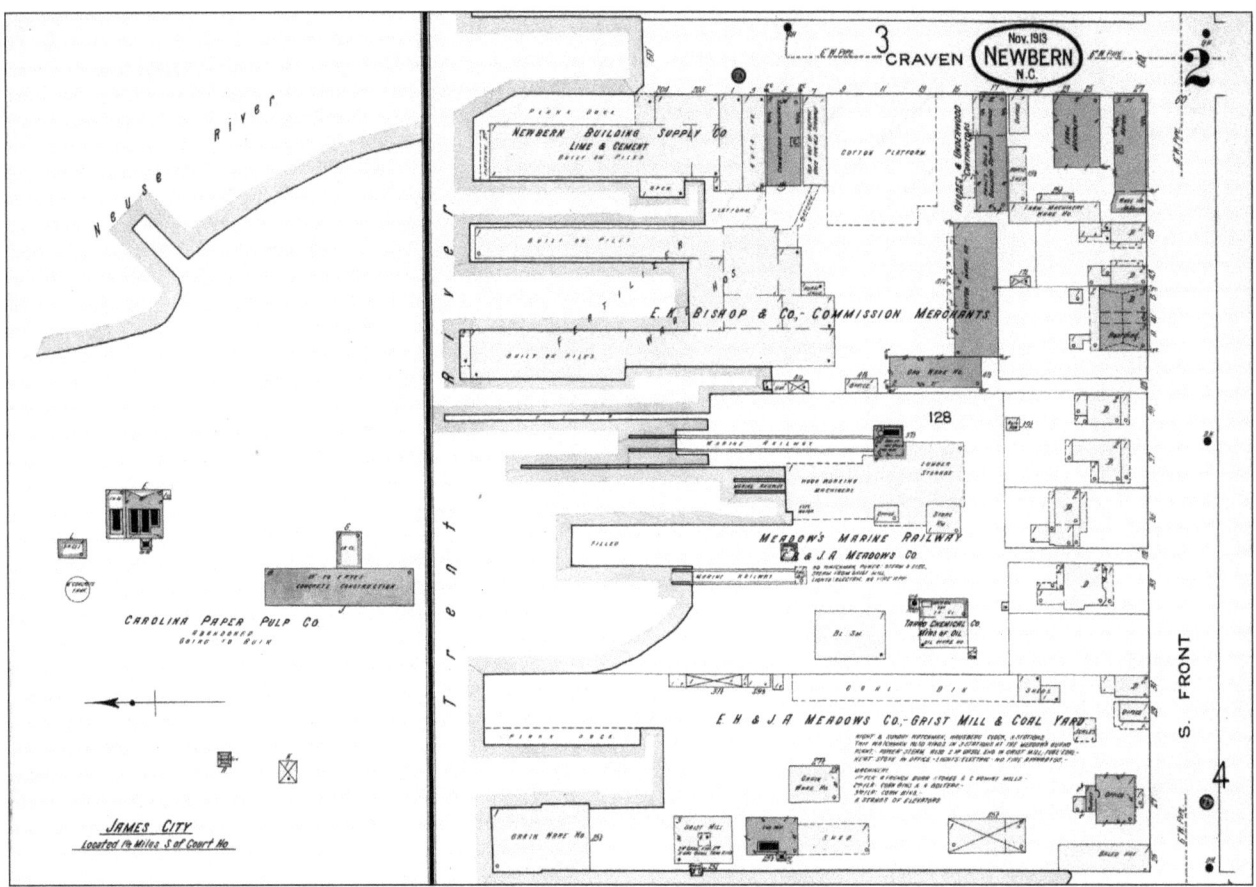

FIGURE 8-8 New Bern waterfront in 1913 showing the location of the Meadows Marine Railway, as depicted on Sanborn map. *Source:* Joyner Library, East Carolina University.

moved to Salter Path. He had a small shop on the edge of Bogue Sound. He and his brother, also a first-class ship carpenter, built houses and even caskets as sidelines to their boatbuilding business.[42] In Beaufort, Bryan Longest and Julius and Logan Whitehurst were the most prolific builders. In 1903, the Rice family sold a waterfront lot to Robert Rice. Robert and Julius Whitehurst formed a partnership and began building vessels at this site.[43]

John F. Bell of Morehead City was the best-known shipbuilder in Carteret County and considered the county's "best carpenter."[44] In 1902, he formed a partnership with C. Manly Wade. Each man was an experienced shipwright, having learned the trade from working with their respective father. Like so many other boat builders, in order to supplement their income, they built houses and did other woodworking. The firm was a success. In 1906, they constructed twelve vessels. In 1908, the firm incorporated and established a sawmill and lumber business. However, in 1916, the partnership was dissolved because of financial difficulties and Wade moved to Charlottesville, Virginia. That same year Charles S. Wallace, owner of various enterprises including fishing interests in Morehead City, negotiated a partnership with Bell. Wallace had a fleet of menhaden vessels that frequently needed repairs and he planned to add to the fleet. The Bell-Wallace Company would continue in operation until shortly after World War II.[45]

The Panic of 1893 and resulting economic slowdown affected the New Bern ship and boat building industry. Only three vessels were launched in the city before 1898, but recovery soon followed. In the decade before 1898, the port's shipbuilding establishments built seventeen documented vessels; two schooners, two barges, and thirteen gasoline tow or freight boats. There were no prominent builders. In 1900, F. T. Gaskill built a steamboat but there is no evidence he constructed others.[46] In addition, there was a considerable amount of boat repair work, most of which was done at the Meadows Shipyard (Figure 8).

In 1892, Howard sold his shipyard and marine railways to his son-in-law, E. A. Meadows. Meadows was a successful local businessman owning, among other property, one of the largest grist mills in the state. As he was not a shipbuilder, he employed master carpenters to carry on the shipyard work. Shortly after taking over the shipyard, Meadows had it "thoroughly repaired and refurnished." The name was changed to Union Point Marine Railway. Thomas Howard's son, James, was employed as superintendent of the shipbuilding facilities.[47] The shipyard caught fire and partially burned in 1896. In 1917, the company contracted to build the wooden hull of a large tug for a Philadelphia firm. The New Bern shipyard was not equipped to install the machinery which included a 1,100-horsepower engine and large Scotch boiler, so the vessel was towed to Norfolk for their installation.[48] The Meadows shipyard would remain in business until World War II.

In 1899, the Goldsboro Chamber of Commerce sought a builder for a steamboat to be used in trade between that city and New Bern. In the 1880s, an occasional steamboat made such a journey during high water, but frequent low water made the business unprofitable. The Chamber launched a campaign and raised funds to construct the vessel. Unable to find a Neuse River shipbuilder, they eventually obtained an agreement with a Washington builder. *Goldsboro* was launched in 1901 but was never a success.

In 1895, the Corps of Engineers moved its depot and repair yard from Washington to New Bern, locating it at Union Point, the confluence of the Neuse and Trent Rivers. The Corps built vessels at the Washington facility and planned to do the same in New Bern. At least one snag boat and the steamer *Trent* were built at the New Bern yard.[49]

Washington ship and boat building activities were similar to that of New Bern. Few new vessels were constructed in the small port town during the 1890s, and only thirteen documented vessels were built there between 1900 and the outbreak of World War I. Nearly all were barges or gasoline-powered craft. By far, the best known of these was *James Adams Floating Theater*, a showboat, completed in 1913 (see Figure 17).

Washington shipbuilder Joseph Farrow was still launching vessels in 1900. During the last few years of his life, he lived with his son-in-law William M. Chauncey. Chauncey, the only shipbuilder of note, inherited the shipbuilding interests in 1906 when Farrow died at the age of eighty-four. Chauncey and his brother ran a livery for several years before he entered the shipbuilding business. The 1880 census listed him as a "horseman." At some time in the early 1890s he began to work for Farrow, probably after he married his daughter. In 1896, he was listed in Branson's *North Carolina Directory* as a block and pump maker. In 1899, Farrow made him a partner in the shipbuilding business. The 1910 census listed Chauncey as a shipyard foreman. However, he was negotiating contracts as well as superintending construction as early as 1900.

Chauncey negotiated a contract to build a barge for the Norfolk and Southern Railroad, but the railroad was dissatisfied with the barge's construction. A settlement was worked out. However, the railroad's general manager made it clear that he was not happy with the Washington shipyard's work: He said, "As to business that we do with Mr. Chauncey in the future [it] will be governed by the character of his work." In 1911, Chauncey claimed to have $75,000 in contracts, but whether this was new construction or repairs is not known.[50] In a letter to the Norfolk and Southern's general manager, Chauncey mentioned having a health problem.[51] In November 1916, Joseph Farrow's surviving children, concerned about Chauncey's declining health and its effect on the family's property including the shipyard and marine railway, negotiated an agreement with Chauncey's son William Allen Chauncey "to protect and preserve the property." The property was preserved in the family name, but as W. A. Chauncey was a businessman and not a shipbuilder, no vessel construction or repairs were carried out at the shipyard after 1917.[52]

In Washington, T. H. B Myers died in 1906 and A.W. Styron went out of business prior to 1910. Styron's last vessel was laid down in 1905, but never completed. Ironically, it was being built on the wharf of T.H.B. Myers.[53] David Liddon, probably the best known local shipwright, moved to Beaufort where he died in 1921.[54] W. A. Holtzschites and his brother, both ship carpenters, came to Washington from Newport News, Virginia. W.A. Holtzschites was a recognized ship builder and designer. The two brothers worked for Chauncey, but left the town before 1910.[55]

In the small town of Belhaven, B.R. White and his brother, along with J. R. Smith, were the most noteworthy boat builders. In 1915, Romulus Krause advertised for boat repairs and building. No documented vessels were built there between 1893 and 1899, but twenty-one were launched between 1899 and 1915. About half were small wooden sloops, the remainder were gasoline powered vessels, one steamer, and one yacht. Boat building in the Hyde County area has had a long tradition, but much of its history is unknown. Ralph Hodges was the best-known boat builder prior to World War I. He and other builders and fishermen constructed many vessels, the majority under five tons.[56]

The Albemarle Sound area produced few vessels during this period. Two steamers were constructed at Hertford on the Perquimans River. *Lakewood* was launched in 1895, and *Belvidere* the following year. The designer and construction superintendent of *Lakewood*, E. S. Willis, was from New England.[57]

The most productive areas in the northeast portion of the North Carolina coast were Elizabeth City and the Outer Banks. As elsewhere in the state, few vessels were built during the 1890s. The 1901 Industrial Edition of the Elizabeth City *Economist* noted that shipbuilding, including repairs, had "practically died out in the city." However, three years later Elizabeth City had four shipyards, more than any other community in the state. Twenty-six vessels were constructed in the port between

1902 and 1915. The *Economist* attributed it to the growing canal traffic. Thomas Hayman, E.S. Willey, William Pailin, James Snell, and George M. Scott were the most prominent shipyard and marine railway owners during the 1890s and into the twentieth century. In 1895, George M. Scott built a large marine railway. Scott was a prominent businessman who opened an insurance firm in the city, founded the Citizens Bank, and owned the Albemarle Lumber Company.[58] The Willey and Scott establishments concentrated on ship repairs. Their railways were large enough to haul several at one time. In 1900, Scott hired three ship carpenters, including a master shipwright, from Berkeley, Virginia to operate his shipyard, but the arrangement proved unsuccessful. Scott and Willey were partners briefly before Willey purchased Scott's railway in 1901.[59] In 1905, Willey requested a permit from the Corps of Engineers to operate this railway as it was beyond the designated harbor line in Elizabeth City.[60] The Corps approved his request. In addition, Willey leased the Pailin Railway for several years.

Pailin's marine railway, which according to Alan Hayman was "a pretty big outfit," went through several operators and owners. It remained closed for some time before Willey leased it. Willey gave up the lease and, in 1903, Palin hired W. H. Roberts, a "well known shipbuilder," to run the yard. Pailin died in 1907. The railway then came under the control of S.D. Barnes and Abe Haskett, and in 1912, under W. P Skinner and C. H. Bailey. It is not mentioned in the 1916 report on the state's labor statistics and had evidently gone out of business.[61] In 1917, Willey sold the yard he acquired from Scott to R. B. Cotter. Willey was in ill health, and he died in 1920.

James Snell had been in ship construction since before the Civil War. He died on June 4, 1904. As he had no heirs, his property, including his shipbuilding facilities, was sold at public auction.[62] In 1907, P.F. Ives purchased the Snell Railways for his two children, P. F. Ives, Jr., and Elizabeth, who were both minors. They petitioned the Corps of Engineers for permission to operate the railways that were beyond the Elizabeth City port line on the Pasquotank River, which was considered navigable water, but did not get permission to operate the shipbuilding facilities.

In 1907, Thomas Hayman leased the property. Hayman was the son of a Tyrrell County farmer who migrated to Elizabeth City, where he developed his skills as a ship carpenter in one of the local yards. The Tyrrell County 1880 census lists Thomas Hayman, age ten, as a farm laborer. How he obtained the capital necessary to start a shipbuilding business is unknown, but he is mentioned in the *Economist* in 1901 as operating a marine railway. J. B. Fearing and Hayman became partners in a shipyard sometime after 1901. Fearing was not a shipbuilder. He was a local businessman who purchased property in 1896, on which the shipyard would be located.[63] Hayman became a most successful shipbuilder. He constructed a

FIGURE 8-9 Thomas Beauregard Hayman. *Source:* Museum of the Albemarle.

large number of vessels including several for the federal government. He was highly respected by officials of the Life Saving Service. "There is only one first class builder in Elizabeth City, T.B. Hayman," a local Life Saving officer wrote the superintendent. Later, when the Life Saving Service decided to rebuild the supply boat *Carolina*, a local official wrote, "Hayman's yard . . . is the best place to have the work done as he has the best workmen."[64] He was also a self-taught marine architect who was granted a patent for one of his vessels. As was typical for shipbuilders, he engaged in other business activities. He purchased the Albemarle Machine Shops, which became known as the Albemarle Iron Works, and also farmed. In 1913, he even ran for Alderman (Figure 9).[65]

There were other shipbuilding facilities near Elizabeth City. John Williams operated a shipyard directly across the river from the city.[66] A Corps of Engineers officer mentioned the Foster Shipyard located just outside the city.

Vessels were still constructed in Camden County, but in decreasing numbers. As on Roanoke Island, shad boats were still being built by Camden County builders. The best-known builder was Alvirah Wright.[67] There are no documented vessels listed for Camden County between 1893 and 1915.

The Outer Banks produced more documented vessels than any other area in the state. Construction sites were scattered throughout the area. With few exceptions, the builders of most of these vessels, as well as those not documented, are unknown. Washington Creef's sons, George Jr. and Ben, owned and operated a shipyard and railway in Manteo where they built and repaired vessels. W. O. Dough was another Manteo builder. Primarily, he built small fishing and racing craft including shad boats. He trained his five sons in the boat building trade. S. S. Midgett was known for his skill in building skiffs and other small boats.[68]

Boat building migrated from the port communities to isolated sites in rural areas. The industry "moved ... from the larger shipyards ... to the local small community 'backyard', where instead of building the large ocean going schooners it became more popular to build smaller 'in shore' vessels in the 5 to 10 ton range."[69] In addition to significant boat building activities in rural areas, considerable boat and shipbuilding still took place in port communities such as Wilmington, Washington, and Elizabeth City.

The 1905 Manufacturing Census lists North Carolina as having only twelve ship or boat building establishments, including five marine railways, employing approximately 200 workers.[70] The 1910 Manufacturing Census lists only ten shipyards for the state, employing sixty-three workers.[71] Unfortunately, the U.S. Census Bureau did not provide criteria for defining ship and boat building establishments or how the number of establishments was determined. A cursory examination of records indicates more than twice that many existed, and there were probably more. The number of shipyards and marine railways continued to increase throughout the period.

In 1905 Wilmington surpassed the other port communities in shipbuilding. The Samuel Skinner Shipyard, with two marine railways, was the largest in the state and the only private shipbuilding enterprise in Wilmington with a marine railway. In 1893, Skinner's son Louis took a gang of twenty carpenters and caulkers to St. Louis, Missouri, to build over one hundred sixty-foot scows for the Corps of Engineers.[72]

In 1901, Samuel Skinner turned his shipyard and marine railway over to Louis who added a copper workshop to the already impressive establishment. In 1906, Louis purchased the property on which the shipbuilding firm was located. He planned to expand the facility by adding a 1,000-ton railway as well as other up-to-date equipment. Subsequently, Louis and several local businessmen organized a new company, the Cape Fear Marine Railway Company, to take the place of the Skinner shipbuilding firm. In 1911, the company upgraded its railway to work on vessels over one thousand tons, purchased some 600 feet of adjacent waterfront property, and added several buildings, including a foundry, machine shop, boiler rooms, and a pattern loft.[73] The Cape Fear Marine Railway remained in business until the property was sold to Broadfoot Iron Work in 1918. During more than thirty years, the Skinners built dozens of vessels from scows to steamboats. There were two other small facilities in Wilmington, the Whitlock Ship Repair Yard and the Cummings Mill Boatyard. Cummings specialized in the construction of naphtha and steam launches.[74]

In 1905, the Wilmington Iron Works announced plans to establish a large shipyard on Eagle Island across the river from Wilmington. The proposed site was the former Beery shipyard. The Iron Works built and repaired ship machinery which included rebuilding the steamboat *A. P. Hurt* after it burned in 1913. The vessel was subsequently renamed *C. W. Lyon*. The president of the Iron Works was E. P. Bailey, who had an engineering degree from North Carolina Agricultural and Mechanical College (North Carolina State University), and not only planned the yard but supervised its construction.[75] Although the opening of the yard was delayed for several years, a joint stock company was incorporated under the name Wilmington Marine Railway and Shipyard. However, the Iron Works retained management and control of the proposed shipbuilding facility. In 1911, a contract was let with H. S. Crandall and Sons, to erect a railway and drydock. Crandall's company was the most experienced in the country in erecting marine railways. Marine railways were usually angled with the lower end under the water so that vessels on their cradle could be lifted from the water. The one built by the Wilmington Iron Works used plans provided by Crandall to lower the railway cradle into the water, tow the vessel onto it, and then lift it out of the water on an even keel and onto the railway. When completed, the Wilmington Marine Railway included two railways, boiler and powerhouse, joiner shop, mold loft, and forge shop.[76] The establishment repaired its first vessel in May 1912.

In the 1890s, Garcia's Boatyard was the most distinctive boatbuilding establishment on the Wilmington waterfront. Manuel Garcia, a native of Portugal, built small boats in Southport before moving to Wilmington in the early 1890s.[77] He leased property at Northrop's Mill, where he designed and constructed an impressive number of vessels including steam tugs, sailing vessels, whaleboats, and yachts. He specialized in pleasure and small commercial craft. His reputation as a boat builder was widely known. Many of his vessels were built for out of state interests. In 1899, Garcia built what newspapers called a boat factory at the foot of Queen Street. Unfortunately, the promising business did not last long. He died in 1901, and the factory went out of business. One contemporary account declared that Garcia "probably constructed more pleasure and river commercial boats for the lower Cape Fear than any other man now living."[78]

Wilmington had one other shipyard. It was owned and operated by the U.S. Army Corps of Engineers. A site near the railroad was leased in 1895 and may have been the location of a marine railway.[79] A number of flats and scows were built there until the facility was moved to Eagle Island in 1910. Not all ship and boat building establishments in the Cape Fear region were located in Wilmington. Southport had a small boatyard and marine railway. Steamboats were still built at Point Caswell and elsewhere on the Black River. In 1914, *Thelma*, the last steamboat to operate on the Cape Fear River, was constructed at Point Caswell.[80]

Although vessels were built in the small settlements "down east," only a few established facilities have been documented in Carteret County. Around 1910, Mildon Willis opened a boat building works near Marshallberg. The Zeph Willis boatyard was in Williston until it went out of business in 1911. In 1905, the Whitehurst and Rice Shipyard and Marine Railway, which was incorporated the following year, opened in Beaufort.[81] The 1904 Sanborn map for Carteret County shows the W. V. Goffrey Boat Building Works on the Newport River. By 1915, Ob Willis had erected a marine railway along the channel in Morehead City. It was large enough to lift the torpedo boat *Winslow* for extensive repairs.[82] The Gordon Canfield Planing Mill in Morehead City, incorporated in 1907, had a small boat yard. A few vessels, primarily lumber barges, were constructed there until World War I.[83] John Bell and Company was the largest shipbuilding establishment in the county. In partnership with C. R. Wade, Bell opened it for business in 1902. The company was incorporated in 1908, providing needed capital to install a marine railway and make other improvements. In 1916, Wade resigned from the company and sold his interests to Charles S. Wallace. The Bell-Wallace Company continued in operation until after World War II.[84]

The J.A. Meadows Steam Marine Railway and Shipyard was the only active shipbuilding facility in New Bern until 1910. Twice that year, the Meadows facility caught fire and was seriously damaged. The facilities were rebuilt and Meadows remained in business for many years. In 1911, the firm advertised in Wilmington newspapers, "Boat Builders by Contract or Journey Work." The advertisement cited pleasure craft as "our specialty."[85] However, as mentioned earlier, the company mainly profited from repair work until after World War I. J.V. Blades, owner of a large New Bern lumber company, established the New Bern Marine Railway at Union Point. No vessels were built there, but the railway continued to operate into the 1920s.[86]

Little is known about the boat and shipbuilding history of Pamlico County. There is no record of any vessels being constructed in Pamlico County after its formation from Craven and Beaufort Counties in 1872. Although small craft, particularly fishing boats, were probably built in the county, the two established shipbuilding facilities were noted for repairing vessels. In 1901, the New Bern *Daily Journal* reported a marine railway was to be built in Oriental. Three years later, W. G. Dixon, a New Bern shipbuilder, moved there and built a railway. In 1911, D.C. McCotter erected a railway at Vandemere on Bay River.[87]

There were two marine railways in Washington; one managed by William Chauncey, and another belonged to the Moss Planing Mill. The mill, which started in 1895, erected a marine railway in 1901. The railway was incorporated as the Mutual Machine Company. It advertised vessel construction, but nearly all work was in repair. The railway remained operational for a number of years. However, the 1916 Sanborn map shows only the Chauncey facility.[88] The Moss Planing Mill remained in business until the property was sold to the town in 2007. Both railways were small, designed to lift vessels 300 tons or under. Initially, the Farrow and Chauncey Railway lifted vessels by means of a mule circling a turnstile. Eventually, the mule was replaced by a gasoline engine.

The only other marine railway was in Belhaven. James J. White moved to Belhaven in 1910 and established the Belhaven Marine Railways, described as a large shipyard, which he operated until his death in 1948. Previously, White had operated a shipyard at Mount Pleasant in Hyde County. The 1915 Sanborn map lists a marine railway in Belhaven owned by the Interstate Co-Operative Company.[89]

Except for a small shipyard operated in Edenton by W. C. Waff in 1915, the only established shipbuilding facilities in the northeastern section of the state were in Elizabeth City and on the Outer Banks. In 1905, Elizabeth City had four shipyards and marine railways. However, Alan Hayman, a shipbuilder and son of a shipbuilder, listed five: the Hayman and Fearing, E. S. Willey, James Snell, Pailin Marine Railway, and John W. Williams Railway located on Goat Island.[90] During the years prior to the outbreak of World War I, considerable change occurred in ownership, operation, and location of these establishments. Thomas Hayman moved his ship and boat building operations three times before 1913. Hayman's partnership with Fearing was short lived. In 1907, he leased the Snell railway and shipbuilding site, and in 1913 he leased a site on Charles Creek where he stayed in business for the remainder of his professional life. As mentioned earlier, the Snell property was purchased by P.I. Ives, who leased it to Hayman in 1907. The property was later sold to R. B. Cotter.[91]

In 1912, the local newspaper announced that J. R. Hunt of Troy, New York was going to establish a large shipbuilding facility at Elizabeth City to construct large barges. The editor enthusiastically reported that the facility would produce fifteen to twenty barges a year.[92] The 1912-1913 city directory lists the Hunt facility located on Knob's Creek. The 1914 Sanborn map shows Hunt's Barge Building Works at the same location.

In 1902, Creef and Creef, the sons of George Washington Creef, owned and operated the only marine railway in Manteo on Roanoke Island (Figure 10). In 1906, E. R. Daniels and W. L. Meekins erected a railway

CHAPTER 8 THE INDUSTRIAL ERA, 1893–1914   241

FIGURE 8-10 George Washington Creef. *Source:* Outer Banks History Center.

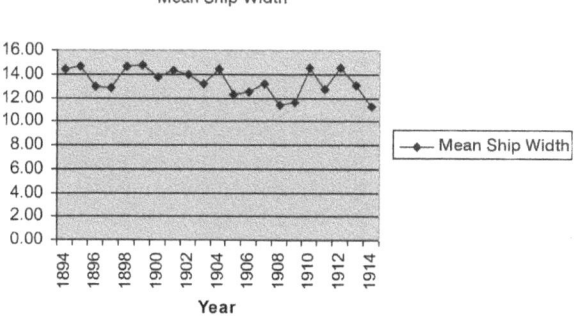

FIGURE 8-11 Vessel width during the Industrial Era shows a slight decrease. *Source:* Author's database.

in Wanchese. Daniels later sold out to Meekins, who still operated the railway in 1916. The Wanchese shipbuilding facility specialized in skiffs and small boats. The Creefs claimed they had an average of three vessels under repair on their railway "all the time."[93]

Along the coastline, just about every community of any size engaged in shipping and shipbuilding and had one or more iron works and foundries that forged and repaired machinery and fittings. The Wilmington Iron Works monopolized the marine forging and repair business in the Cape Fear region. Washington had the Mutual Machine Company, the New Bern Iron Works and Supply Company was in New Bern, and Beaufort had the Barbour Machine Works. In 1904, the U.S. Army complained about the high prices for machine work in New Bern saying, "New Bern has but one machine shop and is too remote from surrounding towns to obtain competition." Consequently, the Corps of Engineers leased land and established a small repair facility.[94] Two shipbuilders in Elizabeth City were also proprietors of iron works. Hayman owned the Albemarle Machine Shop, and the North Carolina Iron Works was owned by George Scott. However, the Elizabeth City Iron Works was by far the largest and most successful in Elizabeth City. It was founded by Joseph F. Sanders who acquired the North Carolina Iron Works from George Scott in 1905.[95]

In contrast to national trends, North Carolina primarily continued to produce wooden vessels. In 1915, a Charlotte newspaper claimed that shipbuilding timber was plentiful, particularly pine in eastern North Carolina, and this gave an advantage to the state's builders. However, at times adequate lumber was difficult to obtain. Driftwood was frequently used in vessel construction on the Outer Banks and elsewhere in state waters. According to the North Carolina Geological and Economic Survey, there were three firms that provided planking for boats.[96] Some wood, such as mahogany, used in yacht construction, had to be imported.

VESSEL DESCRIPTIONS

Between 1894 and 1914, vessel types were consistent with those of the later nineteenth century, but there were marked differences. Variation in beam (width) continued its erratic pattern, but overall, vessels tended to become narrower (Figure 11). Depth, meaning the depth of the hull, remained essentially the same (Figure 12). However, after the turn of the century, depth of vessels tended to increase slightly. This may have been the result of improved, deeper channels. Vessel length was consistent due to the nature of the waters, canals, and the demands of navigation (Figure 13). Most of the vessels built in the state were approximately fifty feet in length regardless of type. However, the beam/depth (width/depth) ratio during the period tended to decline considerably, demonstrating that vessel draft increased as beam narrowed (Figure 14), In part, this must be the result of navigational improvements, primarily by the Corps of Engineers. Equally significant, screw-type vessels required greater draft compared to sternwheel or sidewheel steamers.

As might be expected, the correlation of volume and length indicates a strong positive relationship (Figure 15). The same is the case for beam and depth as related to volume or tonnage. This indicates that vessel design had stabilized into set types in coastal North Carolina.

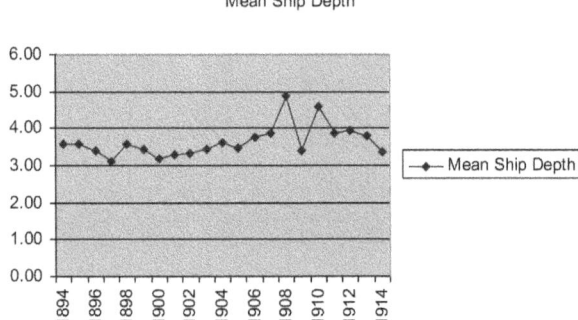

FIGURE 8-12 Vessel depth during the Industrial Period shows a slightly increasing trend. *Source:* Author's database.

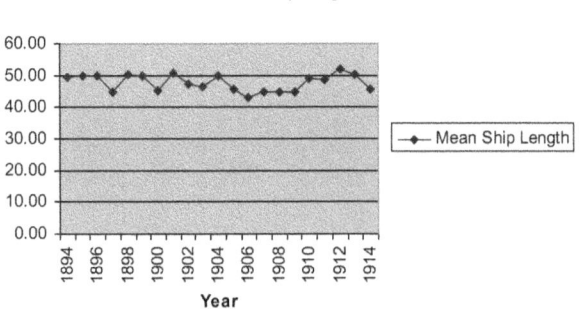

FIGURE 8-13 Vessel length during the Industrial Period shows little change. *Source:* Author's database.

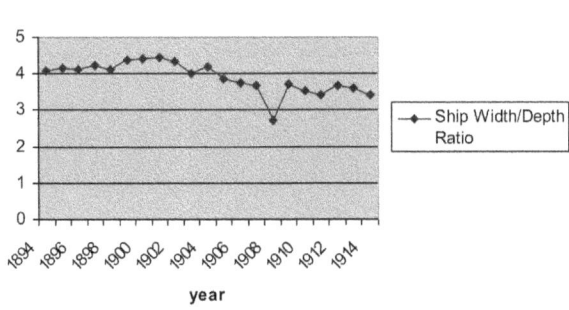

FIGURE 8-14 Vessel width/depth ratio shows a slight decrease, indicating a shallower draft as compared to width during the Industrial Era. *Source:* Author's database.

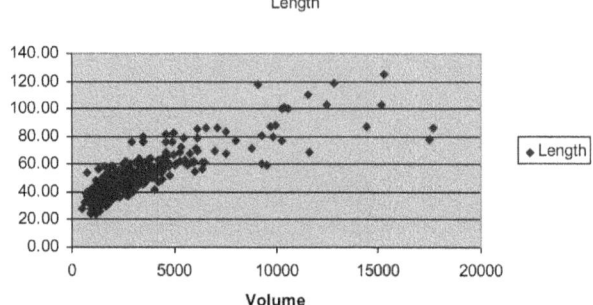

FIGURE 8-15 Scattergram showing a positive relationship between vessel volume and length, very similar to that of the Expansion Period. *Source:* Author's database.

Steamboat Building

The building of river steamers, other steam-powered craft, and many gasoline-powered vessels were the most noticeable changes. Wooden non-documented craft such as skiffs and shad boats continued to be constructed in large numbers. Although in 1916 several large sailing vessels were constructed in Wilmington, government reports indicate that North Carolina's shipbuilding industry primarily produced small sailing ships. By 1916, steel vessels were replacing sailing boats on coastal routes.[97] Railroads built bridges to replace less efficient car floats. Merchants often opposed them, fearing they would hinder water transportation. In Morehead City, Kinston, and Washington, the Corps of Engineers held hearings concerning proposed bridges.

In Washington, opponents of the bridge stressed the importance of sailing vessels that brought products to town. A local shipper of fish wrote that the bridge "would damage my business and all other businesses in this city for the sail boat trade is a big feeder to trade."[98] At the end of the nineteenth century, there were thirty-five steamers and steam tugs, fifty sailing vessels, and at least forty-three barges servicing the port. However, the following year, the steamboat *Alma* was withdrawn from service "for want of sufficient patronage." As early as 1902, the Old Dominion Steamship Company reduced its service on the Tar and Pamlico Rivers. In 1905, the company sold its vessels and permanently suspended river service. After the railroads arrived only three steamers, reduced to two in 1908, continued to ply the river. In 1907, a railroad was completed from Raleigh to Washington. That same year, the Norfolk and Southern finally reached the city. In 1914, the *Washington Daily News* reported, "since the town has two railway lines running in and out, steamboats are practically unknown except for a few tug boats owned by local mills."[99] Of course, the port's shipbuilding industry was adversely affected. In 1905, Styron, who had laid down a new steamboat, could not finish it, indicating

FIGURE 8-16 The steamboat *Howard* loaded down to the gunnels at the dock in New Bern in 1900. It appears that function is more important than beauty. *Source:* Author's files.

"There is no market in the town of Washington for the sale of steamboats."[100] The last steamboats completed in the city, *Goldsboro* and *Ghio* were launched in 1901-1902. Both constructed by Chauncey, *Ghio* was to run on the Roanoke River, and *Goldsboro* was to carry freight on the Neuse River (Figure 16).

Between 1900 and 1905, Washington businessmen incorporated four steamboat lines, all of which were to build steamboats. None were successful.[101] Styron laid down a large steamer at Leechville on the Pamlico estuary for one of the companies. It is not known if the vessel was completed.[102]

Although river steamers were disappearing at a fairly rapid rate, remote areas with no railroad connections continued to depend on them. Steamboat companies were organized by local businessmen and contracted to build the needed vessels. Contentnea Creek residents continued to depend upon water transportation. At least one new steamboat for this trade was built early in the century.[103] In 1912-1913, two were built in the northeast portion of the coast, one in Elizabeth City and a second on the Scuppernong River. They were intended to link the Outer Banks and Tyrrell County with Elizabeth City. The completion of the Norfolk and Southern Railroad to Elizabeth City eliminated most of the passenger traffic. Norfolk and other eastern ports traded by rail, although freight was still being carried through the Chesapeake and Albemarle Canal.[104]

Fairfield, on Lake Mattamuskeet, was the construction site of the steamboat *Alma*. There was no possibility of obtaining railroad service and the town was desperate to get their produce to markets. Consequently, local merchants organized the Fairfield and Elizabeth City Steamboat Company and contracted to have a steamer built. After an eventful launching shortly after Christmas in 1900, the vessel was towed to Elizabeth City for the installation of her machinery. Unfortunately, she was destroyed by fire in 1903.[105]

The Cape Fear River and its tributaries were the sole region of the state where numerous steamboats continued to be built. The vessels serviced communities that had no rail connection. In 1902, the steamboat *Franklin Pearce* was constructed at Shallotte in Brunswick County to carry freight and passengers to and from Wilmington.[106] Nine river steamers were built in Wilmington between 1893 and 1915, the last one, *A.P. Hurt II*, in 1915. All were designed for the upstream trade on the Cape Fear River and its tributaries. Fourteen steamboats and steam flats were also constructed elsewhere for this trade, the majority at sites on the Black River. Three were built at Clear Run in Sampson County at the head of navigation. Seven were constructed at Point Caswell, which had long been an important steamboat building center. *Thelma*, launched in 1914, was the last steamer built at that site. As early as 1903, a Wilmington newspaper captioned an article "The Dying Town of Point Caswell on the Black River." Although it survived a number of years, it eventually became a ghost town.[107] *Anne B.* was built at Bladen in Bladen County in 1900, and *Duplin* in Duplin County in 1904. It has been suggested that the opening of the Cape Fear and Yadkin Railroad in 1890, which paralleled the Black River had little effect on transportation on that river. Alternatively, it may have been the reduced market in naval stores that contributed to its decline. The Corp of Engineers continued dredging in the Black River until 1910.[108]

During the first decade of the twentieth century, tow and tug boats built in the state continued to be powered by steam. Of seventeen documented tug and tow boats constructed during the period, six were powered by gasoline engines, the remainder steam. Those built after 1913 were all gasoline, including diesel powered vessels. Building sites were scattered throughout the east from Southport to Elizabeth City.[109]

Building Pleasure Craft

The introduction of naphtha and gasoline engines revolutionized the boating industry. At the beginning of the twentieth century, recreational boating was generally a sport for the rich. There were, of course, exceptions to this, particularly in the definition of what was a recreational vessel. It was not uncommon for individuals to build small craft for their own use, including recreation. Along the North Carolina coast, hundreds of families had skiffs and other small boats for general use, including recreation. However, a boat constructed just for recreation was another matter. In 1904, there were approximately 15,000 pleasure or recreational watercraft in the United States. By 1910, there were 400,000. Not all of these boats were motorized, but a large majority were powered by mechanical means.[110]

No information has been obtained as to the number of pleasure or recreation vessels built in North Carolina. In the 1890s, steam and later internal combustion powered yachts and other pleasure boats began to be constructed by North Carolina shipbuilders. Manuel Garcia built several in Wilmington. In 1899, he announced plans to establish a "boat factory" specializing in constructing pleasure craft, but he died before the factory could be completed and placed in operation.[111] Small vessels were often constructed for hunting clubs, particularly in the Currituck Sound area.[112] Small steam launches were built as well as miscellaneous steam powered craft simply described as boats. *Tadpole* was perhaps the most unusual steamboat built in North Carolina. Constructed in Gates County, the forty-foot vessel was built on the lines of a dugout periauger. A pleasure and workboat, *Tadpole* navigated the Chowan and Meherrin Rivers for several years.[113]

Small craft built for racing were far more numerous. Prior to the twentieth century, boat racing was popular in the state, and it continued into the new century. Often, races involved work and fishing boats rather than those constructed just for racing. Shad boat races were not uncommon in the sounds. As noted in correspondence from Salvo, "At odd times between the catches of fish our fishermen are enjoying the sport of boat racing."[114] Nonetheless, vessels were being constructed for the specific purpose of racing. Thomas Hayman, a renowned shipbuilder in Elizabeth City, was a leading advocate in this enterprise. He entered his first motor boat in the 1912 races, and by 1915 had perfected a boat named *Slide,* which he claimed was the fastest boat in its class in the world. He substantiated his claims by winning races in Elizabeth City, Manteo, Norfolk, and even the Great Lakes. He then patented the boat with the intention of manufacturing "a craft of this type on an extended scale."[115] However, he never mass-produced the *Slide*-type vessel, although he did continue racing for a number of years.

Building Commercial Fishing Boats

Commercial fishing continued to be a profitable industry in eastern North Carolina. A great number of boats were constructed but few were documented. Most of the boats were for fishing, with a few for particular fisheries. Menhaden, oyster, herring, and shad required specialized types of vessels which all had become common prior to the twentieth century. Menhaden vessels evolved into a tugboat type craft with an extra high bow, engine and boiler located in the stern, and mid-ships low to "facilitate transfer of fish from net" and purse boats.[116] Skipjacks, equipped with dredges, were the most popular oyster boats. Introduced in the 1880s in the Chesapeake Bay area, the type migrated to North Carolina. There were two types of oyster dredgers introduced into North Carolina waters, the two-sail bateau or skipjack, and the three-sail vessel or bugeye. Most of them were located and probably built in the Pamlico River area. In 1915, Ralph Hodges, a Hyde County fisherman, farmer, and shipbuilder, launched the skipjack *Ada Mae*. Not all North Carolina boats were skipjacks. Sharpies and other small boats were employed in oystering.[117] The number of skipjacks built in North Carolina is not known but they are mentioned in personal accounts. Shrimping became increasingly profitable early in the century, but it was not until the introduction of the otto trawl that shrimp trawlers developed as a type sometime before World War I.[118]

Building Ships for the Government

In the past, North Carolina boat and shipbuilders had been successful in obtaining contracts with government agencies and this continued into the twentieth century. A large number of contracts for small boats were made with the Life-Saving Service, and after its merger with the Revenue Cutter Service in 1915, the United States Coast Guard. All surfboats and lifeboats for North Carolina stations were constructed by North Carolina builders. Three vessels were built in the state to carry supplies to the various stations, one at Avon, a second at Elizabeth City, and a third in Morehead City. A number of motor skiffs and dories were also built under contract. Thomas Hayman of Elizabeth City was most successful in obtaining contracts for these craft.[119]

The U.S. Army Corps of Engineers continued to contract with local shipbuilders in the state for various vessels. The Corps maintained its policy of either hiring local labor to construct vessels in their yards at New Bern and Wilmington or contracting with the lowest bidder. At times, the lowest bidder was from outside the state.[120]

Louis Skinner's marine railways in Wilmington, and John F. Bell Company in Morehead City, were the most successful contractors with the Corps. Skinner, like his father before him, built and repaired a number of vessels for the engineers. He received a contract in 1907 to construct two scows, the last work that he did for the Corps. He asked for and received a sixty-day extension to his contractual date of completion because of difficulty in obtaining lumber and labor. In November he wrote, "labor in the country is employed in the harvesting of the cotton crop." Skinner never bid on another Corps boatbuilding proposal. In 1913, the District Engineer in Wilmington wrote that no builder in Wilmington or vicinity had bid on proposed Corps vessels for several years.[121] The Skinner firm went out of business in 1913.

Between 1913 and 1915, the John F. Bell Company received three contracts. In 1913, the company was awarded a contract to build the hull of the launch *Olive*. So, "There are a number of boats of [the type proposed by the Company] . . . in use in, and around, Morehead City by pilots and fishermen, who have found them to be extremely sea-worthy. They are used for going off to the bar and in making the run down to Cape Lookout and they are capable of doing this in rough weather when either of our present launches would be unable to make the trip." The following year, the company received a contract to build the survey boat *Neuse*.[122]

The *Neuse* is interesting in that its construction indicates that the Corps of Engineers was willing to take a chance with the Morehead Company. The Mathis Yacht Building Company of Camden, New Jersey was the second bidder. Mathis, a well-respected boatbuilding firm, protested awarding the bid to John F. Bell Company, saying, "We claim that the lowest bidder is not properly equipped to turn out the joiner work on this boat, as per specifications even when forced to do so by an inspector."[123] The Wilmington District engineer agreed that the Morehead City company was not as experienced as the New Jersey firm in building a vessel of this type, as "This company has constructed boats at its plant at Morehead City in considerable numbers, and satisfactorily to their customers to the best of my knowledge. Their plant is not as well equipped for finishing work as most northern plants and it is lacking in experience in constructing the type of boat required by our specifications." Curiously, he admitted that Bell's work probably would not be as good as that of Mathias: "maintenance and repair charges on the woodwork would begin to accrue much earlier in the use of the Morehead City Boat." Nonetheless, he recommended its acceptance and the Chief of Engineers agreed. The Corps did employ an experienced boatbuilder as an inspector for the motorboat. The *Neuse* was launched in April 1915. Catherine Wade, daughter of company co-owner C.M. Wade, broke a bottle of Neuse River water over the bow at the launching.[124]

Mathis may well have been right. The Corps of Engineers probably should have paid more attention to the negative aspects of the District Engineers' report. The company's next contract proved to be a disaster. It had successfully bid on a motor dredge tender for the Corps of Engineers Galveston District.[125] There were seven bidders, including Bell. The company's bid was late in arriving at the Galveston District office but was accepted based on its date of mailing. In October, Bell informed the District Engineer that the vessel could not be completed on time because various metal fittings, the propeller, and other parts had not been received. It was later revealed that the company was broke and could not even collect cash on delivery parts at the train depot. In January 1916, Wade wrote that the company was unable to complete the work and requested that the government take it over. This was done and the tender *E. M. Hartrick*, originally named *La Porte*, was completed and reached Galveston in April. The surety company sued. John Bell Company had to go into receivership, and Wade, who was blamed for the difficulties, resigned. The Corps' inspector for the vessel wrote, "This is the worst mess I have ever been up against."[126] In 1917, Charles Wallace, a local businessman, paid off the debts and became a partner. The name of the company was changed to Bell-Wallace.

Auxiliary Craft

A variety of miscellaneous vessels were built for federal, state, and local service. In 1910, Bell constructed a powerboat for the federal laboratory on Pivers Island. The company also constructed a gas screw boat for the state's fisheries patrol. Otis Doe built the fisheries patrol vessel *Chowan* in Manteo. In Beaufort, White and Rice constructed an "auxiliary boat." In 1905, the first gasoline-powered fire boat in the state was constructed in Wilmington. New ferries were usually built by shipbuilders. Two were built in Elizabeth City for the Pasquotank River.[127]

Flats, lighters, scows, and barges remained an important means of transportation. For well over a hundred years, these non-powered craft linked hamlets and communities on streams that were not navigable by other vessels. Few barges and similar craft were documented, even those that were engaged in coastal and canal transportation. Treasury Department regulations only documented the towing vessel. With the construction of bridges across most of the waterways, railroads no longer contracted for car floats. Lumber had replaced naval stores as the cargo. Barge building became a lucrative enterprise for shipbuilders after the Civil War. In 1899, the Farrow shipyard in Washington constructed eight barges. Myers and Styron were also building barges in the port. The same was true in the other shipbuilding centers. Even the Hertford County community of Tunis had a small firm building four barges at a time.[128] Many barges were quite large. One built by Myers was 155 feet in length, and the four Tunis vessels were each 164 feet long. The largest was *Charles G. Blades*. Built on the Neuse River, the lumber barge, at an estimated 800 tons, was between 175 and 180 feet long. The large barges often attracted large sizeable crowds for their launching. In New Bern, elementary school children were allowed to attend the ceremony. The bridge across the Neuse River was lined with people and around 200 invited guests were on board as the barge slid into the river.[129] Lumber companies such as Blades, Roper, and Fleetwood and Jackson, employed the state's shipyards to build these vessels. In Washington, Chauncey contracted for the construction of two 130-foot barges for the Interstate Cooperate Company. In New Bern, Meadows built one similar in size for a Philadelphia firm.[130] In the latter decades of the nineteenth century, lumber companies such as Blades often built their own vessels by hiring qualified labor. The Swansboro Lumber Company built several steam towboats and lighters. In 1900, the company constructed a number of double decked scows for freighting lumber to vessels off the bar at Bogue Inlet.[131]

Barges were constructed for a variety of purposes. In Wilmington, locally-built barges were used to carry cargo back and forth from the city to a factory upstream, as excursion barges to transport passengers up and down the river, and for the Diamond Steamboat and Wrecking Company to aid in removing items from wrecked vessels.[132]

The "Infernal" Combustion Engine

The first decade and a half of the twentieth century was the beginning of a new era in water transportation and recreation, mostly due to the internal combustion engine's rapid dominance. While steamboat construction declined, gasoline-powered vessels were launched in ever increasing numbers. Due to the complexity of the internal combustion engine, different mechanics had to become available for maintenance and repairs. The more complicated the engine, the more maintenance it required. In 1900, only five gasoline vessels and one naphtha vessel were documented in North Carolina. In 1905, there were twelve. By 1914, fifteen of the eighteen documented vessels built in the state were gasoline-powered. Between 1900 and 1918, a total of 165 documented gasoline powered vessels (over five tons) were constructed in the state. A large percentage of them were classified as fishing vessels. The use of gasoline engines in fishing vessels was a major factor in the development of the state's ocean fishing industry.

The application of the internal combustion engine to propel watercraft was developed during the 1880s. By the twentieth century, they were commonly used for small craft and larger vessels. The engines were usually inboard, as contrasted to outboard. The two-cylinder outboard gasoline-powered engine was developed in 1909 by Ole Evinrude, a Norwegian-American inventor. Shortly afterwards, the outboard was introduced in North Carolina. There were a number of different engines, inboard and outboard, used on North Carolina-built vessels All were shipped in from out-of-state. The best-known engines were Fairbanks-Morse, Lathrop, Bridgeport, Regal, Clifton, Sterling, Globe, and Fulton. International Harvester and Wolverine Motor Works of Michigan also provided gasoline engines and other machinery parts for North Carolina-built vessels. A few naphtha-powered vessels were built in North Carolina, but gasoline engines were considered more efficient and safer. The larger vessels were usually equipped with twin engines.[133] Communities began to recognize the value of gasoline-powered vessels. The November 19, 1916 issue of the *Kinston Daily News* read, "Kinston Wants a Gasboat Line," and added "Little Chance of Getting Steamers."[134]

Gasoline-powered vessels were built in shipyards by professional workers and throughout the state by non-professionals. They ranged from small skiffs and motor boats to large vessels designed to carry passengers and freight. *Janie L.* was built in Vanceboro in 1905, and *Lenoir* was built in Kinston. She was hauled to Kinston from the building site eight miles on a wagon drawn by four mules.[135] The *Estella* was built at Old Trap in Camden County. Southport, which had gained a reputation for constructing small sailing pilot boats, fishing and racing craft, quickly turned to building motor-powered small craft.[136] The *Wonder*, built at Point Caswell, could carry up to eighty passengers. The *Nydia*, constructed in Washington was seventy-five feet long and carried passengers and freight to and from Hyde County. Five were built in Washington, and eight in Swansboro. A number of menhaden boats were both sail and gasoline-powered. Announcing the launching of the yacht *Smart Set*, a Wilmington newspaper described her as a "steam gasoline yacht" which also carried a full set of sails. Similar confusion characterized the description of *Waterlily* constructed in Elizabeth City by Thomas Hayman. Termed a "steamer" by a local paper, she was a gasoline powered sidewheeler, as noted by a local official, "the first one of the kind seen in this port."[137]

Sails

Sailing vessels were still integral to the coastal economy. At hearings held by the Corps of Engineers in Washington and New Bern, businessmen testified that the bulk of their downstream trade came by way of small sailing craft.[138] Dead rise skiffs were still the primary means of transportation for many families along the coast. Sharpies and shad boats were still in demand and used primarily for fishing. Sharpies were often used for both fishing and freighting.[139]

Between 1893 and 1902, sailing ships and boats comprised the vast majority of documented vessels, with thirty-four constructed in 1902 alone. After that, the number began to steadily decline. In 1905, twelve out of twenty-eight were powered by sail, and in 1908, only four out of thirty-two. In 1909, two were built, but none the following two years. Only one per year over the subsequent few years a few sloops, one brig, and the rest schooners. By 1905, sailboat construction was almost at an end.[140] After 1900, newspapers rarely reported the construction of sailing vessels. A significant but unknown number of large and small sailing vessels were converted to gasoline power during these years. One recent study listed eighty-six boats, either built or home ported in Carteret County between 1900 and 1917, that were converted to gasoline power.[141]

Showboats or Floating Theaters

Floating theaters, or showboats, were among the most unusual vessels built in North Carolina. Floating theaters were not unusual early in the twentieth century, but were generally found on freshwater streams, particularly the Mississippi River and its tributaries. Classified as folk institutions by the *Encyclopedia Britannica*, they carried culture to isolated parts of the country. Showboats were an attraction eagerly anticipated by all communities situated on a water course.[142]

The first floating theaters along the Atlantic seaboard were constructed in North Carolina. In 1914, C. H. Sanderlin, an Elizabeth City businessman, built what he called a floating movie house. Motion pictures were becoming popular throughout the country. Sanderlin's idea was to turn a barge into a floating theater which could be towed to small hamlets and communities that did not have movie houses. Named *Floating Movies*, the 454-ton vessel was launched in 1915.[143] The success of the venture is unknown.

A second floating theater built in the state had considerable public exposure and was highly successful. In fact, *James Adams Floating Theatre* is probably the best known, or certainly one of the best known, vessels built in North Carolina (Figure 17). In 1924, author Edna Ferber heard about the "floating theatre" and traveled to Bath and Washington to spend several days gathering information about it. This was part of her research for writing the novel *Show Boat*, which in time, became the basis for Jerome Kern's musical by that name, and subsequently the basis for at least two movie versions.

In 1913, before designing his vessel, Adams, who knew little about navigation on the eastern seaboard, interviewed seamen and others experienced with area waters. He generated detailed plans of the superstructure which would house the theater. Adams then contracted with William Chauncey's shipyard in Washington to build the floating theater. Chauncey employed a "large force of carpenters" to build the vessel. Adams selected a good bit of the lumber himself. He insisted that the vessel be extremely sturdy. Large beams were used, "heavy thirty-two planks across the bottom, a skin four inches thick, and drift bolted every two feet with twenty-seven inch bolts."[144] The showboat was 128 feet in length, weighed 436 tons, carried a crew and cast of thirty-two, and seated nearly 700. When launched, Adams christened her *Estelle*. He later changed the name to *Playhouse*, and it was under that name that she was enrolled. Subsequently, Adams had "*James Adams Floating Theatre*" painted on her superstructure and she was popularly known by that name for the next eighteen years. Adams purchased two tugs to tow the barge from site to site.

The *James Adams Floating Theatre* did not mark the end of wooden vessel construction in North Carolina. In 1913, the year that the *Floating Theatre* was launched, sixteen documented vessels were listed. One was a yacht, one a schooner, two were river steamers, and the remainder were gasoline-powered vessels built for canal and inland trade. Small fishing and recreational craft built of wood continued to be constructed in the state after World War II. Even a few steamers, primarily tugboats, were launched. The era of commercial sailing vessels plying the Atlantic coast and West Indies had almost disappeared. However, the European crisis and the outbreak of World War I prolonged the practicability of building wooden oceanic cargo vessels throughout the nation, including North Carolina.

Notes

1. Alan D. Watson, *Wilmington: Port of North Carolina*, 119.
2. Elizabeth City *Weekly Advance*, Jan. 17, 1913; Also see *(New Bern)*

FIGURE 8-17 The James Adams Floating Theater. Source: State Archives of North Carolina.

Daily Journal, January 25, 1910: (New Bern) *Daily Journal,* January 30, February 27, March 20, 1910; Richard E. Prince, *Norfolk Southern Railroad, Old Dominion Line, and Connections,* 125, 196.

3. Hearings, April 7, 1909, Entry 1118, Box 105, Record Group 77, Records of the Office of the Chief of Engineers, NARA.

4. *Kinston Free Press,* May 12, 1915; Quinn to Chief, Corps of Engineers, March 12, 1900, Patrick to Chief Engineers, March, 1911, file 24421, RG77, Records of the Office of the Chief of Engineers, NARA.

5. *Elizabeth City Weekly Advance,* January 17, 1913.

6. United States Army Corps of Engineers, *Annual Report of the Chief of Engineers to the Secretary of War for the Year 1906,* 249, 255, 1150.

7. Wilson Angley, "A History of Ocracoke Inlet and Adjacent Areas."

8. Corp of Engineers report for North Carolina, entries 1113, Box 97, RG77, Records of the Office of the Chief of Engineers, NARA-Atlanta. See also New Bern Chamber of Commerce Minutes, February 13, and June 12, 1900, New Bern Chamber of Commerce Records, ECU.

9. Minutes, New Bern Chamber of Commerce Records, May 17, 1899, ECU. For the port's trade see various documents and letters in Entry 1113, Box 32, RG77, Records of the Office of the Chief of Engineers, NARA.

10. Quoted in January 7, 1907, Entry 102, file 59943 RG77: Records of the Office of the Chief of Engineers, NARA; *New Bern Sun,* July 30, 1908; Burwick to Lucas, June 30, 1900, RG77: Records of the Office of the Chief of Engineers, NARA; (Raleigh) *News and Observer,* November 17, 1907; 1906 hearings and hearings, April 7, 1909, E102, file 11264, RG77, Records of the Office of the Chief of Engineers, NARA.

11. The Panic of 1893 and the depression that followed were responsible for much of this decline. Charles Hoffman, *The Depression of the Nineties: An Economic History,* 118.

12. William N. Still Jr., "The Shipbuilding Industry in Washington, North Carolina," in Joseph F. Steelman, ed., *Of Tar Heel Towns, Shipbuilders, Reconstructionists and Alliancemen: Papers in North Carolina History,* 46.

13. Occasionally the building of a ferry is mentioned in a local paper. See the (New Bern) *Daily Journal,* April 26, 1894.

14. (Wilmington) *Morning Star,* September 7, 1883; Marcus B. Simpson and Sallie W. Simpson, *Whaling on the North Carolina Coast,* 44; United States Census Office, *Twelfth Census of the United States, Taken in the Year 1900,* vol. X: *Manufactures, Part IV: Special Reports on Selected Industries,* 224, 226, 232, 227, 236.

15. *Wilmington Evening Dispatch,* February 9, 1906; (Wilmington *Messenger*), November 14, December 17, 1905. The New Bern Iron Works originally got a contract to build one of the two vessels, but had to back out of the work. Reportedly, when asked if local labor would be used, the president of the company replied in the positive if it was available. (Wilmington) *Morning Star,* August 23, 1916; *Newbernian,* November 21, 1916, March 17, 1917; *Elizabeth*

City Daily Advance, March 15, 29, June 16, 1917.

16. The Census on Manufacturing for 1905-06 does not give a total number of wooden boats under five tons for North Carolina; instead, North Carolina is included in "all other states." U.S. Department of Commerce and Labor, Bureau of the Census, *Census on Manufactures: 1905, Bulletin 81: Shipbuilding*, 19.

17. Entry 103, File 10091/30, RG77, Records of the Office of the Chief of Engineers, NARA.

18. It is possible that an article in the (Windsor *Ledger*), dated January 30, 1896, mentioning the establishment of an extensive shipbuilding plant in the city was referring to the Jewell enterprise.

19. (Weldon) *Roanoke News*, May 14, 1909.

20. (Greenville) *King's Weekly*, December 20. 1895; (New Bern) *Weekly Journal*, January 2, 1896. The Edgecombe County Public Library in Tarboro holds a few documents of E. V. and R. A. Zoeller, the owners of the oil company. The records include a few photographs and documents concerning the *Shiloh*. See also the Tar River Oil Company Records, ECU, and Christopher P. McCabe, "The Development and Decline of Tar-Pamlico River Maritime Commerce and its Impact upon Regional Settlement Patterns," 163-165.

21. Robert Zoeller, "Steamboating on the Tar," *The State*, XI (February 5, 1944), 1; Henry Clark Bridgers Jr., "Steamboats on the Tar," 200-201, manuscript copies in the Henry Clark Bridgers Jr. Papers, ECU Manuscript Collection and the Outer Banks History Center, Manteo, N.C.. Some repair records for the *Tarboro* are in the Henry Clark Bridgers Jr. Papers, ECU.

22. *Census on Manufactures: 1905, Bulletin 81: Shipbuilding*, 19. In general, only midwestern states ranked lower than North Carolina.

23. See, for example, Wade (Business Manager for John F. Bell Company of Morehead City) to Davis, December 16, 1912, History Place, Morehead City. Shipyards often had to sue for compensation for work done on a particular vessel. These suits usually were heard in Federal district courts. For example, see *Willey vs. Steamer* Guide, Box 7, Meadows vs Gas Boat *Juanita*, Box l, and Meadows vs Gas Boat *Fannie Brevard*, Box 2, District Court of the United States for the Eastern District of North Carolina, Admiralty, Record Group 21, Records of the District Courts of the United States, NA-Atlanta. See also Tillman lien filed on the schooner *Mary*, January 30, 1901, copy in the William E. Clarke Papers, ECU.

24. (New Bern) *Weekly Journal*, August 16, 1894; (New Bern) *Weekly Journal*, September 21, 1897, September 12, 1899, August 8, October 4, 1901; (New Bern *Daily Journal*), October 5, 1910. Others were quite busy. Creef and Creef marine railway in Manteo averaged three vessels a week "all the time and from two to six waiting." (Elizabeth City) *Tar Heel*, June 27, 1902; October 24, 1902; May 29, 1903.

25. For changes in ownership and management of these yards see (Elizabeth City) *Economist*, July 27, 1900; (Elizabeth City) *Daily Economist*, August 25, 1905; (Raleigh) *North Carolinian*, November 20, 1902; *Elizabeth City Tar Heel*, January 10, February 20, March 7, April 10, 1902, November 23, 1906, January 28, 1910. These newspapers carried notices of repairs at the other yards.

26. *Kinston Free Press*, August 8, 1889; Rodman note, December 15, 1899, Rodman Papers, ECU; (New Bern) *Weekly Journal*, December 26, 1894, (New Bern) *Daily Journal*, May 31, 1883; *Southport Leader*, January 21, 1892. Repairs of sail boat *Robert E. Lee* cited in (Wilmington) *Morning Star*, April 20, 1898.

27. Department of Commerce and Labor, Bureau of the Census, *Census on Manufactures: 1905, Bulletin 81: Shipbuilding*, 28-29.

Again, although extremely useful, census statistics are incomplete. Some coastal counties, such as Brunswick and Currituck, list no boat makers or ship carpenters, although a sizeable number of residents were involved in maritime activities. Moreover, returns do not include the hundreds of fishermen scattered along the coast who built their own boats, at times using family members as workers. Periodically, newspapers report watercraft being constructed by individuals who are not identified as ship or boat carpenters.

28. (New Bern) *Daily Journal*, November 19, 1909; *Elizabeth City Weekly Advance*, February 9, 1912; *New Bern Sun*, July 22, 1908; *Twenty-Ninth Annual Report of the Department of Labor and Printing of the State of North Carolina, 1915*, 62-63; *Thirtieth Annual Report of the Department of Labor and Printing of the State of North Carolina, 1916*, 120-121.

29. Edward R. Fearing and Gloria J. Berry, *An Elizabeth City Album: A Journey Through Time*.

30. (Elizabeth City) *Economist*, November 22, 1901. Hayman also had the unwanted distinction of being the only North Carolina shipbuilder to have his workers strike for better wages.

31. *Elizabeth City Tar Heel*, August 22, 1902; (Elizabeth City) *Daily Economist*, August 19, 1905. In 1915 Hayman employed seven workers.

32. Oral interview of Alan Hayman with Still, 1975, copy in authors' possession. Hayman said "the guys on the Outer Banks were energetic builders."

33. (Greenville) *Eastern Reflector*, November 25, 1898; (Wilmington) *Morning Star*, November 19, 1898; (Wilmington) *Messenger*, November 19, 1898.

34. North Carolina Department of Labor and Printing, *Annual Report of the Department of Labor and Printing of the State of North Carolina*, 29 (1915), 30 (1916), 156-157; *Wilmington Dispatch*, September 9, 1916.

35. Tony P. Wrenn, *Wilmington, North Carolina: An Architectural and Historical Portrait*, 271; Wilmington *Morning Star*, September 12, 1896; November 6, 7, 8, 1907; *Wilmington Dispatch*, November 6, 1907. Samuel Skinner moved to Jacksonville, Florida in 1905 where he died.

36. (Wilmington *Morning Star*, November 14, 1902; March 19, 1920, *Wilmington Dispatch*, August 24, 1917. Other shipbuilders in Wilmington at the time included John Barker, B. H. Stephens, J. "Buck" Cooper, Jim Brinkley, and John Allen Lewis. *Wilmington Morning Star*, April 29, 1906; *Wilmington Dispatch*, July 7, 1910; G. N. Dunn, "Wilmington Shipyard Sites, 1860-1870," copy in the Underwater Archaeology Unit, Fort Fisher, N.C.

37. Wilson Angley, "An Historical Overview of the Black River in Southeastern North Carolina," 40-42, Historical Research Office, North Carolina Office of Archives and History, Raleigh.

38. Bill Reaves, *Southport (Smithville): A Chronology*, II:252.

39. (New Bern) *Daily Journal*, July 15, 20, 1897; White Oak River Corporation Account Book, May 1898, Carteret County Court Records, SANC; (New Bern) *Weekly Journal*, June 2, 1899; William N. Still, Jr., "Shipbuilding and Boatbuilders in Swansboro, 1800-1950," 11; (New Bern) *Daily Journal*, May 11, 1893.

40. Tucker Littleton, *A Civilian History of the Camp Lejeune Area from Earliest Settlement to 1940*, 159; Brown to Kellum, January 17, 1906, Onslow County Miscellaneous Papers, SANC; Still, "Shipbuilding and Boatbuilders in Swansboro, 1800-1950," *Tributaries*, 5 (October 1995), 11; information provided by Tucker Littleton.

41. (Morehead City) *Carteret County News-Times*, July 27, 1980;

North Carolina Bureau of Labor Statistics, *Annual Report of the Bureau of Labor Statistics*, 11 (1897),56. Hall built at least one vessel for the Corps of Engineers. Chadbourn to Stanton, April 26, 1895, RG77, Records of the Office of the Chief of Engineers, NARA-Atlanta; (Beaufort) *Weekly Record*, March 24, 1887.

42. *Researcher*, XVI (Summer, 2000), 11; XVIII (Spring, 2002), 7-8, XX (Summer, 2004), 19-21; information provided to the authors by Wayne Willis, 2006; Carteret County Death Certificates, Carteret County Courthouse, Beaufort, N.C.; William Willis Case File, New Bern District Court Records, RG21: Records of the District Courts of the United States, NARA-Atlanta; contract between Edward Willis and I.J. Davis, May 4, 1890, William C. Clarke Papers, ECU.

43. Carteret County Deed Book, 25, 355, SANC; Merchants Mercantile Agency, *The Credit Experience Guide Being Compiled Reports Upon Those Who Obtain Credit . . . Ayden, Elm City, Freemont . . . North Carolina District*, 438.

44. (New Bern) *Daily Journal*, September 19, 1895.

45. George Wallace to Still, March 18, 1976; oral interview with George Wallace, July 1976; Certificate of Incorporation, 1909, Carteret County Courthouse, Beaufort, N.C.; R. D. W. Connor, *North Carolina: Rebuilding an Ancient Commonwealth*, III:121-122; (Raleigh) *News and Observer*, June 16, 1907. See also Carteret County Deed Book 25, January 6, 1903, September 1914, 190-191, SANC. Evidently Bell and Wade borrowed money in the belief they would get a government contract. They did not get it.

46. *Wilmington Evening Dispatch*, November 11, 1900. See also the (New Bern) *Daily Journal*, April 2, 1902 for C. H. Hall building and owning a large vessel. Also, a Captain Dixon built the steamboat *Uncle Ben* at the foot of Pollock Street. (New Bern) *Daily Journal*, January 18, 1902.

47. Howard to Meadows, Craven County Deed Book 106, 484-485, SANC; (New Bern) *Weekly Journal*, September 15, 1892; August 7, 8, 1895; (New Bern) *Weekly Journal* April 19, 1902. The son of a house carpenter, Meadows, like his father-in-law, served as mayor of New Bern. He died in 1907, the most prominent businessman in the city. (New Bern) *Daily Journal*, June 4, 1907; *Goldsboro Weekly Argus*, June 6, 1907; *Branson's North Carolina Business Directory, 1890*, 217; John D. Whitford Papers; *Historical and Descriptive Review of the State of North Carolina*, I:90; *New Bern City Directory, 1893*, 5. *Branson's Directory* for 1872 listed Meadows as manufacturing soda water. 69. For Howard's estate papers, see Craven County Estate Papers, SANC; (Wilmington) *Messenger*, May 13, 1896.

48. *Morning New Bernian*, January 26, 1917.

49. *Washington Progress*, May 14, 1895; (Wilmington) *Morning Star*, May 9, 1895; Chadbourn to Lucas, August 1, 1899, RG77: Records of the Office of the Chief of Engineers, NARA-Atlanta.

50. *Washington Progress*, May 4, 1911; King to Rodman, February 22, 1900, William Blount Rodman Papers, ECU. See also King to Rodman, December 18, 1899, January 1, 22, 1900; Chauncey to King, December 1, 1899; February 15, 1900, all in the Rodman Papers, ECU; *Branson's North Carolina Business Directory, 1897*.

51. For the last three years of his life, Chauncey built no vessels, at least none that were documented. In 1917, he agreed to work at a government shipyard in Charleston, but his illness prevented it. He had Bright's disease or nephritis, a kidney ailment. He died of the disease in 1918. *Washington Daily News*, January 12, 31, 1918; *Washington Progress*, January 17, 1918; death certificate dated January 12, 1918, Beaufort Record of Deeds, Beaufort County Courthouse, Washington, N.C.

52. Agreement, November 1916, Beaufort County Deed Book 196, 84-85, SANC; Still, "Shipbuilding Industry in Washington, North Carolina," 46-47. There is some confusion on the ownership of the property. A document dated April 1, 1902 indicates that the Mutual Machine Company owned the property on which the Farrow shipbuilding facilities were located and leased it to him and later to Chauncey. Copy of Indenture in the Rodman Papers, ECU. The Mutual Machine Company owned the Myers Shipyard property as well as Chauncey's.

53. *Chauncey and B.G. Moss trading as Moss Planning Mill vs. Virginia Carolina Transportation Company*, April 1908, Beaufort County Court Records, Beaufort County Courthouse, Washington, N.C.

54. *Beaufort News*, March 17, 1921.

55. (Washington) *Gazette-Messenger*, June 1, 1904. The brothers are listed in the 1900 census but not the 1910 census.

56. *Washington Daily News*, February 26, 1975.

57. (Hertford) *Eastern Courier*, June 27, 1895, May 28, 1896; see also April 17, June 5, July 31, 1985, July 9, 1896; (New Bern) *Daily Journal*, June 1, 1897.

58. J. Howard Stevens, *Albemarle, People and Places*, 451; (Elizabeth City) *Economist*, May 4, 1900.

59. Willey to Secretary of War, May 16, 1908, Entry 103, Box 1585, RG77, Records of the Office of the Chief of Engineers, NARA; Willey was also spelled Wiley. (Elizabeth City) *Economist*, November 22, 1901; (Elizabeth City) *Fisherman and Farmer*, April 21, September 8, 13, 1899.

60. The request was the result of a complaint from a tugboat company owner that the marine railway was illegally located. A law was passed in 1890 establishing harbor boundaries in the country and identifying obstructions beyond the harbor boundaries. Railways that extended into the water were included as obstructions. There is a large file including the requests for permission, as well as detailed response by Corp of Engineers officers in Entry 103, Box 1585, file 65569, RG77: Records of the Office of the Chief of Engineers, NARA. See also (Elizabeth City) *Fisherman and Farmer*, February 23, 1900; (Elizabeth City *Economist*), November 22, 1901; North Carolina Department of Labor and Printing, *Annual Report of the Department of Labor and Printing of the State of North CarolinaStatistics*, 30 (1916):158-159. For the location of these yards, see Stevens, *Albemarle, People and Places*. Willey owned a second shipyard and marine railway located on Riverside Drive within the city limits.

61. (Elizabeth City) *Tar Heel*, August 22, 1902, July 31, 1903; *Elizabeth City Advance*, May 11, 1915; (Elizabeth City) *Economist*, August 28, 1903; Pasquotank County Deed Book 28 (1905), 450, Book 50, 9, 443, SANC; Stevens, *Albemarle, People and Places*, 141-144; information from Barbara Snowden, Currituck.

62. Pasquotank County Estate Papers, SANC.

63. The only lead we have is a 1903 photograph with the caption, "Hayman & Fearing Shipyard." Fearing to Culpepper, September 10, 1896, Pasquotank County Deed Book 17, 371, SANC; written communication from Allan H. Hayman to authors, 1976.

64. Miller to Lellan, July 28, 1913, Henning to General Superintendent, April 7, 1913, Box 794, Record Group 26, Records of the United States Coast Guard (USCG), NARA.

65. Assistant Inspector, U.S. Coast Guard, Elizabeth City to Commandant Coast Guard, June 30, 1916, Box 793, RG26, Records of the United States Coast Guard, NARA; USS *Myrtle* File, Ships History Division, Naval Historical Center, Washington, D.C.; *Elizabeth City Weekly Advance*, September 15, 1911; (Elizabeth

City) *Economist*, August 31, 1900; April 26, 1901; communication from Tom Butchko, July 20, 2006, and Alan Hayman to authors, 1976.

66. Williams advertised May 29, 1902 in the (Elizabeth City) *Tar Heel*.

67. (Norfolk) *Virginian-Pilot*, February 26, 1996.

68. *Elizabeth City Tar Heel*, January 17, 27, 1902; (Elizabeth City) *Independent*, January 7, 1921; July 31, 1925; Angel Ellis Khoury, *Manteo: A Roanoke Island Town*, 77.

69. Sonny Williamson, *Sailing with Grandpa*.

70. Department of Commerce and Labor, Bureau of the Census, *Census on Manufactures: 1905, Bulletin 81: Shipbuilding*, 22.

71. *Thirteenth Census of the United States taken in the Year 1910, Vol. X: Manufactures, 1909: Reports for Principal Industries* (1913), 914-915; Department of Commerce and Labor, Bureau of the Census, *Census on Manufactures: 1905, Bulletin 81: Shipbuilding*, 22, 28-29. After 1898 and until 1913, the annual reports of the state's Bureau (later Department) of Labor and Printing ignores shipbuilding firms. The one exception to this is the John Bell Company of Morehead City. The 1905 *Annual Report of the Bureau of Labor and Printing of the State of North Carolina* (vol. 18) mentions boatbuilding in Wilmington.

72. (Wilmington) *Messenger*, May 5, 1893, December 14, 1899; (Wilmington) *Morning Star*, November 8, 1907, August 12, 1883, September 12, 1896, March 13, 1898; Claude V. Jackson III, *The Cape Fear-Northeast Cape Fear Rivers Comprehensive Study: A Maritime History and Survey of the Cape Fear and Northeast Cape Fear Rivers, Wilmington Harbor, North Carolina*, I: 226-229.

73. *Wilmington Dispatch*, November 20, 1906; August 29, November 18, 1911; (Wilmington) *Morning Star*, November 21, 1906; January 10, 1907; September 13, November 30, 1911, February 28, 1912 New Hanover Deed Book 51, 229-230, SANC; Dunn, "Wilmington Shipyard Sites." In March 1912, Louis Skinner wrote that the expansion was "on hold" because of difficulties in obtaining required permission from adjacent property owners as well as the Corps of Engineers. Skinner to Sticker, Entry 103, file 84724, RG77, Records of the Office of the Chief of Engineers, NARA. The original Skinner shipyard and marine railway had been leased. Samuel Skinner died in 1907.

74. *Wilmington Evening Dispatch*, April 14, 1904; Jackson, *Cape Fear-Northeast Cape Fear Rivers Comprehensive Study*, 233.

75. Wilmington Iron Works unpublished history, Wilmington Iron Works Records, ECU; (Wilmington) *Messenger*, November 14, 1905; Dunn, "Wilmington Shipyard Sites.,"

76. Plant Equipment and Capacity Statements, Entry 235, Record Group 32: Records of the U.S. Shipping Board, NARA; (Wilmington) *Morning Star*, July 14, 1912; *Wilmington Dispatch*, May 20, August 29, September 12, 17, 23, October 2, 6, 1911; Bailey to Stickle, September 21, 1911, Entry 103, File 29679, RG77, Records of the Office of the Chief of Engineers, NARA. See also records of the Wilmington Iron Works, particularly its manuscript history, and E.S. Martin to Bailey, May 1, 1914, February 9, 1916, Bailey to Martin, February 6, 1914, Certificate, February 16, 1916, Wilmington Iron Works Records, ECU.

77. Newspapers frequently gave his forename as Emanuel, but census records and his will have it as Manuel.

78. Quoted in Jackson, *Cape Fear-Northeast Cape Fear Rivers Comprehensive Study*, I:225. See also Susan S. Carson, *Joshua's Dream: A Town with Two Names: A Story of Old Southport*, 58-59; Marilyn Lessin, "Emanuel Garcia," in Susan S. Carson and Jon B. Lewis, eds., *Joshua's Legacy: Dream Makers of Old Southport*, 82-84; Garcia File, Series II, Reaves Collection, New Hanover County Public Library, Wilmington; (Wilmington) *Morning Star*, August 28, 1898, September 15, 1899, February 5, 1901; *Wilmington Evening Dispatch*, September 13, 25, 1899, February 3, 1901; (Wilmington) *Messenger*, September 13, 23, 1899.

79. See Harris to Stanton, August 31, 1895, Entry 1116, RG77, Records of the Office of the Chief of Engineers, NARA-Atlanta; *Wilmington Morning Star*, December 10, 1908.

80. Bladen County Heritage Book Committee, *Bladen County Heritage, North Carolina*, 1:86; (Wilmington) *Messenger*, May 20, 1902; Angley, "An Historical Overview of the Black River in Southeastern North Carolina."

81. *Annual Report of the Department of Labor and Printing of the State of North Carolina*, 30 (1916): 120-121. See also Samuel L. Daniels, "Marshallberg. The Beginning," 4; Wayne Willis interview, August 9, 2006, copy in possession of authors.

82. Virginia Pou Doughton, *Tales of the New Atlantic Hotel, 1880-1933*, 45.

83. Articles of Incorporation, August 26, 1907, Book 1, 136-137, Carteret County Courthouse, Beaufort, includes construction of boats as one of its purposes. See also note on the Canfield Planing Mill provided by Wayne Willis, copy in possession of authors.

84. Aleeze Lefferts, H.C. Lay and C. W. Lewis, *Carteret County: Economic and Social*, 61; *Morehead City Coaster*, October 13, 1913, copy in the Frank C. Salisbury Collection, ECU; George Wallace to Still, March 18, 1976, copy in possession of authors; George Wallace oral interview, July 1976, copy in possession of authors; manuscript on boatbuilding in the Frank C. Salisbury Papers, ECU; William N. Still Jr., "Wooden Ship Construction in North Carolina in World War II," *NCHR*, 70, 1 (January 2000): 34-53. The Sanborn map of 1908 indicates that Bell did not have a marine railway at the time.

85. (Wilmington) *Morning Star*, January 5, 1911. In 1915 Meadows wrote the Corps of Engineers that they "were in position and proposed to build wooden boats." To Chief of Engineers, July 4, 1915, RG77, Records of the Office of the Chief of Engineers, NARA.

86. Victor Jones to Still, May 15, 2006. Jones, a staff member of the Craven County Public Library, consulted various city directories. For the fires see the (New Bern) *Daily Journal*, January 9, 10, April 12, 1910; *New Bern Sun Journal*, April 12, 1940. Morton's Railway was located in North Harlowe. (New Bern) *Weekly Journal*, March 10, 1905.

87. *Washington Progress*, February 9, 1911; Marion W. Hardy, *I Remember When "Oriental,"* 64; (New Bern) *Weekly Journal*, July 10, 1901.

88. Mutual Machine Company indenture, April 1, 1903, William Blount Rodman Papers, ECU; *Washington Gazette-Messenger*, June 16, 1901; (Raleigh) *News and Observer*, November 17, 1907.

89. Possibly White organized the Belhaven Marine Railways in Belhaven in 1901. See Charles O. Boyette, Cynthia M. Heath, and the Belhaven Centennial Commission, *Belhaven: The First 100 Years: "Beautiful Harbor,"* 11-12; Also see *High Tides: Hyde County Historical Society Journal, North Carolina*, no. 3 (Spring 1987).

90. For Williams see (Elizabeth City) *Tar Heel*, May 19, 1902; Lou Overman and Edna M. Shannonhouse, *Pasquotank Historical Society: Year Book*, 3:95.

91. Still interview with Alan Hayman, March 1975; Thomas R. Butchko, *On the Shores of the Pasquotank*, 56. Snell died in 1904 and the shipbuilding property was purchased by P. H. Ives. (Elizabeth City) *Independent*, January, 1920. See also *Lizzie Ives et*

al. vs. Charles Gring, February 17, 1909, Supreme Court of North Carolina, 150 N.C. 137, S.E. 609, 1909 N.C. Lexis 7.

92. *Elizabeth City Weekly Advance,* February 9, 1912.

93. (Elizabeth City) *Tar Heel*, January 27, 1902; November 23, 1906.

94. Johnson to Chief of Engineers, Entry 103, file 36209, RG77, Records of the Office of the Chief of Engineers, NARA.

95. Judgment File, April 20, 1905, Civil Action Files, Beaufort County Courthouse, Washington, N.C.; *Elizabeth City Advance,* October 13, 1911, June 25, 1915; (Elizabeth City) *Independent*, March 15, 1918; *New Bern Iron Works vs. The Gas Boat "Fannie Brevard,"* Admiralty Records, Box 2, New Bern, District Court of the United States for the Eastern District of North Carolina, RG21, Records of the District Courts of the United States, NARA-Atlanta.

96. (Wilmington) *Messenger,* October 12, 1901; Roger E. Simmons, *Wood-Using Industries of North Carolina*, 66; Skinner to Brown, November 22, 1907, Entry 103, file 64887, RG77, Records of the Office of the Chief of Engineers, NARA. The three firms were not listed.

97. As one shipping owner said after announcing that steel cargo ships would now service New Bern and other North Carolina ports, "For many years. . . all freight from Baltimore to New Bern [was carried] . . . by sailing craft, which cannot keep up a schedule." *Morning New Bernian*, November 11, 1916 (quote), October 20, 1916.

98. Hearings, January 4, 1906, Entry 102, File 11264, RG77, Records of the Office of the Chief of Engineers, NARA. There is considerable documentation in this file and others in Record Group 77 concerning bridges and shipping.

99. *Washington Daily News,* August 11, 1914; *Washington Progress,* March 23, 1907; McCabe, "Development and Decline of Tar-Pamlico River Maritime Commerce and Its Impact Upon Regional Settlement Patterns," 160, 165-166.

100. Quoted in Still, "Shipbuilding Industry in Washington North Carolina," 46; *Washington Progress,* July 27, 1905; August 1, 1907. In 1908 Styron's wife and the owner of the unfinished steamboat sued the steamboat company for payment of construction up to the date it was ended, October Term, 1908, copy in Civil Action Papers, Beaufort County Superior Court Records Beaufort County Courthouse, Washington, N.C. The suit was dismissed.

101. Copies of the incorporation papers in Beaufort County Records of Incorporation, I, Beaufort County Courthouse, Washington, N.C.

102. *Washington Progress,* April 5, 1900. For the *Ghio,* see (Weldon) *Roanoke News,* May 24, 1901; *Washington Progress,* June 20, 1901; (Scotland Neck) *Commonwealth,* March 20, 1902, and Bridgers, "Steamboats on the Tar," 210-211. In contrast to most conversions, the *Ghio* was changed from screw to stern wheel. For the *Goldsboro,* see the (Wilmington) *Messenger,* August 22, 1900; *Kinston Daily Free Press,* August 23, 1900; *Goldsboro Weekly Argus,* June 21, July 19, August 30, 1900, January 24, 31, May 2, 1901; (New Bern) *Weekly Journal,* July 17, 1900, January 18, 1901. The *Goldsboro* was seized in 1905 by Federal marshals as the owners could not pay repair bills. (New Bern) *Weekly Journal,* May 9, 1905.

103. (New Bern) *Daily Journal,* January 18, 1902; (Greenville) *Eastern Reflector,* July 15, 1902.

104. *Elizabeth City Weekly Advance,* July 19, 1912, January 10, March 11, 1912; Edward R. Outlaw Jr., *Old Nag's Head,* 42-43.

105. Bridgers, "Steamboats on the Tar," 211-212; *Washington Progress,* September 17, 1900; January 17, 1901; (Elizabeth City) *Fisherman and Farmer,* April 25, May 30, 1901.

106. (Wilmington) *Messenger,* March 2, August 2, 1902; (Wilmington) *Morning Star,* February 21, March 7, June 20, 1902; March 22, 1905; *Wilmington Evening Dispatch,* March 1, May 30, June 14, 1902.

107. *Wilmington Evening Dispatch,* September 22, August 13, 1903; April 1, July 23, 1904. For steamers built on the Black River, see *Wilmington Evening Dispatch,* May 12, 1902, April 20, November 9, 1907, November 1, 1913; (Wilmington) *Morning Star,* February 26, March 12, 1901, February 27, November 6, 21, December 25, 1903, April 1, 1904, October 27, November 9, 1907, March 1, 1908; (Wilmington) *Messenger,* March 29, 1900; F. Roy Johnson, *Riverboating in Lower Carolina,* 87-96; Cora Bass, *Sampson County Yearbook,* 1956-1957, 141; Angley, "An Historical Overview of the Black River in Southeastern North Carolina," 37-47; Thomas R. Butchko, *An Inventory of Historic Architecture, Sampson County, North Carolina,* 37; Roy Johnson Collection, SANC. For Wilmington, see *Wilmington Evening Dispatch,* September 4, 1902, August 21, 1915; (Wilmington) *Morning Star,* August 19, 1900, February 6, 1903.

108. Johnson, *Riverboating in Lower Carolina,* 81-82; Bass, *Sampson County Yearbook,* 141.

109. The nomination form for the National Register of Historic Places for Eagle Island, across the river from Wilmington, lists two tugs built for Stone Towing Company at Southport in 1915. See also (New Bern) *Daily Journal,* January 24, 1901; *Bayboro Sentinel,* August 8, 1906; *Wilmington Evening Dispatch,* June 30, 1903; (Elizabeth City) *Tar Heel,* April 4, 1902; *Morning New Bernian,* January 26, 27, 1917.

110. Joseph E. Choate, "Recreational Boating: The Nation's Family Sport," *Annals of the American Academy of Political and Social Science,* no. 313 (September 1957), 109-110.

111. (Wilmington) *Messenger,* September 13, 1899, June 16, 1898, March 29, 1894; Jackson "notes" Underwater Archaeology Branch, Fort Fisher, N.C.; (Wilmington) *Morning Star,* April 29, 1908, June 4, 1916; *Elizabeth City Daily Advance,* September 1, 1911; (New Bern) *Daily Journal,* February 22, 1901; (Morehead City) *Carteret County News-Times,* May 24, 1954, quoting notice in May 21, 1915 newspaper.

112. *Elizabeth City Daily Advance,* January 20, 1917; "Record of Movements," for AB23 formerly *Gadwell,* 1, Register of Coast Guard for 1935, RG26: Records of the United States Coast Guard, NARA. This boat was built by George Creef in 1913 for the Pine Island Gunnery Club and sold to the Coast Guard as a cable boat in 1924.

113. F. Roy Johnson, *Tales from Old Carolina,* 132-133; *Murfreesboro Enquirer,* March 21, 1878. For New Bern and the Neuse River, see (New Bern) *Weekly Journal,* September 25, 1900; *Kinston Free Press,* May 29, 1690; *Goldsboro Carolina Messenger,* June 12, 1894.

114. (Elizabeth City) *Tar Heel,* September 20, 1901, March 21, July 14, 1902. See also Joel G. Hancock, *Strengthened by the Storm,* 15, and the Joel Grant Hancock Collection, ECU.

115. *Elizabeth City Daily Advance,* July 9, 1915. See also *Elizabeth City Weekly Advance,* October 11, 1912; *Elizabeth City Advance,* July 16, August 31, 1915; July 7, 1916. The patent was granted. A copy of his proposal and drawing of the boat is in the Patent Office records, available on the web.

116. Roy Leon Greer, "The Menhaden Industry of the Atlantic Coast: Appendix III to the Report of the U.S. Commissioner of Fisheries for 1914," Bureau of Fisheries Document No. 811 (April 1915):1-27.

117. (Elizabeth) City *Tar Heel,* June 4, 1902; Michael B. Alford,

Traditional Work Boats of North Carolina, 23; Camden Watts, "The *Ada Mae*: An Old Friend Returns to Washington," *Opus* (1998): 4-8; Gordon Watts Jr., "*Ada Mae*: North Carolina's Only Surviving Skipjack," manuscript copy in possession of the authors.

118. William N. Still, Jr. "A Nickel a Bucket: A History of the North Carolina Shrimping Industry," *American Neptune* XLVII (Fall 1987):260.

119. Hening to General Superintendent, April 7, 1913, Miller to Lellan, July 28, 1913, Chadwick to Commandant, Coast Guard, August 5, 1915, Burch to Commandant, July 18, 1916, Box 794; Superintendent, Elizabeth City to Commandant, August 15, 1915, Creef Brothers to Chadwick, May 25, 1916, Box 795; Assistant Inspector, Elizabeth City Station to Commandant, June 30, 1916, Box 793; and Memo, 1915; Assistant Inspector, Elizabeth City Station to Commandant, June 30, 1916, Box 793, Records of the United States Coast Guard, NARA; *Elizabeth City Tar Heel*, January 29, 1909; *Wilmington Evening Dispatch*, May 22, 1911.

120. Memo for contract, December 1916, Entry 103, file 100256, RG77 Records of the Office of the Chief of Engineers, NARA. For vessels built at the Corps yards see Johnston to Chief of Engineers, Entry 103, file 36204; Johnston to Chief, October 31, 1905, Entry 103, file 36209; Lucas to Chief, September 9, 1902, Entry 103, file 30266; Brown to Chief, January 21, 1910, Entry 103, file 74851, all in RG77: Records of the Office of the Chief of Engineers, NARA; (New Bern) *Weekly Journal*, March 27, 1900; (Wilmington) *Messenger*, January 30, 1900.

121. Memo, Wilmington District Office, November 22, 1913, Entry 103, file 90048, and Skinner to Brown, August 1, November 22, 1907, Entry 103, RG77, Records of the Office of the Chief of Engineers, NARA.

122. Chief of Engineers to Bell Company, May 10, 1913, Box 83653, RG77, Records of the Office of the Chief of Engineers, NARA-Atlanta. Wade, a co-owner, pointed out that there were differences between local vessels and what the engineers required, such as an enclosed cabin. Wade to Engineers, February 11, 1913; Peterson to Stickle, February 14, 1913, in Box 83653, RG77, Records of the Office of the Chief of Engineers, NARA-Atlanta.

123. Robinson to Chief of Engineers, October 8, 1914, copy in Entry 103, file 90048, RG77, Records of the Office of the Chief of Engineers, NARA. This file also contains an abstract of the ten companies that bid on the *Neuse*. All but the John F. Bell Company were well known yacht and small boat builders in the northeastern United States.

124. (Morehead City) *Carteret County News-Times*, April 16, 1954, quoting article in the April 16, 1915 issue. There is an extensive file on the building of the *Neuse*, including various documents quoted and cited above, in Entry 103, file 90048, RG77, Records of the Office of the Chief of Engineers, NARA. In the file is a letter dated February 15, 1916 from the Commissioner, Bureau of Fisheries, requesting blue prints and information on the *Neuse*, as he believed that "said vessel the type they needed."

125. For the bid and acceptance see reports dated February 23, 1915, March 4, 8, 1915, entry 103, file 95281, RG77, Records of the Office of the Chief of Engineers, NARA.

126. McDonough to Wilcox, February 1, 1916, Entry 103, file 97337, RG77, Records of the Office of the Chief of Engineers, NARA. The file contains considerable correspondence and other material concerning the troubled project. See also (Morehead City) *Carteret County News Times*, April 22, 1954, citing an April 1916, newspaper article. The file suggests that the John F. Bell Company was simply unable to handle a construction project of this type.

127. (Elizabeth City) *Tar Heel*, April 2, 11, 1902; (Wilmington) *Semi-Weekly Messenger*, September 15, 1905.

128. (Edenton) *Fisherman and Farmer*, August 2, 1889. See also (Murfreesboro) *Index*, May 18, 1888; (Raleigh) *News and Observer*, December 17, 1899; *Washington Progress*, July 16, 1889; *Washington Daily News*, August 21, 1974; Styron deed, May 18, 1878, Beaufort County Deed Book 44, 446, Deed Book 77, 480, SANC.

129. (New Bern) *Weekly Journal*, January 18, 1901; September 11, November 27, 1900, January 15, 1901; (Edenton) *Fisherman and Farmer*, September 13, 1900.

130. *Morning New Bernian*, February 15, 1917, December 15, 1916; *Charlotte Daily Observer*, April 20, 1912; (Elizabeth City) *Tar Heel*, June 27, 1902, April 4, 1902; *Washington Progress*, March 22, 1900; Patrick to Commissioner of Navigation, April 14, 1906, Bureau of Navigation Correspondence, 1884-1934, Box 503, file 40991, Record Group 41, Records of the Bureau of Marine Inspection and Navigation, NARA.

131. (Wilmington) *Messenger*, May 29, 1900; (New Bern) *Daily Journal*, April 12, 1901.

132. This vessel was nicknamed *"Jim Crow"* evidently because the workers were black. *Kinston Free Press*, May 20, 1903; (Wilmington *Messenger*), August 17, 1900; (Wilmington) *Morning Star*, February 28, 1906.

133. *Eastern Carolina Transportation Company v. Fairbanks Morse Company*, September 1907, Pasquotank Superior Court, Pasquotank County Records, SANC; *Wolverine Motor Works v. Gas boat "Nydia,"* 1903, U.S. District Court, In Admiralty, Eastern District of North Carolina, RG21: Records of the District Courts of the United States, NARA-Atlanta; *Wilmington Evening Dispatch*, July 30, 1910; (Wilmington) *Semi-Weekly Messenger*, April 28, 1906; *Southport Herald*, May 28, 1908; (Wilmington) *Morning Star*, June 20, 1902, September 25, 1906. William Luther Paul is usually given the credit for installing the first marine gas engine on Core Sound. Grayden Paul wrote that, early in the twentieth century, his father took a stationary naphtha engine and adapted it for a boat. Mrs. Fred Hill, ed., *Historic Carteret County, North Carolina, 1663-1975*, 86; Pat Dula Davis and others, *Heritage of Carteret County North Carolina*, I, 35-36; Ralph E. Lambrecht, "A Wisconsin Legend: Ole Evinrude And His Out Board Motor," *Wisconsin Magazine of History* 89, no. 3 (Spring 2006):17-28.

134. *Kinston Morning News*, November 19, 1916.

135. Kinston *Daily Free Press*, January 16, February 26, March 4, 9, 19, 22, May 9, 1904; *New Bern Sun*, September 14, 1908.

136. Reaves, *Southport (Smithville): A Chronology*, II:192. See also *Southport Herald*, May 28, 1908; (Elizabeth City) *Independent*, February 25, 1914; *Washington Progress*, September 10, 1914.

137. (Wilmington) *Morning Star*, July 14, 1914. See also *Elizabeth City Daily Advance*, July 14, 1914. For other gasoline-powered vessels, see the *Kinston Progress*, April 2, 1903; (Wilmington) *Evening Dispatch*, October 6, 1902, April 7, 1904, March 30, 1905, November 9, 1907, April 22, 1910, *Washington Progress*, January 16, 1904, September 19, 1907; information on the *Sickle* provided by Wayne Willis and Core Sound Waterfowl Museum, Harkers Island, N.C.

138. File 1118, Entry 103, RG77, Records of the Office of the Chief of Engineers, NARA; (New Bern) *Daily Journal*, October 5, 1900; (Morehead City) *Carteret County News-Times*, May 6, 1960.

139. (Wilmington) *Messenger*, February 8, May 18, 1902; Frank Taylor, "The Historical American Merchant Marine Survey," *American Neptune*, 71; Kay Holt Roberts Stephens, *Judgment Land: the Story of Salter Path*, 1:85, 93; Willis to Still, October 11,

1988, copy in possession of authors; Alphonso Manuscript, Core Sound Waterfowl Museum, Harkers Island, N.C.

140. Williamson, *Sailing with Grandpa*, 3. Williamson was referring to merchant sail evidently being those engaged in the coastwise trade.

141. Sonny Williamson and Steve Goodwin, *Maritime Reflections of Carteret County, North Carolina*. Wayne Willis in a manuscript dated October 10, 2005, claimed that the *Sickle*, built in 1912 by his grandfather in Williston, was the only sharpie to be designed for gasoline power. Information provided by the Core Sound Waterfowl Museum, Harkers Island, N.C. The bugeye *Hattie Creef*, probably the best-known vessel constructed in Manteo, was converted from sail to gasoline power in 1905. Donald and Carol McAdoo, *Reflections of the Outer Banks*, 80.

142. The *Floating Theatre* was the brainchild of James Adams. He and his wife had been circus performers and owners of a vaudeville show. Adams visited a small showboat in a West Virginia town and it became the inspiration for creating a saltwater floating theater. Because of its association with Ferber, the vessel has accumulated considerable literature. See particularly, C. Richard Gillespie, *The James Adams Floating Theatre* which includes a good bibliography and notes. For background on floating theaters, see Philip Graham, *Showboats* and A. Hughlett Mason, *History of Steam Navigation to The Eastern Shore of Virginia*, 55-58. An article published in the (Salisbury, Maryland) *News and Advertiser* includes information from an interview with a former engineer of one of the towboats of the floating theater. Copy of article in possession of the authors.

143. (New Bern) *Daily Journal*, September 16, 1914.

144. Quoted in Gillespie, *James Adams Floating Theatre*, 18. See also *Washington Progress*, November 13, 1913. Her strength would enable the theater in later years to survive storms and even being sunk.

Chapter 9

Prologue to the Future

When our research began many years ago, little thought was given to its outcome. However, we did plan for the research to reveal in a comprehensive manner, that North Carolina was a maritime state, which is contrary to what some scholars thought. We learned very early on that thousands of people were involved in the building of ships and boats, and many thousands more were provisioning the builders, the owners, the captains and their crews. The previous chapters reveal that the coastal area, if not other parts of the Tarheel state, were in fact, maritime oriented. Surely, we have proven Goldenberg incorrect in stating that during colonial times there has been very little shipbuilding south of the Chesapeake Bay. This research substantiates that a significant amount of shipbuilding continued from colonial times throughout the proceeding historical eras. Further, we have learned that there is more than just shipbuilding involved in being part of a maritime environment. It is everything about going down to the sea in ships or boats.

Now that we know considerably more about the shipbuilding history of North Carolina, it is time to culminate this maritime saga. We have chosen the close of the Great War as an ending point even though it is somewhat arbitrary and thought to have little meaning. But, for the purpose of congruence, World War I does offer an end to a conflict and also the beginning of a new era. With the completion of our research effort we offer a peek of the shipbuilding activity during the war to end all wars. Then, a summation of the shipbuilding database as presented through six historical eras to emphasize the importance of shipbuilding in the Old North State. Finally, there is a brief look into the future.

Shipbuilding during the Great War, 1914–1918

From 1914 to 1917, the conflict was pretty much contained in the European arena. This includes the North Atlantic Ocean, the Mediterranean Sea, and the Middle East. There was little concern in North Carolina about places like Serbia, or people named Ferdinand or Sophia. When sides were finally defined, the United States was found assisting Great Britain and their allies with war materials. On the other side, Germany in particular, did not like the United States supplying their enemy. During this time, Germany declared war on the shipping coming from the United States. Several merchant ships from the United States were sunk by German U-boats. When the *Lusitania* was sunk, President Wilson could no longer sustain American neutrality.

In May 1916, R. Lawrence Smith received a contract to construct two large, four-masted schooners at the Wilmington Iron Works shipyard (Figure 1). Smith was a wealthy and prominent Long Island, New York businessman who made his fortune in manufacturing incubators. He also owned a large horse farm near Smithtown, New York, a ranch in Montana, and a phosphate mine in Florida. During World War I, he acquired a steamship line and three shipyards, two of which were in Wilmington. During the war, he shipped thousands of horses and mules to Europe. The Wilmington Iron Works was the contractor for the two ships, but the work was actually done by the Wilmington Marine Railway Company, a separate corporation.[1]

Smith had nine-wooden hulled vessels under construction in his three shipyards. In 1914, the outbreak of World War I spurred a boom for the nation's shipping and shipbuilding interests. In 1916, the fear of becoming officially involved in the conflict prompted Congress to pass legislation creating the United States Shipping Board, to oversee the nation's merchant marine, including all new construction. More ships were needed, and because the country's steel-building facilities were overtaxed, shipping interests turned to the construction of wooden vessels (Figure 2).

Although the Wilmington Iron Works had been in the ship and boat building and repair business for decades, it had no experience in constructing vessels of the type and size needed. This was typical of the shipbuilding establishments south of New England. The schooners were to be 232 feet in length, with a weight of approximately 1,394 gross tons.[2] John Ryan, superintendent of shipbuilding for the Wilmington Iron Works, supervised construction of the two vessels (Figure 3). Local ship and house carpenters were employed. Materials ordered included 1.5 million feet of North Carolina pine and Oregon pine from the Pacific coast. The Iron Works produced the metal fittings excluding the anchor.[3]

Early in July 1916, the scaffolding and launch ways were completed and the keels were laid. The two schooners were scheduled to be turned over to Smith in November, but the company requested and received two extensions. Inexperience of the workforce and difficulty in acquiring materials were responsible for the delays. Smith became increasingly unhappy. In April 1917, an agreement was reached and he took over completion of the two schooners. Smith was allowed to use the Wilmington Marine Railway facilities to complete the schooners. By that date, he already owned the Wilmington Wooden Shipbuilding Company.[4]

Smith sent Arthur P.S. Naul to Wilmington to oversee the project. Naul was general manager for Smith's various enterprises. He knew nothing about shipbuilding but was an excellent organizer. Smith hired a Maine master shipbuilder, Nelson Ingalls, to superintend the completion of the schooners. Although Smith sent Naul, Ingalls, and a few other employees to Wilmington, the bulk of his labor force remained local. Smith's second shipyard, located at Hilton just north of the city limits, became the site for training his workers. They were primarily house carpenters.[5] Launched in the fall of 1917, the schooners were involved in the Atlantic trade during

FIGURE 9-1 *Commack* at Eagle Island in the Port of Wilmington. To the left, is Smith's yacht which served as a temporary home for Naul and family. *Source:* Author's file.

FIGURE 9-2 *Hauppaugue* going down the ways on October 17, 1917. Note the way starting to smolder from the friction. This four-masted vessel was built near the end of the sail era, as steamships were taking over the shipping lanes. *Source:* Author's file.

FIGURE 9-3 The *Hauppaugue* fully laden with feldspar from quarries in the North Carolina mountains, pulling away from the dock, and going to sea. She is loaded nine inches below her Plimsoll marks. *Source:* Author's file.

World War I. The *Hauppaugue* was damaged by a German U-boat. Renamed *Alice Pendelton*, she continued carrying cargo, primarily lumber, until abandoned in Noank, Connecticut in the 1940s. The *Commack* was struck from the role of United States Merchant Vessels in the 1920s and scrapped. They were the last, and probably the only, four-masted schooners built in North Carolina.[6]

At the Naul Shipbuilding Company in Hilton, Smith and his associates took over an uncompleted 1,500-ton schooner. This vessel was never completed, and during the 1917 strike, the plant was closed down permanently. Naul planned to build another shipyard on the Northeast Cape Fear River, but no others were ever built there.[7] Nevertheless, volatility continued in the ship and boat building industry, including Wilmington and many coastal communities.

Shortly after the United States entered the war, the U.S. Shipping Board created the Emergency Fleet Corporation to build vessels. The corporation contracted for thousands of vessels in shipyards throughout the nation. New shipbuilding facilities were established to build these vessels. North Carolina participated in this endeavor. New yards were established in New Bern, Morehead City, and Wilmington.

These establishments would build wooden, steel and concrete vessels. The new facilities were at times rather elaborate, especially one in Wilmington that constructed large merchant vessels. A yard in New Bern was designated to construct concrete vessels of 154 feet in length, and designed to link railheads with coastal fortifications, but various problems such as the shallow water of the Neuse and Trent rivers, the lack of adequate housing for the shipbuilders, and other factors persuaded the company to move the facility to Wilmington. There were other problems with respect to steel vessels in Wilmington; not only mechanics had to be brought in, but so did the steel.

Also in 1917, the federal government acquired a number of pre-WWI built North Carolina vessels for patrol and other duties. The fifty-four foot *Gretchen* was built in Belhaven in 1902 by White, and the *Myrtle*, built by Thomas Hayman, was launched in 1915 in Elizabeth City. The *Marija* was approximately fifty percent completed in 1917 when purchased by the U.S. Navy. A forty-seven-foot motor boat was constructed in Wilmington by Edgar Young. The *Commander* was a sixty-one foot vessel built by Bell-Wallace of Morehead City for the Sheepshead Bay Brothers of Brooklyn, New York, as an excursion boat on the Hudson River. The navy used the converted motor boat at the Brooklyn Navy Yard as a tender for 110 foot subchasers, as well as for work with the Rockaway Naval Air Station.[8]

TABLE 9-1 SHIP DIMENSIONS, VOLUMES, AND TONNAGE OVER SIX HISTORICAL ERAS

Era	Length	Width	Depth	W/D Ration	Volume	Tonnage
Colonial	64	20.33	8.33	2.49	8,816	44.61
Federal	60.87	20.19	6.04	3.39	5,863	76.93
Ante Bellum	62.17	18.33	5.7	3.33	6,286	70.03
Civil War	46.89	13.23	3.53	4.12	1,393	44.9
Expansion	47.47	13.55	3.6	3.89	2,094	25.52
Pre-WWI	48.99	13.85	3.68	3.94	2,535	26.44

Source: Author's database.

The war ended before many of the vessels built for the emergency could be completed and launched. Some were never completed. For example, the concrete vessels were completed but were considered of little uses for peacetime operations, being employed as Coast Guard receiving vessels, breakwaters, and one as a seafood restaurant. The steel ships were completed and would carry cargoes around the world for years. The emergency yards were then closed. Most shipyard workers, many from out of state, were discharged.

With the end of the war, North Carolina experienced a revolution in shipbuilding. The state's ship and boat builders continued to construct wooden vessels, even when the national trend was toward steel. By World War I steamboats and wooden sailing vessels no longer dominated inland and oceanic trade. A few wooden and even steel ships were laid down in 1917-1918. After the war, builders were primarily concerned with building small fishing and pleasure craft. This continued throughout the twentieth century.

SHIPBUILDING DATA THROUGH SIX ERAS

Wars, economic cycles, innovations in various technologies, environmental conditions, and other factors resulted in sustained but volatile growth of North Carolina's shipbuilding industry. Almost constant adaptations in hull design and rigging account for much of the success in the development of North Carolina water transport. Modification of the schooner into the Carolina Sharpie is one example; introduction of the retractable centerboard is another. However, of all the adaptations, use of the gasoline engine on sailing vessels was the most important for local populations.

Ship dimension data clearly demonstrates the adaptation of hull design to the shallow waters of coastal North Carolina (Table 1). Over six historical eras, average length decreased approximately fifteen feet, and width (beam) decreased almost seven feet. These changes relate directly to navigating shoal waters, narrow streams, and canals.

Many shipwrights, migrating from New England and northwestern Europe to North Carolina, came from deepwater ports. Traditionally, they built vessels that had fairly deep drafts, where the draft is the vertical distance from the keel to the hull's waterline, which is usually less than the depth of the hull. Consequently, they had to adjust their designs to accommodate local waters. Average depth of the vessel's hull built during the colonial era was 8.33 feet, and steadily decreased to 3.68 feet by the beginning of World War I. This is a manifestation of the need to navigate shallow waters and canals despite the hundreds of thousands of dollars spent on dredging channels to a navigable depth of at least nine feet. The width/depth ratio of the hull clearly shows the relationship between greater hull width and increasingly shallow hull depth.

The most important and obvious adaptation in ship dimensions is the consistent decline in hull depth in order to avoid the danger of grounding (Figure 4). Average depth of the hull decreased 4.65 feet and is particularly significant as it relates to other dimensions. However, the decrease in average vessel tonnage is also significant (Figure 5). Over the study period, average decrease in tonnage was 18.17 tons with a particularly dramatic decrease of 40.49 tons from the Federal period to just before World War I.

Coastal North Carolina waters required vessels with a shallow draft and limited length. Navigating the ebb

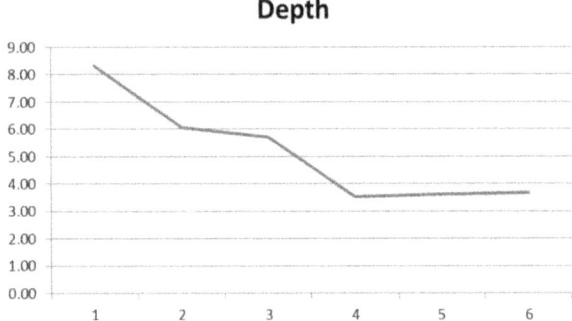

FIGURE 9-4 Decrease in ship depth over successive eras, showing the adaptability of vessels to the shallow waters of inlets and sounds. *Source:* Author's database.

Era 1   Colonial (Chapter 2)
Era 2   Federal (Chapter 3)
Era 3   Antebellum (Chapters 4 and 5)
Era 4   Civil War (Chapter 6)
Era 5   Expansion (Chapter 7)
Era 6   Industrial (Chapter 8)

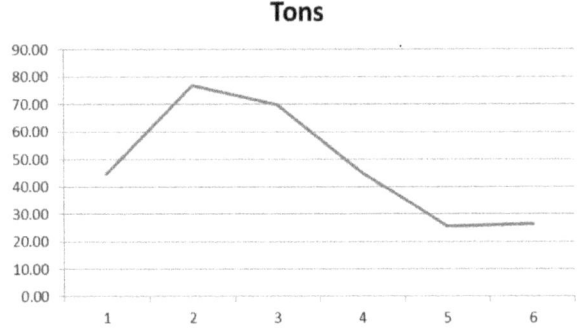

FIGURE 9-5 Decrease in ship tonnage over successive eras, and the adjustment toward smaller vessels, a reflection of shallow waters and small ports. *Source:* Author's database.

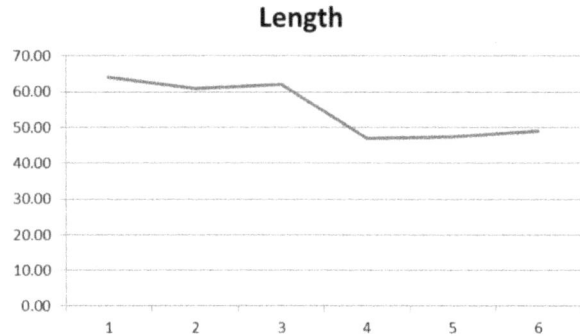

FIGURE 9-6 Decrease in average vessel length over six eras, revealing a likely adjustment to navigational conditions *Source:* Author's database.

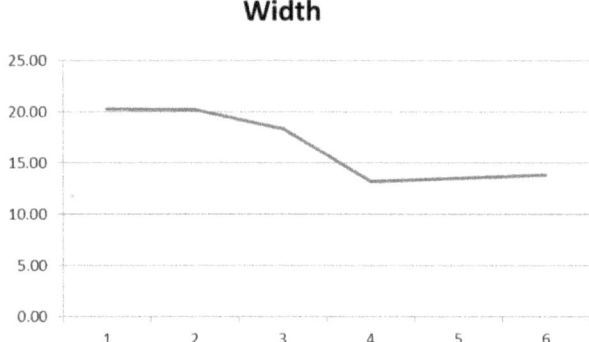

FIGURE 9-7 Decrease in width over six eras, showing an adaption to coastal North Carolina waters. *Source:* Author's database.

bar, the winding inlet channel, flood bar, sounds, streams, and canals involved sharp turns, as the thalweg (greatest consistent depth of a water course) tends to have an even greater meandering (Figure 6). Over the six eras of the study period, average vessel length decreased 15.01 feet. A vessel fifty feet in length is quite small compared to those using deepwater mid-Atlantic and New England ports, and North Carolina's primary trade was with the West Indies. Average width or beam decreased 6.48 feet, from 20.33 to 13.85 feet. During the antebellum period, decrease in beam was 5.10 feet. This, too, was probably due to necessities of navigation (Figure 7).

As might be expected, average vessel volume and tonnage decreased in proportion with hull dimensions. From the colonial through the pre-World War I eras, average vessel volume decreased 5,281 tons, from 8,816 tons to 2,535 tons. The decrease of 3,751 tons during the antebellum period is particularly significant as there was a large decrease in average vessel length, beam, and draft as well. A great deal of change occurred during the Civil War. Average vessel volume increases prior to the war, declines during the war, and increases again during the Expansion Period (Figure 8). In part, this was due to the advent of the steamboat, as much of their cargo was stowed above deck. However, in general, the vessels were smaller due to the economies of scale in relation to types of cargo. The steamboat data seems to bear this out (Figure 9). In 1818, the first steamboat documented as being built in the state, *Henrietta*, had a much deeper draft (six feet) than those that followed. Small hinterlands meant smaller streams, smaller ports, and smaller ports meant smaller vessels, particularly in shallow North Carolina waters.

At first, the steamboat was a boon for inland waterway shippers. Eventually, it gave way to railroads and then to highways. Steamboats had a difficult time competing with government-subsidized railroads. Later, railroads had difficulty competing with motor transportation as

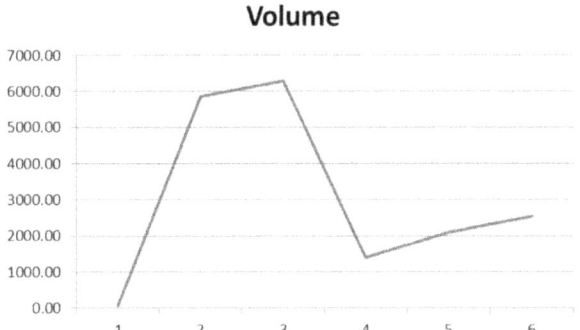

FIGURE 9-8 Average vessel volume before, during, and after the Civil War. *Source:* Author's database.

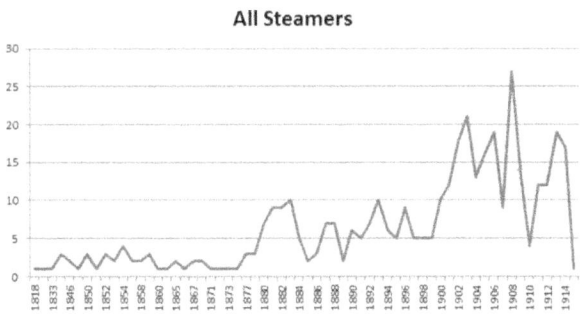

FIGURE 9-9 Number of North Carolina steamers built over four eras. The progression to steam from the traditional sail was slow, but deliberate. *Source:* Author's database.

roads and highways were subsidized by the government. When the *Henrietta* first plied the Cape Fear River, canals were being built to supplement riverine and intercoastal traffic. A charter for the Mohawk and Hudson Railroad was granted in 1826, and the first locomotive in the United States was built in 1830. During the antebellum period, 28 steamboats were built in North Carolina; 20 of these ranging between 40 and 264 tons, were built on the Cape Fear River. Through the Civil War, only three steamboats were built. During the Expansion Era, 97 were built. Of the 385 steamboats built in North Carolina, 257 were built during the pre-World War I era, 173 of which were gas-powered vessels. The gasoline engine was introduced in 1894, and the naphtha-powered vessel in 1899.

Over six eras, vessel design in North Carolina was adapted owing to unique and often treacherous conditions by reducing length, beam, and draft. Smaller vessels could navigate more efficiently and safely than larger vessels, particularly vessels with sails. Increasing values of the width-depth ratio substantiates the adaptation which, concurrently, resulted in a decrease in volume and tonnage.

Conclusion: The Importance of Shipbuilding

Shipbuilding has never been a major industry in the Tarheel state, but an important one. Agriculture, predominately tobacco, cotton and corn, has always been the basis of the state's economy. But naval stores were the chief export during much of the nineteenth century. The Old North State built vessels engaged in foreign and coastal trade carrying these stores and lumber to the West Indies and northeastern ports. True, this trade was also transported by ships constructed elsewhere, but the majority of them were too large to pass through the shallow inlets and inland waters to North Carolina ports. The shipbuilding industry in North Carolina has always been more important than has been generally recognized. Throughout the state's history, ship and boat building were conducted at approximately 300 sites, where almost 4,000 documented vessels were built, with many more undocumented vessels not counted. The shipbuilding sites moved about to locations offering the best timber and the best labor force. The types of vessels built went from small kunners, canoes, and skiffs to large sailing vessels such as schooners and brigs, from steamboats to government vessels such as revenue cutters, to privateers and iron-clad war ships. Pleasure craft became increasingly popular in the latter 1800s. At the same time as the competition from railroad and large iron steamers, the dependence on coastal vessels declined. The building of steamboats declined as well. There were more than 270 people engaged in this profession who called themselves shipwrights in the colonial period to hundreds, perhaps thousands, more, who worked in shipbuilding throughout the remainder of our study period up to 1918.

Shipbuilding has proven its importance as demonstrated in the foregoing chapters, being a major part of the state's overall economy throughout its history. Thus, the maritime economic activity and the importance of building ships and boats cannot be denied.

Anticipating the Future

Toward the latter part of the nineteenth century, there were slight indications of what kind of future activities would be in the maritime area of the Tarheel state: More yachts were being built, as the coastal area was increasing in crop production, particularly hybrid corn, but also becoming more populated, especially with waterfront development. Also, the seafood and fisheries industry continued to grow.

The yacht *Roma*, built in Beaufort in 1897, shown on the cover, is not documented, but is part of the future of coastal Carolina, north of the Cape Fear. Of course, we know today of the goodly number of pleasure boats being built from Wanchese to Wilmington, or from New Bern to High Point, as well as Greenville and Elizabeth City. The building of pleasure craft was slow from the beginning, and coped with the rather volatile highs and lows of the economy, just as the shipbuilding had done in the past. But, it has survived through the years, and has even flourished at times. The industry tended to continue as technology improved. Today, in the Pamlico River near Washington, it is not too unusual to observe a high performance 'cigar' skimming the waters at well over a hundred miles per hour. This is reminiscent of a Grice built sharpie winning a race on the Albemarle Sound in the 1800s.

Most, if not all of the Carolina ports north of the Cape Fear, had outlying farming areas producing fruits and vegetables along with hogs and chickens. This was in addition to the fisheries and their processing facilities. In the Elizabeth City and Edenton vicinity growing potatoes was a specialty. In the New Bern area blueberry farms were important. In the Beaufort area numerous vegetables, such as onions, were grown. Around Wilmington the production of chickens was noted. These hinterlands provided for the provisioning of ships, and this developed into the hospitality industry of today. It might even be said that a certain 'down east' cuisine developed as well. Need the reader be reminded of a lunch on the waterfront of some grilled king mackerel, fries, slaw and hush puppies?

Through the years, as leisure time became more prevalent, the coast became more and more attractive; not only to live near the water, but for recreation as well. The permanent inhabitants knew the maritime environment well. Most everyone had access to a boat or the water. Most, if not all, ports were maritime-oriented. Some ports became larger than others, but none the size of Charlestown or Norfolk. Those ports had deeper water, larger harbors, and larger hinterlands. Before Morehead City became a state port in 1950, Wilmington was the only deep water port in North Carolina.

When World War I ended in 1918, economic expansion was expected. The previous era was anticipated to continue, but with a different emphasis. That is, pleasure craft construction had to answer the demand of those with more leisure time. Trawlers for fishing had to meet the demand of the seafood industry. Sport fishermen needed fast boats to get out into the Gulf Stream. And last, but not least, more seafood was needed to feed growing populations to the north and on the coast, where many had second homes, used particularly in the summertime. More local restaurants appeared to feed the thousands of beach goers. It is very likely a very large majority of all these people do not know about the history of coastal North Carolina or its shipbuilding legacy. Our heritage continues, however, with boatbuilding, marine repair work, commercial fishing, sport fishing, regattas and races, and the museums devoted to our maritime history. Not to mention the beach: as we all go down to the sea in ships and boats!

Notes

1. Bailey to Judge Roundtree, Nov 26, 1919, Wilmington Iron Works Records, ECU. Arthur Naul to Still, n.d., copy in authors' possession.
2. Paul Morris, *Four-Masted Schooners of the East Coast* (Orleans, Mass: Lower Cape Publishing, 1975), 25. This is the official weight. Newspapers and other publications often referred to them as weighing 2,000 tons.
3. *Wilmington Dispatch*, July 11, 1916. (Wilmington) *Morning Star*, July 9, 1916.
4. A copy of the agreement, dated April 28, 1917, is in the Wilmington Iron Works Records, ECU. Smith evidently blamed Ryan for the delays as he had included in the agreement a proviso whereby Ryan was not to set foot on the premises of the shipyard. A Wilmington newspaper article said that the contract was terminated "Due to a change in specifications for the length of the ships." The Wilmington Iron Works records do not substantiate this. See (Wilmington) *Star-News*, May 9, 1976.
5. William N. Still, Jr., "Shipbuilding in North Carolina: The World War I Experience," *American Neptune,* 41 (July 1981), 201. Naul's son said that approximately forty "all house carpenters" provided the workforce but he did not state in which yard. In fact, later, when they went on strike for a raise, Smith refused to grant one because they were not ship, but house carpenters. Barbara R. Reed, "The Tale of a Tough Four-Master," *National Fisherman*, (April 1968), 12. See also Naul to Chappelle, October 2, 1952, copy in authors' possession.
6. Jackson, *The Cape Fear—Northeast Cape Fear Rivers Comprehensive Study*: A Maritime History and Survey of the Cape Fear and Northeast Cape Fear River, Wilmington Harbor, North Carolina, Vol. I. Maritime History (Underwater Archaeology Branch, Kure Beach, North Carolina, 1996), 236.
7. There has been confusion over these two yards. In fact, Naul in his letter to Still, put the two together. This is clearly not correct. The unpublished history of the Wilmington Iron Works states, "Mr. Smith tried to get a new yard established at Hilton just above the Railroad Bridge. They made a start, but the yard was soon abandoned." Wilmington Iron Works Records, ECU. Jackson, *The Cape Fear—Northeast Cape Fear Rivers Comprehensive Study*, 238-239.
8. Jean Wort, "M/V Commander," *Sea History,* 75 (Autumn 1995), 19. Brief sketches of these boats can be found in the volumes of the *Dictionary of Naval Fighting Ships*. Additional information including photographs can be found under their names in the Ships Histories Section, Naval Historical Center, Washington, DC.

Appendices

Appendix A: Alphabetical List of Ships

Name of Ship	Type of Ship	Shipbuilding Location	Year	Tons	Length	Width	Depth
A AND M	SCHOONER	WILMINGTON	1894	11	48.6	12.2	3.6
A. AND H. HADDOCKS	SCHOONER	ELIZABETH CITY	1828	74	67.5	19.83	6.42
A. FRANCIS	SHARPIE	ATLANTIC	1890	5	42.2	10	2.9
A. WINEY	SCHOONER	HUNTING QUARTERS	1869	16.95			
A.B. COVINGTON	SCREW STEAMER	WASHINGTON	1893	56.84	63.6	17.4	7.2
A.B.C. HILL	SCHOONER	ATLANTIC	1899	9	43	13	3
A.C. PATE	SLOOP	EDENTON		8			
A.C. WILLIAMS	SCHOONER	ELIZABETH CITY	1860	65.29	73.5	16.33	5.66
A.J. JOHNSON	PADDLE-WHEEL STEAMER	CLEAR RUN	1899	51	72	21	3.5
A.J. MARINE	SCHOONER	WASHINGTON	1873	35	60.9	17.7	5.1
A.M.P. WHEDBEE	SCHOONER	ELIZABETH CITY	1854	55.7	72.5	16.66	5.08
A.P. HURT	STEAMBOAT	WILMINGTON	1860	85	118	18	6
ABBIE ELIZABETH	SHARPIE	BOGUE	1891	11	47.6	13	3.4
ABERDEEN	SCHOONER	BEAUFORT	1750	50			
ABIGAIL	SCHOONER	CURRITUCK NARROWS	1809	32	46.5	16.62	5.12
ABNER P. NEALE	SCHOONER	HYDE COUNTY	1828	66	60	20	6.5
ABRAHAM DRUCKER	BARGE	WASHINGTON	1882	178.45			
ABRAHAM LINCOLN	SCHOONER	BEAUFORT	1888	7	35.6	9.3	2.7
ACME	BARGE	BUFFALO CITY	1889	45.9			
ACORN	BRIG	WASHINGTON	1769	70			
ACTIVE	SCHOONER	CARTERET COUNTY	1819	32.13	48	15.2	5.17
ACTIVE	SCHOONER	HATTERAS		7			
ACTIVE	SCHOONER	NORTH CAROLINA	1771	15			
ACTOR	SCHOONER	WASHINGTON	1847	59	66.6	19.6	5
ADA	SCHOONER	STRAITS	1867	35			
ADA BOZMAN	SHARPIE	ROSE BAY	1901	6	38.5	13.5	3
ADA FOSTER	SHARPIE	SMYRNA	1891	7	44	11.9	3.3
ADAMANT	BRIG	PLANK BRIDGE	1811	156	24	23	10.58
ADAMANTINE	SCHOONER	WILMINGTON		43			
ADAMENT	SCHOONER	HATTERAS	1872	7.98			
ADDIE	SCHOONER	WILMINGTON	1885	55.15	76.4	19.4	8.1
ADDIE HENRY	SCHOONER	NEW BERN	1864	72.73			
ADDIE L.	SCHOONER	BEAUFORT	1900	6	38	11	2

Name of Ship	Type of Ship	Shipbuilding Location	Year	Tons	Length	Width	Depth
ADDIE MAY	SCHOONER	SOUTHPORT	1900	18	44	16	4
ADEL	SCHOONER	LOCKWOODS FOLLY	1900	6	42.5	12.5	2.8
ADELE	SCHOONER	WILMINGTON	1892	7.28	39.5	10.5	2.8
ADELIA	SCHOONER	ONSLOW COUNTY	1826	86	63	21.08	7.75
ADELINE	BRIG	WASHINGTON	1842	177			
ADELLE	SCREW STEAMER	NEW BERN	1904	46	71	18	6.9
ADIEL	SCHOONER	WILMINGTON		29			
ADMIRAL	SCHOONER	BEAUFORT	1899	29	61	19	4
ADVANCE	SCHOONER	HATTERAS		9			
ADVENTURE	PIRAQUA	BATH	1725				
ADVENTURE		NORTH CAROLINA	1717				
ADVENTURE	SCHOONER	NORTH CAROLINA	1771	25			
ADVENTURE	BRIG	NORTH CAROLINA	1795	125.17	63.5	21.75	10.87
ADVENTURE	BRIG	NORTH CAROLINA	1799	105			
ADVENTURE	SCHOONER	SMYRNA	1881	35.25			
ADVENTURER	SHARPIE	LAKE LANDING	1899	8	45.8	15.4	3.6
ADVOCATE	SCHOONER	STRAITS OF CARTERET	1822	31	48	16	5
AGENORA	SCHOONER	COLUMBIA	1826	105			
AGILE	SCHOONER	STRAITS OF CARTERET	1860	51.42	65	19.58	5.83
AGNES	SCHOONER	HUNTING QUARTERS	1869	14.33	40	13.5	3.9
AGNES	BRIG	MARTIN COUNTY	1795	95			
AGNES	GAS SCREW	MOREHEAD CITY	1908	5	32	8.4	3.7
AGNES	GAS SCREW	MOREHEAD CITY	1909	36	55	18	3.2
AGNES F.	GAS SCREW	WASHINGTON	1914	56	56	14	4.3
AGNES H. WARD	SCHOONER	ONSLOW COUNTY	1853	43	51	18	4
AGNES McLEAN	SCHOONER	ONSLOW COUNTY	1850	27	40	15	4
AGNES T.	SCHOONER	BLADES	1907	15	45	13	6
AGNEW	SCHOONER	SMYRNA	1899	19	53	16	3.9
ALABAMA	PADDLE STEAMER	IVANHOE	1913	34	36	15	3.5
ALABAMA	SCHOONER	NEW BERN	1832	88	68	21	7
ALBATROSS	SCREW STEAMER	BELHAVEN	1901	15	42	13.7	3
ALBEMARLE	PADDLE STEAMER	AVOCA	1888	7.86	56.5	11.88	2

Name of Ship	Type of Ship	Shipbuilding Location	Year	Tons	Length	Width	Depth
ALBEMARLE	SHIP	BERTIE COUNTY	1794	230			
ALBEMARLE	SCHOONER	HERTFORD	1831	50			
ALBEMARLE	DREDGE	WASHINGTON	1893	72	60	24	5
ALBERT	SHARPIE	HAVELOCK	1888	11	50	10.2	3
ALBERTA	GAS SCREW	MARSHALLBERG	1913	5	35	8.3	3.2
ALBIN	SCHOONER	SWANSBORO	1839	24	45.58	14.5	4.42
ALBION	SCHOONER	CAMDEN	1805	109	75	21	8
ALBION	SCHOONER	WILMINGTON		28			
ALERT	SCHOONER	CARTERET COUNTY	1816	45	50	16	6
ALERT	SCHOONER	COINJOCK	1827	26.3			
ALERT	SHARPIE	LENOXVILLE	1887	12	48	16	4
ALERT	BRIG	PORT ROANOKE	1769	105			
ALEXANDER	BRIG	CARTERET COUNTY	1826	172	80	25	10
ALEXANDER	SCHOONER	CRAVEN COUNTY	1843	61	64	18.83	5.92
ALEXANDER	SLOOP	NORTH CAROLINA	1788	47	53	17	6
ALEXANDER CHESHIRE	SCHOONER	EDENTON	1841	54	64	16	5
ALFONZO	GAS SCREW	WILLISTON	1911	21	55	16	3.6
ALFRED DORLAN	SLOOP	ELIZABETH CITY		7			
ALGER	SLOOP	DAVIS	1902	6	37.8	12.8	3
ALGERIA	SCHOONER	BEAUFORT	1881	10.17			
ALICE	SCHOONER	BAY RIVER	1882	9	43.2	15	4.7
ALICE	SCHOONER	BEAUFORT		9			
ALICE	SLOOP	BELHAVEN	1902	5	47	25.6	3.5
ALICE	SCHOONER	CURRITUCK COUNTY	1873	23.24			
ALICE	SCHOONER	HYDE COUNTY	1856	44	58	17	5
ALICE	SCHOONER	NEW BERN	1880	12.53			
ALICE	SCREW STEAMER	TAR LANDING	1903	45	76	14	3.3
ALICE	SHARPIE	WASHINGTON	1894	11	44.6	13.2	2.8
ALICE	SCHOONER	CRAWFORD	1873	32	48.4	16.6	4.3
ALICE DUDLEY	SCHOONER	WASHINGTON	1867	23	55	16	4
ALICE GIBSON	SCHOONER	WINTON	1858	79	80	17	6
ALICE HILL	SCHOONER	PORTSMOUTH	1869	21.34			
ALICE M. BRADLEY	SLOOP	BELHAVEN	1902	9	47	15	3.5
ALLEN GRIST	SCHOONER	BEAUFORT COUNTY	1845	46	59	17	5
ALLEN JONES	SCHOONER	ONSLOW COUNTY	1816	63.56	57.75	17.66	7.25
ALLIANCE	BRIG	NORTH CAROLINA	1788	80			

Name of Ship	Type of Ship	Shipbuilding Location	Year	Tons	Length	Width	Depth
ALLIE	SCREW STEAMER	NEW BERN	1902	7	44	12	3
ALLIE DUDLEY	SCHOONER	PORTSMOUTH	1867	23	55	16	4.4
ALLIGATOR	SCHOONER	PINEY GROVE	1826	43	54	19.5	5
ALMA	SCREW STEAMER	FAIRFIELD	1901	165	110	21	5
ALMA	GAS SCREW	MANTEO	1908	12	48	10	2.4
ALMA	STEAMER	WASHINGTON	1897	11.35	41	13	2.3
ALMA GRAY	GAS SCREW	MOREHEAD CITY	1909	14	56	14	3
ALMA WHITE	SHARPIE	MOUNT PLEASANT	1899	10	52.6	16.5	3.8
ALMARINE	SCHOONER	NEW BERN		9			
ALMILDA	SCHOONER	BEAUFORT	1851	37	27	16	6
ALONZO	SCHOONER	CARTERET COUNTY	1848	98	72.5	22	7.17
ALONZO	SCHOONER	NEW BERN	1833	117	73	22	8
ALONZO TUALANE	SCHOONER	SMYRNA	1890	5	42.2	15	4.3
ALPHA	SCHOONER	WASHINGTON	1826	136			
ALPHA	SCREW STEAMER	WASHINGTON	1887	233.45	121.1	23.5	8.6
ALPHA AND OMEGA	SCHOONER	MARTIN COUNTY	1818	84	22	20	6
ALPHEUS	SCHOONER	ELIZABETH CITY	1826	85			
ALPHEUS	SCHOONER	FORBESVILLE	1827	72	61	22	6.5
ALPHONSO	SHARPIE	WILLISTON	1911	21	55.5	16.7	3.6
ALSON MILLER	SCHOONER	KINNAKEET	1908	8	44	13	3
ALTEIRO	GAS SCREW	WASHINGTON	1903	13	34.9	9.6	4.7
ALVA	SCHOONER	ELIZABETH CITY	1902	27	55.1	21.3	5.1
ALWILDA	SCHOONER	BEAUFORT	1851	37	27	16	6
AMANDA	SCHOONER	HYDE COUNTY	1810	78			
AMANDA CLIFFORD	SCHOONER	HYDE COUNTY	1855	23	45	14	4
AMARYLLIS	SLOOP	NORTH CAROLINA	1789	201			
AMELIA	SCHOONER	BAY RIVER	1825	44	49.66	17.83	6.08
AMELIA	BRIG	ELIZABETH CITY	1831	274			
AMELIA	SCHOONER	NEW TOPSAIL	1789	47			
AMELIA	SCHOONER	NORTH CAROLINA	1789	65			
AMERICAN COASTER	SCHOONER	CURRITUCK NARROWS	1811	54	54	18	6.58
AMERICAN COASTER	SCHOONER	STRAITS OF CORE	1829	89	67	29	7
AMERICAN EAGLE	SCHOONER	HATTERAS	1875	9.76			
AMERICAN EAGLE	SLOOP	RANSOMVILLE	1895	12.99	37.7	15.6	4.5
AMERICAN HERO	SLOOP	COINJOCK BAY	1825			9	
AMERICAN LADY	SCHOONER	INDIAN TOWN	1822	24	34	14.17	4.75
AMERICAN LADY	SCHOONER	POWELLS POINT	1820	56	62	19.5	5.17

Name of Ship	Type of Ship	Shipbuilding Location	Year	Tons	Length	Width	Depth
AMITABLE ADELLE	BRIG	NORTH CAROLINA	1797	152			
AMITY	SCHOONER	NELSON BAY	1888	5.67	31.6	10.7	2.9
AMY	SLOOP	NORTH CAROLINA	1789	65			
ANACONDA	SCHOONER	KINNAKEET	1894	15	41.2	14	3.5
ANACONDA	SCHOONER	WASHINGTON	1838	63	60	18	
ANDREW JACKSON	SCHOONER	CURRITUCK SOUND	1816	55.73	54.42	18.58	6.33
ANDREW WURFLEIN	SCHOONER	WASHINGTON		15			
ANGELIA AND SUSAN	SCHOONER	FALLS CREEK	1807	108			
ANGELICA	SCHOONER	ELIZABETH CITY		34			
ANGELINE	SCHOONER	CARTERET COUNTY	1851	82	70.33	21.66	6.25
ANGENARO	SCHOONER	CARTERET COUNTY	1833	65	59.33	18.58	6
ANGENORA	SCHOONER	COLUMBIA	1826	105	59	22	7
ANN	BRIG	BERTIE COUNTY	1796	121			
ANN	SCHOONER	CARTERET COUNTY	1818	48	60	17	6
ANN	SCHOONER	NORTH CAROLINA	1744	10			
ANN	BRIG	NORTH CAROLINA	1767	97			
ANN	BRIG	NORTH CAROLINA	1770	50			
ANN	BRIG	NORTH CAROLINA	1776	130			
ANN	SCHOONER	NORTH CAROLINA	1803	108			
ANN	SLOOP	PORT BATH	1747	25			
ANN	SCHOONER	STRAITS OF CARTERET	1829	37	52.11	16.66	5
ANN AND MARTIN	SCHOONER	NORTH CAROLINA	1803	108			
ANN AND SARAH	SLOOP	BATH COUNTY	1730	40			
ANN AND SARAH	BRIG	PORT BATH	1732	65			
ANN BRYAN	SCHOONER	VANDEMERE	1885	8	36.5	12.3	3.5
ANN C. DAVENPORT	SCHOONER	TYRRELL COUNTY	1851	48	64	17	4
ANN C. WILLIAMS	SCHOONER	ELIZABETH CITY	1851	68	80	17	5
ANN E. BARY	SCHOONER	WILMINGTON	1848	49	57	17	5
ANN E. DAVENPORT	SCHOONER	CROSS LANDING	1857	56	74	17	4
ANN ELIZA	SCHOONER	LITTLE RIVER	1810	109			
ANN ELIZA	SLOOP	OCRACOKE		8			
ANN FRANCIS	SCHOONER	FAYETTEVILLE	1826		93	15	

Name of Ship	Type of Ship	Shipbuilding Location	Year	Tons	Length	Width	Depth
ANN G. SIKES	SCHOONER	ELIZABETH CITY	1854	66	74	17	5
ANN H. SIM	SLOOP	PLYMOUTH	1846	31	47	16	4
ANN HALSEY	SCHOONER	TYRRELL COUNTY	1847	46	59	17	5
ANN HOWARD	SCHOONER	OCRACOKE	1821	70	64	20	6
ANN HUNTER	SCHOONER	ELIZABETH CITY	1843	54.75	71.5	17	5
ANN HYMAN	SCHOONER	NEW BERN	1841	155	85	24	9
ANN JANE	SCHOONER	SWANSBOROUGH	1839	39	57	18	4
ANN MARIA	SCHOONER	CARTERET COUNTY	1842	133			
ANN MARIA	SCHOONER	CARTERET COUNTY	1848	25	46.75	15.25	4.25
ANN MARIA JONES	SHIP		1803	284			
ANN MARIE	SCHOONER	STRAITS OF NORTH RIVER	1823	101	70	20	8
ANN OF NORTH CAROLINA	SCHOONER	PASQUOTANK	1701	10			
ANN SPARROW	SCHOONER	SMITHS CREEK	1833	23	44	14	4
ANNA	SCHOONER	BATH	1861	16.56			
ANNA	SLOOP	ELIZABETH CITY		11			
ANNA	SHIP	HYDE COUNTY	1805	210.65	84	24.83	11.66
ANNA	SCHOONER	NORTH CAROLINA	1755	20			
ANNA	SHARPIE	SHALLOTTE	1889	8	44	11.6	3.1
ANNA	SCREW STEAMER	WILMINGTON	1894	28.57	60	12.6	4.7
ANNA	SCHOONER	WILMINGTON		17			
ANNA A. HOLTON	SCHOONER	WILMINGTON	1866	136	89	23	7
ANNA BELL	SLOOP	BEAUFORT	1883	5.78			
ANNA BELL	SCHOONER	HUNTING QUARTERS	1883	5	28.9	10.5	2.6
ANNA BELL	SCHOONER	WILMINGTON		10			
ANNA ELIZABETH	SCHOONER	NORTH RIVER	1889	6	47	12.1	3
ANNA FRANCIS	SCHOONER	ELIZABETH CITY	1842	50.52	66.5	15.58	5.42
ANNA LEA	SLOOP	HARLOWE	1892	6	40.3	11.1	3.2
ANNA LOUISA	SCHOONER	ELIZABETH CITY	1842	43.14	59.5	17.25	4.83
ANNA MARIA	SCHOONER	NIXTON	1786	92	67	20	8
ANNABELLA	BRIG	NORTH CAROLINA	1764	100			
ANNE	SCHOONER	NORTH CAROLINA	1798	58			
ANNE	SLOOP	SMITHS CREEK	1778	20			
ANNE DAVIS	SCHOONER	CARTERET COUNTY	1853	38	56	17.83	4.5
ANNE THOMAS	SCHOONER	OCRACOKE	1893	12.23	43	12	3

Name of Ship	Type of Ship	Shipbuilding Location	Year	Tons	Length	Width	Depth
ANNGHEN	SCHOONER	KINNAKEET	1888	11	39.6	14.3	4
ANNIE B.	SCHOONER	BEAUFORT	1883	7.29			
ANNIE B.	SCREW STEAMER	MILL CREEK	1911	9	52	10	3.4
ANNIE C. THOMAS	SCHOONER	HATTERAS	1884	5.52			
ANNIE C. THORN	SCHOONER	HATTERAS	1884	5.52	40	12.5	3.25
ANNIE COLE	SCHOONER	ELIZABETH CITY		7			
ANNIE COLTON	SLOOP	EDENTON		5			
ANNIE DAVIS	SCHOONER	CARLISLE	1853	38			
ANNIE DAVIS OF WASHINGTON	SCHOONER	CARTERET COUNTY	1859	38	56	17	
ANNIE E.	SCHOONER	MARIBEL	1904	13	47.5	14.8	5.1
ANNIE EDWARD	SCHOONER	ELIZABETH CITY	1900	25	52	19	4.8
ANNIE ELWOOD	SLOOP	MOUNT PLEASANT	1903	7	34	15	2.8
ANNIE F. WAHAB	SCHOONER	NEW BERN	1877	32.46			
ANNIE FAIR	SCHOONER	BEAUFORT	1901	8	41	11	3
ANNIE FARROW	SCHOONER	OCRACOKE	1868	39.56			
ANNIE G. MIDGETT	SCHOONER	CORE SOUND	1874	28.86			
ANNIE LENA WHITE	SCHOONER	LAKE LANDING	1899	13	45	16	3.1
ANNIE LOIS	GAS SCREW	COLUMBIA	1908	9	31	7.8	7
ANNIE M. MOORE	SCHOONER	HYDE COUNTY	1874	21.59			
ANNIE M. TURNER	SCHOONER	COINJOCK	1894	7	40	13	2.6
ANNIE MAY	SLOOP	BELHAVEN	1900	7	40	13	2.8
ANNIE MOORE	SCHOONER	SMYRNA	1889	5	41.2	14.1	3.4
ANNIE THOMAS	SHARPIE	OCRACOKE	1893	11	43	12.8	3.6
ANNIE TODD	SCHOONER	ELIZABETH CITY		5			
ANNIE W. DOXEY	SCHOONER	CURRITUCK COUNTY	1876	23	57	15	3.1
ANNIE WALLACE	SCHOONER	ELIZABETH CITY	1882	40.61			
ANNIS	GAS SCREW	BEAUFORT	1913	15	42	10	3.6
ANTELOPE	SCHOONER	HYDE COUNTY	1805	98			
ANTELOPE	SCHOONER	TYRRELL COUNTY	1816	23.19	45	15	4
ANTILOPE	SCHOONER	BROWNS INLET	1811	37.81	55	17.25	4.66
APPRENTICE	SCHOONER	CURRITUCK NARROWS	1826	59	55	18.66	6.83
APPRENTICE BOY	SCHOONER	CURRITUCK NARROWS	1817	30	48	16.33	4.66
ARA AND SARAH	SLOOP	BATH COUNTY	1730	40			
ARAB	SCHOONER	CARTERET COUNTY	1853	48	62.17	17.66	5.08
ARAB	SCHOONER	NEW BERN	1841	68	65	19	6
ARAND M.	SHARPIE SCHOONER	WILMINGTON	1894	11.42	48.6	12.2	3.6

Name of Ship	Type of Ship	Shipbuilding Location	Year	Tons	Length	Width	Depth
ARCADIA	SCHOONER	BEAUFORT	1897	9	45	13	2.8
ARETE ELLIS	SCHOONER	SMITH CREEK	1823	40	48.42	15.75	6.25
ARGO	SCHOONER	CLUBFOOT CREEK	1816	95.52	66.08	20.58	6.58
ARGUOTUS MOORE	SCHOONER	EDENTON	1851	67	73	17	5
ARGUS	SCHOONER	BEAUFORT	1824	83.85	68.42	19.92	7
ARGYLE	SCHOONER	BRUNSWICK COUNTY	1879	14	48.4	13.7	3.7
ARIEL	SCHOONER	BEAUFORT	1828	23	46.5	13.66	4.25
ARIEL	SCHOONER	CARTERET COUNTY	1826	81	66	20	7
ARIEL	SCHOONER	CRAVEN COUNTY	1829	122			
ARIEL	SCHOONER	WASHINGTON	1825	94	69	20	
ARK	STERN-WHEEL STEAMER	MURFREESBORO	1888	143.03	96.6	24.3	6.5
ARMENCY	SCHOONER	CARTERET COUNTY	1840	22	43.58	14.46	2.17
ARRIVAL	SCHOONER	BEAUFORT	1865	7.28			
ARTS AND SCIENCE	SCHOONER	MARTIN POINT	1811	39	52.17	18.58	5
ASSIST	SCHOONER	STUMPY POINT	1841	24	44	14	4
ASTOR	SCHOONER	WASHINGTON	1847	59	66	19	5
ATALANTA	SCHOONER	PERQUIMANS COUNTY	1801	62			
ATLANTIC	SCHOONER	ARENUSE CREEK	1807	130	76	20	9
ATLANTIC	SCHOONER	CEDAR ISLAND	1822	29	46.5	15.66	4.75
ATLANTIC	SLOOP	CURRITUCK NARROWS	1826	26	42.58	15.5	4.83
ATLANTIC	SCHOONER	MANTEO	1905	14	60	15.7	2.8
ATLANTIC	GAS SCREW	MOREHEAD CITY	1903	14	51	12.6	3.2
ATLANTIC	SCHOONER	SMYRNA	1888	5	42	10.8	2.9
ATLANTIC	GAS SCREW	WILMINGTON	1906	14	50	11.2	3
ATLAS	SCHOONER	HYDE COUNTY	1828	35	49	15.83	5
ATLASS	SCHOONER	CARTERET COUNTY	1835	21	46.17	12.5	4
AUGUST FLOWER	SLOOP	ELIZABETH CITY	1892	9	34	12	3
AUGUSTA	SCHOONER	WILMINGTON	1897	15	45	12	3.7
AUGUSTA M.	SHARPIE	SMYRNA	1899	8	46.6	14	3
AUGUSTUS MOON	SCHOONER	EDENTON	1851	67	73	17	5
AUNT SUE	SCREW STEAMER	NEW BERN	1903	37	70	19	4.6
AURORA	SCHOONER	BEAUFORT	1882	8.2			
AURORA	SCHOONER	GOOSE CREEK	1798	93			
AURORA	SCREW STEAMER	WASHINGTON	1894	98.72	103	22.9	5.3

Name of Ship	Type of Ship	Shipbuilding Location	Year	Tons	Length	Width	Depth
AVOCA	STEAMER	AVOCA	1902	9	56.6	11.8	1.9
B.D. LUCE	SCHOONER	MOREHEAD CITY	1902	7	45	12	2.7
B.J. CHRISTIAN	SHCOONER	WASHINGTON		8			
B.L. PERRY	SCHOONER	CARTERET COUNTY	1849	127			
B.M. VAN DUZEN	GAS SCREW	MANTEO	1906	10	42	13	3
B.S. PERRY	SCHOONER	CARTERET COUNTY	1849	127	77	23	8
BABE	SCHOONER	MITCHELL CREEK	1889	8	40.2	11.4	3.2
BABY LOUISE	GAS SCREW	COLINGTON	1908	9	30	9	6.2
BALTIMORE	SCHOONER	BAY RIVER	1828	42	56	21	4
BALTIMORE	SCHOONER	CARTERET COUNTY	1848	43	62.66	17.42	4.66
BARNEY	SCREW STEAMER	WASHINGTON	1893	19.88	53.6	12	3.5
BARTER	SCHOONER	WILMINGTON	1883	28	65	16	3
BATCHELOR	SLOOP	NORTH CAROLINA	1754	10			
BATCHLOR	SLOOP	HYDE PRECINCT	1734	7			
BATH PACKET	BRIG	BATH	1763	80			
BAY RIVER	SLOOP	BAY RIVER	1824	50	50	17	6
BEAUFORT	SLOOP	NORTH CAROLINA	1742	35			
BEAUFORT	SCHOONER	NORTH CAROLINA	1793	92	63	19	9
BEAUFORT	BARGE	WASHINGTON	1883	385.5			
BEAUFORT	SCREW STEAMER	WASHINGTON	1883	188			
BEE	SCHOONER	BEAUFORT	1849	110			
BEE	SCREW STEAMER	STRAWHORN LANDING	1905	16	54	10.9	3
BELINDA	SCHOONER	MURFREESBORO	1794				
BELL	BRIG	NORTH CAROLINA	1768	35			
BELLE	BRIG	BEAUFORT COUNTY	1833	158	82.33	24.66	9.33
BELLE	SCHOONER	HATTERAS		6			
BELLE	SCHOONER	ONSLOW COUNTY	1854	28	52.5	14	4
BELSEY	SLOOP		1772	20			
BELVIDERE	SIDE-WHEEL STEAMER	HERTFORD COUNTY	1896	29.84	80	14.5	3
BEN MIDGETT	SCHOONER	NEW BERN	1850	58			
BENEFIT	SLOOP	NORTH RIVER	1893	7	39.7	11.5	2.7

Name of Ship	Type of Ship	Shipbuilding Location	Year	Tons	Length	Width	Depth
BENJAMIN	BRIG	NORTH CAROLINA	1778	100			
BENJAMIN BLANEY	SCHOONER	SMITHVILLE	1808	54	51	18	6
BENJAMIN F. HANKS	SCHOONER	BEAUFORT COUNTY	1847	97	76	22	6
BENJAMIN HARRISON	SCHOONER	CHICAMICOMICO BANK	1830	58	57	19	6
BENJAMIN MAITLAND	SCHOONER	PLYMOUTH	1853	57	73	17	5
BENNETT	GAS STEAMER	BELHAVEN	1907	14	38	11	3.9
BERKLEY MACHINE WORKS	GAS SCREW	BELHAVEN	1913	13	50	10	6.4
BERNICE CREE		MOREHEAD CITY	1899	9	46	13	3
BERTHA L. MORTON	SCHOONER	MOREHEAD CITY	1900	10	46	13	3
BERTHA W.	GAS STEAMER	VANCEBORO	1906	11	47	13	4.6
BERTIE	SCHOONER	BERTIE COUNTY	1788	91			
BERTIE	GAS SCREW	MOREHEAD CITY	1904	11	47	13.09	3
BERTIE	SCHOONER	SMYRNA	1899	12	47	14	3
BERTIE	SCREW STEAMER	WINDSOR	1872	57.98	68.4	14.2	4.6
BESSIE	SCHOONER	NEW BERN	1880	5.65			
BESSIE	SCHOONER	WASHINGTON	1880	6	36	10.2	2.6
BESSIE	SLOOP	WASHINGTON	1883	8	33.4	10.9	2.5
BESSIE	SCHOONER	WILMINGTON	1881	47.6	63.7	21.2	6.7
BESSIE AND ELLIS	SHARPIE	NEW BERN	1888	9	44.2	13.1	2.9
BESSIE D	SHARPIE	SMYRNA	1891	7	44.1	11.5	3
BESSIE HELLEN	SCHOONER	BEAUFORT	1902	7	40	12	2.4
BESSIE MAY	SCHOONER	HARLOWE	1890		45	13	3.5
BESSIE MOORE	SHARPIE	SMYRNA	1891	5	45.8	12.4	3
BESSIE ROBERTS	SCHOONER	MOREHEAD CITY	1900	8	41	11	2
BEST	SCHOONER	CURRITUCK	1855	83			
BETSEY	SCHOONER	ADAMS CREEK	1792	55			
BETSEY	SCHOONER	BEAUFORT	1810	118.28	71	22	8.83
BETSEY	SCHOONER	CHOWAN COUNTY	1777	90			
BETSEY	SCHOONER	CRAVEN COUNTY	1806	121			
BETSEY	SCHOONER	CURRITUCK	1796	55			
BETSEY	SCHOONER	CURRITUCK	1855	83			
BETSEY	SCHOONER	CURRITUCK COUNTY	1794	25.14	43.83	14.08	4.75
BETSEY	SCHOONER	CURRITUCK COUNTY	1815	25	43	14	4
BETSEY	SCHOONER	MOUSE HARBOR	1783	8			
BETSEY	SCHOONER	MOUSE HARBOR	1785	8			

Name of Ship	Type of Ship	Shipbuilding Location	Year	Tons	Length	Width	Depth
BETSEY	SCHOONER	NEW BERN	1795	94			
BETSEY	SCHOONER	NEW BERN	1809	33			
BETSEY	SCHOONER	NEW RIVER	1809	33	52.33	15.66	5
BETSEY	SLOOP	NORTH CAROLINA	1758	8			
BETSEY	BRIG	NORTH CAROLINA	1760	35			
BETSEY	BRIG	NORTH CAROLINA	1768	35			
BETSEY	SCHOONER	NORTH CAROLINA	1773	35			
BETSEY	SCHOONER	NORTH CAROLINA	1788	60			
BETSEY		NORTH CAROLINA		70			
BETSEY	SCHOONER	PEARCES CREEK	1832	23	44	14	4
BETSEY	BRIG	PORT ROANOKE	1771	50			
BETSEY	SCHOONER	SWANSBOROUGH	1786	68			
BETSEY	SLOOP	TYRRELL COUNTY	1793	49			
BETSEY	SCHOONER		1798	27			
BETSEY AND PATSEY	SCHOONER	CURRITUCK COUNTY	1804	27			
BETSEY AND SALLY	BRIG	BEAUFORT	1802	170.7	74.5	23.75	11.29
BETSEY FULSHIRE	SCHOONER	SLOCUM CREEK	1802	109			
BETSY	SCHOONER	ADAMS CREEK	1812	24	43	13	4
BETSY	SCHOONER	BEARS CREEK	1794	86			
BETSY	SCHOONER	CURRITUCK COUNTY	1785	30	48	15	5
BETSY	BRIGANTINE	NORTH CAROLINA	1762	35			
BETSY	SCHOONER	NORTH CAROLINA	1764	10			
BETSY	SCHOONER	NORTH CAROLINA	1769	10			
BETSY	SLOOP	NORTH CAROLINA	1772	20			
BETSY	SCHOONER	NORTH CAROLINA	1774	40			
BETSY	SCHOONER	NORTH CAROLINA	1786	18			
BETSY	SCHOONER	NORTH CAROLINA	1788	6			
BETSY	BRIG	NORTH CAROLINA	1800	113			
BETSY	SCHOONER	NORTH CAROLINA		80			

Name of Ship	Type of Ship	Shipbuilding Location	Year	Tons	Length	Width	Depth
BETSY	BRIG	PORT ROANOKE	1777	50			
BETSY	BRIG	PORT ROANOKE	1771	50			
BETSY	BRIG	PORT ROANOKE	1774	80			
BETSY	SCHOONER	SWANSBOROUGH	1800	110			
BETSY AND HANNAH	SCHOONER	BEAUFORT	1792	85			
BETSY AND NANCY	SCHOONER	COINJOCK BAY	1824	26	45	15.5	4.5
BETSY B. GLOUCET	SCHOONER	BEAUFORT	1828	128	74	22	
BETSY COTTON	SCHOONER	CHOWAN COUNTY	1804	41.88	50	16.83	5.92
BETSY COX	SCHOONER	SWANSBOROUGH	1800	110			
BETTIE	SHARPIE	DAVIS	1891	7	44.6	11.5	3.3
BETTIE	PADDLE-WHEEL STEAMER	ELIZABETH CITY	1884	64.45			
BETTIE	SIDE-WHEEL STEAMER	NEW BERN	1865	117			
BETTIE A. BUNCH	SCHOONER	BERTIE COUNTY	1875	9	41.8	12.2	2.7
BETTY	PADDLE-WHEEL	NORTH CAROLINA		5			
BETTY C. BELL	SLOOP	CRAWFORD		17			
BEULAH BENTON	SCHOONER	STRAITS	1872	37	56.2	19.4	4.6
BILL ARP	SCHOONER	BELHAVEN	1903	9	38	13	2.8
BIRDIE ESTELL	GAS SCREW	SHILOH	1908	12	49	10	6.04
BIVALVE	SHARPIE	BEAUFORT	1892	11	53.2	15.6	3.7
BIZ	PADDLE-WHEEL STEAMER	WILMINGTON	1881	11.54			
BLACK EYED SUSAN	SCHOONER	NEW RIVER	1818	27	52	14	4
BLACK HAWK	SHCOONER	ELIZABETH CITY		10			
BLACK RIVER	SCREW STEAMER	STRAWHORN LANDING	1907	8	52	11	2.8
BLACK RIVER	SIDE-WHEEL STEAMER	WILMINGTON	1854	67	94	16	4
BLACK SQUALL	SCHOONER	NEW BERN	1855	59			
BLADEN	PADDLE-WHEEL STEAMER	WILMINGTON	1881	132.32			
BLAKELY	SCHOONER	CHOWAN COUNTY	1817	67	58.08	18	7
BLAKELY	SCHOONER	NEW RIVER	1816	100	67	23	7
BLANCH	SCHOONER	BEAUFORT	1899	10	46	13	3
BLANCHE	SCREW STEAMER	NEW BERN	1883	67.87	81	17.2	3.3
BLANCHE	SCHOONER	SMYRNA	1902	7	41	11	2

Name of Ship	Type of Ship	Shipbuilding Location	Year	Tons	Length	Width	Depth
BLANCHE	SHARPIE	STRAITS	1892	10	48.2	14.8	3.8
BLANCHE	GAS SCREW	WILLISTON	1914	8	36	9.6	2.4
BLONDELLE	SHARPIE	WILLISTON	1904	10	44	12.7	2.8
BLOOMER	SHARPIE	MOREHEAD CITY	1893	6	42.8	11.4	2.3
BOB AND ALICE	SHIP	BATH	1734	150			
BONITO	SCREW STEAMER	LENOXVILLE	1882	33.22			
BOSS		NORTH CAROLINA	1756	8			
BOUNTY	SCHOONER	NEW BERN	1846	135	80	23	8
BRANT	SCHOONER	ROANOKE ISLAND	1892	23	60	18.7	4.6
BRAVO	SLOOP	CRAVEN COUNTY	1842	25	46	17	4
BRIDGEPORT	GAS SCREW	MOREHEAD CITY	1911	10	37	11	3.1
BRIDGET AND LYDIA	SCHOONER	NORTH CAROLINA	1762	15			
BRITANIA	SCHOONER	HYDE COUNTY	1816	60	57.5	18.17	6
BROAD BILL	BARGE	MOREHEAD CITY	1901	5			
BROKEN MERCHANT	SLOOP	NORTH CAROLINA	1788	65			
BROOKLYN	SCHOONER	SMYRNA	1899	15	49	15	2.6
BROOKS	SCHOONER	CARTERET COUNTY	1832	50	60.25	16.58	5.75
BROTHERS	SCHOONER	CARTERET COUNTY	1851	24	47.7	15	4
BROTHERS	SCHOONER	NORTH CAROLINA	1800	86			
BRUCE	SCREW STEAMER	WASHINGTON	1898	10.62	39	11	3.42
BRUTAS	BRIG	BEAUFORT	1804	143			
BUCK	SCREW STEAMER	WILMINGTON	1897	29	50	11	4.3
BUCKSKIN	SLOOP	NORTH CAROLINA	1742	8			
BUENA VISTA	BRIG	WASHINGTON	1849	188	94	25	8
BUFFALO BILL	SLOOP	EDENTON	1879	8.78			
BUG	GAS STEAMER		1906	10	36	9.6	4.4
BURDETT	BRIG	SWANSBOROUGH	1827	299	97	27	13
BUTTERFLY	BRIG	NORTH CAROLINA	1743	40			
C. CARROLL	SCHOONER	CARTERET COUNTY	1846	26	47.17	16	4.25
C. HAY	SHARPIE	WHITE OAK RIVER	1890	12	50.6	14.2	3.3

Name of Ship	Type of Ship	Shipbuilding Location	Year	Tons	Length	Width	Depth
C. STOVER	SCHOONER	CARTERET COUNTY	1840	109	73	20	7
C. WASHINGTON COLYER	GAS SCREW	MOREHEAD CITY	1913	43	61	19	5.6
C.A. JOHNSON	SCHOONER	WASHINGTON		68			
C.B. GLOVER	SCHOONER	CARTERET COUNTY	1847	38	55	16	4
C.C. ISABELL	GAS SCREW	BELHAVEN	1905	10	49	11	5.9
C.D. MOFFITT	SCHOONER	SHALLOTTE	1899	15	51	14	3
C.H. CULPEPPER	SCHOONER	ELIZABETH CITY	1857	80.08	88	17	5.75
C.L. COBB	SCHOONER	HATTERAS		17			
C.T. HERMAN	SCHOONER	SHALLOTTE	1903	13	49	13	3
C.W. GRANDY	BOAT	CAMDEN COUNTY	1853	35.35	75	13.25	4
C.W. LYON	PADDLE-WHEEL STEAMER	WILMINGTON	1905	98	118	18.4	4.2
CADER	SLOOP	NORTH CAROLINA	1750	35			
CALDWELL	STEAMER	BEAUFORT	1859	51	65	21.5	4.33
CALEB	SCHOONER	TYRRELL COUNTY	1797	42			
CALEB NICHOL	SCHOONER	NEW RIVER	1833	80			
CALO	SCHOONER	NORTH CAROLINA	1774	20			
CAMDEN	SCHOONER	CAMDEN COUNTY	1831	44	55	17	5
CAMDEN	BRIG	NORTH CAROLINA	1788	75			
CAMDEN UNION	SCHOONER	CAMDEN COUNTY	1860	40.58			
CAMILLE	SIDE-WHEEL STEAMER	MANTEO	1885	21.31	64	12	2.6
CAPER	SCHOONER	HYDE COUNTY	1850	9.5	37.7	12.7	3.6
CAPTAIN DICK	GAS SCREW	BEAUFORT	1910	37	62	18	4.7
CAPTAIN SAM H.	GAS SCREW	BEAUFORT	1908	6	32	9.2	2.8
CAPTOLIA	SCHOONER	CAMDEN	1879	10.48			
CARAWAY	SCHOONER	ELIZABETH CITY	1847	56			
CARITA	SCHOONER	MOREHEAD CITY	1905	11	45	13	3
CARL	SLOOP	BEAUFORT	1902	7	36	12	2.3
CARL T.	GAS SCREW	BEAUFORT	1905	12	48	12.8	2.5
CARNIE	SCREW	STRAITS	1867	35			
CAROLINA	SLOOP	BATH	1731	60			
CAROLINA	SCHOONER	BATH	1874		101	23.8	8.7

Name of Ship	Type of Ship	Shipbuilding Location	Year	Tons	Length	Width	Depth
CAROLINA	SCHOONER	BEAUFORT COUNTY	1882	117.26			
CAROLINA	SCHOONER	CARTERET COUNTY	1857	50			
CAROLINA	SCHOONER	CARTERET COUNTY	1858	57	66.33	19.33	5
CAROLINA	SLOOP	CURRITUCK	1730	35			
CAROLINA	BRIG	EDENTON	1787				
CAROLINA	BRIGANTINE	ELIZABETH CITY	1820	80			
CAROLINA	SCHOONER	ELIZABETH CITY	1852	40			
CAROLINA	CANAL BOAT	ELIZABETH CITY	1912	100			
CAROLINA	SLOOP	NORTH CAROLINA	1767	30			
CAROLINA	BRIG	NORTH CAROLINA	1767	90			
CAROLINA	BRIG	NORTH CAROLINA	1788	70			
CAROLINA	SCHOONER	PORT ROANOKE	1751	40			
CAROLINA	SCHOONER	SMYRNA	1882	18.7			
CAROLINA	PADDLE-WHEEL STEAMER	SNOW HILL	1883	39.28			
CAROLINA	SCREW STEAMER	VANCEBORO	1893	79.95	84	23	4
CAROLINA	BRIG	WASHINGTON	1810				
CAROLINA	SHIP		1783				
CAROLINA ADVENTURE	SLOOP	NORTH CAROLINA	1722	15			
CAROLINA VENTURE	SLOOP	EDENTON	1722	22			
CAROLINA VIRGINIA	SCHOONER	CARTERET COUNTY	1854	61	64.58	22	5
CAROLINE	SCHOONER	BEAUFORT	1817	75			
CAROLINE	SCHOONER	CARTERET COUNTY	1816	74	64.5	19.75	6.17
CAROLINE	SCHOONER	CARTERET COUNTY	1846	21	45	13.66	4.33
CAROLINE	SCHOONER	EDENTON	1858	94	81	21	6
CAROLINE	SCHOONER	ELIZABETH CITY	1852	40.23	52	16.83	4.17
CAROLINE	SLOOP	ELIZABETH CITY		6			
CAROLINE	SCHOONER	HYDE COUNTY	1827	39	50	16	5
CAROLINE	BRIG	NEW RIVER	1834	200			
CAROLINE	SNOW	NORTH CAROLINA	1733	80			

Name of Ship	Type of Ship	Shipbuilding Location	Year	Tons	Length	Width	Depth
CAROLINE V. CASEY	SCHOONER	TYRRELL COUNTY	1853	122			
CAROLYN	SCHOONER	BEAUFORT	1899	15	48	14	3.6
CARPENTERS SON	SCHOONER	CURRITUCK COUNTY	1836	80			
CARPENTERS SON	SCHOONER	SWANSBOROUGH	1810	85	63	19	8
CARPENTERS SONS	SCHOONER	CURRITUCK COUNTY	1817	74.24	65.58	20	6.58
CARRAWAY	SCHOONER	ELIZABETH CITY	1847	56	69	17	5
CARRIE	GAS SCREW	ATLANTIC	1909	6	39	9	2.4
CARRIE	SHARPIE	CURRITUCK COUNTY	1890	8	38.5	13.6	3
CARRIE	SCHOONER	STRAITS	1867	34.75			
CARRIE	SLOOP	SWANSBORO	1900		37	11	2.6
CARRIE B.	SCHOONER	ELIZABETH CITY		7			
CARRIE B. BELLE	SCHOONER	AVON	1906	12	47	13	3
CARRIE DYE	SCHOONER	ELIZABETH CITY		25			
CARRIE GRANNIS	SCHOONER	SMYRNA	1904	11	47	11	3
CARRIE RAE	SCHOONER	NEW BERN	1882	16.52	40.7	15.4	4
CARRIE REEL	SCHOONER	NEW BERN	1882	11.9			
CARTARET	SCHOONER	NORTH CAROLINA	1803	91			
CARTERET	SCHOONER	CARTERET COUNTY	1829	29	47.08	15.58	4.66
CASSANDER	SCHOONER	BEAUFORT		5			
CASSANDRA	SCHOONER	NEW BERN	1848	149	80	23	9
CATHARINE	SCHOONER	BEAUFORT	1836	10			
CATHARINE	SLOOP	ELIZABETH CITY		7			
CATHARINE AND JANE	SCHOONER	SLADE CREEK	1817	101	72	21	7
CATHELEEN	SHARPIE	WILLISTON	1898	11	46	16.5	4
CATHERINE	SCHOONER	BEAUFORT	1835	98			
CATHERINE	SCHOONER	NEW BERN	1855	86.14	84.5	22.5	6.4
CATHERINE	BRIG	NORTH CAROLINA	1802	198			
CATHERINE	SCHOONER	WHITE OAK RIVER	1806	76.49	59.58	18.83	8
CATHERINE	SCREW STEAMER	WILMINGTON	1908	31	60	16	4.8
CATHERINE JANE	SCHOONER	ONSLOW COUNTY	1849	21	43	13	4
CATHERINE M.	GAS SCREW	MOREHEAD CITY	1906	9	44	12	2.4
CATHLEEN	SCHOONER	SMYRNA	1898	16	46	16	4
CATO	SCHOONER	NORTH CAROLINA	1774	20			

Name of Ship	Type of Ship	Shipbuilding Location	Year	Tons	Length	Width	Depth
CECIL	SCHOONER	BEAUFORT	1872	11.06			
CECIL	SCHOONER	MOUNT PLEASANT	1899	17	49	18	5
CENTENNIAL	SCHOONER	BEAUFORT	1876	14	48.9	13.4	3.2
CERES	SHIP	BAY RIVER	1801	241			
CERES	SCHOONER	NORTH CAROLINA	1800	60			
CERES	BOAT	PASQUOTANK COUNTY	1855	46.63	65	13.33	5.83
CERRIN TRYALL	SLOOP	NORTH CAROLINA	1728	3			
CHALLENGE	SLOOP	CAPE LOOKOUT	1883	6.69			
CHAMPION	SCHOONER	BAY RIVER	1848	9.57	42.3	12	3.25
CHAMPION	SCHOONER	CARTERET COUNTY	1852	35	54.58	17	4.42
CHANCE	SCHOONER	WILMINGTON	1793	29			
CHARITY	SCHOONER	PLYMOUTH	1848	61	74	16	5
CHARLES	SCHOONER	BEAUFORT	1869	33.46			
CHARLES	PADDLE-WHEEL STEAMER	EDENTON	1883	10.02			
CHARLES	SIDE-WHEEL STEAMER	ELIZABETH CITY	1883	10.82	56	11	3
CHARLES ADDAMS	SCHOONER	PLYMOUTH	1852	56	72	17	5
CHARLES AND LEWIS	SCHOONER	HYDE COUNTY	1806	122			
CHARLES FISHER	BARGE	WASHINGTON	1880	99.46			
CHARLES HAYS	SCHOONER	WASHINGTON	1817	81	64	19	7
CHARLES LEROY	SHARPIE	SMYRNA	1899	11	53.7	15.4	3.7
CHARLES M. MCCLEES	SCHOONER	TYRRELL COUNTY	1854	112	81	24	6
CHARLES M. WHITLOCK	SCREW STEAMER	POINT CASWELL	1901	49	82	14	4
CHARLES MOLES	SCHOONER	BEAUFORT COUNTY	1833	33	51	14	5
CHARLES S. WALLACE	SHARPIE	MOREHEAD CITY	1899	10	46	12	2.7
CHARLES S. WALLACE	GAS SCREW	MOREHEAD CITY	1902	13	54.5	13	3.6
CHARLES THOMAS	SCHOONER	SMITHVILLE	1873	30			
CHARLESTON	SCHOONER	CARTERET COUNTY	1845	93	70	22	7
CHARLESTON PACKET	BRIG	PITT COUNTY	1810	153			
CHARLIE	GAS SCREW	LENOXVILLE	1913	29	63	16	4.2
CHARLIE RAPER	SCHOONER	EDENTON	1881	15.42			
CHARLOTTE	SLOOP	CARTERET COUNTY	1788	32			

Name of Ship	Type of Ship	Shipbuilding Location	Year	Tons	Length	Width	Depth
CHARLOTTE	SCHOONER	CARTERET COUNTY	1829	23.55	45.83	14.5	4.17
CHARLOTTE	SCHOONER	MARTIN COUNTY	1793	59			
CHARLOTTE	SLOOP	NORTH CAROLINA	1769	20			
CHARLOTTE	BRIG	NORTH CAROLINA	1800	129			
CHARLOTTE	SCHOONER	NORTH CAROLINA	1800	76			
CHARLOTTE	BRIG	SMITH CREEK	1816	148			
CHARLOTTE ANN	SCHOONER	BEAUFORT	1851	88	72	22.58	6.33
CHARLOTTE ANN PIGOTT	SCHOONER	STRAITS	1874	27	52	17.5	5.2
CHARLOTTE CAASE		WILMINGTON	1904	9	49.1	14	4.5
CHARLOTTE CORDAY	SCHOONER	SMITH CREEK	1816	114	76	23	7
CHARLOTTE FARQUHAR	SLOOP	WILMINGTON	1818	47	56	16	5
CHARLOTTE GOOSE	GAS SCREW	WILMINGTON	1904	13	47	13	3.4
CHARLOTTE MADISON	SLOOP	COINJOCK	1815	34.26	42.5	16	6.17
CHARMER	SCHOONER	STRAITS	1901	20	55	16	4
CHARMING BETSEY	SLOOP	CURRITUCK	1730	15			
CHARMING BETSEY	BRIG	NORTH CAROLINA	1779	100			
CHARMING BETSEY	BRIG	PORT ROANOKE	1771	50			
CHARMING BETSEY	SCHOONER	SWANSBOROUGH	1788	72.5			
CHARMING NANCY	SCHOONER	LITTLE RIVER	1750	15			
CHARMING PATSEY	SCHOONER	NORTH CAROLINA	1779	100			
CHARMING PATSY	BRIG	NORTH CAROLINA	1775	100			
CHARMING PEGGY	SCHOONER	NORTH CAROLINA	1764	50			
CHARMING POLLY	BRIG	BATH	1770	70			
CHARMING POLLY	SCHOONER	NORTH CAROLINA	1771	10			
CHARMING POLLY	BRIG	NORTH CAROLINA		30			
CHAS. McLEESE	SCHOONER	TYRRELL COUNTY	1854	113	82	24	7
CHASE	SHARPIE	MOREHEAD CITY	1903	7	40.8	11.5	2.5
CHASE	SCHOONER	SMITHVILLE	1823	104.28	74	19	8.42
CHATHAM	SIDE-WHEEL STEAMER	FAYETTEVILLE	1852	235			

APPENDIX A: ALPHABETICAL LIST OF SHIPS

Name of Ship	Type of Ship	Shipbuilding Location	Year	Tons	Length	Width	Depth
CHATHAM	SIDE-WHEEL STEAMER	NEW BERN	1850	57	101	14	4
CHATHAM	BRIG	NORTH CAROLINA	1795	132			
CHAUNCEY ROY	SCHOONER	BEAUFORT	1893	6	44	10.7	2.6
CHAUNCEY T.	SCHOONER	SHALLOTTE	1904	16	53	17	3.5
CHERUBIM	SCHOONER	BEAUFORT	1900	10	45	13	2.6
CHOWAN	SIDE-WHEEL STEAMER	COLERAIN	1889	10.78	57.3	12.6	2.5
CHOWAN PACKET	SCHOONER	NORTH CAROLINA		30			
CHRISTIANA CAROLINA	SCHOONER	NEW RIVER	1831	33	52	16	4
CHRISTINA	SCHOONER	BEAUFORT		5			
CICERO	SCHOONER	CARTERET COUNTY	1851	108	72.25	22	7.83
CINDERELLA	SCHOONER	PLYMOUTH	1831	88			
CITY OF STELLA	SCOW	STELLA	1890	31.93			
CLARA ESTELL	SCHOONER	NORTH HARLOWE	1898	12	45	13.7	3.6
CLARENCE H.	SCHOONER	SHALLOTTE	1901	17	54	14	4
CLARENDON	SIDE-WHEEL STEAMER	WILMINGTON	1833	140	103	18	7
CLARISSA BONNER	BRIG	DURHAM CREEK	1834	139	81	23	8
CLAUDE	SLOOP	ELIZABETH CITY	1903	5	35.2	11.7	2.6
CLAUDIA AND MARY	SCHOONER	CAMDEN COUNTY	1831	47	58	17	5
CLAY FOREMAN	SCREW STEAMER	ELIZABETH CITY	1902	35	62	15	6.4
CLEM	SCHOONER	SMYRNA	1891	5	44.4	11.1	2.8
CLEOPATRA	PADDLE-WHEEL STEAMER	COLERAIN	1884	26.7			
CLIFFORD PERIN	SCHOONER	BEAUFORT	1900	13	45	14	3
CLINTON L. GUIRKIN	SCHOONER	HARKER'S ISLAND	1871	33.11			
CLIPPER	SCHOONER	BEAUFORT		9			
CLYDE	SHIP	HYDE COUNTY	1803	234.64	91.58	24.5	11.83
COASTER	SCHOONER	CARTERET COUNTY	1807	48	58	16	5
COASTER	SCHOONER	MOREHEAD CITY	1902	5	39	10	2.4
COASTER	SCHOONER	TYRRELL COUNTY	1816	20.72	42.66	14.08	4.08
COERINE	SCHOONER	PLYMOUTH	1857	180			

Name of Ship	Type of Ship	Shipbuilding Location	Year	Tons	Length	Width	Depth
COLER	SCHOONER	BEAUFORT	1903	7	42	12	2.5
COLLECTOR	SCHOONER	CARTERET COUNTY	1815	74	65.33	20.17	6.58
COLLECTOR	SCHOONER	HYDE COUNTY	1824	75	62.75	20.42	6
COLLECTOR	SCHOONER	POWELLS POINT	1821	32	48.2	14.4	4.66
COLONEL BOUGARD	SCHOONER	FEDERAL POINT	1905	7	38	10	2.6
COLONEL MCRAE	SCHOONER	WILMINGTON	1840	89	70	21	6
COLUMBIA	SCHOONER	BELHAVEN	1901	15	50	15	3
COLUMBIA	GAS SCREW	COLUMBIA	1908	6	26	8	6.6
COLUMBIA	SCHOONER	ELIZABETH CITY	1839	48	59	17	5
COLUMBIA	GAS SCREW	SMYRNA	1906	21	53	17	3.6
COLUMBIA	SCHOONER	STRAITS OF CARTERET	1823	72	43	14	5
COLUMBIA	SHARPIE	WILLISTON	1906	21	53.5	17.8	3.6
COLUMBIA	SLOOP	WYSOCKING	1903	8	41	16	2.7
COLVILLE	PADDLE-WHEEL STEAMER	WILMINGTON	1877	139.55	78	15	5
COMET	SCHOONER	CARTERET COUNTY	1817	49	55.5	15.75	6.42
COMET	SCHOONER	CARTERET COUNTY	1819	41	55	15.75	6.42
COMET	SCHOONER	CARTERET COUNTY	1853	34	52.83	17.08	4.5
COMET	SCHOONER	CARTERET COUNTY	1857	9.9	37.1	11.1	3.2
COMET	SCHOONER	PLYMOUTH	1838	102	70	22	7.66
COMET	SCHOONER	WASHINGTON	1842	130	80	23	8
COMFORT	GAS SCREW	NEW BERN	1908	116	103	21	7
COMMERCE	SCHOONER	BEAUFORT	1828	25	47.75	15.5	4.08
COMMERCE	SCHOONER	ELIZABETH CITY	1800	72			
COMMERCE	SCHOONER	NEW BERN		13			
COMMERCE	SCHOONER	NORTH CAROLINA	1799	102			
COMMODATOR	SCHOONER	CURRITUCK COUNTY	1817	26.3	47.17	13.92	4.58
COMMODORE	SCHOONER	BEAUFORT	1899	27	61	18	4
CONCORD	SCHOONER	CURRITUCK NARROWS	1813	60.59	61	19.17	6
CONSOLATION	SCHOONER	CURRITUCK COUNTY	1824	58.15	61.25	20.5	5.5
CONSTANCE	SCHOONER	BELHAVEN	1903	18	45	17	4
CONSTELLATION	BRIG	BEAUFORT	1800	160			
CONSTITUTION	SLOOP	NEW BERN	1827	28			
CONSTITUTION	SLOOP	WYSOCKING	1903	11	42	15	3.2

Name of Ship	Type of Ship	Shipbuilding Location	Year	Tons	Length	Width	Depth
CONTENTNEA	SCREW STEAMER	BELLS FERRY	1877	71.02			
CONVOY	SCHOONER	CURRITUCK COUNTY	1826	28	37	16	4.5
CONVOY	SCHOONER	HYDE COUNTY	1825	73	65	20	6
CONVOY	SCHOONER	LENOXVILLE	1886	13	46.4	16.1	4
COOCH		BEAUFORT	1899	13	58.7	17.4	4.1
CORA	SCHOONER	CEDAR ISLAND	1867	12.19			
CORA	SCHOONER	NEW BERN	1845	64	64	16	6
CORA	SCHOONER	NEW BERN	1850	77	77	19.66	5.75
CORA	SCHOONER	WASHINGTON	1881	175.02	86	23	7.8
CORA MANLY	SCHOONER	EDENTON	1846	60	73	17	5
CORAL	SCHOONER	HATTERAS		5			
COREY	SCHOONER	NORTH CAROLINA	1800	60			
CORN PLANTER	SCHOONER	CURRITUCK NARROWS	1818	69	45.08	21	7
CORRIN	GAS SCREW	CAROLINA CITY	1905	7	33	9	4.6
CORRINE	SCHOONER	BEAUFORT	1881	14.05			
COTTON PLANT	SIDE-WHEEL STEAMER	FAYETTEVILLE	1828	119	105	16	7
COTTON PLANT	SCHOONER	WASHINGTON	1826	116	74	22	8
COURTNEY	SCHOONER	PASQUOTANK COUNTY	1852	69	76	17	5.9
COURTNEY	STERN-WHEEL STEAMER	WILMINGTON	1892	66.72	75.7	20.3	4
CRAFTSMAN	SCREW	WANCHESE	1909	7	37	9	3
CRANSTON	SHIP	NORTH CAROLINA	1753	120			
CRAVEN	SCHOONER	SMITHS CREEK	1820	96	67	21	7
CRINOLINE	SCHOONER	EDENTON	1858	87.88	81	24	6
CROATAN	SIDE-WHEEL STEAMER	ELIZABETH CITY	1887	17.05	60.6	10.6	2.6
CROATAN	BARGE	NEW BERN	1901	416			
CROESUS	SCREW STEAMER	WILMINGTON	1896	36	25	12	3
CUMBERLAND	PADDLE-WHEEL STEAMER	FAYETTEVILLE	1871	120.88			
CUMBERLAND	SCREW STEAMER	MANTEO	1882	119.17	124	21.5	7.5
CUMMING	SCHOONER	NORTH CAROLINA	1788	65			

Name of Ship	Type of Ship	Shipbuilding Location	Year	Tons	Length	Width	Depth
CURIOSITY	SCHOONER	CURRITUCK COUNTY	1839	37	52	17	4.83
CURLEW	PADDLE-WHEEL STEAMER	BERTIE COUNTY	1880	7.26			
CURRAN	SCHOONER	CARTERET COUNTY	1839	34	54.58	15.5	5.5
CURRAN	SCHOONER	NEW BERN	1867	23			
CURTIS MATILDA	SLOOP	COLINGTON	1883	6.06	39.75	11.1	2.8
CYGNET	SCHOONER	CARTERET COUNTY	1826	76	62	19.83	7
CYGNET	SCHOONER	STRAITS OF CARTERET	1794	135	70	21	9
CYRUS	SCHOONER		1813	53			
D.B. WADE	SCHOONER	MOREHEAD CITY	1902	9	43	12	2.7
D.C. WILLIS	SCHOONER	BEAUFORT	1875	15	45	13	3
D.H. PENTON	GAS SCREW	MOREHEAD CITY	1911	12	42	10	4
D.P. WOODBURY	SCHOONER	SMITHVILLE	1848	32	45	18	4
D.V. SESSOMS	SCHOONER	ELIZABETH CITY	1853	45.1	63.75	17.17	4.66
D.W. BAGLEY	SCHOONER	PLYMOUTH	1851	120	81	23	7
D.W. SANDERS	SCHOONER	BEAUFORT	1855	159	85.5	26.25	7.92
DAISY	GAS SCREW	SMYRNA	1901	12	45	16	3.3
DALE	SCHOONER	ATLANTIC	1905	11	45	13	4.5
DAMSEL	SCHOONER	POWELLS POINT	1805	23.33	41.5	16	4.33
DANIEL	GAS SCREW	WIT	1907	18	51.3	18	3.9
DANIEL BELL	SCHOONER	MOREHEAD CITY	1889	11	54.3	14.2	3.7
DANIEL CRESSIE	SLOOP	BELHAVEN	1901	15	45	17	3.9
DANIEL G. FOWLE	SCHOONER	SMYRNA	1889	17	60	15	4.6
DANIEL WEBSTER	SCHOONER	BEAUFORT		24			
DAPHINE	SCHOONER	CARTERET COUNTY	1797	37.01	50	16.5	4.33
DAPHNE	YACHT	BELHAVEN	1913	10	36	8	2.6
DARE	SCHOONER	ELIZABETH CITY		6			
DAUNTLESS	SLOOP	CAPE BANKS	1891	9.11	44	12	2.8
DAUNTLESS	SCHOONER	SMYRNA	1876	14.61	41.1	14.1	4.2
DAUNTLESS	SCREW STEAMER	SOUTH MILLS	1891	44.09	78.6	13.2	3.7
DAVID	SCHOONER	HYDE COUNTY	1741	40			
DAVID	SCHOONER	OCRACOKE		14			
DAVID H. SINMORD	SCHOONER	NEW BERN	1845	156	84	24	9
DAVID IRELAND	SCHOONER	CARTERET COUNTY	1854	153	88.5	25	8
DAVID J. DAY	SCHOONER	CRAVEN COUNTY	1848	106	71	22	8
DAVIS	SCHOONER	NORTH CAROLINA	1801	78			

Name of Ship	Type of Ship	Shipbuilding Location	Year	Tons	Length	Width	Depth
DEB	SCHOONER	NEW BERN		6			
DEBORAH	SCHOONER	WASHINGTON	1822	68	66	20	5.92
DECATUR	SCHOONER	CURRITUCK COUNTY	1819	24	44	14.6	4.6
DEFENDER	SLOOP	RIVER LANDING	1896	8	37	15.3	3.5
DEFENDER	SHARPIE	SMYRNA	1902	10	44	12.6	3
DEFIANCE	SCHOONER	FRANK CREEK	1827	36	51	15.1	5
DEFIANCE	GAS SCREW	MOREHEAD CITY	1903	6	38	9.8	2.4
DEFIANCE	SCHOONER	SMYRNA	1883	9.65	38.5	12	3.3
DELIA	BRIG	MARTIN COUNTY	1798	122			
DELIGHT	SCHOONER	MARTIN POINT	1823	56	47.58	19	6.08
DELIGHT	SCHOONER	PORT ROANOKE	1727	20			
DELMAR	SCHOONER	NEW BERN		73			
DELTA	SCHOONER	HYDE COUNTY	1878	7.11			
DENOBIA	SCHOONER	NEW BERN	1845	26	46	15	4
DEPENDENT	GAS SCREW	WASHINGTON	1912	14	55	14	4
DESPATCH	SCHOONER	BEAUFORT	1823	57	52	17.42	6
DESPATCH	SCHOONER	BOGUE INLET	1823	35.64	52	17.46	4.66
DEWEY	SCHOONER	SMYRNA	1898	20	59	16	4
DEXTER	SCHOONER	HATTERAS	1880	6.43	34	9.4	3
DEZWAY	GAS SCREW	BLOUNTS CREEK	1908	13	32	11	2.8
DEZZIE B. ONSLOW	SCHOONER	HATTERAS	1877	28.46			
DIADEM	SCHOONER	SOUTH RIVER	1892	9.62	47.3	12.7	3.1
DIAMOND	SCHOONER	ALBEMARLE	1881	9			
DIAMOND	SCHOONER	NORTH CAROLINA	1774	30			
DIAMOND A	PADDLE-WHEEL STEAMER	AVOCA	1881	8.66	52.2	11.9	2.3
DIAMOND C	PADDLE-WHEEL STEAMER	AVOCA	1881	9.32	56	13.1	2.1
DIANA	BRIG	CARTERET COUNTY	1807	160			
DIANA	SHIP	CORE SOUND	1795	200	83	23	
DICK	SCHOONER	NEW BERN	1795	75			
DICKIE BIRD	SCHOONER	MOREHEAD CITY	1892	5	41.5	11.5	2.8
DICTATOR	SLOOP	WOODVILLE	1884	9	35.9	13.4	3.7
DILLIGENCE	SLOOP	NORTH CAROLINA	1722	12			
DIME	SCHOONER	NEW BERN		10			
DIME	SCHOONER	STRAITS	1868	7.81	39.8	10.5	2.8
DISPATCH	SCHOONER	NORTH CAROLINA	1764	30			

Name of Ship	Type of Ship	Shipbuilding Location	Year	Tons	Length	Width	Depth
DISPATCH	BRIG	NORTH CAROLINA	1788	100			
DISPATCH	SCHOONER	NORTH CAROLINA	1802	68			
DISPATCH	BRIG	PERQUIMANS COUNTY	1786	151			
DIXIE	SCREW STEAMER	GOLDSBORO	1895	29.55	55	16.3	3.8
DIXIE	GAS SCREW	KITTY HAWK	1906	8	40	8	2.9
DIXIE	GAS SCREW	NEW BERN	1908	10	36	9.8	4.9
DIXON SWINDELL	SCHOONER	CARTERET COUNTY	1850	43	62.42	17.17	4.58
DOLLY VARDEN	SCHOONER	SMITHVILLE	1873	23.59			
DOLPHIN	SCHOONER	BAY RIVER	1856	7	37.2	11	2.8
DOLPHIN	SLOOP	BEAUFORT	1845	37	57	17.9	
DOLPHIN	SCHOONER	BEAUFORT	1845	73			
DOLPHIN	SLOOP	BEAUFORT COUNTY	1845	33	47	17	5
DOLPHIN	SCHOONER	CARTERET COUNTY	1843	92	71	21	7
DOLPHIN	SCHOONER	CARTERET COUNTY	1851	51	66	17	5
DOLPHIN	PADDLE-WHEEL STEAMER	COLERAIN	1896	10.03	54	12	1.09
DOLPHIN	SLOOP	ELIZABETH CITY		8			
DOLPHIN	GAS SCREW	MOREHEAD CITY	1903	7	37	11	2.7
DOLPHIN	SCHOONER	NELSON BAY	1872	7.42	31.8	10	13
DOLPHIN	SCHOONER	NEW BERN	1806	39			
DOLPHIN	SCHOONER	NEW BERN	1865	9	40.6	11.5	3.3
DOLPHIN	SCHOONER	NEW BERN	1866	11.07			
DOLPHIN		NORTH CAROLINA	1754	35			
DOLPHIN	SCHOONER	NORTH CAROLINA	1770	17			
DOLPHIN	SLOOP	NORTH CAROLINA	1773	12			
DOLPHIN	SCHOONER	NORTH CAROLINA	1786	10			
DOLPHIN	SCHOONER	NORTH CAROLINA	1788	18			
DOLPHIN	SCHOONER	PAMLICO		9			
DOLPHIN	SCHOONER	WASHINGTON		6			
DOLPHIN	PADDLE-WHEEL STEAMER	WILMINGTON	1891	15.3	58.5	10.7	2.5

Name of Ship	Type of Ship	Shipbuilding Location	Year	Tons	Length	Width	Depth
DOLPHINE	SCHOONER	CARTERET COUNTY	1845	93	71	22	7
DOMESTIC	SCHOONER	NEW BERN		13			
DONALD H. WARNER	SLOOP	BELHAVEN	1900	9	43	14	3
DORA	SCHOONER	BELHAVEN	1899	20	53	16	4
DORCAS AND ELIZA	SCHOONER	EDENTON	1849	28	47	15	4
DOREEN AND HANNAH	SLOOP	WILMINGTON	1746	14			
DORIE B.	SCHOONER	PINEY POINT	1888	5	32.1	9.2	2.9
DOROTHY	GAS SCREW	ELIZABETH CITY	1908	14	50	12	6.5
DOVE	BRIG	BRUNSWICK	1773	95			
DOVE	SCHOONER	ELIZABETH CITY		7			
DOVE	SLOOP	NORTH CAROLINA	1756	5			
DREADNAUGHT	SHARPIE	OCRACOKE	1888	8	36	12.2	3.6
DRED	SCHOONER	BEAUFORT		5			
DRUDGE	SCHOONER	NORTH CAROLINA	1749	20			
DUNCAN	SCHOONER	COLINGTON	1904	6	32	11	3
DUNCAN MCRAE	SIDE-WHEEL STEAMER	WILMINGTON	1835	215			
DUNLUCE	SHIP	NORTH CAROLINA	1761	125			
DUPLIN	PADDLE-WHEEL STEAMER	CHINQUAPIN	1904	59	69	20	3.8
E AND S	SCHOONER	WILMINGTON	1895	7.35	43.5	9.5	2.8
E. AND M. J. SIMPSON	SCHOONER	EDENTON	1857	50			
E. CHARLEY	SCHOONER	HUNTING QUARTERS	1876	8	40.5	12.8	3.7
E. FRANCES	SCHOONER	ELIZABETH CITY		12			
E. FRANCIS	SCHOONER	CORE SOUND	1857	15	41	14	3
E. FRANCIS	SCHOONER	HARBOR ISLAND	1871	30			
E. HUBBS	SCHOONER	DARE COUNTY	1874	24			
E. PERKINS	BRIG	CONWAYBORO	1854	176			
E. PETERSON	SCHOONER	BLOUNTS CREEK	1891	8	34	10.7	3
E. WHEELER	SCHOONER	PINEY POINT	1881	11.23	38.5	13	3.1
E.A. HARVIS	SCHOONER	POINT CASWELL	1895	107			
E.A. HAWES	PADDLE-WHEEL STEAMER	POINT CASWELL	1895	106.99	78.4	18.8	3.7
E.B. DANIELS	SCHOONER	ROANOKE ISLAND	1899	16	60	14	3.4
E.B. SHULL	SCHOONER	BEAUFORT	1898	9	42	12	3.2

Name of Ship	Type of Ship	Shipbuilding Location	Year	Tons	Length	Width	Depth
E.K. BISHOP	SCREW STEAMER	NEW BERN	1902	44	71	19	4.5
E.K. WILLIS	SCHOONER	OCRACOKE	1893	15	46	12	4
E.L. MYER	SCHOONER	HATTERAS	1869	18	45	15	4
E.M. SHORT	SCREW STEAMER	WASHINGTON	1899	27	52	14	3.7
E.M. TILLEY	SCHOONER	WASHINGTON	1891	15.05	53	17.5	3.7
E.M.J. BETTY	SCHOONER	HATTERAS	1868	25.05	50.6	15.8	5.2
E.R. DANIELS	BRIGANTINE	ROANOKE ISLAND	1899	16	60	14	3
E.W. BRADLEY	SCHOONER	NEW BERN	1840	83	69	21	7
EAGLE	SCHOONER	BAY RIVER	1834	44.79	63.33	17.92	5.58
EAGLE	BRIG	BEAUFORT	1792	104			
EAGLE	BRIG	CRAVEN COUNTY	1800	135			
EAGLE	SCHOONER	CRAWFORD		12			
EAGLE	SCHOONER	ELIZABETH CITY	1842	60.51	75.5	17.5	5.33
EAGLE	SCHOONER	MOREHEAD CITY	1901	9	43	11.7	2
EAGLE	GAS SCREW	MOREHEAD CITY	1907	26	57	13	3.9
EAGLE	SNOW	NORTH CAROLINA	1752	112			
EAGLE	SCHOONER	NORTH CAROLINA	1798	72			
EARL	SCHOONER	TYRRELL COUNTY	1793	66			
EARL GRANVILLE	SNOW	PERQUIMANS COUNTY	1749	60			
EARLE	SCHOONER	SMYRNA	1892	14.5	51.2	14.4	3.3
EARLINE	GAS SCREW	BEAUFORT	1910	14	46	15	3
ECLIPSE	SCHOONER	BEAUFORT	1823	31	52	15	5
ECORSE	SCREW STEAMER	ELIZABETH CITY	1908	52	60	18	8.6
EDENTON	SCHOONER	CARTERET COUNTY	1832	28	51	13	4
EDENTON	SCHOONER	EDENTON	1789	65			
EDGECOMBE	SCREW STEAMER	LEECHVILLE	1877	52.9			
EDINBURGH	BRIG	WILMINGTON	1762	65			
EDITH	SCHOONER	HATTERAS	1896	23.72	52.6	14.8	3.9
EDITH CLARK	SLOOP	LOWLAND	1908	6	28	11	3
EDMOND PARKIM	SCREW STEAMER	NEW BERN	1898	20.88	60	16.3	5.2
EDMUND D. MCNAIR	SIDE-WHEEL STEAMER	WASHINGTON	1835	71	83	16	5
EDMUND F. HANKS	PADDLE-WHEEL	PLYMOUTH	1848	42	58	17	4.1

Name of Ship	Type of Ship	Shipbuilding Location	Year	Tons	Length	Width	Depth
EDNA	SLOOP	HARKER'S ISLAND	1890	5.53	36.4	10	2.8
EDNA	SCHOONER	SMYRNA	1903	9	43	12	3
EDWARD	BRIG	NORTH CAROLINA	1773	60			
EDWARD B. DUDLEY	SCHOONER	SMITHVILLE	1837	25	45	13	5
EDWARD G. WILLIAMS	SCHOONER	ELIZABETH CITY	1832	49	61	17	5
EDWARD R. GILMAN	GAS SCREW	MOREHEAD CITY	1909	14	58	14	2.5
EDWARD STANLEY	SCHOONER	BEAUFORT COUNTY	1838	21	42	14	4
EDWARD TILLETT	BRIG	CURRITUCK COUNTY	1845	170	87	24	9
EDWIN	BRIG	BEAUFORT COUNTY	1811	162	78	25	
EDWIN	SCHOONER	BERTIE COUNTY	1907	11	43	12	2.5
EDWIN	SCHOONER	CARTERET COUNTY	1853	68	70.75	20.5	5.42
EDWIN & SAMUEL	SCHOONER	CARTERET COUNTY	1854	30	44.92	16.17	4.42
EFFIE M. GILLIKIN	SLOOP	NORTH CAROLINA	1728	10			
EFFIE M. GILLIKIN	SCHOONER	SMYRNA	1900	16	50	16	3.6
EIXON SWINDELL	SCHOONER	CARTERET COUNTY	1850	83	62	17	5
ELDRIDGE	SCOW	STELLA	1892	30.25			
ELGIN	SCHOONER	WASHINGTON	1891	41.64	59	16	4
ELI HOGH	SCHOONER	BEAUFORT COUNTY	1832	110	73	22	7
ELIHU A. WHITE	SCHOONER	BEAUFORT	1890	11.48	46	13.8	3.2
ELIJAH	SCHOONER	PLYMOUTH	1833	40	63	15	3.1
ELIJAH PIGOT	SCHOONER	CARTERET COUNTY	1807	128			
ELIJAH PIGOTT	SCHOONER	CARTERET COUNTY	1835	44	57	17.6	5.2
ELIPSE	SCHOONER	BEAUFORT	1823	36	52	15	5
ELISHA WATERS	SCHOONER	WASHINGTON	1857	134			
ELIZ. AND JOSANNA	SLOOP	NORTH CAROLINA	1729	25			
ELIZA	SCHOONER	CRAVEN COUNTY	1800	99			
ELIZA	BRIG	CRAVEN COUNTY	1806	140.58	75.25	22.83	9.5
ELIZA	SCHOONER	CURRITUCK COUNTY	1812	80	61	21	7
ELIZA	SCHOONER	JARROTS BAY	1821	67	62	19	6
ELIZA	SCHOONER	NORTH CAROLINA	1785	113	76	19	8
ELIZA	BRIG	NORTH CAROLINA	1793	114			

Name of Ship	Type of Ship	Shipbuilding Location	Year	Tons	Length	Width	Depth
ELIZA	BRIG	WILMINGTON	1824	181	81	22	11
ELIZA & DORCAS	SCHOONER	OCRACOKE	1816	68	57	19	7
ELIZA AND SUSAN	SHIP	WILMINGTON	1833	316			
ELIZA ANN	SCHOONER	BERTIE COUNTY	1815	51.52	64	17.08	5.33
ELIZA ANN	SCHOONER	CARTERET COUNTY	1814	96.43	67.92	20.83	8.08
ELIZA ANN	SLOOP	CURRITUCK COUNTY	1826	28	46.5	16	4.5
ELIZA ANN WALKER	SCHOONER	TYRRELL COUNTY	1841	39	44	17	5
ELIZA ELLEN	SLOOP	HATTERAS	1883	9.92	42.5	12.5	3.6
ELIZA LORD	BRIG	SWANSBOROUGH	1810	159			
ELIZABETH	SCHOONER	BEAUFORT	1850	84	72	23	6
ELIZABETH	SCHOONER	CARTERET COUNTY	1848	49	62	17.6	5.3
ELIZABETH	SCHOONER	CRAVEN COUNTY	1841	33	51	17	5
ELIZABETH	SCHOONER	EDENTON	1788	60			
ELIZABETH	BRIG	FAYETTEVILLE	1829	115	77	19	8
ELIZABETH	SCHOONER	HUNTING QUARTERS	1883	11.72	39	13	3.5
ELIZABETH	SCHOONER	MARTIN COUNTY	1792	31	47	13	5
ELIZABETH		NEW BERN	1910	90	40	9.4	5.8
ELIZABETH	SLOOP	NORTH CAROLINA	1712				
ELIZABETH	SHALLOP	NORTH CAROLINA	1726	4			
ELIZABETH		NORTH CAROLINA	1734	70			
ELIZABETH	BRIG	NORTH CAROLINA	1748	75			
ELIZABETH	SLOOP	NORTH CAROLINA	1752	10			
ELIZABETH	SCHOONER	PORTSMOUTH	1826	75	61	20	7
ELIZABETH	SCHOONER	ROANOKE	1770	45			
ELIZABETH AND SARAH	SCHOONER	NORTH CAROLINA	1741	12			
ELIZABETH AND SUSANNA	SLOOP	NORTH CAROLINA	1729	25			
ELIZABETH ANN	SCHOONER	CARTERET COUNTY	1842	92	72	21	6
ELIZABETH COWELL	SCHOONER	CURRITUCK COUNTY	1853	120			
ELK	SIDE-WHEEL STEAMER	WILMINGTON	1892	19.88	58	11.2	3
ELLA	SCHOONER	BEAUFORT	1856	31	52.5	16	4.33

Name of Ship	Type of Ship	Shipbuilding Location	Year	Tons	Length	Width	Depth
ELLA	SCHOONER	BEAUFORT	1862	13.74	29.04	9.01	3.03
ELLA	SCHOONER	ELIZABETH CITY		24			
ELLA	SCHOONER	KINNAKEET	1883	7.07	36.5	13.9	3.8
ELLA	SCHOONER	NEW BERN	1880	6.31	37	12	3.1
ELLA	SIDE-WHEEL STEAMER	WASHINGTON	1888	30.9	54.4	12.2	5.4
ELLA	SCHOONER	WILMINGTON	1850	91.69	68.75	22.17	7.08
ELLA CREEF	SCHOONER	MANTEO	1884	8.79	37	14	3
ELLA CROSBY	SCHOONER	ROANOKE ISLAND	1894	16.51	60.7	16.3	3.4
ELLA G	GAS SCREW	KITTY HAWK	1906	9	36	10	6.4
ELLA GRAY	SLOOP	SMYRNA	1892	8.16	44.2	11.4	2.7
ELLA HORTON	SCHOONER	MOREHEAD CITY	1888	6.81	42.4	10	3
ELLA MAE	SLOOP	CROATAN	1902	6	32	11	3
ELLA MAY	SCHOONER	HATTERAS	1873	8.36	42	12.8	3.2
ELLA MAY	SCHOONER	SMYRNA	1894	8.8	43.2	12	3
ELLA MAY	GAS SCREW	WEEKSVILLE	1908	5	30	8	5.8
ELLA MYRTLE	SCHOONER	STRAITS	1898	20	48	17	4.4
ELLA R. HILL	SCHOONER	BEAUFORT	1873	71.86	71.4	23	6.6
ELLA S. HENDERSON	SLOOP	BELHAVEN	1902	9	47	15.8	3.5
ELLA T. NELSON	SCHOONER	MOREHEAD CITY	1902	9	47	15	2.6
ELLEN DOUGLAS	SCHOONER	CARTERET COUNTY	1834	88	67.66	20.42	7.33
ELLES S.	SCREW STEAMER	NEW BERN	1904	87	69	21	8
ELLINOR	SCHOONER	OTTER CREEK	1777				
ELMSLEY	SCHOONER	CURRITUCK NARROWS	1801	20			
ELOISE	SCHOONER	NEW BERN	1908	38	59	18	9
ELOISE	SCREW STEAMER	WASHINGTON	1913	71	67	15	4.9
ELSIE		NORTH CAROLINA	1888	5	47	11	6
ELSIE	STEAM LAUNCH	WILLIAMSTON	1880	4.9	46	10	6
ELSIE W.	GAS SCREW	BELHAVEN	1910	14	40	12	6.3
EMANDELL	GAS SCREW	ELIZABETH CITY	1913	11	43	11	3.1
EMBLEM	SCHOONER	BEAUFORT		32			
EMELINE	SCHOONER	CARTERET COUNTY	1853	34	51.83	17.17	4.58
EMELINE	SCHOONER	HOG ISLAND	1871	10.64	37.3	13.3	3.5
EMELINE	SCHOONER	HYDE COUNTY	1839	32	48	15	
EMELINE	SCHOONER	STRAITS OF CARTARET	1823	35	50.17	15.92	5

Name of Ship	Type of Ship	Shipbuilding Location	Year	Tons	Length	Width	Depth
EMERALD	SCHOONER	BACON	1818	105	79	20	7
EMERALD	SCHOONER	GAR BACON	1818	92	69.17	20.75	6.66
EMERALD	SCHOONER	HATTERAS	1869	10.31	37	13.3	3.7
EMILE AND ELIZA	SCHOONER	CURRITUCK SOUND	1816	57.22	47.25	19.33	4.87
EMILIE	SCHOONER	BEAUFORT	1866	11.4	41	13.4	3.4
EMILIE	SCHOONER	BEAUFORT	1880	9.07			
EMILY	SCHOONER	BEAUFORT	1850	145			
EMILY	SCHOONER	CRAVEN COUNTY	1851	85	72	21.25	6.42
EMILY	SCHOONER	DAILYS LANDING	1814	48.63	54	17.03	6
EMMA	SLOOP	DAVIS	1868	13	39	13	3
EMMA	SLOOP	ELIZABETH CITY	1868	13.62	39	13	3
EMMA	SLOOP	ELIZABETH CITY		5			
EMMA	SCHOONER	NEW BERN		12			
EMMA	SCREW STEAMER	WILMINGTON	1899	18	58	13	4.5
EMMA AND ELIZABETH	SCHOONER	NEW BERN	1853	119			
EMMA ELIZABETH	SCHOONER	NEW BERN	1858	112	91	23	6
EMMA J.	SHARPIE	DAVIS	1905	10	42	13	3.2
EMMA JULIA	SCHOONER	CARTERET COUNTY	1842	99	71	22	8
EMMA S.	SCHOONER	NEW BERN	1893	7.04	33	11	3.7
EMMELINE	SCHOONER	HYDE COUNTY	1819	84	64	20	7
EMPIRE	SCHOONER	ELIZABETH CITY	1847	57	70	17	5
EMPIRE	SCHOONER	ELIZABETH CITY	1857	61	72	17	5
EMPRESS	GAS SCREW	ATLANTIC	1914	10	38	8.2	2.9
EMPRESS	GAS SCREW	WIT	1911	6	33	9	2.7
EMULAUS	SCHOONER	JARROTS BAY	1826	96	68	21	8
ENCORE	SCHOONER	CEDAR ISLAND	1875	16.63	42.3	14.6	4.1
ENCORE	SCHOONER	SWAN QUARTER	1833	48	52	17	5
ENDEAVER	SLOOP	NORTH CAROLINA	1725	5			
ENDEAVOR		NORTH CAROLINA	1789	60			
ENDEAVOR	SCHOONER	ROANOKE	1753	10			
ENDEAVOUR		LITTLE RIVER	1720				
ENDEAVOUR	SCHOONER	NORTH CAROLINA	1786	10			
ENDEAVOUR	SCHOONER	PORT ROANOKE	1753	10			
ENERGY	SLOOP	NEW BERN		29			
ENID AND THOMAS	SCHOONER	NORTH CAROLINA	1728	10			

Name of Ship	Type of Ship	Shipbuilding Location	Year	Tons	Length	Width	Depth
ENTERED APPRENTICE	SLOOP	CURRITUCK NARROWS	1826	59	55	18.08	6.1
ENTERPRISE	SCREW STEAMER	CAMDEN COUNTY	1879	51	77.3	14.5	8
ENTERPRISE	BRIG	CARTERET COUNTY	1821	94			
ENTERPRISE	SLOOP	CURRITUCK COUNTY	1825	21	44	14	4
ENTERPRISE	SCHOONER	ELIZABETH CITY		7			
ENTERPRISE	SCHOONER	NEW RIVER	1859	37	51.75	18	4
ENTERPRISE	SCHOONER	STRAITS OF CARTERET	1821	77.2	67	21.66	6.37
ENTERPRISE	SLOOP	SWANSBOROUGH	1830	31	50	15	4
ERAH	GAS SCREW	ATLANTIC	1914	9	40	9	3.9
ERNEST	SCHONER	BEAUFORT		14			
ESSEN	SCHOONER	STRAITS OF CARTERET	1828	45	52	19	6
ESSEX	SCHOONER	CEDAR ISLAND	1868	10.47			
ESSEX	SCHOONER	HUNTING QUARTERS	1887	22.35	49.6	17	4.6
ESSEX	SCHOONER	ROANOKE ISLAND	1819	58.75	59.42	18.5	6.25
ESTELLE	SCHOONER	WASHINGTON	1892	10.97	35	11.6	3.8
ESTHER	SCHOONER	NEW TOPSAIL	1792	46			
ESTHER	SLOOP	TYRRELL COUNTY	1815	54.78	54	18.75	6.5
ESTHER	SCHOONER		1890	11	41.7	11.6	2.2
ESTHER MAY	SCHOONER	SOUTHPORT	1899	9	41	11	3.4
ETHEL	SCHOONER	LOWLAND	1894	10.72	37.8	12	3.2
ETHEL	SCHOONER	WASHINGTON	1901	98	119	27	4
ETHEL P. NELSON	SCHOONER	ELIZABETH CITY	1901	13	59	17	5
ETHEL P. NELSON	SCHOONER	MOREHEAD CITY	1904	13	47	13.9	3
ETHER	SCHOONER	NEW BERN	1902	16	47	15	4.6
ETHER M. WRIGHT	SCHOONER	ELIZABETH CITY	1901	22	59	17.9	5.3
ETTA	SCHOONER	SWANSBOROUGH	1870	37.83			
ETTA T. WESTON	SCHOONER	WASHINGTON	1884	12	38.2	12.2	3.2
EUDORA T. WALLACE	SCHOONER	MOREHEAD CITY	1901	6	39	12	3
EUGENE	SCHOONER	CARTERET COUNTY	1846	27	50	15	4
EUGENE	SCHOONER	ELIZABETH CITY	1865	20.05	50	15.04	4.1
EUGENE	SLOOP	KITTY HAWK	1891	8.27	30	9.5	3.4
EUGENE	SCHOONER	SWANSBORO	1833	95	68	21	7
EUGENIE	SCHOONER	HATTERAS	1869	6			
EUGENIE	SCHOONER	SMYRNA	1904	11	46	13	2.7
EULA C.	SLOOP	WYSOCKING	1909	6	35.2	13.5	3.4

Name of Ship	Type of Ship	Shipbuilding Location	Year	Tons	Length	Width	Depth
EULA K.	SCHOONER	ELIZABETH CITY	1902	13	50	16	4.6
EUNICE	GAS SCREW	ELIZABETH CITY	1907	12	43	13	4
EUNICE REYNOLDS	SCHOONER	BRUNSWICK COUNTY	1877	35.55	55	22	5
EUREKA	SCHOONER	NEW BERN	1881	6.28			
EURORA T. WALLACE	SHARPIE	MOREHEAD CITY	1901	6	39.8	12	3
EVA	GAS SCREW	BELHAVEN	1908	13	50	13	3
EVA M.	SLOOP	BELHAVEN	1903	7	31	13	3
EVA MAY	SCHOONER	SMYRNA	1899	17	53	15	3.3
EVA PEARL	SCHOONER	MOREHEAD CITY	1905	10	47	14	2.6
EVELENE	SCHOONER	HATTERAS	1876	8.16	36.4	12.3	3.6
EVELINE	SCHOONER	WASHINGTON	1884	19.93	43.06	17.2	4.4
EVELYN	SLOOP	SMYRNA	1891	6.25	43.7	11	2.9
EVERGREEN	SIDE-WHEEL STEAMER	FAYETTEVILLE	1846	160	121	22	6
EVILENA	SCHOONER	HATTERAS	1876	8.16	36		
EXCELSIOR	SCREW STEAMER	WILMINGTON	1884	33.26			
EXCHANGE	SCHOONER	NEW BERN	1833	149	78	24	9
EXERTION	SCHOONER	CRAVEN COUNTY	1807	71			
EXPERIMENT	BRIG	BEAUFORT	1792	107			
EXPERIMENT	SCHOONER	BEAUFORT COUNTY	1808	103	79.5	22	6.8
EXPERIMENT	SLOOP	BRUNSWICK	1773	12			
EXPERIMENT	SCHOONER	JARROTS BAY	1824	45	56	19	5
EXPRESS	SCHOONER	HYDE COUNTY	1848	27	48	15	4
EXPRESS	SLOOP	WASHINGTON		22			
EXPRESS	SCHOONER	WASHINGTON		9			
EXTENUATE	SCHOONER	ELIZABETH CITY		38			
F AND F	SCREW STEAMER	WILMINGTON	1892	24.11	53.4	13.2	3.8
F. MICHELSON	SCHOONER	STRAITS	1825	113	69	22	9
F.J. BROWER	SCHOONER	NORTH CAROLINA	1850	25.24	49.5	14.75	4
F.L. KING	SCHOONER	CARTERET COUNTY	1837	20	40.5	13.66	5
F.M. ISABELLA	SCHOONER	KINNAKEET	1883	9.13	41	12.1	2.8
FAIR	SCHOONER	HYDE COUNTY	1859	20	39	13	4.58
FAIR	SCHOONER	WASHINGTON		20			
FAIR AMERICAN	SHIP	CRAVEN COUNTY	1797	162.5	75	22.83	11
FAIR AMERICAN	SCHOONER	CRAVEN COUNTY	1805	113	75	21	8
FAIR AMERICAN		HERTFORD	1779	170			
FAIR AMERICAN	SCHOONER	NEW BERN	1800	113			

Name of Ship	Type of Ship	Shipbuilding Location	Year	Tons	Length	Width	Depth
FAIR AMERICAN	SCHOONER	PASQUOTANK RIVER	1810				
FAIR AMERICAN	BRIG	PERQUIMANS COUNTY	1798	149			
FAIR AMERICAN	BRIG	SMITHS CREEK	1797	139	75	22	10
FAIR OF WASHINGTON	SCHOONER	HYDE COUNTY	1859	20	39	14	
FAIR PLAY	SCHOONER	HERTFORD COUNTY	1796	117			
FAIRFIELD	SCHOONER	STRAITS	1867	39.29	61.9	18.7	4.9
FAIRY	SIDE-WHEEL STEAMER	NEW BERN	1851	54	81	15	4
FAME	BRIG	SWANSBOROUGH	1794	95.5			
FANCY	SCHOONER	NORTH CAROLINA	1795	59			
FANNIE	SCHOONER	BEAUFORT	1888	6.46	41.4	9.9	2.4
FANNIE	SCHOONER	SMYRNA	1886	7.95	44.2	10.3	2.6
FANNIE BREVARD	SLOOP	NORTH RIVER	1894	9.15	48	13	3.6
FANNY	SCHOONER	CRAVEN COUNTY	1807	53			
FANNY	SCHOONER	CRAVEN COUNTY	1817	96	67	21	8
FANNY	SLOOP	NEW BERN	1785	50			
FANNY	SLOOP	NORTH CAROLINA	1751	13			
FANNY	BRIG	NORTH CAROLINA	1773	90			
FANNY	BRIG	NORTH CAROLINA	1788	40			
FANNY	SCHOONER	NORTH CAROLINA	1793	31			
FANNY	SCHOONER	NORTH CAROLINA	1795	59			
FANNY	SCHOONER	NORTH CAROLINA		15			
FANNY	BRIG	PUNGO	1789	67			
FANNY	SCHOONER	ROANOKE ISLAND	1796	47.36	42	17.5	6.25
FANNY AND PATSY	SCHOONER	COINJOCK BAY	1816	66.06	59.66	21	6.33
FANNY LEE	SCHOONER	BEAUFORT	1850	91			
FANNY LUTTERLOH	SIDE-WHEEL STEAMER	FAYETTEVILLE	1852	50	100	15	3.5
FARMER	SCHOONER	CHOWAN COUNTY	1802	70			
FARMER	SCHOONER	EDENTON	1802	70			
FARMER	SCHOONER	NEW RIVER	1831	44	45	17	5

Name of Ship	Type of Ship	Shipbuilding Location	Year	Tons	Length	Width	Depth
FARMER	PADDLE-WHEEL STEAMER	WILMINGTON	1903	99	101	21	4.9
FARMERS DAUGHTER	SCHOONER	POWELLS POINT	1816	63.7	59	19	6
FARMERS FANCY	SCHOONER	NORTH CAROLINA	1811	19.24	37.08	14.08	4.58
FAV0RITE	BRIG	CURRITUCK COUNTY	1827	118.33	68.5	22	9.25
FAVORITE	SCHOONER	SMYRNA	1886	9.09	34	11.6	3
FAVOURITE	SCHOONER	COINJOCK BAY	1801	73			
FAWN	SCREW STEAMER	SWANSBORO	1900	42	76	16	4
FAYETTEVILLE	SIDE-WHEEL STEAMER	FAYETTEVILLE	1852	264			
FEDERALIST	SCHOONER	CHOWAN COUNTY	1810	48.64	52	17.33	6.42
FERRATA	SCHOONER	SMITHVILLE		36			
FILENA	SCHOONER	KITTY HAWK	1893	26.29	54	17	3.4
FIRE FLY	SCHOONER	NEW BERN	1849	123			
FIRST ADVENTURE	SLOOP	CAPE FEAR RIVER	1727	10			
FISH HAWK	PADDLE-WHEEL STEAMER	EDENTON	1893	13.15	55.8	13.2	2.1
FISH HAWK	GAS SCREW	MOREHEAD CITY	1901	11	45	12	3
FISH HAWK	SLOOP	NEW BERN	1819	24.2	39.92	13	5.17
FISHERMAN	PADDLE-WHEEL STEAMER	EDENTON	1883	11.66			
FLASH	SCHOONER	BEAUFORT	1875	9.19	37.4	12.2	3.4
FLASH	SLOOP	WILMINGTON		17			
FLORA	SCHOONER	BEAUFORT		8			
FLORA	BRIG	ELIZABETH CITY	1831	158	96.58	24.92	13.58
FLORA	SCHOONER	WASHINGTON		14			
FLORENCE	SCHOONER	BEAUFORT	1872	38.87			
FLORENCE	SCREW STEAMER	NEW BERN	1883	8.58			
FLORENCE	SCHOONER	NEW BERN		39			
FLORENCE	SLOOP	NEW BERN		7			
FLORENCE	SLOOP	PAMLICO	1878	6.81			
FLORENCE	SCREW STEAMER	WASHINGTON	1896	20	48	12	4
FLORENCE	GAS SCREW	WILLISTON	1913	10	36	10	3
FLORENCE ELSIE	SLOOP	DAVIS	1900	7	34	14	3
FLORIDA	SCHOONER	NORTH CAROLINA	1765	40			

Name of Ship	Type of Ship	Shipbuilding Location	Year	Tons	Length	Width	Depth
FLOSSIE D. LEE	SCHOONER	DURHAM CREEK	1895	18.55	47	14.9	4.5
FLY	SCHOONER	BEAUFORT	1833	20	46	12.83	3.92
FLY	SLOOP	HERTFORD	1902	5	39.6	11.4	2.7
FLYING FISH		NORTH CAROLINA	1760	15			
FLYING FISH	SLOOP	NORTH CAROLINA	1789	35	51	17	4
FODARALYT	BRIG	NORTH CAROLINA	1797	119			
FORBES AND HUBBARD	SCHOONER	OLD TRAP	1902	7	40	13.7	3
FORETOMAN	SCHOONER	LANCASTER	1797	53			
FORT LANDING	SCHOONER	TYRRELL COUNTY	1815	36.63	49.17	16	5.5
FOUR BROTHERS	SCHOONER	CHURCHES ISLAND	1824	23	43	15	4
FOX	SCREW STEAMER	ELIZABETH CITY	1861	13.82	44.3	9.8	1
FOX	SCHOONER	SMITHS CREEK	1828	20	43	13.75	4
FRANCES	SLOOP	NORTH CAROLINA	1772	60			
FRANCES	SCHOONER	WASHINGTON	1850	123	78	24	8
FRANCES	STEAMER	WASHINGTON	1896	20.16	48	12	4
FRANCES ANN	SCHOONER	WASHINGTON	1847	41	54.75	17.37	5
FRANCES ANN	SCHOONER	WINDSOR CREEK	1819	70	64	18	7
FRANCES CANADY	SCHOONER	CARTERET COUNTY	1834	58	63.25	17.58	6.08
FRANCES D. KENNEDY	SCHOONER	OCRACOKE ISLAND	1828	99	69	23	7
FRANCES J. DANIELS	SCHOONER	SMYRNA	1899	15	50	15	3.6
FRANCES NIXON	BRIG	PERQUIMANS COUNTY	1798	153			
FRANCIS	SLOOP	NORTH CAROLINA	1773	16			
FRANCIS JARVIS	BRIG	BEAUFORT	1820	137			
FRANCIS MARION	SCHOONER	BEAUFORT	1866	7	38.6	11	3.6
FRANCIS WITHERS	SCHOONER	STRAITS OF CARTERET	1829	69	69.42	18.83	6
FRANK	SLOOP	NEW RIVER	1886	5.94	38.5	10.6	2.8
FRANK PIGOT	SCHOONER	CARTERET COUNTY	1867	9.46	36	10	2.5
FRANK SESSOMS	PADDLE-WHEEL STEAMER	WILMINGTON	1894	79.31	86.6	22.8	3.6
FRANKLIN	SCHOONER	BEAUFORT COUNTY	1839	122	75	22	8
FRANKLIN		EDENTON	1778	50			

Name of Ship	Type of Ship	Shipbuilding Location	Year	Tons	Length	Width	Depth
FRANKLIN	SCHOONER	EDENTON	1785	104	70	19	8
FRANKLIN	SCHOONER	NORTH CAROLINA	1788	60			
FRANKLIN	SCHOONER	PERQUIMANS COUNTY	1799	93			
FRANKLIN	SCHOONER	STRAITS OF CORE SOUND	1825	81	63	20.75	7
FRANKLIN	SCHOONER	WASHINGTON	1820	92	69	2.6	7
FRANKLIN D. BELL	SCHOONER	AVON	1900	6	33	11	3
FRANKLIN PIERCE	SCREW STEAMER	SHALLOTTE	1902	36	57	16	4.2
FRED B. RICE	BRIG	WILMINGTON		253			
FRED W. JONES	SCHOONER	NEW BERN	1850	11.22	45.4	12.2	3.5
FREDDIE	SCHOONER	SMYRNA	1889	15.13	55.2	13.8	3.5
FREDERICK	SCHOONER	SWANSBOROUGH	1797	113			
FREDERICK LUNDY	GAS SCREW	MOREHEAD CITY	1912	45	61	19	5
FREEDOM	SCHOONER	CURRITUCK COUNTY	1813	27	44	14.66	4.1
FREEDOM	SCHOONER	MARE POINT	1794	26			
FREEDOM	SCHOONER	NORTH CAROLINA	1789	18			
FREEMAN ELLIS	SCHOONER	NORTH CAROLINA	1803	79			
FREEMASON	SHIP	NORTH CAROLINA	1753	132			
FREEMONT	SCHOONER	BAY RIVER	1848	278	103	28	10
FRIEND	SCHOONER	SMITHVILLE	1833	22	41	13	4
FRIENDS	BRIG	EDENTON	1781	50			
FRIENDS	SCHOONER	PORTSMOUTH		12			
FRIENDSHIP		BATH	1762	10			
FRIENDSHIP	SLOOP	BEAUFORT	1788	33			
FRIENDSHIP	SCHOONER	BEAUFORT	1846	31	51.25	15.83	4.42
FRIENDSHIP	SLOOP	CRAVEN COUNTY	1795	39	54	18	5
FRIENDSHIP	SCHOONER	CURRITUCK BANKS	1812	50	54	14.9	6
FRIENDSHIP	SCHOONER	HARKERS ISLAND	1828	34	51	16.25	4.83
FRIENDSHIP	BRIG	NORTH CAROLINA	1764	60			
FRIENDSHIP	SNOW	NORTH CAROLINA	1765	60			
FRIENDSHIP	SCHOONER	NORTH CAROLINA	1788	18			
FRIENDSHIP OF BEAUFORT	SLOOP	CARTERET COUNTY	1789	41	50	16	6
FULFORD	SCHOONER	BEAUFORT	1832	37	51.5	16.75	5.17

Name of Ship	Type of Ship	Shipbuilding Location	Year	Tons	Length	Width	Depth
G.F. DERICKSON	SCREW STEAMER	ELIZABETH CITY	1894	27.3	51	16	3.3
G.R. DIXON	SCREW	WASHINGTON	1854	209	16	27	8
G.W. WILLIAMS	SLOOP	HARLOWE	1904	6	38	9.9	2.5
GALLATIN	SCHOONER	SMITHFIELD	1813	54	51	17	8
GASPER	SCHOONER	PORT ROANOKE	1761	30			
GAZELLE	SCHOONER	NEW BERN	1892	46	60	14	5
GAZETTE	SLOOP	EDENTON	1750	35			
GEM	SLOOP	JARVISBURG	1884	6	23	11.8	2.6
GENERAL A. JACKSON	SLOOP	CURRITUCK COUNTY	1816	62	59	19	7
GENERAL BROWN	SCHOONER	BERTIE COUNTY	1815	89	70	20	6
GENERAL EHRINGHAUS	SCHOONER	ELIZABETH CITY	1853	105			
GENERAL GEORGE THOM	STEAM LAUNCH	WASHINGTON	1893	24	73	12.5	4.6
GENERAL GREEN	SCHOONER	NORTH CAROLINA	1788	100			
GENERAL H. G. WRIGHT	SNAG BOAT	WILMINGTON	1882	100	102	20	5
GENERAL HARRISON	SCHOONER	TYRRELL COUNTY	1841	26	45	14	4
GENERAL IREDELL	SCHOONER	PLYMOUTH	1822	98	71.5	22	7
GENERAL JACKSON	BRIG	CLUBFOOT CREEK	1812	192.69	70.33	24.42	11.75
GENERAL JACKSON	SCHOONER	CURRITUCK SOUND	1816	38.45	43	17	5
GENERAL JACKSON	SCHOONER	SMITHVILLE	1828	28	49	16.6	4.17
GENERAL SHIELDS	SCHOONER	NEW BERN		95			
GENERAL TAYLOR	SCHOONER	BEAUFORT		14			
GENERAL TAYLOR	SCHOONER	PORTSMOUTH	1849	22	46.5	13.17	4
GENERAL WASHINGTON	SHIP	EDENTON	1785	198			
GENERAL WASHINGTON	BRIG	NORTH CAROLINA	1788	125			
GENERAL WHITING	SCHOONER	WILMINGTON		12			
GENEVA MOORE	SCHOONER	STRAITS	1898	20	50	16	4.3
GENOA	SCHOONER	BEAUFORT		8			
GEORGE	SCHOONER	HYDE COUNTY	1800	124			
GEORGE	BRIG	NORTH CAROLINA	1786	135			
GEORGE	SCHOONER	NORTH CAROLINA	1800	120			
GEORGE DEVEREAUX	BRIG	SMITHS CREEK	1810	110	68	21	8
GEORGE HENRY	SCHOONER	CURRITUCK COUNTY	1847	112	77	23	7

Name of Ship	Type of Ship	Shipbuilding Location	Year	Tons	Length	Width	Depth
GEORGE HENRY	SCHOONER	HYDE COUNTY	1817	101	72	21	7
GEORGE L. LYON	GAS SCREW	MOREHEAD CITY	1904	8	43	11	2.7
GEORGE LORING	BRIG	ELIZABETH CITY	1828	136	76.5	22.83	9
GEORGE M. IVES	GAS SCREW	MOREHEAD CITY	1901	8	43	11	3.1
GEORGE PEABODY	SCHOONER	BEAUFORT		12			
GEORGE PICKETT	SCHOONER	CURRITUCK	1816	68	57.25	20.5	7
GEORGE POLLOCK	SCHOONER	CARTERET COUNTY	1832	96	71.25	21.42	7.42
GEORGE R. DIXON	SCHOONER	WASHINGTON	1855	206			
GEORGE ROBERTS	GAS SCREW	MOREHEAD CITY	1912	33	59	18	4.7
GEORGE SLOVER	SCHOONER	SMYRNA	1900	22	53	18	4
GEORGE W. DILL	SCHOONER	BEAUFORT	1865	112.67			
GEORGE W. RODGERS	SCHOONER	TYRRELL COUNTY	1834	47	66	16	5
GEORGE WASHINGTON	SCHOONER	CHURCHES ISLAND	1816	30.37	52	16.75	4.75
GEORGE WASHINGTON	SCHOONER	CURRITUCK NARROWS	1822	32	45	16.25	5.25
GEORGE WASHINGTON	SCHOONER	OCRACOKE	1823	48	57	18	6
GEORGE WASHINGTON	SLOOP	TYRRELL COUNTY	1815	54.79	54	18.75	6
GEORGE WASHINGTON	BRIG	WASHINGTON	1811	96			
GEORGIA	SCHOONER	LAUNCH	1857	38.22			
GEORGIA	GAS SCREW	MOREHEAD CITY	1902	9	41	12	2.8
GEORGIA A. GASKINS	GAS SCREW	ELIZABETH CITY	1903	13	51	14	3.4
GEORGIA BELLE	SCHOONER	MOREHEAD CITY	1885	7.36	42.6	10.6	2.8
GEORGIA T.	SCHOONER	SWANSBORO	1904	19	55	16	3
GEORGIANNA	SCHOONER	ELIZABETH CITY	1853	51	66	15	5
GERTIE		MOREHEAD CITY	1888		41.5		
GERTIE LORD	SCHOONER	MOREHEAD CITY	1888	6.21	41.6	10.4	2.9
GERTRUDE	GAS SCREW	BELHAVEN	1911	12	44	9	6.9
GERTRUDE	SCHOONER	MOREHEAD CITY	1895	9.09	43.6	11.2	3
GERTRUDE	SHARPIE	WIT	1902	15	48.6	15.1	3.8
GIDEON SPARROW	SCHOONER	SMITHS CREEK	1816	42	54	17.58	5.42
GILT EDGE	SCHOONER	HATTERAS	1888	10.74	40	13.8	3.3
GLADIATOR OF WASHINGTON	SLOOP	OCRACOKE	1851	21	39	15	3.58
GLADYS	GAS SCREW	BEAUFORT	1901	24	59	17	3.8
GLADYS	GAS SCREW	WIT	1908	9	33	9	4.26
GLEANER	SCHOONER	ADAMS CREEK	1813	190	67	22	8.75
GLEANER	SCHOONER	PLYMOUTH	1820	72	66	20	6
GLIDE	SCHOONER	NEW BERN	1898	11.46	46	13	3

Name of Ship	Type of Ship	Shipbuilding Location	Year	Tons	Length	Width	Depth
GLIDE	SCHOONER	WASHINGTON	1892	7.55	30	11.6	3
GLOBE	BRIG	ELIZABETH CITY	1830	97.75	83.5	24	11.33
GLOBE	SCHOONER	STRAITS OF CARTERET	1835	110	71	22	7
GOERNINE	SCHOONER	WILLIAMSTON	1857	180	97	24	8
GOLD HUNTER	SCHOONER	CARTERET COUNTY	1856	77	67.83	21.75	6.42
GOLD HUNTER	SCHOONER	CRAVEN COUNTY	1811	113	71	22	8
GOLD LEAF	SCHOONER	BEAUFORT	1875	13.62	42	13.7	3.5
GOLD LEAF	SCHOONER	HATTERAS	1867	15.78	46	15	3.7
GOLD MINE	SCHOONER	ATLANTIC	1891	11.93	39.4	13.9	3.6
GOLDEN ROD	PADDLE-WHEEL STEAMER	AVOCA	1893	14.15	50.7	10.6	2.9
GOLDSBORO	GAS SCREW	MOREHEAD CITY	1909	6	33	9	2.8
GOLDSBORO	SCREW STEAMER	WASHINGTON	1901	99	100	20.6	5
GOOD HOPE	SCHOONER	ELIZABETH CITY	1850	66	74	17	5
GOOD INTENT	SCHOONER	CARTERET COUNTY	1805	45	51	17	6
GOOD INTENT	SCHOONER	CHOWAN COUNTY	1788	72	62	17	7
GOOD INTENT	SCHOONER	NORTH CAROLINA	1780	8			
GOOD INTENT	SCHOONER	NORTH CAROLINA	1788	65			
GOOD INTENT	SLOOP	NORTH CAROLINA	1789	54.5	54.25	17	6.92
GOOD INTENT	SCHOONER	PASQUOTANK	1747	25			
GOODWIN	SCHOONER	CEDAR ISLAND	1867	12.17	40.3	12.7	3.6
GORDON	GAS SCREW	WILLISTON	1912	34	55	17.6	4.5
GOSPEL SHIP JOSEPH	GAS SCREW	WIT	1909	14	37	13	3
GOVENOR VANCE	SCHOONER	STRAITS	1876	17.38	42.9	14.3	3.6
GRACE GARNET	SCHOONER	EDENTON	1844	36	60	17	4
GRACE M. WALLACE	GAS SCREW	MOREHEAD CITY	1904	12	45	13	2.8
GRACIE	SCHOONER	SMYRNA	1893	7.86	44.6	11.3	2.6
GRACY	BRIG	NORTH CAROLINA	1795	139			
GRANARY	SCHOONER	HYDE COUNTY	1838	30	45	16	5
GRANGER	SLOOP	ELIZABETH CITY		8			
GREENCOCK	BRIG	NORTH CAROLINA	1765	70			
GREENFIELD	PADDLE-WHEEL STEAMER	DRUMMONDS	1887	8.38	56.9	11.5	1.9

Name of Ship	Type of Ship	Shipbuilding Location	Year	Tons	Length	Width	Depth
GREENVILLE	SCHOONER	HYDE COUNTY	1835	137	77	20	8
GRETCHEN	GAS SCREW	BELHAVEN	1902	11	42	12	3
GREYHOUND	PERRI-ANGER	MACHAPONGO RIVER	1727	3			
GREYHOUND	SCHOONER	NORTH CAROLINA	1771	12			
GREYHOUND	PERRI-AUGER	PASQUOTANK	1745	6			
GRUNCOCK	SCHOONER	NORTH CAROLINA	1765	70			
GUARD	SCHOONER	HYDE COUNTY	1847	22	42	14	4.5
GUERNSEY	SLOOP	EDENTON	1734	65			
GUIDE	SCHOONER	STRAITS OF CORE SOUND	1836	44	56	17	5
GUION	GAS SCREW	SMYRNA	1909	6	33	8	2.8
GUY	GAS SCREW	ELIZABETH CITY	1905	12	57	10	2.2
H. AND V. ROYAL		LOCKWOODS FOLLY	1903	14	47	14.7	3.9
H. HILL	SCHOONER	HUNTING QUARTERS	1889	7.82	36	10.5	3
H.B. LANE	SCHOONER	NEW BERN	1888	10.51	42	13.4	3.7
H.E. LEWIS	SCHOONER	TYRRELL COUNTY	1850	46	62	17	4.92
H.F. OSBORNE	SLOOP	ELIZABETH CITY		12			
H.G. WRIGHT	SNAG BOAT	WILMINGTON	1882	100	102	20.6	5
H.H. THOMPSON	SCHOONER	NEW BERN	1857	86	84	23	8
H.N.W.S. NAPOLEON	SCHOONER	NEW BERN	1857	193	120	28	8
H.P. BROWN	SCHOONER	AVON	1894	18.45	45	13.4	3.6
HADDIE BLANCH	GAS SCREW	SOUTHPORT	1901	15	46	14	3.5
HALCYONE	SIDE-WHEEL STEAMER	FAYETTEVILLE	1867	92.29			
HALCYONE	GAS SCREW	MOREHEAD CITY	1903	10	44	12	2.7
HALIFAX	SLOOP	PORT ROANOKE	1775	15			
HALLIFAX	SNOW	NORTH CAROLINA	1755	100			
HAMET RYAN	SCHOONER	EDENTON	1855	90	77	22	6
HAMPTON	BARGE	ELIZABETH CITY	1914	25.7			
HANNAH	BRIG	BEAUFORT	1827	150	77	24	9
HANNAH	SLOOP	NORTH CAROLINA	1759	45			
HANNAH	SCHOONER	SMYRNA	1891	5.83	35	10.06	3.3
HANNAH	BRIG	WILMINGTON	1773	100			
HANNAH WOOD	SCHOONER	SWANSBORO		11			
HANYEEN	SCHOONER	WASHINGTON	1856	48	55	16	5

Name of Ship	Type of Ship	Shipbuilding Location	Year	Tons	Length	Width	Depth
HAPPY COUPLE	SCHOONER	ELIZABETHTOWN	1805	130			
HAPPY COUPLE	SCHOONER	ROANOKE ISLAND	1799	30			
HAPPY GO LUCKY	SCHOONER	BLOUNTS CREEK	1888	7	34	9.5	4
HAPPY LUKE	BRIG	BATH	1734				
HAPPY RETURN	SCHOONER	HYDE COUNTY	1804	26	34	13	5
HAPPY RETURN	SLOOP	NORTH CAROLINA	1763	10			
HARBINGER	BRIG	SMITHS CREEK	1810	199			
HARIETT ELIZA	SCHOONER	CURRITUCK	1826	80	66.92	22.17	7
HARMINE	SCHOONER	BEAUFORT	1798	68			
HARMIT HARKER	SCHOONER	OCRACOKE	1848	23	46	14	4
HARMONY	SCHOONER	NORTH CAROLINA	1786	79			
HARNETT	SCHOONER	NORTH CAROLINA	1788	10			
HAROLD CLARK	SLOOP	BELHAVEN	1900	5	43	14.7	3
HARRIET	SCHOONER	CARTERET COUNTY	1826	42	52.25	17.58	5.5
HARRIET	SCHOONER	NORTH CAROLINA	1791	75			
HARRIET ANDERSON	SCHOONER	WINTON	1827	55			
HARRIET RYAN	SCHOONER	EDENTON	1855	90	77	22	6
HARRIOT	SCHOONER	NORTH CAROLINA	1798	45			
HARRY S.	SCHOONER	RIVERDALE	1893	5.51	35	8.5	2.6
HARTWOOD	BRIG	NORTH CAROLINA	1752	40			
HARVEST	SCHOONER	LOCKWOODS FOLLY	1891	25.99	54.6	17	4.4
HATTIE	SCREW STEAMER	SOUTH MILLS	1888	14.27	55.5	10	2.2
HATTIE	SCHOONER	WASHINGTON		14			
HATTIE A. PETERSON	SLOOP	HATTERAS	1889	8.11	33.5	12.3	3.5
HATTIE A. PITTMAN	SLOOP	HATTERAS	1889	8.11	33.5	12.3	3.5
HATTIE CREEF	GAS SCREW	ROANOKE ISLAND	1901	24	57	16	3
HATTIE D.	SCHOONER	SMYRNA	1886	7			
HATTIE ELLEN	SLOOP	SWAN QUARTER	1906	7	33	12.7	2.8
HATTIE RHEA	SCHOONER	SOUTHPORT	1888	21.03	57	15	5.3
HATTON	SCHOONER	COLUMBIA		15			
HAVANA	SCHOONER	BEAUFORT	1874	12	38.5	12.8	3.6
HAVEN		BEAUFORT		8			
HAWK	SCHOONER	BEAR BANKS	1795	50	59	16	6

Name of Ship	Type of Ship	Shipbuilding Location	Year	Tons	Length	Width	Depth
HAWK	BRIG	CAPE FEAR		60			
HAWK	BRIG	NORTH CAROLINA	1774	100			
HAZARD	SCHOONER	NORTH CAROLINA	1799	119			
HAZARD	SCHOONER	PRINCETON	1795	96.6	66	20	8.6
HAZARD	SCHOONER	ROANOKE ISLAND	1796	35			
HAZEL	GAS SCREW	ELIZABETH CITY	1905	9	42	12	4
HAZEL	SCREW STEAMER	WILMINGTON	1909	38	76	15	4
HAZEL P. HAWKINS	SCHOONER	MOREHEAD CITY	1900	9	44	12	2.8
HEBERNIA	SCHOONER	ADAMS CREEK	1812	22	42	12	4
HECTOR	SCHOONER	NORTH CAROLINA	1800	105			
HELEN	SHIP	HYDE COUNTY	1814	227	87	20	11
HELEN	BRIG	HYDE COUNTY	1818	217.5	86	24	12
HELEN	SCHOONER	MARSHALLBERG	1902	7	40	12	3
HELEN AND ALMA	SCHOONER	ELIZABETH CITY	1904	32	58	21.9	3.6
HELEN JANE	SCHOONER	BEAUFORT		7			
HELEN SMITH	SCREW STEAMER	EDENTON	1870	14.94	45.2	9	5.8
HELLENE	SLOOP	BELHAVEN	1912	6	28	11	3.2
HENERY BATEMAN	SLOOP	OCRACOKE	1826	31	49	17	5
HENRIETTA	SCHOONER	BEAUFORT	1855	92			
HENRIETTA	SCHOONER	BEAUFORT COUNTY	1820	87	71	23	6
HENRIETTA	SCHOONER	CARTERET COUNTY	1824	91	72	22	7
HENRIETTA	SCHOONER	CRAVEN COUNTY	1803	50			
HENRIETTA	SCHOONER	CRAVEN COUNTY	1848	160	85	24	8.83
HENRIETTA	SIDE-WHEEL STEAMER	FAYETTEVILLE	1818	152	119	20	6
HENRIETTA	SLOOP	HYDE COUNTY	1811	69			
HENRIETTA		SMITHS CREEK	1848	175	175	24.66	
HENRIETTA HILL	SCHOONER	NEW BERN		52			
HENRY	SLOOP	BEAUFORT	1830	60	58.83	20.33	5.17
HENRY	SLOOP	EDENTON	1752				
HENRY	SCHOONER	NORTH CAROLINA	1803	39			
HENRY	SLOOP	OCRACOKE	1824	30	48	16	4
HENRY AND THOMAS	SCHOONER	MARTIN COUNTY	1851	53	64	17	5
HENRY AND WILLIAM	SCHOONER	BERTIE COUNTY	1805	60			
HENRY BATMAN	SLOOP	OCRACOKE	1838	30	48.5	16	4

Name of Ship	Type of Ship	Shipbuilding Location	Year	Tons	Length	Width	Depth
HENRY CLAY	SCHOONER	ELIZABETH CITY	1829	89	71.66	21.83	6.66
HENRY CLAY	SCHOONER	NEW BERN		13			
HENRY KING	SCHOONER	EDENTON	1810	42.38	50.08	16.75	6
HENRY MARTIN	SCHOONER	ELIZABETH CITY	1839	30.45	50.66	16.75	4.25
HENRY SEAWELL	SHIP	ELIZABETH CITY	1811	256.2	90.17	24.88	13.08
HENRY W. GRADY	SCHOONER	STRAITS	1892	7.52	34.8	11.5	3.3
HENRY WARING	SCHOONER	OCRACOKE	1824	100	72	22	7
HENRY WESTERMAN	SCHOONER	SMITHVILLE	1875	15.24	45	16.8	4.8
HERBERT A. CREEF	SLOOP	MANTEO	1907	7	36	14	3
HERBERT M	SCREW STEAMER	WILMINGTON	1902	30	52	13	4
HERCULES	SCHOONER	CARTERET COUNTY	1792	42	52	16	6
HERMIT	SCHOONER	CARTERET COUNTY	1808	41	55	16.17	5
HERNDON	SCHOONER	WASHINGTON	1857	144	88	24	7
HERO	GAS SCREW	ATLANTIC	1908	9	38	9	2.5
HERO	SCHOONER	CARTERET COUNTY	1816	62	60	18.5	6.66
HERO	BRIG	EDENTON	1781	50			
HERO	SCHOONER	TYRRELL COUNTY	1806	23.67	38	13.83	4.75
HERTFORD	SCHOONER	NORTH CAROLINA	1758	8			
HESTER	SCHOONER	NORTH CAROLINA	1788	50			
HESTER ANN	SCHOONER	SMYRNA	1885	12.35	39.2	13.7	4.2
HETTIE E	GAS SCREW	MARSHALLBERG	1909	13	58	11	3
HETTY	BRIG	HYDE COUNTY	1805	151			
HIGH PRIEST	SCHOONER	CURRITUCK COUNTY	1842	58	60	20	5
HILDA	GAS SCREW	COINJOCK	1906	8	35	12	3
HIRAM	SLOOP	MARTIN COUNTY	1788	80			
HIRAM	BRIG	PLYMOUTH	1823	114	74	21	8
HIRAM		ROANOKE RIVER	1777	50			
HOBSON	SHARPIE	AVON	1899	6	36	14	3
HOLT	SLOOP	MOREHEAD CITY	1898	6	41	10	2.6
HOLTON	BRIG	ADAMS CREEK	1807	203			
HOME	SCHOONER	CARTERET COUNTY	1856	26	48.5	14.92	4.25
HONEY	SCHOONER	CURRITUCK COUNTY	1807	37	46.5	16.5	5.33
HONYEEN	SCHOONER	WASHINGTON	1856	48	55	16	5
HOPE	BRIG	BEAUFORT COUNTY	1806	127			

Name of Ship	Type of Ship	Shipbuilding Location	Year	Tons	Length	Width	Depth
HOPE	BRIG	BEAUFORT COUNTY	1816	127	79	22	8
HOPE	SCHOONER	CARTERET COUNTY	1816	71	62	19	7
HOPE	SCHOONER	HABSCAN	1794	100			
HOPE	SCHOONER	HYDE COUNTY	1820	48	52	19	6
HOPE	SCHOONER	NARROW SHORE	1816	22.59	41.5	15.33	4.33
HOPE	SNOW	NORTH CAROLINA	1775	80			
HOPE	SCREW STEAMER	POINT CASWELL	1902	9	54	10	3.3
HOPE	SLOOP	WASHINGTON	1790	18			
HOPE	SLOOP	WILMINGTON	1749	25			
HOPEWELL	SLOOP	PERQUIMANS RIVER	1740	8			
HORNET	BRIG	SMITHS CREEK	1806	190			
HORNET	SCHOONER	SMITHS CREEK	1816	68	61.5	16.83	6.58
HORNET	SLOOP	WASHINGTON	1848	11.27			
HORSE	SCHOONER	BEAUFORT	1828	50	58	17	5
HORTON CORWIN JR.	GAS SCREW	EDENTON	1908	7	39	7.8	6.4
HOWARD	SCHOONER	NEW BERN	1852	148	88	26	8
HOWARD	SCHOONER	NEW BERN	1887	75.63	92.03	18.06	4.05
HOWARD W.	SCHOONER	ELIZABETH CITY	1892	15.03	35	13	4
HUGH	SCHOONER	SMYRNA	1881	15.74	47.6	14.2	3.4
HUGH CHISHOLM	SCHOONER	COLUMBIA	1852	65	78	17	5
HUGH W. COLLINS	SCHOONER	EDENTON	1850	58	73	17	5
HUMMINGBIRD	SCHOONER	BERTIE COUNTY	1811	63	67	17	6
HUNTER	SCHOONER	ADAMS CREEK	1821	22	33.5	13.66	4.5
HUNTER	SCHOONER	CRAVEN COUNTY	1811	113			
HUNTER	SLOOP	MARTIN COUNTY	1787	87	65	20	7
HUNTER	SLOOP	NORTH CAROLINA	1788	60			
HUNTER	BRIG	NORTH CAROLINA	1799	109			
HUNTER	BRIG	SWANSBORO	1799	109.65	67.5	19.25	9.66
HUNTER	SCHOONER	SWANSBOROUGH	1815	78	63.66	19	7.5
HUNTRESS	BRIG	PASQUOTANK COUNTY	1849	155			
HUSTLER	SLOOP	BEAUFORT	1905	7	35	13	4
HYDE	BRIG	NORTH CAROLINA	1794	128.23	71.75	23.5	9
I HOPE	SCHOONER	WASHINGTON		16			
I.C. DOBBIN	SCHOONER	CURRITUCK COUNTY	1853	104	73	22	7

Name of Ship	Type of Ship	Shipbuilding Location	Year	Tons	Length	Width	Depth
I.C. MANSON	SCHOONER	CARTERET COUNTY	1852	28	49.42	16.33	4.17
I.C. PETTYJOHN	SCHOONER	MARTIN COUNTY	1838	45	61	16	5
I.L. DURAND	SCHOONER	NEW BERN	1835	111	77	20	7
I.T. WILLIS	SCHOONER	CARTERET COUNTY	1857	20	45	14.33	3.66
IDA	SCHOONER	BEAUFORT		12			
IDA	SCHOONER	PINEY POINT	1873	10.31	35.5	12.3	3.4
IDA	SCHOONER	WASHINGTON		5			
IDA	SLOOP	WILMINGTON	1878	7.1			
IDA L. EATON	SLOOP	SMYRNA	1891	6.68	44.3	11.9	2.9
IDA V.	SCHOONER	SWAN QUARTER	1899	18	44	14	3
IDA AND LYNDA	SLOOP	NORTH CAROLINA	1749				
IDA MAY	SLOOP	MOREHEAD CITY	1888	19.02	52	14	3.4
ILLMA	SCHOONER	BEAUFORT	1897	7	38	14	2.5
IMP	SCHOONER	ELIZABETH CITY	1898	9	54	11	2.9
INDEPENDENCE	SCHOONER	CARTERET COUNTY	1853	57	64.08	20.17	5.33
INDEPENDENCE	SLOOP	CURRITUCK INLET	1830	37	54	17.33	4.66
INDEPENDENCE	SLOOP	NELSON BAY	1885	5.41	39	9.8	2.8
INDEPENDENCE	SHIP	NORTH CAROLINA	1801	223			
INDEPENDENCE	SCHOONER	PASQUOTANK COUNTY	1853	59	70	16	5.66
INDEPENDENCE	SCHOONER	PUNGO RIVER	1802	97			
INDEPENDENCE	SCHOONER	WASHINGTON	1847	84	72	22	6
INDEPENDENCE	SCHOONER	WOODBURN	1856	40.53	64.48	20.13	4.92
INDEX	GAS SCREW	SMYRNA	1900	18	53	16.7	3.6
INDIA	SHARPIE	MOREHEAD CITY	1902	6	43.6	11.6	2.4
INDIA L.	GAS SCREW	JACKSONVILLE	1905	11	37	12.8	5.8
INDIAN HUNTER	SHIP	CRAVEN COUNTY	1805	300			
INDIAN QUEEN	SCHOONER	MARTIN COUNTY	1833	39			
INDIGENCE	SCHOONER	CRAVEN COUNTY	1805	100			
INDUSTRY	SCHOONER	BEAUFORT	1792	31	54	14	4
INDUSTRY	SCHOONER	BRUNSWICK	1772	20			
INDUSTRY	SCHOONER	CARTERET COUNTY	1804	23			
INDUSTRY	SCHOONER	CARTERET COUNTY	1806	54			
INDUSTRY	SCHOONER	CARTERET COUNTY	1811	30	50	14	4
INDUSTRY	SCHOONER	CONWAYBORO	1857	171			
INDUSTRY	SCHOONER	HATTERAS	1867	11.01	41.25	12.75	3.9

Name of Ship	Type of Ship	Shipbuilding Location	Year	Tons	Length	Width	Depth
INDUSTRY	SLOOP	HYDE COUNTY	1838	23	40	13	5
INDUSTRY	SCHOONER	NEW BERN	1867	11.59	41.03	12.9	3.9
INDUSTRY	SCHOONER	NORTH CAROLINA	1769	8			
INDUSTRY	SCHOONER	NORTH CAROLINA	1801	91			
INDUSTRY	SCHOONER	SOUTH RIVER	1816	121	71	22	8
INDUSTRY	SCHOONER	WASHINGTON	1812	125	97	27	13
INPH LIBBY	SCHOONER	ELIZABETH CITY	1844	39	59	16	4.9
INTREPID	SCHOONER	HYDE COUNTY	1800	91.3	75	19	7.17
INTREPID	SCHOONER	VANDEMERE	1896	5.97	30	11.6	3.2
INTREPID	SCHOONER	WASHINGTON		11			
IODINE	SCHOONER	HUNTING QUARTERS	1866	9.14	40.4	11.1	2.8
IONA		NEW BERN	1877	8.78			
IONE	SCHOONER	BEAUFORT		5			
IONE	SCHOONER	NEW BERN	1845	156			
IONE	SCHOONER	WASHINGTON		11			
IOV	SCHOONER	BEAUF0RT		5			
IOWA	SCHOONER	BEAUFORT	1898	15	53	15	3
IOWA	SCHOONER	CARTERET COUNTY	1850	41	57.92	17.66	4
IOWA	SCHOONER	SMITHVILLE		26			
IOWN	SCHOONER	ATLANTIC	1891	6.27	34.7	10.5	3.2
IRMA DARLING	SCHOONER	NEW BERN	1894	12.46	36	12	4
ISAAC W. HUGHES	SCHOONER	NEW BERN	1849	127	79	24	8
ISABEL	SCHOONER	BEAUFORT	1857	86	75	21	6
ISABEL	GAS SCREW	SOUTHPORT	1905	14	50	13	3.9
ISABELLA	BRIG	BEAUFORT	1807	134			
ISABELLA	SCHOONER	CARTERET COUNTY	1842	112	75.42	22.25	7.66
ISABELLA	SCHOONER	CARTERET COUNTY	1857	86	75	21.75	6.08
ISABELLA	SCHOONER	NEW BERN	1881	14.02	46	13	3.3
ISABELLA	GAS SCREW	WASHINGTON	1896	13	56	11.5	3.6
ISABELLA ELLIS	SCREW	NEW BERN	1858	68			
ISABELLA M. SAWYER	SCHOONER	KINNAKEET	1886	8.42	36.3	12.6	3.4
ISAIAH	SCHOONER	CORE SOUND	1826	45	57	18	5
IVALON	SCHOONER	BEAUFORT	1891	13.58	51.8	13.5	3
IVY	SCHOONER	SMYRNA	1899	11	46	13	3
IVY	SCHOONER	WASHINGTON	1891	9.14	35.4	10.2	3
J. HILLES	BARGE	WASHINGTON	1890	295.44			
J. HOPE	SCHOONER	CRAVEN COUNTY	1846	23	47	15	3.83

Name of Ship	Type of Ship	Shipbuilding Location	Year	Tons	Length	Width	Depth
J.A. LEVENSALER	SCHOONER	WASHINGTON		21			
J.C. ADELINE	SCHOONER	ELIZABETH CITY	1849	26.11	47	16	4.17
J.C. ALLEN	SHARPIE	SHALLOTTE	1901	15	49.8	13.7	3.9
J.C. CALHOUN	SCHOONER	ELIZABETH CITY	1842	59.55	70.5	17.42	5.42
J.C. DOBBINS	SCHOONER	CURRITUCK COUNTY	1853	104.76	73	23.25	7.5
J.D. MASON	SCHOONER	HUNTING QUARTERS	1882	11.56			
J.D. PIGOTT	SCHOONER	SHALLOTTE	1895	10.39	46.5	12.5	3.1
J.D. PORTER	SCHOONER	SHALLOTTE	1903	9	40	12	3.2
J.E. BENNETT	GAS SCREW	NEW BERN	1913	33	64	18	3.3
J.E. HOVAH	SCHOONER	ATLANTIC	1901	6	36	10	2.9
J.F. MORRIS	SCHOONER	HUNTING QUARTERS	1883	14.07	41.5	13.8	3.7
J.G. MANSON	SCHOONER	CARTERET COUNTY	1852	28	49	16	4
J.H. DAVIS	SCHOONER	HUNTING QUARTERS	1874	13.27	37	11	3.3
J.H. POTTER	SCHOONER	NORTH RIVER	1875	12.69	42.1	13.8	3.9
J.J. GRANDY	SCHOONER	ELIZABETH CITY	1847	56.53	65.66	17.25	5.25
J.J. MORROW	SCHOONER	HATTERAS	1876	35.95			
J.J. TAYLOR	SCHOONER	HUNTING QUARTERS	1883	10.59	37.1	12.6	3.5
J.J. WOLFENDEN	SCHOONER	NEW BERN	1877	11	45	15	4.2
J.L. DURANT	SCHOONER	NEW BERN	1835	111	78	21	8
J.P. WHEDBEE	SCHOONER	BEAUFORT	1849	80	70	22	6
J.P. WHEDBEE	SCHOONER	OCRACOKE	1848	177			7
J.R. CONDON	SCHOONER	MANTEO	1902	9	44	14	3
J.R. DIXON	GAS SCREW	ATLANTIC	1914	11	41	9.6	3.3
J.T. MAY QUEEN	SCHOONER	WASHINGTON	1877	14.49			
J.T. WILLIS	SCHOONER	BEAUFORT	1865	17.78	50.7	14.9	4.3
J.W. LATHROP	SCHOONER	SOUTHPORT	1909	14	49	14	3.5
J.W. MAITLAND	SCHOONER	PLYMOUTH	1857	230			
JACK	SCHOONER	CORE BANKS	1789	22			
JACK AND JUDY	SCHOONER	NORTH CAROLINA	1751	35			
JACK DOWNING	SCHOONER	SWANSBOROUGH	1835	25	46	13	4
JACK TIER	SHARPIE	BEAUFORT	1902	7	32	13	3.4
JAMAICA	SLOOP	NORTH CAROLINA	1728	8			
JAMES	BARGE	BEAUFORT	1908	8			
JAMES	BRIG	ELIZABETH CITY	1826	150.45	67.25	21.25	10.5
JAMES	SLOOP	NORTH CAROLINA	1749	35			

Name of Ship	Type of Ship	Shipbuilding Location	Year	Tons	Length	Width	Depth
JAMES	SCHOONER	NORTH CAROLINA	1761	5			
JAMES	SCHOONER	PASQUOTANK COUNTY	1788	45			
JAMES AND WILLIAM	BRIG	BEAUFORT COUNTY	1803	150			
JAMES BUCHANAN	SCHOONER	LOCKWOODS FOLLY	1856	37	57	17	4
JAMES CROW	SCHOONER	WILMINGTON	1837	31	53	16	4
JAMES DAVIS	SCHOONER	CARTERET COUNTY	1857	23	46.75	14.5	4
JAMES E. BROWN	GAS SCREW	BUFFALO CITY	1908	8	31	8	7
JAMES F. DAVENPORT	SCHOONER	COLUMBIA	1851	91	67	21	7
JAMES F. MCKEE	SLOOP	SMITHVILLE	1826	67	58	19	7
JAMES H. SMITH	SCHOONER	BEAUFORT COUNTY	1823	37	51	15	5.5
JAMES L. CRANE	SCHOONER	WASHINGTON		7			
JAMES MCKINLEY	SCHOONER	SMITHS CREEK	1811	86.76	66.08	20.42	7.5
JAMES MONROE	SCHOONER	CARTERET COUNTY	1819	69	61	19	6.83
JAMES MONROE	SCHOONER	EDENTON	1817	104.48	68	19.92	8.83
JAMES MURDOCK	BRIG	BAY RIVER	1808	160			
JAMES OF VIRGINIA	BRIGANTINE	NORTH CAROLINA	1688	4			
JAMES RAYMOND	SHARPIE	STRAITS	1899	7	42.2	11.8	2.7
JAMES RUMLEY	SCHOONER	SMYRNA	1877	11.46	42.9	13.6	3.4
JAMES STEWART	BRIG	NIXONTON	1799	133			
JAMES T. EASTON	TUG	WILMINGTON	1891	31	55	14	7
JAMES W. HINTON		ELIZABETH CITY	1856	75	82	17	5
JAMES W. SMITH	SCHOONER	ELIZABETH CITY	1853	70	78	17	5
JAMES WILLIAM	BRIG	BEAUFORT COUNTY	1803	150			
JANATS ELIZA	SCHOONER	JARROTTS BAY	1822	66	62	19	6.5
JANE	SCHOONER	BEAUFORT	1823	166	79	22	10
JANE	BRIG	CARTERET COUNTY	1823	165	79.5	22	10
JANE	SCHOONER	CURRITUCK NARROWS	1821	28	46	15.83	4.58
JANE	SCHOONER	NEW BERN	1829	22	41	13	
JANE	SCHOONER	NEW BERN	1845	156	84	24	9
JANE	SCHOONER	NORTH CAROLINA	1799	58			
JANE	SHIP	NORTH CAROLINA	1800	433			
JANE	SCHOONER	NORTH RIVER	1812	128	71.83	22.92	9.17

Name of Ship	Type of Ship	Shipbuilding Location	Year	Tons	Length	Width	Depth
JANE AND ELIZA	BRIG	SWANSBORO	1795	88.55	60.5	1883	9
JANE AND MARY	SLOOP	NORTH CAROLINA	1714	15			
JANE CAMPBELL	SCHOONER	WASHINGTON	1857	146			
JANE FISHER	SCHOONER	CARTERET COUNTY	1856	32	50	16	4
JANE FISHER	SCHOONER	ELIZABETH CITY	1856	25.52			
JANE MCKINLAY	SCHOONER	SMITHS CREEK	1811	86	66	12	7
JANE W. SMITH	SCHOONER	ELIZABETH CITY	1853	70	78	17	5
JANET	GAS SCREW	ATLANTIC	1912	10	47	10	3.4
JANET	SHIP	NORTH CAROLINA	1766	180			
JANET ANN	SCHOONER	BEAUFORT		12			
JANIE	SCHOONER	SMYRNA	1888	9.67	44.1	11.5	3
JANIE	SCHOONER	SNEADS FERRY	1903	11	41	13	2.9
JANIE BERRY		STRAITS	1894	29.15	50	18.4	3.6
JANNIE	SHIP	NORTH CAROLINA	1766	200			
JARVIS BROWN AND CO.	SCHOONER	CARTERET COUNTY	1816	69	60	18	7.5
JAS. W. HINTON	SCHOONER	ELIZABETH CITY	1856	75	82	17	5
JASON	BRIG	SMITHS CREEK	1817	160			
JAUNITY	SCREW STEAMER	HARDINGS BRIDGE	1912	19	62	14	3
JAY	SCHOONER	CRAVEN COUNTY	1836	24	54	12.66	3.92
JEANNETTE	SCHOONER	NEW BERN		12			
JENNIE	SLOOP	LENOXVILLE	1890	6	41.7	10.3	2.6
JENNIE ALICE	SCHOONER	ELIZABETH CITY		43			
JENNIE HUNTER	SCHOONER	ELIZABETH CITY	1856	80.68	87.5	17	5.82
JENNIE LIND	SCHOONER	NEW BERN		11			
JENNY	SLOOP	BERTIE COUNTY	1786	56			
JENNY	SLOOP	NORTH CAROLINA	1788	60			
JENNY LIND	SCHOONER	NEW BERN	1856	47	59	17	4
JEREMIAH	SLOOP	EDENTON	1743	30			
JESSE ARTHUR	SLOOP	SMYRNA	1891	6.09	42.6	11.2	2.8
JESSIE M. BELL	SCHOONER	BEAUFORT	1892	13.36	49.2	13.6	3.9
JESSIE PALIN	SCHOONER	ELIZABETH CITY		12			
JEWETT C. STEPHENS	BARGE	DURHAM CREEK	1862	119			
JOANNA	SHIP	NIXONTON	1796	284			
JOE	SLOOP	ATLANTIC	1897	14	39	16	3
JOE ANN	SLOOP	COLUMBIA		7			
JOE FLANNER	SCHOONER	WILMINGTON	1858	77	65	19	7
JOHH DAWSON	BARK	WILMINGTON	1850	173			

Name of Ship	Type of Ship	Shipbuilding Location	Year	Tons	Length	Width	Depth
JOHN	SCHOONER	BEAUFORT	1795	64	56	17	8
JOHN	BRIG	CARTERET COUNTY	1829	144	76	23	9.5
JOHN	BRIG	CHOWAN COUNTY	1797	150			
JOHN	SCHOONER	HALIFAX	1804	108			
JOHN	SCHOONER	HYDE COUNTY	1872	8	40	11	2
JOHN	SCHOONER	NEW BERN	1808	87.42	60	20.5	8.5
JOHN	SCHOONER	NORTH CAROLINA	1789	80			
JOHN	SCHOONER	NORTH CAROLINA		15			
JOHN	SCHOONER	WHITE ROCK	1793	83			
JOHN A. BEMBY	SCHOONER	CHOWAN COUNTY	1838	38	51	17	5
JOHN A. BURGES	SCHOONER	ELIZABETH CITY	1857	70	75	17	6
JOHN A. GAMBREL	SCHOONER	ELIZABETH CITY	1849	128	81	22	8
JOHN A. TAYLOR	SCHOONER	WILMINGTON	1852	70			
JOHN ALLEN	SCHOONER	CURRITUCK SOUND	1811	67.48	64	20	6.17
JOHN AND CATHERINE	SLOOP	NORTH CAROLINA	1715	50			
JOHN AND CECIL	SCHOONER	BEAUFORT	1885	5.79	41	10.03	2.2
JOHN AND DAVID	SHIP	BATH	1731	100			
JOHN AND DAVID	SCHOONER	HYDE COUNTY	1751	40			
JOHN AND HANNA	SCHOONER	NORTH CAROLINA	1760	15			
JOHN ARMSTEAD	SCHOONER	PLYMOUTH	1815	118	72	21	9
JOHN B.	SCHOONER	SMYRNA	1888	8.18	44	11	3.1
JOHN BARTLET	SCHOONER	ELIZABETH CITY	1829	105.66	70.33	21.66	8.07
JOHN BENJA	SCHOONER	HATTERAS		8			
JOHN BENSON	BARK	CRAVEN COUNTY	1846	215			
JOHN BOTTY		BEAUFORT	1755	15			
JOHN BOUSHILL	SCHOONER	EDENTON	1849	54	70	17	5
JOHN BRYAN	SCHOONER	PLYMOUTH	1827	98	72	21	7
JOHN BURGUIN	BRIG	SMITHVILLE	1810	163	77	23	11
JOHN BURNEY	SCHOONER	LOWER BROAD CREEK	1815	40	57	17	5
JOHN C. BAKER	SCHOONER	SMITHVILLE	1833	27	48	13	4
JOHN C. COCKY	SCHOONER	EDENTON	1848	43	63	17	4
JOHN C. DAVIS	SLOOP	STRAITS	1890	6.23	32.4	12.02	3.5
JOHN C. PETTYOHN	SCHOONER	MARTIN COUNTY	1838	45	61	16	5
JOHN CHRISTOL	BARGE	WASHINGTON	1882	178.45			

Name of Ship	Type of Ship	Shipbuilding Location	Year	Tons	Length	Width	Depth
JOHN DAWSON	PADDLE-WHEEL STEAMER	FAYETTEVILLE	1858	50			
JOHN DAWSON	PADDLE-WHEEL STEAMER	WILMINGTON	1880	83.41			
JOHN DOYLE	SLOOP	BAY RIVER	1824	50	50.25	17.92	6
JOHN DREW	SHIP	BERTIE COUNTY	1804	231			
JOHN E. BROWN	SHIP	BUFFALO CITY	1909	80	31	8	7
JOHN ELLIS	SCHOONER	NORTH CAROLINA	1802	95			
JOHN F. BELL		MOREHEAD CITY	1903	12	43	11	3.2
JOHN G. COCKEY	SCHOONER	EDENTON	1848	43	63	17	4
JOHN GRAY BLOUNT	SCHOONER	HYDE COUNTY	1830	134	76	24	8
JOHN GRIFFITH	SCHOONER	WILMINGTON	1879	11.67			
JOHN H. HAUGHTON	SIDE-WHEEL STEAMER	WILMINGTON	1854	54			
JOHN H. KUCK	SCHOONER	SHALLOTTE	1895	16.05	51.6	13.6	3.8
JOHN H. SMALL	SCREW STEAMER	MANTEO	1906	49	68	19.2	4.4
JOHN HUGHES	SCHOONER	NEW BERN	1834	94	65	20	8
JOHN JAMES	SCHOONER	ELIZABETH CITY		39			
JOHN JONES	SCHOONER	SOUTH RIVER	1810	66			
JOHN L. DURAND	SCHOONER	NEW BERN	1835	120			
JOHN L. JONES	SCHOONER	COLUMBIA	1850	41			
JOHN LITTLE	SCHOONER	TYRRELL COUNTY	1814	20.31	42.08	13.33	4.25
JOHN M. ROBERTS	SCHOONER, SQ. STERN	GATES COUNTY	1834	67			
JOHN MYERS	SCHOONER	STRAITS OF CORE	1828	99	71	21	7.7
JOHN PERRY	SCHOONER	BEAUFORT COUNTY	1845	44	61	19	5
JOHN PUGH	SCHOONER	CARTERET COUNTY	1833	22	49.75	12.75	4.25
JOHN ROBERTS	SCHOONER	CHOWAN COUNTY	1874	25			
JOHN RODMAN	SCHOONER	HYDE COUNTY	1816	51	56.8	16.8	6
JOHN S. BRYAN	SCHOONER	PLYMOUTH	1827	98			
JOHN STANLEY	SCHOONER	BEAUFORT	1836	91	70.5	21	7
JOHN STANLEY	SCHOONER	CRAVEN COUNTY	1812	51.55	55.75	18.25	6
JOHN STONEY	SCHOONER	ADAMS CREEK	1815	89	65.83	21.25	7.5
JOHN STOREY	BRIG	WILMINGTON	1847	124			
JOHN W. MAITLAND	SCHOONER	PLYMOUTH	1857	230			
JOHN WALLACE	SCHOONER	HYDE COUNTY	1812	96	42.6	16	4

Name of Ship	Type of Ship	Shipbuilding Location	Year	Tons	Length	Width	Depth
JOHN WILLIS	SCHOONER	NORTH CAROLINA	1809	105			
JOHNIE	SLOOP	SWANSBORO	1889	6	40	9.6	2.4
JOHNNY		BEAUFORT	1866	10			
JOHNSTON	BRIG	NORTH CAROLINA	1770	60			
JOLLY A. SAILOR	SCHOONER	CARTERET COUNTY	1811	44	54	18	5
JOLLY BACCHAS	SCHOONER	PASQUOTANK	1804	82			
JOLLY BATCHELOR	BRIG	NORTH CAROLINA	1764	50			
JOLLY ROVER	SLOOP	PERQUIMANS COUNTY	1800	37			
JOLLY SAILOR	SCHOONER	CARTERET COUNTY	1811	38.4	43.08	18.08	4.75
JOLLY SAILOR	SCHOONER	CURRITUCK COUNTY	1807	50	55	18.33	6
JON R	SCREW STEAMER	JACKSONVILLE	1907	9	41	11	6
JONA MAN	SCHOONER	ELIZABETH CITY	1812	94	69.25	22.5	7.75
JONATHAN JACOCKS	SCHOONER	BERTIE COUNTY	1807	283			
JONE	SCHOONER	NEW BERN	1845	156	84.08	24.08	8.83
JONES	GAS SCREW	MARSHALLBERG	1911	22	60	17	3.7
JOSEPH	BRIG	NORTH CAROLINA	1762	60			
JOSEPH	SCHOONER	NORTH CAROLINA	1777	81			
JOSEPH	BRIG	SMITHS CREEK	1812	137	77.11	23	8.83
JOSEPH	SCHOONER	SWANSBORO	1891	20	51	16.8	3.5
JOSEPH AND JAMES	BRIG	HYDE COUNTY	1801	124			
JOSEPH AND JUDA	SCHOONER	QUISTSNA	1751	35			
JOSEPH AND LYDIA	SCHOONER	CHOWAN COUNTY	1749	20			
JOSEPH ANN	SCHOONER	BEAUFORT	1845	37	55	17.33	4.58
JOSEPH BUTLER	SCHOONER	BAY RIVER	1847	256	102	29	
JOSEPH H. NEFF	SCHOONER	BRUNSWICK COUNTY	1873	9.8			
JOSEPH HARVEY	BRIG	PERQUIMANS RIVER	1798	126			
JOSEPH I. WILLIAMS	SCHOONER	MILL BROOK	1847	107	78	24	6
JOSEPH IRWIN	BRIGANTINE	MILL BROOK	1847	107			
JOSEPH KING	SCHOONER	BEAUFORT	1820	36.13	52	15	5.42
JOSEPH LIBBY	SCHOONER	ELIZABETH CITY	1844	30	49	15	4.75
JOSEPH M. MILES	SCHOONER	NEW BERN		16			

Name of Ship	Type of Ship	Shipbuilding Location	Year	Tons	Length	Width	Depth
JOSEPH POTTS	SLOOP	BEAUFORT COUNTY	1843	32	50	16	4
JOSEPH RAMSEY	SCHOONER	TYRRELL COUNTY	1855	63	80	17	4.92
JOSEPH YOUNG	SLOOP	ELIZABETH CITY		8			
JOSEPHINE	SCHOONER	ELIZABETH CITY	1841	45	58	17	5
JOSEPHINE	GAS SCREW	MOREHEAD CITY	1913	36	55	15	4.5
JOSEPHINE	SLOOP		1875	8.18	36.7	14.4	3.8
JOSIAH	SCHOONER	NORTH CAROLINA	1768	15			
JOSIAH COLLINS	SHIP	TYRRELL COUNTY	1795	259			
JOSIE	SCREW STEAMER	SOUTH CREEK	1886	10.6	39.7	9.6	3
JOSIE D.	SCHOONER	LOCKWOODS FOLLY	1904	16	50	15	3.6
JOSIE HAVENS	SCHOONER	CORE SOUND	1867	10.1			
JUANITA	SCHOONER	HARDINGS BRIDGE	1912	19			
JULIA	SCHOONER	ADAMS CREEK	1825	20	42	13.25	4.42
JULIA	SCHOONER	BEAUFORT	1866	8.5	38.5	10.9	3
JULIA	SCHOONER	BEAUFORT	1872	5	32.1	10	2.4
JULIA	SCHOONER	BEAUFORT	1882	5.44	32.1	10	2.4
JULIA	SCHOONER	JARRETTS BAY	1860	8	38.5	10.9	3.1
JULIA	SCREW STEAMER	NEW BERN	1896	7	45	11	3.5
JULIA	BRIG	NORTH CAROLINA	1788	100			
JULIA	SCHOONER	SMYRNA	1898	11.6	49	14.3	3.5
JULIA AND NANCY	SCHOONER	NEW BERN	1841	97	71	21	7
JULIA AND SALLY	SCHOONER	HYDE COUNTY	1806	96			
JULIA ANN	SCHOONER	COINJOCK	1821	36	48.6	17	2.25
JULIA ANN	SCHOONER	CURRITUCK COUNTY	1848	81	67	20	6
JULIA F. HILL	SCHOONER	CORE SOUND	1883	10.17	44.8	12.8	3.3
JULIA FRANCES	BRIG	BEAUFORT	1825	111	73	23	8
JULIA FRANCES	SCHOONER	CARTERET COUNTY	1847	155	83	23.1	8.92
JULIA SELDEN	SCHOONER	ELIZABETH CITY		33			
JULIA TELFAIR	SCHOONER	WASHINGTON	1842	96			
JULIA W. BELL	SCHOONER	MOREHEAD CITY	1890	14.91	52.3	14.2	3.7
JULIAN DEWEY	GAS SCREW	SMYRNA	1902	26	61	17	3.6
JULIAN J. FLEETWOOD	SCREW STEAMER	HERTFORD	1896	38	70	14.6	6

Name of Ship	Type of Ship	Shipbuilding Location	Year	Tons	Length	Width	Depth
JULIANA	SLOOP	NORTH CAROLINA	1738	20			
JULIUS PRINGLE	SCHOONER	BEAUFORT	1829	94	65.33	21.66	7.92
JULLIAN AND JOHN	SLOOP	EDENTON	1746	10			
JUNE	SLOOP	PORT ROANOKE	1772	25			
JUSTIN	SCHOONER	WASHINGTON COUNTY	1808	116			
K.M. THOMAS	SCHOONER	SOUTH CREEK	1890	5.44	32.3	10.2	2.4
K.S. BURNEY	SLOOP	CARTERET COUNTY	1851	33	52	17	5
K.T. WILLIS	SCHOONER	SHACKELFORD BANKS	1895	13	46	14.2	3.6
KATE	SCHOONER	CARTERET COUNTY	1851	26	49.4	14.8	4.2
KATE	SLOOP	ELIZABETH CITY	1877	8.48			
KATE	PERRIANGER	NORTH CAROLINA	1728	5			
KATE	SCHOONER	PLYMOUTH	1846	55	71	17	5
KATE	SCHOONER	SWANSBORO		18			
KATE	SCHOONER	WILMINGTON		17			
KATE KINNEY	SCHOONER	ELIZABETH CITY	1855				
KATE MCLAURIN	SIDE-WHEEL STEAMER	FAYETTEVILLE	1859	54	112	17	3
KATE STAVRO	SCHOONER	EDENTON	1859	62	77	17	5.2
KATHLEEN	SCHOONER	MOREHEAD CITY	1904	11	46	12	2.5
KATIE ESTELL		BELHAVEN	1900	5	32	13.5	3.8
KATRINA	GAS SCREW	EDENTON	1903	8	33	7	6.1
KATY EDWARDS	SCHOONER	SWANSBORO	1874	18			
KENER	BRIG	NORTH CAROLINA	1782	107	76	20	8
KENNNETH PAGE	SLOOP	BELHAVEN	1902	9	47	15	3
KEYPORT	SCHOONER	ELIZABETH CITY	1870	52.33	63.1	22.7	5
KEYSTONE	SCHOONER	PLYMOUTH		14			
KIMBERLY	SCHOONER	NEW BERN	1834	138	80	22.5	8
KING BIRD	SCHOONER	NORTH CAROLINA	1761	20			
KING CRAB	SLOOP	KERSHAW	1894	11	42	12	3.7
KING FISHER	GAS SCREW	DUCK CREEK	1914	8	35	10	3.2
KINGSTON	SLOOP	NORTH CAROLINA	1764	25			
KINSTON	PADDLE-WHEEL STEAMER	NEW BERN	1882	102.55	120	23	4
KIT SANFORD	SCHOONER	JUDITHS	1886	8	41.8	13	3.2

Name of Ship	Type of Ship	Shipbuilding Location	Year	Tons	Length	Width	Depth
KITCH	SCHOONER	CORE SOUND	1812	35	52	15	5
KITTY FLOWERS	SCHOONER	HYDE COUNTY	1824	26	41	14	5
KORET	PADDLE-WHEEL STEAMER	BULL POND	1880	8.84	50	11.1	2.2
L. DAYTON	SCHOONER	NORTH RIVER	1888	6.48	34	11	3.4
L. JONES	SCHOONER	COLUMBIA	1850	41	60	17	4
L. T. WILLIS	SCHOONER	CARTERET COUNTY	1857	20	45	14	4
L. WARREN	SCHOONER	CARTERET COUNTY	1856	68	71.5	22.25	5
L. WITT	SLOOP	PELETIER	1907	12	44	14	3
L.D. LAMB	SCHOONER	PASQUOTANK COUNTY	1849	58	71	17	5
L.D. STARKE	SCHOONER	PASQUOTANK COUNTY	1853	25	40	13	4.9
L.H. CUTLER	SCREW STEAMER	SWIFT CREEK	1882	42.6	84	19.2	3.9
L.S. LUCUS	SCHOONER	SMITHVILLE	1837	39	52	15	5
LA VICTOIRE	SHIP	NORTH CAROLINA	1778	120			
LACEY	SCHOONER	WIT	1902	9	43	14	2.7
LADY ANTRIM	SCHOONER	MANTEO	1885	11.1	42	14	3.8
LADY ATRIM	SCHOONER	EDENTON	1857	87.11	81.6	22.3	6.6
LADY GRANT	SCHOONER	ATLANTIC	1891	10.92	38.3	13.7	3.5
LADY GRAY	SCHOONER	BEAUFORT		8			
LADY JANE	SLOOP	NELSON BAY		6.26	26	11	3
LADY OF THE LAKE	SCHOONER	SMITHS CREEK	1819	64	60	19.33	6.58
LADY WASHINGTON	SLOOP	BAY RIVER	1821	24	48.25	17.33	5
LADY WASHINGTON	SCHOONER	CRAVEN COUNTY	1808	42	43	17	5
LADY WHEDBEE	SCHOONER	CURRITUCK COUNTY	1843	52	64	17	5
LAFAYETTE	BRIG	BEAUFORT	1824				
LAKEWOOD	SCREW STEAMER	HERTFORD	1895	74.51	80.8	19.8	5.8
LALA G.	SCHOONER	ATLANTIC	1913	20	52	15	3.03
LANCEAN	SCHOONER	CURRITUCK NARROWS	1827	59	58	18.66	6.42
LANUCK	SCHOONER	NORTH CAROLINA	1744	15			
LARK	SCHOONER	BELLS BUOY	1788	92			
LARK	SCHOONER	EDENTON	1788	60			
LARTHENA	SCHOONER	KNOTTS ISLAND	1816	43.77	56	18	5.33
LAS PAISLEY	BRIG			80			

Name of Ship	Type of Ship	Shipbuilding Location	Year	Tons	Length	Width	Depth
LAST SHIFT	SCHOONER	NORTH CAROLINA	1771	16			
LATTIE	SCHOONER	SMYRNA	1893	8.91	44.8	12.3	2.8
LAURA	SCHOONER	CARTERET COUNTY	1845	29	51	15.83	4.33
LAURA	SCREW STEAMER	GOLDSBORO	1886	27	70	16.7	2.4
LAURA	SCHOONER	NEW BERN	1867	8.96			
LAURA ANN JANE	SCHOONER	NEW BERN	1875	7.83			
LAURA B. BANKS	SCHOONER	POWELLS POINT	1887	7.8	36.8	11.4	3.4
LAURA D.	SHARPIE	SOUTHPORT	1890	29	65.4	16.3	3.7
LAURA E. JOHNSON	SCHOONER	NEW BERN	1854	190	102	26	8
LAURA GERTRUDE	SCHOONER	BEAUFORT	1855	315	117	27.83	10.75
LAURA J.	SCHOONER	NORTH RIVER	1882	10.04			
LAURA M. TREE	SLOOP	ELIZABETH CITY		6			
LAUREL	SLOOP	BEAUFORT	1725	6			
LAVENIA	SCHOONER	ONSLOW COUNTY	1854	33	42.83	16	4
LAVINIA	SCHOONER	ELIZABETH CITY	1830	93	72.75	21.75	6.83
LAVINIA THOMAS	SCHOONER	STRAITS	1873	12.08	39.1	12.5	3.7
LAWRENCE	SCHOONER	COLUMBIA	1849	47	66	20	4
LAWRENCE	BRIG	NORTH CAROLINA	1816	101			
LE CHARMONT	BRIG	EDENTON		167			
LEADER	SCHOONER	SOUTH RIVER	1897	6.08	40	10.9	2.8
LEAH	SLOOP	SOUTHPORT	1893	7.2	35.7	11.2	2.7
LEBANON	SCHOONER	BERTIE COUNTY	1807	27	46	15	4
LEDGER	SCHOONER	CURRITUCK COUNTY	1820	70	39	16	5
LEDIA STAR	SHARPIE	TURNIGAN BAY	1891	6	32.2	10.6	2.8
LELA MAY	SCHOONER	PAMLICO	1886	7.78	42.4	12.6	3.5
LEMORA ISABEL	SCHOONER	SHALLOTTE	1849	30	48	16	5
LENA	SCHOONER	OCRACOKE	1873	24.61	54.8	16.8	4.5
LENA	GAS SCREW	SWANSBORO	1902	11	47	14	2
LENA VIRGINIA	SCREW STEAMER	LEECHVILLE	1900	21	46	12	3
LENOIR	GAS SCREW	KINSTON	1904	7	32	8	2.4
LENORA ISABEL	SCHOONER	SHALLOTTE	1849	30	48	16	4.5
LEO	SCHOONER	SOUTHPORT	1891	11.33	41	13.5	3.1
LEOLA	SCHOONER	HUNTING QUARTERS	1891	5.83	30	9	3
LEOLA B. GASKILL	SCHOONER	WIT	1904	24	57	18	4
LEONE WHITE	SLOOP	LAKE LANDING	1891	34.06	57	17	4.4
LEONORA	SCHOONER	ELIZABETH CITY	1903	13	44	14	4

Name of Ship	Type of Ship	Shipbuilding Location	Year	Tons	Length	Width	Depth
LEONORA C.	SCHOONER	AVON	1899	6	36	12.6	3.8
LEOPARD	SCHOONER	BEAUFORT	1825	24	44	14	4
LEOPARD	SCHOONER	CURRITUCK COUNTY	1808	55	57	18	6
LETHA	GAS SCREW	ATLANTIC	1905	6	37	9.5	2.2
LETHA	SCHOONER	PORTSMOUTH	1892	5.86	32	11	2.6
LEVANT	SLOOP	CEDAR HAMMOCK	1829	31	44	17	5
LEVIATHAN	SCHOONER	RUMLEY HAMMOCK	1858	24	45	13.33	3.92
LEVY D. TILLETT	SCHOONER	CURRITUCK COUNTY	1845	31	49	15	4
LEWIS	BRIG	SWANSBORO	1796	121			
LEWIS WILLIAMS	SHIP	NORTH CAROLINA	1801	222			
LIBERTY	SCHOONER	CURRITUCK COUNTY	1811	43	50.58	10.66	6
LIDA CARR	SLOOP	BEAUFORT	1888	8.46	41.4	9.9	2.4
LILLIA STAR	SCHOONER	TURNIGAN BAY	1891	6.04	32.3	10.6	2.8
LILLIAN	SCHOONER	BEAUFORT	1867	18	52.3	13.7	3.4
LILLIAN	SCREW STEAMER	ELIZABETH CITY	1905	18	48	12	4.2
LILLIAN	GAS SCREW	ELIZABETH CITY	1908	7	30	8	6.9
LILLIAN	GAS SCREW	FALKLAND	1904	15	56	15	2.9
LILLIAN	SCHOONER	HATTERAS	1889	7.35	36.6	11.4	3.1
LILLIAN	SCHOONER	SMYRNA	1892	9.29	45.4	12.9	3.1
LILLIAN	STEAMER	WILMINGTON	1865	55	84	17	3
LILLIAN LUGILLIAL	SCHOONER	DURANTS NECK	1895	8.64	45	12.5	3
LILLIE	SLOOP	SMYRNA	1890	6.64	43.6	10.7	2.7
LILLIE BELL	SCHOONER	MOREHEAD CITY	1886	7.54	43.2	10	2.6
LILLIE PEARL	SCHOONER	BEAUFORT	1900	11	45	12	3
LILLIE V.	SCHOONER	LOCKWOODS FOLLY	1899	5	37	10	2.5
LILLIN BELL	SCHOONER	MOREHEAD CITY	1886	8	41		
LILLY MAY	SLOOP	COLINGTON	1889	8.93	34.2	12.6	3.6
LILY	SCHOONER	CEDAR ISLAND	1884	5.61	28	10.2	2.5
LILY	GAS SCREW	WILMINGTON	1903	14	50	10	3
LILY P.	SCHOONER	KINNAKEET	1895	9.26	34	14	3.4
LIMA	SCHOONER	CRAVEN COUNTY	1826	31	48.66	16.58	4.58
LINIE B.	SCHOONER	NORTH RIVER	1890	6.28	42.5	10.5	3
LION	SCHOONER	ELIZABETH CITY	1841	35	50	16	4
LION	SCHOONER	NEW BERN	1830	47	54	17	5
LISBON	PADDLE-WHEEL STEAMER	POINT CASWELL	1887	82.4	77	18.6	4

Name of Ship	Type of Ship	Shipbuilding Location	Year	Tons	Length	Width	Depth
LISBON	PADDLE-WHEEL STEAMER	POINT CASWELL	1908	49	85	16	4.5
LITTLE CHARLES	SCHOONER	POWELLS POINT	1817	38	51.66	17.66	5
LITTLE CHARLIE	SCHOONER	NEW BERN		9			
LITTLE DICK	SCHOONER	NORTH CAROLINA	1771	16			
LITTLE DOVE	SCHOONER	NEW BERN	1867	8.89			
LITTLE FOX	SCHOONER	POWELLS POINT	1799	20.42	41	14	4.25
LITTLE FRANK	BRIG	CRAVEN COUNTY	1802	160	76	23	10
LITTLE GEORGE	SCHOONER	BEAUFORT COUNTY	1820	25	43	14	4
LITTLE JIM	SCHOONER	MOREHEAD CITY	1897	12	42	13	2.7
LITTLE JOHN	SCHOONER	BEAUFORT COUNTY	1819	29	49	15	4
LITTLE JOHN	SCHOONER	CARTERET COUNTY	1815	64	62	18.5	6.42
LITTLE JOHN	SCHOONER	CURRITUCK COUNTY	1815	22.89	41.3	14.4	4.9
LITTLE JOHN	SCHOONER	PASQUOTANK RIVER	1813	74	64	20	6.83
LITTLE JOHN	SCHOONER	SWANSBOROUGH	1810	15	48	10	3
LITTLE KELLEN	SHIP	NORTH CAROLINA	1764	100			
LITTLE MART	SCHOONER	FULCHERS LANDING	1903	17	44	13	4
LITTLE PATRICK	BRIG	NORTH CAROLINA	1763	60			
LITTLE POLLY	SCHOONER	NORTH CAROLINA	1768	15			
LITTLE ROBERT	SLOOP	NORTH CAROLINA	1773	20			
LITTLE SALLY	SCHOONER			6			
LITTLE SAMPSON	SCHOONER	KINNAKEET	1885	7.08	32	12.6	3.4
LITTLE SISTER	SCHOONER	SMYRNA	1893	6.32	42.3	11.2	2.3
LITTLE WINNIE	SCHOONER	WILMINGTON	1876	23.08			
LIVE OAK	SCHOONER	CARTERET COUNTY	1805	117			
LIVE OAK	BRIG	SWANSBOROUGH	1800	140			
LIVELY	SCHOONER	BEAUFORT	1865	5.88			
LIVELY	SCHOONER	CARTERET COUNTY	1802	28	49.5	14.33	4.66
LIVELY	SCHOONER	NORTH CAROLINA	1777	40			
LIZZARD	SCHOONER	NORTH CAROLINA	1788	15			
LIZZIE	SLOOP	SMYRNA	1890	11.2	40.7	10.6	2.6

Name of Ship	Type of Ship	Shipbuilding Location	Year	Tons	Length	Width	Depth
LIZZIE ALICE	SHARPIE	SHALLOTTE	1890	7	31.2	11.5	3.1
LIZZIE B.	SLOOP	HARKERS ISLAND	1896	6.85	40.42	11	2.5
LIZZIE BLADES	SCREW STEAMER	NEW BERN	1897	19	49	13	3.7
LIZZIE BURRUS	SCREW STEAMER	NEW BERN	1888	155.42	89.7	20.2	4.9
LIZZIE F. STOWE	SCHOONER	GOOSE CREEK ISLAND	1882	17.71	42.5	16.6	4.2
LIZZIE HAULMON	SCHOONER	ELIZABETH CITY	1888	9.8	42.6	12.2	3.2
LIZZIE WALLACE	BARGE	ELIZABETH CITY	1882	181			
LOCKIE	SCHOONER	PANTEGO	1894	6.78	42	10	3.2
LOCUST	SCHOONER	PLYMOUTH	1846	54	63	17	5.8
LODGE	SCHOONER	CURRITUCK COUNTY	1820	20	39	13	4
LOLA	SCHOONER	STARKEYS CREEK	1897	7	40	11	3
LONIE BUREN	SHARPIE	KINNAKEET	1902	8	46.4	15.6	3.1
LOO GOLDTHWAITE	SCHOONER	NEW BERN	1873	16.51			
LOOKOUT	GAS SCREW		1906	13	24	13	3
LORD HYDE		CAPE FEAR	1768				
LORENA	SCHOONER	CORE SOUND	1884	16.83	48	14.8	3.6
LORENA D.	SCHOONER	BEAUFORT	1901	14	48	15	3
LORENZO	SCHOONER	SWANSBORO	1864	15	42	14.6	4.7
LOTTIE	SCHOONER	SMYRNA	1893	9	45	12	3
LOU C. ROSS	SCHOONER	KITTY HAWK	1909	7	40	10	2.1
LOU WILLIS	SCHOONER	SMYRNA	1876	15.33	42.9	13.8	4.3
LOUISA	SCHOONER	BEAUFORT COUNTY	1852	170	98	25	7
LOUISA	SCHOONER	CURRITUCK COUNTY	1818	20	40.92	14	4.33
LOUISA	SCHOONER	CURRITUCK COUNTY	1819	56	54	19	6
LOUISA	SCHOONER	NEW BERN	1869	11.55	41	14.8	3.5
LOUISA	SCHOONER	SMYRNA	1872	6.11	31.6	10.6	2.7
LOUISA ANN	SCHOONER	HYDE COUNTY	1828	30	44	15	5
LOUISA FRANCIS	SCHOONER	CARTERET COUNTY	1866	94.94	72	21.9	5.8
LOUISA WYATT	SLOOP	BELHAVEN	1902	11	34	14	3.3
LOUISE	SCHOONER	WILMINGTON	1881	47.67	66.4	20.2	6.4
LOUISE F. HARPER	SCHOONER	HARKERS ISLAND	1887	62.15	80.1	22.5	9.2
LOUISE MOREHEAD	SLOOP	MOREHEAD CITY	1886	5.32	39	10.3	2.3
LOVE D. COBB	SCHOONER	BEAUFORT	1860	23.44	45	16.5	4.2
LOVELY	BRIG	NORTH CAROLINA	1770	70			
LU RAY	GAS SCREW	MARINES	1906	14	50	12	4.2

Name of Ship	Type of Ship	Shipbuilding Location	Year	Tons	Length	Width	Depth
LUBENTIA	BRIG	NORTH CAROLINA	1794	135	72	23	10
LUCENT	SCHOONER	CURRITUCK COUNTY	1849	95	72	21	7
LUCIE	SCHOONER	BRUNSWICK COUNTY	1891	10.95	45.1	11.7	3.5
LUCIEN	SCHOONER	BEAUFORT	1857	87	72	23	4.66
LUCILLE	GAS SCREW	ELIZABETH CITY	1903	9	36	15	2.8
LUCK	SCHOONER	NEW BERN		39			
LUCRETIA	SCHOONER	CURRITUCK COUNTY	1851	22.7			
LUCRETTA	SCHOONER	OCRACOKE	1871	22.17	50	15.2	4.2
LUCY	SCHOONER	ADAMS CREEK	1816	129	72	22	9
LUCY	SCHOONER	CAMDEN COUNTY	1779	100			
LUCY	SCHOONER	WASHINGTON	1856	26	48	16	3
LUCY C. HOLMES	SCHOONER	BEAUFORT	1855	98	73	23	6.25
LUCY MAY	SCHOONER	SMYRNA	1904	12	48	11	3
LUCY OF WASHINGTON	SCHOONER	WASHINGTON	1856	26	48	16	3
LUCY RAY	SCHOONER	BELLS ISLAND	1891	9.81	41.7	13.5	3.5
LULA	SLOOP	STARKEYS CREEK	1897	7	40	11.2	2.7
LULA BELMONT	SLOOP	DAVIS	1902	6	39.3	13	
LUNA	SCHOONER	CARTERET COUNTY	1826	31	49	17	5
LUPTON	SCHOONER	HOG ISLAND	1876	8.81	35.9	12.5	3.2
LURA MAE	SHARPIE	AVON	1900	5	36	12.7	2.7
LURANIA	SLOOP	NORTH CAROLINA		60			
LURARIA	SLOOP	CAMDEN	1784	79			
LURENA	SCHOONER	SMYRNA	1899	8	41	12	3
LUSANIA	SCHOONER	CAMDEN	1784	79			
LUTHER B. MAY	SHARPIE	AVON	1903	6	40	12.7	2.8
LUTHER G.	GAS SCREW	MARINES	1912	17	42	13	3.6
LUVENIA RICHARD	SCHOONER	MITCHELL CREEK	1895	13.74	46	15	3.2
LYCURGUS	SLOOP	CURRITUCK COUNTY	1830	30	49	17.4	4.4
LYDA GERTRUDE	BARGE	JORDAN CREEK	1905	12			
LYDIA	PADDLE-WHEEL STEAMER	ELIZABETH CITY	1880	9.69	56	11.5	2.4
LYDIA	SCHOONER	HERTFORD	1799	91	63	20.75	8.25
LYDIA	SCHOONER	NORTH CAROLINA	1755	25			

Appendix A: Alphabetical List of Ships

Name of Ship	Type of Ship	Shipbuilding Location	Year	Tons	Length	Width	Depth
LYDIA	BRIG	NORTH CAROLINA	1788	102	71	23	7
LYDIA	BRIG	NORTH CAROLINA	1796	169			
LYDIA A. WILLIS	SCHOONER	BEAUFORT	1876	18.34	49.7	15.8	4.9
LYDIA G.	GAS SCREW	ATLANTIC	1914	7	39	9	3.1
LYDIA L. LEWIS	SCHOONER	CAMDEN COUNTY	1847	51	61	17	5.8
M. CARRIE	SCHOONER	HUNTING QUARTERS	1875	17	40.2	14.4	4.2
M. ESTELLE	SCHOONER	HUNTING QUARTERS	1876	11	40	13.5	3.2
M. FRANCES	SCHOONER	STRAITS	1882	9.21	38.9	12.9	3.4
M. LUPTON	GAS SCREW	WHARTONSVILLE	1914	29	61	15	3.4
M. PLATT	SCHOONER	CRAVEN COUNTY	1848	106	71	22	8
M.A. SHANKLIN	SCHOONER	SMYRNA	1907	11	46	13	2.9
M.A. STRYON	SCHOONER	CARTERET COUNTY	1854	48	62	16	5.5
M.B. DAVIS	GAS SCREW	DAVIS	1913	18	53	15.9	3.1
M.B. ROBERSON	SCHOONER	BEAUFORT	1833	97	71.75	21.17	7.42
M.C. ADAMS	GAS SCREW	MOREHEAD CITY	1912	9	35	7.8	3
M.C. CRAMMER	SCHOONER	SWANSBORO	1853	22.61			
M.C. ETHRIDGE		PLYMOUTH	1859	144	94	24	7
M.C. HILL	SCHOONER	HUNTING QUARTERS	1897	8	42	11.6	3.1
M.G. WALSTEIN	SCHOONER	ROANOKE ISLAND	1894	16.57	47	16	4
M.J. MESSENGER	SCHOONER	PASQUOTANK	1858	71			
M.K. GERTRUDE	GAS SCREW	ATLANTIC	1914	8	40	9	2
M.P. IVEY	SCHOONER	ELIZABETH CITY	1847	60.51	75.25	17.25	5.08
M.R. ZIMMERMAN	SCHOONER	EDENTON	1852	55	71	17	5
MABEL	SCHOONER	SHALLOTTE	1892	19.35	48.2	15.3	3.8
MABEL E. HORTON	GAS SCREW	MANTEO	1905	8	40	10	2.2
MABELL	SCHOONER	BEAUFORT	1876	16.87	48	14.7	3.6
MADDALENA	SHIP	HYDE COUNTY	1810	253			
MADELINE	GAS SCREW	MOREHEAD CITY	1910	29	58	17	4.8
MADISON◼S BARGE	SCHOONER	ELIZABETH CITY	1827	84	67	21	7
MADORA	SCHOONER	SMYRNA	1888	14.17	47	13.8	3.4
MAGGIE	SLOOP	DARE COUNTY	1877	11.07	37.3	14	3.3
MAGGIE	SCHOONER	SMYRNA	1902	8	44	12	2.5
MAGGIE	SCOW	STELLA	1893	30.35			
MAGGIE	SCHOONER	SWANSBORO	1867	17	50.4	14	3.1
MAGGIE	PADDLE-WHEEL STEAMER	WILMINGTON	1890	53.47	76.1	19.3	3.4

Name of Ship	Type of Ship	Shipbuilding Location	Year	Tons	Length	Width	Depth
MAGGIE ANDREWS	SCHOONER	WIT	1901	9	47	13	3
MAGGIE BEAMAN	SLOOP	WYSOCKING	1906	9	40	15	2.7
MAGGIE BELL	SCHOONER	ELIZABETH CITY		8			
MAGGIE C.	SCHOONER	BEAUFORT	1868	12.9	45	13	3.9
MAGGIE E. DAVIS	SCHOONER	HATTERAS	1899	9	51	16	3.9
MAGGIE ETTER	SCHOONER	CHICAMICOMICO	1883	8.27	35.6	10.8	3.3
MAGGIE H. LANE	SCREW STEAMER	VANCEBORO	1895	24.79	57	13	3.5
MAGGIE J.	SCHOONER	KINNAKEET	1876	8.4	38.4	14	3
MAGGIE J. A.	SCHOONER	KINNAKEET	1894	10.47	36	14.5	3.1
MAGGIE W. WADE	SCHOONER	MOREHEAD CITY	1901	9	43	13	2.4
MAGNOLIA	STEAMER	FAYETTEVILLE	1855	56	110	16.8	4
MAGNOLIA	SCHOONER	HUNTING QUARTERS	1876	10.17	38.1	12.1	3.4
MAGNOLIA	GAS SCREW	WASHINGTON	1903	14	50	11	3.9
MAJOR FISHER	SCHOONER	BEAUFORT		12			
MAJORIE	SCHOONER	BEAUFORT	1906	6	37	11.8	2.4
MALVINA	SCHOONER	HYDE COUNTY	1814	74	63	17	7
MAMIE C. DANIELS	SCHOONER	MOREHEAD CITY	1896	9.32	43.8	11.4	2.8
MAMIE LEWIS	GAS SCREW	SNEADS FERRY	1905	8	37	11	5.3
MANGROVE	SHARPIE	WIT	1902	6	42	14	3
MANIE CARLIS	SCHOONER	ROANOKE ISLAND	1893	20.95	54	13	3.3
MANISTEE	SCHOONER	WIT	1897	12	43	14	3.2
MANISTER	SCHOONER	WILMINGTON	1897	8	35	13.8	4.2
MANLY	SCHOONER	SMYRNA	1905	10	45	13	2.4
MANNER	SCHOONER	CARTERET COUNTY	1819	40	48	17	5
MANTEO	SLOOP	ELIZABETH CITY	1874	9.95	32.5	13.9	3.7
MANTEO	SLOOP	SMYRNA	1890	7.08	43.3	10.8	2.8
MANTEO	SCHOONER	WASHINGTON	1845	147	81	23	8
MANUMIT	SCHOONER	HYDE COUNTY	1840	33	49	16	5
MARA DAUGH	SCHOONER	ROANOKE ISLAND	1804	39	50	17	6
MARBLEHEAD	SCHOONER	SMYRNA	1898	15	48	14	3.2
MAREY MARIAH	SCHOONER	CURRITUCK COUNTY	1836	43	44	17	5
MARGARET	SCHOONER	BERTIE COUNTY	1816	30	49	15	4.9
MARGARET	SCHOONER	POPLAR POINT	1831	98.56	69.66	20.92	7.83
MARGARET	SCHOONER	SMITHS CREEK	1810	106	71.66	22	7.83
MARGARET A. BRUSH	SLOOP	ELIZABETH CITY		12			
MARGARET ANN	SLOOP	EDENTON	1877	8.2	36.6	15.2	3.6
MARGARET BLOUNT	SCHOONER	CURRITUCK COUNTY	1846	27	46	15	4.7

Name of Ship	Type of Ship	Shipbuilding Location	Year	Tons	Length	Width	Depth
MARGARET JANE	SCHOONER	BAY RIVER	1843	6.68	30.8	11.1	3
MARGARET JANE	SCHOONER	BEAUFORT	1844	21	42	14.83	4.08
MARGARET MEADE	SCHOONER	ELIZABETH CITY	1811	117.68	77	20.66	8.33
MARGARET O'NEIL	SCHOONER	NEW BERN		13			
MARGARETTE	SCREW STEAMER	ELIZABETH CITY	1903	22	48	13	5
MARGERET Y. DAVIS	SCHOONER	SMITHVILLE	1847	36	41	14	5
MARGIE	STEAMER	WASHINGTON	1883	85.95			
MARIA	SCHOONER	CARTERET COUNTY	1833	51	58	17.5	5.83
MARIA	SCHOONER	CORE SOUND	1819	32	48	15	5
MARIA	SCHOONER	CURRITUCK	1827	80	62	20	7
MARIA	SLOOP	CURRITUCK COUNTY	1821	29	49	17	4.33
MARIA	SCHOONER	NEW BERN	1823	59	55	18	6.42
MARIA	SHIP	ONSLOW COUNTY	1798	288			
MARIA	SCHOONER	STRAITS	1898	28	55	20	4
MARIA ANN	SCHOONER	EDENTON		17			
MARIA ANN	SCHOONER	NEW BERN		8			
MARIAM	SCHOONER	SOUTH MILLS	1874	48.54			
MARIE	SIDE-WHEEL STEAMER	WASHINGTON	1894	121.24	85.8	26.8	7.7
MARIEL DEEN	GAS SCREW	CURRITUCK	1914	20	52	14	3.5
MARIES	SLOOP	NORTH CAROLINA	1789	65			
MARIETTA	SCHOONER	BEAUFORT	1840	12.48	44	13.6	3.8
MARIETTA	SCHOONER	BEAUFORT		14			
MARINER	SCHOONER	CARTERET COUNTY	1819	40	48.75	17	5.92
MARION	GAS SCREW	BELHAVEN	1906	10	51	12.9	2.6
MARION	SCHOONER	ONSLOW COUNTY	1842	36	55	17	5
MARION TEMPLE	SCHOONER	CLUBFOOT CREEK	1889	23.22	54	15.5	3.3
MARJORIE	SHARPIE	BEAUFORT	1906	6	37	11.8	2.4
MARTHA	SCHOONER	BEAUFORT	1841	95			
MARTHA	SCHOONER	BEAUFORT	1875	52.95			
MARTHA	SCHOONER	CARTERET COUNTY	1851	91	73	22.25	6.58
MARTHA A.	SLOOP	BRIDGEBORO		12			
MARTHA ANN	SCHOONER	NEW BERN	1846	72	58.5	15.17	3.5
MARTHA ANN	SLOOP	PLYMOUTH	1850	25	47	16	3.92

Name of Ship	Type of Ship	Shipbuilding Location	Year	Tons	Length	Width	Depth
MARTHA ANN CARTWRIGHT	SCHOONER	ELIZABETH CITY	1853	59.13	71.75	17.33	5.25
MARTHA COOK	SCHOONER	WILLIAMSTON	1855	188			
MARTHA D.	SCHOONER	PLYMOUTH	1846	57	65	17	5
MARTHA D. THOMAS	SHARPIE	SMYRNA	1896	7	46.3	12.3	3.5
MARTHA DAVIS	SCHOONER	STRAITS	1868	17.3	44	15.2	3.5
MARTHA EMILY	SCHOONER	WASHINGTON		7			
MARTHA H. STEVENS	SCHOONER	CARTERET COUNTY	1849	52	59	16	5
MARTHA H. STYRON		OCRACOKE	1849	46	62	16.09	5
MARTHA J.	SCHOONER	BEAUFORT	1874	10	38.2	12.2	3.3
MARTHA JONES	SLOOP	INDIAN TOWN	1830	20	38	14	4.66
MARTHA M. FOWLE	SCHOONER	WASHINGTON	1842	67	65	19	6
MARTHA MAHOO	SCHOONER		1833				
MARTHA MOORE	SCHOONER	BEAUFORT COUNTY	1855	188	103	25	8
MARTHA OF NORTH CAROLINA	SCHOONER	NORTH CAROLINA	1698	6			
MARTHA SKINNER	SCHOONER	ELIZABETH CITY	1850	173	95	25.01	8
MARTHA WASHINGTON	SCHOONER	NEW BERN		8			
MARTHIS D. THOMAS	SCHOONER	SMYRNA	1896	11	46.3	12.3	3.5
MARTILDA	SCHOONER	CARTERET COUNTY	1823	27	47	15	4.9
MARTIN	SCHOONER	NORTH CAROLINA	1773	25			
MARTIN	SCHOONER	NORTH CAROLINA	1802	78			
MARY	SCHOONER	ADAMS CREEK	1815	81	63.83	19.92	7.5
MARY	SCHOONER	BEAUFORT	1824	34	51	16	4.75
MARY	SCHOONER	BEAUFORT	1846	87	70.5	22	6.58
MARY	SCHOONER	CARTERET COUNTY	1819	38.44	54	15	5
MARY	SCHOONER	CARTERET COUNTY	1826	126	71	23.5	9
MARY	SCHOONER	CARTERET COUNTY	1838	83	68.58	20.66	6.83
MARY	SCHOONER	CARTERET COUNTY	1851	37	54.5	17.08	4.66
MARY	SCHOONER	CRAVEN	1815	81			
MARY	SCHOONER	CRAVEN COUNTY	1830	28	46	16	4
MARY	SCHOONER	CURRITUCK COUNTY	1807	52	54	18	6
MARY	SCHOONER	CURRITUCK COUNTY	1817	52	54	18.5	6

Name of Ship	Type of Ship	Shipbuilding Location	Year	Tons	Length	Width	Depth
MARY	BRIGANTINE	EDENTON	1800	88			
MARY	SCHOONER	ELIZABETH CITY	1844	48.13	65.92	16.92	4.92
MARY	SCHOONER	NEW BERN	1878	7.95	36.5	11.1	3.1
MARY	SCHOONER	NORTH CAROLINA	1745	70			
MARY	SLOOP	NORTH CAROLINA	1749	20			
MARY	SCHOONER	NORTH CAROLINA	1750	10			
MARY	SCHOONER	NORTH CAROLINA	1752	5			
MARY	SCHOONER	NORTH CAROLINA	1775	25			
MARY	SLOOP	NORTH CAROLINA	1780	82	62	20	7
MARY	SLOOP	NORTH CAROLINA	1788	58			
MARY	SCHOONER	NORTH RIVER	1800	59			
MARY	SCHOONER	SMITH CREEK	1816	70	62.42	19.83	6.66
MARY	SCHOONER	SMITH CREEK	1822	98	94	21	7
MARY	SCHOONER	SOUTHPORT	1903	21	55	16	4.8
MARY	SCHOONER	STRAITS	1875	8.02	37.8	11.8	3
MARY	SCHOONER	STRAITS		24.5	54	15.08	4.04
MARY	SCHOONER	STRAITS OF CORE SOUND	1822	25	45	15	4
MARY	SCHOONER	TURNERS CREEK	1874	29.43	53.7	17.8	4.2
MARY	SCHOONER	TYRRELL COUNTY	1834	47	66	16	5
MARY	BRIG	TYRRELL COUNTY	1795	107			
MARY	SCHOONER	WASHINGTON	1847	71	68	20	5
MARY A. GILDERSLEEVE	SCHOONER	ELIZABETH CITY		71			
MARY A. PENDER	SCHOONER	BEAUFORT	1850	40	62	17	4
MARY ABIGAIL	SCHOONER	CARTERET COUNTY	1850	33	51.5	17.5	4.6
MARY ADAMS	SCHOONER	BEAUFORT COUNTY	1818	28	43.92	15.17	4
MARY AGNES	SCHOONER	BEAUFORT	1903	6	37	10	2.4
MARY AMMA	SCHOONER	NEW BERN	1858	2	2		
MARY AND ELIZABETH	SCHOONER	LOCKWOODS FOLLY	1799	30.59	46.5	14.33	5.33
MARY AND ELLEN	SLOOP	EDENTON		15			
MARY AND FRANCES	SCHOONER	PLYMOUTH		13			
MARY AND SUSAN	SCHOONER	HAMILTON	1849	125.34	85.5	24.25	6.92

Name of Ship	Type of Ship	Shipbuilding Location	Year	Tons	Length	Width	Depth
MARY ANN	SCHOONER	ADAMS CREEK	1809	95			
MARY ANN	SCHOONER	BAY RIVER	1827	61	59	19	6
MARY ANN	SCHOONER	CAPE FEAR	1753				
MARY ANN	SCHOONER	ELIZABETH CITY	1827	39	50.33	19.83	4.92
MARY ANN	SCHOONER	HYDE COUNTY	1817	23	43	14	4
MARY ANN	SCHOONER	HYDE COUNTY	1841	34	48	16	5
MARY ANN	BRIG	NORTH CAROLINA	1796	114			
MARY ANN	SCHOONER	NORTH CAROLINA	1798	69			
MARY ANN	SLOOP	POPLAR POINT	1820	68			
MARY ANN REBECCA	SCHOONER	HATTERAS	1871	18.38	53	14	5
MARY B.	GAS SCREW	EAST LAKE	1906	7	34	8	6.8
MARY BEAR	SCHOONER	WILMINGTON		16			
MARY BELL	SCHOONER	BEAUFORT	1899	18	51	15	4
MARY BELL		NORTH RIVER	1891	8			
MARY BELO	SCREW STEAMER	NEW BERN	1904	9	45	11	4
MARY BROWNRIGS	SCHOONER	NORTH CAROLINA	1802	56			
MARY BRYAN	SCHOONER	BEAUFORT COUNTY	1860	21	44	15	4
MARY BRYAN OF WASHINGTON	SCHOONER	BEAUFORT	1860	95	46	16	
MARY C. CRAMNER	SCHOONER	COLUMBIA	1853	60	72	17	4.42
MARY C. CRANMER	SCHOONER	SWANSBORO	1853	34	53	17.2	4.5
MARY C. HOOVER	SCHOONER	BEAUFORT COUNTY	1854	206	101	27	8
MARY C. SUMMER	SCHOONER	EDENTON	1857	55	69	17	5
MARY CAROLINE	SCHOONER	TYRRELL COUNTY	1834	47	66	16	5
MARY D.	SCHOONER	PINEY POINT	1880	7.55	33.5	12	3.1
MARY D.	SCHOONER	PINEY POINT	1885	7.55	33.5	12	3.1
MARY D. HAYMAN	SCHOONER	EDENTON	1853	163	95	25	7
MARY D. ZIMMERMAN	SCHOONER	PLYMOUTH	1850	55			
MARY DUERS	SCHOONER	EDENTON	1854	52			
MARY E.	SCHOONER	BEAUFORT	1905	10	45	12	2.5
MARY E. BURRUS	SLOOP	ENGLEHARD	1905	6	32.1	15.8	3.6
MARY E. HOOVER	SCHOONER	BEAUFORT COUNTY	1853	206	101	27	8
MARY E. PAMROLE	SCHOONER	WASHINGTON	1853	150	88	24	8
MARY E. PARMERLE OF WASHINGTON	SCHOONER	WASHINGTON	1853		88	24	
MARY E. QUEEN	SCHOONER	PINEY POINT	1865	8.59	30.6	11.4	3.4
MARY E. REEVES	SCHOONER	DAVIS	1891	9.28	45.5	12.3	3.1

Name of Ship	Type of Ship	Shipbuilding Location	Year	Tons	Length	Width	Depth
MARY E. ROBERTS	SCREW STEAMER	CHOWAN COUNTY	1873	120.66	93.4	16.5	6.1
MARY ELIZA	SCHOONER	BERTIE COUNTY	1814	92	71	20	7
MARY ELIZA	SCHOONER	CURRITUCK	1841	53			
MARY ELIZA	SCHOONER	PLYMOUTH	1828	42	61	15	5
MARY ELIZA SMALL	SCHOONER	BIG FLATTY CREEK	1890	25.18	51.2	20	4
MARY EMMA	SCHOONER	NEW BERN	1858	31	58	15	4
MARY FLEETWOOD	SCHOONER	NEW BERN	1879	10.02	44	12.3	4.4
MARY FLUHUR	SCHOONER	NEW BERN	1879	10	44.4	14.3	4.4
MARY FRANCIS	BRIG	BAY RIVER	1802	176			
MARY FRANCIS	SCHOONER	CARTERET COUNTY	1844	110	71.83	22.5	8.08
MARY FRANCIS	SCHOONER	MOUNT PLEASANT	1833	26	44	14	4
MARY FRAZIER	SCHOONER	WASHINGTON		6			
MARY HOLLAND	SCHOONER	PORTSMOUTH		6			
MARY J. HAYNIE	SCHOONER	ELIZABETH CITY	1902	11	52	20	3.6
MARY J. SANDERMAN	SCHOONER	ELIZABETH CITY	1840	41	54	16	5
MARY JANE	SCHOONER	BEAUFORT COUNTY	1843	24	46.17	17.92	4.42
MARY JANE	SCHOONER	CARTERET COUNTY	1838	81	66	21	7
MARY JANE	SCHOONER	ELIZABETH CITY		15			
MARY JANE FORSHA	SLOOP	COLINGTON	1888	7.83	36.6	14	3.2
MARY JANE KENNEDY	SCHOONER	ELIZABETH CITY	1856	71.9	81.5	17.33	5.54
MARY K.	SLOOP	MOUNT PLEASANT	1907	10	38	14	3.3
MARY L.	SCHOONER	NEW BERN	1899	12	39	12	3.9
MARY LEE	SCHOONER	SUPPLY	1906	18	51	14	3.8
MARY LOUISA	SCHOONER	ELIZABETH CITY	1854	94.11	84	23.3	7.6
MARY LOUISA	SCHOONER	TYRRELL COUNTY	1850	34	55	16	4
MARY LYDIA	SCHOONER	NORTH BANKS	1816	33.57	51.75	15.83	4.75
MARY M.	SLOOP	MOREHEAD CITY	1902	8	42	12.6	2
MARY MARIAH	SCHOONER	CURRITUCK	1836	43	44	17	5
MARY MAYBIRD	SCHOONER	HUNTING QUARTERS	1897	5	34	10	2.5
MARY MCKAY	SCHOONER	BROAD CREEK	1819	34	47.33	15.92	5.42
MARY QUEEN	SCHOONER	NEW BERN	1902	23	58.7	16	4.4
MARY R. ZIMMERMAN	SCHOONER	EDENTON	1850	55	71	17	5
MARY RILEY	SCHOONER	BEAUFORT		7			
MARY RUFFIN	SCHOONER	MOREHEAD CITY	1891	9.96	47.2	13.1	3.1
MARY S.	SCHOONER	CORE SOUND	1875	24.2	49	16.6	4.2

Name of Ship	Type of Ship	Shipbuilding Location	Year	Tons	Length	Width	Depth
MARY S. MIZELL	SCHOONER	PLYMOUTH	1863	49	76	17	5
MARY SUSAN	SCHOONER	HAMILTON	1849	12	85	24	6
MARY SUSAN NORRIS	SCHOONER	ELIZABETH CITY		8			
MARY T. SANDERSON	SCHOONER	ELIZABETH CITY	1840	41	54	16	5
MARY THERESA	SCHOONER	NEW BERN		94			
MARY THOMAS	SCHOONER	MOREHEAD CITY	1891	9.98	47.5	13.4	2.6
MARY TURNER	SCHOONER	WINDSOR	1803	56			
MARY WHEELER	SCHOONER	STRAITS	1873	27.86	50.7	18.2	4.5
MARY WINEFRED	SCHOONER	PLYMOUTH	1844	45	64	16	5
MARY WINYFRED	SCHOONER	PLYMOUTH	1804	40	64	16	
MARY WOOD	SCHOONER	EDENTON	1859	96	87	21	5
MARYON SPARROW	SCHOONER	SMITHS CREEK	1816	70	62	20	7
MARY'S ANN, BETTY	SCHOONER	NORTH CAROLINA	1763	15			
MASCOT	GAS SCREW	ELIZABETH CITY	1906	5	25	7	6.6
MASCOT	SCREW STEAMER	NEW BERN	1906	33	57	14	8
MATILDA	BRIG	NORTH CAROLINA	1800	133			
MATILDA	BRIG	SMITHS CREEK	1821	135			
MATILDA	SCHOONER	STRAITS OF CARTERET	1823	27	47	15	4
MATTAMUSKEET	SCREW STEAMER	FAIRFIELD	1897	31	57	13	3.6
MATTHEW VAN DU-SEN	SCHOONER	NEW BERN		10			
MATTIE	SCHOONER	BEAUFORT	1866	15.79	48	13.5	3.8
MATTIE MAY	SCHOONER	HATTERAS	1891	7.8	36	10.8	3.4
MATTIE MAY	SCHOONER	OCRACOKE	1895	15	44.5	15.4	3.7
MATTIE O		SMYRNA	1890		43.5		
MAUD	SCHOONER	BEAUFORT	1886	7.09	40.7	10.6	2.4
MAUD	SCHOONER	BEAUFORT	1898	13	44	14	3.2
MAUD	SLOOP	MOREHEAD CITY	1888	6.05	41.3	10.1	2.9
MAUD AND REG	GAS SCREW	WASHINGTON	1905	12	54	13	3.9
MAUD GRANNIS	SLOOP	BELHAVEN	1900	9	43	14.7	3
MAVA DOUGH	SCHOONER	ROANOKE ISLAND	1804	38.56	50	16.66	5.5
MAY	SHARPIE	BEAUFORT	1887	13	44.6	12.6	3.2
MAY	SCHOONER	SOUTHPORT	1887	13.54	44.6	12.6	3.2
MAY BELL	PADDLE-WHEEL STEAMER	GRIFTON	1892	63.57	80	20	3.6
MAY BELL	SCHOONER	NORTH RIVER	1891	10.77	46.5	12.9	3.9
MAY FLOWER	SCHOONER	HARLOWE	1890	10	46	13.3	3.5

Name of Ship	Type of Ship	Shipbuilding Location	Year	Tons	Length	Width	Depth
MAY FLOWER	SCHOONER	NEW BERN	1880	10.78	49.2	13.8	3.6
MAY FRANCIS	SCHOONER	CARTERET COUNTY	1844	110	71	22	8
MAY QUEEN	SHARPIE	NEW BERN	1902	13	58.7	16.6	4.4
MAY QUEEN	SCHOONER	SWANSBORO	1866	11.51	44	12.8	3.1
MAYFLOWER	SCHOONER	CRAWFORD		11			
MAYFLOWER	SCHOONER	GOOSE CREEK ISLAND	1880	12.51	49.2	13.8	3.5
MAYFLOWER	SCHOONER	HARLOWE	1890	10.52	46	13.3	3.5
MAYFLOWER	SCREW STEAMER	POINT CASWELL	1904	92	87	18	6.2
MECKLENBERG	SCHOONER	WASHINGTON	1855	137	93	72	7
MEDAD PLATT	SCHOONER	CRAVEN COUNTY	1848	106			
MELISSA	SCHOONER	CURRITUCK COUNTY	1830	102	70	22.6	7.8
MELISSA HOLLAND	SCHOONER	CARTERET COUNTY	1849	31	49	17.5	4.42
MELISSA OF WASHINGTON	SCHOONER	CARTERET COUNTY	1842	21	42	14	4
MELVILLE	SCHOONER	HATTERAS	1875	12.5	38.3	13.2	4
MELVILLE	SCHOONER	WASHINGTON	1845	112	78	22	7
MELVIN	SCHOONER	NEW BERN	1873	10	95	25.7	7.7
MELVIN	SCHOONER	NEW BERN	1874	111			
MELVIN MORRIS	SCHOONER	SMYRNA	1884	9.34	39.1	12.1	3.8
MELVINA	SCHOONER	MARTIN COUNTY	1849	55	63	17	5.83
MELVINA	SCHOONER	NEW BERN	1872	6.32	27.5	12.4	2.9
MELVINA	SCHOONER	WASHINGTON COUNTY	1849	55	63	17	5.83
MELVIRA	SCHOONER	BEAUFORT	1839	58	63	19	6
MENA BRANCH	SCHOONER	MOREHEAD CITY	1886	5.63	39.9	10	2.6
MENHADEN	GAS SCREW	MOREHEAD CITY	1911	28	55	18	4.3
MENTOR	SCHOONER	CARTERET COUNTY	1816	89.57	60.5	19.5	7.92
MERLE	GAS SCREW	MOREHEAD CITY	1913	8	33	9	3.5
MERMAID	SCHOONER	NORTH CAROLINA	1788	9			
MERMAID	PADDLE-WHEEL STEAMER		1882	9.26	53.2	11	2.5
MERRY WAVE	PADDLE-WHEEL STEAMER	EDENTON	1880	8.49	49.8	11.1	1.9
MESSENGER	SCHOONER	NORTH CAROLINA	1799	78			
MESSENGER	SCREW STEAMER	WILMINGTON	1892	14.67	44.6	9.9	3

Name of Ship	Type of Ship	Shipbuilding Location	Year	Tons	Length	Width	Depth
METEOR	SHARPIE	SMYRNA	1902	13	44.2	12.5	3.2
MIANTONOMIAH	BARK	BAY RIVER	1849	427	116	28	15
MIDAS	SCHOONER	BEAUFORT	1816	47	55	17	6
MIDDLETON	SCHOONER	HYDE COUNTY	1840	37	53	15	5
MIDGETT	SCHOONER	NEW BERN	1850	33	52	16	4.6
MILDRED	SCHOONER	MOREHEAD CITY	1892	6.44	40.9	10.4	2.8
MILDRED MAY	SCHOONER	ELIZABETH CITY	1902	59	80	22	5.6
MILISSA	SCHOONER	CURRITUCK	1830	102	70	22.5	7.66
MILKMAID	SCHOONER	NORTH CAROLINA	1728	5			
MILLY	SCHOONER	NORTH CAROLINA	1804	86			
MILLY RHODES	SCHOONER	EDENTON	1877	9.15	43.9	12.9	2.6
MILTON SELBY OF WASHINGTON	SCHOONER	HYDE COUNTY	1854	33	54.5	15.58	4.5
MINA PERRY	SCHOONER	SMYRNA	1899	18	54	15	3.9
MINERVA	SHIP	BEAUFORT	1806	239	84	25	8
MINERVA	SCHOONER	CARTERET COUNTY	1840	84	68.17	20.66	6.92
MINERVA	SCHOONER	NORTH CAROLINA	1796	113			
MINERVA	BRIG	PITT COUNTY	1807	99			
MINERVA	SCHOONER	WASHINGTON	1881	18.53	45	14.4	4
MINERVA	BRIG		1788	177			
MINERVA L. WEDMAN	SCHOONER	WASHINGTON		85			
MINNIE	SCHOONER	SMYRNA	1883	12.51	40	14.1	3.8
MINNIE	SCHOONER	TURNERS CREEK	1883	16.45	47.6	15.6	3.7
MINNIE AND MAUD	SCHOONER	ELIZABETH CITY	1902	20	51	18	4.4
MINNIE G.	SCHOONER	SHALLOTTE	1888	10.6	44	12.9	3.5
MINNIE WARD	SCHOONER	SWANSBORO	1873	15	49.7	13.3	3.4
MISSOURI	SCHOONER	ATLANTIC	1900	11	40	13	3
MISSOURI	SCHOONER	KINNAKEET	1888	15.64	44.2	15.2	4
MISSOURI	SCHOONER	SMYRNA	1901	18	56	16	3.3
MISSOURI ANN LUTHER	SCHOONER	NEW BERN	1872	14.04			
MITALDA	SCHOONER	CRAVEN COUNTY	1809	114	74	22.58	8
MITALDA	SCHOONER	STRAITS OF CURRITUCK	1823	27	47	15	4
MODERATOR	SCHOONER	CURRITUCK COUNTY	1816	20	40	13	4
MODOC	SLOOP	WILMINGTON		21			
MOHAWK	GAS SCREW	SOUTHPORT	1909	13	44	11	3.3
MOHAWK	SCHOONER	TYRRELL COUNTY	1810	45.58	50.75	17.66	6.1

Name of Ship	Type of Ship	Shipbuilding Location	Year	Tons	Length	Width	Depth
MOLLEY B.	SCHOONER	SWANSBORO	1866	12	44.9	12.8	3.2
MOLLIE	SHARPIE	HATTERAS	1891	8	34.5	10.2	2.6
MOLLIE L. FARMER	SCREW STEAMER	BETHEL	1890	21.54	51	15	3.8
MOLLY	SLOOP	NORTH CAROLINA	1729	40			
MOLLY	SLOOP	NORTH CAROLINA	1754	15			
MOLLY	SCHOONER	NORTH CAROLINA	1784	98			
MOLLY AND BETSY	SCHOONER	ROANOKE	1765	50			
MONEY MAKER	GAS SCREW	SMITH MILLS	1908	28	65	15	4.6
MONTERA	SCHOONER	CARTERET COUNTY	1857	20	40	13.92	4.33
MONTEREY	SCHOONER	PLYMOUTH		48			
MONUMENT	SCHOONER	HYDE COUNTY	1840	45			
MORSE OF BEAUFORT	SCHOONER	BEAUFORT	1828	50	58.17	17.5	5
MOSQUITO HAWK	SCHOONER	NORTH CAROLINA	1772	10			
MOT	GAS SCREW	VANCEBORO	1912	36	64	16	3.2
MOUNT GALLANT	SCHOONER	NORTH CAROLINA	1758	8			
MULBERRY	SCHOONER	NEW BERN	1821	24	41.75	12.42	5.42
MYRTIE	GAS SCREW	WASHINGTON	1902	10	39	10	3.5
MYRTLE	SHARPIE	SMYRNA	1901	13	50.2	16.5	4
MYRTLE	SCHOONER	WASHINGTON	1903	26	50	16	4
MYSTERY	SCHOONER	SHALLOTTE	1894	5.72	37.4	9.7	2.4
MYSTERY	SCHOONER	STRAITS	1876	32.41	55.8	18.7	4.5
MYSTERY	GAS SCREW	WASHINGTON	1900	13	45	13	4.1
MYSTIC	STEAMER	NEW BERN	1866	180			
N. ESTELLE	GAS SCREW	MANNS HARBOUR	1914	15	43	12	3.6
N.J. MERCEDES	SCHOONER	AVON	1901	7	33	14	3
N.P. WOODBURY	SCHOONER	SMITHVILLE	1848	32	45	18	4
NABOB	SCHOONER	PORT ROANOKE	1775	10			
NAN	SCHOONER	CARTERET COUNTY	1819	29	46	14	5
NANCY	SCHOONER	BEAUFORT	1828	35	52.42	16.25	5.17
NANCY	SCHOONER	BEAUFORT	1838	35	52	16	4.83
NANCY	SCHOONER	CURRITUCK COUNTY	1769	13			
NANCY	SCHOONER	CURRITUCK COUNTY	1805	21	46	14.5	3.92
NANCY	SCHOONER	CURRITUCK COUNTY	1814	21.78	55		

Name of Ship	Type of Ship	Shipbuilding Location	Year	Tons	Length	Width	Depth
NANCY	SCHOONER	NORTH CAROLINA	1778	70			
NANCY	SLOOP	NORTH CAROLINA	1785	35			
NANCY	SCHOONER	NORTH CAROLINA	1788	10			
NANCY	BRIG	NORTH CAROLINA	1796	85			
NANCY	SCHOONER	NORTH CAROLINA	1802	36			
NANCY	SCHOONER	ORCHARD CREEK	1800	53			
NANCY	SCHOONER	ROANOKE ISLAND	1801	41.37	53.75	16.25	5.5
NANCY AND BETSY	SCHOONER	CROOKED CREEK	1817	39	51.66	17.75	5.08
NANCY AND BETSY	SCHOONER	POWELLS POINT	1821	21	41.5	14.65	4.33
NANCY AND POLLY	SCHOONER	NORTH BANKS	1798	30	52	15	4.5
NANCY AND SABRINA	SCHOONER	CURRITUCK INLET	1827	35	50	17	5
NANCY AND SUKEY	SHIP	NORTH CAROLINA	1767	85			
NANCY ANNE	SHARPIE	WILMINGTON	1887	15.15	48	13	3.6
NANCY BELL	BRIG	NEW BERN	1803		58	22	
NANCY WHITMELL	SCHOONER	HALIFAX	1804	76			
NANNIE B.	SCREW STEAMER	STELLA	1887	85.45	83	19.2	4.2
NANNIE P. DAVIS	SCHOONER	BEAUFORT	1882	12	49.4	12.6	3.4
NAOMI	SCHOONER	BEAUFORT	1891	15.88	53.6	14	4
NAPOLEON	SCHOONER	NEW BERN	1857	193.48	120	28.2	8.1
NASHVILLE	SCHOONER	STRAITS	1867	6.43	35.8	10.2	2.8
NATHAN DURFREE	SCHOONER	BAY RIVER	1848	250			
NATIVE	SCHOONER	HATTERAS		9			
NATIVE	SCHOONER	HYDE COUNTY	1855	33.48			
NATIVE	SCHOONER	HYDE COUNTY	1856	44	59	17	5
NATIVE	SLOOP	SMYRNA	1892	6.97	40	11.4	2.5
NAUTITUS	SCREW STEAMER	WASHINGTON	1889	46	66	15	4.4
NAVIGATOR	SCHOONER	PINEY GROVE	1830	92	68	2.58	7.42
NEBRASKA	SCHOONER	ELIZABETH CITY	1854	61.55	71	17	5.66
NED WOOD	SCHOONER	EDENTON	1883	8.38	37	12	3
NEDDEEN		GOOSE CREEK ISLAND	1891	12	35	12.5	3.5
NELLIE	SCREW STEAMER	ELIZABETH CITY	1892	12.39	39.1	7.3	3.5
NELLIE	SHARPIE	OCRACOKE	1898	13	47.5	17	3.5
NELLIE	SCHOONER	SWANSBORO	1901	9	42	12.8	2.8

Name of Ship	Type of Ship	Shipbuilding Location	Year	Tons	Length	Width	Depth
NELLIE B.	SCHOONER	SWANSBORO	1899	7	43	12	2
NELLIE B. DEY	SCREW STEAMER	LENOXVILLE	1884	80.88	98	17.5	5
NELLIE B. NEFF	SCHOONER	SMITHVILLE	1874	11.47	38.5	13.3	5
NELLIE BLY	SLOOP	MOREHEAD CITY	1891	5.38	41.9	10.9	3
NELLIE FLORENCE	SLOOP	SMYRNA	1890	6.8	44	11.5	3
NELLIE MAY	GAS SCREW	MOREHEAD CITY	1908	9	38	10	2.8
NELLIE POTTER	SCHOONER	WASHINGTON		29			
NELLIE WADSWORTH	SCHOONER	ELIZABETH CITY	1880	61.42			
NELLIE WATT	SLOOP	BELHAVEN	1885	5	33	22.4	2.4
NELLY AND POLLY	SCHOONER	NORTH CAROLINA	1788	20			
NELSON	SCHOONER	HARKERS ISLAND	1884	19.82	44.5	15.5	4.3
NEMO	GAS SCREW	WIT	1913	14	39	8.7	2
NEPONSIT	GAS SCREW	MOREHEAD CITY	1912	44	61	19	5.5
NEPTUNE	BRIG	NORTH CAROLINA	1765	70			
NEPTUNE	SCHOONER	SMYRNA	1898	12	46	13	3.6
NETA	SHARPIE	ATLANTIC	1896	6	42.2	11.9	3.4
NETA	SCHOONER	BEAUFORT	1900	7	38	10.8	2.6
NETTIE	GAS SCREW	JACKSONVILLE	1908	8	40	10	2.6
NETTIE B. SMITH	SLOOP	BEAUFORT	1897	5	35	11	2.5
NETTIE MAY	SLOOP	BEAUFORT	1905	6	40	11	2.3
NETTIE PIERCE	SCHOONER	BEAUFORT	1890	6	41.6	11	2.9
NETTIE W.	SCREW STEAMER	NEW BERN	1890	36.79	56	15.8	3
NEUSE	PADDLE-WHEEL STEAMER	KINSTON	1876	55.16			
NEUSE	BRIG	SMITHFIELD	1801	135			
NEVA PEARL	SCHOONER	STRAITS	1895	15.48	43.4	16.2	4.5
NEVADA	SCHOONER	SMYRNA	1904	13	45	13	3
NEVADA	SCHOONER	WILMINGTON		30			
NEW BALTIMORE	SCHOONER	NEW BERN		15			
NEW BERN		ADAMS CREEK	1750	168			
NEW BERN	BRIG	ADAMS CREEK	1814	168	79	23	10
NEW BERN	SHIP	NORTH CAROLINA	1750	100			
NEW LIGHT	BRIGANTINE	BEAUFORT	1894	31	56	19	4
NEW WAYNE	SIDE-WHEEL STEAMER	NEW BERN	1850	50			
NEWBURN	SCHOONER	NORTH CAROLINA	1761	20			

Name of Ship	Type of Ship	Shipbuilding Location	Year	Tons	Length	Width	Depth
NILLIE	SCHOONER	OCRACOKE	1898	17.95	47.5	17	3.5
NINA	SCHOONER	MOREHEAD CITY	1896	9.25	43.3	11.8	2.8
NINA	SCREW STEAMER	SWANSBORO	1897	39	82.2	18.2	3.3
NINA DARE	SCHOONER	NORTH RIVER	1892	10.47	45.3	12.7	3.3
NINA G. WALLACE	SCHOONER	MOREHEAD CITY	1901	6	42	11	2.3
NINA M.	SCHOONER	BEAUFORT	1899	14	48	15	3.4
NOAHS ARK	BRIG	NORTH CAROLINA	1788	115			
NOAHS ARK	BRIG	NORTH CAROLINA	1789	65			
NON PAREIL	SCHOONER	CARTERET COUNTY	1799	48			
NONPAREIL	SCHOONER	STRAITS OF CORE	1825	82	63	28	7
NONPLUS	SCHOONER	POWELLS POINT	1826	89.77	72.66	22	
NORMA	GAS SCREW	ATLANTIC	1914	10	38	9	3.6
NORTH CAROLINA	SHIP	BATH	1727	140			
NORTH CAROLINA	SCHOONER	CARTERET COUNTY	1846	148	85	24	8
NORTH CAROLINA	SCHOONER	ELIZABETH CITY	1843	56.19	76.33	17.33	4.58
NORTH CAROLINA	PADDLE-WHEEL STEAMER	FAYETTEVILLE	1859	110	115	22	4.66
NORTH CAROLINA	SCHOONER	MOYOCK LANDING	1818	38	53	18	4.66
NORTH CAROLINA	SHIP	NORTH CAROLINA		201			
NORTH CAROLINA	SLOOP	WILMINGTON		12			
NORTH STATE	SCHOONER	CARTERET COUNTY	1848	35	56.25	16.5	4.42
NORTH STATE	PADDLE-WHEEL STEAMER	FAYETTEVILLE	1870	118.13			
O. COKE	SCHOONER	KINNAKEET	1878	27.44	69.9	17.1	5.4
OCEAN	SCHOONER	GANITY BAY	1827	100	68.5	22.25	7.75
OCEAN BIRD	SCHOONER	HATTERAS	1876	11.33	42	14	4
OCEAN WAVE	SCHOONER	BEAUFORT	1853	153			
OCEAN WAVE	SCHOONER	CAMDEN COUNTY	1853	136	31	24	7
OCEAN WAVE	SHARPIE	GOOSE CREEK ISLAND	1892	6.72	36	10.7	2.2
OCER	SHARPIE						
OCTAVIOUS COKE JR.	PADDLE-WHEEL STEAMER	CHOWAN COUNTY	1883	7.34	48.6	11.5	2.2

Name of Ship	Type of Ship	Shipbuilding Location	Year	Tons	Length	Width	Depth
ODD FELLOW	SCHOONER	CARTERET COUNTY	1847	24	48	13	4
ODY	SHARPIE	HARLOWE	1901	9	41.3	12.3	2.7
OHIO	SCHOONER	OCRACOKE	1857	9.63	42.9	12.4	3.6
OLADEAN	SLOOP	ENGLEHARD	1906	9	35	15.2	2.5
OLIVE BRANCH	BRIG	BEAUFORT	1801	130			
OLIVE BRANCH	SCHOONER	CARTERET COUNTY	1831	27	45	13.42	4.66
OLIVE BRANCH	SCHOONER	TYRRELL COUNTY	1812	32.2	45	15	5.66
OLIVIA	BRIG	NORTH CAROLINA	1802	176.63	82	23.08	10.66
OLIVIA	SCHOONER	WASHINGTON	1839	56	62	19	6
OLIVIA BRICKELL	SCHOONER	OCRACOKE ISLAND	1828	132.34	80.25	24.33	7.75
OLLIE	SCHOONER	MOREHEAD CITY	1894	7	42	11.6	2.7
OLYMPIA	SCHOONER	SMYRNA	1899	14	48	15	3.4
ONLY DAUGHTER	SCHOONER	PASQUOTANK RIVER	1805	63			
ONLY SON	SCHOONER	HATTERAS	1829	28	46	15.42	4
ONO II	GAS SCREW	MOREHEAD CITY	1911	10	53	15	3.7
ONSLOW	BRIG	SWANSBORO	1828	169	78.58	25	10
ONSLOW	BARGE	SWANSBORO	1900	31			
ONSLOW	SCHOONER	WILMINGTON	1845	36.8	55	16.66	4.66
ONSLOW OF SWANS-BOROUGH	SCHOONER	SWANSBOROUGH	1841	130	79	23	8
ONTARIO	SCHOONER	BEAUFORT	1846	63	64.66	20.83	5.58
ONTARIO	SCHOONER	NEW BERN	1857	8.06			
ONTARIO	SCHOONER	WILMINGTON		11			
ONWARD	SCHOONER	ELIZABETH CITY	1867	11.47	42	12.3	3.8
ORADENE	SCHOONER	HUNTING QUARTERS	1874	5.65	30	9.3	3
OREGON	SCHOONER	BEAUFORT	1898	11	45	12	3
OREGON	SCHOONER	HYDE COUNTY	1853	69.01	70.5	21.8	7.3
ORIENT	SCHOONER	ROANOKE ISLAND	1819	20	40.25	13.66	4.33
ORIENTAL	SLOOP	HYDE COUNTY	1887	9.36	32	12.5	3.2
ORTON	BRIG	WILMINGTON	1748	45			
OSBON	SLOOP	KITTY HAWK	1896	5	34	12.6	3
OSCEOLA	SCHOONER	ELIZABETH CITY	1850	64.15	72	17.17	5.58
OSPREY	SCHOONER	HATTERAS	1873	7.95	38	12.5	3.9
OSPREY	SCHOONER	HATTERAS	1893	5	36.9	12.8	3.3
OSTRICH	SCHOONER	NORTH CAROLINA	1788	25			
OTIS D. TERRELL	SCHOONER	PORTSMOUTH	1902	13	46	16	4

Name of Ship	Type of Ship	Shipbuilding Location	Year	Tons	Length	Width	Depth
OTTER	SLOOP	PAMLICO	1703	20			
OYSTER BAY	SCHOONER	OLD TRAP	1899	9	39	12	3
P. AND G. BROWN	SCHOONER	BEAUFORT	1852	21.55	38.83	15.58	4.33
P. MERWIN	SCHOONER	NEW BERN		92			
P.M. WARREN	PADDLE-WHEEL STEAMER	DRUMMOND POINT	1888	6.85	45.2	13.1	2
P.R. PARKER	SLOOP	ELIZABETH CITY		16			
PACIFIC	BRIG	CARTERET COUNTY	1826	121	70.75	22.83	8.83
PACIFIC OF WASHINGTON	SCHOONER	WASHINGTON	1850	80	70.17	23.66	6.25
PACKET	SCHOONER	BEAUFORT		10			
PACKET	SCHOONER	SMYRNA	1876	9.75			
PACTOLUS	SCHOONER	BEAUFORT COUNTY	1843	51	64	17	5
PAISLEY	BRIG	NEW BERN	1800	175			
PALESTINE	SCHOONER	CARTERET COUNTY	1851	45	59.75	17.33	5
PALESTINE	SCHOONER	EDENTON	1845	52	67	17	6
PALESTINE	SCHOONER	STRAITS	1865	7.57	36.9	10.6	2.9
PALLAS	SLOOP	NORTH CAROLINA	1768	35			
PALMER	SCHOONER	HUNTING QUARTERS	1888	7.89	34.5	10.5	3.4
PALMER	BRIG	NORTH CAROLINA	1754	70			
PAMLICO	GAS SCREW	BELHAVEN	1906	14	50	10	2.92
PAMLICO	SCHOONER	CARTERET COUNTY	1835	104	73	22	7
PAMLICO	SCHOONER	PAMLICO	1898	17	56	16.6	3.7
PAMPLICO	SHIP	HYDE COUNTY	1805	259			
PAMPLICO	SCHOONER	STRAITS OF CARTERET	1836	105	71	22	7
PANTHEON	SCHOONER	SWANSBOROUGH	1840	40	58	18	5
PANTHER	SLOOP	NEW BERN	1832	31	46	15	5
PANTHER	SCHOONER	PERQUIMANS COUNTY	1784				
PARAGON	SCHOONER	CARTERET COUNTY	1818	49.6	54	16.42	6.33
PARAGON	SCHOONER	OCRACOKE	1839	34	62	19	5
PARKER	SCHOONER	CARTERET COUNTY	1838	70	66.25	19.5	6.25
PARROTT	SCHOONER	ELIZABETH CITY	1860	11.12			
PARSON BROWN	SCHOONER	BEAUFORT COUNTY	1856	22	45	15	3.66

Name of Ship	Type of Ship	Shipbuilding Location	Year	Tons	Length	Width	Depth
PASQUOTANK	SLOOP	PASQUOTANK COUNTY	1739	40			
PASSENGER	SLOOP						
PAST MASTER	SCHOONER	MARTIN POINT	1825	72	49.75	21.5	6.75
PATHFINDER	SCHOONER	WASHINGTON	1855	328	130	29	9
PATIENCE	SNOW	EDENTON	1751	60			
PATRIARCH	BARK	DAWSONS CREEK	1807	168	81	23	10
PATRICK HENRY	SCHOONER	ELIZABETH CITY		11			
PATRIOT	SCHOONER	CARTERET COUNTY	1850	39	59.5	16.83	4.5
PATRIOT	SCHOONER	STRAITS	1837	44	57	18	4
PATRON	SCHOONER	BEAUFORT	1828	34	50.66	16.5	4.83
PATRON	SCHOONER	CARTERET COUNTY	1852	40	55	17	4
PATRON	SCHOONER	NEW BERN		12			
PATSEY	SCHOONER	CURRITUCK NARROWS	1821	30	40	16	4
PATSEY AND PENELOPE	SCHOONER	BERTIE COUNTY	1809	112			
PATSEY B. BLOUNT	BRIG	BEAUFORT	1828	120	74	22	8
PATSY	SLOOP	NORTH CAROLINA	1788	65			
PATTIE MARTIN	SCHOONER	ELIZABETH CITY	1857	65.21	75.42	17.25	5.5
PATTRAN	SCHOONER	CARTERET COUNTY	1852	40	55.33	17.5	4.83
PATTY	SLOOP	NORTH CAROLINA	1788	30			
PAUL B. CARTER	SCHOONER	WILMINGTON		20			
PAUL JONES	SCHOONER	ONSLOW COUNTY	1814	87	65	20.66	7.66
PAUL PRY	SCHOONER	CARTERET COUNTY	1828	36	50.83	16.42	5
PAULINE	SLOOP	CAPE BANKS	1894	7.03	43	11.5	2.5
PAULINE	SCHOONER	CARTERET COUNTY	1843	60	62.08	19.08	5.92
PAULINE	SHARPIE	WADES SHORE	1887	7	41.9	10.6	2.8
PAULING	SCHOONER	BEAUFORT	1843	66			
PAYNE	SCHOONER	CURRITUCK	1772	10			
PAYNE	SCHOONER	NORTH CAROLINA	1788	12			
PEACE MAKER	SCHOONER	KNOTTS ISLAND	1817	82	63	22.66	7
PEARL	SCHOONER	BEAUFORT		14			
PEARL	SCHOONER	CARTERET COUNTY	1844	29	52	15.7	4
PEARL	SCREW STEAMER	MOREHEAD CITY	1909	8	38	10	2.6

Name of Ship	Type of Ship	Shipbuilding Location	Year	Tons	Length	Width	Depth
PEARL	SCHOONER	PAMLICO		5			
PEARL	SLOOP	POWELLS POINT	1907	8	32	12	4.4
PEARL	SCHOONER	WASHINGTON	1837	55	85	15	4
PEARLIE MAY	SCREW STEAMER	VANCEBORO	1893	58.03	75.6	18	3.2
PEDEE	SCHOONER	CARTERET COUNTY	1831	96	68.66	21.58	7.5
PEGASUS	SCHOONER	CARTERET COUNTY	1811	60	58	17	6.92
PEGGIE		NORTH CAROLINA	1762	150			
PEGGY	SCHOONER	ADAMS CREEK	1795	73	61	19	7
PEGGY	BRIG	NEW BERN	1780	50			
PEGGY	SCHOONER	NORTH CAROLINA	1762	45			
PEGGY	BRIG	NORTH CAROLINA	1768	35			
PEGGY	SLOOP	PITT COUNTY	1776	25			
PEGGY	SCHOONER	POLEY BRANCH	1796	27			
PEGGY	BRIG	PORT ROANOKE	1775	102			
PEGGY AND PAMILA	BRIG	CURRITUCK COUNTY	1814	146	60	24	8
PEGGY TRYON	BRIG	NORTH CAROLINA	1758	70			
PELHAM	GAS SCREW	SMYRNA	1900	9	42	12	2.8
PENDER	SCHOONER	CARTERET COUNTY	1801	104			
PENDER	SCREW STEAMER	SHAKEN	1890	28.05	52.7	14.9	3.4
PENELOPE	BRIG	NORTH CAROLINA	1775	150			
PENELOPE	SCHOONER	NORTH CAROLINA	1796	43	41	16.5	6
PENELOPE	SCHOONER	NORTH CAROLINA	1797	77	78	20	7
PENELOPE	BRIG	NORTH CAROLINA	1800	246			
PERQUIMANS	PADDLE-WHEEL STEAMER	HERTFORD	1891	9.42	52	11	2.9
PERSERVERANCE	BRIG	SMITHS CREEK	1812	212	86	24	11
PERSEVERANCE	SCHOONER	CARTERET COUNTY	1826	88	65.58	20.17	7.75
PET	SCHOONER	BEAUFORT		14			
PETREL	SCHOONER	WASHINGTON	1856	37	71	17.5	4
PETREL	SCHOONER	WASHINGTON	1884	28			
PETREL	SCHOONER	WIT	1903	5	35	10	2.5

Name of Ship	Type of Ship	Shipbuilding Location	Year	Tons	Length	Width	Depth
PEZZIE B. ONSLOW	SCHOONER	HATTERAS	1877	280			
PHENIX	SLOOP	PASQUOTANK	1732	18			
PHEOBE AND JOHN	SCHOONER	NORTH CAROLINA	1768	35			
PHILADELPHIA	SCHOONER	BEAUFORT	1826	88	65	29	8
PHILADELPHIA	SLOOP	NORTH CAROLINA	1774	10			
PHOEBE	SCHOONER	NEW BERN	1799	99			
PHOENIX	SLOOP	PASQUOTANK	1751	18			
PHOENIX	SCHOONER	WASHINGTON	1821	107	69	22	8
PHONICE	SLOOP	NORTH CAROLINA	1743	20			
PICKERING	SCHOONER	CURRITUCK COUNTY	1808	61	58	18	6.66
PIC-NIC	SLOOP	CURRITUCK COUNTY	1883	10			
PIGOT	SCHOONER	CARTERET COUNTY	1816	82	62.66	19.66	7.75
PIGOT	SCHOONER	CARTERET COUNTY	1827	82	62	19	7.75
PILOT'S BRIDE	SCHOONER	NEWPORT	1903	6	36	10	2.5
PINE	SLOOP	BEAUFORT COUNTY	1852	37	49	16	5
PINE OF WILMINGTON	SCHOONER	WASHINGTON	1865	30	49	16	4
PLANET	SCHOONER	CARTERET COUNTY	1846	72	66.25	20.25	6.25
PLANET	SCHOONER	WILMINGTON		13			
PLANTER	SCHOONER	ELIZABETH CITY	1859	105			
PLANTER	SLOOP	HALIFAX COUNTY	1790	54			
PLANTER	SCHOONER	NORTH CAROLINA	1803	104			
PLANTER	SCHOONER	PASQUOTANK COUNTY	1859	97	77	22	6
PLEASURE	BARGE	MAYSVILLE	1909	54			
PLEBE	BRIG	JARRELS BAY	1824	121	76	24	8
PLOUGH BOY	SCHOONER	PONEY ISLAND	1826	21	31.75	15.5	4.25
PLUMEGE	SCHOONER	HARLOWE	1898	6.05	32	12	2.9
PLUNGE	SCHOONER	HARLOWE	1898	8	46	12	3.7
PLYMOUTH	SIDE-WHEEL STEAMER	PLYMOUTH	1835	50			
POINDEXTER D. MURPHY	SCHOONER	CARTERET COUNTY	1839	20	45	13.75	3.75
POLL CARY	BRIG	HALIFAX COUNTY	1794	114			
POLLY	SLOOP	ADAMS CREEK	1789	97	60	21	10

Name of Ship	Type of Ship	Shipbuilding Location	Year	Tons	Length	Width	Depth
POLLY	SCHOONER	BEAUFORT	1786	90	68	20	7
POLLY	SCHOONER	BERTIE COUNTY	1785	105	66	21	8
POLLY	SCHOONER	CURRITUCK	1774	15			
POLLY	SCHOONER	CURRITUCK	1775	25			
POLLY	SCHOONER	HYDE COUNTY	1804	82			
POLLY	SCHOONER	NEW BERN	1779	23			
POLLY	SLOOP	NORTH CAROLINA	1759	40			
POLLY	SCHOONER	NORTH CAROLINA	1760	17			
POLLY	SCHOONER	NORTH CAROLINA	1764	10			
POLLY	SLOOP	NORTH CAROLINA	1767	20			
POLLY	SCHOONER	NORTH CAROLINA	1769	35			
POLLY	BRIG	NORTH CAROLINA	1772	60			
POLLY	SCHOONER	NORTH CAROLINA	1777	10			
POLLY	SLOOP	NORTH CAROLINA	1788	12			
POLLY	SCHOONER	NORTH CAROLINA	1788	62			
POLLY	SCHOONER	NORTH CAROLINA	1788	10			
POLLY	SCHOONER	NORTH CAROLINA	1788	6			
POLLY	SCHOONER	NORTH CAROLINA	1788	60			
POLLY	SLOOP	NORTH CAROLINA	1788	30			
POLLY	SCHOONER	NORTH CAROLINA	1788	8			
POLLY	SLOOP	NORTH CAROLINA	1788	20			
POLLY	SCHOONER	NORTH CAROLINA	1789	79			
POLLY	SCHOONER	NORTH CAROLINA	1796	56			
POLLY	SCHOONER	PERQUIMANS COUNTY	1788	103	74	20	8
POLLY	SLOOP	PORT ROANOKE	1761	30			
POLLY	SHIP	PORT ROANOKE	1776	200			
POLLY	SHIP	PORT ROANOKE	1774	200			
POLLY	SCHOONER	SMITHS CREEK	1796	80			
POLLY	BRIG	TRENT FERRY	1795	113			

Name of Ship	Type of Ship	Shipbuilding Location	Year	Tons	Length	Width	Depth
POLLY AND NANCY	SCHOONER	ADAMS CREEK	1793	53			
POLLY AND NANCY	SCHOONER	COINJOCK BAY	1818	25	45.5	16	4.3
POLLY AND NANCY	SHIP	NORTH CAROLINA	1789	250			
POLLY AND NANCY	SHIP	SWANSBOROUGH	1803	303			
POLLY AND NANCY	SCHOONER	TYRRELL COUNTY	1816	22	44.66	15.42	4
POLLY AND NANCY	SCHOONER	TYRRELL COUNTY	1831	25	45	15	4.25
POLLY AND SALLY	SCHOONER	NORTH CAROLINA	1788	20			
POLLY ASHBY	SCHOONER	COLERTON ISLAND	1820	22.28	42.75	14.75	4.25
POMPEY	SCHOONER	NORTH CAROLINA	1771	5			
POOR MAN'S SHIFT	SCHOONER	NORTH CAROLINA	1728	5			
POST BOY	SCHOONER	WASHINGTON	1823	61	64	19	5
PRECILLA	SCHOONER	EDENTON	1789	100			
PRENTICE BOY	SCHOONER	CURRITUCK NARROWS	1817	30	48	16.33	4.66
PRESIDENT	SLOOP	CURRITUCK	1804	25			
PRETTY GAL	SCREW STEAMER	EDENTON	1879	9.05	51.6	11.6	1.9
PRINCE	SCHOONER	BEAUFORT	1899	31	63	19	4.6
PRINCE	SCHOONER	BEAUFORT	1901	7	37	12	2.6
PRISCELLO ARMISTEAD	BRIG	PLYMOUTH	1811	123	89	23	7
PRISCILLA	SCHOONER	BEAUFORT	1904	7	38	11	2.4
PRISCILLA	SCHOONER	EDENTON	1789	100			
PRISCILLA ANN	SCHOONER	PERQUIMANS COUNTY	1847	50	56	17	5
PROPERTY	SLOOP	NORTH CAROLINA	1728	8			
PROPRIETY	PERRIANGER	NORTH CAROLINA	1722	3			
PROSPERITY	PERRIANGER	ALBEMARLE COUNTY	1723	3			
PROSPERITY	SLOOP	BATH	1728	8			
PROSPERITY	SCHOONER	NORTH CAROLINA	1725	4			
PROSPERITY	SLOOP	NORTH CAROLINA	1742	18			
PRUDENCE	BRIG	NORTH CAROLINA	1781	205			
PURSE	SCHOONER	CARTERET COUNTY	1847	28	49.33	16.42	4.17

Name of Ship	Type of Ship	Shipbuilding Location	Year	Tons	Length	Width	Depth
PYOMINGO	SHIP	HYDE COUNTY	1799	183.16	81	24.5	10.7
QUEEN ANN	SCHOONER	CHOWAN COUNTY	1838	41	67	16	4.2
QUEEN ELIZABETH	SLOOP	NORTH CAROLINA	1741	50			
QUEEN OF THE SOUTH	SCHOONER	BEAUFORT COUNTY	1856	335	133	29	9.6
QUEEN VICTORIA	SCHOONER	BEARDS CREEK	1877	6.34	36.3	10.3	2.8
R. BRUCE MARTIN	SLOOP	EDENTON	1874	13.19	40.2	15.4	4.3
R.C. BEAMON	SCHOONER	HATTERAS	1901	12	44	15.9	2.6
R.E. LEE	SCHOONER	BAYBORO	1892	5.3	30	9.8	2.6
R.E. LEE	SCHOONER	SMYRNA	1883	12.72	44.1	14.2	3.6
R.L. MYERS	SCHOONER	WASHINGTON	1873	44.4			
R.L. MYERS	SCREW STEAMER	WASHINGTON	1885	128.49	118.6	24.8	4.1
R.L. SWINSON	SLOOP	NEW BERN		14			
R.S. BURNEY	SCHOONER	CARTERET COUNTY	1851	33	52.17	16.5	4.5
R.S. DONNELL	SCHOONER	HYDE COUNTY	1858	36	45	16	4.66
R.S. PERRY	SCHOONER	CARTERET COUNTY	1849	127	77.83	23.58	8.08
R.W. BLANCHARD	SLOOP	DAVIS	1902	10	44	14	3
R.W. POWELL	GAS SCREW	WILMINGTON	1911	19	60	13	4.3
R.W. TAYLOR	SCHOONER	MOREHEAD CITY	1899	7	46	13	2.7
R.W. TAYLOR	GAS SCREW	MOREHEAD CITY	1901	12	44	12	4
RACER	SCHOONER	BEAUFORT		22			
RACHAEL ANN	SCHOONER	CARTERET COUNTY	1842	29	50	17	4
RADIANT	SCHOONER	CARTERET COUNTY	1850	38	58.5	17.25	4.42
RAINBOW	SCHOONER	CURRITUCK NARROWS	1818	46	55	18.75	5.25
RAINBOW	SCHOONER	HYDE COUNTY	1801	88			
RAINBOW	SLOOP	NORTH CAROLINA	1766	25			
RALEIGH	SCHOONER	CARTERET COUNTY	1841	67	64	20	6
RALFE	SCHOONER	NORTH CAROLINA	1768	90			
RALLY	SCHOONER	NORTH CAROLINA	1789	20			
RAMBLER	BRIG	CARTERET COUNTY	1815	272	101	26	11
RAMBLER	SCHOONER	NORTH CAROLINA	1789	24			

Name of Ship	Type of Ship	Shipbuilding Location	Year	Tons	Length	Width	Depth
RAMBLER	SCHOONER	PASQUOTANK COUNTY	1797	43			
RANGER	SLOOP	BATH	1731	15			
RANGER	SCHOONER	NORTH CAROLINA	1731	5			
RANGER	SCHOONER	NORTH CAROLINA	1747	20			
RAPID	SCHOONER	SOUTH RIVER	1812	85	61	21	7.92
RAPID	SCHOONER	SOUTH RIVER	1817	85	61.58	21	7.92
RAPIDAN	SCHOONER	WASHINGTON		11			
RAPPAHANNOCK	BARGE	WASHINGTON	1890	295			
RATTLESNAKE	SLOOP	RICE PATH	1886	6.16	39.4	10.5	2.6
RAY	SCHOONER	ELIZABETH CITY	1897	12	52	14	3.4
RAY	SCHOONER	STRAITS	1868	22.57			
REAPER	GAS SCREW	SMYRNA	1907	19	52	16	3.3
REBECCA	BRIG	CAPE FEAR	1730	70	54	21	10
REBECCA	SCHOONER	CARTERET COUNTY	1828	56	59.5	18.25	6
REBECCA	SCHOONER	NORTH CAROLINA	1766	60			
REBECCA	SCHOONER	SMYRNA	1872	32.51	55.3	18.2	4.9
REBECCA AND ELIZABETH	SCHOONER	BEAUFORT	1815	75			
REBECCA AND FREELOVE	SLOOP	NORTH CAROLINA	1735	40			
REBECCA ANN	SCHOONER	STRAITS OF CARTERET	1823	26	41	17	4
REBECCA BELL	SCHOONER	AVON	1901	7	43	13	2
REBECCA HYER	SCHOONER	BEAUFORT	1825	108	69	24	8
REBEKAHE	SCHOONER	BEAUFORT	1847	97	72.17	21.58	7.25
REBEL	SCHOONER	PERQUIMANS RIVER	1782	80			
REBEL EAKE	SCHOONER	BEAUFORT	1847	98	72	22	7
RECOVERY	SHIP	WILMINGTON	1752	80			
RED ROVER	SCHOONER	CARTERET COUNTY	1831	25	47.33	13.33	4.5
RED WOOD	SCHOONER	EDENTON	1883	8.38	36.6	12	3.2
REFUGE	SHARPIE	STELLA	1904	14	52.8	14.9	2.8
REGULATOR	SCHOONER	COINJOCK BAY	1823	40	51.5	18	5.17
REGULATOR	SCHOONER	HATTERAS BANKS	1833	20	39	13	4
REGULATOR	SCHOONER	SMYRNA	1882	43.71	63	20.1	5
RELEASE	SCHOONER	POWELLS POINT	1811	40	39	17.8	5.7
RELIANCE	GAS SCREW	MOREHEAD CITY	1903	6	38	9.9	2.6
RELIEF	SCHOONER	BEAUFORT	1861	11.95			
RELIEF	BRIG	FLOAT BRIDGE	1797	135			

Name of Ship	Type of Ship	Shipbuilding Location	Year	Tons	Length	Width	Depth
RELIEF	SCHOONER	OCRACOKE	1896	12.83	48	14.5	3.66
REMEDY	SCHOONER	SWANSBOROUGH	1820	70	67	19	6
REMITTANCE	BRIG	BEAUFORT	1825	140	77	24	9
RENA B.	SLOOP	SMYRNA	1892	8.03	43.7	11.5	3
RENO	SCHOONER	BEAUFORT		7			
RENWICK	SCHOONER	WASHINGTON	1795	47			
REPUBLICAN	SCHOONER	BERTIE COUNTY	1801	39			
REPUBLICAN	SCHOONER	CARTERET COUNTY	1817	24	43.33	14.5	4.58
RESOLUTION	SCHOONER	COINJOCK	1806	38	54	17	4
RESOLUTION	SCHOONER	EDENTON	1855	62			
RESOLUTION	SCHOONER	NORTH CAROLINA	1788	18			
RESOLUTION	SCHOONER	NORTH CAROLINA	1793	35			
RESOLUTION	SCHOONER	NORTH CAROLINA	1801	96			
RESOLUTION	SCHOONER	ONSLOW COUNTY	1794	34			
RESOLUTION	SCHOONER	PLYMOUTH	1855	62	74	17	5
RESOLUTION	SCHOONER	TYRRELL COUNTY	1814	20	41.66	17.58	4.08
RESOURCE	SCHOONER	NORTH CAROLINA	1779	66			
RESTLESS	SCHOONER	SMYRNA	1888	12.14	45.5	11.9	3
REVOLUTION	SCHOONER	PLYMOUTH	1855	62	70	17	5
RHODA AND MARGARET	SCHOONER	NORTH RIVER	1825	26	45	14	
RICE BIRD	SCHOONER	BRUNSWICK COUNTY	1890	22.28	52	14.8	3.7
RICHARD	BRIG	CARTERET COUNTY	1798	178	77	23	11
RICHARD AND MARY	SCHOONER	CHOWAN COUNTY	1805	60			
RICHARD AND THOMAS	SLOOP	NORTH CAROLINA	1728	10			
RICHARD CATON	SHIP	HYDE COUNTY	1798	270	90	26	13
RICHARD HOPKINS	SLOOP	PLYMOUTH		26			
RICHARD MEADE	BRIG	ELIZABETH CITY	1810	163			
RICHARD MISSKINS	SLOOP	CRAVEN COUNTY	1858	31	42	17	4
RICHARD OF COR-RATUCK	SLOOP	PASQUOTANK	1693	4			
RICHARD OF NORTH CAROLINA	SHALLOP	NORTH CAROLINA	1693	4			
RICHARD WILDER	SCHOONER	ELIZABETH CITY		20			
RICHARD WINSLOW	SCHOONER	HYDE COUNTY	1825	28	44.42	15	5.08

Name of Ship	Type of Ship	Shipbuilding Location	Year	Tons	Length	Width	Depth
RICHMOND	SCHOONER	CARTERET COUNTY	1845	20	46.75	13.17	3.75
RICHMOND	SCHOONER	NORTH CAROLINA	1750	60			
RICHMOND	SCHOONER	WILMINGTON		13			
RICOCHET	SCHOONER	WILMINGTON		59			
RIO	SCHOONER	BEAUFORT	1871	14.26			
RIO	SCHOONER	CARTERET COUNTY	1847	87	69	22	7
RIO GRANDE	SCHOONER	NEW BERN		34			
RIP VAN WINKLE		PLYMOUTH	1833	45	61	16	5
RIPPLE	SCHOONER	BERTIE COUNTY	1908	6	40	11	2.4
RIPPLE	GAS SCREW	MARSHALLBERG	1903	16	45	16	3.4
RIPPLE	GAS SCREW	MOREHEAD CITY	1902	10	47	11	2.7
RISING STATES	BRIG	HERTFORD	1781	90			
RISING STATES	SCHOONER	POWELLS POINT	1827	23	49.5	13	4.08
RISING SUN	SCHOONER	ADAMS CREEK	1824	96	69	21.7	7.7
RISING SUN	SCHOONER	CARTERET COUNTY	1825	37	53	16.75	4.83
RIVAL	SCHOONER	CURRITUCK	1841	35	51	16	5
RIVER QUEEN	SCHOONER	COLINGTON	1895	4.7	38	12.2	3
RIVER QUEEN	PADDLE-WHEEL STEAMER	WILMINGTON	1883	119.58			
ROAM	BARGE	TUNIS	1892	134			
ROAMER	NAPHTHA	BEAUFORT	1899	55	77	26	4
ROAMER	GAS SCREW	MARINES	1902	32	62	18	4.9
ROAMER	SCHOONER	SMYRNA	1901	7	43	12	2.8
ROANOKE	SCHOONER	HUNTING QUARTERS	1820	36	56	17	5
ROANOKE	SCHOONER	NEW BERN	1837	138	77	23	9
ROBERT	SLOOP	CAPE HATTERAS	1777	20			
ROBERT	BRIG	NORTH CAROLINA	1769	105			
ROBERT AND ALICE	SHIP	BATH COUNTY	1734	150			
ROBERT B. POTTER	SCHOONER	SMITHVILLE	1848	70	60	17	7
ROBERT E. LEE	SCHOONER	WILMINGTON	1890	8.22	38	10.9	2.9
ROBERT EDENS	SCHOONER	WILMINGTON	1833	95			
ROBERT H. COWAN	SCHOONER	SOUTHPORT	1872	25.83	46.7	15	6
ROBERT L. HINTON	GAS SCREW	ELIZABETH CITY	1909	9	42	11	6
ROBERT LENOX	SCHOONER	BROAD CREEK	1811	106	68	21	8
ROBERT V. RIDER	SLOOP	HOLLYWOOD	1902	10	36.8	13.2	3.3
ROBINSON	BRIG	NORTH CAROLINA	1753	60			

Name of Ship	Type of Ship	Shipbuilding Location	Year	Tons	Length	Width	Depth
ROLFE	BRIG	NORTH CAROLINA	1768	90			
ROSA	SCREW STEAMER	WILMINGTON	1903	47	66	16	4.4
ROSA B. CORA	SCHOONER	ELIZABETH CITY	1892	17.06	41	13	4
ROSA L. CUMMINGS	SCHOONER	WILMINGTON	1877	12.61			
ROSA OTTO	SCHOONER	WILMINGTON	1902	13	47	12	3.8
ROSA PIERCE	SCHOONER	NORTH RIVER	1893	5.47	40	10.5	2.2
ROSA SCARBOROUGH	SCHOONER	SMITHVILLE	1874	6.29	34.2	11.6	3.7
ROSALIE BEATRICE	SCHOONER	BEACON ISLAND	1853		48	17	4.33
ROSE	SCHOONER	SMITHVILLE	1872	17.02	45.6	15.6	4.1
ROSEBELLE	SCHOONER	SMYRNA	1888	8.84	44.6	11.9	3
ROSE-IN-BLOOM	SCHOONER	CURRITUCK	1829	58	62	20	6.6
ROSETTA	SCHOONER	BEAUFORT	1905	5	39	12	2
ROSLYND	GAS SCREW	SWANSBORO	1903	12	50	12.9	2.7
ROSS	SLOOP	NORTH CAROLINA	1756	8			
ROUGH AND READY	SCHOONER	WASHINGTON	1847	120	77	23	7
ROVER	SLOOP	BEAUFORT		5			
ROVER		WASHINGTON	1914	15	44	11	3.9
ROWAN	SIDE-WHEEL STEAMER	SMITHVILLE	1846	172	130	23	6
ROWENA	SCHOONER	RODANTHE	1882	12.78			
ROXANNE	SCHOONER	KINNAKEET	1878	9.33	42	12	3
ROXIE PITMAN	GAS SCREW	BERTIE COUNTY	1912	16	52	14	4.2
ROYAL EXCHANGE	SHIP	PORT ROANOKE	1772	125			
ROYAL PURPLE	SCHOONER	SMITHVILLE	1846	40	57	18	4
RUBY	BRIG	ROANOKE	1767	90			
RUFUS KING	SCHOONER	SMITHS CREEK	1816	59	58	19.08	6.33
RUSSELL	BRIG	HYDE COUNTY	1790	173			
RUSSELL	SNOW	NORTH CAROLINA	1800	161			
RUTH	SCHOONER	SMYRNA	1894	7.67	43.6	12	2.7
RUTH	SCHOONER	SMYRNA	1897	11	47	13	3.1
RUTH C. WATSON	SCHOONER	MOREHEAD CITY	1896	9.33	43.8	11.4	2.8
RUTH DARLING	SCHOONER	NORTH RIVER	1892	14.27	42.2	15.1	3.6
RUTH J.	SCHOONER	SHALLOTTE	1895	11.81	48.4	12.8	3.1
S. CATHERINE	SCHOONER	CARTERET COUNTY	1851	39	59.75	17	4.42
S. CATHERINE	SCHOONER	EDENTON		35			
S. FRANCIS	SCHOONER	HATTERAS	1868	11.53	40.3	12.5	4.5
S. HYMAN	SCHOONER	CRAVEN COUNTY	1841	24	47	15	4

Name of Ship	Type of Ship	Shipbuilding Location	Year	Tons	Length	Width	Depth
S.C. DOBBIN	SCHOONER	CURRITUCK COUNTY	1853	104	73	22	7
S.H. MCREA	SCHOONER	SCUPPERNONG RIVER	1847	90	74	21	6.83
S.H. SAMPLE	SCHOONER	EDENTON	1851	48	65	17	4.66
S.H. SAMPLE	SCHOONER	EDENTON	1853	40	61	17	4
S.L. ELMYRA	SCHOONER	HATTERAS	1869	18.17	45	15	3.8
S.L. ELMYRA	SCHOONER	HATTERAS	1876	17.38			
S.M. ROLLINS	SHARPIE	BAY RIVER	1891	8	35.5	10.8	3
S.R. POTTER	SCHOONER	SMITHVILLE	1851	110			
S.S. SIMMONS	SLOOP	TYRRELL COUNTY	1844	31	48	17	4
SABINE	SCHOONER	CARTERET COUNTY	1842	94	70	22	7
SABRA	SCHOONER	GARRAT BAY	1826	38.42	50.5	17.42	5.25
SABRA A.	SCHOONER	PINEY POINT	1884	9.31	35.1	11.9	3.3
SADIE	SCHOONER	ATLANTIC	1904	10	44	13	2.7
SADIE D.	SLOOP	NORTH HARLOWE	1904	6	37	10	3.8
SADIE MAY	SHARPIE	SHALLOTTE	1913	9	44	14.5	3
SALAMANDA	SCHOONER	NEW BERN	1814	62	57.5	18.17	7
SALAMANDER	SLOOP	NORTH CAROLINA	1730	40			
SALLEY	SCHOONER	PORT BATH	1745	15			
SALLIE ANN	SCHOONER	NEW BERN	1875	58.89	41.8	12.1	3
SALLIE ANN	SCHOONER	POWELLS POINT	1876	7	33	12	3
SALLIE SMITH	SCHOONER	EDENTON	1856	106			
SALLY	BRIG	BATH	1788	106	71	20	8
SALLY	BRIG	BEAUFORT	1790	165	76	24	10
SALLY	SHIP	CAMDEN	1792	230	85	25	26
SALLY	SCHOONER	CURRITUCK COUNTY	1800	35	52.5	15.83	5
SALLY	SCHOONER	CURRITUCK COUNTY	1802	43	56	17	5
SALLY	SLOOP	EDGECOMBE COUNTY	1803	79			
SALLY	SLOOP	NORTH CAROLINA	1744	12			
SALLY	SLOOP	NORTH CAROLINA	1750	40			
SALLY	BRIG	NORTH CAROLINA	1753	50			
SALLY	SLOOP	NORTH CAROLINA	1757				
SALLY	SLOOP	NORTH CAROLINA	1760	13			

Name of Ship	Type of Ship	Shipbuilding Location	Year	Tons	Length	Width	Depth
SALLY	BRIG	NORTH CAROLINA	1763	50			
SALLY	SLOOP	NORTH CAROLINA	1763	20			
SALLY	SCHOONER	NORTH CAROLINA	1767	25			
SALLY	BRIG	NORTH CAROLINA	1767	60			
SALLY	SLOOP	NORTH CAROLINA	1767	40			
SALLY	SCHOONER	NORTH CAROLINA	1769	45			
SALLY	SCHOONER	NORTH CAROLINA	1770	12			
SALLY	SLOOP	NORTH CAROLINA	1770	10			
SALLY	SCHOONER	NORTH CAROLINA	1779	5			
SALLY	SCHOONER	NORTH CAROLINA	1788	15			
SALLY	SCHOONER	NORTH CAROLINA	1789	30			
SALLY	SCHOONER	NORTH CAROLINA	1796	130			
SALLY	SCHOONER	NORTH CAROLINA		35			
SALLY	BRIG	NORTHAMPTON	1810	34			
SALLY	SCHOONER	ORCHARD CREEK	1801	119			
SALLY	BRIG	PORT ROANOKE	1771	50			
SALLY	SHIP	PORT ROANOKE	1764	170			
SALLY	SCHOONER	PORT ROANOKE	1774	10			
SALLY	SCHOONER	PORTSMOUTH		9			
SALLY	BRIG	WASHINGTON	1802	103			
SALLY AND ANN	SLOOP	NORTH CAROLINA	1766	35			
SALLY AND BETSY	SCHOONER	HERTFORD	1802	53			
SALLY ANN	SCHOONER	BEAUFORT COUNTY	1815	82	62	19	7
SALLY ANN	SCHOONER	CARTERET COUNTY	1855	21	46	14	5
SALLY ANN		NEW BERN	1875	7	41.8	12.1	3
SALLY ANN	SCHOONER	POWELLS POINT	1876	6.65	32.6	12	3
SALLY ANN	SCHOONER	SMITHS CREEK	1825	56	58	19	6
SALLY ANN	SCHOONER	TYRRELL COUNTY	1817	33.39	49.12	16.42	4.92
SALLY ANN OF WASHINGTON	SCHOONER	CARTERET COUNTY	1834	21	46	14	5

Name of Ship	Type of Ship	Shipbuilding Location	Year	Tons	Length	Width	Depth
SALLY BADGER	SCHOONER	EDENTON	1849	131	80	22	8
SALLY GLADDING	SCHOONER	WASHINGTON	1800	57			
SALLY HAVENS	SCHOONER	WASHINGTON	1821	99	73	21	7
SALLY NELSON	SLOOP	SMITHS CREEK	1814	30	40	14	4
SALLY RUFFIN	SCHOONER	NORTH CAROLINA	1798	83			
SALLY SMITH	SCHOONER	EDENTON	1856	106	85	23	6
SALLY SPARROW	SCHOONER	SMITHS CREEK	1815	26	46	14.1	4.1
SALLY W.	SCHOONER	WASHINGTON	1900	7	42.4	13.6	2.7
SALMAGUNDI	SCHOONER	SWANSBOROUGH	1814	62	57	18	7
SAM BEERY	SIDE-WHEEL STEAMER	WILMINGTON	1853	185			
SAM E. EBORN	SCHOONER	WASHINGTON		18			
SAM POTTER	SCHOONER	MARTIN COUNTY	1816	30	51	14	4
SAM R. POTTER	SCHOONER	SMITHVILLE	1851	100			
SAM SIMPSON	SCHOONER	NORTH CAROLINA	1820	61	60.66	18.92	6
SAMPSON	SCHOONER	SMITHS CREEK	1822	53	57.92	18.75	5.83
SAMUEL	SCHOONER	BEAUFORT	1866	18.42	50	13	3
SAMUEL	SCHOONER	BERTIE COUNTY	1804	52.2	57.58	17.83	5.92
SAMUEL	SCHOONER	INDIAN TOWN	1801	48			
SAMUEL	BRIG	SMITHS CREEK	1800	145	86	14	5
SAMUEL AND SARAH	SLOOP	PASQUOTANK	1750	18			
SAMUEL BROWN	BARGE	WASHINGTON	1880	99.46			
SAMUEL C. EBONO OF WASHINGTON	SCHOONER	WASHINGTON	1860	21	48	16	
SAMUEL ECCLES JR.	SCREW STEAMER	HERTFORD COUNTY	1887	41.5	69.6	16.2	6.6
SAMUEL HAYMEN	SCHOONER	NEW BERN		16			
SAMUEL HYMAN	SCHOONER	CRAVEN COUNTY	1841	24	47	15	4
SAMUEL JACKSON	SHIP	BERTIE COUNTY	1801	361			
SAMUEL L. MITCHELL	SCHOONER	BEAUFORT	1845	70			
SAMUEL M. BUCKMAN	SCHOONER	SMYRNA	1889	7.73	44.6	11.5	3
SAMUEL MITCHELL	SCHOONER	WASHINGTON	1846	173	89	25	8
SAMUEL SIMPSON	SCHOONER	CARTERET COUNTY	1820	61	61	19	6
SAMUEL TREADWELL	SCHOONER	CURRITUCK COUNTY	1824	66			
SAN JUAN	SCHOONER	ELIZABETH CITY	1860	105	81	21	6
SANQUIDOR	SLOOP	NORTH CAROLINA	1780	20			
SANTA MARIA	SCHOONER	CURRITUCK COUNTY	1869	8	39.1	11.2	3.2
SANTO MARIA	SCHOONER	EDENTON	1869	8.39			

Name of Ship	Type of Ship	Shipbuilding Location	Year	Tons	Length	Width	Depth
SARA LOUISE	SCREW STEAMER	NEW BERN	1903	63	87	23	7.2
SARAH	SCHOONER	BEAUFORT	1845	43	59	17.33	4.83
SARAH	SCHOONER	BEAUFORT	1878	11.8	41.4	13.3	3
SARAH	SCHOONER	BEAUFORT		13			
SARAH	SCHOONER	BEAUFORT COUNTY	1870	6.66			
SARAH	SCHOONER	BERTIE COUNTY	1732	20			
SARAH	SCHOONER	CAMDEN	1875	6.82	36	12	3
SARAH	SCHOONER	CARTERET COUNTY	1822	71	67.66	19.08	6.66
SARAH	SCHOONER	CARTERET COUNTY	1825	71		19	7
SARAH	SCHOONER	CARTERET COUNTY	1845	42	59	17	5
SARAH	SCHOONER	CARTERET COUNTY	1849	42	59	17.33	4.83
SARAH	SCHOONER	ELIZABETH CITY	1850	65	73	17	6
SARAH	SCHOONER	NEW BERN	1843	67	63	20	6
SARAH	SHALLOP	PASQUOTANK COUNTY	1725	4			
SARAH	SCHOONER	STRAITS	1870	7.01	36.7	10.4	2.8
SARAH	SLOOP	SWANSBORO	1901	6	36	11.9	2.7
SARAH	SCHOONER	WASHINGTON	1846	66	69	20	5
SARAH	BRIG	WILMINGTON	1825	136	71	21	10
SARAH ALLEN	SCHOONER	STRAITS	1888	10.83	39.4	12.5	4.1
SARAH AND ANN	BRIG		1804	160			
SARAH AND MARY	SCHOONER	ELIZABETH CITY	1850	65	73	17	5.9
SARAH AND MARY	SLOOP	NORTH CAROLINA	1714	12			
SARAH ANN	SLOOP	BEAUFORT	1902	5	35	10	2.6
SARAH ANN	SCHOONER	BEAUFORT		29			
SARAH ANN	SCHOONER	CARTERET COUNTY	1828	30	49	15	4
SARAH ANN	SCHOONER	CARTERET COUNTY	1853	39	58.58	17.5	4.42
SARAH ANN	SCHOONER	COINJOCK	1827	41	52.5	18	5.25
SARAH ANN	SCHOONER	GAR BACON	1816	62	60.75	19.66	6.17
SARAH ANN	SCHOONER	WHITE OAK RIVER	1821	32	52.66	15.17	4.5
SARAH ANNA	SCHOONER	JARROTS BAY	1828	73	66	20	7
SARAH DRUMMOND	PADDLE-WHEEL STEAMER	EDENTON	1893	12.87	52	13	2.4
SARAH F. MIDGETTE	SCHOONER	CORE SOUND	1875	23.31	48.8	15.8	4

Name of Ship	Type of Ship	Shipbuilding Location	Year	Tons	Length	Width	Depth
SARAH FRANCES	SCHOONER	NORTH RIVER	1886	8.25	41.4	10.6	2.8
SARAH FRANCIS	SCHOONER	BAY RIVER	1868	18.75	47	14.8	4.5
SARAH GARDNER	SLOOP	NEW BERN		6			
SARAH JANE	SCHOONER	BEAUFORT	1839	104	72	22	8
SARAH JANE	SCHOONER	BEAUFORT	1881	86.12			
SARAH PORTER	SCHOONER	EDENTON	1845	40	63	17	4
SARAH POTTER	SCHOONER	MARTIN COUNTY	1816	30	51	14	4
SARAH VIRGINIA	SCHOONER	NEW BERN		13			
SARAH WEBB	SCHOONER	BEAUFORT		33			
SARAH WILSON	SCHOONER	NORTH RIVER	1892	15.97	50	14.3	3.8
SATILLA	PADDLE-WHEEL SNAGBOAT		1892	195	111	25	5
SATISFACTION	SCHOONER	WILMINGTON	1892	16	35.1	15.6	4.6
SAUCY JACK	SCHOONER	CHURCHES ISLAND	1817	25	37.58	14.58	4.58
SAUCY JACK	SCHOONER	NORTH CAROLINA	1787	35	59	16	5
SAUCY JACK	SCHOONER	NORTH CAROLINA	1788	19			
SAVANNAH	SLOOP	NORTH CAROLINA	1760	15			
SCHLEY	SCHOONER	PORT BATH	1751	15			
SCOTTISH CHIEF	SIDE-WHEEL STEAMER	FAYETTEVILLE	1855	110	123	18	4.75
SCUPPERNONG	SCHOONER	ELIZABETH CITY	1853	71	77	17	5
SCUPPERNONG	DREDGE	NEW BERN	1904	128	78	32	7
SEA BIRD	SLOOP	COLINGTON	1887	9.38	38.2	12.6	3.6
SEA BIRD	SCHOONER	ELIZABETH CITY	1858	92	84	20	6
SEA BIRD	SLOOP	WILMINGTON		9			
SEA FLOWER	SCHOONER	CURRITUCK COUNTY	1799	20.26	46.58	14.33	4.58
SEA FLOWER	SCHOONER	CURRITUCK COUNTY	1818	35	51	16	5
SEA FLOWER	SCHOONER	JARRETTS BAY	1875	9.54	36.1	11.5	3.2
SEA FLOWER	BRIG	NORTH CAROLINA	1730	40			
SEA FLOWER	SCHOONER	NORTH CAROLINA	1788	61			
SEA FLOWER	SLOOP	OREGON MILLS	1872	8.98	38	13	3.2
SEA FOAM	SCHOONER	EDENTON	1882	8.07			
SEA GULL	SLOOP	BEAUFORT	1871	8			
SEA GULL	SLOOP	CRAWFORD		6			
SEA GULL	SLOOP	STRAITS	1871	7.81	30.2	11.5	3.1

Name of Ship	Type of Ship	Shipbuilding Location	Year	Tons	Length	Width	Depth
SEA HORSE	SCHOONER	SMITHS CREEK	1820	124	74	21	9
SEA MONSTER	BOAT	CURRITUCK COUNTY	1855	34.44	85	10.43	4
SEA MONSTER	SCHOONER	ELIZABETH CITY		26			
SEA SERPENT	SCHOONER	WILMINGTON		17			
SEAFLOWER	SCHOONER	NORTH CAROLINA	1730	40			
SEAFLOWER	BRIGANTINE	NORTH CAROLINA	1788	61			
SEAHORSE	SLOOP	NORTH CAROLINA	1743	30			
SEEING	SCHOONER	CURRITUCK COUNTY	1852	158	89	27	2.7
SELECT	SCHOONER	CURRITUCK COUNTY	1833	35	48.5	16	5.33
SELECT	SCHOONER	HUNTING QUARTERS	1866	6.85	33.6	11	2.8
SERPENT	SHIP	BERTIE COUNTY	1799	221	81	24	12
SEVANT	SLOOP	PAMLICO COUNTY	1829		44	16	5
SHADWELL	BRIG	NORTH CAROLINA	1768	40			
SHALLOTTE	GAS SCREW	SHALLOTTE	1911	14	49		
SHAMROCK	SCHOONER	DAVIS	1899	12	49	13	3
SHAMROCK	GAS SCREW	SUPPLY	1913	14	54	14	4
SHAMROCK	GAS SCREW	WINTHROP POINT	1905	9	37	12	4.6
SHELL CASTLE	SCHOONER	CARTERET COUNTY	1815	41	54	16	5
SHELL DRAKE	SCHOONER	OREGON MILLS	1874	24.19	53.4	13.8	4.1
SHENANDOAH	GAS SCREW	ELIZABETH CITY	1907	18	42	16	6
SHIFT		NORTH CAROLINA	1728	5			
SHILOH	SCREW STEAMER	TARBORO	1895	84.59	83	22.6	4
SHOO FLY	PADDLE-WHEEL STEAMER	EDENTON	1880	10.78			
SHUI CHA	GAS SCREW	MOREHEAD CITY	1912	28	56	15	4
SIAM	SCHOONER	ELIZABETH CITY		52			
SICKLE	SHARPIE	WILLISTON	1910	15	47.6	16.1	3
SID PHILLIPS	PADDLE-WHEEL STEAMER	NEW BERN	1902	77	79	18	4.3
SIDNEY	SCHOONER	CURRITUCK COUNTY	1807	47	40.5	16.5	5.33

Name of Ship	Type of Ship	Shipbuilding Location	Year	Tons	Length	Width	Depth
SIDNEY	SCHOONER	ELIZABETH CITY		10			
SIDNEY CUSHIN	BRIG	CRAVEN COUNTY	1807	150	75	22	10
SILENUS	SLOOP	WASHINGTON	1816	70			
SILICIA	SCHOONER	PLYMOUTH	1815	30	52	14	4
SILVER SPRAY	SLOOP	AVON	1905	5	32	13	3.1
SILVER SPRAY	GAS SCREW	MARSHALLBURG	1914	20	52	13	3.8
SISTERS	SCHOONER	HUNTING QUARTERS	1869	7.18	33.9	11.3	2.9
SISTERS	SCHOONER	POWELLS POINT	1826	20	32	14	4.25
SKAVARKY	SCHOONER	PLYMOUTH	1833	46	60.92	16	5
SKIPJACK	SCHOONER	HANOVER CREEK	1855	51	63	19	4.83
SMILIE D.	SLOOP	CORE CREEK	1898	10.07	75.7	12.5	3.1
SMYTH	BRIG	NORTH CAROLINA	1765	80			
SNOW SQUALL	SCHOONER	BEAUFORT COUNTY	1856	27	47	16	4
SNOW STORM	SCHOONER	ELIZABETH CITY	1857	35.91	64	15.75	6
SOLOMON STATUS	BRIG	SWANSBORO	1832	316	96.92	26	15
SOMERSET	SCHOONER	WASHINGTON	1875	29	63.5	24.3	3.7
SOPHIA	BRIG	NORTH CAROLINA	1785	131	80	23	8
SOPHIA AND ELIZA	SCHOONER	ELIZABETH CITY	1828	89	72	22.58	1.66
SOPHIA D.	SCHOONER	CURRITUCK COUNTY	1843	67	73	17	6
SOPHIE WOOD	SCREW STEAMER	EAST LAKE	1891	28.2	63	12	4.1
SOPHY COLLINS	SCHOONER	EDENTON	1849	67	66	20	5.9
SOUTH CAROLINIAN	SCHOONER	CARTERET COUNTY	1835	70	62	20.25	6.7
SOUTH LAKE	SCHOONER	WASHINGTON	1888	24.09	51.6	17.4	4.2
SOUTHAMPTON	SCHOONER	HERTFORD COUNTY	1821	67	59.33	20.66	6.58
SOUTHERN CROSS	SCHOONER	HATTERAS	1876	11.34	56.3	14.3	4.6
SOUTHERNER	SCHOONER	BEAUFORT	1868	17.17	46.4	15.1	4
SOUTHERNER	SCHOONER	CARTERET COUNTY	1852	78	67.5	22.17	6.17
SOUTHERNER	SCHOONER	ELIZABETH CITY	1855	75.21	83	15.75	6.17
SOUTHERNER	SCHOONER	FAYETTEVILLE	1852	51	100	15	3.5
SOUTHERNER	PADDLE-WHEEL STEAMER	FAYETTEVILLE	1854	51	100	15	4
SPECULATION	SHIP	NIXONTON	1806	183.65	82	22.58	11.29
SPECULATOR	SCHOONER	BELLS BAY	1800	109			
SPECULATOR	SCHOONER	NORTH CAROLINA	1798	49			

Name of Ship	Type of Ship	Shipbuilding Location	Year	Tons	Length	Width	Depth
SPEEDWELL	SHALLOP	BERTIE COUNTY	1736	5			
SPEEDWELL	SLOOP	EDENTON	1788	15			
SPEEDWELL	PERRIANGER	NORTH CAROLINA	1726	3			
SPEEDWELL	SLOOP	NORTH CAROLINA	1761	20			
SPORT	SCHOONER	OLD TRAP	1902	6	43	12	3
SPRAY	SCHOONER	CARTERET COUNTY	1858	20	44.66	14.83	3.66
SPRAY	SLOOP	CURRITUCK COUNTY	1895	6.07	31	12	2.8
SPRAY	SCHOONER	ELIZABETH CITY		11			
SPRAY	SCHOONER	STRAITS	1865	17.38	46.4	15.2	4.2
SPRUILL MORSE	SCHOONER	PLYMOUTH	1851	41	59	17	4.66
SPY	SCHOONER	PLYMOUTH	1856	70	74	17	6
SPY	SLOOP	SMYRNA	1889	5.62	29	10.5	3
SQUIRRELL	SNOW	NORTH CAROLINA	1762	100			
ST. ANDREW	SHIP	NORTH CAROLINA	1767	100			
ST. ANDREW	SCHOONER	TYRRELL COUNTY	1737	25			
ST. GEORGE	SLOOP	EDENTON	1739	30			
ST. GEORGE	SLOOP	PORT ROANOKE	1770	10			
ST. JOHN	SCHOONER	CURRITUCK COUNTY	1778	50			
ST. PIERRE	SCHOONER	NEW BERN	1840	110	75	22	8
STAR	SCHOONER	BEAUFORT	1868	10.68	38.3	12	3
STAR	SCHOONER	NEW BERN		6			
STAR	SCHOONER	WILMINGTON		9			
STAR OF WASHINGTON	SCHOONER	HYDE COUNTY	1842	85	74	20	6
STARK ARMISTEAD	SCHOONER	BEAUFORT	1830	82			
STARLIGHT	SCHOONER	HATTERAS	1865	7	30	10	3
STARLIGHT	SCHOONER	NEW BERN		7			
STARTLED FAWN	SCHOONER	ELIZABETH CITY		10			
STATES RIGHTS	SCHOONER	SHALLOTTE	1838	102	73	23	7
STATIRA	SLOOP	WILMINGTON	1829	40	47	18	5
STELLA ALLEN	SCHOONER	MOREHEAD CITY	1902	8	44	12	2.5
STELLA F.	SHARPIE	MOREHEAD CITY	1902	11	44	12.4	2.5
STELLA LEE	SCHOONER	SOUTHPORT	1896	9.38	39	12.5	3.5
STEPHEN S. LEE	SCHOONER	WILMINGTON		18			
STERLING	GAS SCREW	MOREHEAD CITY	1906	13	45	12	3.7
STONEWALL	SCHOONER	BEAUFORT	1875	17.51	48.2	14.4	3.9

Name of Ship	Type of Ship	Shipbuilding Location	Year	Tons	Length	Width	Depth
STYLE	SCHOONER	BATH	1888	6.61	32.6	10.3	2.6
SUCCESS	SCHOONER	AVON	1901	7	46	13	2.7
SUCCESS	SLOOP	NORTH CAROLINA	1733	35			
SUCCESS	SLOOP	NORTH CAROLINA	1744	25			
SUCCESS	SCHOONER	NORTH CAROLINA	1785	89			
SUCCESS	SLOOP	NORTH CAROLINA	1787	40			
SUDIE B.		BOGUE SOUND	1891	30	32	14	3.75
SUDIE D.	SLOOP	CORE CREEK	1891	10.07	45.7	12.5	3.1
SUE	SCREW STEAMER	EDENTON	1881	28.25	53.8	12	3.8
SUE	SCREW STEAMER	EDENTON	1882	18.82			
SUE	SCREW STEAMER	NEW BERN	1898	53	69	18	3.7
SUE CUMMINGS	SCHOONER	ELIZABETH CITY		26			
SUN	PADDLE-WHEEL STEAMER	FAYETTEVILLE	1853	61			
SUNLIGHT		CALABASH	1906	18	50.2	15.5	3.5
SUNNY SOUTH	SCHOONER	CURRITUCK	1870	30.16	55	16	5
SUNNY SOUTH	SCHOONER	MOREHEAD CITY	1891	7.49	44.6	12.3	3.2
SUPERB	BRIG	BROAD CREEK	1816	228	85	25	12
SUPERIOR	SLOOP	EDENTON		5			
SURANA	SLOOP	NORTH CAROLINA	1788	60			
SURMOUNT	SCHOONER	HATTERAS		8			
SURPASS	SCHOONER	CAMDEN COUNTY	1847	58	70	16	5
SURPASS	SCHOONER	CAPE HATTERAS	1840	41	55	17	5
SURPASS	SCHOONER	CARTERET COUNTY	1846	22	52.58	16	4.33
SURPASS	SCHOONER	CORE SOUND	1867	25	52	16	4
SUSAN	SCHOONER	ADAMS CREEK	1822	89	64.5	21.75	7.58
SUSAN	SCHOONER	CAMDEN COUNTY	1846	56	66	17	5
SUSAN	SCHOONER	CARTERET COUNTY	1844	20	48	12	4
SUSAN	SCHOONER	CARTERET COUNTY	1854	20	45	12	4
SUSAN	SCHOONER	GOOSE CREEK ISLAND	1878	19	51	15.7	3.5
SUSAN	SLOOP	HYDE COUNTY	1817	27	43	15.25	5

Name of Ship	Type of Ship	Shipbuilding Location	Year	Tons	Length	Width	Depth
SUSAN	SLOOP	NARROW SHORE	1822	23	41	15	4.66
SUSAN	SCHOONER	PAMLICO	1878	16.9			
SUSAN	SCHOONER	RAYMONDS CREEK	1819	49	52	17.66	6.33
SUSAN	SCHOONER	SWANSBORO	1866	7.33			
SUSAN	SLOOP	WASHINGTON	1816	70.19	65.66	19.66	6.58
SUSAN AND MARY	SCHOONER	ELIZABETH CITY	1850	66			
SUSAN BENJAMIN	SCHOONER	BEAUFORT	1832	80	65.75	20.33	7
SUSAN BRAY	SCHOONER	CURRITUCK COUNTY	1847	121	78	23	7.75
SUSAN CAROLINE	SCHOONER	HATTERAS		12	43.5	12.3	4.2
SUSAN GREGORY	SLOOP	ELIZABETH CITY		20			
SUSAN JANE	SCHOONER	COLUMBIA	1854	114			
SUSAN JANE	SCHOONER	WILMINGTON	1854	116.24	81	23	6.17
SUSANNA	GAS SCREW	MOREHEAD CITY	1900	7	37	10	2
SUSANNAH	SCHOONER	MANTEO	1882	17.16	44.4	19.2	4.2
SUSANNAH	SCHOONER	PERQUIMANS COUNTY	1806	135			
SUSIE	SCHOONER	EDENTON	1882	24.46			
SUSSANNA	SCHOONER	NORTH CAROLINA	1760	15			
SWAN	SCREW STEAMER	NEW BERN	1890	24.32	55	11	3.9
SWAN	SCHOONER	NEW RIVER	1838	59.16	64	18.83	5.66
SWAN	SLOOP	NORTH CAROLINA	1731	6			
SWANNANOA	GAS SCREW	MOREHEAD CITY	1903	13	51	12.3	3.2
SWANSBORO		SWANSBORO	1895	20	54.8	17.4	3
SWANSBORO	BARGE	SWANSBORO	1897	188			
SWANSBOROUGH	SHIP	SWANSBOROUGH	1799	210			
SWEEPSTAKES	SCHOONER	WILMINGTON		28			
SWIFT	SCHOONER	CURRITUCK COUNTY	1795	26			
SWIFT	SCHOONER	NORTH CAROLINA	1782	30			
SWIFT	SCHOONER	NORTH CAROLINA	1789	6			
SWIFT	BRIG	NORTH CAROLINA	1806	189			
SWIFT	SCHOONER	WILMINGTON		10			
T. PICKERING	SCHOONER	CURRITUCK	1816	56	57	18	6
T. PICKERING	SCHOONER	CURRITUCK COUNTY	1808	61	57.66	18.5	6.25
T.C. MITCHELL	SCHOONER	CARTERET COUNTY	1838	99	70.5	22.66	7.33

Name of Ship	Type of Ship	Shipbuilding Location	Year	Tons	Length	Width	Depth
T.D. MURRAY	SCHOONER	WILMINGTON		45			
T.H. SAMPLE	SCHOONER	EDENTON	1851	48	61	17	4
T.H.B. MYERS	SLOOP	WASHINGTON	1873	9			
T.M. TAYLOR	SCHOONER	ATLANTIC	1890	7.08	44	11	2.7
T.M. THOMAS	SCHOONER	BEAUFORT	1873	73	73.7	23	6
T.P. ALSTON	SCHOONER	BEAUFORT	1847	94	71	21.83	7.08
T.R. COBB	SCHOONER	ELIZABETH CITY	1851	65			
TAHOMA	SCREW STEAMER	ELIZABETH CITY	1884	118.44			
TALLAHASSEE	SCHOONER	BEAUFORT	1901	13	48	14.9	2.9
TALMA	BRIG	HYDE COUNTY	1813	145	77	24	8
TAR RIVER	SCREW STEAMER	WASHINGTON	1896	217.14	124.9	23.5	5.2
TARBORO	PADDLE-WHEEL STEAMER	TARBORO	1898	72	77	23	5.8
TARBORO	PADDLE-WHEEL STEAMER	WASHINGTON	1881	143			
TARBOROUGH	SCHOONER	WASHINGTON	1828	93	75	20.75	6
TAYLOR	BARGE	ELIZABETH CITY	1909	82			
TELEGRAPH	SCHOONER	ADAMS CREEK	1816	62	59	19	6
TELEGRAPH	SCHOONER	CARTERET COUNTY	1851	31	52.25	16.42	4.33
TELEGRAPH OF WASHINGTON	SCHOONER	CARTERET COUNTY	1853	20	42	13.5	4
TELESCOPE	SCHOONER	HYDE COUNTY	1857	29	47	16	4
TENIE AND ALICE	SCHOONER	ELIZABETH CITY		65			
THE KATE	SCHOONER	PLYMOUTH	1846	55	71	17	5
THE NORTH CAROLINA	SCHOONER	NEW BERN	1824	140	60	23	10
THE POLLY		CURRITUCK	1779				
THE REBECCA	BRIGANTINE	NORTH CAROLINA	1730	70			
THE SALAMANDER	BRIGANTINE	NORTH CAROLINA	1730	40			
THELMA	SCHOONER	BEAUFORT	1904	12	44	14	3
THELMA	GAS SCREW	MOREHEAD CITY	1902	9	44	12	3
THELMA	PADDLE-WHEEL STEAMER	POINT CASWELL	1913	53	86	19	4
THELMA	GAS SCREW	SMYRNA	1905	10	36	10	4.8
THELMA G.	SCHOONER	KINNAKEET	1903	10	47	16.9	3.4
THEODORE	BARK	ELIZABETH CITY	1832	199			
THERESA	SCHOONER	GERMANTOWN	1877	15.9	45	16.1	3.7

Name of Ship	Type of Ship	Shipbuilding Location	Year	Tons	Length	Width	Depth
THETIS	SCHOONER		1829	50.27			
THOMAS & NANCY	SCHOONER	CARTERET COUNTY	1838	58	61	19	6
THOMAS AND JAMES	BRIG	CAPE FEAR	1749	70			
THOMAS AND TRYALL	SLOOP	PASQUOTANK PRECINCT	1738	20			
THOMAS AND WILLIAM	SCHOONER	BERTIE COUNTY	1805	60			
THOMAS COX	SCHOONER	PLYMOUTH	1822	95	68	21	7
THOMAS H. BLOUNT	SCHOONER	CURRITUCK COUNTY	1817	30	45	16	5
THOMAS JEFFERSON	SCHOONER	CURRITUCK COUNTY	1826	50	55	18	6
THOMAS JEFFERSON	BRIG	WASHINGTON	1801	162			
THOMAS STOW	SCHOONER	CARTERET COUNTY	1832	21	44	34	4
THOMAS THOMAS	SCHOONER	BEAUFORT	1867	43.67	67.4	19.7	5
THOMAS THOMAS	SCHOONER	SMYRNA	1903	6	39	10	2.3
THOMAS UNDERHILL	SCHOONER	CARTERET COUNTY	1838	96	71	21.33	6.92
THOMAS WYNNS	SCHOONER	HERTFORD	1827	92			
THOMAS WYNNS	SCHOONER	HYDE COUNTY	1827	92	67	22	7
THREE BROTHERS	SCHOONER	BACHELOR	1902	11	50	14	3.6
THREE BROTHERS	GAS SCREW	GUM NECK	1908	6	24	6.9	6.9
THREE BROTHERS	SCHOONER	NEW BERN		7			
THREE FRIENDS	SCHOONER	BEAUFORT	1893	5.26	40.4	10.2	2.3
THREE FRIENDS	BRIG	NORTH CAROLINA	1760	50			
THREE FRIENDS	SLOOP	NORTH CAROLINA	1901	20			
THREE MARYS	BRIG	WILMINGTON	1748	40			
THREE POT	GAS SCREW	MOREHEAD CITY	1894	14	45	14	4.2
THREE POT	SCHOONER	MOREHEAD CITY	1894	11.21	37	15	4
THREE SAMUELS	SCHOONER	BEAUFORT	1899	11	46	13.9	3
THREE SISTERS	SCHOONER	COINJOCK	1892	8.77	33	11.6	2.8
THREE SISTERS	SCHOONER	CROW ISLAND	1819	26	47	16	4.17
THREE SISTERS	BRIG	EDENTON	1811	197			
THREE SISTERS	SLOOP	NEW BERN	1788	42	48	16	8
THREE SISTERS	SLOOP	NORTH CAROLINA	1788	10			
THREE TAYLOR	SCHOONER	CROW ISLAND	1819	26	47	16	4.17
THRESSIE	SHARPIE	ATLANTIC	1905	10	45.6	12.6	2.7
TIGER	SCHOONER	NEW BERN	1829	116	70.84	23	8
TILLMAN	SCHOONER	BAY RIVER	1820	112	74	22	8
TIME	SCHOONER	HYDE COUNTY	1833	57	56	20	6

Name of Ship	Type of Ship	Shipbuilding Location	Year	Tons	Length	Width	Depth
TIME	SCHOONER	NEW BERN	1866	11.45	42	13.4	3.5
TIMOTHY PICKERING	SCHOONER	CURRITUCK COUNTY	1808	62	58	19	7
TOM BULL	SCHOONER	CHOWAN COUNTY	1815	36.85	52.83	17	4.83
TOM T	SCREW STEAMER	NEW BERN	1898	38	60	16	5
TOMMY		NORTH CAROLINA	1773	125			
TOMS	SCHOONER	NORTH CAROLINA	1788	26			
TOP	SCHOONER	BEAUFORT	1907	20			
TOPAZ	SCHOONER	CARTERET COUNTY	1850	39	57.8	17	4
TOPSAIL PACKET	SCHOONER	NORTH CAROLINA	1767	30			
TOWN		ATLANTIC	1891	60	35	10	3
TOY	BARGE	BEAUFORT	1907	20			
TOY	GAS SCREW	BEAUFORT	1908	7	28	8	2.2
TOY	SCHOONER	BEAUFORT		14			
TRADER	BOAT	PASQUOTANK COUNTY	1853	25.26	63	13.25	3.29
TRAFALGAR	SCHOONER	WILLIAMSTON	1826	160			
TRAMPOOS	SLOOP	NORTH CAROLINA	1726	12			
TRANSPORT	SCHOONER	WASHINGTON	1838	51	57	18	5
TRAVELER	SCHOONER	CARTERET COUNTY	1856	41	57.83	17.58	4.66
TRAVIS	SCHOONER	NEW BERN	1861	5.5			
TRECO	SCHOONER	CURRITUCK	1895	9.03	42.6	13.7	3
TRENT	SCREW STEAMER	NEW BERN	1882	144.08	109.2	20	5.5
TRENT	SNAG BOAT	NEW BERN	1899	69	70	20	5
TRENT	SCHOONER	TRENT RIVER	1792	71	57	18	8
TRESSIE	SCHOONER	ATLANTIC	1905	10	45	12	2.7
TRIAL	SCHOONER	CRAVEN COUNTY	1810	100	73	23	8.2
TRIAL	SLOOP	NORTH CAROLINA	1759	45			
TRIMMER	SCHOONER	CURRITUCK	1800	80			
TRIMMER	SCHOONER	HYDE COUNTY	1799	84	68	19	7
TRIUMPH	SCHOONER	CARTERET COUNTY	1856	24	47.5	13.92	4.33
TRIUMPH	SCHOONER	ELIZABETH CITY		18			
TRIUMPH	SCHOONER	NEW BERN	1841	55	66	18	5
TRIUMPH	SCHOONER	SWANSBOROUGH	1816	68	61	18.6	7

Name of Ship	Type of Ship	Shipbuilding Location	Year	Tons	Length	Width	Depth
TRUE REPUBLICA	SCHOONER	SNEADS FERRY	1810	29	49	15	4
TRYAL	SLOOP	NORTH CAROLINA	1765	10			
TRYALL	SLOOP	NORTH CAROLINA	1694	4			
TRYALL	PERRIANGER	PORT ROANOKE	1728	3			
TRYON	SCHOONER	BATH	1763	40			
TULIP	BRIG	NORTH CAROLINA	1794	239			
TURPENTINE	SCHOONER	SWANSBOROUGH	1825	118	78	23.25	7.5
TUTEY	BRIG	NORTH CAROLINA	1794	239			
TWO BROTHERS	SCHOONER	BATH	1829	71	60	18	6
TWO BROTHERS	SLOOP	BEAUFORT	1894	6	36.6	9.4	2.4
TWO BROTHERS	SCHOONER	CARTERET COUNTY	1797	59	57	18	7
TWO BROTHERS	SCHOONER	HYDE COUNTY	1817	32	48	16.83	4.83
TWO BROTHERS	SCHOONER	NORTH CAROLINA	1761	45			
TWO BROTHERS	BRIG	NORTH CAROLINA	1770	50			
TWO BROTHERS	BRIG	NORTH CAROLINA	1773	110			
TWO BROTHERS	BRIG	NORTH CAROLINA	1793	111	66	22	9
TWO BROTHERS	SCHOONER	NORTH CAROLINA	1795	70			
TWO BROTHERS	SCHOONER	NORTH CAROLINA	1796	67			
TWO BROTHERS	SCHOONER	NORTH RIVER	1819	39	48	17.42	5.58
TWO BROTHERS	SCHOONER	OCRACOKE	1819	57	56	19	6
TWO BROTHERS	SCHOONER	PLYMOUTH	1841	58	63	17	5
TWO BROTHERS		ROANOKE ISLAND	1904	5	32	10	3
TWO COUSINS	SLOOP	BEAUFORT	1898	10	44	12	2.7
TWO FRIENDS	SLOOP	EDENTON	1789	30			
TWO FRIENDS	SCHOONER	HUNTING QUARTERS	1890	13.15	46.3	13.8	4.3
TWO FRIENDS	SCHOONER	NORTH CAROLINA	1732	20			
TWO NANCY☒S	SCHOONER	NORTH CAROLINA	1803	146			
TWO SISTERS	SCHOONER	CURRITUCK COUNTY	1789	33	50	15	5
TWO SISTERS	SCHOONER	MOUNT PLEASANT	1899	12			

Name of Ship	Type of Ship	Shipbuilding Location	Year	Tons	Length	Width	Depth
TWO SISTERS	SCHOONER	NORTH CAROLINA	1788	16			
TWO SISTERS	SLOOP	NORTH RIVER	1893	7	39	11.1	3.1
U.M. GILLIKIN	GAS SCREW	MOREHEAD CITY	1913	18	42	13	3.6
UNCLE SAM	GAS SCREW	MOREHEAD CITY	1913	43	61	10	5.8
UNCLE SAM	SCREW STEAMER	NEW BERN	1900	80	88	21	5.4
UNION	SCHOONER	BEAUFORT		15			
UNION	SCHOONER	CAPE HATTERAS	1833	41	54	17	5
UNION	SCHOONER	CARTERET COUNTY	1797	17	37	12	4
UNION	SCHOONER	CARTERET COUNTY	1832	20	44	13	3
UNION	SCHOONER	ELIZABETH CITY		14			
UNION	SCHOONER	MATTAMUSKEET	1801	36.71	51.5	15.83	5.25
UNION	BRIG	NORTH CAROLINA	1785	102			
UNION	SCHOONER	PLYMOUTH	1834	76	66.5	19	6.75
UNION	SCHOONER	TYRRELL COUNTY	1816	28.55	48.75	16	4.33
UNION	SCHOONER	WASHINGTON	1795	12	33	10	4
UNION	SIDE-WHEEL STEAMER	WILMINGTON	1850	40	70	13	4
UNION WAVE	SCHOONER	ELIZABETH CITY	1857	111			
UNITED STATES	SCHOONER	CARTERET COUNTY	1828	96	69	21	7
UNITY	SCHOONER	NORTH CAROLINA	1763	20			
UNITY	BRIG	WILMINGTON	1747	80			
URIAH TIMMONS	SCHOONER	SMITHVILLE	1873	22	52	16.5	6
UTILITY	SCHOONER	CARTERET COUNTY	1812	32.6	44.21	14.9	5.9
UTILITY	SCHOONER	STRAITS OF CORE SOUND	1825	49	58	17	6
UXOR	BRIG	CARTERET COUNTY	1827	96.19	67.25	21.46	7.83
UXOR	SCHOONER	STRAITS OF CARTERET	1827	110	68	21	8
V.C. CONKLIN	SCHOONER	JAMESVILLE	1866	16	55	15	3
V.G. MANSON		CARTERET COUNTY	1852	28	49	16	4
VALENTINE	SCHOONER	RICHARD CREEK	1815	45	52	16	10
VALIANT	SLOOP	SMYRNA	1902	10	40	13	3
VALIENT	SCHOONER	CARTERET COUNTY	1820	45.82	54	17.08	4.66

Name of Ship	Type of Ship	Shipbuilding Location	Year	Tons	Length	Width	Depth
VANCEBORO	SCREW STEAMER	VANCEBORO	1888	91.32	93	19.9	4
VANDOLUER	GAS SCREW	BEAUFORT	1901	10	45	13.8	2.8
VARINA	SCHOONER	SMYRNA	1881	16.44	48.6	15.8	3.4
VENICE	SHIP	NORTH CAROLINA	1762	150			
VENNOR	SCHOONER	KINNAKEET	1883	10.42			
VENTURA	YACHT	ATLANTIC	1887	14	44	16	2.8
VENUS	SLOOP	DAVIS	1904	6	34.5	11.4	2.3
VENUS	SCHOONER	HATTERAS	1885	26	62.2	19.1	4.9
VENUS	BRIG	NORTH CAROLINA	1762	150			
VICTORY	SCHOONER	CAPE HATTERAS	1851	31	45	16	5
VICTORY	SCHOONER	STRAITS OF CORE SOUND	1826	24	45	15	4
VIENNA	SCHOONER	CARTERET COUNTY	1853	61	65.5	21.17	5.17
VIGILANT	SCHOONER	NORTH CAROLINA	1802	134			
VIGILANT	SCHOONER	SWANSBORO	1807	51	56	17	6
VINE OAK	SCHOONER	HATTERAS	1872	7	37	11	3
VIOLA	SCHOONER	ELIZABETH CITY	1869	30.64			
VIOLA	GAS SCREW	MOREHEAD CITY	1903	8	39	9.5	2.4
VIOLA	SCHOONER	WILMINGTON	1883	39.44			
VIOLET	SCREW STEAMER	BEAUFORT	1900	14	52	12	3
VIOLET	SCHOONER	NORTH HARLOWE	1901	17	47	12	3.5
VIRGIE MAY	SHARPIE	BEAUFORT	1901	7	45.6	12.5	2.5
VIRGIL	SHARPIE	WIT	1902	12	50.3	14	3.3
VIRGIN CATRENE	SLOOP	NORTH CAROLINA	1766	30			
VIRGINIA	SCHOONER	ELIZABETH CITY	1841	42.56	61	17	4.66
VIRGINIA	SCHOONER	HYDE COUNTY	1812	67	63	14	6
VIRGINIA	SHIP	NORTH CAROLINA	1774	150			
VIRGINIA	SCHOONER	WASHINGTON	1844	31	54	14	4
VIRGINIA	SCHOONER	WASHINGTON COUNTY	1845	23	43	14	3
VIRGINIA CORE	SCHOONER	CARTERET COUNTY	1856	46	62.75	17.5	4.83
VIRGINIA DARE	SCHOONER	HATTERAS	1875	13.72	39	14.4	3.4
VIRGINIA HODGES	SCHOONER	HYDE COUNTY	1835	55	62	19.58	5.25
VIRGINIA HOGES	SCHOONER	TYRRELL COUNTY	1835	55	62	19	5.3
VIRGINIA M.	SHARPIE	ATLANTIC	1896	6	44.6	11.9	2.7

Name of Ship	Type of Ship	Shipbuilding Location	Year	Tons	Length	Width	Depth
VIRGINIA R.	SHARPIE	WIT	1902	5	35.4	12.3	2.7
VIRGINIA SURRITY	SCHOONER	ELIZABETH CITY	1857	100	94	22	7.92
VIRGINITY	SCHOONER	BATH	1725	3			
VOLANT	SCHOONER	CARTERET COUNTY	1847	37	56.33	16.92	4.5
VULCAN	SCHOONER	BEAUFORT	1827	30	48.66	15.75	4.66
W AND T	SHARPIE	SOUTHPORT	1887	15	49.6	14	3
W. H. BUREN	SCHOONER	HUNTING QUARTERS	1883	11.45			
W.C. DOBBIN		CURRITUCK COUNTY	1853	104	73	22	7
W.J. TOWNSEND	SCHOONER	ELIZABETH CITY	1904	40	68	23	4.8
W.J. WALLACE	SCHOONER	MOREHEAD CITY	1902	19	47.8	13	2.7
W.J.B. SHULL	BARGE	BEAUFORT	1906	86			
W.N.H. SMITH	SLOOP	ELIZABETH CITY		28			
W.T. DAGGETT	SCREW STEAMER	PORT CASWELL	1893	33.74	71.4	14.6	3
W.T. RIGGINS	GAS SCREW	MARSHALLBERG	1904	9	46	11	2.4
WACCAMAW NO. 1	STEAM LAUNCH	WILMINGTON	1890	11.6	57	8.5	4
WADE	SCHOONER	NEW BERN	1832	120			
WALKER	SCHOONER	NORTH CAROLINA	1775	12			
WALLY	SCHOONER	LONG CREEK	1817	37	50	15	5
WALTER C. THOMAS	SCHOONER	WILMINGTON	1881	36.3			
WALTER J. DAIL	SCHOONER	PASQUOTANK COUNTY	1851	130	85	24	7.42
WALTON	SCHOONER	BEAUFORT	1874	10	40.2	14.5	3.4
WANETA	GAS SCREW	ATLANTIC	1914	11	39	9.6	4
WASHINGTON	BRIG	BERTIE COUNTY	1790	118			
WASHINGTON	SCHOONER	CARTERET COUNTY	1814	62.55	62	18.42	6.33
WASHINGTON	SCHOONER	CARTERET COUNTY	1839	107	75	22	7
WASHINGTON	SCHOONER	CARTERET COUNTY	1847	20	46.1	12.66	4
WASHINGTON	BRIG	GERMANTOWN	1835	170	81	23	10
WASHINGTON	SCREW STEAMER	WASHINGTON	1881	162.21			
WASHINGTON	SCHOONER	WILMINGTON	1873	172.4			
WASP	SCHOONER	BEAUFORT		5			
WATAUGA	SCHOONER	WASHINGTON	1856	160	99	24	7.5
WATER LILY	GAS PADDLEWHEEL	ELIZABETH CITY	1914	49	64	15	4
WATER LILY	SCHOONER	HATTERAS	1860	11	41.3	12.8	3.4

Name of Ship	Type of Ship	Shipbuilding Location	Year	Tons	Length	Width	Depth
WATUAGA		WASHINGTON	1856	127			
WAVE	SCHOONER	CRAVEN COUNTY	1823	116			
WAVE	SCHOONER	HARLOWE	1902	14	48	14	3.1
WAVE	SCHOONER	PLYMOUTH		14			
WAVE	SCHOONER	STRAITS	1853	32	50.83	17	4.42
WAVE	SCHOONER	WASHINGTON	1848	41	57	17	4
WAVE	SCHOONER	WILMINGTON	1850	92.69	68.75	22.17	7.08
WAVE CREST	SCHOONER	WILMINGTON	1865	300.17			
WAVERLY	SCHOONER	CARTERET COUNTY	1826	87	61.92	21.5	7.92
WAY HAVEN	SCHOONER	SMYRNA	1891	7	44.4	12.1	2.8
WELDON	PADDLE-WHEEL STEAMER	BLUFF POINT	1881	8.64	50.8	12.4	2.2
WELDON	SHARPIE	SMYRNA	1903	10	48.1	14.5	3.4
WE'RE HERE	GAS SCREW	MOREHEAD CITY	1914	9	48	13	2.6
WESLEYAN	SCHOONER	BEAUFORT	1824	29	48	16	5
WEST INDIAN	BRIG	WASHINGTON	1822	104	70	21	8
WHITE WING	SLOOP	SWAN QUARTER	1885	8	33.2	13.6	2.8
WIDOWS SON	SCHOONER	CRAWFORD		30			
WIDOWS SON	SCHOONER	NORTH CAROLINA	1800	91			
WIDOWS SONS	SCHOONER	MARTIN POINT	1816	80.2	66	20.66	6.92
WILD CAT	SCHOONER	CURRITUCK COUNTY	1854	21	46	13.75	3.92
WILLIAM	SCHOONER	BATH	1754	12			
WILLIAM	SLOOP	NORTH CAROLINA	1761	50			
WILLIAM	SLOOP	NORTH CAROLINA	1773	35			
WILLIAM	BRIG	NORTH CAROLINA	1773	130			
WILLIAM	BRIG	NORTH CAROLINA	1774	100			
WILLIAM	BRIG	NORTH CAROLINA	1785	105			
WILLIAM	SCHOONER	NORTH CAROLINA	1798	44			
WILLIAM	SLOOP	NORTH CAROLINA	1802	56			
WILLIAM	BRIG	PORT ROANOKE	1770	100			
WILLIAM	SCHOONER	STRAITS OF CORE SOUND	1825	20	44	13	4
WILLIAM	SCHOONER	WASHINGTON	1791	44			
WILLIAM A. GRAHAM	SCHOONER	ELIZABETH CITY	1851	70	83	17	5

Name of Ship	Type of Ship	Shipbuilding Location	Year	Tons	Length	Width	Depth
WILLIAM A. TURNER	SCHOONER	PLYMOUTH	1829	77.74	65.42	20	6.92
WILLIAM AND MARY	SLOOP	CHURCHES ISLAND	1821	29	46.5		
WILLIAM AND MARY	SLOOP	EDENTON	1746	10			
WILLIAM AND MARY	SHIP	HYDE COUNTY	1805	206			
WILLIAM AND MARY	SHIP	HYDE COUNTY	1805	206			
WILLIAM AND MARY	SCHOONER	INDIAN RIVER	1815	68	60	19	6.75
WILLIAM AND NANCY	SLOOP	CHURCHES ISLAND	1821	29	46.5	17	4.5
WILLIAM AND REBECCA	SCHOONER	PORT BRUNSWICK	1763	8			
WILLIAM B. BLADES, JR	SCREW STEAMER	NEW BERN	1902	62	61	16.7	5.8
WILLIAM B. BURGESS	SCHOONER	PASQUOTANK COUNTY	1850	50	64	17	5
WILLIAM C. BUTLER	SCHOONER	ELIZABETH CITY	1838	104	72	21.5	7.75
WILLIAM CARTER	SLOOP	NORTH CAROLINA	1803	45			
WILLIAM CLARY	BRIG	HERTFORD COUNTY	1802	116			
WILLIAM DEAN	SCHOONER	HYDE COUNTY	1808	88	67	20	7
WILLIAM DUNN	SCHOONER	HYDE COUNTY	1815	88	67	20	7
WILLIAM EATON	SCHOONER	BROAD CREEK	1808	143			
WILLIAM FRANKLIN	BOAT	PASQUOTANK COUNTY	1853	33.41	65	13.5	4.08
WILLIAM FREDERICK	SCHOONER	ELIZABETH CITY	1817	106	69.17	20.83	8.5
WILLIAM G. PRESTON	SCHOONER	CURRITUCK COUNTY	1842	51.51	58	17.33	5.92
WILLIAM GASTON	SCHOONER	SMITHS CREEK	1807	56	56.5	18.75	6.25
WILLIAM GRAY	SCHOONER	BEAUFORT COUNTY	1839	50	56	17	5
WILLIAM H. HARRISON	SCHOONER	HYDE COUNTY	1840	46	49	17	5
WILLIAM H. HOWARD	SCHOONER	CARTERET COUNTY	1850	36	54	17.33	4.58
WILLIAM H. NORTHROP	SCHOONER	WILMINGTON	1859	42	56	16	5
WILLIAM JONES	SCHOONER	HALIFAX COUNTY	1852	43	67	16	4
WILLIAM LITTLEJOHN	SHIP	DALEYS	1798	230			
WILLIAM LUCRAFT	SCHOONER	CARTERET COUNTY	1850	38	59.42	17.33	4.33
WILLIAM M.	SCREW STEAMER	WILMINGTON	1908	87	100	22	4.8
WILLIAM P. BELL	SCHOONER	CARTERET COUNTY	1847	87	68.75	24.66	6.92

Name of Ship	Type of Ship	Shipbuilding Location	Year	Tons	Length	Width	Depth
WILLIAM P. FERRAND	SCHOONER	BEAUFORT	1825	85	67	21	7
WILLIAM P. GURLEY	SCHOONER	ELIZABETH CITY	1857	60.62	72	17.25	5.42
WILLIAM P. MOORE	SCHOONER	CRAVEN COUNTY	1849	95	73	23	7
WILLIAM PENN	BRIG	ELIZABETH CITY	1832	168			
WILLIAM R. SMITH	SCHOONER	HALIFAX COUNTY	1833	51	67	17	5
WILLIAM R. SWIFT	SCHOONER	FORTESQUENT CREEK	1830	43	58	17.58	7
WILLIAM S. COPES	SCHOONER	ELIZABETH CITY	1858	58.55			
WILLIAM SEECRAFT	SCHOONER	CARTERET COUNTY	1850	38	58.42	17.33	4.33
WILLIAM SHAW		WASHINGTON	1850				
WILLIAM T. HARRIS	SCHOONER	BEAUFORT COUNTY	1856	39	52	18	5
WILLIAM W. CHERRY	SCHOONER	BULL POND	1850	59	75	17	5
WILLIE B.	SCHOONER	SWANSBORO	1866	12.55			
WILLIE T.	SCHOONER	KINNAKEET	1883	5.39	34.1	11.3	3
WILLIS	SCHOONER	SMYRNA	1889	7.83	42	10.8	3.2
WILMINGTON	BRIG	NORTH CAROLINA	1769	50			
WILMOT	BRIG	BAY RIVER	1813	216	85.2	25.1	11.8
WINEFRID	BRIG	HALIFAX COUNTY	1792	154			
WINFIELD	SCHOONER	BERTIE COUNTY	1789	55	58	14	6
WINNER	SCHOONER	WILMINGTON	1903	14	46	13	4
WINTHROP	SCREW STEAMER	WINTHROP POINT	1900	39			
WINYAW	SCHOONER	WILMINGTON	1856	48	55	16	5
WOLF	SCHOONER	NEW BERN	1839	25	49	13	4
WONDER	SCREW STEAMER	POINT CASWELL	1907	14	58	9.9	2.8
WORTH BAGLEY	SLOOP	MOREHEAD CITY	1898	7	41	11	2.1
WORTH J.	SCREW STEAMER	ATKINSON	1914	12	55	13	3
WYONA	GAS SCREW	STRAITS	1900	21	53	18.7	4
YELLOW GAL	PADDLE-WHEEL STEAMER	EDENTON	1879	7.66			
YEOPIM	SCREW STEAMER	DRUMMONDS	1881	15.71	61.8	10	5
YONCK	BRIG	BEAUFORT	1779				
YOUNG EAGLE	SCHOOONER	CARTERET COUNTY	1830	24	44.92	14.83	4.5
YOUNG EAGLE	SCHOONER	WASHINGTON	1810	100			
YOUNGER SON	SCHOONER	TYRRELL COUNTY	1816	25.58	42.66	15.82	4.25
YULU N	SCHOONER	BELLE ISLAND	1876	12.2			

Name of Ship	Type of Ship	Shipbuilding Location	Year	Tons	Length	Width	Depth
ZELDA	GAS SCREW	WASHINGTON	1906	13	40	10	3.5
ZELPHIA ANN	SCHOONER	CARTERET COUNTY	1838	9	71.1	20.1	7.1
ZENITH	SCHOONER	CARTERET COUNTY	1857	24	45.5	14.83	4.25
ZENITH	SLOOP	MOUNT PLEASANT	1889	11.49	46	14.7	3
ZENITH	SCHOONER	SWANSBOROUGH	1834	103	71	22	7
ZEORIA	SCHOONER	AVON	1899	10	40	12	2.4
ZEPHANIAH	SCHOONER	ELIZABETH CITY	1855	72.31	82.5	17.33	5.5
ZEPHYR	SCHOONER	SMITHS CREEK	1829	67	62	19	7
ZIYIRA	GAS SCREW	WIT	1911	8	35	8	3.2
ZMORA HILL	SCHOONER	EDENTON	1850	52	67	17	5
	CLIPPER BUILT BRIG	BEAUFORT	1819	200			
	STEAM FLAT	GOLDSBORO	1886	27	70	16.7	2.4
	BRIG	HYDE COUNTY	1816	160	80.58	23.9	9
	SCHOONER	HYDE COUNTY	1816	60	57.5	18	
		MARTIN COUNTY	1788				
	SHIP	NORTH CAROLINA	1747	120			
	SCHOONER	NORTH CAROLINA	1801	38			
		SMITHVILLE	1796		34	14	
	SCHOONER	TYRRELL COUNTY	1806	23.17	38	13.83	4.75

Appendix B: Chronological Dates Ships List

Date	Ship Name	Shipbuilding Location
1688	JAMES OF VIRGINIA	NORTH CAROLINA
1693	RICHARD OF NORTH CAROLINA	NORTH CAROLINA
	RICHARD OF CORRATUCK	PASQUOTANK
1694	TRYALL	NORTH CAROLINA
1698	MARTHA OF NORTH CAROLINA	NORTH CAROLINA
1701	ANN OF NORTH CAROLINA	PASQUOTANK
1703	OTTER	PAMLICO
1712	ELIZABETH	NORTH CAROLINA
1714	JANE AND MARY	NORTH CAROLINA
	SARAH AND MARY	NORTH CAROLINA
1715	JOHN AND CATHERINE	NORTH CAROLINA
1717	ADVENTURE	NORTH CAROLINA
1720	ENDEAVOUR	LITTLE RIVER
1722	CAROLINA VENTURE	EDENTON
	CAROLINA ADVENTURE	NORTH CAROLINA
	DILLIGENCE	NORTH CAROLINA
	PROPRIETY	NORTH CAROLINA
1723	PROSPERITY	ALBEMARLE COUNTY
1725	ADVENTURE	BATH
	VIRGINITY	BATH
	LAUREL	BEAUFORT
	ENDEAVER	NORTH CAROLINA
	PROSPERITY	NORTH CAROLINA
	SARAH	PASQUOTANK COUNTY
1726	ELIZABETH	NORTH CAROLINA
	SPEEDWELL	NORTH CAROLINA
	TRAMPOOS	NORTH CAROLINA
1727	NORTH CAROLINA	BATH
	FIRST ADVENTURE	CAPE FEAR RIVER
	GREYHOUND	MACHAPONGO RIVER
	DELIGHT	PORT ROANOKE
1728	PROSPERITY	BATH
	CERRIN TRYALL	NORTH CAROLINA
	EFFIE M. GILLIKIN	NORTH CAROLINA
	ENID AND THOMAS	NORTH CAROLINA
1728	JAMAICA	NORTH CAROLINA
	KATE	NORTH CAROLINA
	MILKMAID	NORTH CAROLINA
	POOR MAN'S SHIFT	NORTH CAROLINA

Date	Ship Name	Shipbuilding Location
1728	PROPERTY	NORTH CAROLINA
	RICHARD AND THOMAS	NORTH CAROLINA
	SHIFT	NORTH CAROLINA
	TRYALL	PORT ROANOKE
1729	ELIZ. AND JOSANNA	NORTH CAROLINA
	ELIZABETH AND SUSANNA	NORTH CAROLINA
	MOLLY	NORTH CAROLINA
1730	ANN AND SARAH	BATH COUNTY
	ARA AND SARAH	BATH COUNTY
	REBECCA	CAPE FEAR
	CAROLINA	CURRITUCK
	CHARMING BETSEY	CURRITUCK
	SALAMANDER	NORTH CAROLINA
	SEA FLOWER	NORTH CAROLINA
	SEAFLOWER	NORTH CAROLINA
	THE REBECCA	NORTH CAROLINA
	THE SALAMANDER	NORTH CAROLINA
1731	CAROLINA	BATH
	JOHN AND DAVID	BATH
	RANGER	BATH
	RANGER	NORTH CAROLINA
	SWAN	NORTH CAROLINA
1732	SARAH	BERTIE COUNTY
	TWO FRIENDS	NORTH CAROLINA
	PHENIX	PASQUOTANK
	ANN AND SARAH	PORT BATH
1733	CAROLINE	NORTH CAROLINA
	SUCCESS	NORTH CAROLINA
1734	BOB AND ALICE	BATH
	HAPPY LUKE	BATH
	ROBERT AND ALICE	BATH COUNTY
	GUERNSEY	EDENTON
	BATCHLOR	HYDE PRECINCT
	ELIZABETH	NORTH CAROLINA
1735	REBECCA AND FREELOVE	NORTH CAROLINA
1736	SPEEDWELL	BERTIE COUNTY
1737	ST. ANDREW	TYRRELL COUNTY
1738	JULIANA	NORTH CAROLINA
	THOMAS AND TRYALL	PASQUOTANK PRECINCT
1739	ST. GEORGE	EDENTON
	PASQUOTANK	PASQUOTANK COUNTY
1740	HOPEWELL	PERQUIMANS RIVER

Date	Ship Name	Shipbuilding Location
1741	DAVID	HYDE COUNTY
	ELIZABETH AND SARAH	NORTH CAROLINA
	QUEEN ELIZABETH	NORTH CAROLINA
1742	BEAUFORT	NORTH CAROLINA
	BUCKSKIN	NORTH CAROLINA
	PROSPERITY	NORTH CAROLINA
1743	JEREMIAH	EDENTON
	BUTTERFLY	NORTH CAROLINA
	PHONICE	NORTH CAROLINA
	SEAHORSE	NORTH CAROLINA
1744	ANN	NORTH CAROLINA
	LANUCK	NORTH CAROLINA
	SALLY	NORTH CAROLINA
	SUCCESS	NORTH CAROLINA
1745	MARY	NORTH CAROLINA
	GREYHOUND	PASQUOTANK
	SALLEY	PORT BATH
1746	JULLIAN AND JOHN	EDENTON
	WILLIAM AND MARY	EDENTON
	DOREEN AND HANNAH	WILMINGTON
1747	RANGER	NORTH CAROLINA
		NORTH CAROLINA
	GOOD INTENT	PASQUOTANK
	ANN	PORT BATH
	UNITY	WILMINGTON
1748	ELIZABETH	NORTH CAROLINA
	ORTON	WILMINGTON
	THREE MARYS	WILMINGTON
1749	THOMAS AND JAMES	CAPE FEAR
	JOSEPH AND LYDIA	CHOWAN COUNTY
1749	DRUDGE	NORTH CAROLINA
	IDA AND LYNDA	NORTH CAROLINA
	JAMES	NORTH CAROLINA
	MARY	NORTH CAROLINA
	EARL GRANVILLE	PERQUIMANS COUNTY
	HOPE	WILMINGTON
1750	NEW BERN	ADAMS CREEK
	ABERDEEN	BEAUFORT
	GAZETTE	EDENTON
	CHARMING NANCY	LITTLE RIVER
	CADER	NORTH CAROLINA
	MARY	NORTH CAROLINA

Date	Ship Name	Shipbuilding Location
1750	NEW BERN	NORTH CAROLINA
	RICHMOND	NORTH CAROLINA
	SALLY	NORTH CAROLINA
	SAMUEL AND SARAH	PASQUOTANK
1751	PATIENCE	EDENTON
	JOHN AND DAVID	HYDE COUNTY
	FANNY	NORTH CAROLINA
	JACK AND JUDY	NORTH CAROLINA
	PHOENIX	PASQUOTANK
	SCHLEY	PORT BATH
	CAROLINA	PORT ROANOKE
	JOSEPH AND JUDA	QUISTSNA
1752	HENRY	EDENTON
	EAGLE	NORTH CAROLINA
	ELIZABETH	NORTH CAROLINA
	HARTWOOD	NORTH CAROLINA
	MARY	NORTH CAROLINA
	RECOVERY	WILMINGTON
1753	MARY ANN	CAPE FEAR
	CRANSTON	NORTH CAROLINA
	FREEMASON	NORTH CAROLINA
	ROBINSON	NORTH CAROLINA
	SALLY	NORTH CAROLINA
	ENDEAVOUR	PORT ROANOKE
	ENDEAVOR	ROANOKE
1754	WILLIAM	BATH
	BATCHELOR	NORTH CAROLINA
1754	DOLPHIN	NORTH CAROLINA
	MOLLY	NORTH CAROLINA
	PALMER	NORTH CAROLINA
1755	JOHN BOTTY	BEAUFORT
	ANNA	NORTH CAROLINA
	HALLIFAX	NORTH CAROLINA
	LYDIA	NORTH CAROLINA
1756	BOSS	NORTH CAROLINA
	DOVE	NORTH CAROLINA
	ROSS	NORTH CAROLINA
1757	SALLY	NORTH CAROLINA
1758	BETSEY	NORTH CAROLINA
	HERTFORD	NORTH CAROLINA
	MOUNT GALLANT	NORTH CAROLINA
	PEGGY TRYON	NORTH CAROLINA

Date	Ship Name	Shipbuilding Location
1759	HANNAH	NORTH CAROLINA
	POLLY	NORTH CAROLINA
	TRIAL	NORTH CAROLINA
1760	BETSEY	NORTH CAROLINA
	FLYING FISH	NORTH CAROLINA
	JOHN AND HANNA	NORTH CAROLINA
	POLLY	NORTH CAROLINA
	SALLY	NORTH CAROLINA
	SAVANNAH	NORTH CAROLINA
	SUSSANNA	NORTH CAROLINA
	THREE FRIENDS	NORTH CAROLINA
1761	DUNLUCE	NORTH CAROLINA
	JAMES	NORTH CAROLINA
	KING BIRD	NORTH CAROLINA
	NEWBURN	NORTH CAROLINA
	SPEEDWELL	NORTH CAROLINA
	TWO BROTHERS	NORTH CAROLINA
	WILLIAM	NORTH CAROLINA
	GASPER	PORT ROANOKE
	POLLY	PORT ROANOKE
1762	FRIENDSHIP	BATH
	BETSY	NORTH CAROLINA
	BRIDGET AND LYDIA	NORTH CAROLINA
	JOSEPH	NORTH CAROLINA
1762	PEGGIE	NORTH CAROLINA
	PEGGY	NORTH CAROLINA
	SQUIRRELL	NORTH CAROLINA
	VENICE	NORTH CAROLINA
	VENUS	NORTH CAROLINA
	EDINBURGH	WILMINGTON
1763	BATH PACKET	BATH
	TRYON	BATH
	HAPPY RETURN	NORTH CAROLINA
	LITTLE PATRICK	NORTH CAROLINA
	MARY'S ANN, BETTY	NORTH CAROLINA
	SALLY	NORTH CAROLINA
	SALLY	NORTH CAROLINA
	UNITY	NORTH CAROLINA
	WILLIAM AND REBECCA	PORT BRUNSWICK
1764	ANNABELLA	NORTH CAROLINA
	BETSY	NORTH CAROLINA
	CHARMING PEGGY	NORTH CAROLINA
	DISPATCH	NORTH CAROLINA

Date	Ship Name	Shipbuilding Location
1764	FRIENDSHIP	NORTH CAROLINA
	JOLLY BATCHELOR	NORTH CAROLINA
	KINGSTON	NORTH CAROLINA
	LITTLE KELLEN	NORTH CAROLINA
	POLLY	NORTH CAROLINA
	SALLY	PORT ROANOKE
1765	FLORIDA	NORTH CAROLINA
	FRIENDSHIP	NORTH CAROLINA
	GREENCOCK	NORTH CAROLINA
	GRUNCOCK	NORTH CAROLINA
	NEPTUNE	NORTH CAROLINA
	SMYTH	NORTH CAROLINA
	TRYAL	NORTH CAROLINA
	MOLLY AND BETSY	ROANOKE
1766	JANET	NORTH CAROLINA
	JANNIE	NORTH CAROLINA
	RAINBOW	NORTH CAROLINA
	REBECCA	NORTH CAROLINA
	SALLY AND ANN	NORTH CAROLINA
	VIRGIN CATRENE	NORTH CAROLINA
1767	ANN	NORTH CAROLINA
	CAROLINA	NORTH CAROLINA
	CAROLINA	NORTH CAROLINA
	NANCY AND SUKEY	NORTH CAROLINA
	POLLY	NORTH CAROLINA
	SALLY	NORTH CAROLINA
	SALLY	NORTH CAROLINA
	SALLY	NORTH CAROLINA
	ST. ANDREW	NORTH CAROLINA
	TOPSAIL PACKET	NORTH CAROLINA
	RUBY	ROANOKE
1768	LORD HYDE	CAPE FEAR
	BELL	NORTH CAROLINA
	BETSEY	NORTH CAROLINA
	JOSIAH	NORTH CAROLINA
	LITTLE POLLY	NORTH CAROLINA
	PALLAS	NORTH CAROLINA
	PEGGY	NORTH CAROLINA
	PHEOBE AND JOHN	NORTH CAROLINA
	RALFE	NORTH CAROLINA
	ROLFE	NORTH CAROLINA
	SHADWELL	NORTH CAROLINA

Date	Ship Name	Shipbuilding Location
1769	NANCY	CURRITUCK COUNTY
	BETSY	NORTH CAROLINA
	CHARLOTTE	NORTH CAROLINA
	INDUSTRY	NORTH CAROLINA
	POLLY	NORTH CAROLINA
	ROBERT	NORTH CAROLINA
	SALLY	NORTH CAROLINA
	WILMINGTON	NORTH CAROLINA
	ALERT	PORT ROANOKE
	ACORN	WASHINGTON
1770	CHARMING POLLY	BATH
	ANN	NORTH CAROLINA
	DOLPHIN	NORTH CAROLINA
	JOHNSTON	NORTH CAROLINA
	LOVELY	NORTH CAROLINA
	SALLY	NORTH CAROLINA
	SALLY	NORTH CAROLINA
1770	TWO BROTHERS	NORTH CAROLINA
	ST. GEORGE	PORT ROANOKE
	WILLIAM	PORT ROANOKE
	ELIZABETH	ROANOKE
1771	ACTIVE	NORTH CAROLINA
	ADVENTURE	NORTH CAROLINA
	CHARMING POLLY	NORTH CAROLINA
	GREYHOUND	NORTH CAROLINA
	LAST SHIFT	NORTH CAROLINA
	LITTLE DICK	NORTH CAROLINA
	POMPEY	NORTH CAROLINA
	BETSEY	PORT ROANOKE
	BETSY	PORT ROANOKE
	CHARMING BETSEY	PORT ROANOKE
	SALLY	PORT ROANOKE
1772	INDUSTRY	BRUNSWICK
	PAYNE	CURRITUCK
	BETSY	NORTH CAROLINA
	FRANCES	NORTH CAROLINA
	MOSQUITO HAWK	NORTH CAROLINA
	POLLY	NORTH CAROLINA
	JUNE	PORT ROANOKE
	ROYAL EXCHANGE	PORT ROANOKE
	BELSEY	
1773	DOVE	BRUNSWICK
	EXPERIMENT	BRUNSWICK

Date	Ship Name	Shipbuilding Location
1773	BETSEY	NORTH CAROLINA
	DOLPHIN	NORTH CAROLINA
	EDWARD	NORTH CAROLINA
	FANNY	NORTH CAROLINA
	FRANCIS	NORTH CAROLINA
	LITTLE ROBERT	NORTH CAROLINA
	MARTIN	NORTH CAROLINA
	TOMMY	NORTH CAROLINA
	TWO BROTHERS	NORTH CAROLINA
	WILLIAM	NORTH CAROLINA
	WILLIAM	NORTH CAROLINA
	HANNAH	WILMINGTON
1774	POLLY	CURRITUCK
	BETSY	NORTH CAROLINA
	CALO	NORTH CAROLINA
	CATO	NORTH CAROLINA
	DIAMOND	NORTH CAROLINA
	HAWK	NORTH CAROLINA
	PHILADELPHIA	NORTH CAROLINA
	VIRGINIA	NORTH CAROLINA
	WILLIAM	NORTH CAROLINA
	BETSY	PORT ROANOKE
	POLLY	PORT ROANOKE
	SALLY	PORT ROANOKE
1775	POLLY	CURRITUCK
	CHARMING PATSY	NORTH CAROLINA
	HOPE	NORTH CAROLINA
	MARY	NORTH CAROLINA
	PENELOPE	NORTH CAROLINA
	WALKER	NORTH CAROLINA
	HALIFAX	PORT ROANOKE
	NABOB	PORT ROANOKE
	PEGGY	PORT ROANOKE
1776	ANN	NORTH CAROLINA
	PEGGY	PITT COUNTY
	POLLY	PORT ROANOKE
1777	ROBERT	CAPE HATTERAS
	BETSEY	CHOWAN COUNTY
	JOSEPH	NORTH CAROLINA
	LIVELY	NORTH CAROLINA
	POLLY	NORTH CAROLINA
	ELLINOR	OTTER CREEK

Date	Ship Name	Shipbuilding Location
	BETSY	PORT ROANOKE
	HIRAM	ROANOKE RIVER
1778	ST. JOHN	CURRITUCK COUNTY
	FRANKLIN	EDENTON
	BENJAMIN	NORTH CAROLINA
	LA VICTOIRE	NORTH CAROLINA
	NANCY	NORTH CAROLINA
	ANNE	SMITHS CREEK
1779	YONCK	BEAUFORT
	LUCY	CAMDEN COUNTY
	THE POLLY	CURRITUCK
	FAIR AMERICAN	HERTFORD
	POLLY	NEW BERN
	CHARMING BETSEY	NORTH CAROLINA
	CHARMING PATSEY	NORTH CAROLINA
	RESOURCE	NORTH CAROLINA
	SALLY	NORTH CAROLINA
1780	PEGGY	NEW BERN
	GOOD INTENT	NORTH CAROLINA
	MARY	NORTH CAROLINA
	SANQUIDOR	NORTH CAROLINA
1781	FRIENDS	EDENTON
	HERO	EDENTON
	RISING STATES	HERTFORD
	PRUDENCE	NORTH CAROLINA
1782	KENER	NORTH CAROLINA
	SWIFT	NORTH CAROLINA
	REBEL	PERQUIMANS RIVER
1783	BETSEY	MOUSE HARBOR
	CAROLINA	
1784	LURARIA	CAMDEN
	LUSANIA	CAMDEN
	MOLLY	NORTH CAROLINA
	PANTHER	PERQUIMANS COUNTY
1785	POLLY	BERTIE COUNTY
	BETSY	CURRITUCK COUNTY
	FRANKLIN	EDENTON
	GENERAL WASHINGTON	EDENTON
	BETSEY	MOUSE HARBOR
	FANNY	NEW BERN
	ELIZA	NORTH CAROLINA
	NANCY	NORTH CAROLINA

Date	Ship Name	Shipbuilding Location
1785	SOPHIA	NORTH CAROLINA
	SUCCESS	NORTH CAROLINA
	UNION	NORTH CAROLINA
	WILLIAM	NORTH CAROLINA
1786	POLLY	BEAUFORT
	JENNY	BERTIE COUNTY
	ANNA MARIA	NIXTON
	BETSY	NORTH CAROLINA
	DOLPHIN	NORTH CAROLINA
	ENDEAVOUR	NORTH CAROLINA
	GEORGE	NORTH CAROLINA
	HARMONY	NORTH CAROLINA
	DISPATCH	PERQUIMANS COUNTY
	BETSEY	SWANSBOROUGH
1787	CAROLINA	EDENTON
	HUNTER	MARTIN COUNTY
	SAUCY JACK	NORTH CAROLINA
	SUCCESS	NORTH CAROLINA
1788	SALLY	BATH
	FRIENDSHIP	BEAUFORT
	LARK	BELLS BUOY
	BERTIE	BERTIE COUNTY
	CHARLOTTE	CARTERET COUNTY
	GOOD INTENT	CHOWAN COUNTY
	ELIZABETH	EDENTON
	LARK	EDENTON
	SPEEDWELL	EDENTON
	HIRAM	MARTIN COUNTY
		MARTIN COUNTY
	THREE SISTERS	NEW BERN
	ALEXANDER	NORTH CAROLINA
	ALLIANCE	NORTH CAROLINA
	BETSEY	NORTH CAROLINA
	BETSY	NORTH CAROLINA
	BROKEN MERCHANT	NORTH CAROLINA
	CAMDEN	NORTH CAROLINA
	CAROLINA	NORTH CAROLINA
	CUMMING	NORTH CAROLINA
	DISPATCH	NORTH CAROLINA
	DOLPHIN	NORTH CAROLINA
	FANNY	NORTH CAROLINA
	FRANKLIN	NORTH CAROLINA

Date	Ship Name	Shipbuilding Location
1788	FRIENDSHIP	NORTH CAROLINA
	GENERAL GREEN	NORTH CAROLINA
	GENERAL WASHINGTON	NORTH CAROLINA
	GOOD INTENT	NORTH CAROLINA
	HARNETT	NORTH CAROLINA
	HESTER	NORTH CAROLINA
	HUNTER	NORTH CAROLINA
	JENNY	NORTH CAROLINA
	JULIA	NORTH CAROLINA
	LIZZARD	NORTH CAROLINA
	LYDIA	NORTH CAROLINA
	MARY	NORTH CAROLINA
	MERMAID	NORTH CAROLINA
	NANCY	NORTH CAROLINA
	NELLY AND POLLY	NORTH CAROLINA
	NOAHS ARK	NORTH CAROLINA
	OSTRICH	NORTH CAROLINA
	PATSY	NORTH CAROLINA
	PATTY	NORTH CAROLINA
	PAYNE	NORTH CAROLINA
	POLLY	NORTH CAROLINA
	POLLY	NORTH CAROLINA
	POLLY	NORTH CAROLINA
	POLLY	NORTH CAROLINA
	POLLY	NORTH CAROLINA
	POLLY	NORTH CAROLINA
	POLLY	NORTH CAROLINA
	POLLY	NORTH CAROLINA
	POLLY AND SALLY	NORTH CAROLINA
	RESOLUTION	NORTH CAROLINA
	SALLY	NORTH CAROLINA
	SAUCY JACK	NORTH CAROLINA
	SEA FLOWER	NORTH CAROLINA
	SEAFLOWER	NORTH CAROLINA
	SURANA	NORTH CAROLINA
	THREE SISTERS	NORTH CAROLINA
	TOMS	NORTH CAROLINA
	TWO SISTERS	NORTH CAROLINA
1788	JAMES	PASQUOTANK COUNTY
	POLLY	PERQUIMANS COUNTY
	CHARMING BETSEY	SWANSBOROUGH
	MINERVA	

Date	Ship Name	Shipbuilding Location
1789	POLLY	ADAMS CREEK
	WINFIELD	BERTIE COUNTY
	FRIENDSHIP OF BEAUFORT	CARTERET COUNTY
	JACK	CORE BANKS
	TWO SISTERS	CURRITUCK COUNTY
	EDENTON	EDENTON
	PRECILLA	EDENTON
	PRISCILLA	EDENTON
	TWO FRIENDS	EDENTON
	AMELIA	NEW TOPSAIL
	AMARYLLIS	NORTH CAROLINA
	AMELIA	NORTH CAROLINA
	AMY	NORTH CAROLINA
	ENDEAVOR	NORTH CAROLINA
	FLYING FISH	NORTH CAROLINA
	FREEDOM	NORTH CAROLINA
	GOOD INTENT	NORTH CAROLINA
	JOHN	NORTH CAROLINA
	MARIES	NORTH CAROLINA
	NOAHS ARK	NORTH CAROLINA
	POLLY	NORTH CAROLINA
	POLLY AND NANCY	NORTH CAROLINA
	RALLY	NORTH CAROLINA
	RAMBLER	NORTH CAROLINA
	SALLY	NORTH CAROLINA
	SWIFT	NORTH CAROLINA
	FANNY	PUNGO
1790	SALLY	BEAUFORT
	WASHINGTON	BERTIE COUNTY
	PLANTER	HALIFAX COUNTY
	RUSSELL	HYDE COUNTY
	HOPE	WASHINGTON
1791	HARRIET	NORTH CAROLINA
	WILLIAM	WASHINGTON
1792	BETSEY	ADAMS CREEK
	BETSY AND HANNAH	BEAUFORT
	EAGLE	BEAUFORT
	EXPERIMENT	BEAUFORT
	INDUSTRY	BEAUFORT
	SALLY	CAMDEN
	HERCULES	CARTERET COUNTY
	WINEFRID	HALIFAX COUNTY

Date	Ship Name	Shipbuilding Location
1792	ELIZABETH	MARTIN COUNTY
	ESTHER	NEW TOPSAIL
	TRENT	TRENT RIVER
1793	POLLY AND NANCY	ADAMS CREEK
	CHARLOTTE	MARTIN COUNTY
	BEAUFORT	NORTH CAROLINA
	ELIZA	NORTH CAROLINA
	FANNY	NORTH CAROLINA
	RESOLUTION	NORTH CAROLINA
	TWO BROTHERS	NORTH CAROLINA
	BETSEY	TYRRELL COUNTY
	EARL	TYRRELL COUNTY
	JOHN	WHITE ROCK
	CHANCE	WILMINGTON
1794	BETSY	BEARS CREEK
	ALBEMARLE	BERTIE COUNTY
	BETSEY	CURRITUCK COUNTY
	HOPE	HABSCAN
	POLL CARY	HALIFAX COUNTY
	FREEDOM	MARE POINT
	BELINDA	MURFREESBORO
	HYDE	NORTH CAROLINA
	LUBENTIA	NORTH CAROLINA
	TULIP	NORTH CAROLINA
	TUTEY	NORTH CAROLINA
	RESOLUTION	ONSLOW COUNTY
	CYGNET	STRAITS OF CARTERET
	FAME	SWANSBOROUGH
1795	PEGGY	ADAMS CREEK
	HAWK	BEAR BANKS
	JOHN	BEAUFORT
1795	DIANA	CORE SOUND
	FRIENDSHIP	CRAVEN COUNTY
	SWIFT	CURRITUCK COUNTY
	AGNES	MARTIN COUNTY
	BETSEY	NEW BERN
	DICK	NEW BERN
	ADVENTURE	NORTH CAROLINA
	CHATHAM	NORTH CAROLINA
	FANCY	NORTH CAROLINA
	FANNY	NORTH CAROLINA
	GRACY	NORTH CAROLINA

Date	Ship Name	Shipbuilding Location
1795	TWO BROTHERS	NORTH CAROLINA
	HAZARD	PRINCETON
	JANE AND ELIZA	SWANSBORO
	POLLY	TRENT FERRY
	JOSIAH COLLINS	TYRRELL COUNTY
	MARY	TYRRELL COUNTY
	RENWICK	WASHINGTON
	UNION	WASHINGTON
1796	ANN	BERTIE COUNTY
	BETSEY	CURRITUCK
	FAIR PLAY	HERTFORD COUNTY
	JOANNA	NIXONTON
	LYDIA	NORTH CAROLINA
	MARY ANN	NORTH CAROLINA
	MINERVA	NORTH CAROLINA
	NANCY	NORTH CAROLINA
	PENELOPE	NORTH CAROLINA
	POLLY	NORTH CAROLINA
	SALLY	NORTH CAROLINA
	TWO BROTHERS	NORTH CAROLINA
	PEGGY	POLEY BRANCH
	FANNY	ROANOKE ISLAND
	HAZARD	ROANOKE ISLAND
	POLLY	SMITHS CREEK
		SMITHVILLE
	LEWIS	SWANSBORO
1797	DAPHINE	CARTERET COUNTY
	TWO BROTHERS	CARTERET COUNTY
1797	UNION	CARTERET COUNTY
	JOHN	CHOWAN COUNTY
	FAIR AMERICAN	CRAVEN COUNTY
	RELIEF	FLOAT BRIDGE
	FORETOMAN	LANCASTER
	AMITABLE ADELLE	NORTH CAROLINA
	FODARALYT	NORTH CAROLINA
	PENELOPE	NORTH CAROLINA
	RAMBLER	PASQUOTANK COUNTY
	FAIR AMERICAN	SMITHS CREEK
	FREDERICK	SWANSBOROUGH
	CALEB	TYRRELL COUNTY
1798	HARMINE	BEAUFORT
	RICHARD	CARTERET COUNTY
	WILLIAM LITTLEJOHN	DALEYS

Date	Ship Name	Shipbuilding Location
1798	AURORA	GOOSE CREEK
	RICHARD CATON	HYDE COUNTY
	DELIA	MARTIN COUNTY
	NANCY AND POLLY	NORTH BANKS
	ANNE	NORTH CAROLINA
	EAGLE	NORTH CAROLINA
	HARRIOT	NORTH CAROLINA
	MARY ANN	NORTH CAROLINA
	SALLY RUFFIN	NORTH CAROLINA
	SPECULATOR	NORTH CAROLINA
	WILLIAM	NORTH CAROLINA
	MARIA	ONSLOW COUNTY
	FAIR AMERICAN	PERQUIMANS COUNTY
	FRANCES NIXON	PERQUIMANS COUNTY
	JOSEPH HARVEY	PERQUIMANS RIVER
	BETSEY	
1799	SERPENT	BERTIE COUNTY
	NON PAREIL	CARTERET COUNTY
	SEA FLOWER	CURRITUCK COUNTY
	LYDIA	HERTFORD
	PYOMINGO	HYDE COUNTY
	TRIMMER	HYDE COUNTY
	MARY AND ELIZABETH	LOCKWOODS FOLLY
	PHOEBE	NEW BERN
1799	JAMES STEWART	NIXONTON
	ADVENTURE	NORTH CAROLINA
	COMMERCE	NORTH CAROLINA
	HAZARD	NORTH CAROLINA
	HUNTER	NORTH CAROLINA
	JANE	NORTH CAROLINA
	MESSENGER	NORTH CAROLINA
	FRANKLIN	PERQUIMANS COUNTY
	LITTLE FOX	POWELLS POINT
	HAPPY COUPLE	ROANOKE ISLAND
	HUNTER	SWANSBORO
	SWANSBOROUGH	SWANSBOROUGH
1800	CONSTELLATION	BEAUFORT
	SPECULATOR	BELLS BAY
	EAGLE	CRAVEN COUNTY
	ELIZA	CRAVEN COUNTY
	TRIMMER	CURRITUCK
	SALLY	CURRITUCK COUNTY
	MARY	EDENTON

Date	Ship Name	Shipbuilding Location
1800	COMMERCE	ELIZABETH CITY
	GEORGE	HYDE COUNTY
	INTREPID	HYDE COUNTY
	FAIR AMERICAN	NEW BERN
	PAISLEY	NEW BERN
	BETSY	NORTH CAROLINA
	BROTHERS	NORTH CAROLINA
	CERES	NORTH CAROLINA
	CHARLOTTE	NORTH CAROLINA
	CHARLOTTE	NORTH CAROLINA
	COREY	NORTH CAROLINA
	GEORGE	NORTH CAROLINA
	HECTOR	NORTH CAROLINA
	JANE	NORTH CAROLINA
	MATILDA	NORTH CAROLINA
	PENELOPE	NORTH CAROLINA
	RUSSELL	NORTH CAROLINA
	WIDOWS SON	NORTH CAROLINA
	MARY	NORTH RIVER
	NANCY	ORCHARD CREEK
	JOLLY ROVER	PERQUIMANS COUNTY
	SAMUEL	SMITHS CREEK
	BETSY	SWANSBOROUGH
	BETSY COX	SWANSBOROUGH
	LIVE OAK	SWANSBOROUGH
	SALLY GLADDING	WASHINGTON
1801	CERES	BAY RIVER
	OLIVE BRANCH	BEAUFORT
	REPUBLICAN	BERTIE COUNTY
	SAMUEL JACKSON	BERTIE COUNTY
	PENDER	CARTERET COUNTY
	FAVOURITE	COINJOCK BAY
	ELMSLEY	CURRITUCK NARROWS
	JOSEPH AND JAMES	HYDE COUNTY
	RAINBOW	HYDE COUNTY
	SAMUEL	INDIAN TOWN
	UNION	MATTAMUSKEET
	DAVIS	NORTH CAROLINA
	INDEPENDENCE	NORTH CAROLINA
	INDUSTRY	NORTH CAROLINA
	LEWIS WILLIAMS	NORTH CAROLINA
	RESOLUTION	NORTH CAROLINA
		NORTH CAROLINA

Date	Ship Name	Shipbuilding Location
1801	SALLY	ORCHARD CREEK
	ATALANTA	PERQUIMANS COUNTY
	NANCY	ROANOKE ISLAND
	NEUSE	SMITHFIELD
	THOMAS JEFFERSON	WASHINGTON
1802	MARY FRANCIS	BAY RIVER
	BETSEY AND SALLY	BEAUFORT
	LIVELY	CARTERET COUNTY
	FARMER	CHOWAN COUNTY
	LITTLE FRANK	CRAVEN COUNTY
	SALLY	CURRITUCK COUNTY
	FARMER	EDENTON
	SALLY AND BETSY	HERTFORD
	WILLIAM CLARY	HERTFORD COUNTY
1802	CATHERINE	NORTH CAROLINA
	DISPATCH	NORTH CAROLINA
	JOHN ELLIS	NORTH CAROLINA
	MARTIN	NORTH CAROLINA
	MARY BROWNRIGS	NORTH CAROLINA
	NANCY	NORTH CAROLINA
	OLIVIA	NORTH CAROLINA
	VIGILANT	NORTH CAROLINA
	WILLIAM	NORTH CAROLINA
	INDEPENDENCE	PUNGO RIVER
	BETSEY FULSHIRE	SLOCUM CREEK
	SALLY	WASHINGTON
1803	JAMES AND WILLIAM	BEAUFORT COUNTY
	JAMES WILLIAM	BEAUFORT COUNTY
	HENRIETTA	CRAVEN COUNTY
	SALLY	EDGECOMBE COUNTY
	CLYDE	HYDE COUNTY
	NANCY BELL	NEW BERN
	ANN	NORTH CAROLINA
	ANN AND MARTIN	NORTH CAROLINA
	CARTARET	NORTH CAROLINA
	FREEMAN ELLIS	NORTH CAROLINA
	HENRY	NORTH CAROLINA
	PLANTER	NORTH CAROLINA
	TWO NANCYS	NORTH CAROLINA
	WILLIAM CARTER	NORTH CAROLINA
	POLLY AND NANCY	SWANSBOROUGH
	MARY TURNER	WINDSOR
	ANN MARIA JONES	

Date	Ship Name	Shipbuilding Location
1804	BRUTAS	BEAUFORT
	JOHN DREW	BERTIE COUNTY
	SAMUEL	BERTIE COUNTY
	INDUSTRY	CARTERET COUNTY
	BETSY COTTON	CHOWAN COUNTY
	PRESIDENT	CURRITUCK
	BETSEY AND PATSEY	CURRITUCK COUNTY
	JOHN	HALIFAX
	NANCY WHITMELL	HALIFAX
	HAPPY RETURN	HYDE COUNTY
	POLLY	HYDE COUNTY
	MILLY	NORTH CAROLINA
	JOLLY BACCHAS	PASQUOTANK
	MARY WINYFRED	PLYMOUTH
	MARA DAUGH	ROANOKE ISLAND
	MAVA DOUGH	ROANOKE ISLAND
	SARAH AND ANN	
1805	HENRY AND WILLIAM	BERTIE COUNTY
	THOMAS AND WILLIAM	BERTIE COUNTY
	ALBION	CAMDEN
	GOOD INTENT	CARTERET COUNTY
	LIVE OAK	CARTERET COUNTY
	RICHARD AND MARY	CHOWAN COUNTY
	FAIR AMERICAN	CRAVEN COUNTY
	INDIAN HUNTER	CRAVEN COUNTY
	INDIGENCE	CRAVEN COUNTY
	NANCY	CURRITUCK COUNTY
	HAPPY COUPLE	ELIZABETHTOWN
	ANNA	HYDE COUNTY
	ANTELOPE	HYDE COUNTY
	HETTY	HYDE COUNTY
	PAMPLICO	HYDE COUNTY
	WILLIAM AND MARY	HYDE COUNTY
	WILLIAM AND MARY	HYDE COUNTY
	ONLY DAUGHTER	PASQUOTANK RIVER
	DAMSEL	POWELLS POINT
1806	MINERVA	BEAUFORT
	HOPE	BEAUFORT COUNTY
	INDUSTRY	CARTERET COUNTY
	RESOLUTION	COINJOCK
	BETSEY	CRAVEN COUNTY
	ELIZA	CRAVEN COUNTY
	CHARLES AND LEWIS	HYDE COUNTY

Date	Ship Name	Shipbuilding Location
1806	JULIA AND SALLY	HYDE COUNTY
	DOLPHIN	NEW BERN
	SPECULATION	NIXONTON
	SWIFT	NORTH CAROLINA
	SUSANNAH	PERQUIMANS COUNTY
	HORNET	SMITHS CREEK
	HERO	TYRRELL COUNTY
		TYRRELL COUNTY
	CATHERINE	WHITE OAK RIVER
1807	HOLTON	ADAMS CREEK
	ATLANTIC	ARENUSE CREEK
	ISABELLA	BEAUFORT
	JONATHAN JACOCKS	BERTIE COUNTY
	LEBANON	BERTIE COUNTY
	COASTER	CARTERET COUNTY
	DIANA	CARTERET COUNTY
	ELIJAH PIGOT	CARTERET COUNTY
	EXERTION	CRAVEN COUNTY
	FANNY	CRAVEN COUNTY
	SIDNEY CUSHIN	CRAVEN COUNTY
	HONEY	CURRITUCK COUNTY
	JOLLY SAILOR	CURRITUCK COUNTY
	MARY	CURRITUCK COUNTY
	SIDNEY	CURRITUCK COUNTY
	PATRIARCH	DAWSONS CREEK
	ANGELIA AND SUSAN	FALLS CREEK
	MINERVA	PITT COUNTY
	WILLIAM GASTON	SMITHS CREEK
	VIGILANT	SWANSBORO
1808	JAMES MURDOCK	BAY RIVER
	EXPERIMENT	BEAUFORT COUNTY
	WILLIAM EATON	BROAD CREEK
	HERMIT	CARTERET COUNTY
	LADY WASHINGTON	CRAVEN COUNTY
	LEOPARD	CURRITUCK COUNTY
	PICKERING	CURRITUCK COUNTY
	T. PICKERING	CURRITUCK COUNTY
	TIMOTHY PICKERING	CURRITUCK COUNTY
	WILLIAM DEAN	HYDE COUNTY
	JOHN	NEW BERN
	BENJAMIN BLANEY	SMITHVILLE
	JUSTIN	WASHINGTON COUNTY

Date	Ship Name	Shipbuilding Location
1809	MARY ANN	ADAMS CREEK
	PATSEY AND PENELOPE	BERTIE COUNTY
	MITALDA	CRAVEN COUNTY
	ABIGAIL	CURRITUCK NARROWS
	BETSEY	NEW BERN
	BETSEY	NEW RIVER
	JOHN WILLIS	NORTH CAROLINA
1810	BETSEY	BEAUFORT
	FEDERALIST	CHOWAN COUNTY
	TRIAL	CRAVEN COUNTY
	HENRY KING	EDENTON
	RICHARD MEADE	ELIZABETH CITY
	AMANDA	HYDE COUNTY
	MADDALENA	HYDE COUNTY
	ANN ELIZA	LITTLE RIVER
	SALLY	NORTHAMPTON
	FAIR AMERICAN	PASQUOTANK RIVER
	CHARLESTON PACKET	PITT COUNTY
	GEORGE DEVEREAUX	SMITHS CREEK
	HARBINGER	SMITHS CREEK
	MARGARET	SMITHS CREEK
	JOHN BURGUIN	SMITHVILLE
	TRUE REPUBLICA	SNEADS FERRY
	JOHN JONES	SOUTH RIVER
	CARPENTERS SON	SWANSBOROUGH
	ELIZA LORD	SWANSBOROUGH
	LITTLE JOHN	SWANSBOROUGH
	MOHAWK	TYRRELL COUNTY
	CAROLINA	WASHINGTON
	YOUNG EAGLE	WASHINGTON
1811	EDWIN	BEAUFORT COUNTY
	HUMMINGBIRD	BERTIE COUNTY
	ROBERT LENOX	BROAD CREEK
	ANTILOPE	BROWNS INLET
	INDUSTRY	CARTERET COUNTY
	JOLLY A. SAILOR	CARTERET COUNTY
	JOLLY SAILOR	CARTERET COUNTY
	PEGASUS	CARTERET COUNTY
1811	GOLD HUNTER	CRAVEN COUNTY
	HUNTER	CRAVEN COUNTY
	LIBERTY	CURRITUCK COUNTY
	AMERICAN COASTER	CURRITUCK NARROWS

Date	Ship Name	Shipbuilding Location
1811	JOHN ALLEN	CURRITUCK SOUND
	THREE SISTERS	EDENTON
	HENRY SEAWELL	ELIZABETH CITY
	MARGARET MEADE	ELIZABETH CITY
	HENRIETTA	HYDE COUNTY
	ARTS AND SCIENCE	MARTIN POINT
	FARMERS FANCY	NORTH CAROLINA
	ADAMANT	PLANK BRIDGE
	PRISCELLO ARMISTEAD	PLYMOUTH
	RELEASE	POWELLS POINT
	JAMES MCKINLEY	SMITHS CREEK
	JANE MCKINLAY	SMITHS CREEK
	GEORGE WASHINGTON	WASHINGTON
1812	BETSY	ADAMS CREEK
	HEBERNIA	ADAMS CREEK
	UTILITY	CARTERET COUNTY
	GENERAL JACKSON	CLUBFOOT CREEK
	KITCH	CORE SOUND
	JOHN STANLEY	CRAVEN COUNTY
	FRIENDSHIP	CURRITUCK BANKS
	ELIZA	CURRITUCK COUNTY
	JONA MAN	ELIZABETH CITY
	JOHN WALLACE	HYDE COUNTY
	VIRGINIA	HYDE COUNTY
	JANE	NORTH RIVER
	JOSEPH	SMITHS CREEK
	PERSERVERANCE	SMITHS CREEK
	RAPID	SOUTH RIVER
	OLIVE BRANCH	TYRRELL COUNTY
	INDUSTRY	WASHINGTON
1813	GLEANER	ADAMS CREEK
	WILMOT	BAY RIVER
	FREEDOM	CURRITUCK COUNTY
	CONCORD	CURRITUCK NARROWS
1813	TALMA	HYDE COUNTY
	LITTLE JOHN	PASQUOTANK RIVER
	GALLATIN	SMITHFIELD
	CYRUS	
1814	NEW BERN	ADAMS CREEK
	MARY ELIZA	BERTIE COUNTY
	ELIZA ANN	CARTERET COUNTY
	WASHINGTON	CARTERET COUNTY

Date	Ship Name	Shipbuilding Location
1814	NANCY	CURRITUCK COUNTY
	PEGGY AND PAMILA	CURRITUCK COUNTY
	EMILY	DAILYS LANDING
	HELEN	HYDE COUNTY
	MALVINA	HYDE COUNTY
	SALAMANDA	NEW BERN
	PAUL JONES	ONSLOW COUNTY
	SALLY NELSON	SMITHS CREEK
	SALMAGUNDI	SWANSBOROUGH
	JOHN LITTLE	TYRRELL COUNTY
	RESOLUTION	TYRRELL COUNTY
1815	JOHN STONEY	ADAMS CREEK
	MARY	ADAMS CREEK
	REBECCA AND ELIZABETH	BEAUFORT
	SALLY ANN	BEAUFORT COUNTY
	ELIZA ANN	BERTIE COUNTY
	GENERAL BROWN	BERTIE COUNTY
	COLLECTOR	CARTERET COUNTY
	LITTLE JOHN	CARTERET COUNTY
	RAMBLER	CARTERET COUNTY
	SHELL CASTLE	CARTERET COUNTY
	TOM BULL	CHOWAN COUNTY
	CHARLOTTE MADISON	COINJOCK
	MARY	CRAVEN
	BETSEY	CURRITUCK COUNTY
	LITTLE JOHN	CURRITUCK COUNTY
	WILLIAM DUNN	HYDE COUNTY
	WILLIAM AND MARY	INDIAN RIVER
	JOHN BURNEY	LOWER BROAD CREEK
	JOHN ARMSTEAD	PLYMOUTH
	SILICIA	PLYMOUTH
	VALENTINE	RICHARD CREEK
	SALLY SPARROW	SMITHS CREEK
	HUNTER	SWANSBOROUGH
	ESTHER	TYRRELL COUNTY
	FORT LANDING	TYRRELL COUNTY
	GEORGE WASHINGTON	TYRRELL COUNTY
1816	LUCY	ADAMS CREEK
	TELEGRAPH	ADAMS CREEK
	MIDAS	BEAUFORT
	HOPE	BEAUFORT COUNTY
	MARGARET	BERTIE COUNTY

Date	Ship Name	Shipbuilding Location
1816	SUPERB	BROAD CREEK
	ALERT	CARTERET COUNTY
	CAROLINE	CARTERET COUNTY
	HERO	CARTERET COUNTY
	HOPE	CARTERET COUNTY
	JARVIS BROWN AND CO.	CARTERET COUNTY
	MENTOR	CARTERET COUNTY
	PIGOT	CARTERET COUNTY
	GEORGE WASHINGTON	CHURCHES ISLAND
	ARGO	CLUBFOOT CREEK
	FANNY AND PATSY	COINJOCK BAY
	GEORGE PICKETT	CURRITUCK
	T. PICKERING	CURRITUCK
	GENERAL A. JACKSON	CURRITUCK COUNTY
	MODERATOR	CURRITUCK COUNTY
	ANDREW JACKSON	CURRITUCK SOUND
	EMILE AND ELIZA	CURRITUCK SOUND
	GENERAL JACKSON	CURRITUCK SOUND
	SARAH ANN	GAR BACON
	BRITANIA	HYDE COUNTY
	JOHN RODMAN	HYDE COUNTY
		HYDE COUNTY
		HYDE COUNTY
	LARTHENA	KNOTTS ISLAND
	SAM POTTER	MARTIN COUNTY
	SARAH POTTER	MARTIN COUNTY
	WIDOWS SONS	MARTIN POINT
	HOPE	NARROW SHORE
	BLAKELY	NEW RIVER
	MARY LYDIA	NORTH BANKS
	LAWRENCE	NORTH CAROLINA
	ELIZA & DORCAS	OCRACOKE
	ALLEN JONES	ONSLOW COUNTY
	FARMERS DAUGHTER	POWELLS POINT
	CHARLOTTE	SMITH CREEK
	CHARLOTTE CORDAY	SMITH CREEK
	MARY	SMITH CREEK
	GIDEON SPARROW	SMITHS CREEK
	HORNET	SMITHS CREEK
	MARYON SPARROW	SMITHS CREEK
	RUFUS KING	SMITHS CREEK
	INDUSTRY	SOUTH RIVER

Date	Ship Name	Shipbuilding Location
1816	TRIUMPH	SWANSBOROUGH
	ANTELOPE	TYRRELL COUNTY
	COASTER	TYRRELL COUNTY
	POLLY AND NANCY	TYRRELL COUNTY
	UNION	TYRRELL COUNTY
	YOUNGER SON	TYRRELL COUNTY
	SILENUS	WASHINGTON
	SUSAN	WASHINGTON
1817	CAROLINE	BEAUFORT
	COMET	CARTERET COUNTY
	REPUBLICAN	CARTERET COUNTY
	BLAKELY	CHOWAN COUNTY
	SAUCY JACK	CHURCHES ISLAND
	FANNY	CRAVEN COUNTY
	NANCY AND BETSY	CROOKED CREEK
	CARPENTERS SONS	CURRITUCK COUNTY
	COMMODATOR	CURRITUCK COUNTY
	MARY	CURRITUCK COUNTY
	THOMAS H. BLOUNT	CURRITUCK COUNTY
	APPRENTICE BOY	CURRITUCK NARROWS
	PRENTICE BOY	CURRITUCK NARROWS
	JAMES MONROE	EDENTON
	WILLIAM FREDERICK	ELIZABETH CITY
	GEORGE HENRY	HYDE COUNTY
	MARY ANN	HYDE COUNTY
	SUSAN	HYDE COUNTY
	TWO BROTHERS	HYDE COUNTY
	PEACE MAKER	KNOTTS ISLAND
	WALLY	LONG CREEK
	LITTLE CHARLES	POWELLS POINT
	CATHARINE AND JANE	SLADE CREEK
	JASON	SMITHS CREEK
	RAPID	SOUTH RIVER
	SALLY ANN	TYRRELL COUNTY
	CHARLES HAYS	WASHINGTON
1818	EMERALD	BACON
	MARY ADAMS	BEAUFORT COUNTY
	ANN	CARTERET COUNTY
	PARAGON	CARTERET COUNTY
	POLLY AND NANCY	COINJOCK BAY
	LOUISA	CURRITUCK COUNTY
	SEA FLOWER	CURRITUCK COUNTY

Date	Ship Name	Shipbuilding Location
1818	CORN PLANTER	CURRITUCK NARROWS
	RAINBOW	CURRITUCK NARROWS
	HENRIETTA	FAYETTEVILLE
	EMERALD	GAR BACON
	HELEN	HYDE COUNTY
	ALPHA AND OMEGA	MARTIN COUNTY
	NORTH CAROLINA	MOYOCK LANDING
	BLACK EYED SUSAN	NEW RIVER
	CHARLOTTE FARQUHAR	WILMINGTON
1819		BEAUFORT
	LITTLE JOHN	BEAUFORT COUNTY
	MARY MCKAY	BROAD CREEK
	ACTIVE	CARTERET COUNTY
	COMET	CARTERET COUNTY
	JAMES MONROE	CARTERET COUNTY
	MANNER	CARTERET COUNTY
	MARINER	CARTERET COUNTY
	MARY	CARTERET COUNTY
1819	NAN	CARTERET COUNTY
	MARIA	CORE SOUND
	THREE SISTERS	CROW ISLAND
	THREE TAYLOR	CROW ISLAND
	DECATUR	CURRITUCK COUNTY
	LOUISA	CURRITUCK COUNTY
	EMMELINE	HYDE COUNTY
	FISH HAWK	NEW BERN
	TWO BROTHERS	NORTH RIVER
	TWO BROTHERS	OCRACOKE
	SUSAN	RAYMONDS CREEK
	ESSEX	ROANOKE ISLAND
	ORIENT	ROANOKE ISLAND
	LADY OF THE LAKE	SMITHS CREEK
	FRANCES ANN	WINDSOR CREEK
1820	TILLMAN	BAY RIVER
	FRANCIS JARVIS	BEAUFORT
	JOSEPH KING	BEAUFORT
	HENRIETTA	BEAUFORT COUNTY
	LITTLE GEORGE	BEAUFORT COUNTY
	SAMUEL SIMPSON	CARTERET COUNTY
	VALIENT	CARTERET COUNTY
	POLLY ASHBY	COLERTON ISLAND
	LEDGER	CURRITUCK COUNTY

Date	Ship Name	Shipbuilding Location
1820	LODGE	CURRITUCK COUNTY
	CAROLINA	ELIZABETH CITY
	ROANOKE	HUNTING QUARTERS
	HOPE	HYDE COUNTY
	SAM SIMPSON	NORTH CAROLINA
	GLEANER	PLYMOUTH
	MARY ANN	POPLAR POINT
	AMERICAN LADY	POWELLS POINT
	CRAVEN	SMITHS CREEK
	SEA HORSE	SMITHS CREEK
	REMEDY	SWANSBOROUGH
	FRANKLIN	WASHINGTON
1821	HUNTER	ADAMS CREEK
	LADY WASHINGTON	BAY RIVER
	ENTERPRISE	CARTERET COUNTY
	WILLIAM AND MARY	CHURCHES ISLAND
	WILLIAM AND NANCY	CHURCHES ISLAND
	JULIA ANN	COINJOCK
	MARIA	CURRITUCK COUNTY
	JANE	CURRITUCK NARROWS
	PATSEY	CURRITUCK NARROWS
	SOUTHAMPTON	HERTFORD COUNTY
	ELIZA	JARROTS BAY
	MULBERRY	NEW BERN
	ANN HOWARD	OCRACOKE
	COLLECTOR	POWELLS POINT
	NANCY AND BETSY	POWELLS POINT
	MATILDA	SMITHS CREEK
	ENTERPRISE	STRAITS OF CARTERET
	PHOENIX	WASHINGTON
	SALLY HAVENS	WASHINGTON
	SARAH ANN	WHITE OAK RIVER
1822	SUSAN	ADAMS CREEK
	SARAH	CARTERET COUNTY
	ATLANTIC	CEDAR ISLAND
	GEORGE WASHINGTON	CURRITUCK NARROWS
	AMERICAN LADY	INDIAN TOWN
	JANATS ELIZA	JARROTS BAY
	SUSAN	NARROW SHORE
	GENERAL IREDELL	PLYMOUTH
	THOMAS COX	PLYMOUTH
	MARY	SMITH CREEK

Date	Ship Name	Shipbuilding Location
1822	SAMPSON	SMITHS CREEK
	ADVOCATE	STRAITS OF CARTERET
	MARY	STRAITS OF CORE SOUND
	DEBORAH	WASHINGTON
	WEST INDIAN	WASHINGTON
1823	DESPATCH	BEAUFORT
	ECLIPSE	BEAUFORT
	ELIPSE	BEAUFORT
	JANE	BEAUFORT
	JAMES H. SMITH	BEAUFORT COUNTY
	DESPATCH	BOGUE INLET
	JANE	CARTERET COUNTY
	MARTILDA	CARTERET COUNTY
	REGULATOR	COINJOCK BAY
	WAVE	CRAVEN COUNTY
	DELIGHT	MARTIN POINT
	MARIA	NEW BERN
	GEORGE WASHINGTON	OCRACOKE
	HIRAM	PLYMOUTH
	ARETE ELLIS	SMITH CREEK
	CHASE	SMITHVILLE
	EMELINE	STRAITS OF CARTARET
	COLUMBIA	STRAITS OF CARTERET
	MATILDA	STRAITS OF CARTERET
	REBECCA ANN	STRAITS OF CARTERET
	MITALDA	STRAITS OF CURRITUCK
	ANN MARIE	STRAITS OF NORTH RIVER
	POST BOY	WASHINGTON
1824	RISING SUN	ADAMS CREEK
	BAY RIVER	BAY RIVER
	JOHN DOYLE	BAY RIVER
	ARGUS	BEAUFORT
	LAFAYETTE	BEAUFORT
	MARY	BEAUFORT
	WESLEYAN	BEAUFORT
	HENRIETTA	CARTERET COUNTY
	FOUR BROTHERS	CHURCHES ISLAND
	BETSY AND NANCY	COINJOCK BAY
	CONSOLATION	CURRITUCK COUNTY
	SAMUEL TREADWELL	CURRITUCK COUNTY
	COLLECTOR	HYDE COUNTY
	KITTY FLOWERS	HYDE COUNTY

Date	Ship Name	Shipbuilding Location
1824	PLEBE	JARRELS BAY
	EXPERIMENT	JARROTS BAY
	THE NORTH CAROLINA	NEW BERN
	HENRY	OCRACOKE
	HENRY WARING	OCRACOKE
	ELIZA	WILMINGTON
1825	JULIA	ADAMS CREEK
	AMELIA	BAY RIVER
	JULIA FRANCES	BEAUFORT
	REBECCA HYER	BEAUFORT
	REMITTANCE	BEAUFORT
	WILLIAM P. FERRAND	BEAUFORT
	LEOPARD	BEAUFORT
	RISING SUN	CARTERET COUNTY
	SARAH	CARTERET COUNTY
	AMERICAN HERO	COINJOCK BAY
	ENTERPRISE	CURRITUCK COUNTY
	CONVOY	HYDE COUNTY
	RICHARD WINSLOW	HYDE COUNTY
	PAST MASTER	MARTIN POINT
	RHODA AND MARGARET	NORTH RIVER
	SALLY ANN	SMITHS CREEK
	F. MICHELSON	STRAITS
	NONPAREIL	STRAITS OF CORE
	FRANKLIN	STRAITS OF CORE SOUND
	UTILITY	STRAITS OF CORE SOUND
	WILLIAM	STRAITS OF CORE SOUND
	TURPENTINE	SWANSBOROUGH
	ARIEL	WASHINGTON
	SARAH	WILMINGTON
1826	PHILADELPHIA	BEAUFORT
	ALEXANDER	CARTERET COUNTY
	ARIEL	CARTERET COUNTY
	CYGNET	CARTERET COUNTY
	HARRIET	CARTERET COUNTY
	LUNA	CARTERET COUNTY
	MARY	CARTERET COUNTY
	PACIFIC	CARTERET COUNTY
	PERSEVERANCE	CARTERET COUNTY
	WAVERLY	CARTERET COUNTY
	AGENORA	COLUMBIA
	ANGENORA	COLUMBIA

Date	Ship Name	Shipbuilding Location
1826	ISAIAH	CORE SOUND
	LIMA	CRAVEN COUNTY
	HARIETT ELIZA	CURRITUCK
	CONVOY	CURRITUCK COUNTY
	ELIZA ANN	CURRITUCK COUNTY
	THOMAS JEFFERSON	CURRITUCK COUNTY
	APPRENTICE	CURRITUCK NARROWS
	ATLANTIC	CURRITUCK NARROWS
	ENTERED APPRENTICE	CURRITUCK NARROWS
	ALPHEUS	ELIZABETH CITY
	JAMES	ELIZABETH CITY
	ANN FRANCIS	FAYETTEVILLE
	SABRA	GARRAT BAY
	EMULAUS	JARROTS BAY
	HENERY BATEMAN	OCRACOKE
	ADELIA	ONSLOW COUNTY
	ALLIGATOR	PINEY GROVE
	PLOUGH BOY	PONEY ISLAND
	ELIZABETH	PORTSMOUTH
	NONPLUS	POWELLS POINT
	SISTERS	POWELLS POINT
	JAMES F. MCKEE	SMITHVILLE
	VICTORY	STRAITS OF CORE SOUND
	ALPHA	WASHINGTON
	COTTON PLANT	WASHINGTON
	TRAFALGAR	WILLIAMSTON
1827	MARY ANN	BAY RIVER
	HANNAH	BEAUFORT
	VULCAN	BEAUFORT
	PIGOT	CARTERET COUNTY
	UXOR	CARTERET COUNTY
	ALERT	COINJOCK
	SARAH ANN	COINJOCK
	MARIA	CURRITUCK
	FAV0RITE	CURRITUCK COUNTY
	NANCY AND SABRINA	CURRITUCK INLET
	LANCEAN	CURRITUCK NARROWS
	MADISON'S BARGE	ELIZABETH CITY
	MARY ANN	ELIZABETH CITY
	ALPHEUS	FORBESVILLE
	DEFIANCE	FRANK CREEK
	OCEAN	GANITY BAY
	THOMAS WYNNS	HERTFORD

Date	Ship Name	Shipbuilding Location
1827	CAROLINE	HYDE COUNTY
	THOMAS WYNNS	HYDE COUNTY
	CONSTITUTION	NEW BERN
	JOHN BRYAN	PLYMOUTH
	JOHN S. BRYAN	PLYMOUTH
	RISING STATES	POWELLS POINT
	UXOR	STRAITS OF CARTERET
	BURDETT	SWANSBOROUGH
	HARRIET ANDERSON	WINTON
1828	BALTIMORE	BAY RIVER
	ARIEL	BEAUFORT
	BETSY B. GLOUCET	BEAUFORT
	COMMERCE	BEAUFORT
	HORSE	BEAUFORT
	MORSE OF BEAUFORT	BEAUFORT
	NANCY	BEAUFORT
	PATRON	BEAUFORT
	PATSEY B. BLOUNT	BEAUFORT
	PAUL PRY	CARTERET COUNTY
	REBECCA	CARTERET COUNTY
	SARAH ANN	CARTERET COUNTY
	UNITED STATES	CARTERET COUNTY
	A. AND H. HADDOCKS	ELIZABETH CITY
	GEORGE LORING	ELIZABETH CITY
	SOPHIA AND ELIZA	ELIZABETH CITY
	COTTON PLANT	FAYETTEVILLE
	FRIENDSHIP	HARKERS ISLAND
	ABNER P. NEALE	HYDE COUNTY
	ATLAS	HYDE COUNTY
	LOUISA ANN	HYDE COUNTY
	SARAH ANNA	JARROTS BAY
	FRANCES D. KENNEDY	OCRACOKE ISLAND
	OLIVIA BRICKELL	OCRACOKE ISLAND
	MARY ELIZA	PLYMOUTH
	FOX	SMITHS CREEK
	GENERAL JACKSON	SMITHVILLE
	ESSEN	STRAITS OF CARTERET
	JOHN MYERS	STRAITS OF CORE
	ONSLOW	SWANSBORO
	TARBOROUGH	WASHINGTON
1829	TWO BROTHERS	BATH
	JULIUS PRINGLE	BEAUFORT
	CARTERET	CARTERET COUNTY

Date	Ship Name	Shipbuilding Location
1829	CHARLOTTE	CARTERET COUNTY
	JOHN	CARTERET COUNTY
	LEVANT	CEDAR HAMMOCK
	ARIEL	CRAVEN COUNTY
	ROSE-IN-BLOOM	CURRITUCK
	HENRY CLAY	ELIZABETH CITY
	JOHN BARTLET	ELIZABETH CITY
	ELIZABETH	FAYETTEVILLE
	ONLY SON	HATTERAS
	JANE	NEW BERN
	TIGER	NEW BERN
	SEVANT	PAMLICO COUNTY
	WILLIAM A. TURNER	PLYMOUTH
	ZEPHYR	SMITHS CREEK
	ANN	STRAITS OF CARTERET
	FRANCIS WITHERS	STRAITS OF CARTERET
	AMERICAN COASTER	STRAITS OF CORE
	STATIRA	WILMINGTON
	THETIS	
1830	HENRY	BEAUFORT
	STARK ARMISTEAD	BEAUFORT
	YOUNG EAGLE	CARTERET COUNTY
	BENJAMIN HARRISON	CHICAMICOMICO BANK
	MARY	CRAVEN COUNTY
	MILISSA	CURRITUCK
	LYCURGUS	CURRITUCK COUNTY
	MELISSA	CURRITUCK COUNTY
	INDEPENDENCE	CURRITUCK INLET
	GLOBE	ELIZABETH CITY
	LAVINIA	ELIZABETH CITY
1830	WILLIAM R. SWIFT	FORTESQUENT CREEK
	JOHN GRAY BLOUNT	HYDE COUNTY
	MARTHA JONES	INDIAN TOWN
	LION	NEW BERN
	NAVIGATOR	PINEY GROVE
	ENTERPRISE	SWANSBOROUGH
1831	CAMDEN	CAMDEN COUNTY
	CLAUDIA AND MARY	CAMDEN COUNTY
	OLIVE BRANCH	CARTERET COUNTY
	PEDEE	CARTERET COUNTY
	RED ROVER	CARTERET COUNTY
	AMELIA	ELIZABETH CITY

Date	Ship Name	Shipbuilding Location
1831	FLORA	ELIZABETH CITY
	ALBEMARLE	HERTFORD
	CHRISTIANA CAROLINA	NEW RIVER
	FARMER	NEW RIVER
	CINDERELLA	PLYMOUTH
	MARGARET	POPLAR POINT
	POLLY AND NANCY	TYRRELL COUNTY
1832	FULFORD	BEAUFORT
	SUSAN BENJAMIN	BEAUFORT
	ELI HOGH	BEAUFORT COUNTY
	BROOKS	CARTERET COUNTY
	EDENTON	CARTERET COUNTY
	GEORGE POLLOCK	CARTERET COUNTY
	THOMAS STOW	CARTERET COUNTY
	UNION	CARTERET COUNTY
	EDWARD G. WILLIAMS	ELIZABETH CITY
	THEODORE	ELIZABETH CITY
	WILLIAM PENN	ELIZABETH CITY
	ALABAMA	NEW BERN
	PANTHER	NEW BERN
	WADE	NEW BERN
	BETSEY	PEARCES CREEK
	SOLOMON STATUS	SWANSBORO
1833	FLY	BEAUFORT
	M.B. ROBERSON	BEAUFORT
	BELLE	BEAUFORT COUNTY
	CHARLES MOLES	BEAUFORT COUNTY
	UNION	CAPE HATTERAS
	ANGENARO	CARTERET COUNTY
	JOHN PUGH	CARTERET COUNTY
	MARIA	CARTERET COUNTY
	SELECT	CURRITUCK COUNTY
	WILLIAM R. SMITH	HALIFAX COUNTY
	REGULATOR	HATTERAS BANKS
	TIME	HYDE COUNTY
	INDIAN QUEEN	MARTIN COUNTY
	MARY FRANCIS	MOUNT PLEASANT
	ALONZO	NEW BERN
	EXCHANGE	NEW BERN
	CALEB NICHOL	NEW RIVER
	ELIJAH	PLYMOUTH
	RIP VAN WINKLE	PLYMOUTH

Date	Ship Name	Shipbuilding Location
1833	SKAVARKY	PLYMOUTH
	ANN SPARROW	SMITHS CREEK
	FRIEND	SMITHVILLE
	JOHN C. BAKER	SMITHVILLE
	ENCORE	SWAN QUARTER
	EUGENE	SWANSBORO
	CLARENDON	WILMINGTON
	ELIZA AND SUSAN	WILMINGTON
	ROBERT EDENS	WILMINGTON
	MARTHA MAHOO	
1834	EAGLE	BAY RIVER
	ELLEN DOUGLAS	CARTERET COUNTY
	FRANCES CANADY	CARTERET COUNTY
	SALLY ANN OF WASHINGTON	CARTERET COUNTY
	CLARISSA BONNER	DURHAM CREEK
	JOHN M. ROBERTS	GATES COUNTY
	JOHN HUGHES	NEW BERN
	KIMBERLY	NEW BERN
	CAROLINE	NEW RIVER
	UNION	PLYMOUTH
	ZENITH	SWANSBOROUGH
	GEORGE W. RODGERS	TYRRELL COUNTY
1834	MARY	TYRRELL COUNTY
	MARY CAROLINE	TYRRELL COUNTY
1835	CATHERINE	BEAUFORT
	ATLASS	CARTERET COUNTY
	ELIJAH PIGOTT	CARTERET COUNTY
	PAMLICO	CARTERET COUNTY
	SOUTH CAROLINIAN	CARTERET COUNTY
	WASHINGTON	GERMANTOWN
	GREENVILLE	HYDE COUNTY
	VIRGINIA HODGES	HYDE COUNTY
	I.L. DURAND	NEW BERN
	J.L. DURANT	NEW BERN
	JOHN L. DURAND	NEW BERN
	PLYMOUTH	PLYMOUTH
	GLOBE	STRAITS OF CARTERET
	JACK DOWNING	SWANSBOROUGH
	VIRGINIA HOGES	TYRRELL COUNTY
	EDMUND D. MCNAIR	WASHINGTON
	DUNCAN MCRAE	WILMINGTON
1836	CATHARINE	BEAUFORT
	JOHN STANLEY	BEAUFORT

Date	Ship Name	Shipbuilding Location
1836	JAY	CRAVEN COUNTY
	MARY MARIAH	CURRITUCK
	CARPENTERS SON	CURRITUCK COUNTY
	MAREY MARIAH	CURRITUCK COUNTY
	PAMPLICO	STRAITS OF CARTERET
	GUIDE	STRAITS OF CORE SOUND
1837	F.L. KING	CARTERET COUNTY
	ROANOKE	NEW BERN
	EDWARD B. DUDLEY	SMITHVILLE
	L.S. LUCUS	SMITHVILLE
	PATRIOT	STRAITS
	PEARL	WASHINGTON
	JAMES CROW	WILMINGTON
1838	NANCY	BEAUFORT
	EDWARD STANLEY	BEAUFORT COUNTY
	MARY	CARTERET COUNTY
	MARY JANE	CARTERET COUNTY
1838	PARKER	CARTERET COUNTY
	T.C. MITCHELL	CARTERET COUNTY
	THOMAS & NANCY	CARTERET COUNTY
	THOMAS UNDERHILL	CARTERET COUNTY
	ZELPHIA ANN	CARTERET COUNTY
	JOHN A. BEMBY	CHOWAN COUNTY
	QUEEN ANN	CHOWAN COUNTY
	WILLIAM C. BUTLER	ELIZABETH CITY
	GRANARY	HYDE COUNTY
	INDUSTRY	HYDE COUNTY
	I.C. PETTYJOHN	MARTIN COUNTY
	JOHN C. PETTYOHN	MARTIN COUNTY
	SWAN	NEW RIVER
	HENRY BATMAN	OCRACOKE
	COMET	PLYMOUTH
	STATES RIGHTS	SHALLOTTE
	ANACONDA	WASHINGTON
	TRANSPORT	WASHINGTON
1839	MELVIRA	BEAUFORT
	SARAH JANE	BEAUFORT
	FRANKLIN	BEAUFORT COUNTY
	WILLIAM GRAY	BEAUFORT COUNTY
	CURRAN	CARTERET COUNTY
	POINDEXTER D. MURPHY	CARTERET COUNTY
	WASHINGTON	CARTERET COUNTY
	CURIOSITY	CURRITUCK COUNTY

Date	Ship Name	Shipbuilding Location
1839	COLUMBIA	ELIZABETH CITY
	HENRY MARTIN	ELIZABETH CITY
	EMELINE	HYDE COUNTY
	WOLF	NEW BERN
	PARAGON	OCRACOKE
	ALBIN	SWANSBORO
	ANN JANE	SWANSBOROUGH
	OLIVIA	WASHINGTON
1840	MARIETTA	BEAUFORT
	SURPASS	CAPE HATTERAS
	ARMENCY	CARTERET COUNTY
	C. STOVER	CARTERET COUNTY
1840	MINERVA	CARTERET COUNTY
	MARY J. SANDERMAN	ELIZABETH CITY
	MARY T. SANDERSON	ELIZABETH CITY
	MANUMIT	HYDE COUNTY
	MIDDLETON	HYDE COUNTY
	MONUMENT	HYDE COUNTY
	WILLIAM H. HARRISON	HYDE COUNTY
	E.W. BRADLEY	NEW BERN
	ST. PIERRE	NEW BERN
	PANTHEON	SWANSBOROUGH
	COLONEL MCRAE	WILMINGTON
1841	MARTHA	BEAUFORT
	RALEIGH	CARTERET COUNTY
	ELIZABETH	CRAVEN COUNTY
	S. HYMAN	CRAVEN COUNTY
	SAMUEL HYMAN	CRAVEN COUNTY
	MARY ELIZA	CURRITUCK
	RIVAL	CURRITUCK
	ALEXANDER CHESHIRE	EDENTON
	JOSEPHINE	ELIZABETH CITY
	LION	ELIZABETH CITY
	VIRGINIA	ELIZABETH CITY
	MARY ANN	HYDE COUNTY
	ANN HYMAN	NEW BERN
	ARAB	NEW BERN
	JULIA AND NANCY	NEW BERN
	TRIUMPH	NEW BERN
	TWO BROTHERS	PLYMOUTH
	ASSIST	STUMPY POINT
	ONSLOW OF SWANSBOROUGH	SWANSBOROUGH

Date	Ship Name	Shipbuilding Location
1841	ELIZA ANN WALKER	TYRRELL COUNTY
	GENERAL HARRISON	TYRRELL COUNTY
1842	ANN MARIA	CARTERET COUNTY
	ELIZABETH ANN	CARTERET COUNTY
	EMMA JULIA	CARTERET COUNTY
	ISABELLA	CARTERET COUNTY
	MELISSA OF WASHINGTON	CARTERET COUNTY
	RACHAEL ANN	CARTERET COUNTY
1842	SABINE	CARTERET COUNTY
	BRAVO	CRAVEN COUNTY
	HIGH PRIEST	CURRITUCK COUNTY
	WILLIAM G. PRESTON	CURRITUCK COUNTY
	ANNA FRANCIS	ELIZABETH CITY
	ANNA LOUISA	ELIZABETH CITY
	EAGLE	ELIZABETH CITY
	J.C. CALHOUN	ELIZABETH CITY
	STAR OF WASHINGTON	HYDE COUNTY
	MARION	ONSLOW COUNTY
	ADELINE	WASHINGTON
	COMET	WASHINGTON
	JULIA TELFAIR	WASHINGTON
	MARTHA M. FOWLE	WASHINGTON
1843	MARGARET JANE	BAY RIVER
	PAULING	BEAUFORT
	JOSEPH POTTS	BEAUFORT COUNTY
	MARY JANE	BEAUFORT COUNTY
	PACTOLUS	BEAUFORT COUNTY
	DOLPHIN	CARTERET COUNTY
	PAULINE	CARTERET COUNTY
	ALEXANDER	CRAVEN COUNTY
	LADY WHEDBEE	CURRITUCK COUNTY
	SOPHIA D.	CURRITUCK COUNTY
	ANN HUNTER	ELIZABETH CITY
	NORTH CAROLINA	ELIZABETH CITY
	SARAH	NEW BERN
1844	MARGARET JANE	BEAUFORT
	MARY FRANCIS	CARTERET COUNTY
	MAY FRANCIS	CARTERET COUNTY
	PEARL	CARTERET COUNTY
	SUSAN	CARTERET COUNTY
	GRACE GARNET	EDENTON
	INPH LIBBY	ELIZABETH CITY

Date	Ship Name	Shipbuilding Location
1844	JOSEPH LIBBY	ELIZABETH CITY
	MARY	ELIZABETH CITY
	MARY WINEFRED	PLYMOUTH
	S.S. SIMMONS	TYRRELL COUNTY
	VIRGINIA	WASHINGTON
1845	DOLPHIN	BEAUFORT
	DOLPHIN	BEAUFORT
	JOSEPH ANN	BEAUFORT
	SAMUEL L. MITCHELL	BEAUFORT
	SARAH	BEAUFORT
	ALLEN GRIST	BEAUFORT COUNTY
	DOLPHIN	BEAUFORT COUNTY
	JOHN PERRY	BEAUFORT COUNTY
	CHARLESTON	CARTERET COUNTY
	DOLPHINE	CARTERET COUNTY
	LAURA	CARTERET COUNTY
	RICHMOND	CARTERET COUNTY
	SARAH	CARTERET COUNTY
	EDWARD TILLETT	CURRITUCK COUNTY
	LEVY D. TILLETT	CURRITUCK COUNTY
	PALESTINE	EDENTON
	SARAH PORTER	EDENTON
	CORA	NEW BERN
	DAVID H. SINMORD	NEW BERN
	DENOBIA	NEW BERN
	IONE	NEW BERN
	JANE	NEW BERN
	JONE	NEW BERN
	MANTEO	WASHINGTON
	MELVILLE	WASHINGTON
	VIRGINIA	WASHINGTON COUNTY
	ONSLOW	WILMINGTON
1846	FRIENDSHIP	BEAUFORT
	MARY	BEAUFORT
	ONTARIO	BEAUFORT
	SUSAN	CAMDEN COUNTY
	C. CARROLL	CARTERET COUNTY
	CAROLINE	CARTERET COUNTY
	EUGENE	CARTERET COUNTY
	NORTH CAROLINA	CARTERET COUNTY
	PLANET	CARTERET COUNTY
	SURPASS	CARTERET COUNTY
	J. HOPE	CRAVEN COUNTY

Date	Ship Name	Shipbuilding Location
1846	JOHN BENSON	CRAVEN COUNTY
	MARGARET BLOUNT	CURRITUCK COUNTY
	CORA MANLY	EDENTON
	EVERGREEN	FAYETTEVILLE
	BOUNTY	NEW BERN
	MARTHA ANN	NEW BERN
	ANN H. SIM	PLYMOUTH
	KATE	PLYMOUTH
	LOCUST	PLYMOUTH
	MARTHA D.	PLYMOUTH
	THE KATE	PLYMOUTH
	ROWAN	SMITHVILLE
	ROYAL PURPLE	SMITHVILLE
	SAMUEL MITCHELL	WASHINGTON
	SARAH	WASHINGTON
1847	JOSEPH BUTLER	BAY RIVER
	REBEKAHE	BEAUFORT
	REBEL EAKE	BEAUFORT
	T.P. ALSTON	BEAUFORT
	BENJAMIN F. HANKS	BEAUFORT COUNTY
	LYDIA L. LEWIS	CAMDEN COUNTY
	SURPASS	CAMDEN COUNTY
	C.B. GLOVER	CARTERET COUNTY
	JULIA FRANCES	CARTERET COUNTY
	ODD FELLOW	CARTERET COUNTY
	PURSE	CARTERET COUNTY
	RIO	CARTERET COUNTY
	VOLANT	CARTERET COUNTY
	WASHINGTON	CARTERET COUNTY
	WILLIAM P. BELL	CARTERET COUNTY
	GEORGE HENRY	CURRITUCK COUNTY
	SUSAN BRAY	CURRITUCK COUNTY
	CARAWAY	ELIZABETH CITY
	CARRAWAY	ELIZABETH CITY
	EMPIRE	ELIZABETH CITY
	J.J. GRANDY	ELIZABETH CITY
	M.P. IVEY	ELIZABETH CITY
	GUARD	HYDE COUNTY
1847	JOSEPH I. WILLIAMS	MILL BROOK
	JOSEPH IRWIN	MILL BROOK
	PRISCILLA ANN	PERQUIMANS COUNTY
	S.H. MCREA	SCUPPERNONG RIVER
	MARGERET Y. DAVIS	SMITHVILLE

Date	Ship Name	Shipbuilding Location
1847	ANN HALSEY	TYRRELL COUNTY
	ACTOR	WASHINGTON
	ASTOR	WASHINGTON
	FRANCES ANN	WASHINGTON
	INDEPENDENCE	WASHINGTON
	MARY	WASHINGTON
	ROUGH AND READY	WASHINGTON
	JOHN STOREY	WILMINGTON
1848	CHAMPION	BAY RIVER
	FREEMONT	BAY RIVER
	NATHAN DURFREE	BAY RIVER
	ALONZO	CARTERET COUNTY
	ANN MARIA	CARTERET COUNTY
	BALTIMORE	CARTERET COUNTY
	ELIZABETH	CARTERET COUNTY
	NORTH STATE	CARTERET COUNTY
	DAVID J. DAY	CRAVEN COUNTY
	HENRIETTA	CRAVEN COUNTY
	M. PLATT	CRAVEN COUNTY
	MEDAD PLATT	CRAVEN COUNTY
	JULIA ANN	CURRITUCK COUNTY
	JOHN C. COCKY	EDENTON
	JOHN G. COCKEY	EDENTON
	EXPRESS	HYDE COUNTY
	CASSANDRA	NEW BERN
	HARMIT HARKER	OCRACOKE
	J.P. WHEDBEE	OCRACOKE
	CHARITY	PLYMOUTH
	EDMUND F. HANKS	PLYMOUTH
	HENRIETTA	SMITHS CREEK
	D.P. WOODBURY	SMITHVILLE
	N.P. WOODBURY	SMITHVILLE
	ROBERT B. POTTER	SMITHVILLE
	HORNET	WASHINGTON
	WAVE	WASHINGTON
	ANN E. BARY	WILMINGTON
1849	MIANTONOMIAH	BAY RIVER
	BEE	BEAUFORT
	J.P. WHEDBEE	BEAUFORT
	B.L. PERRY	CARTERET COUNTY
	B.S. PERRY	CARTERET COUNTY
	MARTHA H. STEVENS	CARTERET COUNTY
	MELISSA HOLLAND	CARTERET COUNTY

Date	Ship Name	Shipbuilding Location
1849	R.S. PERRY	CARTERET COUNTY
	SARAH	CARTERET COUNTY
	LAWRENCE	COLUMBIA
	WILLIAM P. MOORE	CRAVEN COUNTY
	LUCENT	CURRITUCK COUNTY
	DORCAS AND ELIZA	EDENTON
	JOHN BOUSHILL	EDENTON
	SALLY BADGER	EDENTON
	SOPHY COLLINS	EDENTON
	J.C. ADELINE	ELIZABETH CITY
	JOHN A. GAMBREL	ELIZABETH CITY
	MARY AND SUSAN	HAMILTON
	MARY SUSAN	HAMILTON
	MELVINA	MARTIN COUNTY
	FIRE FLY	NEW BERN
	ISAAC W. HUGHES	NEW BERN
	MARTHA H. STYRON	OCRACOKE
	CATHERINE JANE	ONSLOW COUNTY
	HUNTRESS	PASQUOTANK COUNTY
	L.D. LAMB	PASQUOTANK COUNTY
	GENERAL TAYLOR	PORTSMOUTH
	LEMORA ISABEL	SHALLOTTE
	LENORA ISABEL	SHALLOTTE
	BUENA VISTA	WASHINGTON
	MELVINA	WASHINGTON COUNTY
	ELIZABETH	BEAUFORT
	EMILY	BEAUFORT
	FANNY LEE	BEAUFORT
1850	MARY A. PENDER	BEAUFORT
	WILLIAM W. CHERRY	BULL POND
	DIXON SWINDELL	CARTERET COUNTY
	EIXON SWINDELL	CARTERET COUNTY
	IOWA	CARTERET COUNTY
	MARY ABIGAIL	CARTERET COUNTY
	PATRIOT	CARTERET COUNTY
	RADIANT	CARTERET COUNTY
	TOPAZ	CARTERET COUNTY
	WILLIAM H. HOWARD	CARTERET COUNTY
	WILLIAM LUCRAFT	CARTERET COUNTY
	WILLIAM SEECRAFT	CARTERET COUNTY
	JOHN L. JONES	COLUMBIA
	L. JONES	COLUMBIA
	HUGH W. COLLINS	EDENTON

Date	Ship Name	Shipbuilding Location
1850	MARY R. ZIMMERMAN	EDENTON
	ZMORA HILL	EDENTON
	GOOD HOPE	ELIZABETH CITY
	MARTHA SKINNER	ELIZABETH CITY
	OSCEOLA	ELIZABETH CITY
	SARAH	ELIZABETH CITY
	SARAH AND MARY	ELIZABETH CITY
	SUSAN AND MARY	ELIZABETH CITY
	CAPER	HYDE COUNTY
	BEN MIDGETT	NEW BERN
	CHATHAM	NEW BERN
	CORA	NEW BERN
	FRED W. JONES	NEW BERN
	MIDGETT	NEW BERN
	NEW WAYNE	NEW BERN
	F.J. BROWER	NORTH CAROLINA
	AGNES McLEAN	ONSLOW COUNTY
	WILLIAM B. BURGESS	PASQUOTANK COUNTY
	MARTHA ANN	PLYMOUTH
	MARY D. ZIMMERMAN	PLYMOUTH
	H.E. LEWIS	TYRRELL COUNTY
	MARY LOUISA	TYRRELL COUNTY
	FRANCES	WASHINGTON
	PACIFIC OF WASHINGTON	WASHINGTON
	WILLIAM SHAW	WASHINGTON
	ELLA	WILMINGTON
	JOHH DAWSON	WILMINGTON
	UNION	WILMINGTON
	WAVE	WILMINGTON
1851	ALMILDA	BEAUFORT
	ALWILDA	BEAUFORT
	CHARLOTTE ANN	BEAUFORT
	VICTORY	CAPE HATTERAS
	ANGELINE	CARTERET COUNTY
	BROTHERS	CARTERET COUNTY
	CICERO	CARTERET COUNTY
	DOLPHIN	CARTERET COUNTY
	K.S. BURNEY	CARTERET COUNTY
	KATE	CARTERET COUNTY
	MARTHA	CARTERET COUNTY
	MARY	CARTERET COUNTY
	PALESTINE	CARTERET COUNTY
	R.S. BURNEY	CARTERET COUNTY

Date	Ship Name	Shipbuilding Location
1851	S. CATHERINE	CARTERET COUNTY
	TELEGRAPH	CARTERET COUNTY
	JAMES F. DAVENPORT	COLUMBIA
	EMILY	CRAVEN COUNTY
	LUCRETIA	CURRITUCK COUNTY
	ARGUOTUS MOORE	EDENTON
	AUGUSTUS MOON	EDENTON
	S.H. SAMPLE	EDENTON
	T.H. SAMPLE	EDENTON
	ANN C. WILLIAMS	ELIZABETH CITY
	T.R. COBB	ELIZABETH CITY
	WILLIAM A. GRAHAM	ELIZABETH CITY
	HENRY AND THOMAS	MARTIN COUNTY
	FAIRY	NEW BERN
	GLADIATOR OF WASHINGTON	OCRACOKE
	WALTER J. DAIL	PASQUOTANK COUNTY
	D.W. BAGLEY	PLYMOUTH
	SPRUILL MORSE	PLYMOUTH
	S.R. POTTER	SMITHVILLE
	SAM R. POTTER	SMITHVILLE
	ANN C. DAVENPORT	TYRRELL COUNTY
1852	P. AND G. BROWN	BEAUFORT
	LOUISA	BEAUFORT COUNTY
	PINE	BEAUFORT COUNTY
	CHAMPION	CARTERET COUNTY
	I.C. MANSON	CARTERET COUNTY
	J.G. MANSON	CARTERET COUNTY
	PATRON	CARTERET COUNTY
	PATTRAN	CARTERET COUNTY
	SOUTHERNER	CARTERET COUNTY
	V.G. MANSON	CARTERET COUNTY
	HUGH CHISHOLM	COLUMBIA
	SEEING	CURRITUCK COUNTY
	M.R. ZIMMERMAN	EDENTON
	CAROLINA	ELIZABETH CITY
	CAROLINE	ELIZABETH CITY
	CHATHAM	FAYETTEVILLE
	FANNY LUTTERLOH	FAYETTEVILLE
	FAYETTEVILLE	FAYETTEVILLE
	SOUTHERNER	FAYETTEVILLE
	WILLIAM JONES	HALIFAX COUNTY
	HOWARD	NEW BERN
	COURTNEY	PASQUOTANK COUNTY

Date	Ship Name	Shipbuilding Location
1852	CHARLES ADDAMS	PLYMOUTH
	JOHN A. TAYLOR	WILMINGTON
1853	ROSALIE BEATRICE	BEACON ISLAND
	OCEAN WAVE	BEAUFORT
	MARY E. HOOVER	BEAUFORT COUNTY
	C.W. GRANDY	CAMDEN COUNTY
	OCEAN WAVE	CAMDEN COUNTY
	ANNIE DAVIS	CARLISLE
	ANNE DAVIS	CARTERET COUNTY
	ARAB	CARTERET COUNTY
	COMET	CARTERET COUNTY
	EDWIN	CARTERET COUNTY
	EMELINE	CARTERET COUNTY
	INDEPENDENCE	CARTERET COUNTY
	SARAH ANN	CARTERET COUNTY
	TELEGRAPH OF WASHINGTON	CARTERET COUNTY
	VIENNA	CARTERET COUNTY
	MARY C. CRAMNER	COLUMBIA
	ELIZABETH COWELL	CURRITUCK COUNTY
	I.C. DOBBIN	CURRITUCK COUNTY
	J.C. DOBBINS	CURRITUCK COUNTY
	S.C. DOBBIN	CURRITUCK COUNTY
	W.C. DOBBIN	CURRITUCK COUNTY
	MARY D. HAYMAN	EDENTON
	S.H. SAMPLE	EDENTON
	D.V. SESSOMS	ELIZABETH CITY
	GENERAL EHRINGHAUS	ELIZABETH CITY
	GEORGIANNA	ELIZABETH CITY
	JAMES W. SMITH	ELIZABETH CITY
	JANE W. SMITH	ELIZABETH CITY
	MARTHA ANN CARTWRIGHT	ELIZABETH CITY
	SCUPPERNONG	ELIZABETH CITY
	SUN	FAYETTEVILLE
	OREGON	HYDE COUNTY
	EMMA AND ELIZABETH	NEW BERN
	AGNES H. WARD	ONSLOW COUNTY
	INDEPENDENCE	PASQUOTANK COUNTY
	L.D. STARKE	PASQUOTANK COUNTY
	TRADER	PASQUOTANK COUNTY
	WILLIAM FRANKLIN	PASQUOTANK COUNTY
	BENJAMIN MAITLAND	PLYMOUTH
	WAVE	STRAITS
	M.C. CRAMMER	SWANSBORO

Date	Ship Name	Shipbuilding Location
1853	MARY C. CRANMER	SWANSBORO
	CAROLINE V. CASEY	TYRRELL COUNTY
	MARY E. PAMROLE	WASHINGTON
	MARY E. PARMERLE OF WASHINGTON	WASHINGTON
	SAM BEERY	WILMINGTON
1854	MARY C. HOOVER	BEAUFORT COUNTY
	CAROLINA VIRGINIA	CARTERET COUNTY
	DAVID IRELAND	CARTERET COUNTY
	EDWIN & SAMUEL	CARTERET COUNTY
	M.A. STRYON	CARTERET COUNTY
	SUSAN	CARTERET COUNTY
	SUSAN JANE	COLUMBIA
	E. PERKINS	CONWAYBORO
	WILD CAT	CURRITUCK COUNTY
	MARY DUERS	EDENTON
	A.M.P. WHEDBEE	ELIZABETH CITY
	ANN G. SIKES	ELIZABETH CITY
	MARY LOUISA	ELIZABETH CITY
	NEBRASKA	ELIZABETH CITY
	SOUTHERNER	FAYETTEVILLE
	MILTON SELBY OF WASHINGTON	HYDE COUNTY
	LAURA E. JOHNSON	NEW BERN
	BELLE	ONSLOW COUNTY
	LAVENIA	ONSLOW COUNTY
	CHARLES M. MCCLEES	TYRRELL COUNTY
	CHAS. McLEESE	TYRRELL COUNTY
	G.R. DIXON	WASHINGTON
	BLACK RIVER	WILMINGTON
	JOHN H. HAUGHTON	WILMINGTON
	SUSAN JANE	WILMINGTON
1855	D.W. SANDERS	BEAUFORT
	HENRIETTA	BEAUFORT
	LAURA GERTRUDE	BEAUFORT
	LUCY C. HOLMES	BEAUFORT
	MARTHA MOORE	BEAUFORT COUNTY
	SALLY ANN	CARTERET COUNTY
	BEST	CURRITUCK
	BETSEY	CURRITUCK
	SEA MONSTER	CURRITUCK COUNTY
	HAMET RYAN	EDENTON
	HARRIET RYAN	EDENTON
	RESOLUTION	EDENTON
	KATE KINNEY	ELIZABETH CITY

Date	Ship Name	Shipbuilding Location
1855	SOUTHERNER	ELIZABETH CITY
	ZEPHANIAH	ELIZABETH CITY
	MAGNOLIA	FAYETTEVILLE
	SCOTTISH CHIEF	FAYETTEVILLE
	SKIPJACK	HANOVER CREEK
	AMANDA CLIFFORD	HYDE COUNTY
	NATIVE	HYDE COUNTY
	BLACK SQUALL	NEW BERN
	CATHERINE	NEW BERN
	CERES	PASQUOTANK COUNTY
	RESOLUTION	PLYMOUTH
	REVOLUTION	PLYMOUTH
	JOSEPH RAMSEY	TYRRELL COUNTY
	GEORGE R. DIXON	WASHINGTON
	MECKLENBERG	WASHINGTON
	PATHFINDER	WASHINGTON
	MARTHA COOK	WILLIAMSTON
1856	DOLPHIN	BAY RIVER
	ELLA	BEAUFORT
	PARSON BROWN	BEAUFORT COUNTY
	QUEEN OF THE SOUTH	BEAUFORT COUNTY
	SNOW SQUALL	BEAUFORT COUNTY
	WILLIAM T. HARRIS	BEAUFORT COUNTY
	GOLD HUNTER	CARTERET COUNTY
	HOME	CARTERET COUNTY
	JANE FISHER	CARTERET COUNTY
	L. WARREN	CARTERET COUNTY
	TRAVELER	CARTERET COUNTY
	TRIUMPH	CARTERET COUNTY
	VIRGINIA CORE	CARTERET COUNTY
	SALLIE SMITH	EDENTON
	SALLY SMITH	EDENTON
	JAMES W. HINTON	ELIZABETH CITY
	JANE FISHER	ELIZABETH CITY
	JAS. W. HINTON	ELIZABETH CITY
	JENNIE HUNTER	ELIZABETH CITY
	MARY JANE KENNEDY	ELIZABETH CITY
	ALICE	HYDE COUNTY
	NATIVE	HYDE COUNTY
	JAMES BUCHANAN	LOCKWOODS FOLLY
	JENNY LIND	NEW BERN
	SPY	PLYMOUTH
	HANYEEN	WASHINGTON

Date	Ship Name	Shipbuilding Location
1856	HONYEEN	WASHINGTON
	LUCY	WASHINGTON
	LUCY OF WASHINGTON	WASHINGTON
	PETREL	WASHINGTON
	WATAUGA	WASHINGTON
	WATUAGA	WASHINGTON
	WINYAW	WILMINGTON
	INDEPENDENCE	WOODBURN
1857	ISABEL	BEAUFORT
	LUCIEN	BEAUFORT
	CAROLINA	CARTERET COUNTY
	COMET	CARTERET COUNTY
	I.T. WILLIS	CARTERET COUNTY
	ISABELLA	CARTERET COUNTY
	JAMES DAVIS	CARTERET COUNTY
	L.T. WILLIS	CARTERET COUNTY
	MONTERA	CARTERET COUNTY
	ZENITH	CARTERET COUNTY
	INDUSTRY	CONWAYBORO
	E. FRANCIS	CORE SOUND
	ANN E. DAVENPORT	CROSS LANDING
	E. AND M.J. SIMPSON	EDENTON
	LADY ATRIM	EDENTON
	MARY C. SUMMER	EDENTON
	C.H. CULPEPPER	ELIZABETH CITY
	EMPIRE	ELIZABETH CITY
	JOHN A. BURGES	ELIZABETH CITY
	PATTIE MARTIN	ELIZABETH CITY
	SNOW STORM	ELIZABETH CITY
	UNION WAVE	ELIZABETH CITY
	VIRGINIA SURRITY	ELIZABETH CITY
	WILLIAM P. GURLEY	ELIZABETH CITY
	TELESCOPE	HYDE COUNTY
	GEORGIA	LAUNCH
	H.H. THOMPSON	NEW BERN
	H.N.W.S. NAPOLEON	NEW BERN
	NAPOLEON	NEW BERN
	ONTARIO	NEW BERN
	OHIO	OCRACOKE
	COERINE	PLYMOUTH
	J.W. MAITLAND	PLYMOUTH
	JOHN W. MAITLAND	PLYMOUTH
	ELISHA WATERS	WASHINGTON

Date	Ship Name	Shipbuilding Location
1857	HERNDON	WASHINGTON
	JANE CAMPBELL	WASHINGTON
	GOERNINE	WILLIAMSTON
1858	CAROLINA	CARTERET COUNTY
	SPRAY	CARTERET COUNTY
	RICHARD MISSKINS	CRAVEN COUNTY
	CAROLINE	EDENTON
	CRINOLINE	EDENTON
	SEA BIRD	ELIZABETH CITY
	WILLIAM S. COPES	ELIZABETH CITY
	JOHN DAWSON	FAYETTEVILLE
	R.S. DONNELL	HYDE COUNTY
	EMMA ELIZABETH	NEW BERN
	ISABELLA ELLIS	NEW BERN
	MARY AMMA	NEW BERN
	MARY EMMA	NEW BERN
	M.J. MESSENGER	PASQUOTANK
	LEVIATHAN	RUMLEY HAMMOCK
	JOE FLANNER	WILMINGTON
	ALICE GIBSON	WINTON
1859	CALDWELL	BEAUFORT
	ANNIE DAVIS OF WASHINGTON	CARTERET COUNTY
	KATE STAVRO	EDENTON
	MARY WOOD	EDENTON
	PLANTER	ELIZABETH CITY
	NORTH CAROLINA	FAYETTEVILLE
	KATE MCLAURIN	FAYETTIVILLE
	FAIR	HYDE COUNTY
	FAIR OF WASHINGTON	HYDE COUNTY
	ENTERPRISE	NEW RIVER
	PLANTER	PASQUOTANK COUNTY
1859	M.C. ETHRIDGE	PLYMOUTH
	WILLIAM H. NORTHROP	WILMINGTON
1860	LOVE D. COBB	BEAUFORT
	MARY BRYAN OF WASHINGTON	BEAUFORT
	MARY BRYAN	BEAUFORT COUNTY
	CAMDEN UNION	CAMDEN COUNTY
	A.C. WILLIAMS	ELIZABETH CITY
	PARROTT	ELIZABETH CITY
	SAN JUAN	ELIZABETH CITY
	WATER LILY	HATTERAS
	JULIA	JARRETTS BAY
	AGILE	STRAITS OF CARTERET

Date	Ship Name	Shipbuilding Location
1860	SAMUEL C. EBONO OF WASHINGTON	WASHINGTON
	A.P. HURT	WILMINGTON
1861	ANNA	BATH
	RELIEF	BEAUFORT
	FOX	ELIZABETH CITY
	TRAVIS	NEW BERN
1862	ELLA	BEAUFORT
	JEWETT C. STEPHENS	DURHAM CREEK
	MARY S. MIZELL	PLYMOUTH
1864	ADDIE HENRY	NEW BERN
	LORENZO	SWANSBORO
1865	ARRIVAL	BEAUFORT
	GEORGE W. DILL	BEAUFORT
	J.T. WILLIS	BEAUFORT
	LIVELY	BEAUFORT
	EUGENE	ELIZABETH CITY
	STARLIGHT	HATTERAS
	BETTIE	NEW BERN
	DOLPHIN	NEW BERN
	MARY E. QUEEN	PINEY POINT
	PALESTINE	STRAITS
	SPRAY	STRAITS
	PINE OF WILMINGTON	WASHINGTON
	LILLIAN	WILMINGTON
	WAVE CREST	WILMINGTON
1866	EMILIE	BEAUFORT
	FRANCIS MARION	BEAUFORT
	JOHNNY	BEAUFORT
	JULIA	BEAUFORT
	MATTIE	BEAUFORT
	SAMUEL	BEAUFORT
	LOUISA FRANCIS	CARTERET COUNTY
	IODINE	HUNTING QUARTERS
	SELECT	HUNTING QUARTERS
	V.C. CONKLIN	JAMESVILLE
	DOLPHIN	NEW BERN
	MYSTIC	NEW BERN
	TIME	NEW BERN
	MAY QUEEN	SWANSBORO
	MOLLEY B.	SWANSBORO
	SUSAN	SWANSBORO
	WILLIE B.	SWANSBORO
	ANNA A. HOLTON	WILMINGTON

Date	Ship Name	Shipbuilding Location
1867	LILLIAN	BEAUFORT
	THOMAS THOMAS	BEAUFORT
	FRANK PIGOT	CARTERET COUNTY
	CORA	CEDAR ISLAND
	GOODWIN	CEDAR ISLAND
	JOSIE HAVENS	CORE SOUND
	SURPASS	CORE SOUND
	ONWARD	ELIZABETH CITY
	HALCYONE	FAYETTEVILLE
	GOLD LEAF	HATTERAS
	INDUSTRY	HATTERAS
	CURRAN	NEW BERN
	INDUSTRY	NEW BERN
	LAURA	NEW BERN
	LITTLE DOVE	NEW BERN
	ALLIE DUDLEY	PORTSMOUTH
	ADA	STRAITS
	CARNIE	STRAITS
	CARRIE	STRAITS
	FAIRFIELD	STRAITS
	NASHVILLE	STRAITS
	MAGGIE	SWANSBORO
	ALICE DUDLEY	WASHINGTON
1868	SARAH FRANCIS	BAY RIVER
	MAGGIE C.	BEAUFORT
	SOUTHERNER	BEAUFORT
	STAR	BEAUFORT
	ESSEX	CEDAR ISLAND
	EMMA	DAVIS
	EMMA	ELIZABETH CITY
	E.M.J. BETTY	HATTERAS
	S. FRANCIS	HATTERAS
	ANNIE FARROW	OCRACOKE
	DIME	STRAITS
	MARTHA DAVIS	STRAITS
	RAY	STRAITS
1869	CHARLES	BEAUFORT
	SANTA MARIA	CURRITUCK COUNTY
	SANTO MARIA	EDENTON
	VIOLA	ELIZABETH CITY
	E.L. MYER	HATTERAS
	EMERALD	HATTERAS
	EUGENIE	HATTERAS

Date	Ship Name	Shipbuilding Location
1869	S.L. ELMYRA	HATTERAS
	A. WINEY	HUNTING QUARTERS
	AGNES	HUNTING QUARTERS
	SISTERS	HUNTING QUARTERS
	LOUISA	NEW BERN
	ALICE HILL	PORTSMOUTH
1870	SARAH	BEAUFORT COUNTY
	SUNNY SOUTH	CURRITUCK
	HELEN SMITH	EDENTON
	KEYPORT	ELIZABETH CITY
	NORTH STATE	FAYETTEVILLE
	SARAH	STRAITS
	ETTA	SWANSBOROUGH
1871	RIO	BEAUFORT
	SEA GULL	BEAUFORT
	CUMBERLAND	FAYETTEVILLE
	E. FRANCIS	HARBOR ISLAND
	CLINTON L. GUIRKIN	HARKER'S ISLAND
	MARY ANN REBECCA	HATTERAS
	EMELINE	HOG ISLAND
	LUCRETTA	OCRACOKE
	SEA GULL	STRAITS
1872	CECIL	BEAUFORT
	FLORENCE	BEAUFORT
	JULIA	BEAUFORT
	ADAMENT	HATTERAS
	VINE OAK	HATTERAS
	JOHN	HYDE COUNTY
	DOLPHIN	NELSON BAY
	MELVINA	NEW BERN
	MISSOURI ANN LUTHER	NEW BERN
	SEA FLOWER	OREGON MILLS
	ROSE	SMITHVILLE
	LOUISA	SMYRNA
	REBECCA	SMYRNA
	ROBERT H. COWAN	SOUTHPORT
	BEULAH BENTON	STRAITS
	BERTIE	WINDSOR
1873	ELLA R. HILL	BEAUFORT
	T.M. THOMAS	BEAUFORT
	JOSEPH H. NEFF	BRUNSWICK COUNTY
	MARY E. ROBERTS	CHOWAN COUNTY
	ALICE	CRAWFORD

Date	Ship Name	Shipbuilding Location
1873	ALICE	CURRITUCK COUNTY
	ELLA MAY	HATTERAS
	OSPREY	HATTERAS
	LOO GOLDTHWAITE	NEW BERN
	MELVIN	NEW BERN
	LENA	OCRACOKE
	IDA	PINEY POINT
	CHARLES THOMAS	SMITHVILLE
	DOLLY VARDEN	SMITHVILLE
	URIAH TIMMONS	SMITHVILLE
	LAVINIA THOMAS	STRAITS
	MARY WHEELER	STRAITS
	MINNIE WARD	SWANSBORO
	A.J. MARINE	WASHINGTON
	R.L. MYERS	WASHINGTON
	T.H.B. MYERS	WASHINGTON
	WASHINGTON	WILMINGTON
1874	CAROLINA	BATH
	HAVANA	BEAUFORT
	MARTHA J.	BEAUFORT
	WALTON	BEAUFORT
	JOHN ROBERTS	CHOWAN COUNTY
	ANNIE G. MIDGETT	CORE SOUND
	E. HUBBS	DARE COUNTY
	R. BRUCE MARTIN	EDENTON
	MANTEO	ELIZABETH CITY
	J.H. DAVIS	HUNTING QUARTERS
	ORADENE	HUNTING QUARTERS
	ANNIE M. MOORE	HYDE COUNTY
	MELVIN	NEW BERN
	SHELL DRAKE	OREGON MILLS
	NELLIE B. NEFF	SMITHVILLE
	ROSA SCARBOROUGH	SMITHVILLE
	MARIAM	SOUTH MILLS
	CHARLOTTE ANN PIGOTT	STRAITS
	KATY EDWARDS	SWANSBORO
	MARY	TURNERS CREEK
1875	D.C. WILLIS	BEAUFORT
	FLASH	BEAUFORT
	GOLD LEAF	BEAUFORT
	MARTHA	BEAUFORT
	STONEWALL	BEAUFORT
	BETTIE A. BUNCH	BERTIE COUNTY

Date	Ship Name	Shipbuilding Location
1875	SARAH	CAMDEN
	ENCORE	CEDAR ISLAND
	MARY S.	CORE SOUND
	SARAH F. MIDGETTE	CORE SOUND
	AMERICAN EAGLE	HATTERAS
	MELVILLE	HATTERAS
	VIRGINIA DARE	HATTERAS
	M. CARRIE	HUNTING QUARTERS
	SEA FLOWER	JARRETTS BAY
	LAURA ANN JANE	NEW BERN
	SALLIE ANN	NEW BERN
	SALLY ANN	NEW BERN
	J.H. POTTER	NORTH RIVER
	HENRY WESTERMAN	SMITHVILLE
	MARY	STRAITS
	SOMERSET	WASHINGTON
	JOSEPHINE	
1876	CENTENNIAL	BEAUFORT
	LYDIA A. WILLIS	BEAUFORT
	MABELL	BEAUFORT
	YULU N	BELLE ISLAND
	ANNIE W. DOXEY	CURRITUCK COUNTY
	EVELENE	HATTERAS
	EVILENA	HATTERAS
	J.J. MORROW	HATTERAS
	OCEAN BIRD	HATTERAS
	S.L. ELMYRA	HATTERAS
	SOUTHERN CROSS	HATTERAS
	LUPTON	HOG ISLAND
	E. CHARLEY	HUNTING QUARTERS
	M. ESTELLE	HUNTING QUARTERS
	MAGNOLIA	HUNTING QUARTERS
	MAGGIE J.	KINNAKEET
	NEUSE	KINSTON
	SALLIE ANN	POWELLS POINT
	SALLY ANN	POWELLS POINT
	DAUNTLESS	SMYRNA
	LOU WILLIS	SMYRNA
	PACKET	SMYRNA
	GOVENOR VANCE	STRAITS
	MYSTERY	STRAITS
	LITTLE WINNIE	WILMINGTON

Date	Ship Name	Shipbuilding Location
1877	QUEEN VICTORIA	BEARDS CREEK
	CONTENTNEA	BELLS FERRY
	EUNICE REYNOLDS	BRUNSWICK COUNTY
	MAGGIE	DARE COUNTY
	MARGARET ANN	EDENTON
	MILLY RHODES	EDENTON
	KATE	ELIZABETH CITY
	THERESA	GERMANTOWN
	DEZZIE B. ONSLOW	HATTERAS
	PEZZIE B. ONSLOW	HATTERAS
	EDGECOMBE	LEECHVILLE
	ANNIE F. WAHAB	NEW BERN
	IONA	NEW BERN
	J.J. WOLFENDEN	NEW BERN
	JAMES RUMLEY	SMYRNA
	J.T. MAY QUEEN	WASHINGTON
	COLVILLE	WILMINGTON
	ROSA L. CUMMINGS	WILMINGTON
1878	SARAH	BEAUFORT
	SUSAN	GOOSE CREEK ISLAND
	DELTA	HYDE COUNTY
	O. COKE	KINNAKEET
	ROXANNE	KINNAKEET
	MARY	NEW BERN
	FLORENCE	PAMLICO
	SUSAN	PAMLICO
	IDA	WILMINGTON
1879	ARGYLE	BRUNSWICK COUNTY
	CAPTOLIA	CAMDEN
	ENTERPRISE	CAMDEN COUNTY
	BUFFALO BILL	EDENTON
	PRETTY GAL	EDENTON
	YELLOW GAL	EDENTON
	MARY FLEETWOOD	NEW BERN
	MARY FLUHUR	NEW BERN
	JOHN GRIFFITH	WILMINGTON
1880	EMILIE	BEAUFORT
	CURLEW	BERTIE COUNTY
	KORET	BULL POND
	MERRY WAVE	EDENTON
	SHOO FLY	EDENTON
	LYDIA	ELIZABETH CITY
	NELLIE WADSWORTH	ELIZABETH CITY

Date	Ship Name	Shipbuilding Location
1880	MAYFLOWER	GOOSE CREEK ISLAND
	DEXTER	HATTERAS
	ALICE	NEW BERN
	BESSIE	NEW BERN
	ELLA	NEW BERN
	MAY FLOWER	NEW BERN
	MARY D.	PINEY POINT
	BESSIE	WASHINGTON
	CHARLES FISHER	WASHINGTON
	SAMUEL BROWN	WASHINGTON
	ELSIE	WILLIAMSTON
	JOHN DAWSON	WILMINGTON
1881	DIAMOND	ALBEMARLE
	DIAMOND A	AVOCA
	DIAMOND C	AVOCA
	ALGERIA	BEAUFORT
	CORRINE	BEAUFORT
	SARAH JANE	BEAUFORT
	WELDON	BLUFF POINT
	YEOPIM	DRUMMONDS
	CHARLIE RAPER	EDENTON
	SUE	EDENTON
	EUREKA	NEW BERN
	ISABELLA	NEW BERN
	E. WHEELER	PINEY POINT
	ADVENTURE	SMYRNA
	HUGH	SMYRNA
	VARINA	SMYRNA
	CORA	WASHINGTON
	MINERVA	WASHINGTON
	TARBORO	WASHINGTON
	WASHINGTON	WASHINGTON
	BESSIE	WILMINGTON
	BIZ	WILMINGTON
	BLADEN	WILMINGTON
	LOUISE	WILMINGTON
	WALTER C. THOMAS	WILMINGTON
1882	ALICE	BAY RIVER
	AURORA	BEAUFORT
	JULIA	BEAUFORT
	NANNIE P. DAVIS	BEAUFORT
	CAROLINA	BEAUFORT COUNTY
	SEA FOAM	EDENTON

Date	Ship Name	Shipbuilding Location
1882	SUE	EDENTON
	SUSIE	EDENTON
	ANNIE WALLACE	ELIZABETH CITY
	LIZZIE WALLACE	ELIZABETH CITY
	LIZZIE F. STOWE	GOOSE CREEK ISLAND
	J.D. MASON	HUNTING QUARTERS
	BONITO	LENOXVILLE
	CUMBERLAND	MANTEO
	SUSANNAH	MANTEO
	CARRIE RAE	NEW BERN
	CARRIE REEL	NEW BERN
	KINSTON	NEW BERN
	TRENT	NEW BERN
	LAURA J.	NORTH RIVER
	ROWENA	RODANTHE
	CAROLINA	SMYRNA
	REGULATOR	SMYRNA
	M. FRANCES	STRAITS
	L.H. CUTLER	SWIFT CREEK
	ABRAHAM DRUCKER	WASHINGTON
	JOHN CHRISTOL	WASHINGTON
	GENERAL H. G. WRIGHT	WILMINGTON
	H.G. WRIGHT	WILMINGTON
	MERMAID	
1883	ANNA BELL	BEAUFORT
	ANNIE B.	BEAUFORT
	CHALLENGE	CAPE LOOKOUT
	MAGGIE ETTER	CHICAMICOMICO
	OCTAVIOUS COKE JR.	CHOWAN COUNTY
	CURTIS MATILDA	COLINGTON
	JULIA F. HILL	CORE SOUND
	PIC-NIC	CURRITUCK COUNTY
	CHARLES	EDENTON
	FISHERMAN	EDENTON
	NED WOOD	EDENTON
	RED WOOD	EDENTON
	CHARLES	ELIZABETH CITY
1883	ELIZA ELLEN	HATTERAS
	ANNA BELL	HUNTING QUARTERS
	ELIZABETH	HUNTING QUARTERS
	J.F. MORRIS	HUNTING QUARTERS
	J.J. TAYLOR	HUNTING QUARTERS
	W. H. BUREN	HUNTING QUARTERS

Date	Ship Name	Shipbuilding Location
1883	ELLA	KINNAKEET
	F.M. ISABELLA	KINNAKEET
	VENNOR	KINNAKEET
	WILLIE T.	KINNAKEET
	BLANCHE	NEW BERN
	FLORENCE	NEW BERN
	DEFIANCE	SMYRNA
	MINNIE	SMYRNA
	R.E. LEE	SMYRNA
	CAROLINA	SNOW HILL
	MINNIE	TURNERS CREEK
	BEAUFORT	WASHINGTON
	BEAUFORT	WASHINGTON
	BESSIE	WASHINGTON
	MARGIE	WASHINGTON
	BARTER	WILMINGTON
	RIVER QUEEN	WILMINGTON
	VIOLA	WILMINGTON
1884	LILY	CEDAR ISLAND
	CLEOPATRA	COLERAIN
	LORENA	CORE SOUND
	BETTIE	ELIZABETH CITY
	TAHOMA	ELIZABETH CITY
	NELSON	HARKERS ISLAND
	ANNIE C. THOMAS	HATTERAS
	ANNIE C. THORN	HATTERAS
	GEM	JARVISBURG
	NELLIE B. DEY	LENOXVILLE
	ELLA CREEF	MANTEO
	SABRA A.	PINEY POINT
	MELVIN MORRIS	SMYRNA
	ETTA T. WESTON	WASHINGTON
	EVELINE	WASHINGTON
	PETREL	WASHINGTON
	EXCELSIOR	WILMINGTON
	DICTATOR	WOODVILLE
1885	JOHN AND CECIL	BEAUFORT
	NELLIE WATT	BELHAVEN
	VENUS	HATTERAS
	LITTLE SAMPSON	KINNAKEET
	CAMILLE	MANTEO
	LADY ANTRIM	MANTEO
	GEORGIA BELLE	MOREHEAD CITY

Date	Ship Name	Shipbuilding Location
1885	INDEPENDENCE	NELSON BAY
	MARY D.	PINEY POINT
	HESTER ANN	SMYRNA
	WHITE WING	SWAN QUARTER
	ANN BRYAN	VANDEMERE
	R.L. MYERS	WASHINGTON
	ADDIE	WILMINGTON
1886	MAUD	BEAUFORT
	LAURA	GOLDSBORO
		GOLDSBORO
	KIT SANFORD	JUDITHS
	ISABELLA M. SAWYER	KINNAKEET
	CONVOY	LENOXVILLE
	LILLIE BELL	MOREHEAD CITY
	LILLIN BELL	MOREHEAD CITY
	LOUISE MOREHEAD	MOREHEAD CITY
	MENA BRANCH	MOREHEAD CITY
	FRANK	NEW RIVER
	SARAH FRANCES	NORTH RIVER
	LELA MAY	PAMLICO
	RATTLESNAKE	RICE PATH
	FANNIE	SMYRNA
	FAVORITE	SMYRNA
	HATTIE D.	SMYRNA
	JOSIE	SOUTH CREEK
1887	VENTURA	ATLANTIC
	MAY	BEAUFORT
	SEA BIRD	COLINGTON
	GREENFIELD	DRUMMONDS
	CROATAN	ELIZABETH CITY
	LOUISE F. HARPER	HARKERS ISLAND
	SAMUEL ECCLES JR.	HERTFORD COUNTY
	ESSEX	HUNTING QUARTERS
	ORIENTAL	HYDE COUNTY
	ALERT	LENOXVILLE
	HOWARD	NEW BERN
	LISBON	POINT CASWELL
	LAURA B. BANKS	POWELLS POINT
	MAY	SOUTHPORT
	W AND T	SOUTHPORT
	NANNIE B.	STELLA
	PAULINE	WADES SHORE
	ALPHA	WASHINGTON

Date	Ship Name	Shipbuilding Location
1887	NANCY ANNE	WILMINGTON
	ALBEMARLE	AVOCA
	STYLE	BATH
	ABRAHAM LINCOLN	BEAUFORT
	FANNIE	BEAUFORT
	LIDA CARR	BEAUFORT
	HAPPY GO LUCKY	BLOUNTS CREEK
	MARY JANE FORSHA	COLINGTON
	P.M. WARREN	DRUMMOND POINT
	LIZZIE HAULMON	ELIZABETH CITY
	GILT EDGE	HATTERAS
	ALBERT	HAVELOCK
	PALMER	HUNTING QUARTERS
	ANNGHEN	KINNAKEET
	MISSOURI	KINNAKEET
	ELLA HORTON	MOREHEAD CITY
	GERTIE	MOREHEAD CITY
	GERTIE LORD	MOREHEAD CITY
	IDA MAY	MOREHEAD CITY
	MAUD	MOREHEAD CITY
	ARK	MURFREESBORO
	AMITY	NELSON BAY
	BESSIE AND ELLIS	NEW BERN
	H.B. LANE	NEW BERN
	LIZZIE BURRUS	NEW BERN
1888	ELSIE	NORTH CAROLINA
	L. DAYTON	NORTH RIVER
	DREADNAUGHT	OCRACOKE
	DORIE B.	PINEY POINT
	MINNIE G.	SHALLOTTE
	ATLANTIC	SMYRNA
	JANIE	SMYRNA
	JOHN B.	SMYRNA
	MADORA	SMYRNA
	RESTLESS	SMYRNA
	ROSEBELLE	SMYRNA
	HATTIE	SOUTH MILLS
	HATTIE RHEA	SOUTHPORT
	SARAH ALLEN	STRAITS
	VANCEBORO	VANCEBORO
	ELLA	WASHINGTON
	SOUTH LAKE	WASHINGTON

Date	Ship Name	Shipbuilding Location
1889	ACME	BUFFALO CITY
	MARION TEMPLE	CLUBFOOT CREEK
	CHOWAN	COLERAIN
	LILLY MAY	COLINGTON
	HATTIE A. PETERSON	HATTERAS
	HATTIE A. PITTMAN	HATTERAS
	LILLIAN	HATTERAS
	H. HILL	HUNTING QUARTERS
	BABE	MITCHELL CREEK
	DANIEL BELL	MOREHEAD CITY
	ZENITH	MOUNT PLEASANT
	ANNA ELIZABETH	NORTH RIVER
	ANNA	SHALLOTTE
	ANNIE MOORE	SMYRNA
	DANIEL G. FOWLE	SMYRNA
	FREDDIE	SMYRNA
	SAMUEL M. BUCKMAN	SMYRNA
	SPY	SMYRNA
	WILLIS	SMYRNA
	JOHNIE	SWANSBORO
	NAUTITUS	WASHINGTON
1890	A. FRANCIS	ATLANTIC
	T.M. TAYLOR	ATLANTIC
	ELIHU A. WHITE	BEAUFORT
	NETTIE PIERCE	BEAUFORT
	MOLLIE L. FARMER	BETHEL
	MARY ELIZA SMALL	BIG FLATTY CREEK
	RICE BIRD	BRUNSWICK COUNTY
	CARRIE	CURRITUCK COUNTY
	EDNA	HARKER'S ISLAND
	BESSIE MAY	HARLOWE
	MAY FLOWER	HARLOWE
	MAYFLOWER	HARLOWE
	TWO FRIENDS	HUNTING QUARTERS
	JENNIE	LENOXVILLE
	JULIA W. BELL	MOREHEAD CITY
	NETTIE W.	NEW BERN
	SWAN	NEW BERN
	LINIE B.	NORTH RIVER
	PENDER	SHAKEN
	LIZZIE ALICE	SHALLOTTE
	ALONZO TUALANE	SMYRNA
	LILLIE	SMYRNA

Date	Ship Name	Shipbuilding Location
1890	LIZZIE	SMYRNA
	MANTEO	SMYRNA
	MATTIE O	SMYRNA
	NELLIE FLORENCE	SMYRNA
	K.M. THOMAS	SOUTH CREEK
	LAURA D.	SOUTHPORT
	CITY OF STELLA	STELLA
	JOHN C. DAVIS	STRAITS
	J. HILLES	WASHINGTON
	RAPPAHANNOCK	WASHINGTON
	C. HAY	WHITE OAK RIVER
	MAGGIE	WILMINGTON
	ROBERT E. LEE	WILMINGTON
	WACCAMAW NO. 1	WILMINGTON
	ESTHER	
1891	GOLD MINE	ATLANTIC
	IOWN	ATLANTIC
	LADY GRANT	ATLANTIC
	TOWN	ATLANTIC
	S.M. ROLLINS	BAY RIVER
	IVALON	BEAUFORT
	NAOMI	BEAUFORT
	LUCY RAY	BELLS ISLAND
	E. PETERSON	BLOUNTS CREEK
	ABBIE ELIZABETH	BOGUE
	SUDIE B.	BOGUE SOUND
	LUCIE	BRUNSWICK COUNTY
	DAUNTLESS	CAPE BANKS
	SUDIE D.	CORE CREEK
	BETTIE	DAVIS
	MARY E. REEVES	DAVIS
	SOPHIE WOOD	EAST LAKE
	NEDDEEN	GOOSE CREEK ISLAND
	MATTIE MAY	HATTERAS
	MOLLIE	HATTERAS
	PERQUIMANS	HERTFORD
	LEOLA	HUNTING QUARTERS
	EUGENE	KITTY HAWK
	LEONE WHITE	LAKE LANDING
	HARVEST	LOCKWOODS FOLLY
	MARY RUFFIN	MOREHEAD CITY
	MARY THOMAS	MOREHEAD CITY
	NELLIE BLY	MOREHEAD CITY

Date	Ship Name	Shipbuilding Location
1891	SUNNY SOUTH	MOREHEAD CITY
	MARY BELL	NORTH RIVER
	MAY BELL	NORTH RIVER
	ADA FOSTER	SMYRNA
	BESSIE D	SMYRNA
	BESSIE MOORE	SMYRNA
	CLEM	SMYRNA
	EVELYN	SMYRNA
	HANNAH	SMYRNA
	IDA L. EATON	SMYRNA
	JESSE ARTHUR	SMYRNA
	WAY HAVEN	SMYRNA
	DAUNTLESS	SOUTH MILLS
	LEO	SOUTHPORT
	JOSEPH	SWANSBORO
	LEDIA STAR	TURNIGAN BAY
	LILLIA STAR	TURNIGAN BAY
	E.M. TILLEY	WASHINGTON
	ELGIN	WASHINGTON
	IVY	WASHINGTON
	DOLPHIN	WILMINGTON
	JAMES T. EASTON	WILMINGTON
1892	R.E. LEE	BAYBORO
	BIVALVE	BEAUFORT
	JESSIE M. BELL	BEAUFORT
	THREE SISTERS	COINJOCK
	AUGUST FLOWER	ELIZABETH CITY
	HOWARD W.	ELIZABETH CITY
	NELLIE	ELIZABETH CITY
	ROSA B. CORA	ELIZABETH CITY
	OCEAN WAVE	GOOSE CREEK ISLAND
	MAY BELL	GRIFTON
	ANNA LEA	HARLOWE
	DICKIE BIRD	MOREHEAD CITY
	MILDRED	MOREHEAD CITY
	GAZELLE	NEW BERN
	NINA DARE	NORTH RIVER
	RUTH DARLING	NORTH RIVER
	SARAH WILSON	NORTH RIVER
	LETHA	PORTSMOUTH
	BRANT	ROANOKE ISLAND
	MABEL	SHALLOTTE
	EARLE	SMYRNA

Date	Ship Name	Shipbuilding Location
1892	ELLA GRAY	SMYRNA
	LILLIAN	SMYRNA
	NATIVE	SMYRNA
	RENA B.	SMYRNA
	DIADEM	SOUTH RIVER
	ELDRIDGE	STELLA
	BLANCHE	STRAITS
	HENRY W. GRADY	STRAITS
	ROAM	TUNIS
	ESTELLE	WASHINGTON
	GLIDE	WASHINGTON
	ADELE	WILMINGTON
	COURTNEY	WILMINGTON
	ELK	WILMINGTON
	F AND F	WILMINGTON
	MESSENGER	WILMINGTON
	SATISFACTION	WILMINGTON
	SATILLA	
1893	GOLDEN ROD	AVOCA
	CHAUNCEY ROY	BEAUFORT
	THREE FRIENDS	BEAUFORT
	FISH HAWK	EDENTON
	SARAH DRUMMOND	EDENTON
	OSPREY	HATTERAS
	FILENA	KITTY HAWK
	BLOOMER	MOREHEAD CITY
	EMMA S.	NEW BERN
	BENEFIT	NORTH RIVER
	ROSA PIERCE	NORTH RIVER
	TWO SISTERS	NORTH RIVER
	ANNE THOMAS	OCRACOKE
	ANNIE THOMAS	OCRACOKE
	E.K. WILLIS	OCRACOKE
	W.T. DAGGETT	PORT CASWELL
	HARRY S.	RIVERDALE
	MANIE CARLIS	ROANOKE ISLAND
	GRACIE	SMYRNA
	LATTIE	SMYRNA
	LITTLE SISTER	SMYRNA
	LOTTIE	SMYRNA
	LEAH	SOUTHPORT
	MAGGIE	STELLA
	CAROLINA	VANCEBORO

Date	Ship Name	Shipbuilding Location
1893	PEARLIE MAY	VANCEBORO
	A.B. COVINGTON	WASHINGTON
	ALBEMARLE	WASHINGTON
	BARNEY	WASHINGTON
	GENERAL GEORGE THOM	WASHINGTON
1894	H.P. BROWN	AVON
	TWO BROTHERS	BEAUFORT
	NEW LIGHT	BEAUFORT
	PAULINE	CAPE BANKS
	ANNIE M. TURNER	COINJOCK
	G.F. DERICKSON	ELIZABETH CITY
	KING CRAB	KERSHAW
	ANACONDA	KINNAKEET
	MAGGIE J. A.	KINNAKEET
	ETHEL	LOWLAND
	OLLIE	MOREHEAD CITY
	THREE POT	MOREHEAD CITY
	THREE POT	MOREHEAD CITY
	IRMA DARLING	NEW BERN
	FANNIE BREVARD	NORTH RIVER
	LOCKIE	PANTEGO
	ELLA CROSBY	ROANOKE ISLAND
	M.G. WALSTEIN	ROANOKE ISLAND
	MYSTERY	SHALLOTTE
	ELLA MAY	SMYRNA
	RUTH	SMYRNA
	JANIE BERRY	STRAITS
	ALICE	WASHINGTON
	AURORA	WASHINGTON
	MARIE	WASHINGTON
	A AND M	WILMINGTON
	ANNA	WILMINGTON
	ARAND M.	WILMINGTON
	FRANK SESSOMS	WILMINGTON
1895	RIVER QUEEN	COLINGTON
	TRECO	CURRITUCK
	SPRAY	CURRITUCK COUNTY
	LILLIAN LUGILLIAL	DURANTS NECK
	FLOSSIE D. LEE	DURHAM CREEK
	DIXIE	GOLDSBORO
	LAKEWOOD	HERTFORD
	LILY P.	KINNAKEET
	LUVENIA RICHARD	MITCHELL CREEK

Date	Ship Name	Shipbuilding Location
1895	GERTRUDE	MOREHEAD CITY
	MATTIE MAY	OCRACOKE
	E.A. HARVIS	POINT CASWELL
	E.A. HAWES	POINT CASWELL
	AMERICAN EAGLE	RANSOMVILLE
	K.T. WILLIS	SHACKELFORD BANKS
	J.D. PIGOTT	SHALLOTTE
	JOHN H. KUCK	SHALLOTTE
	RUTH J.	SHALLOTTE
	NEVA PEARL	STRAITS
	SWANSBORO	SWANSBORO
	SHILOH	TARBORO
	MAGGIE H. LANE	VANCEBORO
	E AND S	WILMINGTON
1896	NETA	ATLANTIC
	VIRGINIA M.	ATLANTIC
	DOLPHIN	COLERAIN
	LIZZIE B.	HARKERS ISLAND
	EDITH	HATTERAS
	JULIAN J. FLEETWOOD	HERTFORD
	BELVIDERE	HERTFORD COUNTY
	OSBON	KITTY HAWK
	MAMIE C. DANIELS	MOREHEAD CITY
	NINA	MOREHEAD CITY
	RUTH C. WATSON	MOREHEAD CITY
	JULIA	NEW BERN
	RELIEF	OCRACOKE
	DEFENDER	RIVER LANDING
	MARTHA D. THOMAS	SMYRNA
	MARTHIS D. THOMAS	SMYRNA
	STELLA LEE	SOUTHPORT
	INTREPID	VANDEMERE
	FLORENCE	WASHINGTON
	FRANCES	WASHINGTON
	ISABELLA	WASHINGTON
	TAR RIVER	WASHINGTON
	CROESUS	WILMINGTON
1897	JOE	ATLANTIC
	ARCADIA	BEAUFORT
	ILLMA	BEAUFORT
	NETTIE B. SMITH	BEAUFORT
	RAY	ELIZABETH CITY
	MATTAMUSKEET	FAIRFIELD

Date	Ship Name	Shipbuilding Location
1897	M.C. HILL	HUNTING QUARTERS
	MARY MAYBIRD	HUNTING QUARTERS
	LITTLE JIM	MOREHEAD CITY
	LIZZIE BLADES	NEW BERN
	RUTH	SMYRNA
	LEADER	SOUTH RIVER
	LOLA	STARKEYS CREEK
	LULA	STARKEYS CREEK
	NINA	SWANSBORO
	SWANSBORO	SWANSBORO
	ALMA	WASHINGTON
	AUGUSTA	WILMINGTON
	BUCK	WILMINGTON
	MANISTER	WILMINGTON
	MANISTEE	WIT
1898	E.B. SHULL	BEAUFORT
	IOWA	BEAUFORT
	MAUD	BEAUFORT
	OREGON	BEAUFORT
	TWO COUSINS	BEAUFORT
	SMILIE D.	CORE CREEK
	IMP	ELIZABETH CITY
	PLUMEGE	HARLOWE
	PLUNGE	HARLOWE
	HOLT	MOREHEAD CITY
	WORTH BAGLEY	MOREHEAD CITY
	EDMOND PARKIM	NEW BERN
	GLIDE	NEW BERN
	SUE	NEW BERN
	TOM T	NEW BERN
	CLARA ESTELL	NORTH HARLOWE
	NELLIE	OCRACOKE
	NILLIE	OCRACOKE
	PAMLICO	PAMLICO
	CATHLEEN	SMYRNA
	DEWEY	SMYRNA
	JULIA	SMYRNA
	MARBLEHEAD	SMYRNA
	NEPTUNE	SMYRNA
	ELLA MYRTLE	STRAITS
	GENEVA MOORE	STRAITS
	MARIA	STRAITS
	TARBORO	TARBORO

Date	Ship Name	Shipbuilding Location
1898	BRUCE	WASHINGTON
	CATHELEEN	WILLISTON
	A.B.C. HILL	ATLANTIC
	HOBSON	AVON
	LEONORA C.	AVON
	ZEORIA	AVON
	ADMIRAL	BEAUFORT
	BLANCH	BEAUFORT
	CAROLYN	BEAUFORT
	COMMODORE	BEAUFORT
	COOCH	BEAUFORT
	MARY BELL	BEAUFORT
	NINA M.	BEAUFORT
	PRINCE	BEAUFORT
	ROAMER	BEAUFORT
	THREE SAMUELS	BEAUFORT
	DORA	BELHAVEN
	A.J. JOHNSON	CLEAR RUN
	SHAMROCK	DAVIS
	MAGGIE E. DAVIS	HATTERAS
	ADVENTURER	LAKE LANDING
	ANNIE LENA WHITE	LAKE LANDING
	LILLIE V.	LOCKWOODS FOLLY
1899	BERNICE CREE	MOREHEAD CITY
	CHARLES S. WALLACE	MOREHEAD CITY
	R.W. TAYLOR	MOREHEAD CITY
	ALMA WHITE	MOUNT PLEASANT
	CECIL	MOUNT PLEASANT
	TWO SISTERS	MOUNT PLEASANT
	MARY L.	NEW BERN
	TRENT	NEW BERN
	OYSTER BAY	OLD TRAP
	E.B. DANIELS	ROANOKE ISLAND
	E.R. DANIELS	ROANOKE ISLAND
	C.D. MOFFITT	SHALLOTTE
	AGNEW	SMYRNA
	AUGUSTA M.	SMYRNA
	BERTIE	SMYRNA
	BROOKLYN	SMYRNA
	CHARLES LEROY	SMYRNA
	EVA MAY	SMYRNA
	FRANCES J. DANIELS	SMYRNA
	IVY	SMYRNA

Date	Ship Name	Shipbuilding Location
1899	LURENA	SMYRNA
	MINA PERRY	SMYRNA
	OLYMPIA	SMYRNA
	ESTHER MAY	SOUTHPORT
	JAMES RAYMOND	STRAITS
	IDA V.	SWAN QUARTER
	NELLIE B.	SWANSBORO
	E.M. SHORT	WASHINGTON
	EMMA	WILMINGTON
1900	MISSOURI	ATLANTIC
	FRANKLIN D. BELL	AVON
	LURA MAE	AVON
	ADDIE L.	BEAUFORT
	CHERUBIM	BEAUFORT
	CLIFFORD PERIN	BEAUFORT
	LILLIE PEARL	BEAUFORT
	NETA	BEAUFORT
	VIOLET	BEAUFORT
	ANNIE MAY	BELHAVEN
	DONALD H. WARNER	BELHAVEN
1900	HAROLD CLARK	BELHAVEN
	KATIE ESTELL	BELHAVEN
	MAUD GRANNIS	BELHAVEN
	FLORENCE ELSIE	DAVIS
	ANNIE EDWARD	ELIZABETH CITY
	LENA VIRGINIA	LEECHVILLE
	ADEL	LOCKWOODS FOLLY
	BERTHA L. MORTON	MOREHEAD CITY
	BESSIE ROBERTS	MOREHEAD CITY
	HAZEL P. HAWKINS	MOREHEAD CITY
	SUSANNA	MOREHEAD CITY
	UNCLE SAM	NEW BERN
	EFFIE M. GILLIKIN	SMYRNA
	GEORGE SLOVER	SMYRNA
	INDEX	SMYRNA
	PELHAM	SMYRNA
	ADDIE MAY	SOUTHPORT
	WYONA	STRAITS
	CARRIE	SWANSBORO
	FAWN	SWANSBORO
	ONSLOW	SWANSBORO
	MYSTERY	WASHINGTON

Date	Ship Name	Shipbuilding Location
1900	SALLY W.	WASHINGTON
	WINTHROP	WINTHROP POINT
1901	J.E. HOVAH	ATLANTIC
	N.J. MERCEDES	AVON
	REBECCA BELL	AVON
	SUCCESS	AVON
	ANNIE FAIR	BEAUFORT
	GLADYS	BEAUFORT
	LORENA D.	BEAUFORT
	PRINCE	BEAUFORT
	TALLAHASSEE	BEAUFORT
	VANDOLUER	BEAUFORT
	VIRGIE MAY	BEAUFORT
	ALBATROSS	BELHAVEN
	COLUMBIA	BELHAVEN
	DANIEL CRESSIE	BELHAVEN
	ETHEL P. NELSON	ELIZABETH CITY
	ETHER M. WRIGHT	ELIZABETH CITY
	ALMA	FAIRFIELD
	ODY	HARLOWE
	R.C. BEAMON	HATTERAS
	BROAD BILL	MOREHEAD CITY
	EAGLE	MOREHEAD CITY
	EUDORA T. WALLACE	MOREHEAD CITY
	EURORA T. WALLACE	MOREHEAD CITY
	FISH HAWK	MOREHEAD CITY
	GEORGE M. IVES	MOREHEAD CITY
	MAGGIE W. WADE	MOREHEAD CITY
	NINA G. WALLACE	MOREHEAD CITY
	R.W. TAYLOR	MOREHEAD CITY
	CROATAN	NEW BERN
	THREE FRIENDS	NORTH CAROLINA
	VIOLET	NORTH HARLOWE
	CHARLES M. WHITLOCK	POINT CASWELL
	HATTIE CREEF	ROANOKE ISLAND
	ADA BOZMAN	ROSE BAY
	CLARENCE H.	SHALLOTTE
	J.C. ALLEN	SHALLOTTE
	DAISY	SMYRNA
	MISSOURI	SMYRNA
	MYRTLE	SMYRNA
	ROAMER	SMYRNA

Date	Ship Name	Shipbuilding Location
1901	HADDIE BLANCH	SOUTHPORT
	CHARMER	STRAITS
	NELLIE	SWANSBORO
	SARAH	SWANSBORO
	ETHEL	WASHINGTON
	GOLDSBORO	WASHINGTON
	MAGGIE ANDREWS	WIT
1902	AVOCA	AVOCA
	THREE BROTHERS	BACHELOR
	BESSIE HELLEN	BEAUFORT
	CARL	BEAUFORT
	JACK TIER	BEAUFORT
	SARAH ANN	BEAUFORT
	ALICE	BELHAVEN
	ALICE M. BRADLEY	BELHAVEN
	ELLA S. HENDERSON	BELHAVEN
	GRETCHEN	BELHAVEN
	KENNNETH PAGE	BELHAVEN
	LOUISA WYATT	BELHAVEN
	ELLA MAE	CROATAN
	ALGER	DAVIS
	LULA BELMONT	DAVIS
	R.W. BLANCHARD	DAVIS
	ALVA	ELIZABETH CITY
	CLAY FOREMAN	ELIZABETH CITY
	EULA K.	ELIZABETH CITY
	MARY J. HAYNIE	ELIZABETH CITY
	MILDRED MAY	ELIZABETH CITY
	MINNIE AND MAUD	ELIZABETH CITY
	WAVE	HARLOWE
	FLY	HERTFORD
	ROBERT V. RIDER	HOLLYWOOD
	LONIE BUREN	KINNAKEET
	J.R. CONDON	MANTEO
	ROAMER	MARINES
	HELEN	MARSHALLBERG
	B.D. LUCE	MOREHEAD CITY
	CHARLES S. WALLACE	MOREHEAD CITY
	COASTER	MOREHEAD CITY
	D.B. WADE	MOREHEAD CITY
	ELLA T. NELSON	MOREHEAD CITY
	GEORGIA	MOREHEAD CITY
	INDIA	MOREHEAD CITY

Date	Ship Name	Shipbuilding Location
1902	MARY M.	MOREHEAD CITY
	RIPPLE	MOREHEAD CITY
	STELLA ALLEN	MOREHEAD CITY
	STELLA F.	MOREHEAD CITY
	THELMA	MOREHEAD CITY
	W.J. WALLACE	MOREHEAD CITY
	ALLIE	NEW BERN
	E.K. BISHOP	NEW BERN
	ETHER	NEW BERN
	MARY QUEEN	NEW BERN
	MAY QUEEN	NEW BERN
	SID PHILLIPS	NEW BERN
	WILLIAM B. BLADES, JR	NEW BERN
	FORBES AND HUBBARD	OLD TRAP
	SPORT	OLD TRAP
	HOPE	POINT CASWELL
	OTIS D. TERRELL	PORTSMOUTH
	FRANKLIN PIERCE	SHALLOTTE
	BLANCHE	SMYRNA
	DEFENDER	SMYRNA
	JULIAN DEWEY	SMYRNA
	MAGGIE	SMYRNA
	METEOR	SMYRNA
	VALIANT	SMYRNA
	LENA	SWANSBORO
	MYRTIE	WASHINGTON
	HERBERT M	WILMINGTON
	ROSA OTTO	WILMINGTON
	GERTRUDE	WIT
	LACEY	WIT
	MANGROVE	WIT
	VIRGIL	WIT
	VIRGINIA R.	WIT
1903	LUTHER B. MAY	AVON
	COLER	BEAUFORT
	MARY AGNES	BEAUFORT
	BILL ARP	BELHAVEN
	CONSTANCE	BELHAVEN
	EVA M.	BELHAVEN
	KATRINA	EDENTON
	CLAUDE	ELIZABETH CITY
	GEORGIA A. GASKINS	ELIZABETH CITY
	LEONORA	ELIZABETH CITY

Date	Ship Name	Shipbuilding Location
1903	LUCILLE	ELIZABETH CITY
	MARGARETTE	ELIZABETH CITY
	LITTLE MART	FULCHERS LANDING
	THELMA G.	KINNAKEET
	H. AND V. ROYAL	LOCKWOODS FOLLY
	RIPPLE	MARSHALLBERG
	ATLANTIC	MOREHEAD CITY
	CHASE	MOREHEAD CITY
	DEFIANCE	MOREHEAD CITY
	DOLPHIN	MOREHEAD CITY
	HALCYONE	MOREHEAD CITY
	JOHN F. BELL	MOREHEAD CITY
	RELIANCE	MOREHEAD CITY
	SWANNANOA	MOREHEAD CITY
	VIOLA	MOREHEAD CITY
	ANNIE ELWOOD	MOUNT PLEASANT
	AUNT SUE	NEW BERN
	SARA LOUISE	NEW BERN
	PILOT'S BRIDE	NEWPORT
	C.T. HERMAN	SHALLOTTE
	J.D. PORTER	SHALLOTTE
	EDNA	SMYRNA
	THOMAS THOMAS	SMYRNA
	WELDON	SMYRNA
	JANIE	SNEADS FERRY
	MARY	SOUTHPORT
	ROSLYND	SWANSBORO
	ALICE	TAR LANDING
	ALTEIRO	WASHINGTON
	MAGNOLIA	WASHINGTON
	MYRTLE	WASHINGTON
	FARMER	WILMINGTON
	LILY	WILMINGTON
	ROSA	WILMINGTON
	WINNER	WILMINGTON
	PETREL	WIT
	COLUMBIA	WYSOCKING
	CONSTITUTION	WYSOCKING
1904	SADIE	ATLANTIC
	PRISCILLA	BEAUFORT
	THELMA	BEAUFORT
	DUPLIN	CHINQUAPIN
	DUNCAN	COLINGTON

Date	Ship Name	Shipbuilding Location
1904	VENUS	DAVIS
	HELEN AND ALMA	ELIZABETH CITY
	W.J. TOWNSEND	ELIZABETH CITY
	LILLIAN	FALKLAND
	G.W. WILLIAMS	HARLOWE
	LENOIR	KINSTON
	JOSIE D.	LOCKWOODS FOLLY
	ANNIE E.	MARIBEL
	W.T. RIGGINS	MARSHALLBERG
	BERTIE	MOREHEAD CITY
	ETHEL P. NELSON	MOREHEAD CITY
	GEORGE L. LYON	MOREHEAD CITY
	GRACE M. WALLACE	MOREHEAD CITY
	KATHLEEN	MOREHEAD CITY
	ADELLE	NEW BERN
	ELLES S.	NEW BERN
	MARY BELO	NEW BERN
	SCUPPERNONG	NEW BERN
	SADIE D.	NORTH HARLOWE
	MAYFLOWER	POINT CASWELL
	TWO BROTHERS	ROANOKE ISLAND
	CHAUNCEY T.	SHALLOTTE
	CARRIE GRANNIS	SMYRNA
	EUGENIE	SMYRNA
	LUCY MAY	SMYRNA
	NEVADA	SMYRNA
	REFUGE	STELLA
	GEORGIA T.	SWANSBORO
	BLONDELLE	WILLISTON
	CHARLOTTE CAASE	WILMINGTON
	CHARLOTTE GOOSE	WILMINGTON
	LEOLA B. GASKILL	WIT
1905	DALE	ATLANTIC
	LETHA	ATLANTIC
	THRESSIE	ATLANTIC
	TRESSIE	ATLANTIC
	SILVER SPRAY	AVON
	CARL T.	BEAUFORT
	HUSTLER	BEAUFORT
	MARY E.	BEAUFORT
	NETTIE MAY	BEAUFORT
	ROSETTA	BEAUFORT
	C.C. ISABELL	BELHAVEN

Date	Ship Name	Shipbuilding Location
1905	CORRIN	CAROLINA CITY
	EMMA J.	DAVIS
	GUY	ELIZABETH CITY
	HAZEL	ELIZABETH CITY
	LILLIAN	ELIZABETH CITY
	MARY E. BURRUS	ENGLEHARD
	COLONEL BOUGARD	FEDERAL POINT
	INDIA L.	JACKSONVILLE
	LYDA GERTRUDE	JORDAN CREEK
	ATLANTIC	MANTEO
	MABEL E. HORTON	MANTEO
	CARITA	MOREHEAD CITY
	EVA PEARL	MOREHEAD CITY
	MANLY	SMYRNA
	THELMA	SMYRNA
	MAMIE LEWIS	SNEADS FERRY
	ISABEL	SOUTHPORT
	BEE	STRAWHORN LANDING
	MAUD AND REG	WASHINGTON
	C.W. LYON	WILMINGTON
	SHAMROCK	WINTHROP POINT
1906	CARRIE B. BELLE	AVON
	MAJORIE	BEAUFORT
	MARJORIE	BEAUFORT
	W.J.B. SHULL	BEAUFORT
	MARION	BELHAVEN
	PAMLICO	BELHAVEN
	SUNLIGHT	CALABASH
	HILDA	COINJOCK
	MARY B.	EAST LAKE
	MASCOT	ELIZABETH CITY
	OLADEAN	ENGLEHARD
	DIXIE	KITTY HAWK
	ELLA G	KITTY HAWK
	B.M. VAN DUZEN	MANTEO
	JOHN H. SMALL	MANTEO
	LU RAY	MARINES
	CATHERINE M.	MOREHEAD CITY
	STERLING	MOREHEAD CITY
	MASCOT	NEW BERN
	COLUMBIA	SMYRNA
	MARY LEE	SUPPLY
	HATTIE ELLEN	SWAN QUARTER

Date	Ship Name	Shipbuilding Location
1906	BERTHA W.	VANCEBORO
	ZELDA	WASHINGTON
	COLUMBIA	WILLISTON
	ATLANTIC	WILMINGTON
	MAGGIE BEAMAN	WYSOCKING
	BUG	
	LOOKOUT	
1907	TOP	BEAUFORT
	TOY	BEAUFORT
	BENNETT	BELHAVEN
	EDWIN	BERTIE COUNTY
	AGNES T.	BLADES
	EUNICE	ELIZABETH CITY
	SHENANDOAH	ELIZABETH CITY
	JON R	JACKSONVILLE
	HERBERT A. CREEF	MANTEO
	EAGLE	MOREHEAD CITY
	MARY K.	MOUNT PLEASANT
	L. WITT	PELETIER
	WONDER	POINT CASWELL
	PEARL	POWELLS POINT
	M.A. SHANKLIN	SMYRNA
	REAPER	SMYRNA
	BLACK RIVER	STRAWHORN LANDING
	DANIEL	WIT
1908	HERO	ATLANTIC
	CAPTAIN SAM H.	BEAUFORT
	JAMES	BEAUFORT
	TOY	BEAUFORT
	EVA	BELHAVEN
	RIPPLE	BERTIE COUNTY
	DEZWAY	BLOUNTS CREEK
	JAMES E. BROWN	BUFFALO CITY
	BABY LOUISE	COLINGTON
	ANNIE LOIS	COLUMBIA
	COLUMBIA	COLUMBIA
	HORTON CORWIN JR.	EDENTON
	DOROTHY	ELIZABETH CITY
	ECORSE	ELIZABETH CITY
	LILLIAN	ELIZABETH CITY
	THREE BROTHERS	GUM NECK
	NETTIE	JACKSONVILLE
	ALSON MILLER	KINNAKEET

Date	Ship Name	Shipbuilding Location
1908	EDITH CLARK	LOWLAND
	ALMA	MANTEO
	AGNES	MOREHEAD CITY
	NELLIE MAY	MOREHEAD CITY
	COMFORT	NEW BERN
	DIXIE	NEW BERN
	ELOISE	NEW BERN
	LISBON	POINT CASWELL
	BIRDIE ESTELL	SHILOH
	MONEY MAKER	SMITH MILLS
	ELLA MAY	WEEKSVILLE
	CATHERINE	WILMINGTON
	WILLIAM M.	WILMINGTON
	GLADYS	WIT
1909	CARRIE	ATLANTIC
	JOHN E. BROWN	BUFFALO CITY
	ROBERT L. HINTON	ELIZABETH CITY
	TAYLOR	ELIZABETH CITY
	LOU C. ROSS	KITTY HAWK
	HETTIE E	MARSHALLBERG
	PLEASURE	MAYSVILLE
	AGNES	MOREHEAD CITY
	ALMA GRAY	MOREHEAD CITY
	EDWARD R. GILMAN	MOREHEAD CITY
	GOLDSBORO	MOREHEAD CITY
	PEARL	MOREHEAD CITY
	GUION	SMYRNA
	J.W. LATHROP	SOUTHPORT
	MOHAWK	SOUTHPORT
	CRAFTSMAN	WANCHESE
	HAZEL	WILMINGTON
	GOSPEL SHIP JOSEPH	WIT
	EULA C.	WYSOCKING
1910	CAPTAIN DICK	BEAUFORT
	EARLINE	BEAUFORT
	ELSIE W.	BELHAVEN
	MADELINE	MOREHEAD CITY
	ELIZABETH	NEW BERN
	SICKLE	WILLISTON
1911	GERTRUDE	BELHAVEN
	JONES	MARSHALLBERG
	ANNIE B.	MILL CREEK
	BRIDGEPORT	MOREHEAD CITY

Date	Ship Name	Shipbuilding Location
1911	D.H. PENTON	MOREHEAD CITY
	MENHADEN	MOREHEAD CITY
	ONO II	MOREHEAD CITY
	SHALLOTTE	SHALLOTTE
	ALFONZO	WILLISTON
	ALPHONSO	WILLISTON
	R.W. POWELL	WILMINGTON
	EMPRESS	WIT
	ZIYIRA	WIT
1912	JANET	ATLANTIC
	HELLENE	BELHAVEN
	ROXIE PITMAN	BERTIE COUNTY
	CAROLINA	ELIZABETH CITY
	JAUNITY	HARDINGS BRIDGE
	JUANITA	HARDINGS BRIDGE
	LUTHER G.	MARINES
	FREDERICK LUNDY	MOREHEAD CITY
	GEORGE ROBERTS	MOREHEAD CITY
	M.C. ADAMS	MOREHEAD CITY
	NEPONSIT	MOREHEAD CITY
	SHUI CHA	MOREHEAD CITY
	MOT	VANCEBORO
	DEPENDENT	WASHINGTON
	GORDON	WILLISTON
1913	LALA G.	ATLANTIC
	ANNIS	BEAUFORT
	BERKLEY MACHINE WORKS	BELHAVEN
	DAPHNE	BELHAVEN
	M.B. DAVIS	DAVIS
	EMANDELL	ELIZABETH CITY
	ALABAMA	IVANHOE
	CHARLIE	LENOXVILLE
	ALBERTA	MARSHALLBERG
	C. WASHINGTON COLYER	MOREHEAD CITY
	JOSEPHINE	MOREHEAD CITY
	MERLE	MOREHEAD CITY
	U.M. GILLIKIN	MOREHEAD CITY
	UNCLE SAM	MOREHEAD CITY
	J.E. BENNETT	NEW BERN
	THELMA	POINT CASWELL
	SADIE MAY	SHALLOTTE
	SHAMROCK	SUPPLY
	ELOISE	WASHINGTON

Date	Ship Name	Shipbuilding Location
1913	FLORENCE	WILLISTON
	NEMO	WIT
1914	WORTH J.	ATKINSON
	EMPRESS	ATLANTIC
	ERAH	ATLANTIC
	J.R. DIXON	ATLANTIC
	LYDIA G.	ATLANTIC
	M.K. GERTRUDE	ATLANTIC
	NORMA	ATLANTIC
	WANETA	ATLANTIC
	MARIEL DEEN	CURRITUCK
	KING FISHER	DUCK CREEK
	HAMPTON	ELIZABETH CITY
	WATER LILY	ELIZABETH CITY
	N. ESTELLE	MANNS HARBOUR
	SILVER SPRAY	MARSHALLBURG
	WE'RE HERE	MOREHEAD CITY
	AGNES F.	WASHINGTON
	ROVER	WASHINGTON
	M. LUPTON	WHARTONSVILLE
	BLANCHE	WILLISTON
	IOV	BEAUF0RT
	ALICE	BEAUFORT
	CASSANDER	BEAUFORT
	CHRISTINA	BEAUFORT
	CLIPPER	BEAUFORT
	DANIEL WEBSTER	BEAUFORT
	DRED	BEAUFORT
	EMBLEM	BEAUFORT
	ERNEST	BEAUFORT
	FLORA	BEAUFORT
	GENERAL TAYLOR	BEAUFORT
	GENOA	BEAUFORT
	GEORGE PEABODY	BEAUFORT
	HAVEN	BEAUFORT
	HELEN JANE	BEAUFORT
	IDA	BEAUFORT
	IONE	BEAUFORT
	JANET ANN	BEAUFORT
	LADY GRAY	BEAUFORT
	MAJOR FISHER	BEAUFORT
	MARIETTA	BEAUFORT
	MARY RILEY	BEAUFORT

Date	Ship Name	Shipbuilding Location
1914	PACKET	BEAUFORT
	PEARL	BEAUFORT
	PET	BEAUFORT
	RACER	BEAUFORT
	RENO	BEAUFORT
	ROVER	BEAUFORT
	SARAH	BEAUFORT
	SARAH ANN	BEAUFORT
	SARAH WEBB	BEAUFORT
	TOY	BEAUFORT
	UNION	BEAUFORT
	WASP	BEAUFORT
	MARTHA A.	BRIDGEBORO
	HAWK	CAPE FEAR
	HATTON	COLUMBIA
	JOE ANN	COLUMBIA
	BETTY C. BELL	CRAWFORD
	EAGLE	CRAWFORD
	MAYFLOWER	CRAWFORD
	SEA GULL	CRAWFORD
	WIDOWS SON	CRAWFORD
	A.C. PATE	EDENTON
	ANNIE COLTON	EDENTON
	LE CHARMONT	EDENTON
	MARIA ANN	EDENTON
	MARY AND ELLEN	EDENTON
	S. CATHERINE	EDENTON
	SUPERIOR	EDENTON
	ALFRED DORLAN	ELIZABETH CITY
	ANGELICA	ELIZABETH CITY
	ANNA	ELIZABETH CITY
	ANNIE COLE	ELIZABETH CITY
	ANNIE TODD	ELIZABETH CITY
	BLACK HAWK	ELIZABETH CITY
	CAROLINE	ELIZABETH CITY
	CARRIE B.	ELIZABETH CITY
	CARRIE DYE	ELIZABETH CITY
	CATHARINE	ELIZABETH CITY
	DARE	ELIZABETH CITY
	DOLPHIN	ELIZABETH CITY
	DOVE	ELIZABETH CITY
	E. FRANCES	ELIZABETH CITY
	ELLA	ELIZABETH CITY

Date	Ship Name	Shipbuilding Location
1914	EMMA	ELIZABETH CITY
	ENTERPRISE	ELIZABETH CITY
	EXTENUATE	ELIZABETH CITY
	GRANGER	ELIZABETH CITY
	H.F. OSBORNE	ELIZABETH CITY
	JENNIE ALICE	ELIZABETH CITY
	JESSIE PALIN	ELIZABETH CITY
	JOHN JAMES	ELIZABETH CITY
	JOSEPH YOUNG	ELIZABETH CITY
	JULIA SELDEN	ELIZABETH CITY
	LAURA M. TREE	ELIZABETH CITY
	MAGGIE BELL	ELIZABETH CITY
	MARGARET A. BRUSH	ELIZABETH CITY
	MARY A. GILDERSLEEVE	ELIZABETH CITY
	MARY JANE	ELIZABETH CITY
	MARY SUSAN NORRIS	ELIZABETH CITY
	P.R. PARKER	ELIZABETH CITY
	PATRICK HENRY	ELIZABETH CITY
	RICHARD WILDER	ELIZABETH CITY
	SEA MONSTER	ELIZABETH CITY
	SIAM	ELIZABETH CITY
	SIDNEY	ELIZABETH CITY
	SPRAY	ELIZABETH CITY
	STARTLED FAWN	ELIZABETH CITY
	SUE CUMMINGS	ELIZABETH CITY
	SUSAN GREGORY	ELIZABETH CITY
	TENIE AND ALICE	ELIZABETH CITY
	TRIUMPH	ELIZABETH CITY
	UNION	ELIZABETH CITY
	W.N.H. SMITH	ELIZABETH CITY
	ACTIVE	HATTERAS
	ADVANCE	HATTERAS
	BELLE	HATTERAS
	C.L. COBB	HATTERAS
	CORAL	HATTERAS
	JOHN BENJA	HATTERAS
	NATIVE	HATTERAS
	SURMOUNT	HATTERAS
	SUSAN CAROLINE	HATTERAS
	LADY JANE	NELSON BAY
	ALMARINE	NEW BERN
	COMMERCE	NEW BERN
	DEB	NEW BERN

Date	Ship Name	Shipbuilding Location
1914	DELMAR	NEW BERN
	DIME	NEW BERN
	DOMESTIC	NEW BERN
	EMMA	NEW BERN
	ENERGY	NEW BERN
	FLORENCE	NEW BERN
	FLORENCE	NEW BERN
	GENERAL SHIELDS	NEW BERN
	HENRIETTA HILL	NEW BERN
	HENRY CLAY	NEW BERN
	JEANNETTE	NEW BERN
	JENNIE LIND	NEW BERN
	JOSEPH M. MILES	NEW BERN
	LITTLE CHARLIE	NEW BERN
	LUCK	NEW BERN
	MARGARET O'NEIL	NEW BERN
	MARIA ANN	NEW BERN
	MARTHA WASHINGTON	NEW BERN
	MARY THERESA	NEW BERN
	MATTHEW VAN DUSEN	NEW BERN
	NEW BALTIMORE	NEW BERN
	P. MERWIN	NEW BERN
	PATRON	NEW BERN
	R.L. SWINSON	NEW BERN
	RIO GRANDE	NEW BERN
	SAMUEL HAYMEN	NEW BERN
	SARAH GARDNER	NEW BERN
	SARAH VIRGINIA	NEW BERN
	STAR	NEW BERN
	STARLIGHT	NEW BERN
	THREE BROTHERS	NEW BERN
	BETSEY	NORTH CAROLINA
	BETSY	NORTH CAROLINA
	BETTY	NORTH CAROLINA
	CHARMING POLLY	NORTH CAROLINA
	CHOWAN PACKET	NORTH CAROLINA
	FANNY	NORTH CAROLINA
	JOHN	NORTH CAROLINA
	LURANIA	NORTH CAROLINA
	NORTH CAROLINA	NORTH CAROLINA
	SALLY	NORTH CAROLINA
	ANN ELIZA	OCRACOKE
	DAVID	OCRACOKE

Date	Ship Name	Shipbuilding Location
1914	DOLPHIN	PAMLICO
	PEARL	PAMLICO
	KEYSTONE	PLYMOUTH
	MARY AND FRANCES	PLYMOUTH
	MONTEREY	PLYMOUTH
	RICHARD HOPKINS	PLYMOUTH
	WAVE	PLYMOUTH
	FRIENDS	PORTSMOUTH
	MARY HOLLAND	PORTSMOUTH
	SALLY	PORTSMOUTH
	FERRATA	SMITHVILLE
	IOWA	SMITHVILLE
	MARY	STRAITS
	HANNAH WOOD	SWANSBORO
	KATE	SWANSBORO
	ANDREW WURFLEIN	WASHINGTON
	B.J. CHRISTIAN	WASHINGTON
	C.A. JOHNSON	WASHINGTON
	DOLPHIN	WASHINGTON
	EXPRESS	WASHINGTON
	EXPRESS	WASHINGTON
	FAIR	WASHINGTON
	FLORA	WASHINGTON
	HATTIE	WASHINGTON
	I HOPE	WASHINGTON
	IDA	WASHINGTON
	INTREPID	WASHINGTON
	IONE	WASHINGTON
	J.A. LEVENSALER	WASHINGTON
	JAMES L. CRANE	WASHINGTON
	MARTHA EMILY	WASHINGTON
	MARY FRAZIER	WASHINGTON
	MINERVA L. WEDMAN	WASHINGTON
	NELLIE POTTER	WASHINGTON
	RAPIDAN	WASHINGTON
	SAM E. EBORN	WASHINGTON
	ADAMANTINE	WILMINGTON
	ADIEL	WILMINGTON
	ALBION	WILMINGTON
	ANNA	WILMINGTON
	ANNA BELL	WILMINGTON
	FLASH	WILMINGTON
	FRED B. RICE	WILMINGTON

Date	Ship Name	Shipbuilding Location
1914	GENERAL WHITING	WILMINGTON
	KATE	WILMINGTON
	MARY BEAR	WILMINGTON
	MODOC	WILMINGTON
	NEVADA	WILMINGTON
	NORTH CAROLINA	WILMINGTON
	ONTARIO	WILMINGTON
	PAUL B. CARTER	WILMINGTON
	PLANET	WILMINGTON
	RICHMOND	WILMINGTON
	RICOCHET	WILMINGTON
	SEA BIRD	WILMINGTON
	SEA SERPENT	WILMINGTON
	STAR	WILMINGTON
	STEPHEN S. LEE	WILMINGTON
	SWEEPSTAKES	WILMINGTON
	SWIFT	WILMINGTON
	T.D. MURRAY	WILMINGTON
	LAS PAISLEY	
	LITTLE SALLY	
	OCER	
	PASSENGER	

Appendix C: Deciphering Names of Shipbuilding Locations

Place names with respect to where ships were built are not always what they seem. There is reason for concern. The various spellings of place names were, at times, difficult to match and sometimes certain locations could not be found. Also, there were instances where there were several locations having the same name. With respect to spelling, all place names were checked against gazetteers and changed to the current spelling. If correctly spelled the original names were kept. In the case of place names not found, after a check with the gazetteers, the names only were deleted from the database. It is likely that some of the place names deleted were for plantations rather than a hamlet or village. Several records did not have place names, but were kept in the database.

At times there were instances when the same place name could be found in several locations. For example, there are fourteen Mill Creeks, eight Broad Creeks, seven Goose Creeks, and so forth. Sometimes the location was not known as a shipbuilding site at a certain point in time and was eliminated. In other instances the most predominant shipbuilding site was used and other locations were eliminated. Some place names appearing in the records were located too far from any water course to be considered for inclusion and were eliminated. In all cases, the place name used for the period of history in which it occurred was not necessarily used. For example, Camden was known as Jonesborough in 1792, and then Plank Bridge, and then changed again to Camden in 1840. Finally, general place names such as Hyde Precinct or Bath County involve large areas. In such cases the place was eliminated from being placed on the shipbuilding location map, or a geographic location was chosen.

Place Names of Coastal North Carolina

Adams Creek–There are two Adams Creeks in the eastern part of the state, one a tributary of the Neuse River, and the other a tributary of the Pamlico River. The latter is not mentioned by in William S. Powell and Michael Hill, *The North Carolina Gazetteer* (revised edition, 2010). There were nineteen ships built on Adams Creek, but a significant break in shipbuilding exists between 1795 and 1807. Consequently, the five ships built between 1750 and 1795 were assumed to be constructed on Adams Creek near Bath, an early settlement on Bath Creek. The remaining ships being built between 1807 and 1825 were assumed to be constructed on Adams Creek downstream from New Bern, a very active port during this period. Later, the Adams Creek Canal was built to connect the creek with the Newport River, and became a part of the Intracoastal Waterway.

Albemarle–Ships, it is recorded, were built in Albemarle and Albemarle County. However, no such community existed in the coastal area. Albemarle County ceased to exist after 1668 when it was divided into precincts known as Chowan, Currituck, Pasquotank and Perquimans. For shipbuilding purposes, Albemarle Sound is used for as a general shipbuilding location.

Avoca–A plantation in Bertie County near the confluence of the Chowan River and the Roanoke River with the Albemarle Sound, near Salmon Creek. Black Walnut Point is nearby and is used to locate the shipbuilding location for the plantation.

Bacon–Unknown, but there is a Garbacon Creek, a tributary of the Neuse River, and likely a shipbuilding site.

Bath County–Bath, located between Bath Creek and Back Creek which are tributaries of the Pamlico estuary, was an important colonial village and the center of activity. Bath County, established in 1696, no longer exists as such. Consequently, Bath is used for all shipbuilding locations for Bath County.

Bear Banks–Bear Banks is now a part of Brown's Island since an inlet was closed. Bear Inlet which remains is used for the shipbuilding location.

Beards Creek–There is a Beard Creek which is a tributary of the Neuse River and a Beards Creek which is a settlement on Beard Creek which is no longer as significant as it was in the colonial era. Beard Creek is used for the shipbuilding location.

Bears Creek–There are numerous Bear Creeks in eastern North Carolina, but no Bears Creek. For mapping purposes, Bear Creek in Onslow County is used as it appears on the Moseley map of 1733, and flows into Brown's Sound; it was formerly known as Deep Creek.

Beaufort Town–Beaufort Town is synonymous with the Town of Beaufort.

Belle Island–There are several Bell Islands, but no Belle Island. The Bell Island in Currituck County is used as it is named and located on several colonial era maps.

Bell's Bay–Bell Bay in Hyde County is used.

Bell's Buoy–Bells Point in Carteret County is used.

Bell's Ferry–Grifton is used as it is the more recent name for Bell's Ferry on Contentnea Creek.

Bell's Island–Bells Island in Carteret County is used.

Bethel–A settlement in Perquimans County is used rather than the town in Pitt County.

Blue Rock–Not located in the coastal area or used for mapping a shipbuilding site, although there is a Blue Hill or Bare Hill, a dune on Hatteras Island, east of the village of Hatteras. It could also be a name for a plantation.

Bluff Point–There are four Bluff Points, but the one in Chowan County appears to be the most significant as it is near Edenton and is located on the 1733 Moseley map.

Bridgeboro–Not listed or used for mapping shipbuilding sites, although there is a Bridgeton, not settled until 1900, on the Neuse River across from New Bern.

Broad Creek–There are numerous Broad Creeks in eastern North Carolina. Which ones were important as shipbuilding sites is unknown. But the Broad Creek in Pamlico County is the most likely shipbuilding location as it flows into the Neuse River and is on the 1733 Moseley map. It is also known locally as Lower Broad Creek.

Bull Pond–This location is not listed. However, there is a Bull Bay in Tyrrell County, and it is used as a shipbuilding site as it is near the Scuppernong River and Albemarle Sound with a depth of fourteen feet.

Burlington–While this community is not located in coastal North Carolina, it is located on the Haw River which is a tributary of the Cape Fear River. But, the likelihood of shipbuilding is practically nil. Also, this could be a name for a plantation.

Cape Banks–Cape Banks is not listed, but is assumed to be the Outer Banks, probably a portion of Hatteras Island. Buxton is used for the shipbuilding location.

Cape Fear–The settlement on the Cape Fear River is used for this location.

Cape Lookout–The settlement on Cape Lookout is used for this location.

Carlisle–Carlisle is not listed, but it is assumed to be the site once known as Carlile Island which is now Colington Island.

Carolina City–No longer exists, but was once located in Carteret County, so Carteret County is used as its general location.

Cedar Island–There are several Cedar Islands, but the one used is located in Carteret County and can be found on the 1729 Moll map.

Chicamacomico Bank–This is now Pea Island and was used as a shipbuilding site.

Churches Island–None listed, but there is a Church Island which is known today as Piney Island in Currituck County, and is used as the shipbuilding site.

Clearrun–Not listed, but there is a Clear Run settlement and stream in Sampson County, part of the Black River drainage area, and within the Cape Fear River system. The settlement was used for the shipbuilding site.

Conwaysboro or Conwayboro–This location is not listed, so Conway in Northampton County is use for this shipbuilding location, yet a fair distance from the Meherrin River, a tributary of the Chowan River.

Core Sound Banks–Core Banks is used for this location.

Crawford–Not listed, so Crawford Creek in Beaufort County is used for the shipbuilding site. Also, this could be a name for a plantation.

Crooked Creek–There are three streams with the same name in the coastal area in Beaufort, Camden, and Hyde Counties. The Beaufort location is used for the shipbuilding site.

Currituck Banks–Currituck Light is used for this shipbuilding location.

Currituck Inlet–Currituck Light is used for this shipbuilding location.

Currituck Narrows–Currituck Sound is used for this shipbuilding location.

Daily's Landing–Not listed, but there was a Daily's Creek in Lenoir County, a tributary of the Neuse River. The present Daileys Creek is used for this shipbuilding site. Also, this could be a plantation site.

Daleys–A colonial shipbuilding site not found in the *United States Geological Service Gazetteer*; it could be a plantation.

Drummonds–Not listed and could be a plantation site, but Drummonds Point is used for this shipbuilding site.

Duck Creek–There are numerous Duck Creeks, so the one in Onslow County is used for this shipbuilding site, as it flows into Farnell Bay and known as early as 1744.

Falls Creek–Falls Creek is located in Cumberland County and flows into the Cape Fear River. The site of Falls Creek School is used for the shipbuilding site.

Forbesville–This location was near Elizabeth City on the Pasquotank River, so Elizabeth City is used for the shipbuilding site.

Frank Creek–Not listed, so Franktown in Onslow County, between Jenkins Swamp and Juniper Swamp which drain into the New River, is used for the shipbuilding site.

Ganity Bay–A shipbuilding site during the Expansion Era, but not in the *USGS Gazetteer*.

Garrat Bay–A shipbuilding site during the Expansion Era, but not in the *USGS Gazetteer*.

Gar Bacon–Not listed, so Garbacon Creek which flows into the Neuse River is used for the shipbuilding site. Also, see Bacon.

Goose Creek–There are many Goose Creeks. The Camden County settlement known as Goose Creek is used, as others are merely creeks.

Habscam–Not known to exist in the coastal area, but could be a plantation.

Hardings Bridge–This is not listed as such, so Hardys Bridge in Lenoir County is used for the shipbuilding site, as it is near the Neuse River.

Harlow–Harlowe is used for the shipbuilding site.

Hog Island–There are several islands by this name, but the one in Carteret County appears on the 1733 Moseley map, and was also known as Whale Camp Point.

Hunting Quarter–Sometimes known as Hunting Quarters. The present site of Atlantic is used for this location. Four islands make up Hunting Quarter which was near Hog Island and Hunting Quarter Inlet in the 1730s. It was also the summer settlement of the Core Indians.

Indian River–The colonial shipbuilding site is not known to exist.

Indian Town Old Landing–Not listed; consequently Indian Town in Camden County is used for the shipbuilding site. Indiantown is another spelling.

Ivanhoe–Settlement is located on the Black River in Sampson County.

Jarretts Bay–Listed as Jarrett Bay. Spellings also include Jarrots Bay and Jarrotts Bay, also possibly Jarrels Bay where a ship was built during the Expansion Era.

Judiths–Not listed; consequently Judith Island in Hyde County is used as the shipbuilding site.

Kinnekeet–This is known as Kinnakeet. The site used for this location is Avon which is nearby.

Lake Landing–Not listed as such; Lake Landing Township in Hyde County is used for the shipbuilding location.

Lancaster–Settlement is located in Edgecombe County, perhaps on the Tar River or one of its tributaries. This could be a plantation site.

Launch–Known as The Launch, the shipbuilding site is on Tull Bay in Currituck County, which is used for the location. It appears to be a major colonial shipbuilding site.

Lennoxville–Lenoxville is used for the shipbuilding site which was near Lenox Point, once known as Titus Point, in Carteret County east of Beaufort.

Little River–There are several Little Rivers. The Little River in Perquimans and Pasquotank Counties, which flows into Albemarle Sound, is identified on the 1657 Comberford map as the Yeopim River but shown on the 1671 Ogilby map correctly.

Lockwood Folly or Lockwoods Folly–Lockwood Folly is used with the location being Lockwood Folly Inlet as the shipbuilding site.

Lower Broad Creek–Broad Creek in Pamlico County is used as this shipbuilding site. Also, see Broad Creek.

Lowland or Lowlands–Lowland is used.

Machapongo River–Pungo River is used.

Mare York–Not listed, consequently Mare Point in Beaufort County is used.

Mill Brook–Mill Branch, of which there are several, in Brunswick County is used.

Mill or Mills Creek–Mill Creek, of which there are several, in Carteret County is used.

Mitchell or Mitchells Creek–Mitchell Creek, of which there are several, in Craven County is used.

Mount Pleasant–Site located in Hyde County on the Middletown quadrangle is used.

Murfreesboro–Located in Hertford County on the Meherrin River.

Narrow Shore–Narrow Shore is not listed. This is assumed to be The Narrows on the Newport River, so the Newport River is used for the shipbuilding site.

Nelson, Nelson's or Nelsons Bay–Nelson Bay on Core Sound in Carteret County is used for the shipbuilding site.

New Topsail–New Topsail Inlet is used for the shipbuilding site.

Nixon, Nixton or Nixon's Town–Town, now known as Nixonton on Little River in Pasquotank County, is used for the shipbuilding site.

North Carolina–Many ships were recorded as being built in North Carolina during the colonial era. These ships could have been built anywhere and the exact location for the shipbuilding sites are unknown. Therefore no latitude and longitude are given and consequently are not on the maps in this study.

North River–Settlement in Carteret County on the North River. However, the North River in Pasquotank County was known to have significant shipbuilding activity.

Old Trap–Located in Camden County, an old settlement dating back to the 1650s, and the center of much maritime activity, including a grog shop, hence the name "trap." The coordinates for Wharf Bay are used to locate the shipbuilding site.

Oregon Mills–A shipbuilding site during the Industrial Era, but the location is unknown.

Otter Creek–There are two Otter Creeks in the coastal plain, one flowing into the Tar River and one flowing into the Neuse River. There is also an Otter Creek in Hyde County which is a bay, and the one used for this shipbuilding site.

Pamlico–The settlement is used for the shipbuilding site rather than the river or the sound or the county or the township.

Pearce's Creek–Not listed, consequently Pearce Landing in Lenoir County on the Neuse River is used for the shipbuilding location.

Perquimans County and River–This spelling is used rather than Perquimons.

Piney Grove–Piney Grove Landing in Hyde County is used for the shipbuilding site.

Piney Point–The point or cape in Carteret County is used for the shipbuilding location.

Plank Bridge–This is the old name or another name for the settlement of Camden, so the site of Camden is used for the location of shipbuilding.

Port Bath–Bath is used.

Port Roanoke–Edenton is used.

Portsmouth–Portsmouth Island is used as a general shipbuilding site.

Potts Point–The location is not listed.

Powell's Point–The settlement, not the point or cape, is used as a shipbuilding site.

Princeton–Once known as Pitch Landing, the settlement on the Meherrin River in Hertford County is near Murfreesboro, and is used as a shipbuilding site.

Quistsney–The name is not listed, but Quistna is listed and used as a shipbuilding site in Bertie County. This is also known as Grabtown. The Tuscarora Indians were known to have used this site. It appears to be on the Cashie River.

Smith Creek–Likely at one time also known as Smiths Creek.

Tunis–A shipbuilding site during the Industrial Era.

White Rock–A colonial shipbuilding site, probably a plantation.

Windsor Creek–Not found in the *USGS Gazetteer*.

References

Payne, Roger L. *Place Names of the Outer Banks*. N.p.: T. A. Williams, 1986.

Powell, William S., and Michael Hill. *The North Carolina Gazetteer*. Revised edition. Chapel Hill: University of North Carolina Press, 2010.

United States Geological Survey. *Gazetteer and Maps*.

Appendix D: Colonial Shipbuilders and Shipwrights

The dates beside the shipbuilder names does not indicate when they first arrived in North Carolina, but rather when a shipbuilder is first mentioned in available records. According to the deed books from which much of this information is derived, the majority listed themselves as shipwrights rather than shipbuilders.

Name	Date	Location
Keele, Thomas	1666	Pasquotank County
Davenport, Richard	1685	Albemarle (boatbuilder)
Veedam, William & Johan	1680	Roanoke River
Barkely, William	1691	Perquimans County
Watts, John	1698	Perquimans County
Fox, John	1700	Chowan County (originally from Virginia)
Bodett, Jacob	1700	North Side of Pamlico River, Bath District
Royal, Marmaduke	1700	Carteret County (Cape Lookout)
Blount, Thomas	1702	Plymouth (also blacksmith)
Evans, Thomas	1703	Perquimans County (boatwright)
(name not legible)	1704	Hyde County
Chapman, Ralph	1704	Moved to Rhode Island
Meagar, Charles	1707	Bath
Powell, William	1703–1708	Oriental, Beaufort District
Harding, Thomas	1717–1724	Bath
Midgett, Mathew	1712	Tyrrell County (shipyard owner, then cattle ranch owner)
Goodgroom, Alex	1712	Craven County
Godby, Cary	1712–1713	Chowan (Salmon Creek)
Bell, George	1713	Beaufort
Forts, Charles	1715	Edenton
Sharpe, William	1715	Chowan County, Hertford
Avery, John	1715	Bath (Hyde County)
Wright, Joseph	1716	VA/NC disputed area, later Gates County
Alban, Richard	1716	Chowan County
Hackett, Joseph	1717	Pasquotank County
Downing, William	1718	Albemarle (originally part of Chowan, now Washington County)
Williams, Edward	1718	Pasquotank County (canoe builder)
Outlaw, Edward	1720	Chowan (from VA)
Smith, William	1717–1729	Pasquotank County
Pugh, Francis	1720s	Bertie County
Smith, John	1723	Pasquotank County
Rowan, Mathew	1720	Bath
Smith, Thomas	1720	Hyde (Hyde Precinct treasurer)
Bodett, Isaac	1720	
Browning, Edward	1720	Chowan County
Sillington, Eleizer	1725	Bath
Kemphall, John	1726	
McDonough, Michael	1729	Hyde County
Brian, John	1730	
Avoca, Thomas	1732	Pasquotank County
Everett, Henry	1732	Bath
Stanton, Henry	1732	Carteret County (Newport River)
Gilbert, Thomas	1732	Chowan County

Borden, William	1732	Beaufort (Newport River)
Keen, Richard	1733	Wilmington
Harker, Ebenezer	1736	Bath
Grafton, Samuel	1736	Edenton
Pringle, Alexander	1736	Craven County
Avery, John	1738	Hyde County
Dyer, Michael	1737	New Hanover County
Rigsby, William	1739	Wilmington
Jammerson, James	1739	Perquimans County
Jones, Zachariah	1739	Pasquotank County
Fox, Nicholas	1739	Wilmington
Payne, Thomas	1740s	Brunswick County
Smeeth, David	1740s	Brunswick County
Johnson, Arthur	1741	Craven County (came from South Carolina)
Reed, George	1742	Chowan County
Parker, Thomas	1742	Pasquotank County
Toppin, William	1743	Chowan County
Stephens (Stevens), Thomas	1743	Chowan County
Grainger, Josiah	1743–1778	Wilmington (carpenter)
Wells, Robert	1743–1778	Wilmington
Bell, John	1744	Pasquotank County
Verden, John	1745	Chowan County
Borden, William	1746	Carteret County
Bows, Joseph	1746	Craven County
Howard, Francis	1746	Chowan County
Nash, Josiah	1746	Pasquotank, Camden County
Doughty, John	1748	Wilmington
Currell, William	1749	Chowan County
Parker, Elisha	1750	Edenton
Newby, Thomas	1750	Pasquotank County
Russell, Benjamin	1751	Hyde County (purchased John Avery's land and presumably his shipyard)
Lester, Robert	1752	Onslow County
Nowell, Thomas	1752	Tyrrell County
Cherry, John	1753	Tyrrell County
Haly, William	1753	Bertie County
Ball, Richard	1753	Bertie County
Nowe, Peter	1753	Beaufort
Walpoole, Robert	1753	Beaufort
Perry, John	1754	Chowan County
Miller, Abel	1754	Chowan County, Perquimans County, 1770
Jasper, Jonathan	1755–1760s	Hyde County (Pungo River), Beaufort County
Scott, William	1757	Bertie County
Ivey, Samuel	1757	Pasquotank County
Russell, Robert	1758	Tyrrell County
Neil, William	1758	New Hanover County
Fowler, David	1758	New Hanover County
Smith, Thomas	1758	Hyde County (bought land for timber and part owner of sawmill in 1763)
Matthias, Nathaniel	1759	Chowan County
Corbett, Archibald	1759	Chowan County
Mohun, Hezekiah	1759	Bertie County
Walker, John	1760	New Hanover County
Stone, Benjamin	1760	New Hanover County
Ashburne, Edward	1760	Pasquotank County, Perquimans County
Ashburne, Nicholas	1760	Pasquotank County, Perquimans County
Dawson, Richard	1760	Bertie County

Towne, Daniel	1760	Edenton
Weymouth, John	1761	Craven County
Thomas, John	1761–1773	Hyde County (Pungo River)
Wallace, William	1761	Tyrrell County (from Norfolk)
Taylor, Thomas	1761	Tyrrell County
Grimes, Thomas	1761	Tyrrell County
Manning, Markham	1761	Tyrrell County
Smith, Samuel	1761	Hyde County
Cleeves, John	1761	Hyde County
Tucker, John	1761	Perquimans County
Sparrow, Samuel	1761	Craven County
Bell, Lancelot	1761	Pasquotank County, Perquimans County
Williamson, John	1761	Craven County
Mason, Zacheriah	1762	Chowan County, Currituck County
Polson, William	1762	Halifax County
Grant, Thomas	1760–1762	Halifax County, Edenton
Scott, William	1762	Perquimans County
Harper, William	1762	Chowan County
Every, George	1763	Pitt County (Beaufort County)
Bell, Benjamin	1763	New Hanover County
Bell, Joshua	1763	Hyde County
White, James	1764	Carteret County
Masson, William	1765	Bertie County
Wells, Robert	1766	Wilmington
Gaines, Thomas	1766	Tyrrell County
Streeter, Thomas	1766	Chowan County
Philips,	1766	Beaufort County
Williams, Hatten	1758–1767	Perquimans County
Nichols, Nicholas	1767	Currituck County
Moore, Cornelius	1767	Perquimans County (shipyard owner)
Guyer, Josiah	1767	Perquimans County (sold shipyard to Moore)
Moore, Thomas	1767	New Hanover County
Griffin, James	1767	Onslow County
Butler, Francis	1768	Chowan County
Green, William	1769	Onslow County
Russell, William	1769	Hyde County (mariner bought land from Jonathan Jasper who made out his will, 1770)
Walpole, Robert	1769	Carteret County (Beaufort)
Slade, Jerimah	1769–1771	Beaufort County, Hyde County (plantation owner)
Mounts, Luke	1770s	Pitt County, Beaufort County (mariner)
Jasper, Israel	1770s	Beaufort County
Pigot, Elijah	1770s	Carteret County
Simpson, Obediah	1770s	New Hanover (Tory who fled in 1776)
Law, David	1771	Wilmington
Bell, Joseph	1771	Beaufort County
Newby, Jesse	1771	Edenton
Moore, Cornelius	1771	Edenton (shipyard at Nixonton, Perquimans County)
Wilder, Michael	1771	Chowan County
Smith, Samuel	1771	Hyde County (Mouse Harbor)
Fuller, John	1772	Carteret County
Williams, Francis	1773	Chowan County
Simons, John	1774	Bertie County
Hunter, Abraham	1774	Wilmington
Mitchell, John	1774	New Hanover County
Smith, John	1774	Hyde County
Massey, Adrian	1775	Tyrrell County
Gray, William	1775	Bertie County

Williams, Joseph	1775	Perquimans County
Bell, John	1775	Hyde County
Fortescue, John	1775	Hyde County (Pungo)
Tooley, Adam	1777	Otter Creek (probably Craven County)
Ogden,	1776	Craven County
Pew, Robert	1777	Carteret County
Baily, Thomas	1777	Bertie County
Evert, Henry	1778	Beaufort County
King, John	1778	Craven County
Sparrow, Francis	1778	Craven County
Morse, John	1779	Onslow County, Carteret County
Boon, Lawrence	1778	Carteret County
Sparrow, Roderick	1778	Craven County
Cowell, John	1779	Currituck County
Tuley, Henry	1783	Pamlico County (Pungo Creek) Hyde County
Dyer, Judah	1783	Onslow County (Swansboro)
Armistead, Isaac	n.d.	Northampton County

www.ingramcontent.com/pod-product-compliance
Lightning Source LLC
Chambersburg PA
CBHW041409300426
44114CB00028B/2962